Cases of the UNESCO Committee on Conventions and Recommendations

The Raoul Wallenberg Institute Series of Intergovernmental Human Rights Documentation

VOLUME 5

The titles published in this series are listed at *brill.com/raou*

Cases of the UNESCO Committee on Conventions and Recommendations

Communications examined under the 104 EX/Decision 3.3 Procedure of the Executive Board (1978–1988)

VOLUME 1

Communications filed 1978–1981

Edited by

Leif Holmström

With an Introduction by

Abdulqawi A. Yusuf and Béatrice Dupuy

In cooperation with

UNESCO Office International Standards and Legal Affairs

TUTA SUB AEGIDE PALLAS · 1683 ·

BRILL
NIJHOFF

LEIDEN | BOSTON

ISBN 978-90-04-39028-7 (hardback, volume 1)
ISBN 978-90-04-16878-7 (hardback, set)
ISBN 978-90-04-35403-6 (e-book)

This book is printed on acid-free paper and produced in a sustainable manner.

Printed by Printforce, the Netherlands

CONTENTS

FOREWORD
By Audrey Azoulay
Director-General of UNESCO

INTRODUCTION
By Abdulqawi A. Yusuf and Béatrice Dupuy

ACKNOWLEDGEMENT
By Leif Holmstrom

A. PRELUDE xxvii
B. HISTORICAL BACKGROUND xxviii
C. THE DISTINCTIVE FEATURES OF THE "104 PROCEDURE" xxx
1. Cooperation, dialogue and conciliation xxx
2. The quest for a satisfactory solution xxxi
3. Voluntary cooperation of the States concerned xxxii
4. Confidentiality of the procedure xxxiii
5. A non-confrontational procedure xxxiii
D. ACHIEVEMENTS xxxiv
1. A wide spectrum of cases considered and resolved xxxv
2. An effective delivery of results over the years xxxv
E. ATTEMPTS AT REFORM xxxviii
F. CONCLUSION xxxviii

UNESCO COMMITTEE ON CONVENTIONS AND RECOMMENDATIONS
Communications examined under the 104 EX/Decision 3.3
Procedure of the Executive Board filed 1978–1981 1

No. 2/78 *Romania*
Transylvanian populations in Romania 3
Spring 1979 session 3
No. 10/78 *Uruguay*
Armando Germinal González Ferrando 5
Spring 1979 session 5
No. 11/78 *Argentina*
María Ernestina Giachetti 7
Spring 1979 session 7

No. 12/78	*Israel*					
	Abdul Jawad Saleh – Palestinian Human Rights Committee for the Defence of War and Political Prisoners					9
	Spring 1979 session	9	Autumn 1979 session	11		
	Spring 1980 session	13	Autumn 1980 session	16		
	Spring 1981 session	23	Autumn 1981 session	32		
	Spring 1982 session	43	Autumn 1982 session	54		
	Spring 1983 session	62	Autumn 1983 session	66		
	Spring 1984 session	67	Autumn 1984 session	70		
	Spring 1985 session	72	Autumn 1985 session	75		
	Spring 1986 session	76	Autumn 1986 session	79		
	Spring 1987 session	81	Autumn 1987 session	84		
	Spring 1988 session	89	Autumn 1988 session	92		
	Spring 1989 session	95	Autumn 1989 session	98		
	Spring 1990 session	101	Autumn 1990 session	103		
	Spring 1991 session	105	Autumn 1991 session	108		
No. 21/78	*Union of Soviet Socialist Republics and Ukrainian Soviet Socialist Republic*					
	Yuri Orlov et al.					111
	Spring 1979 session	111	Autumn 1979 session	112		
	Spring 1980 session	113				
No. 25/78	*Chile*					
	The situation of human rights in Chile in the fields of education, science, culture and information					115
	Autumn 1978 session	115	Spring 1979 session	120		
	Autumn 1979 session	121	Spring 1980 session	124		
	Autumn 1980 session	130	Spring 1981 session	138		
No. 26/78	*Argentina*					
	Elsa Alicia Nocent					147
	Autumn 1978 session	147	Spring 1979 session	148		
	Autumn 1979 session	149				
No. 31/78	*Argentina*					
	César Antonio Minué					151
	Spring 1979 session	151				
No. 33/78	*Argentina*					
	Manuel Alberto Santamaría					153
	Autumn 1979 session	153	Spring 1980 session	154		
No. 37/78	*United Kingdom*					
	Children of nomadic Gypsies					157
	Spring 1979 session	157	Autumn 1979 session	159		

No. 38/78	*Switzerland*				
	Ved Kalra				161
	Autumn 1978 session	161			
No. 41/78	*Spain*				
	José Candeas García				163
	Spring 1979 session	163			
No. 47/78	*Uruguay*				
	Eduardo Anselmo Viera				165
	Spring 1979 session	165	Autumn 1979 session	166	
	Spring 1980 session	167			
No. 49/78	*Argentina*				
	Ricardo Rodríguez Anido				169
	Spring 1979 session	169	Autumn 1979 session	170	
	Spring 1980 session	171			
No. 50/78	*Argentina*				
	Juan Carlos Aguirre				173
	Autumn 1979 session	173			
No. 51/78	*Argentina*				
	Fernando de Hallgarten				175
	Spring 1979 session	175	Autumn 1979 session	176	
No. 53/78	*Argentina*				
	Abel Héctor Mateu				177
	Spring 1979 session	177			
No. 54/78	*Chile*				
	Arturo Montes Larrain				179
	Spring 1979 session	179	Autumn 1979 session	180	
	Spring 1980 session	181	Autumn 1980 session	182	
	Spring 1981 session	184			
No. 56/78	*Chile*				
	Jorge Triviño Puelpan				189
	Spring 1981 session	189			
No. 57/78	*Chile*				
	Luis Pueller				191
	Spring 1979 session	191	Autumn 1979 session	192	
	Spring 1980 session	192	Autumn 1980 session	192	
	Spring 1981 session	193			
No. 59/78	*Chile*				
	Gustavo Adolfo Quintana Muñoz				195
	Autumn 1979 session	195	Spring 1980 session	196	
	Autumn 1980 session	196	Spring 1981 session	196	

No. 60/78 *Argentina*
Mario César Clar and Sergio Andrés Clar 197
Spring 1979 session 197 Autumn 1979 session 198
No. 63/78 *Argentina*
Alejandro Enrique Gutiérrez Penette 201
Spring 1979 session 201 Autumn 1979 session 201
No. 64/78 *Chile*
Juan Patricio Cleary Zambón 203
Spring 1979 session 203 Autumn 1979 session 203
Spring 1980 session 204 Autumn 1980 session 205
Spring 1981 session 205
No. 65/78 *Federal Republic of Germany*
Karl Wilhelm Ströder 207
Spring 1979 session 207
No. 66/78 *Chile*
Olga Victoria Morris Barrios 209
Autumn 1979 session 209
No. 67/78 *Chile*
Jorge Orlando Inostrosa Béjares and Rodrigo Mellado 211
Spring 1979 session 211 Autumn 1979 session 211
No. 68/78 *Argentina*
Luis Alberto Verdú Espinosa 213
Spring 1979 session 213
No. 69/78 *Argentina*
Néstor Hugo Cherry 215
Spring 1979 session 215
No. 71/78 *Argentina*
Daniel Gorosito 217
Spring 1979 session 217 Autumn 1979 session 217
Spring 1980 session 218
No. 72/78 *Chile*
Elwin Ayamante 221
Spring 1979 session 221 Autumn 1979 session 222
Spring 1980 session 222 Autumn 1980 session 223
Spring 1981 session 223
No. 74/78 *Argentina*
Perla Elizabeth Schneider 225
Spring 1979 session 225 Autumn 1979 session 225

No. 75/78 *Argentina*
José Carlos Prat-Salvucci 227
Spring 1979 session 227 Autumn 1979 session 227
Spring 1980 session 229
No. 79/78 *Argentina*
Julia Natividad Huarque 231
Spring 1979 session 231 Autumn 1979 session 232
No. 80/78 *Argentina*
Juan José Laso 233
Spring 1979 session 233
No. 81/78 *Argentina*
Guillermo Horacio White 235
Spring 1979 session 235
No. 82/78 *Argentina*
María Cristina Mattioli de Totterau 237
Spring 1979 session 237
No. 83/78 *Argentina*
Rodolfo Omar Rodríguez Echavarría 239
Spring 1979 session 239
No. 84/78 *Argentina*
Oscar Rubén Manzur 241
Spring 1979 session 241
No. 90/79 *Union of Soviet Socialist Republics and Ukrainian Soviet Socialist Republic*
Vadime Delaunay et al. 243
Spring 1979 session 243
No. 92/79 *Yugoslavia*
Milovan Djilas 245
Autumn 1979 session 245
No. 94/79 *Yugoslavia*
Mihajlo Mihajlov 247
Spring 1979 session 247 Autumn 1979 session 247
No. 95/79 *Yugoslavia*
Nikola Novaković 251
Autumn 1979 session 251
No. 96/79 *Argentina*
María Inés Muchiutti 253
Spring 1979 session 253 Autumn 1979 session 253

No. 97/79 *Argentina*
Analía Egle María Minetti 255
Spring 1979 session 255 Autumn 1979 session 255
Spring 1980 session 257

No. 98/79 *Argentina*
Mariano Alejandro Ramiro Martínez 259
Spring 1979 session 259

No. 103/79 *Uruguay*
José Luis Massera 261
Spring 1979 session 261 Autumn 1979 session 262
Spring 1980 session 264 Autumn 1980 session 267
Spring 1981 session 270 Autumn 1981 session 274
Spring 1982 session 280 Autumn 1982 session 287
Spring 1983 session 288 Autumn 1983 session 290
Spring 1984 session 292

No. 104/79 *Argentina*
Violation of human rights in the sectors of education, science, culture and information 295
Spring 1979 session 295 Autumn 1979 session 295
Spring 1980 session 300 Autumn 1980 session 302
Spring 1981 session 304 Autumn 1981 session 307

No. 105/79 *Argentina*
Julia Angélica Brocca de Herrero 315
Autumn 1979 session 315 Spring 1980 session 315

No. 106/79 *Argentina*
Gustavo Marcelo Juárez and María Gabriela Juárez 317
Spring 1979 session 317 Autumn 1979 session 317
Spring 1980 session 318

No. 108/79 *Uruguay*
Hiber Conteris 321
Autumn 1979 session 321 Spring 1980 session 322

No. 109/79 *Paraguay*
Carmen Lara Castro 325
Autumn 1979 session 325

No. 110/79 *Paraguay*
Virgilio Barreiro 327
Autumn 1979 session 327 Spring 1980 session 328

No. 111/79 *Argentina*
Héctor Alberto González 331
Autumn 1979 session 331

No. 112/79 *Argentina*
Marcelo E. Vensentini and Rosalba Vensentini 333
Spring 1980 session 333
No. 113/79 *Argentina*
Federico Eduardo Álvarez Rojas 335
Autumn 1979 session 335 Spring 1980 session 336
No. 115/79 *United States of America*
Vachel Lindsay 339
Autumn 1979 session 339
No. 117/79 *Romania*
A. Dan Vilcu 341
Autumn 1979 session 341 Spring 1980 session 342
No. 123/79 *Romania and Yugoslavia*
Djoka Stojanović 345
Autumn 1979 session 345
No. 124/79 *Poland*
Zygmunt Elbiński 347
Spring 1980 session 347
No. 125/79 *Argentina*
Juan Carlos Suárez 349
Autumn 1979 session 349
No. 126/79 *Morocco*
Eddimaoui Lahbib 353
Spring 1980 session 353
No. 127/79 *Argentina*
María Cristina García Suárez 355
Spring 1980 session 355
No. 129/79 *Argentina*
Oscar Ernesto Cocca Astrada 357
Autumn 1979 session 357 Spring 1980 session 358
No. 132/79 *Union of Soviet Socialist Republics*
Georgi Mikhailov 359
Autumn 1979 session 359
No. 133/79 *Nicaragua*
Vilma Núñez de Escorcia 361
Autumn 1979 session 361
No. 134/79 *Chile*
Abelardo Castro Hidalgo 363
Autumn 1979 session 363 Spring 1980 session 364
Autumn 1980 session 364 Spring 1981 session 364

No. 137/79 *Argentina*
Jorge Víctor Sznaider 365
Autumn 1979 session 365 Spring 1980 session 365

No. 143/79 *Argentina*
Jacinto Rubén Montenegro 367
Autumn 1979 session 367 Spring 1980 session 367

No. 144/79 *Denmark*
Kai Mogens H. Lång 369
Autumn 1979 session 369

No. 145/79 *Lao People's Democratic Republic*
Khamkhing Souvanlasy 371
Autumn 1979 session 371 Spring 1980 session 372
Autumn 1980 session 372 Spring 1981 session 374
Autumn 1981 session 376 Spring 1982 session 379
Autumn 1982 session 383 Spring 1983 session 384
Autumn 1983 session 385 Spring 1984 session 386
Autumn 1984 session 387 Spring 1985 session 388
Autumn 1985 session 390 Spring 1986 session 392
Autumn 1986 session 394

No. 146/79 *Uruguay*
Alfonso Avelino Fernández Cabrelli 397
Spring 1980 session 397

No. 149/79 *Union of Soviet Socialist Republics*
Mstislav Rostropovich and Galina Vishnevskaya 399
Autumn 1979 session 399 Spring 1980 session 400
Autumn 1980 session 402

No. 150/79 *Czechoslovakia*
Václav Havel and Otta Bednářová 405
Spring 1980 session 405 Autumn 1980 session 407
Spring 1981 session 410 Autumn 1981 session 416
Spring 1982 session 423 Autumn 1982 session 429
Spring 1983 session 431

No. 154/79 *Argentina, Chile and Uruguay*
Anatole Boris Julien Grisona and Eva Lucia Julien Grisona 433
Autumn 1979 session 433 Spring 1980 session 435
Autumn 1980 session 436

No. 155/79 *Indonesia*
Irzadi Mirwan 439
Spring 1980 session 439

No. 169/79	*Uruguay*					
	Missing children					441
	Spring 1980 session	441				
No. 173/79	*Guyana*					
	Janet Jagan					443
	Spring 1980 session	443	Autumn 1980 session	443		
	Spring 1981 session	445	Autumn 1981 session	447		
	Spring 1982 session	450	Autumn 1982 session	456		
	Spring 1983 session	458	Autumn 1983 session	459		
	Spring 1984 session	461	Autumn 1984 session	464		
No. 175/79	*France*					
	Lorella Sini					467
	Spring 1980 session	467				
No. 176/79	*Argentina*					
	Klaus Zieschank					469
	Spring 1980 session	469				
No. 177/79	*Argentina*					
	Juan Ángel Nughes					471
	Spring 1980 session	471				
No. 178/79	*Argentina*					
	Norberto Rey Ortalda					473
	Spring 1980 session	473				
No. 179/79	*Argentina*					
	Betina Tarnopolsky					475
	Spring 1980 session	475				
No. 180/79	*Argentina*					
	Fausto Augusto Carillo Rodríguez					477
	Spring 1980 session	477				
No. 181/79	*Argentina*					
	Hugo Tarnopolsky					479
	Spring 1980 session	479				
No. 182/79	*Argentina*					
	Blanca Edith Edelberg de Tarnopolsky					481
	Spring 1980 session	481				
No. 184/79	*El Salvador*					
	Jaime Bairés					483
	Spring 1980 session	483	Autumn 1980 session	484		
No. 189/80	*Poland*					
	Deaf-mute children in Poland					485
	Autumn 1980 session	485				

No. 190/80	*Argentina*	
	Sara Elba Grande	487
	Spring 1980 session 487	
No. 191/80	*Union of Soviet Socialist Republics*	
	Situation of religious activities in the USSR	489
	Spring 1980 session 489 Autumn 1980 session 491	
	Spring 1981 session 495	
No. 193/80	*Guatemala*	
	Teachers and students in Guatemala	501
	Autumn 1980 session 501 Spring 1981 session 503	
	Autumn 1981 session 507	
No. 195/80	*Union of Soviet Socialist Republics*	
	Andrei Sakharov	513
	Autumn 1980 session 513 Spring 1981 session 517	
	Autumn 1981 session 525 Spring 1982 session 534	
No. 196/80	*Denmark*	
	Kai Mogens H. Lång	547
	Autumn 1980 session 547	
No. 197/80	*Chile*	
	Ernesto Ottone Fernández	551
	Spring 1981 session 551	
	Autumn 1981 session 552	
No. 200/80	*Spain*	
	Emilio Mansera Conde	557
	Spring 1980 session 557	
No. 203/80	*Yugoslavia*	
	Vladimir Bonačić et al.	559
	Spring 1980 session 559	
No. 205/80	*German Democratic Republic*	
	Michael Haugk	561
	Autumn 1980 session 561	
No. 209/80	*Union of Soviet Socialist Republics*	
	Yosif Z. Begun	563
	Spring 1980 session 563 Autumn 1980 session 565	
No. 210/80	*Yugoslavia*	
	Kadri Osmani	569
	Autumn 1980 session 569	
No. 211/80	*Argentina*	
	Carlos Alberto Pérez and Mirta Silber de Pérez	571
	Autumn 1980 session 571	

No. 218/80 *Colombia and Uruguay*
Alba Nelda González Sousa 573
Autumn 1980 session 573
No. 220/80 *Argentina*
Disappearance of scientists and doctors in Argentina 575
Autumn 1980 session 575
No. 221/80 *Romania*
Remus Radina 577
Autumn 1980 session 577
No. 222/80 *Uruguay*
Elena Beatriz Vasilskis Castro 579
Autumn 1980 session 579
No. 223/80 *Romania*
The violation of human rights of the Hungarian minority in Romania 581
Autumn 1980 session 581
No. 224/80 *Argentina*
Graciela Esther Arabaolasa 585
Autumn 1981 session 585
No. 233/80 *United States of America and Israel*
Ziad Abu Eain 587
Autumn 1980 session 587
No. 238/80 *Yugoslavia*
Mihajlo Mihajlov 591
Autumn 1980 session 591
No. 241/80 *Argentina*
Antonio Satutto and María Cristina Ortiz 593
Autumn 1980 session 593
No. 242/80 *Union of Soviet Socialist Republics*
Victor Brailovski et al. 595
Spring 1981 session 595 Autumn 1981 session 603
Spring 1982 session 611 Autumn 1982 session 625
No. 247/80 *Romania*
Gheorghe Calciu-Dumitreasa 631
Autumn 1980 session 631
No. 261/80 *Yugoslavia*
Zlatko Matkovič 633
Spring 1981 session 633
No. 264/80 *France*
Zien Al Smail 635
Spring 1981 session 635

No. 266/80	*Argentina*					
	Elba Aurora Martínez de Larrea					637
	Spring 1981 session	637				
No. 267/80	*Chile*					
	Pedro Segundo Ahumada Pizarro					639
	Spring 1981 session	639	Autumn 1981 session	640		
	Spring 1982 session	642				
No. 269/80	*Republic of Korea*					
	Mong Yong Lee					647
	Spring 1981 session	647				
No. 270/80	*Argentina*					
	Juan Carlos Higa					653
	Spring 1981 session	653				
No. 271/80	*Zaire*					
	Taba and Kifuema					655
	Spring 1981 session	655	Autumn 1981 session	656		
No. 273/80	*Chile*					
	Eduardo Novoa Monreal					659
	Spring 1981 session	659	Autumn 1981 session	660		
	Spring 1982 session	662				
No. 274/80	*France*					
	Simon Malley					667
	Autumn 1980 session	667	Spring 1981 session	668		
No. 276/80	*El Salvador*					
	Miguel Ángel García et al.					671
	Spring 1981 session	671	Autumn 1981 session	673		
	Spring 1982 session	678	Autumn 1982 session	678		
	Spring 1983 session	687	Autumn 1983 session	688		
	Spring 1984 session	690	Autumn 1984 session	691		
	Spring 1985 session	694	Autumn 1985 session	697		
	Spring 1986 session	701	Autumn 1986 session	704		
	Spring 1987 session	710	Autumn 1987 session	712		
	Spring 1988 session	714	Autumn 1988 session	717		
	Spring 1989 session	720	Autumn 1989 session	722		
	Spring 1990 session	724				
No. 277/80	*Yugoslavia*					
	Vladimir Bonačić et al.					727
	Spring 1981 session	727				
No. 279/80	*Republic of Korea*					
	Kim Chi ha et al.					731
	Spring 1981 session	731				

No. 281/80 *Uruguay*

Julio Castro 733

Autumn 1981 session 733 Autumn 1987 session 736

No. 283/80 *El Salvador*

Arrest and persecution of teachers in El Salvador 739

Spring 1981 session 739 Autumn 1981 session 739

Spring 1982 session 739 Autumn 1982 session 739

Spring 1983 session 740 Autumn 1983 session 740

Spring 1984 session 740 Autumn 1984 session 740

Spring 1985 session 740 Autumn 1985 session 740

Spring 1986 session 740 Autumn 1986 session 741

Spring 1987 session 741 Autumn 1987 session 741

Spring 1988 session 741 Autumn 1988 session 741

Spring 1989 session 741 Autumn 1989 session 741

Spring 1990 session 742

No. 289/80 *Argentina*

Juan Takara 743

Spring 1981 session 743

No. 290/80 *Cuba*

Armando Valladares Pérez 745

Spring 1981 session 745

No. 291/80 *Argentina*

Claudio Nicolás Grandi et al. 749

Spring 1981 session 749

No. 293/80 *Argentina*

Isabel Hernando de Pelloli 751

Spring 1981 session 751

No. 303/80 *Union of Soviet Socialist Republics*

Vladimir Feltsman and Victor Suslin 753

Spring 1981 session 753 Autumn 1981 session 754

No. 305/80 *India*

Govind Prasad 755

Spring 1981 session 755 Autumn 1981 session 756

No. 306/80 *El Salvador*

Arrest and persecution of teachers in El Salvador 759

Spring 1981 session 759 Autumn 1981 session 759

Spring 1982 session 759 Autumn 1982 session 759

Spring 1983 session 759 Autumn 1983 session 760

Spring 1984 session 760 Autumn 1984 session 760

Spring 1985 session 760 Autumn 1985 session 760

Spring 1986 session 760 Autumn 1986 session 760

Spring 1987 session 761 | Autumn 1987 session 761
Spring 1988 session 761 | Autumn 1988 session 761
Spring 1989 session 761 | Autumn 1989 session 761
Spring 1990 session 761

No. 307/80 *Yugoslavia*
Tomislav Krsmanović 763
Spring 1981 session 763

No. 309/80 *United Kingdom*
Dominic de Graft Aidoo 765
Spring 1981 session 765

No. 312/80 *Senegal*
Repression against teachers, active members of the Syndicat unique et démocratique des enseignants du Sénégal 767
Spring 1981 session 767

No. 314/80 *Guinea*
Barry Abdoulaye et al. 769
Spring 1981 session 769

No. 316/80 *Israel*
Tareq Ya'qoub Ashomali 771
Spring 1981 session 771

No. 317/81 *Guatemala*
Alaíde Foppa 773
Spring 1981 session 773 | Autumn 1981 session 775
Autumn 1987 session 777 | Spring 1988 session 778

No. 319/81 *Argentina and Paraguay*
Antonio Maidana 781
Spring 1981 session 781 | Autumn 1981 session 783
Spring 1982 session 785 | Autumn 1982 session 788
Autumn 1987 session 789 | Spring 1988 session 790

No. 321/81 *Chile*
Victor Xavier Tiznado Rosas 791
Spring 1981 session 791 | Autumn 1981 session 792
Spring 1982 session 795 | Autumn 1982 session 798
Spring 1983 session 799 | Autumn 1983 session 801

No. 322/81 *Bolivia*
Violations of human rights in Bolivia following the events of 17 Juky 1980 803
Spring 1981 session 803 | Autumn 1981 session 805
Spring 1982 session 812 | Autumn 1982 session 824
Spring 1983 session 825

No. 323/81 *Chile*
Gracia Barrios Rivadeneira 827
Spring 1981 session 827 Autumn 1981 session 828
Spring 1982 session 829
No. 324/81 *Chile*
José Balmes Parramón 831
Spring 1981 session 831
No. 325/81 *Chile*
Marco Antonio Peña Pérez 833
Spring 1981 session 833 Autumn 1981 session 834
Spring 1982 session 836
No. 327/81 *Chile*
Concepción Balmes 839
Spring 1981 session 839
No. 328/81 *Union of Soviet Socialist Republics*
Georgij Danilovich Parkhomenko 841
Spring 1981 session 841
No. 334/81 *Union of Soviet Socialist Republics*
Mykola Danilovich Rudenko 843
Spring 1981 session 843 Autumn 1981 session 847
Spring 1982 session 850
No. 342/81 *Union of Societ Socialist Republics*
Iosef Samsonovich Irlin 857
Autumn 1981 session 857
No. 345/81 *Union of Societ Socialist Republics*
Yosif Ziselevich Begun 861
Spring 1981 session 861
No. 346/81 *Union of Societ Socialist Republics*
Victor Brailovski 865
Spring 1981 session 865 Autumn 1981 session 865
Spring 1982 session 865 Autumn 1982 session 865
Autumn 1983 session 866 Spring 1984 session 867
No. 347/81 *Guatemala*
Alaíde Foppa 869
Spring 1981 session 869 Autumn 1981 session 869
Autumn 1987 session 869 Spring 1988 session 869
No. 348/81 *Chile*
Jorge Domingo Martínez Quezada and Irma del Carmen Flores Fajardo 871
Autumn 1981 session 871

No. 352/81 *Union of Societ Socialist Republics*
Vasyl Semenovich Stus 873
Autumn 1981 session 873 Spring 1982 session 879
Autumn 1982 session 886
No. 353/81 *Union of Societ Socialist Republics*
Yuli Kosharovsky 893
Spring 1982 session 893 Autumn 1982 session 899
No. 354/81 *Czechoslovakia*
Karel Soukup 903
Autumn 1981 session 903
No. 356/81 *Chile*
Violeta Isabel Cereceda Parra 907
Autumn 1981 session 907 Spring 1982 session 909
Autumn 1982 session 911 Spring 1983 session 913
No. 359/81 *Bolivia*
Jorge Baldibieso et al. 915
Autumn 1981 session 915 Spring 1982 session 915
Autumn 1982 session 915 Spring 1983 session 915
No. 361/81 *Paraguay*
Andrés Centurión et al. 917
Autumn 1981 session 917 Spring 1982 session 919
No. 369/81 *Argentina*
Alberto Horacio Giusti 923
Autumn 1981 session 923
No. 370/81 *Uruguay*
José Luis Massera 925
Spring 1982 session 925 Autumn 1982 session 925
Spring 1983 session 925 Autumn 1983 session 925
Spring 1984 session 926
No. 371/81 *Egypt*
Ahmed Fouad Negm 927
Autumn 1981 session 927 Spring 1982 session 929
No. 372/81 *Argentina*
Antonio Satutto 933
Autumn 1981 session 933
No. 375/81 *Romania*
Constantin Munteanu 935
Spring 1982 session 935
No. 378/81 *Romania*
Religious persecution in Romania 937
Spring 1982 session 937 Autumn 1982 session 945

No. 379/81	*Union of Societ Socialist Republics*					
	Vladimir Feltsman					947
	Autumn 1981 session	947				
No. 381/81	*Uruguay*					
	Raúl Noel Martínez Machado					951
	Spring 1982 session	951				
No. 385/81	*Union of Societ Socialist Republics*					
	Anatoly Koryagin					955
	Autumn 1981 session	955	Spring 1982 session	959		
No. 386/81	*Egypt*					
	Ahmed Fouad Negm					965
	Autumn 1981 session	965	Spring 1982 session	965		
No. 390/81	*El Salvador*					
	Edgar Mauricio Vellejo					967
	Spring 1982 session	967	Autumn 1982 session	967		
	Spring 1983 session	967	Autumn 1983 session	967		
	Spring 1984 session	968	Autumn 1984 session	968		
	Spring 1985 session	968	Autumn 1985 session	968		
	Spring 1986 session	968	Autumn 1986 session	968		
	Spring 1987 session	968	Autumn 1987 session	969		
	Spring 1988 session	969	Autumn 1988 session	969		
	Spring 1989 session	969	Autumn 1989 session	969		
	Spring 1990 session	969				
No. 392/81	*Yugoslavia*					
	Milovan Djilas					971
	Spring 1982 session	971	Autumn 1982 session	975		
	Spring 1983 session	976	Autumn 1983 session	982		
	Spring 1984 session	983	Autumn 1984 session	985		
	Spring 1985 session	987	Autumn 1985 session	989		
	Spring 1986 session	990	Autumn 1986 session	991		
	Spring 1987 session	993				
No. 396/81	*Chile*					
	Jaime Fernando Rovira Soto					997
	Spring 1982 session	997	Autumn 1982 session	999		
	Spring 1983 session	1001	Autumn 1983 session	1003		
No. 397/81	*Bolivia*					
	Violation of human rights in Bolivia					1005
	Autumn 1981 session	1005	Spring 1982 session	1005		
	Autumn 1982 session	1005	Spring 1983 session	1005		

No. 398/81 *Cuba*
Armando Valladares 1007
Spring 1982 session 1007
No. 399/81 *Czechoslovakia*
Rudolf Battěk 1013
Spring 1982 session 1013
No. 403/81 *Chile*
Gloria Pinto de Manríquez 1017
Spring 1982 session 1017 Autumn 1982 session 1019
No. 404/81 *Chile*
Hugo Muñoz 1023
Spring 1982 session 1023
No. 406/81 *Italy*
Luciano Ferrari Bravo 1025
Spring 1982 session 1025
No. 407/81 *Bolivia*
Jorge Baldibieso et al. 1029
Spring 1982 session 1029 Autumn 1982 session 1029
Spring 1983 session 1029
No. 409/81 *Union of Soviet Socialist Republics*
Anatoly Shcharansky 1031
Spring 1982 session 1031 Autumn 1982 session 1034
No. 417/81 *Argentina*
Eduardo Federico Llosa 1037
Spring 1982 session 1037
No. 418/81 *Union of Societ Socialist Republics*
Victor Brailovski 1043
Spring 1982 session 1043 Autumn 1982 session 1043
No. 421/81 *Yugoslavia*
Vlado Gotovac 1045
Spring 1982 session 1045 Autumn 1982 session 1047
Spring 1983 session 1047
No. 422/81 *Argentina*
Mario Jaime Zaraceansky 1049
Spring 1982 session 1049
No. 425/81 *Yugoslavia*
Sabedin Haljiti et al. 1051
Spring 1982 session 1051 Autumn 1982 session 1057
Spring 1983 session 1057

No. 426/81 *Union of Societ Socialist Republics*
Vladimir Borisov 1059
Spring 1982 session 1059
No. 429/81 *Portugal*
Mário Jorge de Graça Estêvão 1061
Spring 1982 session 1061

ANNEXES

I. **104 EX/DECISION 3.3**
Study of the procedures which should be followed in the examination of cases and questions which might be submitted to Unesco concerning the exercise of human rights in the spheres of its competence, in order to make its action more effective: Report of the Working Party of the Executive Board (104 EX/3) 1063

II. **STANDARD LETTER**
Standard letter sent by the Director of the Office of International Standards and Legal Affairs to the authors of communications examined under 104 EX/Decision 3.3 1069

III. **FORM FOR COMMUNICATIONS**
Form for communications concerning human rights to be submitted to UNESCO 1071

IV. **PROCEDURAL PRACTICE**
Procedural Practice of the Committee on Conventions and Recommendations 1075

V. **TABLES OF COMMUNICATIONS**

(*a*) Communications examined under the 104 EX/Decision 3.3 Procedure of the Executive Board filed 1978–1981 (States concerned) 1087

(*b*) Communications examined under the 104 EX/Decision 3.3 Procedure of the Executive Board filed 1978–1981 (Cases) 1095

(*c*) Communications submitted under the 77 EX/Decision 8.3 Procedure of the Executive Board finally examined under the 104 EX/Decision 3.3 Procedure (States concerned) 1103

Foreword

I have great pleasure in welcoming the publication of this collection of communications that the Committee on Conventions and Recommendations of the UNESCO Executive Board (the "Committee") dealt with during the first ten years of its existence, from 1978 to 1988.

UNESCO's Member States established the Committee in 1978 as one of the permanent subsidiary bodies of its Executive Board to enhance the Organization's action in the promotion and protection of human rights within the scope of its mandate. This mandate derives primarily from Article I.1 of UNESCO's Constitution which provides, *inter alia*, that the purpose of the Organization is to "contribute to peace and security by promoting collaboration among the nations through education, science and culture in order to further universal respect [...] for the human rights and fundamental freedoms, which are affirmed for the peoples of the world, without distinction [...] by the Charter of the United Nations".

The Committee is unique among other United Nations entities dealing with the protection of human rights because of its specific nature: it undertakes its action in the spirit of international cooperation, conciliation and mutual understanding. The Executive Board made this clear when it established the Committee's terms of reference in 1978 (104 EX/Decision 3.3), by stating "UNESCO should not play the role of an international judicial body".

Instead, by means of its cooperative and conciliatory action among UNESCO's Member States, the Committee endeavors to improve the situation and alleviating the suffering of individuals whose rights have allegedly been violated, as well as to restore their rights where they have been denied. It thus combines the humanitarian approach with that of human rights protection.

To fulfill its purpose, the Committee examines communications submitted by individuals, groups of individuals or non-governmental organizations concerning cases and questions of violations of human rights falling within UNESCO's fields of competence, namely: the right to education (Article 26 of the Universal Declaration of Human Rights); the right to share in scientific advancement and its benefits (Article 27 of the Universal Declaration of Human Rights); the right freely to participate in the cultural life of the community (Article 27 of the Universal Declaration of Human Rights); the right to information, including freedom of opinion and expression (Article 19 of the Universal Declaration of Human Rights).

One of the main features of the Committee is that it conducts its work through private deliberations and consultations with the concerned governments. The confidentiality of its discussions has thus led to successful results based on practical solutions to individual cases.

Given the confidential nature of its work, as is the case for all documents issued for the private meetings of UNESCO's Executive Board, the communications examined by the Committee can only be accessible 20 years after their examination. The Wallenberg Institute of Human Rights and Humanitarian Law has thus taken the opportunity to make the communications examined during the first decade of the Committee's work publicly available.

The cases presented in this volume give ample examples of the unique features of the Committee and provide a rich and varied picture of the results it has achieved over the period covered by these cases (1978–1988).

I am confident that the opening of the Committee's deliberations and the manner in which it examines the communications and adopts its decisions will be of great interest to scholars, policy-makers, practitioners and students working in the area of human rights protection. I wish to commend the Wallenberg Institute for undertaking this task on the occasion of the fortieth anniversary of the Committee and of the seventieth anniversary of the Universal Declaration of Human Rights, both of which are being celebrated this year.

Audrey Azoulay
Director-General of UNESCO

Introduction

Abdulqawi A. Yusuf and Béatrice Dupuy***

1 Prelude

Forty years ago, the Executive Board of UNESCO adopted by its decision 104 EX/3.3 a new procedure for dealing with communications submitted to the Organization on alleged violations of human rights within the Organization's fields of competence, namely education, science, culture and communication. The examination of these communications was entrusted by the decision to one of the subsidiary organs of the Executive Board, the Committee on Conventions and Recommendations (CR). The procedure, established under that decision, which is simply known as the "104 Procedure" has since then become the principal tool of UNESCO for dealing with complaints related to specific cases involving human rights in the Organization's fields of competence.

To mark the 40th anniversary of this UNESCO human rights procedure, the Raoul Wallenberg Institute of Human Rights and Humanitarian Law took the initiative to publish this book, which for the first time since the establishment of the procedure, will make known to the public the cases examined from 1978 to 1988 by the Executive Board's Committee on Conventions and Recommendations. This initiative, which deserves to be commended and welcomed, coincides also with the 70th anniversary of the Universal Declaration of Human Rights, which is equally being celebrated in UNESCO throughout 2018.

The confidential nature of the UNESCO "104 Procedure" had so far prevented the publication of the specific cases considered by the Committee and the concrete results achieved by it. However, in accordance with Rule 29 of the Rules of Procedure of the Executive Board, which provides that "Private documents shall normally be made accessible to the public after a period of twenty years", and in conformity with the decision taken by the Board in May 2005 which confirmed the application of this Rule to the confidential documents of the Committee, it has now become possible to make the documents of the CR relating to the first ten years of its existence accessible to the public. The fact that the Raoul Wallenberg Institute has taken advantage of this to bring the work of

* President of the International Court of Justice and former Director of the Office of International Standards and Legal Affairs of UNESCO.

** Former Secretary of the Committee on Conventions and Recommendations of UNESCO from 1994 to 2014

 | DOI:10.1163/9789004354036_002

the Committee to a much wider public is both opportune and timely in view of the 40th anniversary of the "104 Procedure" and the need to make better known the activities and achievements of the UNESCO Committee on Conventions and Recommendations on this important aspect of its work.

2 Historical Background

The Constitution of the UNESCO declares in its Article I, as one of the purposes of the Organization,: "to contribute to peace and security by promoting collaboration among the nations through education, science and culture in order **to further universal respect for justice, for the rule of law and for the human rights and fundamental freedoms which are affirmed for the peoples of the world, without distinction of race, sex, language or religion, by the Charter of the United Nations**" (emphasis added). Thus, human rights has been at the heart of UNESCO's mandate since its creation. However, it took the Organization a long time to establish formal procedures for examining specific complaints related to human rights in the fields of its competence.

The UNESCO Executive Board took its first decisions on the need to establish a mechanism for the examination of complaints related to human rights as early as 1952. Noting that communications alleging violations of certain human rights, in particular educational and cultural rights, were being sent to the Organization by private individuals or associations and that no procedure had been defined at UNESCO for taking action on such communications, the Board decided that the Director-General should transmit such complaints to the Chairperson of the Executive Board.[1] The Chairperson thus began to examine these complaints in consultation with other members of the Bureau of the Executive Board and submitted to the Board those complaints which seemed to call for action of some kind. Although it was understood that the Board would review the matter after a short while, the question was not examined further until the 77th session of the Board in 1967 when a new decision, known as "Decision 8.3", was adopted. Statistics prepared at that time showed that a total of 72 complaints had been transmitted between 1960 and 1967 to the Chairperson of the Board. The Bureau of the Board, however, gradually stopped taking note of the communications transmitted to the Chairperson of the Board, who dealt directly with the communications with the support of the Secretariat.

Decision 8.3 established a new procedure for handling communications on individual cases involving human rights and provided that they would be

1 30 EX/Decision 11.

submitted to the Special Committee on Discrimination in Education. The main characteristic of this new procedure was that the Director-General and not the Committee was responsible for deciding whether a communication received fell within the scope of Decision 8.3.

While continuing to implement Decision 8.3, the Committee kept reviewing also a number of questions concerning its procedure and methods of work among which was the length of the period it took to examine the cases, the information to be included in communications and the confidential nature of the discussions within the Committee. As a result of this continuous review, it gradually became clear that improvements needed to be made to this procedure in order to render its action more effective.

The turning point came in 1976, when the General Conference through 19 C/Resolution 6.113 and 19 C/Resolution 12.1 concerning UNESCO's responsibilities in the field of human rights, requested the Director-General "to study the procedures which should be followed in the examination of cases and questions which might be submitted to UNESCO concerning the exercise of human rights in the spheres to which its competence extends, in order to make its action more effective".

Following a preliminary examination of a comprehensive study prepared by the Secretariat at its 102nd session,[2] the Board decided to set up a Working Party to prepare a report "containing suggestions regarding the procedures to be followed in future (proposing several alternatives whenever necessary)".[3] The proposals of the Working Party enabled the Board to adopt, at its 104th session in 1978,[4] the current procedure laid down in 104 EX/Decision 3.3 under which examination of communications is entrusted to the Executive Board's Committee on Conventions and Recommendations.

However, the Board did not formally decide, at the time, to abolish the earlier procedure laid down by 77 EX/Decision 8.3.

Therefore, despite the introduction of the 104 Procedure, the procedure laid down in 77 EX/Decision 8.3 continued to be applied to communications still pending before the Committee until the 108th session (September 1979) at which time the Committee decided to examine all the 10 outstanding communications concerning 4 countries under the new procedure, thus doing away with the previous procedure.

---

2 Document 102 EX/19.

3 102 EX/Decision 5.6.2.

4 Among the members of the Working Party were Professors T. Buergenthal (United States of America) and N. Karthashkin (Russian Federation), and Mr Paulo E. de Berrêdo Carneiro (Brazil). It must be noted that Karel Vasak, then Director of the Division of human rights and of peace, played a decisive role in the establishment of this procedure.

3 The Distinctive Features of Procedure 104

In establishing the 104 Procedure, the Board laid down in its decision certain principles that had to be observed in the implementation of the procedure and in the examination of communications submitted to the Committee. First and foremost among these principles is the one enunciated in paragraph 7 of the decision which states that "UNESCO, basing its efforts on moral considerations and its specific competence, should act in a spirit of international cooperation, conciliation and mutual understanding". A second principle of equal importance is contained in paragraph 8 of the decision which recognizes the important role of the Director-General in "initiating consultations, in conditions of mutual respect, confidence and confidentiality, to help reach solutions to particular problems concerning human rights". These principles continue to inform and inspire the work of the Committee on Conventions and Recommendations in carrying out its mandate concerning communications on alleged violations of human rights in UNESCO's fields of competence. They also underlie the distinctive features of the procedure which have been developed over the years both through practice as well as through the implementation of these principles.

3.1 *Cooperation, Dialogue and Conciliation*

The Committee endeavours to deal with communications submitted to it through confidential exchange of views with the representatives of the governments concerned by the complaints. The individual cases are discussed among government representatives, in the presence of a representative of the concerned country, in a spirit of mutual cooperation, dialogue and reconciliation. As stated in paragraph 7 of the decision establishing the 104 Procedure, the Committee does not "play the role of an international judicial body". It does not therefore have the authority to condemn the governments concerned for violation of human rights nor to sanction them. Its decisions are neither of an accusatory nature nor are they meant to determine whether a violation of human rights has occurred. They are mainly geared towards finding a concrete solution to the problem and providing a relief to the victim. As paragraph 7 of 104 EX/Decision 3.3 specifies, UNESCO's efforts in dealing with human rights are based on "moral considerations and its specific competence". The Committee members often recall that the main thrust of the procedure is purely for humanitarian reasons and that the Committee considers with the governments concerned what might be done to improve the lot or at least minimize the ordeals of the victims and to find a satisfactory solution to their problems.

Therefore, the Committee mainly relies on dialogue with the governments concerned and uses its persuasive powers and discreet diplomatic approach to convince them to resolve the issues raised in the communications. Its role may therefore be characterized as consisting of fact-finding, mediation and conciliation in issues concerning human rights in the fields of competence of UNESCO.

3.2 *The Quest for a Satisfactory Solution*

The quest for a satisfactory solution generally implies that the Committee may examine a case during several sessions and defer its consideration until it receives additional information, as part of its fact-finding mission, or obtains a positive response from the government concerned resulting in the resolution of the case. The continuous consideration of the case by the Committee until a positive solution is found constitutes some sort of peer pressure on the government concerned whose representatives to UNESCO will continue to be invited to appear before the Committee to discuss the case and to engage in a dialogue with its members. It may also provide additional time and fresh opportunities to the concerned governments to find a satisfactory solution to the problem.

The search for a satisfactory solution is not limited only to the dialogue between the Committee and the representatives of the governments concerned, but it also includes the authors of the communications who have to keep the Committee informed of all developments concerning the case. Both in the phase of examination of the communication as to its admissibility, as well as in the phase of its examination as to its merits, the fact-finding mission of the Committee is facilitated by constant dialogue and correspondence with the author of the communication and with the government concerned. This enables the Committee to take decisions in light of the current status and evolution of the case and to keep abreast of all developments concerning it through different channels of information. It also provides an opportunity for the Committee, pending a satisfactory settlement of the case, to try to ameliorate the situation of the victims through humanitarian appeals.

Therefore, the Committee usually makes appeals for clemency to the authorities concerned, or tries to obtain from the government concerned the improvement of the conditions of confinement of the victim, or expresses to the government concerned its deep concern regarding the state of health of the victim and requests it to allow him to receive appropriate medical treatment. The Committee may also sometimes consider, that given the limited information available or lack of information on the communication, direct contacts on the ground may help to make progress towards the satisfactory settlement of the case. In such situations, it may recommend sending a mission to the country with the concurrence of the authorities.

The fact of remaining seized of the communication, once it is admitted for examination as to its merit, and until such time as a satisfactory solution is achieved, distinguishes the UNESCO 104 Procedure from those of other UN bodies and makes this continuous dialogue with the government concerned and the author of the communication one of its most original characteristics.

3.3 *Voluntary Cooperation of the States Concerned*

The UNESCO 104 Procedure was conceived as a cooperative procedure, agreed among all the Member States of the Organization, on a voluntary non-binding manner. It is not a treaty-based procedure, but a decision adopted by the Executive Board of UNESCO at the behest and with the support of the General Conference of the Organization where all Member States are represented. It therefore enjoys the approval of all Member States, and such approval does not have to be obtained each time a communication concerning a Member State has to be examined by the Committee. As such, it may be considered as a consensual instrument created to monitor the observance of human rights lying within the field of competence of UNESCO, namely the right to education, the right to benefit from scientific progress, the right to participate freely in cultural life, and the right to information, including freedom of opinion and expression.

Thus, under the 104 Procedure a complaint may be made against a Member State precisely because it is a Member of UNESCO that has voluntarily accepted and approved the terms of the procedure. The voluntary cooperation of the government concerned is therefore presumed and is most often provided to the Committee once a communication is submitted. The success of the work of the Committee depends entirely on this voluntary cooperation by the State concerned by the communication. The government of the State concerned is therefore always invited to send a representative to the Committee in order to address the CR, reply to the allegations made by the author of the communication and engage in a dialogue with members of the Committee. The Committee itself does not question the information provided by the government, but invites the author of the communication to provide comments in a confidential manner. If an author of a communication brings to the attention of the Committee information, which contradicts that provided by the government, the members of the Committee have the right to raise these contradictions with the representative of the government within the framework of the confidentiality afforded by the procedure. Since this kind of frank dialogue and cooperation with the government concerned can only be obtained thanks to the confidentiality of the meetings, including the deliberations and documents of the Committee, the meetings of the Committee are closed to the public and the media, and its documents are solely distributed to its members. There is also a long-standing practice in the Executive Board that Member States of the Board, not members of the Committee, should refrain from attending its meetings as observers. In any case, the documents of the Committee are not provided to such Member States of the Board.

3.4 *Confidentiality of the Procedure*

Confidentiality is a cornerstone of the Committee's work. It is also one of the most important contributing factors to its effectiveness. This was well understood by the drafters of 104 Procedure. Indeed, it appears that consensus over the necessity of preserving confidentiality made it possible for the conflicting views, tendencies and interests of the Member States of the Executive Board to be accommodated at the stage of the preparatory work which eventually led to the adoption of 104 EX/Decision 3.3 unopposed. Thanks to this confidentiality, the various actors – the author of the communication, the government concerned and the Committee – can engage in a frank and comprehensive dialogue and exchange views on the facts of the case as well as possible solutions to it without public exposure. It also allows the Committee to negotiate a satisfactory outcome to the case with the government concerned in a confidential manner without the Committee or the author of the communication being able to claim publicly credit for it.

There is no doubt that due to its confidentiality, the 104 Procedure has proven to become very effective and to secure an almost general acceptance.[5] It also underpins the wide-spread recognition by all Member States of UNESCO of the moral authority of the Committee. Many government representatives would have either declined to appear before the Committee or been less forthcoming in providing information to it and exchanging views with it on a specific case, if it were not for the confidential nature of the procedure. In view of the confidentiality of the procedure, the Committee meets strictly *in camera* and the members are expected to respect, and have always respected, the confidential nature of the information submitted to the Committee. However, in some exceptional situations, the Committee may decide to ask the Executive Board to examine a communication in a public meeting, in particular when the dialogue with the authorities of the State concerned has been unsatisfactory. Until now, this decision was taken only with respect to communications concerning two Member States.

5 P.M. Eisemann, *Quelques observations sur une procédure discrète de promotion des droits de l'homme: la « procédure 104 » de l'UNESCO*, in "L'homme dans la société internationale, Mélanges en hommage au Professeur Paul Tavernier", ed. Jean-François Akandji-Kombé, Bruylant, 2013, pp. 707–732; K.J. Partsch and K. Hüfner, "UNESCO Procedures for the Protection of Human Rights", in *Human Rights: International Protection, Monitoring Enforcement*, Ashgate & UNESCO, 2003; M. Paszkowski, "Evocation of An "Unknown" Procedure concerning Human Rights Protection by UNESCO", in "Karel Vasak *Amicorum Liber, Human Rights at the Dawn of the Twenty-First Century*", p. 713, Bruylant, 1999.

3.5 *A Non-confrontational Procedure*

Another specific advantage of the procedure that should be noted is the regular communication between the author of the communication and the government concerned, through the Committee and the Secretariat, thus creating an indirect dialogue in which information is exchanged on the case in a confidential and non-confrontational manner. This process affords both parties to comment on each others views through the Committee, thus strengthening the role of mediation of the Committee which ensures confidentiality to the entire process. Should the author of a communication violate this confidential exchange of information, it is the practice of the Committee to strike the communication from its roster.

Even if the Committee never invites the author of a communication to appear before it, the latter is first informed that the form containing the communication sent to the Secretariat was submitted to the government concerned and to all the members of the Committee, with explicit mention of the identity of the author and the victim. Then the author is informed of the decision taken by the Committee after each session of the CR by a letter from the Secretariat. To ensure the effectiveness of the procedure, it is essential that the author submits his or her views on the declarations made by the representative of the government during the CR session, replies to the requests from the Committee for further information, and keeps it informed of relevant developments in the situation of the victim. The authors particularly appreciate this possibility of constant communication and exchange of information through the Committee which does not exist in the other procedures of the United Nations system.

In the same way, any additional information received from the author and the decision taken by the Committee and its report are transmitted to the government concerned so that it can put forward its point of view and make its comments and engage in a dialogue with the Committee, which meets for this purpose twice a year. As long as the case is not solved, the State is considered accountable to the Committee on the case under examination, and is expected to expose the measures taken by its government for action on the requests by the Committee which could, as we have seen, launch humanitarian appeals and call for a satisfactory solution to the problem.

4 Achievements

The effectiveness of the 104 Procedure and its unique approach to the consideration of alleged violations of human rights in the fields of competence of UNESCO is shown by the relatively high number of cases which have found a satisfactory resolution. The results obtained by the Committee over the years are indeed encouraging and testify to the appropriateness and efficiency of its methods of work.

4.1 *A Wide Spectrum of Cases Considered and Resolved*

The Committee has so far examined more than 600 communications in the fields of competence of UNESCO. Those that have been effectively settled concern a variety of cases such as the following:

- Cases concerning the release of teachers, students, scientists, researchers, artists, writers and journalists.
- Cases concerning the authorization to leave the State in question to study abroad.
- Cases concerning the reinstatement of professors who had previously been prevented to teach; and cases concerning persons belonging to minorities who were not allowed to have education in their own language, or situations where schools were closed by the government, whereby teachers were dismissed.
- Cases concerning the possibility of resuming the publication of a prohibited publication or broadcast or the authorization to publish again, and cases of journalists and writers whose publications were banned for so-called "security reasons".
- Cases concerning the possibility to leave or to return to one's own country or to resume an employment after imprisonment or to resume the exercise of professional activities.
- Cases concerning procedures for admission to universities considered to discriminate against certain minorities.

4.2 *An Effective Delivery of Results Over the Years*

The Committee has successfully resolved most of the cases submitted to it over the thirty years of its existence. From 1978 until 2017, the Committee has examined 602 communications in over 85 countries,[6] of which 400 were considered settled; while the 202 remaining cases concern communications that were either considered inadmissible or whose examination has been suspended or is still under way. The results concerning alleged victims or groups of alleged victims may be broken down as follows:

---

6 On the basis of the composition of UNESCO's electoral groups, the repartition of Member States concerned by communications is the following: Group I (Western States): 15 countries – Group II (States of Eastern Europe): 12 – Group III (Latin America and the Caribbean): 15 – Group IV (Asia and the Pacific): 16 – Group V (a) (African States): 15 – Group V (b) (Arab States): 12.

	1978–1988	1989–2017	Total
released before completion of sentence	99	132	231
authorized to leave their country to go to study or teach	20	1	21
authorized to return to their country	33	2	35
able to resume their employment or activity falling within UNESCO's fields of competence	20	10	30
able to resume a banned publication or broadcast programme	6	8	14
able to resume normal life following a cessation of threats	2	3	5
able to benefit from changes in certain education laws which were discriminatory towards ethnic or religious minorities	3	13	16
able to obtain passports and/or grants, or to receive diplomas	4	8	12
able to resume studies	1	8	9

It is to be noted that during the period 1978–1988, the Committee received a lot of communications relating to the enforced or involuntary disappearance of persons. At its 108th session,[7] it decided as follows:

> "In the case of communications, declared admissible, concerning enforced or involuntary disappearance of persons as a result of action imputed to law enforcement authorities or similar organizations, whether or not it is established that such persons were, or were not, deprived of freedom at the time of their disappearance, if the Committee has not obtained sufficient information about the fate of the missing persons from the governments concerned, the Committee agrees, without prejudice to the important role of the Director-General mentioned in paragraph of 104 EX/Decision 3.3:
>
> (a) to keep such communications on the list of communications pending which is held by the Secretariat;

7 108 EX/38 PRIV., pp. 2–3, para. 11 et Seq.

(b) to request the governments concerned to devote appropriate resources to searching for such persons, in accordance with the recommendations made to them by the General Assembly in its resolution 33/173, and to keep UNESCO informed of any new development concerning each case of disappearance which is brought to the attention of the organization;

(c) to place these communications once more on its agenda when additional information is sent to UNESCO by the governments concerned, the authors of the communications, the family and friends of the missing persons or the competent humanitarian organizations, and in any case to do so every year at one of its sessions".

At the 109th session, after the United Nations Commission on Human Rights had set up a working group to examine the enforced or involuntary disappearance of persons,[8] the Committee decided to ask the Director-General "to bring to the attention of the United Nations working group the communications to which the Committee had decided to apply the special procedure on missing persons and of all other outstanding communications concerning alleged cases of enforced or involuntary disappearances. It was agreed that, without relinquishing its competence over the different communications concerned, the Committee would defer examination of them for a period of one year, i.e. while the working group was sitting, with the exception of those communications concerning disappearances said to have occurred within the last two years, and that it would subsequently examine them in the light of the deliberations of the said working group. In these exceptional cases, the Committee has been always kept informed of the progress made by the working group of the Commission on Human Rights in examining questions of disappearances".[9]

Even in these difficult cases, the action of UNESCO has shown that it is possible to obtain concrete results thanks to dialogue undertaken with Member States in a spirit of international co-operation, conciliation and mutual understanding.

---

8 On 29 February 1980, the United Nations Commission on Human Rights adopted resolution 20 (XXXVI) relating to the question of missing and disappeared persons. That resolution provided for the establishment of a working group consisting of five members, to serve as experts in their individual capacities, "to examine questions relevant to enforced or involuntary disappearances of persons". Resolution 20 (XXXVI) stipulated, inter alia, that "the working group, in carrying out its mandate, shall seek and receive information from governments, intergovernmental organizations, humanitarian organizations and other reliable sources".

5 Attempts at Reform

For the past 40 years, several attempts to reform the procedure were considered. The first one was in 1985, when the General Conference asked the Executive Board to conduct an evaluation of the procedure and, if necessary, to review it in the light of the results achieved and the experience gained. The long debates that followed this resolution did not result in the modification of either the procedure or of the terms of reference of the Committee.

Then, in 1993, the Committee members proposed to change the name of the Committee in order to render more explicit the Committee's concern with human rights. For historical reasons, the Committee's name does not in any way indicate that it deals with human rights issues. Indeed, the original mandate of the Committee was the monitoring of the implementation of various UNESCO's standard-setting instruments. This still continues to be part of the mandate of the Committee, to which the 104 Procedure had been added as the second aspect of its work. Several possible formulations were proposed that would highlight the Committee's two tasks, i.e. the monitoring of the implementation of standard-setting instruments and the examination of communications alleging violations of human rights. However, none of them met with enough support to lead to an actual change of name.

On the other hand, certain improvements have been made over the years to the methods of work of the Committee.[10] These concern, among others, the presentation of working documents, the formulation of the decisions of the Committee, decision-making on the admissibility of communications, dealing with the lack of cooperation on the part of the government concerned, the opportunity to create a mechanism for taking action in case of extreme urgency in between Board sessions, and making the Committee's existence better known. Most recently, the Committee has introduced further improvements to its methods of work regarding the selection of communications, the application of criteria for admissibility, the management of speaking time allotted to the various speakers, the cooperation between the Committee and other UN human rights bodies, the role of the Director-General and the role of the Chairperson of the Committee.[11]

---

9 109 EX/52 PRIV., Annex I, pp. 1–2.

10 See document 204 EX/CR/2, Procedural Practice of the Committee reproduced in this book: Volume 2, Annex 2.

11 See document 156 EX/52, para. 9–10, document 171 EX/61, para. 16–18, document 185 EX/49, para. 3–5, document 196 EX/36, para. 4–18, and see also document 204 EX/CR/2 reproduced in this book.

6 Conclusion

It is not easy to cover in an introduction such as this one the life and work of the UNESCO Committee on conventions and recommendations. This would require a book by itself in view of the richness of its activities, the uniqueness' of its approach and its methods of work, and the importance of its achievements. It is however hoped that all these characteristics will come through in a more concrete manner through the cases presented in this book which cover the first ten years of the existence of the Committee. A perusal of these cases will hopefully provide a better and more comprehensive picture of how the Committee functions and how it approaches its unique task of providing solutions to human rights issues falling within the fields of competence of UNESCO in a cooperative manner and through a sustained dialogue with the authors of communications and the governments concerned. This is indeed the best way to make the work and the achievements of the Committee and its 104 Procedure better known to a much wider public.

Acknowledgement

In the present publication, cases of the UNESCO Committee on Conventions and Recommendations are made easily accessible to the public for the first time ever. By 1988, the 104 EX/Decision 3.3 procedure of the Executive Board had been in operation for 10 years. In 2008, in accordance with the 20-year confidentiality rule of procedure that is binding on the Committee, it seemed appropriate to publish the cases filed during the first 10 years of the new procedure and thereby to give prominence to the achievements of the Committee in the promotion and protection of human rights in UNESCO's fields of competence. In 2008, the 60th anniversary of the Universal Declaration of Human rights was also commemorated. However, the task of compiling, editing and making ready for publication these cases was in fact far more complex and time-consuming than could have been expected. Regrettably, the project has been considerably delayed.

Originally the intention was to publish all communications examined by the Committee under the 104 EX/Decision 3.3 procedure, filed in the years 1978 to 1988, in a single volume. However, it transpired that this was difficult to achieve, because the sessional reports of the Committee were so extensive that the cases had to be compiled in two volumes. Consequently, communications filed in 1978 to 1981 are published in the present volume and those filed in 1982 to 1988 in a companion volume. However, only communications that have reached the stage of being presented to the Committee for examination, and thus are reported cases, have been included. Altogether 357 communications are included in the two volumes.

The communications are arranged in chronological order under their respective communication No. and with all relevant texts presented sesion by session or with reference to other communications. The aim of the editor was to give a correct, consistent and user-friendly presentation of the cases considered by the Committee. To that end obvious typing errors and inconsistencies have been corrected, including those concerning names of persons and places. Other amendments in the text have been placed between square brackets. Reference to documents in the text has been placed in footnotes, normally only where it is made for the first time. Finally, the Organization's old acronym – UNESCO – has been kept when used in the original text. Annexed are tables of communications arranged under "States concerned" and "Cases", respectively. In the present volume, there is also a table related to communications submitted under the 77 EX/Decision 8.3 procedure of the Executive Board finally examined under the 104 EX/Decision 3.3 procedure. Those communications fall outside the scope of this publication.

Annexed to the present volume are also some basic texts with relevant background information: the text of 104 EX/Decision 3.3 approved by the Executive Board on 26 April 1978; the standard letter sent by the Director of International Standards and Legal Affairs to the authors of communications; the form for communications; and the procedural practice of the Committee. The three latter texts are reproduced from a UNESCO document submitted in 2018.

I am grateful for the generous support of the UNESCO Office of International Standards and Legal Affairs, without which this project could not have been successfully carried out. I have had free access to all relevant documents. Mr Abdulqawi A. Yusuf, President of the International Court of Justice and Former Director of the Office, and Ms Béatrice Dupuy, Former Secretary of the Committee, have given me invaluable advice and encouragement. They have also contributed to the present volume with an informative introduction to the 104 EX/ Decision 3.3 procedure and the work of the Committee in dealing with communications submitted under that procedure. Furthermore, I wish to extend my sincere thanks to Ms Audrey Azoulay, the Director-General of UNESCO for her kind foreword to the present publication. Finally, I wish to acknowledge Ms Linda Hiltmann for her dedicated work as research assistant in the project, funded by a grant from UNESCO.

Leif Holmström

former Director of the Raoul Wallenberg Institute
of Human Rights and Humanitarian Law

UNESCO
COMMITTEE ON CONVENTIONS AND RECOMMENDATIONS

Communications

**Examined under the 104 EX/Decision 3.3
Procedure of the Executive Board
filed 1978-1981**

No. 2/78

Concerning *Romania*
Case of *Transylvanian populations in Romania*

Communication of 2 May 1978 submitted by
Joseph Szén and Kálmán Domotor

Spring 1979 session of the Committee on Conventions and Recommendations (107th session of the Executive Board)[1]

145. This communication concerns the situation of certain national groups living in Romania whose rights in the fields of education, science, culture and communication are alleged to have been violated as a result of a policy of discrimination on linguistic grounds.

146. The Director of the Division of Human Rights and Peace said that the memorandum containing the essentials of the allegations made in this communication had been prepared by the "European Committee for the Protection of Human Rights in Romania" for the Meeting of representatives of States which had taken part in the Conference on Security and Co-operation in Europe, held in Belgrade (October 1977 - March 1978).

147. The representative of the Romanian Government put the position of his government, which is stated in a written document sent to Unesco with a letter dated 23 April 1979 from [the] acting Permanent Delegate to Unesco of the Socialist Republic of Romania [...].[2] He particularly drew to the Committee's attention the fact that the author of the communication, having no connection with Romania could not have any reliable knowledge of the situation obtaining there. It was, furthermore, the opinion of the Romanian Government that the communication offered no shred of evidence for the allegations that it contained and did not indicate whether domestic remedies had been used. The memorandum on which the communication was based

[1] See document 107 EX/PRIV.31, paras. 145-149; see also documents 107 EX/CR/PROC. HR/1 and Annex.
[2] See document 107 EX/CR/PROC.HR/1 Annex.

drew all its material from articles disseminated through the media. It was also in flagrant contradiction with the principles of the Charter of the United Nations, in that it called into question the territorial integrity and the inviolability of the frontiers of a State. In conclusion, the representative of the government concerned requested that the communication be declared inadmissible because it did not comply with the conditions listed in paragraph 14 (*a*) (ii), (v) and (ix) of 104 EX/Decision 3.3.

148. Several members of the Committee expressed their satisfaction with the reply of the Romanian Government and proposed that the communication should be declared inadmissible. In addition to the conditions of admissibility that the representative of the Romanian Government had indicated were not met, one member of the Committee considered that the communication lacked moderation in that its language was offensive.

149. The Committee *decided*, following discussion, to declare the communication inadmissible.

No. 10/78

Concerning *Uruguay*
Case of *Armando Germinal González Ferrando*

Communication of 5 April 1978 submitted by
Armando Germinal González Ferrando

Spring 1979 session of the Committee on Conventions and Recommendations (107th session of the Executive Board)[1]

168. The author of this communication is a Uruguayan sculptor who complains of having been arrested arbitrarily and tortured, of having been debarred from the ceremony for the unveiling of a monumental statue of the national hero which he had spent 15 years making, and of having undergone other harassment before being able to leave the country.

169. The representative of the Government of Uruguay indicated to the Committee, both orally and in his letter of 19 April 1979 [...][2] that any allegation concerning physical ill-treatment was rejected by his government and that the name of the person concerned had not been passed over as creator of the statue of José Artigas.

170. Given that the matters alleged by the author of the communication did not clearly seem to fall within the fields of competence of Unesco and that they dated back a considerable time, the Committee *decided* to declare the communication inadmissible.

---

[1] See document 107 EX/PRIV.31, paras. 168-170; see also documents 107 EX/CR/PROC. HR/2 and Annex.
[2] See document 107 EX/CR/PROC.HR/2 Annex.

No. 11/78

Concerning *Argentina*
Case of *María Ernestina Giachetti*

Communication of 17 May 1978 submitted by
María Antonia González de Giachetti

Spring 1979 session of the Committee on Conventions and Recommendations (107th session of the Executive Board)[1]

64. The communication concerns the disappearance of the daughter, aged 28, of the author of the communication, on 6 May 1978 in the centre of Buenos Aires. The representative of the government.concerned, emphasized - as he had already done in his letter of 18 April 1979 to the Director of the Division of Human Rights and Peace [...][2] - the fact that the profession, activity and status of the alleged victim did not fall within Unesco's fields of competence.

65. It was noted in this connection that the author of the communication had not answered the question contained in the communication form which concerned the connection between the alleged violation and the Organization's fields of competence. Some Committee members expressed the opinion that the communication should therefore not be deemed admissible, whereas other members felt that the author of the communication should have an opportunity to bring to the attention of the Committee information which would enable it to determine whether there was any connection between the alleged violation and the Organization's fields of competence. Several Committee members noted that in cases like these the Secretariat should make greater efforts to obtain the information the Committee required in order to decide on the admissibility of communications.

66. It was also noted during the discussion that, when the author of a communication was informed that the communication was not admissible because it did not meet the

[1] See document 107 EX/PRIV.31, paras. 64-67; see also documents 107 EX/CR/PROC.HR/3 and Annex.
[2] See document 107 EX/CR/PROC.HR/3 Annex.

condition stipulated in paragraph 14 (*a*) (iii) of 104 EX/Decision 3.3, he was entitled to address another communication to the Secretariat containing the information that was lacking.

67. Taking these considerations into account, the Committee *decided* that the communication was inadmissible because it showed no evidence of any connection between the alleged violation and the fields of Unesco's competence. A few members of the Committee said that a decision against admissibility in this particular case should not be considered as a precedent binding on the Committee.

No. 12/78

Concerning *Israel*
Case of *Abdul Jawad Saleh - Palestinian Human Rights Committee for the Defence of War and Political Prisoners* [*]

Communication of 2 June 1978 submitted by
Abdul Jawad Saleh

Spring 1979 session of the Committee on Conventions and Recommendations (107th session of the Executive Board)[1]

138. The author of this communication, who is Head of the Palestinian Human Rights Committee for the Defence of War and Political Prisoners and a member of the PLO's Executive Committee, alleges the violation by the State of Israel and the military authorities in the occupied territories of human rights, including those in the fields of education and culture. The above-mentioned Committee had sent the Secretariat several packets of documents which the latter had briefly summarized, including more especially those points which seemed at first sight to come within the Committee's terms of reference. The whole file was made available by the Secretariat, to the members of the Committee who were able to consult the various documents in it.

139. The representative of the Government of Israel reiterated his government's position as set out in its letters of 27 December 1978 and 23 February 1979, stressing that [this communication] did not concern violations of human rights coming within Unesco's competence, and, to the extent that it emanated from an organization publicly committed to the destruction of a Member State of Unesco, that it was motivat-

[*] Alternatively, this communication was being referred to as case of *Abdul Jawad Saleh, Palestinian Human Rights Committee for the Defence of War and Political Prisoners*. From the Committee's spring 1988 session, it was being referred to as case of *Violations of human rights in the fields of education, science, culture and information in the Arab territories occupied by Israel* and from its autumn 1989 session as case of *Violations of human rights in the fields of education, science, culture and information in the occupied territories*.

[1] See document 107 EX/PRIV.31, paras. 138-144; see also document 107 EX/CR/PROC. HR/31.

ed exclusively by political considerations and did not, therefore, comply with the condition of admissibility laid down in paragraph 14 (*a*) (iii) of 104 EX/Decision 3. 3. Moreover, his government rejected as wholly unjustified and without foundation the allegation of violations of human rights. He therefore requested the Committee to declare the communication inadmissible.

140. One member of the Committee pointed out that the author of the communication had submitted it as "Head of the Palestinian Human Rights Committee for the Defence of War and Political Prisoners", as an alleged victim and as the representative of other alleged victims, and that in any case, the Palestine Liberation Organization, as the only legitimate representative of the Palestinian people, was fully qualified to submit such a communication.

141. The same member considered that the communication merited the Committee's attention, and regretted that the Secretariat had not been able to reproduce the details contained in the documentation submitted by its author. The Director of the Division of Human Rights and Peace pointed out that none of the information contained in the hundred pages of documentation received by the Secretariat had been prepared with a view to its submission to Unesco, and that the Secretariat had listed the items of information contained in the documents to enable the Committee to reach a decision on the admissibility of the communication. He considered that there was no doubt that the communication was admissible and in conclusion proposed that the Committee, in accordance with Rule 29 of the Rules of Procedure of the Executive Board should ask the author of the communication to appear before it to present his evidence.

142. Another member of the Committee considered that the information given by the Secretariat in paragraphs 4 and 6 of the summary [...][2] was sufficient for the Committee to be able to declare the communication admissible.

143. Another member of the Committee was of the opinion that if individual cases were at issue, the purpose of the communication was not clear.

144. Recalling that several members had expressed the wish for more detailed information on the facts alleged in the documentation supplied by the author of the communication, the Chairman proposed and the Committee *decided* to suspend examination of the admissibility of this communication pending the preparation by the Secretariat of a fuller summary of the allegations on the basis of information which should be requested of the author of the communication and submitted first to the government concerned. One member of the Committee wished to emphasize that he

---

[2] See document 107 EX/CR/PROC.HR/31.

had only very regretfully subscribed to the consensus since, in his view, there was no doubt about the admissibility of the communication.

Autumn 1979 session of the Committee on Conventions and Recommendations (108th session of the Executive Board)[3]

170. The author of the communication, "Head of the Palestinian Human Rights Committee for the Defence of War and Political Prisoners" and member of the Executive Committee of the PLO, alleges the violation of human rights in the fields of education, science, culture and communication, claimed to have been committed in the territories occupied by the State of Israel.

171. The Director of the Division of Human Rights and Peace recalled that at its [spring 1979] session the Committee had decided to defer consideration of the admissibility of that communication until the Secretariat had prepared a fuller summary of the allegations, on the basis of the data which were to be requested from the author of the communication and submitted beforehand to the government concerned [...].[4] He informed the Committee that, to date, the author of the communication had not supplied the information requested, but had sent to the Secretariat several new documents concerning his communication. The whole collection currently amounted to 65 documents, totalling some 490 pages, which had been summarized by the Secretariat. That summary, distributed to the Committee [...],[5] had been communicated to the government concerned and to the author of the communication. The latter had endorsed the summary in question and had designated the observer of the PLO to Unesco as his representative for the continuation of the procedure in connection with that communication.

172. The representative of the government concerned reiterated the position of her government concerning the communication, a position which had been described to the Committee at its [spring 1979] session, and also in the letter from the Permanent Delegate of Israel, dated 10 September 1979 [...].[6] According to her government, the communication did not concern violations of human rights falling within Unesco's spheres of competence, and, inasmuch as it originated from an organization publicly committed to the destruction of a Member State of Unesco, the communication was motivated solely by considerations of a political nature, and did not, therefore, comply with the condition of admissibility laid down in paragraph 14 (*a*) (iii) of 104 EX/

[3] See document 108 EX/38 PRIV., paras. 170-177; see also documents 108 EX/CR/PROC. HR/1 and Add.3 and 9.
[4] See document 107 EX/PRIV.31, para. 144 (*supra*, pp. 10-11).
[5] See document 108 EX/CR/PROC.HR/1 Add.3.
[6] See document 108 EX/CR/PROC.HR/1 Add.9.

Decision 3.3. She stated in that connection that the author of the communication was a member of the Executive Committee of the Palestine Liberation Organization (PLO) and that the Committee on behalf of which he had approached Unesco was also a member of the PLO. In support of those statements she quoted Articles 6, 15 and 19 of the PLO Charter.

173. She also stressed that Unesco had sent a special mission to investigate the situation of education, science and culture in the territories in question and that the report of that mission would be submitted to the Executive Board; consequently, she suggested that the Committee should not decide on the communication's admissibility before being informed of the opinion of the Executive Board on the findings of that mission. She drew the Committee's attention to the fact that co-operation between her government and the mission was assured. She considered, finally, that the communication formed part of the weapons of the political war being waged against her country.

174. A member of the Committee expressed the view that the government concerned had not produced any new information, and considered that the communication was admissible because the documents submitted by the author, as summarized by the Secretariat, seemed to indicate, firstly, that human rights belonging to Unesco's spheres of competence had indeed been violated in the case in question. In that connection he mentioned several examples of facts analysed in the communication. He added that, with regard to massive, systematic and flagrant violations resulting from a policy of aggression, occupation and racialism, the Committee should consider that the communication concerned a "question" in the sense of paragraph 18 of 104 EX/Decision 3.3. With regard to the mission that had travelled to the occupied territories, he considered that it had no bearing on the terms of reference of the Committee, whose task was to examine individual communications relating to violations of human rights.

175. Regarding the capacity of the author of the communication, several members of the Committee pointed out that the PLO enjoyed the status of an observer with Unesco and other international organizations, and that, at any rate, the author also claimed to be a victim and to be a person with reliable knowledge of the alleged violations. Some members of the Committee took the view that the political affiliation of the author acting in that capacity did not affect the admissibility of the communication. One member considered that, since the author had not supplied the information that the Secretariat had requested of him, the Committee should wait for further clarifications before taking a decision on the admissibility of the communication. He drew the Committee's attention to the fact that many documents provided by the author had no connection with Unesco, and that others were manifestly ill-founded; a number of documents, on the other hand, contained serious allegations, and it was

for that reason that the author should supply the information which the Committee had considered necessary at its [spring 1979] session. Another member stated that those parts of the communication which did not belong to Unesco's spheres of competence could be eliminated from it, as had been done in the case of [another communication].[7]

176. One Committee member expressed doubts on the admissibility of the communication, and thought that there was a risk of duplication between the Committee and the Executive Board. Another member, while noting that the communication had political overtones, recalled that paragraph 14 (*a*) (iii) of 104 EX/Decision 3.3 excluded only communications "motivated exclusively by other considerations" (than considerations relating to respect for human rights). Another member stated that it was difficult to disregard the political aspect of the communication, particularly since the objection raised by the government concerned was, precisely, to the political affiliation of the author.

177. After discussion, and at the Chairman's suggestion, the Committee *decided* to declare the communication admissible, with the reservation that the Secretariat should be instructed, in collaboration with the author, to review the communication in order to eliminate from it any component which did not fall within Unesco's spheres of competence, and to ensure that the communication came within the context of 104 EX/Decision 3.3.

Spring 1980 session of the Committee on Conventions and Recommendations (109th session of the Executive Board)[8]

261. In this communication, the author, who was the Head of the Palestinian Human Rights Committee for the Defence of War and Political Prisoners as well as a member of the Executive Committee of the PLO, alleged the violation of human rights in the fields of education, science, culture and information by the State of Israel in the occupied territories.

262. At its [autumn 1979] session, the Committee had decided to declare the communication admissible, with the reservation that the Secretariat should be instructed, in collaboration with the author, to review the communication in order to eliminete from it any component which did not fall within Unesco's spheres of competence,

---

[7] See document 105 EX/49 PRIV., paras. [83a] (*infra*, p. 118) and 90 (*infra*, pp. 119-120), communication No. 25/78 concerning *Chile*, case of *The situation of human rights in Chile in the fields of education, science, culture and information*.
[8] See document 109 EX/52 PRIV., paras. 261-271; see also documents 109 EX/CR/HR/1 and Add.

and to ensure that the communication came within the context of 104 EX/Decision 3.3.[9]

263. The Secretariat informed both the author of the communication and the government concerned, of the Committee's decision. In accordance with the instructions of the Committee, the communication was revised and presented to the Committee at its present session [...].[10] This document constituted a résumé of 65 documents (490 pages) which had been presented to the Secretariat.

264. The representative of the Israeli Government informed the Committee that her government had received this document late, i.e. less than 30 days before the Committee's session, and emphasized that it was an established rule of the Committee to provide such documents to governments at least 30 days before its sessions. She further indicated that the working language of her country was English and that the document had been sent to her in French, which had made it impossible for her government's experts to study it. The Israeli representative thus requested the Committee to defer its examination of the substance of this communication until its next session, so as to permit her government to study the documentation with appropriate care.

265. The representative of the Director-General explained to the Committee that the only version of the aforementioned document which had been available at the time of the mailing, had been the French version. After discussion, the Committee *decided*, in response to the request of the Israeli Government, to defer until its next session the continuation of its examination of the substance of this communication.

266. The Chairman then informed the Committee that by a letter dated 14 February 1980, the author of the communication had requested the Committee to authorize him to address it, in conformity with the provision of paragraph 14 (*g*) of 104 EX/ Decision 3.3. The Chairman drew the Committee's attention to the fact that it was for the Committee to decide whether or not it should request the Executive Board to authorize it to hear the author of the communication.

267. Certain members of the Committee felt that the request should be responded to favourably, since the presence of Mr Saleh, as a representative of the victims and a victim hinself, would permit an in-depth examination of the communication. Other members felt that since the procedure in question was only foreseen for "exceptional circumstances", the Committee would not be in a position to decide whether or not the circumstances were "exceptional", and thus justifying the taking of the floor by

[9] See document 108 EX/38 PRIV., para. 177 (*supra*, p. 13).
[10] See document 109 EX/CR/HR/1 Add.

the authors of the communication, until it had examined the substance of the communication.

268. One member of the Committee expressed the view that the circumstances were manifestly "exceptional" and warranted the appearance of the author of the communication, because Mr A. J. Saleh's testimony could shed valuable light on the enormous amount of documentation submitted to the Committee, especially since the communication in question was, in that member's opinion, one where it was difficult to assess at a glance whether it was concerned with a set of "cases" or with a "question" within the meaning of decision 104 EX/Decision 3.3.

269. Another member of the Committee said that, while he took due note of paragraph 14 (*g*) of 104 EX/Decision 3.3, Unesco should not become a forum for confrontation between authors of communications and the governments concerned and that it was important not to create a precedent which might prove to be dangerous. He also hoped that emphasis would be placed rather more on effective collaboration between the Organization and those governments.

270. The representative of the Director-General pointed out to the Committee that this was the first time that it found itself presented with such a request. The possibility of addressing the Committee was governed by a reference to the Rules of Procedure of the Executive Board ([Rule] 29); it could only be exercised within very narrow limits and only after express authorization by the Executive Board. Nothing was specified about the modalities for exercising this possibility but it was clear that its purpose was definitely not to organize a contradictory debate between the author of a communication and the representative of the government concerned.

271. After a lengthy discussion, the Committee *decided* to take a decision at the next session on the request presented to it by the author of the communication and to request its Chairman to ask the Chairman of the Executive Board to plan for the possibility of an additional session of the Committee during the next session of the Executive Board. This supplementary session would be convened if the Committee was of the opinion, after having examined the substance of [this communication], that it was justified in responding favourably to the request formulated by the author of the communication in conformity with paragraph 14 (*g*) of 104 EX/Decision 3.3.

No. 12/78 **Israel**

Autumn 1980 session of the Committee on Conventions and Recommendations (110th session of the Executive Board)[11]

270. The author of the communication, "Head of the Palestinian Human Rights Committee for the Defence of War and Political Prisoners" and member of the Executive Committee of the PLO, alleges the violation of human rights in the fields of education, science, culture and communication, claimed to have been committed in the territories occupied by the State of Israel.

271. The following matters referred to in the communication seem, at first sight, to come within the Committee's terms of reference:

arrest and torture of nine schoolchildren;

arrest of a photographer, and alleged torture by the police and confiscation of his photographs and money;

arrest and detention for one month of a journalist for participating in a student demonstration;

condemnation of conditions in the Nevé-Tirza Women's Prison and, in particular, of the suppression of information and culture, and the ban placed on the receiving of certain books and newspapers, etc.

272. At its [spring] 1979 session, the Committee decided to hold over consideration of the admissibility of this communication until the Secretariat had prepared a fuller summary of the allegations, on the basis of the data which were to be requested from the author of the communication and submitted beforehand to the government concerned.[12]

273. At the [autumn] 1979 session, the author had still not supplied the information requested, but had sent to the Secretariat several new documents concerning his communication. All these documents had been summarized by the Secretariat. That summary was distributed to the Committee, communicated to the government concerned and to the author of the communication, and is reproduced immediately after the communication form. The author of the communication had endorsed the summary in question and had designated the observer of the PLO to Unesco as his repre-

---

[11] See document 110 EX/40 PRIV., paras. 270-299; see also documents 110 EX/CR/HR/1 and Add.3.

[12] See document 107 EX/PRIV.31, para. 144 (*supra*, pp. 10-11).

sentative for the continuation of the procedure in connection with that communication.

274. At the [autumn] 1979 session, the representative of the government concerned maintained that the communication did not concern violations of human rights falling within Unesco's spheres of competence, and that, inasmuch as it originated from an organization publicly committed to the destruction of a Member State of Unesco, it was motivated solely by considerations of a political nature, and did not, therefore, comply with the condition of admissibility laid down in paragraph 14 (*a*) (iii) of 104 EX/Decision 3.3. The representative of the government concerned stated in that connection that the author of the communication was a member of the Executive Committee of the Palestine Liberation Organization (PLO) and that the Committee on behalf of which he had approached Unesco was also a member of the PLO. In support of these statements she quoted Articles 6, 15 and 19 of the PLO Charter.

275. She also stressed that Unesco had sent a special mission to investigate the situation of education, science and culture in the territories in question and that the report of that mission would be submitted to the Executive Board; consequently, she suggested that the Committee should not decide on the communication's admissibility before being informed of the opinion of the Executive Board on the findings of that mission. She drew the Committee's attention to the fact that co-operation between her government and the mission was assured. She considered, finally, that the communication formed part of the weapons of the political war being waged against her country.

276. A member of the Committee expressed the view that the government concerned had not produced any new information, and considered that the communication was admissible because the documents submitted by the author, as summarized by the Secretariat, seemed to indicate, firstly, that human rights belonging to Unesco's spheres of competence had indeed been violated in the case in question. In that connection he mentioned several examples of facts analysed in the communication. He added that, with regard to massive, systematic and flagrant violations resulting from a policy of aggression, occupation and racialism, the Committee should consider that the communication concerned a "question" in the sense of paragraph 18 of 104 EX/Decision 3.3. With regard to the mission that had travelled to the occupied territories, he considered that it had no bearing on the terms of reference of the Committee, whose task was to examine individual communications relating to violations of human rights.

277. Regarding the capacity of the author of the communication, several members of the Committee pointed out that the PLO enjoyed the status of an observer with Unesco and other international organizations, and that, at any rate, the author also

claimed to be a victim and to be a person with reliable knowledge of the alleged violations. Some members of the Committee took the view that the political affiliation of the author acting in that capacity did not affect the admissibility of the communication. One member considered that, since the author had not supplied the information that the Secretariat had requested of him, the Committee should wait for further clarifications before taking a decision on the admissibility of the communication. He drew the Committee's attention to the fact that many documents provided by the author had no connection with Unesco, and that others were manifestly ill-founded; a number of documents, on the other hand, contained serious allegations, and it was for that reason that the author should supply the information which the Committee had considered necessary at its [spring 1979] session. Another member stated that those parts of the communication which did not belong to Unesco's spheres of competence could be eliminated from it, as had been done in the case of [another communication].

278. One Committee member expressed doubts on the admissibility of the communication, and thought that there was a risk of duplication between the Committee and the Executive Board. Another member, while noting that the communication had political overtones, recalled that paragraph 14 (*a*) (iii) of 104 EX/Decision 3.3 excluded only communications "motivated exclusively by other considerations" (than considerations relating to respect for human rights). Another member stated that it was difficult to disregard the political aspect of the communication, particularly since the objection raised by the government concerned was, precisely, to the political affiliation of the author.

279. After discussion, and at the Chairman's suggestion, the Committee decided to declare the communication admissible, with the reservation that the Secretariat should be instructed, in collaboration with the author, to review the communication in order to eliminate from it any component which did not fall within Unesco's spheras of competence, and to ensure that the communication came within the context of 104 EX/Decision 3.3.[13]

280. In a letter dated 3 December 1979, in accordance with the Committee's instructions, the Secretariat informed the author of the communication of the Committee's decision. For its part, the Israeli Goverment has also been informed of the foregoing, in a letter dated 11 December 1979.

[13] See document 108 EX/38 PRIV., para. 177 (*supra*, p. 13).

Israel **No. 12/78**

281. In accordance with the Committee's instructions, the communication was revised and submitted to the Committee at its [spring 1980] session [...].[14] That document was a summary of the 65 documents (490 pages) presented to the Secretariat.

282. The representative of the Israeli Government informed the Committee that her government had received this document late, i.e. less than 30 days before the Committee's session, and emphasized that it was an established rule of the Committee to provide such documents to governments at least 30 days before its sessions. She further indicated that the working language of her country was English and that the document had been sent to her in French, which had made it impossible for her government's experts to study it. The Israeli representative thus requested the Committee to defer its examination of the substance of this communication until its next session, so as to permit her government to study the documentation with appropriate care.

283. The representative of the Director-General explained to the Committee that the only version of the aforementioned document which had been available at the time of mailing, had been the French version. After discussion, the Committee decided, in response to the request of the Israeli Government, to defer until its next session the continuation of its examination of the substance of this communication.[15]

284. The Chairman then informed the Committee that by a letter dated 14 February 1980, the author of the communication had requested the Committee to authorize him to address it, in conformity with the provision of paragraph 14 (*g*) of 104 EX/ Decision 3.3. The Chairman drew the Committee's attention to the fact that it was for the Committee to decide whether or not it should request the Executive Board to authorize it to hear the author of the communication.

285. Certain members of the Committee felt that the request should be responded to favourably, since the presence of Mr Saleh, as a representative of the victims and a victim hinself, would permit an in-depth examination of the communication. Other members felt that since the procedure in question was only foreseen for "exceptional circumstances", the Committee would not be in a position to decide whether or not the circumstances were "exceptional", and thus justifying the taking of the floor by the authors of the communication, until it had examined the substance of the communication.

286. One member of the Committee expressed the view that the circumstances were manifestly "exceptional" and warranted the appearance of the author of the commu-

[14] See document 109 EX/CR/HR/1 Add.

[15] See document 109 EX/52 PRIV., para. 265 (*supra*, p. 14).

nication, because Mr A. J. Saleh's testimony could shed valuable light on the enormous amount of documentation submitted to the Committee, especially since the communication in question was, in that member's opinion, one where it was difficult to assess at a glance whether it was concerned with a set of "cases" or with a "question" within the meaning of decision 104 EX/Decision 3.3.

287. Another member of the Committee said that, while he took due note of paragraph 14 (*g*) of 104 EX/Decision 3.3, Unesco should not become a forum for confrontation between authors of communications and the governments concerned and that it was important not to create a precedent which might prove to be dangerous. He also hoped that emphasis would be placed rather more on effective collaboration between the Organization and those governments.

288. The representative of the Director-General pointed out to the Committee that this was the first time that it found itself presented with such a request. The possibility of addressing the Committee was governed by a reference to the Rules of Procedure of the Executive Board ([Rule] 29); it could only be exercised within very narrow limits and only after express authorization by the Executive Board. Nothing was specified about the modalities for exercising this possibility but it was clear that its purpose was definitely not to organize a contradictory debate between the author of a communication and the representative of the government concerned.

289. After a lengthy discussion, the Committee decided to take a decision at the next session on the request presented to it by the author of the communication and to request its Chairman to ask the Chairman of the Executive Board to plan for the possibility of an additional session of the Committee during the next session of the Executive Board. This supplementary session would be convened if the Committee was of the opinion, after having examined the substance of [this communication], that it was justified in responding favourably to the request formulated by the author of the communication in conformity with paragraph 14 (*g*) of 104 EX/Decison 3.3.[16]

290. The author of the communication and the Israeli Government were duly informed by the Secretariat of the Committee's decisions.

291. At its present session the Committee decided that it would first hear the statement of the representative of the Government of Israel before deciding whether or not to invite the author of the communication to appear before the Committee to provide additional information on the case.

---

[16] *Ibidem*, para. 271 (*supra*, p. 15).

Israel **No. 12/78**

292. The Israeli representative presented to the Committee the position of his government [...].[17] He requested the Committee to reconsider its decision, taken at its [autumn 1979] session, to admit the communication since his government continued to feel that it was inadmissible for several reasons. The Israeli representative stated that the communication did not comply with paragraphs 14 (*a*) (iii) and 14 (*a*) (v) - (ix) of 104 EX/Decision 3.3. He emphasized that the author was a member of a terrorist organization and thus did not have the necessary "clean hands" to submit a communication.

293. If the decision to admit the case was irreversible, he said, the communication should nevertheless be dismissed since it was unfounded and frivolous, as an examination of the facts would show. On a point of procedure he stressed that documents Nos. (i) - (x) were dated 1979 and were thus outside the scope of the communication which was submitted in 1978. Furthermore, the documents had not been forwarded to the Israeli Government and could thus not be considered by the Committee.

294. As to the facts alleged in the communication, they were either untrue or distorted, the Israeli representative said; far from encouraging students or pupils to drop out or from preventing the development of higher education in the areas in question, it was precisely the Government of Israel which enabled the establishment of institutions of higher learning in the administered areas. Arab education and culture have greatly expanded and flourished in the administered areas due to the encouragement and assistance they have been receiving throughout from the Israeli authorities, he said. He went on to present statistics to illustrate this point. The Israeli representative requested that the case be dismissed.

295. A member of the Committee commented that the author of the communication had submitted it in several capacities. In any event, the Committee member stated, he was now convinced that the communication concerned a question in the sense of 104 EX/Decision 3.3 and that it would be more appropriate for it to be considered by the Executive Board or the General Conference where a solution might be more readily found, than before the Committee. He felt obliged to respond to the Israeli representative's statement however, since he felt that the occupying forces appeared not to wish to respect international law. He stated that Arab demonstrations in the occupied areas always started peacefully but only became violent when the forces of authority appeared. He also wondered how a student could have been killed by a stray bullet when it was known that the Israeli army was excellently trained.

296. The fact that education was encouraged and growing in the occupied areas was a relative question, he said, since it might well be that the progress might have been

[17] See document 110 EX/CR/HR/1 Add.3.

much more rapid had the area not been occupied, and he cited the progress of his own country. Finally, it was pointed out, the existence of a decree which placed all educational institutions under military control was of itself a reason to treat this communication very seriously. The matter should be treated as a question, he said, and should be handled in accordance with the Committee's procedural decision on questions which it was expected to take at its next session when it would have before it the Secretariat's study on such matters. He went on to draw the Committee's attention to a document recently addressed to the Director-General which was related to the present communication, and which contained new and important information, but which had not yet been forwarded to the Committee. The Committee member raised the queation as to whether it might not be possible to send a fact-finding mission to the territories in question so that the facts could definitely be determined.

297. In response to questions the representative of the Director-General explained that there was no possibility of appeal once the Committee decided to admit a communication. He clarified that once a communication was admitted the necessary procedure to follow was either to dismiss it after a friendly solution to the problem had been arrived at or to dismiss it in accordance with subparagraph (*j*) of paragraph 14 or to submit a report to the Executive Board. In that connection, he pointed out that there existed, in the relevant [104 EX/Decision 3.3], the possibility of submitting one or more separate reports to the Executive Board on the various cases before the Committee.

298. As to the question concerning a fact-finding mission, the representative of the Director-General stated that though not expressly mentioned in the said decision, such missions were a well-established working method for other international human rights organs.

299. The Committee members agreed that the decision to admit the communication was irreversible, and during the exchange of views a consensus emerged that, given the need to determine in the light of the new information provided whether the communication concerned a case or a question, it would be best for the Committee to consider the communication more closely at its next session when it would be in a position to examine the Director-General's relevant study. It was so *decided*.

Israel **No. 12/78**

Spring 1981 session of the Committee on Conventions and Recommendations (112th session of the Executive Board)[18]

454. The author of the communication, "Head of the Palestinian Human Rights Committee for the Defence of War and Political Prisoners" and member of the Executive Committee of the PLO, alleges the violation of human rights in the fields of education, science, culture and communication, claimed to have been committed in the territories occupied by the State of Israel.

455. The following matters referred to in the communication seem, at first sight, to come within the Committee's terms of reference:

arrest and torture of nine schoolchildren;

arrest of a photographer, and alleged torture by the police and confiscation of his photographs and money;

arrest and detention for one month of a journalist for participating in a student demonstration;

condemnation of conditions in the Nevé-Tirza Women's Prison and, in particular, of the suppression of information and culture, and the ban placed on the receiving of certain books and newspapers, etc.

456. At its [spring] 1979 session, the Committee had decided to hold over consideration of the admissibility of this communication until the Secretariat had prepared a fuller summary of the allegations, on the basis of the data which were to be requested from the author of the communication and submitted beforehand to the government concerned.[19]

457. At the [autumn] 1979 session, the author had still not supplied the information requested, but had sent to the Secretariat several new documents concerning his communication. All these documents had been summarized by the Secretariat. That summary was distributed to the Committee, communicated to the government concerned and to the author of the communication. The author of the communication had endorsed the summary in question and had designated the observer of the PLO to Unesco as his representative for the continuation of the procedure in connection with that communication.

---

[18] See document 112 EX/30 PRIV., paras. 454-492; see also document 112 EX/CR/HR/1.
[19] See document 107 EX/PRIV.31, para. 144 (*supra*, pp. 10-11).

No. 12/78 **Israel**

458. At that [autumn] 1979 session, the representative of the government concerned had maintained that the communication did not concern violations of human rights falling within Unesco's fields of competence, and that, inasmuch as it originated from an organization publicly committed to the destruction of a Member State of Unesco, it was motivated solely by considerations of a political nature, and did not, therefore, comply with the condition of admissibility laid down in paragraph 14 (*a*) (iii) of 104 EX/Decision 3.3. The representative of the government concerned had stated in that connection that the author of the communication was a member of the Palestine Liberation Organization (PLO) and that the Committee on behalf of which he had approached Unesco was also a member of the PLO. In support of these statements she had quoted Articles 6, 15 and 19 of the PLO Charter.

459. She had also stressed that Unesco had sent a special mission to investigate the situation of education, science and culture in the territories in question and that the report of that mission would be submitted to the Executive Board; consequently, she had suggested that the Committee should not decide on the communication's admissibility before being informed of the opinion of the Executive Board on the findings of that mission. She had drawn the Committee's attention to the fact that co-operation between her government and the mission was assured. She considered, finally, that the communication formed part of the weapons of the political war being waged against her country.

460. A member of the Committee had expressed the view that the government concerned had not produced any new information, and considered that the communication was admissible because the documents submitted by the author, as summarized by the Secretariat, seemed to indicate, firstly, that human rights belonging to Unesco's spheres of competence had indeed been violated in the case in question. In that connection he had mentioned several examples of facts analysed in the communication. He had added that, with regard to massive, systematic and flagrant violations resulting from a policy of aggression, occupation and racism, the Committee should consider that the communication concerned a "question" in the sense of paragraph 18 of 104 EX/Decision 3.3. With regard to the mission that had travelled to the occupied territories, he considered that it had no bearing on the terms of reference of the Committee, whose task was to examine individual communications relating to violations of human rights.

461. Regarding the capacity of the author of the communication, several members of the Committee had pointed out that the PLO enjoyed the status of an observer with Unesco and other international organizations, and that, in any case, the author had also claimed to be a victim and to be a person with reliable knowledge of the alleged violations. Some members of the Committee had taken the view that the political affiliation of the author acting in that capacity did not affect the admissibility of the

communication. One member considered that, since the author had not supplied the information that the Secretariat had requested of him, the Committee should wait for further clarifications before taking a decision on the admissibility of the communication. He had drawn the Committee's attention to the fact that many documents provided by the author had no connection with Unesco, and that others were manifestly ill-founded; a number of documents, on the other hand, contained serious allegations, and it was for that reason that the author should supply the information which the Committee had considered necessary at its [spring 1979] session. Another member had stated that those parts of the communication which did not belong to Unesco's spheres of competence could be eliminated from it, as had been done in the case of [another communication].

462. One Committee member had expressed doubts on the admissibility of the communication, and thought that there was a risk of duplication between the Committee and the Executive Board. Another member, while noting that the communication had political overtones, had recalled that paragraph 14 (*a*) (iii) of 104 EX/Decision 3.3 excluded only communications "motivated exclusively by other considerations" (than consideration relating to respect for human rights). Another member had stated that it was difficult to disregard the political aspect of the communication, since the objection raised by the government concerned was, precisely, to the political affiliation of the author.

463. After discussion, and on the proposal of the Chairman, the Committee had decided to declare the communication admissible, with the reservation that the Secretariat should be instructed, in collaboration with the author, to review the communication in order to eliminate from it any component which did not fall within Unesco's spheres of competence, and to ensure that the communication came within the context of 104 EX/Decision 3.3.[20]

464. In a letter dated 3 December 1979, in accordance with the Committee's instructions, the Secretariat had informed the author of the communication of the Committee's decision. For its part, the Israeli Government had also been informed of the foregoing, in a letter dated 11 December 1979.

465. In accordance with the Committee's instructions, the communication had been revised and submitted to the Committee at the [spring] 1980 session [...].[21] That document was a summary of the 65 documents (490 pages) presented to the Secretariat.

---

[20] See document 108 EX/38 PRIV., para. 177 (*supra*, p. 13).

[21] See document 109 EX/CR/HR/1 Add.

No. 12/78 **Israel**

466. At that [spring] 1980 session, the representative of the Israeli Government had informed the Committee that her government had received this document late, i.e. less than 30 days before the Committee's session, and had emphasized that it was an established rule of the Committee to provide such documents to governments at least 30 days before its sessions. She had further indicated that the working language of her country was English and that the document had been sent to her in French, which had made it impossible for her government's experts to study it. The Israeli representative had thus requested the Committee to defer its examination of the substance of this communication until its next session, so as to permit her government to study the documentation with appropriate care.

467. The representative of the Director-General had explained to the Committee that the only version of the aforementioned document which had been available at the time of mailing, had been the French version. After discussion, the Committee had decided, in response to the request of the Israeli Government, to defer until its next session the continuation of its examination of the substance of this communication.[22]

468. The Chairman had then informed the Committee that by a letter dated 14 February 1980, the author of the communication had requested the Committee to authorize him to address it, in conformity with the provision of paragraph 14 (*g*) of 104 EX/Decision 3.3. The Chairman had drawn the Committee's attention to the fact that it was for the Committee to decide whether or not it should request the Executive Board to authorize it to hear the author of the communication.

469. Certain members of the Committee had felt that the request should be responded to favourably, since the presence of Mr Saleh, as a representative of the victims and a victim himself, would permit an in-depth examination of the communication. Other members had felt that since the procedure in question was only foreseen for "exceptional circumstances", the Committee would not be in a position to decide whether or not the circumstances were "exceptional", and thus justifying the taking of the floor by the authors of the communication, until it had examined the substance of the communication.

470. One member of the Committee had expressed the view that the circumstances were manifestly "exceptional" and warranted the appearance of the author of the communication, because Mr Saleh's testimony could shed valuable light on the enormous amount of documentation submitted to the Committee, especially since the communication in question was, in that member's opinion, one where it was difficult to assess at a glance whether it was concerned with a set of "cases" or with a "question" within the meaning of decision 104 EX/Decision 3.3.

[22] See document 109 EX/52 PRIV., para. 265 (*supra*, p. 14).

Israel **No. 12/78**

471. Another member of the Committee had said that, while he took due note of paragraph 14 (*g*) of 104 EX/Decision 3.3, Unesco should not become a forum for confrontation between authors of communications and the governments concerned and that it was important not to create a precedent which might prove to be dangerous. He had also hoped that emphasis would be placed rather more on effective collaboration between the Organization and those governments.

472. The representative of the Director-General had pointed out to the Committee that this was the first time that it found itself presented with such a request. The possibility of addressing the Committee was governed by a reference to the Rules of Procedure of the Executive Board ([Rule] 29); it could only be exercised within very narrow limits and only after express authorization by the Executive Board. Nothing was specified about the modalities for exercising this possibility but it was clear that its purpose was definitely not to organize a contradictory debate between the author of a communication and the representative of the government concerned.

473. After a lengthy discussion, the Committee had decided to take a decision at the next session on the request presented to it by the author of the communication and to request its Chairman to ask the Chairman of the Executive Board to plan for the possibility of an additional session of the Committee during the next session of the Executive Board. This supplementary session would be convened if the Committee was of the opinion, after having examined the merits of [this communication], that it was justified in responding favourably to the request formulated by the author of the communication in conformity with paragraph 14 (*g*) of 104 EX/Decision 3.3.[23]

474. At its [autumn] 1980 session the Committee had decided that it would first hear the statement of the representative of the Government of Israel before deciding whether or not to invite the author of the communication to appear before the Committee to provide additional information on the case.

475. The Israeli representative had presented to the Committee the position of his government, set out in the form of a letter dated 22 August 1980. He had requested the Committee to reconsider its decision, taken at the [autumn 1979] session, to admit the communication since his government continued to feel that it was inadmissible for several reasons. He had stated that the communication did not comply with paragraphs 14 (*a*) (iii) and 14 (*a*) (v) - (ix) of 104 EX/Decision 3.3. He had emphasized that the author was a member of a terrorist organization and thus did not have the necessary "clean hands" to submit a communication.

---

[23] *Ibidem*, para. 271 (*supra*, p. 15).

476. If the decision to admit the case was irreversible, he had said, the communication should nevertheless be dismissed since it was ill-founded and frivolous, as an examination of the facts would show. On a point of procedure he had stressed that documents Nos. (i) - (x) were dated 1979 and were thus outside the scope of the communication which was submitted in 1978. Furthermore, the documents had not been forwarded to the Israeli Government and could thus not be considered by the Committee.

477. As to the facts alleged in the communication, they were either untrue or distorted, the Israeli representative had said; far from encouraging students or pupils to drop out or from preventing the development of higher education in the areas in question, it was precisely the Government of Israel which had enabled the establishment of institutions of higher learning in the administered areas. Arab education and culture had greatly expanded and flourished in the administered areas owing to the encouragement and assistance they had been receiving throughout from the Israeli authorities, he said. He had gone on to present statistics to illustrate this point. The Israeli representative had requested that the case be dismissed.

478. A member of the Committee had commented that the author of the communication had submitted it in several capacities. In any event, the Committee member had stated, he was by then convinced that the communication concerned a question in the sense of 104 EX/Decision 3.3 and that it would be more appropriate for it to be considered by the Executive Board or the General Conference where a solution might be more readily found, than before the Committee. He felt obliged to respond to the Israeli representative's statement, however, since he felt that the occupying forces appeared not to wish to respect international law. He had stated moreover that Arab demonstrations in the occupied areas always started peacefully but only became violent when the forces of authority appeared. He had also wondered how a student could have been killed by a stray bullet when it was known that the Israeli army was excellently trained.

479. The fact that education was encouraged and growing in the occupied areas was a relative question, he had said, since it might well be that the progress might have been much more rapid had the area not been occupied, and he cited the progress of his own country. Finally, it had been pointed out, the existence of a decree which placed all educational institutions under military control was of itself a reason to treat this communication very seriously. The matter should be treated as a question, he said, and should be handled in accordance with the Committee's procedural decision on questions which it was expected to take at its next session when it would have before it the Secretariat's study on such matters. He had gone on to draw the Committee's attention to a document recently addressed to the Director-General which was related to the present communication, and which contained new and im-

portant information, but which had not yet been forwarded to the Committee. The Committee member had raised the question as to whether it might not be possible to send a fact-finding mission to the territory in question so that the facts could be determined.

480. In response to questions the representative of the Director-General had explained that there was no possibility of appeal once the Committee decided to admit a communication. He had clarified that once a communication was admitted the necessary procedure to follow was either to dismiss it after a friendly solution to the problem had been arrived at or to dismiss it in accordance with subparagraph (*j*) of paragraph 14 or to submit a report to the Executive Board. In that connection, he had pointed out that there existed, in the relevant [104 EX/Decision 3.3], the possibility of submitting one or more separate reports to the Executive Board on the various cases before the Committee.

481. As to the question concerning a fact-finding mission, the representative of the Director-General had stated that though not expressly mentioned in the said decision, such missions were a well-established working method for other international human rights organs.

482. The Committee members had agreed that the decision to admit the communication was irreversible, and during the exchange of views a consensus had emerged that, "given the need to determine in the light of the new information provided whether the communication concerned a case or a question, it would be best for the Committee to consider the communication more closely at its next session when it would be in a position to examine the Director-General's relevant study". It was so decided at the [autumn 1980] session.[24]

483. The document addressed to the Director-General, referred to in paragraph 479 above, was sent to the government concerned on 20 January 1981, in the three language versions (Arabic, English and French) in which it was received by the Secretariat.

484. The representative of the Government of Israel opened his case at the present session by pleading the Committee's incompetence to deal with the matter. He pointed out that the document referred to in the preceding paragraph had been used by the Director-General in presenting to the General Conference in Belgrade a report which had led to a resolution condemning Israel on the basis of allegations presented as fact [...].[25] He stressed the fact that since the General Conference had already tak-

---

[24] See document 110 EX/40 PRIV., para. 299 (*supra*, p. 22).
[25] See document 21 C/5 Approved, sect. 14, p. XXIV.

en a decision on the communication - in his view, in violation of the procedures laid down in 104 EX/Decision 3.3, which specifically stated that the examination of communications should be confidential - the Committee, a body emanating from the Executive Board, was precluded from "judging" once again a case that had already been "judged" by a higher authority.

485. The representative of the Director-General pointed out that the passage from the report to which the representative of the Israeli Government had referred could not be regarded as a breach of the secret procedure for the examination of communications. This very issue, when raised at Belgrade, had been the subject of a reply by the representative of the Director-General, and he proposed that this reply should be read out. Furthermore, the document in dispute did not legally constitute a communication within the meaning of 104 EX/Decision 3.3, since it was merely one item of information, among others, from the communication pending before the Committee. The Director-General had simply informed the General Conference in a few lines that he had received a complaint from the Chairman of the "Committee for the Defence of Palestinian Human Rights under Israeli Occupation" (among other complaints) and that this complaint, several pages in length, had been transmitted to the Committee on Conventions and Recommendations to be examined in the context of communication No. 12/78, in accordance with the procedure laid down in 104 EX/ Decision 3.3. Under these circumstances, the General Conference had been unable to take a position on the substance of the communication, which remained before the Committee.

486. A few members of the Committee pointed out that Unesco was not a court of law, but that it was using its good offices to seek a solution. In these circumstances, the communication should be considered in conformity with the established procedure.

487. No longer insisting on the plea of incompetence raised by him *in limine litis*, the representative of the Israeli Government then addressed the substance of the matter, recalling his government's position as presented to the [autumn] 1980 session. He then emphasized that Israel acted in conformity with international law, that it had not destroyed any schools, that it had not undertaken mass deportations of teachers, that it had not ruled and would not rule the occupied territories by terror, that it had administered them in accordance with the relevant legal and humanitarian regulations, that it was perfectly possible for any injured party to seek redress against military action regarded as illegal (in this respect Israel applied British jurisprudence) and that everything possible had been done to contribute to the development of education and technical instruction. He concluded by stressing the fact that it had been no part of his intention to argue a case before the Committee, since the sole purpose of the obscure allegations in the communication, in his opinion, was to

incite Unesco to adopt a political attitude and play a part hostile to Israel. With regard to paragraph 14 (*j*) and (*k*) of 104 EX/Decision 3.3, he stated that his government was ready to accept any useful and fruitful suggestion.

488. A member of the Commitee pointed out that detailed examination of the documents annexed to the communication clearly showed that there were, in fact, a number of inaccuracies and some incoherence in the facts put forward. On the principle that, in the state of generalized warfare prevailing in that region of the Middle East, the only way forward was by co-operation, he proposed that a friendly solution should be sought in the spirit of paragraph 14 (*k*) of 104 EX/Decision 3.3.

489. Another member of the Committee pointed out that the communication raised two kinds of problem:

(i) a problem relating to the administration of educational establishments: in this respect, there were no international standards prescribing the percentage of pupils or students to be admitted to a school or university;

(ii) a problem relating to order, security and justice: in this respect, it seemed doubtful whether the case fell within Unesco's fields of competence.

490. This being so, the solution was purely and simply to apply paragraph 14 (*j*) of 104 EX/Decision 3.3 and dismiss the communication once and for all.

491. Two other members of the Committee took the view that it was paragraph 18 of that decision that should be applied (consideration of the communication by the Executive Board and the General Conference in public meetings), since the allegations concerned events that had occurred in an occupied country.

492. After an exchange of views and on the proposal of its Chairman, the Committee *decided* to request the Executive Board to invite the Director-General to determine whether, since the allegations of violations of human rights had been declared admissible, there were grounds for applying paragraph 14 (*k*) of 104 EX/Decision 3.3, on the understanding that the Committee would resume its consideration of the substance of the communication once it had examined the study on the procedural aspects of a "question" as defined in 104 EX/Decision 3.3.

No. 12/78 **Israel**

Autumn 1981 session of the Committee on Conventions and Recommendations (113th session of the Executive Board)[26]

482. The author of the communication, "Head of the Palestinian Human Rights Committee for the Defence of War and Political Prisoners" and member of the Executive Committee of the PLO, alleges the violation of human rights in the fields of education, science, culture and communication, said to have been committed in the territories occupied by the State of Israel.

483. The following matters referred to in the communication seem, at first sight, to come within the Committee's terms of reference:

arrest and torture of nine schoolchildren;

arrest of a photographer, and alleged torture and confiscation of his photographs and money by the police;

arrest and detention for one month of a journalist for participating in a student demonstration;

condemnation of conditions in the Nevé-Tirza Women's Prison and, in particular, of the suppression of information and culture, and the ban placed on the receiving of certain books and newspapers, etc.

484. At its [spring] 1979 session, the Committee decided to hold over consideration of the admissibility of this communication until the Secretariat had prepared a fuller summary of the allegations, on the basis of the data which were to be requested from the author of the communication and submitted beforehand to the government concerned.[27]

485. At the [autumn] 1979 session, the author had still not supplied the information requested, but had sent to the Secretariat several new documents concerning his communication. All these documents had been summarized by the Secretariat. That summary was distributed to the Committee and communicated to the government concerned and to the author of the communication. The author of the communication endorsed the summary in question and designated the observer of the PLO to Unesco as his representative for the continuation of the procedure in connection with that communication.

---

[26] See document 113 EX/38 PRIV., paras. 482-527; see also documents 113 EX/CR/HR/1 and Add.2.

[27] See document 107 EX/PRIV.31, para. 144 (*supra*, pp. 10-11).

Israel **No. 12/78**

486. At that [autumn] 1979 session, the representative of the government concerned maintained that the communication did not concern violations of human rights falling within Unesco's spheres of competence, and that, inasmuch as it originated from an organization publicly committed to the destruction of a Member State of Unesco, it was motivated solely by considerations of a political nature, and did not, therefore, comply with the condition of admissibility laid down in paragraph 14 (*a*) (iii) of 104 EX/Decision 3.3. She stated in that connection that the author of the communication was a member of the Executive Committee of the Palestine Liberation Organization (PLO) and that the Committee on behalf of which he had approached Unesco was also a member of the PLO. In support of these statements she quoted Articles 6, 15 and 19 of the PLO Charter.

487. She also pointed out that Unesco had sent a special mission to investigate the situation of education, science and culture in the territories in question and that the report of that mission would be submitted to the Executive Board; consequently, she suggested that the Committee should not decide on the communication's admissibility before being informed of the opinion of the Executive Board on the findings of that mission. She drew the Committee's attention to the fact that co-operation between her government and the mission was assured. She considered, finally, that the communication formed part of the weaponry of the political war being waged against her country.

488. A member of the Committee expressed the view that the government concerned had not produced any new information, and considered that the communication was admissible because the documents submitted by the author, as summarized by the Secretariat, seemed at first sight to indicate that human rights belonging to Unesco's spheres of competence had indeed been violated in the case in question. In that connection he mentioned several examples of facts analysed in the communication. He added that, with regard to massive, systematic and flagrant violations resulting from a policy of aggression, occupation and racialism, the Committee should consider that the communication concerned a "question" in the sense of paragraph 18 of 104 EX/Decision 3.3. With regard to the mission that had travelled to the occupied territories, he considered that it had no bearing on the terms of reference of the Committee, whose task was to examine individual communications relating to violations of human rights.

489. Regarding the capacity of the author of the communication, several members of the Committee pointed out that the PLO enjoyed the status of an observer with Unesco and other international organizations, and that, at any case, the author had also described himself as a victim and a person with reliable knowledge of the alleged violations. Some members of the Committee took the view that the political affiliation of the author acting in that capacity did not affect the admissibility of the

communication. One member considered that, since the author had not supplied the information that the Secretariat had requested of him, the Committee should wait for further clarifications before taking a decision on the admissibility of the communication. He drew the Committee's attention to the fact that many documents provided by the author had no connection with Unesco and that others were manifestly ill-founded; a number of documents, on the other hand, contained serious allegations, and it was for that reason that the author should supply the information which the Committee had considered necessary at its [spring 1979] session. Another member stated that those parts of the communication which did not belong to Unesco's spheres of competence could be eliminated from it, as had been done in the case of [another communication].

490. One Committee member expressed doubts on the admissibility of the communication and thought that there was a risk of duplication between the Committee and the Executive Board. Another member, while noting that the communication had political overtones, recalled that paragraph 14 (*a*) (iii) of 104 EX/Decision 3.3 excluded only communications "motivated exclusively by other considerations" (than considerations relating to respect for human rights). Another member stated that it was difficult to disregard the political aspect of the communication, since the objection raised by the government concerned was, precisely, to the political affiliation of the author.

491. After discussion, and on the proposal of the Chairman, the Committee decided to declare the communication admissible, with the reservation that the Secretariat should be instructed, in collaboration with the author, to review the communication in order to eliminate from it any component which did not fall within Unesco's spheres of competence, and to ensure that the communication came within the scope of 104 EX/Decision 3.3.[28]

492. In a letter dated 3 December 1979, in accordance with the Committee's instructions, the Secretariat informed the author of the communication of the Committee's decision. The Israeli Goverment was also informed of the foregoing, in a letter dated 11 December 1979.

493. In accordance with the Committee's instructions, the communication was revised and submitted to the Committee at the [spring] 1980 session [...].[29] That document was a summary of the 65 documents (490 pages) presented to the Secretariat.

---

[28] See document 108 EX/38 PRIV., para. 177 (*supra*, p. 13).
[29] See document 109 EX/CR/HR/1 Add.

494. At that [spring] 1980 session, the representative of the Israeli Government informed the Committee that her government had received that document late, i.e. less than 30 days before the Committee's session, and emphasized that it was an established rule of the Committee to provide such documents to governments at least 30 days before its sessions. She further indicated that the working language of her country was English and that the document had been sent to her in French, which had made it impossible for her government's experts to study it. The Israeli representative thus requested the Committee to defer its examination of the substance of this communication until its next session, so as to permit her government to study the papers with the appropriate care.

495. The representative of the Director-General explained to the Committee that the only version of the aforementioned document which had been available at the time of mailing had been the French version. After discussion, the Committee decided, in response to tho request of the Israeli Govennent, to defer until its next session the continuation of its examination of the substance of this communication.[30]

496. The Chairman then informed the Committee that, by a letter dated 14 February 1980, the author of the communication had requested the Committee to authorize him to address it, in conformity with the provision of paragraph 14 (*g*) of 104 EX/ Decision 3.3. The Chairman drew the Committee's attention to the fact that it was for the Committee to decide whether or not it should request the Executive Board to authorize it to hear the author of the communication.

497. Certain members of the Committee felt that the request should be granted, since the presence of Mr Saleh, as a representative of the victims and a victim himself, would permit an in-depth examination of the communication. Other members felt that since the procedure in question was specified only for "exceptional circumstances", the Committee would not be in a position to decide whether or not the circumstances were "exceptional", and thus justified the taking of the floor by the authors of the communication, until it had examined the substance of the communication.

498. One member of the Committee expressed the view that the circumstances were manifestly "exceptional" and warrranted the appearance of the author of the communication, because Mr A. J. Saleh's testimony could shed valuable light on the enormous amount of documentation submitted to the Committee, especially since the communication in question was, in that member's opinion, one where it was difficult to assess at a glance whether it was concerned with a set of "cases" or with a "question" within the meaning of decision 104 EX/Decision 3.3.

---

[30] See document 109 EX/52 PRIV., para. 265 (*supra*, p. 14).

499. Another member of the Committee said that, while he took due note of paragraph 14 (*g*) of 104 EX/Decision 3.3, Unesco should not become a forum for confrontation between authors of communications and the governments concerned and that it was important not to create a precedent which might prove dangerous. He had also expressed the hope that emphasis would be placed rather more on effective collaboration between the Organization and those governments.

500. The representative of the Director-General pointed out to the Committee that this was the first time it had received such a request. Permission to address the Committee could be granted under the Rules of Procedure of the Executive Board ([Rule] 29); it could be exercised only within very narrow limits and after express authorization by the Executive Board. Nothing was specified about the ways in which such permission could be exercised, but it was clear that its purpose was definitely not to organize a contradictory debate between the author of a communication and the representative of the government concerned.

501. After a lengthy discussion, the Committee decided to take a decision at the next session on the request presented to it by the author of the communication and to request its Chairman to ask the Chairman of the Executive Board to plan for the possibility of an additional session of the Committee during the next session of the Executive Board. This supplementary session would be convened if the Committee was of the opinion, after having examined the substance of [this communication], that it was justified in granting the request formulated by the author of the communication in conformity with paragraph 14 (*g*) of 104 EX/Decision 3.3.[31]

502. At its [autumn] 1980 session, the Committee decided that it would first hear the statement of the representative of the Government of Israel before deciding whether or not to invite the author of the communication to appear before the Committee to provide additional information on the case.

503. The Israeli representative presented to the Committee the position of his government, set out in the form of a letter dated 22 August 1980. He requested the Committee to reconsider its decision, taken at [its autumn 1979] session, to admit the communication, since his government continued to feel that it was inadmissible on several counts. He stated that the communication did not comply with paragraphs 14 (*a*) (iii) and 14 (*a*) (v) - (ix) of 104 EX/Decision 3.3. He emphasized that the author was a member of a terrorist organization and thus did not have "sufficiently clean hands" to submit a communication.

---

[31] *Ibidem*, para. 271 (*supra*, p. 15).

Israel **No. 12/78**

504. Even if the decision to admit the case was irreversible, he said, the communication should nevertheless be dismissed since it was ill-founded and frivolous, as an examination of the facts would show. On a point of procedure he stressed that documents (i) - (x) were dated 1979 and were thus outside the scope of the communication which was submitted in 1978. Furthermore, the documents had not been forwarded to the Israeli Government and could thus not be considered by the Committee.

505. As to the facts alleged in the communication, they were either untrue or distorted, the Israeli representative said; far from encouraging students or pupils to drop out or from preventing the development of higher education in the areas in question, it was precisely the Government of Israel which had made possible the establishment of institutions of higher learning in the administered areas. Arab education and culture had greatly expanded and flourished in the administered areas owing to the encouragement and assistance they had been receiving throughout from the Israeli authorities, he said. He went on to present statistics to illustrate this point. The Israeli representative requested that the case be dismissed.

506. A member of the Committee commented that the author of the communication had submitted it in several capacities. In any event, the Committee member stated, he was by then convinced that the communication concerned a question in the sense of 104 EX/Decision 3.3 and that it would be more appropriate for it to be considered by the Executive Board or the General Conference where a solution might be more readily found, than before the Committee. He felt obliged to respond to the Israeli representative's statement, however, since he felt that the occupying forces appeared not to wish to respect international law. He stated moreover that Arab demonstrations in the occupied areas always started peacefully but became violent only when the forces of authority appeared. He also wondered how a student could have been killed by a stray bullet when it was known that the Israeli army was excellently trained.

507. The fact that education was encouraged and growing in the occupied areas was a relative question, he said, since it might well be that the progress might have been much more rapid had the area not been occupied, and he cited the progress of his own country. Finally, it was pointed out, the existence of a decree which placed all educational institutions under military control was of itself a reason to treat this communication very seriously. The matter should be treated as a question, he said, and should be handled in accordance with the Committee's procedural decision on questions which it was expected to take at its next session when it would have before it the Secretariat's study on such matters. He went on to draw the Committee's attention to a document recently addressed to the Director-General which was related to the present communication and contained new and important information but

had not yet been forwarded to the Committee. The Committee member raised the question as to whether it might not be possible to send a fact-finding mission to the territory in question so that the facts could be determined.

508. In response to questions, the representative of the Director-General explained that there was no possibility of appeal once the Committee decided to admit a communication. He explained that once a communication was admitted the necessary procedure to follow was either to dismiss it after a friendly solution to the problem had been arrived at or to dismiss it in accordance with subparagraph (*j*) of paragraph 14 or to submit a report to the Executive Board. In that connection, he pointed out that there existed, in 104 EX/Decision 3.3, the possibility of submitting one or more separate reports to the Executive Board on the various cases before the Committee.

509. As to the question concerning a fact-finding mission, the representative of the Director-General stated that, though not expressly mentioned in the decision, such missions were a well-established working method for other international human rights organs.

510. The Committee members agreed that the decision to admit the communication was irreversible, and during the exchange of views a consensus emerged that, "given the need to determine in the light of the new information provided whether the communication concerned a case or a question, it would be best for the Committee to consider the communication more closely at its next session, when it would be in a position to examine the Director-General's relevant study". It was so decided at the [autumn 1980] session.[32]

511. The document addressed to the Director-General, referred to in paragraph 507 above, was sent to the government concerned on 20 January 1981, in the three language versions (Arabic, English and French) in which it was received by the Secretariat.

512. The representative of the Government of Israel opened his case at the [spring 1981 session] by pleading the Committee's incompetence to deal with the matter. He pointed out that the document referred to in the preceding paragraph had been used by the Director-General in presenting to the General Conference in Belgrade a report which had led to a resolution condemning Israel on the basis of allegations presented as fact [...].[33] He stressed the fact that since the General Conference had already taken a decision on the communication - in his view, in violation of the procedures laid down in 104 EX/Decision 3.3, which specifically stated that the exami-

[32] See document 110 EX/40 PRIV., para. 299 (*supra*, p. 22).
[33] See document 21 C/5 Approved, sect. 14, p. XXIV.

nation of communications should be confidential - the Committee, a body emanating from the Executive Board, was precluded from "judging" once again a case that had already been "judged" by a higher authority.

513. The representative of the Director-General pointed out that the passage of the report to which the representative of the Israeli Government had referred could not be regarded as a breach of the secret procedure for the examination of communications. That very issue, when raised at Belgrade, had been the subject of a reply by the representative of the Director-General, and he proposed that that reply should be read out. Furthermore, the document in dispute did not legally constitute a communication within the meaning of 104 EX/Decision 3.3, since it was merely one item of information, among others, from the communication pending before the Committee. The Director-General had simply informed the General Conference in a few lines that he had received a complaint from the Chairman of the "Committee for the Defence of Palestinian Human Rights under Israeli Occupation" (among other complaints) and that that complaint, several pages in length, had been transmitted to the Committee on Conventions and Recommendations to be examined in the context of communication No. 12/78, in accordance with the procedure laid down in 104 EX/ Decision 3.3. Under these circumstances, the General Conference had been unable to take a position on the substance of the communication, which remained before the Committee.

514. A few members of the Committee pointed out that Unesco was not a court of law but was using its good offices to seek a solution and that the communication should therefore be examined in accordance with the procedure laid down for that purpose.

515. No longer insisting on the plea of incompetence raised by him *in limine litis*, the representative of the Israeli Government had addressed the substance of the matter, recalling his government's position as presented to the [spring] 1980 session. He went on to emphasize that Israel acted in conformity with international law, that it had not destroyed any schools, that it had not undertaken mass deportations of teachers, that it had not ruled and did not rule the occupied territories by terror, that it had administered and was administering them in accordance with the relevant legal and humanitarian regulations, that it was perfectly possible for any injured party to seek redress against military action regarded as illegal (in this respect Israel applied British jurisprudence) and that everything possible had been done to contribute to the development of education and technical instruction. He concluded by stressing the fact that it had been no part of his intention to argue a case before the Committee, since the sole purpose of the obscure allegations in the communication, in his opinion, was to incite Unesco to adopt a political attitude and play a part hostile to Israel.

With regard to paragraph 14 (*j*) and (*k*) of 104 EX/Decision 3.3, he stated that his government was ready to accept any useful and fruitful suggestion.

516. A member of the Commitee pointed out that detailed examination of the documents annexed to the communication clearly showed that there were, in fact, a number of inaccuracies and some incoherence in the facts put forward. On the principle that, in the state of generalized warfare prevailing in that region of the Middle East, the only way forward was by co-operation, he proposed that a friendly solution should be sought in the spirit of paragraph 14 (*k*) of 104 EX/Decision 3.3.

517. Another member of the Committee pointed out that the communication raised two kinds of problem:

> a problem relating to the administration of educational institutions: in that respect, there were no international standards prescribing the percentage of pupils or students to be admitted to a school or university;
>
> a problem relating to order, security and justice: in that respect, it seemed doubtful whether the case fell within Unesco's fields of competence.

518. That being so, the solution was purely and simply to apply paragraph 14 (*j*) of 104 EX/Decision 3.3 and dismiss the communication once and for all.

519. Two other members of the Committee took the view that it was paragraph 18 of that decision that should be applied (consideration of the communication by the Executive Board and the General Conference in public meetings), since the allegations concerned events that had occurred in an occupied country.

520. After an exchange of views and on the proposal of its Chairman, the Committee decided to request the Executive Board to invite the Director-General to determine whether, since the allegations of violations of human rights had been declared admissible, there were grounds for applying paragraph 14 (*k*) of 104 EX/Decision 3.3, on the understanding that the Committee would resume its consideration of the substance of the communication once it had examined the study on the procedural aspects of a "question" as defined in 104 EX/Decision 3.3.[34]

521. On the occasion of the present session, the Permanent Delegate of Israel to Unesco had sent the Secretariat a letter dated 3 September [1981],[35] in which she indicated that her government would be happy to inform the Committee of positive

---

[34] See document 112 EX/30 PRIV., para. 492 (*supra*, p. 31).

[35] See document 113 EX/CR/HR/1 Add.2.

developments in the administered areas in matters within the fields of competence of Unesco. She added that her government would furnish additional information during the next session, thereby demonstrating its efforts to reach a friendly resolution of the issues in question in the hope that the Committee might be able to conclude that the allegations made in this communication were without basis.

522. At the session, the representative of the Director-General said that the latter had twice discussed the matter with the representative of the Government of Israel and was willing, should the Committee so desire, to make further representations; the Committee should, however, stipulate whether he should continue his discussions by making specific suggestions in the spirit of 104 EX/Decision 3.3, paragraph 14 (*k*), or whether he should decide that a friendly solution appeared impossible and so submit the matter to the Executive Board.

523. The representative of the Government of Israel emphasized the spirit of co-operation his government had shown since the start of the affair. He said that in the joint undertaking of the search for a friendly solution, Israel was playing its part by establishing schools, universities and colleges where none had existed before and maintaining order and security in the territories concerned. He considered that Israel was in fact doing more than the minimum required by international law and making quantitative and qualitative improvements in education. He then recalled that his government had communicated to the Committee information and statistical data proving that the author's allegations were unjustified [...].[36] He also referred to a brochure entitled "The rule of law in the areas administered by Israel" - distributed to the members of the Committee - and more particularly to that passage in it dealing with the Supreme Court. He indicated that each citizen, should he believe that any of his rights have been violated, might seek redress from that Court, that the numbers of persons exercising that right of appeal had risen greatly since the start of Israeli administration, and that in respect of complaints submitted by residents in the areas concerned, the Court applied local law, international law and the concepts of justice. Thence it was clear that Israel was not content to maintain normal day-to-day life, but sought to bring about a situation in which the local populace might express its will. The rule of law in the territories made any systematic violation of human rights impossible. Another example might be drawn from higher education: prior to the Israeli administration there had been no universities, while since then four had been established, the number of students was increasing annually by 22 per cent, and 1,150 students from other regions had been admitted: agricultural and polytechnical colleges had also been established by the Israeli administration. The representative of the Israeli Government concluded that such results in education were spectacular and clearly demonstrated that the Government of Israel constantly endeav-

[36] See document 112 EX/CR/HR/1, annex V.

oured to promote education in every practical way. Lastly, he confirmed his government's intention to provide the Committee with a fresh report reviewing the development of the situation so as to reach a friendly solution of the communication.

524. One member of the Committee said that there could be no talk of a friendly solution, not because the Committee was hostile towards the idea but because the facts themselves prevented it, and that consequently the Committee could only resort to the provisions of 104 EX/Decision 3.3, paragraph 18: that is, transmit the communication to the Executive Board.

525. All other members of the Committee who spoke subsequently in the debate called for continuing efforts to find a friendly solution: two felt that applying the provisions of paragraph 18 would mean that the Committee had exhausted the possibilities of a friendly solution, which was not the case, particularly as the Committee was awaiting other documents and information. One of them even added that before invoking paragraph 18, it was necessary both to exhaust the opportunities contained in paragraph 14 (*k*) and furthermore to meet the conditions laid down in paragraph 15 of the decision in question. He emphasized that the facts of the communication had never been examined. He said that there was no automatic expiration of the Director-General's efforts to find a friendly solution. Two other members held that the Director-General should be allowed to follow the development of the situation and asked to keep the Committee informed. Two members argued that on humanitarian grounds it was unwise to make a political issue of the education of people living in the territories concerned; one stipulated that it was in the interest of the populations concerned for the dialogue with the Israeli authorities to continue, and that this would enable the Committee to remain informed about and alert to the way in which courses were being conducted in actual practice. Consequently, the most advantageous decision was not to open a political debate that would exceed the terms of reference of the Committee and Unesco, but rather to maintain the communication on the Committee's agenda, to receive information from the Israeli Government and to allow the Director-General to pursue his search for a friendly settlement.

526. While agreeing with the solution put forward by the previous speakers, one member said that he could not allow the representative of the Israeli Government to say that the rule of law prevailed in the occupied territories while the preamble to the brochure he had just distributed to members of the Committee contested the very validity of the resolutions adopted by the organizations of the United Nations. Lastly, a member returned to the floor to urge that the Israeli Government's remarks contained in [the document referred to in paragraph 523 above][37] be examined at the next session.

---

[37] *Ibidem*.

Israel **No. 12/78**

527. Since the great majority of speakers had called for the communication to be maintained on the Committee's agenda in the hope that the action taken in the spirit of 104 EX/Decision 3.3, paragraph 14 (*k*), might be successful, the Chairman proposed and the Committee *decided*:

(i) to suspend examination of this communication;

(ii) to ask the Executive Board to request the Director-General to pursue his consultations with the government concerned and on this occasion, to attempt to reach a friendly settlement under the terms of paragraph 14 (*k*) of 104 EX/ Decision 3.3;

(iii) to advise the State concerned that the Committee would be glad to receive all relevant information on the development of the situation with which the communication dealt.

Spring 1982 session of the Committee on Conventions and Recommendations (114th session of the Executive Board)[38]

711. The author of the communication, "Head of the Palestinian Human Rights Committee for the Defence of War and Political Prisoners" and member of the Executive Committee of the PLO, alleges the violation of human rights in the fields of education, science, culture and communication, claime to have been committed in the territories occupied by the State of Israel.

712. At its [spring] 1979 session, the Committee decided to hold over consideration of the admissibility of this communication until the Secretariat had prepared a fuller summary of the allegations, on the basis of the data which were to be requested from the author of the communication and submitted beforehand to the government concerned.[39]

713. For the [autumn] 1979 session, the Secretariat prepared a summary of the author's allegations which was distributed to the Committee and communicated to the government concerned and to the author of the communication. The author of the communication endorsed the summary in question and designated the observer of the PLO to Unesco as his representative for the continuation of the procedure in connection with that communication.

---

[38] See document 114 EX/38 PRIV., paras. 711-763; see also documents 114 EX/CR/HR/1 and Add.

[39] See document 107 EX/PRIV.31, para. 144 (*supra*, pp. 10-11).

No. 12/78 **Israel**

714. After discussion, and on the proposal of the Chairman, the Committee decided to declare the communication admissible, with the reservation that the Secretariat should be instructed, in collaboration with the author, to review the communication in order to eliminate from it any component which did not fall within Unesco's spheres of competence, and to ensure that the communication came within the context of 104 EX/Decision 3.3.[40]

715. In accordance with the Committee's instructions, the communication was revised and submitted to the Committee at the [spring] 1980 session [...].[41] That document was a summary of the 65 documents (490 pages) presented to the Secretariat.

716. At the [spring] 1980 session, the Committee, at the request of the Israeli Government, decided to continue detailed consideration of this communication at its next session.[42]

717. The Chairman had then informed the Committee that by a letter dated 14 February 1980, the author of the communication had requested the Committee to authorize him to address it, in conformity with the provision of paragraph 14 (*g*) of 104 EX/Decision 3.3. The Chairman drew the Committee's attention to the fact that it was for the Committee to decide whether or not it should request the Executive Board to authorize it to hear the author of the communication.

718. Certain members of the Committee felt that the request should be responded to favourably, since the presence of Mr Saleh, as a representative of the victims and a victim himself, would permit an in-depth examination of the communication. Other members felt that since the procedure in question was only foreseen for "exceptional circumstances", the Committee would not be in a position to decide whether or not the circumstances were "exceptional", and thus justifying the taking of the floor by the authors of the communication, until it had examined the substance of the communication.

719. One member of the Committee expressed the view that the circumstances were manifestly "exceptional" and warranted the appearance of the author of the communication, because Mr A. J. Saleh's testimony could shed valuable light on the enormous amount of documentation submitted to the Committee, especially since the communication in question was, in that member's opinion, one where it was difficult to assess at a glance whether it was concerned with a set of "cases" or with a "question" within the meaning of 104 EX/Decision 3.3.

---

[40] See document 108 EX/38 PRIV., para. 177 (*supra*, p. 13).
[41] See document 109 EX/CR/HR/1 Add.
[42] See document 109 EX/52 PRIV., para. 265 (*supra*, p. 14).

Israel **No. 12/78**

720. Another member of the Committee said that, while he took due note of paragraph 14 (*g*) of 104 EX/Decision 3.3, Unesco should not become a forum for confrontation between authors of communications and the governments concerned and that it was important not to create a precedent which might prove to be dangerous. He also hoped that emphasis would be placed rather more on effective collaboration between the Organization and those governments.

721. The representative of the Director-General pointed out to the Committee that this was the first time that it had been presented with such a request. The possibility of addressing the Committee was governed by a reference to the Rules of Procedure of the Executive Board ([Rule] 29); it could only be exercised within very narrow limits and only after express authorization by the Executive Board. Nothing was specified about the way in which this possibility was to be exercised but it was clear that its purpose was definitely not to organize a debate between the author of a communication and the representative of the government concerned.

722. After a lengthy discussion, the Committee decided to take a decision at its next session on the request presented to it by the author of the communication and to request its Chairman to ask the Chairman of the Executive Board to plan for the possibility of an additional session of the Committee during the next session of the Executive Board. This supplementary session would be convened if the Committee was of the opinion, after examining the substance of [this communication], that it was justified in responding favourably to the request made by the author of the communication in conformity with paragraph 14 (*g*) of 104 EX/Decision 3.3.[43]

723. At its [autumn] 1980 session, the Committee decided that it would first hear the statement of the representative of the Government of Israel before deciding whether or not to invite the author of the communication to appear before the Committee to provide additional information on the case.

724. The Israeli representative presented to the Committee the position of his government, set out in the form of a letter dated 22 August 1980 [...].

725. If the decision to admit the case was irreversible, he said, the communication should nevertheless be dismissed since it was unfounded and frivolous, as an examination of the facts would show. On a point of procedure he stressed that documents Nos. (i) - (x) were dated 1979 and were thus outside the scope of the communication which was submitted in 1978. Furthermore, the documents had not been forwarded to the Israeli Government and could thus not be considered by the Committee.

---

[43] *Ibidem*, para. 271 (*supra*, p. 15).

726. As to the facts alleged in the communication, they were either untrue or distorted, the Israeli representative said; far from encouraging students or pupils to drop out or from preventing the development of higher education in the areas in question, it was precisely the Government of Israel which enabled the establishment of institutions of higher learning in the administered areas. Arab education and culture had greatly expanded and flourished in the administered areas due to the encouragement and assistance they had been receiving throughout from the Israeli authorities, he said. He went on to present statistics to illustrate this point. The Israeli representative requested that the case be dismissed.

727. A member of the Committee commented that the author of the communication had submitted it in several capacities. In any event, the Committee member stated, he was now convinced that the communication concerned a question in the sense of 104 EX/Decision 3.3 and that it would be more appropriate for it to be considered by the Executive Board or the General Conference where a solution might be more readily found, than before the Committee. He felt obliged to respond to the Israeli representative's statement however, since he felt that the occupying forces appeared not to wish to respect international law. He stated that Arab demonstrations in the occupied areas always started peacefully but only became violent when the forces of authority appeared. He also wondered how a student could have been killed by a stray bullet when it was known that the Israeli army was excellently trained.

728. The fact that education was encouraged and growing in the occupied areas was a relative question, he said, since it might well be that the progress might have been much more rapid had the area not been occupied, and he cited the progress of his own country. Finally, it was pointed out, the existence of a decree which placed all educational institutions under military control was of itself a reason to treat this communication very seriously. The matter should be treated as a question, he said, and should be handled in accordance with the Committee's procedural decision on questions which it was expected to take at its next session when it would have before it the Secretariat's study on such matters. He went on to draw the Committee's attention to a document recently addressed to the Director-General which was related to the present communication, and which contained new and important information, but which had not yet been forwarded to the Committee. The Committee member raised the question as to whether it might not be possible to send a fact-finding mission to the territory in question so that the facts could definitely be determined.

729. In response to questions, the representative of the Director-General explained that there was no possibility of appeal once the Committee had decided to admit a communication. He explained that once a communication was admitted, the necessary procedure to follow was either to dismiss it after a friendly solution to the problem had been arrived at or to dismiss it in accordance with subparagraph (*j*) of para-

graph 14, or to submit a report to the Executive Board. In that connection, he pointed out that there existed, in the relevant [104 EX/Decision 3.3], the possibility of submitting one or more separate reports to the Executive Board on the various cases before the Committee.

730. As to the question concerning a fact-finding mission, the representative of the Director-General stated that though not expressly mentioned in the said decision, such missions were a well-established working method for other international human rights organs.

731. The Committee members agreed that the decision to admit the communication was irreversible, and during the exchange of views a consensus emerged that, given the need to determine, in the light of the new information provided, whether the communication concerned a case or a question, it would be best for the Committee to consider the communication more closely at its next session when it would be in a position to examine the Director-General's relevant study. It was so decided.[44]

732. At the [spring 1981 session], the representative of the Israeli Government addressed the substance of the matter, recalling his government's position as presented to the [autumn] 1980 session. He went on to emphasize that Israel acted in conformity with international law, that it had not destroyed any schools, that it had not undertaken mass deportations of teachers, that it had not ruled and did not rule the occupied territories by terror, that it had administered and was administering them in accordance with the relevant legal and humanitarian regulations, that it was perfectly possible for any injured party to seek redress against military action regarded as illegal (in this respect Israel applied British jurisprudence) and that everything possible had been done to contribute to the development of education and technical instruction. He concluded by stressing the fact that it had been no part of his intention to argue a case before the Committee, since the sole purpose of the obscure allegations in the communication, in his opinion, was to incite Unesco to adopt a political attitude and play a part hostile to Israel. With regard to paragraph 14 (*j*) and (*k*) of 104 EX/ Decision 3.3, he stated that his government was ready to accept any useful and fruitful suggestion.

733. A member of the Committee pointed out that detailed examination of the documents annexed to the communication clearly showed that there were, in fact, a number of inaccuracies and some inconsistencies in the facts put forward. On the principle that, in the state of generalized warfare prevailing in that region of the Middle East, the only way forward was by co-operation, he had proposed that a friendly solution should be sought in the spirit of paragraph 14 (*k*) of 104 EX/Decision 3.3.

---

[44] See document 110 EX/40 PRIV., para. 299 (*supra*, p. 22).

734. Another member of the Committee pointed out that the communication raised two kinds of problems:

> a problem relating to the administration of educational establishments: in this respect, there were no international standards prescribing the percentage of pupils or students to be admitted to a school or university;
>
> a problem relating to order, security and justice: in this respect, it seemed doubtful whether the case fell within Unesco's fields of competence.

735. This being so, the solution was purely and simply to apply paragraph 14 (*j*) of 104 EX/Decision 3.3 and dismiss the communication once and for all.

736. Two other members of the Committee took the view that it was paragraph 18 of that decision that should be applied (consideration of the communication by the Executive Board and the General Conference in public meetings), since the allegations concerned events that had occurred in an occupied country.

737. After an exchange of views and on the proposal of its Chairman, the Committee decided to request the Executive Board to invite the Director-General to determine whether, since the allegations of violations of human rights had been declared admissible, there were grounds for applying paragraph 14 (*k*) of 104 EX/Decision 3.3, on the understanding that the Committee would resume its consideration of the substance of the communication once it had examined the study on the procedural aspects of a "question" as defined in 104 EX/Decision 3.3.[45]

738. For the [autumn 1981 session], the Permanent Delegate of Israel to Unesco sent the Secretariat a letter dated 3 September [1981], in which she indicated that her government would be happy to inform the Committee of positive developments in the administered areas in matters within the fields of competence of Unesco. She added that her government would provide additional information during the next session, thereby demonstrating its efforts to reach a friendly resolution of the issues in question in the hope that the Committee might be able to conclude that the allegations made in that communication were without basis.

739. At that session, the representative of the Director-General said that the Director-General had twice discussed the matter with the representative of the Government of Israel and was willing, should the Committee so desire, to make further representations; the Committee should, however, stipulate whether he should continue his discussions by making specific suggestions in the spirit of 104 EX/Decision 3.3,

---

[45] See document 112 EX/30 PRIV., para. 492 (*supra*, p. 31).

paragraph 14 (*k*), or whether he should decide that a friendly solution appeared impossible and so submit the matter to the Executive Board.

740. The representative of the Government of Israel emphasized the spirit of co-operation his government had shown since the start of the affair. He said that in the joint undertaking of the search for a friendly solution, Israel was playing its part by establishing schools, universities and colleges where none had existed before and maintaining order and security in the territories concerned. He considered that Israel was in fact doing more than the minimum required by international law and making quantitative and qualitative improvements in education. He then recalled that his government had communicated to the Committee information and statistical data proving that the author's allegations were unjustified [...]. He also referred to a brochure entitled "The rule of law in the areas administered by Israel" - distributed to the members of the Committee - and more particularly to that passage in it dealing with the Supreme Court. He indicated that each citizen, should he believe that any of his rights have been violated, might seek redress from that Court, that the numbers of persons exercising that right of appeal had risen greatly since the start of Israeli administration, and that in respect of complaints submitted by residents in the areas concerned, the Court applied local law, international law and the concepts of justice. Thence it was clear that Israel was not content to maintain normal day-to-day life, but sought to bring about a situation in which the local populace might express its will. The rule of law in the territories made any systematic violation of human rights impossible. Another example might be drawn from higher education: prior to the Israeli administration there had been no universities, while since then four had been established, the number of students was increasing annually by 22 per cent, and 1,150 students from other regions had been admitted: agricultural and polytechnical colleges had also been established by the Israeli administration. The representative of the Israeli Government concluded that such results in education were spectacular and clearly demonstrated that the Government of Israel constantly endeavoured to promote education in every practical way. Lastly, he confirmed his government's intention to provide the Committee with a fresh report reviewing the development of the situation so as to reach a friendly solution of the communication.

741. One member of the Committee said that there could be no talk of a friendly solution, not because the Committee was hostile towards the idea but because the facts themselves prevented it, and that consequently the Committee could only resort to the provisions of 104 EX/Decision 3.3, paragraph 18 - that is, transmit the communication to the Executive Board.

742. All other members of the Committee who spoke subsequently in the debate called for continuing efforts to find a friendly solution. Two felt that applying the provisions of paragraph 18 would mean that the Committee had exhausted the possi-

bilities of a friendly solution, which was not the case, particularly as the Committee was awaiting other documents and information. One of them even added that before invoking paragraph 18, it was necessary both to exhaust the opportunities contained in paragraph 14 (*k*) and furthermore to meet the conditions laid down in paragraph 15 of the decision in question. He emphasized that the facts of the communication had never been examined. He said that there was no automatic expiration of the Director-General's efforts to find a friendly solution. Two other members held that the Director-General should be allowed to follow the development of the situation and asked to keep the Committee informed. Two members argued that on humanitarian grounds it was unwise to make a political issue of the education of people living in the territories concerned. One said that it was in the interest of the populations concerned for the dialogue with the Israeli authorities to continue, and that this would enable the Committee to remain informed about and alert to the way in which courses were being conducted in actual practice. Consequently, the most advantageous decision was not to open a political debate that would exceed the terms of reference of the Committee and Unesco, but rather to maintain the communication on the Committee's agenda, to receive information from the Israeli Government and to allow the Director-General to pursue his search for a friendly settlement.

743. While agreeing with the solution put forward by the previous speakers, one member said that he could not allow the representative of the Israeli Government to say that the rule of law prevailed in the occupied territories while the preamble to the brochure he had just distributed to members of the Committee contested the very validity of the resolutions adopted by the organizations of the United Nations. Lastly, a member returned to the floor to urge that the Israeli Government's remarks contained in [the document referred to in paragraph 740] be examined at the next session.

744. Since the great majority of speakers had called for the communication to be maintained on the Committee's agenda in the hope that the action taken in the spirit of 104 EX/Decision 3.3, paragraph 14 (*k*), might be successful, the Chairman proposed and the Committee decided:[46]

(i) to suspend the examination of that communication;

(ii) to ask the Executive Board to request the Director-General to pursue his consultations with the government concerned and on this occasion, to attempt to reach a friendly settlement under the terms of paragraph 14 (*k*) of 104 EX/ Decision 3.3;

---

[46] See document 113 EX/38 PRIV., para. 527 (*supra*, p. 43).

(iii) to advise the State concerned that the Committee would be glad to receive all relevant information on the development of the situation with which the communication dealt.

745. The Secretariat duly contacted the author of the communication and the government concerned as directed by the Committee.

746. On 22 April 1982, the Secretariat received from the Permanent Delegation of Israel to Unesco a letter and a document [...].[47]

747. At the Committee's present session, the representative of the Israeli Government reminded the Committee that his government had presented to the Committee at previous sessions specific answers to the allegations in this communication in the form of legal and factual information.

748. [A document][48] was being presented to the Committee at its present session as a comprehensive report on the education situation in the occupied territories. The Israeli representative went on to cite various data from the report, e.g. while the area had had a population growth of 23 per cent, there had been in the area a growth of the student body of 85 per cent. Furthermore there had been a marked rise in school attendance and there was no longer any illiteracy among the young people.

749. Another significant factor had been the growth of vocational educational schools he said; they were free of charge and offered a wide variety of courses. The Israeli representative pointed out that while the statistics might appear somewhat dry, they did accurately reflect the situation and the progress that had been and was being made. Under certain circumstances, he went on to say, there had been some violent agitation, and it had been necessary to restore order through force. He added that unfortunately, certain elements wished to inflame the situation and to seek publicity for themselves. Despite their agitation, however, they did not succeed in preventing the populace from seeking and obtaining education. There was no systematic violation of human rights in the territories, the Israeli delegate explained, nor could there be since Israel assured that the rule of law prevailed there.

750. The elements for a friendly solution were thus present here, the Israeli representative stated.

---

[47] See document 114 EX/CR/HR/1 Add.
[48] *Ibidem.*

No. 12/78 **Israel**

751. A Committee member informed the Committee that his government wished the communication to be considered as coming within the scope of paragraph 18 of [104 EX/Decision 3.3].

752. Another Committee member felt that the information which had been presented by the Israeli Government was impressive, and he indicated that it would be useful to forward this information to the authors of the communication for eventual comments.

753. It was the view of another Committee member that the comments of the Israeli representative had shown that the Israeli Government was not really concerned with respecting Unesco's interest in education. He stated that statistics were meaningless if a student did not have the proper atmosphere in which to learn. Soldiers surrounded schools, there were curfews, and it was impossible to study in such an atmosphere he said. From the media one could learn about Israel's violent actions against students, the Committee member stated, and he felt that the communication was clearly admissible.

754. The view was then expressed by a Committee member that it was important to remember that the political aspects of this case were not within Unesco's scope of competence. He stated that the communication contained very vague allegations, and that though these allegations did in fact raise certain questions coming within Unesco's areas of interest, the Israeli Government had clearly and fully replied to the allegations and the communication should thus be dismissed as not warranting further action, in accordance with paragraph [14] (*j*) of [104 EX/Decision 3.3].

755. Another Committee member felt that the educational situation in a country could not be examined outside of its political context. The document which had been submitted to Unesco by the Israeli Government bore the imprint of the abnormal situation in the occupied territories and, in fact, the document even revealed that it had been prepared by the Defense Ministry of Israel, he said. He further stated that the right to self-determination was one of the key elements of the United Nations Charter, and that this right was not being respected in the present situation. The educational situation in the occupied territories needed to be seen in the context of the relevant international instruments, he said.

756. A previous speaker then insisted that there were indeed special circumstances there since it was a case of an occupied territory. He thus felt that the Committee should not feel confined to the terms of its usual procedures. Furthermore the statistics were not that impressive, he said, since progress would have taken place in any event over such a long 15-year period. Finally he raised a question as to why Arab teachers were being paid less than their counterparts in the territories.

Israel **No. 12/78**

757. By way of clarification the representative of the Director-General explained that this communication had already been declared admissible by the Committee and that the Committee was at its present session at the stage of the examination of the substance thereof and the seeking of a friendly solution.

758. The question of whether this communication constituted a case or a question, i.e. a series of cases, had not yet been broached by the Committee and thus it was not yet in a position to decide whether or not paragraph 18 of [104 EX/Decision 3.3] applied.

759. Several Committee members expressed their doubts as to the appropriateness of applying paragraph 18. One member stated that he had on several occasions expressed his preference for considering this communication as a case rather than as a question since experience had shown that successful solutions and/or the obtaining of humanitarian assistance were much more likely if communications were examined as individual cases by the Committee. He felt that the Committee should keep the case before it and seek a solution rather than take the simple way out by either dismissing it or passing it on to another Unesco organ. In this same vein, another view was expressed that even before the Committee could decide whether this case constituted a case or a question it would have to address itself to examining the validity of the specific allegations made therein. Other members felt that it was important to settle the case in a friendly manner within the present Committee context and that the best way to do this was to continue to express concern for the educational situation in the territories and to seek the good offices of the Director-General.

760. In response to various questions the Israeli delegate explained that the large percentage of the students cited in the statistics was indeed local, the others being from Israel and other nearby areas. As concerned the vocational schools the number 47,000 represented the overall graduation figure while 3,477 represented the number of graduates in 1981 only. Furthermore the Israeli delegate went on to explain, Israel was not trying to hide the fact that there was a military occupation involved here; had it tried to do so it would no doubt have been accused of attempting annexation. He also explained that the lower wages for the Arab teachers was due to the simple fact that they taught a fewer number of hours; this was so because the teaching system was anchored to the systems in Jordan and Egypt, both of which had shorter schedules than that in Israel, and salaries were obviously linked to the hours of teaching.

761. The view was expressed by a Committee member that whenever there was a foreign occupation the natives tended to view the occupiers as being persons without a heart, this was a fact of life, he said and as long as the war situation that existed in the territories continued to exist, Unesco was likely to have such complaints before

it. But the Committee needed to be effective, he said, and should thus apply the previously mentioned paragraph 18 procedure.

762. Another Committee member stated that he, as one who had spent a year in Gaza and was thus in a position to judge, was pleased to see the considerable progress reflected by the report. He felt that if the paragraph 18 procedure were applied it would take the Committee far from the possibility of a friendly solution.

763. After further debate, the Committee *decided*:

> (i) to suspend examination of the substance of the communication but to keep it on its agenda in conformity with paragraph 14 (*h*) of 104 EX/Decision 3.3;
>
> (ii) to transmit the fresh information provided by the government concerned to the author of the communication and to request him to submit any comments and information that might help the Committee to arrive at a decision as to whether it was appropriate in that particular case to apply the provisions of paragraph 14 (*j*) or paragraph 18 of 104 EX/Decision 3.3;
>
> (iii) to ask the Executive Board to request the Director-General to pursue, in the meantime, his consultations with the government concerned in an attempt to bring about a friendly solution under the terms of paragraph 14 (*k*) of 104 EX/Decision 3.3 and to provide it, at its next session, with all the information he deemed possible and appropriate.

Autumn 1982 session of the Committee on Conventions and Recommendations (115th session of the Executive Board)[49]

420. The author of the communication, "Head of the Palestinian Human Rights Committee for the Defence of War and Political Prisoners" and member of the Executive Committee of the PLO, alleges the violation of human rights in the fields of education, science, culture and communication, claimed to have been committed in the territories occupied by the State of Israel.

421. At its spring 1979 session, the Committee decided to hold over consideration of the admissibility of this communication until the Secretariat had prepared a fuller summary of the allegations, on the basis of the data which were to be requested from

[49] See document 115 EX/28 PRIV., paras. 420-459; see also document 115 EX/CR/HR/1.

the author of the communication and submitted beforehand to the government concerned.[50]

422. For the autumn 1979 session, the Secretariat prepared a summary of the author's allegations which was distributed to the Committee and communicated to the government concerned and to the author of the communication. The author of the communication endorsed the summary in question and designated the observer of the PLO to Unesco as his representative for the continuation of the procedure in connection with that communication.

423. After discussion, the Committee decided to declare the communication admissible, with the reservation that the Secretariat should be instructed, in collaboration with the author, to review the communication in order to eliminate from it any part which did not fall within Unesco's spheres of competence, and to ensure that the communication came within the context of 104 EX/Decision 3.3.[51]

424. In accordance with the Committee's instructions, the communication was revised and submitted to the Committee at the spring 1980 session [...].[52] This document was a summary of the 65 documents (490 pages) presented to the Secretariat.

425. At the spring 1980 session, the Committee, at the request of the Israeli Government, decided to continue detailed consideration of this communication at its next session.[53]

426. After a lengthy discussion, the Committee decided to take a decision at its next session on the request presented to it by the author of the communication and to request its Chairman to ask the Chairman of the Executive Board to plan for the possibility of an additional session of the Committee during the next session of the Executive Board. This supplementary session would be convened if the Committee was of the opinion, after examining the substance of [this communication], that it was justified in responding favourably to the request made by the author of the communication in conformity with paragraph 14 (*g*) of 104 EX/Decision 3.3.[54]

427. At its autumn 1980 session, the Committee decided that it would first hear the statement of the representative of the Government of Israel before deciding whether or not to invite the author of the communication to appear before the Committee to provide additional information on the case. The Israeli representative presented to

---

[50] See document 107 EX/PRIV.31, para. 144 (*supra*, pp. 10-11).
[51] See document 108 EX/38 PRIV., para. 177 (*supra*, p. 13).
[52] See document 109 EX/CR/HR/1 Add.
[53] See document 109 EX/52 PRIV., para. 265 (*supra*, p. 14).
[54] *Ibidem*, para. 271 (*supra*, p. 15).

the Committee the position of his government, set out in the form of a letter dated 22 August 1980 [...].

428. If the decision to admit the case was irreversible, he said, the communication should nevertheless be dismissed since it was unfounded and frivolous, as an examination of the facts would show. On a point of procedure he stressed that documents Nos. (i) - (x) were dated 1979 and were thus outside the scope of the communication which was submitted in 1978. Furthermore, the documents had not been forwarded to the Israeli Government and could thus not be considered by the Committee.

429. As to the facts alleged in the communication, they were either untrue or distorted, the Israeli representative said; far from encouraging students or pupils to drop out or from preventing the development of higher education in the areas in question, it was precisely the Government of Israel which enabled the establishment of institutions of higher learning in the administered areas. Arab education and culture had greatly expanded and flourished in the administered areas due to the encouragement and assistance they had been receiving throughout from the Israeli authorities, he said. He went on to present statistics to illustrate this point. The Israeli representative requested that the case be dismissed.

430. A member of the Committee commented that the author of the communication had submitted it in several capacities. In any event, the Committee member stated, he was now convinced that the communication concerned a question in the sense of 104 EX/Decision 3.3 and that it would be more appropriate for it to be considered by the Executive Board or the General Conference where a solution might be more readily found, than before the Committee. He felt obliged to respond to the Israeli representative's statement however, since he felt that the occupying forces appeared not to wish to respect international law. He stated that Arab demonstrations in the occupied areas always started peacefully but only became violent when the forces of authority appeared. He also wondered how a student could have been killed by a stray bullet when it was known that the Israeli army was excellently trained.

431. The Committee members agreed that the decision to admit the communication was irreversible, and during the exchange of views a consensus emerged that, given the need to determine, in the light of the new information provided, whether the communication concerned a case or a question, it would be best for the Committee to consider the communication more closely at its next session when it would be in a position to examine the Director-General's relevant study. It was so decided.[55]

---

[55] See document 110 EX/40 PRIV., para. 299 (*supra*, p. 22).

Israel **No. 12/78**

432. At the [spring 1981 session], the representative of the Israeli Government addressed the substance of the matter, recalling his government's position as presented to the [autumn] 1980 session. He went on to emphasize that Israel acted in conformity with international law, that it had not destroyed any schools, that it had not undertaken mass deportations of teachers, that it had not ruled and did not rule the occupied territories by terror, that it had administered and was administering them in accordance with the relevant legal and humanitarian regulations, that it was perfectly possible for any injured party to seek redress against military action regarded as illegal (in this respect Israel applied British jurisprudence) and that everything possible had been done to contribute to the development of education and technical instruction. He concluded by stressing the fact that it had been no part of his intention to argue a case before the Committee, since the sole purpose of the obscure allegations in the communication, in his opinion, was to incite Unesco to adopt a political attitude and play a part hostile to Israel. With regard to paragraph 14 (*j*) and (*k*) of 104 EX/Decision 3.3, he stated that his government was ready to accept any useful and fruitful suggestion.

433. A member of the Committee pointed out that detailed examination of the documents annexed to the communication clearly showed that there were, in fact, a number of inaccuracies and some inconsistencies in the facts put forward. On the principle that, in the state of generalized warfare prevailing in that region of the Middle East, the only way forward was by co-operation, he had proposed that a friendly solution should be sought in the spirit of paragraph 14 (*k*) of 104 EX/Decision 3.3.

434. After an exchange of views and on the proposal of its Chairman, the Committee decided to request the Executive Board to invite the Director-General to determine whether, since the allegations of violations of human rights had been declared admissible, there were grounds for applying paragraph 14 (*k*) of 104 EX/Decision 3.3, on the understanding that the Committee would resume its consideration of the substance of the communication once it had examined the study on the procedural aspects of a "question" as defined in 104 EX/Decision 3.3.[56]

435. For the autumn 1981 session, the Permanent Delegate of Israel to Unesco sent the Secretariat a letter dated 3 September [1981], in which she indicated that her government would be happy to inform the Committee of positive developments in the administered areas in matters within the fields of competence of Unesco. She added that her government would provide additional information during the next session, thereby demonstrating its efforts to reach a friendly resolution of the issues in question in the hope that the Committee might be able to conclude that the allegations made in that communication were without basis.

---

[56] See document 112 EX/30 PRIV., para. 492 (*supra*, p. 31).

436. At that session, the representative of the Director-General said that the Director-General had twice discussed the matter with the representative of the Government of Israel and was willing, should the Committee so desire, to make further representations; the Committee should, however, stipulate whether he should continue his discussions by making specific suggestions in the spirit of 104 EX/Decision 3.3, paragraph 14 (*k*), or whether he should decide that a friendly solution appeared impossible and so submit the matter to the Executive Board.

437. The representative of the Government of Israel emphasized the spirit of co-operation his government had shown since the start of the affair. He said that in the joint undertaking of the search for a friendly solution, Israel was playing its part by establishing schools, universities and colleges where none had existed before and maintaining order and security in the territories concerned. He considered that Israel was in fact doing more than the minimum required by international law and making quantitative and qualitative improvements in education. He then recalled that his government had communicated to the Committee information and statistical data proving that the author's allegations were unjustified [...]. He also referred to a brochure entitled "The rule of law in the areas administered by Israel" - distributed to the members of the Committee - and more particularly to that passage in it dealing with the Supreme Court. He indicated that each citizen, should he believe that any of his rights have been violated, might seek redress from that Court, that the numbers of persons exercising that right of appeal had risen greatly since the start of Israeli administration, and that in respect of complaints submitted by residents in the areas concerned, the Court applied local law, international law and the concepts of justice.

438. One member of the Committee said that there could be no talk of a friendly solution, not because the Committee was hostile towards the idea but because the facts themselves prevented it, and that consequently the Committee could only resort to the provisions of 104 EX/Decision 3.3, paragraph 18 - that is, transmit the communication to the Executive Board. All other members of the Committee who spoke subsequently in the debate called for continuing efforts to find a friendly solution.

439. Since the great majority of speakers had called for the communication to be maintained on the Committee's agenda in the hope that the action taken in the spirit of 104 EX/Decision 3.3, paragraph 14 (*k*), might be successful, the Chairman proposed and the Committee decided:[57]

(i) to suspend examination of that communication;

[57] See document 113 EX/38 PRIV., para. 527 (*supra*, p. 43).

(ii) to ask the Executive Board to request the Director-General to pursue his consultations with the government concerned and on this occasion, to attempt to reach a friendly settlement under the terms of paragraph 14 (*k*) of 104 EX/ Decision 3.3;

(iii) to advise the State concerned that the Committee would be glad to receive all relevant information on the development of the situation with which the communication dealt.

440. On 22 April 1982, the Secretariat received from the Permanent Delegation of Israel to Unesco a letter and a document [...].

441. At the Committee's spring 1982 session, the representative of the Israeli Government reminded the Committee that his government had presented to the Committee at previous sessions specific answers to the allegations in this communication in the form of legal and factual information.

442. [The document referred to in paragraph 440 above] was being presented to the Committee at [that] session as a comprehensive report on the education situation in the occupied territories. The Israeli representative went on to cite various data from the report, e.g. while the area had had a population growth of 23 per cent, there had been in the area a growth of the student body of 85 per cent. Furthermore there had been a marked rise in school attendance and there was no longer any illiteracy among the young people.

443. Another significant factor had been the growth of vocational educational schools he said; they were free of charge and offered a wide variety of courses. The Israeli representative pointed out that while the statistics might appear somewhat dry, they did accurately reflect the situation and the progress that had been and was being made. Under certain circumstances, he went on to say, there had been some violent agitation, and it had been necessary to restore order through force. He added that unfortunately, certain elements wished to inflame the situation and to seek publicity for themselves. Despite their agitation, however, they did not succeed in preventing the populace from seeking and obtaining education. There was no systematic violation of human rights in the territories, the Israeli delegate explained, nor could there be since Israel assured that the rule of law prevailed there. The elements for a friendly solution were thus present here, the Israeli representative stated.

444. A Committee member informed the Committee that his government wished the communication to be considered as coming within the scope of paragraph 18 of [104 EX/Decision 3.3]. Another Committee member felt that the information which had been presented by the Israeli Government was impressive, and he indicated that it

would be useful to forward this information to the authors of the communication for eventual comments.

445. Several Committee members expressed their doubts as to the appropriateness of applying paragraph 18. One member stated that he had on several occasions expressed his preference for considering this communication as a case rather than as a question since experience had shown that successful solutions and/or the obtaining of humanitarian assistance were much more likely if communications were examined as individual cases by the Committee. He felt that the Committee should keep the case before it and seek a solution rather than take the simple way out by either dismissing it or passing it on to another Unesco organ. In this same vein, another view was expressed that even before the Committee could decide whether this case constituted a case or a question it would have to address itself to examining the validity of the specific allegations made therein. Other members felt that it was important to settle the case in a friendly manner within the present Committee context and that the best way to do this was to continue to express concern for the educational situation in the territories and to seek the good offices of the Director-General.

446. The view was expressed by a Committee member that whenever there was a foreign occupation the natives tended to view the occupiers as being persons without a heart, this was a fact of life, he said and as long as the war situation that existed in the territories continued to exist, Unesco was likely to have such complaints before it. But the Committee needed to be effective, he said, and should thus apply the previously mentioned paragraph 18 procedure.

447. After further debate, the Committee decided:[58]

> (i) to suspend examination of the substance of the communication but to keep it on its agenda in conformity with paragraph 14 (*h*) of 104 EX/Decision 3.3;
>
> (ii) to transmit the fresh information provided by the government concerned to the author of the communication and to request him to submit any comments and information that might help the Committee to arrive at a decision as to whether it was appropriate in that particular case to apply the provisions of paragraph 14 (*j*) or paragraph 18 of 104 EX/Decision 3.3;
>
> (iii) to ask the Executive Board to request the Director-General to pursue, in the meantime, his consultations with the government concerned in an attempt to bring about a friendly solution under the terms of paragraph 14 (*k*) of 104

[58] See 114 EX/38 PRIV., para. 763 (*supra*, p. 54).

EX/Decision 3.3 and to provide it, at its next session, with all the information he deemed possible and appropriate.

448. The Secretariat has as yet received no further information.

449. At the autumn 1982 session, the representative of the Israeli Government reminded the Committee that this communication had been before the Committee since 1978. Her government had provided at successive sessions information from the legal, conceptual and factual points of view. At the [autumn 1980] session, every allegation had been carefully answered; at the [spring 1981] session the legal aspects had been explained and the rule of law in the occupied territories had been shown; and at the [autumn 1981] session practical information on the educational systems had been presented.

450. Israel had thus co-operated in a friendly way to show in a very detailed manner the progress which had taken place in the territories in question. This information, in the form of a document, had been sent to the author of the communication for comments, and Israel had been waiting for the responses and comments requested of the author.

451. The Israeli representative went on to say that Israel had always been co-operative with the Committee even though it felt that the communication in question had been submitted with ulterior motives. The lack of a reply from the author cast further doubt on the motivations of the author, and the evidence also showed that the communication was ill-founded and submitted in bad faith. Her government requested that examination of this communication be discontinued.

452. Several Committee members felt that the only logical course would be for the Committee to maintain this communication on its agenda, in accordance with paragraph 14 (*h*) of 104 EX/Decision 3.3, so as to allow the author sufficient time to reply.

453. A Committee member stated that the arguments presented by the Israeli Government did not stand up; there was no proof presented of the author's bad faith or ulterior motives. The Committee member wondered whether the author had received the document which was to have been sent to him. He also pointed out that Unesco itself had evidence of the problems faced by the Palestinians, since Unesco had sent a mission to look into such matters.

454. The representative of the Director-General informed the Committee that the Secretariat had sent the document in question to the author at his Beirut address under cover of an explanatory letter on 11 June 1982 by registered mail, with a copy to

the Palestinian Liberation Organization (PLO) observer mission at Unesco. The letter to the Government of Israel had been sent somewhat later, on 23 June.

455. A Committee member wondered how one could speak of bad faith in this case; was Unesco in bad faith when it had corroborated the facts concerning the situation in the occupied territories? What was happening there contradicted the assertions of the Israeli Government.

456. Another Committee member felt that the author was now a twofold victim: he was a victim of the violence of the Israeli invasion of Beirut and he was also thereby prevented from answering the letter sent to him.

457. It was felt by another Committee member that the underlying conflict giving rise to this communication was not within Unesco's jurisdiction. As for that part of the communication which did concern Unesco, he felt that paragraph 14 (*j*) of 104 EX/Decision 3.3, concerning dismissal for not warranting further action, would have been the paragraph to apply, but in the interest of maintaining a consensus he was willing to accept a further suspension of the communication.

458. Another Committee member stated that the concerns of her government were well known and she felt that the least the Committee could do was to keep this communication on its agenda and ask for more information.

459. The Committee then *decided* to apply paragraph 14 (*h*) and to suspend the examination of this communication until its next session.

Spring 1983 session of the Committee on Conventions and Recommendations (116th session of the Executive Board)[59]

286. The author of the communication, "Head of the Palestinian Human Rights Committee for the Defence of War and Political Prisoners" and member of the Executive Committee of the PLO, alleges the violation of human rights in the fields of education, science, culture and communication, claimed to have been committed in the territories occupied by the State of Israel.

287. At the spring 1979 session, the Committee decided to hold over consideration of the admissibility of this communication until the Secretariat had prepared a fuller summary of the allegations, on the basis of the data which were to be requested from

[59] See document 116 EX/48 PRIV., paras. 286-306; see also document 116 EX/CR/HR/1.

the author of the communication and submitted beforehand to the government concerned.[60]

288. For the autumn 1979 session, the Secretariat prepared a summary of the author's allegations which was distributed to the Committee and communicated to the government concerned and to the author of the communication. The author of the communication endorsed the summary in question and designated the observer of the PLO to Unesco as his representative for the continuation of the procedure in connection with that communication.

289. After discussion, the Committee decided to declare the communication admissible with the reservation that the Secretariat should be instructed, in collaboration with the author, to review the communication in order to eliminate from it any part which did not fall within Unesco's spheres of competence and to ensure that the communication came within the context of 104 EX/Decision 3.3.[61]

290. In accordance with the Committee's instructions, the communication was revised and submitted to the Committee at the spring 1980 session [...].[62] This document was a summary of the 65 documents (490 pages) presented to the Secretariat.

291. At the spring 1980 session, the Committee, at the request of the Israeli Government, decided to continue detailed consideration of this communication at its next session.[63]

292. After a lengthy discussion, the Committee decided to take a decision at its next session on the request presented to it by the author of the communication and to request its Chairman to ask the Chairman of the Executive Board to plan for the possibility of an additional session of the Committee during the next session of the Executive Board. This supplementary session would be convened if the Committee was of the opinion, after examining the substance of [this communication], that it was justified in responding favourably to the request made by the author of the communication in conformity with paragraph 14 (*g*) of 104 EX/Decision 3.3.[64]

293. At the autumn 1980 session, the Committee decided that it would first hear the statement of the representative of the Government of Israel before deciding whether or not to invite the author of the communication to appear before the Committee to provide additional information on the case. The Israeli representative presented to

[60] See document 107 EX/PRIV.31, para. 144 (*supra*, pp. 10-11).
[61] See document 108 EX/38 PRIV., para. 177 (*supra*, p. 13).
[62] See document 109 EX/CR/HR/1 Add.
[63] See document 109 EX/52 PRIV., para. 265 (*supra*, p. 14).
[64] *Ibidem*, para. 271 (*supra*, p. 15).

the Committee the position of his government, set out in the form of a letter dated 22 August 1980 [...].

294. The Committee members agreed that the decision to admit the communication was irreversible, and during the exchange of views a consensus emerged that, give the need to determine, in the light of the new information provided, whether the communication concerned a case or a question, it would be best for the Committee to consider the communication more closely at its next session when it would be in a position to examine the Director-General's relevant study. It was so decided.[65]

295. At the spring and autumn 1981 sessions, the Committee decided to request the Executive Board to invite the Director-General to explore the possibility of applying paragraph 14 (*k*) of 104 EX/Decision 3.3.[66]

296. At the Committee's spring 1982 session the representative of the Israeli Government presented to the Committee a comprehensive report entitled "Education and Culture in Judaea, Samaria and the Gaza District". The Committee decided to transmit this report to the author of the communication and to request him to submit to the Committee comments and information thereon.[67]

297. At the autumn 1982 session, the Committee decided to maintain the communication its agenda so as to allow the author additional time to reply.[68]

298. At the Committee's present session the representative of the Israeli Government again reminded the Committee that Israel had always co-operated with Unesco in a friendly way, even though it felt that the communication in question was ill-founded and submitted with ulterior motives. She pointed out that her government had provided at successive sessions information from the legal, conceptual, and factual points of view. At the autumn 1980 session, every allegation had been thoroughly refuted, at the spring 1981 session the legal aspects had been explained and the rule of law in the occupied territories had been demonstrated; at the autumn 1981 session, practical information on the education system had been presented. The Israeli representative went on to point out to the Committee that a document showing in great detail the progress which had taken place in the territories in question had been sent to the author for comment by Unesco almost a year ago and no reply had been received.

---

[65] See document 110 EX/40 PRIV., para. 299 (*supra*, p. 22).

[66] See documents 112 EX/30 PRIV., para. 492 (*supra*, p. 31), and 113 EX/38 PRIV., para. 527 (ii) (*supra*, p. 43), respectively.

[67] See document 114 EX/38 PRIV., para. 763 (ii) (*supra*, p. 54).

[68] See document 115 EX/28 PRIV., para. 459 (*supra*, p. 62).

Israel **No. 12/78**

299. The Israeli representative said that at the Committee's autumn 1982 session she had asked that consideration of this case be discontinued under paragraph 14 (*j*) of [104 EX/Decision 3.3].

300. The Israeli representative stated that, as still no reply had been received since the last session of the Committee, it was clear that the author had not only lost interest but had no reply to make. The lack of a reply to two letters gave further evidence of the ill-founded nature of the communication, she said, and she asked that consideration of it be discontinued under paragraph 14 (*j*) of [104 EX/Decision 3.3].

301. The Israeli representative subsequently informed the Committee that it had become known that the author of the communication had recently been ousted from the PLO. This was an indication that those who had at one time supported this communication no longer considered the author to be qualified to speak for them.

302. Certain members of the Committee expressed the view that the author, as well as the PLO, had had more than ample time to comment upon the information which had been sent to them and that, given their complete lack of response, the Committee should strike this case from its list. One of these members pointed out that the authors would not thereby be prevented from submitting a new communication if they so desired. Another member felt the author should be clearly warned that the communication would be dropped if he still did not reply.

303. Other members of the Committee felt that the lack of a reply was perfectly understandable in light of the horrible events which had taken place over the past months in Lebanon, and that the author should be given more time to reply. One of these Committee members felt that this case still qualified for treatment under paragraph 18 of 104 EX/Decision 3.3. Another member stated that words could not describe the gravity of the events in Lebabon, but that one should not let one's feelings affect one's objectivity. He supported the proposal to give the author one more chance and a clear warning, before striking the communication off.

304. In reply to a question the representative of the Director-General explained the careful steps which the Secretariat had taken to mail the correspondence to the author and his representatives, in accordance with his instructions; he further explained that the author had indeed submitted the communication in a multiple capacity, which was possible under the Committee's procedures.

305. A feeling emerged among many of the Committee members that the author should be given a clear warning that his communication would no longer be considered if he did not provide the reply which had been requested of him.

306. The Committee thus *decided* to:

(i) request the Secretariat to once again send appropriate information to the author;

(ii) give the author one last opportunity to reply, if he so wished;

(iii) re-examine the case at the next session only in the event of the author providing this reply.

Autumn 1983 session of the Committee on Conventions and Recommendations (117th session of the Executive Board)[69]

208. The author of the communication, Head of the Palestinian Human Rights Committee for the Defence of War and Political Prisoners and former member of the Executive Committee of the PLO, alleges violations of human rights in the fields of education, science, culture and communication, claimed to have been committed in the territories occupied by the State of Israel.

209. This Communication has been on the Committee's agenda since [the spring 1979 session].

210. At its [spring 1983] session, the Committee had noted that the author had not yet communicated to it his comments on the report entitled "Education and culture in Judaea, Samaria and the district of Gaza" furnished by the Government of Israel at the spring 1982 session and sent to Mr Abdul Jawad Saleh after that session. Consequently, the Committee had decided to send him that document once again in order to give him one last chance to reply, and to resume consideration of the case at the present session only if that reply was forthcoming.[70]

211. On 7 September 1983, the Secretariat received from Mr Abdul Jawad Saleh a document in Arabic accompanied by 36 annexes in Arabic and English.

212. At the present session the representative of the Government of Israel informed the Committee that he had received a copy of that document on 13 September 1983 and that he stood by his letter of 12 September 1983 [...][71] in which he stated that

---

[69] See document 117 EX/18 PRIV., paras. 208-214; see also documents 117 EX/CR/HR/1 and Add.4.
[70] See document 116 EX/48 PRIV., para. 306 (*supra*, p. 66).
[71] See document 117 EX/CR/HR/1 Add.4.

the Committee should conclude its consideration of this communication given that in his view the condition set by it, i.e. the reply from the author, had not been met.

213. However, Committee members who contributed to a brief discussion on the communication declared themselves in favour of postponing consideration of the communication in order to allow the Secretariat time to make a résumé of the document sent by the author.

214. As a consequence, the Committee *decided* to suspend consideration of this communication until the spring 1984 session.

Spring 1984 session of the Committee on Conventions and Recommendations (119th session of the Executive Board)[72]

217. The author of the communication, Head of the Palestinian Human Rights Committee for the Defence of War and Political Prisoners and former member of the Executive Committee of the PLO alleges violations of human rights in the fields of education, science, culture and communication, claimed to have been committed in the territories occupied by the State of Israel. This communication has been on the Committee's agenda since [the spring 1979 session].

218. About five days before the [autumn 1983] session of the Committee, the Secretariat received from the author of the communication a document in Arabic accompanied by 36 annexes in Arabic and English. Committee members who contributed to a brief discussion on the communication declared themselves in favour of postponing consideration of the communication in order to allow the Secretariat time to make a résumé of the document sent by the author. As a consequence, the Committee decided to suspend consideration of the communication until its spring 1984 session.[73]

219. Introducing the communication to the Committee, the Legal Adviser stated that in the past the Committee, in its examination of the communication, had always benefited from the presence of a representative of the Israeli Government but that at the Committee's present session, the government concerned would not be represented for reasons indicated in the Israeli Permanent Delegate's letter of 2 March 1984 addressed to the Director-General [...].[74] In answer to a question from a member of the Committee who wanted to know if the latest document submitted by the author indi-

---

[72] See document 119 EX/35 PRIV., paras. 217-225; see also documents 119 EX/CR/HR/1 and Add.

[73] See document 117 EX/18 PRIV., para. 214 (*supra*, p. 67).

[74] See document 119 EX/CR/HR/1 Add.

cated whether or not available internal remedies had been exhausted, the Legal Adviser explained that the communication had gone beyond the admissibility stage and that, for that reason, the issue of the exhaustion of internal remedies was not pertinent unless the Committee wanted to consider it within the context of the examination of the substance of the communication. Another member of the Committee expressed regret over the Committee's previous decision by which the communication was declared admissible.

220. A member of the Committee declared that, in his view, it would be difficult for the Committee to make progress in its examination of the communication without the presence of a representative of Israel. Several other members agreed. One member remarked in this connection that the communication appeared to him to raise a "question" rather than an individual "case" and added that a question would be extremely difficult to examine without the co-operation of the government concerned. Observing that the Committee had in the past received the collaboration of the Government of Israel, another member suggested that this government must be informed that it could be in its own interest to resume its co-operation with the Committee because the latest document submitted by the author of the communication contained certain allegations which the Committee could hardly ignore. He proposed that in the meantime, the Committee should set up a working group to compare the report entitled "Education and culture in Judaea, Samaria and the district of Gaza" furnished by the Government of Israel at the spring 1982 session of the Committee and the latest document submitted by the author and which constitutes his comments on that report.

221. Another member however, expressed reservations over this proposal. He suggested the Committee should try and find out why the Israeli authorities were this time withholding their co-operation from the Committee. To this end, he proposed a brief adjournment to enable the Secretariat to invite the Permanent Delegate of Israel to come to the meeting of the Committee. Many members of the Committee deplored the fact that the Israeli Government was not represented. In a general remark in this connection, a member expressed the hope that governments concerned with communications submitted to the Committee would appreciate that the procedure and the work of the Committee provided them with a useful and elegant pretext for rectifying things which might have gone wrong as far as the respect for internationally recognized human rights was concerned.

222. All the members of the Committee who spoke on the communication strongly deplored both the tone and the substance of the letter of 2 March 1984 sent by the Permanent Delegate of Israel. In particular, they found disrespectful the allegation that in its handling of the communication concerned, the Committee had allowed itself to be "manipulated". The collective reaction of the Committee was that all the

allegations made against it in the letter were manifestly ill-founded and unjustified. Consequently, the Committee categorically rejected and repudiated them. Some members suggested that the Israeli Permanent Delegate be requested to withdraw his letter. Others proposed that the offensive parts of the letter should be expunged from the records of the Committee relating to the communication. While fully endorsing the collective reaction of the Committee to the tone and substance of the letter in question, other members however counselled that the Committee should take a forward-looking approach to the examination of the communication and suggested all avenues should be explored in order to obtain the future co-operation of the Israeli authorities in the examination of the communication. Some members proposed in this connection that the Director-General should be requested to use his good offices with the view to securing for the Committee the collaboration of the Israeli Government.

223. In answer to a question from a member of the Committee, the Legal Adviser referred to paragraph 14 (*e*) of [the] Executive Board's [104 EX/Decision 3.3] which provided that "representatives of governments concerned may attend meetings of the Committee in order to provide additional information or to answer questions from members of the Committee on either admissibility or the merits of the communication". He said it was quite clear from this text that no government was under any obligation to send a representative to the Committee during its discussion of a communication which concerned that government. The Legal Adviser added however that, in the past, the Committee had always insisted that it needed the co-operation of the governments concerned in order to discharge effectively the responsibilities incumbent upon it by virtue of the aforementioned [104 EX/Decision 3.3]. Reiterating that this was the first time that the Government of Israel was not lending its help to the Committee in the examination of the communication in question he suggested that perhaps the Committee might wish to ask the Executive Board to request the Director-General to use his good offices with the view to getting the Israeli authorities to resume their co-operation with the Committee so as to enhance the chances of an amicable solution being found to the problems raised by the communication. Remarking that the Permanent Delegate had indicated clearly in his letter why his government was no longer going to co-operate with the Committee, a member of the Committee proposed that a special report should be prepared and sent by the Committee to the Executive Board. Another member however expressed reservations over this proposal because, in his opinion, the Committee would have to do more in respect of the examination of the communication before the Executive Board could usefully be seized with a special report on it.

224. A member of the Committee suggested that the appropriate context in which the examination of the communication should be placed was the Middle East situation which had given rise to much concern. He stated that it was no secret that ten-

sion in that area was caused by Israel's occupation of Arab territories and its policy of terror and repression. According to that member, settlement of the case in question was not possible without an equitable settlement of the Palestinian problem. Recalling the success that the Committee had achieved in the past in helping to obtain solutions to alleged violations of human rights involving individuals, another member remarked that in the case concerning the violation of the human rights of a whole people, that is the Palestinian people, the Committee appeared to him to be less effective. He said this was a contradiction which raised for him personally an issue of conscience.

225. At the end of its discussion of the communication, the Committee *decided*:

(i) to take note of all of the items of information provided by the author of the communication;

(ii) to take note of the position of the government concerned expressed in its letter dated 2 March 1984, the wording of which it proposed to reconsider at the next session;

(iii) to request the Executive Board to invite the Director-General to inform the government concerned of the very great importance attached by the Committee to that government's continued co-operation in the examination of the communication;

(iv) to request the government concerned to forward to the Committee, in time for the next session, any useful information relating to the new material submitted by the author of the communication;

(v) to resume examination of the substance of this communication at its [autumn 1984] session.

Autumn 1984 session of the Committee on Conventions and Recommendations (120th session of the Executive Board)[75]

204. The author of the communication, Head of the Palestinian Human Rights Committee for the Defence of War and Political Prisoners and former member of the Executive Committee of the PLO, alleges violations of human rights in the fields of education, science, culture and communication, claimed to have been committed in the

[75] See document 120 EX/15 PRIV., paras. 204-208, see also document 120 EX/CR/HR/1.

territories occupied by the State of Israel. This communication has been on the Committee's agenda since [the spring 1979 session].

205. Introducing the communication, the Legal Adviser stated that there was no new development concerning it. He added that the Secretariat had, in accordance with the constant practice, informed the Permanent Delegation of Israel that the examination of the communication would be resumed by the Committee at its present session, but there had been no reaction from the Delegation as to the willingness of the Israeli authorities to be represented before the Committee.

206. Several members of the Committee noted that the latest information document submitted to the Committee by the authors of the communication [contains] serious substantive allegations of violations of human rights which fall squarely within Unesco's fields of competence, especially those violations concerning students, teachers and educational institutions in the occupied territories. Reference was also made to the tragic incidents that had taken place at Sabra and Chatila. These members emphasized that these allegations called for serious and responsible explanations from the authorities of the Member State concerned which, for this reason, should have ensured its representation before the Committee. In this connection, one member of the Committee, pointing out that the effectiveness of the Committee's action depended on the co-operation of all Member States concerned, expressed the fear that if the lack of co-operation from the Israeli authorities were to produce a demonstration effect on other States, the work of the Committee could be totally paralysed. He added that it was important for the Executive Board's attention to be drawn to this potentially alarming situation.

207. Noting the nature of the allegations contained in the communication, two members of the Committee expressed the view that if the co-operation of the State concerned remained not forthcoming, the communication might have to be handled within the framework of paragraph 18 of 104 EX/Decision 3.3 which indicates how questions of alleged massive, systematic or flagrant violations of human rights should be dealt with. Other members indicated that perseverance was an essential part of the Committee's moral force and expressed the hope that the new government in the Member State concerned would show more willingness than its predecessor to co-operate with the Committee. In this connection, they suggested that the Executive Board should be asked to request the Director-General to emphasize once again to the Israeli authorities the extreme importance that the Committee attached to a resumption of their co-operation in the examination of the communication concerned.

No. 12/78 **Israel**

208. The Committee:

(i) *Noting* yet again the absence of the government concerned, which did not feel obliged to send a representative for reasons that are given in its letter of 2 March 1984 but that the Committee is unable to accept;

(ii) *Deeply regrets* this refusal to co-operate on the part of the Israeli Government;

(iii) *Asks* the Executive Board to request the Director-General to impress on the Israeli Government the extreme importance attached by the Committee to the co-operation of States concerned by communications, such co-operation being the very essence of Unesco's constitutional provisions and vital in the light of the new information submitted by the author of the communication, to which the government concerned has never replied;

(iv) *Decides* to resume examination of the substance of this communication at its next session, when it firmly hopes it will have the co-operation of the Israeli Government;

(v) *Asks* the Executive Board to request the Director-General to continue his humanitarian representations, in line with paragraph 14 (*k*) of 104 EX/Decision 3.3;

(vi) *Requests* the Executive Board to consider, at such time as it considers appropriate, the problem facing the Committee as a result of the refusal of certain governments to co-operate, thus making it impossible for the Committee to carry out the task assigned to it by the Executive Board in 104 EX/Decision 3.3.

Spring 1985 session of the Committee on Conventions and Recommendations (121st session of the Executive Board)[76]

210. The author of the communication, Head of the Palestinian Human Rights Committee for the Defence of War and Political Prisoners and former member of the Executive Committee of the PLO, alleges violations of human rights in the fields of education, science, culture and communication, claimed to have been committed in the territories occupied by the State of Israel. This communication has been on the Committee's agenda since [the spring 1979 session].

---

[76] See document 121 EX/46 PRIV., paras. 210-217; see also document 121 EX/CR/HR/1.

Israel **No. 12/78**

211. Introducing the communication, the Legal Adviser stated that there was no new development concerning it, except the fact that the Secretariat had just received from the Permanent Delegate of the Member State concerned a letter dated 2 May 1985 by which he re-stated his government's position with respect to the communication concerned.

212. The representative of the government himself read out to the Committee a copy of this letter, in which he explained that the decision of his government to authorize him to appear before the Committee at its current session had been inspired, first and foremost, by consideration of and in deference to the appeal for co-operation made to his government by the Director-General as well as to the views of the Committee's members. This, the letter added, should not, however, be construed as having detracted from or, indeed, disposed of the most serious reservations of the government concerned regarding past examination of the communication, nor of its disapprobation of the departure which its retention on the Committee's agenda had come to symbolize from procedures laid down by the Executive Board's 104 EX/Decision 3.3. The representative of the government concerned stated further in his letter that his government felt it was incumbent upon it to clarify, once again, its conviction that both the substance and the language of the communication in question were totally inadmissible in view of its ill-founded, hostile and highly objectionable nature. He alluded to the document entitled "Report on the Israeli occupation and its effects on cultural and educational institutions in the occupied territories" which was submitted by the author in September 1983 [...][77] and stated that his government considered the information contained in that document was equally inadmissible.

213. The representative of the government concerned concluded his letter with the following statement: "My authorities are deeply convinced that the removal, from the Committee's agenda, of this obnoxious communication, following seven years of unproductive deliberations, will make an important contribution to a spirit of reconciliation and constructive dialogue, in keeping with the true ideals of Unesco, which is so vital to its future growth".

214. In his oral remarks before the Committee, the representative of the government concerned indicated that his appearance before the Committee was part of a confidence-building process that was evolving on the part of his government with respect to the work of the Committee. He urged the Committee not to continue indefinitely with the examination of the communication in question and more so since, according to him, available domestic remedies had not been exhausted.

---

[77] See document 119 EX/CR/HR/1.

No. 12/78 **Israel**

215. A member declared that if the communication in question had occupied the attention of the Committee for a long time, it was entirely the result of the intransigence of the government concerned which was denying the right of a whole people to education. In particular, he pointed out the refusal of the government to reopen schools, universities and other educational institutions closed down in the occupied Arab territories. One other member remarked that not long ago the armed forces of the government concerned had occupied part of Lebanon. He added that although the armed forces were withdrawing from the area of Lebanon occupied by them, hundreds of people, including teachers arrested by the government concerned, were still languishing in Israeli gaols. Another member of the Committee declared that, in his opinion, the end of the problems raised by the communication would not be in sight until the people concerned once again had the right to exercise their sovereignty over their land now occupied by a foreign invader. Several members of the Committee declared that they wanted the communication to continue to occupy the Committee's attention and that accordingly further examination of its substance should be deferred to the autumn 1985 session of the Committee, it being understood that in the meantime the Director-General should be requested by the Executive Board to continue his humanitarian action with a view to contributing to obtain a solution to the problems raised by the communication. A member of the Committee queried whether the communication did not rather raise a "question" that required to be dealt with in accordance with paragraph 18 of [104 EX/Decision 3.3].

216. Two members of the Committee stated that they saw in the presence of the representative of the government an encouraging sign for the resumption of a dialogue between the Committee and that government. While agreeing that the presence of the representative of the government concerned was to be appreciated, another member expressed his regret that although present, the representative of the government was not willing to engage in a dialogue with members of the Committee. Another member declared his wish to see friendly relations established in the Middle East region and urged all those who were interested in peace in that region to work towards it in an amicable manner.

217. At the end of its discussion, the Committee *decided*:

(i) to request the Executive Board to ask the Director-General to continue his humanitarian action with a view to seeking peaceful solutions to the serious problems raised by the communication;

(ii) to keep the communication on its list.

Israel **No. 12/78**

Autumn 1985 session of the Committee on Conventions and Recommendations (122nd session of the Executive Board)[78]

161. The author of the communication, Head of the Palestinian Human Rights Committee for the Defence of War and Political Prisoners and former member of the Executive Committee of the PLO, alleges violations of human rights in the fields of education, science, culture and communication, claimed to have been committed in the territories occupied by the State of Israel. This communication has been on the Committee's agenda since [the spring 1979 session]. At its present session, the Committee was informed that no new information had been received either from the author of the communication or from the government concerned.

162. Observing that the government concerned had not sent a representative to the meeting of the Committee, a member of the Committee declared that if this government had nothing to feel responsible for as far as the allegations contained in the communications were concerned, it should have sent a representative to co-operate with the Committee through a dialogue. This member added that, in his view, the communication invoked cases of violations of certain minimum human rights of the whole of the Palestinian people and declared that such violations greatly disturbed the conscience of all humanity. Associating themselves with the foregoing remarks, some members indicated that to a certain extent the communication might well be considered as raising a "question" rather than isolated cases of alleged violations of human rights coming within the Organization's fields of competence. A number of members of the Committee indicated their regret over the absence of any representative of the government concerned during the Committee's discussion of the communication and expressed the hope that, at its next session, the Committee would be able to count on the co-operation of the government so as to resume a constructive dialogue on the allegations contained in the communication in question. One member, however, stated in this connection that in the past there had been occasional replies or information provided by the government concerned. Evoking in a general manner the importance that the Committee attaches to representation of governments before the Committee during the examination of communications concerning them, a member of the Committee suggested that the Executive Board should examine, at such time as it considers appropriate, the problem created for the Committee by the fact that some governments refuse to co-operate with it, thereby making it impossible for the Committee to carry out the task entrusted to it by the Executive Board in 104 EX/Decision 3.3. Another member of the Committee stated for his part that the problem of some countries' not sending representatives to the Committee could only be examined properly on a case to case basis because while the absence

[78] See document 122 EX/21 PRIV., paras. 161-163; see also document 122 EX/CR/HR/1.

of representation of some countries manifested the refusal of the governments concerned to co-operate with the Committee in its work, for some other countries, the absence of representation might well be for legitimate reasons.

163. After an exchange of views, the Committee adopted the following *decision*:

(i) Noting once again the absence of the government concerned;

(ii) Noting with regret that no new, constructive development concerning this communication has been recorded since the last session,

(iii) Deeply regrets the refusal of the government concerned to co-operate with the Committee;

(iv) Requests the Executive Board, in view of the seriousness of the alleged violations, to ask the Director-General to continue his humanitarian action with a view to seeking a satisfactory solution to the serious problems raised by the communication, in accordance with 104 EX/Decision 3.3, paragraph 14 (*k*);

(v) Requests the Executive Board to examine, at such time as it considers appropriate, the problem created for the Committee by the fact that some governments refuse to co-operate with it, thereby making it impossible for the Committee to carry out the task entrusted to it by the Executive Board in 104 EX/Decision 3.3;

(vi) Decides to keep the communication on its list.

Spring 1986 session of the Committee on Conventions and Recommendations (124th session of the Executive Board)[79]

153. The author of the communication, Head of the Palestinian Human Rights Committee for the Defence of War and Political Prisoners and former member of the Executive Committee of the PLO, alleges violations of human rights in the fields of education, science, culture and communication, claimed to have been committed in the territories occupied by the State of Israel. This communication has been on the Committee's agenda since [the spring 1979 session]. At its present session, the Committee was informed by the Secretariat that the situation remained the same as it was during the autumn 1985 session in the sense that no new information concerning the

[79] See document 124 EX/3 PRIV., paras. 153-157; see also document 124 EX/CR/HR/1.

allegations contained in the communication had been received either from the author of the communication or from the government concerned.

154. On her part, the Chairperson told the Committee that she had had a telephone conversation regarding the communication with the Permanent Delegate of Israel and that the latter had told her that the competent authorities of Israel were of the view that they had already brought to the attention of the Committee at some of its previous sessions all the information they considered relevant to the examination and the disposal of the communication and that they felt no useful purpose would be served by sending a representative to the Committee's present session. Several other members of the Committee expressed their regret over the fact that once again the government concerned had not sent a representative in order to provide additional information or to answer questions from members of the Committee on the merits of the communication. Recalling that the State concerned had always sent representatives to the Programme Commission of the Executive Board during the Commission's discussion of questions concerning educational and cultural institutions in the occupied Arab territories, one member declared that the Committee should perhaps be asking itself questions as to why the same government has on several occasions refused to be represented at the Committee during the examination of the communication in question. Another member advanced a guess that perhaps the government concerned was withholding its co-operation with the Committee because that government felt that the Committee's decision to declare the communication admissible had regrettably been arrived at in a hasty manner. The Chairperson stated that as the Committee had decided in favour of the admissibility of the communication, it would not be advisable for it to reopen that matter.

155. In reply to a question by a member of the Committee, the representative of the Director-General informed the Committee that in pursuance of [23 C/Resolution 27] adopted by the General Conference at its twenty-third session, the Director-General is to appoint a leading academic personality with responsibility for conducting a comprehensive study of the conditions in which academic freedoms are guaranteed and exercised in the occupied Arab territories, and to prepare a report to be submitted to the Executive Board. She said that the documents [...],[80] on the basis of which the aforesaid resolution was adopted, contained allegations some of which were, in their essential particulars, of the same nature as the allegations mentioned in the communication under discussion. She proposed that, with the view to contributing to facilitate the work of the Committee, a comparative study could be made of allegations that appear both in these documents and in the communication concerned. It was also proposed by a member of the Committee that the study should, as far as possible, take into consideration relevant information that may be made available by

[80] See documents 23 C/22 and Add.1 and 2.

appropriate human rights organs of the United Nations and the International Labour Organisation. Another member stated that the study to be prepared should take into account also the information which the Member State concerned has so far put at the disposal of the Committee.

156. With regard to the mission foreseen by the aforementioned [23 C/Resolution 27], some members of the Committee suggested that the mission's terms of reference could perhaps be extended so as to enable it to gather also relevant information concerning the alleged violations of human rights that are invoked in the communication before the Committee. The representative of the Director-General declared in this connection that, in her opinion, since the terms of reference of the envisaged mission had been laid down by the General Conference itself, it would not be appropriate for either the Committee or even the Executive Board to extend their scope or otherwise modify them. While concurring with this opinion, several members of the Committee declared that the mission concerned could, to the extent possible and compatible with its terms of reference, gather information regarding the alleged violations of human rights contained in the communication with which the Committee is seized.

157. After the discussion the Committee took the following *decision*:

The Committee,

(i) Notes once again, with regret, the absence of a representative of the government concerned;

(ii) Notes that the government concerned has been represented before another organ of the Executive Board dealing with questions related to developments affecting the situation of educational institutions in the occupied Arab territories, but has declined to be represented before the Committee;

(iii) Notes with regret that no new, constructive development concerning this communication has been recorded;

(iv) Requests once again the Executive Board to examine, at such time as it considers appropriate, the problem created for the Committee by the fact that some governments refuse to co-operate with it, thereby making it impossible for the Committee to carry out the task entrusted to it by the Executive Board in 104 EX/Decision 3.3;

(v) Requests the Secretariat to prepare a study that would help to facilitate the Committee's consideration of the alleged violations of human rights mentioned in the communication;

(vi) Requests the Executive Board, in view of the seriousness of the alleged violations, to ask the Director-General to continue his humanitarian action with a view to seeking a satisfactory solution to the serious problems raised by the communication;

(vii) Defers consideration of the communication to its next session.

Autumn 1986 session of the Committee on Conventions and Recommendations (125th session of the Executive Board)[81]

180. The author of the communication, Head of the Palestinian Human Rights Committee for the Defence of War and Political Prisoners and former member of the Executive Committee of the PLO, alleges violations of human rights in the fields of education, science, culture and communication, claimed to have been committed in the Arab territories occupied by the State of Israel. This communication has been on the Committee's agenda since [the spring 1979 session]. Among the documents made available to the Committee at its present session was a study [...][82] which, pursuant to the request made by the Committee at its spring 1986 session, the Secretariat had prepared in order to facilitate examination by the Committee of the human rights violations alleged in the communication. This document presented, in particular, a chronological antecedent of the communication up to the Committee's present session which had been extracted by the Secretariat mainly from documentation of about 800 pages submitted to the Organization by the author of the communication and by the government concerned as well as from previous reports of the Committee.

181. Taking the floor at the Committee's present session the representative of the government concerned recalled that the last time his government had been represented before the Committee was at its spring 1985 session and that on that occasion the representative of the government had informed the Committee that he had been authorized by his government to appear before the Committee primarily in deference to the appeal for co-operation made to his government by the Director-General and to the views expressed by members of the Committee. He added that his presence before the Committee at its present session was in the same spirit and with the ob-

[81] See document 125 EX/3 PRIV., paras. 180-184; see also documents 125 EX/CR/HR/1 and Add.
[82] See document 125 EX/CR/HR/1 Add.

jective of dispelling any suggestion of non-co-operation with the Committee that some of its members might be led to make in respect of his government. He declared however that it was the considered position of his government that all that needed to be said by it on the communication and the allegations contained therein had been already stated by its representatives at a number of the Committee's previous sessions and that, for this reason, his government believed that no useful purpose would be served by its participation in the discussion of the substance of the communication concerned. It was recalled in this connection that over the reiterated objections formulated by the government concerned, the Committee decided at its autumn 1979 session to declare the communication in question admissible.

182. The Chairperson expressed her regret that the representative of the government concerned was under instructions not to stay on at the meeting and participate in the discussion of the substance of the communication. After reiterating very briefly the reason that led his government to take this decision, the representative of the government took leave of the Committee.

183. Several members stated that in the light of the position of the government concerned in respect of the discussion of the substance of the communication, it would be helpful to the Committee to defer to its next session the consideration of the communication in the hope that, on that occasion, it would, with the authorization of the Executive Board, have at its disposal the report to be submitted by the leading academic personality that, in pursuance of 23 C/Resolution 27, the Director-General had appointed with responsibility for conducting a comprehensive study of the conditions in which academic freedoms were guaranteed and exercised in the occupied Arab territories. It was agreed by members of the Committee that in that case, the Secretariat should prepare for the Committee a document giving references to parts of the mission's report that might relate to some of the allegations contained in the communication concerned.

184. At the end of the discussion, the Committee *decided*:

(i) to thank the government concerned for sending a representative;

(ii) to express its regret over the decision of the government concerned not to engage with the Committee in a discussion of the substance of the communication in question;

(iii) to appeal to the government concerned to reconsider its position in order to accept at the Committee's next session a dialogue with it in respect of the substance of the communication;

(iv) to request:

(*a*) the Executive Board to make available to it the report that may be submitted to the Board concerning the mission foreseen under 23 C/Resolution 27;

(*b*) the Secretariat to prepare a document indicating references to those parts of that report that might also relate to some of the allegations contained in the communication concerned;

(v) to defer consideration of the communication to its spring 1987 session.

Spring 1987 session of the Committee on Conventions and Recommendations (126th session of the Executive Board)[83]

204. The author of the communication, who was Head of the Palestinian Human Rights Committee for the Defence of War and Political Prisoners and a former member of the Executive Committee of the PLO, has alleged violations of human rights in the fields of education, science, culture and communication, claimed to have been committed in the Arab territories occupied by the State of Israel. This communication has been on the Committee's agenda since the spring 1979 session. Among the documents made available to the Committee at its present session was a study [...][84] which, pursuant to the request made by the Committee at its spring 1986 session, the Secretariat had prepared in order to facilitate examination by the Committee of the human rights violations alleged in the communication.

205. Taking the floor, the representative of the government concerned stated that his predecessors had already replied to all possible questions of the Committee, that the allegations made were based on political considerations and that the Committee should therefore cease this twice-yearly exercise in politicization.

206. One member of the Committee declared that he saw no point in participating in a discussion in which the representative of the "Zionist entity" was taking part. He wondered what credence could be given to the statements of that representative. The member pointed out that there were daily reports of acts of aggression and repression against women and children in Palestine and the occupied Arab territories and against educational institutions in the occupied Arab territories, the most recent of which was the closure - yet again - of Bir-Zeit University by the occupation forces in the course of which young students were murdered. In his view, a large number of

[83] See document 126 EX/3 PRIV., paras. 204-215; see also document 126 EX/CR/HR/1.
[84] See document 125 EX/CR/HR/1 Add.

cases should be submitted to the Committee rather than a single case and he added that "it was indecent, even immoral, to hear the representative of a system that was the very negation of any concept of human rights defy and contest the authority of the Committee in regard to initiatives it had taken which were, in truth, far from matching up to the seriousness of the acts committed".

207. Following this statement, the representative of the government concerned withdrew, declaring that he could not conduct a discussion with the Committee under such conditions in spite of his respect for it.

208. The Chairperson expressed her regret at this decision by the representative of the government concerned and said that if he stayed he would be able to witness for himself the humanitarian nature of the Committee's work, the purpose of which was to try to put a stop to violations of human rights including the right to life and liberty.

209. Several members of the Committee also expressed their regret at this decision. They believed that the representative of the government concerned had chosen to avoid a discussion on the substance of the matter rather than provide a relevant explanation to the Committee. According to these members, his attitude demonstrated that the government concerned had no real wish to co-operate with the Committee. As the Committee had already waited nine years, it was now time, in their view, to apply the procedure provided for in paragraph 18 of 104 EX/Decision 3.3 which dealt with the examination of "questions". It was the view of these members that the Committee was actually confronted with a "question" of massive, systematic and flagrant violations of human rights and fundamental freedoms resulting from the occupation by Israel of foreign territory. One member of the Committee stated that, in view of the fact that no result had been obtained on the subject of the communication, which had been before the Committee for 10 years, he believed the time had come to review the Committee's work since its establishment. As in other organizations, including the United Nations itself, Unesco should reconsider its current activities with a view to enhancing their effectiveness and ensuring tangible results. As he saw it, the Committee should therefore consider whether it had fulfilled its mandate, and if necessary review or change it.

210. At this point, the representative of the Director-General drew attention to the fact that, in his oral report to the present session of the Executive Board, the Director-General had informed it of his decision, in agreement with Father Boné, to postpone the submission of his provisional report to the Board until the autumn session in the hope that the Israeli authorities would be good enough to authorize that distinguished person to visit the occupied Arab territories. Regarding the procedure laid down in paragraph 18 of 104 EX/Decision 3.3 she drew the Committee's attention to

the procedure which it had established at its [spring 1983] session [...][85] whereby it had first to "designate" the communication as constituting a case of massive, systematic and flagrant violation of human rights and then ask the Executive Board if it intended to examine it as a "question".

211. Some members of the Committee considered that as Father Boné's mission was under way and his report, which the Committee intended to use, was not yet available, it would be better to wait until it was completed and appeal to the Government of Israel to do everything within its power to enable that distinguished person to visit the occupied territories and also to obtain in good time whatever assistance was necessary for carrying out his mission.

212. Certain other members of the Committee doubted whether such an appeal would be heard. They emphasized that, in any case, Father Boné's terms of reference did not cover all aspects of the communication. In their view, the Committee should forthwith apply paragraph 18 of 104 EX/Decision 3.3 in the interests of credibility and effectiveness.

213. One member observed that the Committee could not launch an appeal directly but only make a recommendation to the Executive Board, asking it to do so or to request the Director-General to make use of his good offices. In this connection, the Chairperson considered that it would be quite in order to launch an appeal as this would still be a recommendation addressed by the Committee to the Executive Board and when the Board endorsed that recommendation it would become a decision to be implemented in the usual way.

214. While supporting the idea of launching an appeal in accordance with the appropriate procedure, certain other members of the Committee believed that it should be viewed as a final attempt on the part of the Committee which was now prepared to consider recourse to the procedure laid down in paragraph 18 of EX/Decision 3.3 at its next session.

215. Following consideration of the communication and the expression of reservations on the part of one of its members, the Committee *decided*:

(i) to express its dissatisfaction at the lack of information from the government concerned at the present session;

(ii) to express, in emphatic terms, its wish that, through the good offices of the Executive Board and the Director-General, the government concerned

---

[85] See document 116 EX/48 PRIV., paras. 334-340 and annex II.

make prompt efforts to facilitate Father Boné's task so that he may complete his mission before the end of the current academic year;

(iii) to inform the government concerned that should the relevant report of Father Boné, based on the co-operation requested, and all the other information - particularly information from the government concerned - in relation to this communication not be available to the Committee at its next session, it would have no option but to envisage applying the procedure provided for in paragraph 18 of 104 EX/Decision 3.3, namely, to consider describing the communication as a "question" which could lead to its consideration by the Executive Board in public meetings;

(iv) to resume consideration of this communication at its autumn 1987 session.

Autumn 1987 session of the Committee on Conventions and Recommendations (127th session of the Executive Board)[86]

146. The author of the communication, who is Head of the Palestinian Human Rights Committee for the Defence of War and Political Prisoners, alleges violations of human rights in the fields of education, science, culture and communication, claimed to have been committed in the territories occupied by Israel. This communication has been on the Committee's agenda since the spring 1979 session.

147. At its autumn 1986 session, the Committee requested the Executive Board to place at its disposal the report of the mission provided for in 23 C/Resolution 27 relating to the conditions in which academic freedoms are guaranteed and exercised in the occupied territories.[87] The Board agreed to that request in 125 EX/Decision 3. 2.

148. At its spring 1987 session, the Committee expressed the wish that, through the good offices of the Executive Board and the Director-General, the government concerned would make prompt efforts to facilitate the task of the leading academic personality, Father Boné, appointed to undertake the planned mission.[88]

---

[86] See document 127 EX/3 PRIV., paras. 146-165; see also documents 127 EX/CR/HR/1 and Add.

[87] See document 125 EX/3 PRIV., para. 184 (iv) (*a*) (*supra*, p. 81).

[88] See document 126 EX/3 PRIV., para. 215 (ii) (*supra*, pp. 83-84).

149. That mission has been accomplished, and the Committee has had at its disposal the report by Father Boné [...].[89]

150. In accordance with the wish expressed by the Committee at its autumn 1986 session, the Secretariat has prepared [a document][90] mentioning the parts of the report which might also be relevant to some of the allegations contained in the communication.

151. At the present session, the representative of the government concerned stated that the Committee had already been considering the case for nine years and that Israel had always displayed a constructive willingness to co-operate by replying to all possible questions, orally and in writing, and to all requests for clarification. He added that it was in the same spirit that everything had been done to facilitate the task of Father Boné who had, moreover, in his report, thanked the Israeli authorities for their unfailing collaboration, which was tangible and undeniable proof of their willingness to co-operate and a logical consequence of the fact that they had nothing to hide. The representative of the government concerned felt that after so many years of investigations, the Committee should end its consideration of the communication.

152. Several members of the Committee expressed their satisfaction that it had proved possible for Unesco to send a representative to the occupied territories and for the report of the mission to be drawn up in time. They congratulated Father Boné on the objectivity and constructive nature of the document. Some of those members considered that since Israel had not attempted to conceal the facts from that leading personality, the facts to be taken into consideration were accordingly the ones related in his mission report. Certain other members were of the opinion that the report marked an important stage in the discussion and opened up new possibilities of finding a solution. Certain other members pointed out that the report as a whole would be examined by the Programme and External Relations Commission of the Executive Board and by the Board itself, and that the Committee should therefore examine only the extent to which the report dealt with the alleged violations of human rights (falling within Unesco's fields of competence) contained in the communication. Still other members wondered whether, in view of Father Boné's recommendations, it was possible to hope for action to be taken on that remarkable report.

153. Taking the floor again, the representative of the government concerned stated that Israel had nothing to hide but that it was inconceivable that a sovereign State should be constantly inspected for reasons which often lay outside Unesco's purview. In his opinion, if the Committee were to regard the report as merely a stage in

[89] See document 127 EX/8.
[90] See document 127 EX/CR/HR Add.

its consideration of the communication, a new series of discussions lasting several years might well begin. As regards the hoped-for future co-operation, he affirmed that whenever a request was in keeping with the spirit of the Organization, the latter would always find Israel co-operative. He made a point of observing that certain facts alleged in the communication dated back to 1967, i.e. to 20 years previously, and that the specific individual cases originally referred to had already been settled long before that was true, for example, of the cases concerning closures of universities and students arrested, since those institutions had been reopened and the persons concerned had been freed; moreover, contrary to the allegations made, students wishing to leave the occupied territories or Israel itself to register in another university - in particular, as mentioned by the author of the communication, that of Beirut - could do so freely. With respect to the complaint about general policy, he considered that since the matter had been raised in Father Boné's report, it would be the task of other specific organs of Unesco - the Programme and External Relations Commission, the Executive Board or the General Conference - to discuss it. According to the representative of the government concerned, the communication, having been thus voided of its substance, should be struck from the Committee's list.

154. In the view of certain members of the Committee, Father Boné's observations on the violations of human rights in Unesco's fields of competence showed that the basic problems had not been settled; on the contrary, the report had merely opened the discussion. They pointed out that it was the first time that the international community had had such a report before it, a report which, in the opinion of one member, proved that it was appropriate to apply paragraph 18 of 104 EX/Decision 3.3 relating to the consideration of a "question", as envisaged in the Committee's decision at its [spring 1987] session: the accusation no longer concerned a student, a teacher, an institution or censorship but the situation as a whole in the occupied territories. The same speaker referred in particular to paragraph 15.4 of Father Boné's report, entitled "Academic freedom and the destruction of cultural or national identity". It seemed to him that the rapporteur had found that there was no academic freedom in those territories, and that the occupation authorities, through repression, threats and military decisions, had undermined the cultural identity of a people. He considered that the Committee should reinforce the recommendations of Father Boné and make sure that Unesco was able to play its role to the full. That opinion was shared by other members of the Committee.

155. The Chairwoman reminded the Committee of the terms of the decision it had taken at its [spring 1987] session, according to which "should the relevant report of Father Boné, based on the co-operation requested, and all the other information - particularly information from the government concerned - in relation to this communication not be available to the Committee at its next session, it would have no option but to envisage applying the procedure provided for in paragraph 18 of 104 EX/

Decision 3.3, namely, to consider describing the communication as a 'question' which could lead to its consideration by the Executive Board in public meetings".[91] She therefore felt that that possibility had now been ruled out. In any case, the Committee could, after its discussion at the present autumn session, take any decision that it considered appropriate.

156. A few members of the Committee asked for clarifications on questions relating to the censorship of works in Arabic or of books containing the word "Palestine", the attitude of the Israeli authorities *vis-à-vis* the Council for Higher Education and the problem of vocational training that could lead to job opportunities on the labour market in the occupied territories.

157. The representative of the government concerned replied that nothing proved that the facts alleged in Father Boné's report were true: various persons had replied to Father Boné's questions and he had merely noted their answers; it was one thing to mention in the statistics, for example, that a university had been closed, but to identify the person responsible for that closure was another. In support of his argument, he related the circumstances surrounding the closure of Al-Najah University a week previously, a measure decided by its President, an eminent Arab professor, because of the opposition between two groups of students who were trying to impose their ideology on the others. He also referred to paragraph 16.2 (6) of Father Boné's report to the effect that "assistance should be provided to the academic authorities in their university financing efforts, enabling them to maintain the university's independence *vis-à-vis* too strongly political liberation movements, in order to reduce, as far as possible, charges of collaboration with subversion and terrorism and, consequently, the repressive measures which could be associated therewith".

158. With regard to cultural identity, the representative of the government concerned maintained that Israel had helped to safeguard this by assisting in the establishment of universities which had not previously existed and by not attempting to impose Israeli curricula.

159. With regard to the censorship of certain works, he stated that it arose from the necessity to avoid stirring up hatred and discord. To illustrate his argument he quoted a few passages from two books intended for pupils in the fourth and the first years of primary education, and raised the question whether cutting out a few paragraphs or forbidding the circulation of *Mein Kampf* in order to safeguard the innocence of young children truly constituted censorship. He rejected as untrue the claim that a work had been banned simply because it contained the word "Palestine".

[91] See document 126 EX/3 PRIV., para. 215 (iii) (*supra*, p. 84).

160. On the subject of the labour market, he acknowledged that there was indeed a problem for university graduates, but pointed out that the phenomenon was common to all countries, including Israel. He assured members that, in any case, every effort had been made to find an appropriate solution, particularly in the fields of agronomy and tourism.

161. Regarding the Council for Higher Education, he offered to check the matter with the authorities of his country.

162. Some members of the Committee who then took the floor observed that Father Boné's report did not say that the universities had become hotbeds of subversion and that the university authorities had lost control over their institutions. In their view, the facts reported showed that the attacks on both individual and collective rights and freedoms, in particular academic rights and freedoms, the right to cultural identity and the right to work, were undeniable; however, it was a noteworthy fact that the spirit of co-operation shown by the parties concerned appeared to be genuine, and the Committee should, in consequence, take a fresh approach to that delicate matter in order to succeed in re-establishing those rights and freedoms in the occupied territories, to safeguard and improve the atmosphere of understanding recently achieved and to avoid pitfalls of a political nature.

163. One member of the Committee inquired whether it would not be advisable to make public the figures and statistics relating to the violated rights mentioned in the report, since to do so would certainly help to bring about a reduction in violations of that type.

164. Lastly, another member of the Committee stressed that the colonial era was over and that that should also be true for Palestine and the occupied territories.

165. Following a long exchange of views, and after the Committee had been informed by the Secretariat of the receipt, on 23 September 1987, of a document from the author of the communication, the Committee *decided*:

(i) to thank the representative of the government concerned for his attendance and his co-operation;

(ii) to welcome with satisfaction the objective and constructive report prepared by Father Boné, the leading academic personality appointed by the Director-General in accordance with 23 C/Resolution 27 of the General Conference;

(iii) to call the attention of the Executive Board to the interdependence between the specific problems referred to the Committee and the wider problems relating to education on which Father Boné had reported;

(iv) to recommend, therefore, to the Executive Board that it explore with the relevant parties the possible ways in which Unesco, by facilitating and improving constructive co-operation, could assist, the Palestinian educational institutions in playing their rightful educational roles in the development of the area, the preservation of its cultural heritage for posterity and the pursuit of knowledge in collaboration with others;

(v) to urge the Executive Board to seize the opportunity afforded by Father Boné's mission and the support that it had received to maintain and increase the momentum thus given towards peaceful intellectual collaboration under the auspices of Unesco;

(vi) to recommend that the members of the Executive Board take account of the present recommendation when the Board comes to adopt a decision on item 5.2.1 of its agenda;

(vii) having received, on 23 September 1987, a new document written in Arabic from the author of the communication, which document had to be translated into the working languages and which could not be distributed and communicated before the end of the present session, to resume consideration of the communication at its spring 1988 session.

Spring 1988 session of the Committee on Conventions and Recommendations (129th session of the Executive Board)[92]

146. This communication, whose author is Head of the Palestinian Human Rights Committee for the Defence of War and Political Prisoners, alleges violations of human rights in the fields of competence of Unesco in the Arab territories occupied by Israel. The communication has been on the Committee's agenda since [the spring 1979 session]. At its [autumn 1987] session, the Committee was unable to examine a letter from the author of the communication in which he described the policy allegedly pursued by Israel to undermine the cultural identity of the Palestinian people: closure of universities; repressive measures against teachers (surveillance and house arrest), students (expulsion, denial of exit visas for purposes of enrolment in universities abroad), the media (closure, press censorship, expulsion, imprisonment, pre-

[92] See document 129 EX/3 PRIV., paras. 146-154; see also document 129 EX/CR/HR/1.

ventive detention of journalists, both local and foreign), theatres (closure, censorship of plays, arrest of persons working in the theatre), books (banking), researchers, research centres and their directors (preventive detention, censorship of research work, closure of centres), schools (closure, searches), schoolchildren (harassment, drugs), school curricula (obsolete, outdated, purged of Palestinian content, irrelevant to the needs of contemporary society), the Palestinian cultural heritage (setting fire to mosques, excavations) and religion (desecration, Judaization of holy places).

147. One member of the Committee considered that many grave events, confirming those reported in the communication, had occurred since the preceding session. Father Boné's report had been largely overtaken by events inasmuch as the entire Palestinian people were now victims of attempted cultural destruction and extermination. For all these reasons, that member of the Committee supported the proposal to apply paragraph 18 of 104 EX/Decision 3.3.

148. Replying to the questions of one member of the Committee, the representative of the government concerned said that Palestinian students had not been prevented from going abroad to study, but that, as in all countries, passport and other formalities had to be completed. Journalists, the press and theatres had been subjected to censorship only when they posed serious threats to security: when they fomented violence, for example. He strongly denied the accusations against Israel, pointing out that immoderate language did not encourage understanding between peoples, and asked the Committee to strike off its list this communication which had been on it for 10 years.

149. One member of the Committee objected to the concept of a "civilized people" mentioned by the representative of the government concerned. It was a concept that needed to be challenged with the utmost vigour, particularly in 1988 within the precinct of Unesco.

150. Several Committee members, maintaining that this was a case of massive, systematic and flagrant violations of human rights which were being perpetrated repeatedly and growing more serious every day, and giving examples of these violations, asked that the matter be referred to the Executive Board for public debate in plenary meeting in accordance with paragraph 18 of 104 EX/Decision 3.3. Moreover, a permanent solution to the worsening situation in the occupied Arab territories could only be found at an international conference attended by all the parties concerned, so that the Palestinian people might recover their inalienable and imprescriptible rights.

151. A number of members of the Committee, while recognizing that the situation had worsened in the occupied territories, maintained that only a political solution would suffice.

Israel **No. 12/78**

152. Some Committee members pointed out that if the Committee referred this communication to the Executive Board for public debate, it would not be able to consider it any further nor to reinstate it on its list. In any case, the Executive Board would have an opportunity to discuss the situation in the occupied territories at its 130th session, when Father Boné would submit a further report on the conditions in which academic freedoms were guaranteed and exercised in those territories, including Jerusalem and the Golan Heights. The Executive Board would have another opportunity to consider this situation at its present session at the time of the oral report of the Director-General.

153. Some members of the Committee considered that the application of paragraph 18 of 104 EX/Decision 3.3 was not incompatible with further consideration of the communication by the Committee at [its autumn 1988 session].

154. After an exchange of views, the Committee *decided*:

(i) to thank the representative of the government concerned for his attendance and co-operation;

(ii) to express its deep concern regarding the general deterioration of the situation in the occupied Arab territories as described in the communication submitted to it and in the statements that it had heard in the course of its discussion on the matter;

(iii) to stress the urgent need to put an end to that situation;

(iv) to urge the Executive Board, which will have an opportunity to consider the situation in the occupied Arab territories from a more general angle in plenary meeting, to launch an appeal for a just and equitable solution to this problem to be sought with the help of all the parties concerned;

(v) to resume consideration of this communication at [its autumn 1988 session].

No. 12/78 **Israel**

Autumn 1988 session of the Committee on Conventions and Recommendations (130th session of the Executive Board)[93]

173. This communication, whose author is the Head of the Palestinian Human Rights Committee for the Defence of War and Political Prisoners and a former member of the Executive Committee of the PLO, is at the stage of examination of substance. It alleges violations of human rights in Unesco's fields of competence in the Arab territories occupied by Israel. The communication has been on the Committee's agenda since the [spring 1979 session], and was declared admissible at [the autumn 1979] session.[94]

174. During the Committee's [spring 1982 session], the Government of Israel submitted a consolidated report on the situation of education in the occupied territories, entitled "Education and culture in Judaea, Samaria and the Gaza District - 1967/1981" [...].[95]

175. The Committee decided to send on this document to the author of the communication, requesting him to comment on it.[96]

176. Immediately before the [autumn 1983 session], the author of the communication sent the Secretariat a document in Arabic entitled "Report on the Israeli occupation and its consequences for cultural and educational institutions in the occupied territories", together with 36 annexes in Arabic and English. This document dealt with the following questions:

> the general situation in the occupied territories;
> school curricula and textbooks;
> the educational situation in schools on the West Bank;
> higher education;
> vocational training;
> schoolchildren and students;
> the brain drain;
> education for Palestinians in Israel;
> impairment of freedoms;
> collective sanctions and their effects on the educational process;
> the rise of Fascism.

---

[93] See document 130 EX/3 PRIV., paras. 173-185; see also document 130 EX/CR/HR - Israel.
[94] See document 108 EX/38 PRIV., para. 177 (*supra*, p. 13).
[95] See document 114 EX/CR/HR/1 Add.
[96] See document 114 EX/38 PRIV., para. 763 (ii) (*supra*, p. 54).

Israel **No. 12/78**

177. At its [autumn 1987 session], the Committee examined the report of an academic personality appointed by the Director-General to carry out a study on the conditions under which academic freedoms are exercised in the occupied Arab territories [...].[97] It made a number of recommendations to the Executive Board.[98]

178. At the [spring 1988] session, the Committee examined a letter from the author of the communication in which he commented on the policy allegedly followed by Israel with a view to undermining the bases of the Palestinian people's cultural identity.

179. At that session the representative of the Israeli Government considered that the Committee should put an end to the examination of communication, which had already gone on for 10 years, since all clarifications had been provided and the individual and specific cases originally invoked had long since been settled.

180. The Committee had expressed its deep concern regarding the general deterioration of the situation in the occupied Arab territories and stressed the urgent need to put an end to it. It urged the Executive Board to launch an appeal for a just and equitable solution with the help of all the parties concerned.[99] The Executive Board launched this appeal in 129 EX/Decision 8.11.

181. At the present session, the representative of the government concerned pointed out that Israel had always co-operated with the Committee, and intended to continue the dialogue. He expressed his conviction that in a calm atmosphere it would be possible to solve in Israel the problems of a country in which different cultures, different peoples and different religions existed side by side. In his view, Israel had taken particular care to develop the educational institutions, but they had sometimes become centres of political unrest. The authorities had been forced to react. Conversations were taking place with the Director-General with regard to the mission of Father Boné and that of two senior officials of the Organization, proposed by the Director-General in pursuance of [24 C/Resolution] 25 of the General Conference at its twenty-fourth session. There was a good chance that these conversations might produce results and that the missions would take place, but the troubles which had disturbed the territories during the last ten months, particularly in the educational institutions, had not been conducive to easing the situation. However, as soon as an agreement was reached with the Director-General, the Executive Board would be informed.

---

[97] See document 127 EX/8.
[98] See document 127 EX/3 PRIV., para. 165 (*supra*, pp. 88-89).
[99] See document 129 EX/3 PRIV., para. 154 (ii), (iii) and (iv) (*supra*, p. 91).

No. 12/78 **Israel**

182. Some members of the Committee expressed their satisfaction that the dialogue was continuing between Israel and Unesco and they hoped that tangible results might be obtained with regard to the educational and cultural institutions in order to prepare the ground for a comprehensive political settlement.

183. Other members of the Committee, while noting that the question of the educational and cultural institutions in the occupied Arab territories was included on the agenda of the Executive Board, thought that the Committee should not on that account, relinquish its examination of the communication, and that it should take initiatives of its own. They thought that the Committee should acknowledge the fact that the situation, instead of improving, was becoming worse and that, moreover, Israel was persisting in not responding to the steps taken by the Director-General to gain authorization for the missions of Father Boné and of the two senior officials of the Organization. They suggested that the Committee should inform the Executive Board of its grave concern at the massive and flagrant violations of human rights in the occupied Arab territories, and that it should request the Board to launch a new appeal for an attempt to be made to find a just and equitable solution to this problem.

184. It was pointed out that since the whole matter was already before the Executive Board it was difficult for the Committee to take initiatives of its own. As a subsidiary body of the Executive Board it was only possible for it to act through the Board itself. However, the Committee could request the Board to launch a new appeal to Israel to apply in the occupied territories the provisions of humanitarian law, in particular the fourth Geneva Convention relative to the Protection of Civilian Persons in Time of War, and the fundamental norms regarding human rights, especially the Universal Declaration of Human Rights. The Executive Board might also reiterate its appeal to all the parties concerned that they give effect to [129 EX/Decision] 8. 11, which it adopted at its 129th session, and to [24 C/Resolution] 25 adopted by the General Conference at its twenty-fourth session.

185. After an exchange of views, the Committee *decided*:

(i) to thank the representative of the government concerned for his attendance and for his co-operation;

(ii) to express once again its intense concern at the fact that, instead of improving, the situation regarding human rights in the occupied territories was continuing to deteriorate;

(iii) to request the Executive Board to reiterate its urgent appeal to the government concerned to apply the Geneva Conventions (1949) in the occupied territories, in particular the fourth Convention relative to the Protection of Civilian Persons in Time of War, and the Hague Convention (1954), as well as the general principles of international law and the fundamental norms regarding human rights, particularly the Universal Declaration of Human Rights;

(iv) to request the Executive Board to urge the government concerned to cooperate effectively with the Director-General with a view to implementing [24 C/Resolution] 25 adopted by the General Conference at its twenty-fourth session and [129 EX/Decision] 8.11 adopted by the Executive Board at its 129th session;

(v) to resume consideration of this communication at [its spring 1989 session].

Spring 1989 session of the Committee on Conventions and Recommendations (131st session of the Executive Board)[100]

205. This communication, submitted by Mr Abdul Jawad Saleh, the Head of the Palestinian Human Rights Committee for the Defence of Prisoners of War and Political Prisoners, is at the stage of examination as to its substance. Placed on the Committee's agenda at the [spring 1979 session] and declared admissible at the [autumn 1979] session,[101] it alleges violations of human rights in the fields of education, science, culture and communication in the territories occupied by Israel.

206. A short recapitulation of the main points covered in the examination of this communication at previous sessions of the Committee is contained in the report of the Committee's [autumn 1988] session [...].

207. At [the autumn 1988] session, the representative of the government concerned, after stating that it was still Israel's intention to continue the dialogue, informed the Committee that conversations were taking place regarding the mission of two senior Unesco officials proposed by the Director-General in pursuance of 24 C/Resolution 25 concerning educational and cultural institutions in the Arab occupied territories, adopted by the General Conference at its twenty-fourth session, and regarding the mission of Father Boné (the person who had been appointed by the Director-General to carry out a study on the situation regarding the exercise of academic freedoms in those territories).

---

[100] See document 131 EX/3 PRIV., paras. 205-215; see also document 131 EX/CR/HR/ISR.
[101] See document 108 EX/38 PRIV., para. 177 (*supra*, p. 13).

No. 12/78 **Israel**

208. The Committee, having noted that the human rights situation in the occupied territories was continuing to deteriorate, then decided *inter alia*:[102]

> to request the Executive Board to reiterate its urgent appeal to the government concerned to apply the Geneva Conventions (1949) in the occupied territories, in particular the fourth Convention relative to the Protection of Civilian Persons in Time of War, and the Hague Convention (1954), as well as the general principles of international law and the fundamental norms regarding human rights, particularly the Universal Declaration of Human Rights;
>
> to request the Executive Board to urge the government concerned to co-operate effectively with the Director-General with a view to implementing 24 C/ Resolution 25 and 129 EX/Decision 8.11 [...].[103]

209. The Committee's wishes were reflected in [130 EX/Decision] 5.2.1 adopted by the Executive Board at its 130th session.

210. On 31 October 1988 (one week after the Committee had examined the communication), the Secretariat received from Mr Abdul Jawad Saleh a letter expressing the author's disappointment at Unesco's lack of firmness, which in his view, together with the attitude of other international organizations and governments, was encouraging the Israeli occupation authorities to intensify their repression. In his letter he expressed the belief that, in view of the circumstances, the time had come for Unesco to develop new policies and procedures to enable it to solve the unforeseen problems raised by such prolonged occupation. He described how the statements made to the Committe by the representative of the Government of Israel distorted the facts in several connections: in connection with the censorship imposed by Israel, which was part of a systematic policy to prevent the Palestinians from expressing their cultural identity; in connection with the repeated closing and reopening of educational institutions, which were part of a systematic policy to destroy the education process with a view to rendering the new generations of Palestinians powerless; and in connection with the ill-treatment inflicted upon Palestinian children, of whom thousands had been beaten, blinded, paralysed, maimed, traumatized, hundreds imprisoned, and some killed in cold blood, especially during the last 10 months of the Palestinian popular Intifada. The Intifada was a spontaneous Palestinian uprising by an oppressed people rejecting a *status quo* imposed by prolonged occupation, so as to force the Israelis to agree, to take into account the political rights of the Palestinians. He also described the encouragement of drug addiction, in order to neutralize the young generations; and lastly, he described the efforts of the Israeli authorities,

---

[102] See document 130 EX/3 PRIV., para. 185 (iii) and (iv) (*supra*, pp. 94-95).
[103] See document 129 EX/CR/HR/1, annexes I and II.

on the pretext of a specious interpretation of the Geneva Convention to the effect that the only obligation was to preserve the situation which existed before the occupation, to prevent any modernization of curricula and any introduction of scientific innovation in the field of education, and to obscure the reality of the changes being made by the Israeli authorities in the legal and constitutional status of the occupied territories through the adoption of a large number of military orders under which the occupied territories are governed. Mr Abdul Jawad Saleh, the author of the communication, considered that it had become absolutely necessary for Unesco to develop new policies and procedures to establish machinery for the protection of the educational, cultural and social rights of Palestinians in the grip of continuing occupation. It was not only a question of condemning the Israeli violations, but of resuscitating machinery which would guarantee the normal and effective functioning of the education system of the Palestinian people and their cultural institutions, enforce their right to express their cultural identity, and also ensure respect for their dignity.

211. The annexes to that letter, which are drafted in Arabic and amount to 90 pages in all, had not been reproduced.

212. One member of the Committee considered that it was not possible to consider the communication without those annexes, since the annexes dealt with the individual aspects of the communication and the Committee could only examine individual cases. He requested postponement of the examination of the communication until the Committee had received the annexes translated into all its working languages.

213. That request was supported by several members, though some speakers pointed out that the annexes contained only lists of names of victims and cultural or educational institutions which had been closed in the occupied territories; that they did not constitute a new communication; that the Committee had decided to resume consideration of the communication at this session; that the human rights situation had deteriorated still further in the occupied territories, and that the Committee could not remain passive and let events take their course; that the victims of violations should not be made to suffer the consequences of an oversight by the Secretariat; and that the postponement of consideration of the communication might create a dangerous precedent which could jeopardize the work of the Committee.

214. After an exchange of views, the Committee *decided*:

(i) to reassert its specific original authority to examine this communication, even though the situation in the occupied territories was being discussed simultaneously in other bodies of the Executive Board, its task being to seek solutions to individual cases;

(ii) to reiterate, as at its [autumn 1988] session, its intense concern at the fact that the human rights situation in the occupied Arab territories was continuing to deteriorate;

(iii) to postpone examination of this communication until its next session, considering that it was impossible to discuss the case without knowledge of the annexes to the letter of October 1988 from Mr Abdul Jawad Saleh, the author of the communication;

(iv) to express its surprise and regret that the Secretariat had not considered it appropriate to make these annexes available in the working languages of the Committee, and to invite the Secretariat to translate them for the next session and to communicate them to the members of the Committee before that session;

(v) to resume consideration of this communication at its [autumn 1989 session].

215. One member of the Committee expressed the gravest reservations with regard to this decision, as he thought that the only way in which the Committee could fulfill its mandate was to examine this communication in all its aspects so as to help solve this grievous problem. He considered that a pretext had been found to postpone examination of the communication, and that the reasons put forward were not valid as the postponement of the question meant that the victim would suffer from the effects of an oversight by the Secretariat. That member of the Committee stated therefore that he did not consider himself bound by the Committee's decision, which ran the risk of disrupting the Committee's functioning. He also stated that he would reiterate his reservations at the appropriate time.

Autumn 1989 session of the Committee on Conventions and Recommendations (132nd session of the Executive Board)[104]

164. This communication has been on the Committee's agenda since the [spring 1979 session]. It is at the stage of examination as to its substance. It alleges violations of human rights in the fields of education, science, culture and communication in the occupied Arab territories. [...].[105]

[104] See document 132 EX/3 PRIV., paras. 164-170; see also document 132 EX/CR/HR/ISR.
[105] For background documentation, see documents 114 EX/CR/HR/1 and 125 EX/CR/HR/1 Add.

Israel **No. 12/78**

165. At its 129th session, on the Committee's recommendation, the Executive Board launched an appeal to all the parties concerned to seek a just and equitable solution to the general situation in the occupied Arab territories, and at the [autumn 1988] session the Committee, having noted the deterioration in the human rights situation in those territories, requested the Executive Board to reiterate its appeal.[106]

166. At the [spring 1989] session, having reasserted its specific original authority to examine this communication, even though the situation in the occupied territories was being discussed simultaneously in other bodies of the Executive Board, the Committee considered that its task was to seek solutions to individual cases. Accordingly, it requested that translations should be made of the annex to a letter from the author of the communication, the effect of which was to individualize that communication. It reiterated once again its intense concern at the fact that the human rights situation in the occupied Arab territories was continuing to deteriorate.[107]

167. At the present session, the representative of the government concerned, commenting on the information contained in the annex to the above-mentioned letter from the author of the communication, pointed out that the educational establishments whose closure was criticized had been shut for short periods and had long since been reopened, that the pupils and students arrested, who were reported to have been sentenced to terms of imprisonment, had been sentenced for equally short periods and then released, and, finally, that the accusations levelled against the Israeli authorities in regard to drugs were wholly without foundation, drug addiction being a phenomenon common to many countries, one which was extremely worrying for the Israeli authorities as indeed it was for other countries and which they were self-evidently endeavouring to combat, rather than to encourage, as was claimed. In reply to questions, the representative of the government concerned assured the Committee that he would endeavour to identify all those in detention who were reported to be awaiting trial, and to find out what had become of them and what they had been accused of, provided that the four parts of the names of those persons were indicated. He stated that it was in his view unlikely that under Israeli law people could remain for very long in detention without trial.

168. One member of the Committee pointed out that, since the Committee had first begun hearing the successive representatives of the government concerned, no relevant information had ever been obtained.

169. The Committee confirmed its concern to deal with individual cases of violations of human rights, without encroaching upon areas falling within the competence

---

[106] See document 130 EX/3 PRIV., para. 185 (ii) and (iii) (*supra*, pp. 94-95).
[107] See document 131 EX/3 PRIV., para. 214 (i), (iv) and (ii), respectively (*supra*, pp. 97-98).

of other bodies, such as the Executive Board, which had before it a report on educational and cultural institutions in the occupied Arab territories. Nevertheless, it was helpful for it to be able to have an overall view of the situation when individual violations occurred within a more general context.

170. After an exchange of views, the Committee *decided*:

(i) to thank the representatives of the government concerned for their attendance and their co-operation;

(ii) to express once again its intense concern at the increasing violations of human rights in the occupied Arab territories;

(iii) to remind the government concerned of Article 71 of the Geneva Convention relative to the Protection of Civilian Persons in Time of War of 12 August 1949 which requires of the Occupying Power in the occupied territories that it bring to trial accused persons who are prosecuted by it as rapidly as possible, and further provides that no sentence shall be pronounced by the competent courts of the Occupying Power except after a regular trial;

(iv) to ask the government concerned to provide precise information regarding the cases of the pupils and students mentioned by the author of the communication as still awaiting trial;

(v) to request the author of the communication to update it, recording only cases of persons whose rights continue to be violated;

(vi) to request the Executive Board again to exhort the government concerned to co-operate with the Director-General for the purpose of effectively implementing 24 C/Resolution 25 and 129 EX/Decision 8.11 relating to the educational and cultural institutions in the occupied Arab territories and the aggravation of the situation in those territories;

(vii) to resume consideration of this communication at its [spring 1990 session].

Israel **No. 12/78**

Spring 1990 session of the Committee on Conventions and Recommendations (134th session of the Executive Board)[108]

191. This communication is at the stage of examination as to its substance. It has been on the Committee's agenda since the [spring 1979 session]. It alleges violations of human rights in the fields of education, science, culture and communication in the occupied Arab territories. [...].[109]

192. At its 129th session, on the Committee's recommendation, the Executive Board launched an appeal to all the parties concerned to seek a just and equitable solution to the general situation in the occupied Arab territories, and at the [autumn 1988] session the Committee, having noted the deterioration in the human rights situation in those territories, requested the Executive Board to reiterate its appeal.[110]

193. At the [spring 1989] session the Committee, having reasserted its own initial competence to examine this communication, even though the situation in the occupied territories was being discussed simultaneously in other bodies of the Executive Board, came to the conclusion that its task was to seek solutions to individual cases. Accordingly, it requested that translations should be made of the annex to a letter from the author of the communication, the effect of which was to individualize that communication. It reiterated once again its intense concern at the fact that the human rights situation in the occupied Arab territories was continuing to deteriorate.[111]

194. At the [autumn 1989] session, the representative of the Government of Israel, commenting on the information contained in the annex to the letter from the author of the communication, pointed out that the educational establishments whose closure was criticized had been shut for short periods and had long since been reopened, that the pupils and students arrested, who were reported to have been sentenced to terms of imprisonment, had been sentenced for equally short periods and then released, and, finally, that the accusations levelled against the Israeli authorities in regard to drugs were wholly without foundation. He assured the Committee that he would endeavour to identify all those in detention who were reported to be awaiting trial, and to find out what had become of them and what they had been accused of, provided that the four parts of the names of those persons were given.

---

[108] See document 134 EX/3 PRIV., paras. 191-199; see also document 134 EX/CR/HR/ISR.
[109] For background documentation, see documents 114 EX/CR/HR/1 and 125 EX/CR/HR/1 Add.
[110] See document 130 EX/3 PRIV., para. 185 (ii) and (iii) (*supra*, pp. 94-95).
[111] See document 131 EX/3 PRIV., para. 214 (i), (iv) and (ii), respectively (*supra*, pp. 97-98).

No. 12/78 **Israel**

195. The Committee confirmed its concern to deal with individual cases of violations of human rights, without encroaching upon areas falling within the competence of other bodies, such as the Executive Board, which had before it a report on educational and cultural institutions in the occupied Arab territories. Nevertheless, it was helpful for it to be able to have an overall view of the situation when individual violations occurred within a more general context.[112]

196. The Committee requested the Government of Israel to provide precise information regarding the cases of the pupils and students mentioned by the author of the communication as still awaiting trial. It requested the author of the communication to update it so as to include only cases of persons whose rights continued to be violated.[113]

197. At the present session, the representative of the government admitted that he had no additional information concerning this communication, since he had not received the particulars regarding the identity of the alleged victims that had been requested. However, he reiterated his government's concern to co-operate with the Committee.

198. The Committee noted the failure of the author of the communication to reply to its request, but considered that it was up to the government to state the reasons for the detentions and to reveal the identity of the persons they were holding.

199. Following an exchange of views the Committee *decided*:

(i) to thank the representative of the government concerned for his attendance and his co-operation;

(ii) to express once again its intense concern at the increasing violations of human rights in the occupied Arab territories;

(iii) to remind the government concerned of Article 71 of the Geneva Convention relative to the Protection of Civilian Persons in Time of War of 12 August 1949 which requires of the Occupying Power in the occupied territories that it bring to trial accused persons who are prosecuted by it as rapidly as possible, and further provides that no sentence shall be pronounced by the competent courts of the Occupying Power except after a regular trial;

---

[112] See document 132 EX/3 PRIV., para. 169 (*supra*, pp. 99-100).
[113] *Ibidem*, para. 170 (iv) and (v) (*supra*, p. 100).

(iv) to express its regrets that the government concerned had not yet provided precise information regarding the cases of the pupils and students mentioned by the author of the communication as still awaiting trial;

(v) to request the government concerned once again for this information;

(vi) to request the author of the communication to update it, recording only cases of persons whose rights continue to be violated;

(vii) to resume consideration of this communication at its [autumn 1990 session].

Autumn 1990 session of the Committee on Conventions and Recommendations (135th session of the Executive Board)[114]

140. This communication is at the stage of examination of substance. It has been on the Committee's agenda since the [spring 1979 session]. It alleges violations of human rights in the fields of education, science, culture and communication in the occupied Arab territories. [...].[115]

141. At its 129th session, on the Committee's recommendation, the Executive Board launched an appeal to all the parties concerned to seek a just and equitable solution to the general situation in the occupied Arab territories, and at the [autumn 1988] session the Committee, having noted the deterioration in the human rights situation in those territories, requested the Executive Board to reiterate its appeal.[116]

142. At the [spring 1989] session, the Committee, having reasserted its own initial competence to examine this communication, even though the situation in the occupied territories was being discussed simultaneously in other bodies of the Executive Board, came to the conclusion that its task was to seek solutions to individual cases. Accordingly, it requested that translations be made of the annex to a letter from the author of the communication, the effect of which was to individualize that communication. It reiterated once again its intense concern at the fact that the human rights situation in the occupied Arab territories was continuing to deteriorate.[117]

[114] See document 135 EX/3 PRIV., paras. 140-148; see also document 135 EX/CR/HR/ISR.
[115] For background documentation, see documents 114 EX/CR/HR/1 and 125 EX/CR/HR/1 Add.
[116] See document 130 EX/3 PRIV., para. 185 (ii) and (iii) (*supra*, pp. 94-95).
[117] See document 131 EX/3 PRIV., para. 214 (i), (iv) and (ii), respectively (*supra*, pp. 97-98).

No. 12/78 **Israel**

143. At the [autumn 1989] session, the representative of the government concerned, commenting on the information contained in the annex to the letter from the author of the communication, pointed out that the educational establishments whose closure was criticized had been shut for short periods and had long since been reopened, that the pupils and students arrested, who were reported to have been sentenced to terms of imprisonment, had been sentenced for equally short periods and then released, and, finally, that the accusations levelled against the Israeli authorities in regard to drugs were wholly without foundation. He assured the Committee that he would endeavour to identify all those in detention who were reported to be awaiting trial, and to find out what had become of them and what they had been accused of, provided that the four parts of the names of those persons were given.

144. The Committee confirmed its concern to deal with individual cases of violations of human rights, without encroaching upon areas falling within the competence of other bodies, such as the Executive Board, which had before it a report on educational and cultural institutions in the occupied Arab territories. Nevertheless, it was helpful for it to be able to have an overall view of the situation when individual violations occurred within a more general context.[118]

145. The Committee requested the government concerned to provide precise information regarding the cases of the pupils and students mentioned by the author of the communication as still awaiting trial. It requested the author of the communication to update it so as to include only cases of persons whose rights continued to be violated.[119]

146. At the [spring 1990] session, the Committee noted the failure of the author of the communication to reply to its request, but considered that it was up to the government to state the reasons for the detentions and to reveal the identity of the persons it was holding.[120]

147. At the present session, the representative of the government concerned said that, as at the [spring 1990] session, she had no additional information concerning this communication, since she had not received the particulars that her government needed in order to identify the alleged victims. However, she reiterated her government's concern to co-operate with the Committee. She added that ICRC was systematically informed by her government of arrests in the occupied territories. The representatives of ICRC could meet and converse with the persons in detention.

148. After an exchange of views, the Committee *decided*:

---

[118] See document 132 EX/3 PRIV., para. 169 (*supra*, pp. 99-100).
[119] *Ibidem*, para. 170 (iv) and (v) (*supra*, p. 100).
[120] See document 134 EX/3 PRIV., para. 198 (*supra*, p. 102).

(i) to thank the representative of the government concerned for her attendance and co-operation;

(ii) to recall the decision it had adopted at its [spring 1990] session and in particular to request the author of the communication to update it, recording only cases of persons whose rights continue to be violated and taking care to indicate the four parts of their names;

(iii) to resume consideration of this communication at its [spring 1991 session].

Spring 1991 session of the Committee on Conventions and Recommendations (136th session of the Executive Board)[121]

175. This communication is at the stage of examination of substance. It has been on the Committee's agenda since the [spring 1979 session]. It alleges violations of human rights in the fields of education, science, culture and communication in the occupied Arab territories. [...].[122]

176. At its 129th session, on the Committee's recommendation, the Executive Board launched an appeal to all the parties concerned to seek a just and equitable solution to the general situation in the occupied Arab territories, and at the [autumn 1988] session the Committee, having noted the deterioration in the human rights situation in those territories, requested the Executive Board to reiterate its appeal.[123]

177. At the [spring 1989] session, the Committee, having reasserted its own initial competence to examine this communication, even though the situation in the occupied territories was being discussed simultaneously in other bodies of the Executive Board, came to the conclusion that its task was to seek solutions to individual cases. Accordingly, it requested that translations be made of the annex to a letter from the author of the communication, the effect of which was to individualize that communication. It reiterated once again its intense concern at the fact that the human rights situation in the occupied Arab territories was continuing to deteriorate.[124]

178. At the [autumn 1989] session, the representative of the government concerned, commenting on the information contained in the annex to the letter from the author

[121] See document 136 EX/3 PRIV., paras. 175-187; see also document 136 EX/CR/HR/ISR.
[122] For background documentation, see documents 114 EX/CR/HR/1 and 125 EX/CR/HR/1 Add.
[123] See document 130 EX/3 PRIV., para. 185 (ii) and (iii) (*supra*, pp. 94-95).
[124] See document 131 EX/3 PRIV., para. 214 (i), (iv) and (ii), respectively (*supra*, pp. 97-98).

of the communication, pointed out that the educational establishments whose closure was criticized had been shut for short periods and had long since been reopened, that the pupils and students arrested, who were reported to have been sentenced to terms of imprisonment, had been sentenced for equally short periods and then released, and, finally, that the accusations levelled against the Israeli authorities in regard to drugs were wholly without foundation. He assured the Committee that he would endeavour to identify all those in detention who were reported to be awaiting trial, and to find out what had become of them and what they had been accused of, provided that the four parts of the names of those persons were given.

179. The Committee confirmed its concern to deal with individual cases of violations of human rights, without encroaching upon areas falling within the competence of other bodies, such as the Executive Board, which had before it a report on educational and cultural institutions in the occupied Arab territories. Nevertheless, it was helpful for it to be able to have an overall view of the situation when individual violations occurred within a more general context.[125]

180. The Committee requested the government concerned to provide precise information regarding the cases of the pupils and students mentioned by the author of the communication as still awaiting trial. It requested the author of the communication to update it so as to include only cases of persons whose rights continued to be violated.[126]

181. At the [spring 1990] session the Committee noted the failure of the author of the communication to reply to its request but considered that it was up to the government to state the reasons for the detentions and to reveal the identities of the persons it was holding. It expressed once again its intense concern at the increasing violation of human rights in the occupied Arab territories.[127]

182. At the [autumn 1990] session the representative of the government concerned said that, as at the [spring 1990] session, she had no additional information concerning this communication, since she had not received the particulars her government needed to identify the alleged victims. However, she reiterated her government's concern to co-operate with the Committee. She added that the ICRC was systematically informed by her government of arrests in the occupied territories. The representatives of the ICRC could meet and talk to people in detention.

183. The Committee reiterated the decision it had adopted at its [spring 1990] session and in particular requested the author of the communication to update it, includ-

---

[125] See document 132 EX/3 PRIV., para. 169 (*supra*, pp. 99-100).
[126] *Ibidem*, para. 170 (iv) and (v) (*supra*, p. 100).
[127] See document 134 EX/3 PRIV., paras. 198 and 199 (ii), respectively (*supra*, p. 102).

ing only cases of persons whose rights continued to be violated and taking care to state the four parts of their names.[128]

184. At the present session, the representative of the government concerned reaffirmed her government's concern to co-operate with the Committee but regretted that she was unable to provide it with any additional information because of the vagueness of the allegations and the fact that it was impossible to identify the alleged victims. She requested the Committee to strike the communication from its list.

185. Some members questioned the usefulness of a communication dating back so far, at a time when the human rights situation in the occupied Arab territories was a matter of growing concern. It seemed necessary to update the communication; examination of the 1979 communication seemed absurd, and the submission of a new communication appeared to be required.

186. One member felt that the 1979 communication was not necessarily out of date since it had been brought up to date in 1985 and even in 1988. One member wondered whether the silence on the part of the author of the communication was not quite simply due to the fact that all trace of him had been lost. Several members wished the Secretariat to conduct investigations into the Palestinian Human Rights Committee [for the Defence of War and Political Prisoners] and into the fate of the alleged victims who were the subject of the communication by approaching the Permanent Observer for Palestine to UNESCO and other sources in Jordan.

187. After an exchange of views, the Committee *decided*:

(i) to thank the representatives of the government concerned for their attendance and co-operation;

(ii) to invite its secretariat to make all the necessary efforts to trace the author of the communication, to inform it of what had become of the Palestinian Human Rights Committee and to collect information on the fate of the alleged victims;

(iii) to resume consideration of this communication at its [autumn 1991 session].

[128] See document 135 EX/3 PRIV., para. 148 (ii) (*supra*, p. 105).

No. 12/78 **Israel**

Autumn 1991 session of the Committee on Conventions and Recommendations (137th session of the Executive Board)[129]

144. This communication is at the stage of examination of substance. It has been on the Committee's agenda since the [spring 1979 session]. It alleges violations of human rights in the fields of education, science, culture and communication in the occupied Arab territories. [...].[130]

145. At its 129th session, on the Committee's recommendation, the Executive Board launched an appeal to all the parties concerned to seek a just and equitable solution to the general situation in the occupied Arab territories and at the [autumn 1988] session the Committee, having noted the deterioration in the human rights situation in those territories, requested the Executive Board to reiterate its appeal.[131]

146. At subsequent sessions, the Committee reasserted its own initial competence to examine this communication, even though the situation in the occupied territories was being discussed simultaneously in other bodies of the Executive Board, pointing out that its task was to seek solutions to individual cases. It reiterated its intense concern at the fact that the human rights situation in the occupied Arab territories was continuing to deteriorate.[132] It requested the government concerned to provide precise information regarding the cases of the pupils and students mentioned by the author of the communication as still awaiting trial. It requested the author of the communication to update it so as to include only cases of persons whose rights continued to be violated.[133] Noting the failure of the author of the communication to reply to its request, it nevertheless took the view that it was up to the government concerned to state the reasons for the detentions and to reveal the identity of the persons it was holding.[134]

147. The representative of the government concerned pointed out that the educational establishments whose closure was criticized by the author of the communication had been shut for short periods and had long since been reopened, that the pupils and students arrested, who were reported to have been sentenced to terms of imprisonment, had been sentenced to equally short periods and then released, and, finally, that the accusations levelled against the Israeli authorities in regard to drugs were

[129] See document 137 EX/3 PRIV., paras. 144-150; see also document 137 EX/CR/HR/ISR.
[130] For background documentation, see documents 114 EX/CR/HR/1, 125 EX/CR/HR/1 Add, 131 EX/CR/HR/ISR and 132 EX/CR/HR/ISR.
[131] See document 130 EX/3 PRIV., para. 185 (ii) and (iii) (*supra*, pp. 94-95).
[132] See e.g. document 131 EX/3 PRIV., para. 214 (i) and (ii) (*supra*, pp. 97-98).
[133] See e.g. document 132 EX/3 PRIV., para. 170 (iv) and (v) (*supra*, p. 100).
[134] See e.g. document 134 EX/3 PRIV., para. 198 (*supra*, p. 102).

wholly without foundation. He assured the Committee that he would endeavour to identify all those in detention who were reported to be awaiting trial and to find out what had become of them and what they had been accused of, provided that he was given all four parts of their names. As matters stood, he was unable to provide the Committee with additional information owing to the vagueness of the allegations and the impossibility of identifying the alleged victims.

148. At the [spring 1991] session, some members questioned the usefulness of a communication dating back so far, at a time when the human rights situation in the occupied Arab territories was a matter of growing concern. It seemed necessary to update the communication. Examination of the 1979 communication seemed absurd and the submission of a new communication appeared to be required. Faced with silence on the part of the author of the communication, the Committee decided to invite its Secretariat to make all the necessary efforts to trace both him and the Palestinian Human Rights Committee [for the Defence of War and Political Prisoners] and to obtain information on what had become of the alleged victims mentioned in the communication.[135]

149. At the present session, in view of the futility of its efforts and the fact that the communication seemed to have lost all topical relevance, the Committee felt it had no alternative but to suspend its examination *sine die*.

150. After an exchange of views, the Committee *decided*:

(i) to thank the representative of the government concerned for his attendance and co-operation;

(ii) to invite its Secretariat to continue its efforts to trace the author of the communication;

(iii) to keep the communication on its list but to resume consideration of it only on receiving information that would enable it to pursue its task.

---

[135] See document 136 EX/3 PRIV., paras. 187 (ii) (*supra*, p. 107).

No. 21/78

Concerning *Union of Soviet Socialist Republics and Ukrainian Soviet Socialist Republic*
Case of *Yuri Orlov* et al.*

Communication of 10 June 1978 submitted by
Vladimir Maximov and Vadime Delaunay

Spring 1979 session of the Committee on Conventions and Recommendations (107th session of the Executive Board)[1]

158. The authors of this communication claim that violations of the right to freedom of opinion and expression and the exchange of information, guaranteed by Article 19 of the Universal Declaration of Human Rights, have been committed in respect of the alleged victims, who are respectively a physicist, a journalist, a biologist, a historian, a writer and a professor of history, and who have received long prison sentences.

159. The representative of the Government of the USSR considered that the communication merely contained attacks on his government and cast aspersions on his country. The alleged victims had been sentenced for their anti-Soviet activities, under the relevant articles of the Penal Code of the RSFSR. After giving the Committee detailed information about the anti-Soviet activities of each of the alleged victims and of the sentences passed against them, he requested in conclusion that the Committee declare the communication inadmissible.

160. Several members of the Committee expressed the view that the information provided by the authors of the communication was insufficient to enable the Committee to decide upon the admissibility of the communication. Other members, while holding that it was not for the Committee to pronounce upon the legislation of a Member State, took the view that there was a relationship between the alleged vio-

---

* Case of *Yuri Orlov, Sergey Kovalev, Alexander Ginsburg, Victoras Piatkus, Mykola Rudenko and Alexis Tikhy.*

[1] See document 107 EX/PRIV.31, paras. 158-162; see also document 107 EX/CR/PROC.HR/4.

lations of human rights and Unesco's fields of competence and that, at first sight, the communication appeared admissible.

161. One member of the Committee expressed the view, that the conditions listed in subparagraphs (i), (ii), (iii), (iv), (v) and (ix) of paragraph 14 (*a*) of 104 EX/Decision 3.3 had been met in the case under review, while particulars should be requested of the author regarding the stipulation in subparagraph (vi). Subject to that reservation, the communication appeared to be admissible. Another member thought that conditions (i), (ii), (iv) and (vii) had been met, while further information was needed about the conditions stated in subparagraphs (iii), (v), (vi) and (ix). Other members of the Committee held the communication to be inadmissable.

162. In view of the vague or inadequate character of the information supplied by the authors, the Committee *decided* to suspend consideration of the admissibility of the communication pending more detailed information that the Secretariat was instructed to seek from the authors.

Autumn 1979 session of the Committee on Conventions and Recommendations (108th session of the Executive Board)[2]

210. The authors of this communication claim that violations of the right to freedom of opinion and expression and the exchange of information have been committed in respect of the alleged victims, who are respectively a physicist, a journalist, a biologist, a historian, a writer and a professor of history and who have received long prison sentences.

211. The Director of the Division of Human Rights and Peace recalled that at its [spring 1979] session the Committee had decided to defer consideration of the admissibility of this communication, pending more detailed information concerning the allegations put forward, which the Secretariat was instructed to seek from the authors.[3] He informed the Committee that no information from the authors of the communication had been received by the Secretariat in response to the Committee's request.

211a. Having drawn the Committee's attention to the absence of supplementary information from the authors of the communication, the representative of the government concerned proposed reiterating the reasons which he had presented during the

---

[2] See document 108 EX/38 PRIV., paras. 210-213; see also document 108 EX/CR/PROC.HR/ 1.

[3] See document 107 EX/PRIV.31, para. 162 (*supra*, p. 112).

[spring 1979 session], that this communication be removed from the Committee's a-genda.

212. Several members of the Committee pointed out that one of the alleged victims, Mr Ginsburg, was now resident abroad. Another speaker suggested that a second letter, this time with acknowledgement of receipt, should be sent to the authors of the communication, informing them that the Committee would be unable to continue consideration of their communication unless the information requested reached the Secretariat before the next session of the Committee.

213. After discussion on the proposal of the Chairman, the Committee *decided* to suspend consideration of the admissibility of the communication and *instructed* the Secretariat duly to inform the authors that their communication would be removed from the Committee's agenda if the information requested did not reach the Secretariat before the Committee's next session.

Spring 1980 session of the Committee on Conventions and Recommendations (109th session of the Executive Board)[4]

134. The authors of this communication claim that violations of the right to freedom of opinion and expression and the exchange of information have been committed in respect of the alleged victims, who are respectively a physicist, a journalist, a biologist, a historian, a writer and a professor of history and who have received long prison sentences.

135. The representative of the Director-General recalled that at its [spring and autumn 1979] sessions the Committee had decided to defer consideration of the admissibility of this communication, pending more detailed information concerning the allegations put forward, which the Secretariat was instructed to seek from the authors.[5] On 8 April 1980 the authors had sent a letter providing some of the additional information requested.

136. The representative of the Soviet Government reiterated his government's position that the communication did not fulfil the conditions of admissibility set forth in 104 EX/Decision 3.3. He stated that the communication did not meet the condition concerning internal remedies, and that, furthermore, he had checked with the Soviet authorities and learned that no remedies had been filed. In addition, it was felt that

[4] See document 109 EX/52 PRIV., paras. 134-139; see also documents 109 EX/CR/HR/2 and Add.4.

[5] See documents 107 EX/PRIV.31, para. 162 (*supra*, p. 112) and 108 EX/38 PRIV., para. 213 (*supra*, p. 113), respectively.

the communication was offensive to the Soviet legal system: these cases having been tried in accordance with judicial procedures, Unesco should not involve itself with such domestic affairs of the USSR.

137. Some of the Committee members emphasized that the criteria relating to "offensiveness" referred to the language used by the authors of communications and the making of allegations by itself could not be considered offensive, otherwise no case could be presented to the Committee. It vas also pointed out by these members of the Committee that by virtue of principles of international law, and particularly the United Nations Charter, the Helsinki Agreement, and the United Nations Human Rights Covenants which the USSR had ratified, it was definitely established that human rights matters were no longer the purely domestic affairs of States. They did regret, however, that no information had been provided by the authors concerning their efforts to use domestic remedies.

138. Upon being asked about this latter question, the representative of the Director-General explained that the question of attempted domestic remedies had been specifically put to the authors of the communication in the letter addressed to them by the Secretariat.

139. In view of the fact that the authors had not answered the question concerning efforts made to exhaust domestic remedies, the Committee *decided* to declare the communication inadmissible in accordance with paragraph 14 (*a*) (ix) of 104 EX/ Decision 3.3.

No. 25/78

Concerning *Chile*
Case of *The situation of human rights in Chile in the fields of education, science, culture and information* *

Communication of 30 June 1978 submitted by
World Federation of Teachers' Unions

Autumn 1978 session of the Committee on Conventions and Recommendations (105th session of the Executive Board)[1]

74. [...] Communication from the World Federation of Teachers' Unions [WFTU] concerning "The situation of human rights in Chile in the fields of education, science, culture and information".

75. The Chairman noted that the above-mentioned communication dated 30 June 1978 had been transmitted to the goverment on 18 August 1978 after Mr Daniel Monteux, the permanent representative of [WFTU] to Unesco, had, on 8 August 1978, signified his agreement to that step. He drew attention to the fact that in a letter dated 12 September 1978 [...][2] the Permanent Delegate of Chile to Unesco had stated that, in view of the short time that had elapsed between the date when the communication was transmitted to his government and the date of the Committee's session, his government had not been able to examine the communication, particularly with reference to the conditions of admissibility. The Committee nevertheless decided that it was competent to consider the character and admissibility of the communication. To avoid similar difficulties in future, it was decided that the government concerned should be given one month from the time when the communication affecting it had been transmitted to the Permanent Delegate to Unesco. It was further agreed that communications and all correspondence relating to them should, if possi-

---

* At the Committee's spring 1979 session, this communication was being referred to as case of *Situation of human rights in Chile in the fields of education, science, culture and information* and from its autumn 1979 session as case of *Situation of human rights in Chile in the spheres of education, science, culture and communication*.
[1] See document 105 EX/49 PRIV., paras. 74-91; see also document 105 EX/CR/PROC.HR/1.
[2] See document 105 EX/CR/PRIV/INF.2, annex 1.

ble, normally be addressed to the Permanent Delegates to Unesco of the States concerned.

76. The Chairman pointed out that the communication from [WFTU] referred not only to individual cases of alleged violations of human rights but also to measures creating a situation that was alleged to be contrary to human rights in fields falling within Unesco's competence. The Committee therefore had to decide whether the communication constituted a "case" or a "question" within the meaning of paragraph 10 of 104 EX/Decision 3.3.

77. The Director of the Division of Human Rights and Peace drew the Committee's attention to the fact that, in this connection, nearly all legal systems, as well as the accepted rules of international law, recognized three distinct procedural stages: (i) legal definition of the facts referred to the organ in question (in this instance, the question was whether they constituted a "case" or a "question") and (ii) decisions as to competence and admissibility. It should be noted, however, that paragraph 14 of 104 EX/Decision 3.3 dealt with these last two procedural aspects together. He explained that it was usual for the organ to which the matter was referred to rule first of all on the definition of the facts.

78. Several members of the Committee were of the opinion that the communication clearly constituted a "question", whereas other members considered that the matter could not be decided before the Committee had examined the allegations contained in the communication. Some members, moreover, declared that in their opinion the communication was neither a "case" nor a "question" but a political document based on newspaper articles. The Chairman concluded that the communication contained allegations to the effect that, in the country concerned, there might exist a "question" as defined by the rules of procedure. The Committee would have to approach the examination of the communication with this in mind, but a definite decision on this question could be taken by the Committee only after un examination of the substance of the communication.

79. At the Chairman's suggestion, the Committee agreed to begin by examining the communication from the point of view of admissibility. The representative of the government concerned reiterated the position expounded in the letter dated 17 September 1978 and added that, in any event, the communication seemed to him to be inadmissible as not meeting the conditions specified in paragraph 14 (*a*) (v) to (x) of 104 EX/Decision 3.3. He went on to draw the Committee's attention to the highly relevant fact, in his government's view, that a fact-finding group of the United Nations Commission on Human Rights had been authorized to carry out a mission in Chile; he considered that the Committee should not examine the [WFTU] communication until after the fact-finding group's report had been published.

Chile **No. 25/78**

80. The Director of the Division of Human Rights and Peace informed the Committee that the Working Party of the Executive Board that had drawn up 104 EX/Decision 3.3 had discussed the question of whether the fact that a communication had also been referred to another international human rights organ should constitute grounds for inadmissibility; after lengthy discussion of the matter, the Working Party had decided that it should not. He also informed the Committee that the fact-finding group of the Commission on Human Rights was in the process of completing its report, which would very probably be signed on 23 September 1978. The Chairman of the Committee pointed out, in the same connection, that the communication form showed that [WFTU] had submitted the communication in question "simultaneously" to the International Labour Organisation (ILO).

81. With regard to paragraph 14 (*a*) (i) of 104 EX/Decision 3.3, there was no doubt that the condition of admissibility was satisfied.

82. Concerning the condition contained in paragraph 14 (*a*) (ii), certain members of the Committee expressed doubts as to whether the organization from which the communication originated had "reliable knowledge" of the alleged violations, since the communication was not only based on newspaper articles but also contained vastly exaggerated figures, particularly in respect of the number of exiled Chileans. The latter point was also emphasized by the representative of the Chilean Government. Several members of the Committee made the point, however, that the communication was also based on official information issued by the Chilean Government and even on extracts from the Official Gazette of the Republic of Chile.

[82a.] The Director of the Division of Human Rights and Peace drew the Committee's attention to the fact that all legal systems make a presumption of good faith and that it would be reasonable to apply the same rule to the condition of admissibility contained in paragraph 14 (*a*) (ii). Clearly, however, the governments involved should also benefit by that rule.

[82b.] At the Chairman's suggestion, the Committee agreed that the above-mentioned condition had also been met.

83. With regard te the condition mentioned in paragraph 14 (*a*) (iii), whereby the communication must concern violations of human rights falling within Unesco's competence and must not be motivated exclusively by other considerations, several nembers of the Committee drew attention to the political nature of the communication, which, in their opinion, pursued objectives far removed from any desire to see human rights safeguarded in Chile. The majority of the Committee members, however, did not share this point of view.

No. 25/78 **Chile**

[83a.] Several members of the Committee cited parts of the document submitted by [WFTU] that did not concern Unesco's fields of competence. In this connection, the Director of the Division of Human Rights and Peace informed the Committee that it was in no way required to declare the communication as such admissible or inadmissible, but was free to judge certain parts of the communication inadmissible while accepting other parts. At the Chairman's suggestion, the Committee decided to consider the above-mentioned condition as having been met, on the understanding that the Secretariat would delete those parts of the communication that did not fall within Unesco's competence.

84. With regard to paragraph 14 (*a*) (iv), the Committee as a whole was of the opinion that the condition set out therein was satisfied.

[84a.] The Committee as a whole was of the same opinion regarding the condition contained in paragraph 14 (*a*) (v), since the communication did not appear to be manifestly ill-founded; some members of the Committee nevertheless considered that the communication did not contain relevant evidence.

85. With regard to the condition specified in paragraph 14 (*a*) (vi) there were no reservations or objections.

86. As mentioned above, some members of the Committee were of the opinion that the condition contained in paragraph 14 (*a*) (vii) was not satisfied, since the communication was based exclusively on information disseminated through the mass media; other members of the Committee, however, pointed to passages in the communication based on information from other sources. The majority of Committee members took the view that the condition had been met in this case.

87. The Committee recognized on the whole that the condition contained in paragraph 14 (*a*) (viii) was fulfilled, the communication having been addressed to Unesco within a reasonable time-limit.

88. A long discussion took place on the subject of the condition specified in paragraph 14 (*a*) (ix) regarding the prior exhausting of available domestic remedies. The Chairman of the Committee made it clear that it was not necessary for the available domestic remedies actually to have been exhausted since it was sufficient for an indication to be given of whether an attempt had been made to exhaust them. The Director of the Division of Human Rights and Peace stated, moreover, that the reference was to purely domestic remedies, i.e. those provided for in the national legal system and therefore exclusive of any approaches of an international character; furthermore, the remedies in question must be effective, i.e. they must be juridical or judicial means provided for within the domestic judicial system for redressing the al-

leged violation. One member of the Committee remarked that the author of the communication did not really respond to the question that was put to him with regard to paragraph 14 (*a*) (ix), because he spoke of external remedies and not of domestic remedies. Nevertheless, the same member was of the opinion that this objection should not be considered as a reason of inadmissibility. Some members of the Committee were of the opinion that for "cases" all possible attempts should be made to fully exaust all available domestic remedies in keeping with paragraph 14 (*a*) (ix) of 104 EX/Decision 3.3. Moreover, they seriously doubted whether the rule was applicable to the "questions" referred to in paragraph 10 (*b*) of 104 EX/Decision 3.3.

[88a.] It was noted, however, in that connection, that recourse to a constitutional court with reference to a law or to some other text of a general character could likewise be envisaged even in respect of a question within the meaning of paragraph 10 (*b*) of the decision.

[88b.] The Chairman concluded by saying that it appeared from the discussion that the condition relative to the exhaustion of domestic remedies had been satisfied.

89. In respect of the condition set forth in paragraph 14 (*a*) (x), it was generally agreed that the communication related to matters that had not yet been settled. However, it was in connection with that condition that the Committee had examined the situation created by the fact that the same communication had been submitted by [WFTU] to ILO and that the fact-finding group of the Commission on Human Rights would shortly be submitting its report to the United Nations General Assembly. At the suggestion of the Chairman, it was agreed that the Secretariat should gather all information relevant not only to ILO's possible examination of the same communication so as to avoid any overlapping, but also to the report of the fact-finding group of the Commission on Human Rights.

90. After examining the ten conditions of admissibility laid down in paragraph 14 (*a*) of 104 EX/Decision 3.3, the Chairman of the Committee noted that the Committee was, by and large, in agreement that the communication concerned was admissible and in conformity with the provisions of paragraph 14 of 104 EX/Decision 3.3, provided, however that the Secretariat was asked to re-examine the communication with a view to deleting any parts of it that were outside Unesco's fields of competence. The Secretariat was also entrusted with the tasks of:

> (i) notifying the author of the communication and the government concerned of the above-mentioned decision of the Committee, in conformity with paragraph 14 [...] of 104 EX/Decision 3.3;

(ii) transmitting a copy of the revised communication, as provided for above, to the Government of Chile while requesting it to forward to the Committee all relevant information concerning the substance of the matter, and asking the author of the communication for any additional information that he deemed useful;

(iii) contacting the Secretariat of ILO in order to agree on an appropriate division of work concerning the communication.

91. Lastly, the Committee *decided*:

(i) to examine the substance of the allegations made by the author of the communication at its [spring 1979 session];

(ii) to postpone to that [session], following fuller acquaintenance with the substance of the allegations, the final decision on the question as to whether the communication constituted a case or a question within the meaning of paragraph 10 of 104 EX/Decision 3.3.

Spring 1979 session of the Committee on Conventions and Recommendations (107th session of the Executive Board)[3]

185. This communication had been declared admissible by the Committee at its [autumn 1978] session, subject to re-examination of the communication by the Secretariat with a view to deleting any parts that were outside Unesco's fields of competence.[4]

186. The material submitted to the Committee comprised: (i) correspondence about the communication with its author since the adoption by the Committee of its report on its [autumn 1978] session; (ii) correspondence with the Government of Chile concerning that communication since the adoption of the report; (iii) a note on the question as examined by ILO and on the report of the fact-finding group of the United Nations Commission on Human Rights; and (iv) the text of the communication revised by the Secretariat.

---

[3] See document 107 EX/PRIV.31, paras. 185-192; see also documents 107 EX/CR/PROC. HR/5 and Annex.

[4] See document 105 EX/49 PRIV., para. 90 (*supra*, pp. 119-120).

Chile **No. 25/78**

187. Furthermore, the Permanent Delegate of Chile to Unesco [...] had conveyed observations on the communication to the Secretariat under cover of a letter of 28 March 1979 [...].[5]

188. The representative of the Government of Chile presented the observations of his government and repeated his contention that the conditions of admissibility had not been met in the case under review and that, in particular, the communication contained no mention of domestic remedies.

189. As to the substance of the communication, he considered that it was irresponsible and prompted by political passion. He quoted several examples to illustrate the point.

190. He then presented the detailed observations of his government on the various allegations. Several members of the Committee felt that the information supplied by the Government of Chile should be passed on to the author of the communication in order that the Committee might have a reply from him.

191. One member of the Committee drew its attention to the fact that the communication concerned a "question" within the meaning of 104 EX/Decision 3.3, paragraph 10, which should be examined as such by the Executive Board. Another member proposed that the Committee give itself time to reflect on the most suitable method for considering communications concerning "questions".

192. In conclusion, the Committee *decided* to keep the communication on its agenda, to instruct the Secretariat to communicate to the members of the Committee the written observations of the government concerned on the substance of the communication, together with the text of the remarks of the representative of that government to the Committee on that question, and to re-examine the various substantive and procedural problems arising in that connection at its next [session].

Autumn 1979 session of the Committee on Conventions and Recommendations (108th session of the Executive Board)[6]

313. This communication submitted to Unesco by the World Federation of Teachers' Unions [WFTU] was declared admissible by the Committee at its [autumn] 1978 session, the Secretariat being at the same time invited to re-examine the com-

[5] See document 107 EX/CR/PROC.HR/5 Annex.
[6] See document 108 EX/38 PRIV., paras. 313-325; see also documents 108 EX/CR/PROC. HR/2 and Add.1.

munication with a view to deleting from it any parts that were outside Unesco's fields of competence.[7]

314. At its [spring 1979] session the Committee, in accordance with 104 EX/Decision 3.3, had initiated its examination of the merits of the allegations declared admissible. Following that examination, the Committee had decided to keep the communication on its agenda, to instruct the Secretariat to communicate to the members of the Committee the written observations of the government concerned on the substance of the communication, together with the text of the remarks of the representative of that government to the Committee on that question [...],[8] and to re-exanine the various substantive and procedural problems arising in that connection at the present session.[9]

315. The Director of the Division of Human Rights and Peace indicated that the Secretariat had kept the author of the communication informed of the various decisions of the Committee, but that [WFTU] had not submitted any further comments or information to the Secretariat.

316. The representative of the Chilean Government recalled that he had challenged the admissibility of the communication, mainly because there had been no recourse to available domestic remedies and because the communication had been prompted exclusively by political passion. This latter point was confirmed, according to the Chilean representative, by the fact that [WFTU] had not replied to the Secretariat's requests for information and had not submitted any data that would enable the allegations it had made in 1978 to be brought up to date.

317. Concerning the exhaustion of domestic remedies, the Director of the Division of Human Rights and Peace pointed out that, according to paragraph 14 (*a*) (ix) of 104 EX/Decision 3.3, the author of the communication had only to indicate whether an attempt had been made to exhaust available domestic remedies. In addition, according to the general principles of international law, the rule that domestic remedies should first be exhausted applied only if those available were effective and adequate in regard to the allegations put forward.

318. The representative of the Chilean Government repeated, in regard to the merits of [WFTU's] allegations, the information that he had given at the [spring 1979] session, as evidence that the allegations were groundless or had become so. He cited for example the fact that under a new law universities and secondary schools would enjoy autonomous status.

---

[7] See document 105 EX/49 PRIV., para. 90 (*supra*, pp. 119-120).
[8] See document 108 EX/CR/PROC.HR/2 Add.1.
[9] See document 107 EX/PRIV.31, para. 192 (*supra*, p. 121).

Chile **No. 25/78**

319. In the opinion of the Chilean representative, the Committee's examination of the merits of [WFTU's] communication had amply demonstrated that it did not warrant further action, and he consequently suggested that it be dismissed in accordance with paragraph 14 (*j*) of 104 EX/Decision 3.3.

320. One member of the Committee considered that the improvements made in the educational situation in Chile pointed to the effectiveness of the efforts undertaken at international level on behalf of human rights in that country, but that considerable problems remained, as seemed to be illustrated by some of the facts set forth in the communication. In his opinion, the Committee could express its vievs forthwith as to the merits; he was also of the opinion that what vas involved was a "question" within the meaning of paragraph 10 of 104 EX/Decision 3.3.

321. Another member drew the Committee's attention to the reports and decisions of the United Nations Commission on Human Rights and the General Assembly concerning the situation of human rights in Chile. Despite a few improvements, the human rights situation in Chile was still, in his view, a matter of great concern.

322. Several members of the Committee raised the question whether, in the context of 104 EX/Decision 3.3, the matter under review represented a "case" or a "question". Some members considered that what was involved was manifestly a "question", while others were of the opinion that, before deciding on this point, it was desirable to know the various aspects of the procedure to be followed with regard to "question", and suggested that the Secretariat be instructed to prepare a study on this subject.

323. The Chairman recalled that the Committee was no longer concerned with the admissibility of the communication but that, after examining the merits of the allegations contained therein, its task was to bring about a friendly solution, in accordance with paragraph 14 (*k*) of 104 EX/Decision 3.3.

324. In the light of the foregoing discussion, the Committee *decided*:

[i] to instruct the Secretariat to prepare a study on all aspects of the procedure for the examination of a "question";

[ii] to bring up to date the factual data contained in the communication, on the basis of the information to be requested from [WFTU], which will be transmitted to the government concerned for its observations;

[iii] to request the Director-General to enter into contact with the government concerned with a view to proceeding, if appropriate, in accordance with the provisions of paragraph 14 (*k*) of 104 EX/Decision 3.3;

[iv] to determine at its next session the form and content of its report to the Executive Board on this communication, and to decide in particular whether it relates to a "question" by virtue of the large number of individual cases involved;

[v] to appeal to the Chilean Government to continue to take measures to help foster respect for human rights in Unesco's fields of competence.

325. One member of the Committee, while subscribing to the above decision, taken by consensus, considered that the communication under review concerned a "question" and that the Committee should have dealt with it as such, in accordance with the relevant provisions of 104 EX/Decision 3.3.

Spring 1980 session of the Committee on Conventions and Recommendations (109th session of the Executive Board)[10]

236. This communication was subnitted to Unesco by the World Federation of Teachers' Unions [WFTU] and concerns "the situation of human rights in Chile in the spheres of education, science, culture and communication". The Committee examined the communication at its [autumn 1978 session] and recorded the results of this initial examination in its report to the Executive Board [...].

237. The Committee had declared the communication admissible, on condition that the Secretariat be instructed to re-examine the communication with a view to deleting from it any parts that were outside Unesco's fields of competence.[11] The text of the revised communication was given after the communication form, together with the written observations of the Chilean Government and the text of the remarks made by the representative of that government to the Committee at its [spring] 1979 session.

238. At its [autumn 1978] session, the Committee also entrusted the Secretariat with the tasks of "(i) notifying the author of the communication and the government concerned of the above-mentioned decision; (ii) transmitting a copy of the revised communication, as provided for above, to the Government of Chile while requesting it to

[10] See document 109 EX/52 PRIV., paras. 236-260; see also documents 109 EX/CR/HR/1 and 109 EX/CR/HR/4.
[11] See document 105 EX/49 PRIV., para. 90 (*supra*, pp. 119-120).

forward to the Committee all relevant information concerning the substance of the matter, and asking the author of the communication for any additional information that he deemed useful; (iii) contacting the Secretariat of ILO in order to agree on an appropriate division of work concerning the communication".[12]

239. Lastly, the Committee decided "(i) to examine the substance of the allegations made by the author of the communication, at its [spring 1979 session]; (ii) to postpone to that [session], following fuller acquaintance with the substance of the allegations, the final decision on the question as to whether the communication constituted a case or a question within the meaning of paragraph 10 of 104 EX/Decision 3.3".[13]

240. At its [spring] 1979 session the Committee, in accordance with 104 EX/Decision 3.3, had initiated its examination of the merits of the allegations declared admissible. Following that examination, the Committee had decided to keep the communication on its agenda, to instruct the Secretariat to communicate to the members of the Committee the written observations of the government concerned on the substance of the communication, together with the text of the remarks of the representative of that government to the Committee on that question [...][14] and to re-examine the various substantive and procedural problems arising in that connection at the [autumn] 1979 session.[15]

241. [At the autumn 1979 session], the representative of the Director-General indicated that the Secretariat had kept the author of the communication informed of the various decisions of the Committee, but that [WFTU] had not submitted any further comments or information to the Secretariat.

242. The representative of the Chilean Government recalled that he had challenged the admissibility of the communication mainly because there had been no recourse to available domestic remedies and because the communication had been prompted exclusively by political passion. This latter point was confirmed, according to the Chilean representative, by the fact that [WFTU] had not replied to the Secretariat's requests for information and had not submitted any data that would enable the allegations it had made in 1978 to be brought up to date.

243. The representative of the Chilean Government repeated, in regard to the merits of [WFTU's] allegations, the information that he had given at the [spring] 1979 session, as evidence that the allegations were groundless or had become so. He cited for

---

[12] *Ibidem*.
[13] *Ibidem*, para. 91 (*supra*, p. 120).
[14] See document 108 EX/CR/PROC.HR/2 Add.1.
[15] See document 107 EX/PRIV.31, para. 192 (*supra*, p. 121).

example the fact that under a new law universities and secondary schools would enjoy autonomous status.

244. In the opinion of the Chilean representative, the Committee's examination of the merits of [WFTU's] communication had amply demonstrated that it did not warrant further action, and he consequently suggested that it be dismissed in accordance with paragraph 14 (*j*) of 104 EX/Decision 3.3.

245. One member drew the Committee's attention to the reports and decisions of the United Nations Commission on Human Rights and the General Assenfuly concerning the situation of human rights in Chile. Despite a few improvements, the human rights situation in Chile was still, in his view, a matter of great concern.

246. Several members of the Committee raised the question whether, in the context of 104 EX/Decision 3.3, the matter under review represented a "case" or a "question". Some members considered that what was involved was manifestly a "question", while others were of the opinion that, before deciding on this point, it was desirable to know the various aspects of the procedure to be followed with regard to a "question", and suggested that the Secretariat be instructed to prepare a study on this subject.

247. The Chairman recalled that after examining the merits of the allegations contained therein, the task of the Committee was to bring about a friendly solution, in accordance with paragraph 14 (*k*) of 104 EX/Decision 3.3.

248. In the light of the foregoing discussion, the Committee decided:[16]

> [i] to instruct the Secretariat to prepare a study on all aspects of the procedure for the examination of a "question";
>
> [ii] to bring up to date the factual data contained in the communication, on the basis of the information to be requested from [WFTU], which would be transmitted to the government concerned for its observations;
>
> [iii] to request the Director-General to enter into contact with the government concerned with a view to proceeding, if appropriate, in accordance with the provisions of paragraph 14 (*k*) of 104 EX/Decision 3.3;

---

[16] See document 108 EX/38 PRIV., para. 324 (*supra*, pp. 123-124).

[iv] to determine the form and content of its report to the Executive Board on this communication, and to decide in particular whether it related to a "question" by virtue of the large number of individual cases involved;

[v] to appeal to the Chilean Government to continue to take measures to help foster respect for human rights in Unesco's fields of competence.

249. In a letter dated 12 November 1979, the Secretariat requested [WFTU] to forward to it any further information that might shed light on that contained in the revised communication. In view of the fact that no reply had been received to that letter, a registered letter of reminder was sent to [WFTU] dated 12 February 1980. No reply has yet been received.

250. In a letter dated 20 November 1979, the Deputy Director-General suggested to the Chilean Foreign Affairs Minister that an exploratory examination be made into the possibilities of reaching a friendly solution that would help discussions on the communication from [WFTU] at the present session of the Committee, in the spirit of paragraph 14 (*k*) of 104 EX/Decision 3.3. This letter was followed by discussions and further exchanges of letters.

251. By a letter dated 31 March 1980 [...],[17] the Deputy Director-General transmitted to the Chilean authorities a list of suggestions formulated with a view to giving effect to paragraph 14 (*k*) of 104 EX/Decision 3.3. By a letter dated 10 April 1980 [...][18] the Ambassador of Chile to Unesco forwarded his government's comments on the aforementioned suggestions.

252. At the Committee's present session, the representative of the Chilean Government reiterated his government's position and reviewed the progress which had been made. He informed the Committee that as regards the right of Chileans to return and live in their country, the delegation of Chile agrees to propose to its government that the cases of persons exercising an activity connected with Unesco's fields of competence, who have not been convicted of an ordinary offence or who have been convicted of a non-extraditable offence in countries having the same legal systems as Chile and who are at present prevented from returning, should be reviewed with a view to giving favourable effect to the Director-General's representations in order to facilitate the reintegration of such persons in the normal life of their country. In all such cases, the Director-General would notify those concerned, through the competent bodies under his authority, of their prior obligation to prove that they have attempted to exhaust domestic remedies, whether administrative or judicial, as provid-

[17] See document 109 EX/CR/HR/4, annex I.

[18] *Ibidem*, annex II.

ed in subparagraph 14 (*a*) (ix) of 104 EX/Decision 3.3. Likewise, if the Director-General's representations are successfull, Unesco would impress upon those concerned the moral obligation which they incur to respect the laws in force in Chile. The relevant representations would be made through normal existing channels, and in particular through the intermediary of the Permanent Delegation of Chile. The first cases to be delt with would be those of the eight Chilean nationals referred to in the Director-General's letter of 29 November 1979. He has also informed the Committee that as a result of the humanitarian representations made by Unesco, two out of these eight persons have received authorization to return to Chile, for a period of 60 days, in order to regularize their situation.

253. As concerned the situation of primary and secondary education, the Chilean representative stated, firstly, that primary and secondary school curricula contain nothing that might be interpreted as contrary to human rights or to the international obligations contracted by Chile in these matters. In any case, in order to clear up this matter once and for all and to make plain our good faith and concern to co-operate, we herewith reiterate the request formulated on 14 January 1980 with a view to securing Unesco's collaboration in order to implement the Presidential Directives in regard to education. In this way, the expert appointed by Unesco, in addition to providing specialized technical assistance, would be in a position to check whether the curricula comply with the international obligations contracted by Chile in this matter, and to formulate where appropriate such suggestions as he considers relevant. As this expert would inform both Unesco and the consulting government, the matter at issue would be fully covered..

254. With regard to the situation of Chilean universities, work was proceeding on the drafting of the general law on the universities. In the light of the progress achieved to date, it could be said that provision was being made with regard to all matters referred to under this heading, so that once the abovmentioned law is enacted, Chilean universities would attain full autonomy, establishing their own governing bodies, providing extensive facilities for research and, lastly, ensuring that the specific purposes of these centres of learning are fully achieved. The delegation of Chile would keep Unesco constantly informed in this connection.

255. On the matter of the transfer of lecturers and teachers, the representative of the Chilean Government wished to clarify the existing situation. In accordance with Chilean legislation (Statutory Decree No. 960 of 1960 concerning the Civil Service), teachers who are government employees, that is, who serve in the public education system, may be transferred for administrative reasons relating to their service (promotion, termination of duties, etc.) or as a result of disciplinary measures, in the latter case upon completion of a procedure laid down in great detail in the above-mentioned recent legislation. The Chilean delegation will transmit the texts of the legis-

lation in question to the Secretariat. In any case, while considering that the procedure referred to envisages all the norms of the Unesco Recommendation governing this matter, the Chilean delegation has no objection to the formal incorporation of the Recommendation in it.

256. As regards the expulsion of students and dismissal of teachers, a preliminary distinction had to be made in this connection: both secondary and university establishments in Chile were divided into two major groups: public and private. The State could only impose administrative regulations upon the former, its responsibility in the latter case being limited to ensuring in general terms that curricula and syllabuses are complied with. For example, the Catholic universities had their own statutes, approved by the competent authorities of the Vatican; similarly, their rectors were appointed with the Vatican's approval.

257. With regard to public university establishments, their respective statutes all provide for expulsion as an ultimate and extreme disciplinary measure, applicable upon completion of a procedure which affords the opportunity to provide evidence on behalf of those concerned and to refer the case to various authorities in the event of serious penalties being imposed. This was also borne out by the relevant laws and regulations.

258. Finally, the Chilean representative fully agreed about the expediency of maintaining a continuous dialogue with the Director-General with a view to solving the problems that may arise, thereby giving full effect to the principle of co-operation which had been a constant feature of its relations with Unesco.

259. Several members of the Committee expressed their satisfaction that considerable progress had been made on these matters and emphasized the importance of noting the Director-General's actions and the Chilean authorities's spirit of friendly dialogue and willingness to co-operate. Other members of the Committee while noting that certain problems still remained, expressed the view that given the often slow and frustrating work in human rights matters, the achievements here had been quite notable, and that congratulations for the Director-General and the Committee itself were appropriate. One member of the Committee exrressed his scepticism about the co-operation of the Chilean authorities and about the value of the procedures adopted.

260. The Committee *decided*:

> (i) to continue to review with the Chilean authorities the progress made for the settlement of the present communication;

(ii) to examine at its next session the study on all aspects of the procedure for the examination of a "question", which the Secretariat has been instructed to prepare.

Autumn 1980 session of the Committee on Conventions and Recommendations (110th session of the Executive Board)[19]

235. This communication was submitted to Unesco by the World Federation of Teachers' Unions [WFTU] and concerns "the situation of human rights in Chile in the spheres of education, science, culture and communication". The Committee examined the communication at its [autumn 1978 session] and indicated the results of this initial examination in its report to the Executive Board [...].

236. The Committee had declared the communication admissible, on condition that the Secretariat be instructed to re-examine the communication with a view to deleting from it any parts that were outside Unesco's fields of competence.[20] The text of the revised communication is given after the communication form, together with the written observations of the Chilean Government and the text of the remarks made by the representative of that government to the Committee at its [spring] 1979 session.

237. At its [autumn 1978] session, the Committee also entrusted the Secretariat with the tasks of "(i) notifying the author of the communication and the government concerned of the above-mentioned decision; (ii) transmitting a copy of the revised communication, as provided for above, to the Government of Chile while requesting it to forward to the Committee all relevant information concerning the substance of the matter, and asking the author of the communication for any additional information that he deemed useful; (iii) contacting the Secretariat of ILO in order to agree on an appropriate division of work concerning the communication".[21]

238. Lastly, the Committee decided "(i) to examine the substance of the allegations made by the author of the communication, at its [spring 1979 session]; (ii) to postpone to that [session], following fuller acquaintance with the substance of the allegations, the final decision on the question as to whether the communication constituted a case or a question within the meaning of paragraph 10 of 104 EX/Decision 3.3".[22]

239. At its [spring] 1979 session the Committee, in accordance with 104 EX/Decision 3.3, had initiated its examination of the merits of the allegations declared ad-

[19] See document 110 EX/40 PRIV., paras. 235-269; see also document 110 EX/CR/HR/1.
[20] See document 105 EX/49 PRIV., para. 90 (*supra*, pp. 119-120).
[21] *Ibidem*.
[22] *Ibidem*, para. 91 (*supra*, p. 120).

missible. Following that examination, the Committee had decided to keep the communication on its agenda, to instruct the Secretariat to communicate to the members of the Committee the written observations of the government concerned on the substance of the communication, together with the text of the remarks of the representative of that government to the Committee on that question [...][23] and to re-examine the various substantive and procedural problems arising in that connection at the [autumn] 1979 session.[24]

240. The Director of the Division of Human Rights and Peace indicated at that time that the Secretariat had kept the author of the communication informed of the various decisions of the Committee, but that [WFTU] had not submitted any further comments or information to the Secretariat.

241. The representative of the Chilean Government recalled that he had challenged the admissibility of the communication, mainly because there had been no recourse to available domestic remedies and because the communication had been prompted exclusively by political passion. This latter point was confirmed, according to the Chilean representative, by the fact that [WFTU] had not replied to the Secretariat's requests for information and had not submitted any data that would enable the allegations it had made in 1978 to be brought up to date.

242. The representative of the Chilean Government repeated, in regard to the merits of [WFTU's] allegations, the information that he had given at the [spring] 1979 session, as evidence that the allegations were groundless or had become so. He cited for example the fact that under a new law universities and secondary schools would enjoy autonomous status.

243. In the opinion of the Chilean representative, the Committee's examination of the merits of [WFTU's] communication had amply demonstrated that it did not warrant further action, and he consequently suggested that it be dismissed in accordance with paragraph 14 (*j*) of 104 EX/Decision 3.3.

244. Several members of the Committee raised the question whether, in the context of 104 EX/Decision 3.3, the matter under review represented a "case" or a "question". Some members considered that what was involved was manifestly a "question", while others were of the opinion that, before deciding on this point, it was desirable to know the various aspects of the procedure to be followed with regard to a "question", and suggested that the Secretariat be instructed to prepare a study on this subject.

---

[23] See document 108 EX/CR/PROC.HR/2 Add.1.

[24] See document 107 EX/PRIV.31, para. 192 (*supra*, p. 121).

No. 25/78 **Chile**

245. The Chairman recalled that the Committee was no longer concerned with the admissibility of the communication but that, after examining the merits of the allegations contained therein, its task was to bring about a friendly solution, in accordance with paragraph 14 (*k*) of 104 EX/Decision 3.3.

246. In light of the foregoing discussion, the Committee had decided:[25]

[i] to instruct the Secretariat to prepare a study on all aspects of the procedure for the examination of a "question";

[ii] to bring up to date the factual data contained in the communication, on the basis of the information to be requested from [WFTU], which will be transmitted to the government concerned for its observations;

[iii] to request the Director-General to enter into contact with the government concerned with a view to proceeding, if appropriate, in accordance with the provisions of paragraph 14 (*k*) of 104 EX/Decision 3.3;

[iv] to determine at its next session the form and content of its report to the Executive Board on this communication, and to decide in particular whether it relates to a "question" by virtue of the large number of individual cases involved;

[v] to appeal to the Chilean Government to continue to take measures to help foster respect for human rights in Unesco's fields of competence.

247. By a letter dated 20 November 1979, the Deputy Director-General suggested to the Chilean Foreign Affairs Minister that an exploratory examination be made into the possibilities of reaching a friendly solution that would help discussions on the communication from [WFTU] at [the spring 1980] session of the Committee, in the spirit of paragraph 14 (*k*) of 104 EX/Decision 3.3. This letter was followed by discussions and further exchanges of letters.

248. In a letter dated 31 March 1980 [...], the Deputy Director-General transmitted to the Chilean authorities a list of suggestions formulated with a view to giving effect to paragraph 14 (*k*) of 104 EX/Decision 3.3. By a letter dated 10 April 1980 [...] the Ambassador of Chile to Unesco forwarded his government's comments on the aforementioned suggestions.

---

[25] See document 108 EX/38 PRIV., para. 324 (*supra*, pp. 123-124).

Chile **No. 25/78**

249. At the Committee's [spring 1980] session, the representative of the Chilean Government reiterated his government's position and reviewed the progress which had been made. He informed the Committee that as regards the right of Chileans to return and live in their country, the delegation of Chile agrees to propose to its government that the cases of persons exercising an activity connected with Unesco's fields of competence, who had not been convicted of an ordinary offence or who had been convicted for a non-extraditable offence in countries having the same legal system as Chile and who are at present prevented from returning, should be reviewed with a view to giving favourable effect to the Director-General's representations in order to facilitate the reintegration of such persons in the normal life of their country. In all such cases, the Director-General would notify those concerned, through the competent bodies under his authority, of their prior obligation to prove that they have attempted to exhaust domestic remedies, whether administrative or judicial, as provided in subparagraph 14 (*a*) (ix) of 104 EX/Decision 3.3. Likewise, if the Director-General's representations are successful, Unesco would impress upon those concerned the moral obligation which they incur to respect the laws in force in Chile. The relevant representations would be made through normal existing channels, and in particular through the intermediary of the Permanent Delegation of Chile. The first cases to be dealt with would be those of the eight Chilean nationals referred to in the Director-General's letter of 29 November 1979. He also informed the Committee that as a result of the humanitarian representations made by Unesco, two out of these eight persons have received authorization to return to Chile, for a period of 60 days, in order to regularize their situation.

250. As concerned the situation of primary and secondary education, the Chilean representative stated, firstly, that primary and secondary school curricula contain nothing that might be interpreted as contrary to human rights or to the international obligations contracted by Chile in these matters. In any case, in order to clear up this matter once and for all and to make plain our good faith and concern to co-operate, we herewith reiterate the request formulated on 14 January 1980 with a view to securing Unesco's collaboration in order to implement the Presidential Directives in regard to education. In this way, the expert appointed by Unesco, in addition to providing specialized technical assistance, would be in a position to check whether the curricula comply with the international obligations contracted by Chile in this matter, and to formulate where appropriate such suggestions as he considers relevant. As this expert would inform both Unesco and the consulting government, the matter at issue would be fully covered.

251. With regard to the situation of Chilean universities, work was proceeding on the drafting of the general law on the universities. In the light of the progress achieved to date, it could be said that provision was being made with regard to all matters referred to under this heading, so that once the above-mentioned law is en-

acted, Chilean universities would attain full autonomy, establishing their own governing bodies, providing extensive facilities for research and, lastly, ensuring that the specific purposes of these centres of learning are fully achieved. The delegation of Chile would keep Unesco constantly informed in this connection.

252. On the matter of the transfer of lecturers and teachers, the representative of the Chilean Government wished to clarify the existing situation. In accordance with Chilean legislation (Statutory Decree No. 960 of 1960 concerning the Civil Service), teachers who are government employees, that is, who serve in the public education system, may be transferred for administrative reasons relating to their service (promotion, termination of duties, etc.) or as a result of disciplinary measures in the latter case upon completion of a procedure laid down in great detail in the above-mentioned recent legislation. The Chilean delegation would transmit the texts of the legislation in question to the Secretariat. In any case, while considering that the procedure referred to envisages all the norms of the Unesco Recommendation governing this matter, the Chilean delegation has no objection to the formal incorporation of the Recommendation in it.

253. As regards the expulsion of students and dismissal of teachers, a preliminary distinction had to be made in this connection: both secondary and university establishments in Chile were divided into two major groups: public and private. The State could only impose administrative regulations upon the former, its responsibility in the latter case being limited to ensuring in general terms that curricula and syllabuses were complied with. For example, the Catholic universities had their own statutes, approved by the competent authorities of the Vatican; similarly, their rectors were appointed with the Vatican's approval.

254. With regard to public university institutions, their respective statutes all provide for expulsion as an ultimate and extreme disciplinary measure, applicable upon completion of a procedure which affords the opportunity to provide evidence on behalf of those concerned and to refer the case to various authorities in the event of severe penalties being imposed. This was also borne out by the relevant laws and regulations.

255. Finally, the Chilean representative fully agreed about the expediency of maintaining a continuous dialogue with the Director-General with a view to solving the problems that might arise, thereby giving full effect to the principle of co-operation which had been a constant feature of its relations with Unesco.

256. Several members of the Committee expressed their satisfaction that considerable progress had been made on these matters and emphasized the importance of noting the Director-General's actions and the Chilean authorities' spirit of friendly dia-

logue and willingness to co-operate. Other members of the Committee while noting that certain problems still remained, expressed the view that given the often slow and frustrating work in human rights matters, the achievements here had been quite notable, and that congratulations for the Director-General and the Committee itself were appropriate. One member of the Committee expressed his scepticism about the co-operation of the Chilean authorities and about the value of the procedures adopted.

257. The Committee decided at its [spring 1980] session:[26]

(i) to continue to review with the Chilean authorities the progress made for the settlement of the present communication;

(ii) to examine at its next session the study on all aspects of the procedure for the examination of a "question", which the Secretariat was instructed to prepare.

258. The representative of the Director-General added to the introductory summary of the foregoing that the Director-General had recently been apprised of the problem of the expulsion of students from universities and the fact that they had been placed under house arrest.

259. The representative of the Chilean Government recalled that despite numerous requests made of him, the author of the communication had never supplied any proof in support of his allegations and that his government had nevertheless always complied with all the suggestions of the Director-General. He added that he would not reopen the question of the right of Chileans to return to their country since it had been covered elsewhere.[27] With regard to the other points raised by the author, however, an expert had been appointed by Unesco at the request of his government and had been instructed to carry out an on-the-spot check of the validity of the author's allegations. That internationally reputed expert, Professor Ricardo Marín Ibañez, who had been able to act in complete freedom and go wherever he wished, had provided the speaker with the fullest possible documentary material on his mission and had authorized the speaker to inform the Committee of his conclusions.

260. With regard to the allegation that education was under military control, Professor Ibañez had observed that all the authorities responsible for educational matters were civilians and that most of them had continued unchanged at their posts over the previous 10 years. Two facts only might possibly leave scope for interpretation: the

---

[26] See document 109 EX/52 PRIV., para. 260 (*supra*, pp. 129-130).

[27] See document 110 EX/40 PRIV., paras. 45-56 (*infra*, pp. 182-184), communication No. 54/78 concerning *Chile*, case of *Arturo Montes Larrain*.

traffic police [were] authorized to teach the highway code in schools; and the police, under agreements with Interpol, provided optional courses on the prevention of traffic in drugs.

261. As to the claim that curricula were contrary to international commitments assumed by Chile regarding human rights, Professor Ibañez had found the accusation groundless since, on the contrary, curricula were very liberal in Chile and were aimed at making pupils think for themselves.

262. The criticism levelled at the Chilean Government that it was transferring to the private sector certain educational functions which were matters for the State was based on the existence of a pilot plan aimed at making local firms responsible for technical and vocational education, in order to avoid a situation where pupils leaving specialist schools were unable to find work with firms in their region specializing in branches not covered in schools.

263. Despite the contention of the authors of the communication, the Chilean education system was not elitist. Professor Ibañez had noted that the education budget represented 22 per cent of the total budget and that the government's policy was aimed rather at assisting the poorest pupils and students. The previous imbalance between higher education and the other levels of education had been reduced by means of a partial budgetary transfer from primary and secondary education to university education.

264. On the subject of the transfer of teachers, it was true that the Minister of Education was empowered to post teachers for a year to institutions situated in isolated areas which, owing to their remoteness, did not possess their proper complement of teachers. Facilities for appeal were furthermore available in such cases. The situation had not changed since 1931, when any teacher had to have spent a certain period in the provinces as a prerequisite for promotion.

265. With regard to the transfer of school administration to municipal authorities, the expert found it hard to grasp the problem. Those concerned were still the administrative authorities of the State and, since it was centralized, the education system could only be made more effective by an increase in the powers of the local authorities.

266. He added that his government had endeavoured most scrupulously to respect the agreement concluded with the Director-General and to collaborate as efficiently as possible with the Committee. He consequently considered that the communication should be struck off the list; or [WFTU] should be requested to provide proof in

support of the allegations, failing which the communication would be struck off the list.

267. Many members of the Committee made a point of expressing their satisfaction to the representative of the Chilean Government and welcomed the spirit of co-operation displayed by his government in regard to the Committee. Several members were in favour of striking the communication off the list, some because they considered they had been sufficiently informed, others on account of the "fourfold silence" of [WFTU], and still others since they did not feel responsible for permanent supervision of the conditions governing education in Chile. On the other hand, some members wished to study the report by Professor Ibañez before reaching a decision and therefore to postpone examination of the communication to the next session. Most members nevertheless concurred in noting and deeply regretting the silence of [WFTU].

268. The representative of the Director-General emphasized the following three points:

(i) [WFTU] had never answered any letter from the Secretariat, which had not been used as an argument by the Chilean Government, so that it was not raising that as an objection. However, since the procedure under way before the Committee was not a trial, no excessive role should be afforded the author of the communication, whose silence should not be a determining factor in the Committee's decision;

(ii) the precedent constituted by the appointment of an expert at the invitation of a government concerned was a noteworthy feature;

(iii) two courses were open to the Committee: either, in pursuance of paragraph 14 (*j*) of 104 EX/Decision 3.3, to reject the communication because it did not seem, after examination of the substance of the matter, to deserve further action; or to decide to draw up a report on the matter and transmit it to the Executive Board.

269. After a brief exchange of views, the Committee *decided* to postpone further examination of the communication to the next session.

No. 25/78 **Chile**

Spring 1981 session of the Committee on Conventions and Recommendations (112th session of the Executive Board)[28]

415. This communication was submitted to Unesco by the World Federation of Teachers' Unions [WFTU] and concerns "the situation of human rights in Chile in the spheres of education, science, culture and communication". The Committee examined the communication at its [autumn 1978 session] and indicated the results of this initial examination in its report to the Executive Board [...].

416. The Committee had declared the communication admissible, on condition that the Secretariat be instructed to re-examine the communication with a view to deleting from it any parts that were outside Unesco's fields of competence.[29]

417. At its [autumn] 1978 session, the Committee also entrusted the Secretariat with the tasks of "[...] (ii) transmitting a copy of the revised communication, as provided for above, to the Government of Chile while requesting it to forward to the Committee all relevant information concerning the substance of the matter, and asking the author of the communication for any additional information that he deemed useful; (iii) contacting the Secretariat of ILO in order to agree on an appropriate division of work concerning the communication".[30]

418. Lastly, the Committee decided "(i) to examine the substance of the allegations made by the author of the communication, at its [spring 1979 session]; (ii) to postpone to that [session], following fuller acquaintance with the substance of the allegations, the final decision on the question as to whether the communication constituted a case or a question within the meaning of paragraph 10 of 104 EX/Decision 3.3".[31]

419. At its [spring] 1979 session the Committee, in accordance with 104 EX/Decision 3.3, had initiated its examination of the merits of the allegations declared admissible. Following that examination, the Committee had decided to keep the communication on its agenda, to instruct the Secretariat to communicate to the members of the Committee the written observations of the government concerned on the substance of the communication, together with the text of the remarks of the representative of that government to the Committee on that question [...][32] and to re-examine

---

[28] See document 112 EX/30 PRIV., paras. 415-[453a]; see also documents 112 EX/CR/HR/1 and Add.
[29] See document 105 EX/49 PRIV., para. 90 (*supra*, pp. 119-120).
[30] *Ibidem*.
[31] *Ibidem*, para. 91 (*supra*, p. 120).
[32] See document 108 EX/CR/PROC.HR/2 Add.1.

the various substantive and procedural problems arising in that connection at the [autumn] 1979 session.[33]

420. The representative of the Director-General had indicated that the Secretariat had kept the author of the communication informed of the various decisions of the Committee, but that [WFTU] had not submitted any further comments or information to the Secretariat.

421. The representative of the Chilean Government recalled that he had challenged the admissibility of the communication, mainly because there had been no recourse to available domestic remedies and because the communication had been prompted exclusively by political passion. This latter point was confirmed, according to the Chilean representative, by the fact that [WFTU] had not replied to the Secretariat's requests for information and had not submitted any data that would enable the allegations it had made in 1978 to be brought up to date.

422. The representative of the Chilean Government repeated, in regard to the merits of [WFTU's] allegations, the information that he had given at the [spring] 1979 session, as evidence that the allegations were groundless or had become so. He cited for example the fact that under a new law universities and secondary schools would enjoy autonomous status.

423. In the opinion of the Chilean representative, the Committee's examination of the merits of [WFTU's] communication had amply demonstrated that it did not warrant further action, and he consequently suggested that it be dismissed in accordance with paragraph 14 (*j*) of 104 EX/Decision 3.3.

424. Several members of the Committee raised the question whether, in the context of 104 EX/Decision 3.3, the matter under review represented a "case" or a "question". Some members considered that what was involved was manifestly a "question", while others were of the opinion that, before deciding on this point, it was desirable to know the various aspects of the procedure to be followed with regard to a "question", and suggested that the Secretariat be instructed to prepare a study on this subject.

425. The Chairman recalled that the Committee was no longer concerned with the admissibility of the communication but that, after examining the merits of the allegations contained therein, its task was to bring about a friendly solution, in accordance with paragraph 14 (*k*) of 104 EX/Decision 3.3.

---

[33] See document 107 EX/PRIV.31, para. 192 (*supra*, p. 121).

No. 25/78 **Chile**

426. In the light of the foregoing discussion, the Committee decided:[34]

[i] to instruct the Secretariat to prepare a study on all aspects of the procedure for the examination of a "question";

[ii] to bring up to date the factual data contained in the communication, on the basis of the information to be requested from [WFTU], which will be transmitted to the government concerned for its observations;

[iii] to request the Director-General to enter into contact with the government concerned with a view to proceeding, if appropriate, in accordance with the provisions of paragraph 14 (*k*) of 104 EX/Decision 3.3;

[iv] to determine at its [next] session the form and content of its report to the Executive Board on this communication, and to decide in particular whether it relates to a "question" by virtue of the large number of individual cases involved;

[v] to appeal to the Chilean Government to continue to take measures to help foster respect for human rights in Unesco's fields of competence.

427. In a letter dated 20 November 1979, the Deputy Director-General suggested to the Chilean Foreign Affairs Minister that an exploratory examination be made into the possibilities of reaching an amicable solution that would help discussions on the communication from [WFTU] at the [spring 1980] session of the Committee, in the spirit of paragraph 14 (*k*) of 104 EX/Decision 3.3.

428. In a letter dated 31 March 1980, the Deputy Director-General transmitted to the Chilean authorities a list of suggestions formulated with a view to giving effect to paragraph 14 (*k*) of 104 EX/Decision 3.3. By a letter dated 10 April 1980 the Ambassador of Chile to Unesco forwarded his government's comments on the aforementioned suggestions.

429. At the Committee's [spring 1980 session], the representative of the Chilean Government reiterated his government's position and reviewed the progress which had been made. He informed the Committee that as regards the right of Chileans to return and live in their country, the delegation of Chile agreed to propose to its government that the cases of persons exercising an activity connected with Unesco's fields of competence, who had not been convicted of an ordinary offence or who had been convicted for a non-extraditable offence in countries having the same legal sys-

---

[34] See document 108 EX/38 PRIV., para. 324 (*supra*, pp. 123-124).

tem as Chile and who were at present prevented from returning, should be reviewed with a view to giving favourable effect to the Director-General's representations in order to facilitate the reintegration of such persons in the normal life of their country. In all such cases, the Director-General would notify those concerned, through the competent bodies under his authority, of their prior obligation to prove that they had attempted to exhaust domestic remedies, whether administrative or judicial, as provided in subparagraph 14 (*a*) (ix) of 104 EX/Decision 3.3. Likewise, if the Director-General's representations were successful, Unesco would impress upon those concerned the moral obligation which they incurred to respect the laws in force in Chile. The relevant representations would be made through normal existing channels, and in particular through the intermediary of the Permanent Delegation of Chile. The first cases to be dealt with would be those of the eight Chilean nationals referred to in the Director-General's letter of 29 November 1979. He also informed the Committee that as a result of the humanitarian representations made by Unesco, two out of these eight persons had received authorization to return to Chile, for a period of 60 days, in order to regularize their situation.

430. As concerned the situation of primary and secondary education, the Chilean representative stated, firstly, that primary and secondary school curricula contained nothing that might be interpreted as contrary to human rights or to the international obligations contracted by Chile in these matters. In any case, in order to clear up this matter once and for all and to make plain its good faith and concern to co-operate, the Chilean Government reiterated the request formulated on 14 January 1980 with a view to securing Unesco's collaboration in order to implement the Presidential Directives in regard to education. In this way, the expert appointed by Unesco, in addition to providing specialized technical assistance, would be in a position to check whether the curricula complied with the international obligations contracted by Chile in this matter, and to formulate where appropriate such suggestions as he considered relevant. As that expert would inform both Unesco and the consulting government, the matter at issue would be fully covered.

431. With regard to the situation of Chilean universities, work was proceeding on the drafting of the general law on the universities. In the light of the progress achieved to date, it could be said that provision was being made with regard to all matters referred to under this heading, so that once the above-mentioned law was enacted, Chilean universities would attain full autonomy, establishing their own governing bodies, providing extensive facilities for research and, lastly, ensuring that the specific purposes of these centres of learning were fully achieved. The delegation of Chile would keep Unesco constantly informed in this connection.

432. On the matter of the transfer of lecturers and teachers, the representative of the Chilean Government wished to clarify the existing situation. In accordance with

Chilean legislation (Statutory Decree No. 960 of 1960 concerning the Civil Service), teachers who were government employees, that is, who served in the public education system, might be transferred for administrative reasons relating to their service (promotion, termination of duties, etc.) or as a result of disciplinary measures in the latter case upon completion of a procedure laid down in great detail in the above-mentioned recent legislation. The Chilean delegation would transmit the texts of the legislation in question to the Secretariat. In any case, while considering that the procedure referred to envisaged all the norms of the Unesco Recommendation governing this matter, the Chilean delegation had no objection to the formal incorporation of the Recommendation in it.

433. As regards the expulsion of students and dismissal of teachers, a preliminary distinction had to be made in this connection: both secondary and university establishments in Chile were divided into two major groups: public and private. The State could only impose administrative regulations upon the former, its responsibility in the latter case being limited to ensuring in general terms that curricula and syllabuses were complied with. For example, the Catholic universities had their own statutes, approved by the competent authorities of the Vatican; similarly, their rectors were appointed with the Vatican's approval.

434. With regard to public university establishments, their respective statutes all provided for expulsion as an ultimate and extreme disciplinary measure, applicable upon completion of a procedure which afforded the opportunity to provide evidence on behalf of those concerned and to refer the case to various authorities in the event of severe penalties being imposed. This was also borne out by the relevant laws and regulations.

435. Finally, the Chilean representative fully agreed about the expediency of maintaining a continuous dialogue with the Director-General with a view to solving the problems that might arise, thereby giving full effect to the principle of co-operation which had been a constant feature of its relations with Unesco.

436. Several members of the Committee expressed their satisfaction that considerable progress had been made on these matters and emphasized the importance of noting the Director-General's actions and the Chilean authorities' spirit of friendly dialogue and willingness to co-operate. Other members of the Committee while noting that certain problems still remained, expressed the view that given the often slow and frustrating work in human rights matters, the achievements here had been quite notable, and that congratulations for the Director-General and the Committee itself were appropriate. One member of the Committee expressed his scepticism about the co-operation of the Chilean authorities and about the value of the procedures adopted.

437. The Committee therefore decided:[35]

(i) to continue to review with the Chilean authorities the progress made for the settlement of the present communication;

(ii) to examine at its next session the study on all aspects of the procedure for the examination of a "question", which the Secretariat was instructed to prepare.

438. At the [spring] 1980 session, the representative of the Director-General added to the introductory summary of the foregoing that the Director-General had recently been apprised of the problem of the expulsion of students from universities and the fact that they had been placed under house arrest.

439. The representative of the Chilean Government recalled that despite numerous requests made of him, the author of the communication had never supplied any proof in support of his allegations and that his government had nevertheless always complied with all the suggestions of the Director-General. He added that he would not reopen the question of the right of Chileans to return to their country since it had been covered elsewhere. With regard to the other points raised by the author, however, an expert had been appointed by Unesco at the request of his government and had been instructed to carry out an on-the-spot check of the validity of the author's allegations. That internationally reputed expert, Professor Ricardo Marín Ibañez, who had been able to act in complete freedom and go wherever he wished, had provided the speaker with the fullest possible documentary material on his mission and had authorized the speaker to inform the Committee of his conclusions.

440. With regard to the allegation that education was under military control, Professor Ibañez had observed that all the authorities responsible for educational matters were civilians and that most of them had continued unchanged at their posts over the previous 10 years. Two facts only might possibly leave scope for interpretation: the traffic police [were] authorized to teach the highway code in schools; and the police, under agreements with Interpol, provided optional courses on the prevention of traffic in drugs.

441. As to the claim that curricula were contrary to international commitments assumed by Chile regarding human rights, Professor Ibañez had found the accusation groundless since, on the contrary, curricula were very liberal in Chile and were aimed at making pupils think for themselves.

---

[35] See document 109 EX/52 PRIV., para. 260 (*supra*, pp. 129-130).

No. 25/78 **Chile**

442. The criticism levelled at the Chilean Government that it was transferring to the private sector certain educational functions which were matters for the State was based on the existence of a pilot plan aimed at making local firms responsible for technical and vocational education, in order to avoid a situation where pupils leaving specialist schools were unable to find work with firms in their region specializing in branches not covered in schools.

443. Despite the contention of the authors of the communication, the Chilean education system was not elitist. Professor Ibañez had noted that the education budget represented 22 per cent of the total budget and that the government's policy was aimed rather at assisting the poorest pupils and students. The previous imbalance between higher education and the other levels of education had been reduced by means of a partial budgetary transfer from primary and secondary education to university education.

444. On the subject of the transfer of teachers, it was true that the Minister of Education was empowered to post teachers for a year to institutions situated in isolated areas which, owing to their remoteness, did not possess their proper complement of teachers. Facilities for appeal were furthermore available in such cases. The situation had not changed since 1931, when any teacher had to have spent a certain period in the provinces as a prerequisite for promotion.

445. With regard to the transfer of school administration to municipal authorities, the expert found it hard to grasp the problem. Those concerned were still the administrative authorities of the State and, since it was centralized, the education system could only be made more effective by an increase in the powers of the local authorities.

446. He added that his government had endeavoured most scrupulously to respect the agreement concluded with the Director-General and to collaborate as efficiently as possible with the Committee. He consequently considered that the communication should be struck off the list; or [WFTU] should be requested to provide proof in support of the allegations, failing which the communication would be struck off the list.

447. Many members of the Committee made a point of expressing their satisfaction to the representative of the Chilean Government and welcomed the spirit of co-operation displayed by his government in regard to the Committee. Several members were in favour of striking the communication off the list, some because they considered they had been sufficiently informed, others on account of the "fourfold silence" of [WFTU], and still others since they did not feel responsible for permanent supervision of the conditions governing education in Chile. On the other hand, some

members wished to study the report by Professor Ibañez before reaching a decision and therefore to postpone examination of the communication to the next session. Most members nevertheless concurred in noting and deeply regretting the silence of [WFTU].

448. The representative of the Director-General emphasized the following three points:

(i) [WFTU] had never answered any letter from the Secretariat, which had not been used as an argument by the Chilean Government, so that it was not raising that as an objection. However, since the procedure under way before the Committee was not a trial, no excessive role should be afforded the author of the communication, whose silence should not be a determining factor in the Committee's decision;

(ii) the precedent constituted by the appointment of an expert at the invitation of a government concerned was a noteworthy feature;

(iii) two courses were open to the Committee: either, in pursuance of paragraph 14 (*j*) of 104 EX/Decision 3.3, to dismiss the communication because it did not seem, after examination of the merits of the matter, to warrant further action; or to decide to draw up a report on the matter and transmit it to the Executive Board.

449. After a brief exchange of views, the Committee decided to defer further examination of the communication to the present session, pending receipt of the expert's report referred to above.[36]

450. That report reached the Secretariat on 4 May 1981, accompanied by a letter from the Permanent Delegate of Chile. The texts of the letter and of the second part of the report by Professor Ricardo Marin Ibañez were reproduced in [a Committee document].[37]

451. The representative of the Chilean Government drew attention to the spirit of co-operation which his government had always displayed in this matter and which had culminated in the initiative which it had taken to invite an expert appointed by Unesco to visit the country. He stated that the first part of the expert's report was of a technical nature intended to advise the Chilean Government on educational reforms and that the second part was for the attention of the Committee on Conven-

[36] See document 110 EX/40 PRIV., para. 269 (*supra*, p. 137).
[37] See document 112 EX/CR/HR/1 Add.

tions and Recommendations. There had been a delay in communicating this second part because Mr Ibañez had wished to have the statistics included in his report approved by other international organizations so that they should not appear as reflecting his personal opinion. The representative of the Chilean Government read out long extracts from the report [...],[38] showing the inaccuracy of the allegations contained in the communication, the essential aspects of which he had already brought to the attention of the Committee at the [autumn 1980] session.

452. He added that, in his opinion, the Committee was now in a position to understand the false nature of the accusations brought against his government, and he reminded the Committee that the co-operation given by his government should be contrasted with the attitude of [WFTU], which, after having made certain statements, had never confirmed them and had remained silent for more than three years. Consequently, [WFTU] was now totally discredited in the eyes of his government and in future the Chilean Government would not agree to reply to communications from that organization.

453. After a brief exchange of views and bearing in mind the contents of the report by the expert appointed by Unesco, the Committee *decided* that in accordance with the provisions of paragraph 14 (*j*) of 104 EX/Decision 3.3, the communication, after having been examined as to its merits, did not warrant further action.

[453a.] One member of the Committee expressed reservations with regard to this decision.

[38] *Ibidem.*

No. 26/78

Concerning *Argentina*
Case of *Elsa Alicia Nocent*

Communication of 26 June 1978 submitted by
Elsa R. Gelatti de Nocent

Autumn 1978 session of the Committee on Conventions and Recommendations (105th session of the Executive Board)[1]

92. The Chairman summarized the communication, pointing out that it involved the disappearance of a student, the daughter of the author of the communication, whose disapperance took place under circumstances which, in the author's view, were contrary to human rights within the fields of Unesco's competence.

93. The representative of the government emphasized, first of all, that the authorities of his country had been only recently informed of the said communication and that, consequently, they had not had sufficient time to carry out the necessary investigation. He observed, however, that that preliminary investigation showed that the student in question had not been arrested, since her name was not included in any of the lists of persons who had been apprehended.

94. In reference to the first point made by the representative of the government, the Chairman confirmed that, henceforth, the government concerned had at its disposal a time-limit of one month before the Committee examined the communication concerning it.

95. At the Chairman's request, the Director of the Division of Human Rights and Peace noted that at first glance, the admissibility of the communication in question seemed to conflict with the conditions of admissibility as stipulated in paragraph 14 (iii) and (viii); with regard to the condition stipulated in (ii), it would, in fact, appear questionable whether the alleged disappearance had any connection with the human rights falling within the competence of Unesco: it seemed, nevertheless, that inasmuch as the matter concerned a student, this question could be decided upon only

[1] See document 105 EX/49 PRIV., paras. 92-96; see also document 105 EX/CR/PROC.HR/1.

after a more thorough examination of the substance of the allegations. As to the condition stipulated in (viii), what was involved was the objection made by the government concerned, which considered that the communication had not been submitted to it within a reasonable time-limit, inasmuch as two years had elapsed since the student's disappearance. Lastly, he drew the Committee's attention to the fact that the Inter-American Commission on Human Rights had likewise been notified of this matter.

96. Considering that the question of whether the matter fell within Unesco's spheres of competence could be determined only after thorough study and persuaded that the author of the communication had exerted untiring efforts to find her missing daughter - which was evidence of her deep concern in the matter - the Committee, at the Chairman's suggestion, agreed to declare [the communication] admissible. It *decided*, therefore, to ask:

> [i] the government concerned to submit supplementary information on the merits of the communication,
>
> [ii] the author of the communication to supply any further information that she might possess regarding the motives for the disappearance of the student or for her apprehension;
>
> [iii] the Secretariat to contact the Inter-American Commission on Human Rights to find out whether it had taken any action on the matter brought to its attention by the author of the communication.

Spring 1979 session of the Committee on Conventions and Recommendations (107th session of the Executive Board)[2]

193. This communication concerns the disappearance on 16 December 1976 of a woman student at the [National University of La Plata]. The Committee had examined it at its [autumn 1978] session and declared it admissible.[3] Since that decision, the Secretariat had, at the Committee's request, contacted the government concerned, the author of the communication and the Secretariat of the Inter-American Commission on Human Rights, which had informed the Secretariat that the Commission had referred the case to the Argentine Government but had not been able to establish where Miss Nocent was.

---

[2] See document 107 EX/PRIV.31, paras. 193-196; see also documents 107 EX/CR/PROC. HR/6 and Annex.

[3] See document 105 EX/49 PRIV., para. 96 (*supra*, p. 148).

Argentina **No. 26/78**

194. The representative of the Argentine Government informed the Committee that he had been unable to ascertain the whereabouts of the person concerned, just as the Organization of American States had not been able to discover where she was. He added that he had personally checked to see that the Argentine authorities had carried out investigations, but in vain. He also pointed out that the two-and-a-half years which had elapsed since the alleged disappearance was a more than reasonable period for dropping consideration of the case unless fresh information became available.

195. Some members of the Committee spoke of the need to adopt a special procedure for cases of disappearance, guided by General Assembly resolution 33/173.

196. Pending consideration by the Committee of the draft of such a procedure [...],[4] the Committee *decided* to keep the case of Elsa Alicia Nocent on its agenda and to continue seeking a solution consistent with respect for human rights.

Autumn 1979 session of the Committee on Conventions and Recommendations (108th session of the Executive Board)[5]

289. This communication, which concerns the disappearance on 16 December 1976 of a woman student at the National University of La Plata, was declared admissible at the Committee's [autumn 1978 session].[6] In the absence of further information from the Argentine Government, the Committee had decided at its [spring 1979] session to keep this case on its agenda and to continue seeking a solution consistent with respect for human rights.[7] It is to be noted that at that time the Committee had not yet adopted the special procedure for cases of missing persons.

290. It was recalled that, following the Committee's request, the Secretariat had contacted the Inter-American Commission on Human Rights, which had replied that the case of Miss Nocent had been registered on 20 February 1978 and that the Argentine Government had informed the Commission that there was no record of the person in question and that it had no knowledge of her whereabouts.

291. The Argentine representative repeated this information and stated that the authorities of his country had given a great deal of attention to this case. He added that the Inter-American Commission on Human Rights, which was conducting an inquiry in Buenos Aires, would no doubt give information in its report on the present state

---

[4] See document 107 EX/PRIV.31, para. 29.
[5] See document 108 EX/38 PRIV., paras. 289-294; see also document 108 EX/CR/PROC.HR/2.
[6] See document 105 EX/49 PRIV., para. 96 (*supra*, p. 148).
[7] See document 107 EX/PRIV.31, para. 196 (*supra*, p. 149).

of investigations. He emphasized the wide-ranging character of the facilities granted by his government to the Inter-American Commission on Human Rights, pointing out that in Argentina there was a collective awareness of the problem of human rights but that terrorism thwarted the government's efforts.

292. The Director of the Division of Human Rights and Peace informed the Committee that the author of the communication had sent a letter to Unesco on 2 August 1979, received on 7 September 1979, but that this letter provided no new elements.

293. One member of the Committee expressed the wish that the Committee make use of the report to be prepared by the Inter-American Commission on Human Rights.

294. On the Chairman's proposal, the Committee *decided* to apply the special procedure concerning communications relating to missing persons, adopted on 10 September 1979 [...].[8]

---

[8] See document 108 EX/38 PRIV., para. 16.

No. 31/78

Concerning *Argentina*
Case of *César Antonio Minué*

Communication of 11 July 1978 submitted by
Juana Jacinta Gómez de Minué

Spring 1979 session of the Committee on Conventions and Recommendations (107th session of the Executive Board)[1]

68. The communication concerns the disappearance of the son of the author of the communication, a university employee who was allegedly abducted on 16 July 1976. The representative of the government concerned considered that the communication did not establish a sufficiently clear connection with Unesco's fields of competence since it did not state what position the alleged victim held at the university. Some Committee members noted that since the alleged victim was 24 years old he could very well have begun his studies, as indicated on the communication form, and that in any case his work could be considered as being directly related to the work of an educational institution.

69. Following discussion, the Committee observed that the communication was ambiguous on that point and that the information it had at its disposal did not appear to be sufficient to establish a link with Unesco's fields of competence. While recognizing that the author could furnish the requisite information in a subsequent communication, the Committee *decided* that the communication as drafted by the author was inadmissible.

[1] See document 107 EX/PRIV.31, paras. 68-69; see also documents 107 EX/CR/PROC.HR/7 and Annex.

No. 33/78

Concerning *Argentina*
Case of *Manuel Alberto Santamaría*

Communication of 18 July 1978 submitted by
Elena Montecchiari de Santamaría

Autumn 1979 session of the Committee on Conventions and Recommendations (108th session of the Executive Board)[1]

29. This communication concerns the disappearance of the son of the author of the communication, a student of law in La Plata, aged 22, who was reportedly arrested on 10 April 1917 in Buenos Aires by individuals identified as belonging to the armed forces.

30. The representative of the government concerned pointed out that there was not sufficient proof that Mr Santamaría was a student. He noted, in addition, that the place of residence of the person concerned was several hundred kilometres away from the La Plata Law Faculty. He considered that there should be a connection between the occupation of an alleged victim and Unesco's spheres of competence and that, if he was indeed a student, it could of course be presumed that such a connection existed; however, in the present case it had not been demonstrated that the alleged victim had student status.

31. The representative of the Government of Argentina also stated that the Inter-American Commission on Human Rights of the Organization of American States (OAS) was currently studying Mr Santamaría's case and that, for this reason, the case would not be closed if the Committee were to declare it inadmissible.

32. Concerning the distance between the place of residence and the place of study of the alleged victim, one member of the Committee pointed out that this factor did not necessarily call into question Mr Santamaría's student status, in view of the mobility of young people at the present time.

---

[1] See document 108 EX/38 PRIV., paras. 29-35; see also document 108 EX/CR/PROC.HR/1.

33. As regards the investigation being conducted by the Inter-American Commission on Human Rights, the Director of the Division of Human Rights and Peace stated that the Secretariat could, as it had done in other cases, request information from the Secretariat of the Inter-American Commission on Human Rights and transmit it to the Committee.

34. One member of the Committee raised the question of whether the alleged facts could be imputed to the government concerned. The Chaiman pointed out that the question of imputability would necessarily be dealt with when a communication was being examined as to its merits but that it did not need to be dealt with during the consideration of admissibility. The same member of the Committee expressed his concern as to the connection between the alleged violation and Unesco's spheres of competence. It was pointed out that if the information available at the time of the examination as to the merits served to invalidate the presumption based on the occupation of the alleged victim, the Committee could go back on its decision and no longer examine the communication.

35. In the light of the foregoing, the Committee *decided* that the communication was admissible and *instructed* the Secretariat to collect information enabling the alleged victim's student status to be verified and ask OAS to inform it of the result of the examination of this case by the Inter-American Commission on Human Rights.

Spring 1980 session of the Committee on Conventions and Recommendations (109th session of the Executive Board)[2]

194. The author of this communication complained of the disappearance of her son on 10 April 1977. The alleged victim had been reportedly abducted by persons allegedly identified as belonging to the armed forces.

195. At its [autumn] 1979 session, the Committee had examined the admissibility of this communication. The representative of the government concerned had stated that there was not sufficient evidence that Mr Santamaría was a student, and that the Inter-American Commission on Human Rights of the Organization of American States (OAS) was already studying Mr Santamaría's case. The Committee had decided that there was enough of a prima facie case to declare the case admissible.[3]

196. At its present session, the Committee began its examination of the substance of the case.

---

[2] See document 109 EX/52 PRIV., paras. 194-198; see also document 109 EX/CR/HR/1.
[3] See document 108 EX/38 PRIV., para. 35 (*supra*, p. 154).

Argentina **No. 33/78**

197. The representative of the Argentine Government stated that his government had been conducting an extensive search for this person but had not been able to find a trace of him. He was on their missing persons list. He reminded the Committee that there were legal proceedings going on in regard to this case, which was also being examined by the Inter-American [Commission on Human Rights] of the OAS.

198. The Committee *decided* to suspend the examination of the case and to ask the OAS to inform it of the result of its examination.

No. 37/78

Concerning *United Kingdom*
Case of *Children of nomadic Gypsies*

Communication of 21 July 1978 submitted by
Thomas Alan Acton

Spring 1979 session of the Committee on Conventions and Recommendations (107th session of the Executive Board)[1]

150. This communication, which is submitted by the Secretary of the National Gypsy Education Council, alleges, on the basis of Article 3 of the Convention against Discrimination in Education, that the local authorities in the United Kingdom discriminate against the children of nomadic Gypsies. The author briefly describes the general situation which existed in this respect in the Borough of Croydon in 1977 and he further mentions the case of Mary Delaney, alleging that this case also called into question the rights of some 5,000 other children of nomadic Gypsies.

151. The reply of the United Kingdom Government [...][2] described in particular the general responsibilities of the Department of Education and Science and of Local Education Authorities, together with the policy followed regarding the education of children of Gypsies in the United Kingdom.

152. The representative of the United Kingdom Government introduced his government's reply to the Committee, stating how seriously the communication had been taken by his government. If a case of discrimination had nevertheless occurred, British law offered sufficient and adequate means of redress; in the case under consideration, if the Department of Education and Science had been presented with sufficient evidence that the children of nomadic Gypsies had been denied admission to school in Croydon, that Department would have stepped in accordingly. He therefore considered that the condition contained in 104 EX/Decision 3.3, paragraph 14 (*a*) (ix),

---

[1] See document 107 EX/PRIV.31, paras. 150-157; see also documents 107 EX/CR/PROC. HR/8 and Annex.

[2] See document 107 EX/CR/PROC.HR/8 Annex.

relating to the exhaustion of domestic remedies, had not been met and that, on those grounds, the communication should be regarded as inadmissible.

153. Several members of the Committee were of the opinion that certain points in the communication remained obscure but that, on the whole, the United Kingdom offered the means of guaranteeing the right to education without discrimination even though, as could happen in other countries, a decision taken locally might depart from the position of the central government.

154. With regard to the exhaustion of domestic remedies, it was pointed out that condition (ix) of paragraph 14 (*a*) of 104 EX/Decision 3.3 merely stipulated that the communication must "indicate whether an attempt has been made to exhaust available domestic remedies ...", which did not mean that the remedies must have been exhausted. The attempts made in this respect, including a complaint under the Race Relations Act, are described in part IV of the communication form and in the letters of 11 August 1977 and 25 August 1978.

155. As to the other conditions of admissibility, several members of the Committee considered that they had in that particular case been met, without prejudice to any position the Committee might adopt on the merits of the communication.

156. Other members thought that the communication should be regarded as inadmissible because, as pointed out by the representative of the United Kingdom Government, the legal remedies open to the people concerned had not been used. Some members felt that a clear indication should be given to the author of the communication as to what legal remedies were available.

157. After discussing the matter, the Committee *decided* to suspend examination of the admissibility of the communication pending information (*a*) on the outcome of the Bill mentioned in the reply of the United Kingdom Government; (*b*) on the utilization, by the alleged victims, of the legal remedies mentioned by the representative of the United Kingdom Government as not having been exhausted, to which the Secretariat was instructed to draw the attention of the author of the communication; (*c*) on whether admission to school had in fact been denied to the children of nomadic Gypsies; and on any other matter deemed appropriate both by the government concerned and by the author of the communication.

United Kingdom **No. 37/78**

Autumn 1979 session of the Committee on Conventions and Recommendations (108th session of the Executive Board)[3]

205. The Director of the Division of Human Rights and Peace summarized the stage reached in the procedure concerning the communication submitted by Dr T. A. Acton, Secretary of the National Gypsy Education Council, relating to alleged discrimination in education by the local authorities of the United Kingdom, particularly those in the Borough of Croydon, against the children of nomadic Gypsies. He recalled that at its [spring 1979] session the Committee had requested the Secretariat to obtain further information from the author of the communication and the Government concerned, and had meanwhile deferred consideration of the admissibility of the communication [...].[4]

206. The relevant information was sent to Unesco by the author on 17 July 1979 and by the government concerned on 19 July 1979. In his letter of 17 July, the author replied to various points raised in the government's written comments and formally expressed the wish to withdraw his communication. At the same time he expressed warm thanks to Unesco for its action, which he considered had been highly effective. In a letter dated 4 September 1979, the Pemanent Delegate of the United Kingdom informed the Secretariat that his government was in favour of the request for withdrawal of the communication submitted by the author.

207. The Director of the Division of Human Rights and Peace stated that the Committee was not bound to accept the author's request, as the withdrawal of the communication should be studied from the point of view of constituting a "friendly solution" under the terms of paragraph 14 (*k*) of 104 EX/Decision 3.3. According to these provisions, the friendly solution should "advance the promotion of the human rights falling within Unesco's fields of competence".

208. The Chairman stressed that the Committee's decision to accept the author's request for withdrawal could in no way constitute a precedent for the automatic acceptance of such requests by the Committee, as the latter might wish, in other cases, to assure itself that no constraint was being put upon the author of the communication.

---

[3] See document 108 EX/38 PRIV., paras. 205-209; see also document 108 EX/CR/PROC.HR/1

[4] See document 107 EX/PRIV.31, para. 157 (*supra*, p. 158).

No. 37/78 **United Kingdom**

209. The Committee *decided* to accept the author's request to withdraw his communication and therefore considered the matter settled.[5]

[5] For additional information, se documents 109 EX/52 PRIV., para. 293, and 109 EX/CR/HR/INF.3.

No. 38/78

Concerning *Switzerland*
Case of *Ved Kalra*

Communication of 19 July 1978 submitted by
Ved Kalra

Autumn 1978 session of the Committee on Conventions and Recommendations (105th session of the Executive Board)[1]

97. The Chairman of the Committee pointed out that the communication concerned a dispute between a foreign student and a private educational establishment in Switzerland.

98. The representative of the government drew the attention of the Committee to the fact that the Institut des méthodes de direction des entreprises was a private institution which did not come under the Federal Government and that, this being so, he doubted that the subject of the communication fell within Unesco's competence. In any case, however, he felt that the communication was clearly ill-founded, particularly in view of the fact that the author of the communication had the opportunity of seeking legal remedy through the appropriate channels.

99. At the request of the Chairman of the Committee, the Director of the Division of Human Rights and Peace observed that among the human rights alleged by the author of the communication to have been violated, only the right to education fell within Unesco's competence. In that respect, it was to be wondered whether the communication, in its present form, was not manifestly ill-founded.

100. Concerning the State's responsibility for acts of private law, or in this case, the acts of a private educational establishment, the Chairman of the Committee stressed that it was not necessary for the alleged violation of human rights to have been committed by the State; it was enough for it to be charged with such a violation since it was the State's responsibility to guarantee human rights on its territory.

---

[1] See document 105 EX/49 PRIV., paras. 97-102; see also document 105 EX/CR/PROC.HR/1.

No. 38/78 **Switzerland**

101. The Committee *decided* that the communication was not admissible as such, since it did not satisfy the conditions as set forth in paragraph 14 (*a*) (iii) and (v) of 104 EX/Decision 3.3.

102. The representative of the government concerned, drawing the conclusion from a communication which, in his opinion, did not merit the Committee's attention, suggested that in future the Committee might empower its secretariat to reject communications whose authors were mentally unbalanced or which were manifestly ill-founded. The Director of the Division of Human Rights and Peace suggested that the Chairman be consulted before any such decision was taken. It was so *decided.* It was moreover *agreed* that communications of little importance need not be transmitted to the Minister of Foreign Affairs under cover of a letter from the Director-General, but that they could be sent merely with a covering letter from the Secretariat to the Permanent Delegate to Unesco of the country concerned.

No. 41/78

Concerning *Spain*
Case of *José Candeas García*

Communication of 6 August 1978 submitted by
Partido Socialista de Gibraltar

Spring 1979 session of the Committee on Conventions and Recommendations (107th session of the Executive Board)[1]

135. The author of the communication claims that there has been a violation of Articles 12 and 13 of the International Covenant on Civil and Political Rights committed against a Portuguese evangelical pastor, who is said to have been arrested by the Spanish secret police on 11 November 1977 and expelled to Portugal, whereas the alleged victim had been residing from birth in the town from which he was expelled.

136. The representative of the Government of Spain, who presented his government's position [...],[2] considered that the communication should be declared inadmissible because it did not concern the fields of competence of Unesco, in addition to which the relevant domestic remedies had not been exhausted.

137. After several members of the Committee had spoken in support of the analysis made by the representative of the government concerned, the Committee *decided* to declare the communication inadmissible.

---

[1] See document 107 EX/PRIV.31, paras. 135-137; see also documents 107 EX/CR/PROC. HR/9 and Annex.
[2] See document 107 EX/CR/PROC.HR/9 Annex.

No. 47/78

Concerning *Uruguay*
Case of *Eduardo Anselmo Viera**

Communication of 14 August 1978 submitted by
Eduardo Anselmo Viera

Spring 1979 session of the Committee on Conventions and Recommendations (107th session of the Executive Board)[1]

171. The author of the communication alleges that several articles of the Universal Declaration of Human Rights and the International Covenant on Civil and Political Rights were violated by the closing down, on 28 November 1973, of the newspaper "El Popular", of which he was the director, as well as by the arrest and torture inflicted on the personnel of the said newspaper.

172. In his letter of 19 April 1979 [...][2] and orally before the Committee, the representative of the government concerned indicated that the person concerned had been charged on 24 April 1975 by the presiding Military Judge of the Fifth Session (Turno) for an offence under paragraphs 2 and 3 of article 38 of the military Penal Code, entitled "Offences prejudicial to the morale of the Army". On 28 August 1975 he was released on bail, but on 12 September 1977 was arrested for having failed to report to the competent authorities within the time-limit laid down under the system of release on bail. It was the opinion of the representative of the government concerned that the communication did not fulfil the conditions stipulated in paragraph 14 (*a*) (vi) and (ix) of 104 EX/Decision 3.3.

173. Certain members of the Committee noted that the author of the communication was no longer in his country: the Committee did not believe, however, that this consideration in itself entitled it to declare the communication inadmissible.

---

* From the Committee's autumn 1979 session, this communication was being referred to as case of *The newspaper "El Popular"*.
[1] See document 107 EX/PRIV.31, paras. 171-177; see also documents 107 EX/CR/PROC. HR/10 and Annex.
[2] See document 107 EX/CR/PROC.HR/10 Annex.

No. 47/78 **Uruguay**

174. Other members were of the opinion that the case directly concerned the fields of competence of Unesco, inasmuch as it concerned measures taken against a newspaper. For several members, the author's use of certain terms could not be accepted by the Committee: in that respect it was pointed out that paragraph 14 (*a*) (vi) allowed the Committee to examine a communication which contained parts offensive to a government "if it meets all other criteria of admissibility, after the exclusion of the offensive or abusive parts".

175. With respect to the use of domestic remedies, several members were not satisfied with the author's statement that he had not had recourse to the courts in view of the regime in his country. In answer to a question put to him, the Director of the Division of Human Rights and Peace stated that, in international law, the use of available domestic remedies should be effective and adequate in order for the person concerned to be obliged to use them. But the opinion of the person concerned on the effectiveness and adequacy, or otherwise, of the remedies in question did not exempt him from that obligation. Replying to another question, he stated that, except for the American Convention on Human Rights, which contained a provision limiting its application to physical persons, human rights normally benefited both physical and artificial persons, and therefore, in the case of freedom of information, could be applied to a newspaper.

176. Certain members of the Committee observed that, in any case, the information provided by the author was insufficient.

177. In conclusion, the Committee *decided* to instruct the Secretariat to request the author of the communication to be more specific in the indications which he gave, and to draw his attention to the fact that his communication should not contain offensive terms.

Autumn 1979 session of the Committee on Conventions and Recommendations (108th session of the Executive Board)[3]

222. The author of this communication claims violation of Articles 3 and 9 of the Universal Declaration of Human Rights, and of Articles 7, 9, 15 and 18 of the International Covenant on Civil and Political Rights, in respect of the closing down on 28 November 1973, of the newspaper "El Popular" of which he was the director. He also claims that newspaper staff were detained and tortured. After examining the communication at its [spring 1979] session, the Committee had decided to instruct the

[3] See document 108 EX/38 PRIV., paras. 222-224; see also documents 108 EX/CR/PROC. HR/1 and Add.2.

Secretariat to request the author to be more specific in the indications which he gave and to draw his attention to the fact that his communication should not contain offensive terms.[4]

223. The Director of the Division of Human Rights and Peace said that the author of the communication, Mr Eduardo Anselmo Viera, had replied to the Committee's request in a letter dated 10 August 1979, received by Unesco on 21 August 1979 [...].[5] The representative of Uruguay, to whom the letter had been transmitted only a short time before the meeting of the Committee, requested that, in those circumstances, consideration of the communication should be deferred until the next session, so as to give him an opportunity to collect information from his government in regard to the contents of Mr Viera's letter.

224. In viev of the request made by the Uruguayan Government, the Committee *decided* to defer consideration of the admissibility of the communication until its next session.

Spring 1980 session of the Committee on Conventions and Recommendations (109th session of the Executive Board)[6]

173. The author alleges that Articles 3 (the right to life, liberty and security of person) and 9 (the prohibition of arbitrary arrest, detention or exile) of the Universal Declaration of Human Rights, and Articles 7 (torture), 9 (arbitrary arrest or detention), 15 (legality of penalties) and 18 (freedom of thought) of the International Covenant on Civil and Political Rights, were violated by the closing down, on 28 November 1973, of the newspaper "El Popular", of which he was the director. It is alleged that members of the staff of the paper were detained and tortured.

174. After examining the communication at its [spring 1979 session], the Committee had decided to instruct the Secretariat to request the author to be more specific in the indications which he gave and to draw his attention to the fact that his communication should not contain offensive terms.[7]

175. The author of the communication had replied to the Committee's request in a letter received by Unesco on 21 August 1979. The representative of Uruguay, to which the letter had been transmitted only a short time before the meeting of the

[4] See document 107 EX/PRIV.31, para. 177 (*supra*, p. 166).
[5] See document 108 EX/CR/PROC.HR/1 Add.2.
[6] See document 109 EX/52 PRIV., paras. 173-178; see also documents 109 EX/CR/HR/2 and Add.6.
[7] See document 107 EX/PRIV.31, para. 177 (*supra*, p. 166).

Committee, had requested that, in those circumstances, consideration of the communication should be deferred until the next session, so as to give him an opportunity to collect information from his government with regard to the contents of Mr Viera's letter. The Committee had so decided.[8]

176. The representative of the Uruguayan Government stated that this case had been tried and judged in accordance with the Uruguayan laws on the press prohibiting the advocating of violence and subversive activities. Furthermore, the persons involved had not even attempted to use the domestic remedies available. The representative pointed out that this was an old case, dating back to 1973. The Inter-American Commission on Human Rights had already examined the case and shelved it. The Uruguayan representative was of the opinion that the case was inadmissible.

177. A member of the Committee reminded the meeting that duplication was no justification for declaring inadmissible a communication submitted to Unesco. Several members felt that the lack of an attempt to use domestic remedies and the late date of submission of this communication disqualified it.

178. After discussion, the Committee *decided* to declare this communication inadmissible in accordance with paragraph 14 (*a*) (viii) of 104 EX/Decision 3.3.

---

[8] See document 108 EX/38 PRIV., para. 224 (*supra*, p. 167).

No. 49/78

Concerning *Argentina*
Case of *Ricardo Rodríguez Anido**

Communication of 30 August 1978 submitted by
Ricardo Rodríguez Anido

Spring 1979 session of the Committee on Conventions and Recommendations (107th session of the Executive Board)[1]

70. The author of the communication complains of the violation of freedom of thought and freedom of opinion and expression which allegedly resulted from the arbitrary detention of his son in the prison of Córdoba since 16 November 1977, when he was a student at the University of Córdoba.

71. The representative of the government concerned noted that although the alleged victim was an electro-mechanical technician he was also a student, and concluded that under those conditions the communication could be considered admissible. On behalf of the Committee, the Chairman thanked the representative of the government concerned for his co-ooperation.

72. It was noted, however, that while, as a result of the declaration of the representative of the government concerned, it was to be presumed in similar cases that the communication concerned Unesco's fields of competence, the Committee itself, regardless of the position of the government concerned, could still question its admissibility. One Committee member stressed that in his opinion the number of hours devoted to studies should not be a determining factor, since financial circumstances often compel a person to devote the larger part of the day to remunerative work, even though he can properly be considered a student.

---

* At the Committee's spring 1980 session, this communication was being referred to as case of *Ricardo Manuel Rodrigues Anido*.

[1] See document 107 EX/PRIV.31, paras. 70-73; see also documents 107 EX/CR/PROC.HR/11 and Annex.

No. 49/78 **Argentina**

73. In view of the foregoing, the Committee *decided* to declare the communication admissible.

Autumn 1979 session of the Committee on Conventions and Recommendations (108th session of the Executive Board)[2]

295. The author of this communication complains of the violation of freedom of thought and freedom of opinion and expression which has allegedly resulted from the arbitrary detention of his son in the prison of Córdoba since 16 November 1977, when he was a student at the University of Córdoba.

296. This communication was declared admissible at the [spring 1979] session of the Committee,[3] with the result that, at its present session, it proceeded to examine the merits of the allegations declared admissible.

297. The representative of the government concerned informed the Committee that, according to the investigations made in his country, the alleged victim was a technician against whom legal proceedings had reportedly been instituted, but the Argentine representative was unable to give any details concerning the outcome of those proceedings. In reply to a question put by the Chairman, the representative of the Argentine Government confirmed that the name of the person in question did not appear on the lists of persons imprisoned in his country. He reiterated his view that the communication should not have been declared admissible as the alleged victim's occupation of technician had no connection with Unesco's fields of competence.

298. One member of the Committee recalled that other communications concerning students simultaneously exercising an occupation not directly connected with Unesco had been kept on the Committee's agenda until such time as the Secretariat could obtain further details concerning the student status of the alleged victims.

299. On the Chairman's proposal, the Committee *decided* to keep the communication on its agenda and *instructed* the Secretariat again to request the author to supply further details concerning the student status of the alleged victim.

---

[2] See document 108 EX/38 PRIV., paras. 295-299; see also document 108 EX/CR/PROC.HR/2.
[3] See document 107 EX/PRIV.31, para. 73 (*supra*, p. 170).

Argentina **No. 49/78**

Spring 1980 session of the Committee on Conventions and Recommendations (109th session of the Executive Board)[4]

199. The author of this communication complained of the violation of freedom of thought and freedom of opinion and expression which had allegedly resulted from the arbitrary detention of his son in the prison of Córdoba since 16 November 1977, when he was a student at the University of Córdoba.

200. This communication had been declared admissible at the Committee's [spring] 1979 session,[5] with the result that at its [autumn] 1979 session, it proceeded to examine the merits of the allegations declared admissible.

201. The representative of the government concerned had informed the Committee that, according to the investigations made in his country, the alleged victim had been a technician against whom legal proceedings had reportedly been instituted, but the Argentine representative was unable to give any details concerning the outcome of those proceedings. In reply to a question put by the Chairman, the representative of the Argentine Government had confirmed that the name of the person in question did not appear on the lists of persons imprisoned in his country. He reiterated his view that the communication should not have been declared admissible as the alleged victim's occupation of technician had no connection with Unesco's fields of competence.

202. One member of the Committee had recalled that other communications concerning students simultaneously exercising an occupation not directly connected with Unesco had been kept on the Committee's agenda until such time as the Secretariat could obtain further details concerning the student status of the alleged victim.

203. On the Chairman's proposal, the Committee had decided to keep the communication on its agenda and had instructed the Secretariat again to request the author to supply further details concerning the student status of the alleged victim.[6]

204. These details were requested from the author by the Secretariat in a letter dated 19 November 1979. The Argentine Goverment was also informed of the Committee's decision in a letter dated 4 December 1979. A letter of reminder had been sent to the author of the communication by registered mail on 5 February 1980.

---

[4] See document 109 EX/52 PRIV., paras. 199-207; see also document 109 EX/CR/HR/1.
[5] See document 107 EX/PRIV.31, para. 73 (*supra*, p. 170).
[6] See document 108 EX/38 PRIV., para. 299 (*supra*, p. 170).

No. 49/78 **Argentina**

205. The representative of the Argentine Government reiterated his government's position at the Committee's present session.

206. A member of the Committee raised the question as to whether the alleged victim had received the letter addressed to him. The representative of the Director-General explained that up to now the Secretariat had been sending only two letters to the alleged victims but that if the Committee felt it advisable, a third letter with return receipt requested could be sent.

207. The Committee *decided* to suspend the examination of the substance of this case and to instruct the Secretariat to send the author of the communication a letter with return receipt requested asking for more information about the alleged link between the violation and Unesco's fields of competence. It further *instructed* the Secretariat, in general, to request return receipts so that it could be ascertained whether or not the letters had been received by the addressees.

No. 50/78

Concerning *Argentina*
Case of *Juan Carlos Aguirre*

Communication of 17 June 1978 submitted by
Noemi Ester Giacomini de Aguirre

Autumn 1979 session of the Committee on Conventions and Recommendations (108th session of the Executive Board)[1]

36. The author of this communication alleges that several articles of the Universal Declaration of Human Rights and of the Declaration of the Rights of Man and the Citizen have been violated through the abduction of her husband, a carpenter, on 2 June 1977. The author claims that Unesco is competent to deel with this matter by virtue of the provisions of Articles 14, 17 and 18 of the Argentine Constitution.

37. The representative of the government concerned considered that owing to the fact that the alleged victim was a carpenter and was engaged in no intellectual activity having any bearing on the circumstances of the disappearance, it was not possible for a connection to be established with Unesco's spheres of competence.

38. After discussion the Committee *decided* to declare the communication inadmissible since it did not show a connection between the alleged violation and Unesco's spheres of competence and consequently did not fulfil the condition laid down in paragraph 14 (*a*) (iii) of 104 EX/Decision 3.3. The Chairman noted that it was open to the author subseqently to supply proof of a connection between the alleged violation and one of Unesco's fields of competence and that the Committee would then be able to examine this case anew.

---

[1] See document 108 EX/38 PRIV., paras. 36-38; see also document 108 EX/CR/PROC.HR/1.

No. 51/78

Concerning *Argentina*
Case of *Fernando de Hallgarten*

Communication of 15 August 1978 submitted by
Paz Cionfrini de Hallgarten

Spring 1979 session of the Committee on Conventions and Recommendations (107th session of the Executive Board)[1]

74. The author of the communication complains of the disappearance of his son on 26 August 1976, when he was a student and was working in the building trade.

75. The representative of the government concerned considered the communication inadmissible as the author had failed to mention either the name of the university in which the alleged victim supposedly studied or his field of studies. One Committee member asked whether an inquiry had been made by the government concerned which established that the person in question was not a student. The representative of the government concerned replied in the negative, noting that such an inquiry was not appropriate at the time when the admissibility of the communication was under examination.

76. Several Committee members considered that it would be desirable for the Secretariat to complete the files concerning each case and submit a synopsis of all the available facts to the Committee. The Director of the Division of Human Rights and Peace expressed the view that if the Committee so desired the Secretariat could gather additional information in cases where it was clear that such information was lacking in the files, but without undertaking anything that could be regarded as a real preliminary inquiry.

77. After agreeing to request the Secretariat to take the action suggested above, the Committee *decided* to suspend examination of the admissibility of this communica-

[1] See document 107 EX/PRIV.31, paras. 74-77; see also documents 107 EX/CR/PROC.HR/12 and Annex.

tion pending receipt of the additional information that the Secretariat had been instructed to obtain from the author of the communication.

Autumn 1979 session of the Committee on Conventions and Recommendations (108th session of the Executive Board)[2]

39. This communication concerning the disappearance, on 26 August 1976, of the son of the author of the communication, was examined for the first time by the Committee at its [spring 1979] session [...]. The examination of the communication's admissibility was then suspended pending further information regarding the alleged victim's occupation, which the Secretariat was instructed to obtain.[3]

40. The Director of the Division of Human Rights and Peace informed the Committee that no further information had been received by the Secretariat.

41. The representative of the Argentine Government informed the Committee that his government had not discovered any grounds for believing that Mr Hallgarten was a student but that, on the contrary, his name had been found on the list of building workers. According to him, the alleged victim had abandoned his studies after secondary school. In addition, the case had been referred to several international organizations, including the Red Cross and the United Nations. In the absence of any proof of the alleged victim's student status, he considered that the communication was inadmissible.

42. Several members of the Committee were concerned about a hasty decision of inadmissibility being taken by the Committee while further information could be requested from the author of the communication. The latter might have encountered difficulties in communicating with the Secretariat.

43. On the proposal of its Chairman, the Committee *decided* to declare this communication inadmissible. It was specified, however, that, in accordance with established practice, the author would be notified of the decision and of the reasons for it and would be able to submit the case to the Committee again on the basis of further information.

---

[2] See document 108 EX/38 PRIV., paras. 39-43; see also document 108 EX/CR/PROC.HR/1.

[3] See document 107 EX/PRIV.31, para. 77 (*supra*, pp. 175-176).

No. 53/78

Concerning ***Argentina***
Case of ***Abel Héctor Mateu***

Communication of 10 September 1978 submitted by
Nélida Isabel Pérez de Mateu

Spring 1979 session of the Committee on Conventions and Recommendations (107th session of the Executive Board)[1]

78. The communication concerns the disappearance on 1 July 1978 of the author's husband, who is a manual worker. [The] representative of the government concerned was of the opinion that no connection could be established between the activities of the alleged victim and Unesco's fields of competence.

79. The members of the Committee as a whole shared this view, but several of them, referring to the author's letter of 10 September 1978, which touched them deeply from the human standpoint, wondered whether, out of purely humanitarian considerations, it might not be possible to ask the Director-General to intercede on humanitarian grounds in accordance with paragraph 8 (*b*) of 104 EX/Decision 3.3.

80. Other Committee members felt that even action of a humanitarian character could hardly be contemplated, when it was perfectly clear that the communication did not fall within Unesco's fields of competence.

81. Finally, the Committee *decided* to declare [the communication] inadmissible and to ask its Chairman to inform the Director-General about the discussion which had taken place, it being understood that the views expressed during the discussion were to be attributed only to those members of the Committee who had expressed them.

[1] See document 107 EX/PRIV.31, paras. 78-81; see also document 107 EX/CR/PROC.HR/32.

No. 54/78

Concerning *Chile*
Case of *Arturo Montes Larrain*

Communication of 21 September 1978 submitted by
Arturo Montes Larrain

Spring 1979 session of the Committee on Conventions and Recommendations (107th session of the Executive Board)[1]

119. The author of this communication considers that he is a victim of the violation of his right to return to his country and consequently, of his right to exercise his profession as a university teacher and research worker. Living as an exile in Switzerland since January 1974, he claims to have asked the Minister of the Interior, through the Chilean Embassy in Paris, in November 1976 and again in April 1978, to be allowed to return to Chile.

120. The representative of the Government of Chile raised the general problem of the return of exiles to their country. According to the terms of Article 4 of the International Covenant on Civil and Political Rights which Chile had ratified, it was possible for States parties to the Covenent to derogate from their obligations thereunder in time of public emergency which threatened the life of the nation and the existence of which was officially proclaimed. In point of fact, the Government of Chile had derogated from Article 12, paragraph 4, of the Covenant, which was specifically concerned with the right of a person to enter his own country. Notwithstanding the suspension of that right, 90 per cent of the applications to return to the country submitted after the adoption of the amnesty law of 1978 had been given favourable consideration, but the right of return was refused to those representing a danger to public order and to common law criminals, such applications being examined on a case-by-case basis.

[1] See document 107 EX/PRIV.31, paras. 119-122; see also document 107 EX/CR/PROC.HR/13.

No. 54/78 **Chile**

121. With regard to the case of Mr Arturo Montes Larrain, the representative of the government concerned said that he did not know the reasons for the refusal given and offered to make inquiries to find out whether a solution could be reached.

122. The Committee accepted the offer made by the representative of the government concerned and accordingly *decided* to defer consideration of the case until the outcome of those inquiries was known.

Autumn 1979 session of the Committee on Conventions and Recommendations (108th session of the Executive Board)[2]

125. The author of this communication, a university teacher, considers that his right to return to his country and, consequently, his right to exercise his profession, which is that of university teacher and research worker, have been violated. Living as an exile in Switzerland since January 1974, he claims that in November 1976 and later in April 1978, he put in a request to the Minister of the Interior, through the Chilean Embassy in Paris, for permission to return to Chile; these requests were reportedly turned down.

126. The Director of the Division of Human Rights and Peace recalled that at its [spring 1979] session the Committee had decided to suspend examination of the case until the outcome of the inquiries which the representative of the government concerned proposed to make was known.[3]

127. The representative of the government concerned pointed out that under the terms of Article 4 of the International Covenant on Civil and Political Rights, his government hed derogated from Article 12, [paragraph] 4, of that Covenant, which concerns precisely a person's right to enter his own country. Notwithstanding the suspension of this right, most of the applications to return to Chile filed after the proclamation of the amnesty law adopted in 1978 had been favourably dealt with. The reason for the refusal in the case of Mr Montes Larrain was the political campaign conducted abroad by the author of the communication.

128. The representative of the Chilean Government further informed the Committee that in accordance with the jurisprudence of the Supreme Court of Chile, there was available to Mr Montes Larrain a domestic remedy ("recurso de amparo"), under which an appeal could be made against the legality of the Minister of the Interior's decision rejecting the application to return to Chile, with a view to its rescission.

---

[2] See document 108 EX/38 PRIV., paras. 125-129; see also document 108 EX/CR/PROC.HR/1.

[3] See document 107 EX/PRIV.31, para. 122 (*supra*, p. 180).

129. The Committee accordingly *decided* to suspend examination of the admissibility of this communication, and *instructed* the Secretariat to inform its anthor of the availability of a domestic remedy ("recurso de amparo") with the competent national legal authorities.

Spring 1980 session of the Committee on Conventions and Recommendations (109th session of the Executive Board)[4]

81. As these communications[5] all contain the common element of persons complaining that they are prevented from returning to their native Chile by the authorities there, the Committee decided to consider them together.

82. At its [autumn 1979] session, the Committee had decided to suspend consideration of these cases so that the authors could be informed of the domestic remedy ("recurso de amparo") which the representative of the Chilian Government had said was available to them.[6] The Committee had instructed the Secretariat to inform the authors about the aforementioned domestic remedy and asked the Director-General to appeal to the Chilean authorities to seek a humanitarian solution to these cases.

83. The representative of the Chilean Government expressed once again his government's willingness to co-operate with Unesco and again explained the existence of administrative and judicial remedies for persons seeking to return to Chile. The authorities considered it essential that persons at least try these approaches first. Furthermore, the representative explained that he had had consultations with the Deputy Director-General and subsequently with the Legal Adviser in order to find ways to bring humanitarian assistance to the persons wishing to return.

84. The representative of the Chilean Government explained that a procedure had been elaborated for allowing a return to Chile for 60 days of two of the persons concerned in order that they might personally attend to their cases and gain a pennanent stay. It had been emphasized to the persons concerned that the measures were taken on humanitarian grounds, and that they might eventually serve as precedents for re-

---

[4] See document 109 EX/52 PRIV., paras. 81-85; see also document 109 EX/CR/HR/2.

[5] Communications No. 54/78 concerning *Chile*, case of *Arturo Montes Larrain*, No. 57/78 concerning *Chile*, case of *Luis Pueller*, No. 59/78 concerning *Chile*, case of *Gustavo Adolfo Quintana Muñoz*, No. 64/78 concerning *Chile*, case of *Juan Patricio Cleary Zambón*, No. 72/78 concerning *Chile*, case of *Elwin Ayamante Bórquez*, and No. 134/78 concerning *Chile*, case of *Abelardo Castro Hidalgo*.

[6] See document 108 EX/38 PRIV., para. 129 (*supra*, p. 181), para. 133 (*infra*, p. 192), para. 136 (*infra*, p. 195), para. 141 (*infra*, p. 204), para. 153 (*infra*, p. 222) and para. 157 (*infra*, p. 364), respectively.

solving similar cases as long as the Chilean laws were respected and no incidents occurred.

85. After discussion,[7] the Committee *decided* to take note of the measures announced by the representative of the Chilean Government and to re-examine the various communications at its next session, while at the same time requesting the Executive Board to ask the Director-General to encourage a humanitarian solution for the cases in question.

Autumn 1980 session of the Committee on Conventions and Recommendations (110th session of the Executive Board)[8]

45. As these communications[9] all contain the common element of persons complaining that they are prevented from returning to their native Chile by the authorities there, the Committee decided to consider them together.

46. At its [autumn 1979 session], the Committee had decided to suspend consideration of these cases so that the authors could be informed of the domestic remedy ("recurso de amparo") which the representative of the Chilian Government had said was available to them.[10] The Committee had instructed the Secretariat to inform the authors about the aforementioned domestic remedy and asked the Director-General to appeal to the Chilean authorities to seek a humanitarian solution to these cases.

47. The representative of the Chilean Government explained that a procedure had been elaborated for allowing a return to Chile for 60 days of two of the persons concerned in order that they might personally clarify their cases and gain a permanent stay. It had been emphasized to the persons concerned that the measures were taken on humanitarian grounds, and that they might eventually serve as precedents for re-

---

[7] See also document 109 EX/52 PRIV., para. 252 (*supra*, pp. 127-128), communication No. 25/78 concerning *Chile*, case of *Situation of human rights in Chile in the spheres of education, science, culture and communication*; the communications were examined together, with a view to finding a friendly solution which might be applied to them.

[8] See document 110 EX/40 PRIV., paras. 45-56; see also document 110 EX/CR/HR/2.

[9] Communications No. 54/78 concerning *Chile*, case of *Arturo Montes Larrain*, No. 57/78 concerning *Chile*, case of *Luis Pueller*, No. 59/78 concerning *Chile*, case of *Gustavo Adolfo Quintana Muñoz*, No. 64/78 concerning *Chile*, case of *Juan Patricio Cleary Zambón*, No. 72/78 concerning *Chile*, case of *Elwin Ayamante Bórquez*, and No. 134/78 concerning *Chile*, case of *Abelardo Castro Hidalgo*.

[10] See document 108 EX/38 PRIV., para. 129 (*supra*, p. 181), para. 133 (*infra*, p. 192), para. 136 (*infra*, p. 195), para. 141 (*infra*, p. 204), para. 153 (*infra*, p. 222) and para. 157 (*infra*, p. 364), respectively.

solving similar cases as long as the Chilean law were respected and no incidents occurred.

48. The two persons selected by the Chilean authorities to be allowed to return to Chile for 60 days were duly informed of the government's offer, and one of the two persons, Mr Luis Pueller Bravo, thereupon wrote to the Director-General to ask what guarantees of safety he would have and whether Unesco would provide protection for him. Through an exchange of letters the Chilean authorities informed the Director-General that in their opinion all possible guarantees had already been provided and that it was not for Mr Pueller Bravo to doubt that Chile would not abide by the arrangement which it had worked out.

49. With the agreement of the Chilean authorities, the reassurances set fourth in their letter were made known to Mr Pueller Bravo, who subsequently informed the Secretariat that he planned to accept the government's offer to return for 60 days. He said that he planned to leave for Chile on 18 August [1980] and that he would keep Unesco informed of his progress

50. At its present session, the Committee was informed by the Chilean representative that his government had not yet heard from either of the two persons in question. He stated that this apparent lack of interest on their part was seriously complicating matters, and was frustrating the government's efforts to co-operate on this question.

51. The Chilean representative further informed the Committee that similar authorizations to return would soon be issued to other persons desiring them, in addition to the 120 persons who had already been so authorized and whose names would be provided to the Committee.

52. Several members of the Committee expressed their appreciation to the Chilean representative for the spirit of co-operation which his government was showing and emphasized the importance of noting the positive developments in the case while at the same time continuing to work for a friendly solution with the Chilean Government. One member of the Committee felt that forcing the persons involved to make a long and expensive journey for the sake of clarifying certain formalities could not be considered as being a helpful step on the part of the authorities.

53. In response to another question the Chilean representative explained [...] that the required steps were reasonable legal or administrative formalities and not arbitrary ones. He went on to state that the six people of the cases before the Committee were in a special category due to Unosco's interest in them, and that they were being exempted from the usually required appeals procedure.

No. 54/78 **Chile**

54. In reponse to another question the Chilean representative explained that once a person who was allowed to return to clarify his situation succeeded in doing so, he was free to stey on in the country without first having to leave again or having to complete other formalities.

55. When the possibility was raised that Mr Gustavo Adolfo Quintana Muñoz might not have accepted the offer to return to Chile for financial reasons, the Chilean representative explained that it was possible for such persons to obtain an airline ticket on loan from the Chilean Consulate which could be paid back later in Chile.

56. After discussion the Committee *decided* to maintain these six cases on its agenda and to request the Chilean authorities to accord to the other four persons involved the same authorization to return to Chile that had already been granted to Messrs. Pueller Bravo and Quintana Muñoz. The Committee also *decided* to ask the Executive Board to request the Director-General to bring these cases to the attention of the United Nations High Commissioner for Refugees for assistance, financial and otherwise, in order to facilitate their return to Chile.

Spring 1981 session of the Committee on Conventions and Recommendations (112th session of the Executive Board)[11]

49. As these communications[12] all contained the common element of persons complaining that they were prevented from returning to their native Chile by the authorities there, the Committee decided to consider them together.

50. At its [autumn 1979 session], the Committee decided to suspend consideration of these cases so that the authors could be informed of the domestic remedy ("recurso de amparo") which the representative of the Chilean Government said was available to them.[13] The Committee instructed the Secretariat to inform the authors about the aforementioned domestic remedy and asked the Director-General to appeal to the Chilean authorities for assistance in finding a humanitarian solution to these cases.

---

[11] See document 112 EX/30 PRIV., paras. 49-64; see also document 112 EX/CR/HR/2.

[12] Communications No. 54/78 concerning *Chile*, case of *Arturo Montes Larrain*, No. 57/78 concerning *Chile*, case of *Luis Pueller*, No. 59/78 concerning *Chile*, case of *Gustavo Adolfo Quintana Muñoz*, No. 64/78 concerning *Chile*, case of *Juan Patricio Cleary Zambón*, No. 72/78 concerning *Chile*, case of *Elwin Ayamante Bórquez*, and No. 134/78 concerning *Chile*, case of *Abelardo Castro Hidalgo*.

[13] See document 108 EX/38 PRIV., para. 129 (*supra*, p. 181), para. 133 (*infra*, p. 192), para. 136 (*infra*, p. 195), para. 141 (*infra*, p. 204), para. 153 (*infra*, p. 222) and para. 157 (*infra*, p. 364), respectively.

Chile **No. 54/78**

51. At the Committee's [autumn 1980 session], the representative of the Chilean Government expressed his government's willingness to co-operate with Unesco and reaffirmed the existence of administrative and judicial remedies for persons seeking to return to Chile. The authorities considered it essential that persons should at least try these approaches first. Furthermore, the representative explained that he had had consultations with the Deputy Director-General, and subsequently with the Legal Adviser, in order to find ways of providing humanitarian assistance to persons wishing to return.

52. The representative of the Chilean Government also explained that a procedure had been worked out for allowing a return to Chile for 60 days of two of the persons concerned in order that they might personally clarify their cases and gain permission for permanent residence. It had been emphasized to the persons concerned that the measures had been taken on humanitarian grounds, and that they might eventually serve as precedents for resolving similar cases as long as Chilean law was complied with and no incidents occurred.

53. At the [autumn 1980] session the Committee was informed by the Chilean representative that his government had not yet heard from either of the two persons in question. He stated that this apparent lack of interest on their part was seriously complicating matters and was frustrating the government's efforts to co-operate on this question.

54. The Chilean representative further informed the Committee that similar authorizations to return would soon be issued to other persons desiring them, in addition to the 120 persons who had already been so authorized and whose names would be provided to the Committee.

55. After discussion, the Committee at its [autumn 1980] session decided to maintain these six cases on its agenda, and to request the Chilean authorities to accord to the other four persons involved the same authorization to return to Chile as had already been granted to Mr Pueller Bravo and Mr Quintana Muñoz. The Committee also decided to ask the Executive Board to request the Director-General to bring these cases to the attention of the United Nations High Commissioner for Refugees for assistance, financial and otherwise, in order to facilitate their return to Chile.[14]

56. The Director-General did so by a letter dated 16 January 1981 and the United Nations High Commissioner for Refugees replied giving details on procedures which could be used to obtain the financial aid required.

---

[14] See document 110 EX/40 PRIV., para. 56 (*supra*, p. 184).

57. As regards the persons concerned:

> Mr Arturo Montes has stated that he applied to the Chilean Consultate in Paris on 27 October 1980 with a view to obtaining authorization to go to Chile for two months in order to prepare for his permanent return;
>
> a letter posted in Santiago on 29 August 1980 has been received by the Director of the Office of International Standards and Legal Affairs from Mr Luis Pueller Bravo, stating that he was taking various steps with a view to settling in Chile. In another letter, dated 24 February 1981, he gives Unesco an account of his return visit to Chile;
>
> Mr Gustavo Adolfo Quintana Muñoz and Mr Abelardo Castro Hidalgo have not given the Secretariat any further information;
>
> Mr Patricio Cleary Zambón has informed the Secretariat in his letter dated 11 November 1980 that he cannot accept that conditions should be laid down for the return of a native Chilean to his country, and that what he desires is not only the right to return but also the right to work and exercise his profession in a normal way;
>
> Mr Elwin Ayamante Bórquez, in a letter dated 9 February 1981, has adopted a position very similar to that of Mr Patricio Cleary Zambón.

58. At the present session of the Committee, the representative of the Chilean Government said he did not have much to add to the updated statement of facts presented in the Committee's working documents.

59. Mr Pueller Bravo had now been given permission to settle definitely and permanently in Chile, for humanitarian reasons.

60. Mr Muñoz had not yet manifested himself, but the government's offer to return to Chile was still open. He said that the High Commissioner for Refugees had explained in a letter to Unesco the procedures to follow to obtain financial assistance to return to Chile. The Chilean representative suggested that this person once again be informed of the possibility of using the United Nations financial aid available to him.

61. As for Messrs. Zambón and Bórquez, the representative stated that his government considered these cases as closed as the persons in question did not wish to take advantage of the government's offer. Also it had recently discovered that these persons had links with international terrorist organizations. They could of course still

resort to the courts in Chile, he said, and the courts would independently decide on the merits of their petition to return versus the government's petition for their exclusion for terrorist activities. The choice was up to them, he said.

62. As for Mr Montes Larrain, the government needed more information from him in order to arrange his return.

63. As concerned Mr Castro Hidalgo, the Chilean representative explained that he simply had not yet made proper use of the domestic remedies available to him.

64. The Committee *decided*, after discussion, to strike out the communications as having been settled.

No. 56/78

Concerning *Chile*
Case of *Jorge Triviño Puelpan*

Communication of 17 October 1978 submitted by
Jorge Triviño Puelpan

Spring 1981 session of the Committee on Conventions and Recommendations (112th session of the Executive Board)[1]

65. The author of the communication (dated 17 October 1978, received by Unesco on 21 August 1980), a photographic reporter and former student in the Faculty of Musical Arts in Chile, describes himself as a victim of the events of 11 September 1973 in his country. He declares that after the official publication of the Amnesty Decree of 19 April 1978, he went to the Chilean Embassy in Paris to request permission to return to his country of origin, with his wife and daughter, for the purpose of exercising his profession; after waiting several months, he received a negative response; and that his most recent efforts, in May 1980, also proved of no avail.

66. After noting, as a matter of principle, that the alleged victim had made no effort to exhaust domestic remedies, the representative of the government concerned informed the Committee that Mr Puelpan had obtained an unconditional authorization to return to Chile.

67. The Committee accordingly *decided* to strike this communication from its list as having been settled.

---

[1] See document 112 EX/30 PRIV., paras. 65-67; see also document 112 EX/CR/HR/3.

No. 57/78

Concerning *Chile*
Case of *Luis Pueller*

Communication of 18 September 1978 submitted by
Luis Pueller

Spring 1979 session of the Committee on Conventions and Recommendations (107th session of the Executive Board)[1]

123. The author of this communication, a Chilean journalist exiled in France since November 1973, is said to have asked the Chilean authorities for permission to return to his country but his request was allegedly rejected by the Chilean Embassy in Paris, without any reasons being given, on 13 September 1978.

124. The representative of the Government of Chile, explained to the Committee that the author of the communication had been condemned for a common law offence and accordingly did not come under the amnesty law of 1978. If the person concerned returned to Chile, he was liable to be brought before the courts. [The representative of the government concerned] said that he would endeavour to find out whether the return of the person concerned could be envisaged.

125. In view of the proposal made by the representative of the government concerned, the Committee *decided* to defer consideration of the case until the outcome of the inquiries was known.

[1] See document 107 EX/PRIV.31, paras. 123-125; see also document 107 EX/CR/PROC.HR/14.

No. 57/78 **Chile**

Autumn 1979 session of the Committee on Conventions and Recommendations (108th session of the Executive Board)[2]

130. The author of this communication, a. Chilean journalist exiled in France, is said to have asked the Chilean anthorities for permission to return to Chile but his request was allegedly rejected by the Chilean Embassy in Paris.

131. The Director of the Division of Human Rights and Peace recalled that at its [spring 1979] session, the Committee had decided to defer consideration of this case until it learnt of the outcome of the representations which the representative of the government concerned had proposed to take.[3]

132. The representative of the government concerned repeated that the author of the communication had been condemned for a common law offence and accordingly did not come under the amnesty law. He pointed out that in any case, the alleged victim could have recourse to existing remedies through the competent administrative and judicial authorities in order to request re-examination of his application for readmission to Chile.

133. On the proposal of the Chairman, the Committee *decided* to defer consideration of the admissibility of the communication and *instructed* the Secretariat to inform the author of the remedies existing in his country through the competent administrative and judicial authorities.

Spring 1980 session of the Committee on Conventions and Recommendations (109th session of the Executive Board)[4]

Autumn 1980 session of the Committee on Conventions and Recommendations (110th session of the Executive Board)[5]

---

[2] See document 108 EX/38 PRIV., paras. 130-133; see also documents 108 EX/CR/PROC. HR/1 and Add.5.

[3] See document 107 EX/PRIV.31, para. 125 (*supra*, p. 191).

[4] See document 109 EX/52 PRIV., paras. 81-85 (*supra*, pp. 181-182), communication No. 54/78 conerning *Chile*, case of *Arturo Montes Larrain*.

[5] See document 110 EX/40 PRIV., paras. 45-46 (*supra*, pp. 182-184), communication No. 54/78 conerning *Chile*, case of *Arturo Montes Larrain*.

Chile **No. 57/78**

Spring 1981 session of the Committee on Conventions and Recommendations (112th session of the Executive Board)[6]

[6] See document 112 EX/30 PRIV., paras. 49-64 (*supra*, pp. 184-187), communication No. 54/78 concerning *Chile*, case of *Arturo Montes Larrain*.

No. 59/78

Concerning *Chile*
Case of *Gustavo Adolfo Quintana Muñoz*

Communication of 27 September 1978 submitted by
Gustavo Adolfo Quintana Muñoz

Autumn 1979 session of the Committee on Conventions and Recommendations (108th session of the Executive Board)[1]

134. The author of this communication, a professor and deputy Secretary-General at the University of Valparaíso, claims that he is the victim of the violation of the right to live and work in his country owing to the fact that his application to return to Chile was reportedly refused.

135. The representative of the government concerned explained that the alleged victim could take advantage of the "recurso de amparo" to request re-examination of his application to return to his country, but in any case he should clearly state whether he left of his own accord or as a result of banishment: in point of fact in cases where a prison sentence had been commuted to banishment, the only remaining possibility was an act of clemency.

136. On the proposal of the Chairman, the Committee *decided* to defer consideration of the admissibility of the communication and *instructed* the Secretariat to inform the author of the statements made by the representative of the government concerned, particularly concerning the existence of a domestic remedy ("recurso de amparo") through the competent judicial authorities in his country.

[1] See document 108 EX/38 PRIV., paras. 134-136; see also document 108 EX/CR/PROC.HR/1.

No. 59/78 **Chile**

Spring 1980 session of the Committee on Conventions and Recommendations (109th session of the Executive Board)[2]

Autumn 1980 session of the Committee on Conventions and Recommendations (110th session of the Executive Board[3]

Spring 1981 session of the Committee on Conventions and Recommendations (112th session of the Executive Board)[4]

---

[2] See document 109 EX/52 PRIV., paras. 81-85 (*supra*, pp. 181-182), communication No. 54/78 conerning *Chile*, case of *Arturo Montes Larrain*.
[3] See document 110 EX/40 PRIV., paras. 45-56 (*supra*, pp. 182-184), communication No. 54/78 conerning *Chile*, case of *Arturo Montes Larrain*.
[4] See document 112 EX/30 PRIV., paras. 49-64 (*supra*, pp. 184-187), communication No. 54/78 conerning *Chile*, case of *Arturo Montes Larrain*.

No. 60/78

Concerning *Argentina*
Case of *Mario César Clar and Sergio Andrés Clar*

Communication of 3 October 1978 submitted by
Elida Sonia Lusardi de Clar

Spring 1979 session of the Committee on Conventions and Recommendations (107th session of the Executive Board)[1]

82. The author of the communication alleges the violation of several articles of the Universal Declaration of Human Rights, by the abduction of two people on 18 May 1977. The representative of the government concerned considered that the occupations engaged in by the victims - one an accountant, the other an employee - were not such that a connection could be established with Unesco's fields of competence. But he said that, since the author of the communication claimed that one of the alleged victims was deprived of the right to complete his studies and the other of the right of freedom of information and expression, he would agree, should the Committee not declare the communication to be inadmissible, that additional information should be requested by the Secretariat.

83. The Committee went on to examine the various ways in which the information obtained by the Secretariat on this case might be supplemented and, in general, on other cases in which the circumstances were similar. Following discussion of the matter, the Committee decided that the letter accompanying the form addressed to the authors of communications ought to explain more fully how the procedures laid down by 104 EX/Decision 3.3 were applied, and in particular should indicate more fully what Unesco's fields of competence were, it being understood that the Secretariat would endeavour to obtain additional information from the authors of communications in cases where it appeared desirable to do so.

84. With regard to [this communication], the Committee *decided* to suspend the examination of its admissibility pending the receipt of the additional information

[1] See document 107 EX/PRIV.31, paras. 82-84; see also documents 107 EX/CR/PROC.HR/ 15 and Annex.

which the Secretariat had been instructed to request of the author of the communication.

Autumn 1979 session of the Committee on Conventions and Recommendations (108th session of the Executive Board)[2]

44. The examination of the admissibility of this communication, which relates to the alleged abduction of the son and husband of the author of the communication on 18 May 1977, was suspended at the [spring 1979] session of the Committee pending the receipt of additional infomation [...].[3] The Director of the Division of Human Rights and Peace recalled that the examination of this case had been suspended on account of the doubts expressed regarding the existence of a connection between the occupations of the alleged victims ("accountant" and "employee") and Unesco's spheres of competence. He stated that, despite its requests, the Secretariat had not received any further information in this connection.

45. The Argentine representative considered that this represented a typical case of inadmissibility. Apart from the doubts regarding a possible connection with Unesco's spheres of competence, he considered it to be hardly credible that the father and son should have disappeared together when they were alleged not to have disappeared from the same place. He also pointed out that both father and son were members of the Communist Party, which was one of the legal political parties in Argentina. He wondered whether "Trotskyists" might not have been involved in the alleged disappearance. In conclusion, the representative of Argentina noted that this case had been referred to the Inter-American Commission on Human Rights which was currently meeting in Buenos Aires.

46. Several members of the Committee noted that the absence of additional information should not necessarily result in a communication being deemed inadmissible, inasmuch as the author was possibly not responsible for his own silence. Other factors (loss of mail, inaccurate or incomplete address, etc.) might account for this lack of information. Some members of the Committee considered that authors of communications should be allowed a longer period of time so as to enable them to supply the additional information requested.

47. The Director of the Division of Human Rights and Peace provided the Committee with detailed information in this connection regarding the approaches made and

---

[2] See document 108 EX/38 PRIV., paras. 44-48; see also document 108 EX/CR/PROC.HR/1.
[3] See document 107 EX/PRIV.31, para. 84 (*supra*, pp. 197-198).

the measures taken in order to contact the authors of communications and obtain further information.

48. As there was no indication of a connection between the alleged victim and Unesco's spheres of competence, the condition for admissibility laid down in paragraph 14 (*a*) (iii) of 104 EX/Decision 3.3 had consequently not been met, and the Committee *decided* to declare this communication inadmissible.

No. 63/78

Concerning *Argentina*
Case of *Alejandro Enrique Gutiérrez Penette*

Communication of 26 September 1978 submitted by
Ruth Mabel Penette de Gutiérrez

Spring 1979 session of the Committee on Conventions and Recommendations (107th session of the Executive Board)[1]

85. According to the communication, the alleged victim, who is a glazier and a student of journalism, was abducted by three policemen on 24 July 1978. The representative of the government concerned was of the opinion that the communication, which contained no details on the activities of the victim, could not be regarded as falling within Unesco's fields of competence.

86. As the person concerned was a student studying in a field in which Unesco was particularly competent and was working so that he could pursue his studies, several members of the Committee considered that the communication fell directly within Unesco's fields of competence. After discussion of the matter, the Committee *decided* to declare the communication admissible.

Autumn 1979 session of the Committee on Conventions and Recommendations (108th session of the Executive Board)[2]

300. This communication, declared admissible at the Committee's [spring 1979 session],[3] concerns a glazier who is also a student of journalism and who was reportedly abducted by three policemen on 24 July 1978. The Committee at its present session proceeded to examine the merits of the allegations declared admissible.

---

[1] See document 107 EX/PRIV.31, paras. 85-86; see also documents 107 EX/CR/PROC.HR/16 and Annex.
[2] See document 108 EX/38 PRIV., paras. 300-302; see also document 108 EX/CR/PROC.HR/2
[3] See document 107 EX/PRIV.31, para. 86 (*supra*, p. 201).

No. 63/78 **Argentina**

301. The Argentine representative explained that in the situation of latent civil war which prevailed in his country at the time of the disappearances, missing persons might in fact have gone into hiding. Following his request for information on 9 June 1979, he had received a reply on 16 June 1979 to the effect that the case of Mr Penette had been referred to Judge Samboni and was at present pending; he could not, however, provide any further details.

302. After discussion, the Committee *decided* to apply in this case the special procedure concerning communications relating to missing persons, adopted on 10 September 1979 [...].[4]

---

[4] See document 108 EX/38 PRIV., para. 16.

No. 64/78

Concerning *Chile*
Case of *Juan Patricio Cleary Zambón*

Communication of 9 October 1978 submitted by
Juan Patricio Cleary Zambón

Spring 1979 session of the Committee on Conventions and Recommendations (107th session of the Executive Board)[1]

126. The author of this communication, who was a teacher in Chile for 17 years and National President of the Teachers' Union (Sindicato Único de la Enseñanza), complains of the violation of his right to return to his country, as he was allegedly informed by the Consul-General of Chile in Frankfurt (Federal Republic of Germany), to whom he had submitted the relevant application.

127. The representative of the Government of Chile deplored the fact that the person concerned had engaged in a campaign against his country's government, when it had, in fact, commuted the sentence that he had received. Although there was every justification for the refusal in the case in point, the representative of the government concerned proposed to make representations in the person's favour.

128. The Committee *decided* to defer consideration of the case until the outcome of the representations was known.

Autumn 1979 session of the Committee on Conventions and Recommendations (108th session of the Executive Board)[2]

137. The author of this communication, a teacher and national president of the teachers' union (Sindicato Único de la Enseñanza), complains of the violation of his

[1] See document 107 EX/PRIV.31, paras. 126-128; see also document 107 EX/CR/PROC.HR/17.
[2] See document 108 EX/38 PRIV., paras. 137-141; see also document 108 EX/CR/PROC.HR/1.

right to return to his country, on the basis of the information communicated to him by the Consul-General of Chile in Frankfurt (Federal Republic of Germany), to whom he had submitted the relevant application.

138. The Director of the Division of Human Rights and Peace recalled that at its [spring 1979] session the Committee had decided to defer consideration of this case until it learnt of the outcome of the action which the representative of the government concerned had proposed to take.[3]

139. The representative of the government concerned pointed out that the sentence passed on the author of the communication for his terrorist activities and for possession of explosives had been commuted to banishment, and that, accordingly, the refusal which had been given was justified and in conformity with the law of his country.

140. One member of the Committee asked for the question of banishment to be clarified, as it was a relatively severe penalty.

141. The representative of the government concerned stated that commutation of the sentence was an act of clemency, and that in the case in point, banishment had replaced imprisonment. He recalled that the Chilean Government had derogated from the provisions of Article 12, paragraph 4, of the International Covenant on Civil and Political Rights which dealt in point of fact with the right of a person to enter his country. After discussion, and with a view to furthering the search for a humanitarian solution in keeping with respect for human rights, in a spirit of international conciliation and co-operation, the Committee *decided* to keep the communication on its agenda and recommended to the Executive Board that it invite the Director-General to carry out consultations which might help to find a humanitarian solution to this and similar cases. Furthermore, the Committee *instructed* the Secretariat to send the author of the communication the text of the sentence passed on him, which the representative of the government concerned had agreed to communicate to the Committee.

Spring 1980 session of the Committee on Conventions and Recommendations (109th session of the Executive Board)[4]

[3] See document 107 EX/PRIV.31, para. 128 (*supra*, p. 203).
[4] See document 109 EX/52 PRIV., paras. 81-85 (*supra*, pp. 181-185), communication No. 54/78 conerning *Chile*, case of *Arturo Montes Larrain*.

Chile **No. 64/78**

Autumn 1980 session of the Committee on Conventions and Recommendations (110th session of the Executive Board)[5]

Spring 1981 session of the Committee on Conventions and Recommendations (112th session of the Executive Board)[6]

[5] See document 110 EX/40 PRIV., paras. 45-56 (*supra*, pp. 182-184), communication No. 54/78 conerning *Chile*, case of *Arturo Montes Larrain*.
[6] See document 112 EX/30 PRIV., paras. 49-64 (*supra*, pp. 184-187), communication No. 54/78 conerning *Chile*, case of *Arturo Montes Larrain*.

No. 65/78

Concerning *Federal Republic of Germany*
Case of *Karl Wilhelm Ströder*

Communication of 9 August 1978 submitted by
Karl Wilhelm Ströder

Spring 1979 session of the Committee on Conventions and Recommendations (107th session of the Executive Board)[1]

61. The author of this communication, a citizen of the Federal Republic of Germany, complains of the violation of the right to education and of the right to live in his country as a result of his allegedly having been declared insane by the authorities of the University of Cologne and expelled from the university. He allegedly left Europe in 1964 under the pressure of that university and was refused admission to a university in Australia, where he had taken up residence, as a result of a letter from the University of Cologne indicating that he was insane.

62. The representative of the Government of the Federal Republic of Germany, called the Committee's attention to the reply addressed by his government to Unesco on 12 April 1979. According to his government, the communication was inadmissible because it did not meet the conditions laid down in paragraphs 14 (*a*) (v), (viii) and (ix): it was manifestly ill-founded, it was not submitted within a reasonable time following the alleged facts and it did not indicate whether an attempt had been made to exhaust available domestic remedies.

63. Being of the opinion that facts dating back 15 years do not warrant examination by the Committee, the latter *decided* to declare the communication inadmissible.

---

[1] See document 107 EX/PRIV.31, paras. 61-63; see also document 107 EX/CR/PROC.HR/33.

No. 66/78

Concerning *Chile*
Case of *Olga Victoria Morris Barrios*

Communication of 12 October 1978 submitted by
Olga Victoria Morris Barrios

Autumn 1979 session of the Committee on Conventions and Recommendations (108th session of the Executive Board)[1]

142. The communication concerns the case of a Chilean lawyer, now a refugee in the Federal Republic of Germany, who claims to be the victim of the violation of her right to live in her country and to exercise her profession freely therein.

143. The representative of the government concerned considered that the exercise of the profession of lawyer did not establish a sufficiently clear connection with the fields of competence of Unesco; furhermore, he failed to understand the reasons which had led the alleged victim to take up voluntary exile and subsequently to apply for amnesty. According to him, the author of the communication would be able to take advantage of the "recurso de amparo" through the competent judicial authorities in her country.

144. On the proposal of the Chairman, the Committee *decided* to declare the communication inadmissible on the grounds that it did not fall within the fields of competence of Unesco, and *instructed* the Secretariat to inform the author of the communication of the existence of a domestic remedy ("recurso de amparo") through the competent judicial authorities in her country.

---

[1] See document 108 EX/38 PRIV., paras. 142-144; see also document 108 EX/CR/PROC.HR/1.

No. 67/78

Concerning *Chile*
Case of *Jorge Orlando Inostrosa Béjares and Rodrigo Mellado*

Communication of 22 October 1978 submitted by
Evemarie Dietrich

Spring 1979 session of the Committee on Conventions and Recommendations (107th session of the Executive Board)[1]

129. The author of this communication complains that the alleged victims, an office worker and a doctor of Chilean nationality, have been refused the right to return to their native country, Chile.

130. The Committee *decided* to defer consideration of the communication until it learnt the outcome of the representations which the representative of the Government of Chile proposed to make on the matter, in order to draw the attention of the competent Chilean authorities to the Committee's interest in the case.

Autumn 1979 session of the Committee on Conventions and Recommendations (108th session of the Executive Board)[2]

145. The author of this communication complains that the alleged victims, an office worker and a doctor of Chilean nationality, have been refused the right to return to their country.

146. The Director of the Division of Human Rights and Peace recalled that at its [spring 1979] session the Committee had decided to defer consideration of this case

---

[1] See document 107 EX/PRIV.31, paras. 129-130; see also document 107 EX/CR/PROC.HR/34.
[2] See document 108 EX/38 PRIV., paras. 145-148; see also document 108 EX/CR/PROC.HR/1

until it had learnt of the outcome of the representations which the representative of the government concerned had proposed to make.[3]

147. The representative of the government concerned stated that applications for re-admission to the country could be made directly to the Ministry of the Interior and, if the answer was negative, there existed a domestic remedy ("recurso de amparo") through the competent judicial authorities. In any event, there appeared to be no connection between the alleged violation and the fields of competence of Unesco.

148. On the proposal of the Chairman, the Committee *decided* to declare the communication inadmissible as it did not fulfil the condition of admissibility provided for in paragraph 14 (*a*) (v) of 104 EX/Decision 3.3, and *instructed* the Secretariat to inform the author of the communication of the existence of a domestic remedy ("recurso de amparo") through the competent judicial authorities in the State concerned.

[3] See document 107 EX/PRIV.31, para. 130 (*supra*, p. 211).

No. 68/78

Concerning *Argentina*
Case of *Luis Alberto Verdú Espinosa*

Communication of 10 November 1978 submitted by
Aurora Zulema Espinosa de Verdú

Spring 1979 session of the Committee on Conventions and Recommendations
(107th session of the Executive Board)[1]

87. This communication refers to the disappearance of the author's son, who is alleged to have been abducted by the police on 20 August 1977. The representative of the government concerned was of the opinion that the case did not fall within the fields of competence of Unesco and that the matter was before the Inter-American Commission on Human Rights.

88. Answering questions raised by various members of the Committee, the Director of the Division of Human Rights and Peace indicated that, as regards international remedies which could be considered as available, the Secretariat would give no advice whatsoever to the author of the communication. It was becoming customary for information to be exchanged between secretariats on the state of the examination of a particular case being dealt with simultaneously by several organizations; and the Committee had requested the Secretariat to do so with respect to [another communication].[2]

89. Since the information available with respect to the condition of admissibility stipulated in paragraph 14 (*a*) (iii) of 104 EX/Decision 3.3 was not sufficient, the Committee *decided* to declare this communication inadmissible.

---

[1] See document 107 EX/PRIV.31, paras. 87-89; see also document 107 EX/CR/PROC.HR/18.

[2] See document 105 EX/49 PRIV., para. 96 [iii] (*supra*, p. 148), communication No. 26/78 concerning *Argentina*, case of *Elsa Alicia Nocent*.

No. 69/78

Concerning *Argentina*
Case of *Néstor Hugo Cherry*

Communication of 26 October 1978 submitted by
Noemí Carmen Geiser de Cherry

Spring 1979 session of the Committee on Conventions and Recommendations (107th session of the Executive Board)[1]

90. The alleged victim is said to have been arrested by the police or military forces on 19 August 1977 and consequently to have been deprived of the right to work, the right to continue his studies and freedom of opinion.

91. As the profession of the alleged victim (electromechanical engineer) had no connection with the fields of competence of Unesco, the Committee *decided* to declare the communication inadmissible.

[1] See document 107 EX/PRIV.31, paras. 90-91; see also documents 107 EX/CR/PROC.HR/19 and Annex.

No. 71/78

Concerning *Argentina*
Case of *Daniel Gorosito*

Communication of 14 November 1978 submitted by
Irma Caballero de Gorosito

Spring 1979 session of the Committee on Conventions and Recommendations (107th session of the Executive Board)[1]

92. The author of this communication complains that her son, a student, has been unjustly detained since January 1976. The representative of the government concerned expressed the opinion that the connection with the fields of competence of Unesco was not established, as the communication did not indicate the name of the university where the person concerned was said to be studying or the connection which allegedly existed between his studies and the reason for the deprivation of his liberty.

93. Having noted that the author of the communication was unable to obtain information on the reasons for her son's detention, and therefore on the possible link between his studies and his detention, the Committee *decided* to suspend examination of the admissibility of this communication pending further information, which the Secretariat has been instructed to obtain from the author of the communication.

Autumn 1979 session of the Committee on Conventions and Recommendations (108th session of the Executive Board)[2]

49. The author of this communication complains that her son, a student, has been unjustly detained since January 1976. The examination of the admissibility of the communication was suspended at the [spring 1979] session of the Committee in order to obtain further information, concerning in particular the reasons for the deten-

[1] See document 107 EX/PRIV.31, paras. 92-93; see also documents 107 EX/CR/PROC.HR/20 and Annex.
[2] See document 108 EX/38 PRIV., paras. 49-53; see also document 108 EX/CR/PROC.HR/1.

tion [...].[3] Since then the Secretariat has applied to the author of the communication but has received no reply.

50. The representative of the Argentine Government stated that it emerged from the dossier built up by his government concerning this case that Mr Gorosito was not a student, and he was of the opinion that the communication was consequently inadmissible.

51. According to several members of the Committee, it was not incumbent on the author of the communication to supply legal proof of the alleged victim's student status. Replying to a question in this connection, the Director of the Division of Human Rights and Peace said that, in accordance with the practice of the Committee, when the occupation of the alleged victim fell within Unesco's fields of competence, it was presumed, during the consideration of admissibility, that there existed a connection between the alleged violation and Unesco's fields of competence. The Chairman recalled that in this particular instance the Committee had decided to suspend the examination of admissibility pending further information, which it still had not received. In his opinion, the Secretariat's effforts to obtain such information should be redoubled.

52. Endorsing the Chairman's opinion, one member of the Committee pointed out that Unesco was the only authority to which this case had been referred.

53. In conclusion, the Committee *decided* to further suspend examination of the admissibility of this communication, *instructed* the Secretariat to renew its efforts so that the Committee might have available to it additional information which would enable it to take a decision at its next session and *invited* the government concerned to supply any relevant information at its disposal regarding this case.

Spring 1980 session of the Committee on Conventions and Recommendations (109th session of the Executive Board)[4]

10. The author of this communication complains that her son has been unjustly detained since January 1976. The examination of the admissibility of this communication had been suspended at the [spring and autumn 1979] sessions of the Committee in order to obtain further information which would enable the Committee to take a

[3] See document 107 EX/PRIV.31, para. 93 (*supra*, p. 217).

[4] See document 109 EX/52 PRIV., paras. 10-12; see also document 109 EX/CR/HR/2.

decision.[5] The Secretariat had been unable to obtain any further reply from the author since the first suspension of this case.

11. The representative of the Argentine Government reiterated the position that his government had taken on this matter, i.e. that this case was not linked with Unesco's fields of competence and that there was no evidence that this person was a student. He also pointed out that there had been no response from the author of the communication in over a year. For these reasons the Argentine authorities felt that the communication should be deemed inadmissible.

12. After a brief debate the Committee *decided* to strike the communication from its list in view of the fact that the author in over a year and a half had not provided information which would have enabled the Committee to take a decision on admissibility.

---

[5] See documents 107 EX/PRIV.31, para. 93 (*supra*, p. 217) and 108 EX/38 PRIV., para. 53 (*supra*, p. 218), respectively.

No. 72/78

Concerning *Chile*
Case of *Elwin Ayamante**

Communication of 14 November 1978 submitted by
Elwin Ayamante Bórquez

Spring 1979 session of the Committee on Conventions and Recommendations (107th session of the Executive Board)[1]

131. The author of this communication, a teacher of basic education and a student at the Southern University of Chile complains that he has been refused the right to return to his country, on the basis of the application he is said to have made to the Chilean Consulate in Paris in June 1978.

132. The representative of the Government of Chile, informed the Committee that the person concerned had been accused of attempted murder ("homocidio frustrado"). The 15-year term of imprisonment to which he had been sentenced had been commuted to banishment.

133. Some members of the Committee were of the opinion that the case in point came within the category of cases of refusal to allow Chilean citizens to return to their country and that, as such, the representative of the government might also envisage making appropriate representations. Although the latter felt that the case did not have the same prospects of success, he agreed to make similar representations.

134. The Committee accordingly *decided* to defer consideration of the communication until the outcome of the representations made by the representative of the Chilean Government was known.

---

* From the Committee's spring 1980 session, this communication was being referred to as case of *Elwin Ayamante Bórquez*.

[1] See document 107 EX/PRIV.31, paras. 131-134; see also document 107 EX/CR/PROC.HR/21.

No. 72/78 **Chile**

Autumn 1979 session of the Committee on Conventions and Recommendations (108th session of the Executive Board)[2]

149. This communication concerns the case of a teacher of basic education and a student at the Southern University of Chile, who complains that he has been refused the right to return to his country, on the basis of the application he is said to have made to the Chilean Consulate in Paris in June 1978.

150. The Director of the Division of Human Rights and Peace recalled that at its [spring 1979] session the Committee had decided to defer consideration of this case until it learnt of the outcome of the representations which the representative of the government concerned had proposed to make.[3]

151. The representative of the government concerned explained that the 15-year term of imprisonment to whch the person concerned had been sentenced for attempted murder had been commuted to banishment, and that, accordingly, the refusal which had been given was in conformity with the law of his country.

152. A member of the Committee raised the question of the torture which the author of the communication had allegedly undergone, but which had not been the subject of any complaint. The Director of the Division of Human Rights and Peace pointed out, in this connection, that other international organizations responsible for considering communications concerning human rights were reluctant, in any case-file, to invoke on their own authority, human rights violations which had not been the subject of a specific complaint.

153. On the proposal of the Chairman, the Committee *decided* to defer consideration of this communication and *instructed* the Secretariat to inform the author that it would be possible for him to make representations to the competent administrative authorities in his country in order to obtain re-examination of the decision concerning his return to Chile.

Spring 1980 session of the Committee on Conventions and Recommendations (109th session of the Executive Board)[4]

---

[2] See document 108 EX/38 PRIV., paras. 149-153; see also document 108 EX/CR/PROC.HR/1.

[3] See document 107 EX/PRIV.31, para. 134 (*supra*, p. 221).

[4] See document 109 EX/52 PRIV., paras. 81-85 (*supra*, pp. 181-182), communication No. 54/78 conerning *Chile*, case of *Arturo Montes Larrain*.

Chile **No. 72/78**

Autumn 1980 session of the Committee on Conventions and Recommendations (110th session of the Executive Board)[5]

Spring 1981 session of the Committee on Conventions and Recommendations (112th session of the Executive Board)[6]

[5] See document 110 EX/40 PRIV., paras. 45-56 (*supra*, pp. 182-184), communication No. 54/78 conerning *Chile*, case of *Arturo Montes Larrain*.
[6] See document 112 EX/30 PRIV., paras. 49-64 (*supra*, pp. 184-187), communication No. 54/78 conerning *Chile*, case of *Arturo Montes Larrain*.

No. 74/78

Concerning *Argentina*
Case of *Perla Elizabeth Schneider*

Communication of 26 October 1978 submitted by
Abraham Schneider

Spring 1979 session of the Committee on Conventions and Recommendations (107th session of the Executive Board)[1]

94. The author of this communication considers that several articles of the Universal Declaration of Human Rights have been violated to the detriment of his daughter, who was alledgedly abducted on 6 December 1977 at a time when she was a third-year psychology student at the University of Córdoba.

95. After discussion, the Committee *decided* to declare this communication admissible.

Autumn 1979 session of the Committee on Conventions and Recommendations (108th session of the Executive Board)[2]

303. This communication, declared admissible at the Committee's [spring] 1979 session,[3] concerns the disappearance on 6 December 1977 of a third-year woman student studying psychology at the University of Córdoba. At its present session the Committee initiated its examination of the merits of the allegations declared admissible.

304. The representative of the Argentine Government considered that the alleged violation was not imputable to his government, which assumed no responsibility in the

---

[1] See document 107 EX/PRIV.31, paras. 94-95; see also documents 107 EX/CR/PROC.HR/ 22 and Annex.
[2] See document 108 EX/38 PRIV., paras. 303-306; see also document 108 EX/CR/PROC.HR/ 2
[3] See document 107 EX/PRIV.31, para. 95 (*supra*, p. 225).

case of persons who had gone into hiding, as could be assumed, according to the Argentine authorities, to have happened in this particular instance. In reply to one member of the Committee, he stated that the authorities could not know the identity of persons who had gone into hiding in 1976-1977, as the State authorities had at that time been unable to keep track of the membership of terrorist groups.

305. One member of the Committee was of the opinion that the search for missing persons should, in such cases, be as extensive and as thorough as a government could reasonably be expected to undertake.

306. After discussion, the Committee *decided* to apply in this case the special procedure concerning communications relating to missing persons, adopted on 10 September 1979 [...].[4]

[4] See document 108 EX/38 PRIV., para. 16.

No. 75/78

Concerning *Argentina*
Case of *José Carlos Prat-Salvucci*

Communication of 14 November 1978 submitted by
María Josefa Salvucci de Prat

Spring 1979 session of the Committee on Conventions and Recommendations (107th session of the Executive Board)[1]

96. The author of this communication complains of the disappearance on 1 January 1977 of her son, a student of economics and a conscripted soldier. The representative of the government concerned pointed out that nothing was known of the university where the person concerned was said to be studying, and that in any case, as he was doing his military service, the alleged victim was normally required to suspend his studies.

97. After discussion, the Committee *decided* to suspend the examinetton of the admissibility of this communication pending further information, which the Secretariat has been instructed to obtain from the author.

Autumn 1979 session of the Committee on Conventions and Recommendations (108th session of the Executive Board)[2]

54. The examination of the admissibility of this communication, which concerns the disappearance on 1 January 1977 of the son of the author of the communication, was suspended at the [spring 1979] session of the Committee until such time as the Secretariat could obtain further information [...].[3] Following the Secretariat's request,

---

[1] See document 107 EX/PRIV.31, paras. 96-97; see also documents 107 EX/CR/PROC.HR/23 and Annex.
[2] See document 108 EX/38 PRIV., paras. 54-61; see also document 108 EX/CR/HR/1.
[3] See document 107 EX/PRIV.31, para. 97 (*supra*, p. 227).

the author, on behalf of the alleged victim, sent a letter and a certificate of university registration for the attention of the Committee [...].[4]

55. The main question, so far as the Committee was concerned, was to what extent Mr Prat could be regarded as a student, considering that he was serving in the armed forces at the time of his disappearance. According to the representative of the government concerned, Mr Prat could not be regarded as a student at the time of his military service, with the result that, in the absence of further information allowing a connection to be established with Unesco's spheres of competence, the Committee should declare the communication inadmissible.

56. A large number of speakers raised the question whether a student who interrupted his studies to perform his compulsory military service forfeited his student status. Several members of the Committee emphasized the fact that conscription into the armed forces in no way modified student status, at least for the requirements of the decision on the admissibility of a communication.

57. The Argentine representative stated that provision was made under Argentine law for students to benefit automatically from deferment and that Mr Prat had not applied for it. He had therefore discontinued his studies of his own free will when he began his military service.

58. The Director of the Division of Human Rights and Peace noted that the question of the connection between the alleged violation and Unesco's spheres of competence recurred fairly often in the Committee's work. The Committee's practice to date had consisted merely in identifying, during the consideration of admissibility, reasons for thinking that such a connection existed, without seeking to obtain proof that such was indeed the case.

59. A few members were opposed to the idea of suspending examination of this case until the next session of the Committee. One member stressed that any doubt should be to the benefit of the victim. Several members emphasized the fact that the Committee had obtained information it had requested and that consequently there was no reason to suspend the consideration of admissibility yet again.

60. In the light of the foregoing discussion and in a spirit of consensus, the Committee *decided* to suspend examination of this communication until the next session and *instructed* the Secretariat to obtain from the United Nations and from the Organization of American States fuller information concerning the stage that had been

---

[4] See document 108 EX/CR/HR/1.

reached, and the conclusions arrived at, in the examination of this case by the competent bodies of those organizations.

61. One member of the Committee stated that he had not wished to upset the consensus achieved within the Committee but that he felt obliged to make a reservation regarding the decision to suspend examination of the admissibility of this communication, which he considered to be admissible.

Spring 1980 session of the Committee on Conventions and Recommendations (109th session of the Executive Board)[5]

13. In this commmication the author complains that her son, a student of economics and a conscripted soldier, disappeared on 1 January 1977. The examination of the admissibility of this case had been deferred for a second time by the Committee at its [autumn 1979] session in order to obtain more information from the author, the United Nations and from the Organization of American States.[6] No reply to the Secretariat's inquiries had been received from either the author or the Organization of American States. The United Nations, in its reply, regretted that it could not be of assistance since its human rights procedures applicable to Argentina dealt with general situations rather than with individual cases.

14. The representative of the Argentine Government reminded the Committee that the person involved in this case had not availed himself of a student deferment from military service and had thus disqualified himself as a student. He also felt that Unesco should not duplicate the work of the Organization of American States which was also considering this case.

15. Several members of the Committee emphasized the fact that the examination of a case by another body did not prevent the Committee from also examining that case, and one of them expressed concern that Mr Prat-Salvucci may have perhaps lost his student status as a result of being drafted.

16. In view of the fact that the report of the Inter-American Commission on Human Rights was due to be published in the near future, the Committee *decided* to defer its decision with the hope that the said report might provide some more information on this case.

---

[5] See document 109 EX/52 PRIV., paras. 13-16; see also document 109 EX/CR/HR/2.

[6] See document 108 EX/38 PRIV., para. 60 (*supra*, pp. 228-229).

No. 79/78

Concerning ***Argentina***
Case of ***Julia Natividad Huarque***

Communication of 30 November 1978 submitted by
Nélida Manuela Rodríguez de Huarque

Spring 1979 session of the Committee on Conventions and Recommendations (107th session of the Executive Board)[1]

98. The author of this communication complains of the abduction from her home on 8 June 1976 of her daughter, a physics graduate. The representative of the government concerned expressed the opinion that the condition appearing in paragraph 14 (*a*) (viii) of 104 EX/Decision 3.3 whereby "the communication must be submitted within a reasonable time-limit following the facts which constitute its subject-matter or within a reasonable time-limit after the facts have become known", was not fulfilled as the alleged violation dated back nearly three years.

99. Several members of the Committee were of the opinion that the notion of a "reasonable time-limit" should be interpreted in the particular context of each case and that the time required to have recourse to available domestic remedies should be taken into account. Other members of the Committee thought that under the circumstances the communication had been submitted within a reasonable time-limit.

100. On the question of recourse to domestic remedies, some members agreed with the representative of the government concerned that certain remedies should, in all cases, be used before the communication could be deemed admissible. Other members thought that the condition appearing in paragraph 14 (*a*) (ix) of 104 EX/Decision 3.3 should not be interpreted in such a way that the prior exhaustion of domestic remedies became a condition of admissibility, since 104 EX/Decision 3.3 did not provide for this to be so, nor was it the intention of the authors of the decision.

---

[1] See document 107 EX/PRIV.31, paras. 98-102; see also documents 107 EX/CR/PROC.HR/24 and Annex.

No. 79/78 **Argentina**

101. Several members of the Committee raised the question of the possibility of duplication with other institutions, as both the United Nations and the Organization of American States had the same case before them. It was pointed out in this connection that litispendence was not regarded as a cause of inadmissibility and that the simultaneous examination of one and the same case by several organizations did not seem, at first sight, to raise any particular problem; it was nevertheless important for international organizations to exchange information on the results of the examination of this case.

102. After discussion, the Committee *decided* to treat the communication as being admissible and to examine it only when the Secretariat had obtained further information from the author and had made inquiries about the results of the examination of this case by other international bodies.

Autumn 1979 session of the Committee on Conventions and Recommendations (108th session of the Executive Board)[2]

307. This communication, declared admissible by the Committee at its [spring] 1979 session,[3] concerns the abduction on 8 June 1976 of a woman physics graduate. At its present session the Committee initiated its examination of the merits of the allegations declared admissible.

308. The representative of the Argentine Government informed the Committee that this case was one of those that would be examined by the Inter-American Commission on Human Rights currently meeting in Buenos Aires, whose report should contain information relating thereto.

309. The Committee *decided* to apply in this case the special procedure concerning communications relating to missing persons, adopted on 10 September 1979 [...].[4] At the same time, it *instructed* the Secretariat to obtain any further information from the Inter-American Commission on Human Rights.

---

[2] See document 108 EX/38 PRIV., paras. 307-309; see also document 108 EX/CR/PROC.HR/2.
[3] See document 107 EX/PRIV.31, para. 102 (*supra*, p. 232).
[4] See document 108 EX/38 PRIV., para. 16.

No. 80/78

Concerning *Argentina*
Case of *Juan José Laso*

Communication of 15 November 1978 submitted by
Angélica M. de Laso

Spring 1979 session of the Committee on Conventions and Recommendations (107th session of the Executive Board)[1]

103. This communication concerns the case of a former student of the Faculty of Economics who was employed by a bank at the time of his disappearance on 23 December 1975 in Córdoba. The representative of the government concerned expressed the opinion that the connection between the alleged facts and the fields of competence of Unesco was not established with sufficient clarity, and that, in any case, too much time had elapsed since the date of the events.

104. Several members of the Committee were of the opinion that flexibility in the interpretation of the condition of admissibility in relation to a reasonable time-limit was desirable, although they thought that the connection with Unesco's fields of competence was not proven. The Committee consequently *decided* to declare the communication inadmissible.

---

[1] See document 107 EX/PRIV.31, paras. 103-104; see also documents 107 EX/CR/PROC. HR/25 and Annex.

No. 81/78

Concerning *Argentina*
Case of *Guillermo Horacio White*

Communication of 28 November 1978 submitted by
María Rosa Saint Girons de White

Spring 1979 session of the Committee on Conventions and Recommendations (107th session of the Executive Board)[1]

105. This communication concerns the disappearance of an office worker on 10 February 1977. The Committee *decided* that in the absence of information which would justify the view that there was a connection with the fields of competence of Unesco, the communication should be considered inadmissible.

[1] See document 107 EX/PRIV.31, para. 105; see also documents 107 EX/CR/PROC.HR/26 and Annex.

No. 82/78

Concerning *Argentina*
Case of *María Cristina Mattioli de Totterau*

Communication of 11 November 1978 submitted by
Eugenio Roberto Mattioli

Spring 1979 session of the Committee on Conventions and Recommendations (107th session of the Executive Board)[1]

106. The author of this communication complains of the disappearance of his daughter, a commercial expert, who is alleged to have been abducted on 27 February 1976. The representative of the government concerned pointed out a contradiction in the communication, which states in one place that the alleged victim is a commercial expert, but elsewhere states, with reference to the relation with the fields of competence of Unesco, that she is a secondary school student.

107. One member of the Committee pointed out that the victim was alledgedly abducted at the same time as her husband, who was a student.

108. After discussion, the Committee *decided* that the communication was inadmissible, as it did not fall within the fields of competence of Unesco.

[1] See document 107 EX/PRIV.31, paras. 106-108; see also documents 107 EX/CR/PROC. HR/27 and Annex.

No. 83/78

Concerning *Argentina*
Case of *Rodolfo Omar Rodríguez Echavarría*

Communication of 7 December 1978 submitted by
Gloria Liliam Echavarría

Spring 1979 session of the Committee on Conventions and Recommendations (107th session of the Executive Board)[1]

109. The alleged victim, a turner, is said to have been arrested on 6 September 1973 and accused of belonging to a political organization that had been declared illegal. Mr Rodríguez Echavarría is alleged to have been tortured and detained, and so prevented from continuing his studies, deprived of access to the media and denied the possibility of engaging in cultural activities.

110. As the connection of the alleged events with the fields of competence of Unesco was not sufficiently well established, the Committee *decided* to declare the communication inadmissible.

---

[1] See document 107 EX/PRIV.31, paras. 109-110; see also documents 107 EX/CR/PROC. HR/28 and Annex.

No. 84/78

Concerning *Argentina*
Case of *Oscar Rubén Manzur*

Communication of 13 December 1978 submitted by
Oscar Rubén Manzur

Spring 1979 session of the Committee on Conventions and Recommendations (107th session of the Executive Board)[1]

92. The author of this communication and his wife are alleged to have been arrested on 10 August 1976 and deprived of their liberty. As there is no information in the communication which enables a connection to be established with the fields of competence of Unesco, the Committee *decided* to declare it inadmissible.

[1] See document 107 EX/PRIV.31, para. 111; see also documents 107 EX/CR/PROC.HR/29 and Annex.

No. 90/79

Concerning *Union of Soviet Socialist Republics and Ukrainian Soviet Socialist Republic*
Case of *Vadime Delaunay* et al.*

Communication of 30 December 1978 submitted by
Vadime Delaunay *et al.*°

Spring 1979 session of the Committee on Conventions and Recommendations (107th session of the Executive Board)[1]

163. The four co-authors of this communication present themselves both as victims and as a group of persons having reliable knowledge of alleged violations of freedom of expression and conscience and of the right to a fair trial for writers, journalists, academy members and ministers of religion who are held to oppose restrictions on these freedoms in the domains of science, culture and information. The dossier transmitted to the Committee contains a discussion by the authors of the communication, of a number of articles in the Soviet Constitution and the Penal Code of the RSFSR, followed by a description of the trials in May and July 1978 of Y. F. Orlov, L. Lukanenko, Z. K. Gamsazhurdia, A. I. Ginzburg, A. B. Shcharansky and V. Piatkus and of the international reactions to these trials.

164. [The representative of the Government of the USSR] expressed his surprise that this communication should have been sent to the Committee, for it had nothing to do with Unesco inasmuch as it consisted entirely of libellous criticisms of the social structure, constitution and legislation of the USSR.

165. Several members of the Committee noted the particular nature of this communication, which questioned the foundations of the regime of government in a Member State, and expressed the opinion that it was not the Committee's task to pronounce judgement on the legislation of a Member State. While sharing this view,

* Case of *Vadime Delaunay, Vladimir Maximov, Vadime Netchaev and Oscar Rabine.*
° Vadime Delaunay, Vladimir Maximov, Vadime Netchaev and Oscar Rabine.
[1] See document 107 EX/PRIV.31, paras. 163-167; see also document 107 EX/CR/PROC.HR/35.

various members thought that, setting aside the parts which were offensive to the regime of the State concerned, the essence of the communication concerned particular cases and fulfilled the conditions of admissibility.

166. The Chairman drew the Committee's attention to paragraph 7 of 104 EX/Decision 3.3 which reads:

> *Considering* that, in matters concerning human rights within its fields of competence, Unesco, basing its efforts on moral considerations and its specific competence, should act in a spirit of international co-operation, conciliation and mutual understanding; and *recalling* that Unesco should not play the role of an international judicial body.

On the basis of this provision, the Chairman believed that the communication as it stood could not be examined, it being understood that the authors of the communication could at a later date present a communication which did not question the foundations of a Member State and whose admissibility the Committee could then consider. The Director of the Division of Human Rights and Peace specified that the reference to paragraph 7 of 104 EX/Decision 3.3, which did not concern the conditions of admissibility, meant for the Secretariat that the communication would not be classed as a "communication" in the sense of the said decision. The Committee *decided* in conclusion to adopt the solution put forward by its Chairman.

167. Following the adoption of this decision, one member of the Committee pointed out that, while not wishing to prevent the Committee's reaching a consensus decision, he believed that this decision could constitute a precedent which went against 104 EX/Decision 3.3.

No. 92/79

Concerning *Yugoslavia*
Case of *Milovan Djilas*

Communication of 9 April 1979 submitted by
Georges Hainaut

Autumn 1979 session of the Committee on Conventions and Recommendations (108th session of the Executive Board)[1]

230. The author of the communication, who is a French citizen and the representative of the Universal Anticollectivist Alliance, alleges that the Yugoslav Government is violating freedom of expression by preventing the publication of any work which questions the regime of that country, as it is alleged to have done in the case of Milovan Djilas. The latter, who is said to have been imprisoned on several occasions, was allegedly called in by the police on 21 March 1979, when he is said to have been given a "last warning" regarding his activities "hostile" to Yugoslavia. The author believes that his communication directly concerns the fields of competence of Unesco, in viev of the violation of the freedom of expression.

231. The Yugoslav representative disputed the admissibility of the communication, firstly because the author did not have reliable knowledge of the alleged violations, as required under paragraph 14 (*a*) (ii) of 104 EX/Decision 3.3, and secondly because the communication, in view of its offensive character, was not in accordance with paragraph 14 (*a*) (vi) of the said decision. Furthermore, the Yugoslav representative stated that his government was not empovered to approve or disapprove of the publication of any work and that the publishing houses were the sole arbiters in the matter. However, the government was entitled to take proceedings against a writer once his work had been published. In reply to a question from a member of the Committee, the Yugoslav representative said that the most recent works of Mr Milovan Djilas had not been published in Yugoslavia, since Yugoslav publishing houses considered that they were not of sufficient interest to the Yugoslav public.

---

[1] See document 108 EX/38 PRIV., paras. 230-233; see also document 108 EX/CR/PROC.HR/1.

No. 92/79 **Yugoslavia**

232. The Chairman felt that it was disturbing that an author could not publish his works in his own country, but he considered that the communication was too vague for the Committee to be able to consider it admissible. He suggested, that the communication be rejected as being manifestly ill-founded.

233. The Committee endorsed the Chairman's opinion and *decided* that the communication was not admissible because it did not fulfil the requirements of paragraph 14 (*a*) (v) of 104 EX/Decision 3.3.

No. 94/79

Concerning *Yugoslavia*
Case of *Mihajlo Mihajlov*

Communication of 27 October 1978 submitted by
Zygmunt Elbiński

Spring 1979 session of the Committee on Conventions and Recommendations (107th session of the Executive Board)[1]

183. At the request of the government concerned, the representative of which was unable to attend the Committee's meeting as he was travelling, with the Director-General, in the disaster areas of his country, the Committee *decided* to defer consideration of the admissibility of the communication to its next session.

Autumn 1979 session of the Committee on Conventions and Recommendations (108th session of the Executive Board)[2]

234. The communication, consideration of the admissibility of which was deferred at the Committee's [spring 1979] session at the request of the government concerned,[3] alleges the violation of human rights as a result of the material, political and moral conditions to which the writer, Mihajlo Mihajlov, has been subjected, following his imprisonment. The author of the communication, who is of Polish nationality, explains that Mr Mihajlov was granted a presidential amnesty in 1977. In 1975, he had been condemned to seven years' imprisonment and was banned from writing and from speaking in public for four years after completion of his sentence, for having published articles deemed hostile to the Yugoslav socialist system. The articles of the Universal Declaration of Human Rights relating to the right to a fair trial, the right to impart information and ideas and the right to work are alleged to have been violated on this score. The author requests that Mihajlov's trial be reviewed and his

[1] See document 107 EX/PRIV.31, para. 183; see also document 107 EX/CR/PROC.HR/37.
[2] See document 108 EX/38 PRIV., paras. 234-240; see also document 108 EX/CR/PROC.HR/1.
[3] See document 107 EX/PRIV.31, para. 183 (*supra*, p. 247).

situation restored by giving him due moral and material satisfaction and that an official declaration be made specifying whether the ban on writing and on speaking in public for four years is maintained or not.

235. The representative of the government concerned considered that the communication was not admissible, firstly, because it did not fulfil the requirements laid down in paragraph 14 (*a*) (x) of 104 EX/Decision 3.3 since, as a result of the presidential amnesty, the problem had already been settled by the Yugoslav State in accordance with respect for human rights. In fact, Mr Mihajlov had been issued with a passport and was travelling abroad with his mother. Furthermore, the communication did not fulfil the condition laid down in paragraph 14 (*a*) (ii) of the said decision, because the author of the communication could not be regarded as being a person having reliable knowledge of the alleged facts, since he himself had admitted that he did not have such knowledge in his reply to part IV of the form for communications. Lastly, the communication was not in accordance with paragraph 14 (*a*) (v) and (vi) in view of its manifestly ill-founded and offensive character. In that connection, he called the Committee's attention to several passages in the communication dated 27 October 1978.

236. At the Committee's request, the Yugoslav representative confirmed that a four-year ban on writing and on speaking in public had indeed been imposed on Mr Mihajlov, as was permitted under Yugoslav law, and that that ban had started to take effect from the time of the amnesty from which he had benefited in 1977.

237. Several members of the Committee welcomed the fact that Mr Mihajlov had been freed, but expressed concern that a celebrated writer could be deprived of the right of expression, which was a human right of particular importance to Unesco. However, some members wondered to what extent the Committee could take action in cases where the domestic law of a State was involveded.

238. The Director of the Division of Human Rights and Peace recalled that paragraph 10 (*b*) of 104 EX/Decision 3.3 provided that Unesco was called upon to examine "questions of massive, systematic or flagrant violations of human rights which result either from a policy contrary to human rights applied *de jure* or *de facto* by a State ...". In point of fact, a *de jure* policy conducted by a State was bound to be in conformity with its national laws. It followed, therefore, that in considering such "questions", the Committee would be required to examine national laws, especially since, in most countries, international legislation pertaining to human rights normally rated more highly than domestic law. As far as individual cases were concerned, although the Committee might not consider that it was empowered to pass judgement on a legislative provision, it was in any event required to examine the consequences of the application of such a provision from the point of view of respect for

human rights. On the other hand, the Director of the Division of Human Rights and Peace wondered whether the Committee should examine a "potential" violation of human rights even before such a violation occurred. Since Mr Mihajlov was out of the country, it was impossible to tell whether the Yugoslav authorities would take proceedings against him on his return, or whether they would decide not to pursue the matter any further, on the basis of the principle that the prosecuting authority is not bound to take action in every case.

239. Lastly, with regard to the condition stipulated in paragraph 14 (*a*) (ii) of 104 EX/Decision 3.3, namely that if the authors of communications are not themselves the alleged victims, they must have reliable knowledge of the violation, he stated that, if the Committee so wished, the Secretariat could ask the authors to provide more precise explanations in such cases. The Chairman considered that the Secretariat was fully authorized to seek such explanations from authors.

240. In view of the information provided by the representative of the government concerned and of the opinions expressed by the members of the Committee, the Committee *decided*, at the Chairman's suggestion, to declare the communication inadmissible since it did not comply with the conditions laid down in paragraph 14 (*a*) (ii) and (v) of 104 EX/Decision. 3.3.

No. 95/79

Concerning *Yugoslavia*
Case of *Nikola Novaković*

Communication of 26 October 1978 submitted by
Zygmunt Elbiński

Autumn 1979 session of the Committee on Conventions and Recommendations (108th session of the Executive Board)[1]

241. The author of this communication, who is of Polish nationality, claims to be acting as a person with reliable knowledge of the alleged violation. He alleges that Articles 5, 10 and 19 of the Universal Declaration of Human Rights and Articles 7, 14 and 19 (2) of the International Covenant on Civil and Political Rights have been violated in the case of Mr Novaković, a pharmacologist of Yugoslav nationality. The latter is alleged to have been arrested by the Yugoslav secret police in March 1977 and kept in solitary confinement for four months before his trial, which resulted in his being sentenced to 12 years' imprisonment and to the confiscation of his property. The author demands that the legel proceedings taken against Mr Novaković be reviewed.

242. The representative of the Yugoslav Government disputed the admissibility of the communication on the grounds that it did not fulfil the conditions stipulated in paragraph 14 (*a*), (iii), (v) and (vi) of 104 EX/Decision 3.3, namely that it did not establish any link between the alleged violation and Unesco's fields of competence, it was manifestly ill-founded and offensive, and was an abuse of the right to submit communications. He quoted several passages of the communication in support of his statements. The Yugoslav representative also considered that the communication violated Article I of the Constitution of Unesco to which paragraph 6 of 104 EX/Decision 3.3 referred. He stated that the person concerned had been sentenced under normal procedure by a Yugoslav court for having violated Articles 109 and 118 of the Yugoslav Penal Code, as a result of having established contacts abroad with or-

[1] See document 108 EX/38 PRIV., paras. 241-243; see also document 108 EX/CR/PROC.HR/1.

No. 95/79 **Yugoslavia**

ganizations hostile to the State and of having disseminated propaganda hostile to the State.

243. After discussion, the Committee *decided* that the communication was inadmissible because it did not fulfil the requirement laid down in paragraph 14 (*a*) (iii) of 104 EX/Decision 3.3, the occupation of the alleged victim giving no grounds for presuming that there was a link with Unesco's fields of competence and there being no other element in the file establishing any such link.

No. 96/79

Concerning *Argentina*
Case of *María Inés Muchiutti*

Communication of 10 January 1979 submitted by
Elena Luisa Muchiutti de Poletta

Spring 1979 session of the Committee on Conventions and Recommendations (107th session of the Executive Board)[1]

112. The alleged victim is a psychologist, who is said to have been arrested on 16 August 1976. The representative of the government concerned pointed out that the alleged facts dated back too far for this communication to be considered admissible. Some members of the Committee considered that the time that had elapsed could be easily explained by the remedies to which recourse had been had, which are enumerated in part IV of the communication form. Other members of the Committee agreed that the alleged facts fell within the competence of Unesco.

113. The Committee consequently *decided* to declare this communication admissible.

Autumn 1979 session of the Committee on Conventions and Recommendations (108th session of the Executive Board)[2]

310. This communication, declared admissible by the Committee at its [spring] 1979 session,[3] concerns the case of a psychologist who is alleged to have been arrested on 16 August 1976. At its present session the Committee initiated its examination of the merits of the allegations declared admissible.

---

[1] See document 107 EX/PRIV.31, paras. 112-113; see also documents 107 EX/CR/PROC. HR/30 and Annex.

[2] See document 108 EX/38 PRIV., paras. 310-312; see also document 108 EX/CR/PROC.HR/ 2.

[3] See document 107 EX/PRIV.31, para. 113 (*supra*, p. 253).

No. 96/79 **Argentina**

311. The representative of the government concerned informed the Committee that the Inter-American Commission on Human Rights was currently investigating this case. He repeated that the alleged victim's name did not figure on any of the lists of persons imprisoned in his country.

312. The Committee *decided* to apply in this case the special procedure concerning communications relating to missing persons, adopted on 10 September 1979 [...],[4] and *instructed* the Secretariat to obtain any further information from the Inter-American Commission on Human Rights.

---

[4] See document 108 EX/38 PRIV., para. 16.

No. 97/79

Concerning *Argentina*
Case of *Analía Egle María Minetti*

Communication of 27 February 1979 submitted by
Helder Pablo Minetti

Spring 1979 session of the Committee on Conventions and Recommendations (107th session of the Executive Board)[1]

114. This communication concerns the disappearance on 7 March 1977 of the alleged victim, who is said to be a student. The representative of the government concerned noted that there was nothing to suggest that there was a relationship between the alleged violation and the fields of competence of Unesco.

115. Several members of the Committee noted that the author of the communication had stated on the relevant form that the occupation of the alleged victim was that of "student" and that he had been entitled to believe that such an indication was sufficient to show the relationship with Unesco's fields of competence. After some discussion, the Committee *decided* to defer consideration of the admissibility of the communication until such time as the Secretariat had obtained the necessary details from the author of the communication as to the link between the alleged facts and Unesco's fields of competence.

Autumn 1979 session of the Committee on Conventions and Recommendations (108th session of the Executive Board)[2]

62. This communication, which the Committee already examined at its [spring 1979] session, concerns the disappearance of the daughter of the author, aged 24, who was reportedly abducted on 6 March 1977 in Rosario, Argentina. At the Com-

---

[1] See document 107 EX/PRIV.31, paras. 114-115; see also document 107 EX/CR/PROC.HR/38.

[2] See document 108 EX/38 PRIV., paras. 62-66; see also documents 108 EX/CR/PROC.HR/1 and Add.4.

mittee's request, the Secretariat asked the author of the communication for fuller information concerning the student status of Miss Minetti and the link between the alleged violation and Unesco's fields of competence. Attached to the reply received by the Secretariat [...][3] were Miss Minetti's enrolment certificates in a secondary school and a college providing courses in shorthand and typing. Miss Minetti's mother also indicates in her letter that her daughter took part in the activities of the Organization of Secondary-School Students, which has the objective of defending students' rights, specifying that a similar organization exists at the university level.

63. The representative of the government concerned did not contest the fact of the alleged victim's having received secondary education, but he considered that such education did not provide grounds for her being regarded as a "student". Since Miss Minetti had completed her secondary education some six years before the alleged abduction and as her shorthand and typing studies could only be regarded as a course of further training outside her working hours, she was not, according to the Argentine representative, a student at the time of her alleged abduction. He added that, in point of fact, Miss Minetti was on the wanted list by virtue of law 24.840 and was considered to be on the run. He was not in a position to state what the charges against her were.

64. Several members of the Committee did not subscribe to the restrictive interpretation of student status proposed by the Argentine representative. Others suggested that the Secretariat might possibly study the criteria governing such status.

65. One member considered that participation by the person concerned in the activities of a students' union or association could constitute grounds for presuming the existence of a link between the alleged abduction and Unesco's fields of competence, thereby rendering the communication admissible. The representative of Argentina replied that all secondary-school students were members of the Organization of Secondary-School Students, but that it was not normal for a person aged 24 to continue to be a member of such an organization. He suggested that the Secretariat request the Unesco Office in Buenos Aires to seek clarification on this subject.

66. The Committee *decided* to suspend examination of the admissibility of this communication until such time as the Secretariat could obtain further details from the author concerning the connection between the alleged victim's participation in the Organization of Secondary-School Students and her abduction, and information from the government concerned regarding the charges against Miss Minetti and the present situation in regard to the efforts being made to establish her whereabouts.

---

[3] See document 108 EX/CR/PROC.HR/1 Add.4.

Argentina **No. 97/79**

Spring 1980 session of the Committee on Conventions and Recommendations (109th session of the Executive Board)[4]

17. The author of this communication alleged that his daughter, a student, was abducted on 7 March 1977 by persons claiming to belong to the security forces of the Rosario Police (Province of Santa Fe) in a street in the town of Rosario. The examination of the admissibility of this communication had been suspended for a seconed time by the Committee at its [autumn 1979] session in order to obtain further information about the alleged victim's activities and her abduction.[5]

18. The representative of the Argentine Government reiterated his government's view that the alleged victim did not warrant Unesco's intervention since the shorthand and typing courses [followed] by her would not qualify her as a "student" in a way that would concern Unesco. He also reminded the Committee that the Argentine authorities were actively searching for this person in connection with a violation of Argentina's law 24.800.

19. A member of the Committee, agreeing with the position of the Argentine Government, stated that the communication failed to satisfy an admissibility requirement in that it did not contain relevant evidence.

20. Another member of the Committee pointed out that the admissibility requirement referred to required only that the communication "appear to" contain relevant evidence, the weighing of the relevance of the evidence being done after the communication was declared admissible. He also reminded the Committee that Unesco's fields of competence definitely covered persons involved in technical and vocational education, as could be seen from Unesco's programme and from its Recommendation on Technical and Vocational Education.

21. In view of the existing precedents the Committee *decided* to declare admissible the communication in question and to apply to it the special procedure for missing persons.[6]

---

[4] See document 109 EX/52 PRIV., paras. 17-21; see also document 109 EX/CR/HR/2.
[5] See document 108 EX/38 PRIV., para. 66 (*supra*, p. 256).
[6] See documents 108 EX/38 PRIV., para. 16, and 109 EX/52 PRIV., annex I, para. 8, and Corr.

No. 98/79

Concerning *Argentina*
Case of *Mariano Alejandro Ramiro Martínez*

Communication of 5 February 1979 submitted by
Lucrecia Ramona Villalonga de Martínez

Spring 1979 session of the Committee on Conventions and Recommendations (107th session of the Executive Board)[1]

116. This communication concerns the case of a photographer who is said to have been abducted on 27 January 1977. Since there was no indication of any relationship between the alleged violation and Unesco's fields of competence, the Committee *decided* to declare the communication inadmissible.

[1] See document 107 EX/PRIV.31, para. 116; see also document 107 EX/CR/PROC.HR/39.

No. 103/79

Concerning *Uruguay*
Case of *José Luis Massera*

Communication of 11 March 1979 submitted by
Jean-Claude Pecker

Spring 1979 session of the Committee on Conventions and Recommendations (107th session of the Executive Board)[1]

178. As stated [elsewhere in] this report,[2] the case of José Luis Massera was the subject of two communications transmitted to the Committee in conformity with 77 EX/ Decision 8.3 [...],[3] communications which the Committee had decided to keep on its agenda [...].[4] Before re-examining these communications according to the former procedure, the Committee thought it preferable to rule on the admissibility of [the present communication]. This communication alleged violation of Articles 19, 26 and 27 of the Universal Declaration of Human Rights, of Articles 13 and 15 of the International Covenant on Economic, Social and Cultural Rights, and of Articles 14, paragraph 3, and 19 of the International Covenant on Civil and Political Rights, concerning Professor Massera, who had been in dentention, together with his wife, since November 1975. Attached to [the communication] was a copy of a petition signed by 3,310 members of scientific and mathematical institutions in 24 countries.

179. By virtue of paragraph 14 (*f*) of 104 EX/Decision 3.3 whereby "the Committee may avail itself of the relevant information at the disposal of the Director-General", the Director of the Division of Human Rights and Peace drew the attention of the Committee to a very full dossier on the case sent to the Director-General by the Interparliamentary Union, which was actively pursuing the case in view of the fact that the person concerned was also a Senator.

[1] See document 107 EX/PRIV.31, paras. 178-182; see also documents 107 EX/CR/PROC. HR/36 and Annex.
[2] *Ibidem*, para. 47.
[3] See document 107 EX/CR/PRIV.1.
[4] See document 105 EX/49 PRIV., para. 60.

No. 103/79 **Uruguay**

180. It is apparent from the information provided by the representative of the Government of Uruguay in his letter of 19 April 1979 [...][5] and orally presented to the Committee, that Mr Massera is charged with "subversive association", an offence penalized under article 60 (V) of the military Penal Code. His dossier, which is at present in the hands of the military judge, is in the process of being communicated to his lawyer. According to a Commission sent by the National Academy of Science of the United States of America, Mr Massera and his wife are in good health, Mr Massera regularly receives his correspondence and is continuing his intellectual work.

181. The Committee, after having examined [the communication] and the reply made by the Uruguayan Government with respect to this case, *decided* to declare this communication admissible and to combine examination of the merits with that of the communications transmitted to the Committee, in accordance with 77 EX/Decision 8.3.

182. Various members of the Committee stressed the importance which many people throughout the world attached to the release of this scholar and expressed the wish that an appeal for that release should be transmitted to the authorities of Uruguay. With a view to the preparation of the examination of the merits of the Massera case at its next session, the Committee *instructed* the Secretariat to request further information from the authors of the communications and from the authorities in Uruguay, and *expressed the hope* that the competent authorities would see their way to exercising clemency towards Mr Massera and his wife.

Autumn 1979 session of the Committee on Conventions and Recommendations (108th session of the Executive Board)[6]

326. At its [spring 1979] session, when the Committee declared this communication admissible, together with the communications on the same case transmitted in accordance with 77 EX/Decision 8.3, it had also instructed the Secretariat to request further information from the authors of the communications and from the Uruguayan authorities, and had expressed the hope that the competent authorities would see their way to exercising clemency towards Mr Massera and his wife.[7]

327. Since that decision, the Secretariat had received a letter from Mr J. Dieudonné, acting on behalf of Mr J.-C. Pecker, the author of the communication, dated 25 Au-

[5] See document 107 EX/CR/PROC.HR/36 Annex.

[6] See document 108 EX/38 PRIV., paras. 326-331; see also documents 108 EX/CR/PROC. HR/2 and Add.2 and 3.

[7] See document 107 EX/PRIV.31, paras. 181-182 (*supra*, p. 262).

gust 1979 [...],[8] reporting information obtained by Mr Dieudonné during a visit to Uruguay in July 1979. According to this information Mr Massera, who had been kept in solitary confinement for one year, had by 25 August 1979 not yet been brought to trial. Except for the after-effects of the fall he suffered in 1975 reportedly due to the fact that he had been roughly handled by soldiers when he was bound hand and foot, he appeared to be in good health, and he had been allowed to consult a lawyer.

328. The Secretariat had also received a letter from the Uruguayan delegation [...][9] stating that Mr Massera was brought before a military trial judge on 22 October 1976; and that he is being held in Penitentiary Establishment No. 1. A medical report on Mr Massera's state of health was enclosed with the letter from the government.

329. The representative of the government concerned expressed the hope that consideration of this case would be deferred to the next session of the Committee, in order to enable his government to study Mr Dieudonné's letter, which it had received only on 11 September. In reply to a question by a member of the Committee, the Director of the Division of Human Rights and Peace confirmed that the letter sent to the government concerned after the [spring 1979] session of the Committee recalled that the Committee had expressed the hope that clemency would be exercised towards Mr Massera and his wife, but that the government had not replied on this point. The Uruguayan representative stated that he had no information to give.

330. Several members of the Committee considered that Unesco should repeat its request for clemency to the Uruguayan authorities.

331. The Committee accordingly *decided* to recommend that the Executive Board request the Director-General to address on its behalf an appeal to the Uruguayan Government to exercise clemency towards Professor Massera and his wife. The Committee also *decided* to resume consideration of the communication at its next session, and to this end *invited* the government concerned to provide it with any relevant information, including its reply to the detailed information contained in Mr Dieudonné's letter of 25 August 1979.

[8] See document 108 EX/CR/PROC.HR/2 Add.2.
[9] See document 108 EX/CR/PROC.HR/2 Add.3.

No. 103/79 **Uruguay**

Spring 1980 session of the Committee on Conventions and Recommendations (109th session of the Executive Board)[10]

279. The author of this communication, a professor at the Collège de France, acting on his own behalf and that of the Comité pour la défense des hommes de science de l'Académie des Sciences (France), alleged violation of Article 19 of the Universal Declaration of Human Rights and of the International Covenant on Civil and Political Rights (freedom of opinion and expression), of Article 26 of the Universal Declaration of Human Rights and Article 13 of the International Covenant on Economic, Social and Cultural Rights (the right to education), and of Article 27 of the Universal Declaration of Human Rights and Article 15 of the International Covenant on Economic, Social and Cultural Rights (the right to participate in cultural life) with respect to the Uruguayan professor of mathematics, José Luis Massera, who has been in prison since November 1975, as has his wife. The author also alleged violation of Article 14, paragraph 3, of the International Covenant on Civil and Political Rights (guarantees in the event of criminal charges). He also pointed out that Professor Massera has been prevented from accepting an invitation to teach in a Paris university.

280. The author enclosed with his communication a copy of a petition signed by 3,310 members of scientific and mathematical institutions in 24 countries. This petition reads as follows:

> We who sign below, mathematicians end scientists of several countries, express our most profound concern for the situation in which the great Uruguayan mathematician José Luís Massera finds himself.
>
> We request of the authorities of Uruguay the prompt release of Dr Massera and his wife and ask that his works created in prison be released also for the use of the scientific community.

281. This communication was declared admissible by the Committee at its [spring] 1979 session. The Committee, at that session, decided to add this communication to those concerning the same case that were pending in accordance with 77 EX/Decision 8.3. It also instructed the Secretariat to request further information from the authors of the communications and from the Uruguayan authorities, and expressed the hope that the competent authorities would see their way to exercising clemency towards Mr Massera and his wife.[11]

---

[10] See document 109 EX/52 PRIV., paras. 279-292; see also documents 109 EX/CR/HR/1 and Add.3.

[11] See document 107 EX/PRIV.31, paras. 181-182 (*supra*, p. 262).

Uruguay **No. 103/79**

282. Before the [autumn] 1979 session, the Secretariat received a letter from Mr. J. Dieudonné acting on behalf of Mr J.-C. Pecker, the author of the communication, dated 25 August 1979, reporting information obtained by Mr Dieudonné during a visit to Uruguay in July 1979. According to this information Mr Massera, who had been kept in solitary confinement for one year, had not yet been brought to trial. Except for the after-effects of the fall he suffered in 1975 reportedly due to the fact that he had been roughly handled by soldiers while he was bound hand and foot, he appeared to be in good health, and he had been allowed to consult a lawyer.

283. The Secretariat had also received a letter from the Uruguayan Delegation stating that Mr Massera was brought before a military trial judge on 22 October 1976, and that he was being held in Penitentiary Establishment No. 1. A medical report on Mr Massera's state of health was enclosed with the letter from the government.

284. The representative of the government concerned expressed the hope that consideration of this case would be deferred to the next session of the Committee, in order to enable his government to study Mr Dieudonné's letter, which it had received only on 11 September. In reply to a question by a member of the Committee, the Director of the Division of Human Rights and Peace confirmed that the letter sent to the government concerned after the [spring 1979] session of the Committee recalled that the Committee had expressed the hope that clemency would be exercised towards Mr Massera and his wife, but that the government had not replied on this point. The Uruguayan representative stated that he had no information to give.

285. Several members of the Committee considered that Unesco should repeat its request for clemency to the Uruguayan authorities.

286. The Committee accordingly decided to recommend that the Executive Board request the Director-General to address on its behalf an appeal to the Uruguayan Government to exercise clemency towards Professor Massera and his wife. The Committee also decided to resume consideration of the communication at its next session, and to this end invited the government concerned to provide it with any relevant information, including its reply to the detailed information contained in Mr Dieudonné's letter of 25 August 1979.[12]

287. On 20 and 28 November 1979 respectively, the Secretariat wrote to the author of the communication and the government concerned.

---

[12] See document 108 EX/38 PRIV., para. 331 (*supra*, p. 263).

No. 103/79 **Uruguay**

288. In a letter dated 28 November 1979, sent to the Minister of Foreign Relations of Uruguay, the Director-General appealed for clemency for Professor Massera and his wife.

289. At its present session, the Committee had before it a letter addressed by the Uruguayan Delegation on 21 April 1980 [...][13] to the Director-General in which the position of the Uruguayan Government was set forth. It stated that:

> (1) The government maintained formal and substantive reservations as to the Committee's competence in the field of human rights, but that it had always co-operated with the Committee out of respect for Unesco.
>
> (2) That Professor Massera, contrary to the allegation that he "had not yet been brought to trial", was as a matter of fact sentenced on 23 July 1979 by the Second Military Court of First Instance to a term of 20 years' imprisonment.
>
> (3) Any decision concerning the case of Mr Massera would have to be taken in a strictly legal context, for which purpose the proper criminal proceedings are being pursued with every legal guarantee by the competent judicial body in accordance with Uruguayan law. The time spent in custody by Mr Massera would be deducted from the sentence finally imposed.
>
> (4) The reason why Mr Messera was imprisoned was not on account of the ideology he professed but on account of the fact that he occupied the post of Secretary-General of a party that had been declared illegal, continuing to operate covertly after its proscription and maintaining close relations with the military apparatus of that party, the ultimate aim of which was to take over power by illegal means.
>
> (5) As for Mrs Martha Valentini de Massera, she was released in August 1979 by order of the competent judicial body in whose custody she had been held up to that time.

290. The Representative of the Uruguayan Government reiterated to the Committee the position outlined in the aforementioned letter.

291. Several members of the Committee felt that it was important to take note of the fact that Mrs Massera had been released and hoped that a simlar attitude might be adopted *vis-à-vis* Professor Massera himself.

---

[13] See document 109 EX/CR/HR/1 Add.3.

Uruguay **No. 103/79**

292. After discussion, the Committee *decided* to recommend the Executive Board to ask the Director-General to address on its behalf, once again, an appeal to the Uruguayan Government to exercise clemency and ensure the rapid release of Professor Massera, and to continue his own efforts in this matter.

Autumn 1980 session of the Committee on Conventions and Recommendations (110th session of the Executive Board)[14]

312. The author of this communication, a professor at the Collège de France, acting on his own behalf and that of the Comité pour la défense des hommes de science de l'Académie des Sciences (France), alleges violation of Article 19 of the Universal Declaration of Human Rights and of the International Covenant on Civil and Political Rights (freedom of opinion and expession), of Article 26 of the Universal Declaration of Human Rights and Article 13 of the International Covenant on Economic, Social and Cultural Rights (the right to education), and of Article 27 of the Universal Declaration of Human Rights and Article 15 of the International Covenant on Economic, Social and Cultural Rights (the right to participate in cultural life) with respect to the Uruguayan professor of mathematics, José Luis Massera, who has been in prison since November 1975, as has his wife. The author also alleges violation of Article 14, paragraph 3, of the International Covenant on Civil and Political Rights (guarantees in the event of criminal charges). He also points out that Professor Massera has been prevented from accepting an invitation to teach in a Paris university.

313. This communication was declared admissible by the Committee at its [spring] 1979 session. The Committee, at that session, decided to add this communication to those concerning the same case that were pending in accordance with 77 EX/Decision 8.3. It also instructed the Secretariat to request further information from the authors of the communications and from the Uruguayan authorities, and expressed the hope that the competent authorities would see their way to exercising clemency towards Mr Massera and his wife.[15]

314. At its [autumn] 1979 session, the Committee decided to recommend that the Executive Board request the Director-General to address on its behalf an appeal to the Uruguayan Government for clemency towards Professor Massera and his wife. The Committee further decided to resume examination of the communication at the [spring 1980] session and for that purpose invited the government concerned to pro-

---

[14] See document 110 EX/40 PRIV., paras. 312-323; see also documents 110 EX/CR/HR/1 and Add.2.

[15] See document 107 EX/PRIV.31, paras. 181-182 (*supra*, p. 262).

vide it with any useful information on the substance of the allegations made by the authors of the communication.[16]

315. In a letter dated 28 November 1979, sent to the Minister of Foreign Relations of Uruguay, the Director-General appealed for clemency for Professor Massera and his wife.

316. At its [spring 1980] session, the Committee had before it a letter of 21 April 1980 addressed by the Uruguyan delegation to the Director-General in which the position of the Uruguayan Goverment was set forth. It stated that:

> (1) the government maintained formal and substantive reservations as to the Committee's competence in the field of human rights, but that it had always co-operated with the Committee out of respect for Unesco;
>
> (2) Professor Massera, contrary to the allegation that he "had not yet been brought to trial", was as a matter of fact sentenced on 23 July 1979 by the Second Military Court of First Instance to a term of 20 years' imprisonment;
>
> (3) any decision concerning the case of Mr Massera would have to be taken in a strictly legal context, for which purpose the proper criminal proceedings are being pursued with every legal guarantee by the competent judicial body in accordance with Uruguayan law. The time spent in custody by Mr Massera would be deducted from the sentence finally imposed;
>
> (4) the reason why Mr Messera was imprisoned was not on account of the ideology he professed but on account of the fact that he occupied the post of Secretary-General of a party that had been declared illegal, continuing to operate covertly after its proscription and maintaining close relations with the military apparatus of that party, the ultimate aim of which was to take over power by illegal means;
>
> (5) as to Mrs Martha Valentini de Massera, she was released in August 1979 by order of the competent judicial body in whose custody she had been held up to that time.

317. Several members of the Committee considered that it was important to take note of the fact that Mrs Massera had been released, and expressed the hope that a similar step would be taken in respect of Professor Massera himself.

---

[16] See document 108 EX/38 PRIV., para. 331 (*supra*, p. 263).

Uruguay **No. 103/79**

318. After discussion, the Committee decided to recommend that the Executive Board request the Director-General to address on its behalf a fresh appeal to the Uruguayan Government to exercise clemency and release Professor Massera soon, and to continue his own efforts in connection with the case.[17]

319. At the present session, the representative of the Uruguayan Government informed the Committee that the Under-Secretary of State for Foreign Affairs of his country had discussed the case of Professor José Luis Massera with the Director-General during the present session.

320. Several members expressed their satisfaction that the request submitted to the Director-General by the Executive Board had culminated in such high-level talks but said they were disappointed that those talks had not been completed. One member asked whether the Committee could obtain additional information on the substance of the exchanges of views and as to when the request for release lodged by the authors of the communication would be heard. One member of the Committee observed that 13 months had elapsed since the ruling of the Court of First Instance and that the date for hearing of the appeal was still not known.

321. The representative of the Director-General said that the Director-General would no doubt wish himself to give an account of his discussions to the Executive Board. It might accordingly be desirable to postpone examination of the communication to the next session.

322. The representative of the Uruguayan Government considered that the Director-General was certainly the person in the best position to give an account of the conversations which had taken place at such a high level.

323. The Committee consequently *decided*:

[i] to take note of the information provided;

[ii] to postpone examination of the substance of this communication to the next session of the Committee;

[iii] to request the Director-General to give the Executive Board any information he deemed desirable on the progress of his humanitarian representations.

---

[17] See document 109 EX/52 PRIV., para. 292 (*supra*, p. 267).

No. 103/79 **Uruguay**

Spring 1981 session of the Committee on Conventions and Recommendations (112th session of the Executive Board)[18]

536. The author of this communication, Jean-Claude Pecker, a professor at the Collège de France, acting on his own behalf and that of the Comité pour la défense des hommes de science de l'Académie des Sciences (France), alleges violation of Article 19 of the Universal Declaration of Human Rights and of the International Covenant on Civil and Political Rights (freedom of opinion and expression), of Article 26 of the Universal Declaration of Human Rights and Article 13 of the International Covenant on Economic, Social and Cultural Rights (the right to education), and of Article 27 of the Universal Declaration of Human Rights and Article 15 of the International Covenant on Economic, Social and Cultural Rights (the right to participate in cultural life) with respect to the Uruguayan professor of mathematics, José Luis Massera, who has been in prison since November 1975, as has his wife. The author also alleges violation of Article 14, paragraph 3, of the International Covenant on Civil and Political Rights (guarantees in the event of criminal charges). He also points out that Professor Massera has been prevented from accepting an invitation to teach in a Paris university.

537. The author encloses with his communication a copy of a petition signed by 3,310 members of scientific and mathematical institutions in 24 countries. This petition, which can be consulted in the Secretariat, reads as follows:

> We, who sign below, mathematicians and scientists of several countries, express our most profound concern for the situation in which the great Uruguayan mathematician José Luis Massera finds himself.
>
> We request of the authorities of Uruguay the prompt release of Dr Massera and his wife and ask that his works created in prison be released also for the use of the scientific community.

538. This communication had been declared admissible by the Committee at its [spring] 1979 session. The Committee, at that session, had decided to add this communication to those concerning the same case that were pending in accordance with 77 EX/Decision 8.3. It had also instructed the Secretariat to request further information from the authors of the communications and from the Uruguayan authorities, and had expressed the hope that the competent authorities would see their way to exercising clemency towards Dr Massera and his wife.[19]

---

[18] See document 112 EX/30 PRIV., paras. 536-557; see also document 112 EX/CR/HR/1.
[19] See document 107 EX/PRIV.31, paras. 181-182 (*supra*, p. 262).

Uruguay **No. 103/79**

539. Before the [autumn] 1979 session, the Secretariat had received from Mr J. Dieudonné, acting on behalf of Mr J.-C. Pecker, a letter dated 25 August 1979, reporting information obtained by Mr Dieudonné during a visit to Uruguay in July 1979. According to this information, Dr Massera, who had been kept in solitary confinement for one year, had not yet been brought to trial. Except for the after-effects of the fall he suffered in 1975 reportedly due to the fact that he had been roughly handled by soldiers while he was bound hand and foot, he appeared to be in good health, and he had been allowed to consult a lawyer.

540. The Secretariat had also received a letter from the Uruguayan Delegation [...] stating that Dr Massera had been brought before a military trial judge on 22 October 1976 and that he was being held in Penitentiary Establishnent No. 1. A medical report on Dr Massera's state of health had been enclosed with the letter from the government.

541. The representative of the government concerned had expressed the hope that consideration of this case would be deferred to the next session of the Committee, in order to enable his government to study Mr Dieudonné's letter, which it had received only on 11 September. In reply to a question by a member of the Committee, the Director of the Division of Human Rights and Peace had confirmed that the letter sent to the government concerned after the [spring] 1979 session recalled that the Committee had expressed the hope that clemency would be exercised towards Dr Massera and his wife, but that the government had not replied on this point. The Uruguayan representative had stated that he had no information to give.

542. Several members of the Committee had considered that Unesco should repeat its request for clemency to the Uruguayan authorities.

543. The Committee had accordingly decided to recommend that the Executive Board request the Director-General to address on its behalf an appeal to the Uruguayan Government to exercise clemency towards Professor Massera and his wife. The Committee had also decided to resume consideration of the communication at the [spring 1980] session, and to this end had invited the government concerned to provide it with any relevant information, including its reply to the detailed information contained in Mr Dieudonné's letter of 25 August 1979.[20]

544. On 20 and 28 November 1979 respectively, the Secretariat wrote to the author of the communication and the government concerned.

---

[20] See document 108 EX/38 PRIV., para. 331 (*supra*, p. 263).

No. 103/79 **Uruguay**

545. In a letter dated 28 November 1979, sent to the Minister of Foreign Relations of Uruguay, the Director-General had appealed to the Uruguayan Government for clemency for Professor Massera and his wife.

546. At the [spring] 1980 session, the Committee had had before it a letter addressed by the Uruguayan delegation on 21 April 1980 to the Director-General in which the position of the Uruguayan Government was set forth. It stated that:

(1) the government maintained formal and substantive reservations as to the Committee's competence in the field of human rights, but that it had always co-operated with the Committee out of respect for Unesco;

(2) Dr Massera, contrary to the allegation that he "had not yet been brought to trial", had, as a matter of fact, been sentenced on 23 July 1979 by the Military Court of First Instance to a term of 20 years' imprisonment;

(3) any decision concerning the case of Dr Massera would have to be taken in a strictly legal context, for which purpose the proper criminal proceedings were being pursued by the competent judicial body with every safeguard provided under Uruguayan law. The time spent in custody by Dr Massera would be deducted from the sentence finally imposed;

(4) Dr Massera had been imprisoned not on account of the ideology he professed but on account of the fact that he occupied the post of Secretary-General of a party that had been declared illegal, continuing to operate covertly after its proscription and maintaining close relations with the military apparatus of that party, the ultimate aim of which was to take over power by illegal means;

(5) as for Mrs Martha Valentini de Massera, she had been released in August 1979 by order of the competent judicial body in whose custody she had been held up to that time.

547. The representative of the Uruguayan Government had reiterated to the Committee the position outlined above.

548. Several members of the Committee had felt that it was important to take note of the fact that Mrs Massera had been released, and had hoped that a similar attitude might be adopted *vis-à-vis* Dr Massera himself.

549. After discussion, the Committee had decided to recommend the Executive Board to ask the Director-General to address on its behalf, once again, an appeal to

the Uruguayan Government to exercise clemency and ensure the rapid release of Dr Massera, and to continue his own efforts in this matter.[21]

550. At the [autumn] 1980 session, the representative of the Uruguayan Government had informed the Committee that the Under-Secretary of State for Foreign Affairs of his country had discussed the case of Dr José Luis Massera with the Director-General during the session.

551. Several members had expressed their satisfaction that the request submitted to the Director-General by the Executive Board had culminated in such high-level talks but had said they were disappointed that those talks had not been completed. One member had asked whether the Committee could obtain additional information on the substance of the exchanges of views and as to when the request for release lodged by the authors of the communication would be heard. One member of the Committee had observed that 13 months had elapsed since the ruling of the Court of First Instance and that the date for hearing of the appeal was still not known.

552. The representative of the Director-General had said that the Director-General would no doubt wish himself to give an account of his discussions to the Executive Board. It might accordingly be desirable to postpone examination of the communication to the next session.

553. The representative of the Uruguayan Government had considered that the Director-General was certainly the person in the best position to give an account of the conversations which had taken place at such a high level.

554. The Committee consequently decided at the [autumn 1980] session:[22]

> [i] to take note of the information provided;
>
> [ii] to postpone examination of the substance of this communication to the next session of the Committee;
>
> [iii] to request the Director-General to give the Executive Board any information he deemed desirable on the progress of his humanitarian representations.

555. At the present session, the representative of the Government of Uruguay declared that:

---

[21] See document 109 EX/52 PRIV., para. 292 (*supra*, p. 267).

[22] See document 110 EX/40 PRIV., para. 323 (*supra*, p. 269).

from the legal point of view, since legal proceedings were continuing, the executive of his country could not intervene, because of the principle of the separation of powers;

from the humanitarian point of view, there might be a possibility of exercising clemency when final judgement had been delivered. An appeal was pending in Dr Massera's case; the exact date of the hearing - which would be held in public with all legal safeguards - was not known, but it would be held during the current year.

556. Some members of the Committee said they did not wish to cast doubt on the soundness of the legal decision concerning the alleged victim but felt it a pity they could not be informed of the date of the hearing.

557. Following an exchange of views, it was soon generally agreed that, since the government concerned had shown itself sensitive and receptive to the appeal made by scientists from all over the world, the Director-General should be asked to continue making personal representations as provided for in paragraph 8 of 104 EX/Decision 3.3 and that this communication should remain on the list in keeping with the spirit of subparagraph 14 (*k*) of that decision. The Committee so *decided*.

Autumn 1981 session of the Committee on Conventions and Recommendations (113th session of the Executive Board)[23]

582. The author of this communication, Jean-Claude Pecker, a professor at the Collège de France, acting on his own behalf and that of the Comité pour la défense des hommes de science de l'Académie des Sciences (France), alleges violation of Article 19 of the Universal Declaration of Human Rights and of the International Covenant on Civil and Political Rights (freedom of opinion and expression), of Article 26 of the Universal Declaration of Human Rights and Article 13 of the International Covenant on Economic, Social and Cultural Rights (the right to education), and of Article 27 of the Universal Declaration of Human Rights and Article 15 of the International Covenant on Economic, Social and Cultural Rights (the right to participate in cultural life) with respect to the Uruguayan professor of mathematics, José Luis Massera, who has been in prison since November 1975, as has his wife. The author also alleges violation of Article 14, paragraph 3, of the International Covenant on Civil and Political Rights (guarantees in the event of criminal charges). He also

[23] See document 113 EX/38 PRIV., paras. 582-610; see also documents 113 EX/CR/HR/1 and Add.

points out that Professor Massera has been prevented from accepting an invitation to teach in a Paris university.

583. The author encloses with his communication a copy of a petition signed by 3,310 members of scientific and mathematical institutions in 24 countries. This petition, which can be consulted in the Secretariat, reads as follows:

> We, who sign below, mathematicians and scientists of several countries, express our most profound concern for the situation in which the great Uruguayan mathematician José Luis Massera finds himself.
>
> We request of the authorities of Uruguay the prompt release of Dr Massera and his wife and ask that his works created in prison be released also for the use of the scientific community.

584. This communication was declared admissible by the Committee at its [spring] 1979 session. The Committee, at that session, decided to add this communication to those concerning the same case that were pending in accordance with 77 EX/Decision 8.3. It also instructed the Secretariat to request further information from the authors of the communications and from the Uruguayan authorities, and expressed the hope that the competent authorities would see their way to exercising clemency to wards Dr Massera and his wife.[24]

585. Before the [autumn] 1979 session, the Secretariat received from Mr J. Dieudonné, acting on behalf of Mr J.-C. Pecker, a letter dated 25 August 1979, reporting information obtained by Mr Dieudonné during a visit to Uruguay in July 1979. According to this information, Dr Massera, who had been kept in solitary confinement for one year, had not yet been brought to trial. Except for the after-effects of the fall he suffered in 1975 reportedly due to the fact that he had been roughly handled by soldiers while he was bound hand and foot, he appeared to be in good health, and he had been allowed to consult a lawyer.

586. The Secretariat also received a letter from the Uruguayan Delegation [...] stating that Dr Massera had been brought before a military trial judge on 22 October 1976 and that he was being held in Penitentiary Establishment No. 1. A medical report on Dr Massera's state of health was enclosed with the letter from the government.

587. The representative of the government concerned expressed the hope that consideration of this case would be deferred to the next session of the Committee, in

---

[24] See document 107 EX/PRIV.31, paras. 181-182 (*supra*, p. 262).

order to enable his government to study Mr Dieudonné's letter, which it had received only on 11 September. In reply to a question by a member of the Committee, the Director of the Division of Human Rights and Peace confirmed that the letter sent to the government concerned after the [spring] 1979 session recalled that the Committee had expressed the hope that clemency would be exercised towards Dr Massera and his wife, but that the government had not replied on this point. The Uruguayan representative stated that he had no information to give.

588. Several members of the Committee considered that Unesco should repeat its request for clemency to the Uruguayan authorities.

589. The Committee accordingly decided to recommend that the Executive Board request the Director-General to address on its behalf an appeal to the Uruguayan Government to exercise clemency towards Professor Massera and his wife. The Committee also decided to resume consideration of the communication at the [spring 1980] session, and to this end invited the government concerned to provide it with any relevant information, including its reply to the detailed information contained in Mr Dieudonné's letter of 25 August 1979.[25]

590. On 20 and 28 November 1979 respectively, the Secretariat wrote to the author of the communication and the government concerned.

591. In a letter dated 28 November 1979, sent to the Minister of Foreign Relations of Uruguay, the Director-General appealed to the Uruguayan Government for clemency for Professor Massera and his wife.

592. At the [spring] 1980 session, the Committee had before it a letter addressed by the Uruguayan delegation on 21 April 1980 to the Director-General in which the position of the Uruguayan Government was set forth. It stated that:

> (1) the government maintained formal and substantive reservations as to the Committee's competence in the field of human rights, but that it had always co-operated with the Committee out of respect for Unesco;
>
> (2) Dr Massera, contrary to the allegation that he "had not yet been brought to trial", had, as a matter of fact, been sentenced on 23 July 1979 by the Military Court of First Instance to a term of 20 years' imprisonment;
>
> (3) any decision concerning the case of Dr Massera would have to be taken in a strictly legal context, for which purpose the proper criminal proceedings

---

[25] See document 108 EX/38 PRIV., para. 331 (*supra*, p. 263).

were being pursued by the competent judicial body with every safeguard provided under Uruguayan law. The time spent in custody by Dr Massera would be deducted from the sentence finally imposed;

(4) Dr Massera had been imprisoned not on account of the ideology he professed but on account of the fact that he occupied the post of Secretary-General of a party that had been declared illegal, continuing to operate covertly after its proscription and maintaining close relations with the military apparatus of that party, the ultimate aim of which was to take over power by illegal means;

(5) as for Mrs Martha Valentini de Massera, she had been released in August 1979 by order of the competent judicial body in whose custody she had been held up to that time.

593. The representative of the Uruguayan Government reiterated to the Committee the position outlined above.

594. Several members of the Committee felt that it was important to take note of the fact that Mrs Massera had been released, and hoped that a similar attitude might be adopted *vis-à-vis* Dr Massera himself.

595. After discussion, the Committee decided to recommend the Executive Board to ask the Director-General to address on its behalf, once again, an appeal to the Uruguayan Government to exercise clemency and ensure the rapid release of Dr Massera, and to continue his own efforts in this matter.[26]

596. At the [autumn] 1980 session, the representative of the Uruguayan Government informed the Committee that the Under-Secretary of State for Foreign Affairs of his country had discussed the case of Dr José Luis Massera with the Director-General during the session.

597. Several members expressed their satisfaction that the request submitted to the Director-General by the Executive Board had culminated in such high-level talks but said they were disappointed that those talks had not been completed. One member asked whether the Committee could obtain additional information on the substance of the exchanges of views and as to when the request for release lodged by the authors of the communication would be heard. One member of the Committee observed that 13 months had elapsed since the ruling of the Court of First Instance and that the date for hearing of the appeal was still not known.

---

[26] See document 109 EX/52 PRIV., para. 292 (*supra*, p. 267).

No. 103/79 **Uruguay**

598. The representative of the Director-General said that the Director-General would no doubt wish himself to give an account of his discussions to the Executive Board. It was accordingly desirable to postpone examination of the communication to the next session.

599. The representative of the Uruguayan Government considered that the Director-General was certainly the person in the best position to give an account of the conversations which had taken place at such a high level.

600. The Committee consequently decided at the [autumn 1980] session:[27]

> [i] to take note of the information provided;
>
> [ii] to postpone examination of the substance of this communication to the next session of the Committee;
>
> [iii] to request the Director-General to give the Executive Board any information he deemed desirable on the progress of his humanitarian representations.

601. At the [spring 1981 session] the representative of the Government of Uruguay declared that:

> (i) justice should be allowed to take its course, as the executive of his country could not intervene because of the principle of the separation of powers;
>
> (ii) the possibility of exercising clemency could not be considered until a final judgement had been delivered; the hearing of the appeal would begin at the earliest opportunity during the current year.

602. After noting that the government concerned had shown itself to be sensitive and receptive to the appeal made by scientists from all over the world, the Committee decided to ask the Executive Board to request the Director-General to continue making personal representations as provided for in paragraph 8 of 104 EX/Decision 3.3 and to maintain this communication on the list in keeping with the spirit of subparagraph 14 (*k*) of that decision.[28]

603. On 27 August 1981 the Secretariat received from Mr Henri Cartan, a member of the Comité pour la défense des hommes de science de l'Académie des Sciences (France) [...], a letter supplying fresh information regarding Dr Massera [...].[29] It was

[27] See document 110 EX/40 PRIV., para. 323 (*supra*, p. 269).
[28] See document 112 EX/30 PRIV., para. 557 (*supra*, p. 274).
[29] See document 113 EX/CR/HR/1 Add.

alleged that, in prison, Dr Massera had been frequently subjected to interrogations and that he had been accused of passing on political instructions outside the prison by making notes in the margin of a book. It was said, however, that Mrs Massera, the only person authorized to send him books, had not done so for a year. It was reported that the mathematician's cell had very often been searched and that each time he had had to set everything in order again so as to avoid being punished.

604. The letter also requested that the date of the trial in an appeal court be made known sufficiently in advance to enable a French lawyer to make arrangements to attend it.

605. At the present session, the representative of the Director-General said that at this point in the representations being conducted by the Director-General it seemed that a person chosen jointly with the government concerned might be allowed to visit Dr Massera. It was the first time that such a prospect had emerged.

606. The representative of the Uruguayan Government confirmed this news, adding that a new President had assumed office in his country and that he had been issued with no further instructions on the matter. For these reasons and because he had only received a copy of Mr Henri Cartan's letter on 1 September 1981, he asked that consideration of the communication be postponed until the next session.

607. Some members of the Committee were in favour of acceding to this request because of the political situation in Uruguay and especially because the statements of the new President seemed to indicate a desire to return to constitutional government in which political parties would have a right to be heard.

608. Other members of the Committee suspected that it might be an attempt to delay examination of the communication and felt that the Committee should voice its concern on this point.

609. One member of the Committee considered that the case might serve as a standard for future procedure; the facts were that a person had been sentenced in accordance with the laws in force in the country; the Committee had found that the communication was admissible and intended to proceed to an examination of substance; the question therefore arose as to the grounds on which the alleged victim had been sentenced: had he been guilty of criminal acts or of acts described as such in violation of human rights?

610. After an exchange of views, the Committee *decided*:

(i) to postpone consideration of the substance of this communication until the next session, first because of the Director-General's representations in pursuance of paragraph 14 (*k*) of 104 EX/Decision 3.3, which seemed to be bearing fruit, and secondly because of the late receipt by the representative of the government concerned of the letter from [Mr Henri Cartan] bringing new information to the notice of the Committee;

(ii) to reaffirm the Committee's deep interest in Dr Massera's case;

(iii) to inform the author of the communication of this decision.

Spring 1982 session of the Committee on Conventions and Recommendations (114th session of the Executive Board)[30]

819. The Committee decided to examine these two communications together,[31] since they concerned the same alleged victim.

820. The author of the first communication is Mr Jean-Claude Pecker, a professor at the Collège de France, acting on his own behalf and that of the Comité pour la défense des hommes de science de l'Académie des Sciences (France). It is already at the stage of examination as to its substance.

821. The second communication is submitted by Mrs Moriana Hernández de Bazzano, acting as the representative of her father-in-law, Mr José Luis Massera.

822. A mathematician and a graduate of the Faculty of Engineering, Montevideo, where he was a professor from 1937 until his arrest in 1975, Mr Massera was the Director of the Laboratory of the Institute of Mathematics and Statistics from 1949 to 1964 and Professor of Higher Mathematics at the Faculty of Arts and Sciences, Montevideo, which bestowed upon him the title of "Professor Emeritus".

[822a.] Mr Massera's works are said to be concerned mainly with differential equations but also to touch on economic, social, political and philosophical issues.

823. Arrested in Montevideo in October 1975 and detained since that time, although his detention is said to have been officially recognized only in January 1976, Mr Massera is alleged to have been placed in solitary confinement in August 1976, ill-

---

[30] See document 114 EX/38 PRIV., paras. 819-849; see also documents 114 EX/CR/HR/1 and 114 EX/CR/HR/3.

[31] Communications No. 103/79 concerning *Uruguay*, case of *José Luis Massera*, and No. 370/81 concerning *Uruguay*, case of *José Luis Massera*.

treated and tortured. It is alleged in particular that he was imprisoned in a cell, situated beneath a staircase, in which it was impossible for him to stand upright. This ill-treatment is said to have had a permanent after-effect, leaving Mr Massera with one leg shorter than the other, as a result of which it is alleged that he has to walk with the help of a stick and special shoes.

[823a.] It was reportedly not until 10 months after his arrest that he was brought to trial before a military examining magistrate on a charge of "subversive association". Mr Massera was subsequently sentenced to 20 years' imprisonment. This sentence is alleged to be higher than the maximum foreseen for the offence with which he was charged.

824. Referring to Article 14 of the International Covenant on Civil and Political Rights, Mrs Hernández de Bazzano lists the guarantees that were not respected in the trial of the alleged victim: a hearing by a competent independent and impartial tribunal, the right to be informed without delay of the charge, the rights of defence, etc. In support of her claim the author quotes the [views adopted by] the United Nations [Human Rights Committee] which considers that, in the case of Mr Massera, Articles 7, 9 (paragraphs 2, 3 and 4), 10 (paragraph 1), 14 (paragraphs 1, 2 and 3) and 25 of he above-mentioned Covenant have been violated.[32]

825. An appeal made to the Commission for the Defence of Individual Rights of the Council of State (a body set up to replace the Uruguayan Parliament, which was dissolved in 1973) has reportedly had no result. The appeal against Mr Massera's conviction is said to be still pending.

[825a.] For the time being, Mr Massera's case is no longer being considered by other intergovernmental organizations.

826. Mrs Hernández de Bazzano wishes to be informed of any reply from the Uruguayan Government so as to be able to submit further information to the Committee in good time. She also expresses the wish that the following documents be requested so that they can be placed on the file:

> the report of the [Human Rights Committee], the two documents distributed at the same time as this report at the thirty-fourth session of the United Nations General Assembly and resolution 34/35 of this high authority;

---

[32] See *Official Records of the General Assembly, Thirty-fourth Session, Supplement No. 40* (A/34/40), annex VII, communication No. 5/1977 (*Luis María Bazzano Ambrosini, Martha Valentini de Massera and José Luis Massera* v. *Uruguay*), views adopted on 15 August 1979.

the various documents containing the information obtained and the decisions taken by the decision-making organs of the Inter-Parliamentary Union in its various working languages: a set of these documents, in French, was communicated to the Secretariat by the Secretary-General of that organization by confidential letter dated 18 December 1981.

827. She requests lastly:

(i) that the Committee declare her communication admissible;

(ii) that, under the provisions of 104 EX/Decision 3.3, paragraph 14 (*k*), Mr Massera be able rapidly to recover his freedom and his rights;

(iii) that Mr Massera's case be dealt with by the Executive Board and the General Conference in public meeting, in pursuance of paragraphs 17 and 18 of the said decision.

828. A biography of Mr Massera and a detailed list of his works are reproduced in Annex A to the communication. A press release from the American Mathematical Society, stating among other things that a petition requesting Mr Massera's release and signed by 3,200 mathematicians from 27 countries has been transmitted to the United Nations, has been placed on the file and is reproduced in Annex B to the communication.

829. [The present communication] was declared admissible by the Committee at its [spring] 1979 session. The Committee, at that session, decided to add this communication to those concerning the same case that were pending in accordance with 77 EX/Decision 8.3. It expressed the hope that the competent authorities would see their way clear to exercising clemency towards Mr Massera and his wife.[33]

830. At the [autumn] 1979 session, the Committee decided to recommend that the Executive Board request the Director-General to address on its behalf an appeal to the Uruguayan Government to exercise clemency towards Professor Massera and his wife. The Committee also decided to resume consideration of the communication at its next session, and to this end invited the government concerned to provide it with any relevant information.[34]

[33] See document 107 EX/PRIV.31, paras. 181-182 (*supra*, p. 262).

[34] See document 108 EX/38 PRIV., para. 331 (*supra*, p. 263).

Uruguay **No. 103/79**

831. In a letter dated 28 November 1979, sent to the Minister of Foreign Relations of Uruguay, the Director-General appealed to the Uruguayan Government for clemency for Professor Massera and his wife.

832. At the [spring] 1980 session, the Committee had before it a letter addressed by the Uruguayan delegation on 21 April 1980 to the Director-General in which the position of the Uruguayan Government was set forth. It stated that:

> (1) the government maintained formal and substantive reservations as to the Committee's competence in the field of human rights, but that it had always co-operated with the Committee out of respect for Unesco;
>
> (2) Mr Massera had been sentenced on 23 July 1979 by the Military Court of First Instance to a term of 20 years' imprisonment;
>
> (3) any decision concerning the case of Dr Massera would have to be taken in a strictly legal context, for which purpose the proper criminal proceedings were being pursued by the competent judicial body with every safeguard provided under Uruguayan law. The time spent in custody by Mr Massera would be deducted from the sentence finally imposed;
>
> (4) Mr Massera had been imprisoned not on account of the ideology he professed but on account of the fact that he occupied the post of Secretary-General of a party that had been declared illegal, continuing to operate covertly after its proscription and maintaining close relations with the military apparatus of that party, the ultimate aim of which was to take over power by illegal means;
>
> (5) as for Mrs Martha Valentini de Massera, she had been released in August 1979 by order of the competent judicial body in whose custody she had been held up to that time.

833. The representative of the Uruguayan Government reiterated to the Committee the position outlined above.

834. After discussion, the Committee decided to recommend the Executive Board to ask the Director-General to address on its behalf, once again, an appeal to the Uruguayan Government to exercise clemency and ensure the rapid release of Mr Massera, and to continue his own efforts in this matter.[35]

---

[35] See document 109 EX/52 PRIV., para. 292 (*supra*, p. 267).

No. 103/79 **Uruguay**

835. At the [autumn] 1980 session, the representative of the Uruguayan Government informed the Committee that the Under-Secretary of State for Foreign Affairs of his country had discussed the case of Dr José Luis Massera with the Director-General during the session.

836. The representative of the Director-General said that the Director-General would no doubt wish himself to give an account of his discussions to the Executive Board. It was accordingly desirable to postpone examination of the communication to the following session.

837. After discussion, the Committee decided:[36]

> [i] to take note of the information provided;
>
> [ii] to postpone examination of the substance of this communication to the Committee's spring [1981] session;
>
> [iii] to request the Director-General to give the Executive Board any information he deemed desirable on the progress of his humanitarian representations.

838. At the [spring 1981 session], the representative of the Government of Uruguay declared that:

> (i) justice should be allowed to take its course, as the executive of his country could not intervene because of the principle of the separation of powers;
>
> (ii) the possibility of exercising clemency could not be considered until a final judgement had been delivered; the hearing of the appeal would begin at the earliest opportunity.

839. After noting that the government concerned had shown itself to be sensitive and receptive to the appeal made by scientists from all over the world, the Committee decided to ask the Executive Board to request the Director-General to continue making personal representations as provided for in paragraph 8 of 104 EX/Decision 3.3 and to maintain this communication on the list in keeping with the spirit of subparagraph 14 (*k*) of that decision.[37]

840. On 27 August 1981 the Secretariat received from Mr Henri Cartan, a member of the Comité pour la défense des hommes de science de l'Académie des Sciences

---

[36] See document 110 EX/40 PRIV., para. 323 (*supra*, p. 269).
[37] See document 112 EX/30 PRIV., para. 557 (*supra*, p. 274).

(France), a letter supplying fresh information regarding Dr Massera. It was alleged that, in prison, Dr Massera had been frequently subjected to interrogations and that he had been accused of passing on political instructions outside the prison by making notes in the margin of a book. It was said, however, that Mrs Massera, the only person authorized to send him books, had not done so for a year. It was reported that the mathematician's cell had very often been searched and that each time he had had to set everything in order again so as to avoid being punished. The letter also requested that the date of the trial in an appeal court be made known sufficiently in advance to enable a French lawyer to make arrangements to attend it.

841. At the [autumn] 1981 session, the representative of the Director-General said that at that point in the representations being conducted by the Director-General, it seemed that a person chosen jointly with the government concerned might be allowed to visit Dr Massera. It was the first time that such a prospect had emerged.

842. The representative of the Uruguayan Government confirmed this news, adding that a new President had assumed office in his country and that he had been issued with no further instructions on the matter. For these reasons and because he had not received a copy of Mr Henri Cartan's letter until 1 September 1981, he asked that consideration of the communication be postponed until the next session.

843. At the conclusion of the debate, the Committee decided:[38]

> (i) to postpone consideration of the substance of this communication until the next session, first because of the Director-General's representations in pursuance of paragraph 14 (*k*) of 104 EX/Decision 3.3, which seemed to be bearing fruit, and secondly, because of the late receipt by the representative of the government concerned of the letter from [Mr Henri Cartan] bringing new information to the notice of the Committee;
>
> (ii) to reaffirm the Committee's deep interest in Dr Massera's case;
>
> (iii) to inform the author of the communication of this decision.

844. Under cover of a confidential letter dated 18 December 1981, the Secretary-General of the Interparliamentary Union communicated to the Secretariat a series of documents concerning the Interparliamentary Conference held in September 1981 in Havana (Cuba), including a resolution by the Interparliamentary Council, adopted unanimously at its 129th session. In that resolution, the Council mentioned:

---

[38] See document 113 EX/38 PRIV., para. 610 (*supra*, pp. 279-280).

(i) the nomination by the Interparliamentary Union of a Member of Parliament from Costa Rica, Mr Cristian Tattenbach, to be an observer at the hearings of the Supreme Military Court of Appeal which is to deal with the case of Mr Massera and of three other Members of Parliament;

(ii) a passage from the report of the United Nations [Human Rights Committee] to the thirty-fourth session of the United Nations General Assembly; [the Committee] considers that the facts of Mr Massera's case reveal violations of the International Covenant on Civil and Political Rights, especially as regards Articles 7, 9 (paragraphs 2, 3, 5), 10 (paragraph 1), 14 (paragraphs 1, 2, 3) and 25; concludes that the State party is under an obligation to secure the strict observance of the provisions of the Covenant and to enable the victim to have access to appropriate legal remedies.

845. At the present session, the representative of the Director-General reported on the progress of the representations made by the latter regarding the possibility of sending a figure of international stature to Uruguay. In agreement with the government of that country, a person had been chosen, but for reasons of a personal nature he had been unable to accept the proposed assignment. The names of two other persons had then been put forward for consideration by the government concerned; a reply was awaited.

846. The representative of the Uruguayan Government confirmed that there had in fact been regular talks between the representative of the Director-General and his country's delegation to Unesco with a view to arranging the mission referred to. He asked for the Committee's understanding concerning his government's delay in replying following the refusal last March by the person initially selected: since contact had to be established at the highest level, appropriate arrangements had to be made.

847. Several Committee members felt that under the circumstances it would be advisable to await the outcome of the Director-General's representations. In order to ensure correct procedure, they considered that [the new communication] should be declared admissible and combined with [the present communication].

848. Two members of the Committee, however, voiced their extreme concern, on humanitarian grounds, over the distressing situation of the alleged victim. They expressed regret that such a simple matter - the selection of a representative of the Director-General to go to Uruguay - should become an involved question. They hoped that the representative of the government concerned would use his good offices to help in solving the case of Mr Massera as he had done in the past in connection with another Uruguayan case.

Uruguay **No. 103/79**

849. Following an exchange of views, the Committee *decided*:

(i) to declare [the new communication] admissible, the alleged facts being the same as those that were the subject of [the present communication];

(ii) to combine the two communications for examination as to substance;

(iii) to wait until the next session for the outcome of the representations made with a view to reaching a friendly solution, having regard to the Committee's deep interest in the case.

Autumn 1982 session of the Committee on Conventions and Recommendations (115th session of the Executive Board)[39]

469. These two communications[40] concern the same person, Mr José Luis Massera, a mathematician, who was arrested in 1975 and sentenced in July 1979 by the Military Court of First Instance to a term of 20 years' imprisonment for having been Secretary-General of a party that had been declared illegal but in which he had nevertheless continued to play an active part in close conjunction with the military wing of that party, the ultimate aim of which was to take over power by illegal means.

470. The first communication was declared admissible by the Committee at its spring 1979 session,[41] and the second at its spring 1982 session.[42] At the latter session the Committee decided to combine them for examination as to substance and to await the outcome of the Director-General's representations in pursuance of paragraph 14 (*k*) of 104 EX/Decision 3.3 of the Executive Board.[43]

471. At the [autumn] 1981 session, it seemed that a person representing the Director-General might be allowed to visit Mr Massera.

472. Negotiations were concluded in January 1982 with the choice of an eminent Spanish figure. For reasons of a personal nature, however, he was unable to accept the proposed assignment. The names of two other persons were then submitted for the approval of the government concerned.

---

[39] See document 115 EX/28 PRIV., paras. 469-477; see also documents 115 EX/CR/HR/1 and Add.

[40] Communications No. 103/79 concerning *Uruguay*, case of *José Luis Massera*, and No. 370/81 concerning *Uruguay*, case of *José Luis Massera*, were being considered together.

[41] See document 107 EX/PRIV.31, para. 181 (*supra*, p. 262).

[42] See document 114 EX/38 PRIV., para. 849 (i) (*supra*, p. 287).

[43] *Ibidem*, para. 849 (ii) and (iii) (*supra*. p. 287).

No. 103/79 **Uruguay**

473. At the autumn 1982 session, after restating his country's unchanging opinion that the communication was inadmissible, the representative of the government concerned informed the Committee that his government felt a visit by a representative of the Director-General to be inadvisable at present because a special representative of the Secretary-General of the United Nations had visited the prisoner in the meantime, had been able to talk to him freely and had ascertained that he was in a normal state of health.

474. Replying to the concern for Mr Massera's state of health expressed by the Société mathématique de France in a letter to the Director-General dated 21 July 1982, the representative of the Uruguayan Government said that according to the most recent information available to him, Mr Massera had received appropriate medical attention. His state of health was entirely normal for a man of his age.

475. In conclusion, the representative of the Uruguayan Government stated that the authorities of his country would, in any case, be prepared to resume the humanitarian procedure being pursued by the Committee.

476. A member of the Committee said that in view of the state of health of the alleged victim, his age, the length of his sentence and his international stature in the scientific field, he warmly welcomed the acceptance by the government concerned of the Director-General's proposal that a responsible person should visit Mr Massera.

477. After a brief exchange of views, the Committee *decided*:

(i) to take note of the willingness of the government concerned to cooperate on the humanitarian level;

(ii) to ask the Executive Board to request the Director-General to proceed with his action along these lines.

Spring 1983 session of the Committee on Conventions and Recommendations (116th session of the Executive Board)[44]

325. The two communications[45] concern the case of Mr José Luis Massera, a mathematician, who was arrested in 1975 and sentenced in July 1979 by the Military Court of First Instance to a term of 20 years' imprisonment for having served as

[44] See document 116 EX/48 PRIV., paras. 325-331; see also document 116 EX/CR/HR/1.
[45] Communications No. 103/79 concerning *Uruguay*, case of *José Luis Massera*, and No. 370/81 concerning *Uruguay*, case of *José Luis Massera*, were being considered together.

Secretary-General of a party that had been declared illegal but in which he had nevertheless continued to militate clandestinely, in close conjunction with the military wing of that party. The first was declared admissible by the Committee at the spring 1979 session,[46] the second at the spring 1982 session.[47]

326. At the spring 1983 session, the Committee continued its consideration of their substance.

327. The Chairman of the Committee reported to members on the mission assigned to him by the Director-General to visit Uruguay and take part in and pursue the humanitarian representations which he had initiated. He stated in particular that he had been able to talk to Mr Massera, his wife, his doctor, his lawyer, the President of the Republic and the principal Uruguayan authorities and that he had been listened to attentively by these authorities as regards the concern he had expressed and the request for a solution to the case which he had formulated in conformity with his mission. He indicated that a report had been submitted to the Director-General.

328. The representative of the government concerned confirmed these statements. He drew the Committee's attention to the content of a recent telegram he had received that described Mr Massera's state of health in detail as well as the appropriate care that he was receiving.

329. After a thoroughgoing discussion, the Committee members were unanimous in expressing their keen satisfaction at what had been done and their hopes with regard to developments in the case and the possibility of a happy outcome. The Committee also considered that in view of the state of negotiations and the importance of ensuring the confidential character of the case, it would not be opportune to inform the authors of the communications more fully of what had been done to date; the case was, indeed, an exemplary one, for it showed the limits of legal recourse (it had been examined by the Human Rights Committee within the framework of the International Covenant on Civil and Political Rights without apparently yielding any result other than the noting of the facts) and was a case in which humanitarian approaches in the context of 104 EX/Decision 3.3 seemed to promise good results: the fact of being able to send a representative of the Director-General to explore potential solutions *in situ* with the authorities of the country was already in itself a constructive step.

330. Taking the floor again, the representative of the Uruguayan Government promised to convey to it the Committee's thanks. Without wishing to prejudge the atti-

---

[46] See document 107 EX/PRIV.31, para. 181 (*supra*, p. 262).
[47] See document 114 EX/38 PRIV., para. 849 (i) (*supra*, p. 287).

tude of the authors of the two communications, and pointing out in passing that very few countries could pride themselves on agreeing to receive on their territory an international mission with complete freedom of movement, he drew the Committee's attention to the risks inherent in the misuse of the information made available to the authors in question.

331. The Committee finally *decided* to suspend consideration of these two communications, pending the receipt of fresh information, and to ask the Secretariat to inform the authors of the communications that the Director-General had taken various steps, including the sending of a special representative to Uruguay, which gave grounds for some hope of a positive outcome.

Autumn 1983 session of the Committee on Conventions and Recommendations (117th session of the Executive Board)[48]

228. Mr Massera, a mathematician and professor in Montevideo, was arrested on 29 October 1975. Detained since then, he was sentenced by the Military Court of First Instance on 23 July 1979 to a term of 20 years' imprisonment for having, according to information provided by the government concerned, served as Secretary-General of a party that had been declared illegal but in which he had nevertheless continued to militate clandestinely, in close conjunction with the military apparatus of that party whose ultimate aim was allegedly to take over power by illegal means [...].[49] His appeal still remained pending before the Supreme Military Tribunal.

229. The two communications[50] concerning him were declared admissible by the Committee at its spring 1979 and spring 1982 sessions respectively.[51]

230. At this autumn 1983 session the Director-General's representative informed the Committee of the status of the humanitarian representations made by the Director-General. In particular, he acquainted the Committee with the substance of the letter from the President of the Eastern Republic of Uruguay dated 12 August 1983, replying to the Director-General's latest appeal for clemency dated 27 July 1983. This letter recalled that since his youth Mr Massera had indulged in anti-national activities and that his conviction was the result of serious offences, subversive associations and an attempt to violate the Constitution (conspiracy followed by preparatory acts);

---

[48] See document 117 EX/18 PRIV., paras. 228-236; see also document 117 EX/CR/HR/1.
[49] See document 109 EX/CR/HR/1 Add.3.
[50] Communications No. 103/79 concerning *Uruguay*, case of *José Luis Massera*, and No. 370/81 concerning *Uruguay*, case of *José Luis Massera*, were being considered together.
[51] See documents 107 EX/PRIV.31, para. 181 (*supra*, p. 262), and 114 EX/38 PRIV., para. 849 (i) (*supra*, p. 287), respectively.

it pointed out that the person concerned was continuing to receive humane and attentive treatment in prison and that his state of health was satisfactory; it also made the point that judges were totally independent in the decisions they made and that one of the conditions for being eligible for early release was completion of at least half of one's sentence; the letter ended by emphasizing that it was not at present possible for the Uruguayan authorities to contemplate a solution that might lead to Mr Massera being freed; enclosed with the letter were the texts of two laws (of 27 March 1980 and 20 May 1983) concerning the system of early release in cases under military jurisdiction (early or conditional release coming within the jurisdiction of the Supreme Military Tribunal).

231. Taking the floor, the representative of the Government of Uruguay said that he had nothing further to add to the statement by the Director-General's representative other than that his government was still prepared to pursue the dialogue that had already been begun.

232. Some Committee members expressed their deep disappointment and profound concern over the fate of the mathematician, who had already been in detention for nearly eight years. According to them, in fact the idea had been to avoid drawing too much attention to the affair so as not to offend the susceptibilities of the government concerned and to ensure that the representations of the Director-General were as effective as possible, but what had been achieved did not seem to match up to the hopes they had had at the spring 1983 session.

233. Other Committee members displayed some optimism, feeling that it was not an everyday occurrence to hear from a head of state during consideration of a communication, and judging that the letter from the President of the Eastern Republic of Uruguay was legal in tone, and that it would be appropriate to continue the dialogue with the government concerned and renew the appeal for clemency.

234. Other Committee members wondered if the process of granting a possible pardon was actually blocked at the moment merely because a final decision had not yet been passed on Mr Massera's appeal to the Supreme Military Tribunal.

235. Following discussion, the Committee *decided*:

(i) to invite the representative of the government concerned to report to the Uruguayan authorities on the Committee's concern that Mr Massera's appeal hearing should begin very soon and on its anxieties on a humanitarian level;

(ii) to request the Executive Board to invite the Director-General to continue his representations and, if he deemed it opportune, to approach the delegation of Uruguay at the forthcoming General Conference in Paris with a view to finding a solution to this matter;

(iii) to resume consideration of [these communications] at its spring 1984 session.

236. The representative of the government concerned promised to bring the Committee's concern to the attention of the authorities in his country. On the conditions in which Mr Massera was being held and his state of health, he told the Committee that they gave no cause for anxiety, as the Chairman of the Committee had certainly been able to establish quite freely when he was on the spot, during his mission to Montevideo last November at the special request of the Director-General.

Spring 1984 session of the Committee on Conventions and Recommendations (119th session of the Executive Board)[52]

232. Mr Massera, a mathematician and professor, was arrested on 29 October 1975. He was sentenced by the Military Court of First Instance on 23 July 1979 to a term of 20 years' imprisonment for having served as Secretary-General of a party that had been declared illegal but in which he had nevertheless continued to militate clandestinely, in close conjunction with the military apparatus of that party whose ultimate aim was allegedly to take over power by illegal means [...].[53]

233. The Committee had declared these communications[54] admissible at its spring [1979 and spring 1982 sessions] respectively.[55] It had been informed at its spring and autumn 1983 sessions by the representative of the Director-General, of the situation of the humanitarian representations made by the latter to the top Uruguayan authorities, in particular the President of the [Eastern] Republic of Uruguay, consisting mainly of a continuing exchange of correspondence and of consultations and a mission to Montevideo by a special envoy, Professor Putzeys-Álvarez, at that time member of the Executive Board and Chairman of the Committee. At the end of the discussions at the [autumn 1983] session, the Committee decided to ask the Executive Board to request the Director-General to continue his representations with a

[52] See document 119 EX/35 PRIV., paras. 232-235; see also documents 119 EX/CR/HR/1 and Add.
[53] See document 109 EX/CR/HR/1 Add.3.
[54] Communications No. 103/79 concerning *Uruguay*, case of *José Luis Massera*, and No. 370/81 concerning *Uruguay*, case of *José Luis Massera*, were being considered together.
[55] See documents 107 EX/PRIV.31, para. 181 (*supra*, p. 262), and 114 EX/38 PRIV., para. 849 (i) (*supra*, p. 287), respectively.

view to finding a solution,[56] which the Director-General did with all possible dispatch.

234. By letter dated 13 March 1983 [...],[57] the President of the [Eastern] Republic of Uruguay informed the Director-General that Mr Massera had finally been sentenced by the court of appellate jurisdiction to 14 years' imprisonment, but had been granted early release on 3 March 1984.

235. The Committee was pleased to hear of this release and took note of it. Considering that the case of this mathematician was thus closed, it *decided* to strike the two communications from its list.

[56] See document 117 EX/18 PRIV., para. 235 (ii) (*supra*, pp. 291-292).
[57] See document 119 EX/CR/HR/1 Add.

No. 104/79

Concerning *Argentina*
Case of *Violation of human rights in the sectors of education, science, culture and information**

Communication of 15 March 1979 submitted by
Jean-Marie Domenach

Spring 1979 session of the Committee on Conventions and Recommendations (107th session of the Executive Board)[1]

117. At the request of the representative of the government concerned, which had only recently received the communication, the Committee *decided* to defer consideration of its admissibility until its next session.

Autumn 1979 session of the Committee on Conventions and Recommendations (108th session of the Executive Board)[2]

67. The Director of the Division of Human Rights and Peace recalled that the Committee, at its [spring 1979] session, had deferred consideration of the admissibility of [this communication] at the request of the government concerned.[3]

68. This communication alleges the violation by the Argentine Republic of Articles 2 (para. 1), 3, 5, 8, 9, 18, 19, 26 and 27 of the Universal Declaration of Human Rights, as well as of [19 C/Resolution] 12.1 adopted by the General Conference at its nineteenth session; in particular, it alleges the application, in the fields of education, science, culture and information, of policies conflicting with the rights guaranteed by the Universal Declaration of Human Rights.

---

* At the Committee's autumn 1979 session and spring and autumn 1980 sessions, this communication was being referred to as case of *Violations of human rights in the sectors of education, science, culture and information*.

[1] See document 107 EX/PRIV.31, para. 117; see also document 107 EX/CR/PROC.HR/40.

[2] See document 108 EX/38 PRIV., paras. 67-86; see also document 108 EX/CR/PROC.HR/1.

[3] See document 107 EX/PRIV.31, para. 117 (*supra*, p. 295).

No. 104/79 **Argentina**

69. The facts alleged include assassinations, "disappearances", cases of detention without due process or trial, mass dismissals for political reasons, the closing down of newspapers, publications and publishing houses, the prohibition of the dissemination and circulation of certain publications, and their destruction. The communication, which contains an analysis of the relevant provisions of the Argentine Constitution and Argentine legislation, alleges the following, in particular: burning of books, closing down of newspapers and publishing houses, prohibition of the dissemination of certain publications, mass dismissals of teachers, imprisonment and sentencing of a group of academics at the National University of the South for ideological offences under Act No. 20840, assassination or disappearance of teachers, researchers, psychiatrists, students, writers and journalists, "impairment of the scientific and cultural heritage of the Argentine nation".

70. The Chairman drew the Committee's attention to the fact that most of the facts described in the communication had occurred in a context of latent civil war. He recalled that the procedure provided for in 104 EX/Decision 3.3 concerned both "cases" and "questions". At the request of the Chairman, the Director of the Division of Human Rights and Peace explained that under the provisions of paragraph 10 of 104 EX/Decision 3.3, the Committee was called upon to examine cases which were individual and specific and two types of question:

> on the one hand, questions which resulted from a policy contrary to human rights, applied *de jure* or *de facto*, and
>
> on the other hand, questions which resulted from an accumulation of individual cases forming a consistent pattern.

71. He pointed out that all communications, whether they concerned "cases" or "questions", had to meet the same conditions of admissibility, namely those enumerated in paragraph 14 (*a*) of 104 EX/Decision 3.3, though naturally the extent to which a particular condition applied would depend on the nature of the "case" or "question" at issue. For instance, the stipulation in paragraph 14 (*a*) (ix) that the communication should indicate whether an attempt had been made to exhaust available domestic remedies could not apply to a communication impugning a policy whose *de jure* application ran counter to human rights when the country where it was applied had no means whereby the constitutional character of its lavs could be tested.

72. As to the stage in the examination of a communication at which the latter should be classified as concerning a "case" or a "question", 104 EX/Decision 3.3 was not explicit on the point. The Committee, when examining [another communication] at

its [autumn] 1978 session, had agreed to defer a decision in that respect until it had completed consideration as to the merits.[4]

73. The procedure to be followed in the examination of "questions" was laid down in paragraph 18 of 104 EX/Decision 3.3, but that provision concerned only the stage at which a communication relating to a question was brought before the Executive Board. What was more, the actual wording used ("should be considered ... in public meetings") did not make it possible to say precisely whether that was an obligation, or a request, or whether it was possible to choose some other method.

74. The representative of the Argentine Government described the exceptional situation which had prevailed in his country, and was at the root of the disappearances. The latter had occurred mainly at a time when the government had not been in a position to control the activities of armed groups of a combined strength of about 15,000, which even possessed an armaments factory of three storeys. That minority had started its terrorist activities after the democratic elections of 1973 and, according to a recent article in the *International Herald Tribune*, it had carried out 3,000 executions.

75. In the opinion of the representative of the Argentine Government, [this communication] should be regarded as inadmissible on the grounds, *inter alia*, that abusive and offensive terms were employed. What was more, the author of the communication passed an unacceptable political judgement on his country, with the result that the communication was not compatible with the principles of Unesco and the United Nations Charter and so did not meet the condition contained in paragraph 14 (*a*) (iv) of 104 EX/Decision 3.3.

76. The accusations brought against Argentina went far beyond the sphere of human rights and served rather as a pretext for impugning the country's constitutional and legal system. Any intervention in the domestic affairs of a country is prohibited under Article I.3 of Unesco's Constitution, a provision which was reiterated in paragraph 6 of 104 EX/Decision 3.3, under which Unesco undertook not to intervene in any matters which were essentially within the domestic jurisdiction of Member States. In addition, it was emphasized in paragraph 7 of 104 EX/Decision 3.3 that Unesco should not play the role of an international judicial body and that it should act in a spirit of co-operation and conciliation. He cited, as a precedent, [a communication] concerning the USSR, which the Committee, at its [spring 1979] session, had not regarded as a communication, on the grounds that it did not correspond to the

[4] See document 105 EX/49 PRIV., para. 91 (ii) (*supra*, p. 120), communication No. 25/78 concerning *Chile*, case of *The situation of human rights in Chile in the fields of education, science, culture and information.*

spirit of paragraph 7,[5] and maintained that the same applied to [the present communication], which should be dealt with accordingly.

77. In the opinion of the representative of the government concerned, the communication did not contain relevant evidence and, on that account, did not meet the condition of admissibility laid down in paragraph 14 (*a*) (v) of 104 EX/Decision 3.3. Besides, the author of the communication was pursuing a political goal and did not have "reliable knowledge" of the situation, as required by paragraph 14 (*a*) (ii) of 104 EX/Decision 3.3. In this regard the Argentine representative referred to two specific accusations contained in the communication: the closing down of periodicals and publishing houses, on the one hand, and the dismissal of a large number of academics, on the other. In so far as the former accusation was concerned, the Argentine representative observed that the Inter-American Press Association had stated in August last that freedom of the press existed in Argentina. As for the dismissal of academics, the Argentine representative explained that the government had been obliged to discharge many teachers for financial reasons, but also by virtue of the anti-terrorist laws (Nos. 21260 and 21274) which required the dismissal of civil servants jeopardizing law and order. Furthermore, some 40 per cent of the names mentioned in the communication were of persons who had already been set free.

78. Several Committee members testified to the moral and intellectual qualities of the author of the communication, Mr J.-M. Domenach, a French writer. His object was purely humanitarian, according to these members, and the wording of the communication was very measured and by no means abusive. One member observed in this regard that a communication relating to human rights always involved implied criticism of the State concerned. Other members considered that if abusive terms figured in the communication they could be expurgated in accordance with paragraph 14 (*a*) (vi) of 104 EX/Decision 3.3.

79. In the view of certain members of the Committee, the very serious situation prevailing in Argentina deserved to receive Unesco's attention for, as was clear from the many communications already examined by the Committee, major problems existed in that country in the spheres of education, science, culture and information. With reference to the supposed precedent set by [the communication] concerning the USSR,[6] it was observed that the author of the communication concerning Argentina quoted the Argentine Constitution in order to show that a particular decision or situation was not in conformity with it - and in that respect his words were carefully weighed - whereas the authors of [the other communication] had been impugning the political and constitutional regime of a country as such.

---

[5] See document 107 EX/PRIV.31, para. 166 (*supra*, p. 244), communication No. 90/79 concerning *Union of Soviet Socialist Republics*, case of *Vadime Delaunay* et al.
[6] *Ibidem*.

80. Several members of the Committee drew attention to the fact that Unesco could not play the role of a judicial body and that it should confine itself to bearing witness to its ethical and moral mission through a policy of co-operating with the governments concerned. One member expressed doubts as to the admissibility of the communication in view of paragraph [14] (*a*) (vi) of 104 EX/Decision 3.3, the only exceptions to the principle of non-intervention in domestic matters, according to the United Nations Charter, being situations which threatened international peace and security. Another member considered, however, that judicial precedents at the International Court of Justice were conducive to a much less restrictive interpretation of Article 2 (7) of the Charter, especially when it was a matter of human rights.

81. Several members emphasized the fact that the author of a communication was not required, during the consideration of admissibility, to bring formal proof of his allegations, paragraph 14 (*a*) (v) of 104 EX/Decision 3.3 stating very clearly that the communication "must appear to contain relevant evidence". One member of the Committee drew attention to a mistake in the Spanish version of this subparagraph, the term "appear" being missing. The Director of the Division of Human Rights and Peace said that, in the light of the preparatory work, there could be no doubt as to the intention of those who had drafted 104 EX/Decision 3.3 and had certainly meant to include the term "appear", as was the case in all the language versions except the Spanish.

82. Another member considered that in a situation such as that obtaining in Argentina the author of the communication would in any case have to collect all the evidence available. In the opinion of certain members it devolved rather upon the State concerned to produce evidence in support of its assertions.

83. With regard to the complex and voluminous nature of this communication, certain members considered it an accumulation of individual cases, whereas others were of the opinion that if the communication were declared admissible, it should be dealt with as a "question" in accordance with paragraph 18 of 104 EX/Decision 3.3. Certain members held that the examination of a "question" should be approached with the greatest caution.

84. Several members observed that for the time being only the admissibility of the communication was involved, and for that purpose the conditions laid down seemed to have been met. Certain members were of the opinion that it would be impossible to declare the communication inadmissible without bringing the credibility of the procedure established by 104 EX/Decision 3.3 into question. Whereas one Committee member held that the matter, which had not been submitted to other authorities, should be submitted to the United Nations, other members were of the opinion that

the existence of other international authorities did not affect the admissibility of the communication within the framework of Unesco's procedures.

85. After detailed examination of the various aspects of the admissibility of this communication, the Committee *decided* to keep the matter on its agenda, *instructed* the Secretariat to ask the author of the communication to submit it in the form of individual cases and *decided* to express an opinion at its next session as to whether the individual cases which would be declared admissible constituted, by reason of their accumulation, a "question" within the terms of paragraph 10 (*b*) of 104 EX/Decision 3.3.

86. Three members of the Committee expressed reservations concerning this decision and two of them regretted that the Committee had not reached a clearer decision as to the admissibility of the communication, which seemed to them to have been established.

Spring 1980 session of the Committee on Conventions and Recommendations (109th session of the Executive Board)[7]

22. This communication alleges the violation by the Argentine Republic of Articles 2 (paragraph 1), 3, 5, 8, 9, 18, 19, 26 and 27 of the Universal Declaration of Human Rights, as well as of [19 C/Resolution] 12.1 adopted by the General Conference at its nineteenth session; in particular, it alleges the application, in the fields of education, science, culture and information, of policies conflicting with the rights guaranteed by the Universal Declaration of Human Rights.

23. The facts alleged included assassinations, "disappearances", cases of detention without due process or trial, mass dismissals for political reasons, the closing down of newspapers, publications and publishing houses, the prohibition of the dissemination and circulation of certain publications, and their destruction. The communication, which contains an analysis of the relevant provisions of the Argentine Constitution and Argentine legislation, alleges the following, in particular: burning of books, closing down of newspapers and publishing houses, prohibition of the dissemination of certain publications, mass dismissals of teachers, imprisonment and sentencing of a group of academics at the National University of the South for ideological offences under Act No. 20840, assassination or disappearance of teachers, researchers, psychiatrists, students, writers and journalists, "impairment of the scientific and cultural heritage of the Argentine nation".

[7] See document 109 EX/52 PRIV., paras. 22-28; see also documents 109 EX/CR/HR/2 and Add.2.

Argentina **No. 104/79**

24. At its [spring] 1979 session the Committee had deferred consideration of the admissibility of this communication at the request of the government concerned.[8]

25. At its [autumn] 1979 session the Committee had deferred consideration of the admissibility of the communication due to the difficulty it had encountered in deciding whether the communication involved "cases" or a "question" and whether this had any bearing on admissibility. At that session the Committee had decided to keep the communication on its agenda and decided to instruct the Secretariat to ask the author of the communication to resubmit it in the form of individual cases.[9]

26. The representative of the government stated that the communication was slanderous, full of errors, and was still in a broadly unmanageable form. The author had not followed the instructions of the Committee and the communication still spoke broadly in terms of hundreds of victims. Furthermore, it was pointed out that of one of the groups of persons allegedly detained 16 out of 24 were free; of the group of psychiatrists four out of seven were free. The Argentine Government felt that the political motivations behind this slanderous communication were clear and considered that it should be declared inadmissible.

27. A member of the Committee stated that the Committee had been close to admitting this case at its [autumn 1979] session. He indicated that since it met the criteria for admissibility, the submission of communications in the form of individual cases not being one of these, it should be admitted and the questions of substance should be dealt with afterwards. Another member of the Committee felt that the communication was manifestly ill-founded and felt that it should be declared inadmissible, it being understood that any subsequent resubmission of the individual cases therein would still be permitted.

28. Several members of the Committee felt that the author had not complied satisfactorily with its request for redrafting the communication and after discussion the Committee *considered* that it could not accept the communication in its present form, and *decided* to ask the Secretariat to inform the author very clearly of its wishes concerning presentation in the form of individual cases and to inform him of those persons named therein who were no longer being detained.

---

[8] See document 107 EX/PRIV.31, para. 117 (*supra*, p. 295).
[9] See document 108 EX/38 PRIV., para. 85 (*supra*, p. 300).

No. 104/79 **Argentina**

Autumn 1980 session of the Committee on Conventions and Recommendations (110th session of the Executive Board)[10]

9. This communication alleged the violation by the Argentine Republic of Articles 2 (paragraph 1), 3, 5, 8, 9, 18, 19, 26 and 27 of the Universal Declaration of Human Rights, as well as of [19 C/Resolution] 12.1 adopted by the General Conference at its nineteenth session; in particular, it alleged the application, in the fields of education, science, culture and information, of policies conflicting with the rights guaranteed by the Universal Declaration of Human Rights.

10. The facts alleged included assassinations, "disappearances", cases of detention without due process or trial, mass dismissals for political reasons, the closing down of newspapers, publications and publishing houses, the prohibition of the dissemination and circulation of certain publications, and their destruction. The communication, which contained an analysis of the relevant provisions of the Argentine Constitution and Argentine legislation alleged the following, in particular: burning of books, closing down of newspapers and publishing houses, prohibition of the dissemination of certain publications, mass dismissals of teachers, imprisonment and sentencing of a group of academics at the National University of the South for ideological offences under Act No. 20840, assassination or disappearence of teachers, researchers, psychiatrists, students, writers and journalists, "impairment of the scientific and cultural heritage of the Argentine nation".

11. At its [spring 1979 session] the Committee deferred consideration of the admissibility of this communication at the request of the government concerned.[11]

12. At its [autumn] 1979 session the Committee deferred consideration of the admissibility of the communication due to the difficulty it had encountered in deciding whether the communication involved "cases" or a "question" and whether this had any bearing on admissibility. At that session the Committee decided to keep the commuication on its agenda and decided to instruct the Secretariat to ask the author of the communication to resubmit it in the form of individual cases.[12]

13. Following that request by the Secretariat, the communication was reformulated by the author and examined by the Committee in its new form at its [spring] 1980 session. At that sessien, the Committee considered that it could not accept the communication in its new form either, and decided to request the Secretariat to inform the author very clearly that it wished the communication to be submitted in the form

---

[10] See document 110 EX/40 PRIV., paras.9-20; see also document 110 EX/CR/HR/2.

[11] See document 107 EX/PRIV.31, para. 117 (*supra*, p. 295).

[12] See document 108 EX/38 PRIV., para. 85 (*supra*, p. 300).

of individual cases, and to indicate the names of the persons mentioned in his communication, although they were no longer detained.[13]

14. The representative of the Director-General informed the Committee that the author of the communication had not answered the request that the Secretariat sent to him on 27 June 1980.

15. The representative of the Argentine Government stated that, in the absence of a reply, he considered that the Committee should strike that communication off its list.

16. A Committee member stressed that the submission of a communication in the form of individual cases was not one of the criteria of admissibility, that other communications in the past had been declared admissible although they had not been submitted in that form, and that, furthermore, at an earlier meeting the Committee had been on the point of declaring this communication admissible; and, lastly, that since the communication concerned some 400 cases, the labour required of the author was considerable, especially since only a short time had elapsed since the [spring 1980] session. Other members of the Committee said that they shared that point of view.

17. Some Committee members expressed the idea that the silence of the author in response to what they considered to be a "twofold decision", since it had been taken [at the autumn 1979 session] and reiterated [at the spring 1980 session], should be interpreted either as a lack of desire that the Committee should continue its examination of the communication, or as an inability to furnish evidence on the cases submitted. It would therefore serve no purpose to burden the list of matters pending by adding to it a communication for which the author did not seek to continue dialogue with the Committee.

18. The representative of the Argentine Government stated that the Committee's striking this communication off its list would not prevent the author from submitting a fresh communication if he considered it appropriate.

19. The representative of the Director-General recalled that according to established jurisprudence in international law, lack of response had no legal significance, and that the proper procedure for the Committee was to grant a period of grace to the author who had failed to respond, and to strike the communication off the list only after a second period of silence on the part of the author of the communication. However, in the present circumstances, the failure to reply had occurred only once, not

---

[13] See document 109 EX/52 PRIV., para. 28 (*supra*, p. 301).

twice, since the author had reformulated his communication for the [spring 1980 session.

20. After discussion, the Committee *decided* to suspend examination of the communication until its next session, and *instructed* the Secretariat to inform the author of the communication clearly that, in the absence of a reply from him to the question posed in paragraph 13 above, the communication would be struck off the Committee's list.

Spring 1981 session of the Committee on Conventions and Recommendations (112th session of the Executive Board)[14]

10. This communication alleged the violation by the Argentine Republic of Articles 2 (paragraph 1), 3, 5, 8, 9, 18, 19, 26 and 27 of the Universal Declaration of Human Rights, as well as of [19 C/Resolution] 12.1 adopted by the General Conference at its nineteenth session; in particular, it alleged the application, in the fields of education, science, culture and information, of policies conflicting with the rights guaranteed by the Universal Declaration of Human Rights.

11. The alleged acts included assassinations, "disappearances", imprisonment without trial or sentence, mass dismissals for political reasons, the closing down of newspapers, publications and publishing houses, prohibition of the dissemination and distribution of certain publications and their destruction. The communication, which contained a summary of the relevant provisions of the Argentine Constitution and Argentine legislation, alleged the following, in particular: burning of books, closing down of newspapers and publishing houses, prohibition of the dissemination of certain publications, mass dismissals of teachers, imprisonment and sentencing of a group of academics at the National University of the South for ideological offences under Act No. 20840, assassination or disappearance of teachers, researchers, psychiatrists, students, writers and journalists, and the "impairment of the scientific and cultural heritage of the Argentine nation".

12. At its [spring 1979 session] the Committee deferred consideration of the admissibility of this communication at the request of the government concerned.[15]

13. At its [autumn] 1979 session the Committee deferred consideration of the admissibility of the communication due to the difficulty it had encountered in deciding whether the communication involved "cases" or a "question" and whether this had

[14] See document 112 EX/30 PRIV., paras.10-24; see also documents 112 EX/CR/HR/2 and Add.2.
[15] See document 107 EX/PRIV.31, para. 117 (*supra*, p. 295).

any bearing on admissibility. At that session the Committee decided to keep the communication on its agenda and decided to instruct the Secretariat to ask the author of the communication to resubmit it in the form of individual cases.[16]

14. By letter dated 15 November 1979, the Secretariat informed the author of the communication of the Committee's decision and requested him to present it in the form of individual cases.

15. By letter received on 27 February 1980, the author of the communication forwarded to the Secretariat, through his representatives, the communication as accordingly reformulated. This was transmitted to the government concerned on 29 February 1980.

16. At the Committee's [spring 1980 session], the representative of the Argentine Government stated that in its new form the communication was slanderous, full of errors, and was still in a broadly unmanageable form. The author had not followed the instructions of the Committee and the communication still spoke broadly in terms of hundreds of victims. Furthermore, it was pointed out that of one of the groups of persons allegedly detained 16 out of 24 had been set free; of the group of seven psychiatrists, four had been released. The Argentine Government felt that the political motivations behind this slanderous communication were clear, and considered that it should be declared inadmissible.

17. A member of the Committee stated that the Committee had been close to admitting this case at its [autumn 1979] session. He also thought that since it met the criteria for admissibility, the submission of cases in an individual form not being one of these, it should be admitted, and the questions of substance should be dealt with afterwards. Another member of the Committee felt that the communication was manifestly ill-founded and considered that it should be declared inadmissible, on the understanding that subsequent resubmission of the individual cases therein would still be permitted.

18. Several members of the Committee noted that the author had not complied satisfactorily with its request for a redrafting of the communication, and after discussion the Committee considered that it could not accept the communication in its present form, and decided to ask the Secretariat to make very clear to the author its wishes concerning the form of the presentation as individual cases, and to inform him of those persons named therein who were no longer being detained.[17]

---

[16] See document 108 EX/38 PRIV., para. 85 (*supra*, p. 300).

[17] See document 109 EX/52 PRIV., para. 28 (*supra*, p. 301).

19. The Secretariat duly informed the author of this decision. Having received no reply by its [autumn 1980 session], the Committee decided to defer examination of this communication, considering that a period of grace should be allowed to elapse before removing it from the list.[18]

20. As he had indicated to the Secretariat in a letter of 5 December 1980, the author again wrote on 10 February 1981 to state that he was submitting certain individual cases to the Committee for examination only in order to comply with the Committee's decisions; in his view, however, these cases were but so many examples of a systematic policy of arrest and abduction, censorship of all expressions of ideas and opinions and repression directed against the teaching, research and medical communities.

21. In support of his assertions, he furthermore quoted four cases of persons reported missing during 1976: Antonio Misetich, Leonora Zimmerman, Horacio Ciafardini and Federico Eduardo Álvarez Rojas (son), the latter also being the subject of [another communication][19] and, in addition, the fact that the Minister of National Education had been authorized by the decrees of March 1976 and March 1980 to exclude teachers from the teaching profession for ideological reasons, as also the banning of a work by Jacques Prévert by a decree of 24 June 1977, the *Diccionario Enciclopedico Salvat* and volumes 2 and 9 of the [*Gran Enciclopedia de Saber*] by a decree of 23 September 1980.

22. The representative of the Argentine Government told the Committee that, since the original communication had still not been presented in the form of individual cases, the author had not, in his view, complied with the Committee's decision and that the communication should accordingly be declared inadmissible. He nevertheless stated his readiness to collaborate with the Committee should it consider it desirable to examine the seven specific cases referred to in the letter of 10 February 1981.

23. One member expressed the view that only the seven specific cases could be examined by the Committee; the representative of the government concerned went on to stress that four of these seven cases concerned persons who had been missing since 1976. Another member than raised the question as to what the Committee could usefully do in regard to the general "question" raised by the author.

24. After a short discussion, the Committee *decided*:

---

[18] See document 110 EX/40 PRIV., para. 20 (*supra*, p. 304).
[19] Communication No. 113/79 concerning *Argentina*, case of *Federico Eduardo Álvarez Rojas*.

(i) In so far as the communication concerned a "question" relating to massive, systematic or flagrant violations of human rights and fundamental freedoms, to declare it inadmissible as being at present manifestly ill-founded under the terms of paragraph 14 (*a*) (v) of 104 EX/Decision 3.3;

(ii) In regard to the specific cases submitted by the author in his letter of 10 February 1981, a distinction should be drawn:

the cases of missing persons involving facts dating back to 1976 would be dealt with in accordance with the decision taken by the Committee concerning communications relating to missing persons,[20] i.e. in the event such cases would be referred back to the Working Group [on Enforced or Involuntary Disappearances] of the United Nations Commission on Human Rights;

the other specific cases concerning teachers allegedly deprived of the right to teach and the banning of certain works would be examined by the Committee at its next session once the author of the communication had supplied the Committee with more detailed allegations in this respect; the Committee accordingly instructed the Secretariat to notify the author of the foregoing.

Autumn 1981 session of the Committee on Conventions and Recommendations (113th session of the Executive Board)[21]

11. This communication in its original form alleged the violation by the Argentine Republic of Articles 2 (paragraph 1), 3, 5, 8, 9, 18, 19, 26 and 27 of the Universal Declaration of Human Rights, as well as of [19 C/Resolution] 12.1 adopted by the General Conference at its nineteenth session; in particular, it alleged the application, in the fields of education, science, culture and information, of policies conflicting with the rights guaranteed by the Universal Declaration of Human Rights.

12. The alleged acts included assassinations, "disappearances", imprisonment without trial or sentence, mass dismissals for political reasons, the closing down of newspapers, publications and publishing houses, prohibition of the dissemination and distribution of certain publications and their destruction. The communication, which contained a summary of the relevant provisions of the Argentine Constitution and Argentine legislation, alleged the following, in particular: burning of books, closing down of newspapers and publishing houses, prohibition of the dissemination of certain publications, mass dismissals of teachers, imprisonment and sentencing of

[20] See document 112 EX/30 PRIV., paras. 558-566.
[21] See document 113 EX/38 PRIV., paras.11-39; see also document 113 EX/CR/HR/2.

a group of academics at the National University of the South for ideological offences under Act No. 20840, assassination or disappearance of teachers, researchers, psychiatrists, students, writers and journalists, and the "impairment of the scientific and cultural heritage of the Argentine nation".

13. Having examined the communication in turn at its [spring and autumn 1979 and spring and autumn 1980 sessions], the Committee decided, at the last of those sessions, to give the author one final chance to answer the letters from the Secretariat asking him to submit his communication in the shape of individual cases, and consequently decided to leave examination of this communication in abeyance, feeling that there were grounds for allowing a period of grace to elapse before striking it from the list.[22]

14. As he had indicated to the Secretariat in a letter of 5 December 1980, the author again wrote on 10 February 1981 to state that he was submitting certain individual cases to the Committee for examination only in order to comply with the Committee's decisions. In his view, however, these cases were but so many examples of a systematic policy of arrest and abduction, censorship of all expression of ideas and opinions and repression directed against the teaching, research and medical communities.

15. In support of his assertions, he furthermore quoted four cases of persons reported missing during 1976: Antonio Misetich, Leonora Zimmerman, Horacio Ciafardini and Federico Eduardo Alvarez Rojas (son), the latter also being the subject of [another communication] and, in addition, the fact that the Minister of National Education had been authorized by the decrees of March 1976 and March 1980 to exclude teachers from the teaching profession for ideological reasons, as also the banning of a work by Jacques Prévert by a decree of 24 June 1977, the *Diccionario Enciclopedico Salvat* and volumes 2 and 9 of the *Gran Enciclopedia de Saber* by a decree of 23 September 1980.

16. At the [spring 1981] session, the representative of the Argentine Government told the Committee that, since the original communication had still not been presented in the form of individual cases, the author had not, in his view, complied with the Committee's decision and that the communication should accordingly be declared inadmissible. He nevertheless stated his readiness to collaborate with the Committee should it consider it desirable to examine the seven specific cases referred to in the letter of 10 February 1981.

---

[22] See document 110 EX/40 PRIV., para. 20 (*supra*, p. 304).

17. One member expressed the view that only the seven specific cases could be examined by the Committee. The representative of the government concerned went on to stress that four of these seven cases concerned persons who had been missing since 1976. Another member then raised the question as to what the Committee could usefully do in regard to the general "question" raised by the author.

18. After a short discussion, the Committee decided:[23]

> (i) in so far as the communication concerned a "question" relating to massive, systematic or flagrant violations of human rights and fundamental freedoms, to declare it inadmissible as being at present manifestly ill-founded under the terms of paragraph 14 (*a*) (v) of 104 EX/Decision 3.3;
>
> (ii) in regard to the specific cases submitted by the author in his letter of 10 February 1981, a distinction should be drawn:
>
> the cases of missing persons involving facts dating back to 1976 would be dealt with in accordance with the decision taken by the Committee concerning communications relating to missing persons, i.e. in the event such cases would be referred back to the Working Group [on Enforced or Involuntary Disappearances] of the United Nations Commission on Human Rights;
>
> the other specific cases concerning teachers allegedly deprived of the right to teach and the banning of certain works would be examined by the Committee at its next session once the author of the communication had supplied the Committee with more detailed allegations in this respect. The Committee accordingly instructed the Secretariat to notify the author of the foregoing.

19. Thus, at the present session, the following matters needed to be examined:

> (*a*) Case of Laws No. 22194 of 14 March 1980, No. 21278 of 29 March 1976 and Article 4 of the university law of 11 April 1980, all relating to the teaching profession

20. According to the author, Law No. 22194 of 14 March 1980, published in the Argentine Official Gazette of 20 March 1980, brought back into force until 31 December 1980 Law No. 21381 of 13 August 1976. This law, of which the validity has been extended several times, authorizes "the Ministry of Culture and Education and the Military Delegate of the Region to declare incompetent to hold a post in private educational establishments - including private universities, whether or not they are

---

[23] See document 112 EX/30 PRIV., para. 24 (*supra*, pp. 306-307).

recognized by the state - any member of the teaching or non-teaching staff who has been dismissed by application of Law No. 21260 ...".

21. Law No. 21260 of 24 March 1976 provides in Article 1:

> Article 1 - It is authorized, as from 31 December 1976, to dismiss, for reasons of security, any member of the permanent, temporary or contractual staff of the naional public administration, the National Congress, decentralized, autonomous bodies, state concerns and state property, special accounts services, social services and any other body under the Executive Authority that is linked in any way with activities of a subversive or anti-social nature.
>
> This provision also applies to those who openly, in concealment or in secret, advocate or instigate such activities.

22. Law No. 21278 of 29 March 1976 deprives staff in private educational establishments of all rights to security. It stipulates in Articles 1 and 2:

> Article 1 - The Ministry of National Culture and Education has the power to suspend totally or partially the status of teachers, with a view to more effecive attainment of the basic objectives of the Military Junta, through which it is intended to form an education system which is consonant with the counry's needs, serves the interests of the nation and consolidates the values and asirations of the Argentine people.
>
> Article 2 - The Ministry of Culture and Education has the power to suspend totally or partially the application of Law No. 20614 and its regulation decrees, relating to stability of employment of teaching staff in private educational establishments.

23. Lastly, Article 4 of the university law of 11 April 1980 published in the Official Gazette of 24 April 1980 prohibits teachers from supporting or disseminating certain political ideas and exercising political activities. It reads as follows:

> Article 4 - It is not acceptable, within the universities, to conduct any activities implying propaganda, indoctrination, proselytizing or agitation of a party politics or trade union nature, or the dissemination of or support for totalitarian or subversive political concepts.
>
> The functions referred to in Articles 45, 49, 52, 55 and 59 of this law and those of the Secretaries of university faculties or departments are incompatible with the exercise of party politics or trade union functions. Anyone fulfil-

ling the above-mentioned duties shall refrain from making public statements linked with party politics or trade union activities.

24. Articles 7, 8, 10, 11, 18, 19, 23 and 27 of the Universal Declaration of Human Rights are alleged to have been violated.

(*b*) Case of the banning of a work by Jacques Prévert

25. Decree No. 1831 of 24 June 1977 published in the Official Gazette of 30 June 1977, of which the text is annexed to the communication, bans the distribution, sale and circulation throughout the national territory of the book by Jacques Prévert entitled: "Tales for naughty children".

26. Articles 19 of the Universal Declaration of Human Rights, 15 of the International Covenant on Economic, Social and Cultural Rights and 19 of the International Covenant on Civil and Political Rights (the right to freedom of opinion and expression and the right to take part in cultural life and enjoy the benefits of scientific progress) are alleged to have been violated.

(*c*) Case of banning of two encyclopedias

27. Decree No. 2038 of 23 September 1980, published in the Official Gazette of 7 October 1980 which is also annexed to the communication, prohibits the distribution, sale and circulation throughout the national territory of the *Diccionario Enciclopedico Salvat* and volumes 2 and 9 of the *Gran Enciclopedia de Saber*, both published by Salvat, in Barcelona.

28. The same articles as in the case of the book by Jacques Prévert are alleged to have been violated.

29. At the present session the representative of the Argentine Government explained that Laws No. 22194 of 14 March 1980 and No. 21278 of 29 March 1976 were no longer in force. He added that subversion in Argentina had started in university circles and that those laws had been necessary to secure the dismissal of teachers known to have engaged in subversive activities. As far as Article 4 of the university law of 11 April 1980 was concerned, it had to be understood in the context of a totally politicized Argentine university system. It was not a question of banning, but rather of permitting university life to continue normally and not to be hampered by political or union activities. That law was consequently to be considered as temporary.

30. As regards Jacques Prévert's book, the representative of the Argentine Government explained that Jacques Prévert's works themselves were not banned, since the author enjoyed considerable success in Argentina. Last year a progovernment newspaper had devoted a long article to the writer. Action had in fact been taken against a tendentious translation in which an unreliable and inaccurate interpretation of the original French text had been given. The ban had had little effect because not only did another translation of the work exist, but the banned edition had been brought out by a small and little-known publisher.

31. As far as the two volumes of the Salvat encyclopedia were concerned, the representative of the Argentine Government explained that Decree No. 2083 had prohibited their distribution, sale and circulation because they contained a tendentious interpretation both of historical facts and of statistics. It was an isolated measure. After going to court, the publishing house Salvat had in any case modified the passages in question. They had also been able to recover the offending volumes and have them distributed outside Argentine territory.

32. One member of the Committee said that he had experienced, and therefore understood, the problem of universities approaching chaos, but he did not consider that such a situation should necessarily lead to the dismissal of teachers. He was of the opinion that the bans on the translation of Jacques Prévert's book and the two volumes of the encyclopedia were in contravention of Article 15 of the International Covenant on Economic, Social and Cultural Rights.

33. All the other members who spoke concerning the laws on teachers felt that the matter should be considered as settled, since those laws were no longer in force. On the other two points, one member felt that it was not up to a government to ban any book whatsoever. Another member, seeing that Argentina had left that period of agitation behind, wondered whether it was not possible to assume that that type of problem would not occur again.

34. The representative of the Argentine Government replied by pointing out that his country's Constitution authorized the government to censor books which were likely to affect public morals, but that the provision was very rarely applied. In the case of Jacques Prévert, the Argentine Government had invoked that law because it felt that the author's thoughts had been betrayed by a deliberately tendentious translation that no one else would defend.

35. One member pointed out that until a work entered the public domain, it was not for the state to act but the author's heirs. He nevertheless understood that the measures in question had been taken during an unusual period. Two members stressed that in situations of tension or social disturbance, it was easier to understand why

governments might take special measures, but this did not mean that they approved them.

36. The Chairman of the Committee then declared that there was a consensus among members as to the way in which the problems in question should be viewed, but he reminded the Committee that it also had to come to a decision on the admissibility of the communication. He thus put three options to the members, which he thought might reflect the opinions expressed:

(*a*) to declare the communication inadmissible on the grounds that the measures in question were based on the need to safeguard law and order as described in Article 19, paragraph 3, of the International Covenant on Civil and Political Rights;

(*b*) to postpone examination of the communication, and to ask the government to justify the decisions it had taken and to communicate to the Committee the translation in question;

(*c*) to declare the communication admissible, but to note that there was no reason for continuing the examination since the situation described by the author had changed, and consequently to follow the provisions of [paragraph] 14 (*j*) [of 104 EX/Decision 3.3].

37. The first solution was opposed by three members; one, because he felt that, in order to adopt it, it would be necessary to have more information on the translation itself so as to determine to what extent it was harmful; another, because he considered it something of an exaggeration to say that a not very widely distributed translation of one of Jacques Prévert's books was likely to endanger a government's security; and the third, because he thought that to take that decision would necessitate questioning the government in greater detail, while, for his part, he considered that no government should have to offer an explanation about the way it used the law and order clause.

38. Three other members were in favour of the second solution, since they felt that a Unesco Committee could not remain indifferent to the contents of a translation, and they expressed a wish for more information from the government. One member then said that whatever that information might be, he found it hard to see what conclusions the Committee could draw from it. He therefore opted for the third solution.

39. After discussion, the members of the Committee chose the third solution. The Committee *decided*, therefore, to declare the communication admissible but, in ac-

cordance with [paragraph] 14 (*j*) of 104 EX/Decision 3.3, not to continue the examination since it did not now appear to merit action.

No. 105/79

Concerning *Argentina*
Case of *Julia Angélica Brocca de Herrero*

Communication of 16 March 1979 submitted by
Julia Llabrés de Brocca

Autumn 1979 session of the Committee on Conventions and Recommendations (108th session of the Executive Board)[1]

87. The communication concerns the case of a woman teacher alleged to have been abducted on 28 March 1976 by a group of armed individuals who claimed that they were members of the police.

88. The representative of the government concerned pointed out that the author of the communication had not specified where the alleged victim had been professionally employed as a teacher, nor had she stated the connection between the alleged violation and the victim's status of teacher.

89. On the proposal of the Chairman, the Committee *decided* to declare the communication admissible, and *instructed* the Secretariat to obtain from the author the necessary information on the victim's profession and the connection between the alleged facts and her status of teacher.

Spring 1980 session of the Committee on Conventions and Recommendations (109th session of the Executive Board)[2]

208. The mother of the alleged victim complains that her daughter, a teacher, was abducted by a group of heavily armed young men who seemed to belong to the armed forces.

---

[1] See document 108 EX/38 PRIV., paras. 87-89; see also document 108 EX/CR/PROC.HR/1.
[2] See document 109 EX/52 PRIV., paras. 208-214; see also document 109 EX/CR/HR/1.

No. 105/79 **Argentina**

209. This communication was first examined by the Committee at its [autumn 1979 session].

210. The representative of the government concerned had pointed out at that time that the author of the communication had not specified where the alleged victim had been professionally employed as a teacher, nor had she stated the connection between the alleged violation and the victim's status of teacher.

211. On the proposal of the Chairman, the Committee had decided to declare the communication admissible, and had instructed the Secretariat to obtain from the author the necesseary information on the victim's profession and the connection between the alleged facts and her status of teacher.[3]

212. In letters dated 30 October and 6 December 1979 respectively, the Secretariat had written to the author of the communication and the Argentine Government. On 5 February 1980, it had sent the author a letter of reminder by registered mail. No reply had been received.

213. At the Committee's present session, the Argentine representative said that his government maintained its position, namely that the substance of this case was ill-founded, and he requested the Committee to strike it off its list.

214. The Committee again *decided* to suspend its consideration of the substance of the communication and to instruct the Secretariat to seek further information from the author of the communication concerning any link between the allegations declared admissible and Unesco's fields of competence.

---

[3] See document 108 EX/38 PRIV., para. 89 (*supra*, p. 315).

No. 106/79

Concerning *Argentina*
Case of *Gustavo Marcelo Juárez and María Gabriela Juárez*

Communication of 19 March 1979 submitted by
Oscar Mario Osvaldo Juárez

Spring 1979 session of the Committee on Conventions and Recommendations (107th session of the Executive Board)[1]

118. At the request of the representative of the government concerned, which had only recently received the communication, the Committee *decided* to defer consideration of its admissibility until its next session.

Autumn 1979 session of the Committee on Conventions and Recommendations (108th session of the Executive Board)[2]

90. The communication concerns the alleged violation of the right to education and the right to individual freedom of the author's two children, pupils at secondary schools. They are said to have been taken from their home by the federal police on 12 August 1977 and 19 April 1978 respectively.

91. The representative of the government concerned considered that the communication did not establish a sufficiently clear connection between the alleged violation and Unesco's fields of competence, since the student status of the alleged victims was not very obvious; however, he was not opposed to the communication being deemed admissible, or to its being held over pending the receipt of further information.

92. On the proposal of the Chairman, the Committee *decided* to declare the communication admissible.

---

[1] See document 107 EX/PRIV.31, para. 118; see also document 107 EX/CR/PROC.HR/41.
[2] See document 108 EX/38 PRIV., paras. 90-92; see also document 108 EX/CR/PROC.HR/1.

No. 106/79 **Argentina**

Spring 1980 session of the Committee on Conventions and Recommendations (109th session of the Executive Board)[3]

215. The author of this communcation had complained of the violation of the right to education and of the right to individual freedom of his two children, pupils at secondary schools. They are said to have been taken away from their home by the federal police.

216. At its [spring] 1979 session, the Committee had decided to defer consideration of the admissibility of this communication to the [autumn 1979] session at the request of the representative of the Argentine Government, which had received the communication only a short time beforehand.[4]

217. At its [autumn] 1979 session, the representative of the government concerned had stated that in its view the communication did not make it possible to establish a sufficiently clear connection between the alleged violation and Unesco's fields of competence, since the student status of the alleged victims was not very obvious, however, he had not been opposed to the communication being declared admissible, or to its being held over pending the receipt of further information.

218. On the proposal of the Chairman, the Committee had decided to declare the communication admissible.[5]

219. The author of the communication and the Government concerned had been informed of this by the Secretariat on 30 October 1979 and 6 December 1979 respectively.

220. In a letter dated 23 January 1980, the author of the communication notified the Committee that the replies provided by the Argentine Government to the [Organization of American States] were "mistaken" and "tendentious". Documents attached to that letter were sent to the Argentine Government on 15 February 1980.

221. The Argentine representative explained to the Committee that the reference to the mistake concerned an error by the Argentine authorities in their letter's reference to the charges for detainment of Mr Juárez; the correct charge, which should have been stated was the avoidance of military service, and not complicity with a fugitive from justice.

---

[3] See documents 109 EX/52 PRIV., paras. 215-223, and Corr.; see also documents 109 EX/CR/HR/1 and Add.2.

[4] See document 107 EX/PRIV.31, para. 118 (*supra*, p. 317).

[5] See document 108 EX/38 PRIV., para. 92 (*supra*, p. 317).

222. According to the Argentine Government, both of these persons were still missing; the search for them would continue, but for the moment there was no new information.

223. The Committee *decided* to apply the special procedure concerning missing persons to the case.[6] In view of the ever-increasing number of cases of this kind referred to it, the Committee noted that the United Nations Commission on Human Rights, at its last session, on 29 February 1980, had adopted resolution 20 (XXXVI) concerning the question of missing or disappeared persons.[7] That resolution provided for the the establishment of a working group consisting of five of its members, to serve in their individual capacities, "to examine questions relevant to enforced or involuntary disappearances of persons". The Committee was of the opinion that dupplication should be avoided, especially since the working group was a body that had been specially established to examine cases of disappearances. It accordingly felt that it was desirable, in the interest of the effectiveness of the mutual efforts, for co-operation to be established between the working group and the Committee. In this regard, the Committee noted that the aformentioned resolution 20 (XXXVI) provides that "the working group, in carrying out its mandate, shall seek and receive information from governments, intergovernmental organizations, humanitarian organizations and other reliable sources". On the basis of a proposal put forward by one of its members [...],[8] the Committee accordingly adopted a decison [...],[9] concerning the modalities of co-operation with the working group of the United Nations Commission on Human Rights responsible for examining questions of disappearances.

[6] See documents 108 EX/38 PRIV., para. 16, and 109 EX/52 PRIV., annex I, para. 8, and Corr.

[7] See *Official Records of the Economic and Social Council, 1980, Supplement No. 3* (E/1980/13 and Corr.1), chap. XXVI, sect. A.

[8] See document 109 EX/CR/HR/5.

[9] See documents 109 EX/52 PRIV., annex I, para. 8, and Corr.

No. 108/79

Concerning *Uruguay*
Case of *Hiber Conteris*

Communication of 25 March 1979 submitted by
Willem Zaal

Autumn 1979 session of the Committee on Conventions and Recommendations (108th session of the Executive Board)[1]

225. The author of this communication complains of the abduction, detention without trial or sentence and torture inflicted on the alleged victim, who is a Protestant minister of religion and a writer. He vas reportedly abducted at Montevideo airport on 2 December 1976, after taking part in a Christian conference for peace in Czechoslovakia.

226. The representative of the government concerned considered that the communication was manifestly ill-founded and therefore inadmissible in that it did not concern human rights, as Mr Conteris had been sentenced by a military tribunal, on 1 March 1979 to 15 years' imprisonment for acts punishable under Articles 150, 132, 137, 346 and 94 of the Penal Code. The author was currently detained in military premises. Moreover, the author gave no proof of the allegations which he put forward. The representative of Uruguay took the view that the communication was merely an attempt to discredit his government.

227. One member of the Committee underlined the difficulty for the Committee to take a decision concerning the communication, the assertions contained in it appearing to contradict those of the representative of Uruguay. Several members thought that the author of the communication should be informed of the statement made by the Uruguayan representative and be given an opportunity to reply, and that meanwhile the communication should be kept on the Committee's agenda for examination at the next session. Other members however preferred to declare it inadmissible, considering that the information provided was sufficient.

---

[1] See document 108 EX/38 PRIV., paras. 225-229; see also document 108 EX/CR/PROC.HR/1.

No. 108/79 **Uruguay**

228. One member raised the question of the possible consequences of creating a precedent by transmitting to the author all the information provided by the government to the Committee, when the Committee had not yet decided on the admissibility of the communication. The Director of the Division of Human Rights and Peace stated that the Committee's established practice was to request the Secretariat to transmit to the author the information presented by the government, in cases where there was doubt within the Committee whether the condition of paragraph 14 (*a*) (v) of 104 EX/Decision 3.3 had been fulfilled or not.

229. In conclusion, the Committee *decided* to suspend consideration of the communication and *instructed* the Secretariat to transmit to the author the information presented by the Government of Uruguay.

Spring 1980 session of the Committee on Conventions and Recommendations (109th session of the Executive Board)[2]

179. The author of this communication, a Dutch national who resides in the Netherlands, claims to be a person with reliable knowledge of the violations committed with regard to the alleged victim, Mr Conteris, who is a minister of religion and a writer. Mr Conteris was reportedly abducted at Montevideo airport on 2 December 1976, after taking part in a Christian conference for peace in Czechoslovakia. Since then he is said to have been held without trial or sentence, and to have been tortured.

180. This communication had been presented to the Committee at its [autumn] 1979 session where it was decided to hold this communication over; the Secretariat had been instructed to transmit to the author the information presented by the Uruguayan Government.[3] The information was made known to the author of the communication in a letter from the Secretariat dated 19 November 1979. Another letter was sent to the author on 12 February 1980. No answers were received from him.

181. The Uruguayan representative re-emphasized his government's earlier position that this case was clearly inadmissible. He pointed out that the author had not submitted any evidence of his allegations and had not responded to requests for additional information. The alleged victim, said the Uruguayan representative, had been found to be a dangerous member of a subversive group and had been tried and sentenced accordingly.

---

[2] See document 109 EX/52 PRIV., paras. 179-183; see also documents 109 EX/CR/HR/2 and Add.6.

[3] See document 108 EX/38 PRIV., para. 229 (*supra*, p. 322).

Uruguay **No. 108/79**

182. In response to a question the Uruguayan representative explained that persons judged by a military tribunal were kept in military prisons and that there had been no relation between his arrest and his return from the overseas conference.

183. In view of the fact that the author of the communication had not responded to the Committee's requests for additional information, the Committee *decided* to strike the communication from its list.

No. 109/79

Concerning *Paraguay*
Case of *Carmen Lara Castro*

Communication of 19 March 1979 submitted by
Alain Cornevaux

Autumn 1979 session of the Committee on Conventions and Recommendations (108th session of the Executive Board)[1]

184. The author of the communication, a French lawyer who describes himself as President of the "Comité français de soutien et de solidarité au peuple paraguayen" alleges the violation of rights recognized by several articles of the Universal Declaration of Human Rights and of the International Covenants on Human Rights, said to have been committed against Mrs Carmen Lara Castro, a former Member of Parliament and founding President of the Commission for the Defence of Human Rights in Paraguay. She is alleged to have been tried in an irregular manner for her activities in furthering the defence of human rights.

185. The representative of the Paraguayan Government, both in his letter of 6 September 1979 [...][2] and in his oral statement before the Committee, claimed that the author's accusations were untruthful. He wished to describe to the Committee the general situation of his country, before dealing with the specific case of Mrs Castro. Since 1954, the beginning of the state of emergency, the Government had been endeavouring to reconstruct the country. At present, the Paraguayan people were enjoying a period of peace and, for the first time, a democratic regime. The government guaranteed all freedoms to political parties and to the media. However, parties and political movements which advocated violence [...][3] were prohibited, and certain other measures had had to be taken in order to safeguard a lasting peace and a strong democracy.

---

[1] See document 108 EX/38 PRIV., paras. 184-187; see also documents 108 EX/CR/PROC. HR/1 and Add.6.
[2] See document 108 EX/CR/PROC.HR/1 Add.6.
[3] Corrigendum as requested by the representative of the government concerned; see documents 109 EX/52 PRIV., para. 293, and 109 EX/CR/HR/INF.2.

No. 109/79 **Paraguay**

186. Regarding [this communication], the Paraguayan representative emphasized the fact that Mrs Castro had never been deprived of freedom and had never been prosecuted for her activities within the Commission for the Defence of Human Rights. In reply to questions put to him by members of the Committee, he stated that there was no trial in process against Mrs Castro, for political or for any other reasons.

187. In the light of the information supplied by the representative of the Government concerned, the Committee *decided* that the communication, being manifestly ill-founded, did not fulfil the condition laid down in paragraph 14 (*a*) (v) of 104 EX/ Decision 3.3 and that, consequently, it was not admissible.

No. 110/79

Concerning *Paraguay*
Case of *Virgilio Barreiro*

Communication of 19 March 1979 submitted by
Alain Cornevaux

Autumn 1979 session of the Committee on Conventions and Recommendations (108th session of the Executive Board)[1]

188. This communication, submitted by Mr Alain Cornevaux, a French lawyer acting in his capacity as President of the "Comité français de soutien et de solidarité au peuple paraguayen", concerns the violation of several articles of the Universal Declaration of Human Rights and of the International Covenant on Civil and Political Rights. It concerns the arrest, on 10 August 1964, at his home in Asunción, of Mr Barreiro, a university professor. Professor Barreiro was allegedly taken to the police headquarters, and subsequently placed in a concentration camp.

189. The representative of Paraguay, who denied all allegations of torture, confirmed that Mr Barreiro was deprived of his freedom. However, that privation of freedom had no connection with his capacity as a professor, nor was it motivated by his political convictions, since, according to the representative of the Paraguayan Government, he shared the ideology of the State and was a member of the Government Party. He had been arrested, in his capacity as a senior official of the central administration of communications, for having revealed State secrets abroad. The affair vas therefore one of conspiracy within the civil service, punishable under Articles 41 and 61 of the Paraguayan Constitution. He had been deprived of freedom under Articles 79 and 80 of the Constitution and the supplementary laws.

190. The representative went on to state that the case was not a common one, nor was it a matter of discrimination in education; it was, rather, an isolated case implicating a person who had attempted to destroy the state of peace that the present government had taken so many years to establish.

[1] See document 108 EX/38 PRIV., paras. 188-193; see also documents 108 EX/CR/PROC. HR/1 and Add.6.

No. 110/79 **Paraguay**

191. Several members of the Committee were disturbed by the fact that the person concerned had not yet been tried and that he was still being detained without trial or indictment after 15 years, a period that the Committee considered excessive. Most of the Committee members who spoke took the view that the connection with Unesco's spheres of competence was clearly established, in view of Mr Barreiro's profession, although one member expressed doubts on that subject.

192. Several members of the Committee stressed the important intellectual and cultural role of Professor Barreiro in Latin America as a whole.

193. At the close of the discussion, the Committee *decided* to declare the communication admissible and to request the Government of Paraguay to supply the Committee with all relevant information on any indictment of Mr Barreiro, and in particular on whether or not he would be tried.

Spring 1980 session of the Committee on Conventions and Recommendations (109th session of the Executive Board)[2]

272. This communication concerned the arrest on 10 August 1964 of Mr Virgilio Barreiro, a university professor. Mr Barreiro is said to have been detained for the past 16 years without having received a trial or having been indicted.

273. At its [autumn 1979] session, the Committee decided to declare this communication admissible and to request the Government of Paraguay to supply the Committee with all relevant information on any indictment of Mr Barreiro, and in particular whether or not he would be tried.[3]

274. The representative of the Director-General informed the Committee that the representative of the Paraguayan Government asked the Committee to defer its examination of the substance of this communication until its next session in view of the fact that he was not yet in possession of the information which the Committee wished to have on this case.

275. Several members of the Committee expressed their concern over the fact that the Paraguayan representative had not come before the Committee to present to it the information which it had requested.

---

[2] See document 109 EX/52 PRIV., paras. 272-278; see also document 109 EX/CR/HR/1.
[3] See document 108 EX/38 PRIV., para. 193 (*supra*, p. 328).

Paraguay **No. 110/79**

276. The Chairman proposed and the Committee *decided*:

[i] to defer the examination of the substance of this communication as per the request of the representative of the Paraguayan Government;

[ii] to request the Government of Paraguay to present its reply to the Committee in writing and to send it sufficiently far in advance of the Committee's next session to allow it to study it with due care; and

[iii] to instruct the Secretariat to request, in the future, the positions of governments concerned in writing, in advance, so that the Committee would have time to study them with due care.

277. When this report was being adopted, the representative of the Director-General informed the Committee that the representative of the Government of Paraguay, by letter dated 19 May 1980, had informed the Director-General that Mr Barreiro had just been released.

278. Several members of the Committee considered that very positive note should be taken of Mr Barreiro's release. The Committee accordingly *decided* that the communication should be deemed as having been settled.

No. 111/79

Concerning *Argentina*
Case of *Héctor Alberto González*

Communication of 5 March 1979 submitted by
Juan Evangelista González

Autumn 1979 session of the Committee on Conventions and Recommendations (108th session of the Executive Board)[1]

93. The communication deels with the abduction of the author's son on 4 August 1976 by a group of armed people who introduced themselves as members of the State security forces.

94. The representative of the government concerned considered that the communication was not admissible, since the student status of the alleged victim was not clearly established, and he stressed that this case had been brought before the Inter-American Commission on Human Rights.

95. On the proposal of the Chairman, the Committee *decided* to declare the communication inadmissible, and *instructed* the Secretariat to inform the author of the communication of the existence of other international authorities.

[1] See document 108 EX/38 PRIV., paras. 93-95; see also document 108 EX/CR/PROC.HR/1.

No. 112/79

Concerning *Argentina*
Case of *Marcelo E. Vensentini and Rosalba Vensentini*

Communication of 20 July 1979 submitted by
Remy Vensentini

Spring 1980 session of the Committee on Conventions and Recommendations (109th session of the Executive Board)[1]

29. The author of the communication complains of the abduction und disappearance of his daughter and the detention of his son, both allegedly students.

30. The representative of the Argentine Government indicated that the author of the communication had only filled out the required questionnaire for his son and not for his daughter. The Argentine Government was thus in a position to provide information only for the case of the son. His case, as it happened, was quite clear: he had been arrested for participating in armed terrorist activities, charged, tried and sentenced before a regular tribunal in accordance with proper legal procedures. The representative of the government stated that there was no link between the arrest and Unesco's areas of competence and that the communication should thus be considered inadmissible as manifestly ill-founded.

31. A member of the Committee stated that in his opinion the facts given about the daughter in a separate letter should have provided some basis for investigation and that the son's student status could serve as a basis for the admissibility of the communication.

32. Other members of the Committee felt that it was clear that the case involved common law crimes and did not involve Unesco's fields of competence. They felt, however, that the author should be given the opportunity of sending in a questionnaire concerning the case of his daughter.

---

[1] See document 109 EX/52 PRIV., paras. 29-33; see also document 109 EX/CR/HR/3.

No. 112/79 **Argentina**

33. The Committee *decided* to declare the communication inadmissible and *instructed* the Secretariat to send the author another questionnaire for the case of his daughter.

No. 113/79

Concerning *Argentina*
Case of *Federico Eduardo Álvarez Rojas*

Communication of 16 March 1979 submitted by
Federico Álvarez Rojas (father)

Autumn 1979 session of the Committee on Conventions and Recommendations (108th session of the Executive Board)[1]

96. This communication concerns the case of a physicist working for the Argentine National Atomic Energy Commission, who is alleged to have been abducted, together with his wife, and consequently prevented. from pursuing his scientific research.

97. The representative of the Argentine Government stated that the alleged victim was well known in Argentina, and that his national authorities were very much concerned at this case. He recalled that the victim's father had brought the case before the federal authorities, and that in addition a federal jury was conducting an inquiry. He stressed that the disappearance of Mr Rojas represented a serious loss of intellectual potential for Argentina.

98. Lastly, the representative of the Argentine Government drew the Committee's attention to the fact that this case was on the list of the 50 priority cases in respect of which the Inter-American Commission on Human Rights was currently trying to obtain information on the spot, in Buenos Aires. He accordingly proposed that consideration of the case be suspended pending receipt by the Secretariat of information on the results of the Commission's inquiry.

99. The Director of the Division of Human Rights and Peace recalled that the fact of a case being submitted to another international body did not affect the conditions of admissibility specified in 104 EX/Decision 3.3, and thus did not prevent the Committee from declaring a communication admissible.

---

[1] See document 108 EX/38 PRIV., paras. 96-100; see also document 108 EX/CR/PROC.HR/1.

100. The Committee accordingly *decided* to declare this communication admissible, and *instructed* the Secretariat:

(*a*) to request additional information from the Argentine Government;

(*b*) to ascertain from the Inter-American Commission on Human Rights the outcome of the inquiry currently under way.

Spring 1980 session of the Committee on Conventions and Recommendations (109th session of the Executive Board)[2]

224. The author of this communication alleges that his son, who had the same name as the author, was deprived of his freedom as a result of himself and his wife being abducted from their home on 1 October 1976 by a heavily armed group, which ransacked the house and stole several objects.

225. The author believes that the connection with the fields of competence of Unesco was established by the fact that the alleged victim was a physicist working for the National Atomic Energy Commission and that the abduction prevents him from pursuing his scientific research in his country and in other countries to which he has been invited.

226. The Committee examined this communication during its [autumn] 1979 session. On that occasion, the representative of the Argentine Government suggested holding over consideration of this case until such time as the Secretariat was in a position to be acquainted with the results of the Inter-American Commission [on] Human Rights inquiry.

227. The Committee had decided to declare this communication admissible, and had instructed the Secretariat:[3]

(*a*) to request additional information from the Argentine Government;

(*b*) to ascertain from the Inter-American Commission on Human Rights the outcome of the inquiry currently under way.

228. In accordance with the Committee's instruction, the Secretariat wrote to the author of the communication (30 October 1979), the Argentine Government (6 Decem-

---

[2] See document 109 EX/52 PRIV., paras. 224-230; see also document 109 EX/CR/HR/1.
[3] See document 108 EX/38 PRIV., para. 100 (*supra*, p. 336).

ber 1979) and the [Organization of American States (OAS)] (9 November 1979). On 18 January 1980, it sent a telegram of reminder to the OAS. No reply had as yet been forthcoming.

229. The representative of the Argentine Government while pointing out some contradictory claims in the communication, agreed that the case was one which involved a scientist and was thus of interest to Unesco. He explained that this person was on his country's list of missing persons, that his government was actively searching for him, but that no results had yet been obtained.

230. The Committee expressed its appreciation for the interest and manifestly willing co-operation of the Argentine authorities on this case and *decided* to follow the same procedure as in the preceding case,[4] i.e. to apply the special procedure on missing persons.[5]

---

[4] See document 109 EX/52 PRIV., para. 223 (*supra*, p. 319), communication No. 106/79 concerning *Argentina*, case of *Gustavo Marcelo Juárez and María Gabriela Juárez*;

[5] See documents 108 EX/38 PRIV., para. 16, and 109 EX/52 PRIV., annex I, para. 8, and Corr.

No. 115/79

Concerning *United States of America*
Case of *Vachel Lindsay*

Communication of 29 March 1979 submitted by
James W. Drought

Autumn 1979 session of the Committee on Conventions and Recommendations (108th session of the Executive Board)[1]

162. The author of this communication, who is Chairman of the Vachel Lindsay Centennial Committee, and who claims to be acting in the threefold capacity of victim, representative of the victim and person with reliable knowledge of the alleged violation, alleges that the United States Government has violated the Constitution of Unesco by depriving the world of information about Mr Lindsay, an American poet born in 1879.

163. He also claims that the American Government has refused any co-operation with the Centennial Committee or any financial aid for projects connected with the celebration of the Lindsay centenary, and that the postal service has interrupted the distribution of information sent out by his Committee.

164. The representative of the government concerned referred to the letter that the Permanent Delegation sent to Unesco on 10 September 1979 and which gave a detailed reply to each of Mr Drought's allegations. According to that information, the government concerned had conducted a detailed inquiry, in connection with the allegations contained in the communication, which covered the postal service, the National Endowment for the Humanities, and the published works of Vachel Lindsay in the United States. The government considered that the allegation concerning the suppression of information distributed by post was without substance and that other allegations, which did not come under the heading of human rights, were also manifestly ill-founded.

---

[1] See document 108 EX/38 PRIV., paras. 162-169; see also documents 108 EX/CR/PROC. HR/1 and Add.7.

No. 115/79 **United States of America**

165. Regarding the requests for a subvention formulated by the Lindsay Centennial Committee, they had, after careful study, been judged as failing to comply with the criteria in force.

166. In any case, refusal of financial aid could not constitute a violation of human rights.

167. The representative of the government concerned pointed out in that connection that the alleged grievances were connected with acts that could not be imputed to his government, and that in no case were they violations of human rights. He stated that Lindsay's memory was still alive in his country, and that the poet's writings were readily available and were even to be found in the anthologies used in secondary education.

168. A member of the Committee was surprised that the government should express doubts about the existence of a "black list" among United States publishers, in view of the well-known history of such lists at the time of McCarthyism. The same member did not intend thereby to pass judgement on the admissibility of the communication, since all the Committee members who had spoken considered it inadmissible.

169. In view of the reply of the Government of the United States of America, the Committee *decided* to declare the communication inadmissible on the ground that it was manifestly ill-founded, and to instruct the Secretariat to send a copy of the government's reply to the author of the communication.

No. 117/79

Concerning *Romania*
Case of *A. Dan Vilcu*

Communication of 10 April 1979 submitted by
A. Dan Vilcu

Autumn 1979 session of the Committee on Conventions and Recommendations (108th session of the Executive Board)[1]

194. The author of this communication claims to be the victim of a violation of his right to benefit from the result of five years of university studies, owing to the fact that the authorities of the country concerned have refused to confer upon him his degree marking the successful completion of his studies in Romania. He is now living in Sweden as a political refugee and claims to have applied repeatedly for the said diploma.

195. The Romanian Government, both in the letter which the Permanent Delegate sent to the Director-General on 7 September 1979 [...][2] and in the oral explanation of its representative before the Committee, states that the diploma may be issued to the holder in person once the latter has paid the Institute's fees.

196. Some members of the Committee asked the Romanian representative if the student could obtain his diploma by correspondence or through the Romanian Embassy in Stockholm. In reply he stated that Mr Vilcu must present himself in person to sign a register, in accordance with the regulations in force. One member of the Committee considered it only natural that the government should demand the payment of the Institute's fees, which represented only part of the sums which the nation had spent in training the student.

197. Several members of the Committee considered that in such a case, Unesco's role should consist in helping the parties to find a solution to the administrative

---

[1] See document 108 EX/38 PRIV., paras. 194-199; see also documents 108 EX/CR/PROC. HR/1 and Add.8.
[2] See document 108 EX/CR/PROC.HR/1 Add.8.

problems involved, and they appealed to the Romanian Government to allow the rules to be applied flexibly in such a way as to enable Mr Vilcu to obtain his diploma from the Romanian Embassy in Sweden or to empower his representative to obtain it at Bucharest.

198. It was suggested that the author should first be informed of the position of the Romanian Government, before the Committee decided on the admissibility of the communication.

199. The Committee *decided*, therefore, to suspend consideration of the case and to instruct the Secretariat to transmit the information contained in the Romanian delegate's letter to the author of the communication.

Spring 1980 session of the Committee on Conventions and Recommendations (109th session of the Executive Board)[3]

123. The author of this communication claims to be victim of a violation of his right to benefit from the result of five years' study, owing to the fact that the authorities of the country concerned refused to confer upon him his degree marking the successful completion of his studies in Romania in July 1977. Since August 1978, he has been living in Sweden as a political refugee. On 5 December 1978 he applied to the Romanian Embassy in Stockholm, the Romanian Minister for Education and the Rector of the Technical College in Bucharest where he carried out his studies, without any result. He states that it is important to be in possession of his degree for his professional situation Sweden.

124. This communication was first presented to the Committee at its [autumn] 1979 session. On that occasion, the representative of the Romanian Government stated that the degree to which Mr Vilcu is entitled could be conferred upon him once he had presented himself in person and reimbursed part of his scholarship. At that meeting a response to questions from the Committee as to whether the student could obtain his dipoloma by correspondence or through the Romanian Embassy in Stockholm, the Romanian representative stated that Mr Vilcu had to present himself in person to sign a register, in accordance with the regulations in force.

125. The Committee had decided to hold this case over and had instructed the Secretariat to forward the information contained in the letter from the Romanian delegate to the author of the communication.[4] The Secretariat sent that information to the au-

[3] See document 109 EX/52 PRIV., paras. 123-129; see also documents 109 EX/CR/HR/2 and Add.

[4] See document 108 EX/38 PRIV., para. 199 (*supra*, p. 342).

thor on 5 November 1979 and, in addition, in a letter dated 12 December 1979, it informed the Romanian Government of the foregoing. No new element had been received since then.

126. At the Committee's present meeting, the representative of the Romanian Government reiterated his government's willingness to confer Mr Vilcu's degree once he presented himself in person and repaid part of his scholarship.

127. One member of the Committee pointed out the fact that Mr Vilcu claimed his parents were making payments to the Romanian authorities for the education he had received and that the Committee might want to examine that point.

128. Other members of the Committee felt that the case was strictly a contractual one between Mr Vilcu and the Romanian Government.

129. Taking note with appreciation of the Romanian representative's spirit of co-operation on this case, the Committee *decided* to declare the communication inadmissible and at the same time *requested* the representative of the government to use his good offices to attempt to find a solution to the problems of distance and expense which hampered Mr Vilcu in his attempt to obtain his degree.

No. 123/79

Concerning *Romania and Yugoslavia*
Case of *Djoka Stojanović*

Communication of 21 May 1979 submitted by
Paulette Stojanović-Le Trionnaire

Autumn 1979 session of the Committee on Conventions and Recommendations (108th session of the Executive Board)[1]

200. The author of this communication complains of the violation of several articles of the Universal Declaration of Human Rights committed in respect of her husband, who is alleged to have been abducted by members of the Yugoslav police on 8 August 1975 in Romania, where he was on holiday, and taken by force to Yugoslavia for the purpose of imprisonment.

201. The representative of the Romanian Government considered that the Committee should not hesitate to declare the communication inadmissible on account of the fact that Mr Stojanović was an electrician by profession, which had no relation to Unesco's fields of competence. The communication did not, therefore, fulfil the condition set out in paragraph 14 (*a*) (iii) of 104 EX/Decision 3.3.

202. The Yugoslav representative shared the view that the communication was not admissible because it had no connection with Unesco's fields of competence.

203. One member of the Committee, while considering the communication not admissible, wished to know whether Mr Stojanović was in fact in Yugoslavia. The representative of the Yugoslav Government replied that he had no information on that point.

204. After discussion, the Committee *decided* that the communication was not admissible because no link with the fields of competence had been established, in accordance with paragraph 14 (*a*) (iii) of 104 EX/Decision 3.3. Moreover, the Com-

---

[1] See document 108 EX/38 PRIV., paras. 200-204; see also document 108 EX/CR/PROC.HR/1 Add.

mittee *instructed* the Secretariat to inform the author of the communication that it was possible to refer the case to other international bodies.

No. 124/79

Concerning *Poland*
Case of *Zygmunt Elbiński*

Communication of 18 April 1979 submitted by
Zygmunt Elbiński

Spring 1980 session of the Committee on Conventions and Recommendations (109th session of the Executive Board)[1]

117. The author of this communication claims that the Polish authorities will not allow him to pursue his scientific work and refuse him the effective remedy of a fair hearing.

118. The representative of the Polish Government stated that the communication was manifestly ill-founded; especially since the author was mentally deranged and wrote thousands of such unfounded communications every year, as the United Nations and the various foreign embassies in Poland could confirm. She asked the Committee not to admit the communication.

119. A member of the Committee felt that since the Committee was not in a position to refute the Polish Government's assertion that the man was insane, the case should be declared inadmissible.

120. Several other members of the Committee considered that there were no signs of insanity in the communication. They further felt that it should not be the Committee's role to request proofs of sanity from the authors which the Committee could present to the governments concerned, and that questions of sanity should be discussed during the examination of substance, not of admissililit y.

121. Another member of the Committee raised the question of the admissibility of the communication in connection with the fact that the events referred to by the author took place 16 years ago.

---

[1] See document 109 EX/52 PRIV., paras. 117-122; see also document 109 EX/CR/HR/3.

No. 124/79 **Poland**

122. The Committee *decided* that the communication was inadmissible in view of the period of time that had elapsed since the alleged events had taken place.

No. 125/79

Concerning *Argentina*
Case of *Juan Carlos Suárez*

Communication of 21 December 1978 submitted by
Teresa Oberti de Suárez

Autumn 1979 session of the Committee on Conventions and Recommendations (108th session of the Executive Board)[1]

101. The communication concerns the alleged violation of a number of human rights resulting from the abduction of the son of the author of the communication. It is stated that before he disappeared Mr Suárez had been a student of architecture at the National University.

102. The representative of the government concerned considered that the alleged victim's student status should first be checked, since, according to the information in the possession of the Argentine Government, and even according to the text of the communication, the victim was reportedly a craftworker in upholstery. On the basis of paragraph 14 (*a*) (v) of 104 EX/Decision 3.3, he argued that the author of the communication had not provided "relevant evidence", and he accordingly proposed that consideration of the communication be held over until such time as its author furnished evidence of Mr Suárez's student status.

103. In reply to a question raised by a member of the Committee, the Director of the Division of Human Rights and Peace recalled that since there was a presumption of bona fides, it was not in accordance with the Committee's practice to ask the author of the communication to furnish evidence of status (such as educational certificates and the like), at least during the consideration of admissibility. Several members of the Committee pointed out that in accordance with the principle that the different parties involved in a case should be on equal terms, which is an essential element of good faith, it was for the Argentine Government to provide evidence in support of its statement.

---

[1] See document 108 EX/38 PRIV., paras. 101-104; see also document 108 EX/CR/PROC.HR/1.

No. 125/79 **Argentina**

104. On the proposal of the Chairman, the Committee *decided* to suspend consideration of the admissibility of the communication and to instruct the Secretariat to obtain additional information from its author.

Spring 1980 session of the Committee on Conventions and Recommendations (109th session of the Executive Board)[2]

34. In this connection, the author complains of the violation of the human rights of her son, an architecture student at the National University, who was reportedly abducted by four armed persons on 19 November 1977.

35. At its [autumn 1979] session the Committee had decided to hold over examination of the communication so that evidence concerning the student status of Mr Suárez could be obtained from the author.[3] The author in her reply stated that documents concerning her son had disappeared at the same time that he had, when his home had been ransacked; she did, however, enclose photocopies of various documents relating to her son's architectural studies.

36. The representative of the government, while agreeing that this was a case concerning a student, stated that he felt that the case should be considered inadmissible for two reasons: first, there was no link between the person's student status and the fact that he was missing. He felt that a person's profession should not automatically lead to Unesco's involvement, otherwise Unesco risked taking on all cases involving missing students and thereby weaken its effectiveness. Second, the case was presently pending before the Inter-American Commission on Human Rights; he thus felt that Unesco should be duplicating the efforts of another body and that this was highly inadvisable.

37. Several Committee members raised questions coneerning two main issues: (1) whether the status of being a student sufficed by itself to establish a link with Unesco's fields of competence; and (2) whether a communication could be examined at the same time by Unesco and another international body.

38. The representative of the Director-General reminded the Committee that, according to its practice, the student status of an alleged victim created, at the stage of the examination of admissibility, a "presumption" of the existence of a link between the alleged violation and the fields of competence of Unesco. Such a presumption, however, could not by itself be considered as a determining factor justifyring the inter-

[2] See document 109 EX/52 PRIV., paras. 34-42; see also document 109 EX/CR/HR/2.
[3] See document 108 EX/38 PRIV., para. 104 (*supra*, p. 350).

vention of the Organization. In effect, the decision declaring a communication admissible constituted only a preliminary step which allowed both the Committee and the goverment concerned to be informed and to take notice of a presumed link between the case examined and Unesco's fields of competence and of the fact that a closer look at the substance of the allegations was called for.

39. As concerned the examination of a communication by another international body, the representative of the Director-General explained that 104 EX/Decision 3.3 was purposely drafted so as to permit the Committee to declare as admissible a communication already being examined by another international body.

40. Responding to questions from Committee members concerning the possibility of obtaining additional information from other international bodies, the representative of the Director-General replied that the Secretariat could attempt to do so, provided that the Committee so instructed it, but could only do so *vis-à-vis* public, official organizations; in any event, the Secretariat can never act so as to provide assistance to authors of communications.

41. In view of the student status of the alleged victim, the Committee *decided* to declare the communication admissible and *instructed* the Secretariat to obtain additional information thereon from the Inter-American Commission on Human Rights. Furthemore, the Committee *instructed* the Secretariat to obtain, in general, additional information for competent international bodies whenever the file on a communication was incomplete or insufficient and such information would enable the Committee to take a decision more readily on the admissibility of the communication.

42. The representative of the Argentine Government formulated a reservation on the decision of the Committee, because: (1) there was no link between the alleged violations and the fields of competence of Unesco; and (2) the case was already before the Inter-American Commission on Human Rights.

No. 126/79

Concerning *Morocco*
Case of *Eddimaoui Lahbib*

Communication of 30 April 1979 submitted by
an Amnesty International group

Spring 1980 session of the Committee on Conventions and Recommendations (109th session of the Executive Board)[1]

114. The authors of the communication, an Amnesty International group in the Federal Republic of Germany, claim that Mr Lahbib, a Moroccan of Sahrawi origin, employee at the Court of Appeal in Rabat, was arrested solely on the basis of his ethnic and cultural origins.

115. The representative of the Moroccan Government stated that the communication did not clearly identify the victim which made it impossible for his government to investigate the case. Other than a name and a vague profession there were no data to go by. He further emphasized that the Moroccan Government had never put any pressure on any ethnic group for cultural, religious or any other reasons.

116. Several members of the Committee felt that the case was not one coming within Unesco's competence and the Committee *decided* to declare it inadmissible as being manifestly ill-founded.

[1] See document 109 EX/52 PRIV., paras. 114-116; see also document 109 EX/CR/HR/3.

No. 127/79

Concerning *Argentina*
Case of *María Cristina García Suárez*

Communication of 7 May 1979 submitted by
Héctor Daniel Bou

Spring 1980 session of the Committee on Conventions and Recommendations (109th session of the Executive Board)[1]

43. In this communication the author complains of the abduction of his wife, an accountant, by a group of armed persons claiming to belong to the security forces.

44. The Committee was of the opinion that this case was not linked to Unesco's fields of competence, and *decided* that the communication would be declared inadmissible in accordance with paragraph 14 (*a*) (iii) of 104 EX/Decision 3.3.

[1] See document 109 EX/52 PRIV., paras. 43-44; see also document 109 EX/CR/HR/3.

No. 129/79

Concerning *Argentina*
Case of *Oscar Ernesto Cocca Astrada*

Communication of 31 May 1979 submitted by
Etelvina Astrada

Autumn 1979 session of the Committee on Conventions and Recommendations (108th session of the Executive Board)[1]

105. The communication concerns the disappearance in May 1977 of the son of the author, a student of psychology in the Faculty of Philosophy and the Arts at Córdoba University.

106. The representative of the government concerned stressed that the communication gave no specific information on the way in which the alleged victim was said to have disappeared; and he drew the Committee's attention to the fact that some days before he disappeared, the alleged victim had expressed the intention of going on a journey, and that the investigations carried out had yielded no result. He accordingly considered that the communication was inadmissible, since there was nothing which could be regarded as imputable to the Argentine State, and in any case the author of the communication had not made use of available domestic remedies.

107. The Director of the Division of Human Rights and Peace stated that it emerged from the preparatory work on 104 EX/Decision 3.3 that there was no question of requiring the claimant to furnish, during the consideration of admissibility, proof of his allegations, but merely evidence on which a conclusion might be reached as to their apparent credibility. Moreover, the stipulation in paragraph 14 (*a*) (ix) of 104 EX/Decision 3.3 did not entail a requirement that the author of the communication should have exhausted all available domestic remedies, but simply that he should indicate whether an attempt had been made to do so.

[1] See document 108 EX/38 PRIV., paras. 105-108; see also document 108 EX/CR/PROC.HR/1.

No. 129/79 **Argentina**

108. Considering that a doubt persisted as to whether the alleged facts could be imputed to the government concerned, the Committee *decided* to suspend consideration of the admissibility of the communication, and *instructed* the Secretariat to request additional information from its author and from the various international organizations before which the case had been brought.

Spring 1980 session of the Committee on Conventions and Recommendations (109th session of the Executive Board)[2]

45. In this communication, the author complains that her son, a student of psychology, has disappeared. At its [autumn 1979] session the Committee had decided to suspend the examination of the case and seek more information from the Organization of American States and also from the author concerning the victim's disappearance.[3] The Secretariat had received no reply to its numerous letters to the author and to the Organization of American States.

46. The representative of the Argentine Government stated that he felt that the case should be struck from the Committee's list given that no new information had been forthcoming. He reminded the Committee that the young man in question had expressed the intention to undertake a journey and in his opinion this was simply a case of a young man who had gone abroad.

47. Since no additional information had been received, the Committee *decided* to strike the communication off its list.

---

[2] See document 109 EX/52 PRIV., paras. 45-47; see also document 109 EX/CR/HR/2.

[3] See document 108 EX/38 PRIV., para. 108 (*supra*, p. 358).

No. 132/79

Concerning *Union of Soviet Socialist Republics*
Case of *Georgi Mikhailov*

Communication of 12 June 1979 submitted by
Irina Baskina

Autumn 1979 session of the Committee on Conventions and Recommendations (108th session of the Executive Board)[1]

214. This communication concerns the case of a teacher alleged to have been arrested and held arbitrarily in March 1979 on the grounds that he supported the Movement of Non-Conformist Painters.

215. The representative of the government concerned explained that the alleged victim had been convicted, in accordance with existing Soviet law, for illicit traffic in paintings, icons and slides.

216. After discussion, the Committee *decided* to declare the communication inadmissible as being manifestly ill-founded, and *instructed* the Secretariat to inform the author of the information provided by the representative of the government concerned.

---

[1] See document 108 EX/38 PRIV., paras. 214-216; see also document 108 EX/CR/PROC.HR/1.

No. 133/79

Concerning *Nicaragua*
Case of *Vilma Núñez de Escorcia*

Communication of 8 June 1979 submitted by
Gerardo Trejos

Autumn 1979 session of the Committee on Conventions and Recommendations (108th session of the Executive Board)[1]

181. The communication concerns the imprisonment, in May 1979, following a summary judgement by a military tribunal, of a woman university professor who was also secretary of the Latin American Federation of University Women Graduates.

182. The Director of the Division of Human Rights and Peace informed the Committee that since receipt of that communication, Mrs Escorcia had been released by the new government of Nicaragua and that she had, moreover, been appointed judge at the Supreme Court.

183. In view of the foregoing, the Committee welcomed the solution that had been found for that case, which was in keeping with respect for human rights and *decided* accordingly to remove the communication from its agenda.

---

[1] See document 108 EX/38 PRIV., paras. 181-183; see also document 108 EX/CR/PROC.HR/1.

No. 134/79

Concerning *Chile*
Case of *Abelardo Castro Hidalgo*

Communication of 7 May 1979 submitted by
Abelardo Castro Hidalgo

Autumn 1979 session of the Committee on Conventions and Recommendations (108th session of the Executive Board)[1]

154. The author of this communication, who has been a political refugee in Sweden since 22 March 1977, claims to be the victim of the violation of several human rights on account of the fact that the Chilean authorities have not given him permission to return to his country.

155. The representative of the government concerned stated that this communication did not warrant consideration by the Committee; firstly, the author of the communication invoked the amnesty law, whereas he had committed no offence such as would enable him to benefit from it; and secondly, Mr Hidalgo was conducting an active campaign abroad against Chile, which had been the reason for refusal of his right to return to Chile. The representative of Chile considered that the Secretariat might ask the author to clarify his administrative position in viev of the fact that he had been neither arrested nor banished, and suggested that he might request clarifications concerning the accusations brought against him. Nevertheless, the government concerned did not object to this communication being declared admissible.

156. According to one member of the Committee, all the conditions of admissibility had been fulfilled in the case in point, and he pointed out that use of the "recurso de amparo" applied to appeals against an administrative act. The consular authorities of Chile in Stockholm had, however, refused to hand over to Mr Hidalgo a document rejecting his application to return to Chile. The representative of the Chilean Government pointed out in this respect that the person concerned could raise the matter with the consular authority which, in turn, had to refer it to the Ministry of the Interi-

[1] See document 108 EX/38 PRIV., paras. 154-157; see also document 108 EX/CR/PROC.HR/1.

or, which was obliged to provide a document confirming its refusal to authorize Mr Hidalgo's return to his country. At that point, Mr Hidalgo could appeal against the legality of the refusal by way of the recourse of "amparo". Since it was important for authors of similar communications to be aware of the available means of redress against a refusal to authorize a return to Chile in cases where the person concerned had left the country of his own free will, or following banishment, commutation of a sentence or the granting of diplomatic asylum, the representative of the Chilean Government agreed, at the request of several members of the Committee, to prepare an appropriate memorandum on the subject which he would submit to the Secretariat.

157. On the proposal of the Chairman, the Committee *decided* to defer consideration of the admissibility of the communication and *instructed* the Secretariat to send the author of the communication the various items of information provided by the representative of the government concerned.

Spring 1980 session of the Committee on Conventions and Recommendations (109th session of the Executive Board)[2]

Autumn 1980 session of the Committee on Conventions and Recommendations (110th session of the Executive Board)[3]

Spring 1981 session of the Committee on Conventions and Recommendations (112th sessions of the Executive Board)[4]

[2] See document 109 EX/52 PRIV., paras. 81-85 (*supra*, pp. 181-182), communication No. 54/78 conerning *Chile*, case of *Arturo Montes Larrain*.
[3] See document 110 EX/40 PRIV., paras. 45-56 (*supra*, pp. 182-184), communication No. 54/78 conerning *Chile*, case of *Arturo Montes Larrain*.
[4] See document 112 EX/30 PRIV., paras. 49-64 (*supra*, pp. 184-187), communication No. 54/78 conerning *Chile*, case of *Arturo Montes Larrain*.

No. 137/79

Concerning *Argentina*
Case of *Jorge Víctor Sznaider*

Communication of 7 June 1979 submitted by
Beatriz Elena Sznaider

Autumn 1979 session of the Committee on Conventions and Recommendations (108th session of the Executive Board)[1]

109. The communication relates to the alleged violation of the right to freedom in respect of the brother of the author of the communication, and of five other young people, who were allegedly abducted on 19 May 1979 by 10 people in plain clothes who claimed to be members of the "security forces". These persons also reportedly seized the whole of Mr Sznaider's literary work.

110. The representative of the Argentine Government pointed out that the communication gave no information on the results of the appeal procedure initiated in June 1979, and that in any case Mr Sznaider's name did not appear on any list of arrested persons. He considered it possible that Mr Sznaider, as a member of a subversive group, had voluntarily gone into hiding. Lastly, he informed the Committee that fresh information on this case would be communicated to it in the very near future.

111. On the proposal of the Chairman, the Committee *decided* to declare the communication admissible.

Spring 1980 session of the Committee on Conventions and Recommendations (109th session of the Executive Board)[2]

231. The author of the communication complains that her brother and five other young people were abducted on 19 May 1979 by 10 people in plain clothes who

[1] See document 108 EX/38 PRIV., paras. 109-111; see also document 108 EX/CR/PROC.HR/1.
[2] See document 109 EX/52 PRIV., paras. 231-235; see also document 109 EX/CR/HR/1.

claimed to be members of the "security forces". These persons also reportedly seized the entirety of Mr Sznaider's literary work.

232. The connection with the fields of competence of Unesco was said to stem from the fact that the alleged victim was a student at the school of mathematics and that he was also connected with literary groups of the Argentine society of writers.

233. The Committee had considered the admissibility of this communication at its [autumn] 1979 session, and had decided to declare it admissible.[3]

234. The Argentine representative stated that his government took the position that the alleged detention, according to information available to it, had not occurred. There was a judge who had just begun looking into this disappearance, and the Argentine representative promised to pass on to the Committee all information as it became available. So far it was only known that not all of these young people had been students, at least one was a political activist; as for Sznaider, his whereabouts were still unknown.

235. The Committee *decided* to again apply the measures it had adopted for the two preceding cases,[4] i.e. to apply the special procedure on missing persons.[5]

---

[3] See document 108 EX/38 PRIV., para. 111 (*supra*, p. 365).
[4] See document 109 EX/52 PRIV., para. 223 (*supra*, p. 319), communication No. 106/79 concerning *Argentina*, case of *Gustavo Marcelo Juárez and María Gabriela Juárez*, and *ibidem*, para. 230 (*supra*, p. 337), communication No. 113/79 concerning *Argentina*, case of *Federico Eduardo Álvarez Rojas*.
[5] See documents 108 EX/38 PRIV., para. 16, and 109 EX/52 PRIV., annex I, para. 8, and Corr.

No. 143/79

Concerning *Argentina*
Case of *Jacinto Rubén Montenegro*

Communication of 29 June 1979 submitted by
Liliana Perales de Montenegro

Autumn 1979 session of the Committee on Conventions and Recommendations (108th session of the Executive Board)[1]

112. The author of the communication complains of the abduction, on 5 January 1977 in Buenos Aires, of her husband, a student of Paraguayan nationality. Mr Montenegro's state of health has reportedly deteriorated since his detention. The author of the communication alleges violation of the right to personal freedom.

113. The Argentine representative stated that as this communication had been forwarded to his government on 10 August 1979, he had been unable to obtain any information regarding the case; he accordingly proposed that the Committee defer consideration thereof to its next session.

[113a.] On the proposal of the Chairman, it was so *decided.*

Spring 1980 session of the Committee on Conventions and Recommendations (109th session of the Executive Board)[2]

48. The complaint set forth in this communication is to the effect that the right of the author's husband to continue his architectural studies has been violated by his arrest and abduction. The author states that no domestic remedies have been undertaken for fear of reprisals. The examination of the communication had been suspended by the Committee at its [autumn 1979] session at the request of the government which

[1] See document 108 EX/38 PRIV., paras. 112-[113a]; see also document 108 EX/CR/PROC. HR/1 Add.
[2] See document 109 EX/52 PRIV., paras. 48-51; see also document 109 EX/CR/HR/2.

had received it only slightly more than a month before the meeting and needed more time to obtain necessary information.[3]

49. The representative of the Argentine Government stated that his government wished to emphasize that the student status of the victim had not been established, that there was no link existing between the alleged violation of human rights and Unesco's fields of competence, and that there had not even been an attempt to use domestic remedies. For these reasons his government felt the communication should be rejected and the author informed that she could use the domestic remedies available to her.

50. The representative of the Director-General explained in response to a query that the Committee's practice required only that there be an attempt to use domestic remedies rather than to exhaust them all, but that according to well-established international practice the person's opinion about the chances of success of a remedy were no excuse for not making any attempt at all.

51. The Committee quickly reached a consensus and *decided* that the communication was not admissible, being manifestly ill-founded, but that, as with other communications, the case could be reconsidered if new elements were presented.

[3] See document 108 EX/38 PRIV., paras. 113-[113a] (*supra*, p. 367).

No. 144/79

Concerning *Denmark*
Case of *Kai Mogens H. Lång*

Communication of 21 June 1979 submitted by
Kai Mogens H. Lång

Autumn 1979 session of the Committee on Conventions and Recommendations (108th session of the Executive Board)[1]

158. This communication concerns the alleged violation of the Unesco Convention against Discrimination in Education (Article 3 (*c*) and (*d*)) and several articles in the International Covenants on Human Rights.

159. The author of the communication, a Swedish student, alleges that since 1975, the Danish university authorities have refused him the stipend provided for under Danish law, claiming that this measure has been taken because of his political convictions. Mr Lång admits he has not exhausted all means of legal redress for financial reasons, but asserts that he has already had recourse to all administrative remedies.

160. The representative of the Danish Government pointed out that this case had been studied by the Danish Ombudsman who had concluded that the person concerned had in no way been the victim of discrimination. The Ombudsman had considered that this student, who had been entitled to a State stipend up to 1975, had had his stipend withdrawn because he no longer sat examinations or attended lectures, and accordingly no longer fulfilled all the conditions provided for in law No. 113 of 9 April 1975 in respect of university grants. The representative of the government concerned stressed the fact that the decision taken concerning Mr Lång was based exclusively on the conditions provided for by the law and that there had been no political, religious, or any other form of discrimination whatsoever against Mr Lång, or against the members of any group whatsoever. He concluded that the com-

[1] See document 108 EX/38 PRIV., paras. 158-161; see also document 108 EX/CR/PROC.HR/1 Add.

munication should be declared inadmissible as it was manifestly ill-founded and did not fulfil the condition concerning exhaustion of domestic remedies.

161. After discussion, the Committee *decided* that this communication was not admissible because it was manifestly ill-founded and consequently did not fulfil the condition stipulated in paragraph 14 (*a*) (v) of 104 EX/Decision 3.3.

No. 145/79

Concerning *Lao People's Democratic Republic*
Case of *Khamkhing Souvanlasy*

Communication of 11 June 1979 submitted by
Zygmunt Elbiński

Autumn 1979 session of the Committee on Conventions and Recommendations (108th session of the Executive Board)[1]

178. The author of the communication, of Polish nationality, describes himself as a person with reliable knowledee of the alleged violations of Articles 5, 9, 10 and 27 of the Universal Declaration of Human Rights, Article 13 (paragraphs 1 and 4) of the International Covenant on Econonic, Social and Cultural Rights, and Articles 9 and 10 of the International Covenant on Civil and Political Rights. The alleged victim, a teacher and former Director-General of the Ministry of Education of the Lao People's Democratic Republic, is said to have been detained since 1975 in a re-education camp. According to the author, no remedy exists against the decisions of the present government, and the case has not been submitted to any other international authority.

179. The Chairman observed that the government concerned was not represented at the meeting and had sent no reply to the Committee. The Director of the Division of Human Rights and Peace said that the presence of a representative of the government concerned was not mandatory, since paragraph 14 (*e*) of 104 EX/Decision 3.3 stipulated that such representatives "may attend meetings of the Committee ..."; however, it was in keeping with the spirit of 104 EX/Decision 3.3 that solutions to problems of human rights should be sought through dialogue with the governments concerned by the communications.

180. At the Chairman's suggestion, the Committee *decided* to postpone discussion of the admissibility of the communication to its next session, and to request the Secretariat to approach the Lao Government once more, it being understood that the

---

[1] See document 108 EX/38 PRIV., paras. 178-180; see also document 108 EX/CR/PROC.HR/ 1 Add.

Committee would in any case take a decision on the admissibility of the communication at its next session.

Spring 1980 session of the Committee on Conventions and Recommendations (109th session of the Executive Board)[2]

111. The alleged victim, Mr Khamkhing Souvanlasy, a teacher, formerly the Director-General of the Ministry of Educaticn of the Lao People's Democratic Republic, is said to have been detained since 1975 in the re-education camp of Sam Neua, province of northeast Lao, after being summoned, together with other officials of the Ministry, to attend a political re-education seminar.

112. This communication was first put before the Committee at its [autumn] 1979 session.

113. The Committee *decided* to take up this case at its next session and *asked* the Director-General to call to the attention of the government concerned the importance the Committee attached to having a representative of the government present during the Committee's examination of the communication.

Autumn 1980 session of the Committee on Conventions and Recommendations (110th session of the Executive Board)[3]

123. The author of this communication, Mr Zygmunt Elbiński, describes himself as a person with reliable knowledge of the alleged violation. The alleged victim, Mr Khamkhing Souvanlasy, teacher, formerly the Director-General of the Ministry of Education of the Lao People's Democratic Republic, is said to have been detained since 1975 in the re-education camp of Sam Neua, province of northeast Lao, after being summoned, together with other officials of the Ministry, to attend a political re-education seminar. According to the author, no remedy exists against the decisions of the present Government of the Lao People's Democratic Republic.

124. This communication was put before the Committee for the first time at its [autumn 1979 session].

125. The Chairman observed on that occasion that the government concerned was not represented at the meeting and had sent no reply to the Committee.

---

[2] See document 109 EX/52 PRIV., paras. 111-113; see also document 109 EX/CR/HR/2.
[3] See document 110 EX/40 PRIV., paras. 123-130; see also document 110 EX/CR/HR/2.

Lao People's Democratic Republic **No. 145/79**

126. At the Chairman's suggestion, the Committee decided to postpone discussion of the admissibility of the communication to its [spring] 1980 session, and to request the Secretariat to approach the Lao Government once more.[4]

127. On 30 October and 17 November 1979 respectively, the Secretariat informed the author of the communication and the government concerned of the Committee's decision.

128. As the Secretariat had received no new information, the Committee decided at its [spring 1980 session] to take a decision at its present session on the admissibility of this communication and to request the Director-General to draw the attention of the government concerned to the importance attached by the Committee to the presence of a representative of the government when the communication was being considered.[5] The Secretariat took the necessary action but received no reply from the Government. Confronted with the silence and absence of the Lao Government for a third consecutive time, the Committee debated whether it would be appropriate for it to take any decision without the presence of the government concerned.

129. After a prolonged discussion, the Committee reached the conclusion that, in view of the fact that its procedures did not require the presence of a government concerned and in view of the fact that a decision concerning admissibility was in no way a judgement of nor a sanction against a government, there was no reason for the Committee not to at least take a decision on admissibility at its present session.

130. Thereupon the Committee *decided*:

(i) to declare the communication admissible, since it fulfilled the applicable requirements; and

(ii) to inform the Executive Board of the lack of co-operation of the Lao Government.

At the same time the Committee emphasized that this decision to admit the communication in no way meant that in the future other communications would automatically be admitted when the government concerned was absent and silent.

---

[4] See document 108 EX/38 PRIV., para. 180 (*supra*, pp. 371-372).
[5] See document 109 EX/52 PRIV., para. 113 (*supra*, p. 372).

No. 145/79 **Lao People's Democratic Republic**

Spring 1981 session of the Committee on Conventions and Recommendations (112th session of the Executive Board)[6]

493. The author of this communication, Mr Zygmunt Elbiński, describes himself as a person with reliable knowledge of the alleged violation. The violation, according to the author, relates to Articles 5, 9, 10 and 27 of the Universal Declaration of Human Rights, Article 13 (paragraphs 1 and 4) of the International Covenant on Economic, Social and Cultural Rights, and Articles 9 and 10 of the International Covenant on Civil and Political Rights.

494. The connection between the alleged violation and Unesco's spheres of competence lies, according to the author, in the fact that the system of education in the re-education camps impairs individual freedom.

495. The alleged victim, Mr Khamkhing Souvanlasy, a teacher, formerly the Director-General of the Ministry of Education of the Lao People's Democratic Republic, is said to have been detained since 1975 in the re-education camp of Sam Neua, province of northeast Lao, after being summoned, together with other officials of the Ministry, to attend a political re-education seminar.

496. According to the author, no remedy exists against the decisions of the present Government of the Lao People's Democratic Republic. The author states that the case has not been submitted to any other international authority.

497. This communication was put before the Committee for the first time at its [autumn 1979 session].

498. The Chairman observed on that occasion that the government concerned was not represented at the meeting and had sent no reply to the Committee. The Director of the Division of Human Rights and Peace said that the presence of a representative of the government concerned was not mandatory, since paragraph 14 (*e*) of 104 EX/Decision 3.3 stipulated that such representatives "may attend meetings of the Committee ..."; however, it was in keeping with the spirit of 104 EX/Decision 3.3 that solutions to problems of human rights should be sought through dialogue with the governments concerned by the communications.

499. At the Chairman's suggestion, the Committee decided to postpone discussion of the admissibility of the communication to its [spring] 1980 session, and to request the Secretariat to approach the Lao Government once more.[7]

---

[6] See document 112 EX/30 PRIV., paras. 493-505; see also document 112 EX/CR/HR/1.

Lao People's Democratic Republic **No. 145/79**

500. On 30 October and 17 November 1979 respectively, the Secretariat informed the author of the communication and the government concerned of the Committee's decision.

501. As the Secretariat had received no new information, the Committee had decided at its [spring 1980 session] to take a decision [at its autumn 1980 session] on the admissibility of the communication, and to request the Director-General to draw the attention of the government concerned to the importance attached by the Committee to the presence of a representative of the government when the communication was being considered.[8] The Secretariat, which took the necessary action, had not received any reply at the time of the [autumn 1980] session.

502. After a prolonged discussion, the Committee then reached the conclusion that, since its procedures did not require the presence of a representative of the government concerned and a decision concerning admissibility was in no way a judgement of, or a sanction against, a government, there was no reason for the Committee not to take a decision at least on the admissibility of the communication.

503. At its [autumn 1980] session, the Committee therefore decided:[9]

> (i) to declare the communication admissible, since it fulfilled the requirements applicable; and.
>
> (ii) to inform the Executive Board of the lack of co-operation of the Lao Government.

At the same time the Committee emphasized that that decision to admit the communication in no way meant that, in the future, other communications would automatically be admitted when the government concerned was absent and silent.

504. The Secretariat duly informed the Government of the Lao People's Democratic Republic of that decision on 24 October 1980 (acknowledgement of receipt of this letter reached the Secretariat on 21 November 1980).

505. The Government of the Lao People's Democratic Republic had not sent a representative to the current session of the Committee. The Committee therefore *decided*:

---

[7] See document 108 EX/38 PRIV., para. 180 (*supra*, pp. 371-372).
[8] See document 109 EX/52 PRIV., para. 113 (*supra*, p. 372).
[9] See document 110 EX/40 PRIV., para. 130 (*supra*, p. 373).

(i) to pospone consideration of the content of this communication until its next session;

(ii) to ask the Executive Board to request the Director-General to urge once again upon the government concerned the importance attached by the Committee to the presence of a representative of that government at the said session, and to stress that, if again no representative appeared, the Committee would be compelled to continue with its business, notwithstanding the absence of a representative.

Autumn 1981 session of the Committee on Conventions and Recommendations (113th session of the Executive Board)[10]

528. The author of this communication, Mr Zygmunt Elbiński, describes himself as a person with reliable knowledge of the alleged violation. The violation, according to the author, relates to Articles 5, 9, 10 and 27 of the Universal Declaration of Human Rights, Article 13 (paragraphs 1 and 4) of the International Covenant on Economic, Social and Cultural Rights, and Articles 9 and 10 of the International Covenant on Civil and Political Rights.

529. The connection between the alleged violation and Unesco's spheres of competence lies, according to the author, in the fact that the system of education in the re-education camps impairs individual freedom.

530. The alleged victim, Mr Khamkhing Souvanlasy, a teacher, formerly the Director-General of the Ministry of Education of the Lao People's Democratic Republic, is said to have been detained since 1975 in the re-education camp of Sam Neua, province of northeast Lao, after being summoned, together with other officials of the Ministry, to attend a political re-education seminar.

531. According to the author, no remedy exists against the decisions of the present Government of the Lao People's Democratic Republic. The author states that the case has not been submitted to any other international authority.

532. This communication was put before the Committee for the first time at its [autumn 1979 session].

533. The Chairman observed on that occasion that the government concerned was not represented at the meeting and had sent no reply to the Committee. The Director

[10] See document 113 EX/38 PRIV., paras. 528-546; see also document 113 EX/CR/HR/1.

of the Division of Human Rights and Peace said that the presence of a representative of the government concerned was not mandatory, since paragraph 14 (*e*) of 104 EX/ Decision 3.3 stipulated that such representatives "may attend meetings of the Committee ..."; however, it was in keeping with the spirit of 104 EX/Decision 3.3 that solutions to problems of human rights should be sought through dialogue with the governments concerned by the communications.

534. At the Chairman's suggestion, the Committee decided to postpone discussion of the admissibility of the communication to its [spring] 1980 session, and to request the Secretariat to approach the Lao Government once more.[11]

535. On 30 October and 17 November 1979 respectively, the Secretariat informed the author of the communication and the government concerned of the Committee's decision.

536. As the Secretariat had received no new information, the Committee had decided at its [spring 1980 session] to take a decision [at its autumn 1980 session] on the admissibility of the communication, and to request the Director-General to draw the attention of the government concerned to the importance attached by the Committee to the presence of a representative of the government when the communication was being considered.[12] The Secretariat, which took the necessary action, had not received any reply at the time of the [autumn 1980] session.

537. After a prolonged discussion, the Committee had reached the conclusion that, since its procedures did not require the presence of a representative of the government concerned and a decision concerning admissibility was in no way a judgement of, or a sanction against, a government, there was no reason for the Committee not to take a decision at least on the admissibility of the communication.

538. At its [autumn 1980] session, the Committee therefore decided:[13]

(i) to declare the communication admissible, since it fulfilled the requirements applicable; and

(ii) to inform the Executive Board of the lack of co-operation of the Lao Government.

---

[11] See document 108 EX/38 PRIV., para. 180 (***supra***, pp. 371-372).
[12] See document 109 EX/52 PRIV., para. 113 (***supra***, p. 372).
[13] See document 110 EX/40 PRIV., para. 130 (***supra***, p. 373).

At the same time the Committee emphasized that that decision to admit the communication in no way meant that, in the future, other communications would automatically be admitted when the government concerned was absent and silent.

539. The Secretariat duly informed the Government of the Lao People's Democratic Republic of that decision on 24 October 1980 (acknowledgement of receipt of this letter reached the Secretariat on 21 November 1980).

540. The Government of the Lao People's Democratic Republic had not sent a representative to the [spring 1981] session. The Committee, in deciding to postpone consideration of the content of this communication until this session, asked the Executive Board to request the Director-General to urge once again upon the government concerned the importance attached by the Committee to the presence of a representative of that government and to stress that, if again no representative appeared, the Committee would be compelled to continue with its business, notwithstanding the absence of a representative.[14]

541. At the present session, the Committee noted that the government concerned had maintained its silence by failing to send a representative.

542. Some members of the Committee considered this to be a deliberate refusal to co-operate on the part of that government, and felt it wise to lay the matter before the Executive Board, particularly since the alleged victim had since 1975 been subjected to a system of re-education and the Committee seemed likely to be faced with a *fait accompli*.

543. The representative of the Director-General said that under the terms of 104 EX/ Decision 3.3, when all attempts to reach a friendly solution had failed, the Committee should draft a specific report (differing from the regular report of the session's work) for submission to the Executive Board. He added that contacts with the Government of the Lao People's Democratic Republic were made through that country's representative to the United Nations in New York.

544. A number of Committee members thought it premature to speak of a deliberate refusal to co-operate on the part of the Government of the Lao People's Democratic Republic, in view of the difficulties encountered by that country which had very few resources. They urged the Committee to show patience, and asked that a further approach be made to obtain that co-operation.

---

[14] See document 112 EX/30 PRIV., para. 505 (*supra*, p. 375-376).

Lao People's Democratic Republic **No. 145/79**

545. One member hoped that a friendly country with contacts with the Lao People's Democratic Republic might advise the latter that it was in its own interest to break its silence and co-operate with the Committee.

546. After an exchange of views, the Committee *decided*:

(i) to suspend examination of this communication as regards its merits until the next session, when it would deal with the drafting of its report to the Executive Board;

(ii) to ask the Executive Board to request the Director-General to send a cable to the Head of State of the Lao People's Democratic Republic informing him of:

(*a*) Unesco's concern over the present case;

(*b*) the obstacles encountered by the Organization in seeking tangible results in view of the absence of a representative of the government concerned;

(*c*) the Organization's wish to secure the co-operation of the government concerned;

(iii) to request the Secretariat to attach a copy of the communication to that cable;

(iv) to advise the author of the communication of this decision.

Spring 1982 session of the Committee on Conventions and Recommendations (114th session of the Executive Board)[15]

764. The author of this communication, Mr Zygmunt Elbiński, describes himself as a person with reliable knowledge of the alleged violation.

765. Mr Khamkhing Souvanlasy, teacher, formerly the Director-General of the Ministry of Education of the Lao People's Democratic Republic, is said to have been detained since 1975 in a camp in Sam Neua, after being summoned, together with other officials of the Ministry, to attend a political re-education seminar.

[15] See document 114 EX/38 PRIV., paras. 764-784; see also document 114 EX/CR/HR/1.

766. According to the author, no remedy exists against the decisions of the present Government of the Lao people's Democratic Republic. The author states that the case has not been submitted to any other international authority.

767. This communication was put before the Committee for the first time at its [autumn 1979 session].

768. The Chairman observed that the government concerned was not represented at the meeting and had sent no reply to the Committee.

769. At his suggestion, the Committee decided to postpone discussion of the admissibility of the communication to its [spring] 1980 session, and to request the Secretariat to approach the Lao Government once more.[16]

770. As the Secretariat had received no new information, the Committee decided at its spring 1980 session to take a decision at its next session on the admissibility of the communication, and to request the Director-General to draw the attention of the government concerned to the importance attached by the Committee to the presence of a representative of the government when the communication was being considered.[17]

771. At its autumn 1980 session, after a prolonged discussion, the Committee reached the conclusion that, since its procedures did not require the presence of a representative of the government concerned and a decision concerning admissibility was in no way a judgement of, or a sanction against, a government, there was no reason for the Committee not to take a decision at least on the admissibility of the communication.

772. The Committee decided on that occasion:[18]

(i) to declare the communication admissible, since it fulfilled the requirements applicable; and

(ii) to inform the Executive Board of the lack of co-operation of the Lao Government.

At the same time the Committee emphasized that that decision to admit the communication in no way meant that, in the future, other communications would automatically be admitted when the government concerned was absent and silent.

---

[16] See document 108 EX/38 PRIV., para. 180 (*supra*, pp. 371-372).
[17] See document 109 EX/52 PRIV., para. 113 (*supra*, p. 372).
[18] See document 110 EX/40 PRIV., para. 130 (*supra*, p. 373).

Lao People's Democratic Republic **No. 145/79**

773. At the [spring 1981 session], the Government of the Lao People's Democratic Republic was still not represented. The Committee, when deciding to postpone consideration of the content of this communication until the following session, had asked the Executive Board to request the Director-General to urge once again upon the government concerned the importance attached by the Committee to the presence of a representative of the government and to stress that, if again no representative appeared, the Committee would be compelled to continue with its business, notwithstanding the absence of a representative.[19]

774. At the [autumn 1981 session], the Committee noted that the government concerned was maintaining its silence by failing to send a representative.

775. Some members of the Committee considered this to be a deliberate refusal to co-operate on the part of that government, and felt it wise to lay the matter before the Executive Board, particularly since the alleged victim had since 1975 been subjected to a system of re-education and the Committee seemed likely to be faced with a *fait accompli*.

776. The representative of the Director-General said that under the terms of 104 EX/ Decision 3.3, when all attempts to reach a friendly solution had failed, the Committee should draft a specific report (differing from the regular report of the session's work) for submission to the Executive Board. He added that contacts with the Government of the Lao People's Democratic Republic were made through that country's representative to the United Nations in New York.

777. A number of Committee members thought it premature to speak of a deliberate refusal to co-operate on the part of the Government of Lao People's Democratic Republic, in view of the difficulties encountered by that country which had very few resources.

778. After an exchange of views, the Committee decided:[20]

> (i) to suspend examination of this communication as regards its merits until the present session, at which it will deal with the drafting of its report to the Executive Board;
>
> (ii) to ask the Executive Board to request the Director-General to send a cable to the Head of State of the Lao People's Democratic Republic informing him of:

---

[19] See document 112 EX/30 PRIV., para. 505 (*supra*, p. 375-376).

[20] See document 113 EX/38 PRIV., para. 546 (*supra*, p. 379).

(*a*) Unesco's concern over the present case;

(*b*) the obstacles encountered by the Organization in seeking tangible results in view of the absence of a representative of the government concerned;

(*c*) the Organization's wish to secure the co-operation of the government concerned;

(iii) to request the Secretariat to attach a copy of the communication to that cable;

(iv) to advise the author of the communication of this decision.

779. At the present session the Committee once more noted the lack of reaction on the part of the government concerned.

780. One member of the Committee wondered whether the moment had not come to prepare a specific report accompanied by a special recommendation to the Executive Board.

781. Another member of the Committee, who had the impression that the communication had not reached the Government of the Lao People's Democratic Republic considered that a cautious attitude should be adopted, particularly in view of the fact that no mission had been sent to the country and that the Committee was not sure of the veracity of the alleged facts. He suggested deferring examination of the substance of the communication and suggested that it would be advisable to resort to the procedure of good offices.

782. The representative of the Director-General informed the Committee that it would seem that the government concerned had duly received the Secretariat's communication transmitted in pursuance of paragraphs (ii) and (iii) of the decision taken by the Committee at its [autumn 1981] session. Acknowledgement of the covering letter accompanying the communication appeared in the file; a copy of this letter which had been attached to a copy of the communication and several documents relating to it had been sent to the Permanent Representative of the Lao People's Democratic Republic to the United Nations in New York on 18 January 1982. The representative of the Director-General also read the text of the cable sent by the Director-General to the President of the Lao People's Democratic Republic, calling his attention to the Committee's concern over this matter.

783. Given the fact that, to achieve tangible results, it was of paramount importance to have the co-operation of the government concerned, several members of the Com-

mittee supported the view that the Secretariat should be asked to prepare a draft report for the Executive Board and to send it to the government concerned in order to receive its observations before the next session of the Committee.

784. After an exchange of views, the Committee *decided*:

(i) to emphasize once again the importance that the Committee attaches to the co-operation of the governments concerned by communications and, consequently, to information provided by the Lao Government;

(ii) to advise the government of the Committee's humanitarian concern regarding the present case;

(iii) to request the Secretariat to prepare a draft report on the pending case, for submission to the Executive Board in accordance with paragraph 15 of 104 EX/Decision 3.3, and to send it to the government concerned for any comments that it might consider necessary to make on the text;

(iv) to note with gratitude the offer made by the Chairman of the Committee to assist the Secretariat in preparing the aforementioned draft report.

Autumn 1982 session of the Committee on Conventions and Recommendations (115th session of the Executive Board)[21]

460. These two communications[22] concern one individual, Mr Khamkhing Souvanlasy, described as a teacher and former Director-General in the Lao Ministry of Education, who is said to have been detained in a re-education camp since November 1975.

[460a.] The first communication is already being examined as to its substance, and at the [spring 1982] session the Committee asked the Secretariat to draft a specific report for the Executive Board [...].[23]

[460b.] The second is a new communication.

---

[21] See document 115 EX/28 PRIV., paras. 460-461; see also documents 115 EX/CR/HR/1 and 115 EX/CR/HR/3.

[22] Communications No. 145/79 concerning *Lao People's Democratic Republic*, case of *Khamkhing Souvanlasy*, and No. 480/82 concerning *Lao People's Democratic Republic*, case of *Khamkhing Souvanlasy*, were being considered together.

[23] See document 114 EX/38 PRIV., para. 784 (iii) (*supra*, p. 383); for the draft specific report, see document 115 EX/CR/HR/1.

No. 145/79 **Lao People's Democratic Republic**

461. Being short of time, the Committee *decided* to take note of the draft specific report to the Executive Board on these communications and to resume their examination at the next session.

Spring 1983 session of the Committee on Conventions and Recommendations (116th session of the Executive Board)[24]

316. The two communications[25] concern a teacher, Mr Khamkhing Souvanlasy, who is alleged to have been detained in a re-education camp. The first communication is already at the stage of being examined in detail, while the second is still at the stage of being examined as to its admissibility. Concerning the first communication, the Committee decided at its [spring 1982 session] to prepare a specific report for the Executive Board on account of the repeated absence from its meetings of any representative of the government concerned.[26]

317. At the spring 1983 session, the Government of the Lao People's Democratic Republic was not represented. However, in a letter dated 9 November 1982, the Director of the International Organizations Department of the Lao Ministry of Foreign Affairs informed the Secretariat of his government's initial reactions to [the first communication]:

> the Lao Government categorically rejects the allegations in the communication;
>
> the Lao Government has not been able to send a representative to meetings of the Committee for reasons of a diplomatic nature. It is, in addition, occupied with the economic and social development of the country;
>
> the Lao Government will send further information at a later date.

318. Despite the tone of this letter, the Committee felt that it represented a step forward in the affair and *decided* to defer examination of the two communications pending receipt of further information from the Lao Government.

---

[24] See document 116 EX/48 PRIV., paras. 316-318; see also documents 116 EX/CR/HR/1 and 116 EX/CR/HR/2.

[25] Communications No. 145/79 concerning *Lao People's Democratic Republic*, case of *Khamkhing Souvanlasy*, and No. 480/82 concerning *Lao People's Democratic Republic*, case of *Khamkhing Souvanlasy*, were being considered together..

[26] See document 114 EX/38 PRIV., para. 784 (iii) (*supra*, p. 383).

Lao People's Democratic Republic **No. 145/79**

Autumn 1983 session of the Committee on Conventions and Recommendations (117th session of the Executive Board)[27]

223. Mr Khamkhing, a teacher and former Unesco official, is alleged to have been arrested in November 1975 following the change of political regime in the country, and to be still held in detention in a re-education camp (letter from Amnesty International dated 9 August 1983, which the Director-General's representative read out).

224. The first communication,[28] which has been on the Committee's agenda since its autumn 1979 session, was declared admissible at its autumn 1980 session.[29] The second communication, which was considered for the first time at the autumn 1982 session, has still not been declared admissible, but the Committee has always considered it at the same time as the previous one.

225. The government concerned has never been represented before the Committee, but, in a letter dated 9 November 1982 [...],[30] it had promised while rejecting the allegations appearing in the communication, to provide additional information.

226. Although at this autumn 1983 session there was no new factor enabling the Committee's work to advance, several members were of the view that it would be advisable to make another attempt to apprise the Lao authorities of the Committee's humanitarian concerns and the goal it was pursuing in the promotion of human rights, which was the essential spirit of 104 EX/Decision 3.3.

227. After discussing the matter, the Committee *decided*:

(i) to express to the government in question its humanitarian concern about the situation of Mr Khamkhing Souvanlasy;

(ii) to request the Executive Board to invite the Director-General to make representations in whatever forms he may deem appropriate, taking advantage, if necessary, of the presence of the delegation of the Lao People's Democratic Republic at the forthcoming General Conference in Paris, for the purpose of securing the co-operation of the government concerned;

---

[27] See document 117 EX/18 PRIV., paras. 223-227; see also documents 117 EX/CR/HR/1 and 117 EX/CR/HR/2.

[28] Communications No. 145/79 concerning *Lao People's Democratic Republic*, case of *Khamkhing Souvanlasy*, and No. 480/82 concerning *Lao People's Democratic Republic*, case of *Khamkhing Souvanlasy*, were being considered together.

[29] See document 110 EX/40 PRIV., para. 130 (i) (*supra*, p. 373).

[30] See document 116 EX/CR/HR/1.

(iii) to resume consideration of the two communications at its spring 1984 session.

Spring 1984 session of the Committee on Conventions and Recommendations (119th session of the Executive Board)[31]

228. Mr Khamkhing Souvanlasy, a teacher and former Unesco staff member, was allegedly arrested in November 1975 following the change in the political regime of the country. He is said to be detained in a re-education camp.

229. The first communication[32] was declared admissible at the Committee's autumn 1980 session.[33] The second communication, examined for the first time at the autumn 1982 session, is still at the stage of being examined as to its admissibility.

230. The government concerned has never sent any representative to the Committee. Its only reaction was a letter dated 9 November 1982 [...] in which it rejected as unfounded the allegations contained in [the first communication] and promised to send further information to the Secretariat at a later date.[34]

231. After an exchange of views, the Committee *decided*:

(i) to recommend that the Executive Board appeal urgently to the Government of the Lao People's Democratic Republic to co-operate with the Committee and to inform the government that if it does not effectively participate in the autumn 1984 session, the Committee will be forced to consider the facts alleged in the communications as established and consequently to submit a specific report to the Executive Board;

(ii) to express its humanitarian concern for Mr Khamkhing Souvanlasy.

---

[31] See document 119 EX/35 PRIV., paras. 228-231; see also documents 119 EX/CR/HR/1 and 119 EX/CR/HR/2.

[32] Communications No. 145/79 concerning *Lao People's Democratic Republic*, case of *Khamkhing Souvanlasy*, and No. 480/82 concerning *Lao People's Democratic Republic*, case of *Khamkhing Souvanlasy*, were being considered together.

[33] See document 110 EX/40 PRIV., para. 130 (i) (*supra*, p. 373).

[34] See document 116 EX/CR/HR/1.

Lao People's Democratic Republic **No. 145/79**

Autumn 1984 session of the Committee on Conventions and Recommendations (120th session of the Executive Board)[35]

216. Mr Khamkhing Souvanlasy, a teacher and former Unesco staff member, was allegedly arrested in November 1975 following the change in the political regime of the country, since which time he is said to be detained in a re-education camp.

217. The first communication[36] is at the stage of being considered as to its substance, having been declared admissible by the Committee at its autumn 1980 session.[37] The second communication, placed on the Committee's agenda for the first time at its autumn 1982 session, is still at the stage of being considered as to its admissibility.

218. The government concerned has still not arranged to be represented.

219. Some members of the Committee who spoke were of the opinion that there should be no hurry to submit a specific report to the Executive Board, in view of the complex situation in the Lao People's Democratic Republic, which was having to contend with all kinds of difficulties after the Revolution and which, not so long ago, had had diplomatic problems that had prevented it from sending a representative to the Committee. The others considered that it should be made clear to the Lao Government that the Committee was not setting itself up as an international court, that it sought co-operation with that Government in order to establish whether the allegations made were true, and that the case in question was a human one which had already been hanging fire for several years.

220. After an exchange of views, the Committee *decided*:

(i) without prejudice to the future decision of the Committee, to request the Secretariat to prepare a draft of a specific report on this case for the Executive Board;

(ii) to resume consideration of the two communications at the spring 1985 session, and in particular of the said specific report, either initially or when the Committee has sufficient time to give its attention to them;

---

[35] See document 120 EX/15 PRIV., paras. 216-221; see also documents 120 EX/CR/HR/1 and 120 EX/CR/HR/2.

[36] Communications No. 145/79 concerning *Lao People's Democratic Republic*, case of *Khamkhing Souvanlasy*, and No. 480/82 concerning *Lao People's Democratic Republic*, case of *Khamkhing Souvanlasy*, were being considered together.

[37] See document 110 EX/40 PRIV., para. 130 (i) (*supra*, p. 373).

(iii) to request the Secretariat to spare no effort to explain to the Government of the Lao People's Democratic Republic through the channel of its diplomatic representatives in France the non-judicial character of the procedure for consideration of communications by the Committee, its objectivity and the extremely great importance attached by the Committee to the co-operation of that Government and to the presence of one of its representatives before the Committee.

221. Two members of the Committee expressed doubts as to whether a specific report should be submitted to the Executive Board.

Spring 1985 session of the Committee on Conventions and Recommendations (121st session of the Executive Board)[38]

218. Mr Khamkhing Souvanlasy, a teacher and former Unesco staff member, was allegedly arrested and sent to a re-education camp in November 1975. Since that time, apparently nothing has been heard about him. The first communication[39] is at the stage of being considered as to its substance; the second is still at the stage of being considered as to its admissibility.

219. As at previous sessions of the Committee, the government concerned was not represented. Some members of the Committee who spoke noted that this government had repeatedly had every opportunity to co-operate with the Committee but had not done so, apart from a letter dated 9 November 1982 in which it simply refuted the allegations put forward in [the first communication] without supplying any relevant information. In their view, the procedure should be followed up by submitting a specific report to the Executive Board, as the Committee had contemplated doing at its previous sessions; a draft report had been prepared by the Secretariat at the Committee's request and all the Committee needed to do was to add an appropriate operative paragraph to the draft recommendation with which that draft report concluded. One member felt that it might even be necessary to consider sending a member of the Executive Board on mission to the State concerned, in line with the decision that had been taken during the examination of communications concerning another country.

---

[38] See document 121 EX/46 PRIV., paras. 218-224; see also documents 121 EX/CR/HR/1 and 121 EX/CR/HR/2.

[39] Communications No. 145/79 concerning *Lao People's Democratic Republic*, case of *Khamkhing Souvanlasy*, and No. 480/82 concerning *Lao People's Democratic Republic*, case of *Khamkhing Souvanlasy*, were being considered together.

220. Other members of the Committee mentioned that at its [autumn 1984] session, a few members of the Committee had expressed disagreement about the desirability of preparing a specific report for the Executive Board. They pointed out that the Committee had received no additional information either from the author of the first communication or from the author of the second. They felt that it should be borne in mind that the Lao People's Democratic Republic's diplomatic representation in France was small, that its ambassador was often obliged to be away from Paris, that the country was confronted with many development problems, and that further efforts should be made to establish direct contact with the government concerned while avoiding any radical decision that might leave the impression that it had violated human rights simply because of its failure to provide information.

221. Other members of the Committee felt that if the authors had nothing more to add it was because the problem still remained unsolved and that the government should explain what it was doing in the matter.

222. For their part, these members were convinced that the Government of the Lao People's Democratic Republic had duly received [the two communications], together with all the documents in the file relating to them, and that it was therefore fully informed about the successive stages of the Committee's examination of those communications.

223. Bearing in mind the serious nature of the allegations concerning the violations of Articles 5, 9, 10, 19 and 27 of the Universal Declaration of Human Rights (the right not to be subjected to torture or to cruel, inhuman or degrading treatment or punishment, the right not to be subjected to arbitrary arrest, detention or exile, the right to full equality before the law, the right to freedom of opinion and of expression and the right to participate in the cultural life of the community), of Article 13 (1) and (4) of the International Covenant on Economic, Social and Cultural Rights (the right to education that shall be directed to the full development of the human personality and the sense of its dignity and shall strengthen respect for human rights and fundamental freedoms) and of Articles 9, 10 and 25 (*c*) of the International Covenant on Civil and Political Rights (the right to liberty and security of person, the right not to be deprived of one's liberty except on such grounds as are established by law, the right to be tried within a reasonable time, the right to take proceedings before a court, the right of anyone deprived of his liberty to be treated with humanity and with respect for the inherent dignity of the human person, the right to have access to public service in one's country) these members of the Committee greatly regretted the prolonged silence of the Government of the Lao People's Democratic Republic in the face of such allegations of violations of human rights and expressed their deep concern over the uncertainty regarding the situation of the alleged victim.

No. 145/79 **Lao People's Democratic Republic**

224. Following an exchange of views and subject to reservations expressed by a number of members regarding (i) below, the Committee adopted the following *decision*:

The Committee:

(i) requests the Executive Board to ask the Director-General to use his good offices with the government concerned in order to secure new information and an improvement in the situation of Mr Khamkhing Souvanlasy, renewing the invitation to the said government to co-operate with the Committee;

(ii) decides to resume consideration of the substance of these communications at its autumn 1985 session.

Autumn 1985 session of the Committee on Conventions and Recommendations (122nd session of the Executive Board)[40]

164. Mr Khamkhing Souvanlasy, a teacher and former Unesco staff member, was allegedly arrested and sent to a re-education camp in November 1975. The first communication[41] is at the stage of being considered as to its substance; the second is still at the stage of being considered as to its admissibility.

165. By a letter dated 27 August 1985, Amnesty International indicated that according to the latest information, Mr Khamkhing Souvanlasy has been assigned to enforced residence in Soppane, Sam Neua district, Houa Phan province, where he is said to be working as a teacher.

166. The government concerned has not so far arranged to be represented before the Committee.

167. By a letter dated 30 August 1985 [...],[42] the Permanent Delegate of the Lao People's Democratic Republic to Unesco referred to a letter from his government dated 9 November 1982 [...] in which it categorically rejected "the gratuitous accusations made against it" and considered "that the intrigues of these Committee members" constituted "interference in the domestic affairs" of its country. The Permanent

---

[40] See document 122 EX/21 PRIV., paras. 164-169; see also documents 122 EX/CR/HR/1 and 122 EX/CR/HR/2 and Add.3.

[41] Communications No. 145/79 concerning *Lao People's Democratic Republic*, case of *Khamkhing Souvanlasy*, and No. 480/82 concerning *Lao People's Democratic Republic*, case of *Khamkhing Souvanlasy*, were being considered together.

[42] See document 122 EX/CR/HR/2 Add.3.

Delegate also stated his concern to clarify this matter through personal discussions with the members of the Committee.

168. Several members of the Committee felt that information about the situation of Mr Khamkhing Souvanlasy was still inadequate and that it was not known whether he was working in Soppane as a prisoner or as a free man. Some members regretted that no information had been given to the Committee by the government concerned. Other members were of the opinion that it would be appropriate to consider asking the Executive Board to send one of its members to Vientiane. According to one member of the Committee, no final position should be adopted in regard to the failure of the government concerned to participate or provide information, as account had to be taken of the particular situation of the Lao People's Democratic Republic. One other Committee member expressed surprise at the tone of the letter of 30 August 1985 from the Permanent Delegate. Another member was of the opinion that [the first communication], which was based on information published in the press, was inadmissible in the light of 104 EX/Decision 3.3 and that in any event, neither of these communications, which referred to facts dating back to 1975, had been submitted within a reasonable time-limit, in accordance with the provisions of that decision. Some other Committee members noted that, since there was now a Lao diplomatic representative to Unesco, every possible means should be used to continue and intensify efforts to establish dialogue with the government concerned. They expressed the hope that the apparently improved situation of the alleged victim would develop in the direction of his complete freedom.

169. Following the discussion and after a number of members had expressed reservations about paragraph (ii) below and stressed the fact that a representative of the Lao People's Democratic Republic really had difficulty in meeting members of the Committee during its current session, the Committee *decided*:

(i) to take note of the letter dated 30 August 1985 from the Permanent Delegate of the Lao People's Democratic Republic and of his intention to meet members of the Committee in order to clarify this matter, and of the information provided by the author of [the second communication] in its letter dated 27 August 1985;

(ii) to request the Executive Board to ask the Director-General to continue to use his good offices in order to secure further information and an improvement in the situation of Mr Khamkhing Souvanlasy, renewing the invitation to the government in question to co-operate with the Committee;

(ii) to resume consideration of the substance of these commuications at its next session.

No. 145/79 **Lao People's Democratic Republic**

Spring 1986 session of the Committee on Conventions and Recommendations (124th session of the Executive Board)[43]

158. Mr Khamkhing Souvanlasy, a teacher and former Unesco staff member, was allegedly arrested and sent to a re-education camp in November 1975. The first communication[44] is at the stage of being considered as to its substance; the second is still at the stage of being considered as to its admissibility.

159. By a letter dated 27 August 1985, Amnesty International indicated that according to the latest information, Mr Khamkhing Souvanlasy has been assigned to residence in Soppane, Sam Neua district, Houa Phan province, where he is said to be working as a teacher.

160. The government concerned has not arranged to be represented before the Committee since the communications were placed upon its agenda.

161. After stating the alleged facts, the Chairperson recalled that at the autumn 1985 session of the Committee, the Permanent Delegate of the Lao People's Democratic Republic to Unesco had stated, in a letter dated 30 August 1985 [...], that his government categorically rejected "the gratuitous accusations made against it" and considered that the activities of the Committee members constituted "interference in the domestic affairs" of his country. The Permanent Delegate had also expressed, at the time, his concern to clarify this matter through personal discussions with the members of the Commitee.

162. The Chairperson then informed the Committee that no further information had been received and that the Lao Permanent Delegation had not contacted her.

163. For information, the representative of the Director-General briefly mentioned the different stages in the examination of the two communications, and recalled that at its autumn 1984 session the Committee had asked the Secretariat to prepare a specific draft report for the Executive Board in accordance with paragraph 15 of 104 EX/Decision 3.3, but had not seen fit to take further action at its spring 1985 session.

164. Some members of the Committee considered that as it was a question of human rights, the erroneous interpretation according to which the action taken by the Com-

---

[43] See document 124 EX/3 PRIV., paras. 158-168; see also documents 124 EX/CR/HR/1 and 124 EX/CR/HR/2.

[44] Communications No. 145/79 concerning *Lao People's Democratic Republic*, case of *Khamkhing Souvanlasy*, and No. 480/82 concerning *Lao People's Democratic Republic*, case of *Khamkhing Souvanlasy*, were being considered together.

mittee constituted interference in the domestic affairs of a Member State should not be left unanswered. They stressed that the Committee was not issuing an injunction against a government; it was seeking a dialogue with that government in order to arrive at an amicable solution within the framework of the promotion of human rights. The majority of these members wondered whether the Committee ought not to consider sending a mission to the country concerned to check the information provided by Amnesty International.

165. Other members of the Committee took the view that the right course would be to go back to the idea of preparing a specific draft report to the Executive Board and communicating it to the government concerned in order to obtain its co-operation.

166. In answer to a request for clarification concerning the competence of the Committee in regard to the examination of communications, the Chairperson explained that the Committee's terms of reference were clearly defined in 104 EX/Decision 3. 3: it was competent to examine individual and specific cases as well as "questions" (massive, systematic or flagrant violations of human rights and fundamental freedoms), but in instances of the latter the communications should be transmitted to the Executive Board and the General Conference, which would examine them in public meetings.

167. Other members of the Committee expressed their concern that the lack of contact with the government concerned should not imply a lack of co-operation on its part, and added that in any case dialogue with the Lao authorities had not broken down.

168. After an exchange of views the Committee, on the proposal of the Chairperson, *decided*:

(i) to express its regret once again at the absence of a representative of the government concerned;

(ii) to stress to the government concerned that to date the Committee had acted strictly within its terms of reference as laid down in 104 EX/Decision 3.3;

(iii) to ask the authors of the two communications whether they had any further information at their disposal;

(iv) to ask its Chairperson to attempt to establish dialogue with the Lao authorities;

(v) to resume consideration of the two communications at its next session.

No. 145/79 **Lao People's Democratic Republic**

Autumn 1986 session of the Committee on Conventions and Recommendations (125th session of the Executive Board)[45]

185. Mr Khamkhing Souvanlasy, a teacher and former Unesco staff member, is said to have been arrested and sent to a re-education camp in November 1975. The first communication[46] is at the stage of consideration as to its substance; the second is still at the stage of consideration as to its admissibility.

186. By a letter dated 17 July 1986 [...],[47] Amnesty International said that, according to the latest information available to it, Mr Khamkhing Souvanlasy was still assigned to forced residence for "re-education" at the Soppane work camp in the province of Houa Phanh and that he had been designated to work as a teacher in a school in that camp.

187. The Chairperson informed the Committee that, following its request to her at the previous session to attempt to re-establish dialogue with the Lao authorities,[48] she had received the Permanent Delegate of the Lao People's Democratic Republic on 26 August 1986 and had provided her with all the relevant explanations. She then read out a letter dated 4 September 1986 which she had just received from the Permanent Delegate, in which the Permanent Delegate informed her in substance as follows: Her delegation considered it inadvisable for her to take part in the Committee's proceedings. Nevertheless, she wished to offer certain clarifications regarding the case of Mr Khamkhing Souvanlasy. Mr Souvanlasy had completed his "seminar" a few years previously. It was true that seminars had been organized all over the country at the time of the national liberation, with the aim of re-educating the military personnel and officials most highly compromised under the former regime. They had now ended and those who had completed them had been integrated into the various administrative and productive sectors in accordance with their capabilities and, so far as possible, to suit their convenience. They were not subjected to harassment and they now enjoyed the same rights and freedoms as all other citizens. In contrast to former practice, senior personnel were no longer concentrated in the capital. All were equal and no distinction was made between those from the former regime and those who had emerged from the struggle for national liberation. Mr Khamkhing Souvanlasy was at present working at Houa Phanh as a senior member

[45] See document 125 EX/3 PRIV., paras. 185-189; see also documents 125 EX/CR/HR/1 and 125 EX/CR/HR/2 and Add.
[46] Communications No. 145/79 concerning *Lao People's Democratic Republic*, case of *Khamkhing Souvanlasy*, and No. 480/82 concerning *Lao People's Democratic Republic*, case of *Khamkhing Souvanlasy*, were being considered together.
[47] See document 125 EX/CR/HR/2 Add.
[48] See document 124 EX/3 PRIV., para. 168 (iv) (*supra*, p. 393).

of staff in the secondary education service of that province. He was in good health and was doing his best for the construction of the country in his field of competence.

188. In addition to this information, the Chairperson added that during the discussion she had had with the Lao Permanent Delegate, the Delegate had assured her that Mr Khamkhing Souvanlasy was not in a re-education camp and that he was able to travel freely in the country.

189. After an exchange of views, the Committee *decided*:

(i) to take note of the information provided by the government concerned;

(ii) to consider the two communications settled and to strike them from its list in application of:

104 EX/Decision 3.3, paragraph 14 (*j*), in respect of [the first communication] since that communication did not appear to merit further consideration as to its substance, and

paragraph 14 (*a*) (x) of the same decision in respect of [the second communication] as that communication was no longer relevant.

No. 146/79

Concerning *Uruguay*
Case of *Alfonso Avelino Fernández Cabrelli*

Communication of 4 July 1979 submitted by
Zygmunt Elbiński

Spring 1980 session of the Committee on Conventions and Recommendations (109th session of the Executive Board)[1]

184. In this communication, the author, representing himself as a person with reliable knowledge of the alleged violation, claims that Mr Cabrelli has been detained for his Marxist writings.

185. The representative of the Uruguayan Government informed the Committee that Mr Cabrelli had been released and was now totally free.

186. In these circumstances, the Committee *decided* to strike this case from its list.

[1] See document 109 EX/52 PRIV., paras. 184-186; see also documents 109 EX/CR/HR/3 and Add.4.

No. 149/79

Concerning *Union of Soviet Socialist Republics*
Case of *Mstislav Rostropovich and Galina Vishnevskaya*

Communication of 2 August 1979 submitted by
Mstislav Rostropovich and
Galina Vishnevskaya

Autumn 1979 session of the Committee on Conventions and Recommendations (108th session of the Executive Board)[1]

217. The communication concerns the case of two renowned artists who claim to have been prevented from continuing their artistic activities in the normal way. They also complain that they were deprived of their nationality.

218. Having received the communication only recently, the representative of the government concerned requested the Committee to postpone until its next session consideration of its admissibility.

219. One member of the Committee said that its admissibility was so clear that, even without the reply from the government concerned, the Committee could take a decision at the present session. Another speaker proposed that the admissibility and the merits of the communication should be dealt with together at the Committee's next session.

220. The Director of the Division of Human Rights [and Peace] pointed out that 104 EX/Decision 3.3 contained no provision preventing the Committee from deciding on the admissibility of a communication, even without the reply from the government concerned, but that the decision had been thought out and drafted by the Executive Board in a spirit of dialogue and co-operation with the governments concerned. Moreover, although 104 EX/Decision 3.3 made a distinction between consideration of the admissibility and consideration of the merits of a communication, it did not

[1] See document 108 EX/38 PRIV., paras. 217-221; see also document 108 EX/CR/PROC.HR/ 1 Add.

oblige the Committee to carry out this twofold examination during two successive sessions; that had, however, been the Committee's practice up to now.

221. At the suggestion of the Chairman, the Committee *decided* to defer consideration of the admissibility of the communication until its next session.

Spring 1980 session of the Committee on Conventions and Recommendations (109th session of the Executive Board)[2]

140. The communication concerns the case of two renowned artists who claim to have been prevented from continuing their artistic activities in the normal way and from participating in the cultural life of their country due to their having unjustly been deprived of their nationality.

141. The Committe at its [autumn 1979] session had decided to defer the consideration of the admissibility of the case at the request of the government since the latter had received the communication only a short time before the session.[3]

142. In his review of the case, the representative of the Soviet Government reminded the Committee that paragraph 14 (*a*) (v) of 104 EX/Decision 3.3 required that a communication must not be manifestly ill-founded. It was his view that there were a number of inaccuracies in the communication and that it was quite manifestly ill-founded. By way of illustration he stated that while the authors claimed that attempts had been made to end their musical careers, the record showed that during the period in question they had given hundreds of concerts, had earned large sums of money, and had received professional and press recognition. He also called the Committee's attention to samples of sheet music which he said refuted the authors' claim that their names were being removed from works of music which were said to be dedicated to them. As concerned their allegations of political persecution, the Soviet representative stated that the authors had left the Soviet Union of their own free will. He also pointed to a number of incidents in the personal lives of the authors which he said ought to give rise to doubts about the stability of their personalities and about the motives for their submitting the communication. In view of his presentation, the Soviet representative felt that the communication hed been shown to be manifestly ill-founded, and he asked the Committee to declare it inadmissible for that reason.

---

[2] See document 109 EX/52 PRIV., paras. 140-148; see also document 109 EX/CR/HR/2.

[3] See document 108 EX/38 PRIV., para. 221 (*supra*, p. 400).

Union of Soviet Socialist Republics **No. 149/79**

143. One member of the Committee stated that he felt that the communication was very clearly admissible and tended to think that the information supplied by the representative of the government concerning the private lives of the authors in fact reinforced the authors' allegations of invasion of their privacy. Other members of the Committee felt that the representative's refutations of the authors' assertions had been convincing and favoured declaring the communication inadmissible.

144. Still other members of the Committee stated that, while it was true that the communication had been shown to contain certain inconsistencies, this by itself did not suffice to show that the communication was manifestly ill-founded, and they certainly felt that the communication was not offensive or insulting. Furthermore, they pointed out that the key questions of this communication had not been addressed, i.e. were the authors arbitrarily and without recourse deprived of their nationality and were they at present without the possibility of pursuing their cultural activities in their own country?

145. The representative of the Soviet Government explained to the Committee that there existed a procedure of petition to restore nationality and that the Soviet authorities had received no such petition.

146. The representative of the Director-General confirmed in respect of condition 14 (*a*) (vi) of 104 EX/Decision 3.3 that the prohibition of offensive communications meant that they could not contain offensive or injurious language but that the act of presenting or admitting communications could not in itself be considered as offensive since all communications by their nature contained allegations against the States concerned.

147. After a prolonged debate on the aforementioned issues, the Committee *decided*:

(i) to suspend the examination of the admissibility of this communication;

(ii) to instruct the Secretariat to request the authors of the communication to:

(*a*) indicate the purpose and the aim of their communication;

(*b*) indicate how they have complied with condition 14 (*a*) (ix) of 104 EX/ Decision 3.3;

(c) submit additional information in relation to the facts brought up during the examination of the admissibility of this communication; and

(iii) to request the Secretariat to revise the communication with a view to eliminating those allegations therein which do not concern human rights coming within Unesco's competence.

148. The Soviet representative stated that he accepted this compromise decision with regret.

Autumn 1980 session of the Committee on Conventions and Recommendations (110th session of the Executive Board)[4]

154. This communicaticn concerns the case of two renowned artists who claim to have been prevented from continuing their artistic activities in a nomal way and from participating in the cultural life of their country due to their having unjustly been deprived of their nationality.

155. In his review of the case, the representative of the Soviet Government reminded the Committee that paragraph 14 (*a*) (v) of 104 EX/Decision 3.3 required that a communication must not be manifestly ill-founded. It was his view that there were a number of inaccuracies in the communication and that it was quite manifestly ill-founded. By way of illustration he stated that while the authors claimed that attempts had been made to end their musical careers, the record showed that during the period in question they had given hundreds of concerts, had earned large sums of money, and had received professional and press recognition. He also called the Committee's attention to samples of sheet music which he said refuted the authors' claims that their names were being removed from works of music which were said to be dedicated to them. As concerned their allegations of political persecution, the Soviet representative stated that the authors had left the Soviet Union of their own free will. He also pointed to a number of incidents in the personal lives of the authors which he said ought to give rise to doubts about the stability of their personalities and about the motives for their submitting the communication. In view of his presentation, the Soviet representative felt that the communication had been shown to be manifestly ill-founded, and he asked the Committee to declare it inadmissible for that reason.

156. One member of the Committee stated that he felt that the communication was very clearly admissible and tended to think that the information supplied by the representative of the government concerning the private lives of the authors in fact reinforced the author's allegations of invasion of their privacy. Other members of the

---

[4] See document 110 EX/40 PRIV., paras. 154-164; see also document 110 EX/CR/HR/2.

Committee felt that the representative's refutations of the author's assertions had been convincing and favoured declaring the communication inadmissible.

157. Still other members of the Committee stated that, while it was true that the communication had been shown to contain certain inconsistencies, this by itself did not suffice to show that the communication was manifestly ill-founded, and they certainly felt that the communication was not offensive or insulting. Furthermore, they pointed out that the key questions of this communication had not been addressed, i.e. were the authors arbitrarily and without recourse deprived of their nationality and were they at present without the possibility of pursuing their cultural activities in their own country?

158. The representative of the Soviet Government explained to the Committee that there existed a procedure of petition to restore nationality and that the Soviet authorities had received no such petition.

159. After a prolonged debate on the aforementioned issues, the Committee decided:[5]

(i) to suspend the examination of the admissibility of this communication;

(ii) to instruct the Secretariat to request, the authors of the communication to:

(*a*) indicate the purpose and the aim of their communication;

(*b*) indicate how they have complied with condition 14 (*a*) (ix) of 104 EX/ Decision 3.3;

(*c*) submit additional information in relation to the facts brought up during the examination of the admissibility of this communication; and

(iii) to request the Secretariat to revise the communication with a view to eliminating those allegations therein which do not concern human rights coming within Unesco's competence.

160. The Soviet representative stated that he accepted this compromise decision with regret.

[5] See document 109 EX/52 PRIV., para. 147 (*supra*, pp. 401-402).

No. 149/79 **Union of Soviet Socialist Republics**

161. At its present session the Committee was informed by the representative of the Director-General that the Secretariat had recently received two letters from the victims' attorney.

162. In the first letter, dated 20 August 1980, the attorney requested more time to prepare the redrafted communication requested by the Committee.

163. In the second letter, dated 25 August, the attorney informed the Committee that she had received instructions from her clients to withdraw their communication.

164. After a brief discussion the Committee *decided* to allow the communication to be withdrawn. As it had done in a previous case [...][6] the Committee noted that it was not obligated to accept such requests and that it reserved the right not to accept them if it felt that the authors were acting under duress, that the complaint was of special interest to the Committee, or that there were other appropriate reasons for doing so.

---

[6] See document 108 EX/38 PRIV., para. 209 (*supra*, p. 160), communication No. 37/78 concerning *United Kingdom*, case of *Children of nomadic Gypsies*.

No. 150/79

Concerning *Czechoslovakia*
Case of *Václav Havel and Otta Bednářová**

Communication of 3 August 1979 submitted by
Bernard Andreu *et al.*°

Spring 1980 session of the Committee on Conventions and Recommendations (109th session of the Executive Board)[1]

88. The authors of this communication, ten French lawyers, allege that the right of freedom of thought and the right to impart information and ideas guaranteed by Articles 18 and 19 of the Universal Declaration of Human Rights have been violated in respect of Mr Václav Havel, a writer, and Mrs Otta Bednářová, a former reporter for Czechoslovak television. The latter were members of a committee for the support of persons unjustly prosecuted for their activities for the application of the Helsinki Final Act. They are alleged to have been kept under continual surveillance and to have been subsequently arrested, being thus prevented from exercising their professions, circulating their work and imparting their ideas.

89. The representative of the Czechoslovak Government stated that while his government deeply respected the work of Unesco and the Committee, it felt that this communication threatened the continuing co-operation between the government and Unesco. His government felt that the authors of the communication wanted to misuse Unesco to interfere with the internal affairs of Czechoslovakia. The persons in the group mentioned in the communication were said to have received sums of money from abroad and to have had contacts with émigré and foreign organizations.

[89a.] The group had not registered itself as called for by Czechoslovak legislation; it was an illegal group which collected information on government and police offi-

* From the Committee's spring 1982 session, this communication was being referred to as case of *Václav Havel*.
° Communication submitted by Bernard Andreu, Jean Courturon, Francis Jacob, Daniel Jacoby, Eddy Kenig, Sylviane Mercier, Michel, Louis Pettiti, Roland Rappaport and Mario Stasi.
[1] See document 109 EX/52 PRIV., paras. 88-98; see also document 109 EX/CR/HR/3.

cials, and put pressure on state organs. The representative of the government concerned stated that it was clear that Mr Havel and Ms Bednářová violated Czechoslovak laws and they had been tried and sentenced accordingly. Mr Havel and Mrs Bednářová were sentenced to five and three years of prison respectively.

90. The representative of the government also expressed concern that these matters had found their way into a French newspaper shortly after Unesco received the communication.

91. He went on to say that the complaint relied on unconvincing arguments, was hastily thrown together, and was in fact part of an anti-Czechoslovakia slander campaign. Furthermore, since part of the information was obtained from a newspaper published by a notorious Czech émigré group on the outskirts of Paris, the communication did not satisfy a condition laid down by 104 EX/Decision 3.3. He stated that human rignts were too serious a matter to justify giving consideration to a post office box on the outskirts of the city and asked that the Committee declare the communication inadmissible.

92. In this connection, the representative of the Director-General informed the Committee that the article in the French newspaper referred to by the representative of the Czechoslovak Government had given rise to an inquiry on the part of the Secretariat. It was learned that the newspaper's source had been a press release by the authors of the communication; the authors were immediately informed of the importance of confidentiality in these matters and no further incidents had occured.

93. A member of the Committee stated that in his opinion the relationship between Unesco and Czechoslovakia had nothing to do with a communication before the Committee and that it was inappropriate to evoke that relationship. He further felt that there was no sign of slander in the communication, and noted that, as a matter of fact, he knew some of the lawyers who had submitted the communication and could vouch for their being respectable men. He asked whether the authors had informed Unesco of the recent judgements and whether the representative of the government could provide tbe Committee with copies thereof.

94. Several members of the Committee felt that the communication was clearly admissible. They pointed to the clear link between the alleged victims' professions and the right to impart information and Unesco's competence in those areas. It was emphasized that the communication in fact did not use offensive language and did not rely exclusively on mass media information and that having met all the other admissibility requirements as well, it was admissible. It was also pointed out that human rights were not the exclusive internal affair of states and that the Helsinki Final Act assigned Unesco a specific role in the follow-up procedures thereof.

Czechoslovakia **No. 150/79**

95. One member of the Committee felt that a certain number of irregularities of form warranted a suspension of the examination of the communication. He pointed out that one of the letters reproduced was from a news clipping without being so labelled. Also, there was no indication that the authors bad been designated to represent the victims, and of those ten authors, only one had signed on behalf of all of them. These irregularities, he said, warranted a suspension of the examination of the communication.

96. One of the members of the Committee asked whether all articles critical of the Czechoslovak Government would in general be considered by that government to be subversive. The representative of the government replied that the possibility to criticize did exist in Czechoslovakia but stated that in the present case, the persons involved had been found guilty of transmitting the critical comments to émigré organizations.

97. After discussion, the Committee *decided* to declare the communication admissible, on the understanding that the irregularities of form would be corrected.

98. One member of the Committee stated that he felt obliged to make a reservation concerning this decision as a whole.

Autumn 1980 session of the Committee on Conventions and Recommendations (110th session of the Executive Board)[2]

300. The authors of this communication, ten French lawyers, allege that the right of freedom of thought and to impart infomation and ideas guaranteed by Articles 18 and 19 of the Universal Declaration of Human Rights have been violated in respect of Mr Václav Havel, a writer, and Mrs Otta Bednářová, a former reporter for Czechoslovak television. The latter were members of a committee for the support of persons unjustly prosecuted for their activities compatible with the Helsinki Agreements. They are alleged to have been kept under continual supervision and subsequently arrested, being thus prevented from exercising their professions, circulating their work and imparting their ideas.

301. After discussion, the Committee decided at its [spring 1980] session to declare the communication admissible on the understanding that the irregularities of form would be corrected.[3]

---

[2] See document 110 EX/40 PRIV., paras. 300-311; see also documents 110 EX/CR/HR/1 and Add., Add.4 and 5.
[3] See document 109 EX/52 PRIV., para. 97 (*supra*, p. 407).

302. In this connection the representative of the Director-General drew at its present session the Committee's attention to [a document] which reproduced a letter from the authors by which they had taken appropriate steps to remedy those irregularities.[4] He also pointed out that after the appearance of an information leak on the case appeared in a French newspaper a thorough investigation was undertaken and confirmed that the leak had not emanated from the Secretariat.

303. It was pointed out to the Committee that this was the only case so far where there had been leakage of information, and the question was presented whether the Committee would not wish to follow the example of other international bodies in such matters. When leaks occurred at other bodies, the practice was to warn the authors that the case would be dropped if further information were divulged to the public. The representative of the Director-General also called the Committee's attention to a recent letter from one of the authors of the communication, by which he presented information from the son of one of the alleged victims concerning the state of health of his mother, who was in prison.

304. The representative of the Government of Czechoslovakia stated that he had presented his government's position at the Committee's [spring 1980] session. The Committee had before it a letter from the Deputy Minister of Foreign Affairs of his country which was self-explanatory, he said. He reiterated the assertion that the alleged victims' human rights had not been violated; the alleged victims had not been convicted for writing novels or books but for writing anti-state and subversive literature, circulating it to émigré organizations and a Western radio service and for being members of an illegal organization whose activity is financed from abroad.

305. The Czechoslovak representative expressed his concern over the leak which had occurred and also expressed his view that the Committee should not conduct its work on the basis of mere copies of the documents from the alleged victims, but rather should insist on having the originals of the alleged victim's writings put before it. As for the "Charter 77" newsletter mentioned in the recent letter by one of the authors, the Czech representative said this was an illegal publication in Czechoslovakia and the information presented therein should not be taken seriously by the Committee. He stated that, as to the question of Mrs Bednářová's state of health, it was clear that even though it was true that she had in fact been on an invalidity pension, the social security administration had more recently decided to withdrav the pension. This was done, he said, before the matter at hand arose and because on two occasions the competent commissions, which included medical doctors, pronounced themselves in favour of such a measure and thus confirmed that the state of health of Mrs Bednářová had improved.

---

[4] See document 110 EX/CR/HR/1 Add.

Czechoslovakia **No. 150/79**

306. A member of the Committee expressed concern over the information leak which had occurred. He also expressed the view that the authors were trying to draw the Committee into a political game. In his view the Committee was not allowed to meddle where courts had taken a decision in accordance with the law of the country. He further pointed out that the Committee had previously been willing to have confidence in a state's assurances of a prisoner's sof health, and he suggested that the Committee in this case limit itself to asking the Czechoslovak Government to assure that the woman in question received all the medical attention she needed, including any operations which might be necessary to restore her deteriorated health.

307. Another Committee member also expressed his concern over the leak and was of the opinion that the government concerned was justified in its position that the Committee should not question a case which had been tried in the courts. He went on to state that the Committee's concern should be purely humanitarian. A third Committee member adopted the same position.

308. Many Committee members felt that the reply and attitude of the Czechoslovak representative and his government were disappointing and indicative of a lack of willingness to co-operate with the Committee. The Committee members indicated their surprise and concern over this fact and stated that in their view the laconic reply of the Czechoslovak Government was most unsatisfactory since it provided no new information to the Committee and even went so far as to suggest that the Committee was meddling. It was pointed out that the reply contained no information on the texts of the legislation used to convict the persons involved nor did it provide the texts of the judgements as had been requested by the Committee at its [spring 1980] session. The press leak was unanimously regretted and the suggestion to warn the authors was supported. Similarly the proposal to ask for urgent humanitarian aid for the alleged victims was supported. Committee members reminded the Committee that it had on numerous previous occasions decided that a judgement did not end the Committee's interest in a case; since the Committee was not a trial court, it pursued its interest in respect of human rights before or after judgements.

309. It was pointed out that in becoming members of the United Nations, states gave up the right to insist that human rights were strictly within their domestic affairs, and a decision of the International Court of Justice was mentioned which confirmed this principle. It was stressed that international instruments and general legal and moral principles must take precedence when internal laws do not conform to such principles. The important thing was to work in a co-operative spirit to explore ways to find a friendly solution to problems involving human rights. In this specific matter the main concern was to assure speedy humanitarian intervention to provide urgently needed medical assistance to one of the alleged victims.

No. 150/79 **Czechoslovakia**

310. By way of clarification the representative of the Director-General explained that the Secretariat sent to governments concerned photocopies of all documents received from authors, without modification. For practical reasons the Committee sometimes received condensed versions of communications (which at times contained hundreds of pages) but of course the originals were always available in the file which was at the Committee's constant disposal.

311. After a very lengthy discussion, the Committee *decided*:

(i) to ask the Czechoslovak representative to take note of the Committee's wish that Mrs Bednářová be provided with all necessary medical attention to restore her health;

(ii) to express concern over the information leak which had occurred, to note that the Director-General had established that the leak did not emenate from the Secretariat and to warn the authors that no more leaks should occur;

(iii) to keep the communication on its agenda for further consideration on the basis of 104 EX/Decision 3.3 at its next session.

Spring 1981 session of the Committee on Conventions and Recommendations (112th session of the Executive Board)[5]

506. The authors of this communication, ten French lawyers, allege that the right of freedom of thought and the right to impart information and ideas, guaranteed by Articles 18 and 19 of the Universal Declaration of Human Rights, have been violated in respect of Mr Václav Havel, a writer, and Mrs Otta Bednářová, a former reporter for Czechoslovak television. The latter were members of a committee for the support of persons unjustly prosecuted for activities compatible with the Helsinki Agreements. They are alleged to have been kept under continual supervision and subsequently arrested, being thus prevented from exercising their professions, circulating their work and imparting their ideas.

507. As regards domestic means of redress, Mrs Bednářová is said to have lodged a petition against withdrawal of her disability pension. The Prague Municipal Court is alleged to have confirmed withdrawal thereof in May 1979.

---

[5] See document 112 EX/30 PRIV., paras. 506-535; see also document 112 EX/CR/HR/1.

Czechoslovakia **No. 150/79**

508. The authors of the communication state that the alleged violations have not been submitted to any other international authority concerned with the protection of human rights.

509. At the Committee's [spring] 1980 session, the representative of the Czechoslovak Government had stated that, while his government deeply respected the work of Unesco and the Committee, it felt that this communication threatened the continuing co-operation between the government and Unesco. His government felt that the authors of the communication wanted to misuse Unesco to interfere in the internal affairs of Czechoslovakia. The persons in the group mentioned in the communication were said to have received sums of money from abroad and to have had contacts with émigré and foreign organizations. The group had not registered itself as called for by Czechoslovak legislation; it was an illegal group which collected information on government and police officials and put pressure on state organs. The representative of the government concerned had stated that it was clear that Mr Havel and Mrs Bednářová had violated Czechoslovak laws and they had been tried and sentenced accordingly. Mr Havel and Mrs Bednářová had been sentenced to five and three years' imprisonment respectively.

510. The representative of the government had also expressed concern that these matters had found their way into a French newspaper shortly after Unesco received the communication.

511. He had gone on to say that the complaint relied on unconvincing arguments, was hastily thrown together, and was in fact part of an anti-Czechoslovakia slander campaign. Furthermore, since part of the information was obtained from a newspaper published by a notorious Czech émigré group on the outskirts of Paris, the communication did not satisfy a condition laid down by 104 EX/Decision 3.3. He had stated that human rights were too serious a matter for consideration to be given to information coming only from a post office box on the outskirts of the city and had asked that the Committee declare the communication inadmissible.

512. In that connection, the representative of the Director-General had informed the Committee that the article in the French newspaper referred to by the representative of the Czechoslovak Government had given rise to an inquiry on the part of the Secretariat. It had emerged that the newspaper's source had been a press release by the authors of the communication; the authors had been immediately informed of the importance of confidentiality in these matters and no further incidents had occurred.

513. A member of the Committee had stated that, in his opinion, the relationship between Unesco and Czechoslovakia had nothing to do with a communication before the Committee and that it was inappropriate to bring up that relationship. He had

further felt that there was no sign of slander in the communication, and noted that, as a matter of fact, he knew some of the lawyers who had submitted the communication and could vouch for their being respectable men. He had asked whether the authors had informed Unesco of the recent judgements and whether the representative of the government could provide the Committee with copies thereof.

514. Several members of the Committee had felt that the communication was clearly admissible. They had pointed to the clear link between the alleged victims' professions and the right to impart information and Unesco's competence in those areas. It had been emphasized that the communication in fact did not use offensive language and did not rely exclusively on mass media information and that, having met all the other admissibility requirements as well, it was admissible. It had also been pointed out that human rights were not the exclusive internal affair of states and that the Helsinki Final Act assigned Unesco a specific role in the follow-up procedures thereof.

515. One member of the Committee had felt that a certain number of irregularities of form warranted a suspension of the examination of the communication. He had pointed out that one of the letters reproduced was from a news clipping without being so labelled. Also, there was no indication that the authors had been designated to represent the victims, and of those ten authors, only one had signed on behalf of all of them. These irregularities, he had said, warranted a suspension of the examination of the communication.

516. One of the members of the Committee had asked whether all articles critical of the Czechoslovak Government would in general be considered by that government to be subversive. The representative of the government had replied that the possibility of criticizing did exist in Czechoslovakia but had stated that, in the present case, the persons involved had been found guilty of transmitting the critical comments to émigré organizations.

517. After discussion, the Committee had decided to declare the communication admissible on the understanding that the irregularities of form would be corrected.[6]

518. One member of the Committee had stated that he felt obliged to make a reservation concerning that decision as a whole.

519. The Secretariat had duly informed the authors of the communication and the Czechoslovak Government of the Committee's decision. The authors of the communication had replied to the Secretariat's letter of 23 June 1980 on 29 July 1980.

---

[6] See document 109 EX/52 PRIV., para. 97 (*supra*, p. 407).

Czechoslovakia **No. 150/79**

520. At the [autumn 1980] session, the representative of the Director-General had drawn the Committee's attention to the letter of 29 July [1980] in which the authors indicated that they had taken appropriate steps to remedy the irregularities mentioned. He had also pointed out that, after the appearance of an information leak on the case in a French newspaper, a thorough investigation had been undertaken which confirmed that the leak had not emanated from the Secretariat.

521. The representative of the Government of Czechoslovakia had stated that he had presented his government's position at the Committee's [spring 1980] session. He had reiterated the assertion that the alleged victims' human rights had not been violated; they had not been convicted for writing novels or books but for writing anti-state, subversive literature, circulating it to émigré organizations and a Western radio service, and for being members of an illegal organization whose activity was financed from abroad.

522. The Czechoslovak representative had expressed his concern over the leak that had occurred and also expressed his view that the Committee should not conduct its work on the basis of mere copies of the documents from the alleged victims, but rather should insist on having the originals of the alleged victims' writings put before it. As for the "Charter 77" newsletter, mentioned in the recent letter by one of the authors, the Czech representative had said this was an illegal publication in Czechoslovakia and the information presented therein should not be taken seriously by the Committee. He had stated that, as to the question of Mrs Bednářová's state of health, it was clear that, even though it was true that she had in fact been on an invalidity pension, the social security administration had more recently decided to withdraw the pension. That was done, he had said, before the matter at hand arose and because on two occasions the competent commissions, which included medical doctors, had pronounced themselves in favour of such a measure and thus confirmed that the state of health of Mrs Bednářová had improved.

523. A member of the Committee had expressed concern over the information leak which had occurred. He had also expressed the view that the authors were trying to draw the Committee into a political game. In his view, the Committee was not allowed to meddle where courts had taken a decision in accordance with the law of the country. He had further pointed out that the Committee had previously been willing to have confidence in a state's assurances regarding a prisoner's state of health, and he had suggested that the Committee in this case limit itself to asking the Czechoslovak Government to make sure that the woman in question received all the medical attention she needed, including any operations which might be necessary to restore her health.

524. Another Committee member had also expressed his concern over the leak and had been of the opinion that the government concerned was justified in its view that the Committee should not question a case which had been tried in the courts. He had gone on to state that the Committee's concern should be purely humanitarian. A third Committee member had adopted the same position.

525. Many Committee members had felt that the reply and attitude of the Czechoslovak representative and his government were disappointing and indicative of a lack of willingness to co-operate with the Committee. The Committee members had indicated their surprise and concern over this fact and had stated that, in their view, the laconic reply of the Czechoslovak Government was most unsatisfactory since it provided no new information to the Committee and even went so far as to suggest that the Committee was meddling. It had been pointed out that the reply contained no information on the texts of the legislation used to convict the persons involved nor did it provide the texts of the judgements, as had been requested by the Committee at its [spring 1980] session. The press leak had been unanimously regretted and the suggestion that the authors be warned had been supported. Similarly the proposal to ask for urgent humanitarian aid for the alleged victims had been supported. Some members had reminded the Committee that it had on many previous occasions decided that a judgement did not end the Committee's interest in a case; since the Committee was not a trial court, it pursued its interest in respect of human rights before or after judgements.

526. It had been pointed out that, in becoming members of the United Nations, states gave up the right to insist that human rights were strictly within their domestic affairs, and a decision of the International Court of Justice had been mentioned which confirmed that principle. It had been stressed that international instruments and general legal and moral principles should take precedence when internal laws did not conform to such principles. The important thing was to work in a co-operative spirit to explore ways to find a friendly solution to problems involving human rights. In this specific matter, the main concern was to assure speedy humanitarian intervention to provide urgently needed medical assistance to one of the alleged victims.

527. The representative of the Director-General had explained that the Secretariat had sent to governments concerned photocopies of all documents received from authors, without modification. For practical reasons, the Committee sometimes received condensed versions of communications (which at times ran to hundreds of pages) but the originals were, of course, always available in the file which was at the Committee's constant disposal.

Czechoslovakia **No. 150/79**

528. After a very lengthy discussion, at the [autumn 1980] session, the Committee decided:[7]

> (i) to ask the Czechoslovak representative to take note of the Committee's wish that Mrs Bednářová be provided with all necessary medical attention to restore her health;
>
> (ii) to express concern over the information leak that had occurred, to note that the Director-General had established that the leak did not emanate from the Secretariat and to warn the authors that no more leaks should occur;
>
> (iii) to keep the communication on its agenda for further consideration at its next session on the basis of 104 EX/Decision 3.3.

529. The representative of the government concerned announced at the present session that Mrs Bednářová had been released on 26 September 1980, in accordance with the provisions of the Czechoslovak Penal Code. With regard to the case of Mr Václav Havel, he stated that he had no further information to add, since the person concerned had been sentenced for subversive activities under the current legislation.

530. Several merrbers of the Committee expressed their satisfaction at the release of one of the alleged victims, and wished to thank the Czechoslovak Government.

531. One member of the Committee wondered whether it was not possible to appeal to the clemency of the Czechoslovak Head of State. He hoped that the Director-General might agree, in the spirit of paragraph 14 (*k*) of 104 EX/Decision 3.3, to continue to negotiate through the appropriate channels with a view to arriving at a humanitarian settlement of the case.

532. Several members of the Committee pointed out that, at the [autumn 1980] session, the Committee had had before it all the information necessary to enable it to say that Mr Václav Havel and Mrs Otta Bednářová had been judged and sentenced in accordance with the law, and that concern was now being occasioned by Mrs Bednářová's state of health.

533. However, since Mrs Bednářová had been released, it should be acknowledged that the matter was settled and that the Czechoslovak Government had furnished proof that it was very willing to co-operate with the Committee.

---

[7] See document 110 EX/40 PRIV., para. 311 (*supra*, p. 410).

No. 150/79 **Czechoslovakia**

534. Drawing a parallel with [another communication],[8] one member of the Committee stressed the desirability of issuing an appeal for clemency with regard to the case of Mr Václav Havel.

535. Finally, the Committee:

(i) *Took note* with satisfaction of the release of Mrs Otta Bednářová; and

(ii) *Decided*, pursuant to the provisions of paragraph 14 (*k*) of 104 EX/Decision 3.3, to ask the Executive Board to request the Director-General to take steps with a view to bringing about a friendly solution to the case.

Autumn 1981 session of the Committee on Conventions and Recommendations (113th session of the Executive Board)[9]

547. The authors of this communication, ten French lawyers, allege that the right of freedom of thought and the right to impart information and ideas, guaranteed by Articles 18 and 19 of the Universal Declaration of Human Rights, have been violated in respect of Mr Václav Havel, a writer, and Mrs Otta Bednářová, a former reporter for Czechoslovak television. The latter were members of a committee for the support of persons unjustly prosecuted for activities compatible with the Helsinki Agreements. They are alleged to have been kept under continual supervision and subsequently arrested, being thus prevented from exercising their professions, circulating their work and imparting their ideas.

548. As regards domestic means of redress, Mrs Bednářová is said to have lodged a petition against withdrawal of her disability pension. The Prague Municipal Court is alleged to have confirmed withdrawal thereof in May 1979.

549. The authors of the communication state that the alleged violations have not been submitted to any other international authority concerned with the protection of human rights.

550. At the Committee's [spring] 1980 session, the representative of the Czechoslovak Government stated that, while his government deeply respected the work of Unesco and the Committee, it felt that this communication threatened the continuing co-operation between the government and Unesco. His government felt that the authors of the communication wanted to misuse Unesco to interfere in the internal af-

[8] See document 112 EX/30 PRIV., paras. 536-557 (*supra*, pp. 270-274), communication No. 103/79 concerning *Uruguay*, case of *José Luis Massera*.
[9] See document 113 EX/38 PRIV., paras. 547-581; see also document 113 EX/CR/HR/1.

fairs of Czechoslovakia. The persons in the group mentioned in the communication were said to have received sums of money from abroad and to have had contacts with émigré and foreign organizations. The group had not registered itself as called for by Czechoslovak legislation; it was an illegal group which collected information on government and police officials and put pressure on state organs. The representative of the government concerned stated that it was clear that Mr Havel and Mrs Bednářová had violated Czechoslovak laws and they had been tried and sentenced accordingly. Mr Havel and Mrs Bednářová had been sentenced to five and three years' imprisonment respectively.

551. The representative of the government also expressed concern that these matters had found their way into a French newspaper shortly after Unesco received the communication.

552. He went on to say that the complaint relied on unconvincing arguments, was hastily thrown together, and was in fact part of an anti-Czechoslovakia slander campaign. Furthermore, since part of the information was obtained from a newspaper published by a notorious Czech émigré group on the outskirts of Paris, the communication did not satisfy a condition laid down by 104 EX/Decision 3.3. He stated that human rights were too serious a matter for consideration to be given to information coming only from a post office box on the outskirts of the city and asked that the Committee declare the communication inadmissible.

553. In that connection, the representative of the Director-General informed the Committee that the article in the French newspaper referred to by the representative of the Czechoslovak Government had given rise to an inquiry on the part of the Secretariat. It emerged that the newspaper's source had been a press release by the authors of the communication; the authors had been immediately informed of the importance of confidentiality in these matters and no further incidents had occurred.

554. A member of the Committee stated that, in his opinion, the relationship between Unesco and Czechoslovakia had nothing to do with a communication before the Committee and that it was inappropriate to bring up that relationship. He further felt that there was no sign of slander in the communication, and noted that, as a matter of fact, he knew some of the lawyers who had submitted the communication and could vouch for their being respectable men. He asked whether the authors had informed Unesco of the recent judgements and whether the representative of the government could provide the Committee with copies thereof.

555. Several members of the Committee felt that the communication was clearly admissible. They pointed to the clear link between the alleged victims' professions and the right to impart information and Unesco's competence in those areas. It was em-

phasized that the communication in fact did not use offensive language and did not rely exclusively on mass media information and that, having met all the other admissibility requirements as well, it was admissible. It was also pointed out that human rights were not the exclusive internal affair of states and that the Helsinki Final Act assigned Unesco a specific role in the follow-up procedures thereof.

556. One member of the Committee felt that a certain number of irregularities of form warranted a suspension of the examination of the communication. He pointed out that one of the letters reproduced was from a news clipping without being so labelled. Also, there was no indication that the authors had been designated to represent the victims, and of those ten authors, only one had signed on behalf of all of them.

557. One of the members of the Committee asked whether all articles critical of the Czechoslovak Government would in general be considered by that government to be subversive. The representative of the government replied that the possibility of criticizing did exist in Czechoslovakia but stated that, in the present case, the persons involved had been found guilty of transmitting the critical comments to émigré organizations.

558. After discussion, the Committee decided to declare the communication admissible on the understanding that the irregularities of form would be corrected.[10]

559. One member of the Committee stated that he felt obliged to make a reservation concerning that decision as a whole.

560. The Secretariat duly informed the authors of the communication and the Czechoslovak Government of the Committee's decision. The authors of the communication replied to the Secretariat's letter of 23 June 1980 on 29 July 1980.

561. At the [autumn 1980] session, the representative of the Director-General drew the Committee's attention to the letter of 29 July [1980] in which the authors indicated that they had taken appropriate steps to remedy the irregularities mentioned. He also pointed out that, after the appearance of an information leak on the case in a French newspaper, a thorough investigation had been undertaken which confirmed that the leak had not emanated from the Secretariat.

562. The representative of the Government of Czechoslovakia stated that he had presented his government's position at the Committee's [spring 1980] session. He reiterated the assertion that the alleged victims' human rights had not been violated;

---

[10] See document 109 EX/52 PRIV., para. 97 (*supra*, p. 407).

they had not been convicted for writing novels or books but for writing anti-state, subversive literature, circulating it to émigré organizations and a Western radio service, and for being members of an illegal organization whose activity was financed from abroad.

563. The Czechoslovak representative expressed his concern over the leak that had occurred and also expressed his view that the Committee should not conduct its work on the basis of mere copies of the documents from the alleged victims, but rather should insist on having the originals of the alleged victims' writings put before it. As for the "Charter 77" newsletter, mentioned in the recent letter by one of the authors, the Czech representative said this was an illegal publication in Czechoslovakia and the information presented therein should not be taken seriously by the Committee. He stated that, as to the question of Mrs Bednářová's state of health, it was clear that, even though it was true that she had in fact been on an invalidity pension, the social security administration had more recently decided to withdraw the pension. That was done, he had said, before the matter at hand arose and because on two occasions the competent commissions, which included medical doctors, had pronounced themselves in favour of such a measure and thus confirmed that the state of health of Mrs Bednářová had improved.

564. A member of the Committee expressed concern over the information leak which had occurred. He also expressed the view that the authors were trying to draw the Committee into a political game. In his view, the Committee was not allowed to meddle where courts had taken a decision in accordance with the law of the country. He further pointed out that the Committee had previously been willing to have confidence in a state's assurances regarding a prisoner's state of health, and he had suggested that the Committee in this case limit itself to asking the Czechoslovak Government to make sure that the woman in question received all the medical attention she needed, including any operations which might be necessary to restore her health.

565. Another Committee member also expressed his concern over the leak and was of the opinion that the government concerned was justified in its view that the Committee should not question a case which had been tried in the courts. He went on to state that the Committee's concern should be purely humanitarian. A third Committee member adopted the same position.

566. Many Committee members felt that the reply and attitude of the Czechoslovak representative and his government were disappointing and indicative of a lack of willingness to co-operate with the Committee. The Committee members indicated their surprise and concern over this fact and stated that, in their view, the laconic reply of the Czechoslovak Government was most unsatisfactory since it provided no new information to the Committee and even went so far as to suggest that the Com-

mittee was meddling. It was pointed out that the reply contained no information on the texts of the legislation used to convict the persons involved nor did it provide the texts of the judgements, as had been requested by the Committee at its [spring 1980] session. The press leak had been unanimously regretted and the suggestion that the authors be warned had been supported. Similarly the proposal to ask for urgent humanitarian aid for the alleged victims had been supported. Some members reminded the Committee that it had on many previous occasions decided that a judgement did not end the Committees' interest in a case; since the Committee was not a trial court, it pursued its interest in respect of human rights before or after judgements.

567. It was pointed out that, in becoming members of the United Nations, states gave up the right to insist that human rights were strictly within their domestic affairs, and a decision of the International Court of Justice was mentioned which confirmed that principle. It was stressed that international instruments and general legal and moral principles should take precedence when internal laws did not conform to such principles. The important thing was to work in a co-operative spirit to explore ways to find a friendly solution to problems involving human rights. In this specific matter, the main concern was to assure speedy humanitarian intervention to provide urgently needed medical assistance to one of the alleged victims.

568. The representative of the Director-General explained that the Secretariat sent to governments concerned photocopies of all documents received from authors, without modification. For practical reasons, the Committee sometimes received condensed versions of communications (which at times ran to hundreds of pages) but the originals were, of course, always available in the file which was at the Committee's constant disposal.

569. After a very lengthy discussion the Committee decided:[11]

(i) to ask the Czechoslovak representative to take note of the Committee's wish that Mrs Bednářová be provided with all necessary medical attention to restore her health;

(ii) to express concern over the information leak that had occurred, to note that the Director-General had established that the leak did not emanate from the Secretariat and to warn the authors that no more leaks should occur;

(iii) to keep the communication on its agenda for further consideration at its next session on the basis of 104 EX/Decision 3.3.

---

[11] See document 110 EX/40 PRIV., para. 311 (*supra*, p. 410).

Czechoslovakia **No. 150/79**

570. At the [spring 1981] session, the representative of the Government of Czechoslovakia announced that Mrs Bednářová had been released on 26 September 1980, in accordance with the provisions of the country's Penal Code. With regard to Mr Václav Havel, he stated that he had no further information to add.

571. Several members of the Committee pointed out that at the [autumn 1980] session all the necessary information had been available for the justice of the sentence passed on the two alleged victims to be confirmed and that there was particular concern about Mrs Bednářová's health, but that, since she had been released, it had to be acknowledged that the matter was settled and that the Czechoslovak Government had furnished proof of its willingness to cooperate with the Committee.

572. Other members of the Committee stressed the desirability of issuing an appeal to the Czechoslovak Government for clemency to be shown towards Mr Václav Havel.

573. After an exchange of views, the Committee decided:[12]

> (i) to take note with satisfaction of the release of Mrs Otta Bednářová;
>
> (ii) to ask the Executive Board to request the Director-General to make representations, on humanitarian grounds, with a view to bringing about an amicable solution, in accordance with the provisions of paragraph 14 (*k*) of 104 EX/Decision 3.3.

574. In pursuance of paragraph (ii) of that decision, the Director-General had made the first representations, on humanitarian grounds, to the government concerned by sending to the Czechoslovak Minister of Foreign Affairs a letter dated 22 June 1981.

575. In his reply of 5 September 1981 the Czechoslovak Minister stated that it was difficult for his government to accede to an appeal for clemency: Mr Václav Havel had been sentenced with supporting evidence for subversive activities financed and guided from abroad; disregarding all warnings, the person concerned had, time and time again, engaged in acts of sabotage against his country and had not appreciated the humanitarian measures taken in his favour by the government authorities.

576. One member of the Committee considered that the Committee was in duty bound to respect the rights of a state that, against its will, had not been able to comply with the Committee's wishes. However, since the Committee had requested the

[12] See document 112 EX/30 PRIV., para. 535 (*supra*, p. 416).

Director-General to make representations, he felt that it was advisable to request the Director-General to continue his representations.

577. Another Committee member wished to know what exactly the offences were that Mr Václav Havel was alleged to have committed. He was of the opinion that a visit could be made by a representative of the Director-General to the alleged victim in the same way as was being envisaged in another case pending before the Committee.

578. Taking the floor in order to provide information to the Committee, the representative of the Czechoslovak Government recalled the statements that he had made at the previous sessions, stressing that Mr Václav Havel had not been convicted for his literary writings but for his collaboration with a foreign espionage service.

579. One member of the Committee stated that it was a very subjective matter to decide whether or not activities were subversive: since the competent court had assessed the facts, its decision could not be called into question. He felt that the Committee should confine itself to seeking a humanitarian settlement of this case.

580. Other Committee members endorsed the idea that the Director-General should be requested to continue his representations.

581. After a lengthy exchange of views the Committee *decided*:

(i) to postpone consideration of the substance of the communication until the next session;

(ii) to request the government concerned to state the exact grounds on which Mr Václav Havel had been convicted and to ensure that all such documents as it might consider necessary to enlighten the Committee regarding all the points raised by it in this case be placed in the file, whether they pertained to the origins of the allegations advanced by the authors of the communication or to the information leak regarding consideration thereof by the Committee;

(iii) to ask the Executive Board to request the Director-General to continue to make representations on humanitarian grounds;

(iv) to request the Secretariat to inform the authors of the communication of this decision.

Czechoslovakia **No. 150/79**

Spring 1982 session of the Committee on Conventions and Recommendations (114th session of the Executive Board)[13]

785. The authors of this communication, ten French lawyers, allege that the right of freedom of thought and to impart information and ideas guaranteed by Articles 18 and 19 of the Universal Declaration of Human Rights have been violated in respect of Mr Václav Havel, a writer. The latter was a member of a committee for the support of persons unjustly prosecuted for their activities compatible with the Helsinki Agreements. He is alleged to have been kept under continual supervision and subsequently arrested, being thus prevented from exercising his profession, circulating his works and imparting his ideas.

786. At the [spring] 1980 session, the representative of the Czechoslovak Government stated that while his government deeply respected the work of Unesco and the Committee, it felt that this communication threatened the continuing cooperation between the government and Unesco. His government felt that the authors of the communication wanted to misuse Unesco to interfere with the internal affairs of Czechoslovakia. The persons in the group mentioned in the communication were said to have received sums of money from abroad and to have had contacts with émigré and foreign organizations. The group had not registered itself as called for by Czechoslovak legislation; it was an illegal group which collected information on government and police officials, and put pressure on state organs. The representative of the government concerned maintained that it was clear that Mr Havel had violated Czechoslovak laws and that was why he had been sentenced to imprisonment.

787. The representative of the Czechoslovak government expressed concern that these matters had found their way into a French newspaper shortly after Unesco had received the communication.

788. He went on to say that the complaint relied on unconvincing arguments, was hastily thrown together, and was in fact part of an anti-Czechoslovakia slander campaign. Furthermore, since part of the information was obtained from a newspaper published by a notorious Czech émigré group on the outskirts of Paris, the communication did not satisfy a condition laid down by 104 EX/Decision 3.3. He stated that human rights were too serious a matter to justify giving consideration to information coming from a post office box on the outskirts of the city and asked that the Committee declare the communication inadmissible.

---

[13] See document 114 EX/38 PRIV., paras. 785-818; see also document 114 EX/CR/HR/1.

789. In this connection, the representative of the Director-General informed the Committee that the article in the French newspaper referred to by the representative of the Czechoslovak Government had given rise to an inquiry on the part of the Secretariat. It was learned that the newspaper's source had been a press release by the authors of the communication; the authors were immediately informed of the importance of confidentiality in these matters and no further incidents had occurred.

790. Several members of the Committee pointed to the clear link between the alleged victims' professions and the right to impart information and Unesco's competence in those areas. It was emphasized that the communication in fact did not use offensive language and did not rely exclusively on mass media information and that having met all the other admissibility requirements as well, it was admissible. It was also pointed out that human rights were not the exclusive internal affair of states and that the Helsinki Final Act assigned Unesco a specific role in the Act's follow-up procedures.

791. One member of the Committee felt that a certain number of irregularities of form warranted a suspension of the examination of the communication. He pointed out that one of the letters reproduced was from a news clipping without being so labelled. Also, there was no indication that the authors had been designated to represent the victims, and of those ten authors, only one had signed on behalf of all of them.

792. After discussion, the Committee decided to declare the communication admissible on the understanding that the irregularities of form would be corrected.[14]

793. At the August 1980 session, the representative of the Director-General said that the authors had taken appropriate steps to remedy those irregularities. He also pointed out that after information on the case had been leaked to a French newspaper, a thorough investigation had been undertaken which confirmed that the leak had not emanated from the Secretariat.

794. The representative of the Government of Czechoslovakia expressed his view that the Committee should not conduct its work on the basis of mere copies of the documents from the alleged victims, but rather should insist on having the originals put before it. He said that the "Charter 77" newsletter mentioned by one of the authors of the communication was an illegal publication in Czechoslovakia and the information presented in it should not be taken seriously by the Committee.

---

[14] See document 109 EX/52 PRIV., para. 97 (*supra*, p. 407).

Czechoslovakia **No. 150/79**

795. Some Committee members thought that the government concerned was justified in its position that the Committee should not question a case which had been tried in the courts. They went on to state that the Committee's concern should be purely humanitarian.

796. Many Committee members pointed out that the reply of the representative of the Government of Czechoslovakia contained no information on the legislation used to convict the persons involved nor did it provide the texts of the judgements.

797. The proposal to ask for urgent humanitarian aid for the alleged victim and for his wife, Mrs Otta Bednářová, who had also been arrested and sentenced, was supported. Committee members reminded the Committee that it had on numerous previous occasions decided that a judgement did not end the Committee's interest in a case; since the Committee was not a trial court, it pursued its interest in respect of human rights before or after judgements. It was further pointed out that in becoming members of the United Nations, states gave up the right to insist that human rights were strictly within their domestic affairs. A decision of the International Court of Justice was mentioned which confirmed this principle.

798. After a very lengthy discussion, the Committee decided:[15]

> (i) to ask the representative of the Government of Czechoslovakia to take note of the Committee's wish that Mrs Bednářová be provided with all necessary medical attention to restore her health;
>
> (ii) to express concern over the leak of information which had occurred, to note that the Director-General had established that the leak did not emanate from the Secretariat and to warn the authors that no more leaks should occur;
>
> (iii) to keep the communication on its agenda for further consideration at its next session on the basis of 104 EX/Decision 3.3.

799. At the [spring 1981] session, the representative of the Government of Czechoslovakia announced that Mrs Bednářová had been released on 26 September 1980, in accordance with the provisions of the country's Penal Code. With regard to Mr Václav Havel, he stated that he had no further information to add. Several members of the Committee pointed out that at the [autumn 1980] session all the necessary information had been available for the justice of the sentence passed on the two alleged victims to be confirmed and that there was particular concern about Mrs Bednářová's health, but that, since she had been released, it had to be acknowledged that

[15] See document 110 EX/40 PRIV., para. 311 (*supra*, p. 410).

the matter was settled and that the Czechoslovak Government had given proof of its willingness to co-operate with the Committee.

800. Other members of the Committee stressed the desirability of issuing an appeal to the Czechoslovak Government for clemency to be shown towards Mr Václav Havel.

801. After an exchange of views, the Committee decided:[16]

(i) to take note with satisfaction of the release of Mrs Otta Bednářová;

(ii) to ask the Executive Board to request the Director-General to make representations, on humanitarian grounds, with a view to bringing about an amicable solution, in accordance with the provisions of paragraph 14 (*k*) of 104 EX/Decision 3.3.

802. In pursuance of paragraph (ii) of that decision, the Director-General had made the first representations, on humanitarian grounds, to the government concerned by sending to the Czechoslovak Minister of Foreign Affairs a letter dated 22 June 1981.

803. In his reply of 5 September 1981 the Czechoslovak Minister stated that it was difficult for his government to accede to an appeal for clemency: Mr Václav Havel had been sentenced with supporting evidence for subversive activities financed and guided from abroad; despite warnings, the person concerned had, time and time again, engaged in acts of sabotage against his country and had not appreciated the humanitarian measures taken in his favour by the government authorities.

804. At the [autumn] 1981 session, one member of the Committee had expressed the view that the Committee was in duty bound to respect the rights of a state that, against its will, had not been able to comply with the Committee's wishes. However, since the Committee had requested the Director-General to make representations, he felt that it was advisable to request the Director-General to continue his representations.

805. Another Committee member wished to know what exactly the offences were that Mr Václav Havel was alleged to have committed. He was of the opinion that a visit could be made by a representative of the Director-General to the alleged victim in the same way as was being envisaged in another case pending before the Committee.

---

[16] See document 112 EX/30 PRIV., para. 535 (*supra*, p. 416).

Czechoslovakia **No. 150/79**

806. Taking the floor in order to provide information to the Committee, the representative of the Czechoslovak Government recalled the statements that he had made at the previous sessions, stressing that Mr Václav Havel had not been convicted for his literary writings but for his collaboration with a foreign espionage service.

807. After a lengthy exchange of views the Committee decided:[17]

(i) to postpone consideration of the substance of the communication until the present session;

(ii) to request the government concerned to state the exact grounds on which Mr Václav Havel had been convicted and to ensure that all such documents as it might consider necessary to enlighten the Committee regarding all the points raised by it in this case be placed in the file, whether they pertained to the origins of the allegations advanced by the authors of the communication or to the information leak regarding consideration of the communication by the Committee;

(iii) to ask the Executive Board to request the Director-General to continue to make representations on humanitarian grounds;

(iv) to request the Secretariat to inform the authors of the communication of this decision.

808. In accordance with paragraph (iii) of that decision, the Director-General had in a letter dated 7 January 1982 repeated his appeal for clemency to the Czechoslovak Government.

809. In a reply dated 17 April 1982, the Czechoslovak Minister of Foreign Affairs stated that his government had never hesitated to display a humanitarian attitude whenever the offender recognized his guilt and showed willingness to mend his ways but that, because of Mr Havel's attitude and reluctance to respond to the extreme leniency shown him by the competent authorities, the government found it extremely difficult to show even greater leniency by acceding to an appeal for clemency.

810. At the current session, after recalling the grounds on which Mr Havel had been sentenced (subversive activities in conjunction with foreign circles hostile to the country), the representative of the Czechoslovak Government stated that the Prague court had recently considered, within the framework of the legislation in force, re-

---

[17] See document 113 EX/38 PRIV., para. 581 (*supra*, p. 422).

leasing Mr Havel on parole, inasmuch as he had served half of his sentence, but that he had violated the prison regulations and so made it impossible to show him indulgence. The representative of the Czechoslovak Government added that the government had a duty to defend the state and the citizens, and could consequently do no more.

811. Some Committee members wondered how a person who was not a terrorist and had no weapons could give grounds for fear. They found it somewhat discouraging that a display of indulgence towards such a person should be said to present a danger to the government, and were left with the impression that the situation had somehow been reversed: a government was alleged to be in a position of weakness in respect of an individual armed with a pen in his hand.

812. One Committee member emphasized the great patience and readiness to co- operate with the Committee shown by the Czechoslovak Government. He pointed out that no matter what clemency it had shown, Mr Havel appeared to be unrepentent. In those circumstances, he wondered what else could be asked of the Czechoslovak authorities. He called for the application of paragraph 14 (*j*) of 104 EX/Decision 3.3: "The Committee shall dismiss any communication which, having been found admissible, does not, upon examination of the merits, appear to warrant further action".

813. A Committee member felt that the proper action did not appear to have been taken on paragraph (ii) of the decision adopted by the Committee at its [autumn 1981] session. In his view, the available evidence showed that Mr Havel, a dramatist of repute, had exercised the human rights guaranteed him by the international instruments, that he had been offered permission to leave the country - in other words, to forgo his right of expression - that he had refused to do so, and that he had on those grounds been imprisoned. The member considered that the communication should be kept on the agenda, and that all the information received at the current session should be sent to the authors of the communication to enable them to make their comments known.

814. A member pointed out that [Mr] Pettiti, one of the authors, was the French judge at the European Court of Human Rights. In his view, there was therefore every guarantee of the responsibility and objectivity of the communication. He said that during consideration of previous cases concerning Czechoslovakia it had been stated that no one could be punished for expressing his opinion, but that in the case in point the opposite was clearly true.

815. Replying to a member who wished to know whether it was true that the competent authorities had suggested that the alleged victim should go abroad to work, the

representative of the Czechoslovak Government said that that was so. Mr Havel had been offered that opportunity by the Minister of Culture, but had not accepted it.

816. The representative of the Czechoslovak Government added that Mr Havel had never been told that if he did not leave the country he would be imprisoned. Further, the documents submitted as evidence in the trial of Mr Havel were subversive and against the state; they included more specifically coded material. The case was by no means one of freedom of expression.

817. A Committee member said he had not lost hope: the clemency process initiated by the Czechoslovak Government deserved acknowledgement and acclaim, while the letter that the Minister of Foreign Affairs had sent to the Director-General still left room for a humanitarian approach. In his view, the correct approach was to continue to appeal to the Czechoslovak Government's humanitarian feelings.

818. After a long exchange of views, the Committee *decided*:

(i) to keep the communication on its agenda;

(ii) to make known to the authors of the communication all the information provided by the government concerned;

(iii) taking account of the steps already taken, to request the representative of the government concerned to take note of the Committee's humanitarian concern, and to await the outcome of such an approach designed to secure a friendly solution within the spirit of paragraph 14 (*k*) of 104 EX/Decision 3.3.

Autumn 1982 session of the Committee on Conventions and Recommendations (115th session of the Executive Board)[18]

462. This communication concerns a writer, Mr Václav Havel, described as a member of a committee for the support of persons unjustly prosecuted for their activities in accordance with the Helsinki Agreements, who was sentenced to five years' imprisonment.

463. It was considered by the Committee at the [spring and autumn 1980, spring and autumn 1981 and spring 1982 sessions] (it was declared admissible at the [spring] 1980 session).[19]

[18] See document 115 EX/28 PRIV., paras. 462-468; see also document 115 EX/CR/HR/1.

[19] See document 109 EX/52 PRIV., para. 97 (*supra*, p. 407).

No. 150/79 **Czechoslovakia**

464. At the Committee's request,[20] the Director-General made representations, on humanitarian grounds, to the government concerned, appealing to it for clemency (letters dated 22 June 1981 and 7 January 1982 from the Director-General to the Czechoslovak Minister of Foreign Affairs).

465. The Czechoslovak Government stated that it was difficult to respond to these appeals for the following reasons:

> Mr Havel had been sentenced on good evidence for subversive activities financed and guided from abroad. Despite warnings, the person concerned had, time and time again, engaged in acts of sabotage against his country and had not appreciated the humanitarian measures taken in his favour by the government authorities (letters from the Czechoslovak Minister of Foreign Affairs to the Director-General dated 5 September 1981 and 17 April 1982).
>
> Mr Havel had broken prison regulations; the Prague court, which had considered releasing him on parole under the legislation in force, had been unable to show such clemency.

466. At its spring 1982 session, the Committee decided, "taking account of the steps already taken, to request the representative of the government concerned to take note of the Committee's humanitarian concern, and to await the outcome of such an approach designed to secure a friendly solution within the spirit of paragraph 14 (*k*) of 104 EX/Decision 3.3".[21]

467. At the autumn 1982 session, in response to the above-mentioned decision, the representative of the Czechoslovak Government informed the Committee that the authorities in his country were attending to the matter with patience and goodwill. An appropriate response would be forthcoming.

468. After a brief exchange of views, the Committee *decided*:

> (i) to postpone consideration of the communication until its next session;
>
> (ii) to ask the representative of the government concerned to keep the Committee informed of the decision of the authorities in his country.

---

[20] See documents 112 EX/30 PRIV., para. 535 (ii) (*supra*, p. 416), and 113 EX/38 PRIV., para. 581 (iii) (*supra*, p. 422), respectively.
[21] See document 114 EX/38 PRIV., para. 818 (iii) (*supra*, p. 429).

Czechoslovakia **No. 150/79**

Spring 1983 session of the Committee on Conventions and Recommendations (116th session of the Executive Board)[22]

319. This communication has been examined by the Committee since the spring 1980 session. It concerns the case of a writer sentenced to five years' imprisonment for subversive activities.

320. At the spring 1983 session, the representative of the government concerned informed the Committee that the alleged victim had been released finally on 7 February last and that he had since enjoyed all the rights of a Czechoslovak citizen, particularly as regards the provision of free medical care.

321. One Committee member considered that, although the case was settled, the fact nevertheless remained that Mr Havel, one of the leading figures of the European literary scene, had been sentenced for having exercised his human rights and in particular his right to freedom of expression, and that he had been released solely because he was seriously ill.

322. Replying to this statement, another Committee member stressed the need rather to pay tribute to the generosity of the government concerned and the interest which it had shown in the Committee's work, despite the subversive activities allegedly committed by Mr Havel.

323. While endorsing the view that it was proper to show gratitude to the Czechoslovak authorities, one Committee member expressed the hope that Mr Havel would henceforth be able to contribute without let or hindrance to Czechoslovak and world literature.

324. The communication having been deemed to be settled, the Committee *decided* to strike it from its list in accordance with paragraph 14 (*a*) (x) of 104 EX/Decision 3.3 of the Executive Board.

[22] See document 116 EX/28 PRIV., paras. 319-324; see also document 116 EX/CR/HR/1.

No. 154/79

Concerning *Argentina, Chile and Uruguay*
Case of *Anatole Boris Julien Grisona and Eva Lucia Julien Grisona*

Communication of 6 August 1979 submitted by
Jean-Louis Weil

Autumn 1979 session of the Committee on Conventions and Recommendations (108th session of the Executive Board)[1]

114. The communication concerns the alleged abduction in Argentina, on 26 September 1976, of an Argentine child, aged 4, and a Uruguayan child, aged 6, at the same time as their parents. While the parents were still missing, the two children had been found by their grandmother in Chile, where they were in the process of being adopted by a Chilean couple. According to the author of the communication, who states that he is a person with reliable knowledge of the alleged violations of human rights, there is an established connection between the alleged. violations and Unesco's fields of competence, owing to the fact that the children in question have been separated from their natural cultural environment.

115. The Committee heard in succession the representatives of the three governments regarded by the author of the communication as being concerned.

116. The representative of the Uruguayan Government was of the opinion that there were no grounds for imputing responsibility for the alleged facts to the Uruguayan Government or its employees, that the communication constituted part of a hostile campaign against his government, and that in consequence it was not admissible, since it did not comply with the conditions stipulated in paragraphs 14 (*a*) (iii) and (v) of 104 EX/Decison 3.3.

117. Confining himself solely to the facts alleged to have taken place on Chilean territory, the Chilean representative pointed out that his government had never tried to

[1] See document 108 EX/38 PRIV., paras. 114-124; see also document 108 EX/CR/PROC.HR/1 Add.

cover up this case, which had been widely reported in the Chilean press. He considered that the communication was not very clear, and did not furnish evidence of the allegations it contained. He stated that the two children in question had been found in a park by the police who had placed them in a children's home. However, the doctor had considered that it was not in the children's interest to remain in the home, and it was for this reason that the judge responsible for the case had entrusted them to Dr Larrabeiti pending the result of the investigations undertaken to trace the parents, since to the Chilean legal authorities this appeared to be a case of children who had been abandoned. Notwithstanding the wide publicity given to the case, no one had come forward. Dr and Mrs Larrabeiti had accordingly decided to adopt both children. The adoption procedure, which normally lasts at least two years, in order to enable the natural parents to come forward and oppose it, had been halted when a woman claiming to be their grandmother asked for the custody of the children. It was under these circumstances that the judge had reopened the investigations in order to find out how the children had come to Chile. According to information just received from Chile by the Chilean representative, it appeared that the lawyers acting for Dr Larrabeiti and the grandmother had signed a joint document in which the grandmother recognized that the children had found a home, and stated that she was no longer opposed to their adoption. In the view of the Chilean representative, the communication had no longer any purpose.

118. The Argentine representative stated that his government was only very indirectly concerned by this problem. It appeared that the case involved a Uruguayan national who had crossed into Argentina and had subsequently disappeared. In his view, the communication furnished no concrete evidence, nor did it state what its purpose was. It could not be deemed admissible without further information.

119. Several members of the Committee expressed their concern at the facts alleged in this communication, some of them expressing the view that an additional reason for deeming it admissible was that Unesco was taking part in the International Year of the Child. In their view, children were potentially entitled to all the human rights coming within Unesco's fields of competence, and to certain specific rights stipulated, along with others, in the Declaration of the Rights of the Child. It was pointed out that this was the first time that the Committee had before it a communication relating to the education of minors.

120. Other members considered that a decision should not be taken on the grounds of the emotion aroused by this case, and that it would be dangerous to establish a precedent whereby the Committee would deem admissible any communication concerning children.

Argentina, Chile and Uruguay **No. 154/79**

121. For some members, the connection between the alleged facts and the Organization's fields of competence was too vague for the communication to be declared admissible. It was however pointed out that Article 13 (3) of the International Covenant on Economic, Social and Cultural Rights, and Article 18 (4) of the International Covenant on Civil and Political Rights both dealt with the right of the parents to choose a child's religious and moral education. However, the purpose of the communication was not very clear, since it was not stated whether its author was asking for the grandmother to be given responsibility for discharging the parental functions referred to in the above-mentioned provisions of the Covenants. The Director of the Division of Human Rights and Peace pointed out in this connection that it might be useful for the questionnaire to ask the authors of communications to specify their purpose.

122. Some members of the Committee considered that the children were not really in danger, since they were enjoying home life with adoptive parents. One member stressed that the real victims were not the children, but their missing parents.

123. In the view of some members, this case came exclusively within the purview of private law, in particular the law on family rights.

124. In conclusion, the Committee *decided* to keep this communication on its agenda until such time as the Secretariat obtained fuller information from the author as to its purpose, and from the Chilean Government as to the present situation in regard to the adoption procedure, and in particular as to the reported agreement on this subject between all the parties concerned.

Spring 1980 session of the Committee on Conventions and Recommendations (109th session of the Executive Board)[2]

52. The alleged victims, Anatole Boris Julien Grisona (aged 6 and of Uruguayan nationality) and Eva Lucia Julien Grisona (aged 4 and of Argentine nationality), are said to have been abducted in Argentina (San Martin - Province of Buenos Aires), at the same time as their parents, by a group of persons in uniform on 26 September 1976. The children are said to be staying at the present time with Mr and Mrs Larrabeiti Yañez in Valparaíso, under another identity, with a view to their being adopted.

53. The Committee *decided* to defer consideration of this suspended case, since the Secretariat had received additional information from the [author] of the communica-

---

[2] See document 109 EX/52 PRIV., paras. 52-53; see also document 109 EX/CR/HR/2.

tion only two days before the meeting of the Committee and had not as yet transmitted that information to the States concerned.

Autumn 1980 session of the Committee on Conventions and Recommendations (110th session of the Executive Board)[3]

21. The alleged victims, Anatole Boris Julien Grisona (aged 6 and of Uruguayan nationality) and Eva Lucia Julien Grisona (aged 4 and of Argentine nationality), are said to have been abducted in Argentina (San Martin - Province of Buenos Aires), at the same time as their parents, by a group of persons in uniform on 26 September 1976. The children are said to be staying at the present time with Mr and Mrs Larrabeiti Yañez in Valparaíso, under another identity, with a view to their being adopted.

22. At its [spring 1980] session, the Committee decided to defer consideration of this suspended case, since the Secretariat had received additional information from the [author] of the communication only two days before the meeting of the Committee, and had not as yet transmitted that information to the States concerned.[4] Since then, that information has been brought to the attention of those Governments.

23. The representative of the Chilean Government stated that, although the information contained in [a Committee document][5] was not inaccurate, certain points warranted clarification:

> the document alleging an agreement between the children's grandmother and Mr and Mrs Larrabeiti Yañez was accurate; however, it had not been prepared with a view to the formal and final adoption of the Grisona children, but in order to settle the problem of their legal custody by Mr and Mrs Larrabeiti Yañez;
>
> he had himself spoken with the judge heaing the case, who had not favoured taking the adoption procedure further until he had received fuller information on the fate of the parents; if one or both reappeared, they would obviously take preference; otherwise, the children would be free at the age of fifteen to decide whether or not to remain in Chile, and Mr and Mrs Larrabeiti Yañez couple could then adopt them permanently;
>
> meanwhile, according to the grandmother herself, the children were better off with Mr and Mrs Larrabeiti Yañez than with herself, since they were in a

[3] See document 110 EX/40 PRIV., paras. 21-26; see also document 110 EX/CR/HR/2.
[4] See document 109 EX/52 PRIV., para. 53 (*supra*, pp. 435-436).
[5] See document 110 EX/CR/HR/2.

privileged social environment; she had the right to visit them, and they, themselves had travelled to Uruguay at the beginning of the year to see some of their relatives.

24. The representative of the Chilean Government added that an inquiry was nevertheless in progress on the way in which the children had arrived in Chile, and on that point further information might subsequently emerge.

25. Two members expressed the view that, from both the legal and the human angle, the case was inadmissible. Others considered that the case should not be declared inadmissible, but should be regarded as settled.

26. The Committee *decided* accordingly that the communication was inadmissible, under paragraph 14 (*a*) (x) of 104 EX/Decision 3.3, since it had been settled in accordance with the human rights principles set forth in the Universal Declaration of Human Rights and the International Covenants on Human Rights.

No. 155/79

Concerning *Indonesia*
Case of *Irzadi Mirwan*

Communication of 31 July 1979 submitted by
Zygmunt Elbiński

Spring 1980 session of the Committee on Conventions and Recommendations (109th session of the Executive Board)[1]

107. In this communication the author, a Polish national, alleges the confiscation and banning of a book and the arrest and detainment of one of its co-authors

108. The representative of the Indonesian Government explained to the Committee that the individual in question had been arrested for criminal activities and had been tried and sentenced in accordance with Indonesian law. He was assisted by four well-known lawyers as his defence counsel, and had been subsequently freed since his detainment time was counted toward the one and a half year sentence he received. The representative of the government further indicated that the so-called "book" was actually just a mimeographed pamphlet; it played a minor role in the affair and was still in existence. His government felt it was unjust to accuse it of violating the principles of freedom of opinion and expression, and it considered the communication to be erroneous, fragmentary and inadmissible.

109. Several members of the Committee felt that since the alleged victim was now at liberty, the communication should be struck off the list. Other members felt that the main issue was actually the possibility of circulating information, but that in the light of the facts presented they too felt the communication should be struck from the Committee's list.

110. The Committee so *decided*.

---

[1] See documents 109 EX/52 PRIV., paras. 107-110, and Corr.; see also document 109 EX/CR/HR/3.

No. 169/79

Concerning *Uruguay*
Case of *Missing children*

Communication of 24 October 1979 submitted by
Syndicat National de l'Enseignement Supérieur

Spring 1980 session of the Committee on Conventions and Recommendations (109th session of the Executive Board)[1]

187. The authors of this communication, members of a French teachers' union, protested against the arbitrary arrest, disappearance and torture of Uruguayan children.

188. The Uruguayan representative stated that the communication was totally unfounded, and was simply an atttack whose purpose was to lower the esteem of his country. His government categorically denied such disappearances and felt that the communication, which provided no evidence of such disappearances, was inadmissible.

189. The Committee felt that the communication was too vague and that it did not provide anything concrete for Unesco to go by. The communication was *decided* inadmissible as manifestly ill-founded.

[1] See document 109 EX/52 PRIV., paras. 187-189; see also documents 109 EX/CR/HR/3 and Add.4.

No. 173/79

Concerning *Guyana*
Case of *Janet Jagan*

Communication of 31 August 1979 submitted by
Janet Jagan

Spring 1980 session of the Committee on Conventions and Recommendations (109th session of the Executive Board)[1]

105. The author of this communication, a Guyanese journalist and editor of the only non-governmental daily newspaper in her country, the "Mirror", claims to be the victim of the violation of Articles 18 and 19 of the Universal Declaration of Human Rights, as the newspaper has had to reduce and/or cease its normal publication owing to restrictions by the government on the importation of newsprint. She claims there is in fact a plentiful supply of newsprint in the country.

106. The Committee *decided* to defer the consideration of this case due to the absence of the representative of the Guyanese Government, and *asked* the Director-General to call to the attention of the Government concerned the importance the Committee attaches to having a representative of the government present during the Committee's examination of the communication.

Autumn 1980 session of the Committee on Conventions and Recommendations (110th session of the Executive Board)[2]

107. The author of this communication, a Guyanese journalist and editor of the only non-governmental daily newspaper in her country, the "Mirror", claims to be the victim of the violation of Articles 18 and 19 of the Universal Declaration of Human Rights, as the newspaper has had to reduce and/or cease its normal publication owing to restrictions by the government on the importation of newsprint. She claims there is in fact a plentiful supply of newsprint in the country.

---

[1] See document 109 EX/52 PRIV., paras. 105-106; see also document 109 EX/CR/HR/3.
[2] See document 110 EX/40 PRIV., paras. 107-114; see also document 110 EX/CR/HR/2.

No. 173/79 **Guyana**

108. In 1973 the printers of the newspaper took the case to the competent court alleging an infringement of the Constitution. The court ruled in favour of the claimants on 29 May 1976 but the Appeal Court subsequently, at the close of the appeal proceedings started in 1978, set that verdict aside.

109. At its [spring 1980] session, the Committee decided to suspend consideration of the communication because of the absence of the representative of the Guyanese Government. It requested the Director-Genetal to draw the attention of the government concerned to the importance attached by the Committee to the presence of a representative of the government when the communication was being considered.[3]

110. The representative of the Director-General informed the Committee that the Guyanese High Commission in London had contacted Unesco on 21 August 1980 to inform it that the High Commissioner was in Guyana for the purpose of discussing this affair with the competent government authorities, and that the information requested by the Committee could not be provided for the present session.

111. A Committee member recalled that the Committee had just decided to declare admissible [another communication], although, as in the case of the present communication, the Permanent Representative of that country was not present.[4] He added, however, that three differences should be noted between the two communications: the present communication had come before the Committee for the second time only, and not for the third time, as was the case of that concerning the Lao People's Democratic Republic; regarding the latter, furthemore, it had been decided at the [spring 1980] session that, in any event, a decision on its admissibility would be taken at the present session; lastly, the representative of the Director-General had just stated that the Guyanese Government had responded. Therefore, that member concluded that these considerations prompted him to suggest that the decision on admissibility be deferred until the next session.

112. Numerous members indicated their agreement with this suggestion. One, however; wished to make it clear that if the Committee took such a decision, it should not be inferred that, by so doing, it had established a strict rule whereby the examination of a communication would be automatically deferred if the government concerned had, on the first occasion, refrained from appearing before the Committee. There might, indeed, be cases in which urgency would call for a more rapid decision.

---

[3] See document 109 EX/52 PRIV., para. 106 (*supra*, p. 443).
[4] See document 110 EX/40 PRIV., para. 130 (*supra*, p. 373), communication No. 145/79 concerning *Lao People's Democratic Republic*, case of *Khamkhing Souvanlasy*.

Guyana **No. 173/79**

113. Two members expressed doubts on the very existence of a violation of human rights.

114. After discussion, the Committee *decided* to suspend examination of this case until its next session.

Spring 1981 session of the Committee on Conventions and Recommendations (112th session of the Executive Board)[5]

169. The author of this communication, a Guyanese journalist and editor of the only non-governmental daily newspaper in her country, the "Mirror", claims to be a victim of the violation of Articles 18 and 19 of the Universal Declaration of Human Rights, as the newspaper has had to reduce and even cease its normal publication owing to restrictions by the government on the importation of newsprint. She claims there is in fact a plentiful supply of newsprint in the country.

170. In 1973 those responsible for the newspaper took the case to the proper court, alleging an infringement of the Guyanese Constitution. The court ruled in favour of the claimants on 29 May 1976 but the Appeal Court, at the close of the appeal proceedings started in 1978, set that verdict aside.

171. A memorandum was sent to the United Nations and was dealt with in accordance with the procedure set out in [Economic and Social Council] resolutions 728 F (XXVII), 1235 (XLII) and 1503 (XLVIII).

172. The author of the communication also supplied the Secretariat with two copies of the "Mirror" containing articles exposing the situation in greater detail.

173. At its [spring 1980] session, the Committee decided to suspend consideration of the communication because of the absence of the representative of the Guyanese Government. It requested the Director-General to draw the attention of the government concerned to the importance attached by the Committee to the presence of a representative of the government when the communication was being considered.[6]

174. At the [autumn 1980] session the representative of the Director-General informed the Committee that the Guyanese High Commission in London had contacted Unesco on 21 August 1980 to inform it that the High Commissioner was in Guyana for the purpose of discussing this affair with the relevant government authori-

---

[5] See document 112 EX/30 PRIV., paras. 169-178; see also document 112 EX/CR/HR/2.
[6] See document 109 EX/52 PRIV., para. 106 (*supra*, p. 443).

ties, and that the information requested by the Committee could not be provided in time.

175. After noting the foregoing, the Committee decided to defer examination of the communication to the present session.[7] One member of the Committee, however, wished to make it clear that, if the Committee took such a decision, it should not be inferred that, by so doing, it had established a strict rule whereby the examination of a communication would be automatically deferred if the government concerned had, on the first occasion, refrained from appearing before the Committee. There might, indeed, be cases in which urgency would call for a more rapid decision.

176. Two members expressed doubts on the very existence of a violation of human rights.

177. On 18 November 1980 the Secretariat received two letters from Mrs Janet Jagan:

> One stated that the situation remained unchanged and that the "Mirror" was being forced to reduce not only its circulation but also the number of pages and the frequency of publication. This letter is accompanied by a number of documents by way of proof, including copies of newspapers belonging to, or favourable to the government, and a copy of the "Mirror" (containing very few pages in comparison with the others).
>
> The other letter drew attention to an item published by the "Guyana Chronicle" in its edition of 2 November 1980, giving an account of part of the Committee's discussion at the [autumn 1980] session, in particular the views of one member who reportedly felt that the communication should be declared inadmissible.

178. The government concerned had not indicated why it could not be represented before the Committee at the present session. However, considering that the Guyanese High Commissioner in London had contacted Unesco on two occasions, in August and October 1980, regarding this communication, and in view of the usefulness of co-operation with the government concerned, the Committee *decided*:

> (i) to postpone consideration of the admissibility of the communication to the next session;

---

[7] See document 110 EX/40 PRIV., para. 114 (*supra*, p. 445).

(ii) to ask the Executive Board to request the Director-General to urge upon the Guyanese Government the importance that the Committee attaches to the presence of a representative of the government at that session.

Autumn 1981 session of the Committee on Conventions and Recommendations (113th session of the Executive Board)[8]

257. The author of this communication, a Guyanese journalist and editor of the only non-governmental daily newspaper in her country, the "Mirror", claims to be a victim of the violation of Articles 18 and 19 of the Universal Declaration of Human Rights, as the newspaper has had to reduce and even cease its normal publication owing to restrictions by the government on the importation of newsprint. She claims there is in fact a plentiful supply of newsprint in the country.

258. In 1973 those responsible for the newspaper took the case to the proper court, alleging an infringement of the Guyanese Constitution. The court ruled in favour of the claimants on 29 May 1976 but the Appeal Court, at the close of the appeal proceedings started in 1978, set that verdict aside.

259. At its [spring 1980] session, the Committee decided to suspend consideration of the communication because of the absence of the representative of the Guyanese Government. It requested the Director-General to draw the attention of the government concerned to the importance attached by the Committee to the presence of a representative of the government when the communication was being considered.[9]

260. At the [autumn 1980] session, the representative of the Director-General informed the Committee that the Guyanese High Commission in London had contacted Unesco on 21 August 1980 to inform it that the High Commissioner was in Guyana for the purpose of discussing this affair with the relevant government authorities, and that the information requested by the Committee could not be provided in time.

261. After noting the foregoing, the Committee decided to defer examination of the communication to the next session.[10] One member of the Committee, however, wished to make it clear that, if the Committee took such a decision, it should not be inferred that, by so doing, it had established a strict rule whereby the examination of a communication would be automatically deferred if the government concerned had,

---

[8] See document 113 EX/38 PRIV., paras. 257-273; see also documents 113 EX/CR/HR/2 and Add.5.

[9] See document 109 EX/52 PRIV., para. 106 (*supra*, p. 443).

[10] See document 110 EX/40 PRIV., para. 114 (*supra*, p. 445).

on the first occasion, refrained from appearing before the Committee. There might, indeed, be cases in which urgency would call for a more rapid decision.

262. Two members expressed doubts on the very existence of a violation of human rights.

263. At the [spring 1981] session the Secretariat informed the Committee that on 18 November 1980 it had received two letters from Mrs Janet Jagan:

> One stated that the situation remained unchanged and that the "Mirror" was being forced to reduce not only its circulation but also the number of pages and the frequency of publication. The letter was accompanied by a number of documents by way of proof, including copies of newspapers belonging to or favourable to the government, and a copy of the "Mirror" (containing very few pages in comparison with the others).
>
> The other letter drew attention to an item published by the "Guyana Chronicle" in its edition of 2 November 1980, giving an account of part of the Committee's discussion at the [autumn 1980] session, in particular the views of one member who reportedly felt that the communication should be declared inadmissible.

264. The government concerned was not represented; nor had it indicated why it cculd not be represented before the Committee. However, considering that the Guyanese High Commissioner in London had contacted Unesco on two occasions, in August and October 1980, regarding this communication, and in view of the usefulness of co-operation with the government concerned, the Committee decided:[11]

> (i) to postpone consideration of the admissibility of the communication to the present session;
>
> (ii) to ask the Executive Board to request the Director-General to urge upon the Guyanese Government the importance the Committee attached to the presence of a representative of the government at that session.

265. At its present session the Committee was informed that in a letter dated 23 July 1981 and received by the Secretariat on 4 August 1981, the author of the communication reported that the Government of Guyana had changed its attitude since the [spring 1981] session of the Committee.

---

[11] See document 112 EX/30 PRIV., para. 178 (*supra*, pp. 446-447).

Guyana **No. 173/79**

266. According to this letter, the Government of Guyana has decided, since 14 July 1981, to sell to the New Guyana Company owned by Mrs Jagan two rolls of newsprint per week, thereby enabling her to continue publishing a four-page edition of the "Sunday Mirror" (four pages represent the equivalent of one sheet of ordinary newsprint). However, it is claimed that the price asked was exorbitant: G $3.25 for one pound of newsprint, corresponding to G $6,500 for approximately one ton); in view of the deliveries received in July 1979 at a price of G $0.70 per pound, there has apparently been an increase of about 365 per cent.

267. Mrs Jagan also stated that this small allocation of two rolls of newsprint every week does not enable her company to resume normal publication of the four-page daily "Mirror" and the sixteen-page weekly "Sunday Mirror".

268. This letter was accompanied by the following documents:

a copy of a letter from the New Guyana Company to Guyana National Newspapers expressing surprise at the excessively high price of the newsprint sold to the company;

a copy of a letter from the New Guyana Company to the Guyanese Government's Minister of Trade raising this problem of price and drawing attention to the difficulties thus created for the company;

a copy of the four-page "Sunday Mirror" dated 19 July 1981.

269. The Chairman of the Committee noted that the Guyanese Government was not represented and opened the discussion. One member of the Committee stated that the Committee had been understanding about the difficulties encountered by the government concerned in having itself represented, and that in his view the communication could be considered without the presence of a representative. No objection was raised to that proposal. The same member then turned to the substance of the matter and observed that, in his opinion, the violation of human rights committed by the government regarding the right to transmit information was not too serious, since one of Mrs Jagan's newspapers had resumed publication, albeit with fewer pages and a lower circulation. He further considered that the fact that the price of the newsprint had risen did not lie within the competence of the Committee.

270. Other members took the floor to note an improvement in the situation reported by Mrs Janet Jagan in her original communication, and to suggest that the government concerned should be informed of the wish of the Committee to see the publication continue in its present form and, if possible, in its original form, and receive the necessary supply of newsprint for the purpose.

271. While agreeing with the foregoing, another member wished to highlight the problem of government control of information. Two other members, who were also in agreement with the previous speakers, expressed the desire to remind the government concerned that its repeated absences were a matter of concern to the Committee.

272. One member stated that in his view the sale of newsprint at a prohibitive price could constitute an indirect means of preventing the dissemination of a specific type of information. He therefore considered that the Committee should request the government concerned and the author of the communication to inform it of the resources available to other newspapers. Two members consequently proposed that consideration of the communication be deferred.

273. In view of the various suggestions made and noting that the "Mirror", after a completely silent interval, had been able to resume publication despite a very sharp increase in the price of newsprint, the Committee *decided*:

(i) to defer consideration of the admissibility of this communication to its next session; and meanwhile,

(ii) to request the government concerned and the alleged victim to provide relevant information on the quantities and prices of newsprint available to other newspapers published in Guyana;

(iii) to inform the government concerned that the Committee welcomed the efforts made by that government to permit publication of one of Mrs Janet Jagan's newspapers and that it hoped to see the newspaper continue in its original form; further, that the fact that the government was not represented before the Committee remained a matter of concern and regret for it, in view of the importance it attached to dialogue with the governments concerned by such communications.

Spring 1982 session of the Committee on Conventions and Recommendations (114th session of the Executive Board)[12]

489. The author of this communication, a Guyanese journalist and editor of the only non-governmental daily newspaper in her country, the "Mirror", claims to be a victim of the violation of Articles 18 and 19 of the Universal Declaration of Human Rights, as the newspaper has had to reduce and even cease its normal publication

[12] See document 114 EX/38 PRIV., paras. 489-510; see also document 114 EX/CR/HR/2.

owing to restrictions by the government on the importation of newsprint. She claims there is in fact a plentiful supply of newsprint in the country.

490. In 1973 those responsible for the newspaper took the case to the proper court, alleging an infringement of the Guyanese Constitution. The court ruled in favour of the claimants on 29 May 1976 but the Appeal Court, at the close of the appeal proceedings started in 1978, set that verdict aside.

491. At its spring 1980 session, the Committee decided to suspend consideration of the communication because of the absence of the representative of the Guyanese Government. It requested the Director-General to draw the attention of the government concerned to the importance attached by the Committee to the presence of a representative of the government when the communication was being considered.[13]

492. At the autumn 1980 session, the representative of the Director-General informed the Committee that the Guyanese High Commission in London had contacted Unesco on 21 August 1980 to inform it that the High Commissioner was in Guyana for the purpose of discussing this affair with the relevant government authorities, and that the information requested by the Committee could not be provided in time.

493. After noting the foregoing, the Committee decided to defer examination of the communication to the next session.[14] One member of the Committee, however, wished to make it clear that, if the Committee took such a decision, it should not be inferred that, by so doing, it had established a strict rule whereby the examination of a communication would be automatically deferred if the government concerned had, on the first occasion, refrained from appearing before the Committee. There might, indeed, be cases in which urgency would call for a more rapid decision.

494. Two members expressed doubts as to the very existence of a violation of human rights.

495. At the spring 1981 session, the Secretariat informed the Committee that on 18 November 1980 it had received two letters from Mrs Janet Jagan:

> One stated that the situation remained unchanged and that the "Mirror" was being forced to reduce not only its circulation but also the number of pages and the frequency of publication. The letter was accompanied by a number of documents by way of proof, including copies of newspapers belonging to or

---

[13] See document 109 EX/52 PRIV., para. 106 (*supra*, p. 443).
[14] See document 110 EX/40 PRIV., para. 114 (*supra*, p. 445).

favourable to the government, and a copy of the "Mirror" (containing very few pages in comparison with the others).

The other letter drew attention to an item published by the "Guyana Chronicle" in its edition of 2 November 1980, giving an account of part of the Committee's discussion at the autumn 1980 session, in particular the views of one member who reportedly felt that the communication should be declared inadmissible.

496. The government concerned was not represented; nor had it indicated why it could not be represented before the Committee. However, considering that the Guyanese High Commissioner in London had contacted Unesco on two occasions, in August and October 1980, regarding this communication, and in view of the usefulness of co-operation with the government concerned, the Committee decided:[15]

(i) to postpone consideration of the admissibility of the communication to the next session;

(ii) to ask the Executive Board to request the Director-General to urge upon the Guyanese Government the importance the Committee attached to the presence of a representative of the government at that session.

497. At its autumn 1981 session, the Committee was informed that, in a letter dated 23 July 1981 and received by the Secretariat on 4 August 1981, the author of the communication reported that the Government of Guyana had changed its attitude since the [spring 1981] session of the Committee.

498. According to this letter, the Government of Guyana had decided, since 14 July 1981, to sell to the New Guyana Company owned by Mrs Jagan two rolls of newsprint per week, thereby enabling her to continue publishing a four-page edition of the "Sunday Mirror" (four pages represent the equivalent of one sheet of ordinary newsprint). However, it is claimed that the price asked was exorbitant: \$3.25 (Guyana) for one pound of newsprint, corresponding to \$6,500 (Guyana) for approximately one ton; in view of the deliveries received in July 1979 at a price of \$0.70 (Guyana) per pound, there has apparently been an increase of about 365 per cent.

499. Mrs Jagan also stated that this small allocation of two rolls of newsprint every week does not enable her company to resume normal publication of the four-page daily "Mirror" and the sixteen-page weekly "Sunday Mirror".

---

[15] See document 112 EX/30 PRIV., para. 178 (*supra*, pp. 446-447).

500. The letter was accompanied by the following documents:

> a copy of a letter from the New Guyana Company to Guyana National Newspapers expressing surprise at the excessively high price of the newsprint sold to the company;
>
> a copy of a letter from the New Guyana Company to the Guyanese Government's Minister of Trade raising this problem of price and drawing attention to the difficulties thus created for the company;
>
> a copy of the four-page "Sunday Mirror" dated 19 July 1981.

501. The Chairman of the Committee noted that the Guyanese Government was not represented and opened the discussion. One member of the Committee stated that the Committee had been understanding about the difficulties encountered by the government concerned in having itself represented, and that in his view the communication could be considered without the presence of a representative. No objection was raised to that proposal. The same member then turned to the substance of the matter and observed that, in his opinion, the violation of human rights committed by the government regarding the right to transmit information was not too serious, since one of Mrs Jagan's newspapers had resumed publication, albeit with fewer pages and a lower circulation. He further considered that the fact that the price of the newsprint had risen did not lie within the competence of the Committee.

502. Other members took the floor to note an improvement in the situation as reported by Mrs Janet Jagan in her original communication, and to suggest that the government concerned should be informed of the Committee's wish to see the publication continue in its present form and, if possible, in its original form, and receive the necessary supply of newsprint for the purpose.

503. While agreeing with the foregoing, another member wished to highlight the problem of government control of information. Two other members, who were also in agreement with the previous speakers, expressed the desire that the government concerned should be reminded that its repeated absences were a matter of concern to the Committee.

504. One member stated that in his view the sale of newsprint at a prohibitive price could constitute an indirect means of preventing the dissemination of a specific type of information. He therefore considered that the Committee should request the government concerned and the author of the communication to inform it of the resources available to other newspapers. Two members consequently proposed that consideration of the communication be deferred.

505. In view of the various suggestions made and noting that the "Mirror", after a completely silent interval, had been able to resume publication despite a very sharp increase in the price of newsprint, the Committee decided:[16]

(i) to defer consideration of the admissibility of this communication until the present session; and meanwhile,

(ii) to request the government concerned and the alleged victim to provide relevant information on the quantities and prices of newsprint available to other newspapers published in Guyana;

(iii) to inform the government concerned that the Committee welcomed the efforts made by that government to permit publication of one of Mrs Janet Jagan's newspapers and that it hoped to see the newspaper continue in its original form; further, that the fact that the government was not represented before the Committee remained a matter of concern and regret to it, in view of the importance it attached to dialogue with the governments concerned by such communications.

506. In response to the Committee's request, Mrs Janet Jagan sent the Secretariat a letter, dated 14 January 1982, in which she first of all thanked the Committee for the interest and attention it had shown in the matter of the "Mirror" newspaper. She then went on to explain that the situation of her newspaper had not changed: whereas it was formerly published daily with an enlarged edition on Sunday, it is now published only once a week as a four-page paper and the amount of newsprint supplied makes it impossible to return to the previous situation. The only other newspaper in Guyana is the "Guyana Chronicle" (the "Sunday Chronicle" on Sundays), which is printed and published by the state-owned Guyana National Newspapers Ltd, which supplies newsprint to the "Mirror" at a price of $6,500 (Guyana) per short ton. She mentioned that she had been denied the right to obtain supplies from any other source. Mrs Janet Jagan has learned from the firm which supplies newsprint to the Guyana National Newspapers Ltd, that the present CIF Georgetown price for rolls of newsprint is approximately $2,000 (Guyana) per short ton. She explained that the total cost, with all charges paid, of a short ton of newsprint to the Guyana National Newspapers Ltd, was approximately $2,360 (Guyana) and that consequently, by selling it to her at $6,500 (Guyana) they were making a profit of $4,140 (Guyana) or 175.4 per cent per short ton. She pointed out that a firm in Florida in the United States of America had offered her rolls of newsprint at a price equivalent to $1,500 (Guyana) per short ton FAS (from any seaport)., She added, finally, that since December 1981, her company was being offered only ends newsprint from the Guyana

[16] See document 113 EX/38 PRIV., para. 273 (*supra*, p. 450).

National Newspapers Ltd, and no longer the two rolls per week as reported in her last letter of 23 July 1981.

507. The Committee noted that, although the government had been informed of the decision taken by the Committee at its [autumn 1981] session and, more recently, in accordance with the usual practice, of the fact that this communication had been included in the agenda of the present session, it was still not represented.

508. All the members who spoke stated that they were in favour of the communication's being declared admissible, pointing out that the facts alleged constituted a violation of the freedom of expression that Unesco has always sought to safeguard, more especially where newspapers are concerned. Two members made the point that this case was typical of a situation in which many newspapers might find themselves, certain governments having used or now using the supply of newsprint as a means of exercising prior censorship. One member said he would like the Committee to have standards which could be applied in all similar cases and that, consequently, he hoped that any rules the Committee might adopt to assist the publication of Mrs Janet Jagan's newspaper would also be applied in circumstances where people holding the same opinions as Mrs Janet Jagan might be in authority.

509. All the speakers also regretted the absence of a representative of the Guyanese Government and thought that, if the government found it difficult to be represented, it could at least write to the Secretariat. They hoped that the decision to be taken by the Committee would prompt the government concerned to establish contact with it. One member suggested that, meanwhile, the said government should be asked to consider whether it could take measures to improve the situation of Mrs Janet Jagan's newspaper. Finally, one member asked whether the Director-General himself might not approach the Guyanese Government directly.

510. The Committee accordingly *decided*:

(i) to declare the communication admissible, as satisfying the conditions laid down in 104 EX/Decision 3.3;

(ii) to ask the Executive Board to request the Director-General to inform the Guyanese Government, by any means he might consider appropriate:

(*a*) of the interest taken by Unesco in the fate of Mrs Janet Jagan's newspaper, and of its wish to see an improvement in its situation;

(*b*) of the deep desire on the part of the Organization to obtain its active co-operation, in particular when the substance of the communication is examined at its next session.

Autumn 1982 session of the Committee on Conventions and Recommendations (115th session of the Executive Board)[17]

412. The author of this communication, a Guyanese journalist and editor of the only non-governmental daily newspaper in her country, the "Mirror", claims to be a victim of the violation of Articles 18 and 19 of the Universal Declaration of Human Rights, as the newspaper has had to reduce and even cease its normal publication owing to restrictions by the government on the importation of newsprint. She claims there is in fact a plentiful supply of newsprint in the country.

413. In 1973 those responsible for the newspaper took the case to the proper court, alleging an infringement of the Guyanese Constitution. The court ruled in favour of the claimants on 29 May 1976 but the Appeal Court, at the close of the appeal proceedings started in 1978, set that verdict aside.

414. This communication has been on the Committee's agenda since its spring 1980 session. The government concerned has never sent a representative to appear before the Committee, whereas the author of the communication has kept the Committee regularly informed of developments.

415. At its spring 1982 session, the Committee decided:[18]

(i) to declare the communication admissible, as satisfying the conditions laid down in 104 EX/Decision 3.3;

(ii) to ask the Executive Board to request the Director-General to inform the Guyanese Government, by any means he might consider appropriate:

(*a*) of the interest taken by Unesco in the fate of Mrs Janet Jagan's newspaper, and of its wish to see an improvement in its situation:

(*b*) of the deep desire on the part of the Organization to obtain its active co-operation, in particular when the substance of the communication is examined at its present session.

---

[17] See document 115 EX/28 PRIV., paras. 412-419; see also documents 115 EX/CR/HR/1 and Add.2.

[18] See document 114 EX/38 PRIV., para. 510 (*supra*, pp. 455-456).

Guyana **No. 173/79**

416. On 23 June 1982, the Secretariat contacted both the Guyanese High Commissioner in London and the Minister of Foreign Affairs of Guyana by registered letter with acknowledgement of receipt to inform them of the Committee's decision. Enclosed with the letter to the Minister of Foreign Affairs were copies of all letters sent to Guyana's representative in the United Kingdom since the beginning of the affair. The acknowledgement of receipt was returned from Guyana dated 23 July 1982.

417. At its autumn 1982 session, the Committee was informed in a letter from Mrs Janet Jagan dated 6 August 1982 that she had been happy to learn that her communication had been declared admissible, that the weekly supply of two rolls of newsprint had been reduced to only one roll, that in spite of discussions with the Prime Minister she was still forced to pay 6,500 Guyanese dollars per short ton of newsprint and, finally, that she was considering a further reduction in the circulation of her weekly which at present consisted of only four pages owing to the reduced supplies.

418. All members of the Committee who spoke on the matter expressed serious concern at the fate of Mrs Janet Jagan's newspaper and renewed regret at the failure of the Guyanese Government to send a representative. One of them added that the attitude of the Guyanese Government amounted to more than a mere oversight and it was clear that it had no intention of acceding to the Committee's requests. Under these circumstances and to prevent the efforts of the Committee and of Unesco itself from being frustrated by a government's refusal to co-operate, he proposed that a draft report to the Executive Board should be prepared by the Secretariat and submitted to the Committee. A member of the Committee recalled that when the Committee's report was submitted to the Executive Board, a member of the Board had offered to use his good offices to establish contact with the government concerned, and in view of the continuing absence of the Guyanese Government, he could only support the preceding proposal.

419. The Committee therefore *decided* to ask the Secretariat to draw up a draft specific report for submission to the Executive Board in pursuance of paragraph 15 of 104 EX/Decision 3.3. This draft, together with an appropriate recommendation, will be examined and adopted by the Committee at its next session after being transmitted in advance to the government concerned for its comments and observations.

No. 173/79 **Guyana**

Spring 1983 session of the Committee on Conventions and Recommendations (116th session of the Executive Board)[19]

278. The author of this communication, a Guyanese journalist and editor of the only non-governmental daily newspaper in her country, the "Mirror", claims to be a victim of the violation of Articles 18 and 19 of the Universal Declaration of Human Rights, as the newspaper has had to reduce and even cease its normal publication owing to restrictions by the government of the importation of newsprint. She claims there is in fact a plentiful supply of newsprint in the country.

279. In 1973 those responsible for the newspaper took the case to the proper court, alleging an infringement of the Guyanese Constitution. The court ruled in favour of the claimants on 29 May 1976 but the Appeal Court, at the close of the appeal proceedings started in 1978, set that verdict aside.

280. This communication has been on the Committee's agenda since its spring 1980 session. The government concerned has never sent a representative to appear before the Committee, whereas the author of the communication has kept the Committee regularly informed of developments.

281. At the spring 1982 session, the Committee decided to declare the communication admissible, as satisfying the conditions stipulated by 104 EX/Decision 3.3.[20] It noted, on the one hand, that all the members who had spoken had stated that they were in favour of the communication's being declared admissible, pointing out that the facts alleged constituted a violation of the freedom of expression that Unesco has always sought to safeguard, especially where newspapers are concerned; and on the other, that all the speakers also regretted the absence of a representative of the Guyanese Government and thought that, if the government found it difficult to be represented, it could at least write to the Secretariat.

282. By a letter dated 14 February 1983, Mrs Janet Jagan stated that the situation described in her previous letter had not changed: she was still receiving only one roll of newsprint a week at a price of 6,500 Guyanese dollars per short ton, and the newspaper was still restricted to four pages and its circulation reduced. By a letter dated 8 April 1983, Mrs Janet Jagan informed the Committee that the price of the newsprint supplied to her had been reduced to 5,200 Guyanese dollars per short ton and that she was awaiting a gift of 10 rolls of newsprint for which she had not yet received an import licence.

---

[19] See document 116 EX/48 PRIV., paras. 278-285; see also document 116 EX/CR/HR/1.

[20] See document 114 EX/38 PRIV., para. 510 (i) (*supra*, p. 455).

Guyana **No. 173/79**

283. One member of the Committee suggested that the communication be taken off the Committee's list, since its author did not request that examination be continued. Another member noted that neither did Mrs Janet Jagan express a desire to withdraw her communication, and that in addition, although the price had been reduced, 5,200 Guyanese dollars per short ton remained high compared with the cost price, which according to the letter from Mr C. Jagan dated 21 May 1982 was 2,360 Guayanese dollars per short ton.

284. Two members of the Committee thought that examination of the communication should be continued, while raising this question with the author, if only because the Committee could not find the repeated absences of the government concerned satisfactory.

285. The Committee therefore *decided*:

(i) to continue examining the substance of this communication at the next session,

(ii) to inform the author of the uncertainty caused within the Committee by her letter noting a slight improvement in her situation, and to ask her accordingly whether she wished the Committee to continue examination of her communication,

(iii) to reiterate to the government concerned that its failure to participate in the work of the Committee continued to cause the Committee great concern, for it considered that it was of first importance to secure the active co-operation of the government in question in regard to its examination and analysis of this case.

Autumn 1983 session of the Committee on Conventions and Recommendations (117th session of the Executive Board)[21]

202. The author of this communication, a Guyanese journalist and editor of the only non-governmental daily newspaper in her country, the "Mirror" claims to be a victim of the violation of Articles 18 and 19 of the Universal Declaration of Human Rights, as the newspaper has had to reduce and even cease its normal publication owing to restrictions by the government of the importation of newsprint. She claims there is in fact a plentiful supply of newsprint in the country. This communication

[21] See document 117 EX/18 PRIV., paras. 202-[207a]; see also documents 117 EX/CR/HR/1 and Add.

has been on the Committee's agenda since its spring 1980 session. The government concerned has never sent a representative to appear before the Committee, whereas the author of the communication has kept the Committee regularly informed of developments.

203. At its spring 1983 session, the Committee was informed by Mrs Janet Jagan by a letter dated 8 April 1983 that the price of the newsprint supplied to her had been reduced 6,500 to 5,200 Guyanese dollars per short ton and that she was awaiting a gift of 10 rolls of newsprint for which she had not yet received an import licence. At that session, the Committee decided, *inter alia*, to inform the author of the uncertainty caused within the Committee by her letter noting a slight improvement in her situation, and to ask her accordingly whether she wished the Committee to continue examination of her communication.[22]

204. By letter dated 2 August 1983, Mrs Janet Jagan replied to this question in the affirmative indicating that the reduction in price had only a slight advantage and that the price of $5,200 was still prohibitive. She added that her newspaper continued to be allocated only one roll of newsprint per week and that the result of this restriction and the excessive price continued to have the effect of: (1) preventing the "Mirror" from regaining publication as a daily and Sunday paper, as existed formerly; and (2) preventing the "Mirror"'s former Sunday edition of 16 pages from being resumed.

205. It was proposed that this communication which had already been declared admissible should be examined by the Committee at its current autumn 1983 session, from the standpoint of substance even if a representative of Guyana was not present before the Committee. One member of the Committee expressed some doubt about the usefulness of such an examination and suggested instead that the Executive Board might perhaps be asked to consider the possibility of holding a public debate on the communication. Other members counselled caution in this connection, pointing out that the strength of the procedure laid down by 104 EX/Decision 3.3 was the practice of a humanitarian approach and quiet diplomacy which the implementation of that decision had given rise to; they expressed the fear that a public debate might well have a boomerang effect. It was suggested that the authorities of Guyana should be given another chance to co-operate with the Committee in the examination of the communication concerned.

206. Supporting this suggestion, one member said it was all the more reasonable since Guyana had no diplomatic representation in Paris.

207. At the conclusion of its discussion, the Committee *decided*:

---

[22] See document 116 EX/48 PRIV., para. 285 (ii) (*supra*, p. 459).

(i) to request the Executive Board to invite the Director-General to contact the delegation of Guyana, in particular at the forthcoming General Conference in Paris, with a view to securing the co-operation of the government concerned;

(ii) to request the Secretariat to prepare a specific interim draft report for the Executive Board on this case;

(iii) to resume consideration of this communication at the spring 1984 session.

[207a.] Later on during the Committee's session, the Chairman informed members of the Committee that he had been able to have a discussion with the Permanent Delegate of Guyana who was based outside France but who had come that day to Paris. The Chairman stated that he had communicated the essentials of the Committee's decision to the Permanent Delegate and that the latter had indicated the willingness of his government to co-operate with the Committee.

Spring 1984 session of the Committee on Conventions and Recommendations (119th session of the Executive Board)[23]

208. The author of this communication, a Guyanese journalist and editor of what is alleged to be the only non-governmental daily newspaper in her country, the "Mirror", claims to be a victim of the violation of Articles 18 and 19 of the Universal Declaration of Human Rights, as the newspaper has had to reduce and even cease its normal publication owing to restrictions by the government of the importation of newsprint. She claims there is in fact a plentiful supply of newsprint in the country. This communication has been on the Committee's agenda since its spring 1980 session. The government concerned has never sent a representative to appear before the Committee, whereas the author of the communication has kept the Committee regularly informed of developments.

209. The communication was examined by the Committee for the first time at its spring 1980 session. The Committee declared it admissible at its spring 1982 session.[24] Not having received the co-operation of the government concerned in the examination of the communication at any of its sessions, the Committee decided, at its [autumn 1983] session, *inter alia*, to request the Secretariat to prepare a specific in-

---

[23] See document 119 EX/35 PRIV., paras. 208-216; see also documents 119 EX/CR/HR/1 and Add.
[24] See document 114 EX/38 PRIV., para. 510 (i) (*supra*, p. 455).

terim draft report on the case for the Executive Board and to resume consideration of the case at its spring 1984 session.[25]

210. At the Committee's present session, the member who also represents the Government of Guyana on the Executive Board spoke in his personal capacity on the communication since, according to him, he had not had the benefit of instructions from his government. After having expressed his regret over the fact that his country had not so far given its official views on the communication, he took a preliminary point of objection against the decision taken by the Committee at its spring 1982 session by which the communication was declared admissible. In this connection, he drew attention to the fact that under certain legal systems, the highest courts reserved the right to review or set aside any of their binding decisions if it came to light that a given decision falling into that category was given *per incuriam* or was arrived at on the basis of a substantial error of law.

211. The Legal Adviser recalled in this connection that it had been open to the government concerned to put in an appearance at the appropriate time to urge the Committee not to declare the communication admissible and that the government had not availed itself of the opportunity. He stated that no precedent existed in favour of a possible revision by the Committee of its decision on admissibility adding that, as far as he was aware, none existed also under the practice of other international organs which dealt with cases of alleged violations of human rights. He stated however that if the Committee decided not to reverse its decision on the admissibility of the communication, it would none the less be open to it to reject the communication on an appropriate ground upon completing the examination of its substance.

212. Recalling that in its examination of the communication the Committee had never benefited from the co-operation of the government concerned, several members of the Committee stated that they would not be in favour of either reopening discussion on the issue of admissibility of the communication or reversing the decision already taken by the Committee on that issue.

213. On the substance of the case, the member of the Committee who also represents the government concerned on the Executive Board remarked that the alleged victim of the alleged violation of human rights had taken her case to the highest court, that is, the Court of Appeal and that she had lost the case. He submitted that if the Court of Appeal rejected the case of the alleged victim, then it was reasonable to suppose that the court which enjoys complete independence had concluded there had been no violation of any of the civil liberties and fundamental human rights, including freedom of speech and freedom of expression, which are guaranteed by the Constitution

---

[25] See document 117 EX/18 PRIV., para. 207 (ii) (*supra*, p. 461).

of his country. The member concerned informed the Committee that in all probability, the difficulties the alleged victim was having with respect to her efforts to get additional newsprint and at lower prices arose out of general complex economic problems which his country is currently facing rather than a desire on the part of the competent authorities of his country to squeeze her out of business as a newspaper editor and publisher. He assured the other members of the Committee that freedom of information was fully respected in his country and that anybody had the right to criticize the government either by word of mouth or in print and that, as a matter of fact, a number of people did so. He further stated that newsprint was in such short supply that the national newspapers "The Daily Chronicle" and "The Sunday Chronicle" were forced to reduce not only their sizes but numbers of pages, and a few years ago the national evening paper could no longer be printed.

214. The Legal Adviser explained that in its examination of the communication, the Committee was required to apply international standards in the field of human rights and that for this reason the judgement of the Court of Appeal of the country concerned was not conclusive one way or another. A member of the Committee suggested that perhaps the government concerned might consider the possibility of giving more newsprint to the alleged victim at the expense of government newspapers since the government would no doubt have other means of disseminating its views. Another member raised the possibility of the Committee charging its Chairman with a mission to the country concerned with the view to making a direct humanitarian appeal with the competent authorities of that country. The Legal Adviser stated that there was no precedent for such a mission and that, in his opinion, any decision on a mission like that would have to be taken by the Executive Board itself. At the suggestion of one member, the Committee agreed not to take any action on the specific interim draft report it had before it until its next session.

215. The Legal Adviser before the end of the discussion gave an undertaking to the said member, who represents his Government, that the judgement of the Court of Appeal to which reference was made would be made available to the Committee at its autumn session in the appropriate languages for the purpose of assessing the validity of the complaint made.

216. At the end of its discussion, the Committee *decided*:

(i) to maintain the communication as admissible;

(ii) to suspend the examination of the substance of the communication until its autumn 1984 session;

(iii) to request the member of the Committee who represents the government concerned on the Executive Board to collect and provide to it at its next session maximum information concerning the communication.

Autumn 1984 session of the Committee on Conventions and Recommendations (120th session of the Executive Board)[26]

199. The author of this communication, a Guyanese journalist and editor of what is alleged to be the only non-governmental daily newspaper in her country, the "Mirror", claims to be a victim of the violation of Articles 18 and 19 of the Universal Declaration of Human Rights, as the newspaper has had to reduce and even cease its normal publication owing to restrictions by the government of the importation of newsprint. She claims there is in fact a plentiful supply of newsprint in the country. This communication has been on the Committee's agenda since its spring 1980 session. The communication was examined by the Committee for the first time at its spring 1980 session. The Committee declared it admissible at its spring 1982 session.[27]

200. At the Committee's spring 1984 session, the member who also represents the Government of Guyana on the Executive Board spoke in his personal capacity on the communication since, according to him, he had not had the benefit of instructions from his government. The Committee therefore requested him to collect and provide to it at its present session maximum information concerning the communication.[28]

201. In accordance with this request, the member concerned provided the Committee at its present session with written information [...].[29] In his oral submission to the Committee, he stated that the case brought on behalf of the alleged victim in the Guyanese courts had been examined with utmost thoroughness by the highest court of the land, the Court of Appeal, whose panel of three judges had unanimously come to the conclusion that there had been no infringement of the country's constitutional provisions relating to freedoms of expression and information. He emphasized also that, in rejecting the allegations of *mala fides* and discrimination made against the competent Guyanese authorities, the Court of Appeal, whose judgements are final and conclusive, had held that such import restrictions as had been imposed on the alleged victim and her newspaper were legally legitimate regulatory action in the

---

[26] See document 120 EX/15 PRIV., paras. 199-203; see also documents 120 EX/CR/HR/1 and Add. and Add.2.
[27] See document 114 EX/38 PRIV., para. 510 (i) (*supra*, p. 455).
[28] See document 119 EX/35 PRIV., para. 216 (iii) (*supra*, p. 464).
[29] See document 120 EX/CR/HR/1 Add.2.

country's economy even if indirectly and consequentially they affected freedoms of expression and information. The member of the Committee who also represented the government concerned informed the Committee that another case instituted by the alleged victim in connection with the same allegations previously examined by the Court of Appeal had just been turned down in September 1984 by the Guyanese High Court.

202. Concerning the alleged refusal of the competent authorities to issue import licences for newsprint given free of charge by certain foreign sources, the member concerned stated that government policy was not against donation *per se* of newsprint by foreign sources but rather against such donations only if they were effected on a discriminatory basis, and subject to what is stated in the third and fifth paragraphs of page 9 (English version) of [the document referred to above in para. 201] and what is stated in the last paragraph of page 13 (English version) of the said document, as being the law of Guyana to which reference was made. While finding the explanations offered as generally satisfactory, another member of the Committee expressed reservations about this policy.

203. Having examined all aspects of the communication and after hearing the very detailed explanations provided by the representative of the government concerned, especially as regards judgements rendered in the case by the competent Guyanese courts, the Committee adopted the following *decision*:

The Committee:

(i) Decides, in conformity with paragraph 14 (*j*) of 104 EX/Decision 3.3, that the communication which it had previously declared admissible, no longer appears to warrant further actions upon examination of its merits, and is accordingly dismissed.

(ii) Expresses confidence that the government concerned will continue to take all necessary measures aimed at facilitating the exercise of freedom of expression and information by all the newspapers and other publications in Guyana without discrimination.

No. 175/79

Concerning *France*
Case of *Lorella Sini*

Communication of 18 October 1979 submitted by
Serge Albert Pierre Cappe

Spring 1980 session of the Committee on Conventions and Recommendations (109th session of the Executive Board)[1]

102. The author of this communication complained that the departmental study grant of a student, the daughter of an Italian immigrant worker living in France, had not been renewed because of her Italian nationality. The alleged violation was said to be in violation of French and EEC law.

103. The representative of the French Government expressed his willingness to discuss this case in any way the Committee felt appropriate, but first wanted to mention that the case had recently been settled by the granting of a retroactive scholarship to the student in question.

104. The Committee felt that there was no need to undertake a theoretical debate on the admissibility of a settled case, and *decided* to strike this communication from its list.

---

[1] See document 109 EX/52 PRIV., paras. 102-104; see also document 109 EX/CR/HR/3.

No. 176/79

Concerning *Argentina*
Case of *Klaus Zieschank*

Communication of 21 November 1979 submitted by
Emmy Notter

Spring 1980 session of the Committee on Conventions and Recommendations (109th session of the Executive Board)[1]

54. The author of this communication, acting in her capacity as a representative of a Swiss group of Amnesty International, complains of the disappearance of Mr Zieschank, an Argentine-German dual national.

55. The representative of the Argentine Government stated that Mr Zieschank, a former student, had been working as a mechanic in Argentina; the authors had not alleged any link between the case and Unesco's fields of competence. The Argentine authorities had three agencies looking for this person but could find no trace of him.

56. The Committee felt that Unesco was not competent to examine this case as there was no link between the alleged violation and Unesco's fields of competence, and consequently *decided* that the communication was inadmissible.

---

[1] See document 109 EX/52 PRIV., paras. 54-56; see also document 109 EX/CR/HR/3.

No. 177/79

Concerning *Argentina*
Case of *Juan Ángel Nughes*

Communication of 19 November 1979 submitted by
Olga Antezana de Nughes

Spring 1980 session of the Committee on Conventions and Recommendations (109th session of the Executive Board)[1]

57. The author of this communication, currently residing in Switzerland, complains of the disappearence of her son, a student, after his alleged abduction by four heavily armed persons.

58. The representative of the Argentine Government agreed that that the case involved a student but did not believe the actions allegedly taken against him were related to his student status. He was also of the opinion that since the case had been brought before several other international bodies, it would be inadvisable for Unesco to duplicate their work.

59. Several members of the Committee pointed out that the practice of the Committee was to allow a profession in Unesco's fields of competence to serve as a presumption in favour of admissibility, and that consistency demanded the same in this case. A member of the Committee wondered if it would not be sufficient to ask the Argentine Government to search for the victim.

60. The Committee *decided* to declare the case admissible, to apply to it the special missing persons procedure,[2] and to ask the Argentine authorities to do their best to locate the victim.

---

[1] See document 109 EX/52 PRIV., paras. 57-60; see also document 109 EX/CR/HR/3.
[2] See documents 108 EX/38 PRIV., para. 16, and 109 EX/52 PRIV., annex I, para. 8, and Corr.

No. 178/79

Concerning *Argentina*
Case of *Norberto Rey Ortalda*

Communication of 29 June 1979 submitted by
Irma Luisa Ortalda de Rey

Spring 1980 session of the Committee on Conventions and Recommendations (109th session of the Executive Board)[1]

61. The author of this communication complains of the detention of her son, a doctor and research scientist, who is allegedly being held and ill-treated for holding progressive scientific ideas.

62. The representative of the Argentine Government insisted that this case was flagrantly inadmissible. The person in question was being examined by the authorities because of his armed terrorist activities, not because of his ideas, scientific or otherwise. In fact, this person had already been detained in 1975 under the previous Constitutional government. The representative of the Argentine Government stated that the author of the communication contradicted herself several times; he felt that it was obvious that this communication had nothing to do with Unesco's fields of competence and should not be admitted.

63. Some members of the Committee agreed with the representative of the government concerned that the link with Unesco's fields of competence had not been clearly established, and that the communication contained several inconsistencies.

64. Other members of the Committee felt that the alleged victim's profession should allow him the benefit of a doubt and that the inconsistencies noted in a communication should be examined after its admission. If it were found to be lacking in merit, the case should be dismissed at that subsequent stage.

65. After discussion, the Committee, though leaning toward inadmissibility, *felt* that the author should be accorded a final opportunity to show a link between the case

[1] See document 109 EX/52 PRIV., paras. 61-65; see also document 109 EX/CR/HR/3.

and Unesco's fields of competence and *decided* to suspend the case until its next session. The Committee also *decided* to instruct the Secretariat to prepare for it at its next session a study on the procedure followed hitherto by the Committee with regard to a presumption of the existence of a link with Unesco's fields of competence owing to the exercise of a particular profession by the alleged victim.

No. 179/79

Concerning *Argentina*
Case of *Betina Tarnopolsky*

Communication of 30 July 1979 submitted by
Daniel Tarnopolsky

Spring 1980 session of the Committee on Conventions and Recommendations (109th session of the Executive Board)[1]

66. In his three communications,[2] the author complains of the abduction and disappearance of his sister, father and mother, who were a student, a chemist and an educational psychologist, respectively. The father and mother were allegedly abducted at the same time by armed, hooded persons in plain clothes; the daughter was abducted some hours later by individuals who took her from her grandmother's home.

67. The representative of the Argentine Government stated that there was no reason to believe that there was a link between these cases and the field of culture. Also, since the incidents had taken place four years ago a reasonable time for presentation of the case had passed. The case was further more being investigated by no less than seven judges and was also pending before the Organization of American States. There were thus no grounds nor need to admit this case before Unesco.

68. A member of the Committee pointed out that culture was not the only field of Unesco's compentence; included also were education, science, information and communication. Here a student, a chemist and an educational psychologist were involved, persons clearly falling vithin Unesco's fields of competence. He also re-emphasized the fact that the Committee had purposely not been prevented from examining cases already before other fora, and went on to assert that persons using domestic remedies should not be penalized for doing so on the grounds that such procedures had lasted too long.

---

[1] See document 109 EX/52 PRIV., paras. 66-72; see also document 109 EX/CR/HR/3.

[2] Communications No. 172/79 concerning *Argentina*, case of *Betina Tarnopolsky*, No. 181/79 concerning *Argentina*, case of *Hugo Tarnopolsky*, and No. 182/79 concerning *Argentina*, case of *Blanca Edith Edelberg de Tarnopolsky*.

No. 179/79 **Argentina**

69. The representative of the Director-General, by way of clarification, informed the Committee that in international human rights law it was accepted that the reasonable time-limit for filing a communication be measured as from the date of the decision taken on the domestic remedy. This rule was in the interest of States as well as of the individuals since it encouraged a primary recourse to domestic remedies rather than an immediate rush to international bodies.

70. Other members of the Committee indicated that they considered the occupations of the persons to be sufficient to warrant admission of these communications.

71. After further discussion, the Committee *decided* to suspend consideration of these cases on the understanding that the representative of the Argentine Government would endeavour to obtain additional information.

72. Certain members of the Committee noted that they had agreed to the decision to suspend, rather than to declare admissible these communications with regret and reservations.

No. 180/79

Concerning *Argentina*
Case of *Fausto Augusto Carrillo Rodríguez*

Communication of 18 July 1979 submitted by
María Felicita Giménez de Carrillo

Spring 1980 session of the Committee on Conventions and Recommendations (109th session of the Executive Board)[1]

73. Acting as a representative of the alleged victim who was a lawyer, the author of the communication complains of his abduction and disappearance.

74. The representative of the Argentine Government stated that his government was unable to provide information on this case, as it involved a Paraguayan living in Paraguay.

75. A member of the Committee pointed out that there could be no link with Unesco's fields of competence in the case of this lawyer.

76. After discussion, the Committee *decided* that the communication was inadmissible, as it did not fall within the fields of competence of Unesco.

---

[1] See document 109 EX/52 PRIV., paras. 73-76; see also document 109 EX/CR/HR/3.

No. 181/79

Concerning *Argentina*
Case of *Hugo Tarnopolsky*

Communication of 30 July 1979 submitted by
Daniel Tarnopolsky

Spring 1980 session of the Committee on Conventions and Recommendations (109th session of the Executive Board)[1]

[1] See document 109 EX/52 PRIV., paras. 66-72 (*supra*, pp. 475-476), communication No. 179/79 concerning *Argentina*, case of *Betina Tarnopolsky*.

No. 182/79

Concerning *Argentina*
Case of *Blanca Edith Edelberg de Tarnopolsky*

Communication of 30 July 1979 submitted by
Daniel Tarnopolsky

Spring 1980 session of the Committee on Conventions and Recommendations (109th session of the Executive Board)[1]

[1] See document 109 EX/52 PRIV., paras. 66-72 (*supra*, pp. 475-476), communication No. 179/79 concerning *Argentina*, case of *Betina Tarnopolsky*

No. 184/79

Concerning *El Salvador*
Case of *Jaime Bairés*

Communication of 2 July 1979 submitted by
Bertrand Bellon

Spring 1980 session of the Committee on Conventions and Recommendations (109th session of the Executive Board)[1]

99. This communication concerns Mr Jaime Bairés who is alleged to have been arrested in front of the San Carlos Barracks in San Salvador on 23 February 1979.

100. The alleged victim is reported to have been subjected to torture for two days (burned with a soldering iron, etc.). The author of the communication states that at the time of the events the alleged victim was a teacher at the National University of El Salvador; that he died on 4 March 1979, and that those who assassinated him had mistaken him for his brother Federico, former President of the General Association of Salvadorian University Students.

101. The Committee *decided* to defer consideration of this case to the next session at the request of the representative of the Government of El Salvador.

Autumn 1980 session of the Committee on Conventions and Recommendations (110th session of the Executive Board)[2]

74. The author of this communication, Mr Bertrand Bellon, states that he is the Head of the Education and Research Unit of the University of Paris VIII, where the victim was a student. He alleges that on 23 February 1979, Mr Jaime Bairés was arrested in front of the San Carlos Barracks in San Salvador, and then handed over to the National Guards.

---

[1] See document 109 EX/52 PRIV., paras. 99-101; see also document 109 EX/CR/HR/3.
[2] See document 110 EX/40 PRIV., paras. 74-79; see also document 110 EX/CR/HR/2.

No. 184/79 **El Salvador**

75. The alleged. victim is reported to have been subjected to torture for two days (burned with a soldering iron, etc.). The author of the communication states that at the time of the events the alleged victim was a teacher at the National University of El Salvador; that he died on 4 March 1979, and that those who assassinated him had mistaken him for his brother Federico, former President of the General Association of Salvadorian University Students.

76. The author of the communication states that a demand was lodged on 7 March 1979 with the Public Prosecutor of El Salvador concerning the search for, and punishment of, those guilty of the assassination of Jaime Bairés. He states that at the international level, information has been sent to the International Federation of the Human Rights of Man and to Amnesty International.

77. At the request of the-representative of the Government of El Salvador the Committee decided at its [spring] 1980 session to defer consideration of this case to its present session.[3]

78. The representative of the Government of El Salvador informed the Committee at its present session that this case was one of 30 to 40 cases of violations of human rights which had been denounced before various international human rights bodies, violations which had been perpetrated by the previous regime in El Salvador. He stated that his government deplored the extremely regrettable actions of the former regime, and that he himself had been present at the ceremony organized at the Sorbonne for the presentation *in absentia* of Mr Bairés's [master] thesis.

79. In view of the fact that the victim in question was known to be dead, the Committee *decided* to strike this case from its agenda while at the same time expressing the hope that the Salvador Government would take all appropriate steps to bring the murderers to justice, to provide appropriate aid to the victim's family, and to assure that such violations of human rights were prevented from happening again.

---

[3] See document 109 EX/52 PRIV., para. 101 (*supra*, p. 483).

No. 189/80

Concerning *Poland*
Case of *Deaf-mute children in Poland*

Communication of 10 December 1979 submitted by
Zygmunt Elbiński

Autumn 1980 session of the Committee on Conventions and Recommendations (110th session of the Executive Board)[1]

115. The author of this communication, Mr Zygmunt Elbiński, describes the circumstances under which deaf-mute children at the Przemysl school are allegedly prevented from practising their religion, thereby becoming victims, together with their parents, of a violation of Articles 18 (freedom of thought) and 26 (2) and (3) (right to education) of the Universal Declaration of Human Rights.

116. The representative of the Polish Government stated that in Poland parents were at liberty to give their children whatever religious instruction they pleased and that this principle had been upheld in the present case.

117. All speakers considered that this communication was trivial, unsubstantiated, and should therefore be declared inadmissible.

118. The Committee accordingly *decided* to declare the communication inadmissible since it was mananifestly ill-founded.

---

[1] See document 110 EX/40 PRIV., paras. 115-118; see also documents 110 EX/CR/HR/3 and Add.5.

No. 190/80

Concerning *Argentina*
Case of *Sara Elba Grande*

Communication of 14 January 1980 submitted by
Silvio and Aurora Grande-Rosa y Ibarra

Spring 1980 session of the Committee on Conventions and Recommendations (109th session of the Executive Board)[1]

77. The authors of this communication claim that the security forces of the Argentine Goverment abducted their daughter on 28 July 1976 and thereby violently and arbitrarily interrupted her education at the "Lomas Zamora" Institute.

78. The representative of the Argentine Government stated that this case was almost four years old and had thus not been submittcd within a reasonable period of time. He indicated that the Committee should reject such old cases, otherwise it risked rendering meaningless the criteria provided for by 104 EX/Decision 3.3 concerning the submission of cases within a reasonble time-limit. In his view the case was clearly inadmissible.

79. One membcr of the Committee reiterated that a "reasonable" time-limit meant allowing time for resorting to domestic remedies, and in this case the authors had diligently submitted 17 applications for *habeas corpus*. Another member was of the opinion that a disappearance could be seen as a "continuing" violaion of human rights and that time-limits therefore did not apply. Severel other members of the Committee felt that the case was clearly admissible.

80. The Chairman proposed and the Committee *decided* to declare the communication admissible and to apply to it the special procedure for disappeared persons.[2] Note was taken of the Argentine representative's reservation concerning the application of a "reasonable time-limit" to the case.

---

[1] See document 109 EX/52 PRIV., paras. 77-80; see also document 109 EX/CR/HR/3 Add.
[2] See documents 108 EX/38 PRIV., para. 16, and 109 EX/52 PRIV., annex I, para. 8, and Corr.

No. 191/80

Concerning *Union of Soviet Socialist Republics*
Case of *Situation of religious activities in the USSR*

Communication of 3 December 1979 submitted by
Christian Solidarity International

Spring 1980 session of the Committee on Conventions and Recommendations (109th session of the Executive Board)[1]

149. According to this communication which was presented by "Christian Solidarity International", a non-governmental organization based in Zurich, Switzerland, the USSR is responsible for the violation of Article 1, paragraph 1, of the Constitution of Unesco; of Articles 18, 19 and 26, paragraphs 2 and 3, of the Universal Declaration of Human Rights; of Articles 18, 19 and 26 of the International Covenant on Civil and Political Rights; of the Convention against Discrimination in Education and the Final Act of the Conference on Security and Co-operation in Europe.

150. As concerns the connection between the alleged violations and the fields of competence of Unesco, the author of the communication considers that all those professing Christian religion in the Soviet Union are the victims of flagrant discrimination in all the fields of competence of Unesco.

151. In a 24-page "petition", supplemented by 28 annexes representing some 164 pages of documents, the authors gave examples of coercive measures to this end in the USSR, and distinguished nine categories as follows:

(1) an anti-religious educational system;

(2) religious discrimination against students;

(3) reprisals against relatives;

[1] See document 109 EX/52 PRIV., paras. 149-158; see also document 109 EX/CR/HR/3 Add.

(4) coercive measures against teachers;

(5) occupational isolation;

(6) suppression of the church;

(7) anti-religious campaigns;

(8) anti-religious propaganda;

(9) atheistic society as the ultimate objective.

152. The representative of tbe Soviet Government reminded the Committee that a third party submitting a communication had to have reliable knowledge of the facts and the communication had to contain relevant evidence and could not appear to be manifestly ill-founded. The Soviet representative said that this communication was faulty on both counts, and he proceeded to point out a number of examlples. He stated that whereas the authors claimed that religious groups were restricted to 20 members, Soviet law defined a religious community as consisting of "not less than" 20 members; whereas the authors claimed that there was a law against religious literature, he himself had checked and had found no anti-religious propaganda law. Furthermore, he stated, religious literature was abundantly available as evidenced by some samples he could show to the Committee, in addition, thousands of foreign language bibles had even been imported for use by various non-Russian language groups.

153. The Soviet representative added that.he had spoken to the high religious leaders of the various Russian churches, and they were dismayed by the allegations in the communication. These religious leaders addressed letters to the Director-General which the Soviet delegate read to the Committee. Therein the religious leaders affirmed that, although some ordinary daily problems existed, church/state relations in the Soviet Union were quite normal, and they stated that they felt the communication to be an act counter to their ecumenical goal.

154. In view of the evidence he had presented and given the position of the high religious leaders, the Soviet representative considered the communication to be manifestly ill-founded.

155. A member of the Committee felt that the Soviet representative's presentation was irrefutable and that the Committee should be extremely prudent with a case as complex as this one. Another member of the Committee agreed that the presentation of the Soviet representative should not be doubted and stated that the Committee

should refrain from allowing cases to be accepted on the basis of humanitarian reasons alone.

156. Several members of the Committee stated that at the admissibility stage all that is required for admission is a prima facie case, the merit of the allegations being later examined during the discussion of the substance. It was stated that the central issue appeared to be whether individuals in the USSR encountered unjust restrictions in their daily religious activities and whether they suffered from discrimination on account of their religious convictions in the exercise of rights falling within Unesco's fields of competence. It was noted that the communication mentioned specific individual cases as well as general cases, and that even the letter from one of the high church officials admitted that there were problems of a daily nature in the church.

157. Another member of the Committee stated that he felt the case to be so complex that he was obliged not to take a stand for the moment.

158. The Committee finally *decided*:

(i) to take note of the letters addressed to the Director-General;

(ii) to request the authors of the communication to place the communication within the framework of the provisions of 104 EX/Decision 3.3;

(iii) to request the Secretariat to review the communication in order to determine whether and to what extent the human rights which are invoked therein come within the fields of Uneso's competence;

(iv) to defer the examination of the admissibility of the communication until its next session.

Autumn 1980 session of the Committee on Conventions and Recommendations (110th sessions of the Executive Board)[2]

165. This communication has been presented by "Christian Solidarity International", a non-governmental organization based in Zurich, Switzerland. This organization states that it has reliable knowledge of the violations denounced, the examples of which are based for the most part on information obtained from the Institut Glaube 2. Welt, Zollikon, Switzerland, and from the sources indicated by that Institute.

[2] See document 110 EX/40 PRIV., paras. 165-182; see also document 110 EX/CR/HR/2.

No. 191/80 **Union of Soviet Socialist Republics**

166. According to this communication, the USSR is responsible for the violation of Article 1, paragraph 1, of the Constitution of Unesco; of Articles 18, 19 and 26, paragraphs 2 and 3, of the Universal Declaration of Human Rights; of Articles 18, 19 and 26 of the International Covenant on Civil and Political Rights; of the Convention against Discrimination in Education and the Final Act of the Conference on Security and Co-operation in Europe.

167. As concerns the connection between the alleged violations and the fields of competence of Unesco, the author of the communication considers that all those professing Christian religion in the Soviet Union are the victims of a flagrant discrimination in all the fields of competence of Unesco.

168. In a 24-page "petition" the author gives examples of coercive measures to this end in the USSR, and distinguishes nine categories as follows:

(1) an anti-religious educational system;

(2) religious discrimination against students;

(3) reprisals against relatives;

(4) coercive measures against teachers;

(5) occupational isolation;

(6) suppression of the church;

(7) anti-religious campaigns;

(8) anti-religious propaganda;

(9) atheistic society as the ultimate objective.

169. The authors have attached 28 annexes to the "petition" representing some 164 pages of documents. Most of these annexes provide details on particular cases of alleged violations of human rights.

170. The representative of the Soviet Governmernt reminded the Committee at its [spring 1980] session that a third party submitting a communication had to have reliable knowledge of the facts and the communication had to contain relevant evidence and could not appear to be manitestly ill-founded. The Soviet representative said that this communication was faulty on both counts, and he proceeded to point out a

number of examples. He stated stated that whereas the authors claimed that religious groups were restricted to 20 members, Soviet law defined a religious [community] as consisting of "not less than" 20 members; whereas the authors claimed that there was a law against religious literature, he himself had checked and had found no anti-religious propaganda law. Furthermore, he stated, religious literature was abundantly available as evidenced by some samples he could show to the Committee; in addition, thousands of foreign language bibles had even been imported for use by various non-Russian lingual groups.

171. The Soviet representative added that he had spoken to the high religious leaders of the various Russian churches, and they were dismayed by the allegations in the communication. These religious leaders addressed letters to the Director-General which the Soviet delegate read to the Committee. Therein the religious leaders affirmed that, although some ordinary daily problems existed within the church, church/state relations in the Soviet Union were quite normal, and they stated that they felt the communication to be an act counter to their ecumenical goal.

172. In view of the evidence he had presented and given the position of the high church officials, the Soviet representative considerad the communication to be manifestly ill-founded.

173. A member of the Committee felt that the Soviet representative's presentation was irrefutable und that the Committee should be extremely prudent with a case as complex as this one. Another member of the Committee agreed that the presentation of the Soviet representative should not be doubted and stated that the Committee should refrain from allowing cases to be accepted on the basis of humanitarian reasons alone.

174. Several members of the Committee stated that at the admissibility stage all that is required for admission is a prima facie case, the merit of the allegations being later examined during the discussion of the substance. It was stated that the central issue appeared to be whether individuals in the USSR encountered unjust restrictions in their daily religious activities; it was noted that the communication mentioned specific individual cases as well as general cases, and that even the letter from one of the high church officials admitted that there were problems of a daily nature in the church.

175. Another member of the Committee stated that he felt the case to be so complex that he was obliged not to take a stand for the moment.

No. 191/80 **Union of Soviet Socialist Republics**

176. The Committee finally decided:[3]

(i) to take note of the letters addressed to the Director-General;

(ii) to request the authors of the communication to place the communication within the framework of the provisions of 104 EX/Decision 3.3;

(iii) to request the Secretariat to review the communication in order to determine [whether and] to what extent the human rights which are invoked therein come within the fields of Uneso's competence;

(iv) to defer the examination of the admissibility of the communication until the next [session].

177. The representative of the Director-General informed the Committee at its present session that the Secretariat had so far received no word from the authors of the communication, and he reminded the Committee that the study requested by it in paragraph (iii) of its decision had been postponed until the decicion of the Executive Board is taken at the present session.

178. The representative of the Government of the Soviet Union outlined once again his government's position on this matter, as he had done for the Committee at its [spring 1980] session.

179. Certain members of the Committee expressed the view that the communication should be stricken from the agenda since the authors had not responded to the Committee.

180. Other Committee members felt that it would be unfair and unreasonable to strike the communication on such grounds in view of the exceptionally short time period which had passed since the Committee's [spring 1980] session, and in view of the burdensome task which the Committee had imposed on the authors of the communication.

181. In response to a question about the Committee's procedural practice, the representative of the Director-General informed the Committee that its policy on allowing time for responses had so far been very liberal, for both governments and authors. The Committee had consistently allowed at least a "double silence", i.e. no response for two sessions before striking a communication, and there were at least two prece-

---

[3] See document 109 EX/52 PRIV., para. 158 (*supra*, p. 491).

dents where the Committee had warned the author in question before striking his communication.

182. With a view toward remaining consistent with its procedures, the Committee *decided* to suspend the consideration of the admissibility of this communication until its next session.

Spring 1981 session of the Committee on Conventions and Recommendations (112th session of the Executive Board)[4]

222. This communication has been presented by "Christian Solidarity International", a non-governmental organization based in Zurich, Switzerland. This organization states that it has reliable knowledge of the violations denounced, the examples of which are based for the most part on information obtained from the Institut Glaube 2. Welt, Zollikon, Switzerland, and from the sources indicated by that Institute.

223. According to this communication, the USSR is responsible for the violation of Article 1, paragraph 1, of the Constitution of Unesco; of Articles 18, 19 and 26, paragraphs 2 and 3, of the Universal Declaration of Human Rights; of Articles 18, 19 and 26 of the International Covenant on Civil and Political Rights; of the Convention against Discrimination in Education and the Final Act of the Conference on Security and Co-operation in Europe.

224. As concerns the connection between the alleged violations and the fields of competence of Unesco, the author of the communication considers that all those professing the Christian religion in the Soviet Union are the victims of flagrant discrimination in all the fields of competence of Unesco.

225. In a 24-page "petition" the author gives examples of coercive measures to this end in the USSR, and distinguishes nine categories as follows:

(1) an anti-religious educational system;

(2) religious discrimination against students;

(3) reprisals against relatives;

(4) coercive measures against teachers;

---

[4] See document 112 EX/30 PRIV., paras. 222-247; see also document 112 EX/CR/HR/2.

(5) occupational isolation;

(6) suppression of the church;

(7) anti-religious campaigns;

(8) anti-religious propaganda;

(9) atheistic society as the ultimate objective.

226. The authors have attached 28 annexes to the "petition" representing some 164 pages of documents. Most of these annexes provide details on particular cases of alleged violations of human rights.

227. The representative of the Soviet Government reminded the Committee at the [spring 1980] session that a third party submitting a communication had to have reliable knowledge of the facts and the communication had to contain relevant evidence and could not appear to be manifestly ill-founded. The Soviet representative said that this communication was faulty on both counts, and he proceeded to point out a number of examples. He stated that whereas the authors claimed that religious groups were restricted to 20 members, Soviet law defined a religious community as consisting of "not less than" 20 members; whereas the authors claimed that there was a law against religious literature, he himself had checked and had found no anti-religious propaganda law. Furthermore, he stated, religious literature was abundantly available as evidenced by some samples he could show to the Committee; in addition, thousands of foreign language bibles had even been imported for use by various groups speaking languages other than Russian.

228. The Soviet representative added that he had spoken to the high religious leaders of the various Russian churches, and they were dismayed by the allegations in the communication. These religious leaders had addressed letters to the Director-General which the Soviet delegate read to the Committee. In them, the religious leaders affirmed that, although some everyday problems existed within the church, church/state relations in the Soviet Union were quite normal, and they stated that they felt the communication ran counter to their ecumenical goal.

229. In view of the evidence he had presented, and given the position of the high church officials, the Soviet representative considered the communication to be manifestly ill-founded.

230. One member of the [...] Committee felt that the Soviet representative's presentation was perfectly acceptable and that the Committee should be extremely prudent

with a case as complex as this one. Another member of the Committee agreed that the presentation of the Soviet representative should not be challenged and stated that the Committee should refrain from allowing cases to be accepted on the basis of humanitarian reasons alone.

231. Several members of the Committee stated that at the admissibility stage all that is required for admission is a prima facie case, the merit of the allegations being examined later during the discussion of the substance. It was stated that the central issue appeared to be whether or not individuals in the USSR encountered unjust restrictions in their religious activities and whether or not they were discriminated against in the exercise of rights related to Unesco's fields of competence on account of their religious convictions. It was noted that the communication mentioned specific individual cases as well as general cases, and that even the letter from one of the high church officials admitted that there were day-to-day problems in the church.

232. Another member of the Committee stated that he felt the case to be so complex that he was obliged not to take a stand for the moment.

233. The Committee finally decided:[5]

(i) to take note of the letters addressed to the Director-General;

(ii) to request the authors of the communication to place the communication within the framework of the provisions of 104 EX/Decision 3.3;

(iii) to request the Secretariat to review the communication in order to determine [whether and] to what extent the human rights which are invoked therein come within the fields of Unesco's competence;

(iv) to defer examination of the admissibility of the communication until the next [session].

234. The authors of the communication and the government concerned were duly informed by the Secretariat.

235. The representative of the Director-General informed the Committee at the [autumn 1980] session that the Secretariat had so far received no word from the authors of the communication, and he reminded the Committee that the study requested by it in paragraph (iii) of its decision had been postponed pending a decision by the Executive Board.

---

[5] See document 109 EX/52 PRIV., para. 158 (*supra*, p. 491).

No. 191/80 **Union of Soviet Socialist Republics**

236. Certain members of the Committee expressed the view that the communication should be removed from the agenda since the authors had not replied to the Committee.

237. Other Committee members felt that it would be unfair and unreasonable to strike the communication out on such grounds in view of the exceptionally short period of time which had passed since the Committee's [spring 1980] session, and in view of the burdensome task which the Committee had imposed on the authors of the communication.

238. In response to a question about the Committee's procedural practice, the representative of the Director-General informed the Committee that its policy on allowing time for replies had so far been very liberal, for both governments and authors. The Committee had consistently allowed at least a "double silence", i.e. no reply for two sessions, before striking out a communication, and there were at least two precedents where the Committee had warned the author in question before striking his communication out.

239. With a view to remaining consistent with its procedures, the Committee decided to suspend consideration of the admissibility of this communication until the present session.[6]

240. Replying to the letters from the Secretariat dated 22 July and 29 September 1980, informing him of the decision taken by the Committee at its [spring and autumn 1980] sessions, the author of the communication considers in his letter dated 24 November 1980 that the communication meets all the conditions laid down in 104 EX/Decision 3.3. In his opinion, there is therefore no need to alter the presentation of the communication. In order to clarify the situation, the Secretariat sent him a letter dated 12 January 1981 elucidating one point and asking him to confirm his agreement.

241. At the present session, the representative of the Soviet Government had recalled the arguments he had presented at the [autumn 1980] session concerning the dissemination of the bible and religious literature and the erroneous interpretation of Soviet laws concerning religious groups; he added that the question of the atheization of society was not a problem that concerned Unesco and that the Holy Synod of the Russian Orthodox Church and the Union of Christian Evangelists of the USSR, in their letters to the Director-General, had themselves been at pains to affirm that religious freedom was respected in the USSR and to so inform the Committee on Conventions and Recommendations; and, finally, that although his government was

[6] See document 110 EX/40 PRIV., para. 182 (*supra*, p. 495).

ready to co-operate in the examination of the communication, it was not clear to him how this could be of any use to the Committee since the highest church authorities were satisfied with the existing situation and the authors of the communication themselves showed no evidence of a desire to co-operate, having failed on two occasions to reply to letters from the Secretariat. Accordingly, he felt it preferable to adjourn consideration of the communication.

242. One member expressed the view that the communication contained a series of allegations that constituted a "question" and that though religious activities in the USSR in themselves perhaps did not fall within Unesco's sphere of competence, one thing that certainly did was the use of schools for the purpose of anti-religious indoctrination.

243. In response to questions on that matter, the representative of the Director-General made the following three points:

> that in the letter of acknowledgement which was approved by the Committee and sent by the Secretariat to the authors of the communication, the right to freedom of religion was not mentioned either as a right which fell *per se* within Unesco's sphere of competence or as a right implicit in the exercise of a right protected by Unesco;
>
> that, from another standpoint, although freedom of religion could be regarded as an element of culture, it was not sure that this interpretation was approved by religious organizations;
>
> that, finally, as he pointed out to members of the Committee, the right of parents to ensure the religious and moral education of their children in conformity with their own conviction was provided for in Article 26 (3) of the Universal Declaration of Human Rights, in Article 18 (4) of the International Covenant on Civil and Political Rights and Article 13 (3) of the International Covenant on Economic, Social and Cultural Rights.

244. The representative of the Soviet Government took the floor again and noted that the authors of the communication had first said nothing, had then replied in an unsatisfactory manner to the Committee's request and, finally, had failed to answer it altogether; that they had thereby shown their reluctance to co-operate; that he did not understand why the Committee continued to consider the question when the Soviet religious leadership, which was directly concerned, had asked the Committee not to interfere; and that, lastly, he did not see where this discussion would lead if it were pursued at the level of the Committee or of another Unesco body since, given

the variations existing within the same religious system, enormous contradictions were sure to emerge and would remain unresolved.

245. One member of the Committee said that, in his view, Unesco should only see to it that the principle of religious freedom was respected and should go no further than that; he was supported by another member who came from a secular State and, for that reason, preferred to take no part in a religious discussion. Another member emphasized that the point at issue was alleged violations of human rights guaranteed by the Universal Declaration of Human.Rights and by the two [International] Covenants on Human Rights which had been ratified by the State concerned, allegations that had been presented within the framework of procedures laid down by the Executive Board of Unesco, of which the State concerned was a member, in a communication that was well presented both as to form and content and that, under the circumstances, he saw no reason why the Committee should stop half-way.

246. In his reply to one member who stressed that the problem raised by the communication was not a problem of religion but a problem of religious freedom, the representative of the Soviet Government said that religious freedom was a fundamental principle of the Soviet Constitution. Some members suggested that the author of the communication should be asked to reply to the Secretariat's letter of 12 January 1981 and to clarify his intentions and, should he fail to do so, that the rule of "double silence" be applied and the communication struck out at the next session. Another member reminded the Committee that there was nothing to prevent the author from presenting other communications concerning the cases of persons whose religious freedom had been restricted.

247. The Committee therefore *decided*:

(i) that in so far as the communication raised a "question" about massive violations of religious freedom, it did not fall within spheres of Unesco's competence;

(ii) that with regard to the individual cases cited in the communication, it instructed the Secretariat to remind the author of its letter of 12 January 1981 and to make it clear to him that he was entitled to submit new communications in conformity with 104 EX/Decision 3.3.

No. 193/80

Concerning *Guatemala*
Case of *Teachers and students in Guatemala*

Communication of 2 April 1980 submitted by
Romesh Chandra

Autumn 1980 session of the Committee on Conventions and Recommendations (110th session of the Executive Board)[1]

101. The author of the communication, Mr Romesh Chandra, President of the World Peace Council, claims that attacks have been made on the liberty, security of person and lives of factory and farmer trade union leaders, university students and teachers; in 1970, a teacher and two lawyers were allegedly murdered, and since 1977 many students, lawyers and teachers are claimed to have been kidnapped, injured or killed. On 21 December 1979, a detachment of the Guatemalan Army, the ESA, is said to have totally destroyed, using incendiary bombs, all the facilities of the university campus of Quezaltenango, injuring and killing many people in the course of that operation.

[101a.] On 16 February 1980, the same events apparently recurred at the University of Chiquimula. The life of the Rector of the San Carlos National University of Guatemala, Lic. Saúl Osorio Paz, is allegedly threatened, as is that of several other members of the University, including Mr Leonel Carrillo Reeves, Dean of the Faculty of Chemistry and Mr Romeo Alvarado Polanco, Dean of the Faculty of Law.

102. The representative of the Guatemalan Government explained that the communication did not comply with the conditions of admissibility set forth in 104 EX/Decision 3.3. The flagrant contradictions contained in the communication concerning the dates of the alleged events, and concerning the events themselves, showed that the author did not have reliable knowledge; since they were acts of terrorism, the alleged facts did not fall within Unesco's fields of competence; no relevant proof had been supplied by the author; in suggesting that a fascist organization existed within

[1] See document 110 EX/40 PRIV., paras. 101-106; see also documents 110 EX/CR/HR/3 and Add.4.

the Guatemalan Army, the communication was offensive; there was nothing to indicate that domestic remedies had been sought; the acts of terrorism to which the communication referred had been committed by illegal organizations, and therefore could not be imputed to the government; for all these reasons, the communication should be declared inadmissible.

103. One Conmittee member shared the view of the representative of the Guatemalan Government, but, like most other members who spoke after him, he suggested that humanitarian action should be contemplated; another member took the view that whereas some components of the communication - in particular its reference to the names of trade unionists and workers - did not fall within Unesco's field of competence, the same was not true of the major part of it, which concerned the destruction of unviersities and the murder of teachers and students; at the admissibility stage, it was sufficient that the communication should appear prima facie well-founded; it was the duty of governments to ensure that human rights were respected by all citizens, and therefore to oppose their violation; accordingly the communication was admissible. Several members of the Committee expressed their agreement with that conclusion; some members expressed the desire to be better informed.

104. The representative of the Guatemalan Government said that his government was prepared to grant its full co-operation, and that it was able to provide the Committee with immediate information on Mr Paz, Mr Reeves and Mr Alvarado: the first had requested the Higher Council of the University to grant him leave of absence for an indefinite period and was at present abroad, at liberty to return to his country; the second had concluded his term of office as Acting Rector and was working in his faculty; the third was at present Rector of the University. The Guatemalan Government acknowledged and fulfilled its international obligations concerning human rights, and it was a certainty that those responsible for the regrettable events in question would be prosecuted. Finally, a mission of the Inter-American Commission on Human Rights had been invited by the Government to to visit Guatemala, and was currently preparing a report on the situation of human rights in that country.

105. The Chairman of the Committee observed that during the discussion most of the members had declared themselves in favour of humanitarian intervention, and said that he personally was prepared, as a Guatemalan citizen, to examine the case with his Government; it was also his impression that the conflict between the Committee members in favour of admissibility and those opposed to it might be resolved by a request for further information addessed to the [author] of the communication. Those members who spoke subsequently were in favour of that suggestion.

106. Accordingly, the Committee *decided*:

[i] to request the Executive Board to ask the Director-General to take steps of a humanitarian nature with regard to the individuals mentioned in the communication, whose lives or personal security were threatened, and who seemed by virtue of their activities to fall within Unesco's fields of competence;

[ii] to request its Chairman to act on the same lines in a personal capacity, jointly with the Director-General, and to provide it at its next session with all relevant information that he considered of use in relation to the allegations contained in the communication;

[iii] to inform the author of the communication of the humanitarian measures thereby taken;

[iv] to suspend examination of the admissibility of this communication;

[v] to request the author of the communication to provide, for his part, all relevant information supplementing the allegations put forward concerning the violation of human rights and, to that end, to reformulate the communication so that it might clearly fit in with the procedural stipulations of 104 EX/Decision 3.3;

[vi] to request the Executive Board to ask the Director-General to ask the Inter-American Commission on Human Rights to send him its report on the mission that it was to carry out in Guatemala.

Spring 1981 session of the Committee on Conventions and Recommendations (112th session of the Executive Board)[2]

139. The author of the communication, Mr Romesh Chandra, President of the World Peace Council, claims to be a person with reliable knowledge of the violations described below.

140. According to this communication, attacks have been made on the liberty, lives and security of person of factory and farm workers, trade union leaders and university students and teachers. In 1970, a teacher and two lawyers were allegedly murdered, and since 1977 many students, lawyers and teachers are claimed to have been kidnapped, injured or killed. On 21 December 1979, a detachment of the Guatemalan Army, the ESA, is said to have totally destroyed, using incendiary bombs, all the

[2] See document 112 EX/30 PRIV., paras. 139-154; see also document 112 EX/CR/HR/2.

facilities of the university campus of Quezaltenango, injuring and killing many people in the course of that operation.

141. On 16 February 1980, the same events apparently recurred at the University of Chiquimula. The life of the Rector of the San Carlos National University of Guatemala, Lic. Saúl Osorio Paz, is allegedly threatened, as are the lives of several other members of the University, including Mr Leonel Carrillo Reeves, Dean of the Faculty of Chemistry and Mr Romeo Alvarado Polanco, Dean of the Faculty of Law.

142. At the [autumn 1980] session the representative of the Guatemalan Government explained that the communication did not comply with the conditions of admissibility set forth in 104 EX/Decision 3.3. The flagrant contradictions contained in the communication concerning the dates of the alleged events, and concerning the events themselves, showed that the author did not have reliable knowledge. Since they were acts of terrorism, the alleged facts did not fall within Unesco's fields of competence; no relevant proof had been supplied by the author; in suggesting that a fascist organization existed within the Guatemalan army, the communication was offensive; there was nothing to indicate that domestic remedies had been sought; the acts of terrorism to which the communication referred had been committed by illegal organizations, and therefore could not be imputed to the government, and for all these reasons, the communication should be declared inadmissible.

143. One Committee member shared the view of the representative of the Guatemalan Government, but, like most other members who spoke after him, he suggested that humanitarian action should be contemplated. Another member took the view that whereas some components of the communication - in particular its reference to the names of trade unionists and workers - did not fall within Unesco's field of competence, the same was not true of the major part of it, which concerned the destruction of universities and the murder of teachers and students. At the admissibility stage, it was sufficient that the communication should appear prima facie well founded. It was the duty of governments to ensure that human rights were respected by all citizens, and therefore to oppose their violation. Accordingly, the communication was admissible. Several members of the Committee expressed their agreement with that conclusion, but some members expressed the desire to be better informed.

144. The representative of the Guatemalan Government said that his government was prepared to grant its full co-operation.

145. The Chairman of the Committee observed that during the discussion most of the members had declared themselves in favour of humanitarian intervention, and said that he personally was prepared, as a Guatemalan citizen, to examine the case with his government. It was also his impression that the conflict between the Com-

mittee members in favour of admissibility and those opposed to it might be resolved by a request for further information addressed to the [author] of the communication. Those members who spoke subsequently were in favour of that suggestion.

146. The Committee accordingly decided at its [autumn 1980] session:[3]

> [i] to request the Executive Board to ask the Director-General to take steps of a humanitarian nature with regard to the individuals mentioned in the communication, whose lives or personal security were threatened, and who seemed by virtue of their activities to fall within Unesco's fields of competence;
>
> [ii] to request its Chairman to act on the same lines in a personal capacity, jointly with the Director-General, and to provide it at its next session with all relevant information that he considered of use in relation to the allegations contained in the communication;
>
> [iii] to inform the author of the communication of the humanitarian measures thereby taken;
>
> [iv] to suspend examination of the admissibility of this communication;
>
> [v] to request the author of the communication to provide, for his part, all relevant information supplementing the allegations put forward concerning the violation of human rights and, to that end, to reformulate the communication so that it might clearly fit in with the procedural stipulations of 104 EX/Decision 3.3;
>
> [vi] to request the Executive Board to ask the Director-General to ask the Inter-American Commission on Human Rights to send him its report on the mission that it was to carry out in Guatemala.

147. On 19 August 1980, the Minister of Foreign Affairs sent a telegram to the Deputy Director-General concerning the above-mentioned communication. The text of the telegram is contained in [a Committee document].[4]

148. The Committee's decisions were duly carried out by the Secretariat.

---

[3] See document 110 EX/40 PRIV., para. 106 (*supra*, pp. 502-503).
[4] See document 112 EX/CR/HR/2.

No. 193/80 **Guatemala**

149. On 28 January 1981, the Minister of Foreign Affairs of Guatemala sent to the Director-General of Unesco his government's reply concerning this communication. The text of the letter [...][5] contained the information which had earlier been conveyed orally by the Guatemalan Minister of Foreign Affairs to the Committee's Chairman, and which the latter conveyed to the Committee at its present session.

150. The Chairman explained to the Committee that, in pursuance of that part of the Committee's decision which had been addressed to him, he had conferred with the Director-General and had transmitted a letter from him to his authorities. In January 1981 he had conferred with the Minister of Foreign Affairs of his country and had been informed that Mr Osorio Paz had resigned his post and had left the country using his own passport. He had left of his own free will and was entitled to return to Guatemala whenever he wished. The Chairman went on to say that the Guatemalan authorities informed him that Mr Alvarado Polanco was at present the Dean of the Faculty of Law and Social Science at San Carlos University and was working, and that Mr Polanco had the complete freedom to leave the country if he so wished. The Chairman said he had also spoken with Mr Carrillo Reeves personally, and he had been informed by him that he was having no problem carrying out his functions as Rector of the University of San Carlos.

151. The representative of the Guatemalan Government reminded the Committee that his government had at its [autumn 1980] session presented clear refutations of the allegation in the communication. Furthermore, he said, the communication's author had not complied with the Committee's request to supply further information and to reformulate the communication within the framework required by 104 EX/ Decision 3.3. The Guatemalan representative stated that for these reasons the communication should be dismissed by the Committee.

152. A Committee member expressed the view that there were other aspects of this communication, such as armed military attacks on universities and assassinations of teachers and students, which merited consideration by the Committee.

153. The representative of the Guatemalan Government reminded the Committee that these allegations had been thoroughly discussed and refuted at the Committee's [autumn 1980] session. He again explained that these crimes had been committed by extreme right and left wing clandestine terrorist groups, and that they could not in any way be attributed to the Guatemalan Government.

154. After a brief discussion the Committee *decided*:

---

[5] *Ibidem*.

(i) to take note with satisfaction of the result of the humanitarian representations made on behalf of the three academics;

(ii) to suspend consideration of the admissibility of this communication, reminding its author of the request made to him by the Committee to provide all relevant information supplementing the allegations put forward concerning the violation of human rights and, to that end, to reformulate the communication so that it might clearly fit in with the procedural stipulations of 104 EX/Decision 3.3, and informing him that, if he failed to reply, his communication would be struck off the list of communications.

Autumn 1981 session of the Committee on Conventions and Recommendations (113th session of the Executive Board)[6]

225. The author of the communication, Mr Romesh Chandra, President of the World Peace Council, claims to be a person with reliable knowledge of the violations described below.

226. According to this communication, attacks have been made on the liberty, lives and security of person of factory and farm workers, trade-union leaders and university students and teachers. In 1970, a teacher and two lawyers were allegedly murdered, and since 1977 many students, lawyers and teachers are claimed to have been kidnapped, injured or killed. On 21 December 1979, a detachment of the Guatemalan Army, the ESA, is said to have totally destroyed, using incendiary bombs, all the facilities of the university campus of Quezaltenango, injuring and killing many people in the course of that operation.

227. On 16 February 1980, the same events apparently recurred at the University of Chiquimula. The life of the Rector of the San Carlos National University of Guatemala, Lic. Saúl Osorio Paz, is allegedly threatened, as are the lives of several other members of the University, including Mr Leonel Carrillo Reeves, Dean of the Faculty of Chemistry and Mr Romeo Alvarado Polanco, Dean of the Faculty of Law.

228. At the [autumn 1980] session, the representative of the Guatemalan Government explained that the communication did not comply with the conditions of admissibility set forth in 104 EX/Decision 3.3. The flagrant contradictions contained in the communication concerning the dates of the alleged events, and concerning the events themselves, showed that the author did not have reliable knowledge. Since they were acts of terrorism, the alleged facts did not fall within Unesco's fields of

[6] See document 113 EX/38 PRIV., paras. 225-244; see also document 113 EX/CR/HR/2.

competence; no relevant proof had been supplied by the author; in suggesting that a fascist organization existed within the Guatemalan Army, the communication was offensive; there was nothing to indicate that domestic remedies had been sought; the acts of terrorism to which the communication referred had been committed by illegal organizations, and therefore could not be imputed to the government, and for all these reasons, the communication should be declared inadmissible.

229. One Committee member shared the view of the representative of the Guatemalan Government, but, like most other members who spoke after him, he suggested that humanitarian action should be contemplated. Another member took the view that whereas some components of the communication - in particular its reference to the names of trade unionists and workers - did not fall within Unesco's field of competence, the same was not true of the major part of it, which concerned the destruction of universities and the murder of teachers and students. At the admissibility stage, it was sufficient that the communication should appear prima facie well founded. It was the duty of governments to ensure that human rights were respected by all citizens, and therefore to oppose their violation. Accordingly, the communication was admissible. Several members of the Committee expressed their agreement with that conclusion, but some expressed the desire to be better informed.

230. The representative of the Guatemalan Government said that his government was prepared to grant its full co-operation.

231. The Chairman of the Committee observed that during the discussion most of the members had declared themselves in favour of humanitarian intervention, and said that he personally was prepared, as a Guatemalan citizen, to examine the case with his government. It was also his impression that the conflict between the Committee members in favour of admissibility and those opposed to it might be resolved by a request for further information addressed to the [author] of the communication. Those members who spoke subsequently were in favour of that suggestion.

232. The Committee accordingly decided at its [autumn 1980] session:[7]

> [i] to request the Executive Board to ask the Director-General to take steps of a humanitarian nature with regard to the individuals mentioned in the communication, whose lives or personal security were threatened, and who seemed by virtue of their activities to fall within Unesco's fields of competence;

---

[7] See document 110 EX/40 PRIV., para. 106 (*supra*, pp. 502-503).

[ii] to request its Chairman to act on the same lines in a personal capacity, jointly with the Director-General, and to provide it at its next session with all relevant information that he considered of use in relation to the allegations contained in the communication;

[iii] to inform the author of the communication of the humanitarian measures thereby taken;

[iv] to suspend examination of the admissibility of this communication;

[v] to request the author of the communication to provide, for his part, all relevant information supplementing the allegations put forward concerning the violation of human rights and, to that end, to reformulate the communication so that it might clearly fit in with the procedural stipulations of 104 EX/ Decision 3.3;

[vi] to request the Executive Board to ask the Director-General to ask the Inter-American Commission on Human Rights to send him its report on the mission that it was to carry out in Guatemala.

233. On 19 August 1980 the Guatemalan Minister of Foreign Affairs sent the Deputy Director-General a telegram stating briefly that while it was true that there had been terrorist attacks in some university centres, responsibility for them had been publicly claimed by left and right-wing factions operating clandestinely; and that the Government of Guatemala was waging a constant struggle to maintain peace and respect for human rights and fundamental freedoms.

234. On 28 January 1981 the Minister sent the Director-General a letter containing information recorded by the Chairman of the Committee following an interview with the Minister.

235. At the [spring 1981] session, the Chairman of the Committee said that he had in fact been informed by the Minister of Foreign Affairs of Guatemala that:

Mr Osorio Paz had left the country using his own passport;

Mr Alvarado Polanco was at present carrying out his professional activities as Dean of the Faculty of Law and Social Science at San Carlos University in complete freedom, and could leave the country if he so wished;

Mr Carillo Reeves was the Rector of the University of San Carlos.

No. 193/80 **Guatemala**

236. The Chairman of the Committee even said that he had had the opportunity to speak with Mr Carillo Reeves, who had informed him that he had encountered no problem in carrying out his functions as Rector.

237. The representative of the Guatemalan Government recalled his government's position and pointed out that the author of the communication had not complied with the Committee's request to supply further information and to reformulate the communication within the framework required by 104 EX/Decision 3.3.

238.The Committee finally decided:[8]

(i) to take note with satisfaction of the result of the humanitarian representations made on behalf of the three academics;

(ii) to suspend consideration of the admissibility of this communication, reminding its author of the request made to him by the Committee to provide all relevant information supplementing the allegations put forward concerning the violation of human rights and, to that end, to reformulate the communication so that it might clearly fit in with the procedural stipulations of 104 EX/Decision 3.3, and informing him that, if he failed to reply, his communication would be struck off the list of communications.

239. At the present session, the representative of the government concerned stated that he was not in possession of any new information worthy of record. He insisted that, since the author of the communication had not replied to the repeated requests by the Committee, the case should be struck from the list.

240. One Committee member wondered whether it was possible to take such action in the absence of additional grounds on which to base an appraisal.

241. Another member raised the question of whether the author of the communication had received the letter from the Secretariat informing him of the decision taken by the Committee at the [spring 1981] session.

242. The representative of the Director-General pointed out that the World Peace Council was a very important and well-known organization, that it was unlikely that the letter had not reached Mr Romesh Chandra, and that he himself had had the opportunity to speak about it to a representative of that organization, so that it was difficult to imagine that the author of the communication might be unaware of the Committee's decision.

---

[8] See document 112 EX/30 PRIV., para. 154 (*supra*, pp. 506-507).

Guatemala **No. 193/80**

243. Several members of the Committee considered that the Committee should abide by its decision taken at the [spring 1981] session, bearing in mind the fact that the author of the communication had twice failed to reply: the cooperation of both the government concerned and the author of the communication was necessary.

244. After a discussion on the advantages of systematically sending the authors of communications letters with a request for a formal acknowledgement, and after noting the comments by the representative of the Director-General on the fact that the authors of communications received and filed by the Secretariat were required to follow a procedure laid down in writing, the Committee *decided*:

(i) to strike the communication from the list in application of the rule concerning the failure by the author of the communication to reply on two occasions; and to declare that in any case it was inadmissible as being manifestly unfounded in accordance with the provisions of paragraph 14 (*a*) (v) of 104 EX/Decision 3.3;

(ii) to communicate this decision to the author of the communication;

(iii) to make arrangements for all letters to authors of communications informing them of decisions taken by the Committee to be sent by registered post, accompanied by a request for a formal acknowledgement.

No. 195/80

Concerning *Union of Soviet Socialist Republics*
Case of *Andrei Sakharov*

Communication of 28 February 1980 submitted by
The Lawyers Committee for International Human Rights

Autumn 1980 session of the Committee on Conventions and Recommendations (110th session of the Executive Board)[1]

183. This communication was submitted by a non-governmental organization, "The Lawyers Committee for International Human Rights", which claims to have reliable knowledge of the alleged violations.

184. It alleges that the world-famous physicist, Dr Andrei Sakharov, has been subjected to persecution by the Soviet Government. The first signs of this are said to have appeared as long ago as 1967, when he published two articles expounding his thoughts on the role and future of science and the dangers of nuclear war. His family and friends have reportedly suffered harassment since 1973. The pressures on him and those around him have allegedly been intensified since 1977. On 2 January 1980, he was reportedly arrested, stripped of his honours (Hero of Labour, Order of Lenin, etc.) and exiled to Gorky by decree of the Presidium. He is said to be forbidden all communication, even about science or on purely family matters, especially with foreign countries, and also to be forbidden to leave the town of Gorky.

185. The author of the communication alleges that the USSR took such action so as to make it impossible for Dr Sakharov to pursue his scientific research; to deprive him of self-expression and to prevent him communicating his thoughts on the philosophical, social and political consequences of his work as a physicist; to curtail his activity in the promotion and defence of human rights; and in general to deny him all access to the national and international information and communication media through which he might make known his scientific and philosophical ideas.

---

[1] See document 110 EX/40 PRIV., paras. 183-200; see also document 110 EX/CR/HR/3.

186. As regards recourse to domestic remedies, the author of the communication claims that since Dr Sakharov has not been formally accused of any crime or offence, no verdict has been pronounced aginst which he might appeal. Nevertheless, Dr Sakharov has reportedly protested to the Public Prosecutor against the action taken against him. This case has been raised at the United Nations Commission on Human Rights.

187. The Secretariat has received several letters and cables in support of this communication from various organizations (New York Academy of Sciences, American Association for the Advancement of Science, American Physical Society, Federation of American Scientists, Faculty of Natural Sciences and Mathematics of the University of New York at Buffalo, U.S.A., American Mathematical Society, National Academy of Sciences, Society for Industrial and Applied Mathematics and the Department of Statistics of the University of California, Berkeley, U.S.A.).

188. The representative of the Government of the Soviet Union stated to the Committee at its present session that he intended to prove that this communication was clearly inadmissible.

189. As concerned the first of the two alleged persecutions of Dr Sakharov, one said to have taken place over the past 12 years, the Soviet representative stated that far from being a persecution or ostracism, Mr Sakharov's transfer to the Lebedev Institute in 1969 was a transfer to one of the oldest and most respected institutions in the Soviet Union. The Soviet representative, in quoting a letter from Dr Sakharov wherein the scientist said he intended to do some work in the field of elementary particles, stated to the Committee that this was a clear refutation of the assertion that Dr Sakharov was being ostracized or persecuted.

190. Furthermore, the Soviet representative explained that the allegation that the government had virtually suspended Dr Sakharov's scientific activity could be seen to be untrue by referring to a list prepared by the Soviet Academy of Sciences of the scientific works which Dr Sakharov had published during the period in question.

191. As for the second of the two assertions, which concerned Dr Sakharov's recent "exile" the Soviet representative stated that this was a perfectly legitimate action on the part of the Soviet authorities and did not involve violations of Dr Sakharov's human rights. He stressed that although Dr Sakharov had been awarded a Nobel Peace Prize, his statements on current issues were inconsistent with the interests of peace. If one looked at Dr Sakharov's statements in the press, it was obvious that he was in favour of the use of economic, political and military measures against his own country to prevent its so-called expansion, said the Soviet representative. He went on to

explain that since Dr Sakharov had thus become a threat to national security, the Supreme State authority decided to impose some restrictive measures against him.

192. Dr Sakharov was thus transferred and restricted to the city of Gorky where he is forbidden to contact foreign citizens; however, he is still an active member of the Soviet Academy of Science, is still working and still receives his salary and benefits, it was explained.

193. The Soviet representative stated that such a restriction and limitation taken in the interest of national security could not be seen as a violation of human rights, for paragraph 3 of Article 12 of the International Covenant on Civil and Political Rights allowed the restriction of a person's right of movement for security reasons.

194. He vent on to state that this communication was an attempt to draw the Committee into a political confrontation, which would be detrimental to Unesco's aims. The Committee should not be drawn into such a game and should declare the communication inadmissible.

195. A member of the Committee stated that he felt that Dr Sakharov's views were not really at issue here; however, the fact that he was still allowed to work and receive a salary seemed to show that the communication was ill-founded. Another member of the Committee expressed the viev that the government in question probably had a valid interest in controlling a special scientist with unique knowledge such as Sakharov, who had separated himself from the posture of his government. A third member of the Committee expressed the view that although logic might lead one to the conclusion that the case was admissible, it was not necessarily a good idea to follow the rule of logic, especially in a case such as this one where the state may well have good reasons to take such action against a great scientist.

196. Several members of the Committee felt that the communication was clearly admissible and wondered how national security reasons could be cited as a justification for the actions taken, given that Dr Sakharov's security clearance had been revoked over 10 years ago. It was emphasized that the communication could not be deemed to be ill-founded or without reliable evidence since the Soviet representative did not contest the facts; it was only the interpretation of the facts which he contested and this was a matter to be considered during the discussion of the substance and not during the discussion of admissibility. A member of the Committee stated that the communication clearly satisfied all the conditions for admissibility. He indicated that the communication could not be deemed manifestly ill-founded since a major part of it was based on information coming from Dr Sakharov himself. Reference was made to the complaints made by Dr Sakharov in January 1980 that the Soviet authorities were, *inter alia*, interfering with his right to receive and impart informa-

tion and were preventing him not only from seeing foreigners but also from telephoning and from seeing his grandchildren. Also read to the Committee was Dr Sakharov's assertion that he was and would always be a defender of peace, disarmament and human rights, and that the Soviet press was twisting his views to make it appear otherwise. The Committee member added that there was nothing in the communication which could lead one to think that it was wholly or even partly motivated by political considerations; he pointed out that a broad spectrum of scientific and other organizations bad been alarmed by the case and had protested to the Soviet Government.

197. Another member of the Committee wondered whether it was not more important for the Committee to find friendly solutions than to adhere strictly to its procedures, and he suggested that a decision on admissibility might be postponed while more information was being sought from both the government concerned and the author.

198. Several Committee members objected that such a postponement would be an improper and unjustified avoidance of this communication, which so clearly met the Committee's admissibility requirements and which was of paramount interest to Unesco. They stated that they would have great difficulty accepting such a proposal.

199. The Soviet representative stated that he too would have great difficulty accepting such a proposal since the communication was in his view so clearly inadmissible.

200. After a lengthy discussion and search for a consensus on the matter, the Committee *decided*:

(i) to defer the decision on the admissibility of the communication until its next session;

(ii) to request the Executive Board to ask the Director-General, in the meantime, to supplement by all appropriate means the information available on the facilities provided to Dr Sakharov for continuing his scientific research work under conditions consistent with the provisions of the Unesco Recommendation on the Status of Scientific Researchers.

Union of Soviet Socialist Republics **No. 195/80**

Spring 1981 session of the Committee on Conventions and Recommendations (112th session of the Executive Board)[2]

248. This communication was submitted by a non-governmental organization, "The Lawyers Committee for International Human Rights", which claims to have reliable knowledge of the alleged violations.

249. This communication alleges that the world-famous physicist, Dr Andrei Sakharov, has been subjected to persecution by the Soviet Government. The first signs of this are said to have appeared as long ago as 1967, when he published two articles expounding his thoughts on the role and future of science and the dangers of nuclear war. His family and friends have reportedly suffered harassment since 1973. The pressures on him and those around him have allegedly been intensified since 1977. On 2 January 1980, he was reportedly arrested, stripped of his honours (Hero of Labour, Order of Lenin, etc.) and exiled to Gorky by decree of the Presidium. He is said to be forbidden all communication, even about science or on purely family matters, especially with foreign countries, and also to be forbidden to leave the town of Gorky.

250. The author of the communication alleges that the USSR took such action so as to make it impossible for Mr Sakharov to pursue his scientific research; to deprive him of self-expression and to prevent him communicating his thoughts on the philosophical, social and political consequences of his work as a physicist; to curtail his activity in the promotion and defence of human rights; and in general to deny him all access to the national and international information and communication media through which he might make known his scientific and philosophical ideas.

251. As regards recourse to domestic remedies, the author of the communication claims that since Dr Sakharov has not been formally accused of any crime or offence, no verdict has been pronounced against which he might appeal. Nevertheless, Dr Sakharov has reportedly protested to the Public Prosecutor against the action taken against him.

252. At the Committee's [autumn 1980] session, the representative of the Soviet Government had stated to the Committee that Dr Sakharov had made statements in favour of the use of economic, political and military measures against his own country to prevent its so-called expansion. He went on to explain that since Dr Sakharov

[2] See document 112 EX/30 PRIV., paras. 248-288; see also documents 112 EX/CR/HR/2 and Add.

had thus become a threat to national security, the Supreme State authority decided to impose some restrictive measures against him.

253. Dr Sakharov had thus been transferred and restricted to the city of Gorky where he was forbidden to contact foreign citizens. However, he was still an active member of the Soviet Academy of Sciences, was still working and still received his salary and benefits.

254. The Soviet representative stated that such restrictions and limitations taken in the interest of national security could not be seen as a violation of human rights, for paragraph 3 of Article 12 of the International Covenant on Civil and Political Rights allowed the restriction of a person's right of movement for security reasons.

255. He went on to state that this communication was an attempt to draw the Committee into a political confrontation, which would be detrimental to Unesco's aims. The Committee should not let itself become involved, and should declare the communication inadmissible.

256. A member of the Committee stated that he felt that Dr Sakharov's views were not really at issue here. However, the fact that he was still allowed to work and receive a salary seemed to show that the communication was ill-founded. Another member of the Committee expressed the view that the government in question probably had a valid interest in controlling a special scientist with unique knowledge such as Sakharov, who had dissociated himself from the position of his government. A third member of the Committee expressed the view that although logic might lead one to the conclusion that the case was admissible, it was not necessarily a good idea to follow the rule of logic, especially in a case such as this one where the state might well have good reasons to take such action against a great scientist.

257. Several members of the Committee felt that the communication was clearly admissible and wondered how national security reasons could be cited as a justification for the actions taken, given that Dr Sakharov's security clearance had been revoked over 10 years ago. It was emphasized that the communication could not be deemed to be ill-founded or without reliable evidence since the Soviet representative did not contest the facts. It was only the interpretation of the facts which he contested and this was a matter to be considered during the discussion of the substance and not during the discussion of admissibility. A member of the Committee stated that the communication clearly satisfied all the conditions for admissibility. He indicated that the communication could not be deemed manifestly ill-founded since a major part of it was based on information coming from Dr Sakharov himself. Reference was made to the complaints made by Dr Sakharov in January 1980, the Soviet authorities were, *inter alia*, interfering with his right to receive and impart information

and were preventing him not only from seeing foreigners but also from telephoning and from seeing his grandchildren. Also read to the Committee was Dr Sakharov's assertion that he was and would always be a defender of peace, disarmament and human rights, and the Soviet press was twisting his views to make it appear otherwise. The Committee member added that there was nothing in the communication which could lead one to think that it was wholly or even partly motivated by political considerations. He pointed out that a broad spectrum of scientific and other organizations had been alarmed by the case and had protested to the Soviet Government.

258. A member of the Committee wondered whether it was not more important for the Committee to find amicable solutions than to adhere strictly to its procedures, and he suggested that a decision on admissibility might be postponed while more information was being sought from both the government concerned and the author.

259. Several Committee members objected that such a postponement would be an improper and unjustified avoidance of this communication, which so clearly met the Committee's admissibility requirements and which was of paramount interest to Unesco. They stated that they would have great difficulty accepting such a proposal.

260. The Soviet representative stated that he too would have great difficulty accepting such a proposal since the communication was in his view clearly inadmissible.

261. After a lengthy discussion and search for a consensus on the matter, the Committee at its [autumn 1980] session decided:[3]

(i) to defer the decision on the admissibility of the communication until its next session;

(ii) to request the Executive Board to ask the Director-General, in the meantime, to supplement by all appropriate means the information available on the facilities provided to Dr Sakharov for continuing his scientific research work under conditions consistent with the provisions of the Unesco Recommendation on the Status of Scientific Researchers.

262. The Deputy Director-General brought the Committee's decisions to the knowledge of the Permanent Delegate of the USSR in letters dated 24 October 1980 and 20 January 1981. The Director of the Office of International Standards and Legal Affairs also informed the author of the communication of them in a letter dated 7 October 1980.

---

[3] See document 110 EX/40 PRIV., para. 200 (*supra*, p. 516).

No. 195/80 **Union of Soviet Socialist Republics**

263. On 19 March 1981 the Secretariat received from the author of the communication a letter, dated 2 March 1981, providing additional information.

264. In this letter the author reviewed the 10 conditions of admissibility of [104 EX/ Decision 3.3] and explained how the present communication fulfilled each one of them. The letter also provided updated information on the conditions of Dr Sakharov's confinement, stating, *inter alia*, that he was still prevented from receiving visitors or having contacts with other scientists, that he was still having difficulty with his working conditions and that his recent publications had in fact been prepared before his exile, and that he was still being harassed by secret police.

265. The Secretariat also received, on 11 May 1981, a letter dated 9 May 1981 from the Permanent Delegate of the Soviet Union to Unesco. In this letter, which the representative of the Director-General read to the Committee at its present session, the Permanent Delegate informed the Director-General on behalf of his government that his government intended to supply exhaustive information to the Committee at its present session in reply to the questions posed by it on this case at its [autumn 1980] session. He also recalled the meeting which he and the representative of the Soviet Government before the Committee had recently had with the Director-General, at which meeting they had submitted to him detailed documentation attesting to the fact that Dr A. Sakharov had all means at his disposal to pursue his scientific work in his chosen fields, to have access to the scientific literature necessary for his work, and to be able to publish his works.

266. At its present session, the representative of the Soviet Government reminded the Committee that he had presented to it at its [autumn 1980] session two facts concerning this communication: there were no facts therein reflecting a violation of human rights, and the communication had been manifestly ill-founded. He said that he had shown that Dr Sakharov was not being subjected to harassment or sanctions. A discussion had taken place as to whether or not the Soviet authorities had the right to decide on the resettlement of Dr Sakharov in another city, and he said that this had been justified not only by the importance of Sakharov's scientific information to the state but also by his political activities, which included appeals for economic, social and even military measures against his own country. Attention had been focused on the need to obtain additional information as to the possibilities open to Dr Sakharov to continue his scientific work. This aspect, he said, should be the main focus of the Committee's attention with respect to this case, and he explained that he would demonstrate to the Committee that Dr Sakharov did indeed have these possibilities open to him. He added that the Soviet Government was perfectly willing to co-operate in such an examination. It was explained that Dr Sakharov remained a full-fledged member of the Soviet Academy of Sciences and that he was a co-worker of the Lebedev Institute of Physics, an extremely renowned institution. He had submitted to

the Physics Institute of the Soviet Academy a programme of work for 1981 which had been adopted by the Institute without any amendments.

267. Dr Sakharov was completely free to determine the direction and the topics of his research; this was the first and most important fact in the case, the Soviet representative said.

268. As for the possibility of publishing the results of his research, this possibility was said to be confirmed by the list of his works published after his exile to Gorky. If his scientific productivity of the January 1980 - May 1981 period and the ten-year period preceding his move to Gorky were compared, one saw that it was much higher in the later period.

269. Thirdly, it was mentioned that there was much political propaganda around this case. Furthermore, one of the authors had not completely respected the confidentiality of the case, since he had openly rallied support for Dr Sakharov, the Soviet representative said.

270. As for the allegation that there were no libraries accessible to Dr Sakharov in Gorky and that certain important books were not available there, the Soviet representative stated that he had made a special trip to Gorky to check on these points. He found that the main library there was extremely well stocked and received all the latest journals from around the world. Regional libraries were also available; Dr Sakharov, however, had not applied for the use of the works allegedly unavailable to him. This was of course his prerogative, the Soviet representative said. He pointed out that special funds were made available in the Soviet Union so that scientific institutes could purchase books and journals from all over the world for Soviet scientists.

271. The Soviet representative finally stated that this matter had thus been discussed sufficiently and should be considered as inadmissible.

272. A Committee member stated that after hearing these arguments from the Soviet representative, he got the impression that Gorky was a scientific paradise and that all scientists should try to get themselves exiled there. He felt that Unesco had an obligation to protect geniuses regardless of their specialization or nationality. He stated that Dr Sakharov should be permitted to live and work where he himself chose and should be allowed to express himself as he wished. The Soviet Union should not be overly fearful of expressions of opinion he said, and should not forget the universal aspects of this genius who had so much to contribute to all humanity.

No. 195/80 **Union of Soviet Socialist Republics**

273. The Soviet representative stated that he had adequately addressed the specific question which had been expressed in the Committee's last decision on this case. He said that he was not claiming that Gorky was an ideal place for any scientist. It was clear that Dr Sakharov's resettlement there was not ideal; it was a measure taken by the state in relation to a scientist who had the most important state secrets and who expressed dangerous political opinions. These restrictions did not represent a violation that came within the competence of Unesco, he said.

274. A Committee member felt that this case concerned a person working in Unesco's fields of interest whose professional and personal rights were being violated, and it was thus clearly admissible.

275. Another Committee member stated that the three arguments presented by the Soviet representative did not reply to all aspects of the communication. He said the authors had very logically and convincingly presented the evidence of the communication's fulfilling each of the 10 conditions of admissibility outlined in paragraph 14 (*a*) of [104 EX/Decision 3.3]. The Committee member was of the view that Dr Sakharov had a right to practice his scientific research wherever he wanted, and that the case should thus remain before the Committee.

276. Still another Committee member, while reminding the Committee that it should concern itself with violations of human rights within its fields of competence regardless of the importance or lack of importance of the person involved, stated that it was nevertheless worth noting that Dr Sakharov had made a very significant and positive contribution to the Soviet Union's nuclear and scientific development, and that he had received the highest awards bestowed upon him by that country. It was not the Committee member's intention to make an East-West issue out of this case, and he went on to express the view that there would be far less East-West tension if such suppressions of the right to free expression as in his case were not constantly fuelling that tension. He also wished to offer the observation that it was those persons in the West most interested in friendly co-operation with the Soviet Union, the scientists and researchers, who were the ones most likely to be upset and repulsed by the Soviet Union's action against this great and internationally minded scientist. The Committee member reminded the Committee that it still had before it the question concerning admissibility of this communication, which still had not been answered. Dr Sakharov, he pointed out, was aware of the arguments which had been advanced by the Soviet Union to the effect that his rights as a scientist were not being violated, and he himself had answered these arguments in his letter before the Committee. Sakharov stated that there was no possibility of meeting anyone other than his wife and three other persons, as he was kept under constant surveillance and visitors were not allowed. Sakharov said that he had no contact with other scientists in Gorky, that he had no library nearby, that he had no possibility to telephone, that his radio was

jammed, and that KGB agents illegally entered his flat. Sakharov had further stated that the accusations by the state were clearly ill-founded, since he supported peace disarmament and détente and never revealed any military secrets. Dr Sakharov also said that he expressed his own viewpoints and did not speak for any geopolitical group; he insisted on having a public trial, since he was being punished without any recourse to the courts, which was grossly illegal on the part of the Soviet authorities and contrary to the Soviet Constitution. The Committee member in concluding reflected as to what tremendous courage it must have taken for a person who was at the pinnacle of Soviet society, greatly respected, admired and decorated, to speak openly according to his convictions. It was certain that a thaw in international relations would be welcomed by all countries of the world, he said, and perhaps it was possible that the persons exercising power in the Soviet Union would come to realize that freedom for Dr Sakharov would be a significant gesture on their part towards creating such a thaw.

277. The representative of the Soviet Union said he felt certain that this communication was being used in an East-West confrontation. It was clear that Dr Sakharov had found himself on the wrong side during such a confrontation, a side which ran counter to the interests and security of the Soviet Union. It was clear that there was an Atlantic alliance growing around the defence of Dr Sakharov, he said. He went on to add that Dr Sakharov supported the Pentagon's plans for the modernization of the missile forces in Europe, and that this was not supporting peace, but rather was a defence of the Atlantic Pact. He was even beginning to take the position that accused the KGB of supporting international terrorism. These were aggressive theses which undermined the Soviet Union. It was these positions which required the Soviet authorities to take defensive measures against Sakharov, the representative said. He further stated that if the Committee started to consider Dr Sakharovs' own statements, it could easily be misled, since Sakharov had taken a position on the wrong side.

278. As for the alleged fiancée of the son of Sakharov, the Soviet representative stated that she was in fact the "fiancée" of a man who was already married; he offered that information parenthetically, he said, since he felt that a discussion on this theme would not be fruitful. He stated that there was no violation of human rights here; Dr Sakharov's restriction to Gorky was not really a limitation of his freedom. In any event, he said that a state was allowed to impose certain restrictions in the interest of national security, and the communication was thus clearly inadmissible.

279. A Committee member was of the opinion that rather than refuting the allegations in this communication, the Soviet representative had confirmed them. The case was clearly admissible, and it appeared that the only reason why the Soviet representative did not admit this fact was that he was making a political issue out of it.

280. Another Committee member reminded the Committee that Dr Sakharov had not been involved in scientific work which could be considered as concerning state secrets. The member wondered what could be done here and whether it might not be possible to send someone to visit Dr Sakharov, possibly someone from among those countries which had excellent relations with the East and the West and yet which were none the less extremely disturbed by what was being done to Dr Sakharov.

281. Another Committee member pointed out that his country and others, which were neither in the East or the West, were very concerned by what had happened to Dr Sakharov. He asked the Soviet representative not to think only in terms of geopolitical confrontation, since many states which admired the Soviet Union would like to engage in a friendly debate on the matter of this great scientist. It would probably be useful, he said, for the Director-General to engage in discussions at all levels on behalf of the various Committee members whose concern had clearly been manifested here.

282. Another Committee member felt that the Director-General could perhaps go even further and address an appeal for clemency to the Soviet authorities, in view of the fact that this communication was clearly admissible.

283. The Soviet representative stated that any appeals for clemency could only be applied where there was a punishment being applied. In this case, there had been no punishment, he said, so no appeal was appropriate. He further stated that he felt that any admission of this communication would be unacceptable. He went on to insist that an expression of opinion favouring the installation of NATO missiles aimed at the Soviet Union was a perfectly valid reason for the authorities to send Sakharov to confinement in Gorky.

284. A Committee member then pointed out that under the Committee's procedures for the admissibility of a communication, an admission was not considered to be a presumption of a violation of human rights.

285. It was felt by another Committee member that it was important to admit this case because it was clearly admissible, and because it would also make more evident to the Soviet authorities the concern of this Committee over this case.

286. In agreeing with the position taken by the Soviet representative, another Committee member wished to point out that Dr Sakharov was not really very far from Moscow and that in any event he was not a scientist who was as active in science as were other Soviet scientists. Also, he said, it was unacceptable that Dr Sakharov express views which were against his own country and people. There was clearly political agitation behind this communication, he said, and the Committee should not be

party to such political confrontation. A compromise solution was proposed, which was to suspend the consideration of the admissibility of this communication.

287. The Chairman then stated that a consensus seemed to have developed in the Committee that this communication should not be declared inadmissible and that there was a role to be played by the Director-General in this case.

288. After much discussion, the Committee *decided*:

(i) to take note of the detailed information provided by the representative of the government concerned about the opportunities offered to Andrei Sakharov to continue his scientific research work, and to pass it to the author of the communication;

(ii) taking into account the fact that, in conformity with paragraph 8 (*b*) of 104 EX/Decision 3.3, the Director-General had already entered into consultations with the Soviet authorities, to ask the Executive Board to request the Director-General to continue these consultations and to inform the Committee of their results at the next session;

(iii) to postpone in the interim consideration of the admissibility of the communication and to take the matter up again at the next session in the light of any further information that might be presented, in particular by the author of the communication, with a view to deciding on its admissibility.

Autumn 1981 session of the Committee on Conventions and Recommendations (113th session of the Executive Board)[4]

305. This communication was submitted by a non-governmental organization, "The Lawyers Committee for International Human Rights", which claims to have reliable knowledge of the alleged violations.

306. This communication alleges that the world-famous physicist, Dr Andrei Sakharov, has been subjected to persecution by the Soviet Government. The first signs of this are said to have appeared as long ago as 1967, when he published two articles expounding his thoughts on the role and future of science and the dangers of nuclear war. His family and friends have reportedly suffered harassment since 1973. The pressures on him and those around him have allegedly been intensified since 1977.

[4] See document 113 EX/38 PRIV., paras. 305-342; see also documents 113 EX/CR/HR/2 and Add.6 and 7.

On 2 January 1980, he was reportedly arrested, stripped of his honours (Hero of Labour, Order of Lenin, etc.) and exiled to Gorky by decree of the Presidium. He is said to be forbidden all communication, even about science or on purely family matters, especially with foreign countries, and also to be forbidden to leave the town of Gorky.

307. The author of the communication alleges that the USSR took such action so as to make it impossible for Mr Sakharov to pursue his scientific research; to deprive him of self-expression and to prevent him communicating his thoughts on the philosophical, social and political consequences of his work as a physicist; to curtail his activity in the promotion and defence of human rights; and in general to deny him all access to the national and international information and communication media through which he might make known his scientific and philosophical ideas.

308. As regards recourse to domestic remedies, the author of the communication claims that since Dr Sakharov has not been formally accused of any crime or offence, no verdict has been pronounced against which he might appeal. Nevertheless, Dr Sakharov has reportedly protested to the Public Prosecutor against the action taken against him.

309. The Committee at its [autumn 1980] session decided:[5]

> (i) to defer the decision on the admissibility of the communication until its next session;
>
> (ii) to request the Executive Board to ask the Director-General, in the meantime, to supplement by all appropriate means the information available on the facilities provided to Dr Sakharov for continuing his scientific research work under conditions consistent with the provisions of the Unesco Recommendation on the Status of Scientific Researchers.

310. The Deputy Director-General brought the Committee's decisions to the knowledge of the Permanent Delegate of the USSR in letters dated 24 October 1980 and 20 January 1981. The Director of the Office of International Standards and Legal Affairs also informed the author of the communication of them in a letter dated 7 October 1980.

311. On 19 March 1981 the Secretariat received from the author of the communication a letter, dated 2 March 1981, providing additional information.

---

[5] See document 110 EX/40 PRIV., para. 200 (*supra*, p. 516).

Union of Soviet Socialist Republics **No. 195/80**

312. In this letter the author reviewed the 10 conditions of admissibility of 104 EX/Decision 3.3 and explained how the present communication fulfilled each one of them. The letter also provided updated information on the conditions of Dr Sakharov's confinement, stating, *inter alia*, that he was still prevented from receiving visitors or having contacts with other scientists, that he was still having difficulty with his working conditions and that his recent publications had in fact been prepared before his exile, and that he was still being harassed by secret police.

313. The Secretariat also received, on 11 May 1981, a letter dated 9 May 1981 from the Permanent Delegate of the Soviet Union to Unesco. In this letter, which the representative of the Director-General read to the Committee at its [spring 1981] session, the Permanent Delegate informed the Director-General on behalf of his government that his government intended to supply exhaustive information to the Committee at [the spring 1981] session in reply to the questions posed by it on this case at its [autumn 1980] session. He also recalled the meeting which he and the representative of the Soviet Government before the Committee had recently had with the Director-General, at which meeting they had submitted to him detailed documentation attesting to the fact that Dr A. Sakharov had all means at his disposal to pursue his scientific work in his chosen fields, to have access to the scientific literature necessary for his work, and to be able to publish his works.

314. At its [spring 1981] session the Committee therefore decided:[6]

(i) to take note of the detailed information provided by the representative of the government concerned about the opportunities offered to Andrei Sakharov to continue his scientific research work, and to pass it to the author of the communication;

(ii) taking into account the fact that, in conformity with paragraph 8 (*b*) of 104 EX/Decision 3.3, the Director-General had already entered into consultations with the Soviet authorities, to ask the Executive Board to request the Director-General to continue these consultations and to inform the Committee of their results at the next session;

(iii) to postpone, in the interim, consideration of the admissibility of the communication and to take the matter up again at the next session in the light of any further information that might be presented, in particular by the author of the communication, with a view to deciding on its admissibility.

---

[6] See document 112 EX/30 PRIV., para. 288 (*supra*, p. 525).

No. 195/80 **Union of Soviet Socialist Republics**

315. On 24 August 1981, the Secretariat received a letter from the author of the communication contesting the main arguments put forward by the representative of the Soviet Government.

316. While stressing that it had already provided exhaustive information regarding the violations of the scientist's rights, the Lawyers Committee for International Human Rights said that it now wished to submit additional information based on:

(i) a letter dated January 1981 from Mr Sakharov to Mr Sidney Drell, Deputy Director of the Stanford Linear Accelerator Center, thanking the American physicists for the concern they had shown about his situation: this letter is said to have been published in *The Washington Star* of 2 April 1981;

(ii) a statement by Mr Sakharov dated 17 March 1981 following the alleged theft of his brief-case on 13 March 1981;

(iii) an article entitled "The Responsibility of Scientists" which is said to have been written by Mr Sakharov for an international conference organized in his honour by the New York Academy of Scientists, the American Institute of Physics and the American Physical Society at Rockefeller University on 1 May 1981: this article was reportedly published in *The New York Review of Books* on 25 June 1981.

317. Summing up its point of view, the Lawyers Committee for International Human Rights said that it considered Mr Sakharov's exile to be an infringement of Unesco's Recommendation [on] the Status of Scientific Researchers (20 November 1974) and a violation of the Universal Declaration of Human Rights and the International Covenant on Civil and Political Rights.

318. As exile was, in the opinion of the author of the communication, a form of sentence, it should be pronounced by a court of law and its duration should not exceed five years (in the scientist's case, however, the term of exile would appear to be indefinite). As the academician had not had access to information affecting national security for 13 years, the author asserted that there was no justification for his continued exile. There were no justifiable grounds either for the refusal to issue an exit visa to Elizaveta Alexeyeva, his son's fiancée, who had never in any way been concerned with state secrets.

319. Referring to the international character of the scientist's profession, the author alleged that Mr Sakharov's exile prevented him from participating in the world scientific community.

Union of Soviet Socialist Republics **No. 195/80**

320. As regards the claim of the representative of the Soviet Government to the effect that Mr Sakharov's scientific productivity had increased in the period January 1980 to May 1981, the author pointed out that this was not the case, since the three articles published at the time were reportedly written partly or even entirely before his exile. It added that the scientist had no access to research material and that the theft of his brief-case on 13 March 1981 showed that even if he did have access to scientific literature he was not free to make use of it for his research.

321. The Lawyers Committee for International Human Rights considered that the documents referred to under [paragraph 316] (i), (ii) and (iii) above provided ample proof of the difficulties with which the alleged victim had to contend and which were caused by the Soviet authorities, who continued to isolate him and to prevent him from engaging fully in his scientific pursuits.

322. On 4 September 1981, the Secretariat received from the author of the communication a letter with additional information for the Committee which included the following documents:

(i) As proof of the decline in Mr Sakharov's scientific output [...]:[7] photocopies of three articles published by him in 1980 in "Soviet Physics JETP", as translated by the American Institute of Physics: "Cosmological models of the universe with reversal of time's arrow", "Mass formula for mesons and baryons" and "An estimate of the coupling constant between mesons and baryons".

323. The Lawyers Committee for International Human Rights pointed out that, in a letter addressed to his American colleagues, Mr Sakharov had stated that the second and third of these articles had been written before December 1979. (The author of the communication stated that this letter was of too personal a nature to be submitted in full, but relevant passages could be produced.)

(ii) as proof that restrictions had been placed on Mr Sakharov's correspondence with the West and that all visits to him had been forbidden;

(*a*) copies of various telegrams sent to him on the occasion of his sixtieth birthday and not received; according to the author of the communication, the academician had been unable to telephone or correspond with the members of his family now residing in the United States of America;

[7] See document 113 EX/CR/HR/2 Add.6, para. 1.

(*b*) a copy of Mr Alexander Babyonyshev's sworn statement concerning his alleged visit to Gorky in March 1980 with the intention of visiting Dr Sakharov: on the day of his arrival he had been warned by a member of the KGB, Major Shuvalov, that if he were to attempt to visit the scientist he would be expelled from the town; Dr Sakharov had wanted to see him at the house where he was staying but had been prevented from doing so by those responsible for his surveillance; on the evening of the third day, before leaving Gorky, Babyonyshev had, however, succeeded in seeing Dr Sakharov by climbing through the window of his ground-floor apartment; he had been able to ascertain at first hand that the scientist's wireless receiver had been jammed; when running away from Mr Sakharov's house, having left by the way he had entered, he had been stopped and questioned by the police; the academician had witnessed the scene and gone to his rescue at the police station, outside the door of which he had waited for three hours in perishing cold;

(*c*) a copy of a sworn statement by Mrs Sarra Babyonyshev, who had thought that reports about the ban on visits to Mr Sakharov were exaggerated: when in March 1980 she had gone to Gorky to visit the scientist and his wife, she had been picked up by the police and held for a day before eventually being taken back to the airport, without having even obtained permission to take a walk in the town, because Major Shuvalov had refused to believe that the only reason for her visit was to give the scientist a cake of which he was particulary fond, and because the authorities would not allow her to meet acquaintances in the street.

324. The Lawyers Committee for International Human Rights considered the restrictions imposed on Mr Sakharov on grounds of national security to be unnecessarily strict. It requested the Committee to take steps to enable the academician to regain his freedom, to make full use of his intellectual abilities and to exercise all his rights in accordance with international law.

325. At the Committee's present session the representative of the Soviet Government stated that he felt the authors of the communication were not respecting the confidentiality required by the Committee's proceedings. Many of the letters and telegrams being sent to the Director-General concerning Dr Sakharov showed signs that they were inspired by the authors of the communication. Furthermore, he said, the authors were trying to enter into direct contact with the members of the Committee. The authors did so by sending letters to Committee members via the permanent delegations; thus if the Committee member did not open his own mail, the material became public and confidentiality was breached. Such an act showed a lack of trust in the Secretariat on the part of the authors, and the fact that they asked that their

communication be given "careful consideration" showed that they thought it was not already being given careful consideration.

326. Such an attitude required that serious conclusions be drawn in this regard.

327. The representative of the Director-General made the point that the letter in question was not in fact one which had been sent to the Secretariat and that the Secretariat had had no knowledge of it. He also explained that the Director-General was acutely aware of the importance of confidentiality in the Committee's procedures and that he had on various occasions strongly emphasized to authors the importance of the authors' respecting this rule.

328. A Committee member stated that the confidentiality of the Committee was important, and he felt there was some justification in the Soviet representative's remarks.

329. Another Committee member felt that the mailing in question should not necessarily be seen to be a violation of the Committee's confidentiality since the letters had been specifically addressed to the Committee members.

330. Another Committee member felt that it was not inappropriate for authors to address themselves directly to Committee members or even public officials outside of the Committee. He felt there was no violation of confidentiality in the mailing in question.

331. The Chairman pointed out that the only channel for the Committee to receive documentation was through the Secretariat and that the documentation in question could therefore not be brought into the discussion.

332. Another Committee member felt that the matter of the mailings was not a breach of Committee confidentiality and was in fact a petty issue; he felt it should not sidetrack the Committee from its examination of the case.

333. The Soviet representative thereupon proceeded to address the substantive aspects of the communication. He stated that there were two main questions involved in the case.

334. The first was to what extent the Soviet Union was justified for national security reasons to assign Dr Sakharov to live in the city of Gorky, where his contact with others was limited. He reminded the Committee that Dr Sakharov had been working in fields where he acquired information of high national security importance. He stated that, notwithstanding the authors' claim that Dr Sakharov did not any longer

have such knowledge, this was a question which only the appropriate security authorities of the Soviet Union could judge, not the authors or the Committee.

335. The other question was to what extent sanctions were appropriate against Dr Sakharov for his having made statements contrary to the strategic interests of the Soviet Union. It had been shown that Dr Sakharov had made such statements, for example his statements in favour of the stationing of missiles, aimed at the USSR, on European soil. It appeared that Dr Sakharov still maintained his attitude and the Soviet representative quoted a recent article in *The Washington Post* to emphasize this point. A decision had thus been taken by the highest Soviet authorities to isolate Dr Sakharov, since his views were dangerous and went against the mainstream of the Soviet people's thinking.

336. Nevertheless, Dr Sakharov still had the possibility of continuing his scientific work, the Soviet representative said. He still worked with the prestigious Lebedev Institute, he had the chance to set up his own scientific programme, he still had ample access to library facilities in Gorky, and he still had the possibility of publishing his works. By his own choice he published in the *Journal of Experimental and Theoretical Physics*; in fact everything he had submitted to it had been published. The Soviet representative stated that six members of the French Academy of Sciences and an Australian scientist had confirmed that Dr Sakharov was quite productive despite his situation in Gorky. As to the authors' assertion concerning certain of Dr Sakharov's articles, the articles in question had been submitted to the Soviet journal in a rough form and had to be reworked twice before they could finally be published.

337. The Soviet representative stated that according to many scientists, Dr Sakharov's work in Gorky, especially in baryon studies, was of definite interest to the scientific community.

338. The Soviet delegate conceded that some particular problems might be arising in regard to the provision of scientific supplies, but he felt that the necessary means could always be found to solve such problems.

339. A Committee member stated that top scientists had informed him that Mr Sakharov was one of the most brilliant minds alive in the world today, and that he was paving important new paths on the frontiers of science. However, since the fields of research he was involved in were theoretical, their practical application was not a present possibility and these narrow and highly specialized fields required many more facilities than those which were given him in Gorky. It also seemed totally unrealistic, he said, to claim that Dr Sakharov still possessed any knowledge which could endanger national security, since he had not been working in related fields for

over a decade. Furthermore, on the question of some of the dates of publication of his articles, it seemed most likely that Dr Sakharov was writing about matters which had been taking shape in his mind for years and which he had not been able to put into written form in a short period of time.

340. The Committee member felt that it would be appropriate in the present case to recommend that the Executive Board should ask the Director-General to continue to take appropriate steps in regard to this case.

341. Another Committee member felt that while the Committee could not question the security decisions of Soviet authorities and while the Committee should be careful to look only at matters coming within its competence, it was nevertheless vital that Unesco should manifest its interest in as important a science-related question as this one and that it should continue to monitor the situation, which certainly was a cause for its concern. He went on to say that it was his sincere conviction that if the Soviet authorities could facilitate the Director-General's consultations, the existing mass of anti-Soviet propaganda in the world could probably be considerably deflated. It was his hope that the Soviet authorities could co-operate closely with the Director-General.

342. After discussion, and on the proposal of the Chairman, the Committee *decided*:

(i) to take note of the additional information duly submitted by the author of the communication, while greatly regretting the circulation of the letter of 14 August 1981 among the members of the Committee in ways that did not conform with the provisions of 104 EX/Decision 3.3 and, more particularly, paragraph 14 (*b*) and to direct the Secretariat to draw the attention of the author of the communication to the extreme importance it attaches to the scrupulous respect of the confidential nature of its procedures;

(ii) to take note of the new information provided by the representative of the government concerned regarding the circumstances in which Andrei Sakharov is able to pursue his scientific research in Gorky, the city where he has been placed under house arrest for security reasons;

(iii) to request the Executive Board to invite the Director-General to continue his consultations with the Soviet authorities, in conformity with paragraph 8 (*b*) of 104 EX/Decision 3.3 and, more particularly, with such scientific authorities of the USSR as are able to provide further information on the application of Unesco's Recommendation on the Status of Scientific Researchers, as it relates to the allegations contained in [the present communication].

No. 195/80 **Union of Soviet Socialist Republics**

Spring 1982 session of the Committee on Conventions and Recommendations (114th session of the Executive Board)[8]

526. This communication is submitted by "The Lawyers Committee for International Human Rights", which states itself to be a non-governmental organization with reliable knowledge of the alleged violations.

527. This communication alleges that the world-famous physicist, Dr Andrei Sakharov, has been subjected to persecution by the Soviet Government. The first signs of this are said to have appeared as long ago as 1967, when he published two articles expounding his thoughts on the role and future of science and the dangers of nuclear war. His family and friends have reportedly suffered harassment since 1973. The pressures on him and those around him have allegedly been intensified since 1977. On 2 January 1980, he was reportedly arrested, stripped of his .honours (Hero of Labour, Order of Lenin, etc.) and exiled to Gorky by decree of the Presidium. He is said to be forbidden all communication, even about science or on purely family matters, especially with foreign countries, and also to be forbidden to leave the town of Gorky.

528. The author of the communication alleges that the USSR took such action so as to make it impossible for Mr Sakharov to pursue his scientific research; to deprive him of self-expression and to prevent him communicating his thoughts on the philosophical, social and political consequences of his work as a physicist; to curtail his activity in the promotion and defence of human rights; and in general to deny him all access to the national and international information and communication media through which he might make known his scientific and philosophical ideas.

529. As regards recourse to domestic remedies, the author of the communication claims that since Dr Sakharov has not been formally accused of any crime or offence, no verdict has been pronounced against which he might appeal. Nevertheless, Dr Sakharov has reportedly protested to the Public Prosecutor against the action taken against him.

530. The Committee at its [autumn] 1980 session decided:[9]

(i) to defer the decision on the admissibility of the communication until its next session;

---

[8] See document 114 EX/38 PRIV., paras. 526-579; see also documents 114 EX/CR/HR/2 and Add. and Add.5.

[9] See document 110 EX/40 PRIV., para. 200 (*supra*, p. 516).

(ii) to request the Executive Board to ask the Director-General, in the meantime, to supplement by all appropriate means the information available on the facilities provided to Dr Sakharov for continuing his scientific research work under conditions consistent with the provisions of the Unesco Recommendation on the Status of Scientific Researchers.

531. On 19 March 1981 the Secretariat received from the author of the communication a letter, dated 2 March 1981, providing additional information.

532. In this letter the author reviewed the 10 conditions of admissibility of 104 EX/Decision 3.3 and explained how the present communication fulfilled each one of them. The letter also provided updated information on the conditions of Dr Sakharov's confinement, stating, *inter alia,* that he was still prevented from receiving visitors or having contacts with other scientists, that he was still having difficulty with his working conditions and that his recent publications had in fact been prepared before his exile, and that he was still being harassed by secret police.

533. The Secretariat also received, on 11 May 1981, a letter dated 9 May 1981 from the Permanent Delegate of the Soviet Union to Unesco. In this letter, which the representative of the Director-General read to the Committee at its spring 1981 session, the Permanent Delegate informed the Director-General on behalf of his government that his government intended to supply exhaustive information to the Committee in reply to the questions posed by it on this case at its [autumn 1980] session. He also recalled the meeting which he and the representative of the Soviet Government before the Committee had had with the Director-General, at which meeting they had submitted to him detailed documentation attesting to the fact that Dr Sakharov had all means at his disposal to pursue his scientific work in his chosen fields, to have access to the scientific literature necessary for his work, and to be able to publish his works.

534. At the close of that spring 1981 session the Committee therefore decided:[10]

(i) to take note of the detailed information provided by the representative of the government concerned about the opportunities offered to Andrei Sakharov to continue his scientific research work, and to pass it to the author of the communication;

(ii) taking into account the fact that, in conformity with paragraph 8 (*b*) of 104 EX/Decision 3.3, the Director-General had already entered into consultations with the Soviet authorities, to ask the Executive Board to request the

[10] See document 112 EX/30 PRIV., para. 288 (*supra*, p. 525).

Director-General to continue those consultations and to inform the Committee of their results at its following session;

(iii) to postpone, in the interim, consideration of the admissibility of the communication and to take the matter up again at the next session in the light of any further information that might be presented, in particular by the author of the communication, with a view to deciding on its admissibility.

535. On 24 August 1981, the Secretariat received a letter from the author of the communication contesting the main arguments put forward by the representative of the Soviet Government.

536. While stressing that it had already provided exhaustive information regarding the violations of the scientist's rights, the Lawyers Committee for International Human Rights said that it now wished to submit additional information based on:

(i) a letter dated January 1981 from Dr Sakharov to Mr Sidney Drell, Deputy Director of the Stanford Linear Accelerator Center, thanking the American physicists for the concern they had shown about his situation: this letter is said to have been published in *The Washington Star* of 2 April 1981;

(ii) a statement by Dr Sakharov dated 17 March 1981 following the alleged theft of his brief-case on 13 March 1981;

(iii) an article entitled "The Responsibility of Scientists" which is said to have been written by Dr Sakharov for an international conference organized in his honour by the New York Academy of Scientists, the American Institute of Physics and the American Physical Society at Rockefeller University on 1 May 1981: this article was reportedly published in *The New York Review of Books* on 25 June 1981.

537. Summing up its point of view, the Lawyers Committee for International Human Rights said that it considered Dr Sakharov's exile to be an infringement of Unesco's Recommendation [on] the Status of Scientific Researchers (20 November 1974) and a violation of the Universal Declaration of Human Rights and the International Covenant on Civil and Political Rights.

538. As exile was, in the opinion of the author of the communication, a form of sentence, it should be pronounced by a court of law and its duration should not exceed five years (in the scientist's case, however, the term of exile would appear to be indefinite). As the academician had not had access to information affecting national security for 13 years, the author asserted that there was no justification for his con-

tinued exile. There were no justifiable grounds either for the refusal to issue an exit visa to Elizaveta Alexeyeva, his son's fiancée, who had never in any way been concerned with state secrets.

539. Referring to the international character of the scientist's profession, the author alleged that Dr Sakharov's exile prevented him from participating in the world scientific community.

540. As regards the claim of the representative of the Soviet Government to the effect that Dr Sakharov's scientific productivity had increased in the period January 1980 to May 1981, the author pointed out that this was not the case, since the three articles published at the time were reportedly written partly or even entirely before his exile. It added that the scientist had no access to research material and that the theft of his brief-case on 13 March 1981 showed that even if he did have access to scientific literature he was not free to make use of it for his research.

541. The Lawyers Committee for International Human Rights considered that the documents referred to under [paragraph 536] (i), (ii) and (iii) above provided ample proof of the difficulties with which the alleged victim had to contend and which were caused by the Soviet authorities, who continued to isolate him and to prevent him from engaging fully in his scientific pursuits.

542. On 4 September 1981, the Secretariat received from the author of the communication another letter with additional information for the Committee; it included the following documents:

> (i) As proof of the decline in Mr Sakharov's scientific output [...]: photocopies of three articles published by him in 1980 in "Soviet Physics JETP", as translated by the American Institute of Physics: "Cosmological models of the universe with reversal of time's arrow", "Mass formula for mesons and baryons" and "An estimate of the coupling constant between mesons and baryons".

The Lawyers Committee for International Human Rights pointed out that, in a letter addressed to his American colleagues, Dr Sakharov had stated that the second and third of these articles had been written before December 1979. (The author of the communication stated that this letter was of too personal a nature to be submitted in full, but relevant passages could be produced.)

> (ii) As proof that restrictions had been placed on Dr Sakharov's correspondence with the West and that all visits to him had been forbidden:

(*a*) copies of various telegrams sent to him on the occasion of his sixtieth birthday and not received; according to to the author of the communication, the academician had been unable to telephone or correspond with the members of his family now residing in the United States of America;

(*b*) a copy of Mr Alexander Babyonyshev's sworn statement concerning his alleged visit to Gorky in March 1980 with the intention of seeing Dr Sakharov: on the day of his arrival he had been warned by a member of the KGB, Major Shuvalov, that if he were to attempt to visit the scientist he would be expelled from the town; Dr Sakharov had wanted to see him at the house where he was staying but had been prevented from doing so by those responsible for his surveillance; on the evening of the third day, before leaving Gorky, Babyonyshev had, however, succeeded in seeing Dr Sakharov by climbing through the window of his ground-floor apartment; he had been able to ascertain at first hand that the scientist's wireless receiver had been jammed; when running away from Dr Sakharov's house, having left by the way he had entered, he had been stopped and questioned by the police; the academician had witnessed the scene and gone to his rescue at the police station, outside the door of which he had waited for three hours in perishing cold;

(*c*) a copy of a sworn statement by Mrs Sarra Babyonyshev, who had thought that reports about the ban on visits to Dr Sakharov were exaggerated: when in March 1980 she had gone to Gorky to visit the scientist and his wife, she had been picked up by the police and held for a day before eventually being taken back to the airport, without having even obtained permission to take a walk in the town, because Major Shuvalov had refused to believe that the only reason for her visit was to give the scientist a cake of which he was particularly fond, and because the authorities would not allow her to meet acquaintances in the street.

The Lawyers Committee for International Human Rights considered the restrictions imposed on Dr Sakharov on grounds of national security to be unnecessarily strict. It requested the Committee to take steps to enable the academician to regain his freedom, to make full use of his intellectual abilities and to exercise all his rights in accordance with international law.

543. At the Committee's [autumn 1981 session] the representative of the Soviet Government stated that he felt the authors of the communication were not respecting the confidentiality required by the Committee's proceedings. Many of the letters and telegrams being sent to the Director-General concerning Dr Sakharov showed signs that they were inspired by the authors of the communication. Furthermore, he said, the authors were trying to enter into direct contact with the members of the Com-

mittee. The authors did so by sending letters to Committee members via the permanent delegations; thus if the Committee member did not open his own mail, the material became public and confidentiality was breached. Such an act showed a lack of trust in the Secretariat on the part of the authors, and the fact that they asked that their communication be given "careful consideration" showed that they thought it was not already being given careful consideration.

544. Such an attitude required that serious conclusions be drawn in this regard.

545. The representative of the Director-General made the point that the letter in question was not in fact one which had been sent to the Secretariat and that the Secretariat had had no knowledge of it. He also explained that the Director-General was acutely aware of the importance of confidentiality in the Committee's procedures and that he had on various occasions strongly emphasized to authors the importance of the authors' respecting this rule.

546. A Committee member stated that the confidentiality of the Committee was important, and he felt there was some justification in the Soviet representative's remarks.

547. Another Committee member felt that the mailing in question should not necessarily be seen to be a violation of the Committee's confidentiality since the letters had been specifically addressed to the Committee members.

548. Another Committee member felt that it was not inappropriate for authors to address themselves directly to Committee members or even public officials outside of the Committee. He felt there was no violation of confidentiality in the mailing in question.

549. The Chairman pointed out that the only channel for the Committee to receive documentation was through the Secretariat and that the documentation in question could therefore not be brought into the discussion.

550. Another Committee member felt that the matter of the mailings was not a breach of Committee confidentiality and was in fact a petty issue; he felt it should not sidetrack the Committee from its examination of the case.

551. Addressing the substantive aspects of the communication, the representative of the Soviet Government stated that there were two main questions involved in the case.

552. The first was to what extent the Soviet Union was justified for national security reasons to assign Dr Sakharov to live in the city of Gorky, where his contact with others was limited. He reminded the Committee that Dr Sakharov had been working in fields where he acquired information of high national security importance. He added that this was a question which only the appropriate security authorities of the Soviet Union could judge, not the authors or the Committee.

553. The other question was to what extent sanctions were appropriate against Dr Sakharov for his having made statements contrary to the strategic interests of the Soviet Union. It had been shown that Dr Sakharov had made such statements, for example his statements in favour of the stationing of missiles, aimed at the USSR, on European soil. It appeared that Dr Sakharov still maintained his attitude. The representative of the Soviet Government quoted a recent article in *The Washington Post* to emphasize this point. A decision had thus been taken, he said, by the highest Soviet authorities to isolate Dr Sakharov, since his views were dangerous and went against the mainstream of the Soviet people's thinking.

554. Nevertheless, Dr Sakharov still had the possibility of continuing his scientific work, the representative of the Soviet Government went on. He still worked with the prestigious Lebedev Institute, he had the chance to set up his own scientific programme, he still had ample access to library facilities in Gorky, and he still had the possibility of publishing his works. By his own choice he published in the *Journal of Experimental and Theoretical Physics*; in fact everything he had submitted to it had been published. The representative of the Soviet Government stated that six members of the French Academy of Sciences and an Australian scientist had confirmed that Dr Sakharov was quite productive despite his situation in Gorky. As to the authors' assertion concerning certain of Dr Sakharov's articles, the articles in question had been submitted to the Soviet journal in a rough form and had to be reworked twice before they could finally be published.

555. The representative of the Soviet Government stated that according to many scientists, Dr Sakharov's work in Gorky, especially in baryon studies, was of definite interest to the scientific community.

556. He conceded that some particular problems might be arising in regard to the provision of scientific supplies, but he felt that the necessary means could always be found to solve such problems.

557. A Committee member stated that top scientists had informed him that Dr Sakharov was one of the most brilliant minds alive in the world today, and that he was paving important new paths on the frontiers of science. However, since the fields of research he was involved in were theoretical, their practical application was not a

present possibility and these narrow and highly specialized fields required many more facilities than those which were given him in Gorky. It also seemed totally unrealistic, he said, to claim that Dr Sakharov still possessed any knowledge which could endanger national security, since he had not been working in related fields for over a decade. Furthermore, on the question of some of the dates of publication of his articles, it seemed most likely that Dr Sakharov was writing about matters which had been taking shape in his mind for years and which he had not been able to put into written form in a short period of time.

558. The Committee member felt that it would be appropriate in the present case to recommend that the Executive Board should ask the Director-General to continue to take appropriate steps in regard to this case.

559. Another Committee member felt that while the Committee could not question the security decisions of Soviet authorities and while the Committee should be careful to look only at matters coming within its competence, it was nevertheless vital that Unesco should manifest its interest in as important a science-related question as this one and that it should continue to monitor the situation, which certainly was a cause for its concern. He added that it was his sincere conviction that if the Soviet authorities could facilitate the Director-General's consultations, the existing mass of anti-Soviet propaganda in the world could probably be considerably deflated. It was his hope that the Soviet authorities could co-operate closely with the Director-General.

560. After discussion, and on the proposal of the Chairman, the Committee decided:[11]

(i) to take note of the additional information duly submitted by the author of the communication, while greatly regretting the circulation of the letter of 14 August 1981 among the members of the Committee in ways that did not conform with the provisions of 104 EX/Decision 3.3 and, more particularly, paragraph 14 (*b*) and to direct the Secretariat to draw the attention of the author of the communication to the extreme importance it attaches to the scrupulous respect of the confidential nature of its procedures;

(ii) to take note of the new information provided by the representative of the government concerned regarding the circumstances in which Andrei Sakharov is able to pursue his scientific research in Gorky, the city where he has been placed under house arrest for security reasons;

---

[11] See document 113 EX/38 PRIV., para. 342 (*supra*, p. 533).

(iii) to request the Executive Board to invite the Director-General to continue his consultations with the Soviet authorities, in conformity with paragraph 8 (*b*) of 104 EX/Decision 3.3 and, more particularly, with such scientific authorities of the USSR as are able to provide further information on the application of Unesco's Recommendation on the Status of Scientific Researchers, as it relates to the allegations contained in [the present communication].

561. On 22 March 1982, the Secretariat received a letter from the Lawyers Committee for International Human Rights and a letter from Ms Liza Alexeyeva, both of which appear in [a Committee document].[12]

562. At the Committee's present session the representative of the Soviet Government reminded the Committee that it had at its [autumn 1981] session decided to concentrate on the question as to whether Dr Sakharov was free to continue his scientific activities. That decision had clearly delimited the scope of the inquiry that the Committee would undertake, he said.

563. The Soviet representative explained that Dr Sakharov had in the past months been working on a multifaceted model of the universe and that this study had in fact been finalized in March of this year. The work dealt with fundamental questions of cosmology and had been sent by Dr Sakharov to be published as an article in the scientific *Journal of Experimental and Theoretical Physics*. The Soviet representative circulated a copy of the manuscript and stated that it was planned for publication in 1982. He went on to say that this manuscript irrefutably showed that Dr Sakharov was free to continue his scientific activities, and the fact that the article would be published showed that his ideas were being allowed to circulate.

564. The Soviet representative further explained that Dr Sakharov had the possibility of contacting other scientists and he read a recent letter of Dr Sakharov's in which the scientist mentioned that he had been visited by scientists such as Drs Fainberg, Kalashnikov and Linde and that he looked forward to the visit of others from the Academy of Sciences Institute of Physics. The Soviet representative stated that he had been informed that the scientists in question would be allowed to visit Dr Sakharov at the expense of the Institute.

565. The Soviet representative further explained that the equipment and literature which Dr Sakharov needed for his activities was being duly provided to him by the Soviet authorities and that the results of his work were permitted to be made public. The Soviet representative felt that to the extent that the Committee had been informed of the progress made in the situation of Dr Sakharov the decision taken by it

[12] See document 114 EX/CR/HR/2 Add.

at its [autumn 1981] session had been complied with and that there was no longer any reason to continue the examination of this case.

566. A Committee member stated that he saw no change in the basic problem, i.e. that a scientist had been placed in confinement arbitrarily, without legal proceedings by the authorities, and that his right to pursue his activities had correspondingly been limited.

567. The Committee member raised the question as to what a private letter of Dr Sakharov was doing in a government file. He stated furthermore that the text of that letter showed the exact opposite of what the Soviet representative asserted it did, since it showed that Dr Sakharov hoped that exceptions would be made to the restrictions which existed on visiting possibilities. The Committee member emphasized that Dr Sakharov was a great scientist who needed to be allowed the freedom to pursue his work if he was to make the great contribution of which he was capable to the Soviet Union and the world.

568. The Soviet representative stated that he found himself in a perplexing situation; he wondered if it was worthwhile co-operating with the Committee if it was necessary to submit documentation for every trivial question which was raised. He stated that Dr Sakharov was not in fact "banned" to Gorky; that term was not completely accurate. It was pointed out that the Committee had asked the Soviet scientific organizations to comment on whether or not Dr Sakharov was being allowed to practise his profession, and the photocopy of the article which was going to be published addressed that question directly. The letter which had been read, the Soviet representative said, was an official document sent by Dr Sakharov to the heads of the department of the institute in question. It had been officially received and could thus be officially mentioned. While there were indeed limitations on Dr Sakharov concerning contacts with foreign scientists, there were no such limitations on contacts with Soviet scientists. Dr Sakharov's request to be visited was a normal one and was not a request for exceptions. It was Dr Sakharov who had stated that there had been a change in certain circumstances, which showed that Dr Sakharov himself, no longer wished to inflame the situation.

569. The authors of the communication had distorted the situation the Soviet representative said. The new information which he had submitted totally reported the allegations and the Committee should not allow itself to be drawn into a case of agitation.

570. A Committee member pointed out that whatever term was used the fact was that Dr Sakharov was living under an enforced residence which significantly interfered with his ability to carry out his scientific activities.

571. Another Committee member pointed out that the restrictions imposed on this scientist did indeed go against the provision of the Universal Declaration of Human Rights which set forth the right to freedom of movement and residence within the borders of each state, but the Committee member also indicated that he understood that Dr Sakharov was being allowed to continue his work, which was important for the Soviet Union.

572. The Soviet representative explained that there were indeed a number of restrictions placed on Dr Sakharov but that certain special circumstances existed in this case. These circumstances were within the purview of the State authorities and did not contravene national law. The letter of Dr Sakharov showed that the reasons for earlier restrictions on contacts with Soviet scientists had now disappeared and that indeed visits by scientists would now be even paid for by Soviet authorities.

573. A Committee member raised the question as to whether Dr Sakharov himself was free to go and visit scientists if he wished, and he also pointed out that it was clear that foreign scientists were not being allowed to visit Dr Sakharov.

574. Another Committee member expressed the opinion that the fact that a person was a great thinker did not free that person from the obligations incumbent on all citizens. No right was absolute, he said. He pointed out that the United Nations Human Rights Commission had decided not to pursue this case, and he stated that there was no reason for a Unesco Committee to feel that it should continue its examination of this case when another Committee had decided not to do so.

575. Certain Committee members expressed their appreciation to the Soviet representative for having provided up-to-date information on Dr Sakharov's situation, but doubted that the fact that Dr Sakharov had produced one article showed that he was free of all restrictions in the pursuit of his activities. They felt that the letter presented and the statement made by the Soviet representative, while certainly showing that Dr Sakharov was not entirely prevented from carrying out scientific activities, also definitely showed that significant restrictions on his activities did in fact still exist. For this reason they felt that the Committee's decision on this case taken at its [autumn 1981] session should still be applied.

576. Another Committee member stated that he, as a physicist, was particularly interested in this case, and he was personally aware that the international scientific community was also following the case very closely. He pointed out that scientists were just as human as other persons and that while they were certainly subject to the same laws as other citizens, it might be good to be especially tolerant of them since the nature of their work gave them heavy responsibilities and sometimes led them to make stronger pronouncements than other persons.

Union of Soviet Socialist Republics **No. 195/80**

577. The Soviet representative stated that it had been Dr Sakharov's concern about his daughter-in-law which had led Dr Sakharov himself to refuse the visits of scientists. Since that concern was now past, and since the Committee had already discussed the substance of the case at length, the Soviet representative wondered whether the Committee could not now strike the case from its list.

578. A Committee member felt that the Committee could probably put certain aspects of the case behind it but that since Dr Sakharov was still in enforced residence in Gorky a dropping of the case would not be appropriate.

579. The Committee thereupon *decided*:

(i) to take note of the information which, in response to the requests made and the concerns expressed at its [autumn 1981] session, the representative of the government concerned had provided on Dr Sakharov's recent scientific research and on the opportunities available to him to make contact with scientists in order to continue his scientific research;

(ii) aware of the fact that the communication in issue was submitted as long ago as 1980 and quite a number of circumstances then relevant have in the interim changed, the Committee suspends further consideration of the communication as now formulated; and

(iii) to ask the Director-General to continue his efforts to obtain additional information about the possibilities for Dr Sakharov to pursue his scientific work in accordance with the Recommendation on the Status of Scientific Researchers (20 November 1974) keeping in mind the concern expressed by members of the Committee with regard to this matter.

No. 196/80

Concerning *Denmark*
Case of *Kai Mogens H. Lång*

Communication of 3 November 1979 submitted by
Kai Mogens H. Lång

Autumn 1980 session of the Committee on Conventions and Recommendations (110th session of the Executive Board)[1]

63. This case was submitted to the Committee on Conventions and Recommendations at its [autumn 1979] session, when it decided after discussion that this communication was not admissible.[2] The author of the communication and the Government concerned were informed of the Committee's decision on 30 October 1979 and 17 December 1979 respectively.

64. The author of the communication wrote on 3 November 1979, 1 January and 11 February 1980 to resubmit his case to Unesco, alleging the inaccuracy of the information communicated by the Danish Government, on which the Committee's decision was based.

65. This communication concerns the alleged violation of the Unesco Convention against Discrimination in Education (Article 3 (*c*) and (*d*)) and several articles in the International Covenants on Human Rights.

66. The author of the communication, a Swedish student, alleges that since 1975, the Danish university authorities have refused him the stipend provided for under Danish law, claiming that this measure has been taken because of his political convictions. Mr Lång admits he has not exhausted all means of legal redress for financial reasons, but asserts that he has already had recourse to all administrative remedies.

[1] See document 110 EX/40 PRIV., paras. 63-73; see also document 110 EX/CR/HR/3.
[2] See document 108 EX/38 PRIV., para. 161 (*supra*, p. 370), communication No. 144/79 concerning *Denmark*, case of *Kai Mogens H. Lång*.

No. 196/80 **Denmark**

67. The representntive of the Danish Government pointed out that this case had been studied by the Danish Ombudsman who had concluded that the person concerned had in no way been the victim of discrimination. The Ombudsman had considered that this student, who had been entitled to a State stipend up to 1975, had had his stipend withdrawn because he no longer sat examinations or attended lectures, and accordingly no longer fulfilled all the conditions provided for in law No. 113 of 9 April 1975 in respect of university grants. The representative of the Government concerned stressed the fact that the decision taken concerning Mr Lång was based exclusively on the conditions provided for by the law and that there had been no political, religious or any other form of discrimination whatsoever against Mr Lång, or against the members of any group whatsoever.

68. At the present session, Mr Lång submitted further documents to the Committee, which he claimed would demonstrate that he was the victim of a discriminatory application of the relevant Danish laws and regulations, and that the Ombudsman had refused to consider his case.

69. The representative of the Danish Government stated that he did not consider that the communication contained any new facts. He repeated the information that he had already provided at the [autumn 1979] session, and to support it he quoted a letter addressed to Mr Lång by the Cmbudsman, which clearly established that, contrary to Mr Lång's claims, the former had considered his case, but that he had found no reason to criticize the decision of the Court of Appeal, since Mr Lång had never taken an examination or furnishad proof of his ability to study. The representative of the Danish Government therefore proposed to consider this case inadmissible.

70. All the speakers voiced their agreement that the communication should be declared inadmissible. One speaker wished to call in question the possibility of submitting a further communication when a decision of the Committee had already been taken on the same case. Another stated that he shared that point of view, and that if a communication did not furnish any new facts, it should not be re-examined, but that otherwise it was equitable to do so.

71. The representative of the Director-General stated that it was not a matter of encouraging the authors to submit the same allegations to the Committee more than once, but that, even in the absence of the right of appeal explicitly laid down by 104 EX/Decision 3.3, the doors should not be closed, especially since the Committee, pursuant to 104 EX/Decision 3.3, had the power to oppose any abuse of the right to submit communications (para. 14 (*a*) (vi)). Furthermore, the same practice was current in other international bodies with authority on human rights.

Denmark **No. 196/80**

72. He suggested that the Committee request the Secretariat to urge authors wishing to submit a further communication to ensure that it contained new facts, in the absence of which their communication would be rejected as abusive.

73. The Committee *decided*:

[i] to declare the communication inadmissible as constituting an abuse of the right to submit communications;

[ii] to agree to the examination of communications (concerning a case or a question already submitted to the Committee) which contained new facts;

[iii] to request the Secretariat to urge authors wishing to submit a further communication to ensure that the latter contained new facts, in the absence of which their communication would be declared inadmissible as an abuse of the right to submit communications.

No. 197/80

Concerning *Chile*
Case of *Ernesto Ottone Fernández*

Communication of 18 December 1979 submitted by
Ernesto Ottone Fernández

Spring 1981 session of the Committee on Conventions and Recommendations (112th session of the Executive Board)[1]

68. The author of the communication is a sociologist and President of the World Federation of Democratic Youth (WFDY) , an organization having consultative status (category B) with Unesco. On 5 December 1979 he was allegedly detained at Santiago airport, along with Dr Jaime Pinzón (Colombian Liberal Party Deputy) and Mr Roberto Guerzoni (of the Italian Committee of Youth for International Relations, attached to the Italian Ministry of Foreign Affairs), all three of them members of a WFDY delegation invited to participate in an advisory meeting with ECLA (United Nations Economic Commission for Latin America) and to make contact with various sectors of Chilean youth.

69. The representative of the government concerned informed the Committee that WFDY was an organization which was hostile to the Chilean Government; it was trying to make the Committee believe that ECLA had invited it to a meeting, whereas neither ECLA nor the Unesco Regional Office in Santiago, with which he had been in touch, had any knowledge of such a meeting.

70. From the outset, a number of members of the Committee considered that, given such contradictions between the statements by the author and those of the government regarding the facts, it was necessary to ask the author for additional information on the ECLA meeting.

71. Some members pointed out that the right allegedly violated in the case in question was not the complainant's right to enter his own country, but the right to perform his functions as President of a non-governmental organization having consulta-

[1] See document 112 EX/30 PRIV., paras. 68-74; see also document 112 EX/CR/HR/3.

tive status, category B, with Unesco, and that therefore, in order to determine whether the case fell within Unesco's sphere of competence, better information was needed about the circumstances of the ECLA meeting. Other members considered that the communication was inadmissible from the outset; either because it was not sufficiently precise, or because the author had made no effort to exhaust domestic remedies. Finally, while not contesting the exemplary value of questions of principle, some members questioned whether action by the Committee on a past problem would be meaningful, and observed in that connection that the purpose and aim of the communication had not been specified. One member deplored the lack of courtesy thus shown by authors to Unesco, pointing out that the provision of imprecise and incomplete information lengthened the discussions in the Committee.

72. The representative of the Chilean Government spoke again, stressing that the determining factor in the decision taken by the Chilean authorities was that the author had given a false reason for entering the country, since, according to the information obtained, there was no such ECLA meeting, and that accordingly the measure taken was entirely justified. If the author had really been invited to that meeting, he should be able to produce the written invitation.

73. Thereafter, many members declared themselves in favour of postponing examination of the communication so that, in the meantime, additional information might be requested from the author.

74. The Committee accordingly *decided* to suspend examination of the communication until its next session, and to request the Secretariat to write meanwhile to the author, in order, firstly, to inform him of the existence of other procedures, including those available on the basis of the Headquarters Agreement between ECLA and the Chilean Government, and, secondly, to request him to specify the circumstances of the ECLA meeting, and, if possible, to provide written evidence in support of his statements.

Autumn 1981 session of the Committee on Conventions and Recommendations (113th session of the Executive Board)[2]

108. The author of the communication is a sociologist and President of the World Federation of Democratic Youth (WFDY), an organization having consultative status (category B) with Unesco. On 5 December 1979 he was allegedly detained at Santiago airport, along with Dr Jaime Pinzón (Colombian Liberal Party Deputy) and

---

[2] See document 113 EX/38 PRIV., paras. 108-122; see also documents 113 EX/CR/HR/2 and Add. and Add.8.

Mr Roberto Guerzoni (of the Italian Committee of Youth for International Relations, attached to the Italian Ministry of Foreign Affairs), all three of them members of a WFDY delegation invited to participate in an advisory meeting with ECLA (United Nations Economic Commission for Latin America) and to make contact with various sectors of Chilean youth.

109. At the [spring 1981] session, the representative of the government concerned informed the Committee that WFDY was an organization which was hostile to the Chilean Government; it had been trying to make the Committee believe that ECLA had invited it to a meeting, whereas neither ECLA nor the Unesco Regional Office in Santiago, with which he had been in touch, had any knowledge of such a meeting.

110. From the outset, a number of members of the Committee considered that, given such contradictions between the statements by the author and those of the government regarding the facts, it was necessary to ask the author for additional information on the ECLA meeting.

111. Some members pointed out that the right allegedly violated in the case in question was not the complainant's right to enter his own country, but the right to perform his functions as President of a non-governmental organization having consultative status, category B, with Unesco, and that, therefore, in order to determine whether the case fell within Unesco's sphere of competence, better information was needed about the circumstances of the ECLA meeting. Other members considered that the communication was inadmissible from the outset, either because it was not sufficiently precise, or because the author had made no effort to exhaust domestic remedies. Finally, while not contesting the exemplary value of questions of principle, some members questioned whether action by the Committee on a past problem would be meaningful, and observed in that connection that the purpose and aim of the communication had not been specified. One member deplored the lack of courtesy thus shown by the authors to Unesco, pointing out that the provision of imprecise and incomplete information lengthened the discussions in the Committee.

112. The representative of the Chilean Government spoke again, stressing that the determining factor in the decision taken by the Chilean authorities was that the author had given a false reason for entering the country, since, according to the information obtained, there was no such ECLA meeting, and that accordingly the measure taken was entirely justified. If the author had really been invited to such a meeting, he should be able to produce the written invitation.

113. Thereafter, many members declared themselves in favour of postponing examination of the communication so that, in the meantime, additional information might be requested from the author.

No. 197/80 **Chile**

114. The Committee accordingly decided to suspend examination of the communication until the present session, and to request the Secretariat to write meanwhile to the author, in order, firstly, to inform him of the existence of other procedures, including those available on the basis of the Headquarters Agreement between ECLA and the Chilean Government, and, secondly, to request him to specify the circumstances of the ECLA meeting, and, if possible, to provide written evidence in support of his statements.[3]

115. At the present session, the Committee was informed that the Secretariat had received a letter dated 6 July 1981 from Mr Ottone Fernández [...],[4] in which the author stated, first, that he "found it incomprehensible that a Chilean citizen, in possession of documents perfectly in order, should be required to invoke any reason for entering his country", and, secondly, confirmed that the ECLA meeting referred to had indeed been scheduled to take place; enclosed with the letter were photocopies of the following:

(i) an official communication from ECLA demonstrating, according to the author, the existence of working relations between ECLA and the World Federation of Democratic Youth (WFDY) and mentioning the idea of a visit;

(ii) a telegram referring to consultations in connection with such a visit;

(iii) a cable confirming ECLA's intention to organize the meeting in question.

116. Mr Ottone Fernández also mentioned in his letter that an ECLA official had been present at the airport at the time of his arrival.

117. The representative of the Government of Chile pointed out that by his letter of 6 July 1981 Mr Ottone Fernández had altered his initial communication relating to the alleged violation of the Headquarters Agreement with ECLA, the organization which, it was claimed, had sponsored the meeting to which Mr Ottone Fernández had been on his way, since he was, in fact, raising the problem of his right to return to Chile; the Chilean representative stated that he wished to pursue the question initially raised.

118. In this connection he had a copy of a letter dated 27 August 1981 from ECLA to the Ministry of Foreign Affairs of Chile, in which the Commission indicated that the Days on the Rights and Duties of Youth which had been held in Chile from 7 to

---

[3] See document 112 EX/30 PRIV., para. 74 (*supra*, p. 552).
[4] See document 113 EX/CR/HR/2 Add.

10 December 1979 had enjoyed "neither the patronage nor the co-operation of ECLA, which in fact learned of them only through the Chilean press". He considered therefore that the information placed by the author at the Committee's disposal was false.

119. One member of the Committee stated that if ECLA had learned of the meeting in question only through the Chilean press, it was strange that an ECLA official should have been at the airport when the WFDY delegation had arrived and that the author should have been able to produce the documents referred to above. Consequently, he requested that the letter from ECLA be reproduced and examination of the communication deferred until the end of the session.

120. The representative of the Chilean Government pointed out that the letter in question was signed by the Secretary-General of ECLA and that this, de facto and *de jure*, rendered all other statements or acts by subordinate officials of ECLA null and void. Other members of the Committee also declared themselves to be in favour of postponing examination of the communication.

121. When this communication was again placed on the Committee's agenda, the Committee had at its disposal photocopies of the documents mentioned in Mr Ottone Fernández's letter and of the ECLA letter of 27 August 1981 [...].[5]

122. After studying these documents, the Committee *decided* to declare the communication inadmissible as being manifestly ill-founded in that it did not contain relevant evidence within the meaning of paragraph 14 (*a*) (v) of 104 EX/Decision 3.3.

[5] See document 113 EX/CR/HR/2 Add.8.

No. 200/80

Concerning *Spain*
Case of *Emilio Mansera Conde*

Communication of 30 January 1980 submitted by
Emilio Mansera Conde

Spring 1980 session of the Committee on Conventions and Recommendations (109th session of the Executive Board)[1]

130. The author of this communication alleges that various educational, scientific and cultural rights of the Andalusian people are being systematically violated by the Spanish Government.

131. The representative of the Spanish Government stated that his government found the assertions in the communication to be manifestly ill-founded, especially in light of the national legislation existing in Spain to prevent discrimination against ethnic groups. The representative also pointed out that there had not even been an attempt to exhaust the many domestic remedies which were available in such cases.

132. While pointing to the fact that the conditions for admissibility did not require the exhaustion of all domestic remedies, several members of the Committee agreed that in this case the fact that there had not even been an attempt at such remedies seriously weakened the case for admissibility and stated that they felt the communication was inadmissible, being manifestly ill-founded.

133. After a brief discussion the Committee *decided* that the communication was manifestly ill-founded and therefore inadmissible.

---

[1] See document 109 EX/52 PRIV., paras. 130-133; see also documents 109 EX/CR/HR/3 Add. and Add.2.

No. 203/79

Concerning *Yugoslavia*
Case of *Vladimir Bonačić* et al.[*]

Communication of 5 February 1980 submitted by
Vladimir Bonačić

Spring 1980 session of the Committee on Conventions and Recommendations (109th session of the Executive Board)[1]

190. The author of this communication, presenting himself as a professor of art and information systems of Yugoslav nationality, complains that both he and two other persons whose professions are respectively an information system designer and an architect in computer lighting systems, have been arbitrarily excluded from a project for creating a multi-media, electronic library system for a university library. Since November 1978 the three persons concerned are reported to have been prevented from pursuing their intellectual work on information systems and from publishing on any subject. Other measures are also said to have been taken against them, including criminal charges.

191. The representative of the Yugoslav Government stated that this communication was completely ill-founded and full of misrepresentations. First of all, these persons had not been dismissed; when their design was rejected by the various bodies of the library, they themselves had resigned. Furthermore, the author of the communication was not a professor of art, he was simply a lecturer. Finally, there were no charges or proceedings taken against them and they have not been prevented from working as could be seen from their recent exhibitions in Zagreb and other cities. It was also pointed out that these persons did not resort to available remedies for the alleged violation, but rather addressed themselves to officials who were not competent in labour law.

---

[*] Case of *Vladimir Bonačić, Miroljub Cimerman and Dunya Donassy.*
[1] See document 109 EX/52 PRIV., paras. 190-192; see also documents 109 EX/CR/HR/3 and Add.3.

No. 203/79 **Yugoslavia**

192. The Committee, after brief discussion, came to the conclusion that the affair appeared to be essentially a labour dispute involving professional qualifications and *decided* that it was inadmissible as manifestly ill-founded.

No. 205/80

Concerning *German Democratic Republic*
Case of *Michael Haugk*

Communication of 8 February 1980 submitted by
Suzanne Szydlo

Autumn 1980 session of the Committee on Conventions and Recommendations (110th session of the Executive Board)[1]

119. The author of the communication alleges that Mr Michael Haugk, an electronics engineer, was arrested on 16 March 1978 for criticizing the electoral system and foreign policy of the GDR and sentenced on 22 August 1978 to three years and eight months' detention. According to a former fellow detainee, the prisoner's state of health is very bad.

120. In a letter dated 21 August 1980, the representative of the Government of the GDR informed the Committee that no one named Michael Haugk existed in Karl-Marx-Stadt, that no such trial had taken place on 22 August 1978 and that no such person had been sentenced in the GDR.

121. A consensus very quickly emerged to the effect that the communication was devoid of substance since the alleged victim did not appear to exist.

122. The Committee *decided* to declare the communication inadmissible as being manifestly ill-founded.

[1] See document 110 EX/40 PRIV., paras. 119-122; see also document 110 EX/CR/HR/3.

No. 209/80

Concerning *Union of Soviet Socialist Republics*
Case of *Yosif Z. Begun*

Communication of 22 February 1980 submitted by
American Jewish Committee and
National Conference on Soviet Jewry

Spring 1980 session of the Committee on Conventions and Recommendations (109th session of the Executive Board)[1]

159. This communication submitted by the American Jewish Committee and the National Conference on Soviet Jewry, lists 10 international instruments relating to human rights of which a certain number of provisions are said to have been violated by the USSR. It further quotes the Constitution of the USSR and that of the RSFSR, a number of provisions of which are also said to have been violated.

160. As concerns the connection between the alleged violations and the fields of competence of Unesco, the communication states that the alleged victim is a scientist and a teacher of mathematics and Hebrew. It is stated that the Hebrew language is essential to the survival of Jewish national culture and that by prohibiting Mr Begun from teaching this language, he and other Jews in the USSR are being deprived of basic rights in the fields of education, religion, culture, language and information.

161. Mr Begun, is said to have been deprived of his employment in 1971 after having submitted a request for an exit visa for Israel; since he has been unable to find any other work, he is said to have taken up teaching mathematics and Hebrew. His requests to be registered as a teacher of this language were reportedly turned down and on 3 March 1977 he was allegedly arrested for "parasitic mode of life"; on 1 June 1977 he was reportedly sentenced to exile in Siberia for two years; on his return on 17 May 1978 he is said to have been arrested for having been in illegal residence in Moscow, and was again sentenced to three years' exile in Siberia on 28 June 1978, a sentence which he is still serving. According to the authors of the com-

[1] See document 109 EX/52 PRIV., paras. 159-169; see also document 109 EX/CR/HR/3 Add.

munication, Mr Begun's exile is the direct result of his not being allowed to teach Hebrew.

162. The representative of the Soviet Government informed the Committee that the Jewish communities in the USSR felt that the organizations submitting this communication were interfering with their affairs. The Soviet representative stated that these organizations had participated in anti-Soviet conferences and did not have a friendly attitude toward the Soviet Union. He doubted the sincerity of the communication.

163. Furthermore, he insisted that the communication was based on erroneous contentions. For one thing, Mr Begun's offence was not that he was a Jew or a teacher of Hebrew; it was that he was a parasite, that is to say he was not gainfully employed in a useful activity as was required by the Soviet law. It was known that Mr Begun had lived for many years on funds sent from abroad. Also, it was clear, said the Soviet representative, that Mr Begun could not have been a teacher of Hebrew since he had gone to a technical school and had learned electronics, not Hebrew. In any event, Mr Begun had had only four students and these would not have been sufficient to provide him a living.

164. As for the contention that the teaching of Hebrew was being stifled, this was not true. Furthermore, Hebrew had never been a national language of the Soviet Jewry, their national language having always been Yiddish. The Soviet Union had the greatest respect for the Yiddish language and a tremendous amount of Yiddish literature was published there every year, he said.

165. The Soviet representative summed up by stating that Mr Begun's sentencing had had no relation to his teaching of Hebrew, that there was no link between this case and Unesco's fields of competence, and the communication should therefore be considered as manifestly ill-founded and inadmissible.

166. One Committee member stated that he did not find the communication to be ill-founded but he was not sure what the link with Unesco's fields of competence was.

167. Other Committee members stated that this case contained several clear issues of concern to Unesco, among them the questions whether there had been a violation of the right of a scientist to leave his country, wheher there had been a violation of the right to teach, whether there existed a violation of an ethnic group's right to its own culture, and so on. One of the members indicated concern over the fact that Mr Begun had had a problem-free employment record for 22 years and had been faced with an absolute impossibility of being employed as of the time he had applied for an exit visa to Israel. Furthermore, he stated that it appeared from an official docu-

ment in the file that the Moscow Ministry of Finance had informed Mr Begun that in the USSR Hebrew was taught neither in governmental institutes of higher and intermediate education nor in schools of general education and had therefore specifically refused Mr Begun's attempt to work as a teacher of Hebrew on the grounds that it was not a "useful activity".

168. The representative of the Soviet Government stated that it would serve no purpose to continue to dwell on meaningless contradictions; and he added that Mr Begun had on his own left his electronics job months before applying for his exit visa because he had been afraid he might be refused the visa on national security reasons. As concerned the letter from the Moscow Finance Ministry, the Soviet representative suggested that the Committee not look to those tax authorities as a source of information on what was or was not being taught in the Soviet Union. It was explained that Mr Begun's attempts to teach Hebrew just served as a guise for his parasitism. The Soviet representative stated that it might be appropriate to ask for humanitarian action in this case but that the Committee should not admit it on the basis of the false generalizations it contained.

169. After considerable debate on the above issues the Committee *decided*:

(i) to request the authors of the communication to supplement the information already provided concerning the extent to which the right to teach Hebrew exists in the Soviet Union, and particularly to ask if this right can be exercised by a person who does not have professional teaching qualifications;

(ii) to suspend the examination of the admissibility of this communication;

(iii) to express the wish that a humanitarian solution be applied to this case.

Autumn 1980 session of the Committee on Conventions and Recommendations (110th session of the Executive Board)[2]

201. This communication submitted by the American Jewish Committee and the National Conference on Soviet Jewry, lists 10 international instruments relating to human rights of which a certain number of provisions are said to have been violated by the USSR. It also quotes the Constitution of the USSR and that of the RSFSR, a number of provisions of which are also said to have been violated.

[2] See document 110 EX/40 PRIV., paras. 201-[211a]; see also documents 110 EX/CR/HR/2 and Add.

202. As concerns the connection between the alleged violations and the fields of competence of Unesco, the communication states that the alleged victim is a scientist and a teacher of mathematics and Hebrew. It is stated that the Hebrew language is essential to the survival of Jewish national culture and that by prohibiting Mr Begun from teaching this language, the USSR is depriving him and other Jews in the USSR of basic rights in the fields of education, religion, culture, language and information.

203. Mr Begun is said to have been deprived of his employment in 1971 after having submitted a request for an exit visa for Israel; since he has been unable to find any other work, he is said to have taken up teaching mathematics and Hebrew. His requests to be registered as a teacher of this language were reportedly turned down and on 3 March 1977 he was allegedly arrested for "parasitic mode of life"; on 1 June 1977 he was reportedly sentenced to exile in Siberia for two years; on his return on 17 May 1978 he is said to have been arrested for having been in illegal residence in Moscow, and was again sentenced to three years' exile in Siberia on 28 June 1978, a sentence which he is still serving.

204. At its [spring 1980] session the Committee decided:[3]

(i) to request the authors of the communication to supplement the information already provided concerning the extent to which the right to teach Hebrew exists in the Soviet Union, and particularly to ask if this right can be exercised by a person who does not have professional teaching qualifications;

(ii) to suspend the examination of the admissibility of this communication;

(iii) to express the wish that a humanitarian solution be applied to this case.

205. The representative of the Soviet Goverment informed the Committee that Mr Yosif Begun had been released on 16 August 1980 and was at present preparing to leave the Siberian region; the provisions of paragraph 14 (*a*) (x) of 104 EX/Decision 3.3 were therefore applicable and the matter should be declared settled.

206. A member of the Committee asked whether this meant that Mr Begun would be allowed to live in Moscow with his family and teach Hebrew. Another member pointed out that, as the authors had responded to the questions asked by the Committee, their reply [...][4] should be examined, since the communication raised the

[3] See document 109 EX/52 PRIV., para. 169 (*supra*, p. 565).
[4] See document 110 EX/CR/HR/2 Add.

wider problem of the right of the Jewish minority to benefit from the teaching of Hebrew.

207. It was debated whether the communication constituted a case or a question as defined in 104 EX/Decision 3.3. The representative of the Soviet Government considered that "it was manifestly an individual case that has been settled". A Committee member pointed out that while, formally speaking, the initial communication cited Mr Begun only as the alleged victim, it in fact concerned the status of Hebrew teaching and teachers in general; according to another member, the Committee was in a way confronted with two communications: one concerning the case of Mr Begun, whose situation had now changed, the other relating to a general question which had not yet been settled.

208. The representative of the Director-General stated that although the author in his response to the Committee's request concerning the circumstances under which Hebrew could be taught in the USSR had emphasized the "question" angle of the communication, the form clearly referred to an individual case; the maxim "electa una via non obviam ad alteram" laid down a general legal principle according to which once a particular form of appeal had been chosen, it could not be replaced by another.

209. On the subject of Mr Begun himself, several members expressed concern about his future prospects as a teacher of Hebrew: since his release involved no commitment in that respect, the problem might recur at any moment.

210. The representative of the Director-General recalled that when new facts arose in a case that had been struck off the list and these were brought to the Committee's attention by the author of the communication, the Secretariat, in the absence of the right of appeal provided for in 104 EX/Decision 3.3, would regard this as a new communication, which would be submitted as such for examination by the Committee. Any person or non-governmental organization was at liberty to apprise Unesco of either a case or a question as defined in 104 EX/Decision 3.3.

211. At the proposal of the Chairman, who noted that the members of the Committee were in general agreement as to the individual nature of this communication and that the alleged victim had recovered his freedom, the Committee *decided* to note that the matter raised in this communication had been settled as an individual case and as such should therefore be struck from its list.

211[a]. A member of the Committee stated that he would have to express a reservation concerning this decision.

No. 210/80

Concerning *Yugoslavia*
Case of *Kadri Osmani*

Communication of 12 February 1980 submitted by
Keneth Meisel

Autumn 1980 session of the Committee on Conventions and Recommendations (110th session of the Executive Board)[1]

220. The author of the communication, Mr Keneth Meisel, acting on behalf of the Basel Group of Amnesty International, claims that Mr Kadri Osmani, a teacher, was arrested, judged and imprisoned in 1975 for expressing views favourable to Albanian nationalism and for belonging to an association with Albanian nationalist sympathies. By these actions the Yugoslav Government is alleged to have violated Article 19 (freedom of expression) and 22 (freedom of association) of the International Covenant on Civil and Political Rights and is also alleged to have refused to give information on the conditions of detention and state of health of Mr Kadri Osmani.

221. The representative of the Yugoslav Government considered that this communication was outside Unesco's fields of competence. Mr Kadri Osmani had not been imprisoned as a teacher or for having expressed his ideas but because he had engaged in activities contrary to the interests of the State by advocating the secession of a Yugoslav province.

222. He was consequently arrested in 1970, imprisoned for 10 months and enjoined to refrain from activities detrimental to the territorial integrity of his country. Taking no heed of this warning, he had resumed such activities and was therefore rearrested. He was now in prison and his state of health was satisfactory.

223. A Committee member considered the communication inadmissible but thought that Amnesty International should be informed of the reasons for the Committee's decision. The other speakers supported this position.

---

[1] See document 110 EX/40 PRIV., paras. 220-224; see also document 110 EX/CR/HR/3.

No. 210/80 **Yugoslavia**

224. The Committee therefore *decided* that this communication was inadmissible since it did not fall within Unesco's fields of competence.

No. 211/80

Concerning *Argentina*
Case of *Carlos Alberto Pérez and Mirta Silber de Pérez*

Communication of 19 March 1980 submitted by
María Ventura Figueroa de Pérez

Autumn 1980 session of the Committee on Conventions and Recommendations (110th session of the Executive Board)[1]

27. The author of the communication, Mrs María Ventura Figueroa de Pérez, complains of the abduction and disappearance of her son Carlos Alberto Pérez, a clerk, and of the latter's wife, said to be a writer. The victims are said to have been taken from their home on 12 May 1979 at midnight by a group of men claiming to be security officers. They were with four other persons who were apparently also abducted. Since then, the author of the communication has been unable to obtain any information concerning them.

28. The representative of the Argentine Government stated that in his view this communication did not fall within Unesco's fields of competence: the author's son was a clerk, and, since the communication contained no information concerning the civil status of his wife, nothing proved that she was a writer. The Argentine Association of Writers, which had been contacted, did not know of her in that capacity.

29. One member stated that while the case of Carlos Alberto Pérez was clearly inadmissible, a doubt remained concerning his wife, and further information should be requested from the author regarding her. Certain members took the view that the communication was inadmissible as a whole, some considering the link with Unesco's fields of competence to be non-existent, and others finding it too tenuous. Other members suggested that the Argentine Government be requested to show clemency towards the alleged victims. Finally, several members asked why the case of these missing persons should not be sent to the working group of the United Nations Commission on Human Rights.

---

[1] See document 110 EX/40 PRIV., paras. 27-31; see also document 110 EX/CR/HR/3.

No. 211/80 **Argentina**

30. The representative of the Director-General recalled the content of the Committee's decision on missing persons, taken at the [spring 1980] session,[2] which specified in particular that if their disappearance had occurred after 1 June 1978, it remained subject to examination by the Committee; he stated, however, that if the Committee so desired, it could declare the communication inadmissible and decide as an exceptional measure that, although it was not pending, it would be transmitted to the working group.

31. After a brief exchange of views, the Committee *decided* that the communication was inadmissible, since it was not within Unesco's fields of competence, but that, as an exceptional measure and although it was not pending, it would be transmitted to the working group of the United Nations Commission on Human Rights.

[2] See document 109 EX/52 PRIV., annex I, para. 8, and Corr.

No. 218/80

Concerning *Colombia and Uruguay*
Case of *Alba Nelda González Sousa*

Communication of 24 March 1980 submitted by
Rocío Lezama González

Autumn 1980 session of the Committee on Conventions and Recommendations (110th session of the Executive Board)[1]

57. The author of the communication, Miss Rocío Lezama González, the daughter of the alleged victim, complains that, initially in Uruguay and then in Colombia, her mother Mrs Alba Nelda González Sousa, a pianist, was persecuted on account of having taken part in popular cultural and artistic activities and of belonging to the "musicians" section of the "Broad Front" (a left-wing alliance) subsequently disbanded by the military. The alleged victim is reported to have left her native Uruguay and gone with her family to Argentina. Her son is said to have been abducted in 1976 by the Uruguayan and Argentine police. In 1978, the alleged victim is reported to have gone under an assumed identity to Colombia, where she was arrested on 31 January 1979. It is claimed that she was tortured for 15 days, during which she received neither food nor drink, and that, as a result, she had to be treated in the military hospital. After a year of preventive detention, she was brought before a military tribunal - the Court Martial. The alleged victim together with 160 other people accused of belonging to the 19th of April Movement - is currently avaiting trial by the Court Martial at the "La Picota" prison in Bogotá.

58. The representative of the Colombian Govenment explained that Mrs Sousa had entered Colombia clandestinely in 1978 under an assumed name; she was indeed suspected of having participated in terrorist action and arrested for that reason, but since her links with the terrorist group M19 had not been proven, she was released, and remained under the supervision of the competent Bogotá judge only because of her assumed identity; in Colombia, persons accused of falsification of official documents were liable to expulsion; no country had offered to admit her; Uruguay had not requested her extradition. Mrs Sousa was unable to provide evidence of the tor-

[1] See document 110 EX/40 PRIV., paras. 57-62; see also document 110 EX/CR/HR/3.

tures that she claimed to have suffered; if she could do so, she would, under Colombian law, have all appropriate legal facilities at her disposal.

59. The representative of the Uruguayan Government confirmed that his government had not requested the extradition of this person.

60. Many members took up the point that the mere fact that Mrs Sousa was an artist did not bring this communication within the fields of competence of Unesco; the accusations against her had no bearing on Unesco's activities. Some members suggested that the Committee should contact the Office of the High Commissioner for Refugees through the Secretariat, so that a host country might be sought for Mrs Sousa; one member suggested requesting the Colombian Government to grant this person her freedom until a solution had been found, and to facilitate her departure.

61. The representative of the Colombian Government stated that it was difficult for his country to keep Mrs Sousa, and that he would inform the President of the Republic of Colombia of the Committee's suggestions.

62. At the suggestion of the Chairman, the Committee *decided*:

[i] to declare the communication inadmissible;

[ii] to inform the Colombian Government of the Committee's concern to find for Mrs Sousa a host country which would offer her all necessary safeguards so that she might devote herself to her art;

[iii] to request the Executive Board to ask the Director-General to approach the High Commissioner for Refugees so that he might seek a solution to this case.

No. 220/80

Concerning *Argentina*
Case of *Disappearance of scientists and doctors in Argentina*

Communication of 13 February 1980 submitted by
The Lawyers Committee for International Human Rights

Autumn 1980 session of the Committee on Conventions and Recommendations (110th session of the Executive Board)[1]

32. The auther of the communication alleges that since 1976 numerous scientists, doctors and their families have been abducted, arrested and continue to be held without trial, or else have disappeared without explanation. The Argentine medical profession, which prior to 1976 included some highly qualified members and a total medical force proportionately higher than that of the United States, is said to have found itself as a result - like the whole of the Argentine scientific community - seriously weakened and handicapped in its development by these violations of human rights.

33. Some 20 cases involving named individuals are referred to in detail in this communication by way of illustration of its claims.

34. The representative of the Argentine Government considered that the Committee should not examine this communication, which concerned disappearances that had taken place prior to 1978, and that it should therefore be transmitted to the working group of the United Nations Commission on Human Rights.

35. One member pointed out that one of the missing persons constituted an exception, since he was alleged to have been abducted in August 1978, but that it was nevertheless preferable to refer the entire communication to the aforementioned working group. One member recalled that in so doing the Committee was not deciding not to proceed with the affair, but merely suspending its examination.

---

[1] See document 110 EX/40 PRIV., paras. 32-36; see also document 110 EX/CR/HR/3.

No. 220/80 **Argentina**

36. A consensus in favour of referral to the working group very quickly emerged, and the Committee accordingly *decided* to transmit the cases listed in that communication to the working group of the United Nations Commission on Humen Rights.

No. 221/80

Concerning *Romania*
Case of *Remus Radina*

Communication of 28 March 1980 submitted by
Cicerone Ionitoiu

Autumn 1980 session of the Committee on Conventions and Recommendations (110th session of the Executive Board)[1]

131. The author.of the communication, Mr Cicerone Ionitoiu, a Romanian refugee and former teacher, is acting as a friend and representative of the alleged victim, Mr Radina, a former officer, currently a technician, who is reported to have been sentenced to 16 months' imprisonment for having published in a foreign country, without permission from the Romanian Government, a book relating his recollections of life in prison. This sentence was pronounced at a time when Mr Radina's state of health, seriously impaired by 10 years of prison and hard labour between 1946 and 1964, was such that he could not expect to live for more than two or three more years, on condition, furthermore, that he underwent intensive medical care.

[131a.] The author maintains that rights and freedoms protected by Articles 18 (freedom of thought), 19 (freedom of opinion and expression), and 27 (right to a cultural life) of the Universal Declaration of Human Rights have been violated.

132. The representative of the Government of Romania informed the Committee that the alleged victim, a former officer and technician, had been convicted, for a violation of the press laws of Romania and had been sentenced to 16 months in prison plus a fine. The Bucharest appeals court later lowered the fine to the equivalent of $80.00.

[132a.] The Romanian representative explained to the Committee his government's position that the case did not fall within Unesco's competence since the alleged victim's profession was not related thereto and that it should thus not be admitted.

---

[1] See document 110 EX/40 PRIV., paras. 131-137; see also document 110 EX/CR/HR/3.

No. 221/80 **Romania**

133. Furthermore, it was explained, the person in question had been allowed to leave Romania for France on the second of June of this year.

134. Several Committee members stated that although they felt that a link with Unesco's competence could be seen to exist in the alleged violation of the right to freedom of thought, opinion and expression, the fact that the alleged victim had been freed and allowed to leave the country settled the matter and eliminated the need for discussing its admissibility.

135. Another Committee member agreed that the case did not warrant discussion but expressed concern that a slanderous case such as this one had been forwarded to the Committee by the Secretariat.

136. The representative of the Director-General explained to the Committee that it was impossible for the Secretariat to guess in advance whether communications might be considered as slanderous by States concerned and that even if this were possible it vould be inappropriate for the Secretariat to pre-judge and eliminate cases on behalf of the Committee. He reminded the Committee that its procedures contained a specific provision which enabled it to eliminate portions of communications which were considered to be offensive.

137. The Committee promptly *decided* to dismiss the case as having been settled.

No. 222/80

Concerning *Uruguay*
Case of *Elena Beatriz Vasilskis Castro*

Communication of 26 March 1980 submitted by
Sergio Vasilskis

Autumn 1980 session of the Committee on Conventions and Recommendations (110th session of the Executive Board)[1]

212. The author of the communication, Mr Sergio Vasilskis, complains of the detention of his sister, Elena Beatriz Vasilskis Castro, a student teacher, who was arrested on 4 June 1972. It is alleged that Miss Vasilskis Castro has been cited by the Uruguayan Armed Forces as an example of "the infiltration of the education system by Marxist extremists", and that since her arrest she has suffered serious maltreatment and torture which have caused grave deterioration of her health - partial deafness, vitamin deficiency, Raynaud's disease, etc.; the necessary care having been refused her, as well as the opportunity to continue her studies.

213. The author claims that Articles 9 (protection against arbitrary detention), 10 (right to a fair trial), 11 (presumption of innocence), 18 (freedom of thought) and 19 (freedom of opinion and expression) of the Universal Declaration of Human Rights have been violated.

[213a.] To the author's knowledge there has been no recourse to domestic remedies, since the military counsel appointed by the court has not taken the matter up. However, the author has submitted this case to many important individuals and international organizations

214. The representative of the Uruguayan Government informed the Committee that the alleged victim, Miss Castro, had been a member of the Tupamaro terrorist group and had been directly involved in the murders of several public officials. She had been tried and convicted for these and other violent criminal acts in accordance with Uruguayan law and had had legal counsel provided to assure her defence at trial.

---

[1] See document 110 EX/40 PRIV., paras. 212-219; see also document 110 EX/CR/HR/3.

No. 222/80 **Uruguay**

215. As far as the allegations of lack of proper medical attention were concerned, the Uruguayan representative stated that Miss Castro had been receiving all the medical assistance she needed. He went on to point out that Miss Castro herself in her letters gave clear indications that she was in fact seeing doctors end even consulting medical specialists.

216. Several Committee members felt that the case was clearly inadmissable since the necessary connection with Unesco' s fields of competence was missing.

217. One of the Commttee members indicated strong concern over the possibility that one of Miss Castro's defence lawyers might have been forced to leave the country; the Committee member felt that the case should at least be held over while more information was being sought on this point.

218. The Uruguayan representative emphasized to the Committee that none of Miss Castro's lawyers had been forced off the case and that she had always had a lawyer available to her throughout the proceedings. A Committee member who knew the lawyer alleged to have been forced from the country informed the Committee that the departure was in fact voluntary and had taken place several years after Miss Castro's trial.

219. The Committee, after a further exchange of views, *decided* to declare the communication inadmissible as not being related to Unesco's fields of competence and requested the Uruguayan Government to take any further steps which might be possible, to assure that Miss Castro had and continued to have proper medical attention.

No. 223/80

Concerning *Romania*
Case of *The violation of human rights of the Hungarian minority in Romania*

Communication of 27 March 1980 submitted by
The International Human Rights Law Group and
The Committee for Human Rights in Romania

Autumn 1980 session of the Committee on Conventions and Recommendations
(110th session of the Executive Board)[1]

138. The authors of this communication - "The International Human Rights Law Group" and "The Committee for Human Rights in Romania", two non-governmental organizations - claim to be organizations having reliable knowledge of the alleged violations.

139. The auhors of the communication allege that the members of the Hungarian minority living in Romania are victims of flagrant and persistent violation of their human rights and fundamental freedoms. It is claimed that:

(*a*) they cannot freely enjoy the cultural life of their community: Hungarian writers are prevented from publishing their articles in Hungarian literary journals, the number of books published in Hungarian is very small and the importation of Hungarian books is limited by the government; at present there are only two theatrical companies as compared with six 20 years ago in a region with a dense Hungarian population; students of the Hungarian Actors School are discriminated against; Romanian television presents only three hours of Hungarian language programmes per week, on Monday afternoons during working hours;

(*b*) their rights to information and freedom of expression are curbed: official statistics show a decrease in the frequency of Hungarian language publica-

[1] See document 110 EX/40 PRIV., paras. 138-147; see also documents 110 EX/CR/HR/3 and Add.3.

tions and in the number of pages of Hungarian newspapers, and only Hungarian language newspapers as opposed to Romanian language newspapers have been affected by the restrictions on newsprint;

(*c*) the Romanian Government has a deliberate policy of dispersing Hungarian residents in Romania and of transferring Romanian workers into traditionally Hungarian areas; moreover; it falsifies statistics concerning the Hungarian population in an effort to reduce the actual numerical importance of the Hungarian minority in Romania, distorts historical facts to the advantage of the Romanian population and shows no respect for historical archives and documents of Hungarian origin;

(*d*) in the field of education, statistics show a dramatic decline in the proportion of pupils and students receiving instruction in the Hungarian language; the number of subjects taught in this language are limited and the number of Hungarian students admitted to the university increases at a rate 10 times less than that observed for the total number of admissions; teachers who have tried to preserve their cultural identity or to defend themselves against discriminatory methods of the government have been persecuted, interned and arrested.

140. According to the authors of the communication, Romania is in violation of Articles 1 (3), 55 and 56 of the Charter of the United Nations; Articles 1, 2, 13, 18, 19, 20, 23 (1) and 27 of the Universal Declaration of Human Rights; Articles 2 (1), 18, 19, 22 and 27 of the International Covenant on Civil and Political Rights; Articles 2 (2), 6 (1), 13 and 15 of the International Covenant on Econonic, Social and Cultural Rights; Articles 1 (1), 5 (*d*) (vii), (viii) and (ix), 5 (*e*) (i) and (vi) and 7 of the International Convention on the Elimination of All Forms of Racial Discrimination; Articles 1 and 5 of the Unesco Convention against Discrimination in Education and Articles 1 (1) (*a*) and (3), 2 and 3 (*c*), (*d*) and (*e*) of the International Labour Organisation's Discrimination (Employment and Occupation) Convention.

141. As to the steps taken by the member's of the Hungarian minority, victims of these violations, to exhaust domestic remedies, the authors of the communication allege that those of them who voiced protests were persecuted, imprisoned and often confined to a mental hospital. A typical example is the case of Mr Karoly Kiraly, a party member and a communist, alternate member of the Politburo, who in 1977, submitted three memoranda to the party concerning the forced denationalization of minorities by the Romanian Government. Mr Kiraly was placed under house arrest, expelled from the party and is still subjected to threats and persecutions. He is not allowed to leave the country.

Romania **No. 223/80**

142. The United Nations Commission on Human Rights and Sub-Commission on Prevention of Discrimination and [...] Protection of Minorities were informed of the main lines of this communication, without any notable results. In regard more specifically to the violation of human rights and fundamental freedoms in the fields of education, culture and information, the authors consider that it falls within the sphere of Unesco's competence.

143. The Romanian representative drew the Committee's attention to his government's written reply concerning the matter at hand [...].[2] Therein his government took the position that the communication was inadmissible for several reasons: the information on the matter was unreliable - the authors did not reside in Romania - and was full of errors - e.g. Mr Karoly Kiraly was not being persecuted but was leading a normal life in his native town, as several U.S. congressmen who visited him there could attest; the communication was politically motivated - the authors were linked to anti-Romanian groups and were trying to launch a political campaign to attack Romania's policies; the substance of this communication had already been decided by the Committee when it examined at a previous session another communication which had been considered inadmissible;[3] and finally the case had already been examined in another international forum and rejected.

144. Certain Committee members expressed the view that this communication was an old one being simply resubmitted in a different form and stated that it should not be admitted because it had already been rejected by the Committee.

145. Other Committee members felt that there were new elements being presented but that the communication concerned a question rather than a case, which meant that the Committee could not consider it until it had defined at its next session its policy on questions.

146. Still other Committee members felt that admissibility conditions were probably satisfied since other victims besides Mr Kiraly were being presented, since there was nothing in the communication to indicate that it was complaining about Romanian politics in general rather than about the specific alleged violations of human rights, since there were new elements presented, and since examination of a communication in another forum did not preclude its examination by the Committee. In view of the complexity of the case, however, these Committee members wondered whether it would not be best to ask for more information before taking a decision on admissibility.

---

[2] See document 110 EX/CR/HR/3 Add.3.

[3] See document 107 EX/PRIV.31, para. 149 (*supra*, p. 4), communication No. 2/78 concerning *Romania*, case of *Transylvanian populations in Romania*.

No. 223/80 **Romania**

147. After an exchange of views the Committee *decided* to declare the communication inadmissible as being manifestly ill-founded.

No. 224/80

Concerning *Argentina*
Case of *Graciela Esther Arabaolasa*

Communication of 17 March 1980 submitted by
Pierre Further

Autumn 1981 session of the Committee on Conventions and Recommendations (113th session of the Executive Board)[1]

40. The author of this communication, Mr Pierre Furter, a teacher, of Swiss nationality, explained that Mrs G. E. Arabaolasa, a teacher (employed by the National Directorate of Adult Education) was arrested on 26 April 1977, when she was three months pregnant, and placed at the disposal of the National Executive Power, as provided for under the Argentine Constitution when martial law is in force. She is said to have been brutally interrogated and to have signed a "confession" for fear of losing her child. It is said that she gave birth prematurely to twins on 13 October 1977 in the prison of San Luis.

41. The communication goes on to state that she was sentenced to four years' imprisonment for violating the law on "National Security" and for "illegal association", that in October 1978 she was transferred to the prison of Villa Devoto in Buenos Aires, that she is still there and that she is due for release on 26 April 1981.

42. The author alleges violations of Articles 18 (freedom of thought, conscience and religion), 19 (the right to seek, receive and impart information and ideas) and 20 (the right to freedom of assembly and association) of the Universal Declaration of Human Rights.

43. It is stated that her parents lodged an appeal with the Appeal Court of Mendoza (Cámara Federal de Apelaciones de Mendoza), which in August 1979 confirmed the sentence imposed by the Court of First Instance. It is alleged that she should have been legally entitled to release on parole on 26 December 1979, having served two-thirds of her sentence, but that release was not granted.

---

[1] See document 113 EX/38 PRIV., paras. 40-46; see also document 113 EX/CR/HR/3.

No. 224/80 **Argentina**

44. The purpose and aim of this communication are that Mrs Arabaolasa should be released immediately her sentence expires and allowed to leave Argentina to go to France, a country for which she holds a visa. The author maintains that prisoners frequently remain in prison after the end of their sentence.

45. The representative of the Argentine Government pointed out to the Committee that Mrs Arabaolasa had not been sentenced for being an established teacher but for her subversive activities, and since that was the case the communication was inadmissible. What was more, it was untrue to claim that she had confessed because she had been brutally interrogated and feared losing her child. She had simply signed what she had said during her interrogation. Finally, it was incorrect to say that she had given birth prematurely. This could be disproved merely by counting the months. The author merely wished to move the Committee to pity. In any event, she had been taken care of by the International Red Cross. The Argentine representative also made it clear that in Argentina, after serving a sentence, there was a period of conditional freedom which was designed to prevent people who had been freed from joining up again with their former companions in subversion. He added that the Argentine Government had no case to answer, since it was up to the judicial authorities to decide whether the date for releasing someone from prison should be brought forward or not. He himself had no idea whether Mrs Arabaolasa was now free.

46. Since no member of the Committee wished to take the floor, the Committee *decided*, at the Chairman's proposal, to take note of the information given by the representative of Argentina, to declare the communication inadmissible as it concerned violations which did not enter into Unesco's fields of competence in accordance with paragraph 14 (*a*) (iii) of 104 EX/Decision 3.3, and finally to appeal to the representative of the Argentine Government to use his good offices in that affair and to keep the Committee informed, through the Secretariat, of developments in Mrs Arabaolasa's situation.

No. 233/80

Concerning *United States of America and Israel*
Case of *Ziad Abu Eain*

Communication of 10 April 1980 submitted by
Abdel Munen Baker

Autumn 1980 session of the Committee on Conventions and Recommendations (110th session of the Executive Board)[1]

80. The author of this communication, Mr Abdel Munen Baker, Vice President of the International Union of Students, a non-governmental organization, is acting as a person possessing reliable knowledge of the alleged violation.

81. The author complains that Mr Ziad Abu Eain, a Palestinian student, is being held in Chicago Metropolitan Prison, U.S.A., awaiting extradition to Israel. The alleged victim's state of health - he began a hunger strike on 29 March 1980 - is said to be very critical. He has been admitted to the prison hospital. The Government of Israel alleges that the victim placed an explosive charge in the town of Tiberius on 14 May 1979, whereas a number of witnesses testify that he never left the town of Ramallah on the day of the incident.

82. The author of the communication claims that Articles 18 (freedom of thought), 19 (freedom of opinion and expression), 20 (freedom of association), 26 (right to education) and 27 (right to participate in cultural life) of the Universal Declaration of Human Rights have been violated.

83. The author does not mention whether any recourse has been had to domestic or international remedies.

84. The representative of the Government of the United States drew the Committee's attention to the written statement which presented his government's position on this communication [...].[2]

---

[1] See document 110 EX/40 PRIV., paras. 80-94; see also documents 110 EX/CR/HR/3 and Add.2 and 6.

85. The United States representative explained that the person in question, Mr Ziad Abu Eain was being detained pending a decision by the United States judicial authorities as to whether or not he should be extradited under the terms of a convention between the United States and Israel. He said it was not possible to predict the outcome of the legal remedies which remained to Mr Abu Eain. Concerning the allegation that Mr Abu Eain would not get a fair trial if extradited to Israel, he noted the high standards of justice which prevail in Israel and the Committee's difficulties in dealing with potential human rights violations as had been raised in a previous communication. As to the allegations that Mr Abu Eain's health in prison was in danger, these were untrue, he had been examined by an [Arabic-speaking] physician of his own choosing and had been found to be in normal health.

86. It was the United States Government's view that the communication was inadmissible as failing to comply with several of the admissibility requirements of [104 EX/Decision 3.3]. For one thing the communication did not fall within Unesco's field of competence, since no Unesco-related rights were alleged to be violated and since Mr Ziad was not a student, the United States representative said. The relevant records clearly established the latter fact and Mr Abu Eain so indicated on his visa application to the United States. Furthermore, it was pointed out even if Mr Ziad had been a student, there would still be no link with Unesco's field of competence, since his detention had nothing to do with his occupation, student or otherwise.

87. For another thing, it was pointed out, the communication did not indicate whether an attempt had been made to exhaust available domestic remedies. The United States representative emphasized that the failure to comply with this admissibility requirement of itself sufficed to declare the communication inadmissible.

88. Finally, the point was made that the communication was inadmissible as being manifestly ill-founded since the allegations made were not supported by information presented; there was not even a logical link between them.

89. The representative of the Government of Israel drew the Committee's attention to his country's written reply [...].[3] His government was also of the opinion that no violations of Mr Ziad's human rights could be alleged since the United States courts had not yet taken a decision against him. The demand for Mr Ziad's extradition was legally based on a United States-Israel treaty, currently in force. The Israeli representative also emphasized that the communication was clearly inadmissible for the various reasons already outlined.

---

[2] See document 110 EX/CR/HR/3 Add.2.

[3] See document 110 EX/CR/HR/3 Add.6.

United States of America and Israel **No. 233/80**

90. Several Committee members expressed their certainty that the Committee could not consider the present case since it did not meet several admissibility criteria and since the Committee could not presume a future violation of human rights where none presently existed.

91. One Committee member stated that he had full confidence in the legal procedures of the United States and that he would address solely the humanitarian considerations of the case. He expressed his view that Mr Ziad, if extradited, would not receive fair treatment. Since the [author] of the communication indicated there were serious doubts about Mr Ziad's involvement in the bombings in question, especially since the Israeli authorities allegedly used pressure tactics to obtain the information which supposedly incriminated Mr Abu Eain, this Committee member appealed to the United States authorities to take this element into consideration. He felt that the Committee should postpone its consideration of this case in order to clarify certain parts of the communication.

92. Another member of the Committee felt that there might well be a violation of Mr Ziad's humun rights taking place because the United States was not complying with the United Nations minimum rules concerning the treatment of detainees. Also the political offence clause of the United States-Israel treaty might not be respected. He felt the case should be deferred and more information sought.

93. The United States representative noted to the Committee that the question of guilt or innocence was not being decided in the United States, only the question of extradition. Furhermore, in this connection it was for the United States courts to decide whether or not the political offence clause of the treaty was applicable. The United States representative also emphasized that the matter was being handled in full conformity with the United States laws and Constitution, as well as the international instruments to which the United States was a party.

94. After a lengthy discussion the Committee *decided* to declare the case inadmissible and to express its wish that the United States authorities make certain that Mr. Ziad's human rights were being fully respected and that any humanitarian steps possible be taken on his behalf.

No. 238/80

Concerning *Yugoslavia*
Case of *Mihajlo Mihajlov*

Communication of 11 April 1980 submitted by
The International Human Rights Law Group

Autumn 1980 session of the Committee on Conventions and Recommendations (110th session of the Executive Board)[1]

225. This communication is submitted by a non-governmental organization, "The International Human Rights Law Group", which has its headquarters in New York, U.S.A., and is represented by its Executive Director, Mrs Amy Young-Anawaty, and by Mr Charles E. M. Kolb, a lawyer.

226. The authors of the communication claim to be an organization having reliable knowledge of the alleged violations.

227. According to this communication, the professor and writer Mihajlo Mihajlov was dismissed from his post as professor at the University in 1965 and arrested for publishing articles in the Yugoslav periodical *Delo*. It is claimed that he was subsequently arrested and imprisoned on several occasions for articles published in the Yugoslav and Western press. Following a large period of detention, he is said to have been forbidden to communicate through the press, the radio and the television or to appear in public. This situation still prevails and will continue to do so until November 1981. According to the authors of this communication, Professor Mihajlo Mihajlov, who has been living in the United States of America since 1968, wishes to return to Yugoslavia and to exercise the right to communicate, to publish and to teach. As a result of articles published in the American press he is said to be under order of arrest in Yugoslavia.

228. According to this communication, violations have occurred in respect of Articles 18, 19, 20, 26, 27 and 28 of the Universal Declaration of Human Rights; Articles 2 (1) and 8 (1) of the International Covenant on Civil and Political Rights; Arti-

[1] See document 110 EX/40 PRIV., paras. 225-233; see also document 110 EX/CR/HR/3.

cles 2 (2), 3, 6, 7 [and] 15 of the International Covenant on Economic, Social and Cultural Rights; Articles 3 (*a*) [and] 5 of the Convention and Recommendation against Discrimination in Education; Articles 4 (1) and 7 of the Declaration on the Principles of International Cultural Co-operation; and Articles 1 (3), 55 and 56 of the United Nations Charter.

229. With regard to recourse to domestic remedies the authors of the communication report that appeals have been lodged against the six sentences passed on Professor Mihajlo Mihajlov with all the competent appeal courts of Croatia, Serbia and Vojvodina. Except in two cases, the decisions of the lower court appear simply to have been confimed.

230. The representative of the Yugoslav Government informed the Committee that he had nothing to add to the position which had been previously taken on this matter by his government at the Committee's [autumn] 1979 session [...].[2] He stated that it appeared that the authors wanted Unesco to presume in advance that a violation of human rights might occur in this case.

231. Certain Committee members noted that the allegation of a pending warrant against Mr Mihajlov was a new element in the case and wondered whether it would not be advisable to suspend the consideration of the communication until more information on this new element could be obtained.

232. Other Committee members pointed out that even if it were definitely established that a warrant were pending, one could still only speculate as to whether or not the authorities would use it against Mr Mihajlov if and when he returned to Yugoslavia. Consequently, the communication would still only concern a potential violation of human rights and not an actual violation.

233. In view of the fact that the Committee could only deal with actual and not potential violations of human rights, it was *decided* that the communication would be declared inadmissible.

---

[2] See document 108 EX/38 PRIV., paras. 235-236 (*supra*, p. 248), communication No. 94/79, concerning *Yugoslavia*, case of *Mihajlo Mihajlov*.

No. 241/80

Concerning *Argentina*
Case of *Antonio Satutto and María Cristina Ortiz*

Communication of 3 April 1980 submitted by
José Satutto

Autumn 1980 session of the Committee on Conventions and Recommendations (110th session of the Executive Board)[1]

37. The author of the communication, Mr José Satutto, complains of the abduction and disappearance of his son, Mr Antonio Satutto, a student in the Engineering Faculty, and of the latter's wife, Mrs María Cristina Ortiz, a student in the Institute of Fine Arts.

38. According to the statement submitted, the sister/sister-in-law of the couple was abducted on 26 July 1978 in a street in Mar del Plata and interrogated. Two days later, on 28 July, the owners of the boarding house where Antonio and María Cristina Ortiz were resident and a number of witnesses are said to have seen some 15 masked and armed individuals enter the boarding house and take away Antonio and María Cristina Ortiz. María Rosa Ortiz was apparently released.

39. The author of the communication claims that Articles 9 (arbitrary detention) and 18 (freedom of thought) of the Universal Declaration of Human Rights have been violated.

40. The representative of the Argentine Government indicated to the Committee that there was a serious contradiction in this communication, one which by itself would shed serious doubt on the reliability of the information provided. He pointed out that the alleged victims were said to have been studying in the city of Mar del Plata and were said to have been abducted in the city of La Plata, when in fact the cities were 400 miles apart.

---

[1] See document 110 EX/40 PRIV., paras. 37-44; see also document 110 EX/CR/HR/3.

41. Even more significant, however, was the fact that his government had learned that the alleged victims were not students at the time of the alleged abduction. It had been learned that at that time Mr Satutto was a metalworker and his wife a perfumery shop assistant, both working in La Plata.

42. The Argentine representative asserted that the case was thus clearly inadmissible, which did not mean, however, that his government would not make an effort to look for these missing persons.

43. During its discussion, the Committee reached a consensus that this communication should be declared inadmissible and that, in keeping with the Committee's practice, the author should be informed of the reasons for the Committee's decision.

44. It was so *decided*.

No. 242/80

Concerning *Union of Soviet Socialist Republics*
Case of *Victor Brailovski* et al.*

Communication of 22 April 1980 submitted by
Alfred Kastler

Spring 1981 session of the Committee on Conventions and Recommendations (112th session of the Executive Board)[1]

289. The first of the above-mentioned communications[2] was submitted by Mr Alfred Kastler, a member of the Academy of Science in Paris and a member of the French National Council for Protection of the Rights of Jews in the USSR, a non-governmental organization. It describes him as a person having reliable knowledge of the alleged violations.

290. According to this communication:

(*a*) Since 1972, Mr Victor Brailovski, a cyberneticist, has been denied access to laboratories and libraries and the right to publish in the USSR or participate in international congresses; his mail is intercepted, his telephone cut off, his apartment has been searched on a number of occasions and his scientific documents confiscated.

In 1972, he applied for an emigration visa to Israel. In 1976, he was given permission to emigrate with his son, but he refused to leave without his wife. In order to live, he says, he took part in the seminar of the "Outcasts of Science". He claims to have been unable to seek any legal redress. He is at present reportedly held in Butyrka prison, since his arrest on 13 November 1980.

* Case of *Irina and Victor Brailovski, Vladimir Kislik, Alexandre Lerner and Nahum Meinam.*
[1] See document 112 EX/30 PRIV., paras. 289-334; see also documents 112 EX/CR/HR/3 and Add. and Add.2.
[2] Communications No. 242/80 concerning *Union of Soviet Socialist Republics*, case of *Victor Brailovski* et al., and No. 346/81 concerning *Union of Soviet Socialist Republics*, case of *Victor Brailovski*, were being considered together.

(*b*) Mrs Irina Brailovski, a mathematician, is faced with the same situation as her husband. Some of her most recent work has been published under the names of other researchers.

(*c*) Mr Vladimir Kislik, a nuclear physicist, finds himself in a similar predicament. After applying for an emigration visa to Israel in 1973, he lost his job. His wife and son could have emigrated.

(*d*) Alexandre Lerner, a cyberneticist, has been in exactly the same situation since he applied for an emigration visa in 1971. To continue his scientific activity, he holds a weekly private seminar at home.

(*e*) Nahum Meinam, a mathematician, has been reduced to the same situation since applying for an emigration visa in 1975. Elderly and sick, he is no longer entitled to medical care at the USSR Academy of Sciences' special polyclinic. To continue to live as a man of science, he participates in Mr Victor Brailovski's seminar for the "Outcasts of Science".

291. The second of the above-mentioned communications [...] was submitted by the Greater New York Conference on Soviet Jewry and concerns only Mr Brailovsky. The facts alleged therein are essentially the same as in the other communication but are presented in greater detail. A lengthy report on the alleged violations submitted by the authors was not reproduced for the Committee but is available for consultation in the Secretariat's files, as is a letter, sent in support of this communication, from the brother of the alleged victim.

292. When taking up these two communications, the Committee decided to first discuss the case of Mr Brailovsky by itself, since this case was presented in both communications. Subsequently, the cases of Mrs Brailovsky and Messrs Kislik, Lerner and Meinam [...] were discussed.

A. *Case of Mr Brailovsky*

293. The representative of the Government of the Soviet Union stated to the Committee that preliminary judicial investigations concerning Mr Brailovsky were presently being carried out in Moscow. Mr Brailovsky, it was explained, was being kept under preventive measures and close surveillance, in keeping with the penal procedural code.

294. The Soviet representative went on to say that before conclusions were formulated by the judicial body in question, it was impossible to comment on the case, since the outcome was not certain and the principle of objectivity required that it not

be discussed. He suggested that the case be deferred until the Committee's next session.

295. A member of the Committee stated that since there was an investigation under way, he also felt that the examination of this case should be put off until the next session.

296. Another member of the Committee felt that the position taken by the Soviet Government was a cause for great concern. He indicated that there had been a violation of international human rights standards in this case since 1972 and that Dr Brailoysky had been under arrest for many months. He further indicated that this person was being charged under an article of the Soviet penal code which in effect prohibited the simple circulation of materials, and that during the month that had passed since the arrest, there had already been ample time to make a determination in this case. Instead of a determination, he said, there was persecution; it was a cause of deep concern that a person could be so jailed indefinitely. The Committee member went on to ask whether the Committee might ever get around to examining such a case if it were repeatedly told, session after session, that the investigation by the authorities was still under way.

297. In this case there was a long pattern of harassment which was more than adequate grounds for declaring the case receivable.

298. Another member of the Committee asked why it was necessary to await a court decision since the alleged violation dated back to 1972, among them an exit visa refusal. The other question which presented itself, he said, was why a person who wanted to leave the USSR was not allowed to do so.

299. It was felt by another Committee member that this case was an exemplary one for Unesco; it concerned a scientist and violations within Unesco's competence, presented by a trustworthy witness. Though it might be premature at this session to expect the Soviet representative to go into details, it was nevertheless important to ask within what period of time the Committee could expect a result and what was the basis for the treatment which dated back to 1972.

300. Another Committee member agreed that the case clearly came within Unesco's competence, and he expressed his concern at the period of almost 10 years during which the alleged violations of human rights had taken place; however, he felt it advisable to wait a bit longer since the case was now before a court.

301. It was stated by another Committee member that the case was within Unesco's competence and that it should only be deferred until the next session on the under-

standing that if it had not been favourably resolved by then, the Committee would admit the case and review its substantive aspects. In no event was it to be postponed again.

302. By way of clarification the representative of the Director-General read to the Committee [article 14, paragraph 3 (*c*),] of the [International] Covenant on Civil and Political Rights concerning excessive delays before trials and explained that international practice and jurisprudence related this concept to possible sentences in question, i.e. that one-half of the potential sentence was generally considered the limit of a reasonable delay before being brought to trial.

303. A member of the Committee then stated that despite the respect which the Committee owed the scientist submitting this communication, it was obvious that he was linked with the international Zionist movement. He said that the USSR had given exit visas to tens of thousands of Jews and that if Brailovsky had not been given one, there was probably a good reason.

304. Several Committee members thereupon insisted that the discussion should not be expanded beyond the case at hand, that the authors of communications should not be subjected to personal attacks.

305. In response to a question, the representative of the Director-General explained the difference between examinations concerning admissibility and those concerning substance. While admissibility examinations mainly concerned the question of fulfilment of the criteria outlined in paragraph 14 (*a*) of [104 EX/Decision 3.3] and examinations of substance involved the particular merits of the case, it was nevertheless true that it was necessary to a very limited extent to examine the facts when discussing whether a case was "prima facie" within Unesco's competence or was "manifestly ill-founded". Naturally a decision on admissibility did not mean that the case has been found to be well-founded. It was perfectly possible to declare a case admissible and then later dismiss it as being ill-founded if this was found to be the situation when the facts were more closely examined.

306. It was then stated by a Committee member that while it was clear that the Committee did not plan to intervene in domestic affairs of a country and that this case should be deferred until the next session, the Committee should nevertheless state its wish to the USSR that no efforts should be spared to ensure the respect of human rights and a speedy and favourable resolution in this case.

307. Another Committee member stated that he saw the case as being clearly admissible. There were the events of the nine years which preceded the arrest, and his government was following this case closely.

Union of Soviet Socialist Republics **No. 242/80**

308. Still another Committee member felt that the best course of action lay between immediate admission and indefinite postponement. He proposed that the Committee decide that the admissibility of the case must be examined at the next session, that the Soviet representative be called upon to sensitize his government as to the Committee's strong concern in this case and to ask it to accelerate its proceedings.

309. The Soviet representative emphasized his government's desire to work with the Committee in the spirit of [104 EX/Decision 3.3]. He stated that his government would carefully respect all provisions of its penal code, which he said allowed him to be optimistic about the news he could present to the Committee at its next session. The question of what was a reasonable pre-trial delay was a debatable one, he said, but in any event the applicable penal code would be strictly respected.

310. Thereupon, the Committee *decided*:

(i) to take its decision on admissibility at its next session;

(ii) to call upon the representative of the Soviet Union to sensitize his government as to the concern of the Committee over the case; and

(iii) to appeal to the Soviet Government to accelerate to the fullest extent possible the proceedings in this case.

B. *Case of Mrs Brailovsky, Vladimir Kislik, Alexandre Lerner and Nahum Meinam*

311. The Soviet representative stated to the Committee that the author of this communication, the French National Council for the Protection of Jews in the USSR, was an organ established to interfere in the domestic affairs of another country; it spread misinformation and unfriendly propaganda. He cited the case of an article published in a French newspaper, submitted on behalf of this Council, which alleged the violation of human rights of 163 Soviet Jews and which he had learned to be unfounded by personally checking on those persons in the USSR. Thus it could be seen that this body was unreliable; in any event, he went on to say, the Soviet Jews did not need anyone's protection, and it was deplorable that the leading French scientist who had signed this communication on behalf of the Council had become involved with this group, which tried to complicate things and encouraged the brain drain.

312. The Soviet representative said he had been instructed to ask the representative of the Director-General whether the goal of paragraph 14 (*k*) of 104 EX/Decision

3.3, concerning the finding of an amicable solution, could possibly be met where an author was guided by unfriendly intentions.

313. The representative of the Director-General replied that paragraph 14 (*k*) only became applicable once a communication had been deemed admissible, and once the merits were being examined. However, the spirit of finding a friendly solution ran throughout the text of the decision and such a solution could be found at any time.

314. The Soviet representative stated that his government wanted to co-operate but did so with difficulty in the face of hostile propaganda. As to the facts of the matter, more than 250,000 Soviet Jews had been allowed to leave the country, which was 98.4 per cent of all Jews who asked for permission to leave. The overwhelming majority of Soviet Jews felt they were part of the country, he said, and never even thought of leaving. Also the opportunities to work were excellent for them, and they comprised a significantly high percentage of highly qualified and decorated professionals in the country, he said. Those who were not allowed to leave were so barred due to their having classified information vital to national security; it was explained they could leave once the information became outdated, although this often took years. Such an interdiction was perfectly in keeping with international law, he said.

315. Furthermore, he stated, the other allegations were untrue - these persons did have access to libraries, and if they were not working, it was because they had left their posts. Messrs Lerner and Meinam had retired and received their full pension and they used libraries as was evidenced by their signed reader's application, which the Soviet representative showed the Committee. He also said that Mr Meinam received the most sophisticated and specialized medical treatment free of charge. In any event, these persons had the right to petition and have a periodic review of their visa requests, he said. Thus, the allegations were unfounded and the case was not admissible.

316. A member of the Committee stated that the characteristics of persons or groups submitting communications were not relevant and that cases should be considered on their own merits. All persons and groups of whatever creed or race had an equal right to submit communications; what a group happened to believe or do in a different forum was not material to a case at hand, and there could of course be very good explanations for events in other forums.

317. He went on to point out that the overall question of treatment of Jews in the Soviet Union was not before the Committee; if it were, other authoritative sources could be quoted to contradict the Soviet representative; for example, the statement that a high percentage of Jews asking to leave were allowed to do so could well con-

ceal the fact that many Jews were afraid to ask to leave when they saw what happened in cases such as these.

318. As to the classified data, it was of course impossible for the Committee to judge this, he said, but it could request the authorities to review the cases periodically and frequently to see if the information was outdated yet.

319. Furthermore, the Committee member said, the Soviet representative had not dealt with all the allegations, each case was admissible on its own. Mrs Brailovsky had not retired, she was subject to all sorts of harassment, and this fact had not been dealt with.

320. Also Mr Kislik was 46 and had been subjected to violations of his rights since he was 38 and could not participate or work in his field. It was pointed out that these points had not been dealt with or explained. As for Mr Lerner, his case started when he was 52, long before he retired, it was emphasized. In Mr Meinam's case, it had not been alleged that he did not receive medical aid but that he was denied access to the polyclinic with which he had had an affiliation. It was stated that if in fact access to libraries was possible for two of the victims, this was good but it did not solve the other problems and the other victims' situations, and each case was thus clearly admissible, separately and on its own merits.

321. Another member of the Committee agreed that each case was admissible and pointed out that their access to one library might not meet their needs, and he wondered why these persons were not allowed to continue working in their fields. As for the possibility of petitioning the Advocate-General, the Committee member emphasized that this was not a true remedy as defined by international instruments and was a serious lacuna in Soviet procedure, since the review was within the discretion of the Advocate-General only and was not mandatory and enforceable.

322. Another Committee member, while supporting the admissibility of this case, expressed pessimism about obtaining the helpful co-operation of the government concerned. He wondered whether it would not be more effective, rather than to concentrate on individual cases, to appeal to have national legislation brought into conformity with international norms such as Unesco's.

323. The Soviet representative stated that one should avoid approaching the propagandist smoke screen in this communication. He said he could prove that all four persons had for years had access to a library and stated that he had verified that a phone listing of one of them was correct and not disconnected, as had been alleged. Furthermore, he said, two of these persons received funds from Israel, which was technically illegal, but the authorities were being lenient about this.

324. Also he saw no reason why persons should be allowed to use their phones to transmit information to an institute in Israel and also be paid from abroad. He further felt that the denial of use of a certain polyclinic could not be seen as a sanction.

325. As to the question of emigration visas, he stated that it was not Unesco's competence to become an emigration lobby for Zionists. Although one could sympathize with these people, it was clear that the law had to be upheld.

326. A Committee member stated that although the case in the abstract appeared admissible, the visa refusals based on security knowledge might well be justified. He also feared that political motives might be behind this communication.

327. Several Committee members emphasized that the question of exit visas was not the issue and that this point, which was outside Unesco's competence, should cease to be discussed. The key issue was whether these persons were prevented from working or participating in their scientific fields. These Committee members pointed out that these allegations had still not been dealt with by the Soviet representative.

328. The Soviet representative stated that there were many obstacles in his country to speeding up the emigration process in this case. He also mentioned that the communication's author did not list his purpose and aim on the form, so that if the communication could not be rejected, it should at least be deferred until this point could be clarified by the author.

329. Certain other Committee members also felt it would be useful to ask for more information on that point.

330. Several other Committee members pointed out that it was not a condition of admissibility to fill in all parts of the form, least of all the purpose and aim section. This was no reason to defer consideration, they felt.

331. In response to a question the representative of the Director-General explained that that section of the form existed only since the [autumn 1980] session of the Committee and had only been added to help clarify possible solutions for unusually complex cases. In response to a query as to why the Director-General could not seek more information in such cases on his own initiative, it was explained that the Director-General did not wish to prejudge or take positions on cases going to the Committee.

332. A Committee member stated to the Committee that he felt that the Soviet representative had been the one presenting the facts to the Committee, whereas the author of the communication had only been presenting words. Furthermore, the Committee

member questioned whether any country would allow a nuclear physicist to leave, as was being requested here.

333. Another Committee member stated that his country was one of those in which no restrictions were placed on anyone, of whatever profession, wishing to leave his country in times of peace, but that emigration questions should be seen as irrelevant here so that the main issue of whether these persons were being deprived of their human rights in their own country could be focused on.

334. After a long and involved discussion, the Committee *decided* to suspend consideration of the admissibility of the [communications] on the understanding that [they] would be re-examined at the next session by which time the [authors] of the [communications] - to whom, in accordance with established practice, the information provided by the government concerned at the present session, would have been transmitted - would have clarified the aim and purpose of the [communications] and provided any supplementary information [they] deemed useful.

Autumn 1981 session of the Committee on Conventions and Recommendations (113th session of the Executive Board)[3]

343. The first of the above-mentioned communications[4] was submitted by Mr Alfred Kastler, a member of the Academy of Science in Paris and a member of the French National Council for Protection of the Rights of Jews in the USSR, a non-governmental organization. It describes him as a person having reliable knowledge of the alleged violations.

344. According to this communication:

> (*a*) Since 1972, Mr Victor Brailovski, a cyberneticist, has been denied access to laboratories and libraries and the right to publish in the USSR or participate in international congresses; his mail is intercepted, his telephone cut off, his apartment has been searched on a number of occasions and his scientific documents confiscated.
>
> In 1972, he applied for an emigration visa to Israel. In 1976, he was given permission to emigrate with his son, but he refused to leave without his wife.

[3] See document 113 EX/38 PRIV., paras. 343-365; see also documents 113 EX/CR/HR/2 and Add.2 and 3.

[4] Communications No. 242/80 concerning *Union of Soviet Socialist Republics*, case of *Victor Brailovski* et al., and No. 346/81 concerning *Union of Soviet Socialist Republics*, case of *Victor Brailovski*, were being considered together.

In order to live, he says, he took part in the seminar of the "Outcasts of Science". He claims to have been unable to seek any legal redress. He is at present reportedly held in Butyrka prison, since his arrest on 13 November 1980.

(*b*) Mrs Irina Brailovski, a mathematician, is faced with the same situation as her husband. Some of her most recent work has been published under the names of other researchers.

(*c*) Mr Vladimir Kislik, a nuclear physicist, finds himself in a similar predicament. After applying for an emigration visa to Israel in 1973, he lost his job. His wife and son could have emigrated.

(*d*) Alexandre Lerner, a cyberneticist, has been in exactly the same situation since he applied for an emigration visa in 1971. To continue his scientific activity, he holds a weekly private seminar at home.

(*e*) Nahum Meinam, a mathematician, has been reduced to the same situation since applying for an emigration visa in 1975. Elderly and sick, he is no longer entitled to medical care at the USSR Academy of Sciences' special polyclinic. To continue to live as a man.of science, he participates in Mr Victor Brailovski's seminar for the "Outcasts of Science".

345. The second of the above-mentioned communications [...] was submitted by the Greater New York Conference on Soviet Jewry and concerns only Mr Brailovski. The facts alleged therein are essentially the same as in the other communication but are presented in greater detail. A lengthy report on the alleged violations submitted by the authors was not reproduced for the Committee but is available for consultation in the Secretariat's files, as is a letter, sent in support of this communication, from the brother of the alleged victim.

346. At its [spring 1981] session, the Committee decided to suspend consideration of the admissibility of the communications on the understanding that they would be re-examined at the next session by which time the authors of the communications - to whom, in accordance with established practice, the information provided by the government concerned at the present session, would have been transmitted - would have clarified the aim and purpose of the communications and provided any supplementary information they deemed useful.[5]

[346a.] Once informed of the Committee's decision, the authors sent further information.

---

[5] See document 112 EX/30 PRIV., para. 334 (*supra*, p. 603).

Union of Soviet Socialist Republics **No. 242/80**

347. In a letter dated 9 July 1981, the Greater New York Conference on Soviet Jewry stated that on 17 and 18 June 1981 Mr Brailovski was tried before a repressive court. He was accused of breaking Article 190/1 of the Russian Criminal Code which prohibits the circulation of false information slandering the Soviet state and the social system of the country and, it is alleged, he was sentenced to five years' exile within the country, though it would seem that this sentence was subsequently reduced to three years and three months.

348. The author of the communication considered that, Mr Brailovski being involved with the cultural journal "Jews in the USSR", the sentence given to this scientist was another example of the measures of intimidation directed against him since 1972. He wished it to be clearly understood that the journal in question was an apolitical publication which dealt only with cultural problems, and that consequently there was no question of fabricating false and slanderous information. It should be added that since the examination of the communication by the Committee at its [spring 1981] session, the situation of the alleged victim had grown dramatically worse.

349. The Greater New York Conference on Soviet Jewry would like to see an end to the suffering experienced by Mr Brailovski and his family and hopes that the cyberneticist may be able to resume his scientific, cultural and educational activities in Israel, which is the country of his choice.

350. The French National Council for Protection of the Rights of Jews in the USSR sent two letters to the Secretariat:

351. A. *Letter dated 13 July 1981*

(i) Mr Alfred Kastler stated that, since the communication was first submitted, the situation of the alleged victims had become worse. He cited as an example the arrest and the recent conviction of Messrs Brailovski and Kislik "in circumstances which", he emphasized, "manifestly disregard Soviet law". He considered that the rights proclaimed in Article 15 of the Universal Declaration of Human Rights (right to nationality) and in Article 7 of the Declaration of the Principles of International Cultural Co-operation (broad dissemination of ideas and knowledge) have been violated through "repeated interruptions and attempts to prevent the meetings of seminars of the 'Outcasts of Science'", violations which have particularly affected Messrs Brailovski and Lerner.

(ii) In addition, the author of the communication stated that he had very little time before the date fixed for the Committee's meeting to gather evidence which will refute the statements of the Soviet Government's representative. He pointed out that communications with the USSR are "extremely difficult", but promised nevertheless to produce additional, relevant documents as soon as possible.

(iii) He stated that the aim of his communication was to bring to an end the violations of the rights of the individuals cited as victims.

352. B. *Letter dated 29 July 1981*

Under cover of this letter the following documents were forwarded to the Secretariat:

353. (*a*) *A letter dated 22 July 1981, sent by Mr Kastler to Mr Anatoli Alexandrov, President of the USSR Academy of Sciences*

In this letter, Mr Kastler informs Mr Alexandrov that he has submitted a communication to Unesco concerning Mr and Mrs Brailovski and Messrs Lerner, Meiman and Kislik. He states that, on the basis of the information provided by the individuals concerned and by foreign visitors, these scientists:

no longer have access to their laboratories, to scientific libraries or to research institutes;

are no longer able to attend congresses either in the USSR or abroad;

have had their unofficial meetings disrupted.

In conclusion, Mr Kastler requests the President of the USSR Academy of Sciences to explain these alleged violations of human rights.

354. (*b*) *A dossier on Irina Brailovski*

(1) It contains a brief biography illustrating her brilliant academic career, together with an account of the difficulties she experienced from 1972, when she first requested permission for her family to be able to emigrate, until 18 June 1981, when her husband was sentenced to five years' exile within the country for "spreading anti-Soviet propaganda". (She was able to attend the trial with her son.)

(2) In this dossier mention is made of a declaration by Mr Anatoli Logunov, Rector of the Moscow State University, who is alleged to have said to an astrophysicist from Princeton, on a visit to this city in October 1979, that "the University of Mos-

cow had no objection to the departure of Irina Brailovski and that he would inform the OVIR (the visa office)".

(3) As evidence of some of the harassment to which the alleged victim has been subjected, the dossier also includes the following information:

(i) *a written statement (under oath) by Professor Maurice Bertran Priestley of the University of Manchester, Institute of Science and Technology*, testifying that a scientific meeting at the home of Irina Brailovski was disrupted by the police on 15 March 1981;

(ii) *a written statement by Professor H. Diamant of Umeå University (Sweden)* who claims to have witnessed, on 24 April 1981, the anguish of Irina Brailovski who was totally without news of her imprisoned husband, and on 25 April, the action by the police and the KGB to prevent a seminar being held at her home;

(iii) *a written statement (under oath) bv Mr Claude Deutsch of the Physics Laboratory for Gases and Plasmas (a laboratory associated with the CNRS)*, testifying that on 31 May and 1 June 1980, during his stay in Moscow, the Brailovskis' telephone had been put out of use;

(iv) *an invitation dated April 1978 from Cornell University (Ithaca, New York) to various conferences and consultations and an invitation dated December 1977 to an international symposium at the University of Sheffield.* Irina Brailovski was unable to reply to these invitations.

355. (*c*) *A dossier on Victor Brailovski*

It contains basic information about the person concerned (date of birth, profession, address) and an account of the difficulties which he experienced from his first application to emigrate in 1972, until his conviction for breaking Article 190/1 of the Russian Criminal Code.

356. (*d*) *A dossier on Alexandre Lerner*

[1] It contains a brief biography followed by an account of the difficulties which he experienced from September 1971, when the Soviet authorities intercepted a letter of invitation which was sent by the members of his family living in Israel, and when he submitted an official request to emigrate, until the death of his wife from a heart attack in July 1981.

[2] His daughter Sonia, who had been given permission to emigrate, was able to attend her mother's funeral.

[3] As evidence of some of the difficulties experienced by Mr Lerner, the dossier also includes the following information:

[i] *A written statement (under oath) by Mrs Sonia Levin (née Lerner)*

Confirming the dismissal of her father from the Institute of Cybernetics and from the Moscow Physico-Technical Institute (it is alleged that Mr Lerner was requested to leave the lecture room during his course and, on his refusal, that the students were forced to leave) and also confirming what has already been stated above concerning the interception of the letter of invitation from Israel.

Instancing the failure to forward an invitation sent to her father by the American Mathematical Society in 1978, and also the cutting off of the family telephone in Moscow (No. 137 53 96) for the first time in May 1972 (allegedly under the pretext of the need to carry out repairs on a cable, which then took a year and a half to complete) and then again in 1973, some time after October, until the death of her mother in July 1981. As a result, it is alleged, it was impossible to call an ambulance urgently when her mother fell ill. (In addition, all the telegrams of condolence from Israel and most of the telegrams from Western countries are alleged to have been intercepted.)

[ii] *An invitation to a symposium dated 8 January 1980, sent by IFAC in Toulouse (International Federation of Automatic Control - France) and an invitation dated 11 March 1981 from the University of Paris VII to Mr Lerner to take up a post as associate professor for the university year 1981/1982*, invitations which the scientist was unable to answer.

[iii]. *An open letter bv Mr Lerner, dated 13 August 1979*, protesting against the Soviet authorities' opposition to his accepting an invitation to the 9th Congress of the International Political Science Association in Moscow, and against his replacement by another person.

357. (*e*) *A dossier on Vladimir Kislik*

[1] It lists the harassment experienced by this physicist following his application to emigrate in October 1973: loss of his job at the Institute of Physics in Kiev (where he had been working since 1966); the fact that he has not been able to work for eight years now; the deletion of his name from all scientific publications, the interception

of his mail; threats of arrest and of prosecution for "black-market activities" should he continue to hold scientific seminars in his home; his apartment has been searched; he was arrested in July 1980, freed two weeks later and arrested again in May 1981 and sentenced to three years in a camp for "serious hooliganism".

[2] Following a telephone conversation with Israel in May 1976, it is alleged that his telephone was permanently cut off.

[3] This dossier contains a copy of a letter dated 20 July 1981 from Mr Kislik's lawyer, Mr Daniel Jacobi, protesting against the silence of the USSR Embassy in Paris in response to his request for a visa to visit the USSR in order to defend his client both in the Court of First Instance and on appeal.

358. *(f) A dossier on Nahum Meiman*

[1] After a short biography it gives an account of the difficulties experienced by the mathematician since he applied to emigrate in 1974.

[2] Mr Meiman, it is alleged, was arrested for the first time in November 1976, and again in 1977, though his detention did not last very long. It is alleged that his telephone was cut off after he was arrested for the first time.

[3] In January 1980, it is alleged that the legal authorities forbade him to have anything more to do with the Supervisory Committee for the Application of the Helsinki Agreements.

[4] The scientist's family were apparently given permission to emigrate in 1977.

[5] He is elderly and in poor health and, it is alleged, he now lives alone and the clinic which looked after him for several years has refused to take care of him.

359. At the Committee's present session, the representative of the Soviet Government stated that the contention of the authors that the sentencing of Mr Brailovski was unfair was an unfounded and offensive contention. He went on to explain that the legal provision under which Mr Brailovski has been sentenced was one which prohibited the systematic circulation of defamatory ideas, i.e. ideas which were known to be false by their author. At Mr Brailovski's trial, which had been an open one, it had been shown that Mr Brailovski had been engaged since 1972 in the circulation of materials which he knew to be false and damaging to the reputation of the Soviet system. In those materials, for which he was responsible either as an author or as an editor, it was contended that racism and anti-Semitism were widespread in the Soviet Union. During his trial it had been shown that, under the guise of fighting

anti-Semitism, Mr Brailovski was in fact being chauvinistic and was disseminating anti-Soviet slander. The court had been lenient and had handed down a sentence which did not deprive him of freedom. He had been sentenced to a five-year internal exile, which had been reduced to three years in view of his time served. For these reasons the communication was ill-founded and inadmissible.

360. In reply to questions the Soviet representative stated that there was no punishment in the Soviet Union of persons applying for exit visas. Thousands of Jews were allowed to leave the Soviet Union every year. The Soviet representative pointed out that Mr Brailovski could have left the country long ago but since his wife had not been allowed to leave, for security reasons, he had chosen to stay. As for the term "exile", it meant compulsory settling within the confines of a given administrative region, in which the person was free to circulate, work and live with his family. Under certain exceptional circumstances he could be allowed to exit for brief periods.

361. A Committee member stated that this was a case where a person had been sentenced as a criminal, merely for expressing himself in writing. Such an action could be seen as contrary to the Universal Declaration of Human Rights, he said, and, furthermore, though it was true that libel laws existed throughout the world, they provided for civil penalties not criminal penalties. The question of what was a false statement was a subjective one, he said, and one man's falsehood was sometimes another man's truth. Communist parties throughout the world were constantly making harsh remarks about the countries in which they were located and they were not prosecuted for making such statements. The Committee member felt it important that the Committee's concern for the right to the freedom of expression should be clearly expressed in this case. He went on to say that Mr Brailovski's assertion that there was anti-Semitism in the Soviet Union would by some be seen to be a true statement, and that in any event such a statement could hardly be seen as dangerous enough to warrant criminal penalties; freedom of speech must be seen to include the freedom to criticize rightly or wrongly.

362. Another Committee member felt that it would not be useful to go into comparisons of ideology. However, in practical terms the Committee's concern should be noted in cases such as this where the penalty was disproportionately severe for the acts alleged to have been committed.

363. Another Committee member felt that the Committee should look dispassionately at the facts and realize that certain countries punished acts which others did not consider punishable. Since it appeared that Mr Brailovski was being allowed to work and since the Committee was not competent to help him emigrate or change his sentence, it was not competent in this matter, he said.

Union of Soviet Socialist Republics **No. 242/80**

364. After a lenghty discussion, the Committee *decided*:

(i) to ask the delegate of the government concerned to provide all the necessary information concerning the present status of Mr Brailovski and to request him to make known to the proper authorities the Committee's exclusively humanitarian interest in the cases of the alleged victim and his wife;

(ii) to transmit this information, in conjunction with the other new facts that had appeared in this case, to the authors of the two communications;

(iii) to resume consideration of the admissibility of the two communications at its next session.

365. In considering the cases of the other persons cited in these communications, the Committee *decided* to apply the terms of its aforementioned decision, *mutatis mutandis*, in these cases also, while at the same time stressing that in the case of Mr Meiman, old age was an additional factor which merited humanitarian considerations by the competent Soviet authorities.

Spring 1982 session of the Committee on Conventions and Recommendations (114th session of the Executive Board)[6]

580. The first [of the above-mentioned communications][7] is submitted by Mr Alfred Kastler, a member of the Academy of Science in Paris and member of the French National Council for the Protection of the Rights of Jews in the USSR, a non-governmental organization. It describes him as a person having reliable knowledge of the alleged violations.

581. According to this communication:

(*a*) Since 1972, Mr Victor Brailovski, a cyberneticist, has been denied access to laboratories and libraries and the right to publish in the USSR or participate in international congresses; his mail is intercepted, his telephone cut off, his apartment has been searched on a number of occasions and his scientific documents confiscated.

---

[6] See document 114 EX/38 PRIV., paras. 580-618; see also documents 114 EX/CR/HR/2 and Add and 114 EX/CR/HR/3.

[7] Communications No. 242/80 concerning *Union of Soviet Socialist Republics*, case of *Victor Brailovski* et al., No. 346/81 concerning *Union of Soviet Socialist Republics*, case of *Victor Brailovski*, and No. 418/81 concerning *Union of Soviet Socialist Republics*, case of *Victor Brailovski*, were being considered together.

In 1972, he applied for an emigration visa to Israel. In 1976, he was given permission to emigrate with his son, but he refused to leave without his wife. In order to live, he apparently took part in the seminar of the "Outcasts of Science". He claims to have been unable to seek any legal redress. He is at present reportedly held in Butyrka prison, since his arrest on 13 November 1980.

(*b*) Mrs Irina Brailovski, a mathematician, is faced with the same situation as her husband. Some of her most recent work has been published under the names of other researchers.

(*c*) Mr Vladimir Kislik, a nuclear physicist, finds himself in a similar predicament. After applying for an emigration visa to Israel in 1973, he lost his job. His wife and son could have emigrated. He was reportedly arrested on 19 March 1981 and is stated to be held in Lukyanovka prison.

(*d*) Alexandre Lerner, a cyberneticist, has been in exactly the same situation since he applied for an emigration visa in 1971. To continue his scientific activity, he holds a weekly private seminar at home.

(*e*) Nahum Meiman, a mathematician, has been reduced to the same situation since applying for an emigration visa in 1975. Elderly and sick, he is no longer entitled to medical care at the USSR Academy of Sciences special polyclinic. To continue to live as a man of science, he participates in Mr Victor Brailovski's seminar for the "Outcasts of Science".

582. The second communication [...] was submitted by the Greater New York Conference on Soviet Jewry and concerns only Mr Brailovski. The facts alleged therein are essentially the same as in the previous communication but are presented in greater detail. A lengthy report on the alleged violations submitted by the authors was not reproduced for the Committee but is available for consultation in the Secretariat's files, as is a letter, sent in support of this communication, from the brother of the alleged victim.

583. At the [spring] 1981 session, the Committee decided to suspend consideration of the admissibility of the communications on the understanding that they would be re-examined at the next session by which time the authors of the communications - to whom, in accordance with established practice, the information provided by the government concerned at the present session, would have been transmitted - would

have clarified the aim and purpose of the communications and provided any supplementary information they deemed useful.[8]

584. In a letter dated 9 July 1981, the Greater New York Conference on Soviet Jewry stated that on 17 and 18 June 1981 Mr Brailovski was tried before a repressive court. He was accused of breaking Article 190/1 of the Russian Criminal Code which prohibits the circulation of false information slandering the Soviet state and the social system of the country and, it is alleged, he was sentenced to five years' exile within the country, though it would seem that this sentence was reduced to three years and three months.

585. The author of the communication considered that, Mr Brailovski being involved with the cultural journal "Jews in the USSR", the sentence given to this scientist was another example of the measures of intimidation directed against him since 1972. He wished it to be clearly understood that the journal in question was an apolitical publication which dealt only with cultural problems, and that consequently there was no question of fabricating false and slanderous information. It should be added that since the examination of the communication by the Committee, the situation of the alleged victim had grown dramatically worse.

586. The Greater New York Conference on Soviet Jewry would like to see an end to the suffering experienced by Mr Brailovski and his family and hopes that the cybereticist may be able to resume his scientific, cultural and educational activities in Israel, which is the country of his choice.

587. The French National Council for Protection of the Rights of Jews in the USSR sent two letters to the Secretariat:

A. *Letter dated 13 July 1981*

> (i) Mr Alfred Kastler stated that, since the communication was first submitted, the situation of the alleged victims had become worse. He cited as an example the arrest and conviction of Messrs Brailovski and Kislik in circumstances which he held to be inconsistent with Soviet law. He considered that the rights proclaimed in Article 15 of the Universal Declaration of Human Rights (right to nationality) and in Article 7 of the Declaration of the Principles of International Cultural Co-operation (broad dissemination of ideas and knowledge) have been violated through "repeated interruptions and attempts to prevent the meetings of seminars of the 'Outcasts of Science'".

---

[8] See document 112 EX/30 PRIV., para. 334 (*supra*, p. 603).

(ii) He stated that the aim of his communication was to bring to an end the violations of the rights of the individuals cited as victims.

B. *Letter dated 29 July 1981*

Under cover of this letter the following documents were forwarded to the Secretariat:

(*a*) *A letter dated 22 July 1981, sent by Mr Kastler to Mr Anatoli Alexandrov, President of the USSR Academy of Sciences*

In this letter, Mr Kastler informs Mr Alexandrov that he has submitted a communication to Unesco concerning Mr and Mrs Brailovski and Messrs Lerner, Meiman and Kislik. He states that, on the basis of the information provided by the individuals concerned and by foreign visitors, these scientists:

no longer have access to their laboratories, to scientific libraries or to research institutes;

are no longer able to attend congresses either in the USSR or abroad;

have had their unofficial meetings disrupted.

In conclusion, Mr Kastler requests the President of the USSR Academy of Sciences to explain these alleged violations of human rights.

(*b*) *A dossier on Irina Brailovski*

(1) It contains a brief biography illustrating her brilliant academic career, together with an account of the difficulties she experienced from 1972, when she first requested permission for her family to be able to emigrate, until 18 June 1981, when her husband was sentenced to five years' exile within the country for "spreading anti-Soviet propaganda". (She was able to attend the trial with her son.)

(2) In this dossier mention is made of a declaration by Mr Anatoli Logunov, Rector of the Moscow State University, who is alleged to have said to an astrophysicist from Princeton, on a visit to this city in October 1979, that "the University of Moscow had no objection to the departure of Irina Brailovski and that he would inform the OVIR (the visa office)".

(3) As evidence of some of the harassment to which the alleged victim has been subjected, the dossier also includes the following information:

(i) *a written statement (under oath) by Professor Maurice Bertran Priestly of the University of Manchester, Institute of Science and Technology*, testifying that a scientific meeting at the home of Irina Brailovski was disrupted by the police on 15 March 1981;

(ii) *a written statement by Professor H. Diamant of Umeå University (Sweden)* who claims to have witnessed, on 24 April 1981, the anguish of Irina Brailovski who was totally without news of her imprisoned husband, and on 25 April, the action by the police and the KGB to prevent a seminar being held at her home;

(iii) *a written statement (under oath) by Mr Claude Deutsch of the Physics Laboratory for Gases and Plasmas (a laboratory associated with the CNRS)*, testifying that on 31 May and 1 June 1980, during his stay in Moscow, the Brailovski's telephone had been put out of use;

(iv) *an invitation dated April 1978 from Cornell University (Ithaca, New York) to various conferences and consultations and an invitation dated December 1977 to an international symposium at the University of Sheffield.* Irina Brailovski was unable to reply to these invitations.

(c) A dossier on Victor Brailovski

It contains basic information about the person concerned (date of birth, profession, address) and an account of the difficulties which he experienced from his first application to emigrate in 1972, until his conviction for breaking Article 190/1 of the Russian Criminal Code.

(d) A dossier on Alexandre Lerner

[1] It contains a brief biography followed by an account of the difficulties which he experienced from September 1971, when the Soviet authorities intercepted a letter of invitation which was sent by the members of his family living in Israel, and when he submitted an official request to emigrate, until the death of his wife from a heart attack in July 1981.

[2] His daughter Sonia, who had been given permission to emigrate, was able to attend her mother's funeral.

[3] As evidence of some of the difficulties experienced by Mr Lerner, the dossier also includes the following information:

[i] *A written statement (under oath) by Mrs Sonia Levin (née Lerner)*

Confirming the dismissal of her father from the Institute of Cybernetics and from the Moscow Physico-Technical Institute (it is alleged that Mr Lerner was requested to leave the lecture room during his course and, on his refusal, that the students were forced to leave) and also confirming what has already been stated above concerning the interception of the letter of invitation from Israel.

Instancing the failure to forward an invitation sent to her father by the American Mathematical Society in 1978, and also the cutting off of the family telephone in Moscow (No. 137 53 96) for the first time in May 1972 (allegedly under the pretext of the need to carry out repairs on a cable, which then took a year and a half to complete) and then again in 1973, some time after October, until the death of her mother in July 1981. As a result, it is alleged, it was impossible to call an ambulance urgently when her mother fell ill. (In addition, all the telegrams of condolence from Israel and most of the telegrams from Western countries are alleged to have been intercepted.)

[ii] *An invitation to a symposium dated 8 January 1980, sent by IFAC in Toulouse (International Federation of Automatic Control - France) and an invitation dated 11 March 1981 from the University of Paris VII to Mr Lerner to take up a post as associate professor for the university year 1981/1982*, invitations which the scientist was unable to answer.

[iii] *An open letter by Mr Lerner, dated 13 August 1979*, protesting against the Soviet authorities' opposition to his accepting an invitation to the 9th Congress of the International Political Science Association in Moscow, and against his replacement by another person.

(e) A dossier on Vladimir Kislik

[1] It lists the harassment experienced by this physicist following his application to emigrate in October 1973: loss of his job at the Institute of Physics in Kiev (where he had been working since 1966); the fact that he has not been able to work for eight years now; the deletion of his name from all scientific publications, the interception of his mail; threats of arrest and of prosecution for "black-market activities" should he continue to hold scientific seminars in his home; his apartment has been searched; he was arrested in July 1980, freed two weeks later and arrested again in May 1981 and sentenced to three years in a camp for "serious hooliganism"

[2] Following a telephone conversation with Israel in May 1976, it is alleged that his telephone was permanently cut off.

[3] This dossier contains a copy of a letter dated 20 July 1981 from Mr Kislik's lawyer, Mr Daniel Jacobi, protesting against the silence of the Soviet Embassy in Paris in response to his request for a visa to visit the USSR in order to defend his client both in the Court of First Instance and on appeal.

(f) A dossier on Nahum Meiman

[1] After a short biography it gives an account of the difficulties experienced by the mathematician since he applied to emigrate in 1974.

[2] Mr Meiman, it is alleged, was arrested for the first time in November 1976, and again in 1977, though his detention did not last very long. It is alleged that his telephone was cut off after he was arrested for the first time.

[3] In January 1980, it is alleged that the legal authorities forbade him to have anything more to do with the Supervisory Committee for the Application of the Helsinki Agreements.

[4] The scientist's family were apparently given permission to emigrate in 1977.

[5] He is elderly and in poor health and, it is alleged, he now lives alone and the clinic which looked after him for several years has refused to take care of him.

588. At the Committee's [autumn 1981] session, the representative of the Soviet Government stated that the contention of the authors that the sentencing of Mr Brailovski was unfair, was an unfounded and offensive contention. He went on to explain that the legal provision under which Mr Brailovski has been sentenced was one which prohibited the systematic circulation of defamatory ideas, i.e. ideas which were known to be false by their author. At Mr Brailovski's trial, which had been an open one, it had been shown that Mr Brailovski had been engaged since 1972 in the circulation of materials which he knew to be false and damaging to the reputation of the Soviet system. In those materials, for which he was responsible either as an author or as an editor, it was contended that racism and anti-Semitism were widespread in the Soviet Union. During his trial it had been shown that, under the guise of fighting anti-Semitism, Mr Brailovski was in fact being chauvinistic and was disseminating anti-Soviet slander. The court had been lenient and had handed down a sentence which did not deprive him of freedom. He had been sentenced to a five-year internal exile, which had been reduced to three years in view of his time served. For these reasons the communication was ill-founded and inadmissible.

589. In reply to questions, he stated that there was no punishment in the Soviet Union of persons applying for exist visas. Thousands of Jews were allowed to leave the Soviet Union every year. The representative of the Soviet Government pointed out that Mr Brailovski could have left the country long ago but since his wife had not been allowed to leave, for security reasons, he had chosen to stay. As for the term "exile", it meant compulsory settling within the confines of a given administrative region, in which the person was free to circulate, work and live with his family. Under certain exceptional circumstances he could be allowed to exit for brief periods.

590. A Committee member stated that this was a case where a person had been sentenced as a criminal, merely for expressing himself in writing. Such an action could be seen as contrary to the Universal Declaration of Human Rights, he said, and, furthermore, though it was true that libel laws existed throughout the world, they provided for civil penalties not criminal penalties. The question of what was a false statement was a subjective one, he said, and one man's falsehood was sometimes another man's truth. Communist parties throughout the world were constantly making harsh remarks about the countries in which they were located and they were not prosecuted for making such statements, the Connnittee members had added. The speaker felt it important that the Committee's concern for the right to the freedom of expression should be clearly expressed in this case. He stressed that Mr Brailovski's assertion that there was anti-Semitism in the Soviet Union could be seen by some to be a true statement, but that in any event such a statement could hardly be seen as dangerous enough to warrant criminal penalties; freedom of speech must be seen to include the freedom to criticize rightly or wrongly.

591. Another Committee member felt that it would not be useful to go into comparisons of ideology. However, in practical terms the Committee's concern should be noted in cases such as this where the penalty was disproportionately severe for the acts alleged to have been committed.

592. Another Committee member felt that the Committee should look dispassionately at the facts and realize that certain countries punished acts which others did not consider punishable. Since it appeared that Mr Brailovski was being allowed to work and since the Connnittee was not competent to help him emigrate or change his sentence, it was not competent in this matter, he said.

593. After lengthy discussion, the Committee decided:[9]

(i) to ask the delegate of the government concerned to provide all the necessary information concerning the present status of Mr Brailovski and to re-

[9] See document 113 EX/38 PRIV., para. 364 (*supra*, p. 611).

quest him to make known to the proper authorities the Committee's exclusively humanitarian interest in the cases of the alleged victim and his wife;

(ii) to transmit this information. in conjunction with the other new facts that had appeared in this case, to the authors of the two communications;

(iii) to resume consideration of the admissibility of the two communications at the present session.

594. In considering the cases of the other persons cited in these communications, the Committee decided to apply the terms of its aforementioned decision, *mutatis mutandis*, in these cases also, while at the same time stressing that in the case of Mr Meiman, old age was an additional factor which merited humanitarian considerations by the competent Soviet authorities.[10]

595. On 10 March 1982, the Secretariat received from Mr Alfred Kastler, the author of the connnunication, a letter drawing attention to the aggravation of the situation of the alleged victims. He describes as "deeply shocking" the fact that Mr Brailovski could be convicted for circulating documents stating that "racism and anti-Semitism are widespread in the USSR", since he considers that "to hold opinions and ideas and to express and spread them are human rights which are recognized in the Universal Declaration of Human Rights and reaffirmed in the Helsinki Final Act".

596. In a brief review of the facts concerning the other alleged victims, Mr Kastler states that, having written to the President of the Academy of Sciences of the USSR requesting the latter to confirm or refute the allegations contained in his communication and not having received an answer, he is entitled to interpret this silence as confirmation of the facts he has submitted to the Committee.

597. Five files are annexed to this letter:

[*a*] *File on Irina Brailovski*

The condition of the alleged victim is stated to have deteriorated considerably following the sending of her husband into internal exile and the forced suspension of the seminar which was being held at her place of residence.

The documents contained in this file are identical to those which Mr Kastler transmitted to the Secretariat with his letter of 29 July 1981, whose substance has already been reported in the summary of that communication.

---

[10] *Ibidem*, para. 365 (*supra*, p. 611).

No. 242/80 **Union of Soviet Socialist Republics**

[*b*] *File on Victor Brailovski*

This file contains, in addition to the documents already received by the Secretariat during the [autumn 1981] session, the following supplementary information:

on 24 August 1981 the appeals court confirmed the judgement of the Court of First Instance convicting Mr Brailovski;

in September 1981 Mr Brailovski was transferred by special aeroplane to his place of exile where he found accommodation and work, consisting in the repair of calculators;

lastly, the author of the communication states that on 4 March 1982 he learned that the alleged victim has been ordered not to leave his residence after 7 p.m. He believes that this order conflicts with the "internal exile" regime described by the representative of the Soviet Government at the [autumn 1981] session.

[*c*] *File on Alexandre Lerner*

This file consists of photocopies of all the documents already received by the Secretariat, plus two new documents:

a photocopy of Mr Lerner's letter accepting the offer of a post of associate teacher at Université de Paris VII for the year 1981-1982; (the author of the communication reports that the University authorities have just renewed the offer for the year 1982-1983);

a photocopy of a message from Mr Lerner addressed to the participants in the Eighth Congress of IFAC (International Federation of Automatic Control) informing them of his distressing situation.

[*d*] *File on Vladimir Kislik*

This file contains the following additional information:

in September 1981, Mr Kislik was transferred to a camp at Donetsk (Ukraine); during the transfer he came down with dysentery accompanied by bleeding and was placed in Dniepropetrovsk prison hospital;

in November 1981 he was detained in a camp at Dzerzhinsk;

in January 1982 he was granted "early conditional release subject to assigned employment";

he now resides under surveillance at Jdanov, where he works as a welder and must report to the militia three times a day.

The following items are attached to the file:

a set of photocopies of documents relating to the steps taken by Mr Kislik's lawyers with a view to obtaining a visa for entry into the Soviet Union;

a photocopy of a statement by Mr Paul Kessler, Director of Research at the Centre National de la Recherche Scientifique (CNRS), who had met Mr Kislik at Kiev on 17 April 1980; according to this statement, the alleged victim told his visitor that the authorities had caused him all kinds of annoyance and had prevented foreigners from contacting him; regarding this last point, Mr Kessler indicated that, while he had succeeded in reaching Mr Kislik, he had suffered a number of provocations upon returning to his hotel and, when he had attempted the following day to visit some friends of the physicist, he had been attacked and turned back.

[*e*] *File on Nahum Meiman*

The new document on this file is a written statement by Professor Yves Quéré, a French physicist, who claims to have met Mr Meiman on 9 and 10 January 1982 in the latter's Moscow apartment. He states that Mr Meiman told him that the Soviet authorities had repeatedly denied his requests for an emigration visa, that he had been summoned frequently by the KGB and the magistrate and that his telephone line had been disconnected (on 13 March 1981). The mathematician's health had deteriorated considerably. In order to call a doctor, his wife had to go outside to a public telephone booth, even in very cold weather: she had recently had to go out for this purpose twenty times when the temperature in Moscow was around -30°C.

Professor Quéré ends his statement by pointing out that all Mr Meiman requests is the elementary right to emigrate to a country of his choice and to be reunited with his family.

598. On 19 March 1982, the Secretariat received a letter from the Greater New York Conference on Soviet Jewry arguing that the explanations furnished by the representative of the Soviet Government at the [autumn 1981] session were not in accordance with the facts and that the ill-treatment of Mr Brailovski dated from the time of his first emigration request. The author of the communication states that, according

to the information which he was able to obtain, the conviction of the cyberneticist had been based on unsupported statements: no witness had implicated him directly in any offence. The Greater New York Conference on Soviet Jewry also considers that the penalty imposed on the alleged victim is excessive. The author points out that Mr Brailovski is still deprived of all contact with friends and colleagues.

599. Attached to this letter are photocopies of documents already in the file and photocopies of letters from the Secretariat informing the author of the communication of the decision taken by the Connnittee at preceding sessions.

600. The third communication [...] is a new one which the Committee decided to consider at the same time as the two already pending communications concerning Mr Brailovski.

601. This communication is submitted by Mrs Kay O. Curry and Mrs Amy Young Anawaty on behalf of the International Human Rights Law Group, a non-governmental organization having reliable knowledge of the alleged violations.

602. Mr Victor Brailovski is described as a teacher and a scientist who has worked in the fields of computer science and cybernetics. It is alleged that he lost his job in his own special field in 1972 and that since then he has been deprived of all opportunities to teach and of all access to libraries (his admission card has been confiscated). It is also claimed that his telephone has been cut off, his apartment searched and that his scientific books and his books on Jewish culture have been confiscated, as well as certain of his own works, in particular a manuscript and some articles written for publication in a cultural journal entitled "The Jews in the USSR". It was reportedly the contents of this journal which constituted the main reason for his conviction although it is said that it pursued no political aims; apart from being an expression of Jewish culture, it allegedly contained interviews with two important members of the Human Rights Movement, Messrs Andrei Sakharov and Evgeny Barabanov.

603. He was arrested in Moscow in November 1980 and allegedly accused of having circulated documents which he knew to be false and which slandered the Soviet state and the social system. Sentenced on 18 June 1981 to five years' internal exile - a sentence which is said to be longer than the maximum laid down by the law - he reportedly had his sentence subsequently reduced to 39 months because of the time he had already served. Before his arrest, and in order to keep his scientific knowledge up to date after the loss of his employment, Mr Brailovski allegedly participated or attempted to participate in seminars - when he did not hold them in his own home - which gave him the opportunity to meet colleagues and communicate with them. In this respect too, his rights would not appear to have been recognized.

604. With regard to the means of redress used, the authors wish to state that Mr Brailovski's appeal has not achieved any positive result, the Supreme Court having upheld the previous decision. It is also pointed out that, during the court of first instance proceedings, the friends of the alleged victim were not admitted to the courtroom.

605. With regard to the purpose and aim of this communication, the authors would like the Director-General and the Executive Board to use their good offices to bring about a humanitarian solution in this affair. They also request that Unesco should recommend the Soviet Government to return to Mr Brailovski his library card so that he may use the libraries and carry on with his scientific work. Furthermore, they request that he should receive proper medical treatment. Finally, they request that the communication should be submitted to the Executive Board for its examination.

606. Two documents are appended to the communication:

> (i) a document giving information about the legal status of the "International Human Rights Law Group";
>
> (ii) a document reproducing the articles from international instruments which the authors of the communication consider to have been violated by the Soviet authorities in the case of Mr Brailovski. They are available to members of the Committee in the Secretariat.

607. The Committee at its present session decided to examine the case of Mr Brailovski separately from the other cases.

608. The representative of the Soviet Government stated that he wished to respond to the decision which the Committee took at its [autumn 1981] session. He said that he was certain that the Committee saw that the sentencing of Mr Brailovski had been properly carried out by a Soviet court in accordance with Soviet law. He explained that Mr Brailovski was presently living in internal exile in the Maisyeshlak region in the Kayekstan town of Bencou.

609. The authors were ill-informed about Soviet legislation, the representative said, they did not know that Article 43 of the Criminal Code allowed for less severe sentences in certain cases.

610. The Soviet representative informed the Committee that Mr Brailovski was presently working as one of 13 persons of diverse nationalities, as a calculating machine mechanic. Mr Brailovski himself had selected the working conditions, it was ex-

plained. He worked from 8 a.m. to[11] and after work he read and continued his personal work. He lived in a one-room flat, with certain shared facilities, in conditions typical for the area. The prosecutor of the region had informed the Soviet representative that Mr Brailovski's wife came occasionally to visit for a few days at a time and she brought him scientific and non-scientific reading material. His son also had visited. The author's request for Mr Brailovski's library card to be returned was absurd. The Soviet representative said when Mr Brailovski returned to Moscow he would be able to obtain one on simple application to the library. Furthermore his free time was his own to use as he pleased, it was explained and his wife and children could live with him but they preferred to live in Moscow. It was the view of the Soviet representative that there was no basis for the Committee to concern itself any further with this case.

611. A Committee member expressed appreciation for the information which the Soviet representative had provided, but he went on to point out that Mr Brailovski had been deprived of his liberty for merely publishing and circulating information about Jews in the Soviet Union. Though the Committee was not a tribunal he said, it was nevertheless in a position to offer its comments to the Soviet authorities since the case was within Unesco's competence and thus admissible.

612. Another Committee member concurred with this view and added that Mr Brailovski's problems seemed to have started with his request to emigrate to Israel. This fact should be placed side by side with the scientific aspects of the case, he said.

613. A Committee member felt that Mr Brailovski had been duly sentenced according to Soviet law and that Unesco's competence here was doubtful since Mr Brailovski's so-called intellectual activity predated the events leading to his arrest.

614. It was felt by another Committee member that all 10 conditions of admissibility were met and that the case was therefore admissible.

615. Another Committee member felt that the Committee must come to the conclusion that the case was inadmissible since the Committee could not challenge the national laws of the state concerned.

616. Still another Committee member pointed out that the Committee on several occasions had commented on governmental or court actions when those actions were of concern to Unesco and when the acts concerned did not involve violence. In this case the right to communicate was at issue and this was of prime concern to Unesco.

[11] Omission in the original text.

Union of Soviet Socialist Republics **No. 242/80**

617. Following the proposal of the [Chairman], the Committee then *decided* to ask the Executive Board to invite the Director-General to take action in accordance with paragraph 14 (*k*) of 104 EX/Decision 3.3 to seek a friendly solution to [Mr Brailovski's] case, and to resume consideration of the admissibility of the [case] at its next session.

618. The Committee further *decided* that the above-mentioned decision concerning Mr Brailovski should also be applied to the cases of Messrs Kislik, Lerner and Meiman.

Autumn 1982 session of the Committee on Conventions and Recommendations (115th session of the Executive Board)[12]

232. This communication[13] is submitted by Mrs Kay O. Curry and Mrs Amy Young Anawaty on behalf of the International Human Rights Law Group, a non-governmental organization having reliable knowledge of the alleged violations.

233. Mr Victor Brailovski is described as a teacher and a scientist who has worked in the fields of computer science and cybernetics. It is alleged that he lost his job in his own special field in 1972 and that since then he has been deprived of all opportunities to teach and of all access to libraries (his admission card has been confiscated). It is also claimed that his telephone has been cut off, his apartment searched and that his scientific books and his books on Jewish culture have been confiscated, as well as certain of his own works, in particular a manuscript and some articles written for publication in a cultural journal entitled "The Jews in the USSR". It was reportedly the contents of this journal which constituted the main reason for his conviction although it is said that it pursued no political aims; apart from being an expression of Jewish culture, it allegedly contained interviews with two important members of the Human Rights Movement, Messrs Andrei Sakharov and Evgeny Barabanov.

[233a.] He was arrested in Moscow, in November 1980 and allegedly accused of having circulated documents which he knew to be false and which slandered the Soviet State and the social system. Sentenced on 18 June 1981 to five years' internal exile - a sentence which is said to be longer than the maximum laid down by the law - he reportedly had his sentence subsequently reduced to 39 months because of the time he had already served.

---

[12] See document 115 EX/28 PRIV., paras. 232-262; see also document 115 EX/CR/HR/2.

[13] Communication No. 418/81 concerning *Union of Soviet Socialist Republics*, case of *Victor Brailovski*, considered together with communications No. 242/80 concerning *Union of Soviet Socialist Republics*, case of *Victor Brailovski* et al., and No. 346/81 concerning *Union of Soviet Socialist Republics*, case of *Victor Brailovski*.

[233b.] Before his arrest, and in order to keep his scientific knowledge up to date after the loss of his employment, Mr Brailovski allegedly participated or attempted to participate in seminars - when he did not hold them in his own home - which gave him the opportunity to meet colleagues and communicate with them. In this respect too, his rights would not appear to have been recognized.

234. The authors are of the opinion that there have been violations by the Soviet authorities of Mr Brailovski's human rights, and in particular, of his right to carry on his profession as a scientist, his right to information and communication, his right to freedom of conscience and his right to the freedom of expression of his culture and of his religious beliefs. It would therefore seem that there has been a failure to respect the principles laid down in the Charter of the United Nations, in the Universal Declaration of Human Rights, in the International Covenants on Civil and Political Rights and on Economic, Social and Cultural Rights, in the Helsinki Agreements, in the Convention and Recommendation against Discrimination in Education (Unesco) and in the Declaration of the Principles of International Co-operation (Unesco).

235. With regard to the means of redress used, the authors wish to state that Mr Brailovski's appeal has not achieved any positive result, the Supreme Court having upheld the previous decision. It is also pointed out that, during the court of first instance proceedings, the friends of the alleged victim were not admitted to the courtroom.

236. The case of Mr Brailovski is the subject of two other communications submitted by Mr Alfred Kastler, a member of the Academy of Science in Paris and a member of the French National Council for Protection of the Rights of Jews in the USSR, and by the Greater New York Conference on Soviet Jewry [...].They have been pending before the Committee since the [spring] 1981 session. At the [autumn 1981] session, the Committee requested the representative of the government concerned to provide, at the next session, all the necessary information concerning the present status of Mr Brailovsky and to make known to the appropriate Soviet authorities the Committee's exclusively humanitarian interest in the case of the alleged victim.[14]

237. At the spring 1982 session, the representative of the Soviet Government recalled his country's position regarding the decision taken by the Committee at the autumn 1981 session. He stated that the sentencing of Mr Brailowski had been carried out in accordance with Soviet law. He informed the Committee that at Maisyeshlak, the place of his internal exile, Mr Brailovski was working as a calculating machine mechanic, that he had himself selected his working conditions and that he

[14] See document 113 EX/38 PRIV., para. 364 (i) (*supra*, p. 611).

had opportunities for reading and following his own pursuits, using his leisure time as he pleased.

238. The representative of the Soviet Government said that the prosecutor of the region concerned had informed him that Mrs Brailovski came occasionally to visit her husband, bringing him both scientific and non-scientific reading matter. He added that this cyberneticist's son had also been able to visit his father. According to the Soviet Government's representative, Mr Brailovski's wife and children could come to live with him but had preferred to remain in Moscow.

239. Concerning the request of the International Human Rights Law Group [...] that Mr Brailovski's library card be returned to him, the representative of the Soviet Government stated that Mr Brailovski could obtain one simply by applying to the library when he returned to Moscow.

240. Some Committee members felt that Unesco's competence in the matter was doubtful, since Mr Brailovski's purported intellectual activity pre-dated the events leading to his arrest, and the Committee could in no way challenge the national laws of the country concerned. They had come to the conclusion that the case being examined was inadmissible.

241. Some other Committee members considered the case to be wholly within Unesco's competence because Mr Brailovski's problems appeared to have started with his request for authorization to emigrate to Israel, because he had been deprived of his liberty for merely publishing and circulating information about Jews in the Soviet Union and because what was at issue here was the right to communicate.

242. After an exchange of view, the Committee decided:[15]

> to ask the Executive Board to invite the Director-General to take action in accordance with paragraph 14 (*k*) of 104 EX/Decision 3.3 to seek an amicable solution to Mr Brailovski's case; and to resume consideration of its admissibility at the present session.

243. The Committee further decided that the decision should also be applied to the cases of Messrs Kislik, Lerner and Meiman.[16]

244. On 20 July 1982 the Secretariat received from Mr Alfred Kastler [...] a letter the text of which is reproduced below.

---

[15] See document 114 EX/38 PRIV., para. 617 (*supra*, p. 625).
[16] *Ibidem*, para. 618 (*supra*, p. 625).

245. Enclosed with the letter were sworn statements by Messrs Paul Kessler and Alfred Ramani, two French physicists who recently visited Moscow and Kiev in the Soviet Union from 1 to 8 July 1982.

246. From these statements, the following facts may be noted.

A. *Situation of Victor and Irina Brailovski*

247. Mr Brailovski is still at his place of exile. He was visited in May by his wife, son and daughter, who were not able to stay long on account of the region's extremely severe climate.

248. Mrs Irina Brailovski's opportunities for engaging in her scientific work are severely limited.

B. *Situation of Mr Alexandre Lerner*

249. There has been no improvement in his situation. He is suffering from angina pectoris. He was not able, despite his work on the artificial heart, to attend a congress on cardiology held recently in Moscow.

C. *Situation of Mr Nahum Meiman*

250. His state of health gives cause for alarm. His scientific work is severely limited.

D. *Situation of Mr Vladimir Kislik*

251. Having been conditionally released from the camp at Dzerzhinsk, he was transferred to Zhdanov on 25 January 1982. He worked for a time as a welder. In February he had an accident at work (a broken finger). Since then he has been on lighter duties as a quality-control inspector.

252. Mr Kislik is suffering from a serious heart disease.

253. Mr Ramani states that he has kept up a lengthy correspondence with Mr Kislik. Most of his letters are held up for a long time before reaching their destination; some do not arrive at all. The Soviet postal authorities admit the loss of a number of the letters and have paid him compensation.

254. At the autumn 1982 session, the representative of the Soviet Government pointed out that Mr Kastler in his letter of 15 July conceded that the Soviet representative's statements about Mr Brailovski's working conditions were accurate. The au-

thor did, however, put forward a new assertion, namely that Mr Brailovski's family had found the climate unfavourable for visits and that the daughter had developed an ailment in her limbs. This was a matter for a doctor to look into, the Soviet representative said, and it did not change the fact that Mr Brailovski's family was free to visit him.

255. The author of the parallel communication asserted that Mr Brailovski did not have access to local libraries. This was not true, the Soviet representative said; Mr Brailovski had access just as much as others in the region did. As for Mr Meiman, he was said to be suffering from several health problems, but he was of course a very elderly man, the Soviet representative stated, and his condition consequently could not be seen as being very unusual.

256. As to the assertion that Mr Lerner was dismayed that he had not been invited to a congress of heart specialists, the Soviet representative explained that the organizers of the congress had told him that Mr Lerner's former field of specialization had not been on the agenda of the congress and that they therefore did not invite him. The Soviet representative further explained that Mr Kislik had been transferred to another camp, his conditions of work had been eased and his situation had improved, even though he had had an accident in which he broke his finger. It was then pointed out that the importance of the computer information which Mrs Brailovski possessed had not changed, and the national security restrictions on her emigration possibilities thus remained in force.

257. A Committee member felt that the question of admissibility of this case had to be decided in the negative since the Soviet Union had domestic laws barring emigration for certain security reasons. It was gratifying that the working conditions of the persons involved had been improved, and the Committee member expressed the hope that the Soviet authorities.would continue to keep humanitarian aspects in mind and to allow the persons to work in their fields of competence.

258. A Committee member pointed out that while the Committee could not question the emigration laws and policies of the Soviet Union, it could and should be concerned about the patterns of events which so often followed applications for emigration visas in that country. The fact that the personal situation of these persons could be worse, as the Soviet representative had said, did not excuse the violation of these persons' right to function in their own profession. The Committee member emphasized that to drop this matter now would mean the Committee endorsed the action which had been taken against these persons.

259. Another Committee member felt that this was clearly a matter involving slander, not freedom of expression. If the Committee allowed itself to look at the deci-

sion of the tribunal in question it would be passing judgement on the internal legislation of a country. It was nothing more than the internal application of the penal code of a country and these cases were clearly inadmissible, the Committee member said.

260. The Committee was reminded by certain of its members that it had previously looked at countries' domestic legislation in several other cases. The international normative instruments made it possible to compare the national legislations with the standards of those instruments, and it was right and appropriate to do so. The question arose as to what sort of "intervention" was possible; coercive measures were of course clearly excluded. One Committee member said that the Committee could in fact engage in reviews and dialogues, and another member said that if the Committee did not look at the legislation of all countries in the same manner, it would be guilty of having different standards for different countries.

261. The question was posed by a Committee member as to how 13 letters addressed by registered mail to Mr Kislik could be lost in the Soviet Union. The Soviet representative explained that he felt it would be pointless to review endlessly the requirement that Unesco not interfere in the internal affairs of Member States. The restriction was quite clear, he said. As for the question of letters not reaching their destination in the Soviet Union, this was an administrative matter coming under the Universal Postal Union's competence and should not be examined by Unesco. The allegations that the alleged victims were limited in their professional activities as a result of their desire to emigrate were not true, the Soviet representative said, and he reminded the Committee that he had presented ample evidence to this effect. In the Kislik case, of course, the imprisonment had occurred as a result of a criminal conviction for battery with an automobile.

262. Thereupon, the Committee *decided*:

(i) to ask the Executive Board to invite the Director-General to take, within the scope of paragraph 14 (*k*) of 104 EX/Decision 3.3, all requisite steps, by whatever means he might deem appropriate, to achieve a friendly, humanitarian solution in respect of these communications;

(ii) to resume consideration of the admissibility of these communications at one of its forthcoming sessions, once new facts have been communicated to the Director-General.[17]

[17] See communication No. 346/81 concerning *Union of Soviet Socialist Republics*, case of *Victor Brailovski*.

No. 247/80

Concerning *Romania*
Case of *Gheorghe Calciu-Dumitreasa*

Communication of 16 April 1980 submitted by
Sergiu Grossu

Autumn 1980 session of the Committee on Conventions and Recommendations (110th session of the Executive Board)[1]

148. The author of the communication, Mr Sergiu Grossu, is a journalist and Director of the journal "Catacombes", acting on behalf of the Comité français pour la défense du prêtre roumain Gheorghe Calciu-Dumitreasa which has as its President the writer Virgil Gheoghiu, a former political detainee in Romania condemned on religious grounds.

149. The author of the communication complains of the arrest and condemnation to 10 years imprisonment of the priest Calciu-Dumitreasa.

150. Since 1977, Father Gheorghe Calciu-Dumitreasa, Professor of French and New Testament Studies at the Theological Seminar of Bucharest, has allegedly been subjected to reprisals: threatened following a sermon deploring the destruction of a church of historic value, forbidden to preach in certain places following a sermon against atheism and forbidden to preach at all following a series of lectures in May 1973. Subsequently, he is said to have had his contract as a priest suspended, to have been dismissed from his post as a professor and to have been handed over to the secret police. Pressures are said to have been exerted resulting in his wife losing her job; and a slanderous pamphlet was apparently sent to the tenants of his block. It is claimed that he was tortured following his arrest. His conviction on a criminal charge on 4 May 1979 was apparently upheld on 6 June 1979.

151. The author of the communication claims that Articles 3 (the right to life), 5 (degrading treatment), 12 (the right to privacy), 18 (freedom of thought), 19 (freedom

[1] See document 110 EX/40 PRIV., paras. 148-153; see also document 110 EX/CR/HR/3.

of opinion) and 23 (the right to work) of the Universal Declaration of Human Rights have been violated.

152. The representative of the Romanian Government explained to the Committee that the alleged victim in this case had been tried and convicted for taking part in fascist activities threatening the State. At the time of arrest the person in question had no longer been a teacher or a priest, the representative said, and since the arrest had not been related to this person's former activities there was no link between this case and Unesco's fields of competence.

153. The Committee took note of the Romanian representative's statement and *declared* the communication inadmissible as not falling within Unesco's competence.

No. 261/80

Concerning *Yugoslavia*
Case of *Zlatko Matković*

Communication of 21 June 1980 submitted by
Zlatko Matković

Spring 1981 session of the Committee on Conventions and Recommendations (112th session of the Executive Board)[1]

384. The author of the communication states that he is a physician, head of the clinical pharmacology division of the research department at the Dr Josip Kajfeš Hospital in Zagreb. Having completed advanced training in clinical pharmacology, in March 1976 he requested the competent authority, under the provisions of the law in force in Croatia, to issue him with a document certifying that he was qualified in this field, but this was refused. He claims that since then he has been subjected to various forms of harassment, coming chiefly from the Director of the hospital in which he is professionally employed. He claims furthermore that he submitted his case to the relevant courts, but has been unable to have the decisions given in his favour enforced.

385. The representative of the Yugoslav Government stated that the communication raised two problems: the problem of the certificate claimed by Dr Z. Matković, and the problem of his relationships with the Director of the hospital where he was employed. On the first point, the representative of the Yugoslav Government stated that the award of this diploma was subject to two requirements: completion of a period of resident hospital training and also the passing of an examination, and in fact Dr Z. Matković had not sat this examination. With regard to the second point, he stressed that the problems existing between the author and the Director of the hospital were an internal matter for this institution and could only be solved by the hospital authorities themselves or by the courts.

386. A member of the Committee, who considered that the case was quite straight forward and that there was no need for the representative of the Yugloslav Govern-

[1] See document 112 EX/30 PRIV., paras. 384-387; see also document 112 EX/CR/HR/3.

ment to put forward further arguments, proposed that the communication should be declared inadmissible as being manifestly ill-founded, and this was supported by all the members who subsequently spoke.

387. Consequently, the Committee *decided* to declare the communication inadmissible as being manifestly ill-founded with regard to one of its claims, and as not falling within Unesco's fields of competence with regard to the other, in accordance respectively with subparagraphs 14 (*a*) (v) and (iii) of 104 EX/Decision 3.3.

No. 264/80

Concerning *France*
Case of *Zien Al Smail*

Communication of 26 June 1980 submitted by
Zien Al Smail

Spring 1981 session of the Committee on Conventions and Recommendations (112th session of the Executive Board)[1]

125. The author of the communication, aged 34, of Syrian nationality, is said to have been a student in 1975-1976 at the School of Physiotherapy in Orléans. Having failed his end-of-year examination, he was informed by the Director of the institution that he would have to repeat the year in question, then that he would have to leave the school. Following the intervention of the Ministry of Health in September 1975, he is said to have been readmitted to the school. Having once again failed his end-of-year examination, he is said to have been finally excluded from the institution. Believing that his exclusion was due to the fact that the Director was opposed to the presence of foreigners in the school, he reportedly appealed, without success, to the competent Administrative Court (his claim appears to have been rejected on 10 February 1978) and to the Conseil d'État (claim said to have been rejected on 27 July 1979).

126. Mr Zien Al Smail wishes to be permitted to enrol in a school of physiotherapy.

127. Referring the decision on the admissibility of the communication to the judgement of the Committee, the representative of the government concerned wondered whether the inability to pass an examination constituted a violation of human rights.

128. It rapidly became clear to the Committee that the case was inadmissible: Unesco could not play the part of an examining board or a supranational court of appeal in order to alleviate a student's disappointments in his studies, more particularly since the competent administrative authorities, including the Conseil d'État, had al-

[1] See document 112 EX/30 PRIV., paras. 125-130; see also document 112 EX/CR/HR/3.

ready delivered unfavourable verdicts as to the grounds for his complaints and claims.

129. For those reasons, the Committee *declared* the communication inadmissible in accordance with paragraph 14 (*a*) (v) of 104 EX/Decision 3.3.

130. A Committee member trusted that the French authorities would show indulgence towards the student Zien Al Smail, who wished to be enrolled in another establishment providing an identical course.

No. 266/80

Concerning *Argentina*
Case of *Elba Aurora Martínez de Larrea*

Communication of 19 May 1980 submitted by
Elba Aurora Martínez de Larrea

Spring 1981 session of the Committee on Conventions and Recommendations (112th session of the Executive Board)[1]

25. The author of the communication claims to be a teacher of Spanish language and literature and to be the victim of measures taken against her by the Argentine administrative authorities. The Ministry of Education is said to have forbidden her, by its decision of 23 November 1975, to conduct classes anywhere in the country for a period of five years, without having carried out a preliminary investigation and without giving her a chance to defend herself.

26. The person concerned claims that she had at the time recently passed a competitive examination which gave her the right to teach for a stipulated maximum number of hours per week. It is claimed that, as a result of the ministerial decision, she also forfeited her social security rights and her retirement pension rights. Bearing in mind that she is approaching 50, Mrs Elba Aurora Martínez de Larrea feels that she is the victim of an unjust and inhuman measure, which is in conflict with human rights, with basic Argentine law and with the precepts of the Argentine Constitution.

27. The representative of the government concerned indicated that the author of the communication presented the matter as though the measure complained of constituted a punishment, whereas it was a purely administrative measure taken under a law of 1974 and motivated by budgetary considerations. He added that the person concerned had been entitled to an equitable indemnity at the time when the decision was taken to terminate her teaching duties.

28. Having observed that not only did the facts which had prompted the allegation antedate the introduction of the communication by almost five years (November

[1] See document 112 EX/30 PRIV., paras. 25-28; see also document 112 EX/CR/HR/3.

1975/May 1980) but that the communication itself did not lie within the fields of Unesco's competence (contractual conflict between the administration and the author), the Committee *decided* to declare it inadmissible in accordance with paragraph 14 (*a*) (iii) and (viii) of 104 EX/Decision 3.3.

No. 267/80

Concerning *Chile*
Case of *Pedro Segundo Ahumada Pizarro*

Communication of 24 April 1980 submitted by
Pedro Segundo Ahumada Pizarro

Spring 1981 session of the Committee on Conventions and Recommendations (112th session of the Executive Board)[1]

75. The author of the communication, who is a student, claims to have been victimized by the Chilean university authorities, who are alleged to have expelled him from the faculty where he was studying for having publicly criticized the university and government authorities, with particular reference to price increases for student transport.

76. The representative of the government concerned told the Committee that the student had received an initial warning for having publicly challenged government measures relating to the charges for transport. Instead of applying to the body qualified to deal with such matters, as had been suggested to him in that warning, he had launched a public appeal against the government, which led the university authorities to expel him from the university.

77. One member of the Committee stated clearly that he was in favour of treating the communication as admissible. All the other members who spoke were chiefly concerned to appeal to the spirit of co-operation that the Chilean Government had already shown in the past, urging it to consider on what conditions the student might resume his university studies.

78. While acknowledging that students had a right to education, the representative of the Chilean Government emphasized that they also had a duty to respect their country's institutions; nevertheless, although the Chilean Government was not itself involved, he agreed to intercede personally with the Council of the University from

[1] See document 112 EX/30 PRIV., paras. 75-79; see also document 112 EX/CR/HR/3.

which the student had been expelled, in the hope that he might be given another chance.

79. The Committee accordingly *decided* to take note of the statements made by the representative of the Chilean Government and to resume discussion of the admissibility of this communication at its next session.

Autumn 1981 session of the Committee on Conventions and Recommendations (113th session of the Executive Board)[2]

123. The author of the communication, who is a student, claims to have been victimized by the Chilean university authorities, who are alleged to have expelled him from the faculty where he was studying for having publicly criticized the university and government authorities, with particular reference to price increases for student transport.

124. At the [spring 1981] session of the Committee the representative of the government concerned told the Committee that the student had received an initial warning for having publicly challenged government measures relating to the charges for transport. Instead of applying to the body qualified to deal with such matters, as was suggested to him in that warning, he had launched a public appeal against the government, which led the university authorities to expel him from the university.

125. One member of the Committee stated clearly that he was in favour of treating the communication as admissible. All the other members who spoke were chiefly concerned to appeal to the spirit of co-operation that the Chilean Government had already shown in the past, urging it to consider on what conditions the student might resume his university studies.

126. While acknowledging that students had a right to education, the representative of the Chilean Government emphasized that they also had a duty to respect their country's institutions; nevertheless, although the Chilean Government was not itself involved, he agreed to intercede personally with the Council of the University from which Mr Pizarro had been expelled, in the hope that he might be given another chance.

127. The Committee accordingly decided to take note of the statements made by the representative of the Chilean Government and to resume discussion of the admissibility of this communication at the present session.[3]

---

[2] See document 113 EX/38 PRIV., paras. 123-134; see also document 113 EX/CR/HR/2.

Chile **No. 267/80**

128 At this session, the representative of the Chilean Government explained that while this was a problem of internal university discipline in which it was not for the government to intervene by virtue of the principle of university autonomy, he had nevertheless personally approached the present Rector of the University as he had promised at the [spring 1981] session. The procedure which the student should follow was stated to be the following: he should write to the Rector of the University in order to ask him to reconsider the case, indicating any new facts which could serve to support his request for readmission, and he should then send a copy of that letter to the representative of the Chilean Government at Unesco, who declared his willingness to act as a mediator with the Rector of the University.

129. In the view of two members of the Committee, it was clear that the student concerned had been expelled not for reasons having to do with the university but for reasons having to do with the government. They considered that this might constitute a violation of democratic rights for which the Chilean Government was answerable.

130. The representative of the Chilean Government took the floor again to explain that he had not meant that the Government of Chile was not concerned with the case, but only that it was not responsible for solving a problem which came within the internal competence of the university. He was prepared to make his good offices available none the less.

131. One member pointed out that in higher education two sectors must be distinguished, namely the private and the public. In his own country, for example, actions that were permissible in the private sector were in some cases illegal in the public sector and not even the courts could intervene to settle certain matters that came within the jurisdiction of a private institution; he thus understood the Chilean Government's difficulty with regard to settlement of the problem. Another member remarked that the distinction was not relevant, inasmuch as every government was responsible for violations of human rights within its territory.

132. Many members subsequently stated that the Committee's main task was to try to find a practical solution to the problem. The offer of co-operation made by the representative of the government concerned should, therefore, be accepted, the Secretariat should be asked to notify the student of the possibility thus presented to him, and examination of the communication should be postponed until the next session. Other speakers, while also expressing approval of this solution, stated that they were surprised that the student should be asked to send the Chilean Government representative a copy of his letter to the Rector. One speaker asked whether this was an obli-

[3] See document 112 EX/30 PRIV., para. 79 (*supra*, p. 640).

gation incumbent upon the student; another indicated that such a requirement might dissuade the student from adopting the suggested procedure, since he might find it strange to be asked to send a letter to a representative of the government.

133. The representative of the Chilean Government explained that neither a question of principle nor an obligation was involved, but that if he was to play the role of mediator in the case and help to bring the matter to a satisfactory conclusion, it was important for him to be informed of the terms of the student's petition.

134. The Committee accordingly *decided*:

(i) to resume examination of the admissibility of this communication at the next session;

(ii) to ask the representative of the Chilean Government in the meantime to use his good offices in serving as a mediator with the university authorities;

(iii) to advise the author of the communication of the Chilean Government's offer, suggesting that he write to the Rector of the University to ask him to reconsider the case, indicating any new facts which could serve to support his request for readmission;

(iv) to ask the Chilean Government and the author of the communication to provide the Committee, at its next session, with all the information at their disposal concerning the outcome of this matter.

Spring 1982 session of the Committee on Conventions and Recommendations (114th session of the Executive Board)[4]

400. The author of the communication, who is a student, claims to have been victimized by the Chilean university authorities, who are alleged to have expelled him from the faculty where he was studying for having publicly criticized the university and government authorities, with particular reference to price increases for student transport.

401. At the spring 1981 session, the representative of the government concerned told the Committee that the student had received an initial warning for having publicly challenged government measures relating to the charges for transport. Instead of applying to the body qualified to deal with such matters, as was suggested to him in

[4] See document 114 EX/38 PRIV., paras. 400–415; see also document 114 EX/CR/HR/2.

that warning, he had launched a public appeal against the government, which led the university authorities to expel him from the university.

402. One member of the Committee stated clearly that he was in favour of treating the communication as admissible. All the other members who spoke were chiefly concerned to appeal to the spirit of co-operation that the Chilean Government had already shown in the past, urging it to consider on what conditions the student might resume his university studies.

403. While acknowledging that students had a right to education, the representative of the Chilean Government emphasized that they also had a duty to respect their country's institutions; nevertheless, although the Chilean Government was not itself involved, he agreed to intercede personally with the Council of the University from which Mr Pizarro had been expelled, in the hope that he might be given another chance.

404. The Committee accordingly decided to take note of the statements made by the representative of the Chilean Government and to resume discussion of the admissibility of this communication at the following session.[5]

405. At the autumn 1981 session, the representative of the Chilean Government explained that while this was a problem of internal university discipline in which it was not for the government to intervene by virtue of the principle of university autonomy, he had nevertheless personally approached the present Rector of the University as he had promised at the [spring 1981] session. The procedure which the student should follow was stated to be the following: he should write to the Rector of the University in order to ask him to reconsider the case, indicating any new facts which could serve to support his request for readmission, and he should then send a copy of that letter to the representative of the Chilean Government at Unesco, who declared his willingness to act as a mediator with the Rector of the University.

406. In the view of two members of the Committee, it was clear that the student concerned had been expelled not for reasons having to do with the university but for reasons having to do with the government. They considered that this might constitute a violation of democratic rights for which the Chilean Government was answerable.

407. The representative of the Chilean Government took the floor again to explain that he had not meant that the Government of Chile was not concerned with the case, but only that it was not responsible for solving a problem which came within the in-

[5] See document 112 EX/30 PRIV., para. 79 (*supra*, p. 640).

ternal competence of the university. He was prepared to make his good offices available none the less.

408. One member pointed out that in higher education two sectors must be distinguished, namely the private and the public. In his own country, for example, actions that were permissible in the private sector were in some cases illegal in the public sector and not even the courts could intervene to settle certain matters that came within the jurisdiction of a private institution; he thus understood the Chilean Government's difficulty with regard to settlement of the problem. Another member remarked that the distinction was not relevant, inasmuch as every government was responsible for violations of human rights within its territory.

409. Many members subsequently stated that the Committee's main task was to try to find a practical solution to the problem. The offer of co-operation made by the representative of the government concerned should, therefore, be accepted, the Secretariat should be asked to notify the student of the possibility thus presented to him, and examination of the communication should be postponed until the following session. Other speakers, while also expressing approval of this solution, stated that they were surprised that the student should be asked to send the Chilean Government representative a copy of his letter to the Rector. One speaker asked whether this was an obligation incumbent upon the student; another indicated that such a requirement might dissuade the student from adopting the suggested procedure, since he might find it strange to be asked to send a letter to a representative of the government.

410. The representative of the Chilean Government explained that neither a question of principle nor an obligation was involved, but that if he was to play the role of mediator in the case and help to bring the matter to a satisfactory conclusion, it was important for him to be informed of the terms of the student's petition.

411. The Committee therefore decided:[6]

(i) to resume examination of the admissibility of this communication at the present session;

(ii) to ask the representative of the Chilean Government in the meantime to use his good offices in serving as a mediator with the university authorities;

(iii) to advise the author of the communication of the Chilean Government's offer, suggesting that he write to the Rector of the University to ask him to

---

[6] See document 113 EX/38 PRIV., para. 134 (*supra*, p. 642).

reconsider the case, indicating any new facts which could serve to support his request for readmission;

(iv) to ask the Chilean Government and the author of the communication to provide the Committee, at the present session, with all the information at their disposal concerning the outcome of this matter.

412. On 6 January 1982 the Secretariat received the text of the letter delivered by the author to the Rector of the University of Santiago on 11 December 1981. In this document, Mr Pizarro requested the Rector to reconsider his case, in view of the fact that as a student he had always behaved respectfully towards the members of the university community, and that the fault held against him as the grounds for his expulsion should, according to Rule 15 of the university rules, entail a maximum penalty of expulsion for two academic semesters, a period which had been completed upon the entry into force of the measure taken in this connection.

413. At the present session, the representative of the government concerned stated that he had approached the university authorities; their reaction had been somewhat unenthusiastic but they had nevertheless been willing to listen to what he had to say. The Executive Secretary of the University's Academic Council had acknowledged that the matter was a difficult one, since not only did Mr Pedro Segundo Ahumada Pizarro have a lengthy record, he was also a poor student, his marks in science courses having been below the minimum required by the University. However, the fact that a new Rector had just been appointed might serve to facilitate a review of the situation. Mr Ahumada Pizarro had, in fact, submitted his request on 11 December 1981, but 10 days later, on 21 December, he had been distributing pamphlets against the new Rector, the very person whose indulgence he had been seeking. Consequently, the University authorities had advised the representative of the government that despite their desire to co-operate, they could see no obvious solution, unless Unesco would answer for the future conduct of this student, which was obviously out of the question. The representative of the Chilean Government said that in his view, after the sequence of events described he could not possibly undertake any further action on behalf of the person concerned.

414. One member of the Committee said that in his opinion this was a case of student revolt calling the very operation of the University into question, and that the communication must be declared inadmissible on the grounds that it was manifestly ill-founded. Another member suggested that the student concerned had acted on the spur of the moment and it might well be possible to "rehabilitate" him.

415. After a brief exchange of views, the Committee *decided* to take note of the statements of the representative of the Government of Chile and to declare the com-

munication inadmissible on the grounds that it was manifestly ill-founded under the provisions of paragraph 14 (*a*) (v) of 104 EX/Decision 3.3.

No. 269/80

Concerning *Republic of Korea*
Case of *Mong Yong Lee*

Communication of 24 June 1980 submitted by
Guy Dupré

Spring 1981 session of the Committee on Conventions and Recommendations (112th session of the Executive Board)[1]

193. As both of these communications[2] essentially dealt with the same alleged violations of human rights, which were imputed to the Korean authorities, the Committee decided to consider them at the same time.

194. The author of the first communication, the Secretary-General of the Fédération C.G.T. de l'Éducation, de la Recherche et de la Culture, acting on behalf of his organization, draws attention to grave violations of human rights in South Korea following the popular rising in Kwangju in May 1980 - involving the massacre, torture, arrest and condemnation of a large number of students, university lecturers, teachers, scientists and men of culture.

195. The main case quoted in the communication is that of Mr Mong Yong Lee, a teacher condemned to 20 years' imprisonment for plotting against the security of the state. The explanatory note attached gives the names of other victims:

> Dong Nyum Chung, a student leader, condemned to death;
>
> Eun Koh, a poet, sentenced at the same time as Mr Mong Yong Lee and to the same term of imprisonment;

---

[1] See document 112 EX/30 PRIV., paras. 193-213; see also documents 112 EX/CR/HR/3 and Add.3.
[2] Communications No. 269/80 concerning *Republic of Korea*, case of *Mong Yong Lee*, and No. 279/80 concerning *Republic of Korea*, case of *Kim Chi ha* et al.

No. 269/80 **Republic of Korea**

Tae Hong Kim, President of the Association of South Korean Journalists, arrested under the martial law;

Chi Ha Kim, a poet, imprisoned;

Dae Jung Kim, one of the opposition leaders in South Korea condemned to death (a number of distinguished international figures have intervened to try to save him).

196. The communication also reports the massacre by the army of more than 2,000 students, teachers, intellectuals and citizens in Kwangju; the arrest and condemnation last October of several hundred students; and the suspension of a large number of periodicals.

197. The author of the second communication is Professor of Law at the University of Nice, acting in the capacity of representative of the International Committee of Jurists for Democracy and Human Rights in South Korea, an international non-governmental organization having, he claims, reliable knowledge of the violations of human rights in that country.

198. He lists the namnes of the following people as victims:

Kim Chi ha
Yang Song U
Moon Ik hwan
Chang Ki pyo
Song Ki Sook
Lee Young hee,

who are poets, novelists and a writer, according to a document attached to the communication (Letter to Poets Around the World), which is available to Committee members at the Secretariat; and

Kim Dae Joong
Yoon po-sn

who, according to a White Book also attached to the communication (available to Committee members at the Secretariat), are respectively a former candidate for the presidency, at the time of Mr Park Jung hi, and a former President of Korea; and

Ham suk hun, a believer (according to the same White Book).

199. He cites other victims not mentioned by name:

other clergy
dismissed journalists
dismissed professors.

200. The explanatory letter with appendices provides an overall view of the repression exercised by the governmental authorities (police, the KCIA special police and the army ...) against students and citizens suspected of belonging to groups seeking to overthrow state institutions (violation of the "anti-communist" law and the law on state security).

201. With regard to the students, the author notes that the only thing they demanded was the democratization of education and freedom of expression. Reference is made, in particular, to the events subsequent to the death of Mr Park Jeng hi, specifically between November 1979 and August 1980, including the Kwangju Affair when student strikes and demonstrations turned into political movements, following on government-ordered repressive action, before exploding into a popular riot which, according to the author of the communication, ended in a blood-bath (photocopies of photographs from the world press as evidence thereof are available to Committee members at the Secretariat).

202. The representative of the Korean Government explained to the Committee that the new fifth Republic of Korea had been launched in October 1980 after an overwhelming approval by popular referendum. Martial law had been lifted on 25 January 1981, and the people were again allowed to enjoy all fundamental freedoms.

203. He emphasized that the assassination of President Park had created an exceptional situation. There had been a power vacuum, and martial law had had to be imposed to prevent a North Korean takeover. The riots mentioned in the communications were started by armed infiltrators among the peaceful protesters. He went on to state that no government would condone such a rebellion against it; here the very life and existence of the South Korean Republic had been endangered.

204. Furthermore the criminal courts in his country had turned up concrete evidence that there had been a premeditated plot to overthrow the government, he said. The rioters had been in possession of thousands of arms and explosives. For humanitarian reasons, however, the government had decided to release a large number of the arraigned persons, and the most of the rest were later released on a general amnesty. It was explained that the goal of the government was conciliation and harmony.

205. The representative of the Korean Government went on to assert that the communications were not admissible since they were based exclusively on news media information. While in general not questioning the reliability of the press, the Korean representative said that he had been able to confirm that there had been several articles based on rumours and exaggerations.

206. As for 13 of the alleged victims named, six had been released, six had received commuted sentences, and one had never been arrested. Moreover, this was a purely domestic matter, he said.

207. The Korean representative also mentioned that the various internal remedies available to the alleged victims had not been exhausted.

208. Finally, he stated that the communications were motivated by extraneous considerations, namely propaganda on behalf of North Korea. For these reasons he felt the communication to be clearly inadmissible.

209. Several Committee members thereupon agreed with this view that the case was inadmissible for various reasons.

210. It was pointed out that the sanctions involved in these cases had been imposed for armed criminal acts and were thus not violations of rights falling within Unesco's fields of competence. Other members pointed to the admissibility disqualification resulting from an exclusive reliance on newspaper articles.

211. Other Committee members however, spoke of their sorrow concerning these events, as they had personally followed them closely, and felt there were grave violations of human rights which had been and were being committed. Though these violations perhaps did not fall within Unesco's competence, it was felt that these violations would be severely judged by history and that they cried out for a humanitarian intervention.

212. Another Committee member expressed his fear that there would be serious adverse long-term consequences for the educational system in that country unless conditions were rapidly ameliorated, but he agreed that the case was outside of Unesco's competence.

213. After a brief discussion, the Committee *decided* to declare [these communications] as being inadmissible, firstly because the alleged violations do not fall within Unesco's spheres of competence and, secondly, because - in accordance with Article 4 of the International Covenant on Civil and Political Rights - a state may, in time of

public emergency, derogate from its obligations under that Covenant to the extent strictly required by the exigencies of the situation.

No. 270/80

Concerning *Argentina*
Case of *Juan Carlos Higa*

Communication of 16 July 1980 submitted by
María Antonia Higa

Spring 1981 session of the Committee on Conventions and Recommendations (112th session of the Executive Board)[1]

29. These three communications[2] concern the disappearance of persons. The Committee *decided* to deal with them in pursuance of the decision taken by it concerning communications relating to the cases of missing persons.[3]

---

[1] See document 112 EX/30 PRIV., para. 29; see also documents 112 EX/CR/HR/3 and Add.
[2] Communications No. 270/80 concerning *Argentina*, case of *Juan Carlos Higa*, No. 289/80 concerning *Argentina*, case of *Juan Takara*, and No. 291/80 concerning *Argentina*, case of *Claudio Nicolás Grandi* et al.
[3] See documents 108 EX/38 PRIV., para. 16, 109 EX/52 PRIV., annex I, para. 8, and Corr. and 112 EX/30 PRIV., paras. 558-566.

No. 271/80

Concerning *Zaire*
Case of *Taba and Kifuema*

Communication of 15 July 1980 submitted by
Amnesty International

Spring 1981 session of the Committee on Conventions and Recommendations (112th session of the Executive Board)[1]

409. The author of this communication, Amnesty International (International Secretariat), reports two cases of violations of human rights which, in its view, fall within Unesco's spheres of competence.

410. One concerns Mr Taba (first name probably Alphonse), teacher in a Roman Catholic secondary school. He is alleged to have been arrested on 25 May 1980 and held at the National Search and Investigation Centre (police) in Kinshasa for two weeks. It is claimed that he was beaten morning and night and not given sufficient food. It is reported that he was let out for two days then imprisoned again. It was rumoured that he died in June 1980. His wife is anxious to know what has happened to him.

411. The other case concerns Mr Kifuema (first name unknown), a student at the Higher Institute of Applied Technology, Kinshasa. He is alleged to have been arrested around February - March 1980 on the occasion of the student strike for the payment of grants and better conditions. He is said to have been held in a military camp before being transferred to the National Search and Investigation Centre. In May 1980 it was announced that all the students had been released. Kifuema was not among them, however.

412. Since this communication was transmitted to the government concerned on 13 January 1981 in the language used by its author (English) and on 2 March 1981 in an unofficial French translation, the representative of the Government of Zaire requested that the examination of this communication be deferred until the next ses-

[1] See document 112 EX/30 PRIV., paras. 409-413; see also document 112 EX/CR/HR/3.

sion. He added that a delegation from Amnesty International had been invited to visit Zaire during May this year (1981) and that further information would be made available to the Committee at its next session.

413. Although it was customary for the Secretariat to send the forms and documents which they had received to the government concerned in the language in which they were sent, the Committee, bearing in mind the information provided by the representative of the Government of Zaire, *decided* to defer the examination of the admissibility of this communication until its next session.

Autumn 1981 session of the Committee on Conventions and Recommendations (113th session of the Executive Board)[2]

470. The author of this communication, Amnesty International (International Secretariat), reports two cases of violations of human rights which, in its view, fall within Unesco's spheres of competence.

471. One concerns Mr Taba (first name probably Alphonse), a teacher in a Roman Catholic secondary school. He is alleged to have been arrested on 25 May 1980 and held at the National Search and Investigation Centre (police) in Kinshasa for two weeks. It is asserted that he was beaten morning and night and not given sufficient food. It is reported that he was let out for two days then imprisoned again. It was rumoured that he died in June 1980. His wife is anxious to know what has happened to him.

472. The other case concerns Mr Kifuema (first name unknown), a student at the Higher Institute of Applied Technology, Kinshasa. He is alleged to have been arrested around February-March 1980 on the occasion of the student strike for the payment of grants and better conditions. He is said to have been held in a military camp before being transferred to the National Search and Investigation Centre. In May 1980 it was announced that all the students had been released. Kifuema was not among them, however.

473. Since this communication was transmitted to the government concerned on 13 January 1981 in the language used by its author (English) and on 2 March 1981 in an unofficial French translation, the representative of the Government of Zaire requested that the examination of this communication be deferred until the next session.

---

[2] See document 113 EX/38 PRIV., paras. 470-480; see also document 113 EX/CR/HR/2.

474. Although it was customary for the Secretariat to send the forms and documents which they had received to the government concerned in the language in which they were sent, the Committee, bearing in mind the information provided by the representative of the Government of Zaire, decided to defer the examination of the admissibility of this communication until its next session.[3]

475. At the present session, the representative of the government concerned stated that, as he had already announced at the [spring 1981] session, his government had invited a delegation from Amnesty International to visit Zaire to go into the question of human rights with the authorities. That delegation, consisting of two people, had duly visited Zaire from 16 to 23 July 1981; they had met the representatives of the various authorities in the country, asked all the questions they wanted, visited the prisons and freely questioned the prisoners selected by them from a list they themselves had drawn up, but they had been able to provide no firm information about the two alleged victims.

476. The representative of the Government of Zaire also stated that the government had carried out a thorough inquiry on its own account; the names Taba and Kifuema were known neither at the National Search and Investigation Centre in Kinshasa nor at the educational institutions mentioned in the communication.

477. Without calling the good faith of Amnesty International into question, he wished to draw attention to the unreliability of its informants, who had quite obviously just wanted to discredit his country in the eyes of the world, destabilize it and sabotage its efforts at economic and social recovery. He also pointed out that in May 1980 Amnesty International had published with a great flourish a report depicting Zaire as a land of torture, listing as dead people who were still in power and referring to martyred children when the children in question were in fact in an education centre run by a Belgian priest. In his opinion, the communication was manifestly ill-founded.

478. One member of the Committee considered that the case should be left on the agenda pending the receipt of further information from the author of the communication.

479. Several members of the Committee were of the opinion that the communication contained no pertinent facts: it might be asked, for example, why the author of the communication, who was levelling such grave accusations against a state, had not tried to make contact with the wife of one of the alleged victims, since she was thought to be in France at present, to obtain all the necessary details, such as the first

---

[3] See document 112 EX/30 PRIV., para. 413 (*supra*, p. 656).

name of her husband. It was clear that the communication was based on rumour. One member of the Committee added that he strongly deplored the methods used by Amnesty International in presenting communications, the present case being a striking illustration of those methods.

480. Following an exchange of views, the Committee *decided*:

(i) to declare the communication inadmissible as being manifestly ill-founded, applying the provisions of paragraph 14 (*a*) (v) of 104 EX/Decision 3.3;

(ii) to notify the author of the communication of its decision in accordance with the usual practice.

No. 273/80

Concerning *Chile*
Case of *Eduardo Novoa Monreal*

Communication of 5 August 1980 submitted by
Eduardo Novoa Monreal

Spring 1981 session of the Committee on Conventions and Recommendations (112th session of the Executive Board)[1]

80. The author of the communication, a professor of criminal, legal and social science, complains that he was prohibited by the Chilean Government from returning to his country of origin, while he was abroad in June 1978 in the course of his teaching and research activities. The Chilean authorities are said to have accused him of engaging in political activities, which, he claims, is not the case; he considers that the legitimacy of defending legal positions different from those of the government should be recognized. Furthermore, he has been dismissed from his university post in Chile. He wishes to return to his country and to secure respect for his rights as a university teacher.

81. The representative of the Chilean Government explained that, contrary to the allegations of the author of the communication - and as he himself had already told the Committee on several occasions - administrative and legal procedures existed to deal with situations of that kind. He added that he was holding at the Committee's disposal a list of persons who had availed themselves of such possibilities and had, since the Committee's previous session, been accorded the right to return permanently to their country or the right to reside there temporarily; finally, Mr Novoa Monreal's opposition was not only a matter of doctrine, since he recognized the legitimacy of overthrowing the existing government by non-constitutional means.

82. One member of the Committee proposed that the representative of the Chilean Government be asked whether it might be possible to authorize Mr Novoa Monreal to return temporarily to Chile, so that he might take advantage of the channels of re-

[1] See document 112 EX/30 PRIV., paras. 80-84; see also document 112 EX/CR/HR/3.

dress open to him; another member stated that he thought the communication inadmissible, on the ground that domestic remedies had not been exhausted.

83. After the representative of the Director-General had reminded the Committee of the decisions it had taken in similar situations, where the person concerned, by virtue of his occupation, came within Unesco's field of competence but had not sought redress through existing channels, those members who spoke indicated their willingness to follow those precedents.

84. The Committee accordingly *decided* to suspend consideration of the admissibility of the communication, to issue an appeal to the Chilean Government to examine what measures it might consider feasible, and to request the Secretariat to inform the author of the communication of the means of redress available to him, according to the indications given on the subject by the Chilean Government in its note on "recurso de amparo" (the remedy of *amparo*).

Autumn 1981 session of the Committee on Conventions and Recommendations (113th session of the Executive Board)[2]

135. The author of the communication, a professor of criminal, legal and social science, complains that he was prohibited by the Chilean Government from returning to his country of origin, while he was abroad in June 1978 in the course of his teaching and research activities. The Chilean authorities are said to have accused him of engaging in political activities, which, he claims, is not the case; he considers that the legitimacy of defending legal positions different from those of the government should be recognized. Furthermore, he has been dismissed from his university post in Chile. He wishes to return to his country and to secure respect for his rights as a university teacher.

136. At the [spring 1981] session of the Committee, the representative of the Chilean Government explained that, contrary to the allegations of the author of the communication - and as he himself had already told the Committee on several occasions - administrative and legal procedures existed to deal with situations of that kind. He added that he was holding at the Committee's disposal a list of persons who had availed themselves of such possibilities and had, since the Committee's previous session, been accorded the right to return permanently to their country or the right to reside there temporarily; finally, Mr Novoa Monreal's opposition was not only a matter of doctrine, since he recognized the legitimacy of overthrowing the existing government by non-constitutional means.

---

[2] See document 113 EX/38 PRIV., paras. 135-142; see also document 113 EX/CR/HR/2.

Chile **No. 273/80**

137. One member of the Committee proposed that the representative of the Chilean Government be asked whether it might be possible to authorize Mr Novoa Monreal to return temporarily to Chile, so that he might take advantage of the channels of redress open to him; another member stated that he thought the communication inadmissible, on the ground that domestic remedies had not been exhausted.

138. After the representative of the Director-General had reminded the Committee of the decisions it had taken in similar situations, where the person concerned, by virtue of his occupation, came within Unesco's fields of competence but had not sought redress through existing channels, those members who had spoken indicated their willingness to follow those precedents.

139. The Committee accordingly decided to suspend consideration of the admissibility of the communication, to issue an appeal to the Chilean Government to examine what measures it might consider feasible, and to request the Secretariat to inform the author of the communication of the means of redress available to him, according to the indications given on the subject by the Chilean Government in its note on "recurso de amparo".[3]

140. At the present session, the representative of the Chilean Government declared that it was for the person concerned to avail himself of the existing means of redress and that, in addition to the possibility of administrative redress sought from the author of the administrative decision, there existed judicial remedies that enabled the plaintiff to be informed by the court of the reasons for the decision taken by the government. The representative of the Chilean Government indicated that his government could not do anything more since Mr Novoa Monreal did not appear to have taken advantage of the means of redress open to him.

141. All the members who spoke considered that, in the absence of a reply from the author, and lacking, in particular, any information concerning his use or otherwise of the means of redress available to him, the Committee could not continue its deliberations on this communication.

142. The Committee accordingly *decided* to suspend consideration of this communication, to instruct the Secretariat to write to the author in order to ask him whether or not he had availed himself of the means of redress brought to his notice at the [spring 1981] session or whether he had the intention of so doing, and to make it clear that, in the absence of information from him, the Committee would be obliged to strike his communication off its list at its next session.

---

[3] See document 112 EX/30 PRIV., para. 84 (*supra*, p. 660).

No. 273/80 **Chile**

Spring 1982 session of the Committee on Conventions and Recommendations (114th session of the Executive Board)[4]

416. The author of the communication, a professor of criminal, legal and social science, complains that he was prohibited by the Chilean Government from returning to his country of origin, while he was abroad in June 1978 in the course of his teaching and research activities. The Chilean authorities are said to have accused him of engaging in political activities, which, he claims, is not the case; he considers that the legitimacy of defending legal positions different from those of the government should be recognized. Furthermore, he has been dismissed from his university post in Chile. He wishes to return to his country and to secure respect for his rights as a university teacher.

417. At the spring 1981 session, the representative of the Chilean Government explained that, contrary to the allegations of the author of the communication - and as he himself had already told the Committee on several occasions - administrative and legal procedures existed to deal with situations of that kind. He added that he was holding at the Committee's disposal a list of persons who had availed themselves of such possibilities and had, since the Committee's previous session, been accorded the right to return permanently to their country or the right to reside there temporarily; finally, Mr Novoa Monreal's opposition was not only a matter of doctrine, since he recognized the legitimacy of overthrowing the existing government by non-constitutional means.

418. One member of the Committee proposed that the representative of the Chilean Government be asked whether it might be possible to authorize Mr Novoa Monreal to return temporarily to Chile, so that he might take advantage of the channels of redress open to him; another member stated that he thought the communication inadmissible, on the ground that domestic remedies had not been exhausted.

419. After the representative of the Director-General had reminded the Committee of the decisions it had taken in similar situations, where the person concerned, by virtue of his occupation, came within Unesco's fields of competence but had not sought redress through existing channels, those members who had spoken indicated their willingness to follow those precedents.

420. The Committee accordingly decided to suspend consideration of the admissibility of the communication, to issue an appeal to the Chilean Government to examine

[4] See document 114 EX/38 PRIV., paras. 416-428; see also documents 114 EX/CR/HR/2 and Add.2.

what measures it might consider feasible, and to request the Secretariat to inform the author of the communication of the means of redress available to him, according to the indications given on the subject by the Chilean Government in its note on "recurso de amparo".[5]

421. At the autumn 1981 session, the representative of the Chilean Government declared that it was for the person concerned to avail himself of the existing means of redress and that, in addition to the possibility of administrative redress sought from the author of the administrative decision, there existed judicial remedies that enabled the plaintiff to be informed by the court of the reasons for the decision taken by the government. The representative of the Chilean Government indicated that his government could not do anything more since Mr Novoa Monreal did not appear to have taken advantage of the means of redress open to him.

422. All the members who spoke considered that, in the absence of a reply from the author, and lacking, in particular, any information concerning his use or otherwise of the means of redress available to him, the Committee could not continue its deliberations on this communication.

423. The Committee accordingly decided to suspend consideration of this communication, to instruct the Secretariat to write to the author in order to ask him whether or not he had availed himself of the means of redress brought to his notice at the [spring 1981] session or whether he had the intention of so doing, and to make it clear that, in the absence of information from him, the Committee would be obliged to strike his communication off its list at the present session.[6]

424. On 2 April 1982 the author had sent the Secretariat a long letter setting forth the reasons why he had not sought to avail himself of the means of redress suggested by the representative of the Chilean Government at the [autumn 1981] session. He had stated that under the terms of provisional Article 24 of the Constitution, Chilean citizens who had been forbidden to return to Chile were expressly denied any form of legal recourse; the same article stipulated that an appeal for the review of any such measure could only be submitted to the authority which had taken the decision in question. In that connection, the author had explained that he and a number of other persons had submitted a joint appeal for the review of the measure in question to the Chilean Ambassador to Venezuela. Lastly, the author had emphasized that any Chilean citizen who submitted a request for permission to return through his consulate was required, before such permission could be granted, to sign a special document whereby he recognized the legitimacy of the "military government". Mr Novoa

---

[5] See document 112 EX/30 PRIV., para. 84 (*supra*, p. 660).
[6] See document 113 EX/38 PRIV., para. 142 (*supra*, p. 661).

Monreal had stated that in his view, that requirement was an oppressive measure which constituted a restriction on freedom of thought.

425. At the present session, the representative of the government concerned stated that it was quite clear from Mr Novoa Monreal's letter that he had not properly submitted his application for permission to return. Yet, he said, the procedure was perfectly clear: the person concerned was required to submit to the consulate nearest to his place of residence an individual application for permission to return to Chile. As part of that procedure, he was indeed asked to sign a statement whereby he agreed to abide by the laws of his country; such a requirement was in force in many countries and had never been challenged. The procedure had yielded good results, since in Paris itself 49 such applications, or 50 per cent of those received during 1981, had been approved on those terms. In submitting a joint application, and in not signing the statement referred to above, Mr Novoa Monreal had failed to follow the procedure in force. It was, then, normal that his application could not be considered. In addition, Mr Novoa Monreal had made a legal error in referring, in so far as his own case was concerned, to the terms of provisional Article 24 of the Constitution. The last paragraph of that article did in fact rule out any form of legal remedy in respect of the measures adopted under paragraph (*c*) of the same article, but the decision taken in Mr Novoa Monreal's case had been based on a decree-law of 1974, so that a request for review and an application for *amparo* could have been submitted. It was thus clear that the person concerned had not even attempted to make use of the legal remedies available to him.

426. Most of the speakers said that in their view the communication was inadmissible, since the author had not attempted to exhaust available domestic remedies; they emphasized the need to transmit to him the information provided by the representative of the government concerned. One member, while expressing agreement on the latter point, stated that he hoped that the communication could be left on the Committee's agenda for humanitarian reasons, so that the person concerned would have an opportunity to clarify his situation. Another member stated that he could see no humanitarian problem in the case, but only an exclusively legal problem arising from the fact that Mr Novoa Monreal had not made use of the opportunities available to him and apparently had had no intention of doing so; he also added, as a previous speaker had already remarked, that Mr Novoa Monreal could always submit a-fresh communication if he should see fit to do so.

427. The representative of the Director-General pointed out that all international authorities, and the International Court of Justice in particular, had ruled that a plaintiff's opinion as to the effectiveness or otherwise of a legal remedy did not relieve him of the obligation of resorting to it.

Chile **No. 273/80**

428. The Committee therefore *decided*:

(i) to take note of the statements of the representative of the government concerned and to instruct the Secretariat to transmit them to the author of the communication;

(ii) to declare the communication inadmissible under 104 EX/Decision 3.3, paragraph 14 (*a*) (ix), inasmuch as its author had not attempted to exhaust the domestic remedies available to him.

No. 274/80

Concerning *France*
Case of *Simon Malley*

Communication of 8 August 1980 submitted by
Philippe Waquet

Autumn 1980 session of the Committee on Conventions and Recommendations (110th session of the Executive Board)[1]

95. In his letter dated 11 August 1980, Mr Philippe Waquet, a barrister admitted to plead before the Conseil d'État and the Cour de Cassation, acting in agreement with Mr Jean-Denis Bredin and Mr Paul Prompt, barristers admitted to plead at the Paris Bar, referred to the Director-General a communication concerning France and an alleged violation of the freedom of opinion and expression of Mr Simon Malley, editor of the fortnightly review *Afrique-Asie*, in consequence of the refusal of the French authorities to renew his residence permit. At the same time, Mr Waquet asked the Director-General, "in view of the seriousness of the situation ... [and] if necessary, through the use of emergency procedures", to have the said communication submitted to the Committee on Conventions and Recommendations at the [autumn 1980] session beginning on 25 August 1980.

96. In submitting this request for urgent examination to the Committee on Conventions and Recommendations, the Director-General pointed out that, in accordance with the relevant decision and the established practice of the Committee, the government concerned must be allowed one month between the date when the communication was transmitted to it and the date of the Committee's session. The communication in question had been transmitted to the government concerned on 13 August 1980.

97. The representative of the French Government stated that his government had not been informed sufficiently in advance of this communication, and that in the circumstances he would perhaps be unable to answer all the questions that might be raised. However, he was willing to comply with the Committee's decision concerning the

[1] See document 110 EX/40 PRIV., paras. 95-100; see also document 110 EX/CR/HR/3 Add.

interpretation of a rule that the Committee had laid down for itself, and he stated that he was prepared to examine the case on the basis of emergency procedures if the Committee so decided.

98. All the Committee members who spoke stated that it was not necessary to make an exception to the rule in question. One of the members expressed the wish that the representative of the French Government might use his good offices to ensure that an immediate expulsion order was not served on Mr Malley before the latter had exhausted the domestic remedies available to him.

99. The representative of the French Government replied that at the present stage of events, where no examination of the case had yet been undertaken, it did not seem to him possible to accede to such a request and that in the meantime Mr Mallay had available to him measures of recourse, including possible injunctive relief, which made the aforementioned request unnecessary.

[99a]. He added, however, that he would not fail to inform the relevant authorities of the Committee's exchanges of views on this matter.

100. In conclusion, the Committee *decided*:

> [i] to take note of the willingness of the representative of the Government concerned to take part in the examination of the communication if the Committee had considered it desirable;
>
> [ii] to defer the examination of this case to the next session.

Spring 1981 session of the Committee on Conventions and Recommendations (112th session of the Executive Board)[2]

131. In his letter dated 11 August 1980, Mr Philippe Waquet, a barrister admitted to plead before the Conseil d'État and the Cour de Cassation, acting in agreement with Mr Jean-Denis Bredin and Mr Paul Prompt, barristers admitted to plead at the Paris Bar, referred to the Director-General a communication concerning an alleged violation of the freedom of opinion and expression of Mr Simon Malley, editor of the fortnightly review "Afrique-Asie", in consequence of the refusal of the French authorities to renew his residence permit. At the same time, Mr Waquet asked the Director-General, "in view of the seriousness of the situation ... [and] if necessary, through the use of emergency procedures", to have the said communication submit-

[2] See document 112 EX/30 PRIV., paras. 131-138; see also document 112 EX/CR/HR/2.

ted to the Committee on Conventions and Recommendations at the [autumn 1980] session beginning on 25 August 1980.

132. At the [autumn 1980] session, the representative of the French Government had stated that his government had not been informed sufficiently in advance of this communication (which had been transmitted to it only on 13 August 1980), and that he might be unable to answer all the questions that might be raised. He had stated, however, that he was prepared to examine the case on the basis of an emergency procedure if the Committee so decided.

133. The Committee had then stated that there were no grounds for making an exception to the rule of one month's notice.

134. In conclusion, the Committee had decided:[3]

> [i] to take note of the willingness of the representative of the government concerned to take part in the examination of the communication if the Committee had considered it desirable;
>
> [ii] to defer the examination of this case to the present session.

135. Recalling that the law in respect of immigration and the residence of foreigners in a country was the prerogative of that country's government, the representative of the French Government stated that Mr Malley, who apparently held dual nationality, Egyptian and American, had been the holder of a temporary residence permit which had not been renewed, and subsequently of an authorization to stay in France, valid for three months, which had on several occasions been extended until 1980.

136. The representative of the French Government further stated that while editor of the review "Afrique-Asie", Mr Malley had on several occasions attacked foreign heads of state with which France maintained friendly relations, and had sometimes gone so far as threats and incitement to revolt. He wondered whether any government could tolerate such conduct.

137. Following a detailed analysis of Article 13 of the International Covenant on Civil and Political Rights (an alien lawfully in the territory of a State Party to the present Covenant may be expelled therefrom only in pursuance of a decision reached in accordance with law ...), several Committee members considered that France had not violated the provisions of that international instrument; that since the residence permit had not been extended by the competent authorities, then regardless

---

[3] See document 110 EX/40 PRIV., para. 100 (*supra*, p. 668).

of the alleged victim's activities in the field of information, the journalist in question was no longer "lawfully" in France; that he had not yet exhausted domestic remedies (following the rejection of his plea by the administrative courts, it should be referred to the Conseil d'État before 22 May 1981); and that hence there were no grounds for finding the communication admissible. Several Committee members emphasized that there had been no violation of the right to information, since the party concerned was still free to exercise his profession elsewhere, and the review in question continued to be published.

138. In the light of the provisions of 104 EX/Decision 3.3, paragraph 14 (*a*) (iii) - not related to Unesco's fields of competence - and (ix) - exhaustion of available domestic remedies - the Committee *declared* the communication inadmissible.

No. 276/80

Concerning *El Salvador*
Case of *Miguel Ángel García* et al.*

Communication of 11 June 1980 submitted by
Amnesty International

Spring 1981 session of the Committee on Conventions and Recommendations (112th session of the Executive Board)[1]

113. Amnesty International (International Secretariat), the author of the communication, denounces the violation of human rights committed by the authorities of El Salvador against the following alleged victims:

> Dr Miguel Ángel García and Dr Carlos Ernesto Alfaro Rodríguez: both are said to have been abducted on 15 May 1980 from a hospital in Cojutepeque, accused of having given assistance to left-wing activists; their death is said to have provoked a strike of 600 doctors, supported by other health workers;
>
> Leonel Menéndez Quiroga: a professor at the José Simeón Cañas Central American University, he is said to have been abducted by policemen on 21 May 1980 while under anaesthetic awaiting a surgical operation (extraction of bullets) at the Rosales Hospital;
>
> Ángel Erasmo Figueroa: a biologist, he is said to have been murdered on 18 April 1980 at the Santa Tecla Hospital where he was being treated for bullet wounds;
>
> Héctor Lemus Rosa: of unknown profession, he is said to have been killed recently at the Rosales Hospital by armed men.

---

* Case of *Miguel Ángel García, Carlos Ernesto Alfaro Rodríguez, Leonel Menéndez Quiroga, Ángel Erasmo Figueroa and Héctor Lemus Rosa*. From the Committee's spring 1983 session, this communication was being referred to as case of *Leonel Menéndez Quiroga* and from its spring 1987 session, as case of *Leonel Menéndez Quiroga and others*.

[1] See document 112 EX/30 PRIV., paras. 113-124; see also document 112 EX/CR/HR/3.

No. 276/80 **El Salvador**

114. The aim of Amnesty International's communication is:

to ensure that the perpetrators are brought to trial;

to obtain compensation for the victims' families.

115. [Two other] communications[2] allege the same facts. The first is submitted by the National Association of Salvadorian Teachers (ANDES), the second, by the National Education Federation (FEN, in France). The latter uses a copy of the dossier prepared by the former as the basic document in support of its condemnation of alleged violations of human rights in El Salvador.

116. This dossier contains a summary of facts concerning a hundred or so alleged victims (teachers or students who, it is claimed, were murdered, arrested or abducted between 1971 and 1980). In most cases, each summary is accompanied by an identity photograph.

117. The authors of the two communications denounce the alleged persecution of teachers by the governmental forces of El Salvador, laying particular stress on the fact that these incidents took place in front of their students.

118. They also mention the climate of insecurity reigning in schools and universities. Some educational institutions have apparently been closed down.

119. FEN indicates that such a situation "no doubt goes well beyond Unesco's competence". It would like to have Unesco's reaction to such events as they affect "youth, teachers, education, the right to freedom and culture of a whole nation".

120. Domestic remedies are claimed to have produced no tangible results.

121. The matter is also said to have been referred to the [Organization of American States (OAS)] and the [International Labour Organisation (ILO)].

122. In a letter dated 5 May 1981, the Permanent Delegate of El Salvador to Unesco apologized for being unable to be present during the consideration of the communications, since he had not received in time from his government the detailed information that would enable him to provide the Committee with the necessary explanations.

---

[2] Communications No. 276/80 concerning *El Salvador*, case of *Miguel Ángel García* et al., No. 283/80 concerning *El Salvador*, case of *Arrest and persecution of teachers in El Salvador*, and No. 306/80 concerning *El Salvador*, case of *Arrest and persecution of teachers in El Salvador*, were being considered together.

El Salvador **No. 276/80**

123. Some Committee members maintained that it was not good practice to decide virtually automatically to defer consideration of a communication when the representative of the government concerned failed to appoint a deputy. Certain situations did require urgent consideration, and it was improper to delay consideration of such communications.

124. Noting that deferment of the consideration of a communication to the following session might, in many cases, benefit the alleged victim (in the past, some alleged victims had been released before the following session), and that such deferment might be granted when the Committee felt that the request was not a delaying tactic, the Committee *decided*:

(i) to defer consideration of [the three communications] to the following session;

(ii) to request the Executive Board to invite the Director-General to draw the attention of the government concerned to the importance which the Committee attached to its being fully represented at that session, so that detailed explanations might be provided concerning the allegations contained in the communications.

Autumn 1981 session of the Committee on Conventions and Recommendations (113th session of the Executive Board)[3]

204. The three communications[4] all concern El Salvador. The Committee decided to deal with them jointly.

205. Amnesty International (International Secretariat), the author of the [first] communication, denounces the violation of human rights committed by the authorities of El Salvador against the following alleged victims:

Dr Miguel Ángel García and Dr Carlos Ernesto Alfaro Rodríguez: both are said to have been abducted on 15 May 1980 from a hospital in Cojutepeque, accused of having given assistance to left-wing activists; their death is said to have provoked a strike of 600 doctors, supported by other health workers;

---

[3] See document 113 EX/38 PRIV., paras. 204-224; see also document 113 EX/CR/HR/2.
[4] Communications No. 276/80 concerning *El Salvador*, case of *Miguel Ángel García* et al., No. 283/80 concerning *El Salvador*, case of *Arrest and persecution of teachers in El Salvador*, and No. 306/80 concerning *El Salvador*, case of *Arrest and persecution of teachers in El Salvador*.

No. 276/80 **El Salvador**

Leonel Menéndez Quiroga: a professor at the José Simeón Cañas Central American University, he is said to have been abducted by policemen on 21 May 1980 while under anaesthetic awaiting a surgical operation (extraction of bullets) at the Rosales Hospital;

Ángel Erasmo Figueroa: a biologist, he is said to have been murdered on 18 April 1980 at the Santa Tecla Hospital where he was being treated for bullet wounds;

Héctor Lemus Rosa: of unknown profession; he is said to have been killed recently at the Rosales Hospital by armed men.

206. The aim of Amnesty International's communication is:

to ensure that the perpetrators are brought to trial;

to obtain compensation for the victims' families.

207. The [other] two communications allege the same facts. They are submitted respectively by the National Association of Salvadorian Teachers (ANDES), and by the National Education Federation (FEN, in France). The latter uses a copy of the dossier prepared by the former as the basic document in support of its condemnation of alleged violations of human rights in El Salvador.

208. This dossier contains a summary of facts concerning a hundred or so alleged victims (teachers or students who, it is claimed, were murdered, arrested or abducted between 1971 and 1980). In most cases, each summary is accompanied by an identity photograph.

209. The authors of the two communications denounce the alleged persecution of teachers by the governmental forces of El Salvador, laying particular stress on the fact that these incidents took place in front of their students.

210. They also mention the climate of insecurity reigning in schools and universities. Some educational institutions have apparently been closed down.

211. FEN simply draws attention to: wholesale political assassinations, tortures and violence. It adds that such a situation "no doubt goes well beyond Unesco's competence". It would like to have Unesco's reaction to such events as they affect "youth, teachers, education, the right to freedom and culture of a whole nation".

212. Domestic remedies are claimed to have produced no tangible results.

213. The matter is also said to have been referred to the [Organization of American States (OAS)] and the [International Labour Organisation (ILO)].

214. At the [spring 1981] session, in a letter dated 5 May 1981, the Permanent Delegate of El Salvador to Unesco apologized for being unable to appear before the Committee, since he had not received in time from his government detailed information that would enable him to provide the Committee with the necessary explanations.

215. Noting that the deferment of the consideration of a communication to the following session might, in many cases, benefit the alleged victim and that such deferment might be granted when the Committee felt that the request was not a delaying tactic, the Committee decided:[5]

> (i) to defer consideration of the three communications to the following session;
>
> (ii) to request the Executive Board to invite the Director-General to draw the attention of the government concerned to the importance which the Committee attached to its being fully represented at that session, so that detailed explanations might be provided concerning the allegations contained in the communications.

216. At the present session, the representative of the Government of El Salvador declared that his government sought understanding and co-operation from all international bodies, particularly Unesco. The problems affecting his country were, in fact, extremely complex. For some 50 years now El Salvador had been experiencing violence, which had been caused by extremists, in particular by a small group which had created a climate of rebellion and insurrection, revealing its strength by means of destructive activities. It was in order to provide the nation with a solution to this problem that the army had had recourse to the coup d'état of October 1979. However, the extremists, supplied with arms and given encouragement from abroad, continued their terrorist activities with the aim of overthrowing the government. They had killed public officials, mayors, judges, doctors, teachers and other civilians. The Revolutionary Junta hoped to solve the crisis by strengthening the economy, carrying out agrarian reforms, distributing land to the peasants, nationalizing the banks and certain branches of the economy ... In the political field, it was seeking to establish a dialogue within the country and hold elections so that a Constituent Assembly might draw up a social contract.

---

[5] See document 112 EX/30 PRIV., para. 124 (*supra*, p. 673).

No. 276/80 **El Salvador**

217. With regard to the cases mentioned in the communications, the representative of the Government of El Salvador stated that a special committee had been set up to consider them, but, as in a good number of other cases, the police, the army and the judiciary had not managed to discover the guilty parties, and the investigations had proved fruitless, since no one was prepared to give evidence. He also pointed out that negotiations between the competent authorities and ANDES had recently taken place: as a result a number of measures had been taken on behalf of teachers, in response to their demands and claims.

218. Having regard to the prevailing climate of violence as illustrated by the fact that unidentified bodies were being buried almost every day; people were reported missing, more than 200,000 refugees were living in neighbouring countries, and a considerable number of people were taking part in guerrilla warfare, the representative of the Government of El Salvador considered that the problem raised by the three communications fell outside Unesco's competence, particularly as the alleged facts were not the result of the institutional structure of the state nor of an act of the government against its own people: the victims were killed because of politico-military action and as a result of confrontations between several different factions. After having pointed out that the problem of El Salvador had already been submitted to the United Nations, that a special rapporteur had just been appointed, that a recent report of the International Committee of the Red Cross had fully revealed the true situation, he concluded by stating that the communications should be deemed inadmissible, as his government could not be held responsible for a tragic situation which was not caused by the central administration.

219. Most of the members of the Committee stated that they were deeply concerned at the distress of this country. Whoever was responsible, they were of the opinion that the alleged violations were clear violations of human rights. The communications did not appear to them to be inadmissible. They wondered, however, whether the Committee could take any practical action, given the extent of the alleged violations.

220. Other members of the Committee, while indicating their deep sorrow, expressed themselves satisfied with the statement made with such compassion by the representative of the Government of El Salvador. They pointed out that the latter had not denied the alleged facts and that he had only cast doubt as to whether they could be imputed to his government. They recalled that the Committee was not a court of law and had always attempted to find a friendly solution. Some of them were astonished at the reluctance of the representative of the government concerned to accept that the communications should be declared admissible, for admissibility did not in itself constitute a condemnation and did not imply any form of guilt whatsoever.

El Salvador **No. 276/80**

221. Several members were of the opinion that, following the foreign intervention resulting from the great strategic importance of Latin America in general and also because of the poverty existing in the country, where many different races mingled, El Salvador offered a favourable terrain for violence and that therefore it was difficult to establish where the responsibilities lay. Some members stated that no government could be held responsible for the behaviour of individuals acting outside its control.

222. In order to avoid a mistaken interpretation of his statement, which might give the impression that there was a lack of authority in the country, the representative of the Government of El Salvador stated that the government's authority had been, and was being exercised throughout its territory and that the country was continuing to function; any feeling that there was an absence of authority was due to the fact that it was impossible to solve certain unfortunate cases.

223. The discussion then centred on the responsibility of a state for alleged violations of human rights. In accordance with the principle set out in Article 2 of the International Covenant on Civil and Political Rights, several members were of the opinion that the government concerned could not escape its responsibilities, since any government was responsible for maintaining respect for the human rights of the people who came within its jurisdiction. After pointing out that violence affected all sectors of the population indiscriminately, and that the victims had become involved simply because they were in El Salvador, other members considered that it was not justifiable to hold the government responsible. Several other members considered that despite the limited competence of Unesco, the Organization was in duty bound to help a country which was moved by the desire to put its own house in order.

224. After a long exchange of views, the Committee *decided*:

(i) to defer consideration of the admissibility of the three communications until the following session, while awaiting further information;

(ii) to request the representative of the government concerned to inform the latter of the humanitarian concern of the Committee with regard to the individual cases specifically mentioned in these communications, and to keep the Committee informed of the measures taken to improve the situation of teachers in El Salvador and also of the outcome of the examination of the affair by the United Nations and by the OAS;

(iii) to request the Secretariat to follow the examination of the situation of human rights in El Salvador by the United Nations and by the other international organizations competent in the field of human rights;

(iv) to communicate this decision to the authors of the communications so that they might provide additional information in the light of the development of the situation in El Salvador.

Spring 1982 session of the Committee on Conventions and Recommendations (114th session of the Executive Board)[6]

487. Referring to these four communications,[7] the Permanent Delegate of El Salvador to Unesco sent a letter dated 21 April 1982 to the Secretariat in which he stated that, on account of the political situation in his country, where there was at present a hiatus in the exercise of governmental power, he was not able to provide the Committee with detailed information. He therefore requested that the examination of the communications concerning his country be held over until a later date, when he expected to be able to provide the information required.

488. In accordance with the Committee's practice in similar cases, the Committee *decided* to acquiesce in the request made by the representative of the government concerned and to postpone consideration of the admissibility of these four communications until its next session.

Autumn 1982 session of the Committee on Conventions and Recommendations (115th session of the Executive Board)[8]

84. At the autumn 1981 session, the Committee had on its agenda [three communications],[9] which it decided to deal with jointly.

---

[6] See document 114 EX/38 PRIV., paras. 487-488; see also documents 114 EX/CR/HR/2 and Add.2 and 3 and 114 EX/CR/HR/3.

[7] Communications No. 276/80 concerning *El Salvador*, case of *Miguel Ángel Garcia* et al., No. 283/80 concerning *El Salvador*, case of *Arrest and persecution of teachers in El Salvador*, No. 306/80 concerning *El Salvador*, case of *Arrest and persecution of teachers in El Salvador*, and No. 390/81 concerning *El Salvador*, case of *Edgar Mauricio Vallejo*, were being considered together.

[8] See document 115 EX/28 PRIV., paras. 84-116; see also documents 115 EX/CR/HR/2 and 115 EX/CR/HR/3 Add.

[9] Communications No. 276/80 concerning *El Salvador*, case of *Miguel Ángel Garcia* et al., No. 283/80 concerning *El Salvador*, case of *Arrest and persecution of teachers in El Salvador*, and No. 306/80 concerning *El Salvador*, case of *Arrest and persecution of teachers in El Salvador*.

El Salvador **No. 276/80**

85. Amnesty International (International Secretariat), the author of the [first] communication, denounces the alleged violation of human rights committed by the authorities of El Salvador against the following alleged victims:

> Dr Miguel Ángel García and Dr Carlos Ernesto Alfaro Rodríguez: both are said to have been abducted on 15 May 1980 from a hospital in Cojutepeque, accused of having given assistance to left-wing activists; their death is said to have provoked a strike of 600 doctors, supported by other health workers;
>
> Leonel Menéndez Quiroga: a professor at the José Simeón Cañas Central American University, he is said to have been abducted by policemen on 21 May 1980 while under anaesthetic awaiting a surgical operation (extraction of bullets) at the Rosales Hospital;
>
> Ángel Erasmo Figueroa: a biologist, he is said to have been murdered on 18 April 1980 at the Santa Tecla Hospital where he was being treated for bullet wounds;
>
> Héctor Lemus Rosa: of unknown profession, he is said to have been killed recently at the Rosales Hospital by armed men.

86. The aim of Amnesty International's communication is: to ensure that the perpetrators are brought to trial; to obtain compensation for the victims' families.

87. [The other] two communications which allege the same facts are submitted respectively by the National Association of Salvadorian Teachers (ANDES), and by the National Education Federation (FEN, in France). The latter uses a copy of the dossier prepared by the former as the basic document in support of its condemnation of alleged violations of human rights in El Salvador.

88. This dossier contains a summary of facts concerning a hundred or so alleged victims (teachers or students who, it is claimed, were murdered, arrested or abducted between 1971 and 1980). In most cases, the summary is accompanied by a passport photograph. From the list of 119 names, given [in a Committee document],[10] the Committee was able to see that all had been killed with the exception of the first eight persons on the list, who were known to have been arrested on a particular date.

89. The authors of the two communications denounce the alleged persecution of teachers by the governmental forces of El Salvador, laying particular stress on the fact that these incidents took place in front of their students.

[10] See document 112 EX/CR/HR/3.

90. FEN states that such a situation "no doubt goes well beyond Unesco's competence". It would like to have Unesco's reaction to such events as they affect "youth, teachers, education, the right to freedom and culture of a whole nation".

91. Domestic remedies are claimed to have produced no tangible results. The matter is also said to have been referred to the [Organization of American States (OAS)] and the [International Labour Organisation (ILO)]..

92. At the spring 1981 session, in a letter dated 5 May 1981, the Permanent Delegate of El Salvador to Unesco apologized for being unable to appear before the Committee, since he had not received in time from his government detailed information that would enable him to provide the Committee with the necessary explanations.

93. Noting that the deferment of the consideration of a communication to the following session might, in many cases, benefit the alleged victim and that such deferment might be granted when the Committee felt that the request was not a delaying tactic, the Committee decided:[11]

> (i) to defer consideration of the three communications to the following session;
>
> (ii) to request the Executive Board to invite the Director-General to draw the attention of the government concerned to the importance which the Committee attached to its being fully represented at that session, so that detailed explanations might be provided concerning the allegations contained in the communications.

94. At the autumn 1981 session, the representative of the Government of El Salvador had declared that his government asked all international bodies, particularly Unesco, to be understanding and co-operative. The problems affecting his country were, in fact, extremely complex. For some 50 years El Salvador had been experiencing violence, which had been caused by extremists, in particular by a small group which had created a climate of rebellion and insurrection, revealing its strength by means of destructive activities.

95. With regard to the cases mentioned in the communications, the representative of the Government of El Salvador stated that a special committee had been set up to consider them, but, as in a good number of other cases, the police, the army and the judiciary had not managed to discover the guilty parties, and the investigations had proved fruitless, since no one was prepared to give evidence. He also pointed out

---

[11] See document 112 EX/30 PRIV., para. 124 (*supra*, p. 673).

that negotiations between the competent authorities and ANDES had recently taken place: as a result a number of measures had been taken on behalf of teachers, in response to their demands and claims.

96. Having regard to the prevailing climate of violence as illustrated by the fact that unidentified bodies were being buried almost every day, people were disappearing, while more than 200,000 refugees were living in neighbouring countries, and a considerable number of people were taking part in guerrilla warfare, the representative of the Government of El Salvador considered that the problem raised by the three communications fell outside Unesco's competence. After having pointed out that the problem of El Salvador had already been submitted to the United Nations, that a special rapporteur had just been appointed, that a report of the International Committee of the Red Cross had fully revealed the true situation, he had concluded by stating that the communications should be deemed inadmissible, as his government could not be held responsible for a tragic situation which was not caused by the central administration.

97. Most of the members of the Committee stated that they were deeply concerned at the distress of this country. Whoever was responsible, they were of the opinion that the alleged violations were clear violations of human rights. The communications did not appear to them to be inadmissible. They wondered, however, whether the Committee could take any practical action, given the extent of the alleged violations.

98. Other members of the Committee, while indicating their deep sorrow, expressed themselves satisfied with the statement made with such compassion by the representative of the Government of El Salvador. They pointed out that the latter had not denied the alleged facts and that he had only cast doubt as to whether they could be imputed to his government. They recalled that the Committee was not a court of law and had always attempted to find a friendly solution. Some of them were astonished at the reluctance of the representative of the government concerned to accept that the communications should be declared admissible, for admissibility did not in itself constitute a condemnation and did not imply any form of guilt whatsoever. Some members considered that despite the limited competence of Unesco, the Organization was in duty bound to help a country which was moved by the desire to put its own house in order.

99. After a lengthy exchange of views, the Committee decided:[12]

[12] See document 113 EX/38 PRIV., para. 224 (*supra*, pp. 677-678).

(i) to defer consideration of the admissibility of the three communications until the following session, while awaiting further information;

(ii) to request the representative of the government concerned to inform the latter of the humanitarian concern of the Committee with regard to the individual cases specifically mentioned in these communications, and to keep the Committee informed of the measures taken to improve the situation of teachers in El Salvador and also of the outcome of the examination of the affair by the United Nations and by the OAS;

(iii) to request the Secretariat to follow the examination of the situation of human rights in El Salvador by the United Nations and by the other international organizations competent in the field of human rights;

(iv) to communicate this decision to the authors of the communications so that they might provide additional information in the light of the development of the situation in El Salvador.

100. The Secretariat duly informed the author and the government concerned of the Committee's decision. It also contacted OAS, ILO and the United Nations and received from the latter two organizations the following information:

(*a*) At its 118th session, the Governing Body of [the International Labour Office] approved the 211th report of its Committee on Freedom of Association, paragraphs 403 to 436 of which are devoted to complaints submitted by various trade union organizations against the Government of El Salvador. In its recommendations to the Governing Body, the Committee describes its extreme concern at the seriousness of the allegations and observes that events of this kind had continued to occur after 15 October 1979, the date when the previous government was relieved of office, considers that there is a continuity between the successive governments of a state and deplores the many cases of loss of human life and injury referred to in the complaints. In general the Committee considers that normalization of the trade union situation and of working relations - an essential objective if full respect for human rights is to be guaranteed - and an easing of social tension would be promoted if the government examined the situation of the detainees mentioned by the complainants, with a view to releasing the persons arrested on account of their trade union activities.

(*b*) From the United Nations, the Secretariat received a copy of the interim report submitted by [the Economic and Social Council] to the General Assembly at its thirty-eighth session, dealing with the situation regarding human rights and fundamental freedoms in El Salvador, prepared by Professor José Antonio Pastor Ridruejo, the Special Representative of the Commission on Human Rights in conformity with resolution 32 (XXXVII) of the Commission on Human Rights. The final report was to be submitted to the Commission on Human Rights in February-March 1982. Attached was a copy of resolution 36/155 on the situation of human rights and fundamental freedoms in El Salvador adopted by the General Assembly on 16 December 1981.

101. In reply to the Secretariat's letter, Amnesty International, author of [the first communication], sent to the Organization a letter dated 31 March 1982 [...],[13] according to which "human rights in El Salvador, including those falling within Unesco's competence, continue to be violated systematically and flagrantly on a massive scale". The Secretary-General of Amnesty International also pointed out that he had noted with interest that the Government of El Salvador had created a special committee to examine the cases referred to in [the communication] and that he would very much appreciate receiving any particulars available with respect to this committee and its work.

102. On 15 July 1982 the Secretariat received from Amnesty International a letter [...][14] stating that "the scale of the violations of human rights within Unesco's mandate ... demonstrates the unavailability of real and effective domestic remedies in El Salvador".

103. On 24 June 1982 the Secretariat received, under cover of a letter from the World Confederation of Organizations of the Teaching Profession (WCOTP), a letter from the National Association of Salvadorian Teachers (ANDES), author of [the second communication],[15] in which it expressed its gratitude "for all the measures designed to halt the campaign of 'genocide' against our teacher comrades". On 23 July 1982 WCOTP also transmitted to the Secretariat an extract from the report drawn up by Mr Marc Alain Berberat who had recently had talks with Salvadorians in exile and from which it emerged that the situation in El Salvador had not improved.

104. [A fourth] communication[16] was first submitted to the Committee at its spring 1982 session.

105. The author of the communication, Amnesty International, states that Mr Edgar Mauricio Vallejo, a writer of Salvadorian nationality who is very well known in

[13] See document 114 EX/CR/HR/2 Add.2.
[14] See document 115 EX/CR/HR/2.
[15] *Ibidem*.
[16] Communication No. 390/81 concerning *El Salvador*, case of *Edgar Mauricio Vallejo*.

Central America, was reportedly abducted in the Plaza del Sol in San Salvador on 4 July 1981 by masked men in civilian clothing, who are alleged to have then driven him off in a jeep without number plates.

106. The author of the communication states that the police first acknowledged but later denied that Mr Edgar Mauricio Vallejo was in detention. The case is also stated to have been submitted to the United Nations Working Group on Enforced or Involuntary Disappearances, with no results known yet. The purpose and aim of this communication are to obtain acknowledgement by the Salvadorian authorities of Mr Edgar Mauricio Vallejo's detention and assurances about his treatment. Amnesty International fears in fact, that Mr Edgar Mauricio Vallejo might have been tortured and killed by those who abducted him.

107. At its spring 1982 session, the Committee decided to agree to the request for postponement made by the representative of the government concerned and to defer consideration of the admissibility of the four [communications].[17]

108. The author of [a fifth] communication,[18] Mr Daniel Rétureau, Secretary-General of the World Federation of Teachers' Unions [WFTU], submits a file containing three lists: a list of 137 Salvadorian teachers reported to have been murdered by the armed forces and police of the Government of El Salvador in 1980; another list of 80 teachers reported to have met the same fate in 1981, together with a brief account, against each name, of the circumstances of death; and a third list of 49 Salvadorian teachers reported to have been arrested by the security forces of the Government of El Salvador and to have disappeared, with an indication of the place and date of disappearance in each case. The author's aim is to secure condemnation of the alleged murders and to obtain information on the persons who have been imprisoned or have disappeared.

109. This communication was placed on the Committee's agenda for the first time at this session. The Committee decided to deal jointly with the five communications mentioned above.

110. At the autumn 1982 session, the representative of the Director-General informed the Committee that the assignment of the Special Representative of the United Nations Commission on Human Rights responsible for looking into this situation had been extended for one year and that his report would be submitted to the 39th session of that Commission.

---

[17] See document 114 EX/38 PRIV., para. 488 (*supra*, p. 678).

[18] Communication No. 477/82 concerning *El Salvador*, case of *Violation of human rights in El Salvador*.

El Salvador **No. 276/80**

111. The representative of the Salvadorian Government thanked the Committee for the concern it had shown for the human rights situation in his country; he explained that in order to dispel the climate of violence that reigned in his country, free elections had been held on 28 March 1982 and the international observers invited for the occasion had been able to see that they had taken place under normal conditions, with a very high rate of participation. The Constituent Assembly thus elected had appointed a provisional President, Dr Álvaro Alfredo Magaña, who had no affiliations with any political party and whose aim was to restore peace in the country. A Pact adopted by President Magaña's Cabinet contained seven headings, one of which was "human rights". Accordingly, a Commission had been set up at the beginning of August to see that human rights were respected and to investigate violations that had occurred in the past, in addition, his country was expecting a visit from the Special Representative mentioned by the representative of the Director-General.

112. Under these circumstances, he trusted that the Committee would show understanding and would not dwell too much on the regrettable errors committed in the past but would take notice of the evidence of goodwill shown by the Salvadorian Government. Although he considered that the communications were inadmissible because available domestic remedies had not been exhausted in accordance with the terms of paragraph 14 (*a*) (ix) of 104 EX/Decision 3.3, the representative of the government concerned said he was willing to examine the cases in order to demonstrate his government's goodwill. He therefore went through the list of 217 Salvadorian teachers who had been killed, pointing out that there was no proof that they were all genuine teachers, that in 32 cases those responsible for the deaths had not been identified and that in others, persons in civilian clothing had been held responsible. The latter might quite conceivably have belonged to extreme right-wing paramilitary groups hostile to ANDES, which was, by its own definition, a left-wing organization that had fought against previous governments and remained equally intransigent in its attitude to the present Government of El Salvador. Finally, he was inclined to think that a large number of the missing persons might be in hiding. He added that the list of murdered teachers included two mayors who, as all other mayors, belonged to the party of the government in power and that it seemed odd that the latter should have turned the armed forces and the police against them.

113. He therefore concluded that the communications had been submitted without due consideration and were not backed up by sufficient proof to implicate the responsibility of the Government of El Salvador. He felt that the authors should be asked to furnish more cogent proof if the authorities were to make further headway with their investigations.

No. 276/80 **El Salvador**

114. In referring to the tragic events in El Salvador, some speakers expressed sorrow, others dismay and all expressed regret at the situation and its inherent dangers, which involved the right to life. In view of the complexity of the [communications], one member proposed in order to deal with it more methodically, that the cases should be divided into two categories: one for persons whose death had been established and concerning whom, while deeply regretting the circumstances, he felt that the Committee was powerless to act, so that their case should be dropped from its agenda, and the other for missing persons, concerning whom he suggested that the Director-General should get in touch with the Salvadorian Government which had just declared itself willing to co-operate. Most of the Committee members supported this course of action, noting that since the new Salvadorian Government seemed prepared to throw all the weight of its authority into finding a solution, Unesco was in duty bound to assist it. Some of them added that cases of missing persons could also be submitted to the Working Group on Enforced or Involuntary Disappearances attached to the United Nations Commission on Human Rights.

115. While supporting the idea of intervention by the Director-General, two members considered it the Committee's duty to declare the communications admissible. One member of the Committee thought perhaps that the question might be dealt with in accordance with the terms of paragraph 18 of 104 EX/Decision 3.3. Two other members drew the Committee's attention to reports by the Catholic church to the effect that the violations denounced by the communications were still going on: it had been alleged, for instance, that over 200 people had been murdered between 6 and 19 August 1982; the Archbishop of El Salvador believed that the police and the army of El Salvador were responsible.

116. In the light of these considerations, the Committee, deeply deploring the heavy loss of human life in El Salvador - although expressing no opinion, in the absence of conclusive information, as to the authors of these acts - and regretting that the human rights situation in El Salvador is still a source of grave concern to the international community, *decided*:

(i) to transmit the full text of the statement by the representative of the government concerned to the authors of the [communications], requesting them to provide the Committee with such comments and information as they deem appropriate;

(ii) to delete from their list cases of alleged violation of human rights regarding persons whose death has been established since action by the Committee in such cases would be to no avail;

(iii) to instruct the Secretariat to make available to the Special Representative of the United Nations Commission on Human Rights any information arising from the communications that he might find useful in carrying out his new assignment;

(iv) to ask the Executive Board to request the Director-General to take whatever humanitarian action he considers useful to bring about a friendly solution to the matter set out in the communications and with this end in view to give every assistance to the Salvadorian authorities in ensuring greater respect for human rights, particularly by promoting human rights education;

(v) to ask the representative of the government concerned to submit to the Committee at its next session a general survey of the situation with regard to the human rights of teachers in El Salvador and, in particular, detailed information concerning the individual cases mentioned in the communications.

Spring 1983 session of the Committee on Conventions and Recommendations (116th session of the Executive Board)[19]

66. These five communications[20] denounce violations of human rights which are said to have been committed in El Salvador, particularly with regard to teachers, and to have caused the death or disappearance of a number of people.

67. At this session the Committee had before it two letters from the authors of the communications and a letter from the Permanent Delegation of El Salvador to Unesco (all three summarized or reproduced in [Committee documents]).[21]

68. In its letter the Government of El Salvador informed the Committee that despite the difficult and tragic situation in which the country was placed, an Amnesty Law had been promulgated and had come into force; that general elections were to be held at the end of December and that the education system was operating normally. As regards the communications themselves, the representative of the government in-

[19] See document 116 EX/48 PRIV., paras. 66-71; see also documents 116 EX/CR/HR/2 and Add. and Add.3.

[20] Communications No. 276/80 concerning *El Salvador*, case of *Leonel Menéndez Quiroga*, No. 283/80 concerning *El Salvador*, case of *Arrest and persecution of teachers in El Salvador*, No. 306/80 concerning *El Salvador*, case of *Arrest and persecution of teachers in El Salvador*, No. 390/81 concerning *El Salvador*, case of *Edgar Mauricio Vallejo*, and No. 477/ 82 concerning *El Salvador*, case of *Violation of human rights in El Salvador*, were being considered together.

[21] See documents 116 EX/CR/HR/2 and Add. and Add.3.

dicated that he had received no new information or facts which might be of assistance in the work of the Committee: for that reason - and in accordance with precise instructions from his government - he would refrain from attending the meeting to which he had been invited.

69. All the members who spoke expressed their grave concern at the seriousness of the situation in El Salvador; one of them expressed regret that no information had been provided on the specific practical problems raised by the communications; another suggested that the Director-General be asked to continue his efforts to find a friendly solution. A third member suggested that the decision taken by the Committee should reiterate point (v) of the decision adopted at the [autumn 1982] session.

70. The representative of the Director-General stated that in accordance with the Committee's decision[22] the Director-General had offered his assistance to the Salvadorian Government in ensuring greater respect for human rights, particularly by promoting human rights education; the Permanent Delegate of El Salvador to Unesco had expressed his thanks, but so far appeared not to have taken advantage of the proposal.

71. The Committee therefore *decided*:

(i) to keep these communications on its agenda and to resume the examination of their admissibility at the next session;

(ii) to request the Executive Board to ask the Director-General to continue his efforts to bring about a friendly solution;

(iii) to reiterate its request to the government concerned to submit to it at the next session a general survey of the situation with regard to human rights of teachers in El Salvador and, in particular, detailed information concerning the individual cases mentioned in the communications.

Autumn 1983 session of the Committee on Conventions and Recommendations (117th session of the Executive Board)[23]

80. These five communications[24] denounce violations of human rights which are said to have been committed in El Salvador, particularly with regard to teachers, and to have caused the death or disappearance of a large number of people.

---

[22] See document 115 EX/28 PRIV., para. 116 (iv) (*supra*, p. 687).

[23] See document 117 EX/18 PRIV., paras. 80-83; see also document 117 EX/CR/HR/2.

El Salvador **No. 276/80**

81. The earliest of these communications have been on the agenda of the Committee since its spring 1981 session.

82. At the present session, the Salvadorian Government was not represented. One member of the Committee deplored the absence of a representative of the government concerned, which he considered all the more regrettable in view of the tragic situation affecting the people of El Salvador; he added that the Director-General should be asked to continue his efforts. Two other members of the Committee endorsed this suggestion. The representative of the Director-General stated that the question of human rights in El Salvador was a central concern of the United Nations Commission on Human Rights which, in March 1983 had adopted a resolution reproduced in [a Committee document][25] which provided in particular for the mandate of the Special Representative to be extended for a further year. One member of the Committee suggested that the action of the Committee should be co-ordinated with that of the Commission on Human Rights.

83. Consequently, the Committee *decided* by consensus:

(i) to postpone consideration of the admissibility of these communications until the next session;

(ii) to ask the Executive Board to request the Director-General to continue his efforts to find a friendly solution and to draw the attention of the government to the importance attached to its co-operation with the Committee;

(iii) to repeat its request to the representative of the government concerned to provide it, at its next session; with a comprehensive document on the human rights situation of teachers in El Salvador and, in particular, with detailed information on the individual cases covered by the communications.

---

[24] Communications No. 276/80 concerning *El Salvador*, case of *Leonel Menéndez Quiroga*, No. 283/80 concerning *El Salvador*, case of *Arrest and persecution of teachers in El Salvador*, No. 306/80 concerning *El Salvador*, case of *Arrest and persecution of teachers in El Salvador*, No. 390/81 concerning *El Salvador*, case of *Edgar Mauricio Vallejo*, and No. 477/ 82 concerning *El Salvador*, case of *Violation of human rights in El Salvador*, were being considered together.

[25] See document 116 EX/CR/HR/2.

No. 276/80 **El Salvador**

Spring 1984 session of the Committee on Conventions and Recommendations (119th session of the Executive Board)[26]

88. The five communications[27] mentioned above denounce violations of human rights allegedly perpetrated in El Salvador, against teachers in particular, which are said to have resulted in many deaths and disappearances.

89. The earliest of these communications have been on the Committee's agenda since its spring [1981 session]. In connection with the Committee's examination of the admissibility of these communications since that date, the Salvadorian Government sent a representative to the autumn [1981 and autumn 1982 sessions]. At all other sessions it refrained from doing so, explaining its position in writing.

90. No letter was submitted to the Committee at the present session, and no representative of the Salvadorian Government was present.

91. The Legal Adviser informed the Committee that the matter of the human rights situation in El Salvador continued to hold the attention of the Commission on Human Rights of the United Nations and that the mandate of the Special Representative appointed by the Commission in connection with its examination of the question had again been extended for one year.

92. All the members of the Committee who spoke stated that they were very much concerned about both the attitude of the government involved towards the Committee and the fate of the alleged victims; they thought it necessary to inform the Salvadorian Government of these two causes for concern and request it to make all possible efforts to improve the situation of the individuals mentioned in the communications and inform the Committee about the matter. A member of the Committee stressed the role that could be played in such cases by the Commission on Human Rights of the United Nations, which had a Special Representative on the spot. Another member of the Committee expressed the hope that the new government that was about to take office in El Salvador would take all possible steps to promote action in support of respect for human rights.

---

[26] See document 119 EX/35 PRIV., paras. 88-93; see also document 119 EX/CR/HR/2.

[27] Communications No. 276/80 concerning *El Salvador*, case of *Leonel Menéndez Quiroga*, No. 283/80 concerning *El Salvador*, case of *Arrest and persecution of teachers in El Salvador*, No. 306/80 concerning *El Salvador*, case of *Arrest and persecution of teachers in El Salvador*, No. 390/81 concerning *El Salvador*, case of *Edgar Mauricio Vallejo*, and No. 477/ 82 concerning *El Salvador*, case of *Violation of human rights in El Salvador*, were being considered together.

93. Consequently the Committee *decided*:

(i) to ask the Executive Board to request the Director-General to make urgent approaches to the government concerned so that the latter might in future resume its co-operation with the Committee and present, as the Committee had already requested at its autumn [1982 and spring and autumn 1983 sessions], a comprehensive document on the human rights situation of teachers in El Salvador, in the absence of which the Committee would feel obliged at its next session to submit to the Executive Board a specific report dealing with the facts, which have not yet been disputed, on the basis of the five communications;

(ii) to request the Secretariat to provide all possible assistance to the Special Representative of the Commission on Human Rights of the United Nations in the fulfilment of his mandate;

(iii) to examine these communications at its autumn [1984 session].

Autumn 1984 session of the Committee on Conventions and Recommendations (120th session of the Executive Board)[28]

62. The five communications[29] mentioned above denounce violations of human rights allegedly perpetrated in El Salvador, against teachers in particular, which are said to have resulted in many deaths and disappearances.

63. The earliest of these communications have been on the Committee's agenda since its spring [1981 session]. In connection with the Committee's examination of the admissibility of these communications since that date, the Salvadorian Government sent a representative to the autumn [1981 and autumn 1982 sessions]. At all other sessions it refrained from doing so, explaining its position in writing.

64. No letter had been submitted to the Committee at the [spring 1984] session, and no representative of the Salvadorian Government had been present. Consequently the Committee had decided:[30]

---

[28] See document 120 EX/15 PRIV., paras. 62-69; see also document 120 EX/CR/HR/2.

[29] Communications No. 276/80 concerning *El Salvador*, case of *Leonel Menéndez Quiroga*, No. 283/80 concerning *El Salvador*, case of *Arrest and persecution of teachers in El Salvador*, No. 306/80 concerning *El Salvador*, case of *Arrest and persecution of teachers in El Salvador*, No. 390/81 concerning *El Salvador*, case of *Edgar Mauricio Vallejo*, and No. 477/ 82 concerning *El Salvador*, case of *Violation of human rights in El Salvador*, were being considered together.

(i) to ask the Executive Board to request the Director-General to make urgent approaches to the government concerned so that the latter might in future resume its co-operation with the Committee and present, as the Committee had already requested at its autumn [1982 and spring and autumn 1983 sessions], a comprehensive document on the human rights situation of teachers in El Salvador, in the absence of which the Committee would feel obliged at its next session to submit to the Executive Board a specific report dealing with the facts, which have not yet been disputed, on the basis of the five communications;

(ii) to request the Secretariat to provide all possible assistance to the Special Representative of the Commission on Human Rights of the United Nations in the fulfilment of his mandate;

(iii) to examine these communications at the present session.

65. The Legal Adviser informed the Committee that the Government of El Salvador had notified the Secretary-General of the United Nations that in view of the exceptional situation prevailing in its territory, it had invoked the provisions of Article 4 of the International Covenant on Civil and Political Rights, entitling it to the suspension of certain obligations imposed by that Covenant.

66. At the present session, no letter had been submitted to the Committee by the Government of El Salvador and no representative had been appointed to appear before it.

67. Most of the Committee members considered that in view of the content of the communications and the lack of co-operation of the government concerned, it was essential for the Committee to take firm action so as not to lose its credibility. In this connection, a number of Committee members supported a suggestion by one of them that the Executive Board be asked to send a mission to El Salvador to discuss the matter with the competent authorities, subject, of course, to the prior agreement of the Salvadorian Government. Some members felt that the mission should consist of one or more members of the Executive Board; others considered that it should be a mission of the Director-General himself or his representative; a third group suggested a joint initiative by the Executive Board and the Director-General. One member of the Committee pointed out that a Special Representative of the United Nations Commission on Human Rights for El Salvador had been in office for three years, that he devoted a great deal of time and effort to the matter and drew up a voluminous report each year leading to the adoption of a resolution by the Commis-

[30] See document 119 EX/35 PRIV., para. 93 (*supra*, p. 691).

sion; his mandate had again been extended this year for a further year. The Government of El Salvador was co-operating with the Special Representative, who had never been refused permission to visit a particular region or interview a particular individual. The member concerned stated that, in his view, it would perhaps be going too far to ask the Salvadorian Government to receive and co-operate with two representatives of the United Nations system at one time; the Committee should rather get in touch with the Special Representative, inform him of the motives for its concern and request him to obtain information on the individual cases submitted to it. Two members of the Committee were reluctant to accept such a solution, one considering that the logistic problems referred to would not constitute an obstacle, and the other that the involvement of another international body should not impede specific action by the Committee, and that, moreover, the United Nations Commission on Human Rights was seeking information from which to draw general conclusions regarding the violation or non-violation of human rights, whereas the Committee was concerned with the specific situation of individuals who were suffering or had disappeared. The Legal Adviser noted in this connection that the reports of the Special Representative dealt with the general situation but also with individual cases, but they did not contain specific information on teachers; he also informed the members of the Committee who had raised the question that there were indeed precedents for human rights missions by personal representatives of the Director-General and that the Executive Board frequently resorted to action of this kind in other fields.

68. Several members of the Committee deplored the gravity of the situation in El Salvador, which could only be described as tragic and urged the Committee to abide by the decision it had taken at its [spring 1984] session, since the Salvadorian Government had not responded to the request submitted to it. Some members deeply regretted the silence of the Salvadorian Government; one member considered that the failure of the government concerned to reply implied that the facts alleged in the communications were true and that the communications should therefore be declared admissible.

69. After the discussion, the Committee took the following *decision*:

> The Committee,
>
> Noting that five communications denouncing violations of human rights in Unesco's fields of competence, of which teachers in particular have apparently been the victims, have been referred to it since 1980 by national and international trade unions and other non-governmental organizations,
>
> Noting that the Committee, as early as its autumn 1982 session, requested the government concerned to send it an overall review of the human rights situa-

tion of teachers in El Salvador, but that no such document has yet been communicated to it in spite of repeated requests to that effect,

Declares the five communications admissible, as the allegations contained therein do not prima facie seem manifestly ill-founded;

Taking the view that consideration of the communications thus declared admissible necessitates the Committee's being able to refer to additional information that the government concerned is best able to furnish,

Considering that such additional information is necessary before it can submit any report on the five communications to the Executive Board,

Therefore requests the Executive Board, after consultation with the government concerned and in agreement with it, to commission one of its members to visit El Salvador and, with the assistance of the Director-General or his representative, to initiate or pursue discussions with the government concerned about the allegations made in the five communications;

Decides to resume consideration of those communications at its next session.

Spring 1985 session of the Committee on Conventions and Recommendations (121st session of the Executive Board)[31]

200. These five communications[32] denounce violations of human rights allegedly perpetrated in El Salvador, against teachers in particular, which are said to have resulted in many deaths and disappearances. [The first three communications] have been on the Committee's agenda since its spring 1981 session [...]. At its autumn 1982 session [...], the Committee decided to strike from its list the cases of deceased persons, feeling that representations by it could not, in the event, have any result.[33] The individual cases of missing teachers, writers or students, the overall situation of teachers, and that of school and university institutions still required attention.

[31] See document 121 EX/46 PRIV., paras. 200-209; see also document 121 EX/CR/HR/1.
[32] Communications No. 276/80 concerning *El Salvador*, case of *Leonel Menéndez Quiroga*, No. 283/80 concerning *El Salvador*, case of *Arrest and persecution of teachers in El Salvador*, No. 306/80 concerning *El Salvador*, case of *Arrest and persecution of teachers in El Salvador*, No. 390/81 concerning *El Salvador*, case of *Edgar Mauricio Vallejo*, and No. 477/ 82 concerning *El Salvador*, case of *Violation of human rights in El Salvador*, were being considered together.
[33] See document 115 EX/28 PRIV., para. 116 (ii) (*supra*, p. 686).

El Salvador **No. 276/80**

201. In considering these communications, the Committee had had the co-operation of the government concerned up to its spring 1983 session [...].

202. Since then, that government had had no contact with the Committee either by letter or through an appointed representative.

203. At its autumn 1984 session, the Committee, after declaring the five communications admissible, decided to request the Executive Board, after consultation with the government concerned and in agreement with it, to commission one of its members to visit El Salvador and, with the assistance of the Director-General or his representative, to initiate or pursue discussions with the government concerned about the allegations made in the said communications.[34]

204. In presenting the communications to the Committee at the current session, the representative of the Director-General reminded the meeting of the background to them and stated that the question of the human rights situation in El Salvador was still being considered by the United Nations Commission on Human Rights. The mandate of the Special Representative appointed by that Commission to investigate that question had been successively extended for further periods of one year since 1981, and, most recently by resolution 1985/35 of 13 March 1985.

205. The Chairman of the Executive Board furnished information to the Committee about the proposed mission, which had been approved in principle by that Board. He stated that, immediately after the Board's special session (from 12 to 15 February 1985), on 22 February 1985, he had had an interview with the chargé d'affaires of the Permanent Delegation of El Salvador to Unesco, during which the arrangements for carrying out that mission had been considered. A member of the Board had been ready to visit El Salvador between 15 and 31 March 1985; after consulting his government, the chargé d'affaires had informed the Chairman of the Executive Board, by a letter dated 28 February 1985, that the proposed period coincided with the period of the parliamentary elections in his country; that, on that account, the proposed dates would not allow the government to give the requisite attention to the mission; and that the government would be grateful if other dates could be suggested so that it might examine them with a view to giving due attention to the mission.

206. The Government of El Salvador had thus raised no objection to the mission in principle. It had merely indicated that the dates proposed were not suitable, though without suggesting others.

---

[34] See document 120 EX/15 PRIV., para. 69 (*supra*, pp. 693-694).

No. 276/80 **El Salvador**

207. In the reply he had sent to the chargé d'affaires of El Salvador on 15 March, the Chairman of the Executive Board had made it clear to him that there was plainly not enough time still available before the spring 1985 session of the Committee for the mission to be organized effectively, but that the Board member approached to carry out the mission remained willing to undertake it after the 121st session - if it were maintained in principle by the Executive Board - in July 1985, at the dates felt to be most convenient by the Salvadorian authorities. He had also expressed the hope that the government concerned would send a representative to the Committee's meeting so that it could explain its own point of view on the communications in question. On 22 April 1985, he had received a letter from the chargé d'affaires informing him that the Permanent Delegation of El Salvador considered that the Committee's examination of the communications concerning El Savlador should be postponed until the proposed mission had done its work and that, in the delegation's opinion, it would be premature for El Salvador to be represented at the current meeting of the Committee.

208. Several members of the Committee who spoke expressed their keen regret that the government of the country concerned had not sent a representative to the Committee's meeting. They emphasized the humanitarian aspect of the cases submitted and the urgent need for action to be taken to arrive at an acceptable solution, in view of the seriousness of the allegations made, which were a source of deep concern to them. They stressed the need to maintain the principle of the mission proposed at the Committee's autumn 1984 session. Some of these members were of the opinion that it would even be desirable to request the Executive Board to discuss the matter. They felt that the situation in El Salvador was still extremely disquieting, that there were grounds for speaking genocide, and that as, in their view, the alleged facts taken together constituted a "question" and not simply specific individual cases, they reserved the right to ask for the application of paragraph 18 of 104 EX/Decision 3.3, under which "questions" should be considered by the Executive Board and the General Conference in public meetings.

209. After discussion, the Committee took the following *decision*:

The Committee,

Noting that five communications denouncing violations of human rights in Unesco's fields of competence, of which teachers in particular have apparently been the victims, have been referred to it since 1980 by national and international trade unions and other non-governmental organizations,

Noting that the Committee, as early as its autumn 1982 session, requested the government concerned to send it an overall review of the human rights situation of teachers in El Salvador, but that no such document has yet been communicated to it in spite of repeated requests to that effect,

Recalling that, at its autumn 1984 session, it had declared the five communications admissible, as the allegations contained therein did not prima facie seem manifestly ill-founded;

Taking the view that consideration of the communications thus declared admissible necessitates the Committtee's being able to refer to additional information that the government concerned is best able to furnish,

Considering that such additional information is necessary before it can submit any report on the five communications to the Executive Board,

Accordingly requests the Executive Board to confirm its decision, taken at its 120th session, concerning the mission to be sent to El Salvador and its terms of reference;

Thanks the Chairman of the Executive Board for the efforts he has made in connection with this case and requests him to continue them;

Decides to resume consideration of these communications at its next session.

Autumn 1985 session of the Committee on Conventions and Recommendations (122nd session of the Executive Board)[35]

150. These five communications[36] denounce violations of human rights allegedly perpetrated in El Salvador, against teachers in particular, which are said to have resulted in many deaths and disappearances. [The first three communications] have been on the Committee's agenda since its spring 1981 session [...]. At its autumn 1982 session [...], the Committee decided to strike from its list the cases of deceased persons, feeling that representations by it could not, in the event, have any result.[37]

[35] See document 122 EX/21 PRIV., paras. 150-160; see also document 122 EX/CR/HR/1.

[36] Communications No. 276/80 concerning *El Salvador*, case of *Leonel Menéndez Quiroga*, No. 283/80 concerning *El Salvador*, case of *Arrest and persecution of teachers in El Salvador*, No. 306/80 concerning *El Salvador*, case of *Arrest and persecution of teachers in El Salvador*, No. 390/81 concerning *El Salvador*, case of *Edgar Mauricio Vallejo*, and No. 477/ 82 concerning *El Salvador*, case of *Violation of human rights in El Salvador*, were being considered together.

[37] See document 115 EX/28 PRIV., para. 116 (ii) (*supra*, p. 686).

The individual cases of missing teachers, writers or students, the overall situation of teachers, and that of school and university institutions still required attention.

151. At its autumn 1984 session, the Committee declared these communications admissible and decided to request the Executive Board, after consultation with the government concerned and in agreement with it, to commission one of its members to visit El Salvador and, with the assistance of the Director-General or his representative, to initiate or pursue discussions with the government concerned about the allegations made in the said communications.[38]

152. Informing the Committee of the steps he had taken regarding the undertaking of the planned mission, which already on an earlier occasion it had not been possible to carry out (between the autumn 1984 session and the spring 1985 session), the Chairman of the Executive Board reported the following exchange of correspondence:

153. Immediately after the 121st session of the Board (which was held from 9 May to 21 June 1985), he wrote a letter to the chargé d'affaires of the Permanent Delegation of El Salvador to Unesco on 24 June, communicating to him the relevant passages of the Committee's report and the dates proposed by the Board member approached to carry out the mission. Receiving no reply, he wrote again to the chargé d'affaires, on 15 July 1985. By a letter dated 22 July 1985, the latter informed him that, in view of the absence of the Minister for External Relations of his government, dates other than those proposed would be suggested, but that the members of the mission would be received only in a personal capacity. The Chairman of the Board then replied by letter dated 31 July 1985 that the decision to send a mission to El Salvador had been that of the Board, and that it was not possible to change either its representative nature or its terms of reference. By a telex dated 14 August 1985 and subsequently confirmed by a letter dated 20 August 1985, the chargé d'affaires indicated that his government was prepared to receive the mission, in a personal capacity, on 28, 29 and 30 August 1985. By a letter dated 30 August 1985, confirming an interim letter of 27 August 1985 from the Secretariat of the Board, the Chairman of the Board made it clear once againt that it was not possible to change either the nature or the terms of reference of the mission.

154. Supplementing this information, the member of the Executive Board who had been approached stated, for his part, that he had provided every assurance with regard to the strictly confidential nature of the mission that he had agreed to undertake at the Board's request.

---

[38] See document 120 EX/15 PRIV., para. 69 (*supra*, pp. 693-694).

El Salvador **No. 276/80**

155. Taking the floor, the representative of the Salvadorian Government stated that his presence before the Committee was a proof of his country's willingness to re-establish direct contact with the Committee. He recalled that it was in May 1984 that, for the first time in 50 years of El Salvador's history, a civilian who based his policy on the protection and promotion of human rights had been democratically elected Head of State. He informed the Committee that, in its efforts to ensure respect for these rights, the Salvadorian Government had taken, *inter alia*, the following measures: priority consideration of denunciations of violations of human rights in the country, in particular through the Human Rights Commission of El Salvador, set up in August 1982; strengthening of the institutional structure of that Commission in order to enable it to inspect the premises of the security forces, military garrisons, hospitals and other premises, in cases of inquiries relating to arrested or missing persons; regular inspection of all detention centres; strengthening of the machinery of judicial inquiry in order to guarantee impartiality in trials; disbandment of a rural police unit in charge of intelligence operations (Unidad de Inteligencia de la Policía de Hacienda); establishment of a "Subsecretaria de Seguridad Pública" headed by a member of the Human Rights Commission of El Salvador appointed to keep effective check on the security forces; setting up of a Commission of Inquiry responsible for investigating the nefarious activities of the "Death Squads" and the attacks upon members of the civilian population allegedly perpetrated by the military. The representative of the Salvadorian Government added that the Human Rights Commission of El Salvador had endeavoured to alert the country to the need to respect these rights by conducting a consciousness-raising campaign, particularly among the armed forces, and that the list of alleged victims in the communications in question had been transmitted to that Commission, which had to date succeeded in identifying seven cases, the other persons concerned continuing to be the subject of inquiries as they were not being held in detention centres. The representative also indicated that, for the purposes of the mission to El Salvador of a member of the Executive Board, a working group had been set up and a report was currently being prepared, which, after it had been presented to that member on the occasion of the mission, would be completed and transmitted to Unesco. In this regard, he stated that his government intended to extend every facility to the mission, but to receive it in a personal capacity.

156. Many Committee members expressed their deep concern regarding the human rights situation in El Salvador, which they felt to be of exceptional gravity, involving heinous crimes and many cases of disappearances. They wondered why the government concerned would not agree to receive the mission decided upon by the Executive Board as being a Unesco mission. In their opinion, once the Executive Board had given the mission its mandate, the mission could not but be an official one.

No. 276/80 **El Salvador**

157. One member of the Committee felt that it would have been perfectly understandable if the competent Salvadorian authorities had refused to receive a private mission, but not a mission decided upon by an executive organ of an international organization of which El Salvador was a member. Another Committee member was of the opinion that if the efforts to continue the dialogue with the government concerned through the dispatch of a Board member on an official mission came to nothing it would then be necessary to apply the provisions of paragraph 18 of 104 EX/ Decision 3.3, and lay the question before the Executive Board in a public meeting.

158. While some members of the Committee stated that the respect of human rights in El Salvador still left much to be desired, others acknowledged that there was at present a general trend in El Salvador towards an improvement in the human rights situation, although this trend was still not as marked as might be wished. They were nevertheless astonished by the reluctance of the government concerned to receive the planned mission as operating in an official capacity and reiterated that it was essential for the mission to be carried out as quickly as possible. It was pointed out, in connection with the mission of the Special Representative to El Salvador of the United Nations Commission on Human Rights, that the mandate which he had been given by the terms of the relevant resolution of the Commission clearly showed that he was conducting his mission in an official, representative capacity.

159. Taking the floor again, the representative of the government concerned confirmed that the human rights situation in his country was still not ideal, but added that a mechanism making for stability had begun to operate. He suggested that a problem of terminology might be involved in the question of the mission to El Salvador of a member of the Executive Board, explaining that his government intended to give every assistance to the mission, but meant by the expression "in a personal capacity" that it was not its intention to observe the protocol appropriate to a State representative. In reply to a question, he stated that following the presidential elections of May 1984 and the coming to power of the present President of the Republic of El Salvador an amnesty had been declared.

160. Following an exchange of views, the Committee *decided*:

(i) to take note of the information supplied by the representative of the State concerned;

(ii) to express once again its concern regarding the gravity of the human rights situation in El Salvador, particularly in regard to teachers;

(iii) to request the Executive Board, accordingly, to confirm its decision after consultation with the government concerned and in agreement with it, to commission one of its members to visit El Salvador and, acting on behalf of the Executive Board and with the assistance of the Director-General or his representative, to initiate or pursue discussions with that government about the allegations made in the five communications, a report on the results of the mission, which will be of a confidential nature, being submitted to the Committee on Conventions and Recommendations and to the Executive Board at a private meeting.

Spring 1986 session of the Committee on Conventions and Recommendations (124th session of the Executive Board)[39]

143. These five communications[40] denounce alleged violations of human rights claimed to have been perpetrated in El Salvador against teachers in particular.

144. It was recalled that at its autumn 1984 session, the Committee had declared these five communications admissible and had decided to request the Executive Board, after consultation with the government concerned and in agreement with it, to commission one of its members to visit El Salvador and, with the assistance of the Director-General or his representative, to initiate or pursue discussions with the government concerned about the allegations made in the said communications.[41] Following the acceptance by the Executive Board of the Committee's request for a mission to El Salvador and after appropriate consultations especially with the competent authorities of El Salvador, the then Chairman of the Executive Board [...] designated Mr Gian Franco Pompei (Italy) as the member of the Committee who was to undertake the mission concerned.

145. At its spring 1985 session, the Committee was informed by the Chairman of the Executive Board that while the Government of El Salvador had raised no objection to the mission in principle, it had said that the period between 15 and 31 March 1985 which had been proposed for the mission coincided with the period of parliamentary elections in that country and that for that reason it would not be possible for the gov-

---

[39] See document 124 EX/3 PRIV., paras. 143-152 and annex; see also document 124 EX/CR/HR/1.

[40] Communications No. 276/80 concerning *El Salvador*, case of *Leonel Menéndez Quiroga*, No. 283/80 concerning *El Salvador*, case of *Arrest and persecution of teachers in El Salvador*, No. 306/80 concerning *El Salvador*, case of *Arrest and persecution of teachers in El Salvador*, No. 390/81 concerning *El Salvador*, case of *Edgar Mauricio Vallejo*, and No. 477/82 concerning *El Salvador*, case of *Violation of human rights in El Salvador*, were being considered together.

[41] See document 120 EX/15 PRIV., para. 69 (*supra*, pp. 693-694).

ernment to give requisite attention to the mission. He stated also that the government had not, on its part, suggested any alternative dates.

146. At its 121st session, the Executive Board confirmed its decision, taken at its 120th session, concerning the mission to be sent to El Salvador and its terms of reference. The Chairman of the Executive Board reported to the Committee at its autumn 1985 session of the steps he had taken with the view to enabling the designated member of the Board to carry out the mission. He informed the Committee that in his consultations with the Government of El Salvador he had been told that the competent authorities of that Member State were prepared to receive the mission only in a personal capacity. He said that it was for this reason that the envisaged mission had not taken place because, as he had made clear to the government concerned, the decision to send a mission to El Salvador had been that of the Executive Board and consequently it was not possible for himself to accept a change either in its representative nature or in its terms of reference. At its 122nd session, the Executive Board confirmed again its decision concerning the mission to El Salvador and decided it be entrusted to its mandated representative who, for that purpose, would be acting on behalf of the Executive Board.

147. The Chairman of the Executive Board reported to the Committee at its current session on the consultations he has had with the authorities of El Salvador with a view to giving effect to the decision of the Board concerning the mission to their country. He said that these consultations had not enabled effect to be given to this decision of the Board because the authorities of the Member State concerned had maintained their previous position that the mission would be received in a "personal" and "private" capacity while, on his part, he had confirmed his precedessor's view that since the mission concerned had been decided upon by the Executive Board itself, the Chairman of the Board was not competent to authorize it to take place on a "personal" or "private" basis.

148. The Chairperson and the other members of the Committee who spoke on the communications concerned expressed their regret that Mr Pompei had not been able to undertake the mission because the authorities of El Salvador had offered to receive him in a personal or private capacity and not as a representative of Unesco. They strongly urged the government concerned to reconsider its position in this respect.

149. The representative of the Government of El Salvador declared that there had indeed been some difficulties regarding the status of the mission decided upon by the Executive Board. He said further that his government was prepared to grant the one who will undertake the mission all the necessary diplomatic privileges and facilities and treat the person in the same manner as it had treated other individuals who had

undertaken similar missions on behalf of the United Nations or the International Labour Organisation. One member of the Committee remarked in this connection that the issue at stake was not one of diplomatic privileges or facilities but of accreditation. A number of members of the Committee insisted that it was indispensable that the person undertaking the mission be received by the competent authorities of El Salvador as a mandated representative of the Executive Board if the mission was to have some value for the task that the Committee was called upon to discharge in respect of the five communications concerned. The representative of the Government of El Salvador declared that while the competent authorities of his country were not prepared to consider the mission as official for their own purposes, they were willing to receive the person designated to undertake the mission as a mandated representative of the Executive Board. Note was taken of this statement.

150. At the request of the Chairperson and some other members of the Committee, the representative of the Government of El Salvador agreed to confirm in writing that the envoy of the Executive Board to be entrusted with the envisaged mission would be received by the competent authorities of his country as the mandated representative of the Board and that the person would be given appropriate facilities for carrying out the mission, it being understood that the mission's report would be treated as confidential by the Organization. In this connection, one member of the Committee assured the representative of the government concerned that Mr Pompei who had previously been designated to carry out this mission had, by virtue of his experience and qualifications, all the qualities that would ensure total objectivity in the responsibility which had been entrusted to him in that respect. One member considered that the mission should be entrusted to a current member of the Committee. Mr Pompei's term of office as a member of the Executive Board and consequently of the Committee having come to an end, the same member suggested that the Chairperson should be entrusted with the mission. This proposal having been supported by two members of the Committee, it was decided to recommend to the Executive Board that it designate the Chairperson of the Committee for this mission.

151. The Chairperson declared that should she be in charge of the mission, she would like to be accompanied by another member of the Committee who spoke Spanish and also knew the Latin American region very well. It was proposed that the Chairperson should discuss with the Chairman of the Executive Board the modalities for the implementation of the Board's decision concerning the mission to El Salvador.

152. At the end of its discussion, the Committee *decided*:

(i) to express once again its concern regarding the gravity of the human rights situation in El Salvador, particularly in regard to teachers;

(ii) to request the Executive Board to confirm its decision taken at its 120th, 121st and 122nd sessions concerning the mission to be sent to El Salvador and its terms of reference;

(iii) to recommend to the Executive Board to name, after consultation with the government concerned and in agreement with it, the Chairperson for the said mission;

(iv) to take note of the assurances given to the Committee by the representative of the Government of El Salvador to the effect that the person so commissioned by the Executive Board will be received by the competent authorities of his country as the mandated representative of the Board and given appropriate facilities to enable the envoy to carry out the mission in question in suitable conditions;

(v) to resume consideration of these communications at its next session and consider the report which will be drawn up by the mission on its return from El Salvador.

Autumn 1986 session of the Committee on Conventions and Recommendations (125th session of the Executive Board)[42]

168. The first five communications[43] denounce alleged violations of human rights claimed to have been perpetrated in El Salvador against teachers in particular. At its autumn 1984 session [...] the Committee declared them admissible and requested the Executive Board, after consultation with the government concerned and in agreement with it, to commission one of its members to visit El Salvador. With the assistance of the Director-General or his representative, that member was to initiate or pursue discussions with the government concerned about the allegations made in those communications.[44] After the Executive Board had decided on the mission, consultations were held with the Salvadorian authorities and at its 124th session the

[42] See document 125 EX/3 PRIV., paras. 168-179; see also documents 125 EX/CR/HR/1 and Add.2 and 125 EX/CR/HR/2.
[43] Communications No. 276/80 concerning *El Salvador*, case of *Leonel Menéndez Quiroga*, No. 283/80 concerning *El Salvador*, case of *Arrest and persecution of teachers in El Salvador*, No. 306/80 concerning *El Salvador*, case of *Arrest and persecution of teachers in El Salvador*, No. 390/81 concerning *El Salvador*, case of *Edgar Mauricio Vallejo*, No. 477/82 concerning *El Salvador*, case of *Violation of human rights in El Salvador*, and No. 690/85 concerning *El Salvador*, case of *Filomena Claros de Majano*, were being considered together.
[44] See document 120 EX/15 PRIV., para. 69 (*supra*, pp. 693-694).

Board received assurances that the person undertaking the mission would be received in El Salvador as its representative.

169. The sixth communication concerns Mrs Filomena Claros de Majano. Submitted to the Committee at its spring 1986 session, it is still being considered from the point of view of admissibility. On the Committee's recommendation, the Executive Board decided at its 124th session to include this communication in the mandate of its mission.

170. Mr Gian Franco Pompei (Italy), a former member of the Executive Board, carried out the mission from 21 to 27 July 1986. His report is reproduced in [a Committee document].[45]

171. Mr Pompei noted that under the terms of his mandate he had been asked to initiate or pursue discussions with the government concerned about the allegations made in the six communications and to express the concern of the Committee and the Executive Board about the gravity of the human rights situation in El Salvador, especially as regards teachers and students. He explained that his report reviewed the general human rights situation in the country and described certain new institutions set up to safeguard such rights since the new government had come into power. Specific cases of human rights violations could only be dealt with by placing them in the context of the time at which they were said to have been perpetrated. This context had changed considerably. Mr Pompei said that the Salvadorian authorities had provided him with all the facilities he needed for his mission. They had been highly co-operative and extremely helpful. With regard to the first five communications, he confirmed what the author of [the first communication] had himself stated, namely that the following alleged victims were all dead: Dr Miguel Ángel García, Dr Carlos Ernesto Alfaro Rodríguez, Ángel Erasmo Figueroa and Héctor Lemus Rosa. The place and date of their death was in fact known. The Salvadorian authorities assured Mr Pompei that the fifth alleged victim in this communication, Mr Leonel Menéndez Quiroga, was also dead. Mr Pompei noted that the Committee had decided at its autumn 1982 session [...] "to delete from its list cases of alleged violation of human rights regarding persons whose death has been established since action by the Committee in such cases would be to no avail".[46] As the authors of the communications had asked, in the case of the deceased persons, whether there had been legal proceedings with a view to finding and sentencing the guilty parties and whether the families of the victims had been compensated, Mr Pompei informed the Committee that he had requested information in that connection but had only been able to obtain it for the period after 1982, following the establishment of the government Human

[45] See document 125 EX/CR/HR/1 Add.2.
[46] See document 115 EX/28 PRIV., para. 116 (ii) (*supra*, p. 686).

Rights Commission. There were no records prior to that date, in particular for the years 1979 and 1980 when there had been a very large number of abductions and murders. He had had to fall back on the press cuttings made available by the Commission. Those who had been in power during the hardest and most turbulent period in El Salvador's history were not concerned with human rights. It was during that dark period that the alleged victims in the communications had died or disappeared. Mrs Filomena Claros de Majano had disappeared in January 1984 and the representative of the government concerned had informed the Committee at its [spring 1986] session that the authorities of his country had already undertaken an investigation concerning her case and that the inquiry had been entrusted to the Public Prosecutor at the Supreme Court. Mr Pompei said that the information gathered about the case in El Salvador from the Ministry of Education, the government Human Rights Commission and the Legal Protection Department of the Archbishopric was in line with that provided by the author of [the sixth communication]. He added that he had been informed that the mother of the alleged victim had been assisted by the Legal Department at the Ministry of Education in making a complaint to the legal authorities concerning the abduction of her daughter. He received assurances that the daughter was not being held in any establishment run by the public authorities and that the final results of the Supreme Court inquiry would be communicated to Unesco. In this connection, a note by the Head of the Legal Department of the Ministry of Education of El Salvador and a number of documents provided by the Archbishopric are reproduced as annexes to the mission report. As far as assistance to the families was concerned, Mr Pompei reported that the Minister of Education of El Salvador had given him copies of a decree establishing a system of pensions for the children of the victims of violence where such victims were members of the teaching profession or belonged to the Ministry, and copies of decrees concerning the application of these measures to specific cases. The Minister had assured him that this pension system was being applied in the case of Mrs Filomena Claros de Majano. As contacts had been re-established with the government concerned, Mr Pompei expressed the hope that the government would not fail to provide the Committee with additional information. In reply to questions, he said that he had not met the families of the alleged victims or the officers of the National Association of Salvadorian Educators (ANDES), one of the authors of [the second communication]. In any event, it was appropriate, in his opinion, to recognize that the present government was making a real effort to ensure that those human rights would henceforth be observed. This feeling was shared by a number of members of the Committee.

172. Some other members of the Committee found it difficult to accept in all conscience the unsubstantiated statement that the missing persons were purely and simply deceased. They urged the government concerned to make every effort to clarify the circumstances of the death of the alleged victims, if such was really the case, in order to put an end to the cruel uncertainty of parents who were still hoping to see

their relatives reappear one day. Recalling that at the autumn 1985 session, the representative of the government concerned had mentioned a working group which was responsible at the time for preparing a report on the first five communications, one member asked whether this document could be made available to the Committee. He also wished to know whether the decree of the Minister of Education of El Salvador establishing a system of pensions for the children of persons who had disappeared or been killed, applied not only to the case of Mrs Filomena Claros de Majano but also to the cases of the other alleged victims about whom the Committee was concerned. In addition, confining himself to factual considerations, he pointed out that with regard to:

- [the first communication]: there were no relevant documents attesting, where appropriate, to the death of the five alleged victims. He asked the representative appointed by the Executive Board whether he had documentary evidence of those deaths and, if so, the name of the institution that had provided him with the information;

- [the second and third communications]: in addition to the alleged victims stated to have already been killed, the authors had mentioned the names of eight other persons who had disappeared (Manuel Alberto Rivera, Efraín Arévalo Ibarra, Hipólito Rolando Martínez, Carlos Iván Burgos, María Teresa Hernández Saballos, Agustín Osmín Hernández, Mauricio Evaristo Burgos and Carlos Alberto González) about whom no information had been collected;

- [the fourth communication]: the situation of the alleged victim, Mr Edgar Mauricio Vallejo who had also disappeared, had not been clarified either;

- [the fifth communication]: alongside the list of persons killed, the author of the communication had provided a list of 49 teachers who had reportedly been arrested by the security forces. The case of these alleged victims did not seem to have been dealt with in the mission report either.

173. Two members of the Committee wondered how the Government of El Salvador intended to guarantee respect for human rights and whether it did not consider it advisable for Unesco to assist it in this field.

174. One member of the Committee expressed the view that although the Committee could feel gratified that the Executive Board had, for the first time, been able to send a mission to a Member State concerned by communications alleging human rights violations, the question should none the less be raised as to the extent to which this mission was justified having regard to the results achieved. In his view, the representative appointed by the Executive Board had done all he could, with tact and di-

plomacy, and had succeeded in re-establishing a dialogue with the government concerned, but the additional information sought had not been obtained. He regretted that although Mrs Filomena Claros de Majano had been kidnapped in January 1984, the Salvadorian authorities had still not been able to establish responsibilities in that case and that no fresh information had been added to what the Committee already knew. In addition, according to this member of the Committee, at a time when there was a concern to avoid duplication of effort, it was difficult to understand and to explain the originality of Unesco's mission in relation to a similar mission that the United Nations had just carried out in that same country. This member therefore wished that in the future such superfluous expenditure would be avoided and that information would be sought through the usual means, that is to say, through the representatives of the governments concerned.

175. Other members of the Committee held the view that it was useful, in certain cases, to have recourse to this kind of mission.

176. The representative of the Director-General recalled that in addition to that mission carried out on behalf of the Executive Board, on the Committee's recommendation, two other missions had also been carried out, at the Board's request, by a representative of the Director-General, in December 1979 and November 1982.

177. In his statement, the representative of the government concerned said that the authorities of his country were satisfied with Unesco's mission but that it would have been preferable if it had taken place in 1981 or 1982 since the present government was not responsible for the alleged facts. This government had demonstrated its desire to co-operate with the Organization with a view to throwing light on the fate of the alleged victims, but it was difficult to achieve the desired results because the archives had not been properly kept under preceding governments. With regard to the assistance that Unesco could provide to the Government of El Salvador with a view to developing human rights teaching and the defence of human rights, to which two members of the Committee had alluded, an application to that effect had already been sent to the Organization in December 1985. The representative of the government concerned added that El Salvador intended, within the limits of its slender resources, to heighten national awareness in this matter by means of education.

178. With regard to the decision that the Committee should recommend to the Executive Board, one member, after submitting a draft decision, presented a revised draft decision which, after suggesting that the Board should pay tribute, in a private meeting, to the victims referred to in [the first communication], recommended that the Executive Board should appeal to the authorities of San Salvador for the families of the deceased to be equitably compensated, under the procedures instituted by the present government of that country, and should request the government to provide

relevant information on the fate of the missing persons referred to in [the second to fifth communications]. The idea of launching this appeal was supported by two members of the Committee. Other members of the Committee stated that the communications which the Committee had received included the names of many allegedly deceased victims and that it would not be appropriate to pay tribute to only some while disregarding others. Other members also said that it was not the Committee's practice to recommend such tributes. In regard to the proposed appeal concerning compensation, other members of the Committee considered it out of order, since such a decision would exceed the powers of the Committee. A number of members were of the view that the Executive Board should invite the Director-General to consider the possibilities of offering to the Government of El Salvador assistance with a view to developing human rights teaching. On this point, two members of the Committee stated that the Government of El Salvador had already demonstrated, in word and in deed, that it was prepared to ensure the observance of human rights and that the Committee had no authority to give it advice, the rule being that Unesco should only offer assistance to Member States that requested it. The author of the above-mentioned draft decision agreed to join the consensus that appeared to prevail in favour of another, more concise, draft decision, so long as his proposals were adequately reflected in the report. He regretted, nevertheless, that the Committee had not considered it advisable to proceed further by adopting a decision with more substance that would enable it to make progress in the clarification of the cases in question.

179. At the end of the debate, the Committee adopted the following *decision*:

The Committee,

1. Notes with satisfaction that the Salvadorian Government has shown itself ready to continue to collaborate with it and to make vital information available to it in accordance with the procedure in force;

2. Decides to examine at its next session [the first five communications] together with [the sixth communication] and requests, in particular, the representative of the Salvadorian Government to provide additional information on these communications in the light of the discussions that have taken place;

3. Recommends that the Executive Board should take note of Mr Pompei's report on his mission to El Salvador and express its gratitude to him for the scrupulous conscientiousness and the high degree of competence that he showed in carrying out the task entrusted to him.

No. 276/80 **El Salvador**

Spring 1987 session of the Committee on Conventions and Recommendations (126th session of the Executive Board)[47]

196. These communications[48] denounce alleged violations of human rights claimed to have been perpetrated in El Salvador, mainly against teachers.

197. It was during its autumn [1984 session] that the Committee declared them admissible and requested the Executive Board to commission one of its members to visit El Salvador to engage in or pursue discussions with the government concerned about the allegations made in those communications.[49]

198. That mission was carried out in July 1986 by a representative appointed by the Executive Board [...].[50]

199. The government concerned had not sent a representative to the present session. However, in a letter [...] dated 5 May 1987 to the Secretariat, the Permanent Delegate of El Salvador to Unesco stated that, in spite of the efforts made by the authorities of his country, it had not been possible to gather additional information concerning those communications. He repeated that the authorities were ready to receive a visit by a member of the Executive Board or of the Committee with a view to ending this distressing situation.

200. One member of the Committee expressed surprise at the absence of a representative of the government concerned. She explained that, as a member of the Inter-American Commission [on] Human Rights, she had received a copy of a letter addressed by the Secretary-General of that body to the Director-General concerning the question of dual procedures raised by the Government of El Salvador which had requested the Commission to discontinue consideration of cases which were also the subject of communications currently awaiting consideration by the Committee.

201. The members of the Committee who took part in the ensuing discussion also expressed their regret that the representative of the government had been unable to

---

[47] See document 126 EX/3 PRIV., paras. 196-203; see also document 126 EX/CR/HR/1.

[48] Communications No. 276/80 concerning *El Salvador*, case of *Leonel Menéndez Quiroga and others*, No. 283/80 concerning *El Salvador*, case of *Arrest and persecution of teachers in El Salvador*, No. 306/80 concerning *El Salvador*, case of *Arrest and persecution of teachers in El Salvador*, No. 390/81 concerning *El Salvador*, case of *Edgar Mauricio Vallejo*, and No. 477/82 concerning *El Salvador*, case of *Violation of human rights in El Salvador*, were being considered together.

[49] See document 120 EX/15 PRIV., para. 69 (*supra*, pp. 693-694).

[50] See document 125 EX/CR/HR/1 Add.2.

attend the meeting, in spite of the efforts made to suit his convenience. It was decided that the Chairperson should write to the Permanent Delegate of El Salvador to inform him of those views.

202. While declaring that he fully understood the situation in El Salvador as it had been described during the [autumn 1986] session and also the difficulties encountered by the present government of the country due to the absence of records and of data concerning the events which had occurred before it came to power, one member believed that the Committee should make representations to the Salvadorian authorities and urge them to use all available remedies so as to pursue inquiries to the furthest possible extent. He also pointed out, together with another member of the Committee, that, in the report of the mission carried out by the Executive Board's appointed representative, there was some confusion concerning the number of alleged victims in each communication, who in fact had been far more numerous: a list should therefore be drawn up for the attention of the government concerned. Referring to the existence of a ministerial decree instituting a system of pensions for the children of victims of violence belonging to the teaching profession or the Ministry of Education [...], he considered - although questions of compensation as such did not fall within the Committee's competence - that an appeal should be made to the Government of El Salvador so as to enable the families of victims to receive compensation in the framework of existing national legislation. This aspect of its humanitarian concerns was also expressed by other members of the Committee.

203. After an exchange of views, the Committee *decided*:

(i) to express its regret that it had been unable to benefit from the presence of a representative of the government concerned, and to request the Chairperson to send a letter in those terms to the Permanent Delegation of El Salvador to Unesco;

(ii) to reiterate its previous request to that government for additional information and to ask the Secretariat to send with it a full list of the alleged victims mentioned in the five communications, after striking out the names of deceased persons, in accordance with the decision taken by the Committee at its autumn 1982 session [...];[51]

(iii) taking into account existing Salvadorian legislation, to launch a humanitarian appeal to that government on behalf of the families of the alleged victims, and especially of their children, so that they might receive compensation;

---

[51] See document 115 EX/28 PRIV., para. 116 (ii) (*supra*, p. 686).

(iv) to request the government concerned to be good enough to inform the families of the missing persons of any details which it might communicate to the Committee;

(v) to resume consideration of these five communications at its autumn 1987 session.

Autumn 1987 session of the Committee on Conventions and Recommendations (127th session of the Executive Board)[52]

136. These communications[53] denounce alleged violations of human rights claimed to have been perpetrated in El Salvador, mainly against teachers.

137. It was during its autumn [1984 session] that the Committee declared them admissible and requested the Executive Board to commission one of its members to visit El Salvador to engage in or pursue discussions with the government concerned about the allegations made in those communications.[54]

138. That mission was carried out in July 1986 by a representative appointed by the Executive Board.[55]

139. At the present session, the representative of the government concerned informed the Committee that the appropriate authorities in El Salvador had done everything possible to investigate the cases of the missing persons mentioned in these communications, but that they had not been able to obtain any additional information. He recalled that his government had always shown willingness to co-operate and that it had done so in particular during the mission of the representative of the Executive Board. He requested that, in view of the fact that the events in question had occurred long before the present government had come to power, in view of the efforts which it had made and, in addition, on account of the initiative by the Ministry of National Education to take under its protection the wives and children of the alleged victims, consideration of these communications be formally ended, by

[52] See document 127 EX/3 PRIV., paras. 136-145; see also document 127 EX/CR/HR/1.
[53] Communications No. 276/80 concerning *El Salvador*, case of *Leonel Menéndez Quiroga and others*, No. 283/80 concerning *El Salvador*, case of *Arrest and persecution of teachers in El Salvador*, No. 306/80 concerning *El Salvador*, case of *Arrest and persecution of teachers in El Salvador*, No. 390/81 concerning *El Salvador*, case of *Edgar Mauricio Vallejo*, and No. 477/82 concerning *El Salvador*, case of *Violation of human rights in El Salvador*, were being considered together.
[54] See document 120 EX/15 PRIV., para. 69 (*supra*, pp. 693-694).
[55] See document 125 EX/CR/HR/1 Add.2.

means of an "amnesty", so to speak, for his country. He asked the Committee to understand and support El Salvador's policy in the quest for peace and internal stability. In that connection, he referred to the dialogue entered into by his government with all the opposition factions, armed or otherwise, and the recent signing of a peace agreement in Guatemala.

140. Replying to questions, he stated that assistance to the families of the alleged victims took the form of payment of compensation and assumption of responsibility for the training and education of the children. In addition, he pointed out that full provision was made for the return of missing persons, or of exiles who had "disappeared" for various reasons, under the terms of the above-mentioned peace agreement.

141. Several members of the Committee observed that on the list of missing persons [...],[56] the date of imprisonment of some of those persons and the name of the prison were in some cases mentioned. They thought that further efforts should be made on the basis of this information to take inquiries further in order to determine the fate of those persons, that the lack of information was not adequate justification for the closure of the file and that, on the contrary, further perseverance was needed in the search for information.

142. Taking the floor again, the representative of the government concerned stated that inquiries had been made, but than none of the alleged victims was in prison.

143. Two members of the Committee were of the opinion that it was necessary to take into account not only the substantial amount of additional information provided by the representative of the government concerned, but also the mission report of the representative appointed by the Executive Board, who had drawn attention to the positive determination of the Government of El Salvador to remedy the previous situation concerning human rights, to the difficulties encountered by the competent authorities in obtaining information about the missing persons, given the peculiar circumstances of civil war and armed insurrection prevailing in the country, and also to the remarkable work of the (governmental) commission on human rights to determine what had happened to these persons and whether or not they were dead.

144. One Committee member took the view that it would be advisable for the government concerned to continue its inquiries in particular by getting in touch with the teachers' union and with other organizations to which the missing persons had belonged.

---

[56] See document 127 EX/CR/HR/1, annex II.

145. After an exchange of views, the Committee *decided*:

(i) to thank the representative of the government concerned for attending the meeting and for his co-operation;

(ii) to take note with satisfaction of his statements concerning his government's assumption of responsibility for the families of the alleged victims and for the measures taken on behalf of the children;

(iii) while taking note of the efforts already made, to request the government concerned to continue its inquiries concerning the missing persons by having recourse to all the sources of information, and to clarify the circumstances in which a number of persons, initially detained in a specific prison, had subsequently disappeared;

(iv) to ask the authors of the five communications whether they had any other relevant information;

(v) to resume consideration of the communications at its spring 1988 session.

Spring 1988 session of the Committee on Conventions and Recommendations (129th session of the Executive Board)[57]

132. The first five communications,[58] which were at the stage of examination of substance, denounced violations of human rights alleged to have been perpetrated in El Salvador, mainly against teachers, and which were said to have resulted in the death and disappearance of a large number of people. At its autumn [1982 session], the Committee had decided to strike cases of deceased persons from its list, considering that in those circumstances no intervention it might make could yield any results.[59]

[57] See document 129 EX/3 PRIV., paras. 132-139; see also documents 129 EX/CR/HR/1, 129 EX/CR/HR/1 Inf.1 and 129 EX/CR/HR/2.

[58] Communications No. 276/80 concerning *El Salvador*, case of *Leonel Menéndez Quiroga and others*, No. 283/80 concerning *El Salvador*, case of *Arrest and persecution of teachers in El Salvador*, No. 306/80 concerning *El Salvador*, case of *Arrest and persecution of teachers in El Salvador*, No. 390/81 concerning *El Salvador*, case of *Edgar Mauricio Vallejo*, No. 477/82 concerning *El Salvador*, case of *Violation of human rights in El Salvador*, and No. 690/85 concerning *El Salvador*, case of *Filomena Claros de Majano*, were being considered together.

[59] See document 115 EX/28 PRIV., para. 116 (ii) (*supra*, p. 686).

El Salvador **No. 276/80**

133. The sixth communication still at the stage of consideration of admissibility, concerned the alleged abduction and disappearance of Mrs Filomena Claros de Majano.

134. At the present session, the representative of the government concerned recalled that the cases of persons alleged to have disappeared were related to events which had taken place at a time when his country was going through a period of violence and upheaval. There were no witnesses to these events who might have helped to advance inquiries. Every effort had been made by the Salvadorian authorities to find the people concerned. In any case the present government could not be held responsible for acts to which it had not been a party. The representative of the government concerned then produced a document [...][60] from which it transpired that:

> (i) as regards the [fifth communication]:
>
> Mr Miguel Ángel Ayala Ramírez, Mr Rafael Antonio Carias, Miss Ana Elizabeth Nuñez, Mr Rafael Barrera (or Rafael Américo Barrera Chávez or Cheves), Mr Rigoberto Climaco, Mrs Rosa Mélida Villatoro de Ramírez (currently working for the Ministry of Education as Director of the Teachers' Welfare Department) and Mrs María Luisa Rojas (residing in Mexico as representative of AMES) had been released in 1983 under an amnesty law;
>
> Mr Douglas Mauricio Ramírez, Secretary for University Extension Work of the National University, was currently abroad;
>
> that Mrs Vilma Soto, allegedly abducted in February 1982 and detained in the Ilopango Women's Prison, was in fact, not listed in the records of that prison;
>
> (ii) as regards [the sixth communication], no new information concerning the case of Mrs Filomena Claros was available.

135. Some members of the Committee, while welcoming the mainly reassuring information provided on those cases, expressed surprise that the authorities should have taken so long to obtain it and that so little detail had been given about the situation of the people who had been released.

136. Other members of the Committee expressed their concern about the many cases which had not been elucidated and the inadequacy of the information provided by

[60] See document 129 EX/CR/HR/1 Inf.1.

the government concerned. They also wondered how the system of assistance for the families, especially the children, of alleged victims had been applied.

137. Other members, again, pointed out that positive developments had occurred in the human rights situation in El Salvador, that the humanitarian approach was the only one that the Committee could follow, and that any kind of political judgement should be avoided.

138. Some members of the Committee considered that the first results obtained after eight years of endeavour proved that the Committee had been right to persevere in its consideration of these communications, particularly in the case of missing persons.

139. After an exchange of views, the Committee *decided*:

(i) to thank the representative of the government concerned for his attendance and co-operation;

(ii) to take note with satisfaction of the information that he had provided, especially the details from which it was possible to see the marked progress made in elucidating the position of some of the alleged victims;

(iii) while appreciating the efforts it had made, to request the government concerned, to continue its inquiries concerning the other persons alleged to be missing, particularly the as yet unclarified cases on the list prepared for the Committee at its [autumn 1987 session] and the case of Mrs Filomena Claros de Majanos;

(iv) to request the government concerned to provide the Committee with whatever information it has been able to obtain on this case;

(v) to resume consideration of the cases which had not yet been elucidated at the [next session].

El Salvador **No. 276/80**

Autumn 1988 session of the Committee on Conventions and Recommendations (130th session of the Executive Board)[61]

152. The first five communications[62] denounce violations of human rights alleged to have been committed in El Salvador, against teachers in particular, and to have resulted in the death or disappearance of a large number of persons. They are at the stage of examination of substance, having been declared admissible by the Committee at the [autumn 1984 session].[63]

153. The earliest of these communications have been on the Committee's agenda since the [spring 1981 session]. The most recent, concerning the alleged abduction of Mrs Filomena Claros de Majano, is still at the stage of examination of its admissibility. It has been on the Committee's agenda since the [spring 1986 session].

154. At the [autumn 1982 session], the Committee decided to strike cases of deceased persons from its list, considering that in the circumstances its intervention could no longer yield any results.[64]

155. In July 1986 a mission was carried out in El Salvador by a mandated representative of the Executive Board. The purpose was to initiate or continue dialogue with the government concerned regarding the allegations contained in the communications.

156. The report of that mission stated that no archives existed relating to facts prior to 1982. There remained only a few newspaper cuttings from the period. The report also mentioned a decree issued by the Minister of Education of El Salvador instituting a pension scheme for the children of victims belonging to the teaching profession or to the ministry.

157. At the [spring 1988] session, after taking note with satisfaction of the information provided by the representative of the government concerned, which had re-

---

[61] See document 130 EX/3 PRIV., paras. 152-166; see also document 130 EX/CR/HR - El Salvador.

[62] Communications No. 276/80 concerning *El Salvador*, case of *Leonel Menéndez Quiroga and others*, No. 283/80 concerning *El Salvador*, case of *Arrest and persecution of teachers in El Salvador*, No. 306/80 concerning *El Salvador*, case of *Arrest and persecution of teachers in El Salvador*, No. 390/81 concerning *El Salvador*, case of *Edgar Mauricio Vallejo*, No. 477/82 concerning *El Salvador*, case of *Violations of human rights in El Salvador*, and No. 690/85 concerning *El Salvador*, case of *Filomena Claros de Majano*, were being considered together.

[63] See document 120 EX/15 PRIV., para. 69 (*supra*, pp. 693-694).

[64] See document 115 EX/28 PRIV., para. 116 (ii) (*supra*, p. 686).

vealed that marked progress had been made in elucidating the situation of some of the alleged victims, and while appreciating the efforts made by the Salvadorian authorities, the Committee requested the government concerned to continue its inquiries and to provide it with all available information regarding the persons alleged to be missing and also in respect of Mrs Filomena Claros de Majano.[65]

158. Complying with the Committee's request, the Secretariat compiled a list of as yet unclarified cases. It contains 58 names.

159. Noting once again that for some 10 years his country had been in a state of internal conflict, making it difficult to conduct investigations and to ensure the proper administration of justice, and that the present government bore no responsibility for these matters, the representative of the government concerned assured the Committee that every effort had been made to trace the missing persons, but to no avail. That being so, he requested the Committee to declare the six cases closed. He further noted that his government had requested Unesco's assistance in respect of the teaching of human rights, but that it had not so far obtained any such assistance.

160. The Secretariat was asked to remind the sector concerned of this request.

161. Several members of the Committee, while fully understanding the situation in which the Government of El Salvador found itself, expressed their objections to the cases being declared closed. Further efforts should be made to shed light on the fate of the 58 persons alleged to be missing, and it was important that their cases should not be abandoned.

162. They also expressed disappointment at not having obtained any precise information about the implementation of the system of aid and assistance for the families of the victims which the government claimed it had set up.

163. In the opinion of some members of the Committee, the Committee, while not losing sight of these communications and while keeping them on its list, should deal with them by referring back to the decision taken by it at the [autumn 1979 session], which reads as follows:[66]

> In the case of communications, declared admissible, concerning enforced or involuntary disappearance of persons as a result of action imputed to law enforcement authorities or similar organizations, whether or not it is established that such persons were, or were not, deprived of freedom at the time of their

---

[65] See document 129 EX/3 PRIV., para. 139 (ii) and (iii) (*supra*, p. 716).
[66] See document 108 EX/38 PRIV., para. 16.

disappearance, if the Committee has not obtained sufficient information about the fate of the missing persons from the governments concerned, the Committee agrees, without prejudice to the important role of the Director-General mentioned in paragraph 8 of 104 EX/Decision 3.3:

(*a*) to keep such communications on the list of communications pending which is held by the Secretariat;

(*b*) to request the governments concerned to devote appropriate resources to searching for such persons, in accordance with the recommendations made to them by the General Assembly in its resolution 33/173, and to keep Unesco informed of any new development concerning each case of disappearance which is brought to the attention of the Organization;

(*c*) to place these communications once more on its agenda when additional information is sent to Unesco by the governments concerned, the authors of the communications, the family and friends of the missing persons or the competent humanitarian organizations, and in any case to do so every year at one of its sessions.

164. This formula seemed especially appropriate in that representatives of the United Nations Commission on Human Rights had recently gone to El Salvador, and the term of office of the Special Rapporteur of the Commission for El Salvador had just been extended. The Committee might consequently obtain information from the Commission.

165. Other members of the Committee suggested that the authors of the various communications be informed of the present status of the file and the proposal by the government concerned to declare it closed. This would perhaps prompt the authors to endeavour to collect fresh information.

166. After an exchange of views, the Committee *decided*:

(i) to thank the representative of the government concerned for his attendance and co-operation;

(ii) to ask the authors of these six communications if they had further information to transmit to the Committee;

(iii) to urge the government concerned to continue its inquiries in order to clarify the cases of persons alleged in those communications to have disappeared and to request it to provide it with a list of names of the families of victims in receipt of government aid;

(iv) to request the Secretariat to obtain from the United Nations Commission on Human Rights any available information concerning these allegedly missing persons;

(v) to resume consideration of these six communications at the [next session].

Spring 1989 session of the Committee on Conventions and Recommendations (131st session of the Executive Board)[67]

186. The first five communications[68] are at the stage of being considered as to substance, having been declared admissible by the Committee at the [autumn 1984 session].[69] The earliest of them have been on the Committee's agenda since the [spring 1981] session. The sixth communication dates from the [spring 1986] session and is still at the stage of being considered as to its admissibility.

187. These six communications are being considered together by the Committee since they all concern cases of allegedly missing persons, those of deceased persons having been struck from its list at the [autumn 1982 session] in view of the Committee's feeling that in the circumstances its intervention could no longer yield any results.[70]

188. According to the report of the mission carried out by a mandated representative of the Executive Board in El Salvador in July 1986, the Salvadorian authorities had confirmed that Mr Leonel Menéndez Quiroga [the first communication] had died, but had not produced any document to substantiate that assertion. The report also indicated that no archives existed covering the period prior to 1982. There remained only a few newspaper cuttings from the period. The report also mentioned a decree

---

[67] See document 131 EX/3 PRIV., paras. 186-195; see also document 131 EX/CR/HR/ELS.
[68] Communications No. 276/80 concerning *El Salvador*, case of *Leonel Menéndez Quiroga and others*, No. 283/80 concerning *El Salvador*, case of *Arrest and persecution of teachers in El Salvador*, No. 306/80 concerning *El Salvador*, case of *Arrest and persecution of teachers in El Salvador*, No. 390/81 concerning *El Salvador*, case of *Edgar Mauricio Vallejo*, No. 477/82 concerning *El Salvador*, case of *Alleged violations of human rights in El Salvador*, and No. 690/85 concerning *El Salvador*, case of *Filomena Claros de Majano*, were being considered together.
[69] See document 120 EX/15 PRIV., para. 69 (*supra*, pp. 693-694).
[70] See document 115 EX/28 PRIV., para. 116 (ii) (*supra*, p. 686).

issued by the Minister of Education of El Salvador instituting a pension scheme for the children of victims belonging to the teaching profession or to the ministry.

189. At the [autumn 1988] session, the representative of the government concerned recalled that for some 10 years his country had been in a state of internal conflict and that every effort had been made by the Salvadorian authorities to trace the missing persons, but to no avail. He stated that the present government bore no responsibility for these disappearances. He requested that the six cases be declared closed. He further pointed out that his government had requested Unesco's assistance in respect of the teaching of human rights, but that it had not so far obtained any such assistance.

190. At the time, the Committee decided: (i) to ask the authors of these communications if they had further information to transmit to it; (ii) to urge the government concerned to continue its inquiries in order to clarify the cases of persons alleged to have disappeared and to request it to provide a list of names of the families of victims in receipt of government aid.[71]

191. The Social and Human Sciences Sector of Unesco, the sector concerned by the request made by the Government of El Salvador for assistance in the teaching of human rights, contacted the permanent delegation of that country. The Secretariat also asked the United Nations Commission on Human Rights for information regarding the as yet unclarified cases of the persons alleged in those six communications to have disappeared, forwarding to the Commission for that purpose a list containing a summary of each case. No reply has yet been received.

192. In a letter dated 6 January 1989, the [World Confederation of Organizations of the Teaching Profession, one of the authors of the second communication], made it known that it had not been informed by its Salvadorian member organization of other alleged violations of human rights, but that it was going to consult that organization for confirmation.

193. For its part, Amnesty International, author of [the first, fourth and sixth communications], informed the Secretariat, in a letter dated 7 March 1989, that it had no further information.

194. At the present session, the representative of the government concerned stated that, despite the efforts made, the situation had not progressed. El Salvador was having to contend with a fratricidal war, natural disasters (earthquake, severe drought,

[71] See document 130 EX/3 PRIV., para. 166 (ii) and (iii) (*supra*, pp. 719-720).

etc.), social problems and a serious economic crisis. The Government of President Duarte had co-operated with the Committee to the fullest possible extent.

195. Following an exchange of views, the Committee *decided*:

(i) to thank the representative of the government concerned for his attendance and his co-operation;

(ii) to request that government once again to continue its inquiries in order to clarify the cases of the persons alleged in the six communications to have disappeared and to await information from the United Nations Commission on Human Rights;

(iii) to resume consideration of these communications at its [next session].

Autumn 1989 session of the Committee on Conventions and Recommendations (132nd session of the Executive Board)[72]

148. The first five communications[73] are at the stage of examination of substance, having been declared admissible by the Committee at the [autumn 1984 session].[74] The sixth communication dates from the [spring 1986 session] and is still at the stage of consideration as to its admissibility.

149. These communications concern all the allegedly missing persons listed in [a Committee document].[75] The list contains 58 names. It was drawn up after removing, first, the cases cleared up as a result of information provided by the government concerned and by Amnesty International and, second, deceased persons, following the Committee's decision at the [autumn 1982 session] to remove the latter from the list of alleged victims.[76]

---

[72] See document 132 EX/3 PRIV., paras. 148-156; see also documents 132 EX/CR/HR/ELS and Add.
[73] Communications No. 276/80 concerning *El Salvador*, case of *Leonel Menéndez Quiroga and others*, No. 283/80 concerning *El Salvador*, case of *Arrest and persecution of teachers in El Salvador*, No. 306/80 concerning *El Salvador*, case of *Arrest and persecution of teachers in El Salvador*, No. 390/81 concerning *El Salvador*, case of *Edgar Mauricio Vallejo*, No. 477/82 concerning *El Salvador*, case of *Alleged violations of human rights in El Salvador*, and No. 690/85 concerning *El Salvador*, case of *Filomena Claros de Majano*, were being considered together.
[74] See document 120 EX/15 PRIV., para. 69 (*supra*, pp. 693-694).
[75] See document 130 EX/CR/HR - El Salvador, annex.
[76] See document 115 EX/28 PRIV., para. 116 (ii) (*supra*, p. 686).

El Salvador **No. 276/80**

150. At the [spring 1989] session, the representative of the government concerned informed the Committee that, despite the efforts made, the situation had not changed, no fresh information having been obtained about what had happened to those persons.

151. The Committee decided to request the government once again to continue its inquiries, and to await information from the United Nations Commission on Human Rights.[77]

152. By letter dated 21 July 1989 [...],[78] the United Nations Centre for Human Rights, Geneva, reported that 15 of the alleged victims were also on the list kept by the specialized working group of the Commission on Human Rights, but that the Government of El Salvador had not yet provided any information relating to them.

153. At the present session, the government concerned was not represented.

154. A member of the Committee indicated that as Amnesty International had sent a delegation to El Salvador in 1987, it should perhaps be asked whether it wished to maintain its communications. The same question should also be addressed to the other authors of communications.

155. In this connection, the Chairman read out a letter dated 14 August 1989 in which Amnesty International once again expressed its concern over the fate of the alleged victims.

156. After an exchange of views, the Committee *decided*:

(i) to express its regrets at the absence of any representative of the government concerned;

(ii) to take note of the letter of 14 August 1989 from Amnesty International;

(iii) to ask the authors of the communications whether they wished to maintain them, even in the absence of additional information that would allow the Committee to continue its action;

(iv) to resume consideration of these communications at the [next session].

---

[77] See document 131 EX/3 PRIV., para. 195 (ii) (*supra*, p. 722).
[78] See document 132 EX/CR/HR/ELS Add.

No. 276/80 **El Salvador**

Spring 1990 session of the Committee on Conventions and Recommendations (134th session of the Executive Board)[79]

173. The first five communications[80] are at the stage of examination of substance, having been declared admissible by the Committee at the [autumn 1984 session].[81] The earliest of these have been on the Committee's agenda since the [spring 1981 session]. The sixth communication dates from the [spring 1986 session] and is still at the stage of examination as to its admissibility.

174. These commmunications concern all the allegedly missing persons listed in [a Committee document].[82] This list contains 58 names. It was drawn up after removing, first, the cases settled as a result of information provided by the government concerned and by Amnesty International and, second, deceased persons.

175. At the [spring 1989] session, the representatives of the government concerned informed the Committee that, despite the efforts made, the situation had not changed, no fresh information having been obtained about what had happened to those persons.

176. At the [autumn 1989] session, the United Nations Centre for Human Rights, Geneva, informed the Committee that 15 of the alleged victims were also on the list kept by the specialized working group of the Commission on Human Rights, but that the Government of El Salvador had not provided any information about them.

177. Having expressed its regrets that no representative of the government concerned had been present, the Committee decided to ask the authors of the communications whether they wished to maintain them, even in the absence of additional information that would allow the Committee to continue its action.[83]

---

[79] See document 134 EX/3 PRIV., paras. 173-181; see also document 134 EX/CR/HR/ELS.
[80] Communications No. 276/80 concerning *El Salvador*, case of *Leonel Menéndez Quiroga and others*, No. 283/80 concerning *El Salvador*, case of *Arrest and persecution of teachers in El Salvador*, No. 306/80 concerning *El Salvador*, case of *Arrest and persecution of teachers in El Salvador*, No. 390/81 concerning *El Salvador*, case of *Edgar Mauricio Vallejo*, No. 477/82 concerning *El Salvador*, case of *Alleged violations of human rights in El Salvador*, and No. 690/85 concerning *El Salvador*, case of *Filomena Claros de Majano*, were being considered together.
[81] See document 120 EX/15 PRIV., para. 69 (*supra*, pp. 693-694).
[82] See document 130 EX/CR/HR - El Salvador, annex.
[83] See document 132 EX/3 PRIV., para. 156 (i) and (iii) (*supra*, p. 723).

El Salvador **No. 276/80**

178. By a letter dated 1 December 1989, the World Confederation of Organizations of the Teaching Profession indicted that it wished [the second communication] to be kept on the Committee's agenda. By a letter dated 23 April 1990, Amnesty International stated that although it had not been able to obtain any additional information from the government concerned, it hoped that the Committee would resume examination of these cases at its next session.

179. During the present session, the representative of the government concerned reported on the measures taken by the new government of El Salvador to ensure the defence and promotion of human rights in her country, which was racked by internal strife which, as everyone knew, had resulted in intermittent outbursts of violence. She said that intensive efforts were being made to achieve national reconciliation. She expressed the hope that, in view of the length of time these communciations had been under consideration, the Committee might strike them from its list.

180. Most members of the Committee shared this view. However, one member of the Committee, without opposing the consensus, was reluctant to agree to such a solution, since several of the authors of these communications had stated that they wished them to be kept on the Committee's agenda.

181. After an exchange of views, the Committee *decided*:

(i) to thank the representatives of the government concerned for their attendance and co-operation;

(ii) to strike the communications from its list.

No. 277/80

Concerning *Yugoslavia*
Case of *Vladimir Bonačić* et al.*

Communication of 25 July 1980 submitted by
Vladimir Bonačić

Spring 1981 session of the Committee on Conventions and Recommendations (112th session of the Executive Board)[1]

388. Mr Vladimir Bonačić describes himself as both author of the communication and as victim. He claims to be a professor of art and of information systems. Two persons on his team - Mr Miroljub Cimerman, an "information system designer", and Mrs Dunja Donassy, an "architect of computer lighting systems" - are also described as being victims.

389. The main alleged violation of rights concerns the right to work on a project involving the setting up of a multi-media electronic system for the National and University Library of Zagreb, a project conceived in co-operation with Unesco [...].

390. When the project was rejected by the Yugoslav authorities in September 1978, Mr Vladimir Bonačić's team, it is alleged, was prevented from pursuing its work in the field of information systems, from teaching in the University, from publishing anything at all or producing any original work in computer science. Other measures of harassment - penal proceedings, among them - were, it is claimed, taken against the three alleged victims.

391. At the [spring 1980 session], the Committee examined this case [...].[2] The representative of the Yugoslav Government declared at that time that:

* Case of *Vladimir Bonačić, Miroljub Cimerman and Dunya Donassy*.
[1] See document 112 EX/30 PRIV., paras. 388-402; see also document 112 EX/CR/HR/3.
[2] See document 109 EX/52 PRIV., paras. 190-192 (*supra*, pp. 559-560), communication No. 203/80 concerning *Yugoslavia*, case of *Vladimir Bonačić* et al.

(*a*) the interested parties had not been dismissed from their posts: it was they who had resigned;

(*b*) the author of the communication was not a professor, but a lecturer:

(*c*) no charges had been filed or proceedings engaged against the interested parties;

(*d*) they had not been prevented from working; the exhibitions they had recently organized in Zagreb and other cities were evidence of that fact;

(*e*) they had not attempted to exhaust available domestic remedies; they had addressed themselves to services that were incompetent, by reason of the subject-matter, to adjudicate a labour grievance.

392. Considering that the case amounted to a labour dispute involving their professional qualifications, the Committee declared that [the communication] was not admissible because the complaint was manifestly ill-founded.[3]

393. In July 1980, Mr Vladimir Bonačić sent the Secretariat other documents to establish the validity of his communication. In view of the provisions of paragraph 14 (*a*) (x) of 104 EX/Decision 3.3 and in the light of the additional information, the complainant, although advised that there is no recourse against a decision of the Committee, has introduced a new communication. The latter dated 25 July 1980, again cites the same persons as victims. While it is signed by Mr Bonačić alone, the covering letter and two explanatory letters, dated 1 August and 10 September 1980 respectively, are signed both by him and Mr Miroljub Cimerman.

394. In essence, these are the grounds for the new communication:

> The Committee, it is alleged, was misinformed by the representative of the Yugoslav Government. It would seem that there have been further violations of the human rights and fundamental freedoms of the complainants. After attempts to withstand the harassment of the authorities for two years, Vladimir Bonačić and Miroljub Cimerman were allegedly expelled from the country.

395. Refuting point by point the arguments of the representative of the Yugoslav Government cited above, they supply various documents in substantiation of the following facts:

---

[3] *Ibidem*, para. 192 (*supra*, p. 560).

with reference to point (*a*): they produce two photocopies of documents, dated 17 July 1980, proving that both of them were deprived of employment for one year even though theirs is a much sought-after profession in the labour market [...]; according to a trade union document [...], they are accused of being spies who warrant no assistance;

with reference to point (*c*): they produce two documents, proving that proceedings have been instituted that could lead to prison sentences for political offences;

with reference to point (*d*): they produce a photocopy of a handwritten confidential letter which, they assert, was written by a high official directing that they should be forced to resign, that their work should be appropriated and its authorship attributed to other persons, Party members; the high official in question, who was appointed as the new co-ordinator of all library posts on 23 August 1978, allegedly issued orders on 28 August to Messrs Bonačić and Cimerman and Mrs Donassy to relinquish their duties and to turn over to him all documents concerning the multimedia electronic system they had designed; they apparently refused to do so, even in September 1978, in spite of threats; forced out of the library on 19 September 1978, Mrs Donassy was the first to be stripped of her post; victims of a policy of intimidation, the two other complainants, it seems, finally handed in their resignations; as for the exhibition of some of their work, mentioned by the representative of the Yugoslav Government, what was apparently involved were a few works designed prior to the time when they were the victims of harassment, actually when they were abroad;

with reference to point (*e*): they produce various jurisdictional decisions which led to no positive results as far as they were concerned [...]; representations made to high-level executive authorities were also apparently of no avail [...].

396. As collateral evidence of the harassment to which they were subjected, the complainants produce the written testimony of Professor Bozo Tazak, former Director of a Unesco Centre in Zagreb (International Referral Centre for Information Handling Equipment - IRCHIHE), who was found dead, they say, in mysterious, not to say suspicious, circumstances.

397. The complainants consider that the methods used by the Party, especially as far as they are concerned, are tantamount to the expulsion of undesirable intellectuals from Yugoslavia.

398. It is their wish that the Yugoslav Government should:

put a stop to all penal proceedings against them;

recognize that they hold the rights to their works on computer art, works which they claim have been unduly ascribed to other persons;

pay them the salaries allegedly due for the work done by them in Yugoslavia;

authorize them to enter Yugoslavia, visit it and take care of their families, to see their friends and work as they see fit (they are living at the present time, it seems, in Amsterdam, Holland).

399. Before the representative of the government concerned was invited to speak, a member of the Committee intervened to say that, in his opinion, the terms used by the authors of the communication were unacceptable and the communication was inadmissible; he considered that, by declaring that the decision taken by the Committee on [the previous communication] was arbitrary and without foundation, the authors were displaying an insulting attitude towards the Committee; another member disagreed with this interpretation, being of the opinion that the authors had used acceptable terms in contesting the decision of the Committee, and furthermore he wished to know if the authors were authorized to return to their country.

400. The representative of the Yugoslav Government replied that the parties concerned had left Yugoslavia with their passports in order and could therefore freely return, but that, however, he could not promise them that no legal action would be taken against them.

401. In Yugoslavia, every citizen had the right to bring an action against another citizen. Thus, the Director of the National and University Library of Zagreb had brought an action for libel against the authors of the communication, though the case was still pending because the court concerned had not been able to make contact with the defendants. Mr Bonačić had also instituted proceedings against the Director of this library, but the case had not been settled for the same reasons.

402. After a brief discussion, the Committee *decided* to declare the communication inadmissible as being manifestly ill-founded in conformity with paragraph 14 (*a*) (v) of 104 EX/Decision 3.3.

No. 279/80

Concerning *Republic of Korea*
Case of *Kim Chi ha* et al.*

Communication of 10 June 1980 submitted by
Robert Charvin

Spring 1981 session of the Committee on Conventions and Recommendations (112th session of the Executive Board)[1]

* Case of *Kim Chi ha, Yang Song U, Moon Ik hwan, Chang Ki pyo, Song Ki Sook, Lee Young hee, Kim Dae Joong, Yoon po-sn and Ham suk hun and other clergy, dismissed journalists and dismissed professors.*

[1] See document 112 EX/30 PRIV., paras. 193-213 (*supra*, pp. 647-651), communication No. 269/80 concerning *Republic of Korea*, case of *Mong Yong Lee*.

No. 281/80

Concerning *Uruguay*
Case of *Julio Castro*

Communication of 16 August 1980 submitted by
an Amnesty International group

Autumn 1981 session of the Committee on Conventions and Recommendations (113th session of the Executive Board)[1]

456. Amnesty International, Madrid (Spain) Group I, represented by Mrs Geneviève Perrin, describes itself as a non-governmental organization with reliable knowledge of the violations alleged.

457. Mr Julio Castro, aged 70, educator and journalist and former Unesco official (1952-1954 in Mexico; November 1966 to November 1970 in Ecuador), is alleged to have been arrested on 1 August 1977 and transported in a van to an unknown destination. He is said to have been suffering from cardiac insufficiency. His family allegedly informed the police of his poor state of health. Some time later, the Uruguayan Government is reported to have said that Mr Castro went to Argentina on 22 September 1977. The Argentine Government is stated to have notified the Inter-American Commission on Human Rights on 10 December 1977 that he was not listed among the people who had entered the country, subsequently changing its mind on 2 January 1979. It is believed that Mr Castro is detained in Uruguay or perhaps even died in prison after being tortured.

458. At the time of his disappearance, the family of the alleged victim is said to have made approaches to the police and the government authorities without managing to obtain any positive result.

459. Amnesty International and the Inter-American Commission on Human Rights, to whose notice the case was brought, have apparently not been able to find.a solution.

---

[1] See document 113 EX/38 PRIV., paras. 456-469; see also document 113 EX/CR/HR/3.

No. 281/80 **Uruguay**

460. Under "Purpose and aim of this communication", the author expresses its hope that Unesco will take an interest in the case of this man who has worked for the same objectives as the Organization.

461. Mr Castro's case was the subject of a communication that was submitted by Mr Luis B. Prieto, Chairman of the Culture Commission of the Venezuelan Senate, on 7 September 1977 and dealt with by the Committee under the old procedure.[2] At the [spring and autumn 1978 and spring and autumn 1979] sessions, further information was requested from both the government concerned and the author of the communication. According to information provided by the Uruguayan Government at those sessions, Mr Castro was said to have left Uruguay on 22 September 1977 and to have arrived in Buenos Aires, his arrival apparently being confirmed by a communiqué from the Argentine Ministry of Foreign Affairs. In a letter of 10 July 1979, the Secretariat, on the instructions of the Committee, drew the attention of the author of the communication to the fact that it related only to Uruguay and that the alleged victim was no longer in that country. The Secretariat also pointed out that the procedure laid down in 104 EX/Decision 3.3 allowed for the introduction of a fresh communication implicating Argentina. At its [autumn] 1979 session, the Committee, in the absence of any fresh communication to Unesco from Mr Prieto, decided to delete the affair from its agenda.[3]

462. First of all, the representative of the Uruguayan Government asked whether any provision of 104 EX/Decision 3.3 authorized the reopening of a question already dealt with.

463. The representative of the Director-General, the Legal Adviser, said that there was nothing in the text of 104 EX/Decision 3.3 to prevent the Committee from considering the same facts: that did not constitute grounds for inadmissibility. The authors of the decision had purposely excluded the principle of *non bis in idem* from the list of conditions of inadmissibility.

464. The representative of the Uruguayan Government then read out the text of a document from the Uruguayan authorities stating that the alleged victim was in Buenos Aires on 22 September 1977 as a tourist. He pointed out that the present communication put forward no new evidence.

465. Some members of the Committee considered that it would be useful to ask the author of the communication for further details regarding Mr Castro's present cir-

---

[2] Communication submitted under 77 EX/Decision 8.3.

[3] See document 108 EX/38 PRIV., para. 287.

cumstances, expressions such as "it is believed that" and "perhaps even" being of little help in enlightening the Committee.

466. Other members believed that it would be appropriate to request the Argentine Government to verify whether the alleged victim had left its territory, pointing out incidentally that uncertainty on that point remained since the name "Julio Castro" was very common in Spanish-speaking countries and could be borne by several individuals; the checking of a passenger manifest alone proved nothing in particular.

467. Taking the floor once more, the representative of the government concerned said that when Mr Castro's family had notified the authorities of his absence, he had been searched for, photographs of him had been disseminated by the press and the audio-visual media, but that it had not proved possible to find him.

468. After a wide exchange of views, a consensus emerged that the case in question fell into the framework of cases of missing persons and, as such, should be transmitted, as had been decided at previous sessions,[4] to the Working Group of the United Nations Commission on Human Rights in Geneva.

469. The Committee finally *decided* to request the Secretariat:

(i) to inform the author of the communication that the Committee had already decided to strike the case from its list (at its [autumn] 1979 session), that the communication supplied no new evidence enabling the Committee to consider it in full knowledge of the facts, that the Government of Uruguay had been able to discover that Mr Castro was not on its territory and that the communication therefore concerned the case of a missing person;

(ii) to transmit the case to the United Nations Commission on Human Rights Working Group on Enforced or Involuntary Disappearances [...];

(iii) to treat the present communication henceforth, therefore, in the same way as the other communications on missing persons.

---

[4] See documents 108 EX/38 PRIV., para. 16, 109 EX/52 PRIV., annex I, para. 8, and Corr. and 112 EX/30 PRIV., paras. 558-566.

No. 281/80 **Uruguay**

Autumn 1987 session of the Committee on Conventions and Recommendations (127th session of the Executive Board)[5]

199. The communication in question is [...] submitted by Mrs Geneviève Perrin, on behalf of Amnesty International, Madrid (Spain) Group I. It concerns the case of Mr Julio Castro, an educator and journalist who is said to have been abducted on 1 August 1977 and driven by van to an unknown destination.

200. According to information received from the specialized Working Group of the United Nations Commission on Human Rights, by verbal notes dated 28 August and 15 December 1980 and 7 January 1982 the government concerned stated that Mr Julio Castro had left Uruguay on 22 September 1977 for Buenos Aires (Argentina) on Pluna flight No. 159. The Argentine Ministry of Foreign Affairs reportedly confirmed this information at the time.

201. Owing to the length of the Committee's proceedings on the afternoon of 16 September 1987, the hearing of the Permanent Delegate of Uruguay to Unesco, representing the government concerned, did not take place. One member of the Committee asked the Chairwoman to send a letter to the representative of the Government of Uruguay apologizing on behalf of the Committee for the aforementioned circumstance.

202. Prior to consideration of the communication, on the afternoon of 18 September 1987, the Chairwoman offered her sincere apologies, on behalf of the Committee, for that unfortunate occurrence and also thanked the Permanent Delegate for having so thoughtfully provided the Secretariat with a written statement.

203. In that statement, he had emphasized the desire of the constitutional Government of Uruguay, established after 12 years of military dictatorship, to collaborate with the Committee in its efforts to defend and affirm the existence of human rights. In that respect, his country was party to various universal or regional international instruments and was doing its utmost to make good the moral and material prejudice sustained by the victims of the violations committed under the previous regime. The Uruguay Parliament had granted a broad amnesty to all political prisoners, and commissions of inquiry had been set up to clarify cases of violations of human rights and identify the culprits.

---

[5] See document 127 EX/3 PRIV., paras. 199-208; see also document 127 EX/CR/HR/2, annex II.

Uruguay **No. 281/80**

204. With regard to the case of Mr Julio Castro, the Permanent Delegate stated that the Public Prosecutor, Mr Jorge Sambucetti, had been entrusted with the weighty task of investigating enforced or involuntary disappearances of persons but had not yet completed his work. Any relevant information obtained would be made available to Unesco.

205. The Permanent Delegate stated that his government would shortly be submitting a detailed report to the Commission on Human Rights on all the measures it had adopted to ensure the effective observance of such rights.

206. Taking the floor, one member of the Committee observed that the case of Uruguay was similar to that of Argentina and Bolivia *vis-à-vis* [the United Nations Economic and Social Council and] Commission on Human Rights. The Commission had in fact decided also to terminate consideration of the situation regarding massive and systematic violations of human rights in Uruguay under the procedure governed by [Economic and Social Council] resolution 1503 (XLVIII) [...].[6] The Committee had, at its spring 1987 session taken a similar decision concerning Argentina and Bolivia.[7] The same should apply to Uruguay since democracy had been restored in that country, since considerable efforts had been made by the present government regarding human rights and since competent national authorities had been entrusted with investigating cases of the enforced or involuntary disappearance of persons.

207. Several members of the Committee endorsed that opinion. One of them considered that it would be helpful to be provided with the report mentioned in his statement by the Permanent Delegate of Uruguay to Unesco.

208. After an exchange of views, the Committee *decided*, given the return to democracy and the rule of law in Uruguay and in view of the efforts of the government concerned to clarify the situation of missing persons, to terminate consideration of the communication concerning that country and to strike it from its list.

---

[6] See Commission on Human Rights decision 1985/107 and Economic and Social Council decision 1985/139.
[7] See document 126 EX/3 PRIV., paras. 216-226.

No. 283/80

Concerning *El Salvador*
Case of *Arrest and persecution of teachers in El Salvador*

Communication of 20 August 1980 submitted by National Association of Salvadorian Teachers*

Spring 1981 session of the Committee on Conventions and Recommendations (112th session of the Executive Board)[1]

Autumn 1981 session of the Committee on Conventions and Recommendations (113th session of the Executive Board)[2]

Spring 1982 session of the Committee on Conventions and Recommendations (114th session of the Executive Board)[3]

Autumn 1982 session of the Committee on Conventions and Recommendations (115th session of the Executive Board)[4]

---

* From the Committee's autumn 1983 session, World Confederation of Organizations of the Teaching Profession (WCOTP) was being added as author of this communication.

[1] See document 112 EX/30 PRIV., paras. 113-124 (*supra*, pp. 671-673), communication No. 276/80 concerning *El Salvador*, case of *Miguel Ángel García* et al.

[2] See document 113 EX/38 PRIV., paras. 204-224 (*supra*, pp. 673-678), communication No. 276/80 concerning *El Salvador*, case of *Miguel Ángel García* et al.

[3] See document 114 EX/38 PRIV., paras. 487-488 (*supra*, p. 678), communication No. 276/80 concerning *El Salvador*, case of *Miguel Ángel García* et al.

[4] See document 115 EX/28 PRIV., paras. 84-116 (*supra*, pp. 678-687), communication No. 276/80 concerning *El Salvador*, case of *Miguel Ángel García* et al.

No. 283/80 **El Salvador**

Spring 1983 session of the Committee on Conventions and Recommendations (116th session of the Executive Board) [5]

Autumn 1983 session of the Committee on Conventions and Recommendations (117th session of the Executive Board)[6]

Spring 1984 session of the Committee on Conventions and Recommendations (119th session of the Executive Board)[7]

Autumn 1984 session of the Committee on Conventions and Recommendations (120th session of the Executive Board)[8]

Spring 1985 session of the Committee on Conventions and Recommendations (121st session of the Executive Board)[9]

Autumn 1985 session of the Committee on Conventions and Recommendations (122nd session of the Executive Board)[10]

Spring 1986 session of the Committee on Conventions and Recommendations (124th session of the Executive Board)[11]

---

[5] See document 116 EX/48 PRIV., paras. 66-71 (*supra*, pp. 687-688), communication No. 276/80 concerning *El Salvador*, case of *Leonel Menéndez Quiroga*.
[6] See document 117 EX/18 PRIV., paras. 80-83 (*supra*, pp. 688-689), communication No. 276/80 concerning *El Salvador*, case of *Leonel Menéndez Quiroga*.
[7] See document 119 EX/35 PRIV., paras. 88-93 (*supra*, pp. 690-691), communication No. 276/80 concerning *El Salvador*, case of *Leonel Menéndez Quiroga*.
[8] See document 120 EX/15 PRIV., paras. 62-69 (*supra*, pp. 691-694), communication No. 276/80 concerning *El Salvador*, case of *Leonel Menéndez Quiroga*.
[9] See document 121 EX/46 PRIV., paras. 200-209 (*supra*, pp. 694-697), communication No. 276/80 concerning *El Salvador*, case of *Leonel Menéndez Quiroga*.
[10] See document 122 EX/21 PRIV., paras. 150-160 (*supra*, pp. 697-701), communication No. 276/80 concerning *El Salvador*, case of *Leonel Menéndez Quiroga*.
[11] See document 124 EX/3 PRIV., paras. 143-152 (*supra*, pp. 701-704), communication No. 276/80 concerning *El Salvador*, case of *Leonel Menéndez Quiroga*.

El Salvador **No. 283/80**

Autumn 1986 session of the Committee on Conventions and Recommendations (125th session of the Executive Board)[12]

Spring 1987 session of the Committee on Conventions and Recommendations (126th session of the Executive Board)[13]

Autumn 1987 session of the Committee on Conventions and Recommendations (127th session of the Executive Board)[14]

Spring 1988 session of the Committee on Conventions and Recommendations (129th session of the Executive Board)[15]

Autumn 1988 session of the Committee on Conventions and Recommendations (130th session of the Executive Board)[16]

Spring 1989 session of the Committee on Conventions and Recommendations (131st session of the Executive Board)[17]

Autumn 1989 session of the Committee on Conventions and Recommendations (132nd session of the Executive Board)[18]

---

[12] See document 125 EX/3 PRIV., paras. 168-179 (*supra*, pp. 704-709), communication No. 276/80 concerning *El Salvador*, case of *Leonel Menéndez Quiroga*.
[13] See document 126 EX/3 PRIV., paras. 196-203 (*supra*, pp. 710-712), communication No. 276/80 concerning *El Salvador*, case of *Leonel Menéndez Quiroga and others*.
[14] See document 127 EX/3 PRIV., paras. 136-145 (*supra*, pp. 712-714), communication No. 276/80 concerning *El Salvador*, case of *Leonel Menéndez Quiroga and others*.
[15] See document 129 EX/3 PRIV., paras. 132-139 (*supra*, pp. 714-716), communication No. 276/80 concerning *El Salvador*, case of *Leonel Menéndez Quiroga and others*.
[16] See document 130 EX/3 PRIV., paras. 152-166 (*supra*, pp. 717-720), communication No. 276/80 concerning *El Salvador*, case of *Leonel Menéndez Quiroga and others*.
[17] See document 131 EX/3 PRIV., paras. 186-195 (*supra*, pp. 720-722), communication No. 276/80 concerning *El Salvador*, case of *Leonel Menéndez Quiroga and others*.
[18] See document 132 EX/3 PRIV., paras. 148-156 (*supra*, pp. 722-723), communication No. 276/80 concerning *El Salvador*, case of *Leonel Menéndez Quiroga and others*.

No. 283/80 **El Salvador**

Spring 1990 session of the Committee on Conventions and Recommendations (134th session of the Executive Board)[19]

[19] See document 134 EX/3 PRIV., paras. 173-181 (*supra*, pp. 724-725), communication No. 276/80 concerning *El Salvador*, case of *Leonel Menéndez Quiroga and others*.

No. 289/80

Concerning *Argentina*
Case of *Juan Takara*

Communication of 5 July 1980 submitted by
Norma Beatriz Alba de Takara

Spring 1981 session of the Committee on Conventions and Recommendations
(112th session of the Executive Board)[1]

[1] See document 112 EX/30 PRIV., para. 29 (*supra*, p. 653), communication No. 270/80 concerning *Argentina*, case of *Juan Carlos Higa*.

No. 290/80

Concerning *Cuba*
Case of *Armando Valladares Pérez*

Communication of 30 June 1980 submitted by
Martha L. López de Valladares

Spring 1981 session of the Committee on Conventions and Recommendations (112th session of the Executive Board)[1]

99. Armando Valladares Pérez, the alleged victim, is described as a poet. According to his wife, the author of the communication, he was sentenced, at the age of 23, to 30 years' imprisonment for his political convictions which conflict with those of the government, and has been serving his sentence since 27 December 1960. He is now stricken with paralysis and can only move about in a wheelchair.

100. Mrs Valladares also describes the tragic conditions in which her husband has to live, deprived of drugs and medical care, and the pitiful situation in which his family is vegetating, one of them dismissed from his job, the others deprived of emigration visas for the United States.

101. The rights deemed to have been violated are, principally: the right to freedom of thought, opinion and expression, the right freely to participate in cultural life and the right to share in scientific advancement and its benefits.

102. Mrs Valladares requests:

better treatment for her husband,

adequate medical attention,

permission for the members of his family to leave the country,

and freedom for him to exercise his rights as a poet and a painter.

---

[1] See document 112 EX/30 PRIV., paras. 99-112; see also document 112 EX/CR/HR/3.

No. 290/80 **Cuba**

103. The case had already been considered by the Committee in 1976 in accordance with the procedure laid down by 77 EX/Decision 8.3 of the Executive Board.

104. The representative of the government concerned emphasized that although he was providing explanations, he did not accept the allegations made by the author of the communication. He pointed out that:

> Armando Valladares Pérez had, before his imprisonment, been neither a poet nor a painter;
>
> he had commited an offence against the Cuban State: with others, he had fomented terrorist activities whose purpose had been to prepare an uprising with a view to overthrowing the established order, and he had been found in possession of arms, ammunition and explosives;
>
> he had been condemned to 25 years' imprisonment in accordance with the laws in force not as an intellectual and the author of literary and artistic works, but as a terrorist who had abandoned all professional activities to devote himself exclusively to counter-revolutionary action.

105. The representative of the government concerned further stated that the alleged victim was held under an ordinary prison regime, that he had an individual room in the prison hospital, that he was properly treated by specialists, that he himself refused the treatment offered, except for medicines, and constantly adopted a hostile attitude towards it, and that although a rehabilitation programme existed which in no way required him to abandon his convictions, he persisted in a negative attitude.

106. In reply to a question from a Committee member, the representative of the government concerned indicated that Valladares had not yet completed his sentence, that when he had done so he would not remain in prison, and that under Cuban legislation, all who wished to emigrate were free to do so.

107. Certain Committee members considered that the communication was worded in heart-rending terms, but that in view of the pertinent explanations given by the representative of the government concerned, it appeared difficult to declare the case admissible.

108. Other members pointed out that since Valladares had become a writer after being imprisoned, there could be no question of any retrospective presumption of competence on the part of Unesco. Since the status of a detainee was defined by his sentence, the restrictions imposed on his freedom in no way contradicted human rights, those restrictions being recognized by all countries. No contrary ruling could be

found in the "standard minimum rules for the treatment of prisoners" drawn up under United Nations auspices [...] in 1955, and approved by [the Economic and Social Council]. The fact of having written two books in prison - and their merits could not be taken for granted - was by no means sufficient to create a presumption of competence on the part of the Organization.

109. Other members held that while the justification for Valladares's conviction could not be challenged from the standpoint of Unesco's fields of competence, the sentence he had already served - 21 years of imprisonment - none the less appeared extremely harsh; and that on humanitarian grounds it was to be hoped that the Cuban Government would take account of the feelings expressed in the Committee as to the conditions of his imprisonment and the opportunities available to him for pursuing his activities as a writer.

110. The representative of the Cuban Government pointed out that since the prisoner had acted in conjunction with very resolute terrorists, his case could not be viewed in isolation, and that he must consequently complete his sentence. He stated that while he could pass on to his government the views expressed in the Committee, he could not officially accept a humanitarian appeal on behalf of the prisoner. This opinion was shared by a number of Committee members, who saw in any such appeal an implicit recognition that Cuba had violated a human right, while no accusations could in fact be made against the authorities of that country.

111. After a lengthy debate, a consensus emerged around the following ideas:

(i) that the communication should be declared inadmissible in accordance with paragraph 14 (*a*) (iii) of 104 EX/Decision 3.3; the alleged facts did not fall within Unesco's fields of competence, since there had been no violation of the human rights of either a writer or an artist, Valladares having been sentenced for offences under ordinary law;

(ii) that the author of the communication should be informed that, as the government concerned had shown, Valladares had been offered treatment under satisfactory conditions, but he himself had not been co-operative.

112. The Committee so *decided*.

No. 291/80

Concerning *Argentina*
Case of *Claudio Nicolás Grandi* et al.*

Communication of 22 September 1980 submitted by
Nadine Basile

Spring 1981 session of the Committee on Conventions and Recommendations
(112th session of the Executive Board)[1]

---

* Case of *Claudio Nicolás Grandi, Enrique Daniel Guillen, Elba Eva Acuña de Sáez, Maria Claudia Falcone Méndez, Julio Jorge Gudiño, Rosa Dalia Herrera, Margarita Erlich* et al.

[1] See document 112 EX/30 PRIV., para. 29 (*supra*, p. 653), communication No. 270/80 concerning *Argentina*, case of *Juan Carlos Higa*.

No. 293/80

Concerning *Argentina*
Case of *Isabel Hernando de Pelloli*

Communication of 23 September 1980 submitted by
Isabel Hernando de Pelloli

Spring 1981 session of the Committee on Conventions and Recommendations (112th session of the Executive Board)[1]

30. The author of the communication, who describes herself as a teacher of education, claims to be a victim of the Argentine administrative authorities. According to her account, the directors of the college where she was working informed her in October 1979 of a decision of the Minister of Education to terminate her employment as a teacher in the institution in question, allegedly in the interests of good administration.

31. The author considers that her dismissal without prior notice and without valid grounds constitutes a violation of the right to freedom of thought, right to freedom of expression and opinion.

32. The representative of the government concerned pointed out that the appeal lodged by the author had been rejected. As in the case of Mrs Elba Aurora Martínez de Larrea [...],[2] the decision taken in her respect did not constitute a punishment, for it was an administrative measure dictated by budgetary considerations, in view of the country's economic situation, designed to reduce the number of civil servants, which had been authorized by law and accompanied by compensation calculated on the basis of the number of years of actual service.

33. Several members of the Committee expressed concern regarding the fate of the author of the communication after reading the last sentence of her description of the facts of the claim: "The same resolution prevents me from engaging in any cultural

---

[1] See document 112 EX/30 PRIV., paras. 30-35; see also document 112 EX/CR/HR/3.
[2] *Ibidem*, para. 27 (*supra*, p. 637), communication No. 266/80 concerning *Argentina*, case of *Elba Aurora Martinez de Larrea*.

or teaching activity anywhere in the country". Should this assertion be true, the problem would in their view no longer be a strictly administrative one, and the dismissal of Mrs Hernando de Pelloli would present a difficult problem.

34. In order to remove all ambiguity, the representative of the government concerned read the text of the resolution at issue, from which it emerged:

(i) that the alleged victim was completely free to exercise her activities in fields other than the civil service: indeed, no provision of the resolution prohibited her from working within the national territory;

(ii) that she had the option of seeking legal redress if she considered the administrative authority's decision to be vitiated by irregularities.

35. In the light of the information supplied, itself corroborated by documents in the file kept by the Secretariat, the Committee *decided* to declare the communication inadmissible in accordance with paragraph 14 (*a*) (iii) of 104 EX/Decision 3.3. In its reply to Mrs Hernando de Pelloli, the Secretariat will draw her attention to the fact that the last sentence in her description of the facts of the claim does not correspond to the truth. Should she possess relevant information to the contrary, she would be entitled to submit a further communication.

No. 303/80

Concerning *Union of Soviet Socialist Republics*
Case of *Vladimir Feltsman and Victor Suslin**

Communication of 12 January 1981 submitted by
Yves Haguenauer

Spring 1981 session of the Committee on Conventions and Recommendations (112th session of the Executive Board)[1]

335. In view of the fact that the representative of the Soviet Government had pointed out that the form for communications concerning the case of Victor Suslin had not reached the government concerned within the prescribed time-limit (that is, one month before the Committee meeting), the Committee decided to examine only the case of Vladimir Feltsman at its present session.

336. The author of the communication, Mr Yves Haguenauer, acting in the capacity of a person with reliable knowledge of the facts alleged, drew Unesco's attention to the case of Vladimir Feltsman, a concert pianist, graduate of the Moscow Conservatory and winner of the "Concertino Praga" and "Marguerite Long" international competitions, whose musical activities had, it was claimed, been "abruptly interrupted", whose recordings made for radio and television had been suppressed and whose records had been withdrawn from commercial circuits after he had applied for a visa for Israel in June 1979. Mr Feltsman would like to resume his musical activities in the country of his choice.

337. The representative of the Soviet Government noted that Mr Feltsman was a young pianist who had been refused nothing so that he could develop his talent, that he owned an apartment in a block of flats for artists, that he had been raised in the family of the great composer Feltsman and that, suddenly, he had signified his wish to leave everything, including his mother who was incurably ill, so that he could join his wife's aunt, whom he did not even know, who was living in Israel. As for the al-

* At the Committee's autumn 1981 session, this communication was being referred to as case of *Victor Suslin*.

[1] See document 112 EX/30 PRIV., paras. 335-339; see also document 112 EX/CR/HR/3 Add.

legation that his records had been withdrawn from commercial circuits, the Director of Melodia and the Director of the Promotion and Distribution Department of this firm which had produced six of his recordings had confirmed to the representative of the Soviet Government that they had taken no steps to that effect and that Mr Feltsman's records continued to be distributed normally. As for his musical activities, the representative of the government concerned said that in 1979 Mr Feltsman had contacted the Director of the Moscow State Philharmonic Orchestra and informed him of his intention to leave the USSR. When he was asked whether he would still be able to fulfil his commitments for the year 1980 in the event that his name was included in the programme, his answer was no and his name was accordingly dropped. Then when his departure was delayed, he said that he would like to continue his concert work and although the programme had already been drawn up without him, arrangements were made for his participation in a number of concerts in 1980 - including five in which he performed as a soloist - and in 1981.

338. The members who took part in the discussion came out in favour of inadmissibility since they felt that the Committee could not accede to Mr Feltsman's wish to resume his musical activities in the country of his choice in view of the fact that the right to leave his country was not among the rights falling within fields of Unesco's competence. One member expressed the hope that the Soviet authorities would reexamine Mr Feltsman's request for a visa.

339. After discussion, the Committee *decided* that the communication [in the case of Vladimir Feltsman] was inadmissible on the grounds that it did not fall within Unesco's fields of competence as set forth in paragraph 14 (*a*) (iii) of 104 EX/Decision 3.3.

Autumn 1981 session of the Committee on Conventions and Recommendations (113th session of the Executive Board)[2]

366. In view of the fact that the author of the communication, acting of his own free will, had asked to have the communication withdrawn from the Committee's consideration because Mr Suslin had recently been allowed to leave the Soviet Union, the Committee *decided* to accede to the author's request and struck the communication off its list.

---

[2] See document 113 EX/38 PRIV., para. 366; see also documents 113 EX/CR/HR/2 and Add. 6.

No. 305/80

Concerning *India*
Case of *Govind Prasad*

Communication of 24 October 1980 submitted by
Govind Prasad

Spring 1981 session of the Committee on Conventions and Recommendations (112th session of the Executive Board)[1]

179. The author of the communication, who describes himself as a specialist in physical chemistry and chemical spectroscopy, claims to be the victim of discrimination on account of his origins.

180. In April 1972 he was transferred from his native province of India to take up an appointment as Senior Scientific Assistant in the Regional Research Laboratory of Jormat in Assam. He was able to work normally until the end of 1974 but since then, following the appointment of new officials from Assam itself to run the laboratory, his life and career as a scientist have, by his own account, been constantly and seriously disrupted. Compared with his colleagues from Assam, who (according to the author) are far less well qualified than himself, he is allegedly the least favoured, being relegated to the ranks of the dispensable, his work rejected, his competence denied, obliged to work in fields other than that in which he is specialized, his prospects of advancement blocked, his career in peril, his request for a transfer refused, his accommodation unsuitable, etc.

181. All recourse to higher authorities apparently proved fruitless.

182. The author requests that discrimination on account of caste or regional factors be treated as racial discrimination. He accuses the public authorities of:

violation of the right to equality and justice,

discrimination in the field of scientific work,

[1] See document 112 EX/30 PRIV., paras. 179-185; see also document 112 EX/CR/HR/3.

the author being allegedly deprived of the atmosphere of freedom necessary for such work.

183. This communication was transmitted to the government concerned by letter dated 2 January 1981.

184. The representative of the government concerned made himself available to the Committee on several occasions but, owing to its very full agenda, the Committee was not able to give its attention to the communication until its 14th meeting (12 May 1981, in the evening), at a time when the representative was absent from the meeting room.

185. The Committee therefore *decided* to postpone examination of the admissibility of this communication to the next session.

Autumn 1981 session of the Committee on Conventions and Recommendations (113th session of the Executive Board)[2]

274. The author of the communication, who describes himself as a specialist in physical chemistry and chemical spectroscopy, claims to be the victim of discrimination on account of his origins.

275. In April 1972 he was transferred from his native province of India to take up an appointment as Senior Scientific Assistant in the Regional Research Laboratory of Jormat in Assam. He was able to work normally until the end of 1974 but since then, following the appointment of new officials from Assam itself to run the laboratory, his life and career as a scientist have, by his own account, been constantly and seriously disrupted. Compared with his colleagues from Assam, who (according to the author) are far less well qualified than himself, he is allegedly the least favoured, being relegated to the ranks of the dispensable, his work rejected, his competence denied, obliged to work in fields other than that in which he is specialized, his prospects of advancement blocked, his career in peril, his request for a transfer refused, his accommodation unsuitable, etc.

276. All recourse to higher authorities apparently proved fruitless.

277. The author requests that discrimination on account of caste or regional factors be treated as racial discrimination. He accuses the public authorities of:

[2] See document 113 EX/38 PRIV., paras. 274-283; see also document 113 EX/CR/HR/2.

violation of the right to equality and justice,

discrimination in the field of scientific work,

the author being allegedly deprived of the atmosphere of freedom necessary for such work.

278. At the [spring 1981] session, the representative of the government concerned made himself available to the Committee on several occasions but, owing to its very full agenda, the Committee was not able to give its attention to the communication until its 14th meeting (12 May 1981, in the evening), at a time when the representative was absent from the meeting room.

279. The Committee therefore decided to postpone examination of the admissibility of this communication to the next session.[3]

280. The representative of the Government of India stated at the present session that the affair was a domestic departmental matter, that an official who felt he had been wronged by an administrative measure could take legal proceedings for redress in regard to the violated right, and that the communication should consequently be declared inadmissible.

281. Several members of the Committee took the view that the case indeed did not fall within the competence of Unesco since the issue was an administrative one. They noted that the author of the communication had not sought the domestic remedies available.

282. Some members of the Committee observed that trust should be placed in Indian justice.

283. After a brief discussion, the Committee *decided*:

(i) to declare the communication inadmissible by virtue, in particular, of the provisions of paragraph 14 (*a*) (ix) of 104 EX/Decision 3.3 since no attempt had been made to exhaust available domestic remedies;

(ii) to request the Secretariat to notify Mr Govind Prasad of the decision in accordance with the well-established practice of the Committee.

---

[3] See document 112 EX/30 PRIV., para. 185 (*supra*, p. 756).

No. 306/80

Concerning *El Salvador*
Case of *Arrest and persecution of teachers in El Salvador*

Communication of 10 September 1980 submitted by National Education Federation

Spring 1981 session of the Committee on Conventions and Recommendations (112th session of the Executive Board)[1]

Autumn 1981 session of the Committee on Conventions and Recommendations (113th session of the Executive Board)[2]

Spring 1982 session of the Committee on Conventions and Recommendations (114th session of the Executive Board)[3]

Autumn 1982 session of the Committee on Conventions and Recommendations (115th session of the Executive Board)[4]

Spring 1983 session of the Committee on Conventions and Recommendations (116th session of the Executive Board)[5]

---

[1] See document 112 EX/30 PRIV., paras. 113-124 (*supra*, pp. 671-673), communication No. 276/80 concerning *El Salvador*, case of *Miguel Ángel García* et al.
[2] See document 113 EX/38 PRIV., paras. 204-224 (*supra*, pp. 673-678), communication No. 276/80 concerning *El Salvador*, case of *Miguel Ángel García* et al.
[3] See document 114 EX/38 PRIV., paras. 487-488 (*supra*, p. 678), communication No. 276/80 concerning *El Salvador*, case of *Miguel Ángel García* et al.
[4] See document 115 EX/28 PRIV., paras. 84-116 (*supra*, pp. 678-687), communication No. 276/80 concerning *El Salvador*, case of *Miguel Ángel García* et al.
[5] See document 116 EX/48 PRIV., paras. 66-71 (*supra*, pp. 687-688), communication No. 276/80 concerning *El Salvador*, case of *Leonel Menéndez Quiroga*.

No. 306/80 **El Salvador**

Autumn 1983 session of the Committee on Conventions and Recommendations (117th session of the Executive Board)[6]

Spring 1984 session of the Committee on Conventions and Recommendations (119th session of the Executive Board)[7]

Autumn 1984 session of the Committee on Conventions and Recommendations (120th session of the Executive Board)[8]

Spring 1985 session of the Committee on Conventions and Recommendations (121st session of the Executive Board)[9]

Autumn 1985 session of the Committee on Conventions and Recommendations (122nd session of the Executive Board)[10]

Spring 1986 session of the Committee on Conventions and Recommendations (124th session of the Executive Board)[11]

Autumn 1986 session of the Committee on Conventions and Recommendations (125th session of the Executive Board)[12]

---

[6] See document 117 EX/18 PRIV., paras. 80-83 (*supra*, pp. 688-689), communication No. 276/80 concerning *El Salvador*, case of *Leonel Menéndez Quiroga*.
[7] See document 119 EX/35 PRIV., paras. 88-93 (*supra*, pp. 690-691), communication No. 276/80 concerning *El Salvador*, case of *Leonel Menéndez Quiroga*.
[8] See document 120 EX/15 PRIV., paras. 62-69 (*supra*, pp. 691-694), communication No. 276/80 concerning *El Salvador*, case of *Leonel Menéndez Quiroga*.
[9] See document 121 EX/46 PRIV., paras. 200-209 (*supra*, pp. 694-697), communication No. 276/80 concerning *El Salvador*, case of *Leonel Menéndez Quiroga*.
[10] See document 122 EX/21 PRIV., paras. 150-160 (*supra*, pp. 697-701), communication No. 276/80 concerning *El Salvador*, case of *Leonel Menéndez Quiroga*.
[11] See document 124 EX/3 PRIV., paras. 143-152 (*supra*, pp. 701-704), communication No. 276/80 concerning *El Salvador*, case of *Leonel Menéndez Quiroga*.
[12] See document 125 EX/3 PRIV., paras. 168-179 (*supra*, pp. 704-709), communication No. 276/80 concerning *El Salvador*, case of *Leonel Menéndez Quiroga*.

El Salvador **No. 306/80**

Spring 1987 session of the Committee on Conventions and Recommendations (126th session of the Executive Board)[13]

Autumn 1987 session of the Committee on Conventions and Recommendations (127th session of the Executive Board)[14]

Spring 1988 session of the Committee on Conventions and Recommendations (129th session of the Executive Board)[15]

Autumn 1988 session of the Committee on Conventions and Recommendations (130th session of the Executive Board)[16]

Spring 1989 session of the Committee on Conventions and Recommendations (131st session of the Executive Board)[17]

Autumn 1989 session of the Committee on Conventions and Recommendations (132nd session of the Executive Board)[18]

Spring 1990 session of the Committee on Conventions and Recommendations (134th session of the Executive Board)[19]

---

[13] See document 126 EX/3 PRIV., paras. 196-203 (*supra*, pp. 710-712), communication No. 276/80 concerning *El Salvador*, case of *Leonel Menéndez Quiroga and others*.
[14] See document 127 EX/3 PRIV., paras. 136-145 (*supra*, pp. 712-714), communication No. 276/80 concerning *El Salvador*, case of *Leonel Menéndez Quiroga and others*.
[15] See document 129 EX/3 PRIV., paras. 132-139 (*supra*, pp. 714-716), communication No. 276/80 concerning *El Salvador*, case of *Leonel Menéndez Quiroga and others*.
[16] See document 130 EX/3 PRIV., paras. 152-166 (*supra*, pp. 717-720), communication No. 276/80 concerning *El Salvador*, case of *Leonel Menéndez Quiroga and others*.
[17] See document 131 EX/3 PRIV., paras. 186-195 (*supra*, pp. 720-722), communication No. 276/80 concerning *El Salvador*, case of *Leonel Menéndez Quiroga and others*.
[18] See document 132 EX/3 PRIV., paras. 148-156 (*supra*, pp. 722-723), communication No. 276/80 concerning *El Salvador*, case of *Leonel Menéndez Quiroga and others*.
[19] See document 134 EX/3 PRIV., paras. 173-181 (*supra*, pp. 724-725), communication No. 276/80 concerning *El Salvador*, case of *Leonel Menéndez Quiroga and others*.

No. 307/80

Concerning *Yugoslavia*
Case of *Tomislav Krsmanović*

Communication of 6 October 1980 submitted by
Tomislav Krsmanović

Spring 1981 session of the Committee on Conventions and Recommendations (112th session of the Executive Board)[1]

403. The author of the communication, an economist, describes himself as a victim of the governmental authorities of his country. In a long and rather disconnected account, he maintains that from childhood to adulthood he has been the victim of repression and discrimination and that he only began to defend himself in 1975. Although his health has been seriously affected, he states that he has not been arrested or subjected to any formal punishment. According to him, his troubles are the result of his being a "political misfit". There has been a refusal to make use of his services and skills. He claims that in the various firms where he worked in a study or research capacity he was dismissed or demoted and exposed to the humiliation of being labelled mentally unbalanced. The police allegedly let it be known that he had been forcibly committed to a psychiatric hospital in 1973. His medical report was, apparently, read out before all the workers. He was, he claims, prevented from speaking at certain political meeting or international conferences and from making normal use of the telephone; his domicile was violated without any legal warrant to do so. His wife, brother and sister apparently suffered the consequences of the ill-treatment meted out to him. In September 1978, he says that he published an article on educational reform and a month later, an article on wife-beating. The editor-in-chief of the magazine publishing these articles apparently got into serious trouble for having done so. Since that time, he says, none of his articles have been accepted for publication

404. Mr Tomislav Krsmanović complains that only communist families receive preferential treatment and that he has had no choice but to forgo any legal action because he is subject to all sorts of intimidation.

---

[1] See document 112 EX/30 PRIV., paras. 403-408; see also document 112 EX/CR/HR/3.

No. 307/80 **Yugoslavia**

405. The representative of the Yugoslav Government contested the admissibility of this communication on the grounds that the author was not a victim and did not bring reliable evidence of the violations alleged. He also stated that the communication was not in Unesco's fields of competence.

406. It was explained to the Committee that Mr Krsmanović was presently living as a free citizen in Yugoslavia and that he had never been imprisoned or prosecuted, except for a misdemeanour charge which had been dropped when it became known that he had a mental illness, schizophrenia. He was neither a victim nor did he give specific proof of other violations. Many of the persons he mentioned had in fact been dead for years or did not even exist. The Yugoslav representative explained that this person had for years been sending such generalized allegations to newspapers around the world. This by itself showed that he enjoyed a total freedom of communication.

407. As to the allegation that he was persecuted and repressed by the state, it was explained to the Committee that the judge in the misdemeanour case had had entered on the court records the evidence showing that Mr Krsmanović had been a patient in a mental hospital since 1973. The records showed that he suffered from a form of schizophrenia and was not aware of his illness nor was he responsible for his actions.

408. After a brief discussion the Committee consequently *decided* that this communication could clearly be dismissed as being manifestly ill-founded.

No. 309/80

Concerning *United Kingdom*
Case of *Dominic de Graft Aidoo*

Communication of 13 October 1980 submitted by
Dominic de Graft Aidoo

Spring 1981 session of the Committee on Conventions and Recommendations (112th session of the Executive Board)[1]

214. The author of this communication, who is at present a legal practitioner in Ghana, alleges that Professor Anthony Allott, who had been appointed by London University to assess the quality of his thesis, kept the thesis - the result of two and a half years' research work - for four years and drew on it, allegedly with the connivance of the University, in writing his book "The Limits of Law", which was published by Butterworth and Company Ltd. He is seeking, *inter alia*, financial assistance to enable him to initiate legal proceedings in the British courts.

215. The representative of the United Kingdom Government informed the Committee that Mr de Graft Aidoo had made no effort to exhaust domestic remedies, even though it was possible in the United Kingdom to request financial assistance for that purpose. To obtain financial assistance, a person did not have to be a British citizen; nor did he have to be resident in the United Kingdom: it was enough for him to have only limited means and reasonable grounds for complaint. The representative therefore suggested to the Committee that Mr de Graft Aidoo be informed of that possibility, as explained in a document, setting out the procedure to be followed, which he had left with the Secretariat.

216. After a brief discussion, the Committee *decided* to declare the communication inadmissible, by virtue of paragraph 14 (*a*) (ix) of 104 EX/Decision 3.3, on the grounds that domestic remedies had not been exhausted; and to ask the Secretariat to send Mr de Graft Aidoo the information provided by the representative of the Government of the United Kingdom.

---

[1] See document 112 EX/30 PRIV., paras. 214-216; see also document 112 EX/CR/HR/3.

No. 312/80

Concerning *Senegal*
Case of *Repression against teachers, active members of the Syndicat unique et démocratique des enseignants du Sénégal*

Communication of 20 November 1980 submitted by
World Federation of Teachers' Unions

Spring 1981 session of the Committee on Conventions and Recommendations (112th session of the Executive Board)[1]

217. The World Federation of Teachers' Unions (WFTU), the author of the communication, complains of what it describes as arbitrary acts on the part of the Senegalese Government, which has allegedly taken various administrative or police measures (dismissal, suspension, transfer, prohibition from leaving the country, etc.) to penalize teachers who are members of the Syndicat unique et démocratique des enseignants du Sénégal (SUDES), because they took part in an examinations strike.

218. After reminding the Committee that the political history of his country formed part of a long-standing democratic tradition, the representative of the government concerned described the circumstances in which the members of SUDES had gone on strike, following which the measures mentioned in the communication had been taken against them by his government. He then explained that, at the beginning of 1981, the government had convened what was called the "States General of Education", in which he had been asked to take part. He had himself on that occasion made an appeal both to the government and to SUDES, one effect of which had been the lifting of all penalties imposed on the striking teachers.

219. Lastly, the representative of the government concerned enumerated certain liberal measures his government had just adopted, including a full amnesty for all political and trade union offences and the abolition of the need for an exist visa. On the basis of the new developments that had occurred between the time the communication had been submitted and its examination by the Committee, he therefore empha-

[1] See document 112 EX/30 PRIV., paras. 217-221; see also document 112 EX/CR/HR/3.

sized that, since a solution had been found to the events described, the communication could not, in accordance with the procedure followed by the Committee, be deemed admissible. Several Committee members supported that position.

220. The Director-General's representative having explained that the Committee's past practice in such a case had been not to declare the communication inadmissible but to delete it from the list as having been settled, a consensus in favour of the latter course was quickly reached.

221. The Committee accordingly *decided* to strike this communication off its list as having been dealt with, specifying, at the request of several members of the Committee, that, as usual, the reasons for the decision should be conveyed to the author of the communication, which could if it thought it necessary, submit a further communication in the event of new facts coming to light.

No. 314/80

Concerning *Guinea*
Case of *Barry Abdoulaye* et al.*

Communication of 5 December 1980 submitted by
Nadine Barry

Spring 1981 session of the Committee on Conventions and Recommendations (112th session of the Executive Board)[1]

164. The author of the communication, Mrs Nadine Barry, describes herself as both a representative of the Association of French Families of Political Prisoners in Guinea (AFFPPG), of which she is the President, and a victim. She states that the eight members of the Association are the wives of Guinean university graduates (with the single exception of Mr Keita Noumandian, who was a General) arrested - she alleges - for offences of opinion between 14 October 1968 and 29 August 1972. Four of the eight prisoners were allegedly never tried or sentenced; three were condemned to death and one to penal servitude for life. Since then, the families are said to have received no news of the prisoners, while their representations to the French and Guinean authorities have produced no result.

165. The author of the communication seeks to obtain from the Guinean Government information concerning the present situation of the eight prisoners and the issue of an official death certificate, indicating their place of burial, in the event of decease, basing her case on the right to freedom of expression set forth, *inter alia*, in Article 19 of the Universal Declaration of Human Rights, which she claims extends to the right of [those mentioned in] the communication to receive official information regarding the fate of their husbands.

166. The representative of the government concerned reminded the meeting that on 22 November 1970 his country had witnessed events of exceptional gravity, following which exceptional measures had had to be taken, including the establishment of

* Case of *Barry Abdoulaye, Barry Baba, Camara Balla, Keita Noumandian, Keita Kèmoko, Marof Achaar, Soumah Théodore and Sylla Fodé Saliou.*
[1] See document 112 EX/30 PRIV., paras. 164-168; see also document 112 EX/CR/HR/3.

an emergency court which had been responsible for handling each of the cases under consideration. The persons concerned had taken part in armed aggression against Guinea and the reasons for their arrest had nothing to do with Unesco's fields of competence. The communication was therefore clearly inadmissible.

167. All members who spoke were in favour of declaring the communication inadmissible. Most of them stressed that it was inadmissible because the right to receive information in the sense intended by the author of the communication did not fall within Unesco's fields of competence, since it was not covered by Article 19 of the Universal Declaration of Human Rights. Two members wondered whether, for humanitarian reasons the government could not inform the wives of what had become of their husbands; they none the less supported the decision that the communication should be declared inadmissible.

168. The Committee consequently *decided* to declare this communication inadmissible since it did not fall within Unesco's fields of competence.

No. 316/80

Concerning *Israel*
Case of *Tareq Ya'qoub Ashomali*

Communication of 5 September 1980 submitted by
Committee for the Defence of Palestinian Human Rights
under Israeli Occupation

Spring 1981 session of the Committee on Conventions and Recommendations (112th session of the Executive Board)[1]

186. The Committee for the Defence of Palestinian Human Rights under Israeli Occupation, the author of the communication, draws attention to the case of a Palestinian student who is accused of having thrown stones at military vehicles and at troops and is said to have been arrested on 15 May 1980. It is alleged that he was subjected to serious maltreatment which had grave consequences on his health: rupture of the urinary tract, broken ribs, etc. He was later moved from one hospital to another and underwent several operations. In view of his critical condition, his doctors recommended that he be hospitalized abroad. The Israeli authorities are alleged to have opposed this. On 15 November 1980, he was given a suspended prison sentence of six months and fined 5,000 shekels.

187. The author hopes that immediate action will be taken to enable the victim to receive suitable medical treatment abroad.

188. The representative of the government concerned informed the Committee that the alleged victim was not at present in custody and that he was perfectly free to study, to express his views and to travel - in particular, to travel abroad for medical treatment. He emphasized that Tareq Ya'qoub Ashomali's student status did not establish the slightest link between the act of throwing stones at Israeli troops and Unesco's spheres of competence, that that act constituted an offence, and that the Israeli authorities had a duty to maintain public order and the peace and tranquility of the community. He also refuted the other allegations in the communication, includ-

[1] See document 112 EX/30 PRIV., paras. 186-192; see also documents 112 EX/CR/HR/3 and Add.4.

ing those referring to violations of international instruments relating to human rights. The purpose of the communication, he said, was purely political.

189. Questioned as to the truth of the allegation that the student had been tortured, he said he had been caught by an Israeli soldier and that both had fallen and injured themselves.

190. Some members of the Committee considered that in the case in point there had clearly been a violation of human rights, particularly of Article 7 of the International Covenant on Civil and Political Rights, as it concerned a student whose health had been endangered by beating and torture in his own country and who, by means of a trial and of special endorsements on his travel documents, was being denied freedom to leave his country for the purpose of seeking medical treatment abroad.

191. Other members of the Committee asserted that, although one could not fail to be moved by the tragic human situation described in the communication, consideration should nevertheless be confined to the purpose and aim stated by the author of the communication, who was asking that the alleged victim be enabled to "receive proper medical attention abroad". In their view, since the Israeli Government had announced that the student was entirely free to leave the country, formal note should be taken of that fact and the author of the communication, who was requesting immediate action to save a human life, should be informed. One member of the Committee even suggested that the author of the communication be notified by telegram.

192. The Committee finally *decided*:

[i] to strike the case of the list, on the grounds that the purpose and aim of the communication had been met by the statement made by the representative of the Israeli Government to the effect that the alleged victim was entirely free to leave the country and receive medical attention abroad;

[ii] to ask the Executive Board to request the Director-General to send the author of the communication a telegram informing it of the contents of that statement and asking it to reply, giving details of the further action taken in this affair, on the understanding that such details could, if need be, be brought to the knowledge of the Committee at its next session.

No. 317/81

Concerning *Guatemala*
Case of *Alaíde Foppa*

Communication of 24 December 1980 submitted by
Nicole Dreyfus

Spring 1981 session of the Committee on Conventions and Recommendations (112th session of the Executive Board)[1]

155. The author of [the first communication],[2] Mrs Nicole Dreyfus, barrister, Secretary-General of the "Association française des juristes démocrates", describes herself as a person with reliable knowledge of the alleged violations. [Mrs] Gisèle Halimi, barrister, the author of [the other communication], is acting as the victim's representative and Vice-President of the International Association of Women Writers.

156. Mrs Alaíde Foppa de Solórzano, widow, a renowned Guatemalan poetess and an active defender of the right to culture for women and for the Guatemalan people, is alleged to have been abducted on 19 December 1980 (on 20 December 1980 according to Mrs Dreyfus) in Guatemala City. Her driver is said to have attempted to intervene. Like her, he is reported to have been struck and carried off in the attackers' car. Since the date indicated, neither Alaíde Foppa nor her driver has been seen again.

157. Mrs Dreyfus asks that everything possible should be done to find the alleged victim. For her part, [Mrs] Halimi calls for the "opening of an official inquiry (which the Guatemalan Government has to date refused to undertake)".

158. The representative of the government concerned stated that he had done his utmost to trace Mrs Foppa and her driver, and to discover the identity of those responsible for the abduction so that they might be brought to trial, particularly in view of the fact that the poetess was the sister-in-law of a member of the government.

[1] See document 112 EX/30 PRIV., paras. 155-163; see also document 112 EX/CR/HR/3 Add.
[2] Communications No. 317/81 concerning *Guatemala*, case of *Alaide Foppa*, and No. 347/81 concerning *Guatemala*, case of *Alaide Foppa*, were being considered together.

No. 317/81 **Guatemala**

159. He said that [Mrs] Halimi's allegation concerning the official "silence" on the part of the Guatemalan authorities was untrue: the appointment she had asked for with the Ambassador of Guatemala in Paris had been granted; she herself had cancelled it on the grounds that she had other pressing engagements on the date agreed.

160. Several members of the Committee considered that, in view of the convincing statements made by the representative of the government concerned - statements fully answering the requests put forward by the authors of the communications - the case should be declared inadmissible.

161. Other members of the Committee took the view that, because of the alleged victim's occupation, the presumption of competence on the part of Unesco seemed beyond dispute; the crux of the matter in the case in point was that a person had disappeared - a disappearance occurring in the context of "corpses found", "mass graves", etc. - and that in such dramatic circumstances it was not possible to declare the case inadmissible.

162. Yet other members wished to point out that, while the stated purpose and aim of the communication as formulated were important, they could not be interpreted as being a condition for admissibility additional to those set forth in paragraph 14 (*a*) of 104 EX/Decision 3.3.

163. After a long exchange of views, the Committee *decided*, in conformity with paragraph 14 (*h*) of 104 EX/Decision 3.3, to:

(i) suspend consideration of the two communications;

(ii) inform the government concerned of the concern of the Committee, which would like an inquiry to be conducted with all due dispatch;

(iii) instruct the Secretariat to inform the authors of the two communications of the statements made by the representative of the government concerned, pointing out that he was ready to meet them at the Embassy of Guatemala in Paris.

Guatemala **No. 317/81**

Autumn 1981 session of the Committee on Conventions and Recommendations (113th session of the Executive Board)[3]

245. The author of [the first communication],[4] Mrs Nicole Dreyfus, barrister, Secretary-General of the "Association française des juristes démocrates", describes herself as a person with reliable knowledge of the alleged violations. [Mrs] Gisèle Halimi, barrister, the author of [the other communication], is acting as the victim's representative and Vice-President of the International Association of Women Writers.

246. Mrs Alaíde Foppa de Solórzano, a widow, a renowned Guatemalan poetess and an active defender of the right to culture for women and for the Guatemalan people, is alleged to have been abducted on 19 December 1980 (on 20 December 1980 according to Mrs Dreyfus) in Guatemala City. Her driver is said to have attempted to intervene. Like her, he is reported to have been struck and carried off in the attackers' car. Since the date indicated, neither Alaíde Foppa nor her driver has been seen again.

247. Mrs Dreyfus asks that everything possible should be done to find the alleged victim. For her part, [Mrs] Halimi calls for the "opening of an official inquiry (which the Guatemalan Government has to date refused to undertake)".

248. At the [spring 1981] session, the representative of the government concerned stated that he had done his utmost to trace Mrs Foppa and her driver, and to discover the identity of those responsible for the abduction so that they might be brought to trial, particularly in view of the fact that the poetess was the sister-in-law of a member of the government.

249. He said that [Mrs] Halimi's allegation concerning the official "silence" on the part of the Guatemalan authorities was untrue: the appointment she had asked for with the Ambassador of Guatemala in Paris had been granted; she herself had cancelled it on the grounds that she had other pressing engagements on the date agreed.

250. Several members of the Committee considered that, in view of the convincing statements made by the representative of the government concerned - statements fully answering the requests put forward by the authors of the communications - the case should be declared inadmissible.

---

[3] See document 113 EX/38 PRIV., paras. 245-256; see also document 113 EX/CR/HR/2.
[4] Communications No. 317/81 concerning *Guatemala*, case of *Alaíde Foppa*, and No. 347/81 concerning *Guatemala*, case of *Alaíde Foppa*, were being considered together.

No. 317/81 **Guatemala**

251. Other members of the Committee took the view that, because of the alleged victim's occupation, the presumption of competence on the part of Unesco seemed beyond dispute, that the case in point concerned a person who had disappeared - a disappearance occurring in the context of "corpses found", "mass graves", etc. - and that in such dramatic circumstances it was not possible to declare the case inadmissible.

252. Other members again wished to point out that, while the stated purpose and aim of the communication as formulated were important, they could not be interpreted as being a condition for admissibility additional to those set forth in paragraph 14 (*a*) of 104 EX/Decision 3.3.

253. After a long exchange of views, the Committee decided, in accordance with paragraph 14 (*h*) of 104 EX/Decision 3.3:[5]

(i) to suspend consideration of the two communications;

(ii) to inform the government concerned of the concern of the Committee, which would like an inquiry to be conducted with all due dispatch;

(iii) to instruct the Secretariat to inform the authors of the two communications of the statements made by the representative of the government concerned, pointing out that he was ready to meet them at the Embassy of Guatemala in Paris.

254. In accordance with the Committee's decision in the case of missing persons,[6] the case of Mrs Foppa was brought to the attention of the Working Group [on Enforced or Involuntary Disappearances] of the United Nations Commission on Human Rights, in Geneva.

255. At the present session, the representative of the government concerned stated that the competent authorities of his country had made every effort to find the alleged victim, but in vain. He undertook to provide any further information which might become available. He added that the Guatemalan Embassy in Paris was still ready to hold discussions with the authors of the two communications.

256. After a brief exchange of views, the Committee *decided*:

---

[5] See document 112 EX/30 PRIV., para. 163 (*supra*, p. 774).
[6] See documents 108 EX/38 PRIV., para. 16, 109 EX/52 PRIV., annex I, para. 8, and Corr. and 112 EX/30 PRIV., paras. 558-566.

(i) to keep the two communications on the list, pending information from the Working Group of the United Nations Commission on Human Rights and any further information that might be supplied by the Guatemalan Government;

(ii) to request the Secretariat to inform the authors of both communications of all additional information received at this session.

Autumn 1987 session of the Committee on Conventions and Recommendations (127th session of the Executive Board)[7]

181. The communications in question[8] are [...] submitted [respectively] by Mrs Nicole Dreyfus of the "Association française des juristes démocrates" and [...] by Mrs Halimi, then President of "Choisir" and Vice-President of the International Association of Women Writers, and now Chairwoman of the Committee. They concern Mrs Alaíde Foppa, a writer and teacher, who is said to have been abducted, together with her driver, by a group of armed persons on 19 December 1980 in Guatemala City.

182. At the spring 1981 session, the representative of the government concerned stated that everything possible had been done to trace the alleged victims.

183. In a letter dated 7 September 1987, the Permanent Delegate of Guatemala to Unesco asked, on behalf of his government, for consideration of these two communications to be deferred until a subsequent session since between the receipt of the letter from the Secretariat advising the government of the resumption of consideration by the Committee and the present session, the interval had been too short for the authorities in his country to gather the relevant information in time. Furthermore, the Guatemalan Constitution, in force since January 1986, had instituted the office of a Human Rights Prosecutor, and he was now dealing with the affair. In addition, information from the Working Group of the Commission on Human Rights responsible for studying cases of missing persons might constitute useful background material for continued investigations in Guatemala.

184. Of the members of the Committee who spoke, some, while assuring the Chairwoman of their complete confidence in her integrity and objectivity, wondered whether, in juridical terms, the status of author of a communication was not incompatible with that of Chairwoman of the Committee. In the view of others, since the Committee was not a court, there was no need to apply that principle. It was ob-

---

[7] See document 127 EX/3 PRIV., paras. 181-188; see also document 127 EX/CR/HR/2, annex III.

[8] Communications No. 317/81 concerning *Guatemala*, case of *Alaíde Foppa*, and No. 347/81 concerning *Guatemala*, case of *Alaíde Foppa*, were being considered together.

served that within the Committee, everybody had an interest in respect for human rights, so that there was no distinction between Committee members and authors of communications. Others took the view that in the circumstances, a practical solution should be found by leaving aside [that communication] and considering, for example, only [the communication] submitted by Mrs Nicole Dreyfus.

185. The Chairwoman of the Committee told members that she was ready to withdraw but that, as there was no Vice-Chairman and as the existing rules did not cover the situation, a complicated procedure would have to be followed to enable an ad hoc Chairman to be installed. The procedure had already been used and consisted in having the Chairman of the Executive Board designate a Vice-Chairman, also belonging to the Committee, to serve as the Committee's acting Chairman.

186. Some members of the Committee requested that mention should be made in the present report that it was felt to be necessary to ask the appropriate decision-making bodies to examine the possibility of the Committee's having a Vice-Chairman so that it could, in future, overcome the problem of the Chairman being unable to exercise his functions through incompatibility or unavailability.

187. In that respect, the Chairwoman stated that the problem was shared by other committees and commissions and that the reform would simply involve a minor amendment to Rule 16 (2) of the Rules of Procedure of the Executive Board.

188. After an exchange of views, the Committee *decided* to accede to the request made by the government concerned and to defer consideration of [the two communications] until its spring 1988 session.

Spring 1988 session of the Committee on Conventions and Recommendations (129th session of the Executive Board)[9]

162. The communications in question[10] were [...] concerning the same alleged victim, Mrs Alaíde Foppa, a writer and teacher, who was said to have been abducted, together with her driver, on 19 December 1980 in Guatemala City.

163. The Director-General's representative informed the Committee that at its 42nd session, by resolution 1986/62, the Commission on Human Rights had decided to consider examination of the human rights situation in Guatemala as completed. He

[9] See document 129 EX/3 PRIV., paras. 162-165; see also document 129 EX/CR/HR/2.
[10] Communications No. 317/81 concerning *Guatemala*, case of *Alaíde Foppa*, and No. 347/81 concerning *Guatemala*, case of *Alaide Foppa*, were being considered together.

also pointed out that the Commission, noting the Guatemalan Government's readiness to co-operate actively with it and the government's efforts to ensure full exercise of fundamental freedoms within the country, had also decided to place an advisory service on the protection of human rights at the disposal of that State and for that purpose to appoint an expert to evaluate progress made.

164. After reviewing the various stages of the Committee's examination of these two communications since 1981, the representative of the government concerned outlined the radical political changes that had occurred in his country, particularly as regards human rights. He recalled the reasons that had led the Committee to refer the case of Mrs Alaíde Foppa to the specialized Working Group of the Commission on Human Rights responsible for studying cases of missing persons (avoidance of duplication) and to cease examination of similar communications concerning countries in which democracy and the rule of law had been restored. He also drew the Committee's attention to the prolonged silence of the authors of the two communications and the Committee's practice of striking communications from its list in such an event. He said that the Guatemalan authorities had conducted inquiries on Mrs Foppa's abduction and that these investigations were continuing under the direction of the Human Rights Prosecutor, an office recently instituted under the new Constitution and corresponding to that of Ombudsman. In any event, the case would not be forgotten, since the result of the current inquiries would be communicated to the specialized Working Group of the Commission on Human Rights, which still had the matter before it. In conclusion, he asked the Committee to cease examination of these commtinications.

165. After an exchange of views, the Committee *decided*:

(i) to thank the representative of the government concerned for his attendance and co-operation;

(ii) to cease examination of these two communications and to strike them from its list, in view of the return of democracy and the rule of law to Guatemala, the efforts of the government concerned to elucidate the case of Mrs Alaíde Foppa and the fact that the Working Group of the Commission on Human Rights was continuing its examination of the case.

No. 319/81

Concerning *Argentina and Paraguay**
Case of *Antonio Maidana*

Communication of 13 January 1981 submitted by
Comité français de solidarité et de soutien
au peuple du Paraguay

Spring 1981 session of the Committee on Conventions and Recommendations (112th session of the Executive Board)[1]

36. The author of the communication is the Comité français de solidarité et de soutien au peuple du Paraguay, represented by its President, Mr Alain Cornevaux. This association describes itself as a group of persons having reliable knowledge of the alleged violations.

37. According to the association, Antonio Maidana, a teacher and founder of the Teachers' Federation of Paraguay, after being released in 1977 on completion of a twenty-year prison sentence in Paraguay, took up residence in Argentina at the beginning of 1978. He is alleged to have been abducted in a street in Buenos Aires on 27 August 1980 by a group of individuals in plain clothes, and has been missing since that date. He was reportedly deported to Paraguay in January 1981 by the Argentine authorities, who allegedly handed him over to General Marcial Samaniego, the Minister of Defence.

38. The representative of the Paraguayan Government stated that his government was very concerned about respect for human rights, and that there had been no collusion whatsoever between the Paraguayan and Argentine authorities as regards the abduction of Antonio Maidana. He said that while the allegations in the communication were of a striking nature, they were based on no real foundation.

* From the autumn 1987 session of the Committee, this communication was being referred to as concerning *Paraguay*.
[1] See document 112 EX/30 PRIV., paras. 36-43; see also document 112 EX/CR/HR/3 Add.

39. In turn, the representative of the Argentine Government stated that, following a complaint and an application for a writ of *habeas corpus*, an inquiry had been instituted: Antonio Maidana had not been arrested by the authorities responsible for law and order; no witness had been present at the alleged abduction; according to the daughter of an individual who had disappeared at the same time as Maidana, Maidana and her father had an appointment to meet somewhere in Buenos Aires at the alleged date of the abduction; according to a newspaper report, Maidana had last been seen in Caracas, in Venezuela. The representative of the Argentine Government added that the missing person had never been a teacher in Argentina. He stressed that, since no tangible proof had been furnished by the author of the communication in support of the veracity of the alleged facts, there were no grounds for saying that there had been a violation of human rights by his country's authorities. He stated that, even if the Committee declared this case to be admissible, his government would not agree to participate in considering such a communication.

40. In view of the information thus provided, a member of the Committee wondered how it was possible for the author of the communication to claim reliable knowledge of the alleged facts. In his view, it was clear that the communication had been drawn up without due consideration.

41. The representative of the Director-General drew the Committee's attention to the principle that there is always a presumption of good faith, and said that if it were proved that the author of the communication had not acted in good faith, the provisions of paragraph 14 (*a*) (vi) of 104 EX/Decision 3.3 would apply: the case submitted would be rejected as an abuse of the right to submit communications.

42. Stressing that a presumption of good faith cannot be upheld once proof to the contrary has been furnished, a member of the Committee stated that the case under consideration was a classic example of a communication relating to missing persons.

43. The Committee finally *decided*:

(i) to suspend consideration of the admissibility of the communication;

(ii) to instruct the Secretariat to bring the information supplied by the governments concerned to the knowledge of the author of the communication and to request the author to provide additional information on the present situation of the alleged victim.

Argentina and Paraguay **No. 319/81**

Autumn 1981 session of the Committee on Conventions and Recommendations (113th session of the Executive Board)[2]

47. The author of the communication is the [Comité français de solidarité et de soutien au peuple du Paraguay], represented by its President, Mr Alain Cornevaux. This association describes itself as a group of persons having reliable knowledge of the alleged violations.

48. According to the association, Antonio Maidana, a teacher and founder of the Teachers' Federation of Paraguay, after being released in 1977 on completion of a twenty-year prison sentence in Paraguay, took up residence in Argentina at the beginning of 1978. He is alleged to have been abducted in a street in Buenos Aires on 27 August 1980 by a group of individuals in plain clothes, and has been missing since that date. He was reportedly deported to Paraguay in January 1981 by the Argentine authorities, who allegedly handed him over to General Marcial Samaniego, the Minister of Defence.

49. At the [spring 1981] session, the representative of the Paraguayan Government stated that his government was very concerned about respect for human rights, that there had been no collusion whatsoever between the Paraguayan and Argentine authorities as regards the abduction of Antonio Maidana and that while the allegations in the communication were of a striking nature, they were based on no real foundation.

50. In turn, the representative of the Argentine Government stated that, following a complaint and an application for a writ of *habeas corpus*, an inquiry had been instituted: Antonio Maidana had not been arrested by the authorities responsible for law and order; no witness had been present at the alleged abduction; according to the daughter of an individual who had disappeared at the same time as Maidana, Maidana and her father had an appointment to meet somewhere in Buenos Aires at the alleged date of the abduction; according to a newspaper report, Maidana had last been seen in Caracas, in Venezuela. The representative of the Argentine Government added that the missing person had never been a teacher in Argentina, and that, since no tangible proof had been furnished by the author of the communication in support of the veracity of the alleged facts, there were no grounds for saying that there had been a violation of human rights by his country's authorities. He stated that, even if the Committee declared this case to be admissible, his government would not agree to participate in considering such a communication.

---

[2] See document 113 EX/38 PRIV., paras. 47-59; see also documents 113 EX/CR/HR/2 and Add.4.

51. In view of the information thus provided, a member of the Committee wondered how it was possible for the author of the communication to claim reliable knowledge of the alleged facts. In his view, it was clear that the communication had been drawn up without due consideration.

52. The representative of the Director-General drew the Committee's attention to the principle that there was always a presumption of good faith, and said that if it were proved that the author of the communication had not acted in good faith, the provisions of paragraph 14 (*a*) (vi) of 104 EX/Decision 3.3 would apply: the case submitted would be rejected as an abuse of the right to submit communications.

53. Stressing that a presumption of good faith could not be upheld once proof to the contrary has been furnished, a member of the Committee stated that the case under consideration was a classic example of a communication relating to missing persons.

54. The Committee finally decided:[3]

> (i) to suspend consideration of the admissibility of the communication;
>
> (ii) to instruct the Secretariat to bring the information supplied by the governments concerned to the knowledge of the author of the communication and to request the author to provide additional information on the present situation of the alleged victim.

55. Under cover of a letter dated 15 July 1981, the author of the communication had forwarded to the Secretariat three copies of cables from a press agency (PL) which made it apparent, according to different sources, that the Secretary-General of the Paraguayan Communist Party, Antonio Maidana, was being detained in the Emboscada prison.

56. At the present session, the representatives of the two governments concerned informed the Committee that they had no new information about the facts alleged in that communication. They rejected as inaccurate the latest information provided by the [Comité français de solidarité et de soutien au peuple du Paraguay].

57. The representative of the Argentine Government stressed in particular that there was no joint Argentine-Paraguayan police force operating together. Each country was a sovereign state with its own institutions. In any event, he said, he would not fail to provide the Committee with any other information that could be obtained concerning Antonio Maidana. In reply to a member of the Committee who wished in-

[3] See document 112 EX/30 PRIV., para. 43 (*supra*, p. 782).

vestigations to be carried out on the basis of information claiming that the alleged victim was in Venezuela, he indicated that he would send on to the Secretariat the text of the newspaper article in question.

58. Several members of the Committee expressed their concern regarding the fate of Antonio Maidana, and were of the opinion that the case should be considered as that of a missing person.

59. After discussion, the Committee *decided*:

(i) to suspend consideration of the admissibility of that communication;

(ii) to pass the case on to the Working Group of the United Nations Commission [on] Human Rights at Geneva, which deals with cases of enforced or [involuntary] disappearance of persons;

(iii) to record formally the offer made by both the governments concerned to pass on to the Secretariat any new information relating to the alleged victim;

(iv) to inform the author of the communication of any new facts relating to the case.

Spring 1982 session of the Committee on Conventions and Recommendations (114th session of the Executive Board)[4]

329. The author of the communication is the Comité français de solidarité et de soutien au peuple du Paraguay, represented by its President, Mr Alain Cornevaux. This association describes itself as a group of persons having reliable knowledge of the alleged violations.

330. According to the association, Antonio Maidana, a teacher and founder of the Teachers' Federation of Paraguay, after being released in 1977 on completion of a twenty-year prison sentence in Paraguay, took up residence in Argentina at the beginning of 1978. He is alleged to have been abducted in a street in Buenos Aires on 27 August 1980 by a group of individuals in plain clothes, and has been missing since that date. He is stated to have been deported to Paraguay in January 1981.

[4] See document 114 EX/38 PRIV., paras. 329-346; see also documents 114 EX/CR/HR/2 and Add.4.

No. 319/81 **Argentina and Paraguay**

331. At the spring 1981 session, the representative of the Paraguayan Government stated that his government was very concerned about respect for human rights and that there had been no collusion whatsoever between the Paraguayan and Argentine authorities as regards the abduction of Antonio Maidana.

332. In turn, the representative of the Argentine Government stated that, following a complaint and an application for a writ of *habeas corpus*, an inquiry had been instituted: Mr Antonio Maidana had not been arrested by the authorities responsible for law and order; no witness had been present at the alleged abduction; according to a newspaper report, Mr Maidana had last been seen in Caracas, in Venezuela. The representative of the Argentine Government added that the missing person had never been a teacher in Argentina, that no tangible proof had been furnished by the author of the communication in support of the veracity of the alleged facts, and that there were no grounds for saying that there had been a violation of human rights by his country's authorities.

333. After an exchange of views, the Committee decided:[5]

(i) to suspend consideration of the admissibility of the communication;

(ii) to instruct the Secretariat to bring the information supplied by the governments concerned to the knowledge of the author of the communication and to request the author to provide additional information on the present situation of the alleged victim.

334. Under cover of a letter dated 15 July 1981, the author of the communication forwarded to the Secretariat three copies of cables from a press agency (PL) which made it apparent, according to different sources, that the Secretary-General of the Paraguayan Communist Party, Antonio Maidana, was being detained in the Emboscada prison.

335. At the autumn 1981 session, the representatives of the two governments concerned informed the Committee that they had no new information about the facts alleged in that communication. They rejected as inaccurate the latest information provided by the [Comité français de solidarité et de soutien au peuple du Paraguay].

336. The representative of the Argentine Government stressed in particular that there was no joint Argentine-Paraguayan police force operating together. In reply to a member of the Committee who wished investigations to be carried out on the basis

[5] See document 112 EX/30 PRIV., para. 43 (*supra*, p. 782).

of information claiming that the alleged victim was in Venezuela, he said that he would send on to the Secretariat the text of the newspaper article in question.

337. Several members of the Committee expressed their concern regarding the fate of Mr Antonio Maidana, and were of the opinion that the case should be considered as that of a missing person.

338. After discussion the Committee decided:[6]

(i) to suspend consideration of the admissibility of that communication;

(ii) to pass the case on to the Working Group of the United Nations Commission [on] Human Rights at Geneva, which deals with cases of enforced or involuntary disappearance of persons;

(iii) to record formally the offer made by both the governments concerned to pass on to the Secretariat any new information relating to the alleged victim;

(iv) to inform the author of the communication of any new facts relating to the case.

339. By its letter dated 6 April 1982, the Permanent Delegation of Argentina to Unesco stated that Mr Maidana had been reported to be in Caracas by Oldřich Pospíšil, a political commentator with *Rudé Právo*, the Czechoslovak Communist Party newspaper, in the issue of that paper for 10 April 1981.

340. Additionally, by a letter dated 15 April 1982, the delegation stated that, according to a report published in the daily *Pravda*, in its issue for 21 August 1981, the TASS agency in Buenos Aires had quoted the First Secretary of the Paraguayan Communist Party as saying that Mr Maidana was alive and imprisoned in that country.

341. By a letter dated 19 April 1982, the Secretary-General of a non-governmental organization styled "France-Amérique Latine" stated that he had learnt from a "reliable source" that Mr Maidana was detained in the Fortin Esperanza prison in Argentina.

342. At the current session, referring to the content of the first two letters, the representative of the Argentine Government stated that all the evidence indicated that the alleged victim was not in Argentina.

[6] See document 113 EX/38 PRIV., para. 59 (*supra*, p. 785).

343. So far as the letter from "France-Amérique Latine" was concerned he stated that there was no such prison as Fortin Esperanza, nor even a village of that name. He promised, however, to contact his government to obtain relevant information.

344. For his part, the representative of the Paraguayan Government said that he had nothing to add to the evidence considered at the [spring 1981] session; the authorities in his country knew nothing at all about the fate of the alleged victim.

345. Several Committee members felt it appropriate that the new information provided by the Argentine Government should be brought to the notice of the author of the communication, and that any explanations he might wish to make should be considered at the next session.

346. Following an exchange of views, the Committee so *decided*.

Autumn 1982 session of the Committee on Conventions and Recommendations (115th session of the Executive Board)[7]

9. This communication concerns the case of a missing person, Mr Antonio Maidana, described as a teacher and founder of the Teachers' Federation of Paraguay, who is alleged to have been abducted in a street in Buenos Aires on 27 August 1980 by a group of individuals in plain clothes.

10. It was examined by the Committee for the first time at its spring 1981 session.

11. At its autumn 1981 session, the Committee decided to pass the communication on to the Working Group of the United Nations Commission on Human Rights which deals with cases of enforced or involuntary disappearance of persons.[8]

12. At its spring 1982 session, the Committee was informed by the representative of the Argentine Government that Mr Maidana had been reported by a newspaper (*Rudé Právo*, 10 April 1981) to be in Caracas, Venezuela, and that, according to a report in a daily (*Pravda*, 21 August 1981), he was alive and imprisoned in Paraguay. The representative of the government of that country stated that he knew nothing at all about the fate of the alleged victim.

13. At the autumn 1982 session, no further information had reached the Committee.

---

[7] See document 115 EX/28 PRIV., paras. 9-14; see also document 115 EX/CR/HR/2.
[8] See document 113 EX/38 PRIV., para. 59 (ii) (*supra*, p. 785).

Argentina and Paraguay **No. 319/81**

14. The Committee *decided* to keep the communication on its list and to resume consideration of it when fresh information had been received.

Autumn 1987 session of the Committee on Conventions and Recommendations (127th session of the Executive Board)[9]

194. The communication in question is [...] submitted by the [Comité français de solidarité et de soutien au peuple du Paraguay]. It concerns the case of Mr Antonio Maidana, a teacher, founder of the Teachers' Federation of Paraguay and former General Secretary of the Paraguayan Communist Party, who is said to have been abducted in Buenos Aires, Argentina, on 27 August 1980 and to have been deported to Paraguay in January 1981.

195. According to information received from the specialized Working Group of the United Nations Commission on Human Rights, the Paraguayan Government stated on 12 June 1985 that after his release on 27 January 1977, Mr Antonio Maidana had gone to Sweden. It had later learnt that he had travelled to Moscow and subsequently to the German Democratic Republic. He had not returned to Paraguay.

196. The representative of the government concerned stated that all he could say for the time being was that Mr Antonio Maidana had left Paraguay of his own accord for a third country. Since he had no relevant information to offer, he requested that consideration of the communication should be deferred.

197.One member of the Committee expressed the wish that.the United Nations document drawn up by a special rapporteur on the situation in Paraguay should be added to the file.

198. After an exchange of views, the Committee *decided*:

(i) to thank the representative of the government concerned for his attendance and co-operation;

(ii) to repeat its request for information on the fate of Mr Antonio Maidana;

(iii) to resume consideration of the communication at its spring 1988 session.

---

[9] See document 127 EX/3 PRIV., paras. 194-198; see also document 127 EX/CR/HR/2, annex IV.

No. 319/81 **Argentina and Paraguay**

Spring 1988 session of the Committee on Conventions and Recommendations (129th session of the Executive Board)[10]

171. Mr Antonio Maidana, founder of the Teachers' Federation of Paraguay and former General Secretary of the Paraguayan Communist Party, aged 64 at the time of the events, was, according to the author of the communication, abducted in Buenos Aires on 27 August 1980 by individuals wearing plain clothes.

172. On 12 June 1985 the Paraguayan Government had informed the specialized Working Group of the Commission on Human Rights that after his release on 27 January 1977, Mr Maidana had gone to Sweden. It had later learnt that he had travelled to Moscow and subsequently to the German Democratic Republic. According to the government concerned, he had never returned to Paraguay.

173. The Working Group had considered at its 16th session that this case had been clarified on Paraguay's part.

174. At the present session, after outlining the information already submitted to the Committee, to the effect that Mr Maidana had been traced to Buenos Aires in Argentina, Caracas in Venezuela, Sweden and Central Europe, the representatives of the government concerned considered that their country was in no way responsible for his alleged disappearance.

175. After an exchange of views and taking into account the decision of the specialized Working Group of the United Nations Commission on Human Rights to consider the case in question as clarified by the Paraguayan authorities, the Committee *decided* to strike the communication from its list.

---

[10] See document 129 EX/3 PRIV., paras. 171-175; see also document 129 EX/CR/HR/2.

No. 321/81

Concerning *Chile*
Case of *Víctor Xavier Tiznado Rosas*

Communication of 9 January 1981 submitted by
Víctor Xavier Tiznado Rosas

Spring 1981 session of the Committee on Conventions and Recommendations (112th session of the Executive Board)[1]

85. The author of the communication, Mr Víctor Xavier Tiznado Rosas, a refugee in Belgium since December 1973, complains that the Chilean Ministry of the Interior rejected the request allegedly submitted to it in April 1978 that he might be authorized to return to Chile. The Chilean authorities claimed that their refusal was based on reasons of national security, although it is said that no proceedings had been instituted against Mr Tiznado Rosas and no sentence pronounced on him. He is a doctor by profession, having completed his specialization in clinical biology, and states that he has devoted a great deal of his time to research work which should be continued in his native cultural environment. He says that in January 1981 he submitted another request in the hope of visiting his sick mother, aged 68.

86. The representative of the Chilean Government pointed out that, after the refusal of the author's request in 1978, he had used no means of redress, either administrative or legal; he thought it necessary to inform the author of the existence of such means of redress and of the possibility of requesting permission to return on a provisional basis.

87. When asked whether a refugee of Chilean origin retained his Chilean nationality, the representative of the Chilean Government stated that Chilean nationality was forfeited only in specific cases, which did not include the state of being exiled or a refugee.

88. One member emphasized that, while Mr V. X. Tiznado Rosas was a doctor, he was also a researcher, which fact would suffice, in case of need, to create a presump-

[1] See document 112 EX/30 PRIV., paras. 85-90; see also document 112 EX/CR/HR/3.

tion of competence on the part of Unesco; furthermore, he had repeated his request on 6 January 1981 in order to visit his elderly and ailing mother; the Committee should appeal to the goodwill of the government concerned.

89. The representative of the Chilean Government expressed his willingness to pass on such arguments to his government, and stated that, if the second request were refused, the person concerned could appeal to the appropriate courts.

90. Following a brief exchange of views, the Committee *decided* to suspend consideration of the admissibility of this communication, to inform the author of the means of redress available to him according to the information given by the representative of the Chilean Government, and to appeal to the goodwill of that government in assessing the present case.

Autumn 1981 session of the Committee on Conventions and Recommendations (113th session of the Executive Board)[2]

143. The author of the communication, Mr Víctor Xavier Tiznado Rosas, a refugee in Belgium since December 1973, complains that the Chilean Ministry of the Interior rejected the request allegedly submitted to it in April 1978 that he might be authorized to return to Chile. The Chilean authorities claimed that their refusal was based on reasons of national security, although it is said that no proceedings had been instituted against Mr Tiznado Rosas and no sentence pronounced on him. He is a doctor by profession, having completed his specialization in clinical biology, and states that he has devoted a great deal of his time to research work which should be continued in his native cultural environment. He says that in January 1981 he submitted another request in the hope of visiting his sick mother, aged 68.

144. At the [spring 1981] session of the Committee, the representative of the Chilean Government pointed out that, after the refusal of the author's request in 1978, he had used no means of redress, either administrative or legal; he thought it necessary to inform the author of the existence of such means of redress and of the possibility of requesting permission to return on a provisional basis.

145. When asked whether a refugee of Chilean origin retained his Chilean nationality, the representative of the Chilean Government stated that Chilean nationality was forfeited only in specific cases, which did not include the state of being exiled or a refugee.

---

[2] See document 113 EX/38 PRIV., paras. 143-155; see also documents 113 EX/CR/HR/2 and Add.6.

Chile **No. 321/81**

146. One member emphasized that, while Mr V. X. Tiznado Rosas was a doctor, he was also a researcher, which fact would suffice, in case of need, to create a presumption of competence on the part of Unesco; furthermore, he had repeated his request on 6 January 1981 in order to visit his elderly and ailing mother; the Committee should appeal to the goodwill of the government concerned.

147. The representative of the Chilean Government expressed his willingness to pass on such arguments to his government, and stated that, if the second request were refused, the person concerned could appeal to the appropriate courts.

148. Following a brief exchange of views, the Committee decided to suspend consideration of the admissibility of this communication, to inform the author of the means of redress available to him according to the information given by the representative of the Chilean Government, and to appeal to the goodwill of that government in assessing the present case.[3]

149. On 27 August 1981 the author sent a letter to the Secretariat [...],[4] enclosing a photocopy of the negative reply given by the Chilean Consulate in Antwerp (Belgium) to his request of 6 January 1981 for permission to return to Chile. He added that this reply, for which no reasons were given, was not, in his view, in keeping with the standards laid down by the Chilean Government itself since, in the note drawn up at the request of the Committee on Conventions and Recommendations by the representative of the Chilean Government, it was stated that "the Ministry of the Interior may refuse such authorization for reasons connected with the security of the state, in which case it shall state the reasons for its refusal" (underlined by the author).

150. At the present session the representative of the Chilean Government pointed out to the Committee that, although Mr Tiznado Rosas had been informed of the means of redress available to him, he had not used them. He stated that the best way of resolving such situations was, however, to take advantage of the existing judicial remedies, which could be done on behalf of the person concerned by any person residing in Chile, without it even being necessary to have the assistance of a lawyer. He added lastly that the government was obliged to inform the relevant court of the reasons for its refusal and that, consequently, by applying to that court, the plaintiff would be notified of those reasons.

151. One member of the Committee observed that the Committee was faced here with a case similar to many others, which proceeded as follows: Chilean citizens de-

---

[3] See document 112 EX/30 PRIV., para. 90 (*supra*, p. 792).
[4] See document 113 EX/CR/HR/2 Add.6.

prived of the right to return to their country asked for permission to do so and such permission was refused them by the Chilean Ministry of the Interior, this being notified to them by the Consuls. This decision could be submitted to judicial review in the course of which the person concerned would at least be informed of the reasons for the refusal and possibly obtain authorization to return to Chile. He consequently considered that this procedure was clear and that, at all events, the Committee should suggest to the author of the communication that he avail himself of the judicial means of redress.

152. Other members stated that they would be of the same opinion as the previous speaker were there no new element involved. However, in this particular case, the author had submitted a second request to return in order to go and see his elderly and ailing mother. He recalled that in comparable cases the Chilean Government had granted to those concerned authorization to return for 60 days, thereby enabling them to settle their problems far more easily on the spot, and that financial assistance had even been offered by the Office of the High Commissioner for Refugees in cases where there were financial difficulties standing in the way of this temporary return.

153. The representative of the Chilean Government confirmed that the existence of purely judicial means of redress did not preclude the extraordinary means of redress afforded by recourse to his good offices on humanitarian grounds and that he was prepared to take action along these lines if the Committee so requested him.

154. One member expressed surprise at the fact that a judicial procedure was necessary in order to know the reason for a governmental decision. For the information of the Committee, the representative of the Director-General stated that there was no international normative text that made it binding on government authorities to state the reasons for decisions such as that in question in this communication.

155. After discussion the Committee *decided*:

(i) to suspend consideration of this communication until the next session;

(ii) to appeal to the Chilean Government's spirit of co-operation so that it might consider to what extent it would be possible for it to grant to Mr Tiznado Rosas authorization to return temporarily to Chile, in accordance with the procedure established by it in this matter;

(iii) to inform the author of the need to use the judicial means of redress in order to ascertain the reasons for the refusal with which he had met and to convey to him the tenor of the statements made by the representative of the Chilean Government.

Spring 1982 session of the Committee on Conventions and Recommendations (114th session of the Executive Board)[5]

429. The author of the communication, Mr Víctor Xavier Tiznado Rosas, a refugee in Belgium since December 1973, complains that the Chilean Ministry of the Interior rejected the request allegedly submitted to it in April 1978 that he might be authorized to return to Chile. The Chilean authorities claimed that their refusal was based on reasons of national security, although it is said that no proceedings had been instituted against Mr Tiznado Rosas and no sentence pronounced on him. He is a doctor by profession, having completed his specialization in clinical biology, and states that he has devoted a great deal of his time to research work which should be continued in his native cultural environment. He says that in January 1981 he submitted another request in the hope of visiting his sick mother, aged 68.

430. At the spring 1981 session, the Committee decided to suspend consideration of the admissibility of this communication, to inform the author of the means of redress available to him according to the information given by the representative of the Chilean Government, and to appeal to the goodwill of that government in assessing the present case.[6]

431. On 27 August 1981 the author sent a letter to the Secretariat [...], enclosing a photocopy of the negative reply given by the Chilean Consulate in Antwerp (Belgium) to his request of 6 January 1981 for permission to return to Chile. He added that this reply, for which no reasons were given, was not, in his view, in keeping with the standards laid down by the Chilean Government itself since, in the note drawn up at the request of the Committee on Conventions and Recommendations by the representative of the Chilean Government it was stated that "the Ministry of the Interior may refuse such authorization for reasons connected with the security of the state, in which case it shall state the reasons for its refusal" (underlined by the author).

432. At the autumn 1981 session, the representative of the Chilean Government pointed out to the Committee that, although Mr Tiznado Rosas had been informed of the means of redress available to him, he had not used them. He stated that the best way of resolving such situations was, however, to take advantage of the existing ju-

[5] See document 114 EX/38 PRIV., paras. 429-440; see also document 114 EX/CR/HR/2.
[6] See document 112 EX/30 PRIV., para. 90 (*supra*, p. 792).

dicial remedies, which could be done on behalf of the person concerned by any person residing in Chile, without its even being necessary to have the assistance of a lawyer. He added lastly that the government was obliged to inform the relevant court of the reasons for its refusal and that, consequently, by applying to that court, the plaintiff would be notified of those reasons.

433. One member of the Committee observed that the Committee was faced here with a case similar to many others, which proceeded as follows: Chilean citizens deprived of the right to return to their country asked for permission to do so and such permission was refused them by the Chilean Ministry of the Interior, this being notified to them by the Consuls. This decision could be submitted to judicial review in the course of which the person concerned would at least be informed of the reasons for the refusal and possibly obtain authorization to return to Chile. He consequently considered that this procedure was clear and that, at all events, the Committee should suggest to the author of the communication that he avail himself of the judicial means of redress.

434. Other members stated that they would be of the same opinion as the previous speaker were there no new element involved. However, in this particular case, the author had submitted a second request to return in order to see his elderly and ailing mother. He recalled that, in comparable cases, the Chilean Government had granted to those concerned authorization to return for 60 days, thereby enabling them to settle their problems far more easily on the spot, and that financial assistance had even been offered by the Office of the High Commissioner for Refugees in cases where there were financial difficulties standing in the way of this temporary return.

435. The representative of the Chilean Government confirmed that the existence of purely judicial means of redress did not preclude the extraordinary means of redress afforded by recourse to his good offices on humanitarian grounds and that he was prepared to take action along those lines if the Committee so requested him.

436. One member expressed surprise at the fact that a judicial procedure was necessary in order to know the reason for a governmental decision. For the information of the Committee, the representative of the Director-General stated that there was no international normative text that made it binding on government authorities to state the reasons for decisions such as that in question in this communication.

437. After discussion the Committee decided:[7]

(i) to suspend consideration of this communication until the present session;

---

[7] See document 113 EX/38 PRIV., para. 155 (*supra*, pp. 794-795).

(ii) to appeal to the Chilean Government's spirit of co-operation so that it might consider to what extent it would be possible for it to grant to Mr Tiznado Rosas authorization to return temporarily to Chile, in accordance with the procedure established by it in this matter;

(iii) to inform the author of the need to use the judicial means of redress in order to ascertain the reasons for the refusal with which he had met and to convey to him the tenor of the statements made by the representative of the Chilean Government.

438. At the present session, the representative of the government concerned stated that, so far as he knew, Mr Tiznado Rosas had still not had recourse either to administrative or to judicial means of redress, but had applied to the Consulate again. He thus seemed to have misunderstood the information given him by the Secretariat following the Committee's decision at its [autumn 1981] session. As the Consulate had no authority in such matters, applications for reconsideration had to be sent direct to the Ministry of the Interior in Santiago, the parties concerned requesting permission from that Ministry to return to Chile permanently or, failing that, temporarily. In the event of a refusal, or if no reply were received within a reasonable time-limit (which might be put at about 30 days), they could use the judicial means of redress and file an application for *amparo*. The representative of the government concerned explained that this procedure produced satisfactory/results if it were used correctly.

439. The Chairman of the Committee said that the author of the communication should be given detailed information concerning the procedure and suggested that consideration of the case should therefore be suspended. While agreeing with that proposal, one member pointed out that although the person in question had not exhausted the domestic remedies available, the Committee was not taking a decision on the admissibility of the communication.

440. The Committee therefore *decided*:

(i) to communicate to the author the detailed information supplied by the representative of the Chilean Government;

(ii) to defer consideration of the admissibility of the communication until the next session.

No. 321/81 **Chile**

Autumn 1982 session of the Committee on Conventions and Recommendations (115th session of the Executive Board)[8]

23. This communication concerns the case of a Chilean refugee, Mr Víctor Xavier Tiznado Rosas, a doctor, whose request for permission to return to Chile, made in April 1978, was apparently rejected by the Ministry of the Interior for reasons of national security, and whose second request, made in January 1981, for permission to visit his mother who is sick and very old, also appears to have been rejected.

24. This communication was examined by the Committee for the first time at the spring 1981 session.

25. The representative of the government concerned pointed out at the autumn 1981 session and at the spring 1982 session that Mr Tiznado Rosas had not used the existing means of redress, either administrative or legal, and did not appear to have fully understood the information that he had given him through the Committee and the Secretariat.

26. On 27 July, the Secretariat received from Mr Víctor Xavier Tiznado Rosas a letter, together with a set of documents, from which it emerged that Mr Tiznado Rosas's sister had submitted, on her brother's behalf, an application for *amparo* (enforcement of constitutional rights). This the Appeal Court in Santiago had declared inadmissible on 24 December 1981, a judgement confirmed by the Supreme Court on 5 January 1982.

27. At the autumn 1982 session, the representative of the Chilean Government pointed out that from the information provided by Mr Tiznado Rosas, the Committee could see that such applications were in fact considered. He then said that in March 1981, a new Constitution had come into force in Chile, which extended the scope of application of the remedies existing in cases such as that of Mr Tiznado Rosas. To this, further laws and administrative and judicial jurisprudence had been added. Thus on 12 April 1982, the Supreme Court had adopted a decision which gave the Appeal Courts very strict instructions on how they should deal with such appeals, particularly when evaluating and examining the facts advanced by the Ministry of the Interior with a view to having the decisions which it had taken upheld. He added that his wish to co-operate with the Committee had led him to re-examine and add to the note on applications for *amparo* which he had sent the Secretariat in 1980. He thought therefore that Dr Tiznado Rosas should submit a new application but

[8] See document 115 EX/28 PRIV., paras. 23-28; see also documents 115 EX/CR/HR/2 and Add.

stressed that, if this application were to succeed, it was essential that it should fully comply both in form and substance with all the suggestions contained in this new note and that it should make particular reference to the decision of the Supreme Court. He said that such action was not part of the normal work of a government representative, but he wanted to see that justice was done, although obviously he could not guarantee the success of any such application.

28. Considering that there still existed possible remedies, of which the author of the communication would be informed in the note on this subject written by the representative of the government concerned, the Committee *decided*:

(i) to convey to the author the above-mentioned note and all the information provided by the representative of the Chilean Government;

(ii) to defer consideration of the admissibility of this communication until its next session.

Spring 1983 session of the Committee on Conventions and Recommendations (116th session of the Executive Board)[9]

12. This communication concerns the case of a Chilean refugee, Mr Víctor Xavier Tiznado Rosas, a doctor, whose request for permission to return to Chile, made in April 1978, was apparently rejected by the Ministry of the Interior for reasons of national security, and whose second request, made in January 1981, for permission to visit his mother who is sick and very old, also appears to have been rejected. This communication was examined by the Committee for the first time at the spring 1981 session.

13. The author replied by letter dated 24 February 1983 to the Secretariat's letter informing him of the decision taken by the Committee at its autumn 1982 session. He described the various vain attempts that he had made to have his case considered by the Chilean authorities. With regard to the application for *amparo* in particular, he said that his lawyer had not thought it worth submitting a new application, being of the opinion that it would go the same way as the preceding ones because, in his view, the position of the courts had not changed.

14. At the present session, the representative of the Chilean Government said that he had informed the Committee at the [autumn 1982 session] of the way in which applications for *amparo* were to be submitted, and that in doing so he had actually o-

[9] See document 116 EX/48 PRIV., paras. 12-19; see also document 116 EX/CR/HR/2.

verstepped his role by giving very precise instructions, which the individual concerned, however, apparently preferred to ignore. Lastly, the author's assertion that the commission had declined to consider his case did not make sense because the commission's role had been to establish a procedure and not to settle individuai cases.

15. Two members of the Committee pointed out that, according to Mr Tiznado Rosas himself, he had nothing to do with education [...].[10] He was in fact a doctor and it was hard to see the relevance of the case to Unesco's fields of competence.

16. The representative of the Director-General said that as it was the fifth time that the communication had come before the Committee, it would be difficult at that stage to declare it inadmissible on the grounds of incompetence, especially in view of the fact that the government concerned had not raised that objection *in limine litis* as it might have done.

17. One of the previous speakers took the floor again to say that, in his opinion a decision to suspend a communication was in no way binding on the Committee for the future.

18. The representative of the Chilean Government said that the authorities in his country took a very broad view of the competence of the Committee since they were motivated by the humanitarian aspects of the cases examined rather than by any other consideration.

19. After a brief discussion, the Committee *decided*:

> (i) to defer consideration of the admissibility of the communication until the next session and, in the interim,
>
> (ii) to instruct the Secretariat to inform the author once again of the action he should take, particularly in the light of the statements made by the representative of the government concerned.

---

[10] See document 115 EX/CR/HR/2 Add., para. 5.

Chile **No. 321/81**

Autumn 1983 session of the Committee on Conventions and Recommendations (117th session of the Executive Board)[11]

9. The author of the communication, a doctor and a Chilean refugee, states that the request for permission to return to Chile which he claims to have made in April 1978, was apparently rejected by the Ministry of the Interior for reasons of national security, and that a second request, made in January 1981, for permission to visit his mother who is sick and very old, also appears to have been rejected. This communication was examined by the Committee for the first time at the spring 1981 session.

10. At the present session, the representative of the government concerned said that in this case, as in many others, the author had not exhausted all the remedies available to him, as he had several times been asked to do by the Secretariat of Unesco. He informed the Committee that as a result of measures taken by him personally, Mr V. X. Tiznado had nevertheless been given permission to return to Chile, and that the complainant's name was included on a list of persons authorized to return to Chile which had appeared in the Chilean official gazette for August. He added that that list had been routinely sent to all Chilean Consulates abroad.

11. Mr. Víctor Tiznado Rosas having informed the Secretariat that he had in fact received authorization to return to Chile, the Committee *decided* to consider his case as settled and to strike it from the list of communications.

[11] See document 117 EX/18 PRIV., paras. 9-11; see also document 117 EX/CR/HR/2.

No. 322/81

Concerning *Bolivia*
Case of *Violations of human rights in Bolivia following the events of 17 July 1980**

Communication of 4 August 1980 submitted by
National Committee for the Defence of Democracy
in Bolivia

Spring 1981 session of the Committee on Conventions and Recommendations (112th session of the Executive Board)[1]

44. The National Committee for the Defence of Democracy in Bolivia (CONADE), the author of the communication, supported by Mr Joe Nordman in his capacity as President of the International Association of Democratic Lawyers (a non-governmental organization having consultative status with Unesco) and as a person with reliable knowledge of the alleged facts, since he was on the spot from 11 to 16 August 1980, claims that since the events of 17 July 1980 a large number of political leaders, trade unionists, academics, teachers, clergy and journalists have been arrested, injured, tortured and killed; some are said to have been abducted and to have disappeared. According to the author, not only have political parties and trade unions been banned but violations of human rights in the fields of education, science, culture and information have attained alarming proportions:

(*a*) the universities are said to have been closed and occupied by the army, so that the future of 40,000 students is in jeopardy; several university lecturers, including the Vice-Chancellor of the University of Cochabamba, have allegedly been arrested and others, including the Dean of the La Paz Faculty of Medicine, have been forced to seek safety in flight; the Confederation of Bolivian Universities has apparently been dissolved and its leaders imprisoned

* From the Committee's spring 1982 session, this communication was being referred to as case of *Violations of human rights in Bolivia* and at its spring 1983 session as case of *Alleged violations of human rights in Bolivia*.

[1] See document 112 EX/30 PRIV., paras. 44-48; see also document 112 EX/CR/HR/3.

or driven into exile; scientists and members of the liberal professions have, according to the author, suffered the same fate;

(*b*) works of art, including a fresco by the painter Pantoja, have allegedly been destroyed;

(*c*) the author claims that the radio stations of the Bolivian Labour Confederation (COB) and of the Church have been wrecked, that the press is censored and that most foreign journalists have been arrested and expelled.

45. In a letter dated 4 May 1981 addressed to the Deputy Director-General of Unesco, the Permanent Delegate of Bolivia stated that the file on the communication he had received contained no relevant document involving the provisions of paragraph 14 (*a*) of 104 EX/Decision 3.3, that the photocopies it contained were illegible and that in these circumstances he was not in a position to take part in the work of the Committee.

46. The representative of the Director-General said that the entire contents of the file on the communication had been transmitted to the government concerned in the usual way, and that it was possible that there were photocopies which were difficult to read.

47. While not objecting to the idea of deferring consideration of the communication, a member of the Committee pointed out that, whatever the case might be, such deferment should not constitute a precedent in favour of the governments concerned by communications.

48. After an exchange of views, the Committee *decided*:

(i) to defer consideration of the admissibility of the communication until the next session;

(ii) to ask the Executive Board to request the Director-General to call the attention of the Bolivian Government to the importance attached by the Committee to the presence of its representative, and to inform it that the communication would be examined at the next session even in the absence of any Bolivian representative.

Bolivia **No. 322/81**

Autumn 1981 session of the Committee on Conventions and Recommendations (113th session of the Executive Board)[2]

72. Of the three communications concerning Bolivia,[3] the first was submitted for consideration by the Committee at its [spring 1981] session and the other two are new communications.

73. The National Committee for the Defence of Democracy in Bolivia (CONADE), the author of the [first] communication, supported by Mr Joe Nordman in his capacity as President of the International Association of Democratic Lawyers (a non-governmental organization having consultative status with Unesco) and as a person with reliable knowledge of the alleged facts, since he was on the spot from 11 to 16 August 1980, claims that since the events of 17 July 1980 a large number of political leaders, trade unionists, academics, teachers, clergy and journalists have been arrested, injured, tortured and killed; some are said to have been abducted and to have disappeared. According to the author, not only have political parties and trade unions been banned but violations of human rights in the fields of education, science, culture and information have attained alarming proportions:

(*a*) the universities are said to have been closed and occupied by the army, so that the future of 40,000 students is in jeopardy; several university lecturers, including the Vice-Chancellor of the University of Cochabamba, have allegedly been arrested and others, including the Dean of the La Paz Faculty of Medicine, have been forced to seek safety in flight; the Confederation of Bolivian Universities has apparently been dissolved and its leaders imprisoned or driven into exile; scientists and members of the liberal professions have, according to the author, suffered the same fate;

(*b*) works of art, including a fresco by the painter Pantoja, have allegedly been destroyed;

(*c*) the author claims that the radio stations of the Bolivian Labour Confederation (COB) and of the Church have been wrecked, that the press is censored and that most foreign journalists have been arrested and expelled.

---

[2] See document 113 EX/38 PRIV., paras. 72-107; see also documents 113 EX/CR/HR/2 and 113 EX/CR/HR/3 Add and Add.2.

[3] Communications No. 322/81 concerning *Bolivia*, case of *Violations of human rights in Bolivia following the events of 17 July 1980*, No. 359/81 concerning *Bolivia*, case of *Jorge Baldibieso* et al., and No. 397/81 concerning *Bolivia*, case of *Violation of human rights in Bolivia*, were being considered together.

No. 322/81 **Bolivia**

74. At the [spring 1981] session, in a letter dated 4 May 1981 addressed to the Deputy Director-General of Unesco, the Permanent Delegate of Bolivia stated that the file on the communication he had received contained no relevant document making it possible for him to appear before the Committee in accordance with the provisions of paragraph 14 (*a*) of 104 EX/Decision 3.3.

75. The representative of the Director-General said that the entire contents of the file on the communication had been transmitted to the government concerned in the usual way, and that it was possible that there were photocopies which were difficult to read.

76. After an exchange of views, the Committee decided:[4]

(i) to defer consideration of the admissibility of the communication until the present session;

(ii) to ask the Executive Board to request the Director-General to draw the attention of the Bolivian Government to the importance attached by the Committee to the presence of its representative, and to inform it that the communication would be examined at the next session even in the absence of any Bolivian representative.

77. The author of the [second] communication, Mr Víctor Hugo Nin Saavedra, a student of Bolivian nationality, a delegate of the Bolivian University Confederation and a member of CONADE, describes himself as a person with reliable knowledge of the alleged violations. He is the signatory of the seven communication forms, but in his covering letter of 15 July 1981 he acknowledges receipt of the Secretariat's standard letter of 15 April 1981 on behalf of Mr Jaime Paz Zamora, Vice-President of the Government of National Unity (GUN), who was the initiator of the communication.

A. *Case of Jorge Baldibieso, José Luis Suárez, Gonzalo Barrón and Ricardo Navarro*

78. The author relates that on 15 January 1981, between 4.30 and 5.30 p.m., a commando of regular and paramilitary troops raided a house in La Paz where a secret meeting of opposition leaders, members of the Movement of the Revolutionary Left (MIR) was being held. Finding themselves surrounded, the nine persons present attempted to give themselves up. The soldiers opened fire, wounding some of them, although nobody was armed. The others were arrested, tortured and finally mur-

[4] See document 112 EX/30 PRIV., para. 48 (*supra*, p. 804).

dered. The latter group included: Jorge Baldibieso, an engineer and student leader of the Local University Federation (FUL - ORURO), José Luis Suárez, father of two, a sociologist and a teacher at the University of La Paz and in various military and police institutes, Gonzalo Barrón, father of two, an architect and leader of the Bolivian University Confederation and Ricardo Navarro, who had one daughter and was an engineer, a lecturer at the University of La Paz and leader of the Local University Federation (FUL) of La Paz.

79. The purpose and aim given by the author in all four cases are to induce the Bolivian Military Junta to provide a detailed explanation for the massacre in order to establish where responsibility lies. The Permanent Council of Bishops, Cardinal Clemente Maurer, the 16 bishops of the church hierarchy and the Archbishop of La Paz, Mgr Manrique, are said to have made a similar request to the Military Junta.

80. The author would also like the Executive Board to back the establishment of an independent international commission to look into the circumstances leading to the murders.

B. *Case of Marcelo Quiroga Santa Cruz*

81. According to the author, on 17 July 1980, between 12 and 12.30 p.m., paramilitary commandos in ambulances belonging to the National Social Security Fund surrounded and attacked the headquarters of the trade union, Central Obrera Boliviana (COB), where a meeting of the National Committee for the Defence of Democracy [in Bolivia] (CONADE) was being held. Political, trade union and religious leaders attending the meeting were taken prisoner. When one of the attackers recognized Mr Marcelo Quiroga Santa Cruz, the leader of the Bolivian Socialist Party, he shot him in cold blood. The wounded man was taken to the Miraflores military barracks. Nothing further was heard of him until his death was announced by the Junta in an official communiqué.

82. The purpose and aim of the communication are to demand that the Military Junta provide a clear and detailed account of the circumstances which led to the murder of Mr Marcelo Quiroga Santa Cruz and explain why there was no autopsy and why the body of the victim was not handed over to his relatives.

C. *Case of Elías Rafael Flores*

83. The alleged victim, Mr E. R. Flores, was a sociologist at the University of La Paz. Arrested at the end of September 1980, he was taken first to the Miraflores military prison, then to the Ministry of the Interior and finally to the Departamento de Orden Político (DOP) at the beginning of October. He was last seen by his relatives

at the Ministry of the Interior and by the prisoners sharing his cell in the DOP on 18 October. Since that date his whereabouts are unknown. The military government denies that he is being held officially.

84. The purpose and aim of the communication are to obtain a clear explanation from the military government for the disappearance of Mr E. R. Flores and to request the Executive Board's support for setting up an independent international commission to investigate incidents of this kind which have been a common occurrence in Bolivia since July 1980.

85. As regards these six cases, the space for information concerning domestic remedies sought is left blank in one case (Jorge Baldibieso) and in the other five cases the author claims that it cannot be filled in because the country has no lawfully constituted administration but only a government based on violence.

86. It is stated that no international authority was approached in the first four cases but that the case of Mr Quiroga Santa Cruz was submitted to sessions 127-128 of the Inter-Parliamentary Union and that of Mr. E. R. Flores to Amnesty International.

D. *Silvia Natalia Rivera*

87. Mrs Silvia Natalia Rivera, a sociologist, is said to have been imprisoned and ill-treated (she allegedly suffered a broken rib) between 31 May 1980 and 1 June 1980. On 18 April 1980 she was dismissed from the University where she held the post of assistant professor. According to the author, all her research material - manuscripts, files, books and tape recordings representing five years' research in the field of rural sociology - were confiscated.

88. The representations made by the university authorities apparently led to the release of Mrs Rivera. The action taken by her agent to recover her documents, however, was of no avail.

89. It is stated that no international body was approached concerning the affair.

90. The purpose and aim of the communication are to secure protection for the alleged victim's intellectual right to the confiscated research material and manuscripts to recover the documents in question and to secure respect for freedom of thought in Bolivia.

91. The [third] communication, presented by Mr Joe Nordmann, President of the International Association of Democratic Lawyers and co-author with CONADE (Na-

tional Committee for the Defence of Democracy in Bolivia) of [the first communication], is a continuation of the latter.

92. It includes the following documents:

[1] *A document entitled "Nine months of repression in Bolivia"*

This report, drawn up in March 1981 by the Ad Hoc National Executive Committee of the Permanent Assembly for Human Rights in Bolivia, accuses the authorities of having resorted to repression and terror as instruments of government since the events of 17 July 1980:

Chapter I gives a general description of General García Meza's regime;

Chapter II deals with the destruction of the trade unions, especially the attack on the headquarters of the Central Obrera Boliviana (COB) and the arrest and murder of a number of trade union and political leaders, members of CONADE, clergymen and journalists;

Chapter III describes the harassment and "muzzling" of the written, spoken and audio-visual media, both national and international: attacks on the offices of newspapers and magazines, the destruction or closing-down of radio stations, the arrest or expulsion of journalists, censorship, etc.;

Chapter IV deals with the persecution of religious institutions and the clergy.

[2] *A letter dated 14 April 1981 from the Pemanent Assembly for Human Rights in Bolivia and a letter dated 15 April 1981 from UNITAS (Unión Nacional de Instituciones para el Trabajo de Acción Social) accompanied by a document entitled "Evidence from the Information and Documentation Centre on Bolivia (CIDOB) concerning violations of human rights in that country"*

93. These documents deal with violations of human rights in the field of science, education and culture and, in particular, with the destruction of the CIDOB and the reprisals against persons working there (the Centre was established in 1977 and was officially recognized by the Office of the President of the Republic); the CIDOB asks, *inter alia*, for Unesco's intervention to prevent irreparable damage to the cultural heritage of the Bolivian people.

No. 322/81 **Bolivia**

[3] *A document describing the situation of the Bolivian universities since the events of July 1980*

94. A process of democratization of the universities and a new organizational and administrative policy had been initiated shortly before the events of 17 July 1980. Since then the universities have been occupied by the army, with controls and searches several times a day, constant harassment of the teaching and other staff and of students, an atmosphere of tension and fear, with each individual being required to submit a curriculum vitae covering the past 10 years to the military authorities, mass dismissals, rectors being replaced by military commissars and the future of tens of thousands of students at stake.

[4] *Eight communication forms*

95. Seven of these forms relate to the seven cases described in [the second communication] since they cover the same facts and concern the same alleged victims.

96. The eighth form describes the case of Mr Víctor Hugo Nin Saavedra (author of [the second communication]), who reportedly left Bolivia in normal circumstances on 8 September 1978 to continue his studies.

97. He is said to have renewed his passport at the Bolivian Consulate in Paris in 1979. In June 1980 he mislaid the passport and reported the matter to the Consulate. He was issued with a safe-conduct renewable every three months, pending a decision by the Ministry of the Interior. Some time later, the Ministry sent a cable turning down his application for a new passport and thus preventing him from returning to his country.

98. It is claimed that no domestic means of redress were available.

99. It appears that the matter has not been referred to any international body apart from Unesco.

100. According to the author, the aim and purpose of the communication are to obtain an explanation from the Bolivian Government for its stance on the matter and to have a passport issued on behalf of the alleged victim.

101. At the present session, the Committee noted again that the government concerned had not sent a representative to take part in the discussion concerning the communications.

Bolivia **No. 322/81**

102. Some members of the Committee considered that it was inappropriate to postpone consideration of these communications, firstly because it would be wrong to give the impression of favouring a state that decided not to co-operate with the Committee, and secondly because in the individual cases concerned, the tragic situation of the alleged victims might have worsened in the meantime.

103. One member of the Committee suggested that it might be advisable to declare the three communications automatically admissible and to initiate an examination of their substance at the next session.

104. Some members of the Committee pointed out that a new government had just taken over power in Bolivia. According to the latest information available, there had been an amnesty for political prisoners and a review of the curfew. In addition, the universities had either already been reopened or would be reopened shortly.

105. In practice, the Committee had declared a case automatically admissible on one occasion only, the government concerned having, however, been advised in advance that such a decision would be taken even if it did not send a representative to the Committee's meeting. In any case, a number of Committee members said that the application of 104 EX/Decision 3.3 should not imply any idea of condemnation, since the Committee aspired in all cases to reach a practical solution.

106. After an exchange of views, several members of the Committee stated that consideration of the three communications should in their view, be suspended, and the Committee accordingly *decided*:

> (i) to defer examination of the admissibility of the three communications until such time as the Committee should receive additional information, both from the Government of Bolivia and from the authors of the communications in question;
>
> (ii) to ask the Executive Board to request the Director-General to advise the government concerned, once again, that in the Committee's view it would be most desirable for a representative of that government to attend the next session of the Committee, it being understood that the admissibility of the aforesaid communications would be examined at that session notwithstanding the absence of such a representative.

107. The Committee *took note* of a document received at a late date by the Secretariat [...].[5] This was a letter from the Permanent Delegate of Bolivia to Unesco recall-

[5] See document 113 EX/CR/HR/3 Add.2.

ing the terms of his letter of 4 May 1981 and emphasizing that the communications which had been submitted to the Organization were politically inspired.

Spring 1982 session of the Committee on Conventions and Recommendations (114th session of the Executive Board)[6]

347. These four communications[7] concern alleged violations of human rights in Bolivia following the events of 17 July 1980. The Committee has decided to consider them jointly.[8]

348. The National Committee for the Defence of Democracy in Bolivia (CONADE), the author of the [first] communication, supported by Mr Joe Nordmann in his capacity as President of the International Association of Democratic Lawyers (a non-governmental organization having consultative status with Unesco) and as a person with reliable knowledge of the alleged facts, since he was on the spot from 11 to 16 August 1980, claims that since the events of 17 July 1980 a large number of political leaders, trade unionists, academics, teachers, clergy and journalists have been arrested, injured, tortured and killed; some are said to have been abducted and to have disappeared. According to the author, not only have political parties and trade unions been banned but violations of human rights in the fields of education, science, culture and information have attained alarming proportions:

(*a*) the universities are said to have been closed and occupied by the army, so that the future of 40,000 students is in jeopardy; several university lecturers, including the Vice-Chancellor of the University of Cochabamba, have allegedly been arrested and others, including the Dean of the La Paz Faculty of Medicine, have been forced to seek safety in flight; the Confederation of Bolivian Universities has apparently been dissolved and its leaders imprisoned or driven into exile; scientists and members of the liberal professions have, according to the author, suffered the same fate;

(*b*) works of art, including a fresco by the painter Pantoja, have allegedly been destroyed;

---

[6] See document 114 EX/38 PRIV., paras. 347-399; see also documents 114 EX/CR/HR/2 and Add. and 114 EX/CR/HR/3 Add.
[7] Communications No. 322/81 concerning *Bolivia*, case of *Violations of human rights in Bolivia*, No. 359/81 concerning *Bolivia*, case of *Violations of human rights in Bolivia*, No. 397/81 concerning *Bolivia*, case of *Violations of human rights in Bolivia*, and No. 407/81 concerning *Bolivia*, case of *Violations of human rights in Bolivia*.
[8] See document 114 EX/38 PRIV., para. 36 (*infra*, p. 1029), communication No. 407/81 concerning *Bolivia*, case of *Jorge Baldibieso* et al.

(*c*) the author claims that the radio stations of the Bolivian Labour Confederation (COB) and of the Church have been wrecked, that the press is censored and that most foreign journalists have been arrested and expelled.

349. At the [spring] 1981 session, in a letter dated 4 May 1981 addressed to the Deputy Director-General of Unesco, the Permanent Delegate of Bolivia stated that the file on the communication he had received contained no relevant document.

350. The representative of the Director-General said that the entire contents of the file on the communication had been transmitted to the government concerned in the usual way, and that it was possible that there were photocopies of photocopies which were difficult to read.

351. After an exchange of views, the Committee decided:[9]

(i) to defer consideration of the admissibility of the communication until the following session;

(ii) to ask the Executive Board to request the Director-General to draw the attention of the Bolivian Government to the importance attached by the Committee to the presence of its representative, and to inform it that the communication would be examined at the next session even if no Bolivian representative attended.

352. The author of [the second communication] is Mr Víctor Hugo Nin Saavedra, a student of Bolivian nationality, a delegate of the Bolivian University Confederation and a member of CONADE.

353. The author of [the fourth communication] is Mrs Ruth Navarro, a sociologist of Bolivian nationality.

A. *Case of Jorge Baldibieso, José Luis Suárez, Gonzalo Barrón, Ricardo Navarro and Ramiro Velasco*

354. On 15 January 1981, between 4.30 and 5.30 p.m., a commando of regular and paramilitary troops allegedly raided a house in La Paz where a secret meeting of opposition leaders, members of the Movement of the Revolutionary Left (MIR) was being held. Finding themselves surrounded, the nine persons present reportedly attempted to give themselves up. It is claimed that the soldiers opened fire on some of them, although none was armed. The others were allegedly arrested, tortured and fi-

[9] See document 112 EX/30 PRIV., para. 48 (*supra*, p. 804).

nally murdered. The latter group is said to have included: Jorge Baldibieso, an engineer and student leader of the Local University Federation (FUL-ORURO); José Luis Suárez, father of two, a sociologist and a teacher at the University of La Paz and in various military and police institutes; Gonzalo Barrón, father of two, an architect and leader of the Bolivian University Confederation; Ricardo Navarro, who had one daughter and was an engineer, a lecturer at the University of La Paz and leader of the Local University Federation (FUL) of La Paz; and Ramiro Velasco, an economist and professor at the Catholic University of La Paz.

355. The authors of both communications ask that a detailed explanation of this massacre be provided so that it may be established where responsibility lies.

356. They also wish support to be given for the establishment of an independent international commission to look into the circumstances leading to the event of 15 January 1981.

B. *Case of Marcelo Quiroga Santa Cruz*

357. On 17 July 1980, between 12 and 12.30 p.m. paramilitary commandos in ambulances belonging to the National Social Security Fund allegedly surrounded and seized the headquarters of the trade union, Central Obrera Boliviana (COB), where a meeting of the National Committee for the Defence of Democracy [in Bolivia] (CONADE) was being held. Political, trade union and religious leaders attending the meeting were reportedly taken prisoner. One of the attackers is said to have recognized Mr Marcelo Quiroga Santa Cruz, the leader of the Bolivian Socialist Party, and to have shot him in cold blood. The wounded man was apparently then taken to the Miraflores military barracks. His death was announced, it is claimed, by the Junta in an official communiqué.

358. The authors of both communications ask for a clear and detailed explanation of the circumstances in which Mr Marcelo Quirogo Santa Cruz died. They further wish to know why no autopsy was carried out and why the body was not returned to his family.

C. *Case of Elías Rafael Flores*

359. Mr Elías Rafael Flores, a sociologist at the University of La Paz, was allegedly arrested at the end of September 1980. He is reported to have been taken first to the Miraflores military prison, then to the Ministry of the Interior and finally to the Departamento de Orden Político (DOP) at the beginning of October. He was apparently last seen by his relatives at the Ministry of the Interior and by the prisoners sharing his cell in the DOP on 18 October. Since that date his whereabouts are said to be un-

known. The military government has reportedly denied that he is being held officially.

360. Mr Nin Saavedra requests an explanation of Mr Elías Rafael Flores's disappearance. He also requests the Executive Board's support for the setting up of an independent international commission to investigate incidents of this kind which have been a common occurrence in Bolivia since July 1980.

D. *Case of Silvia Natalia Rivera*

361. Mrs Silvia Natalia Rivera, a sociologist, is said to have been imprisoned and ill-treated (she allegedly suffered a broken rib). This is said to have occurred between 31 May 1980 and 1 June 1980. On 18 April 1980 she was allegedly dismissed from the university where she held the post of assistant professor. According to the author, all her research material - manuscripts, files, books and tape recordings, representing five years' research in the field of rural sociology - was confiscated.

362. The representations made by the university authorities apparently led to the release of Mrs Rivera. The action taken by her agent to recover her research documents, however, was of no avail.

363. Mr Nin Saavedra asks that intellectual rights in the confiscated research material and manuscripts be protected, that the documents be returned to the alleged victim, and that the right to research and freedom of thought in Bolivia be respected.

E. *The Information and Documentation Centre on Bolivia (CIDOB)*

364. It is alleged that, on 28 July 1980, a paramilitary group invaded the headquarters of CIDOB and seized all furniture, equipment and documents on the premises. In a CIDOB document attached to the communication, it is stated that the disappearance of all the centre's property represents an incalculable loss not only to CIDOB but also to the country's cultural heritage, since the ransacked library allegedly contained unique specimens, original documents and manuscripts. Some items of the property, a list of which is attached to the communication, are reportedly now at the Ministry of the Interior, while others have allegedly been destroyed, sold or distributed to those who perpetrated the ransacking. Some members of the staff were allegedly subjected to such harassment that they have chosen to leave the country.

365. Mrs Ruth Navarro requests the Bolivian Government to explain the reasons for the raid and to restore the equipment, documents and archives seized.

No. 322/81 **Bolivia**

366. The Unión Nacional de Instituciones para el Trabajo de Acción Social (UNITAS), of which CIDOB was a member, and the Asamblea Permanente de los Derechos Humanos of Bolivia support this communication through letters addressed to the Committee. The dossier also includes documents containing general information on Bolivia.

367. [The third] communication, presented by Mr Joe Nordmann, co-author with CONADE of [the first communication], is a continuation of the latter. It includes the following documents:

[1] *A document entitled "Nine months of repression in Bolivia"*

368. This report, drawn up in March 1981 by the Ad Hoc National Executive Committee of the Permanent Assembly for Human Rights in Bolivia, accuses the authorities of having resorted to repression and terror as instruments of government since the events of 17 July 1980.

[2] *A letter dated 14 April 1981 from the Permanent Assembly for Human Rights in Bolivia and a letter dated 15 April 1981 from UNITAS (Unión Nacional de Instituciones para el Trabajo de Acción Social) accompanied by a document entitled "Evidence from the Information and Documentation Centre on Bolivia (CIDOB) concerning violations of human rights in that country"*

369. These documents deal with violations of human rights in the fields of science, education and culture and, in particular, with the destruction of the CIDOB and the reprisals against persons working there.

[3] *A document describing the situation of the Bolivian universities since the events of July 1980*

370. A process of democratization of the universities and a new organizational and administrative policy had been initiated shortly before the events of 17 July 1980. Since then the universities have been occupied by the army, with controls and searches several times a day, harassment of the teaching and other staff and of students, an atmosphere of tension and fear, with each individual being required to submit a curriculum vitae covering the past 10 years to the military authorities, mass dismissals, rectors being replaced by soldiers, and the future of tens of thousands of students at stake.

Bolivia **No. 322/81**

[4] *Eight communication forms*

371. Seven of these forms relate to the seven cases described in [the third communication] since they cover the same facts and concern the same alleged victims (Jorge Baldibieso, José Luis Suárez, Gonzalo Barrón, Ricardo Navarro, Marcelo Quiroga Santa Cruz, Elías Rafael Flores and Silvia Natalia Rivera).

372. The eighth form describes the case of Mr Víctor Hugo Nin Saavedra, who reportedly left Bolivia in normal circumstances on 8 September 1978 to continue his studies.

373. He is said to have renewed his passport at the Bolivian Consulate in Paris in 1979. In June 1980 he mislaid the passport and reported the matter to the Consulate. He was issued with a safe-conduct renewable every three months, pending a decision by the Ministry of the Interior. Some time later, the Ministry sent a cable turning down his application for a new passport and thus preventing him from returning to his country. An official of the Bolivian Embassy in Paris is furthermore said to have accused Mr Nin Saavedra of removing property belonging to the Embassy.

374. The author asks the Bolivian Government to explain its stance on the matter, and wishes a passport to be issued to the alleged victim.

375. At the [autumn] 1981 session, the Committee noted for the second time that the government concerned had not sent a representative to take part in the discussion concerning the communications.

376. Some members of the Committee considered that it was inappropriate to postpone consideration of these communications, firstly because it would be wrong to give the impression of favouring a state that decided not to co-operate with the Committee, and secondly because in the individual cases concerned, the tragic situation of the alleged victims might have worsened in the meantime.

377. One member of the Committee suggested that it might be advisable to declare the three communications automatically admissible and to initiate an examination of their substance at the present session.

378. Some members of the Committee pointed out that a new government had just taken over power in Bolivia. According to the latest information available, there had been an amnesty for political prisoners and a review of the curfew. In addition, the universities had either already been reopened or would be reopened shortly.

379. In practice, the Committee had declared a case automatically admissible on one occasion only, the government concerned having, however, been advised in advance that such a decision would be taken even if it did not send a representative to the Committee's meeting. In any case, the application of 104 EX/Decision 3.3 should not imply any idea of condemnation, since the Committee aspired in all cases to reach a practical solution.

380. After an exchange of views, the Committee decided:[10]

> (i) to defer consideration of the admissibility of [the three communications] until such time as the Committee should receive additional information, both from the Government of Bolivia and from the authors of the communications in question;
>
> (ii) to ask the Executive Board to request the Director-General to advise the government concerned, once again, that in the Committee's view it would be most desirable for a representative of that government to attend the present session of the Committee, it being understood that the admissibility of the a-foresaid communications would be examined at that session notwithstanding the absence of such a representative.

381. The Committee finally took note of a document received at a late date by the Secretariat [...]. This was a letter from the Permanent Delegate of Bolivia to Unesco recalling the terms of his letter of 4 May 1981 and emphasizing that the communications which had been submitted to the Organization were politically inspired.[11]

382. On 16 March 1982, the Secretariat received from the author of [the third communication], Mr Joe Nordmann, a letter transmitting three documents containing additional information:

> a copy of the report of the Inter-American Commission on Human Rights, dated 13 October 1981, on the human rights situation in Bolivia;
>
> a copy of a letter submitted by Mrs Marcelo Quiroga Santa Cruz to the [Organization of American States] Commission on Human Rights requesting that an investigation be carried out to establish the circumstances of her husband's death;

[10] See document 113 EX/38 PRIV., para. 106 (*supra*, p. 811).
[11] *Ibidem*, para. 107 (*supra*, p. 811).

a copy of the report by Mr Héctor Gros Espiell, Special Envoy of the United Nations Commission on Human Rights, dated 31 December 1981.[12]

383. Mr Joe Nordmann considers that General Torrelio's government "has been able to improve the human rights situation only at the level of official statements".

384. In writing his report, the Special Envoy took into account all the information which he obtained, including the items contained in the above-mentioned report of the Inter-American Commission on Human Rights. ("The Inter-American Commission on Human Rights has reached the conclusion that the Bolivian Government which assumed power on 17 July 1980 has seriously infringed the rights of the human person recognized by the American Convention on Human Rights ..."; " ... the Commission trusts that this change - the change in the Presidency of the Republic on 4 September 1981 - will lead to more open institutions, reflected in the holding, in the near future, of free general elections with the full participation of the various political parties, so that the Bolivian people may enjoy the benefits of a democratic, representative regime founded on the free expression of the popular will.")[13]

385. With regard to the matters to which these four communications refer, the Special Envoy's report contains the following information:

(*a*) *Concerning [the first communication]*

386. Mr Gros Espiell stated that the universities were reopened in April 1981 and that the competent authorities were preparing draft legislation granting the universities autonomy and establishing definitive regulations for university activities. (The Bolivian Government's comments on Mr Gros Espiell's report confirmed that a bill to this effect was actually in preparation.)

387. Concerning the problems related to information, the Special Envoy stated that he had taken up with the Bolivian authorities the question of the compulsory broadcasting of the state radio programmes. He reproduced in a footnote a passage from an appeal made on 18 July 1980 by the Archbishop of La Paz, Mgr Jorge Manrique, of which the following is an extract:

> ... I request compensation for the damage caused to the Church's broadcasting facilities, their immediate repair and the free expression of ideas on the

[12] See documents E/CN.4/1500 and Corr.1 and Add.1 (comments of the Bolivian Government).
[13] Translated [in the Committee's report] from the French, the authoritative English version not being available.

> airwaves. The premises of the newspaper *Presencia* must be evacuated and the feeedom of its circulation immediately ensured ...[14]

388. According to Mr Gros Espiell, "there is no doubt that serious violations of the right of free expression have taken place since 17 July 1980", and that, even though the most flagrant of these violations have ceased, "the press, radio and television broadcasting of all opinions and points of view are still seriously restricted".[15]

389. On the other hand, the Special Envoy observed that during his stay in Bolivia "the press was able to devote a considerable amount of space to political discussion and analysis" that "the newspapers carried many items on violations of human rights" and that "the visit of the Special Envoy received very wide coverage in the information media". He pointed out, however, that it had "in some cases been stated that these concessions were probably essentially temporary and limited to the period of the Special Envoy's visit". He had nevertheless wished to mention that "a climate of détente and openness prevailed during his visit", which was "in itself a clearly positive factor".[16]

(The comments of the Bolivian Government on the Special Envoy's report which relate to the question of freedom of expression contain the following passage:

> ... On 9 December 1981, the Bolivian Government suspended the system of compulsory broadcasting of the state radio programmes and made it clear that Bolivian broadcasting stations could operate freely provided only that they observed the laws regulating their activities.
>
> Moreover, it is incontrovertible that the government installed on 4 September 1981 has ensured full freedom of expression of the press, and during his visit to Bolivia the Special Envoy was able to observe that this freedom of expression was real.)[17]

390. The Special Envoy stated that he had received a list of persons under house arrest who had been freed or exiled, which list had been transmitted by the Bolivian Government to the [International Labour Organisation (ILO)] on 10 November 1980; comparison of that list with that of the alleged victims named in the communication, provides some information on five of those persons:

---

[14] *Idem.*
[15] *Idem.*
[16] *Idem.*
[17] *Idem.*

(i) Fr Julio Tumiri, priest, is under house arrest (the Special Envoy was able to meet him freely on 24 October 1981 at Cochabamba);

(ii) Cayetano Llobet, sociologist, was freed on 2 November 1980;

(iii) Liber Forti, theatre manager, and Oscar Peña Franco, journalist, have been exiled;

(iv) Gladis Selón Romero, leader of the Federation of Bolivian Women, was freed on 9 October 1980.

391. Mr Gros Espiell stated that the Minister of the Interior had informed him on 22 October 1981 that "there were at present no political prisoners nor any concentration camps in Bolivia and that only six persons were under house arrest"; the Minister's advisors had informed him, moreover, that "the remedy of *habeas corpus* was functioning effectively".[18]

(b) [The three other communications]

392. The many complaints of violation of human rights brought to the attention of the Special Envoy include the complaints concerning six of the nine alleged victims named in these three communications:

Marcelo Quiroga Santa Cruz (deputy and lawyer, leader of the Bolivian Socialist Party);

Ricardo Navarro (teacher);

Luis Suárez (teacher);

Jorge Baldibieso (engineer);

Gonzalo Barrón (leader of the Bolivian University Confederation);

Elías Rafael Flores (sociologist).

393. The Special Envoy described his report as a "comprehensive, objective and balanced evaluation of the facts alleged which takes account of all the information studied, specific circumstances and his on-the-spot observations".[19]

---

[18] *Idem.*
[19] *Idem.*

394. He expressed his belief that serious, massive and persistent violations of human rights had been committed in Bolivia since 17 July 1980. He added, however, that "the situation did not remain completely unchanged between the beginning and the end of the period in question (i.e. from 17 July 1980 to 31 December 1981, the date of preparation of the report)" and that "it would seem that, beginning on 4 September 1981, the date on which the authorities reaffirmed their determination to guarantee respect for human rights, there had been in certain respects a relative improvement".[20]

(The comments of the Bolivian Government on the Special Envoy's report contain several references to the government's will to co-operate with the international community and to its desire to "correct existing anomalies and progressively to guarantee the exercise of human rights" until "the national institutions and the public authority of the state can be fully restored". The Bolivian Government emphasizes, however, that, "it cannot accept the reports submitted by non-governmental organizations, as they are not always based on impartial judgement and analysis but aim rather to give a distorted and harmful picture of the situation in Bolivia".)[21]

395. On 17 March 1982 the Secretariat received a letter from the author of [the second communication], Mr Nin Saavedra, transmitting documents identical to those sent by Mr Joe Nordmann, as well as several articles on violations of human rights in Bolivia which had recently been published in the press. Mr Saavedra considers that there is no difference between the present government and the one that preceded it. He calls for an international mission of inquiry to be sent to Bolivia to make a first-hand report, in the manner of the United Nations Commission on Human Rights, on the present situation concerning human rights falling within the spheres of competence of Unesco and to determine the circumstances of the murder of Mr Marcelo Quiroga Santa Cruz and of the massacre of 15 January 1981.

396. At the present session, the Committee once more regretted the fact that the government concerned was not represented.

397. Several members of the Committee were of the opinion that the four communications concerned cases which prima facie seemed to fall within the fields of competence of Unesco, while others, by reason, for example, of the professions exercised by the alleged victims, seemed possible to declare inadmissible or, because of the death of the alleged victims, seemed not to be particularly deserving of further consideration. It was therefore important to sift them.

---

[20] *Idem.*
[21] *Idem.*

Bolivia **No. 322/81**

398. One member of the Committee observed that most of the cases submitted appeared to be a cry from the heart, and that the Committee should press for the co-operation of the Bolivian Government.

399. After an exchange of views, the Committee *decided*:

(i) to request the Executive Board to ask the Director-General to appeal personally to the Minister of Foreign Affairs of the government concerned in order to obtain, as a matter of the utmost urgency, its co-operation, and to ask its Chairman to do likewise;

(ii) to declare [the first and third communications] admissible, since they concerned infringements of human rights in the fields of education, science, culture and communication;

(iii) to declare [the third and fourth communications] admissible, since they concerned the destruction of the Information and Documentation Centre on Bolivia (CIDOB) and reprisals against persons employed there;

(iv) to declare [the second and third communications] admissible since they concerned the following individual cases:

(1) Silvia Natalia Rivera, sociologist and teacher;

(2) Víctor Hugo Nin Saavedra, student;

(v) to discontinue consideration of the following cases because of the death of the alleged victims:

Jorge Baldibieso, engineer, student leader of the Local University Federation (FUL-ORURO);

José Luis Suárez, sociologist, teacher at the University of La Paz;

Gonzalo Barrón, architect, leader of the Bolivian University Confederation;

Ricardo Navarro, engineer, teacher at the University of La Paz and leader of the La Paz FUL;

Ramiro Velasco, economist and teacher at the Catholic University of La Paz;

No. 322/81 **Bolivia**

Marcelo Quiroga Santa Cruz, leader of the Bolivian Socialist Party, deputy, lawyer and lecturer in economics;

[Second, third and fourth communications]

(vi) to declare [the second and third communications] admissible, since they concerned the case of Elías Rafael Flores, sociologist at the University of La Paz, arrested in September 1980 and missing since 18 October 1980, and to instruct the Secretariat to refer this case, in accordance with normal procedure,[22] to the [Working Group on Enforced or Involuntary Disappearances] of the United Nations Commission on Human Rights;

(vii) to declare inadmissible the remaining allegations contained in [the four communications], on the grounds that they do not fall within the fields of competence of Unesco;

(viii) to begin consideration of the substance of those communications declared admissible at its next session.

Autumn 1982 session of the Committee on Conventions and Recommendations (115th session of the Executive Board)[23]

410. After the representative of the Director-General had presented these communications,[24] the representative of the Bolivian Government made a statement. He then withdrew.

411. After an exchange of views, the Committee *decided* to draw up a specific report concerning these communications for the attention of the Executive Board, which report will be examined by the Committee at its next session.

[22] See documents 108 EX/38 PRIV., para. 16, 109 EX/52 PRIV., annex I, para. 8, and Corr. and 112 EX/30 PRIV., paras. 558-566.
[23] See document 115 EX/28 PRIV., paras. 410-411; see also document 115 EX/CR/HR/1.
[24] Communications No. 322/81 concerning *Bolivia*, case of *Violations of human rights in Bolivia*, No. 359/81 concerning *Bolivia*, case of *Violations of human rights in Bolivia*, No. 397/81 concerning *Bolivia*, case of *Violations of human rights in Bolivia*, and No. 407/81 concerning *Bolivia*, case of *Violations of human rights in Bolivia*, were being considered together.

Bolivia **No. 322/81**

Spring 1983 session of the Committee on Conventions and Recommendations (116th session of the Executive Board)[25]

273. These communications[26] allege that violations of human rights were committed in Bolivia following the military coup on 17 July 1980. The first [communication] has been on the Committee's agenda since the spring 1981 session, the second and third since the autumn 1981 session and the fourth since the spring 1982 session. At the last of these sessions, after noting the repeated absence of any representative of the government concerned, the Committee decided to declare admissible the allegations concerning:[27]

> infringements of human rights in the fields of education, science, culture and communication since the events of 17 July 1980;
>
> the destruction of the Information and Documentation Centre on Bolivia (CIDOB) and the reprisals against persons employed there;
>
> the case of Mrs Silvia Natalia Rivera, a sociologist, who had been imprisoned on 31 May - 1 June 1980, and dismissed from her work at university, and all of whose research material had been confiscated;
>
> the case of Mr Víctor Hugo Nin Saavedra, a student, whose application for a passport allowing him to return to his country was allegedly refused;
>
> the case of Mr Elías Rafael Flores, a socialogist, who disappeared on 18 October 1980 (this case was transmitted to the Working Group of the United Nations Commission on Human Rights on the instructions of the Committee).

274. At the autumn 1982 session, the Permanent Delegate of Bolivia, who appeared before the Committee, made a statement and then left. Given the inadequate partici-

---

[25] See document 116 EX/48 PRIV., paras. 273-277; see also documents 116 EX/CR/HR/1 and Add.

[26] Communications No. 322/81 concerning *Bolivia*, case of *Alleged violations of human rights in Bolivia*, No. 359/81 concerning *Bolivia*, case of *Alleged violations of human rights in Bolivia*, No. 397/81 concerning *Bolivia*, case of *Alleged violations of human rights in Bolivia*, and No. 407/81 concerning *Bolivia*, case of *Alleged violations of human rights in Bolivia*, were being considered together.

[27] See document 114 EX/38 PRIV., para. 399 (ii), (iii), (iv) and (vi) (*supra*, pp. 823-824).

pation of the government concerned, the Committee decided to prepare a specific report for the Executive Board [...].[28]

275. At the present spring 1983 session, in a letter dated 6 May, the Bolivian Minister of Education and Culture informed the Director-General that following the re-establishment of a fully legal state in his country, the government presided over by Dr Hernán Siles Zuazo had completely restored respect for human rights and fundamental freedoms on 10 October 1982. He expressed his government's gratitude for the solidarity shown by the international community, and thanked the Director-General for his action in support of respect for human rights in Bolivia within Unesco's fields of competence. He welcomed the support provided by the Organization in the promotion of human rights and fundamental freedoms, which would be reflected in the establishment of an Institute for the study of human rights, people's rights and peace, and the organization of a symposium which might be held in Bolivia in late 1983. His government was always prepared to co-operate with the Committee, and he apologized to the Committee for the tone and manner adopted by the representative of the previous government at the autumn 1982 session. He also said that in October 1982 his government had set up a commission in charge of studying and clarifying cases of missing persons, and that in November 1982 it had ratified both the International Covenants on Human Rights and the Optional Protocol to the International Covenant on Civil and Political Rights. He concluded by requesting the Executive Board and the Committee to regard the four cases concerning his country as closed in view of the positive new situation prevailing there as regards human rights.

276. The Bolivian Minister sent a copy of the letter to [Mr] Joe Nordmann, President of the International Association of Democratic Lawyers, one of the authors of the four communications. Four documents were annexed to the letter, including a copy of the report dated 13 December 1982 by Professor Héctor Gros Espiell, Special Envoy for the United Nations Commission on Human Rights,[29] and a copy of the Commission's [resolution 1983/33 of 8 March 1983 to cease examination of the human rights situation in Bolivia].

277. In view of the favourable development of the human rights situation in Bolivia, especially as regards human rights within Unesco's fields of competence, a fact that has been confirmed by the information received, and in line with the decision reached by the United Nations Commission on Human Rights, the Committee *decided* to cease examination of these four communications in accordance with paragraph 14 (*j*) of 104 EX/ Decision 3.3.[30]

---

[28] See document 115 EX/28 PRIV., para. 411 (*supra*, p. 824).
[29] See document E/CN.4/1983/22.
[30] See also document 126 EX/3 PRIV., paras. 218, 220 and 225-226.

No. 323/81

Concerning *Chile*
Case of *Gracia Barrios Rivadeneira*

Communication of 14 January 1981 submitted by
Gracia Barrios Rivadeneira

Spring 1981 session of the Committee on Conventions and Recommendations (112th session of the Executive Board)[1]

91. The authors of [the first two communications][2] describe themselves as artists (painters) and former lecturers in the Faculty of Fine Arts of the University of Chile in Santiago; they claim to have been victimized by the authorities of their country, which are alleged to have prevented them from returning to live and work there: on 27 March 1979 for the former, and on 25 July 1977 for the latter. The Chilean Consulate in Paris is said to have issued passports to them marked with the letter "L", thereby preventing them from exercising their right to return to their own country.

92. The author of [the third communication], Mrs Concepción Balmes, claims to have been victimized by the government authorities in her country, who have not authorized her to return there; a negative reply was apparently made to her request to the Embassy of Chile in France. She states that she came to France in 1973 at the age of 16, accompanying her father, and that no warrant has been issued for her arrest and no charge brought against her. She adds that she now has a child of six.

93. These three persons wish to return to Chile to live, work and participate in cultural activities there.

94. Having emphasized that none of these persons had made any effort to exhaust domestic remedies, the representative of the Chilean Government said that the head of the family, José Balmes Parramón, and his daughter, Concepción Balmes, could

---

[1] See document 112 EX/30 PRIV., paras. 91-95; see also document 112 EX/CR/HR/3.

[2] Communications No. 323/81 concerning *Chile*, case of *Gracia Barrios Rivadeneira*, No. 324/81 concerning *Chile*, case of *José Balmes Parramón*, and No. 327/81 concerning *Chile*, case of *Concepción Balmes*, were being considered together.

return to Chile immediately, unconditionally and permanently; that he had not yet received confirmation that the same solution would be adopted for Mr Parramón's wife, but that it was probable; and that this information could be conveyed immediately to the authors of the communications.

95. A consensus rapidly emerged in the Committee, which *decided* to strike out of its list, as having been settled, [the second and third communications], to postpone consideration of the admissibility of [the first communication] until its next session.

Autumn 1981 session of the Committee on Conventions and Recommendations (113th session of the Executive Board)[3]

156. The author of this communication describes herself as an artist (painter) and a former lecturer in the Faculty of Fine Arts of the University of Chile in Santiago; she claims to have been victimized by the authorities of her country, which are alleged to have prevented her from returning there to live, work and participate in cultural activities. On 27 March 1979 the Chilean Consulate in Paris is said to have issued a passport to her marked with the letter "L", thereby preventing her from exercising her right to return to her country.

157. Mrs Gracia Barrios Rivadeneira wants, first, the Chilean authorities to respect her right to live and work in her country and, secondly, expresses a wish to join her family and especially her mother, who is already of a very advanced age.

158. Having emphasized that this person had not made any effort to exhaust domestic remedies, the representative of the Chilean Government said, at the [spring 1981] session, that Mrs Rivadeneira's husband, Mr José Balmes Parramón, and her daughter, Concepción Balmes, had been authorized to return to Chile immediately, unconditionally and permanently; that he had not yet received confirmation that the same solution would be adopted for Mr Parramón's wife, but that it was probable; and that this information could be conveyed immediately to the authors of the communications.

159. A consensus rapidly emerged in the Committee, which decided to postpone consideration of the admissibility of this communication until the present session.[4]

160. At the present session, the representative of the Chilean Government stated that he hoped to have the possibility of settling this case once and for all by the end of

---

[3] See document 113 EX/38 PRIV., paras. 156-162; see also document 113 EX/CR/HR/2.

[4] See document 112 EX/30 PRIV., para. 95 (*supra*, p. 828).

the session of the Committee and that he was awaiting information from the government of his country in this connection.

161. The Committee accordingly decided by consensus to postpone this case until the last day of its [session]. On that occasion the representative of the Chilean Government stated that, in order for a solution to be found to this case, it was necessary for the Secretariat to issue a certificate to him indicating whether or not Mr Triviño Puelpan [...][5] had described himself as the husband of Mrs Concepción Balmes, who was Mrs Gracia Barrios Rivadeneira's own daughter.

162. The Committee *decided* by consensus to postpone consideration of this case until its next session in order to allow the Secretariat to consider the communication from the angle suggested by the representative of the Chilean Government.

Spring 1982 session of the Committee on Conventions and Recommendations (114th session of the Executive Board)[6]

441. The author of this communication describes herself as an artist (painter) and a former lecturer in the Faculty of Fine Arts of the University of Chile in Santiago; she claims to have been victimized by the authorities of her country, which are alleged to have prevented her from returning there to live, work and participate in cultural activities. On 27 March 1979, the Chilean Consulate in Paris is said to have issued a passport to her marked with the letter "L", thereby preventing her from exercising her right to return to her country.

442. Mrs Gracia Barrios Rivadeneira wants, first, the Chilean authorities to respect her right to live and work in her country and, secondly, expresses a wish to join her family and especially her mother, who is already of a very advanced age.

443. Having emphasized that this person had not made any effort to exhaust domestic remedies, the representative of the Chilean Government said, at the spring 1981 session, that Mrs Rivadeneira's husband, Mr José Balmes Parramón, and her daughter, Concepción Balmes, had been authorized to return to Chile immediately, unconditionally and permanently; that he had not yet received confirmation that the same solution would be adopted for Mr Parramón's wife, but that it was probable; and that this information could be conveyed immediately to the authors of the communications.

---

[5] Communication No. 56/78 concerning *Chile*, case of *Jorge Triviño Puelpan*.

[6] See document 114 EX/38 PRIV., paras. 441-449; see also document 114 EX/CR/HR/2.

No. 323/81 **Chile**

444. A consensus rapidly emerged in the Committee, which decided to postpone consideration of the admissibility of this communication until the next session.[7]

445. At the autumn 1981 session, the representative of the Chilean Government stated that, in order for a solution to be found to this case, it was necessary for the Secretariat to issue a certificate to him indicating whether or not Mr Triviño Puelpan [...] had described himself as the husband of Mrs Concepción Balmes, who was Mrs Gracia Barrios Rivadeneira's own daughter.

446. The Committee decided by consensus to postpone consideration of this case until the present session in order to allow the Secretariat to consider the communication from the angle suggested by the representative of the Chilean Government.[8]

447. On 15 September 1981 the Secretariat delivered to the representative of the Chilean Government the letters and documents featuring in the files on the various members of the family and establishing that Mr Triviño Puelpan had indeed described himself as the husband of Mrs Concepción Balmes.

448. At the present session, the representative of the government concerned explained that the way in which the members of the family had presented their case had created some confusion but that the problem had now been settled. As a result of his mediation, Mrs Gracia Barrios Rivadeneira and her daughter, Concepción Balmes, had been received on 19 April last by the Chilean Consul in Paris, who had issued them with a passport enabling them to return permanently to Chile where, in the meanwhile, Mr José Balmes and his son-in-law, Mr Triviño Puelpan, had organized an exhibition.

449. The Committee therefore *decided* under the terms of paragraph 14 (*a*) (x) of 104 EX/Decision 3.3, to strike the communication off the list as having been settled.

[7] See document 112 EX/30 PRIV., para. 95 (*supra*, p. 828).
[8] See document 113 EX/38 PRIV., para. 162 (*supra*, p. 829).

No. 324/81

Concerning *Chile*
Case of *José Balmes Parramón*

Communication of 14 January 1981 submitted by
José Balmes Parramón

Spring 1981 session of the Committee on Conventions and Recommendations (112th session of the Executive Board)[1]

[1] See document 112 EX/30 PRIV., paras. 91-95 (*supra*, pp. 827-828), communication No. 323/81 concerning *Chile*, case of *Gracia Barrios Rivadeneira*.

No. 325/81

Concerning *Chile*
Case of *Marco Antonio Peña Pérez*

Communication of 23 January 1981 submitted by
Marco Antonio Peña Pérez

Spring 1981 session of the Committee on Conventions and Recommendations (112th session of the Executive Board)[1]

96. The author of the communication describes himself as a music teacher, and claims to have been victimized by the government authorities of his country, who, he alleges, have not authorized him to return there. He states that he has submitted two applications for this purpose to the Consultate of Chile in Paris, one in December 1979 and the other in April 1980. He is also said to have requested permission to visit his sister, who was seriously ill, in October 1980. He claims to have received no reply to his requests. He points out that the name Marco Antonio Peña Núñez, which is in no way identical with his own, is recorded on the national list of persons prohibited from returning to the country. He also states that, when his passport was renewed in June 1978, it was marked with the letter "L" (signifying prohibition from re-entering the country).

97. The representative of the government concerned informed the Committee that it was possible that an error, such as that mentioned by the author of the communication, had in fact been made; that he would have to continue his inquiries to establish that for certain; and that he would inform the Committee of his findings.

98. In the circumstances, the Committee *decided* to postpone consideration of the admissibility of this communication until its next session.

---

[1] See document 112 EX/30 PRIV., paras. 96-98; see also document 112 EX/CR/HR/3 Add.

No. 325/81 **Chile**

Autumn 1981 session of the Committee on Conventions and Recommendations (113th session of the Executive Board)[2]

163. The author of the communication describes himself as a music teacher, and claims to have been victimized by the government authorities of his country, who, he alleges, have not authorized him to return there. He states that he has submitted two applications for this purpose to the Consulate of Chile in Paris, one in December 1979 and the other in April 1980. He is also said to have requested permission to visit his sister, who was seriously ill, in October 1980. He claims to have received no reply to his requests. He points out that the name Marco Antonio Peña Núñez, which is in no way identical with his own, is recorded on the national list of persons prohibited from returning to the country. He also states that, when his passport was renewed in June 1978, it was marked with the letter "L" (signifying prohibition from re-entering the country) .

164. At the [spring 1981] session, the representative of the government concerned informed the Committee that it was possible that an error, such as that mentioned by the author of the communication, had in fact been made; that he would have to continue his inquiries to establish that for certain; and that he would inform the Committee of his findings.

165. In the circumstances, the Committee decided to postpone consideration of the admissibility of this communication until the present session.[3]

166. At the present session the representative of the Director-General brought to the knowledge of the Committee a letter addressed by the author to the Secretariat on 1 September 1981. In this letter the author said that the information concerning the possible confusion of names was given to him by the CIMADE, which had the only list known to him of persons prohibited from entering Chile (Decreto escrito No. 92 of 7 March 1980), and in which his name did not appear.

167. The representative of the Chilean Government stated that on inquiry it seemed that there was no mistake in the name and that the person prohibited from entering Chile was indeed Mr Antonio Peña Pérez, but as the aforementioned letter constituted a new element he would like consideration of the case to be deferred to the following session to give him time to ask the competent authorities of his government to reopen the case in the light of that letter.

---

[2] See document 113 EX/38 PRIV., paras. 163-173; see also document 113 EX/CR/HR/2.
[3] See document 112 EX/30 PRIV., para. 98 (*supra*, p. 833).

Chile **No. 325/81**

168. Some members of the Committee considered that it was premature to take such a decision without going more closely into the communication, for if there was no mistake the Committee was faced with the case of a person who was debarred from returning to his country. One Committee member added that if there was no longer any doubt as to the identity of the person, the Chilean authorities could have set some procedure in motion for settling the case.

169. One member of the Committee suggested that the author be told that there was no mistake concerning his identity, that he was therefore the person debarred from returning to Chile and that to remedy such a situation he should avail himself of the judicial means of redress existing for the purpose. The note on the "recurso de amparo" should be sent to him in that connection. The same member hoped that the Chilean Government would do everything possible to inform the Committee at its next session of the action taken in this matter.

170. One member, while stating that he was in perfect agreement with the previous speaker, urged that the author be told clearly to apply to the courts. The representative of the Director-General pointed out that in similar cases the Committee contemplated, alongside the judicial recourse, interceding on humanitarian grounds to have the principle of the reunion of families respected.

171. All subsequent speakers endorsed these suggestions.

172. The representative of the government concerned took a favourable view of the solutions contemplated. However, he expressed the wish that consideration of the communication be deferred to the next session instead of the end of the present session, emphasizing that the delicate and confidential approaches he would have to make in this case could not be made by Telex, but required his presence in Santiago.

173. The Committee therefore *decided*:

(i) to defer consideration of this case to its next session;

(ii) to appeal to the spirit of co-operation of the Chilean Government so that it might consider to what extent it was possible on humanitarian grounds connected with the unity of the family to grant Mr Peña Pérez an authorization to return temporarily in accordance with the procedure already established;

(iii) to ask the representative of the Chilean Government to inform it of the action taken in this matter;

(iv) to tell the author that there did not seem to be any mistake concerning his identity but that, following his letter, the competent Chilean authorities were going to resume their inquiries and that he should in any case avail himself of the existing judicial means of recourse, about which he would be informed by the note on "recurso de amparo".

Spring 1982 session of the Committee on Conventions and Recommendations (114th session of the Executive Board)[4]

450. The author of the communication describes himself as a music teacher, and claims to have been victimized by the government authorities of his country, who, he alleges, have not authorized him to return there. He states that he has submitted two applications for this purpose to the Consulate of Chile in Paris, one in December 1979 and the other in April 1980. He is also said to have requested permission to visit his sister, who was seriously ill, in October 1980. He claims to have received no reply to his requests. He points out that the name Marco Antonio Peña Núñez, which is in no way identical with his own, is recorded on the national list of persons prohibited from returning to the country. He also states that, when his passport was renewed in June 1978, it was marked with the letter "L" (signifying prohibition from re-entering the country).

451. At the spring 1981 session, the representative of the government concerned informed the Committee that it was possible that an error, such as that mentioned by the author of the communication, had in fact been made; that he would have to continue his inquiries to establish that for certain; and that he would inform the Committee of his findings.

452. In the circumstances, the Committee decided to postpone consideration of the admissibility of this communication until the following session.[5]

453. At the autumn 1981 session, the representative of the Director-General brought to the knowledge of the Committee a letter addressed by the author to the Secretariat on 1 September 1981. In that letter, the author said that the information concerning the possible confusion of names was given to him by CIMADE, which had the only list known to him of persons prohibited from entering Chile (Decreto escrito No. 92 of 7 March 1980), and in which his name did not appear.

---

[4] See document 114 EX/38 PRIV., paras. 450-457; see also document 114 EX/CR/HR/2.

[5] See document 112 EX/30 PRIV., para. 98 (*supra*, p. 833).

Chile **No. 325/81**

454. The representative of the Chilean Government stated that, on inquiry, it seemed that there was no mistake in the name and that the person prohibited from entering Chile was indeed Mr Antonio Peña Pérez, but as the aforementioned letter constituted a new element he would like consideration of the case to be deferred to the following session to give him time to ask the competent authorities of his government to reopen the case in the light of that letter.

455. After a brief discussion the Committee decided:[6]

(i) to defer consideration of this case to the present session;

(ii) to appeal to the spirit of co-operation of the Chilean Government so that it might consider to what extent it was possible on humanitarian grounds connected with the unity of the family to grant Mr Peña Pérez an authorization to return temporarily in accordance with the procedure already established;

(iii) to ask the representative of the Chilean Government to inform it of the action taken in this matter;

(iv) to tell the author that there did not seem to be any mistake concerning his identity but that, following his letter, the competent Chilean authorities were going to resume their inquiries and that he should in any case avail himself of the existing judicial means of recourse, about which he would be informed by the note on "recurso de amparo".

456. At the present session, the representative of the government concerned said that this was an example of a case where the procedure he had just mentioned in connection with one of the preceding cases[7] had been properly understood and used to good effect by the person in question. There had been no mistake with regard to identity: Mr A. Peña Pérez had indeed been debarred from returning to Chile but the request for reconsideration that he had sent to the Ministry of the Interior in Santiago had been accepted and he had been authorized to return to Chile unconditionally and permanently. The representative of the Chilean Government felt that this had given the Committee fresh proof of his government's spirit of co-operation and of the effectiveness of the procedure it had established.

457. After discussion, the Committee *decided*:

---

[6] See document 113 EX/38 PRIV., para. 173 (*supra*, pp. 835-836).

[7] See document 114 EX/38 PRIV., para. 438 (*supra*, p. 797), communication No. 321/81 concerning *Chile*, case of *Victor Xavier Tiznado Rosas*.

No. 325/81 **Chile**

(i) to take note of the information supplied by the representative of the government concerned;

(ii) to strike the communication off the list as having been settled, in accordance with the terms of paragraph 14 (*a*) (x) of 104 EX/Decision 3.3.

No. 327/81

Concerning *Chile*
Case of *Concepción Balmes*

Communication of 28 January 1981 submitted by
Concepción Balmes

Spring 1981 session of the Committee on Conventions and Recommendations
(112th session of the Executive Board)[1]

[1] See document 112 EX/30 PRIV., paras. 91-95 (*supra*, pp. 827-828), communication No. 323/81 concerning *Chile*, case of *Gracia Barrios Rivadeneira*.

No. 328/81

Concerning *Union of Soviet Socialist Republics*
Case of *Georgij Danilovich Parkhomenko*

Communication of 29 January 1981 submitted by
Geneviève Laforêt

Spring 1981 session of the Committee on Conventions and Recommendations (112th session of the Executive Board)[1]

340. According to the author of the communication, Mrs Geneviève Laforêt, residing at Corbeil-Essonnes (France), Mr Georgij Danilovich Parkhomenko is a film producer and art photographer who is reduced by present circumstances to working as a lighting-radio technician in a travelling theatrical company. On account of his correspondence with foreign friends and, in particular, since he requested a visa to emigrate to France, all his letters to addresses abroad are alleged to have been systematically intercepted. Only letters written under a false name and posted in Moscow have apparently reached their destinations.

341. The author claims that Article 19 of the Universal Declaration of Human Rights has been violated and hopes that the authorities of Kharkov, the place of residence of the alleged victim, will observe the right to information and to freedom of opinion and expression which has not been recognized. Apparently no steps have been taken recently to exhaust domestic remedies, but in previous years the lodging of a complaint led, it is claimed, to the alleged victim's being summoned to appear before the militia and KGB.

342. The representative of the Soviet Government remarked that despite the most thorough inquiries made of trade unions, unions or associations grouping film-makers, art or press photographers, the name of Mr Georgij Danilovich Parkhomenko could not be found on any membership lists. He added that Mr Parkhomenko had begun working after he had completed secondary school and in 20 years had changed his job 18 times but had never worked either as a film-maker or art photographer; the case did not, therefore, fall within Unesco's fields of competence. Fur-

[1] See document 112 EX/30 PRIV., paras. 340-344; see also document 112 EX/CR/HR/3.

thermore, he wondered why the author of the communication had addressed herself to Unesco to make sure that the correspondence of the alleged victim reached its destination when the Kharkov Central Post Office had confirmed by letter that Mr Parkhomenko had never lodged a complaint although such recourse was available under the Postal Regulations. He therefore felt that the communication was manifestly ill-founded and did not meet the "attempt" criterion laid down in paragraph 14 (*a*) (ix) of 104 EX/Decision 3.3 to exhaust available domestic remedies. He therefore concluded that the communication was inadmissible.

343. All members who took part in the discussion also deemed the communication inadmissible. However, some speakers wished to point out that the only possible grounds for such a decision was the fact that the professional activity of the alleged victim was one which did not fall within fields of Unesco's competence.

344. A consensus having been reached to that effect, the Committee *decided* that the communication was not admissible because it did not fall within Unesco's fields of competence as set out in paragraph 14 (*a*) (iii) of 104 EX/Decision 3.3.

No. 334/81

Concerning *Union of Soviet Socialist Republics*
Case of *Mykola Danilovich Rudenko*

Communication of 14 February 1981 submitted by
International Association for the Defence of Artists
victims of repression

Spring 1981 session of the Committee on Conventions and Recommendations (112th session of the Executive Board)[1]

345. According to AIDA, the International Association for the Defence of Artists victims of repression, the author of the communication Mykola Danilovich Rudenko, a Ukrainian writer and poet, was reportedly arrested in February 1977, in Kiev, and sentenced in June of the same year to seven years in a hard labour camp and five years of internal exile for anti-Soviet propaganda. Prior to his arrest, he was a member of Amnesty International and the President of the Ukrainian branch of the Group for monitoring the Helsinki Agreement. Wounded during the war and now aged 60, he is reported to have greatly suffered from the camp's regime (in Mordovskaya), in particular as a result of the obligation imposed upon him to operate a machine tool. On 19 December 1980, he began a hunger strike for an unlimited period of time.

346. His wife addressed a petition to the President of the Presidium of the Supreme Soviet of the USSR on 25 December 1980, describing her husband's physical and moral destitution and also recording the harassment to which she has been subjected by the police authorities. The alleged victim has been adopted by Amnesty International's French section in Caen, which has launched an urgent appeal on his behalf.

347. The representative of the Soviet Union stated to the Committee that a communication involving this person had already been rejected by the Committee at its [spring 1980] session[2] and that the case should thus not be re-examined. For the

[1] See document 112 EX/30 PRIV., paras. 345-366; see also document 112 EX/CR/HR/3 Add.
[2] See document 109 EX/52 PRIV., para. 139 (*supra*, p. 114), communication No. 21/78 concerning *Union of Soviet Socialist Republics and Ukrainian Soviet Socialist Republic*, case of *Yuri Orlov* et al.

Committee's information, he went on to say that he had checked with the prison doctors and had learned that Mr Rudenko was in the prison hospital after having undergone a two-stage prostate operation. He had undergone the first stage of the operation on 21 December 1980 and the second stage on 23 March 1981, it was explained. The operation had been successfully carried out, he said, and Mr Rudenko was now recuperating satisfactorily in a special part of the prison hospital where he was receiving special treatment. The Soviet representative read out lengthy attestations from the prison doctors and passed them around to the Committee. He concluded by asserting that since there had, in fact, been no hunger strike, and there had been no threat to Rudenko's health, nor any new information to qualify this as a new communication, the communication was inadmissible.

348. The Chairman and other Committee members requested the Soviet representative to provide in the future translations of the Russian documents which he wished to circulate, since to most members they were not understandable.

349. On the matter of the communication a Committee member expressed the view that the case was clearly admissible as being a violation within Unesco's fields of competence. He pointed out that this case was one of those unfortunate and deliberate actions on the part of the Soviet Union to suppress the monitoring of the extent to which it was fulfiling its obligations under the Helsinki Act. Here a member of Amnesty International had been imprisoned for nothing more than the peaceful expression of his views; there had been no violence or armed conspiracy involved here. It was a violation of his right to communicate and the other rights relating to free expression as outlined in the Universal Declaration of Human Rights which came within Unesco's competence.

350. This case clearly satisfied the admissibility requirements of 104 EX/Decision 3. 3, he said, and he further pointed out that this case had not yet been before the Committee for examination of its merits. There was thus no double jeopardy involved here.

351. The Soviet representative took the position that the question of why and how Rudenko was arrested was irrelevant. He stated that the Committee had been asked to end a hunger strike, and since there had never been one, the matter was settled. Unesco could not be a supranational tribunal reviewing various countries' court decisions. He stated that Rudenko had been sentenced according to Soviet law.

352. Another Committee member agreed with this analysis.

353. Several Committee members felt that the part of the communication expressing its purpose as being related to the hunger strike was irrelevant to the communica-

tion's admissibility. They pointed out that the conditions of admissibility did not mention anything about purpose. It was stated that the hunger strike was an added cause of concern, the most urgent one, but that the main concern was the violation of Rudenko's human rights in Unesco's fields of competence, which violations were clearly listed as the main complaints on the form submitted to the Committee. A Committee member emphasized that the act of declaring a communication admissible did not yet signify that it was well-founded. He said that the Committee was not in any way trying to review the Soviet court decisions; the Committee was only interested in using its good offices and in making an appeal. Another Committee member pointed out that since the Committee was not a tribunal, it could look at cases before or after judicial determination by a state and then appeal to executive branches of governments.

354. On the question of resubmission of a communication, the representative of the Director-General explained to the Committee that its decision at its [spring 1980] session concerned a communication, submitted by different authors, which concerned several victims of which one was Rudenko. The decision not to admit the communication had been taken because the authors had provided no information as to whether they had used any domestic remedies. But it was not the same communication as this one, so there was technically no resubmission here, he said.

355. Furthermore, it was explained, the drafters of 104 EX/Decision 3.3 had purposely not included therein the provision that new communications could not be examined if they were substantially the same as previously submitted communications, a provision which existed in procedures used by other organizations. This was a significant change in human rights procedures, and other organizations, including the Organization of African Unity (OAU) in its Charter of Rights of Man and Peoples, had followed Unesco's precedent.

356. Several Committee members expressed their deep concern that persons were punished in the Soviet Union for a simple expression of their opinions and their exercising the right to communicate.

357. The representative of the Soviet Union stated that the discussion of what constituted a crime of opinion ("délit d'opinion") would take the Committee far afield. He said that the Soviet Union did not prohibit criticism or dissidence; what it prohibited was the making of conscious and systematic false statements discrediting the political system of the Soviet Union. Rudenko had not been prosecuted for his literary or artistic works; it was his distribution of writings about strikes which had never taken place which was intolerable and which was against the law.

358. A Committee member supported the view of the Soviet representative and said that the Committee should not concern itself with national legislation, as everyone probably had a different opinion thereon.

359. Another Committee member felt that the complaint was classically ambiguous, since the remedy requested was not really in line with the violations alleged. He felt that the authors should be informed that the hunger strike had ended and that they and the victim should be informed that the remedy requested was consequently no longer concordant with the violations outlined in the communication.

360. It was emphasized by another member of the Committee that international organizations did not intervene in countries' internal affairs *per se* but said that it was a well established fact that when a country requested to become a member of such an organization or ratified or adopted the provisions of an international instrument, it thereby expressed its willingness to uphold the provisions of the Organization's Constitution or of the international instruments, and it consequently opened itself up to certain comparisons of its legislation and its international obligations. He went on to explain that the declaring invalid of a domestic judicial decision would be an intervention and thus inappropriate, whereas a review of a situation in comparison to the minimum international standards of respect for human rights and a subsequent addressing of appeals to a country's executive was perfectly legitimate and appropriate. He pointed out that no country of the world could pretend to be free of human rights violations and that the Committee could make a positive contribution in such cases by at least bringing to the attention of a country's government the Committee's view that a violation had been committed, and by appealing for its correction.

361. After lengthy discussion, and study of the communication with great interest, the Committee *decided* to defer a decision as to its admissibility to the next session.

362. In accordance with the customary procedure, the author of the communication would be informed of the detailed statement made by the representative of the government concerned with regard to the medical care which Mr Rudenko had received and which was still being provided.

363. In the meantime, the representative of the government concerned would, at the request of the Committee, inform the competent authorities of the concern expressed during the meeting with regard to Mr Rudenko's state of health, and of the appropriate humanitarian measures which it had been hoped would be taken in this connection.

364. A Committee member stated that he wished his abstention to go on record since he felt the Executive Board might get the false impression that the Committee had

been concerned only with the state of Mr Rudenko's health, whereas in fact it had also been seriously concerned by the violations of his human rights.

365. Another Committee member declared his astonishment that the Committee had not decided to contact the victim in this case, as it had decided to do in other cases before it.

366. A third Committee member stated that his silence during the debate of this communication should not be construed as an agreement to any particular position.

Autumn 1981 session of the Committee on Conventions and Recommendations (113th session of the Executive Board)[3]

367. According to AIDA, the International Association for the Defence of Artists victims of repression, the author of the communication, Mykola Danilovich Rudenko, a Ukrainian writer and poet, was reportedly arrested in February 1977, in Kiev, and sentenced in June of the same year to seven years in a hard labour camp and five years of internal exile for anti-Soviet propaganda. Prior to his arrest, he was a member of Amnesty International and the President of the Ukrainian branch of the Group for monitoring the Helsinki Agreement. Wounded during the war and now aged 60, he is reported to have greatly suffered from the camp's regime (in Mordovskaya), in particular as a result of the obligation imposed upon him to operate a machine tool. On 19 December 1980, he began a hunger strike for an unlimited period of time.

368. His wife addressed a petition to the President of the Presidium of the Supreme Soviet of the USSR on 25 December 1980, describing her husband's physical and moral destitution and also recording the harassment to which she has been subjected by the police authorities. The alleged victim has been adopted by Amnesty International's French section in Caen, which has launched an urgent appeal on his behalf.

369. At its [spring 1981] session the Committee decided to defer a decision as to admissibility to its next session, to inform in accordance with the customary procedure, the author of the communication of the detailed statement made by the representative of the government concerned with regard to the medical care which Mr Rudenko had received and which was still being provided, and to request the representative of the government concerned to inform the competent authorities of the concern expressed during the meeting with regard to Mr Rudenko's state of health, and of

---

[3] See document 113 EX/38 PRIV., paras. 367-381; see also document 113 EX/CR/HR/2.

the appropriate humanitarian measures which it had been hoped would be taken in this connection.[4]

370. At the Committee's present session the representative of the Soviet Government reminded the Committee that he had at the Committee' [spring 1981] session disproved the contention of the author of this communication that Mr Rudenko was on a hunger strike. He also pointed out that Mr Rudenko's incarceration in a hospital had been undertaken for medical reasons and that he had been kept therein for his recovery; Mr Rudenko had in fact been released on 5 June of this year, his health having been found satisfactory. The Soviet representative said that he had conveyed to the prison camp authorities the Committee's concerns expressed at its [spring 1981] session, and the camp authorities had decided to alleviate the work-load and working hours of Mr Rudenko. Furthermore, he went on to say, since the authors of the communication had under section V of the form asked for Mr Rudenko's release because of his hunger strike, and since Mr Rudenko was in fact neither on a hunger strike nor any longer in hospital confinement, the Committee should terminate its consideration of this case.

371. A Committee member felt that Mr Rudenko's state of health was certainly of concern but that this was not the main issue; it was a question of whether a person could be imprisoned for having expressed his opinions. It was pointed out that Mr Rudenko had distinguished himself in his military service and in his public service work within the Soviet system. The Committee member felt that the imprisonment of Mr Rudenko because he had expressed his political opinions in his writings was a violation of human rights coming within Unesco's fields of competence, that section V of the author's form did not disqualify this communication, and that the Committee should address an appeal to the Soviet representative to use his good offices to see if the case could be reconsidered, especially in view of the fact that Mr Rudenko had already paid a high price in suffering and loss of health.

372. Another Committee member felt that the facts of the case showed that the Soviet Union had been justified in its treatment of Mr Rudenko and indeed had been very humane by providing careful medical treatment for him.

373. It was noted by another Committee member that this victim, who was a great poet and writer, who had loyally served his country, had been in prison since 1977; the Committee member wanted to associate himself with the proposal that the Committee appeal to the Soviet authorities for a reconsideration of the sentence.

---

4 See document 112 EX/30 PRIV., paras. 361-363 (*supra*, p. 846).

374. Another Committee member agreed that the Committee should appeal for a shorter sentence for Mr Rudenko and felt that the authors of the communication should be informed that Mr Rudenko's health was no longer in danger and that his work-load had been lightened.

375. The Soviet representative stated that Mr Rudenko had not been sentenced for his literary activities. He had been sentenced because he had contributed to the distribution of material which was used against the Soviet Union. The Soviet representative said that the Committee could not question the judgement of the Ukrainian High Court, nor could it shorten the sentence. He went on to say that he had in a humanitarian spirit conveyed the wishes of the Committee to the authorities and Mr Rudenko's situation had in fact improved. He felt that a person convicted of criminal activity should not receive special consideration all his life just for health reasons. There was a possibility of favourable treatment for Mr Rudenko, he said, but Mr Rudenko persisted in his wholly insubordinate attitude and thus eliminated this possibility. Since Mr Rudenko was not willing to change his attitude it was he himself who was maintaining his present situation.

376. A.Committee member pointed out that the Committee had not yet been presented with the elements of the crime of which Mr Rudenko had been accused. He asked why Mr Rudenko should not be allowed to associate with a Committee designed to monitor the Helsinki Agreement and why a person should not be allowed to write criticism of his government, as long as he did not commit violent acts. Soviet legislation which prohibited such peaceful expressions and acts was a violation of international human rights norms, he explained. The Committee member felt that the case was clearly admissible and that, if it was not admitted, it should at least be kept on the Committee's agenda and monitored.

377. The Soviet representative stated that his government stood ready to co-operate with the Committee, but he felt that it would be unacceptable to undertake a discussion of Soviet legislation. The legislation in question was not against writings *per se*, but only against those in which the author deliberately twisted facts and slandered the Soviet Union. The Soviet representative stated that in the legal proceedings against Mr Rudenko there had been absolutely no mention of any of Mr Rudenko's activities with a Helsinki watch group.

378. A Committee member felt that the Soviet Union as a party to international covenants could not claim not to have to answer to anyone on questions of human rights; he stated that in the present case there had been a denial of a freedom which the covenants at the most allow to be restricted only somewhat, or only occasionally.

No. 334/81 **Union of Soviet Socialist Republics**

379. It was said by another Committee member that the Committee had to work on the basis of the facts put before it by the authors and the government concerned. If these facts seemed to be divergent, he said, then an attempt must be made to reconcile them; the Committee should not let its methodology sidetrack it. It was suggested that the Committee should use the practical approach.

380. The Soviet representative stated that the Soviet Union had fulfilled all its international obligations and that allegations by Committee members to the contrary were totally unacceptable.

381. After an involved discussion, the Committee *decided*:

(i) to request the Soviet representative to exercise his good offices for humanitarian purposes in this case, as he himself had proposed;

(ii) to inform the authors of the communication of the present situation as regards the victim and also to inform them of the possibility, open to the victim, of receiving more favourable treatment, as explained by the representative of the government concerned;

(iii) to suspend the examination of the admissibility of the present communication.

Spring 1982 session of the Committee on Conventions and Recommendations (114th session of the Executive Board)[5]

619. This communication is submitted by AIDA (International Association for the Defence of Artists victims of repression).

620. Mr Mykola Danilovich Rudenko, a Ukrainian writer and poet, was reportedly arrested in February 1977, in Kiev, and sentenced in June of the same year to seven years in a hard labour camp and five years of internal exile for anti-Soviet propaganda. Prior to his arrest, he was a member of Amnesty International and the President of the Ukrainian branch of the Group for monitoring the Helsinki Agreement. Wounded during the war and now aged 60, he is reported to have greatly suffered from the camp's regime (in Mordovskaya), in particular as a result of the obligation imposed upon him to operate a machine tool. On 19 December 1980, he began a hunger strike for an unlimited period of time.

---

[5] See document 114 EX/38 PRIV., paras. 619-650; see also document 114 EX/CR/HR/2.

621. His wife addressed a petition to the President of the Presidium of the Supreme Soviet of the Union of Soviet Socialist Republics on 25 December 1980, describing her husband's physical and moral destitution and also recording the harassment to which she has been subjected by the police authorities. The alleged victim has been adopted by Amnesty International's French Section in Caen, which has launched an urgent appeal on his behalf.

622. It is claimed that violations have occurred in respect of Articles 18 (freedom of thought, conscience and religion), 19 (freedom of opinion and expression), 20 (freedom of peaceful assembly and association) and 27 (freedom to participate in cultural life and share in scientific advancement) of the Universal Declaration of Human Rights.

623. As to the purpose and aim of the communication, the author requests the immediate release of Mr Rudenko for health reasons.

624. At the [spring] 1981 session the Committee decided to defer a decision as to admissibility to its next session, to inform in accordance with the customary procedure, the author of the communication of the detailed statement made by the representative of the government concerned with regard to the medical care which Mr Rudenko had received and which was still being provided, and to request the representative of the government concerned to inform the competent authorities of the concern expressed during the meeting with regard to Mr Rudenko's state of health, and of the appropriate humanitarian measures which it had been hoped would be taken in this connection.[6]

625. At the [autumn 1981] session the representative of the Soviet Government reminded the Committee that he had at the Committee's [apring 1981] session disproved the contention of the author of this communication that Mr Rudenko was on a hunger strike. He also pointed out that Mr Rudenko's incarceration in a hospital had been undertaken for medical reasons and that he had been kept therein for his recovery. Mr Rudenko had left hospital on 5 June 1981 his health having been found satisfactory. The representative of the Soviet Government said that he had conveyed to the prison camp authorities the Committee's concern and the camp authorities had decided to alleviate the work-load and working hours of Mr Rudenko. Furthermore, he went on to say, since the authors of the communication had under section V of the form asked for Mr Rudenko's release because of his hunger strike, and since Mr Rudenko was in fact neither on a hunger strike nor any longer in hospital confinement, the Committee should terminate its consideration of this case.

---

[6] See document 112 EX/30 PRIV., paras. 361-363 (*supra*, p. 846).

626. A Committee member felt that Mr Rudenko's state of health was certainly of concern but that this was not the main issue; it was a question of whether a person could be imprisoned for having expressed his opinions. It was pointed out that Mr Rudenko had distinguished himself in his military service and in his public service work within the Soviet system. According to the Committee member, the imprisonment of Mr Rudenko because he had expressed his political opinions in his writings was a violation of human rights coming within Unesco's fields of competence. Section V of the author's form, he stated, did not disqualify this communication and the Committee should address an appeal to the representative of the Soviet Government to use his good offices to see if the case could be reconsidered; Mr Rudenko had already paid a high price in suffering and loss of health.

627. Another Committee member felt that the facts of the case showed that the Soviet Union had been justified in its treatment of Mr Rudenko and indeed had been very humane by providing careful medical treatment for him.

628. It was noted by another Committee member that the alleged victim, a great poet and writer who had loyally served his country, had been in prison since 1977; the Committee member wanted to associate himself with the proposal that the Committee appeal to the Soviet authorities for a reconsideration of the sentence.

629. Another Committee member thought that the Committee should appeal for a shorter sentence for Mr Rudenko and felt that the authors of the communication should be informed that Mr Rudenko's health was no longer in danger and that his work-load had been lightened.

630. The representative of the Soviet Government, after observing that Mr Rudenko had not been sentenced for his literary activities but for contributing to the distribution of material which was used against the Soviet Union, said that the Committee could not question the judgement of the Ukrainian High Court, nor could it shorten the sentence. He went on to say that, in his view, a person convicted of criminal activity should not receive special consideration all his life just for health reasons. There was a possibility of favourable treatment for Mr Rudenko, he said, but Mr Rudenko persisted in his wholly insubordinate attitude and thus eliminated this possibility. Since Mr Rudenko was not willing to change his attitude it was he himself who was maintaining his present situation.

631. A Committee member pointed out that the Committee had not yet been presented with the elements of the crime of which Mr Rudenko had been accused. He asked why Mr Rudenko should not be allowed to associate with a Committee designed to monitor the Helsinki Agreement and why a person should not be allowed to write criticism of his government, as long as he did not commit violent acts. Soviet legis-

lation which prohibited such peaceful expressions and acts was a violation of international human rights norms, he explained. The Committee member felt that the case was clearly admissible and that, if it was not admitted, it should at least be kept on the Committee's agenda and monitored.

632. In reply, the representative of the Soviet Government stated that his government stood ready to co-operate with the Committee but that it was unacceptable to undertake a discussion of Soviet legislation, which was not against writings *per se*, but only against those in which the author deliberately twisted facts and slandered the Soviet Union; in the legal proceedings against Mr Rudenko there had been absolutely no mention of any of Mr Rudenko's activities with a Helsinki watch group.

633. A Committee member felt that the Soviet Union as a party to international covenants could not claim not to have to answer to anyone on questions of human rights; he stated that in the present case there had been a denial of a freedom which the covenants at the most allow to be restricted only somewhat, or only occasionally.

634. It was said by another Committee member that the Committee had to work on the basis of the facts put before it by the authors and by the government concerned. If these facts seemed to be divergent, he said, an attempt must be made to reconcile them; the Committee should not let its methodology sidetrack it. It was suggested that the Committee should use the practical approach.

635. The representative of the Soviet Government stated that the Soviet Union had fulfilled all its international obligations and that allegations by Committee members to the contrary were totally unacceptable.

636. After an involved discussion, the Committee decided:[7]

(i) to request the representative of the Soviet Government to exercise his good offices for humanitarian purposes in this case, as he himself had proposed;

(ii) to inform the author of the communication of the present situation as regards the victim and of the possibility, open to the victim, of receiving more favourable treatment, as explained by the representative of the government concerned;

(iii) to suspend the examination of the admissibility of the communication.

---

[7] See document 113 EX/38 PRIV., para. 381 (*supra*, p. 850).

No. 334/81 **Union of Soviet Socialist Republics**

637. On 22 February 1982 the Secretariat received a letter from the author of the communication. According to AIDA:

(i) the conditions under which Mr Rudenko is detained have not been changed;

(ii) the wife of the alleged victim, Mrs Raissa Afanasievna Rudenko, was arrested in April 1981 and sentenced, on 11 September of the same year, to three years at a hard labour camp and five years of internal exile for her action on behalf of her husband;

(iii) shortly before Mrs Rudenko's arrival at her place of detention, in Mordovia, close to that of her husband, he was reportedly transferred to another camp in the Perm area.

638. AIDA asks that Mr and Mrs Rudenko be released and allowed to emigrate to Canada, to the Federal Republic of Germany or to France.

639. The author enclosed with the letter a copy of the record of Mr Rudenko's case prepared by Amnesty International, French Section, Caen. The account of events does not differ from that given above.

640. On the same date the Secretariat also received a letter from Amnesty International, French Section, Caen, transmitting a further copy of the Rudenko case.

641. At the Committee's present session, the representative of the Soviet Government pointed out that this communication was before the Committee for the third time. He explained that the second cycle of examination had commenced when it had been alleged that Mr Rudenko had gone on a hunger strike.

642. A detailed examination of the communication had allowed the Committee to see that the author was either ignorant of the facts or was misinforming the Committee, since it had been shown that at the time of the alleged hunger strike, Mr Rudenko had been in fact in a hospital being given post-surgery intensive care, included intravenous feeding.

[642a.] The Soviet representative went on to state that the request of the Committee formulated at its [autumn 1981] session had been duly carried out by him. He explained that he had obtained a certificate attesting to the fact that after February 1982 Mr Rudenko had received a thorough medical examination. Mr Rudenko was being monitored by doctors in the dispensary, that is to say, monitored by doctors on their own initiative. Mr Rudenko's condition was satisfactory, he said; the spinal nerve compression had improved, his spine movement forward was limited, his blood pressure was slightly high but his breathing was normal.

643. The Soviet representative explained that Mr Rudenko's work schedule had been lightened to four hours of work a day. There was no limit to the medical monitoring provided for him.

[643a.] The Soviet representative felt that this reporting to the Committee fully satisfied the request for humanitarian intervention which the Committee had formulated at its [autumn 1981] session. He added that in his opinion the author was not respecting the rules governing the submission of communications, since [the author] was not respecting completely the confidentiality of the case. A French chapter of Amnesty International, an organization not originally involved with this communication, had circulated information which must have been shared with them by the author. It was for these reasons that the Soviet representative insisted that the examination of this case should not be continued.

644. The representative of the Director-General reminded the Committee that it had taken its previous decision in view of the fact that the statements of the author and the Soviet representative had been completely contradictory and the Committee had thus wanted to allow the author the possibility of submitting further information once [the author] was informed of the Soviet Government's position. In fact, the author had not submitted new information but rather information on a non-related set of facts.

645. The Soviet representative then emphasized that he wished to make it clear that he was in no way accusing the Unesco Secretariat of any improper action; it was clearly the author of the communication who had violated the confidentiality of the case. The Amnesty International chapter had written directly to the Secretariat and in the letter a portion of the Committee's last report was quoted. Obviously, the author had provided the information to them, the Soviet representative said.

646. A Committee member expressed the view that the reason this communication was still before the Committee was because the Committee had never really settled the key question, which was not the question of the equality of the medical attention Mr Rudenko was getting, but rather whether he should be in prison in the first place. Even if there were a violation of confidentiality here, and it was not clear that there was, and even if the medical attention Mr Rudenko was getting was adequate, it was still a surprising situation that the activities of Mr Rudenko should have led him before the courts in the first place and should have resulted in such a lengthy sentence, the Committee member stated. While it was true that the Committee did not review

national legislation of Member States, it could still express to governments its concern and interest, he said.

647. In response to a question from the Soviet representative, the Director-General's representative explained that it was very clear that the author had violated the confidentiality of the communication, having been clearly informed in advance of this confidentiality, and the Secretariat had noted this in the file. It was, however, for the Committee to decide whether or not such a violation constituted an abuse of the right to submit communications as mentioned in paragraph [14 (*a*)] (vi) of [104 EX/Decision 3.3] and thus to strike it from its list, more or less as a sanction.

648. A very lengthy discussion followed on the question of whether or not there had been a breach of confidentiality by the author and, if so, what the consequent action of the Committee should be. Certain Committee members felt that there had been a breach, that the Committee should be very strict since the prestige and co-operation of governments were at stake, and that the communication should be stricken from the Committee's list. Other Committee members felt that there had not been a breach, or at least not a serious one, that in any event the general principles of law required that before a sanction could be applied a clear interdiction of the activity in question would have had to have been made known in advance, and that it would furthermore be morally inappropriate to punish the author in view of the mitigating circumstances. One Committee member stated that the Committee should not examine cases involving questions of national law since this was beyond Unesco's scope and another Committee member felt that the Committee should do so since it was important to ensure that the international norms in Unesco's fields of competence were being respected.

649. A Committee member pointed out that the events of the alleged violations actually took place many years ago and that the question was thus raised as to whether the communication had been submitted in a timely manner.

650. After much debate, the Committee *decided*:

(i) to note that a breach of confidentiality had occured in this case;

(ii) to declare the communication inadmissible because it had not been submitted within a reasonable period of time, as required by paragraph [14 (*a*)] (viii) of [104 EX/Decision 3.3];

(iii) to ask the Secretariat to ensure that the letter sent to the authors of communications clearly explained the need for confidentiality and the consequences of breaches thereof.

No. 342/81

Concerning *Union of Soviet Socialist Republics*
Case of *Iosef Samsonovich Irlin*

Communication of 15 October 1980 submitted by
Iosef Samsonovich Irlin

Autumn 1981 session of the Committee on Conventions and Recommendations (113th session of the Executive Board)[1]

382. Mr Iosef Samsonovich Irlin, aged 47, was both author of the communication and victim of the alleged violations.

383. He was a scientific research worker in the field of medicine, a specialist in oncology and a qualified medical doctor. During 20 years' service, he claims to have written numerous scientific publications or papers, including two monographs dealing with oncological questions. His wife, also a scientific researcher, worked in the field of microbiology.

384. On 9 April 1979, he, his wife and his elderly mother applied for emigration visas for Israel. According to the author, he and his wife were immediately dismissed from their jobs. Mr Irlin was dismissed from the Centre of Oncological Science of the Medical Academy of the USSR. Deprived of a livelihood and of employment, his family has had to endure all kinds of hardship during the past two years. Worn down by uncertainty, depression and deprivation, his mother has suffered a serious decline in health.

385. According to the author, the Irlin family was eventually refused permission to leave the country without a word of explanation.

386. He claims that neither he nor his wife have ever had access in their work to military or state secrets. He feels that in 20 years' service he has fulfilled his obligations to the USSR and that he cannot be accused of adding to the "brain drain" since no use has been made during the past two years either of his own or of his wife's

[1] See document 113 EX/38 PRIV., paras. 382-395; see also document 113 EX/CR/HR/3 Add.

knowledge and professional competence. He adds that if he were to emigrate from the USSR he would be leaving no dependants behind him in the country.

387. The representative of the Soviet Government pointed out to the Committee that the author of the communication was seeking Unesco's support for an emigration from the Soviet Union. He stated that the Committee had on more than one occasion decided that emigration matters were not within its competence and he called upon the Committee to be consistent and to declare this communication inadmissible.

388. A Committee member stated that the communication did not only speak of emigration matters but also mentioned violation of rights concerning the author's possibility of pursuing his scientific work in the Soviet Union. This aspect of the case was definitely within the Committee's competence, he said.

389. Other Committee members felt that the Committee should only address the grievances advanced by the author for a solution. Since in this case the author did not ask the Committee to help protect any rights other than that of emigration the Committee should not take such an unrequested initiative.

390. The representative of the Director-General explained that part V of the questionnaire could under no circumstances be seen as an additional condition of admissibility. As to the question as to whether the Committee could look into violations of which the author does not specifically complain, he said the practice in international bodies varied, but in general the bodies did not usually take the initiative to seek remedies on his behalf.

391. Several Committee members felt that it would be unreasonably legalistic and a loss of time to reject the communication and wait for the author to resubmit his communication with section V revised, and felt that the Committee should at its present session examine the other violations alleged.

392. Several other Committee members felt that the Committee should not jump to conclusions on behalf of the author since the author might well later complain that the Committee was offering him something he had not asked for.

393. The Soviet representative explained that Mr Irlin had left his job at the scientific institute of his own free will. He went on to say that though posts there were filled by secret ballot for five-year periods, the institute could still use certain administrative steps to take him back, but that this depended on Mr Irlin's co-operation.

394. A Committee member pointed out that Mr Irlin said that he had been forced to leave his job after he took steps to request emigration permission.

Union of Soviet Socialist Republics **No. 342/81**

395. Following a discussion, the Committee *decided*:

(i) to declare the communication inadmissible in so far as it concerned the right to emigrate from the USSR which did not fall within Unesco's sphere of competence, on the understanding that the author of the communication could submit a further communication to the Committee alleging the violation of human rights which did fall within Unesco's fields of competence;

(ii) to request the representative of the Soviet Government to inform the authorities of his country of the humanitarian concerns expressed in connection with this communication within the Committee.

No. 345/81

Concerning *Union of Soviet Socialist Republics*
Case of *Yosif Ziselevich Begun*

Communication of 26 February 1981 submitted by
American Jewish Committee

Spring 1981 session of the Committee on Conventions and Recommendations (112th session of the Executive Board)[1]

367. Yosif Ziselevich Begun is described by the American Jewish Committee, the author of the communication, as a scientist and teacher (of mathematics and Hebrew) of Jewish nationality. He is alleged to have taught for several years at a Soviet economic research institute. He was compelled to resign from his post following his application for an exit visa to Israel in April 1971. To earn his living, he gave private tuition in mathematics and Hebrew. In June 1977, he was apparently sentenced for "parasitism" to two years' exile in Magadan Oblast, in Siberia. Having served his sentence, he resumed his family life in Moscow, his birthplace. The competent authorities not having renewed his resident's permit, he was again sentenced, on a charge of violating the relevant regulations, to three years' exile in the same province (June 1978). Having served this second sentence, he was released in August 1980. However, he was allegedly required to live in localities situated more than 100 kilometres from Moscow. He is at present residing in Strunino, a town with a very small Jewish population. As a result, he has great difficulty earning his living as a private teacher of Hebrew, a subject of study not apparently recognized by the Soviet public authorities.

368. Recourse to legal and administrative remedies since his first sentence has produced no positive results.

369. The application recently formulated by Mr Begun and his wife for authorization to emigrate has reportedly been rejected on the ground that, until 1969, his work had given him access to information relating to national security.

---

[1] See document 112 EX/30 PRIV., paras. 367-383; see also document 112 EX/CR/HR/3 Add.

No. 345/81 **Union of Soviet Socialist Republics**

370. The author of the communication states that, in relation to [another communication] concerning the same alleged victim,[2] this is a new communication concerning the continued violation of human rights chiefly involving three facts:

> the discriminatory nature of the Soviet Government's refusal to recognize Mr Begun's Hebrew courses as legitimate;
>
> the banning of Mr Begun from Moscow;
>
> the refusal on the part of the competent authorities to grant exit visas to Mr and Mrs Begun.

371. When [the previous communication] was submitted, in February 1980, Mr Begun was in detention [...].[3] Shortly before the 110th session of the Executive Board, he was freed. At [the autumn 1980] session, the Committee decided "to note that the matter raised in this communication had been settled as an individual case and as such should therefore be struck from its list" [...].[4]

372. At the Committee's present session the representative of the Soviet Union reminded the Committee that it had spent a great deal of time on this case at its [autumn 1980] session, and that he had gone to great lengths to show that the teaching of Hebrew called for highly qualified teachers, that it was not the national language of Soviet Jews, and that it was taught in three universities in the Soviet Union. The case had been settled at the Committee's [autumn 1980] session, he said, and yet the authors were now claiming there were new circumstances in order to resubmit this case. However, it would probably be best to leave Mr Begun alone and let him make his own decisions, the Soviet representative said. Mr Begun now lived in the town of Stronino where he had a job which gave him much spare time to study scientific literature. The security reasons for his visa denial were still valid, the Soviet representative said, and he reminded the Committee that it had already agreed that national security reasons could justify visa denials. There were no new elements or violations in this case, the representative said, and it should be considered as being inadmissible.

373. Two Committee members thereupon expressed their views that the case lay outside Unesco's competence and should not be admitted.

---

[2] Communication No. 209/80 concerning *Union of Soviet Socialist Republics*, case of *Yosif Z. Begun*.

[3] See document 109 EX/52 PRIV., paras. 159-169 (*supra*, pp. 563-565).

[4] See document 110 EX/40 PRIV., para. 211 (*supra*, p. 567).

374. Another Committee member felt that the teaching of Hebrew was an important part of Jewish culture and that there was a clear violation here of both educational and cultural rights, rights with which Unesco was very much concerned.

375. This view was shared by another Committee member, who added that whereas most minorities in the Soviet Union were not culturally discriminated against, this was not true of the Jewish and the German minorities.

376. A Committee member who had been a member of an international committee on minorities stated that in his experience the Soviet Union was always very receptive to appeals concerning exit visas. He had received much mail from persons around the world interested in this case, and he expressed optimism that an appeal on behalf of Mr Begun would not fall on deaf ears.

377. It was the view of another Committee member that if Mr Begun had been denied an exit visa, the Soviet authorities must have had good reasons for denying it, since they routinely allowed large numbers of persons to emigrate. He also felt that the decision whether or not to allow a person to teach on the basis of his qualifications was an administrative one and thus lay outside Unesco's concern.

378. The Soviet representative thereupon emphasized that Mr Begun was not a qualified teacher of Hebrew and had not previously been a teacher of that language.

379. Several Committee members then pointed out that although government authorities of a country could legitimately decide to prevent a teacher from teaching in the public school system on the basis of his qualifications, their interference with the possibility of his teaching privately was a violation of his human rights. One Committee member felt that the Soviet representative was not dealing with the key issues, and he posed two questions: was Mr Begun free to live in Moscow if he so chose, and was Mr Begun free to teach Hebrew privately if he so chose?

380. The Soviet representative stated that some questions could not be answered yes or no and said that the system in the Soviet Union was unlike the system in the West. In order to live in a city one had to have an authorized apartment and since Mr Begun was divorced from his wife, his old apartment was no longer available to him. Also the Soviet Union imposed requirements for teaching qualifications generally, and Mr Begun just did not have the necessary qualifications for teaching Hebrew.

381. A Committee member expressed the view that although violations of human rights might well be involved here, the scope of the question was so large that it would be better debated in other, larger fora outside Unesco.

No. 345/81 **Union of Soviet Socialist Republics**

382. After an involved discussion, the Committee *decided* to declare the communication inadmissible, as it did not concern human rights within Unesco's fields of competence.

383. A Committee member stated that he wished his dissent concerning this decision to be recorded.

No. 346/81

Concerning *Union of Soviet Socialist Republics*
Case of *Victor Brailovski**

Communication of 18 February 1981 submitted by
Greater New York Conference on Soviet Jewry

Spring 1981 session of the Committee on Conventions and Recommendations (112th session of the Executive Board)[1]

Autumn 1981 session of the Committee on Conventions and Recommendations (113th session of the Executive Board)[2]

Spring 1982 session of the Committee on Conventions and Recommendations (114th session of the Executive Board)[3]

Autumn 1982 session of the Committee on Conventions and Recommendations (115th session of the Executive Board)[4]

---

* From the spring 1981 to autumn 1982 sessions, this communication was being referred to as case of *Irina and Victor Brailovski, Vladimir Kislik, Alexandre Lerner and Nahum Meinam*.

1 See document 112 EX/30 PRIV., paras. 289-334 (*supra*, pp. 595-603), communication No. 242/80 concerning *Union of Soviet Socialist Republics*, case of *Victor Brailovski* et al.

2 See document 113 EX/38 PRIV., paras. 343-365 (*supra*, pp. 603-611), communication No. 242/80 concerning *Union of Soviet Socialist Republics*, case of *Victor Brailovski* et al.

3 See document 114 EX/38 PRIV., paras. 580-618 (*supra*, pp. 611-625), communication No. 242/80 concerning *Union of Soviet Socialist Republics*, case of *Victor Brailovski* et al.

4 See document 115 EX/28 PRIV., paras. 232-262 (*supra*, pp. 625-630), communication No. 242/80 concerning *Union of Soviet Socialist Republics*, case of *Victor Brailovski* et al.

No. 346/81 **Union of Soviet Socialist Republics**

Autumn 1983 session of the Committee on Conventions and Recommendations (117th session of the Executive Board)[5]

131. In June 1981 Mr Brailovski, a cyberneticist, was convicted of having circulated documents considered defamatory to the Soviet Union and sentenced to five years of internal exile, the term being reduced to three years on account of the time already served.

132. This case was examined by the Committee at its spring and [autumn 1981 and spring and autumn 1982 sessions]. At the last session the Committee decided *inter alia* to resume consideration of the admissibility of these communications[6] at one of its forthcoming sessions, once new facts had been communicated to the Director-General.[7] On 26 April 1983 the Secretariat received a letter from the author of [the present communication] requesting that examination of the communication be continued, the author maintaining that Mr Brailovski continued to be subjected to harassment and intimidation. It was alleged that the cyberneticist did not have access to scientific literature of the requisite standard in the area to which he has been assigned, and that he could not discuss his scientific ideas with his colleages. He was not allowed to be released before the end of his term, as anticipated, on the grounds that he had arrived at work ten minutes late one day.

133. The representative of the Government of the USSR who is also a member of the Committee informed the Committee that Mr Brailovski was not in prison but serving a term of deportation in the Caspian area of the USSR where he spends his time repairing various pieces of equipment. The representative of the government pointed out that this was not hard labour nor the area of confinement a bad one. He informed the Committee that Mr Brailovski's sentence will be ending in 1984 and expressed the hope that the alleged victim and his family will thereafter enjoy normal life. He indicated also that Mr Brailovski's family have had access to him and will continue to have access to him. Pointing out that the alleged victim's son is currently enrolled in an institute of higher education, the representative of the government concerned stated that this fact demonstrated that there is no discrimination against Jews in the USSR because the student concerned is not the son of just any Jew, but a convicted one.

---

[5] See document 117 EX/30 PRIV., paras. 131-135; see also document 117 EX/CR/HR/2.

[6] Communications No. 242/80 concerning *Union of Soviet Socialist Republics*, case of *Victor Brailovski* et al., No. 346/81 concerning *Union of Soviet Socialist Republics*, case of *Victor Brailovski*, and No. 418/81 concerning *Union of Soviet Socialist Republics*, case of *Victor Brailovski*, were being considered together.

[7] See document 115 EX/28 PRIV., para. 262 (*supra*, p. 630), communication No. 242/80 concerning *Union of Soviet Socialist Republics*, case of *Victor Brailovski* et al.

Union of Soviet Socialist Republics **No. 346/81**

134. Another member of the Committee said that the statement of the representative of the government concerned implied that there was no change in the situation of the alleged victim who was not able to practise his profession because he was banished to an area where it was not possible for him to do so; all this for exercising his freedom of expression.

135. After this brief exchange of views, the Committee *decided* to keep the communication on its roll while expressing the hope that the competent authorities of the USSR would show clemency to Mr Brailovski so that he could resume his activities in the field of science.

Spring 1984 session of the Committee on Conventions and Recommendations (119th session of the Executive Board)[8]

156. Mr Victor Brailovski, a cyberneticist, was sentenced in June 1981 to five years' internal exile for having circulated documents considered defamatory to the Soviet Union, a term which was reduced to three years on account of the time already served.

157. This communication has been on the Committee's roll since its [spring 1981 session].

158. At the present session [...], the representative of the Soviet Government, who is also a member of the Committee, recalled the circumstances of Mr Brailovski's sentence, the very mild regime under which his sentence had been served and the absence of any unfavourable consequences with respect to his family, and in particular the education of his children. He told the Committee that restrictions on the scientist had been lifted and that he had already returned to his Moscow flat, where he was living at the moment. In answer to questions from members of the Committee about Mr Brailovski's career prospects and his freedom of movement, he said that the future of the person concerned depended on himself alone; it was up to him to take the initiative by making approaches to various enterprises and institutions. The judicial decision set no restrictions on his freedom of movement. The Committee nevertheless asked to be kept informed of Mr Brailovski's future professional situation.

159. Following an exchange of views, the Committee *decided* to consider the case of Mr Brailovski as having been settled and to strike the communication from its list.

---

[8] See document 119 EX/35 PRIV., paras. 156-159; see also documents 119 EX/CR/HR/2 and Add.3.

No. 347/81

Concerning *Guatemala*
Case of *Alaíde Foppa*

Communication of 11 March 1981 submitted by
Gisèle Halimi

Spring 1981 session of the Committee on Conventions and Recommendations
(112th session of the Executive Board)[1]

Autumn 1981 session of the Committee on Conventions and Recommendations
(113th session of the Executive Board)[2]

Autumn 1987 session of the Committee on Conventions and Recommendations
(127th session of the Executive Board)[3]

Spring 1988 session of the Committee on Conventions and Recommendations
(129th session of the Executive Board)[4]

---

[1] See document 112 EX/30 PRIV., paras. 155-163 (*supra*, pp. 773-774), communication No. 317/81 concerning *Guatemala*, case of *Alaíde Foppa*.
[2] See document 113 EX/38 PRIV., paras. 245-256 (*supra*, pp. 775-777), communication No. 317/81 concerning *Guatemala*, case of *Alaíde Foppa*.
[3] See document 127 EX/3 PRIV., paras. 181-188 (*supra*, pp. 777-778), communication No. 317/81 concerning *Guatemala*, case of *Alaíde Foppa*.
[4] See document 129 EX/3 PRIV., paras. 162-165 (*supra*, pp. 778-779), communication No. 317/81 concerning *Guatemala*, case of *Alaíde Foppa*.

No. 348/81

Concerning *Chile*
Case of *Jorge Domingo Martínez Quezada and Irma del Carmen Flores Fajardo*

Communication of 17 March 1981 submitted by
Jorge Domingo Martínez Quezada

Autumn 1981 session of the Committee on Conventions and Recommendations (113th session of the Executive Board)[1]

174. At the time of his arrest on 16 September 1973, Mr J. D. Martínez Quezada, of Chilean nationality, married to Mrs Irma del Carmen Flores Fajardo and father of two children, had been employed by the Municipality of Maipú since 1 October 1959 and was leader of the Maipú Municipal Employees' Association and national leader of the Chilean Municipal Employees' Association.

175. Mr Martínez complains of having been arrested, tortured and tried between 18 October and 13 November 1973, of having been dismissed from his post and from his duties as a trade union leader, of having been prevented from teaching and explaining his political ideas, of having been obliged to go into exile and of being prevented, together with his wife, from returning to Chile. He considers that Articles 18 (freedom of thought, conscience and religion) and 19 (the right to receive and impart ideas) of the Universal Declaration of Human Rights have been violated.

176. The domestic remedies he says he has used are two applications to the Chilean authorities made on 10 August 1978 and 20 July 1979 for authorization to return to Chile and approaches made to the Vicaría de la Solidaridad.

177. The purpose and aim of Mr Martínez Quezada's communication are that the Chilean authorities should cease the violations of human rights of which he alleges himself to be the victim and authorize him to return to Chile and to reside there freely in conditions that will not interfere with his human dignity, in full possession of his rights as a citizen.

[1] See document 113 EX/38 PRIV., paras. 174-182; see also document 113 EX/CR/HR/3.

No. 348/81 **Chile**

178. The representative of the Chilean Government drew the attention of the Committee to the reply in writing made by his government concerning this affair [...][2] and confirmed that it considered the communication inadmissible since it did not come within Unesco's spheres of competence, the alleged victim being a municipal employee. He added that the case might concern the International Labour Organisation.

179. All members who subsequently took the floor spoke in favour of the inadmissibility of the communication. Some of them suggested that it be explained to the author that his case fell rather within the competence of the ILO. One member stated that his government was still concerned about the violations of human rights which occurred in Chile.

180. The representative of the Director-General wished to make it clear that individuals did not enjoy the right of direct access to the ILO, that right being restricted to occupational organizations and states. The United Nations, on the other hand, received individual complaints under [Economic and Social Council resolution 1503 (XLVIII)].

181. One member considered that these explanations might be given to the author. Another member observed that the case had already been put before the United Nations and the [Organization of American States]. Yet another member considered that while it was important to explain the grounds for the Committee's decision it was not essential in every case to explain to the authors the existence of other means of recourse.

182. The Committee therefore *decided* to declare the communication inadmissible on the grounds that it did not come within Unesco's competence under the terms of paragraph 14 (*a*) (iii) of 104 EX/Decision 3.3.

[2] See document 113 EX/CR/HR/3.

No. 352/81

Concerning *Union of Soviet Socialist Republics*
Case of *Vasyl Semenovich Stus*

Communication of 16 March 1981 submitted by
The Lawyers Committee for International Human Rights

Autumn 1981 session of the Committee on Conventions and Recommendations (113th session of the Executive Board)[1]

396. This communication was submitted by the Lawyers Committee for International Human Rights, which described itself as a non-governmental organization with reliable knowledge of the alleged violations.

397. Mr Vasyl Semenovich Stus, a Ukrainian of 43, is described as a poet, translator and literary critic whose works have apparently been translated into several languages (Russian, Byelorussian, German, Spanish, French and English) and whose main publications are said to be two collections of poems "Winter Trees", published in Belgium in 1970, and "The Cheerful Cemetery", an essay on Pavlo Tychynu's poetry ("Phenomenon of its Age") and one on that of Volodymyr Svidzinsky ("Feeble Blossoming of the Personality").

398. Mr Stus is said to have protested in 1965 against the government's suppression of Ukrainian literature and culture and to have defended imprisoned people of letters and of culture while he was employed by the State Historical Archive in Kiev. It is alleged that the Soviet authorities confiscated and destroyed his poems, that he was forced to resign from his post and abandon his studies and that he was refused work until the time he was arrested, in January 1972, on a charge of agitation and anti-Soviet propaganda (violation of Article 62 of the Ukrainian Penal Code). It is further alleged that the trial was motivated solely by the fact that his poems had been published abroad and that, as a result, he was condemned to five years' "corrective" imprisonment in labour camps and three years' internal exile. It is reported that he fell seriously ill in 1976. At the end of his prison sentence, he was reportedly banished to Siberia - to the Tenkivsk region, Magadan province, situated some 10,500 kilo-

[1] See document 113 EX/38 PRIV., paras. 396-420; see also document 113 EX/CR/HR/3.

metres from Moscow, where the winters are particularly severe. There, it is stated, he worked in the coal mines. His delicate health was apparently seriously damaged, and it is reported that he had to undergo an operation for a stomach ulcer. He is said to have asked the English Centre of International PEN in 1978 to help him preserve his works from destruction. In August of that year he was reportedly compelled to burn all his correspondence. It is stated that in 1979 he rejoined the Ukrainian group working to promote the implementation of the Helsinki Agreements. He was apparently again arrested on 18 May 1980 and again charged with violating Article 62 of the Penal Code. It is stated that, as a second-time offender, he was condemned in September-October 1980 to 10 years' hard labour and five years' internal exile. He is alleged to have been tortured before trial.

399. It is stated that at present he can publish nothing and that he has been prevented from accepting invitations to teach or lecture on literary subjects in American universities (Harvard, Temple and Illinois).

400. It is alleged that the persecution to which he has been subjected continued throughout his detention, that he was accused of being a Fascist and attacked personally in the press.

401. The representative of the Soviet Government stated that this communication was totally and unconditionally inadmissible. He found it incomprehensible that the jurists submitting this communication should ask for the consideration of the Committee in a case where there had been a court sentence and an upholding of that sentence by a higher court in accordance with Soviet law. He stated that the assertions that Mr Stus's sentencing was for the publishing of his poems outside the country and for his joining the Ukrainian group monitoring the Helsinki Agreement was designed to mislead the Committee. What in fact Mr Stus had done was to write open letters critical of the Soviet system which were published and still are published by foreign nationalistic organizations which are known to be hostile to the Soviet Union.

402. It was a question, he went on to say, of the tenor of Mr Stus's writings. The representative warned that not everything that was put into rhyme should be considered as poetry; verses inciting hatred and calling for violent aggression ran counter to the principles of Unesco and could not be called poetry, he said.

403. The Soviet representative read some of Mr Stus's verses to the Committee and pointed out that Mr Stus described the Soviet Union as a concentration-camp country built on blood and bones. The representative wondered how any country could tolerate such hateful imagery directed against it. In addition, he said, Mr Stus in his prose writings had been perpetrating subversion against the Soviet Union; Mr Stus

called for violent uprising and vengeance for political reasons. For these reasons the communication should be rejected, he said.

404. A Committee member felt that the case at hand came under Article 15 of the [International] Covenant on Economic, Social and Cultural Rights. This Article, he said, unlike Article 19 of the [International] Covenant on Civil and Political Rights could not be limited on national security grounds by the state. He went on to point out that poets in many countries wrote angry verses, and that countries should not censor writers because they wrote things the country finds offensive. Furthermore, he stated, it was totally unfair to punish Mr Stus for the activities of a foreign publishing house.

405. The representative of the Soviet Government stated that Article 20 of the [International] Covenant on Civil and Political Rights prohibited war propaganda and advocacy of national, racial or religious hatred, and in the view of the representative Article 20 supported the results in the case of Mr Stus.

406. Another Committee member felt that there were limits on poetic licence. He felt that hateful works which contained false information such as those written by Mr Stus should not qualify as educational or cultural works, and they would certainly be inappropriate for presentation in schools to children. The fact that a person was a writer did not automatically qualify him for Unesco's competence, certainly not if he committed criminal activities.

407. Another member of the Committee pointed out that Mr Stus's right to teach was not at issue here. The broad issue, he said, was whether the case of a person who had been sentenced under the laws of a country could be examined by the Committee. It was clear that this could be done, he said, and he pointed to the Committee's decision in its previous cases, notably the *Massera* case.[2] He went on to say that the publishing of Mr Stus's poetry by others than himself was irrelevant to the case. The Committee member went on to emphasize that there was not the slighest evidence that Mr Stus had been engaged in violent activities against the state. All Mr Stus had done was use words, he had expressed his feelings, as writers have done over the centuries, he said. This right was protected by the Universal Declaration of Human Rights; Mr Stus indeed had strong nationalistic feelings, but he had a right to express them, it was stated. Also, the Committee member said, it was not fair to judge the totality of Mr Stus's works on the basis of a few quotations. He went on to say that this was a clear case of a person being persecuted merely for expressing himself, and the case was thus clearly admissible.

[2] Communication No. 103/79 concerning *Uruguay*, case of *José Luis Massera*.

408. Another Committee member felt that the Committee's position on national legislation was not completely settled; it was necessary to proceed case by case. While he understood how this kind of poetry could be seen as distasteful to the Soviet Union, he pointed out that some very great poets have been against their governments. He went on to indicate that Mr Stus had not actively worked to overthrow the Soviet Union and that the sentence he had received was a considerably harsh one. The question also arose in this case, he said, as to what weight to give to the various provisions of the international covenants which had been cited.

409. It was the view of another Committee member that [Article 20 of the International Covenant on Civil and Political Rights] cited by the Soviet representative was irrelevant here as there was no racism, war propaganda, etc. in Mr Stus's writings. He further felt that the circulation of false information was not a valid reason for putting someone in gaol.

410. The representative of the Director~General explained that Article 4 of the [International] Covenant on Economic, Social and Cultural Rights did in fact allow certain limitations to all the rights outlined in that Covenant, provided that they were clearly outlined in legislation, were compatible with those rights, and were solely for the purpose of promoting the general welfare in a democratic society. He went on to point out the principle of the indivisibility of human rights and explained that the rights of one Covenant were not hierarchically above those in the other. In fact the cited Article [19, paragraph 3 (*b*), of the International Covenant on Civil and Political Rights] did allow certain restrictions, as did Article 20, the latter being one of the most controversial articles in the Covenants and one to which certain states made reservations upon ratification, but not the state concerned by the present communication. He explained that the states which had not ratified the Covenants would nevertheless be to a certain extent morally bound by their provisions because of the competence of Unesco.

411. A Committee member felt that the communication had deliberately distorted the facts of the case for slanderous purposes. It was an abuse of the right to submit communications and was irreceivable, he said. The claim that Ukrainian cultural activities were being stifled was false, he went on to say, and explained that one person out of ten was involved in cultural activities in that Republic. Millions of books and magazines were published annually, and there were hundreds of writers, painters, etc. who had at their disposal special houses and facilities. There existed ample opportunity to publish critical material and no one was prosecuted for doing so. Mr Stus, he said, had not been prosecuted because of his cultural activities, but rather because he had adopted an anti-state position and had made appeals against the state. The Committee member said that he was officially empowered to say on behalf of the Ukrainian authorities that there had not been any torturing of Mr Stus. Further-

more it was a lie that his works had been burned. The Soviet Union, he said, ranked first in the world for the number of foreign works translated. He stated that as far as the trial was concerned, Mr Stus had had the right to defend himself and had had legal counsel. The Committee member felt that the authors of the communication were trying to push Unesco into interfering in the domestic affairs of the USSR; the Committee could not try to have domestic legislation changed. For all these reasons he felt the case was clearly inadmissible.

412. Another Committee member was of the opinion that few states could tolerate writings such as Mr Stus's. However, though he did not wish to interfere in any domestic affairs, he said that he found the sentence to be quite harsh and pointed out that the simple banning of the writings was the countermeasure other states would have used. He wondered whether it might not be possible for the Committee, without questioning state structures, to call upon the Soviet Union for a review of this situation. Yet another Committee member felt that the works of artists could not be categorized as good or bad and that artists required the freedom to express feelings, for if only certain artists were considered acceptable there would have been far fewer artists throughout history. He felt that the communication fulfilled the requirements for admission and asked what might happen to the defence of universal culture if Unesco refused to examine a case such as this one.

413. The question was raised by a Committee member why the Committee had decided not to question certain cases before it where sentences had been passed out in conformity with national legislation and in the present case was leaning towards questioning the sentencing.

414. It was stated by another Committee member that though there was indeed somewhat of a conflict between the obligation not to interfere in domestic affairs and the obligation to see if international covenants were being respected, the resolution of such a conflict should be seen in a practical and realistic way in terms of what could be achieved in the specific case on a humanitarian or other basis.

415. The representative of the Soviet Government felt that the limitations on expression which exist in Soviet legislation were perfectly in keeping with the Soviet interpretation of the international instruments. As to the sentence, it had been the result of the deep-rooted conviction of the trial court, which was authorized by legislation to pass such a sentence, he said. He felt that it would be contradictory to ask for humanitarian consideration in this case and at the same time to keep the case on the Committee's agenda. He pointed out that the decision was taken by an independent duly constituted court, and that it was not for the Committee to question it.

416. A Committee member felt that an appeal to the Soviet Government would not constitute a judgement or condemnation of the government nor would it be a questioning of the propriety of the court in question. He pointed out that the Committee endeavoured to work towards amicable solutions with the governments involved in the cases before the Committee and in the present case a suspension of a decision on the admissibility and an appeal to the government to perhaps lessen the sentence would not be inappropriate. Even though Mr Stus may have shown extreme indiscretion.in the choice of his language, his sentence was none the less a harsh one.

417. Another Committee member stated that the question at hand was whether or not the communication was admissible. All the conditions of admissibility seemed to be met except the exhaustion of domestic remedies, but since Stus was in prison it would be unreasonable to expect this of him. However, since the actions of Mr Stus would be unacceptable in any country, the admission of the communication might not be appropriate either.

418. A Committee member felt that it was doubtful that the poems of a so-called secondary poet could endanger the Soviet Union. He felt that there had been an over-reaction in this matter; it should not be the role of the state to censor the mere expression of feelings by individuals.

419. It was stressed by several Committee members that a few excerpts would not be sufficient to judge the writings of Mr Stus, and they emphasized the need for the Committee to have before it at its next session a significant amount of Mr Stus's poems, translated into Unesco's working languages.

420. Following a discussion, the Committee *decided*:

(i) to resume consideration of the admissibility of the communication at the next session, and with that in view;

(ii) to request the author of the communication to supply further details on the compatibility of the grievances alleged in the communication with the International Covenants on Human Rights, especially Article 19, paragraph 3, (protection of public order) and Article 20, paragraph 2, (prohibition of any advocacy of national hatred) of the International Covenant on Civil and Political Rights;

(iii) to request the government concerned to supplement the details already supplied, particularly as regards Articles 4 and 15 of the International Covenant on Economic, Social and Cultural Rights and Article 19, paragraph 2, of the International Covenant on Civil and Political Rights.

Union of Soviet Socialist Republics **No. 352/81**

Spring 1982 session of the Committee on Conventions and Recommendations (114th session of the Executive Board)[3]

651. This communication is submitted by the Lawyers Committee for International Human Rights, which describes itself as a non-governmental organization with reliable knowledge of the alleged violations.

652. Mr Vasyl Semenovich Stus, a Ukrainian of 43, is described as a poet, translator and literary critic whose works have apparently been translated into several languages (Russian, Byelorussian, German, Spanish, French and English) and whose main publications are said to be two collections of poems "Winter Trees" , and "The Cheerful Cemetery", an essay on Pavlo Tychynu's poetry ("Phenomenon of its Age") and one on that of Volodymyr Svidzinsky ("Feeble Blossoming of the Personality").

653. Mr Stus is said to have protested in 1965 against the government's suppression of Ukrainian literature and culture and to have defended imprisoned people of letters and of culture while he was employed by the State Historical Archive in Kiev. It is alleged that the Soviet authorities confiscated and destroyed his poems, that he was dismissed from his post and had to abandon his studies and that he was refused work until the time he was arrested, in January 1972, on a charge of agitation and anti-Soviet propaganda (violation of Article 62 of the Ukrainian Penal Code). It is further alleged that his trial was motivated solely by the fact that his poems had been published abroad and that, as a result, he was condemned to five years' "corrective" imprisonment in labour camps and three years' internal exile. It is reported that he fell seriously ill in 1976. At the end of his prison sentence, he was reportedly banished to Siberia - to the Tenkivsk region, Magadan province, situated some 10,500 kilometres from Moscow, where the winters are particularly severe. There, it is stated, he worked in the coal mines. His delicate health was apparently seriously damaged, and it is reported that he had to undergo an operation for a stomach ulcer. He is said to have asked the English Centre of International PEN in 1978 to help him preserve his works from destruction. In August of that year he was reportedly compelled to burn all his correspondence. It is stated that in 1979 he rejoined the Ukrainian group working to promote the implementation of the Helsinki Agreements. He was apparently again arrested on 18 May 1980 and again charged with violating Article 62 of the Penal Code. It is stated that, as a second-time offender, he was condemned in September-October 1980 to 10 years' special labour and five years' internal exile. He is alleged to have been tortured before trial.

---

[3] See document 114 EX/38 PRIV., paras. 651-685; see also document 114 EX/CR/HR/2.

654. It is stated that at present he can publish nothing and that he has been prevented from accepting invitations to teach or lecture on literary subjects in American universities (Harvard, Temple and Illinois).

655. It is alleged that the persecution to which he has been subjected continued througout his detention, that he was accused of being a Fascist and attacked personally in the press.

656. The rights said to have been violated are the right to privacy (Article 12 of the Universal Declaration of Human Rights and Article 17 of the International Covenant on Civil and Political Rights), the right to freedom of opinion and expression (Article 19 of the Covenant), the right freely to participate in cultural life, to enjoy the arts and to share in scientific advancement (Article 27 of the Universal Declaration and Article 15 of the International Covenant on Economic, Social and Cultural Rights) and the right to freedom of peaceful assembly and association (Article 20 of the Universal Declaration).

657. It is stated that Mr Stus has not been able to use any means of redress. The matter has not been submitted to any international authority other than Unesco.

658. The stated purpose and aim of the author's communication is to obtain strong, decisive action from the world community in Mr Stus's defence so that he may recover his safety and freedom of movement and expression.

659. At the [autumn 1981 session] the representative of the Soviet Government stated that this communication was totally and unconditionally inadmissible. He found it incomprehensible that the jurists submitting this communication should ask for the consideration of the Committee in a case where there had been a court sentence and an upholding of that sentence by a higher court in accordance with Soviet law. He stated that the assertions that Mr Stus's sentencing was for the publishing of his poems outside the country and for his joining the Ukrainian group monitoring the Helsinki Agreement was designed to mislead the Committee. What in fact Mr Stus had done, he stated, was to write open letters critical of the Soviet system which were published and still are published by foreign nationalistic organizations known to be hostile to the Soviet Union.

660. It was a question, he went on to say, of the tenor of Mr Stus's writings. The representative warned that not everything that was put into rhyme should be considered poetry; verses inciting hatred and calling for violent aggression ran counter to the principles of Unesco and could not be called poetry, he said.

Union of Soviet Socialist Republics **No. 352/81**

661. The representative of the Soviet Government read some of Mr Stus's verses to the Committee and pointed out that Mr Stus described the Soviet Union as a concentration-camp country built on blood and bones. He wondered how any country could tolerate such hateful imagery directed against it. In addition, he said, Mr Stus in his prose writings had perpetrated subversion against the Soviet Union, calling for violent uprisings and vengeance for political reasons. The communication should therefore be rejected, he said.

662. A Committee member felt that the case at hand came under Article 15 of the [International] Covenant on Economic, Social and Cultural Rights. This Article, he said, unlike Article 19 of the [International] Covenant on Civil and Political Rights could not be limited on national security grounds by the state. He went on to point out that poets in many countries wrote angry verses, and that writers should not be censored because they wrote things the country found offensive. Furthermore, he stated, it was totally unfair to punish Mr Stus for the activities of a foreign publishing house.

663. The representative of the Soviet Government stated that Article 20 of the [International] Covenant on Civil and Political Rights prohibited war propaganda and advocacy of national, racial or religious hatred. In his view, that Article 20 supported the results in the case of Mr Stus.

664. Another Committee member felt that there were limits on poetic licence. He felt that hateful works which contained false information such as those written by Mr Stus should not qualify as educational or cultural works, and they would be inappropriate for presentation in schools to children. The fact that a person was a writer, he added, did not automatically qualify him for Unesco's competence; certainly not if he committed criminal activities.

665. Another member of the Committee pointed out that Mr Stus's right to teach was not at issue here; the problem, he said was whether the case of a person who had been sentenced under the laws of a country could be examined by the Committee. He considered that this could be done in view of the Committee's decisions in its previous cases, notably the *Massera* case. He went on to say that the publishing of Mr Stus's poetry by others than himself was irrelevant to the case; there was not the slightest evidence that Mr Stus had been engaged in violent activities against the state. All Mr Stus had done was use words and express his feelings, like all writers over the centuries, he said, and that right was protected by the Universal Declaration of Human Rights. Mr Stus indeed had strong nationalistic feelings, but he had a right to express them, it was stated; it was not fair to judge the totality of Mr Stus's works on the basis of a few quotations. He went on to say that this was a clear case of a

person being persecuted merely for expressing himself, and the case was thus clearly admissible.

666. Another Committee member felt that the Committee's position on national legislation was not completely settled; it was necessary to proceed case by case. While he understood how this kind of poetry could be seen as distasteful to the Soviet Union, he pointed out that some very great poets have been against their governments. He went on to indicate that Mr Stus had not actively worked to overthrow the Soviet Union and that the sentence he had received was a considerably harsh one. The question also arose in this case, he said, as to what weight to give to the various provisions of the international convenants which had been cited.

667. Another Committee member found that [Article 20 of the International Covenant on Civil and Political Rights] cited by the representative of the Soviet Government was irrelevant here as there was no racism, war propaganda, etc., in Mr Stus's writings. He also felt that the circulation of false information was not a valid reason for putting someone in gaol.

668. The representative of the Director-General explained that Article 4 of the [International] Covenant on Economic, Social and Cultural Rights, did in fact allow certain limitations to all the rights outlined in that Covenant, provided that they were clearly outlined in legislation, were compatible with those rights, and were solely for the purpose of promoting the general welfare in a democratic society. He went on to point out the principle of the indivisibility of human rights and emphasized that the rights set out in one Covenant were not hierarchically above those in the other. In fact the cited Article [19, paragraph 3 (*b*), of the International Covenant on Civil and Political Rights] did allow certain restrictions, as did Article 20, the latter being one of the most controversial articles in the Covenants and one to which certain states had made reservations upon ratification, but not the state concerned by the present communication. The representative of the Director-General considered that the states which had not ratified the Covenants would nevertheless be to a certain extent morally bound by their provisions because of the competence of Unesco.

669. A Committee member stated that the communication had deliberately distorted the facts of the case for slanderous purposes. The claim that Ukrainian cultural activities were being stifled was false, he went on to say, and explained that one person out of ten was involved in cultural activities in the Ukraine; millions of books and magazines were published annually, and there were hundreds of writers, painters, etc., who had at their disposal special houses and facilities; there existed ample opportunity to publish critical material and no one was prosecuted for doing so. Mr Stus, he said, had not been prosecuted because of his cultural activities, but rather because he had adopted an anti-Soviet position and had incited people to oppose the

state. The Committee member said that he was officially empowered to say on behalf of the Ukrainian authorities that there had not been any torturing of Mr Stus. Furthermore it was a lie that his works had been burned. The Soviet Union, he went on, ranked first in the world for the number of foreign works translated. He stated that as far as the trial was concerned, Mr Stus had had the right to defend himself and had had legal counsel. The Committee member felt that the authors of the communication were trying to push Unesco into interfering in the domestic affairs of the Union of Soviet Socialist Republics; the Committee could not try to have domestic legislation changed. For all these reasons he felt the case was clearly inadmissible.

670. Another Committee member was of the opinion that few states could tolerate writings such as Mr Stus's. However, he said that he found the sentence to be quite harsh and pointed out that the simple banning of the writings was the countermeasure other states would have used. He wondered whether it might not be possible for the Committee, without questioning state structures, to call upon the Soviet Union for a review of the case.

671. Yet another Committee member thought that the works of artists could not be categorized as good or bad and that artists required the freedom to express feelings. He felt that the communication fulfilled the requirements for admission and wondered what might happen to the defence of universal culture if Unesco refused to examine a case such as this one.

672. The question was raised by a Committee member why the Committee had decided not to question certain cases before it where sentences had been passed out in conformity with national legislation and in the present case was leaning towards questioning the sentencing.

673. It was stated by another Committee member that though there was indeed something of a conflict between the obligation not to interfere in domestic affairs and the obligation to see if international covenants were being respected, the resolution of such a conflict should be seen in a practical and realistic way in terms of what could be achieved in the specific case on a humanitarian or other basis.

674. Taking the floor once more, the representative of the Soviet Government stated that the limitations on expression which existed in Soviet legislation were perfectly in keeping with the Soviet interpretation of the international instruments, that the sentence passed on Mr Stus had been the result of the deep-rooted conviction of the trial court, and that it would accordingly be contradictory to ask for humanitarian reconsideration in this case and at the same time request that the case be kept on the Committee's agenda.

No. 352/81 **Union of Soviet Socialist Republics**

675. A Committee member felt that an appeal to the Soviet Government would not constitute a judgement or condemnation of the government nor would it be a questioning of the propriety of the court in question. He pointed out that the Committee endeavoured to work towards amicable solutions with the governments involved in the cases before the Committee and in the present case a suspension of a decision on the admissibility and an appeal to the government to perhaps lessen the sentence would not be inappropriate.

676. Another Committee member stated that the question at hand was whether or not the communication was admissible. All the conditions of admissibility seemed to be met except the exhaustion of domestic remedies, but since Stus was in prison it would be unreasonable to expect this of him. However, since the actions of Mr Stus would be unacceptable in any country, the admission of the communication might not be appropriate either.

677. A Committee member felt that it was doubtful that the poems of a so-called secondary poet could endanger the Soviet Union. He felt that there had been an over-reaction in this matter; it should not be the role of the state to censor the mere expression of feelings by individuals.

678. It was stressed by several Committee members that a few excerpts would not be sufficient to judge the writings of Mr Stus, and they emphasized the need for the Committee to have before it at its next session a significant amount of Mr Stus's poems, translated into Unesco's working languages.

679. Following a discussion, the Committee decided:[4]

(i) to resume consideration of the admissibility of the communication at the next session, and, with that in view;

(ii) to request the author of the communication to supply further details on the compatibility of the grievances alleged in the communication with the International Covenants on Human Rights, especially Article 19, paragraph 3, (protection of public order) and Article 20, paragraph 2, (prohibition of any advocacy of national hatred) of the International Covenant on Civil and Political Rights;

(iii) to request the government concerned to supplement the details already supplied, particularly as regards Articles 4 and 15 of the International Cove-

[4] See document 113 EX/38 PRIV., para. 420 (*supra*, p. 878).

nant on Economic, Social and Cultural Rights and Article 19, paragraph 2, of the International Covenant on Civil and Political Rights.

680. The Secretariat has so far received no further information concerning this communication.

681. At the Committee's present session the representative of the Soviet Government stated that the imprisonment of Mr Stus had not been contrary neither to national law nor to international standards and that this had been clearly demonstrated by him at the Committee's [autumn 1981] session. He pointed out that the author of the communication had not provided any new information which could be seen to reply to the Committee's request for further information. The author's reply in this case consisted of broad generalizations and laughable requests. How could Mr Stus be allowed to take up teaching posts abroad when he was serving a prison sentence, the Soviet representative asked. In view of the silence of the author the Committee should strike the conwunication from its list, he said.

682. A Committee member stated that he had expected the Soviet Government to provide translations of Mr Stus's poems so that the Committee could determine whether in fact they were as subversive as they were claimed to be. This was the key question here, he said.

683. The Soviet representative pointed out that the Committee's decision had not called upon the Soviet Government to provide translations of the poems. It was for the author to provide information on elements which had been deemed to be missing. Since he had not done so, the case should be dismissed.

684. In reply to a question the representative of the Director-General explained that as far as the Committee's power of inquiry was concerned, three sources were foreseen. The two main ones were obviously the authors and the governments concerned, but a third, rarely used source, was the "relevant information at the disposal of the Director-General" foreseen by paragraph [14] (*f*) of [104 EX/Decision 3.3].

685. After a brief discussion the Committee *decided* to postpone its consideration of the admissability of this case in view of the interim reply of the authors which indicated that translations of Mr Stus's poems would be sent to the Committee in the near future.

No. 352/81 **Union of Soviet Socialist Republics**

Autumn 1982 session of the Committee on Conventions and Recommendations (115th session of the Executive Board)[5]

263. This communication is submitted by the Lawyers Committee for International Human Rights, which describes itself as a non-governmental organization with reliable knowledge of the alleged violations. Mr Vasyl Semenovich Stus, a Ukrainian of 43, is described as a poet, translator and literary critic whose works have apparently been translated into several languages.

264. Mr Stus is said to have protested in 1965 against the government's suppression of Ukrainian literature and culture and to have defended imprisoned people of letters and of culture while he was employed by the State Historical Archive in Kiev. It is alleged that the Soviet authorities confiscated and destroyed his poems, that he was dismissed from his post and had to abandon his studies and that he was refused work until the time he was arrested, in January 1972, on a charge of agitation and anti-Soviet propaganda (violation of Article 62 of the Ukrainian Penal Code). It is further alleged that his trial was motivated solely by the fact that his poems had been published abroad and that, as a result, he was condemned to five years' "corrective" imprisonment in labour camps and three years' internal exile. It is reported that he fell seriously ill in 1976. At the end of his prison sentence, he was reportedly banished to Siberia - to the Tenkivsk region, Magadan province, situated some 10,500 kilometres from Moscow, where the winters are particularly severe. There, it is stated, he worked in the coal mines. His delicate health was apparently seriously damaged, and it is reported that he had to undergo an operation for a stomach ulcer. He is said to have asked the English Centre of International PEN in 1978 to help him preserve his works from destruction. In August of that year he was reportedly compelled to burn all his correspondence. It is stated that in 1979 he rejoined the Ukrainian group working to promote the implementation of the Helsinki Agreements. He was apparently again arrested on 18 May 1980 and again charged with violating Article 62 of the Penal Code. It is stated that, as a second-time offender, he was condemned in September-October 1980 to 10 years' special labour and five years' internal exile. He is alleged to have been tortured before trial.

265. It is stated that at present he can publish nothing and that he has been prevented from accepting invitations to teach or lecture on literary subjects in American universities (Harvard, Temple and Illinois).

---

[5] See document 115 EX/28 PRIV., paras. 263-292; see also document 115 EX/CR/HR/2.

266. It is alleged that the persecution to which he has been subjected continued throughout his detention, that he was accused of being a Fascist and attacked personally in the press.

267. At the autumn 1981 session, the representative of the Soviet Government stated that this communication was totally and unconditionally inadmissible. He found it incomprehensible that the jurists submitting this communication should ask for the consideration of the Committee in a case where there had been a court sentence and an upholding of that sentence by a higher court in accordance with Soviet law. He stated that the assertions that Mr Stus's sentencing was for the publishing of his poems outside the country and for his joining the Ukrainian group monitoring the Helsinki Agreement was designed to mislead the Committee. What in fact Mr Stus had done, he stated, was to write open letters critical of the Soviet system which were published and still are published by foreign nationalistic organizations known to be hostile to the Soviet Union.

268. The representative of the Soviet Government read some of Mr Stus's verses to the Committee and pointed out that Mr Stus described the Soviet Union as a concentration-camp country built on blood and bones. He wondered how any country could tolerate such hateful imagery directed against it. In addition, he said, Mr Stus in his prose writings had perpetrated subversion against the Soviet Union, calling for violent uprisings and vengeance for political reasons. The communication should therefore be rejected, he said.

269. Another Committee member felt that there were limits on poetic licence. He felt that hateful works which contained false information such as those written by Mr Stus should not qualify as educational or cultural works, and they would be inappropriate for presentation in schools to children. The fact that a person was a writer, he added, did not automatically qualify him for Unesco's competence; certainly not if he committed criminal activities.

270. Another member of the Committee pointed out that Mr Stus's right to teach was not at issue here; the problem, he said was whether the case of a person who had been sentenced under the laws of a country could be examined by the Committee. He considered that this could be done in view of the Committee's decisions in its previous cases, notably the *Massera* case. He went on to say that the publishing of Mr Stus's poetry by others than himself was irrelevant to the case; there was not the slightest evidence, that Mr Stus had been engaged in violent activities against the state. All Mr Stus had done was use words and express his feelings, like all writers over the centuries, he said, and that right was protected by the Universal Declaration of Human Rights. Mr Stus indeed had strong nationalistic feelings, but he had a right to express them, it was stated; it was not fair to judge the totality of Mr Stus's works

on the basis of a few quotations. He went on to say that this was a clear case of a person being persecuted merely for expressing himself, and the case was thus clearly admissible.

271. Another Committee member found that [Article 20 of the International Covenant on Civil and Political Rights] cited by the representative of the Soviet Government was irrelevant here as there was no racism, war propaganda, etc., in Mr Stus's writings. He also felt that the circulation of false information was not a valid reason for putting someone in goal.

272. A Committee member stated that the communication had deliberately distorted the facts of the case for slanderous purposes. The claim that Ukrainian cultural activities were being stifled was false, he went on to say, and explained that one person out of ten was involved in cultural activities in the Ukraine; millions of books and magazines were published annually, and there were hundreds of writers, painters, etc., who had at their disposal special houses and facilities; there existed ample opportunity to publish critical material and no one was prosecuted for doing so. Mr Stus, he said, had not been prosecuted because of his cultural activities, but rather because he had adopted an anti-Soviet position and had incited people to oppose the state. The Committee member said that he was officially empowered to say on behalf of the Ukrainian authorities that there had not been any torturing of Mr Stus. Furthermore it was a lie that his works had been burned. The Soviet Union, he went on, ranked first in the world for the number of foreign works translated. He stated that as far as the trial was concerned, Mr Stus had had the right to defend himself and had had legal counsel. The Committee member felt that the authors of the communication were trying to push Unesco into interfering in the domestic affairs of the Union of Soviet Socialist Republics; the Committee could not try to have domestic legislation changed. For all these reasons he felt the case was clearly inadmissible.

273. Yet another Committee member thought that the works of artists could not be categorized as good or bad and that artists required the freedom to express feelings. He felt that the communication fulfilled the requirements for admission and wondered what might happen to the defence of universal culture if Unesco refused to examine a case such as this one.

274. Taking the floor once more, the representative of the Soviet Government stated that the limitations on expression which existed in Soviet legislation were perfectly in keeping with the Soviet interpretation of the international instruments, that the sentence passed on Mr Stus had been the result of the deep-rooted conviction of the trial court, and that it would accordingly be contradictory to ask for humanitarian reconsideration in this case and at the same time request that the case be kept on the Committee's agenda.

Union of Soviet Socialist Republics **No. 352/81**

275. It was stressed by several Committee members that a few excerpts would not be sufficient to judge the writings of Mr Stus, and they emphasized the need for the Committee to have before it at its next session a significant amount of Mr Stus's poems, translated into Unesco's working languages.

276. Following a discussion, the Committee decided:[6]

> (i) to resume consideration of the admissibility of the communication at the next session, and, with that in view;
>
> (ii) to request the author of the communication to supply further details on the compatibility of the grievances alleged in the communication with the International Covenants on Human Rights, especially Article 19, paragraph 3, (protection of public order) and Article 20, paragraph 2, (prohibition of any advocacy of national hatred) of the International Covenant on Civil and Political Rights;
>
> (iii) to request the government concerned to supplement the details already supplied, particularly as regards Articles 4 and 15 of the International Covenant on Economic, Social and Cultural Rights and Article 19, paragraph 2, of the International Covenant on Civil and Political Rights.

277. At the spring 1982 session, the representative of the Soviet Government stated that the imprisonment of Mr Stus had not been contrary either to national law or to international standards and that this had been clearly demonstrated by him at the Committee's [autumn 1981] session. He pointed out that the author of the communication had not provided any new information which could be seen to reply to the Committee's request for further information. The author's reply in this case consisted of broad generalizations and laughable requests. How could Mr Stus be allowed to take up teaching posts abroad when he was serving a prison sentence, the Soviet representative asked. In view of the silence of the author the Committee should strike the communication from its list, he said.

278. A Committee member stated that he had expected the Soviet Government to provide translations of Mr Stus's poems so that the Committee could determine whether in fact they were as subversive as they were claimed to be. This was the key question here, he said.

279. After a brief discussion the Committee decided to postpone its consideration of the admissibility of this case in view of the interim reply of the authors which indi-

---

[6] See document 113 EX/38 PRIV., para. 420 (*supra*, p. 878).

cated that translations of Mr Stus's poems would be sent to the Committee in the near future.[7] On 10 May 1982 the Secretariat received from the Lawyers Committee for International Human Rights a letter forwarding copies of three of Mr Stus's poems translated into English.

280. At the autumn 1982 session, the representative of the Soviet Government reminded the Committee that Mr Stus had committed acts of incitement to violence and hatred. In his so-called poems Mr Stus criticized the Soviet system, and his writings were likely to provoke negative feelings which could lead to violent acts, the Soviet representative said; Mr Stus had been sentenced under a penal code article designed to punish such acts. In no way was the question one involving a violation of freedom of expression.

281. The authors of this communication had submitted to the Committee three of Mr Stus's poems dating from the mid-nineteen sixties and which in fact did not include destructive elements. But the presentation of harmless writings was merely a trick and had no bearing on the question whether Stus had written other, slanderous works, the Soviet representative said. In his view, the case was clearly inadmissible.

282. Certain Committee members recalled that the Committee had only had excerpts of Mr Stus's poems read to it by the Soviet representative. They pointed out that it would be important for the Committee to see the excerpts in their complete context rather than as isolated phrases. It appeared that Mr Stus was indeed a talented poet whose only "flaw" was that he was a Ukrainian nationalist. The Committee members felt that since it was often possible to take excerpts of a work and give them a different meaning than that originally intended, the Committee should be allowed to see the excerpts in their proper context.

283. The Soviet representative then explained that in each country the concept existed that there could be justifiable limitations on the freedom of speech. Furthermore, he said there were many witnesses at the Stus trial who had testified that he had called on them and others to use all forms of violence against Soviet authorities.

284. The Soviet representative read aloud some excerpts of Mr Stus's poems and said that such writings did not qualify for protection as an exercise of freedom of speech and that Unesco should not concern itself with protecting such slanderous exressions.

285. A Committee member felt that although every country had its own view and legislation in the area of freedom of speech, the Committee was still justified in

---

[7] See document 114 EX/38 PRIV., para. 685 (*supra*, p. 885).

making comments thereon. The mutual respect between Member States of Unesco did not preclude the consideration of cases such as this by the Committee, since the world intellectual community had a certain moral code with which Unesco must be concerned.

286. Another Committee member stated that there existed no liberty without limits and that individuals had to take into consideration the legislation of the country in which they were writing. As for the question of Mr Stus's guilt, this was a question within the competence of the national juridical authorities, and it would be inappropriate for Unesco to attempt to review the court findings. The content of the poems could in fact even run afoul of the legal standards in various countries, but of course standards did change and evolve the Committee member said. There was also the question as to whether Mr Stus's poems were disseminated without his knowledge or collaboration, a question which further complicated an already complex case. The Committee member felt that the best manner to proceed was to entrust the Director-General with taking such steps as he thought appropriate in this case.

287. Certain members of the Committee emphasized that it was not just the poems of Mr Stus which had led to his conviction but mainly his actions inciting violence and hatred. One of the Committee members stated that Mr Stus did not in fact reflect the views of the Ukrainians. The man in the street in the Ukraine did not like the poems of Mr Stus; the Ukraine had many great poets but Stus was not one of them, he said. These Committee members felt that the case was definitely not admissible.

288. Another Committee member emphasized that the Committee still had not been presented with any evidence that Mr Stus had committed any acts of violence against the Soviet Union. He stated that it would be useful to have for the record information as to exactly what it was which had sent Mr Stus to prison the first time and also the second time.

289. Another Committee member made the point that the Committee could now see, thanks to the poems which had been submitted by the authors of the communication that Mr Stus was indeed a poet and came within Unesco's fields of competence. The Committee member also said that while international instruments gave the national authorities a certain discretion in slightly limiting some of the freedoms set forth in those instruments, the international supervisory bodies could review whether that discretion had been properly exercised. That discretion did not allow an absolute suppression of any freedom by the state he said.

290. The Soviet representative emphasized that the Universal Declaration of Human Rights provided that

> In the exercise of his rights and freedoms, everyone shall be subject only to such limitations as are determined by law solely for the purpose of securing due recognition and respect for the rights and freedoms of others and of meeting the just requirements of morality, public order and the general welfare in a democratic society.

The Soviet representative stated that the complex question of "public order" was one which came within the sole competence of the Soviet juridical organs. A Soviet court had decided that Mr Stus's describing the Soviet Union as a large concentration camp and other similar slanderous remarks were insulting and injurious to the Soviet Union. The Soviet representative went on to say that the Committee was more than the sum of its parts and such a Unesco Committee had an obligation to preserve the mutual respect of its Member States.

291. A Committee member felt it would not be useful to go into deep discussion on concepts which varied greatly from culture to culture. He felt that the solution could not be found in confrontation but rather in leaving the matter in the hands of the Director-General for appropriate action.

292. After some further discussion, the Committee *decided*:

> (i) to request the representative of the government concerned to approach the competent authorities on humanitarian grounds with a view to securing a reduction in the sentences of 10 years' imprisonment and five years' assignation to a forced residence, since it was the exercise by Stus, even if it might be deemed improper, of the freedom of expression which is essential to Unesco that was one of the grounds of the proceedings initiated against Stus and of his sentencing, and to inform the Director-General of the result of his approaches;
>
> (ii) not to continue consideration of the admissibility of the present communication.

No. 353/81

Concerning *Union of Soviet Socialist Republics*
Case of *Yuli Kosharovsky*

Communication of 30 March 1981 submitted by
Greater New York Conference on Soviet Jewry

Spring 1982 session of the Committee on Conventions and Recommendations (114th session of the Executive Board)[1]

196. The author of the communication, the Greater New York Conference on Soviet Jewry, claims to be a non-governmental organization with reliable knowledge of the alleged violations.

197. Mr Yuli Kosharovsky, a radio electronics engineer, was employed in a research institute in Sverdlovsk. In the position which he occupied, he was allegedly prohibited by the regulations from leaving the country for a period of three years following termination of his appointment. Wishing to emigrate to Israel, he resigned in May 1971 in order, it is claimed, to comply with this regulation. His first application for authorization to emigrate, formulated in May 1971, allegedly fulfilled all the requisite conditions, but was apparently rejected by the competent authorities on the grounds that he possessed secret information affecting the interests of the state. His many subsequent applications, formulated every six months, were, it is claimed, all rejected. His wife Inna and their two children, Mikhail and Eliezer, were reportedly likewise unable to obtain a visa authorizing them to leave the country. As a result of the rejection of his applications to emigrate, Mr Kosharovsky has allegedly failed to find employment in the scientific field in which he is qualified. The Soviet authorities have reportedly intervened on several occasions in the seminars which he organized for Jewish scientists who had lost their jobs as a result of applying for permission to emigrate, as well as in the Hebrew classes which he taught, as a cultural leader of the Jewish community in the USSR (of the 119 nationalities officially recognized in the USSR, the Jewish nationality reportedly occupies, in terms of its numerical importance, twelfth place).

---

[1] See document 114 EX/38 PRIV., paras. 196-218; see also document 114 EX/CR/HR/3.

198. The difficulties encountered by Mr Kosharovsky allegedly took different forms: disruption of the private lessons and lectures which he gave, direct threats to him (in particular of arrest for parasitism) and pressure upon his students (who were allegedly summonsed on several occasions to the offices of the KGB, where they were asked to stop studying Hebrew with him), repeated detention for short periods either for "hooliganism" or for causing public disorder, or even without any grounds being adduced. During a visit to Moscow by Mr Richard Nixon, for example, he was allegedly placed in custody at the Volokolamsky prison, where he claims to have been subjected to cruel and degrading treatment. The author of the communication considers that this harassment has been such as to prevent the alleged victim from maintaining his scientific knowledge on a par with that of his colleagues, owing to his having lost contact with them. Mr Kosharovsky was allegedly compelled, in order to provide for himself and his family, to work as a night-watchman in a cinema.

199. Various approaches to the administrative and judicial authorities and even to the Party authorities with a view to securing recognition of his rights were reportedly of no avail. In order to prove his good faith, Mr Kosharovsky is alleged to have invited the members of the KGB and of the security forces to attend his Hebrew courses. He reportedly asked the government authorities to provide him with a classroom. The author of the communication stresses that, if he organized his courses in private apartments, this was because it was materially impossible for him to hold them elsewhere. The matter does not appear to have been submitted to any international authority other than Unesco.

200. With regard to the aim and object of the communication, the author asks that the Committee inquire into Mr Kosharovsky's present situation, with particular reference to the violation by the Soviet authorities of his rights in the fields of science, education and culture, and to the refusal to recognize his right to leave the country.

201. On 3 March 1982 the Secretariat received a letter dated 26 February 1982 from the author of the communication referring to the constant "erosion" of the alleged victim's rights. According to the Greater New York Conference on Soviet Jewry, KGB officials are alleged to have recently confiscated Mr Kosharovsky's typewriter and all the materials required for his teaching work.

202. The representative of the Soviet Government stated that two facts were absolutely evident from the communication. First of all it concerned one of those cases of a request for permission to emigrate which the Committee on several previous occasions had decided did not come within its competence. Secondly, the case involved a radio-technologist, which profession could not be said to be linked directly with the field of science. There was nothing in Mr Kosharovsky's background which could be said to bring his case within the fields of competence of Unesco the Soviet

representative said, and for these reasons, he felt that the case should be declared inadmissible by the Committee.

203. A member of the Committee felt that it was important to make a distinction between routine requests for emigration *per se*, and requests which were linked to the fields of competence of Unesco. In this case Mr Kosharovsky had been prevented from being active as a teacher and researcher. His wish was to remain active in his scientific and teaching activities. The question was thus whether this case should not be regarded in the light of a request for emigration in order to enjoy rights falling within Unesco's fields of competence. As to the matter of the qualification of an electronic engineer, the Committee member pointed out that the view concerning engineers had changed over the last century and that engineers in certain fields were today quite often seen as being scientists. Furthermore, Mr Kosharovsky had also conducted research in a scientific institute and thus could even more be seen to be involved in the scientific field. Unesco's competence *vis-à-vis* this case could thus clearly be seen to exist, the Committee member said, and it would be inappropriate to categorically take the position that all emigration cases were outside of the Committee's competence.

204. Another Committee member agreed that the case was clearly within the scope of the Committee's mandate, and this for several reasons. For one, it was clear that the Committee had decided that where a person's opportunity to practise his profession was being blocked by his inability to either return to or leave his country, the case was one which was of interest to Unesco. He went on to say that there was a pattern in the Soviet Union which had become evident to the Committee. Persons requesting permission to emigrate soon found themselves without a job in their field. Furthermore, he said, there was a violation here of the right to teach, since the seminars of Mr Kosharovsky were prohibited, a fact which also concerned his cultural rights. Finally, the Committee member pointed out that the field of electronic engineering could clearly be seen, in the present day and age, to be within the field of science. Thus the case was clearly admissible.

205. Another Committee member agreed that educational and cultural rights were involved here, not just a question of scientific rights. It did not seem right that a person who wished to teach electronics or Hebrew should encounter difficulties. The Committee member felt that the Committee should focus primarily on the question of the violation of Mr Kosharovsky's rights in the USSR. Subsequently, the question of emigration could be addressed, if it was found that he could not practise his profession.

206. The Soviet representative stated that it was clear that this was a case involving emigration purely and simply. He stated that while it was true that the gap between

the exact and applied sciences had been diminished over the past century, it was still true that not every engineer was a scientist, nor was every engineer who worked in an institute a scientist. Activities auxiliary to scientific fields should not be confused with the scientific fields themselves. Mr Kosharovsky's work in the Sverdlovsk institute did not qualify him as a scientist. The Soviet representative stated that there was absolutely no evidence to show that Mr Kosharovsky was teaching or holding seminars in the scientific fields in which he had been trained. Apart from broad assertions in the communication, there was nothing to show that Mr Kosharovsky was conducting seminars in fields in which he had received schooling. Furthermore, the Soviet representative went on to say, the teaching of Hebrew, or any other language, was not a crime. Hebrew was in fact taught in several educational institutions in the Soviet Union even though that language was not really the national language of the Soviet Jews. The overwhelming majority of Soviet Jews used Yiddish. He expressed the view that the Committee at a former session had arrived at the conclusion that a person could not teach without possession of certain qualifications. So it was in the Soviet Union, he said, the teaching of Hebrew was not prohibited, but certain qualifications were required before one could teach. Mr Kosharovsky had the opportunity at present to work as an engineer. However if Mr Kosharovsky did not want to work as an engineer it would not be right to force him to do so. It was explained by the Soviet representative that Mr Kosharovsky was involved in teaching Hebrew in a private capacity to a small group of pupils and that he had not been restricted in this activity. There were no tangible facts in the communication which pointed to restrictions in this regard, and the question of whether he had received telephonic threats were impossible for him to investigate. It was in fact true that the police had visited Mr Kosharovsky's flat, the Soviet representative said, and they did indeed confiscate his typewriter. But this visit had been in strict conformity with the applicable Soviet legislation and involved the need to examine a typewriter which had been suspected of use for criminal activities. It was worth pointing out that only five per cent of the persons applying for emigration were refused that right, and this only because they had been working in fields related to national security. The present case was a simple case of request for emigration, it contained no elements to link it to Unesco's competence and thus was inadmissible, the Soviet delegate stated.

207. A Committee member felt it important to make certain clear distinctions. The colloquial language of some Jews was Yiddish but it was not for all of them. Hebrew, however, as the holy language of the Jews was common to them all, whereas the various colloquial languages were not. As concerned the teaching of Hebrew the question was not whether a person had the qualifications for teaching in a school, but whether he was free to teach privately on a purely voluntary basis without government interference. In the present case it had been shown that agents of the government had interfered with this right to teach, and that students had been intimidated by KGB agents. The Committee member pointed out that the Soviet representa-

tive had not attempted to rebut the assertion that Mr Kosharovsky himself qualified as a scientific worker. Mr Kosharovsky's working in the Sverdlovsk institute was by itself a prima facie case. It was clear that there was a pattern in the Soviet Union in which a person who applied for an exit visa could thereafter not find work in his field. There were several clear allegations of violations in Unesco's fields of competence in this communication and it was thus of interest to the Committee.

208. Another Committee member expressed disappointment that the Soviet representative, who was usually so forthcoming with facts on cases, had not provided more information here. He had not stated what the subjects were of the seminars which he claimed were not scientific ones, nor had he explained why Mr Kosharovsky was among the five per cent refused permission to leave for security reasons, when in fact the applicable regulations blocked emigration for only three years.

209. The Soviet representative reasserted his view that there was no proof in the present case that Mr Kosharovsky's teaching activities had been limited. Furthermore he wished to emphasize that Yiddish was the overwhelmingly predominant language of the Soviet Jews and that there was not one Soviet Jew who spoke the colloquial language of Ladino. He stated that 5,887 persons who had been refused the right to emigrate had in fact been allowed to leave a certain number of years later. The question of how long to make a person wait before granting an emigration visa was a delicate one, he said, since it depended on the degree of secrecy of that person's work. The delay could be three, five, ten years or even more. There existed, of course, a procedure to review the applications every six months, the Soviet representative explained.

210. The Chairman pointed out that during the preceding discussions three main points had been raised. In this regard he felt it would be helpful to ask the representative of the Director-General to provide some illumination on the three points: (1) what was the proper definition of the term "scientist"? (2) what was the international legal view concerning the right to teach? and (3) what was the view as concerned the right to emigrate?

211. The representative of the Director-General replied that as concerned the first question, it would be appropriate to consult Unesco's Recommendation on the status of scientific researchers. Article 1 (*d*) (i) defined scientific researchers as "those persons responsible for investigating a specific domain in science or technology".

212. As for the terms "science" and "technology" they were defined as follows:

> The world "science" signifies the enterprise whereby mankind, acting individually or in small or large groups, makes an organized attempt, by means

of the objective study of observed phenomena, to discover and master the chain of causalities; brings together in a co-ordinated form the resultant sub-systems of knowledge by means of systematic reflection and conceptualization, often largely expressed in the symbols of mathematics; and thereby furnishes itself with the opportunity of using, to its own advantage, understanding of the processes and phenomena occurring in nature and society.

213. "Technology signifies such knowledge as relates directly to the production or improvement of goods or services." The Director-General's representative went on to say that these definitions were the only internationally accepted definitions for those terms and that it was of course for the Committee to decide whether they applied in the case before it.

214. As to the second question, it was clear that in the relevant Article 13 of the United Nations [International] Covenant on Economic, Social and Cultural Rights the right of everyone to education was recognized; however there was no reference whatsoever to a right to teach.

215. As to the question concerning emigration, the Director-General's representative stated that the *Irlin* case was relevant.[2] The Committee's decision there had been "to declare the communication inadmissible in so far as it concerned the right to emigrate from the USSR which did not fall within Unesco's sphere of competence, [on the understanding] that the author of the communication [could] submit a further communication to the Committee alleging the violation of human rights which did fall within Unesco's fields of competence".[3] The representative of the Director-General pointed out that a question was raised by the fact that a person could waive his human rights. In other words a person could waive his right to leave a country by accepting to work in an institute while knowing that this would block his chances for emigration. One could ask in the present case whether Mr Kosharovsky had been informed that his working at the institute would have the consequence of preventing his later emigration.

216. The view was thereupon expressed by a Committee member that the details concerning the various forms of Jewish colloquial languages and other such esoteric details were not material to the main questions in this case. The key matter for the Committee to examine in this case was the treatment which Mr Kosharovsky was receiving. The two things which needed to be decided was whether Mr Kosharovsky was a scientific worker, and it seemed that he was, since he certainly was not merely

---

[2] Communication No. 342/81 concerning *Union of Soviet Socialist Republics*, case of *Iosef Samsonovich Irlin*.

[3] See document 113 EX/38 PRIV., para. 395 (i) (*supra*, p. 859).

a switchboard repairman at the institute, and whether there is any truth to the allegation in this communication.

217. Another Committee member stated that while it was probably true that there was nothing in the Soviet criminal code which said that teaching Hebrew was an offence there was a problem in the Soviet Union that certain government organs sometimes took action against groups or committees outside the bounds of the law. The question of emigration in previous cases had been questions of pure emigration, and the distinction which needed to be made in this case was that the question of emigration here was linked with the fact that Mr Kosharovsky had lost his job and at present was being prevented in the Soviet Union from obtaining one in his field.

218. The Committee, after a lengthy debate, *decided* to adopt the following position. It:

(i) noted that the communication as submitted fell prima facie within Unesco's competence in that it concerned Mr Kosharovsky's alleged inability to work in his special field;

(ii) considered it necessary to have additional information both from the author of the communication and from the government concerned, before arriving at a decision as to admissibility.

Autumn 1982 session of the Committee on Conventions and Recommendations (115th session of the Executive Board)[4]

293. The author of the communication, the Greater New York Conference on Soviet Jewry, claims to be a non-governmental organization with reliable knowledge of the alleged violations.

294. Mr Yuli Kosharovsky, a radio electronics engineer, was employed in a research institute in Sverdlovsk. In the position which he occupied, he was allegedly prohibited by the regulations from leaving the country for a period of three years following termination of his appointment. Wishing to emigrate to Israel, he resigned in May 1971 in order, it is claimed, to comply with this regulation. His first application for authorization to emigrate, formulated in May 1971, alledgedly fulfilled all the requisite conditions, but was apparently rejected by the competent authorities on the grounds that he possessed secret information affecting the interests of the state. His

[4] See document 115 EX/28 PRIV., paras. 293-307; see also documents 115 EX/CR/HR/2 and Add.

many subsequent applications, formulated every six months, were, it is claimed, all rejected. His wife Inna and their two children, Mikhail and Eliezer, were reportedly likewise unable to obtain a visa authorizing them to leave the country. As a result of the rejection of his applications to emigrate, Mr Kosharovsky has allegedly failed to find employment in the scientific field in which he is qualified. The Soviet authorities have reportedly intervened on several occasions in the seminars which he organized for Jewish scientists who had lost their jobs as a result of applying for permission to emigrate, as well as in the Hebrew classes which he taught, as a cultural leader of the Jewish community in the USSR (of the 119 nationalities officially recognized in the USSR, the Jewish nationality reportedly occupies, in terms of its numerical importance, twelfth place).

295. With regard to the aim and object of the communication, the author asks that the Committee inquire into Mr Kosharovsky's present situation, with particular reference to the violation by the Soviet authorities of his rights in the fields of science, education and culture, and to the refusal to recognize his right to leave the country.

296. On 3 March 1982 the Secretariat received a letter dated 26 February 1982 from the author of the communication referring to the constant "erosion" of the alleged victim's rights. According to the Greater New York Conference on Soviet Jewry, KGB officials are alleged to have recently confiscated Mr Kosharovsky's typewriter and all the materials required for his teaching work.

297. At the spring 1982 session, the representative of the Soviet Government stated that two facts were absolutely evident from the communication. First of all it concerned one of those cases of a request for permission to emigrate which the Committee on several previous occasions had decided did not come within its competence. Secondly, the case involved a radio-technologist, which profession could not be said to be linked directly with the field of science. There was nothing in Mr Kosharovsky's background which could be said to bring his case within the fields of competence of Unesco the Soviet representative said, and for these reasons, he felt that the case should be declared inadmissible by the Committee.

298. A Committee member stated that the case was clearly within the scope of the Committee's mandate, and this for several reasons. For one, it was clear that the Committee had decided that where a person's opportunity to practise his profession was being blocked by his inability to either return to or leave his country, the case was one which was of interest to Unesco. He went on to say that there was a pattern in the Soviet Union which had become evident to the Committee. Persons requesting permission to emigrate soon found themselves without a job in their field. Furthermore, he said, there was a violation here of the right to teach, since the seminars of Mr Kosharovsky were prohibited, a fact which also concerned his cultural rights.

Finally, the Committee member pointed out that the field of electronic engineering could clearly be seen, in the present day and age, to be within the field of science. Thus the case was clearly admissible.

299. The Committee, after a lengthy debate, decided to adopt the following position.[5] It:

(i) noted that the communication as submitted fell prima facie within Unesco's competence in that it concerned Mr Kosharovsky's alleged inability to work in his special field;

(ii) considered it necessary to have additional information both from the author of the communication and from the government concerned, before arriving at a decision as to admissibility.

300. On 28 July 1982, the Secretariat received a letter from the Greater New York Conference on Soviet Jewry, providing additional information on the above case for the Committee. The author of the communication considers that the Soviet Government is, in fact, asserting the inadmissibility of the communication solely on the grounds that the alleged facts do not fall within Unesco's fields of competence (application of paragraph 14 (*a*) (iii) of 104 EX/Decision 3.3). The author therefore assumes that the other conditions of admissibility have been met.

301. As for the argument by the representative of the Soviet Government that one of the issues raised by the communication is a problem of emigration, the Greater New York Conference on Soviet Jewry states that the emigration applications of Mr Kosharovsky and of his family are integrally related to the systematic deprivation of his rights as a scientist, a science teacher, a Hebrew teacher and a leader of the Jewish community. It maintains, furthermore, that to consider Mr Kosharovsky only as a "technologist" implied a very narrow reading of the word "science". According to the Greater New York Conference on Soviet Jewry, Mr Kosharovsky's research activities at the institute where he worked constitutes clear evidence of his qualifications as a scientist (according to the author, rejection of Mr Kosharovsky's initial application to emigrate on the grounds that he had access to allegedly secret documents indicates recognition of his status as a scientist).

302. The author further stresses that the refusal of the Soviet authorities to allow Mr Kosharovsky to work in his specialized fields or to participate in informal scientific seminars is atrophying his expertise and constitutes a violation of the right to develop his scientific skills. The Greater New York Conference further claims that the

---

[5] See document 114 EX/38 PRIV., para. 218 (*supra*, p. 899).

campaign of harassment against Mr Kosharovsky has been increasing and he is said to have stopped teaching Hebrew last spring. Finally, it notes that this harassment has recently changed in form: it is alleged that Mr Kosharovsky's apartment has been searched; Hebrew texts, including textbooks, dictionaries and grammar books, as well as other teaching material, are said to have been confiscated; works on Jewish culture, history books and literature connected with the State of Israel and writings concerning the hope for a national Jewish revival were also reportedly seized.

303. At the autumn 1982 session, the representative of the Soviet Government reviewed again the information which he had presented to the Committee at its [spring 1982] session and repeated his view that the question here was a pure emigration question. He explained that Mr Kosharovsky now had the opportunity of working in his professional field and could pursue further his professional studies. The Soviet representative offered his personal services to help Mr Kosharovsky find a job through the appropriate job agency, if Mr Kosharovsky so desired.

304. The Committee then engaged in a lengthy debate on the question as to whether the acceptance of the Soviet representative's offer would require the Committee to drop further corisideration of this case and whether the Soviet representative should be specifically requested to report on the outcome of his action.

305. Certain Committee members felt that consideration of this case should be avoided since it might be damaging for the Committee's reputation and open it to manipulation by ethnic groups.

306. Other Committee members felt that serious allegations of violations within Unesco's fields of competence, including the confiscation of books and educational materials, had not been adequately addressed and still needed careful examination.

307. The Committee finally *decided* as follows. It:

> [i] took note of the information provided on the one hand by the government concerned and, on the other, by the author of the communication;
>
> [ii] deemed the communication to be inadmissible;
>
> [iii] notwithstanding this decision, requested the representative of the government concerned to take whatever steps might enable the alleged victim to find employment and to report to it thereon at its next session, without this formality giving rise to any further discussion as to the substance of the communication on the basis of the information that it now contained.

No. 354/81

Concerning *Czechoslovakia*
Case of *Karel Soukup*

Communication of 30 March 1981 submitted by
Amnesty International

Autumn 1981 session of the Committee on Conventions and Recommendations (113th session of the Executive Board)[1]

295. The author of the communication, Amnesty International (Mr Thomas Hammarberg, International Secretariat), describes itself as a non-governmental organization with reliable knowledge of the alleged violations.

296. Mr Karel Soukup, aged 30, is said to be a musician, song-writer and singer whose songs apparently contained criticism of the government. He is said to be an unofficial member of the Czechoslovak Charter 77 Human Rights Movement and to have been detained on many occasions. His house is said to have been searched and his driving licence confiscated. He was allegedly remanded in custody on 1 July 1980 by order of the Ústí nad Labem District Prosecutor, on a charge of breaching the peace (Article 202, section 1, of the Penal Code) and eventually sentenced to 10 months' imprisonment on 5 November 1980. The offence of which he is said to have been accused apparently arose out of the following incident: having been invited to a wedding, he apparently sang - at the request of the family - 10 old anti-government songs for which he had already been prosecuted in 1976 and which ridiculed the police and contained vulgar expressions; those present, however, were apparently not in the least scandalized.

297. It is reported that the Charter 77 spokesman protested to the Attorney General of the Czechoslovak Socialist Republic on 30 July 1980. On 5 August 1980, 296 people from different parts of the country are said to have signed a petition requesting the release of Mr Karel Soukup. It is reported that the Ústí nad Labem Court of Appeal upheld the sentence passed by the Court of First Instance.

[1] See document 113 EX/38 PRIV., paras. 296-304; see also document 113 EX/CR/HR/3.

No. 354/81 **Czechoslovakia**

298. The purpose and aim of the communication indicated by Amnesty International are that the alleged victim may obtain reparation since domestic remedies have been exhausted and he was due for release on 1 May 1981.

299. The representative of the government concerned stated that the Ministry of Justice of his country had made all the necessary inquiries relating to the present communication and that the investigation had revealed that Mr Karel Soukup had been convicted of criminal offences, to wit, acts of violence and hooliganism.

300. Concerning the incident at the wedding, mentioned by the author of the communication, he said that the event occurred on 26 April 1980. With a friend, Mr Soukup went uninvited into a restaurant where a wedding reception was taking place. There he began to sing obscene songs. The family, who were very shocked, asked the intruders to leave, but in vain. This was what prompted the request for the police to intervene to restore order. Mr Soukup's conviction was thus unrelated to the provisions of the International [Covenants] on Human Rights and the rights of entertainers that would bring it within the sphere of competence of Unesco.

301. Several members of the Committee stated that it was not advisable to have a photograph of the alleged victim circulated since this would be seen as an attempt to influence the decision of the Committee, the person in question being a long-haired, slovenly dressed man.

302. The discussion turned to the question of whether the Committee should shelve the communication or declare it inadmissible on the grounds that Mr Soukup had been freed from prison on 1 May 1981.

303. The prevailing opinion was that the matter should not be shelved just because Mr Soukup had already served his sentence. Mr Soukup might conclude from that that his detention had been illegal.

304. The author of the communication had requested compensation for the alleged victim, a matter that did not fall within the sphere of competence of the Committee as defined in 104 EX/Decision 3.3, even though it was dealt with in Article 9, paragraph 5, of the International Covenant on Civil and Political Rights (anyone who has been the victim of unlawful arrest or detention shall have an enforceable right to compensation). The Committee therefore *decided*:

> (i) to declare the communication inadmissible under the provisions of paragraph 14 (*a*) (iii) and (v) of 104 EX/Decision 3.3 as falling outside Unesco's competence and being manifestly ill-founded, as it adduced no relevant evidence;

(ii) to transmit that decision to the author of the communication, drawing his attention to the fact that, in all cases, the question of compensation for alleged victims was not a matter for the Organization.

No. 356/81

Concerning *Chile*
Case of *Violeta Isabel Cereceda Parra*

Communication of 1 April 1981 submitted by
Violeta Isabel Cereceda Parra

Autumn 1981 session of the Committee on Conventions and Recommendations (113th session of the Executive Board)[1]

183. The author of the communication, Mrs Violeta Isabel Cereceda Parra, of Chilean nationality, born in 1939, author and composer of folk-songs, complains that her requests for permission to return to Chile, addressed to the Chilean Consulate in France in 1977 and 1979, were both refused for undisclosed reasons.

184. The domestic remedies said to have been used are the two requests made to the Chilean Consulate in France. The matter has not been submitted to any other international authority.

185. Mrs Cereceda wishes to be authorized to return freely to her country and to be informed of the reasons for refusal of such authorization.

186. The representative of the Chilean Government observed that after Mrs Cereceda's applications for authorization to return to Chile had been rejected, she had not availed herself of any judicial means of recourse, whereas if she had done so she could have known the grounds for the refusal, since the government was required to communicate to the competent court the grounds for its decision. The representative of the Chilean Government then added that Mrs Cereceda had recently called on the Chilean Consulate in Paris and applied for an authorization to return temporarily and that he saw that as a solution to the problem. He said he was prepared to make representations on his return to Santiago with a view to obtaining for the author an authorization to return for 60 days, which would enable her, if she so desired, to take the necessary steps while there to settle the problem of her definitive return, as had been done in other cases.

---

[1] See document 113 EX/38 PRIV., paras. 183-189; see also document 113 EX/CR/HR/3.

No. 356/81 **Chile**

187. Some members of the Committee considered that under these conditions it was advisable to suspend examination of the admissibility of this communication and to inform the author of the statements of the representative of the Chilean Government. At the same time the representative of the government concerned could be requested to let the Committee know what action was taken in the matter and inform it in due course whether, after this possible period of temporary return, Mrs Cereceda was authorized to reside definitively in Chile. Two members considered that in the presence of a communication which clearly fell within Unesco's spheres of competence, the proposal of the Chilean Government was not satisfactory because it did not correspond with what the author asked, namely, to return freely to her country and to know the reasons for the initial refusal. Since a violation of the fundamental right to return to one's country was involved, the Committee ought to be more exacting and, on the one hand, try to find out the reasons for Mrs Cereceda's being debarred from returning to Chile and, on the other hand, ask the Chilean Government to go further into the question of the definitive return of the person concerned.

188. Other members expressed disagreement on these points. They thought that since an authorization for Mrs Cereceda's temporary return was contemplated, the question of why her previous application met with a refusal no longer arose and that it was advisable to accept the proposal of the representative of the Chilean Government, which would enable the person concerned to return to her country temporarily and to avail herself there of the existing means of recourse in the hope of a favourable outcome.

189. Consequently, taking into account the information supplied concerning the Consulate's interview with Mrs Cereceda and the good offices which the representative of the Chilean Government was ready to provide in seeking a settlement, the Committee *decided*:

(i) to defer consideration of the admissibility of this communication to its next session;

(ii) to take note of the proposal and statements of the representative of the Chilean Government;

(iii) to inform the author of the communication of those statements.

Chile **No. 356/81**

Spring 1982 session of the Committee on Conventions and Recommendations (114th session of the Executive Board)[2]

458. The author of the communication, Mrs Violeta Isabel Cereceda Parra, of Chilean nationality, born in 1939, author and composer of folk-songs, complains that her requests for permission to return to Chile, addressed to the Chilean Consulate in France in 1977 and 1979, were both refused for undisclosed reasons.

459. The domestic remedies said to have been used are the two requests made to the Chilean Consulate in France. The matter has not been submitted to any other international authority.

460. Mrs Cereceda wishes to be authorized to return freely to her country and to be informed of the reasons for refusal of such authorization.

461. At the autumn 1981 session the representative of the Chilean Government observed that after Mrs Cereceda's applications for authorization to return to Chile had been rejected, she had not availed herself of any judicial means of recourse, whereas if she had done so she could have known the grounds for the refusal, since the government was required to communicate to the competent court the grounds for its decision. The representative of the Chilean Government then added that Mrs Cereceda had recently called on the Chilean Consulate in Paris and applied for an authorization to return temporarily and that he saw that as a solution to the problem. He said he was prepared to make representations on his return to Santiago with a view to obtaining for the author an authorization to return for 60 days, which would enable her, if she so desired, to take the necessary steps while there to settle the problem of her definitive return, as had been done in other cases.

462. Some members of the Committee considered that under these conditions it was advisable to suspend consideration of the admissibility of this communication and to inform the author of the statements of the representative of the Chilean Government. At the same time the representative of the government concerned could be requested to let the Committee know what action was taken in the matter and inform it in due course whether, after this possible period of temporary return, Mrs Cereceda was authorized to reside definitively in Chile. Two members considered that in the presence of a communication which clearly fell within Unesco's spheres of competence, the proposal of the Chilean Government was not satisfactory because it did not correspond with what the author asked, namely, to return freely to her country and to know the reasons for the initial refusal. Since a violation of the fundamental right to

[2] See document 114 EX/38 PRIV., paras. 458-469; see also document 114 EX/CR/HR/2.

return to one's country was involved, the Committee ought to be more exacting and, on the one hand, try to find out the reasons for Mrs Cereceda's being debarred from returning to Chile and, on the other hand, ask the Chilean Government to go further into the question of the definitive return of the person concerned.

463. Other members expressed disagreement on these points. They thought that since an authorization for Mrs Cereceda's temporary return was contemplated, the question of why her previous application met with a refusal no longer arose and that it was advisable to accept the proposal of the representative of the Chilean Government, which would enable the person concerned to return to her country temporarily and to avail herself there of the existing means of recourse in the hope of a favourable outcome.

464. Consequently, taking into account the information supplied concerning the Consulate's interview with Mrs Cereceda and the good offices which the representative of the Chilean Government was ready to provide in seeking a settlement, the Committee decided:[3]

(i) to defer consideration of the admissibility of this communication to its present session;

(ii) to take note of the proposal and statements of the representative of the Chilean Government;

(iii) to inform the author of the communication of those statements.

465. On 27 October 1981 the author was informed of the statements made by the representative of the Chilean Government and of the Committee's decision. She replied on 15 December thanking Unesco for its intercession and expressing the hope that her situation would be finally clarified.

466. At the present session, the representative of the government concerned explained that the case of Mrs Cereceda Parra was similar to that of Mr Tiznado Rosas [...]. Mrs Cereceda Parra had approached the Consulate which did not have the power of decision. He therefore suggested that Mrs Cereceda Parra should be informed in the same way as Mr Tiznado Rosas.[4] Questioned on the subject of authorization to return temporarily to Chile, the representative of the Chilean Government stated that the same procedure should be followed. Replying to a member of the Committee, he stated that his humanitarian intercession could only be effective if the situation of

---

[3] See document 113 EX/38 PRIV., para. 189 (*supra*, p. 908).

[4] See document 114 EX/38 PRIV., para. 438 (*supra*, p. 797), communication No. 321/81 concerning *Chile*, case of *Victor Xavier Tiznado Rosas*.

the persons concerned was clear, which was not the case in this instance, despite what was implied in the communication. Consequently, he considered that the only possible course of action was for Mrs Cereceda Parra to request the Ministry of the Interior at Santiago to re-examine her case, if necessary through a lawyer, who needed no special mandat for this purpose.

467. One member suggested that it should be possible for the consulates of countries where a large number of Chileans resided to inform their fellow citizens of the procedure described by the representative of the Chilean Government.

468. When one member emphasized the fact that an author and composer of music was possibly not an expert in administrative procedure and should be given assistance, the representative of the Director-General suggested that detailed explanations should be given to Mrs Cereceda Parra verbally.

469. The Committee therefore *decided*:

(i) to defer consideration of the admissibility of this case to its next session, and in the meantime,

(ii) to request the Secretariat to contact Mrs Cereceda Parra and provide her with detailed information on the procedure she should follow.

Autumn 1982 session of the Committee on Conventions and Recommendations (115th session of the Executive Board)[5]

29. This communication concerns the case of Mrs Violeta Isabel Cereceda Parra, who states herself to be a writer and composer of folk-songs, and whose requests to the Chilean Consulate in France (in 1977 and 1979) for permission to return to her country were rejected.

30. This communication was examined by the Committee for the first time at its autumn 1981 session. The representative of the government concerned pointed out on that occasion that Mrs Cereceda Parra had not made use of the appropriate legal remedies. In view of the fact that she had most recently requested permission for a temporary return, he proposed to offer his good offices in order that this wish might be granted.

[5] See document 115 EX/28 PRIV., paras. 29-36; see also document 115 EX/CR/HR/2.

No. 356/81 **Chile**

31. At the spring 1982 session, the representative of the goverment concerned informed the Committee that his intervention on humanitarian grounds could only be effective if the situation of the persons concerned was clear, which was not so in this particular case. He also suggested that Mrs Cereceda Parra should be informed, in the same way as Mr Víctor Tiznado Rosas [...], of the new remedies which now existed in Chile.

32. On 20 July 1982, the Secretariat received a letter from Mrs Cereceda Parra in which she acknowledged receipt of the Secretariat's letter which had conveyed to her the above-mentioned information. She said that, according to statements made by the Chilean Consulate, her three requests had been passed directly to the Ministry of the Interior. Finally, she added that she would ask a lawyer to undertake the procedures outlined by the representative of the Chilean Government.

33. At the autumn 1982 session, the representative of the government concerned declared that he had no new information concerning this case and that Mrs Cereceda Parra did not appear to have submitted any request. Consequently he could only repeat what he had already said concerning the communication submitted by Mr Tiznado Rosas [...][6] and suggested that his new note on the remedies existing in Chile should be sent to the person concerned.

34. The members who spoke expressed their agreement with this proposal and took the view that the Committee should strike this communication off its list at its next session if Mrs Cereceda Parra did not take up the means of redress of which she had been informed.

35. The representative of the Director-General said that the person concerned did not seem to understand legal matters very well. To help her, the Committee had decided, at its [spring 1982] session, to request the Secretariat to enter into contact with her[7] and it was ready to do the same again on this occasion.

36. The Committee *decided* consequently:

(i) to request the Secretariat to enter into contact with Mrs Cereceda Parra in order to pass on to her the above-mentioned note and all the information provided by the representative of the Chilean Government, and to inform her that if no legal action was taken by her in Chile, the Committee would strike her communication off its list at its next session;

---

[6] *Ibidem*, para. 27 (*supra*, pp. 798-799), communication No. 321/81 concerning *Chile*, case of *Víctor Xavier Tiznado Rosas*.
[7] See document 114 EX/38 PRIV., para. 469 (ii) (*supra*, p. 911).

(ii) to defer consideration of the admissibility of this communication until its next session.

Spring 1983 session of the Committee on Conventions and Recommendations (116th session of the Executive Board)[8]

20. This communication concerns the case of Mrs Violeta Isabel Cereceda Parra, who states herself to be a writer and composer of folk-songs, and whose requests to the Chilean Consulate in France (in 1977 and 1979) for permission to return to her country were rejected.

21. This communication was examined by the Committee for the first time at its autumn 1981 session. At its [autumn 1982 session], the Committee decided to request the Secretariat to enter into contact with Mrs Cereceda Parra in order to pass on to her the above-mentioned note and all the information provided by the representative of the Chilean Government, and to inform her that if no legal action was taken by her in Chile, the Committee would strike her communication off its list at its next session.[9]

22. In accordance with the Committee's decision, the Secretariat arranged a meeting with Mrs Cereceda in Paris on 17 November 1982. On that occasion, she had said she was willing to initiate proceedings through her lawyer in Santiago, Mr Alberto Velásquez.

23. At the present session, the representative of the Chilean Government said that before he left Santiago in early April, he had made a point of inquiring from the Court of Appeal whether Mrs Cereceda Parra had submitted an application, and had been told that she had not.

24. The members of the Committee who took the floor expressed the view that, under those circumstances and in view of the fact that the person concerned could still make use of the remedies of which she had been duly informed, the communication should be struck from the Committee's list.

25. Consequently, the Committee *decided*, in view of the decision which it had taken at the preceding session, to strike this communication from its list because the individual concerned had not used the remedies of which she had been informed.

---

[8] See document 116 EX/48 PRIV., paras. 20-25; see also document 116 EX/CR/HR/2.
[9] See document 115 EX/28 PRIV., para. 36 (i) (*supra*, p. 912).

No. 359/81

Concerning *Bolivia*
Case of *Jorge Baldibieso* et al.*[*]*

Communication of 25 March 1981 submitted by
Víctor Hugo Nin Saavedra

Autumn 1981 session of the Committee on Conventions and Recommendations (113th session of the Executive Board)[1]

Spring 1982 session of the Committee on Conventions and Recommendations (114th session of the Executive Board)[2]

Autumn 1982 session of the Committee on Conventions and Recommendations (115th session of the Executive Board)[3]

Spring 1983 session of the Committee on Conventions and Recommendations (116th session of the Executive Board)[4]

---

[*] Case of *Jorge Baldibieso, José Luis Suárez, Gonzalo Barrón, Ricardo Navarro, Marcelo Quiroga Santa Cruz, Elías Rafael Flores and Silvia Natalia Rivera*. From the Committee's spring 1982 session, this communication was being referred to as case of *Violations of human rights in Bolivia* and at its spring 1983 session as case of *Alleged violations of human rights in Bolivia*.

[1] See document 113 EX/38 PRIV., paras. 72-107 (*supra*, pp. 805-812), communication No. 322/81 concerning *Bolivia*, case of *Violations of human rights in Bolivia following the events of 17 July 1980*.

[2] See document 114 EX/38 PRIV., paras. 347-399 (*supra*, pp. 812-824), communication No. 322/81 concerning *Bolivia*, case of *Violations of human rights in Bolivia*.

[3] See document 115 EX/28 PRIV., paras. 410-411 (*supra*, p. 824), communication No. 322/81 concerning *Bolivia*, case of *Violations of human rights in Bolivia*.

[4] See document 116 EX/48 PRIV., paras. 273-277 (*supra*, pp. 825-826), communication No. 322/81 concerning *Bolivia*, case of *Alleged violations of human rights in Bolivia*.

No. 361/81

Concerning *Paraguay*
Case of *Andrés Centurión* et al.*

Communication of 17 April 1981 submitted by
Victoriano Centurión

Autumn 1981 session of the Committee on Conventions and Recommendations (113th session of the Executive Board)[1]

284. The author of the communication, Victoriano Centurión, a farmer, is the father of two alleged victims.

285. According to him, a peasant demonstration against the injustices of the Paraguayan Government occurred on 8 March 1980. The extremely brutal repression resulted in 10 deaths and numerous injuries. On the same occasion, a large number of people were arrested, while others sought refuge in the Panamanian Embassy in Asunción. The Government of Paraguay defended its action by asserting that the instigators of the demonstration were "hooligans and bandits". Mr Victoriano Centurión's children, Andrés (22) and Luciano (17), sharing in the general indignation of public opinion in the country, denounced the official version of the events at their school in San Lorenzo, since they were also accustomed to selling the produce of the demonstrating peasants in the market. On 17 March, both of the author's children and his nephew, Mr Vidal Martínez (25), who was also attending a literacy course at the Regional Education Centre in San Lorenzo, were arrested and brutally tortured by the police. They were subsequently transferred to Tacumbu prison.

286. According to the author of the communication, "sham legal proceedings" were initiated by the Government of Paraguay, which blocked all means of redress.

287. Amnesty International is said to have been informed of the matter.

---

* Case of *Andrés Centurión, Luciano Centurión and Vidal Martínez.*

[1] See document 113 EX/38 PRIV., paras. 284-294; see also document 113 EX/CR/HR/3 Add.

No. 361/81 **Paraguay**

288. Mr Victoriano Centurión points out that the communication concerns not only his son Andrés but also his other son Luciano and his nephew Vidal Martínez (all of whom were pupils at the San Lorenzo Regional Education Centre, attending the evening literacy course).

289. With regard to the purpose and aim of the communication, the author requests Unesco's intervention with a view to obtaining the release of the three alleged victims so that they can continue their studies (he claims that the victims were imprisoned with common-law offenders and were being treated as such).

290. The representative of the Paraguayan Government stated that the demonstration in question had taken the form of a low-key attempt at a coup d'état. The facts had been related both in the press and in official communiqués. In the confusion a number of persons had been arrested and prosecuted. For the time being, the government could say no more since it was necessary to let justice follow its course.

291. Some members of the Committee considered that the alleged occurrences did not seem to lie within Unesco's fields of competence, despite the status of Mr Andrés Centurión, Mr Luciano Centurión and Mr Vidal Martínez as pupils attending a literacy course; for if communications were viewed from the angle of lifelong education, everybody would be concerned.

292. Several members of the Committee were of the opinion that the author of the communication should be asked for a detailed explanation of the links between the occurrences reported and the fields of competence of the Organization, and that at the same time the government concerned should be asked for additional information since the question of competence should as a rule be decided upon before that of admissibility.

293. After s brief discussion, the Committee *decided*:

(i) to defer consideration of the admissibility of the communication;

(ii) to convey the decision to the author of the communication with a request for further details concerning the alleged occurrences, establishing that a link existed between them and the fields of competence of Unesco, and that the occurrences were neither of a political nor of a criminal nature;

(iii) to request the government concerned to provide additional information on further action taken in connection with the case.

Paraguay **No. 361/81**

294. One member of the Committee wished to make it clear that it would be appropriate to inform the author of the communication that Unesco enjoyed limited competence and that he could take the matter to other broader-based international forums.

Spring 1982 session of the Committee on Conventions and Recommendations (114th session of the Executive Board)[2]

511. The author of the communication, Victoriano Centurión, a farmer, is the father of the first two alleged victims.

512. According to him, a peasant demonstration against the injustices of the Paraguayan Government occurred on 8 March 1980. Its extremely brutal repression had resulted in 10 deaths and numerous injuries. On the same occasion, a large number of people had been arrested. He himself had sought refuge in the Panamanian Embassy in Asunción. The Government of Paraguay had defended its repressive action by asserting that the instigators of the demonstration were "hooligans and bandits". Mr Victoriano Centurión's children, Andrés (22) and Luciano (17), sharing in the general indignation of public opinion in the country had denounced the official version of the events at their school in San Lorenzo, since they were also accustomed to selling the produce of the demonstrating peasants in the market. On 17 March, both of the author's children and his nephew, Mr Vidal Martínez (25), who was also attending a literacy course at the Regional Education Centre in San Lorenzo had been arrested and tortured by the police. They had subsequently been transferred to Tacumbu prison.

513. According to the author of the communication, "sham legal proceedings" were initiated by the Government of Paraguay, which blocked all means of redress. Amnesty International is said to have been informed of the matter.

514. Mr Victoriano Centurión points out that the communication concerns not only his son Andrés but also his other son Luciano and his nephew Vidal Martínez (all of whom were pupils at the San Lorenzo Regional Education Centre, attending the evening literacy course).

515. With regard to the purpose and aim of the communication, the author requests Unesco's intervention with a view to obtaining the release of the three alleged vic-

[2] See document 114 EX/38 PRIV., paras. 511-525; see also documents 114 EX/CR/HR/2 and Add.2.

tims so that they can continue their studies (he claims that the victims were imprisoned with common-law offenders and were being treated as such).

516. At the [autumn 1981] session the representative of the Paraguayan Government stated that the demonstration in question had taken the form of a low-key attempt at a coup d'état. The facts had been related, he added, both in the press and in official communiqués. A number of persons had been arrested and prosecuted. For the time being, the government could say no more since it was necessary to let justice follow its course.

517. Some members of the Committee considered that the alleged occurrences did not seem to lie within Unesco's fields of competence, despite the status of Mr Andrés Centurión, Mr Luciano Centurión and Mr Vidal Martínez as pupils attending a literacy course; for if communications were viewed from the angle of lifelong education, everybody would be concerned.

518. Several members of the Committee were of the opinion that the author of the communication should be asked for a detailed explanation of the links between the occurrences reported and the fields of competence of the Organization, and that at the same time the government concerned should be asked for additional information since the question of competence should as a rule be decided upon before that of admissibility.

519. After a brief discussion, the Committee decided:[3]

(i) to defer consideration of the admissibility of the communication;

(ii) to convey the decision to the author of the communication with a request for further details concerning the alleged occurrences, establishing that a link existed between them and the fields of competence of Unesco, and that the occurrences were neither of a political nor of a criminal nature;

(iii) to request the government concerned to provide additional information on further action taken in connection with the case.

520. One member of the Committee wished to make it clear that it would be appropriate to inform the author of the communication that Unesco enjoyed limited competence and that he could take the matter to other broader-based international forums.

---

[3] See document 113 EX/38 PRIV., para. 293 (*supra*, p. 918).

Paraguay **No. 361/81**

521. On 19 April 1982 the Permanent Delegate of Paraguay to Unesco sent a letter to the Secretariat stating that the author of the communication stood accused of assault, armed attack, the kidnapping of the passengers of a bus and the seizure of their property, which occurred in the administrative area of the town of Caaguazú on 8 March 1980. These acts were a breach of public security and order, clearly defined as a common law crime in the Criminal Law and Constitution of the Republic of Paraguay. The three alleged victims were the subject of the same criminal proceedings. All the accused, who were being held in prison, had chosen their counsel and had made a statement before the competent judge. The signatory of the letter added that the prosecution was following its normal course and that, because of the total independence of the judiciary, the Paraguayan Government could not interfere in any way with the normal course of the proceedings.

522. At the present session the representative of the government concerned confirmed the points made in the aforementioned letter.

523. All the members of the Committee with the exception of one considered that, in view of the fresh information placed at their disposal, which clearly established that the reported occurrences did not lie within Unesco's fields of competence, the communication should be declared inadmissible. They also thanked the representative of the Paraguayan Government for being so good as to provide the information required by the Committee.

524. Expressing his concern that the decisions taken by the Committee should be consistent, one member suggested that the communication should remain pending since the proceedings concerning the alleged victims were in progress. One other member pointed out in this connection that, in other cases where the proceedings against alleged victims had not been initiated or were in progress, the Committee had nevertheless taken a decision as to admissibility; in addition, irrespective of this question of precedent, it was noted that, in the present case, the victims were not being tried on the grounds of their having exercised human rights protected by international covenants but for criminal offences.

525. After discussion the Committee accordingly *decided*:

(i) to declare the communication inadmissible as not concerning violations of human rights falling within Unesco's fields of competence in conformity with 104 EX/Decision 3.3, paragraph 14 (*a*) (iii);

(ii) to request the government to be so good as to notify the Committee, in due course, of the outcome of the proceedings in progress concerning the alleged violations.

No. 369/81

Concerning *Argentina*
Case of *Alberto Horacio Giusti*

Communication of 5 June 1981 submitted by
Committee for solidarity with the relatives of persons detained,
killed or tortured in Argentina for political reasons

Autumn 1981 session of the Committee on Conventions and Recommendations (113th session of the Executive Board)[1]

60. Through its representative Dr Osvaldo De Benedetti, the Committee for solidarity with the relatives of persons detained, killed or tortured in Argentina for political reasons (COSOFAN) alleges that Professor Alberto Horacio Giusti of the Science Faculty at the University of Buenos Aires was arrested on 16 June 1977 by a group of people in plain clothes who said they belonged to the military security forces. He was reportedly thrown roughly into a military vehicle and taken away to an unknown destination. The author calls on the Argentine Government to provide information about the missing person and to arrange for his release.

61. The representative of the Argentine Government said that the relevant authorities in his country had been unable to investigate the whereabouts of the person in question, since the information provided by the author was inadequate and, in particular, there had been no precise indication of the place of arrest. He noted that the case had also been referred to the Inter-American Commission on Human Rights. He finally suggested that, as in other cases of missing persons, the matter should be submitted to the Working Group [on Enforced or Involuntary Disappearances] of the United Nations Commission on Human Rights.

62. A consensus was very quickly reached on this point and the Committee *decided* to deal with the communication in accordance with its decision relating to missing persons.[2]

---

[1] See document 113 EX/38 PRIV., paras. 60-62; see also document 113 EX/CR/HR/3.
[2] See documents 108 EX/38 PRIV., para. 16, 109 EX/52 PRIV., annex I, para. 8, and Corr. and 112 EX/30 PRIV., paras. 558-566.

No. 370/81

Concerning *Uruguay*
Case of *José Luis Massera*

Communication of 10 May 1981 submitted by
Moriana Hernández de Bazzano

Spring 1982 session of the Committee on Conventions and Recommendations (114th session of the Executive Board)[1]

263. The Committee *decided* to combine consideration of this communication with [another communication] concerning the same alleged victim.[2]

Autumn 1982 session of the Committee on Conventions and Recommendations (115th session of the Executive Board)[3]

Spring 1983 session of the Committee on Conventions and Recommendations (116th session of the Executive Board)[4]

Autumn 1983 session of the Committee on Conventions and Recommendations (117th session of the Executive Board)[5]

---

[1] See document 114 EX/38 PRIV., paras. 263 and 819-849 (*supra*, pp. 280-287), communication No. 103/79 concerning *Uruguay*, case of *José Luis Massera*.
[2] Communication No. 103/79 concerning *Uruguay*, case of *José Luis Massera*.
[3] See document 115 EX/28 PRIV., paras. 469-477 (*supra*, pp. 287-288), communication No. 103/79 concerning *Uruguay*, case of *José Luis Massera*.
[4] See document 116 EX/48 PRIV., paras. 325-331 (*supra*, pp. 288-290), communication No. 103/79 concerning *Uruguay*, case of *José Luis Massera*.
[5] See document 117 EX/18 PRIV., paras. 228-236 (*supra*, pp. 290-292), communication No. 103/79 concerning *Uruguay*, case of *José Luis Massera*.

No. 370/81 **Uruguay**

Spring 1984 session of the Committee on Conventions and Recommendations (119th session of the Executive Board)[6]

[6] See document 119 EX/35 PRIV., paras. 232-235 (*supra*, pp. 292-293), communication No. 103/79 concerning *Uruguay*, case of *José Luis Massera*.

No. 371/81

Concerning *Egypt*
Case of *Ahmed Fouad Negm*

Communications of 24 May 1981 submitted by
Patrick Jean Charles Bombal Acampora

Autumn 1981 session of the Committee on Conventions and Recommendations (113th session of the Executive Board)[1]

190. Both communications concern the same alleged victim.[2]

191. The first is submitted by Mr Patrick Jean Charles Bombal Acampora, a manufacturer's representative, and the second, which is more detailed, by AIDA-France (Association internationale de défense des artistes victimes de la répression).

192. They report the case of an Egyptian poet, Mr Ahmed Fouad Negm, aged 52, allegedly detained at present in the Esteqnaf prison, Cairo.

193. The alleged victim is said to have been arrested and imprisoned on several occasions since 1959. He is said to have spent a total of 13 years in prison. In March 1978 he was indicted by a Military Tribunal for having attacked the dignity of the Head of the State through a poem which he read to a university and was sentenced to a year of hard labour. Rather than serve his sentence he preferred to go underground, but he was finally arrested on 29 April 1981. He subsequently went on a hunger strike to protest against the ill-treatment inflicted on him in prison. He may be tried again for two further offences, contempt of court and membership of an illegal organization.

194. AIDA states that Mr Negm's works, in the Arabic spoken by the people, make him a great poet of the Middle East and the Maghrib - four collections of poems published in the Arab world, more than 200 songs sung by a well-known singer, Mr

---

[1] See document 113 EX/38 PRIV., paras. 190-203; see also documents 113 EX/CR/HR/3 and Add.
[2] Communications No. 371/81 concerning *Egypt*, case of *Ahmed Fouad Negm*, and No. 386/81 concerning *Egypt*, case of *Ahmed Fouad Negm*, were being considered together.

Sheick Iman (who is not allowed to sing in Egypt), a record made in France and many pirate recordings.

195. Assisted by a lawyer, Mr Negm appealed against the sentence convicting him in 1978. There would appear to be very little hope of the case being reopened. A former lawyer of the poet is said to have been imprisoned, but it is not known on what grounds.

196. A French lawyer, [Mr] Régis de Castelnau, is reported to have made representations in Egypt on behalf of IADL (International Association of Democratic Lawyers) without achieving any result. [Mr] Joe Nordmann, President of the Association, and Mr Mahmud Amin El Alem, a writer, are said to have denounced the repressive system established in Egypt.

197. In April 1981 AIDA started a press campaign on behalf of the poet. It prepared a petition which was signed by 800 artists and other personalities.

198. In addition to the International Association of Democratic Lawyers, the case was brought to the notice of the French PEN, the International PEN and Amnesty International.

199. Since the poet's works are banned and he is imprisoned for public expression of poetry, it would seem that the following rights proclaimed in the Universal Declaration of Human Rights have been violated: the right to all the fundamental freedoms without distinction of any kind, such as race, language, religion, opinion (Article 2); the right not to be subjected to torture or to cruel, inhuman or degrading treatment (Article 5); the right to freedom of opinion and expression (Article 19); the right freely to participate in the cultural life of the community, to enjoy the arts (Article 27).

200. As to the aim and purpose of the communication, AIDA states that it wishes the sentence delivered by the Military Tribunal to be quashed, the poet to be freed and freedom of expression to be recognized in Egypt.

201. For his part, Mr Acampora requests, in addition to the release of the alleged victim, that the public authorities should lift the ban on the poet's works and that the practice of torturing prisoners should cease.

202. After the substance of the two communications had been made known, the Director-General's representative informed the Committee that the Permanent Delegate of Egypt to Unesco had informed the Secretariat that he had not yet received the

relevant information from his government and consequently requested that consideration of these communications be deferred to the following session.

203. In accordance with established practice, the Committee *decided*:

(i) to acquiesce in the request by the Permanent Delegate of Egypt;

(ii) to request the Executive Board to invite the Director-General to draw the attention of the government concerned to the importance attached by the Committee to the presence of one of its representatives at the next session.

Spring 1982 session of the Committee on Conventions and Recommendations (114th session of the Executive Board)[3]

470. Both communications concern the same alleged victim.[4]

471. The first is submitted by Mr Patrick Jean Charles Bombal Acampora, a manufacturer's representative, and the second, which is more detailed, by AIDA-France (Association internationale de défense des artistes victimes de la répression).

472. They report the case of an Egyptian poet, Mr Ahmed Fouad Negm, aged 52, allegedly detained at present in the Esteqnaf prison, Cairo.

473. The alleged victim is said to have been arrested and imprisoned on several occasions since 1959. He is said to have spent a total of 13 years in prison. In March 1978 he was indicted by a Military Tribunal for having attacked the dignity of the Head of the State through a poem which he read to a university and was sentenced to a year of hard labour. Rather than serve his sentence he preferred to go underground, but he was finally arrested on 29 April 1981. He subsequently went on a hunger strike to protest against the ill-treatment inflicted on him in prison.

474. AIDA states that Mr Negm's works, in the Arabic spoken by the people, make him a great poet of the Middle East and the Maghrib - four collections of poems published in the Arab world, more than 200 songs sung by a well-known singer, Mr Sheick Iman (who is not allowed to sing in Egypt), a record made in France and many pirate recordings.

---

[3] See document 114 EX/38 PRIV., paras. 470-486; see also documents 114 EX/CR/HR/2 and Add.4.

[4] Communications No. 371/81 concerning *Egypt*, case of *Ahmed Fouad Negm*, and No. 386/81 concerning *Egypt*, case of *Ahmed Fouad Negm*, were being considered together.

475. Assisted by a lawyer, Mr Negm appealed against the sentence convicting him in 1978. There would appear to be very little hope of the case being reopened. A former lawyer of the poet is said to have been imprisoned, but it is not known on what grounds.

476. A French lawyer, [Mr] Régis de Castelnau, is reported to have made representations in Egypt on behalf of IADL (International Association of Democratic Lawyers) without achieving any result. [Mr] Joe Nordmann, President of the Association, and Mr Mahmud Amin El Alem, a writer, are said to have denounced the repressive system established in Egypt.

477. AIDA wishes the sentence delivered by the Military Tribunal to be quashed, the poet to be freed and freedom of expression to be recognized in Egypt.

478. For his part, Mr Acampora requests, in addition to the release of the alleged victim, that the public authorities should lift the ban on the poet's works and that the practice of torturing prisoners should cease.

479. At the [autumn] 1981 session the Director-General's representative informed the Committee that the Permanent Delegate of Egypt to Unesco had informed the Secretariat that he had not yet received the relevant information from his government and consequently requested that consideration of these communications be deferred to the following session.

480. In accordance with established practice, the Committee decided:[5]

> (i) to acquiesce in the request of the Permanent Delegate of Egypt;
>
> (ii) to request the Executive Board to invite the Director-General to draw the attention of the government concerned to the importance attached by the Committee to the presence of one of its representatives at the present session.

481. At the present session, the Permanent Delegate of the Arab Republic of Egypt to Unesco, referring to the contents of the letter dated 23 April 1982 which he had sent to the Secretariat, drew attention to the following facts:

> Mr Ahmed Fouad Negm had been sentenced in 1978 to one year's imprisonment for an offence under the ordinary law: incitement to violence; he had escaped from prison some time after being sentenced; rearrested on 29 April 1981, he had had to serve his sentence, his case being certainly aggravated by

[5] See document 113 EX/38 PRIV., para. 203 (*supra*, p. 929).

his escape; he had not gone on hunger strike; he had been receiving the normal treatment given to prisoners, in accordance with the laws in force; he was nearing the end of his sentence;

Mr Bombal Acampora and AIDA, like Mr Negm himself, admitted that he had chosen to "go illegally underground"; no relevant evidence had been produced in the two communications received; in the opinion of the Egyptian authorities, they were improper and ill-founded.

482. One member of the Committee was of the opinion that the only criterion that justified its examination of the two communications was Mr Negm's status as a poet. In his opinion, as the latter had committed a criminal offence, there was no doubt that the case did not fall within Unesco's fields of competence, and should therefore be declared inadmissible in accordance with paragraph 14 (*a*) (iii) of 104 EX/Decision 3.3.

483. Another member of the Committee stated that the central issue was not to ensure that Mr Negm should be released, but to know whether he could exercise his freedom of expression. He expressed some doubt as to whether all his poems encouraged violence. He inquired whether there was in fact a ban on their publication.

484. Another member of the Committee pointed out that freedom of expression should not be used to incite to violence and that the Committee should avoid setting itself up as a court of appeal. Addressing his remarks to the government concerned, he recommended that, so long as Mr Negm complied with the law, he should be free to write and to have his works published.

485. The representative of the Egyptian Government replied that he would, of course, report faithfully to his government all that the members of the Committee had said. He added, speaking in a personal capacity and drawing on his own experience, that he could assure the Committee that Mr Negm's poems, in anthologies and on cassettes, were openly sold in the streets of Cairo.

486. After an exchange of views, the Committee *decided* to declare the two communications inadmissible, as being clearly ill-founded and not containing relevant evidence (paragraph 14 (*a*) (v) of 104 EX/Decision 3.3).

No. 372/81

Concerning *Argentina*
Case of *Antonio Satutto*

Communication of 10 April 1981 submitted by
José Satutto

Autumn 1981 session of the Committee on Conventions and Recommendations (113th session of the Executive Board)[1]

63. The author of the communication, Mr José Satutto, a turner, of Italian nationality, describes himself as father of the victim and as a person having reliable knowledge of the facts alleged. He complains of the disappearance of his son, Mr Antonio Satutto, a student at the Engineering Faculty of Mar del Plata, who was abducted at La Plata on 28 July 1978.

64. According to the statement, Antonio Satutto's sister-in-law, María Rosa Ortiz, was abducted on 26 July 1978 in a street in Mar del Plata and interrogated to discover where her sister and brother-in-law were living. Two days later, on 28 July, in the city of La Plata, the owners of the boarding house where Antonio and María Cristina Ortiz were living, and some witnesses, are said to have seen some 15 masked and armed people enter the boarding house and take Antonio and María Cristina Ortiz away. María Rosa Ortiz was apparently released on the following day.

65. This communication was submitted to the Committee for examination at the [autumn 1980] session [...].[2]

[65a.] The representative of the Argentine Government indicated to the Committee at that time, as mentioned in the report on the session, [...],[3] that:

---

[1] See document 113 EX/38 PRIV., paras. 63-71; see also document 113 EX/CR/HR/3.
[2] Communication No. 241/80 concerning *Argentina*, case of *Antonio Satutto and María Cristina Ortiz.*
[3] See document 110 EX/40 PRIV., paras. 40-41 (*supra*, pp. 593-594).

> ... there was a serious contradiction in this communication, one which by itself would shed serious doubt on the reliability of the information provided. He pointed out that the alleged victims were said to have been studying in the city of Mar del Plata and were said to have been abducted in the city of La Plata, when in fact the cities were 400 miles apart.
>
> Even more significant, however, was the fact that his government had learned that the alleged victims were not students at the time of the alleged abduction. It had been learned that at that time Mr Satutto was a metalworker and his wife a perfumery shop assistant, both working in La Plata.

66. In his further communication, the author explains that Mr Satutto Ortiz and his wife were resident in Mar del Plata, where both of them were studying and working simultaneously. In support of his statement, Mr José Satutto encloses some work certificates and his son's student card, which is stamped "reregistration 1978". He also explains that on 15 March 1978 his son, as expected, received instructions (which are included in the file) to report to the military district of the city of La Plata.

67. Because Mrs Ortiz Satutto was thought to be pregnant and the formalities with the military authorities were taking a long time, the couple settled in La Plata in the boarding house where he was arrested.

68. The author wishes to be informed of the whereabouts of the missing person.

69. The representative of the Argentine Government said that although the student card had a reregistration stamp on it the student in question had not been attending his courses. He added that a number of the facts reported in the communication seemed surprising. He did not understand, for instance, why the alleged victim had been called up by the military district of La Plata, which was not his place of residence and where students were usually called up in July and not in March.

70. The members who spoke felt that the new information which the communication contained seemed to confirm the fact that it fell within Unesco's fields of competence and that, since it concerned a missing person, the Committee's decision on that matter ought to be applied.

71. The Committee consequently *decided* to deal with this communication in accordance with its decision on missing persons.[4]

---

[4] See documents 108 EX/38 PRIV., para. 16, 109 EX/52 PRIV., annex I, para. 8, and Corr. and 112 EX/30 PRIV., paras. 558-566.

No. 375/81

Concerning *Romania*
Case of *Constantin Munteanu*

Communication of 15 June 1981 submitted by
League for the Defence of Human Rights in Romania

Spring 1982 session of the Committee on Conventions and Recommendations (114th session of the Executive Board)[1]

151. This communication is submitted by the League for the Defence of Human Rights in Romania (LDHR.), acting as a non-governmental organization possessing reliable knowledge of the alleged violations.

152. It is alleged that Mr Constantin Munteanu was expelled for political reasons from the faculty where he was studying; it is said that he nevertheless managed to become an engineer by attending evening classes. His application to be accepted as a doctoral candidate was reportedly rejected. Since that time, he is said to have filed 79 requests for permission to leave the country.

153. As for the purpose and aim of the communication, the League states that Mr Munteanu is not the only person to be refused, on political grounds, the possibility of preparing a doctorate or engaging in studies. The author requests that such practices be publicly denounced.

154. Confirming the gist of a letter from the Permanent Delegation of Romania to Unesco, dated 13 April 1982 [...],[2] the representative of the Romanian Government stated that Mr Munteanu had left his country legally on 2 February 1982, and was living with relatives in the United States of America.

155. The matter having thus been settled in accordance with the wishes of the alleged victim, the Committee *decided* to strike the communication from the list.

---

[1] See document 114 EX/38 PRIV., paras. 151-155; see also documents 114 EX/CR/HR/3 and Add.2.
[2] See document 114 EX/CR/HR/3 Add.2.

No. 378/81

Concerning *Romania*
Case of *Religious persecution in Romania*

Communication of 28 June 1981 submitted by
League for the Defence of Human Rights in Romania

Spring 1982 session of the Committee on Conventions and Recommendations (114th session of the Executive Board)[1]

156. This communication is submitted by the League for the Defence of Human Rights in Romania, represented by Mrs Maria Bratianu, Secretary-General, who, in her letter accompanying the communication expresses concern over the disappearance, on 9 March 1979, of Mr Vasile Paraschiv, a Romanian worker and member of the Free Union of Workers of Romania (SLOMR).

157. In the prescribed communication form transmitted to the Secretariat, the author presents information, above all, on "religious persecution in Romania" and identifies the following persons as victims:

A. *Orthodox*

(1) Gheorghe Calciu Dumitreasa:

Priest and lecturer at Bucharest Theological Seminary, he was allegedly dismissed on 17 May 1978, arrested on 10 May 1979 and sentenced to 10 years' imprisonment. At the present time, he is said to be detained in the prison in Aiud.

The case of the alleged victim was the subject of an earlier communication submitted by a journalist acting in the name of the French Committee for the defence of this priest.[2] The Committee on Conventions and Recommendations, at the [autumn 1980 session], declared the communication inadmissible as not falling within

[1] See document 114 EX/38 PRIV., paras. 156-171; see also document 114 EX/CR/HR/3.
[2] Communication No. 247/80 concerning *Romania*, case of *Gheorghe Calciu-Dumitreasa*.

Unesco's competence;[3] the representative of the Romanian Government claimed at that session that at the time of Gheorghe Calciu Dumitreasa's arrest, he was no longer a teacher or a priest and that he had been found guilty of having taken part in fascist activities threatening the state.

(2) Gavrila Stefan:

A priest, allegedly arrested a number of times. He was, it is said, excluded from the clergy and then reinstated as a result of a campaign in the foreign press. He is now, apparently, serving in a parish of Costandoiu (Vrancea).

(3) Dumitru Bejan:

A priest, allegedly placed under forced residence in Hârlau, Moldavia.

(4) Grebenea:

A priest, allegedly placed under forced residence in Piatra Neamt (Moldavia) and prevented from officiating.

(5) Garbulet:

A teacher in Pângarati (Neamt); allegedly persecuted for his religious zeal as an orthodox preacher.

(6) Gheorghe Brasoveanu:

Economist, founding member of the free trade union SLOMR, he allegedly spent several months in a psychiatric hospital for having criticized the nature of relations between church and state.

B. *Adventists*

(1) Ion Balaban:

It is alleged that he was persecuted for his religious beliefs, that he requested authorization to emigrate to Australia, that he was dismissed from his employment and that he has no means of subsistence.

---

[3] See document 110 EX/40 PRIV., para. 153 (*supra*, p. 632).

(2) George Caraivan:

He allegedly spent 10 years in prison for having tried to emigrate in 1955. He was apparently arrested again a few months ago and imprisoned in Poarta Alba for having filed an application for emigration for himself and his wife.

(3) Titu Bujor:

A teacher, he was allegedly dismissed from his post because of his religious beliefs. He apparently also applied for emigration (for himself and his family).

(4) Gheorghe Dan:

A house painter, both he and his family have allegedly been subjected to humiliation and insults. He has apparently applied for permission to emigrate to the Federal Republic of Germany.

(5) Victor Dragulin:

Both he and his family are allegedly victims of religious persecution. He wishes to emigrate to the United States of America.

(6) Gheorghe Mateescu:

An Adventist minister, he was allegedly divested of his functions and his children expelled from school. He also wants to leave the country.

(7) Dumitru Nemesniciuc and Ion Nemesniciuc:

Workers, they were allegedly persecuted for their religious beliefs which prevented them from working on Saturdays. They were even, it is said, imprisoned for five months. They wish to emigrate to the United States of America.

C. *Baptists*

(1) Gheorghe Michescu:

It is alleged that he lost his job because of his religious beliefs, that he was transferred to Timis as an unskilled worker and that his applications for emigration have been refused.

(2) Pavel Ploscariu, Haralambie Ploscariu, Zaharia Ploscariu and members of their families:

Because of the religious persecution they have allegedly been subjected to, they apparently applied for emigration to the United States of America, but to no avail.

(3) Chisar:

He apparently asked for permission to join his wife and daughter abroad, lost his job, was arrested at Timisoara and tortured.

D. *Pentecostalists*

(1) Vasile Bilanca:

He was allegedly persecuted for his religious beliefs and imprisoned for four months in Suceava for having requested permission to emigrate to the United States of America.

(2) Ena Chelaru:

This case seems to be similar to the one above.

(3) Nicolae Damian:

A minister, he was allegedly arrested along with his wife and was the victim of harassment and threats because his house was apparently used as a house of prayer.

(4) Aurel Iovuta:

He was allegedly persecuted, with his family, for a number of years. They wish to emigrate to the United States of America.

(5) Ion Lazareanu:

A preacher, he was, it is alleged, also the victim of persecution and lost his job after seeking authorization to emigrate to the United States of America. He was, it appears, accused of parasitism.

(6) Pavel Marinau:

He and his family were, allegedly, the victims of harassment; they also want to leave for the United States of America.

(7) Lica Poloczar:

It is alleged that he was persecuted for his religious beliefs, that he asked for permission to emigrate to the United States of America and that he was imprisoned for four months in Radauti.

E. *Distribution of the Bible*

(1) Mathias Fackner:

For distributing the Bible, he was allegedly arrested and sentenced to three years' imprisonment on 18 October 1980.

(2) Paul Gross:

For the same reason, he was allegedly sentenced to four years' imprisonment (18 October 1980).

(3) Manfred Herbert:

For the same reason, he was allegedly sentenced to two years' imprisonment.

(4) Gheorghe Hofman:

For the same reason, he was allegedly sentenced to 18 months' imprisonment.

(5) Michael Kloos:

Also for the same reason, he was allegedly sentenced to three years' imprisonment.

158. As for the purpose and aim of the communication, the League wishes the Romanian Government to end the religious persecution of the persons named above and of other persons who are in a similar situation.

159. The representative of the government concerned pointed out that the communication was self-contradictory: the author had begun by referring to the disappearance of a worker who was a member of the Free Union of Workers (SLOMR), Mr Vasile

Paraschiv. Having realized that such a case was inadmissible because it did not fall within Unesco's fields of competence, the author had shifted the communication on to different ground, that of religious persecution, which was something that had never occurred in Romania; in so doing she had revealed her true purpose, namely, the denigration and defamation of that country. The representative of the Romanian Government said that in his view the communication had been prompted by exclusively political considerations and was therefore inadmissible.

160. One member of the Committee recalled that the Committee had discussed the problem of religious persecution at length when examining a communication and that it had decided that the subject did not come within Unesco's competence. Accordingly, and in view of the fact that the case of the worker Vasile Paraschiv also did not fall within the Organization's fields of competence, he considered that the communication submitted by the League for the Defence of Human Rights in Romania was inadmissible.

161. One member of the Committee stated that in his view it was difficult to say that religion was not part of culture, and that most of the individual cases that had been submitted did appear to fall within Unesco's competence.

162. In order to clarify matters for the Committee, the representative of the Director-General stated that while the question of freedom of religion had certainly been discussed on the occasion of the examination of a communication, the Committee had reached no decision as to whether that question fell within the Organization's sphere of competence.

163. In order to prove that the allegations made in the communication were groundless, the representative of the Romanian Government, while explaining that there had been no persecutions for religious activities, belief, or the expression of opinion, provided, by way of examples, information on the following cases:

(1) *Case of Gheorghe Calciu Dumitreasa*:

This person had been sentenced, not because of his religious activities, but because of his activities in connection with efforts to reconstitute Fascist elements in Romania. The Committee had decided once already that the case was inadmissible. Accordingly, the "non bis in idem" principle should be followed.

(2) *Case of Gavrila Stefan*:

The person concerned was officiating without let or hindrance. He was not being subjected to any form of discrimination.

(3) *Cases of Ion Balaban and George Caraivan*:

These persons had left Romania of their own free will.

(4) *Cases of Dumitru Nemesniciuc and Ion Nemesniciuc*:

These persons had been sentenced to several months' imprisonment for disturbing the peace and vandalism. They had been released after serving their sentences.

(5) *Case of Vasile Bilanca*:

This person also had been sentenced to prison for disturbing the peace and vandalism.

(6) *Case of Pavel Marinau*:

This person had already left Romania.

(7) *Cases of Mathias Fackner, Paul Gross, Manfred Herbert, Gheorghe Hofmann and Michael Kloos*:

These five persons had been sentenced to imprisonment for offences against the laws on foreign currency. They had since been released following a measure granting remission of their sentence.

(8) *Case of Gheorghe Mateescu*:

The Romanian Government representative said that while he did not have adequate information at his disposal on this case, the assertion that Mr Mateescu's children had been expelled from school was absurd, since in Romaina no such measure could be taken against the children of any citizen.

164. In that connection, a member of the Committee mentioned that in Romania children are required to attend school.

165. The representative of the Romanian Government added that the reason why he had not provided any details on the other alleged victims was quite simply that they had not been subjected to any persecution.

166. To clarify matters, the Committee *decided* that it would be desirable to examine the facts relating to the alleged victims case by case, gradually eliminating those cases that did not fall within Unesco's fields of competence or were manifestly ill-

founded in that they did not contain relevant supporting evidence, in accordance with the provisions of paragraph 14 (*a*) (iii) and (v). The case of the worker Vasile Paraschiv was dismissed because the author of the communication had not included it in the standard form; the Committee considered that that case was probably inadmissible in any event, on the grounds that it did not fall within Unesco's competence.

167. Following this procedure, the Committee *eliminated* all the other cases except those of Gheorghe Calciu Dumitreasa, Titu Bujor, Gheorghe Mateescu, Gheorghe Michescu and Nicolae Damian.

168. The Committee thus remained with only five cases to examine.

169. (*a*) *Case of Gheorghe Calciu Dumitreasa*:

With reference to the "non bis in idem" principle, the representative of the Director-General pointed out that 104 EX/Decision 3.3 contained no stipulation to the effect that the same case could not be examined twice.

Several members of the Committee wanted to know exactly what charges had been brought against the alleged victim.

Recalling that the individual concerned had been tried and sentenced for having taken part in Fascist activities threatening the state, the representative of the Romanian Government pointed out that there was nothing new in the case, and consequently he did not see any need to re-examine it. He indicated, in passing, that Mr Dumitreasa's health had been well looked after.

After an exchange of views, the Committee finally *declared* the communication inadmissible as being manifestly ill-founded.

170. (*b*) *Cases of Gheorghe Michescu and Nicolae Damian*:

In the absence of relevant evidence furnished by the author of the communication, the Committee *declared* that these two cases were also inadmissible under the provisions of 104 EX/Decision 3.3, paragraph 14 (*a*) (v).

171. (*c*) *Cases of Titu Bujor and Gheorghe Mateescu*:

There appeared to be a link between the alleged facts and Unesco's fields of competence. In order to be able to consider these cases in full knowledge of the facts, the Committee *decided*:

(i) to suspend consideration of these two cases;

(ii) to request the representative of the government concerned to make available to the Committee, at its next session, such information as he might deem appropriate, and also to ask the author of the communication for additional information that would demonstrate that the communication fulfilled all the conditions governing admissibility set forth in 104 EX/Decision 3.3, paragraph 14 (*a*).

Autumn 1982 session of the Committee on Conventions and Recommendations (115th session of the Executive Board)[4]

202. This communication concerns several persons identified by name, who are alleged to have been victims of religious persecution by the Romanian authorities.

203. At the spring 1982 session, the Committee, having examined the individual cases one by one in the light of the explanations given by the representative of the Romanian Government, retained only the cases of Mr Titu Bujor, described as a teacher, and Mr Gheorghe Mateescu, described as an Adventist minister, requesting additional information on those cases before coming to a decision.[5]

204. Confirming the contents of the letter dated 18 August 1982 addressed to the Director-General by the Permanent Delegation of Romania to Unesco [...],[6] the representative of the government concerned, stressing once again that the allegations set out in the communication were biased and groundless, stated that:

> Mr Titu Bujor had applied in April 1980 for permission to emigrate, with his wife and three children: he had obtained satisfaction;
>
> Mr Gheorghe Mateescu, having also received permission to emigrate, had left Romania for the United States of America on 31 May 1982, accompanied by his wife and two children.

205. The representative of the Romanian Government then quoted a series of legal texts and regulations which guarantee freedom of thought, conscience, belief, worship and religion in Romania, and which even provide for sanctions against those who infringe those freedoms.

---

[4] See document 115 EX/28 PRIV., paras. 202-206; see also documents 115 EX/CR/HR/2 and Add.3.

[5] See document 114 EX/38 PRIV., para. 171 (*supra*, pp. 944-945).

[6] See document 115 EX/CR/HR/2 Add.3.

No. 378/81 **Romania**

206. After a brief discussion, the Committee *decided* to delete the communication from its list, as the case of the two alleged victims had been settled in accordance with their wishes.

No. 379/81

Concerning *Union of Soviet Socialist Republics*
Case of *Vladimir Feltsman*

Communication of 26 June 1981 submitted by
Yves Haguenauer and Alexandre Kagan

Autumn 1981 session of the Committee on Conventions and Recommendations (113th session of the Executive Board)[1]

421. A communication, [...],[2] was submitted in January 1981 by Mr Yves Haguenauer, who described himself as a person with reliable knowledge of the alleged violations.

422. According to him, Mr Vladimir Feltsman, a Soviet Jew, well known as a concert pianist, graduate of the Moscow Conservatorium and prize-winner of the international competitions "Concertino Praga" and the "Concours Marguerite Long", who had made a number of recordings widely distributed throughout the world and often given concerts both at home and abroad, had lost his job and been deprived of all professional activity since applying for an emigration visa in June 1979. Invited to the Ukraine for a series of concerts, for which he had been preparing for a long time, he found himself in an impasse: the concerts had been cancelled without his being informed of the fact.

423. At its [spring 1981] session, the Committee decided, after discussion, to declare the case inadmissible, in pursuance of paragraph 14 (*a*) (iii) of 104 EX/Decision 3.3.[3]

424. A further communication concerning Mr Feltsman was submitted by Mr Yves Haguenauer and Mr Feltsman's brother-in-law, Mr Alexandre Kagan, in a letter dated 25 June 1981.

---

[1] See document 113 EX/38 PRIV., paras. 421-438; see also document 113 EX/CR/HR/3 Add.
[2] Communication No. 303/80 concerning *Union of Soviet Socialist Republics*, case of *Vladimir Feltsman and Victor Suslin.*
[3] See document 112 EX/30 PRIV., para. 339 (*supra*, p. 754).

No. 379/81 **Union of Soviet Socialist Republics**

425. While the communication follows the same pattern as above, Mr Haguenauer added further facts and details in the form filled in on 6 July 1981 and signed by him alone:

> Mr Feltsman was unable to respond to numerous offers of concerts or recitals in the West, from the Concertgebouw, Amsterdam, and Carnegie Hall, New York, in particular.
>
> The French authorities, who were responsible for the organization of the "Paris-Moscow" exhibition in Moscow in June 1981, had expressed the wish that Mr Feltsman, as a former prize-winner of the "Concours Marguerite Long" in Paris, should give a concert, as part of the activities planned for the programme of the exhibition. The pianist was not even approached in this connection by the appropriate Soviet authorities.

426. The latter fact was quoted by the authors of the communication as a quite recent example which shows clearly that the vexations to which Feltsman is subjected in the exercise of his art are real and still exist.

427. The authors of the communication explained, moreover, that Mr Feltsman was excluded from the concerts organized by the Philharmonic in the following way: first, it was alleged, he was banned from all concerts; then he obtained a few concerts in remote provinces, where the conditions were deplorable. Two examples were given to illustrate this:

> In Georgia, in December 1980, the piano was unplayable. With the agreement of the local authorities, he had to resign himself to giving no recital.
>
> In the Ukraine, in February 1981, Mr Feltsman was to give five concerts, but when he arrived he found that the concerts had not been announced so he was obliged to return to Moscow without having played there either.

428. Mr Haguenaurer and Mr Kagan noted that the pianist has not actually been able to play in public since June 1979, the time of his first application for an emigration visa.

429. According to them, Mr Feltsman's records were unobtainable in Moscow and the main stores in the provinces. They admitted that they might conceivably be found in some remote spot in the provinces, but they claimed that the records have been removed from the commercial circuits.

430. Finally, they pointed out that the pianist's name has been withdrawn from the encyclopedia of Soviet musicians.

431. As aim and purpose of their communication, the authors state that they wanted Mr Feltsman to be able to resume his brutally interrupted musical activities as soon as possible, and to be able to do so in the country of his choice. All he asked was to be able to join members of his family in Israel, particularly his brother-in-law, Mr Alexandre Kagan, and their aunt.

432. The representative of the Soviet Government stated at the Committee's present session that the author of the communication was part of an organization which acted to lure Soviet musicians out of their country. He reminded the Committee that he had presented to it at its [spring 1981] session much documentation that this pianist was being given ample opportunity to practise his art in the Soviet Union. He went on to emphasize that the right to emigrate was not one within the competence of Unesco and that it was established Committee practice to consider a resubmission of a case already handled by the Committee to be an abuse of the right to submit communications. The few additional facts presented in this resubmission were insignificant and did not make this a new communication, he added. The Soviet representative emphasized that Mr Feltsman's records had not been removed from the Soviet market; the record company Melodia had assured him of this. Nor did he feel it fair on the part of the author to denigrate large Soviet cities, where Mr Feltsman had been allowed to play, as being of no significance simply because they were somewhat distant from Moscow. Furthermore, he added, Mr Feltsman had refused to go on with one of the concert tours, simply because he felt that his appearance had been insufficiently advertised. The Soviet representative went on to say that Mr Feltsman presently had the opportunity for a 32-concert tour in important cities, which was presently being planned by the All Union concert tour authorities. Everything depended on Mr Feltsman's willingness to accept the opportunities open to him, the representative said.

433. Several Committee members agreed that questions of emigration *per se* were not within the competence of the Committee, but one Committee member wondered why the Committee permitted itself to examine questions of immigration into countries and not emigration out of them.

434. The Committee member went on to point out that Mr Feltsman had not played at certain concert opportunities allegedly offered to him because the conditions had in fact been made impossible for him, either through lack of advertising or because of a defective piano. He went on to point out that Mr Feltsman was an extremely gifted pianist and raised the question as to whether the concert tour being drawn up for him was taking into account Mr Feltsman's views.

435. Another Committee member felt that certain important questions remained unanswered. He asked whether Mr Feltsman had indeed been excluded from mention in the encyclopedia of Soviet musicians, whether he had been excluded from the Moscow Philharmonic, and whether the offers to play in the West had been forwarded to him.

436. The representative of· the Soviet Government stated that Mr Feltsman was not being limited in his professional activities, indeed he was being indulged as if he were a whimsical child. The Soviet representative stated that Mr Feltsman was being consulted about his planned concerts, and that they were not being forced on him. He went on to state that he had not looked into the matter of the exclusion of Mr Feltsman's name from the Soviet encyclopedia, but wondered whether one could really view such an inclusion as an automatic right. It appeared to be a case of an exclusion of his name rather than a withdrawal of it. As for the concerts with the Moscow Philharmonic, these were decided by that body, and they were not within the ambit of the Soviet Government. With regard to invitations extended to Soviet musicians by other countries, there was an established administrative procedure by which these were processed in the Soviet Union, and they could thus not have been addressed to Mr Feltsman directly.

437. In response to a question concerning the weight the Committee should assign to the various facts, the representative of the Director-General explained that the Committee had decided at its first session to assume the good faith of the governments which presented information to it. On the other hand the Committee had also decided that it had the right to look at the communication beyond the information which was submitted. He went on to say that 104 EX/Decision 3.3 had a very progressive article in it, [paragraph 14] (*f*), which provided that "the Committee may avail itself of the relevant information at the disposal of the Director-General".

438. After an involved debate, the Committee *decided* to declare the communication inadmissible on the grounds of paragraph 14 (*a*) (x) of 104 EX/Decision 3.3, as having been settled in accordance with the human rights principles set forth in the Universal Declaration of Human Rights and the International Covenants on Human Rights.

No. 381/81

Concerning *Uruguay*
Case of *Raúl Noel Martínez Machado*

Communication of 17 June 1981 submitted by
Víctor Ernesto Martínez Machado

Spring 1982 session of the Committee on Conventions and Recommendations (114th session of the Executive Board)[1]

264. Mr Víctor Ernesto Martínez Machado, a student, describes himself as the representative of Mr Raúl Noel Martínez Machado, a history teacher. According to the allegation, Mr Raúl Noel Martínez Machado was arrested on 16 October 1971 and sentenced to a prison term of nine and a half years. It is said that he was taken to the military hospital in 1977. Reportedly tortured during his arrest, he was again subjected to ill-treatment at the end of 1979. It is alleged that he was transferred from Libertad prison on 26 November 1980, kept in solitary confinement and tortured. In May 1981, his family traced him to Colonia barracks. His prison term came to an end on 16 April 1981.

265. In the documents attached to the letter introducing the communication it is stated that "a military tribunal had been convened inside the Libertad penitentiary with a view to obtaining, through intimidation, testimony for the purpose of retrying Raúl Noel Martínez Machado and other missing persons" and that "there was a precedent for this in the case of Hugo Dermit Barbato, a political prisoner who, having served his term and obtained a visa for Sweden, was transferred to a military unit and tortured to death". It is noted in the communication form, which was completed at a more recent date, that Mr Raúl Noel Martínez Machado was allegedly retried by an "illegal tribunal that was set up in the prison".

266. The author of the communication requests the release of Mr Raúl Noel Martínez Machado (a request is also made in the original dossier for the granting by France of a visa for him) .

---

[1] See document 114 EX/38 PRIV., paras. 264-273; see also document 114 EX/CR/HR/3.

No. 381/81 **Uruguay**

267. The representative of the Uruguayan Government said that, since 1970, his country, which had been enjoying a prolonged period of peace in the framework of genuine democracy, had experienced a powerful current of terrorism: the Tupamaros, in particular, had launched armed attacks in an effort to seize power by force; they had resorted to violence - murder, bomb attacks, kidnapping, etc. - in the same way as the Red Brigades in Italy and other terrorist groups operating in the Federal Republic of Germany had done.

268. The representative of the Uruguayan Government stated that Raúl Noel Martínez Machado had been arrested at the same time as other Tupamaros, that he had been tried and sentenced in accordance with the law (by which the military tribunal was empowered to act) and that the alleged victim's status as a teacher had nothing to do with his terrorist activities. He explained that Mr Machado would probably have been released at the end of his sentence in April 1981, but that the competent authorities had meanwhile discovered a movement to relaunch the Tupamaros which was in conjunction with a group of prisoners, including Mr Machado. That was the reason why he had had to face a retrial.

269. Several members of the Committee were in agreement in recognizing the legitimacy of the struggle of the state concerned against terrorism and the inadmissibility of the communication, in conformity with paragraph 14 (*a*) (iii) of 104 EX/Decision 3.3. They did, however, express their deep concern about the torture to which the alleged victim had reportedly been subjected.

270. One member expressed fear lest Mr Machado's fate were to be the same as that of the political prisoner, Hugo Dermit Barbato, mentioned by the author in his communication.

271. The representative of the Uruguayan Government took the floor once more to reply to the misgivings expressed, and said that the authorities of his country did not torture prisoners, whether Tupamaros or not, and he regretted that by a reversal of the burden of proof a statement to the contrary was so easily accepted. With regard to the case of Hugo Dermit Barbato, he said that he had committed suicide and his death had not been the result of torture.

272. One member of the Committee said that while he was not at all opposed to the Committee demonstrating its feelings at the humanitarian level, he felt obliged to say that he could not accept the facts alleged in the communication.

273. After an exchange of views, the Committee *decided*:

(i) to declare the communication inadmissible since it did not fall within the spheres of Unesco's competence, pursuant to the provisions of paragraph 14 (*a*) (iii) of 104 EX/Decision 3.3;

(ii) to ask the representative of the government concerned to be good enough to take note of the Committee's humanitarian concern.

No. 385/81

Concerning *Union of Soviet Socialist Republics*
Case of *Anatoly Koryagin*

Communication of 23 June 1981 submitted by
American Psychiatric Association

Autumn 1981 session of the Committee on Conventions and Recommendations (113th session of the Executive Board)[1]

439. The American Psychiatric Association (APA), represented by Mr Harold Visotsky, described itself as a non-governmental organization with reliable knowledge of the alleged violations.

440. Mr Anatoly Koryagin, a Soviet psychiatrist aged 42, who is said to have actively opposed the abuse of psychiatry for political purposes, was apparently arrested on 13 February 1981 at Belgorod on his way home to Kharkov, in Ukraine, from Moscow. Some time earlier he had told two Western journalists that there was no medical justification for the forced internment in a psychiatric hospital of the Ukrainian engineer, Mr Alexei Nikitin, who had protested about the conditions of the workers in the coal mines to Western newspaper correspondents. In June 1981 Mr Koryagin was sentenced to seven years' imprisonment and five years' internal exile.

441. In January 1977 a small group of Soviet citizens set themselves up as a Commission to Investigate the Use of Psychiatry for Political Purposes. This Commission managed to issue a number of information bulletins, statements, appeals and open letters on the subject. It was assisted in its task by Dr Koryagin, by another psychiatrist and by a jurist well known in Moscow, Sofia Kallistratova. While gathering information, it is alleged to have given the victims or potential victims advice of a legal and practical nature as to ways of resisting the abuse of psychiatry by the Soviet authorities.

---

[1] See document 113 EX/38 PRIV., paras. 439-455 see also document 113 EX/CR/HR/3 Add.

No. 385/81 **Union of Soviet Socialist Republics**

442. The author of the communication claims that one by one practically all the members of the said Commission were arrested and punished for having dared to uphold the ideals and highest traditions of medicine and psychiatry.

443. Dr Koryagin, by opposing the violation of human rights through psychiatry, has had his own human rights violated.

444. The author of the communication requested Unesco's prompt intervention to help secure the liberation of Mr Koryagin.

445. The various documents attached to the communication include:

446. (*a*) A copy of an English text (probably a translation) supposed to have come from Dr Koryagin:

(1) This text indicates that persons obliged to undergo treatment in ordinary or special psychiatric hospitals show no sign or symptoms of mental illness when examined and that the reason for having joined the ranks of the insane was that they had said things which were regarded as anti-Soviet.

(2) Examples of this kind of patient given in the text are:

> the psychiatrist A. Butko, who tried to swim to Turkey;
>
> the engineer L. Pribytkov, former member of the Communist Party, who renounced his Russian nationality and made several attempts to enter a foreign embassy;
>
> the engineer A. Paskauskien who distributed nationalist tracts;
>
> the electromechanical engineer A. Nikitin (a medical report is annexed to the text).

(3) The different ways in which psychiatry is used for political purposes are described at length.

> (i) At the request of the investigators, persons charged with an anti-Soviet act are subjected to a medical/psychiatric examination and declared insane. They are then forced to undergo treatment in a psychiatric hospital.
>
> (ii) Called up by a military conscription office for examination by a commission, the person concerned is escorted by a policeman to a psychiatric hospi-

tal for observation. It is frequently not a military office but the Executive Committee of the District Soviet or the Town Committee of the Party, or the police, or a body of inspectors in patrol cars that performs this function.

(iii) Sometimes a man is taken to the police station as a result of a quarrel at work or with neighbours. From there he is sent to a psychiatric hospital.

(iv) An order may be issued for a person to be interned in a psychiatric hospital without the person concerned being aware of the fact, on the grounds that he has previously been interned or his state of health has deteriorated - a deterioration which takes the form of increased anti-Soviet activities. This form of internment was used as a preventive measure during the 1980 Olympic Games in particular, persons deemed socially dangerous because suspected of having anti-Soviet tendencies being hospitalized for the duration of the Games.

- Seventy per cent of the persons forcibly hospitalized under such measures are declared psychopathic, the other 30 per cent schizophrenic.

- In the medical files, it is said, the term "paranoid" is frequently used to indicate that there are indubitable signs of that mental illness constituted by the presence of anti-Soviet sentiments.

- The ill-treatment undergone by the so-called patients is mentioned in the text, moreover: injection of neuroleptic substances as punishment, deliberate brutality. The KGB is alleged to have been directly involved in the decision concerning the duration of their confinement in the psychiatric hospitals.

447. (*b*) Photocopies of some press articles.

448. (*c*) A photocopy of a draft resolution of the World Psychiatric Association condemning the negative attitude of the All Union Society of Psychiatrists and Neurologists in the USSR.

449. The representative of the Soviet Government stated that, although he could introduce voluminous data into the discussion of this case, he would for the moment confine himself to addressing the question of the competence of the Committee for this case. He explained that Dr Koryagin was an ordinary practising doctor; he was not by virtue of his profession as a psychiatrist and general practitioner a person coming within Unesco's fields of competence, i.e. education, science, culture or communication. For this reason, the representative said, there was no link with the Committee's competence and the case was thus inadmissible.

No. 385/81 **Union of Soviet Socialist Republics**

450. A Committee member pointed out to the Committee that the profession of a complainant was actually a secondary link to Unesco's fields of competence and that the primary link to look for was the field of activity which might be affected by violations of the human rights of the victim, and that since in this case the field was that of science, the case was admissible.

451. Several Committee members felt that the case was clearly within Unesco's fields of competence, pointing to the fact that psychiatry dealt with the psyche, a key aspect of man which concerned Unesco. One member called to the Committee's attention the fact that the United Nations General Assembly in its resolution 35/130 adopted on 11 December 1980, placed the subject of mental health under the rubric of "Science and technological development".

452. Another Committee member asked what qualifications were required of scientists in the Soviet Union and what qualifications were required of doctors.

453. The Soviet representative explained that Dr Koryagin was a general practitioner in psychiatry and could in no way be seen as a member of the scientific community. He went on to say that the subject of psychiatric hospital policies was such a politicized issue that he feared that if the Committee embarked on a discussion thereof it would be opening a Pandora's box. Western scientists visiting the USSR had on several occasions been invited to formulate their own opinions about certain interned patients, he said, and while the majority did not want to formulate opinions, others confirmed the diagnosis of Soviet doctors. The Soviet representative felt that it would be unwise for the Committee, which did not really have the proper scientific background, to judge the question of the scientific aspects in this case.

454. After further discussion by the Committee, the Soviet representative explained that he in fact did not really have sufficient data to respond fully to the Committee on this matter, due to the receipt of the communication barely a month before.

455. The Committee thereupon *decided*:

(i) to adjourn of the admissibility of the communication; and

(ii) to request the government concerned to place at the Committee's disposal at the next session all necessary information on the measures which may have been taken against Dr Anatoly Koryagin depriving him of his freedom as well as on the complaints of a more general nature formulated in the communication.

Union of Soviet Socialist Republics **No. 385/81**

Spring 1982 session of the Committee on Conventions and Recommendations (114h session of the Executive Board)[2]

686. This communication is submitted by the American Psychiatric Association (APA), which describes itself as a non-governmental organization with reliable knowledge of the alleged violations.

687. Mr Anatoly Koryagin, a Soviet psychiatrist aged 42, who is said to have actively opposed the abuse of psychiatry for political purposes, was apparently arrested on 13 February 1981 at Belgorod on his way home to Kharkov, in Ukraine, from Moscow. Some time earlier he had told two Western journalists that there was no medical justification for the forced internment in a psychiatric hospital of the Ukrainian engineer, Mr Alexei Nikitin, who had protested about the conditions of the workers in the coal mines to Western newspaper correspondents. In June 1981 Mr Koryagin was sentenced to seven years' imprisonment and five years' internal exile.

688. In January 1977 a small group of Soviet citizens set themselves up as a Commission to Investigate the Use of Psychiatry for Political Purposes. This Commission managed to issue a number of information bulletins, statements, appeals and open letters on the subject. It was assisted in its task by Dr Koryagin, by another psychiatrist and by a jurist well known in Moscow, Sofia Kallistratova. While gathering information, it is alleged to have given the victims or potential victims advice of a legal and practical nature as to ways of resisting the abuse of psychiatry by the Soviet authorities.

689. The author of the communication claims that one by one practically all the members of the said Commission were arrested and punished for having dared to uphold the ideals and highest traditions of medicine and psychiatry.

690. The American Psychiatric Association is said to have sent many appeals to the Soviet Government. The Committee on the Abuse of Psychiatry of the World Psychiatric Association contacted the All Union Society of Psychiatrists and Neurologists in the USSR (a member organization of the World Psychiatric Association, WPA) but received no reply.

691. The case has been submitted to other authorities besides the WPA: the Royal College of Psychiatrists in the United Kingdom, Amnesty International, the American Association for the Advancement of Science and the National Academy of Science.

---

[2] See document 114 EX/38 PRIV., paras. 686-709 see also document 114 EX/CR/HR/2.

692. The author of the communication requests Unesco's prompt intervention to secure Dr Koryagin's release.

693. The various documents attached to the communication include:

(*a*) A copy of an English text (probably a translation) supposed to have come from Dr Koryagin:

> (i) This text indicates that persons obliged to undergo treatment in ordinary or special psychiatric hospitals show no sign or symptoms of mental illness when examined and that the reason for having joined the ranks of the insane was that they had said things which were regarded as anti-Soviet.
>
> (ii) Examples of this kind of patient given in the text are:
>
> the psychiatrist A. Butko, who tried to swim to Turkey;
>
> the engineer L. Pribytkov, former member of the Communist Party, who renounced his Russian nationality and made several attempts to enter a foreign embassy;
>
> the engineer A. Paskauskien, who distributed nationalist tracts;
>
> the electromechanical engineer A. Nikitin (a medical report is annexed to the text).
>
> (iii) The different ways in which psychiatry is used for political purposes are described at length.

(*b*) Photocopies of some press articles.

(*c*) A photocopy of a draft resolution of the World Psychiatric Association condemning the negative attitude of the All Union Society of Psychiatrists and Neurologists in the Union of Soviet Socialist Republics.

694. At the [autumn] 1981 session the representative of the Soviet Government stated that, although he could introduce voluminous data into the discussion of this case, he was for the moment confining himself to the question of the competence of the Committee for this case. He explained that Dr Koryagin was an ordinary practising doctor; he was not by virtue of his profession as a psychiatrist and general practitioner a person coming within Unesco's fields of competence, i.e. education, science, culture or communication.

Union of Soviet Socialist Republics **No. 385/81**

695. A Committee member pointed out to the Committee that the profession of a complainant was actually a secondary link to Unesco's fields of competence and that the primary link to look for was the field of activity which might be affected by violations of the human rights of the victim, and that since in this case the field was that of science, the case was admissible.

696. Several Committee members felt that the case was clearly within Unesco's fields of competence, pointing to the fact that psychiatry dealt with the psyche, a key aspect of man which concerned Unesco. One member called to the Committee's attention the fact that the United Nations General Assembly in its resolution 35/130 adopted on 11 December 1980, placed the subject of mental health under the rubric of "Science and technological development".

697. Another Committee member asked what qualifications were required of scientists in the Union of Soviet Socialist Republics and what qualifications were required of doctors.

698. The representative of the Soviet Government explained that Dr Koryagin was a general practitioner in psychiatry and could in no way be seen as a member of the scientific community. He went on to say that the subject of psychiatric hospital policies was such a politicized issue that he feared that if the Committee embarked on a discussion thereof it would be opening a Pandora's box. Western scientists visting the Union of Soviet Socialist Republics had on several occasions been invited to formulate their own opinions about certain interned patients, he said, and while the majority did not want to formulate opinions, others confirmed the diagnosis of Soviet doctors. The representative of the Soviet Government felt that it would be unwise for the Committee, which did not really have the proper scientific background, to judge the question of the scientific aspects in this case.

699. After further discussion by the Committee, the representative of the Soviet Government explained that he in fact did not really have sufficient data to respond fully to the Committee on this matter, since the communication had been received barely a month before.

700. The Committee thereupon decided:[3]

(i) to adjourn of the admissibility of the communication; and

(ii) to request the government concerned to place at the Committee's disposal for the present session all necessary information on the measures which may

[3] See document 113 EX/38 PRIV., para. 455 (*supra*, p. 958).

have been taken against Dr Anatoly Koryagin depriving him of his freedom as well as on the complaints of a more general nature formulated in the communication.

701. On 5 February 1982 the Secretariat received a letter dated 26 January 1982 from the author of the communication. The American Psychiatric Association requests a fuller explanation of the statement by the representative of the Soviet Government at the [autumn 1981] session that Dr Koryagin could not be seen as a member of the scientific community.

702. Attached to the letter is, in addition to copies of the texts annexed to the claim form and mentioned above, a set of photocopies of various publications comprising:

a biography of Dr Koryagin (17 June 1981);

an editorial in "World Medicine" on Dr Koryagin's case (13 June 1981),

an article from "Psychaitric News" (7 August 1981);

two articles from "The Lancet" (13 and 27 June 1981);

an appeal by Amnesty International dated 19 February 1981;

an article from "The Observer" (14 June 1981);

an article from the newspaper "Le Monde" (23 May 1981);

an article from "Cahiers du Samizdat" (Belgium, March/April 1981) reproducing an article by Dr Koryagin, which is the French version of the text in English attached to the communication form and referred to above under (*a*);

three pages of an information bulletin (No. 2, October 1981) of the International Association on Political Use of Psychiatry containing an open letter from Dr Koryagin to the psychiatrists of the world, reportedly written in July 1981; Dr Koryagin regards the sentence passed on him as retaliation against a specialist for merely doing his duty and heeding his conscience; he continues to hold the authorities responsible for using psychiatry as a means of repression.

703. At the present session the representative of the Soviet Government stated that he was ready to furnish the necessary proof to show that the case did not fall within Unesco's fields of competence. Considering that, in accordance with the procedure

laid down in 104 EX/Decision 3.3, there existed a legal relationship between the government and the Committee, but not between the government and the author of the communication, he felt that he did not need to reply to the question asked by the latter in his letter of 26 January 1982. He explained, however, that Mr Koryagin was an ordinary worker and not a scientific worker in the sense that this concept should be understood and this was the reason for his having raised the question of the Committee's lack of competence. He went on to say that the person concerned had been convicted by a competent court at a public hearing for common law offences: incitement to commit acts of violence, circulation of fraudulent material intended to harm the reputation of the Soviet state, deliberate misrepresentation of the activities of doctors in the Union of Soviet Socialist Republics, possession of equipment able to be used for terrorist activities (firearm).

704. One member of the Committee felt that it was of little importance whether or not the alleged victim enjoyed the status of a "scientist". He considered that what was important was that he was a psychiatrist who had had the courage to speak the truth about a serious problem, namely, the use of psychiatry for political ends. In reality, Mr Koryagin had dared to reveal what the authorities did not want to make public and he consequently considered that the accusation brought against him was a way of twisting the facts.

705. Taking the floor again, the representative of the Soviet Government expressed his astonishment at this statement. Mr Koryagin had committed a clearly defined offence; the validity of the accusation had been demonstrated by testimony and proof; the presumption of trust in the information provided by the government concerned was a factor making for co-operation with the Committee; it was inadmissible that there should be talk of an accusation designed to conceal something.

706. One member of the Committee felt that the fact of singling out certain important points in the communication could not be regarded as a criticism since, where he himself was concerned, he felt obliged to act according to his conscience. He proposed that, since the allegations concerned a branch of medicine, the communication might be suitably transmitted to the World Health Organization (WHO).

707. This proposal was supported by several members of the Committee. One of them thought that WHO might contemplate setting up an ad hoc Committee to consider the alleged facts and that this idea of transmitting the communication to WHO might perhaps be a welcome initiative enabling that organization to establish a standing body, similar to the Committee.

No. 385/81 **Union of Soviet Socialist Republics**

708. One member of the Committee wondered what action WHO might be able to take on a communication of this kind since it had no procedure for examining cases of human rights violations.

709. After an exchange of views the Committee *decided* to ask the Executive Board to request the Director-General to transmit the communication to WHO for any action that that organization might feel it should take on the matter within its own field of competence.

No. 386/81

Concerning *Egypt*
Case of *Ahmed Fouad Negm*

Communication of 6 July 1981 submitted by
Association internationale de défense des artistes
victimes de la répression

Autumn 1981 session of the Committee on Conventions and Recommendations (113th session of the Executive Board)[1]

Spring 1982 session of the Committee on Conventions and Recommendations (114th session of the Executive Board)[2]

[1] See document 113 EX/38 PRIV., paras. 190-203 (*supra*, pp. 927-929), communication No. 371/81 concerning *Egypt*, case of *Ahmed Fouad Negm*.
[2] See document 114 EX/38 PRIV., paras. 470-486 (*supra*, pp. 929-931), communication No. 371/81 concerning *Egypt*, case of *Ahmed Fouad Negm*.

No. 390/81

Concerning *El Salvador*
Case of *Edgar Mauricio Vallejo*

Communication of 15 July 1981 submitted by
Amnesty International

Spring 1982 session of the Committee on Conventions and Recommendations (114th session of the Executive Board)[1]

110. The Committee *decided* to combine consideration of this communication with that of [three other communications] concerning the same state.[2]

Autumn 1982 session of the Committee on Conventions and Recommendations (115th session of the Executive Board)[3]

Spring 1983 session of the Committee on Conventions and Recommendations (116th session of the Executive Board)[4]

Autumn 1983 session of the Committee on Conventions and Recommendations (117th session of the Executive Board)[5]

---

[1] See document 114 EX/38 PRIV., paras. 110 and 487-488 (*supra*, p. 678), communication No. 276/80 concerning *El Salvador*, case of *Miguel Ángel García* et al.
[2] Communications No. 276/80 concerning *El Salvador*, case of *Miguel Ángel García* et al., No. 283/80 concerning *El Salvador*, case of *Arrest and persecution of teachers in El Salvador*, and No. 306/80 concerning *El Salvador*, case of *Arrest and persecution of teachers in El Salvador*.
[3] See document 115 EX/28 PRIV., paras. 84-116 (*supra*, pp. 678-687), communication No. 276/80 concerning *El Salvador*, case of *Miguel Ángel García* et al.
[4] See document 116 EX/48 PRIV., paras. 66-71 (*supra*, pp. 687-688), communication No. 276/80 concerning *El Salvador*, case of *Leonel Menéndez Quiroga*.
[5] See document 117 EX/18 PRIV., paras. 80-83 (*supra*, pp. 688-689), communication No. 276/80 concerning *El Salvador*, case of *Leonel Menéndez Quiroga*.

No. 390/81 **El Salvador**

Spring 1984 session of the Committee on Conventions and Recommendations (119th session of the Executive Board)[6]

Autumn 1984 session of the Committee on Conventions and Recommendations (120th session of the Executive Board)[7]

Spring 1985 session of the Committee on Conventions and Recommendations (121st session of the Executive Board)[8]

Autumn 1985 session of the Committee on Conventions and Recommendations (122nd session of the Executive Board)[9]

Spring 1986 session of the Committee on Conventions and Recommendations (124th session of the Executive Board)[10]

Autumn 1986 session of the Committee on Conventions and Recommendations (125th session of the Executive Board)[11]

Spring 1987 session of the Committee on Conventions and Recommendations (126th session of the Executive Board)[12]

---

[6] See document 119 EX/35 PRIV., paras. 88-93 (*supra*, pp. 690-691), communication No. 276/80 concerning *El Salvador*, case of *Leonel Menéndez Quiroga*.
[7] See document 120 EX/15 PRIV., paras. 62-69 (*supra*, pp. 691-694), communication No. 276/80 concerning *El Salvador*, case of *Leonel Menéndez Quiroga*.
[8] See document 121 EX/46 PRIV., paras. 200-209 (*supra*, pp. 694-697), communication No. 276/80 concerning *El Salvador*, case of *Leonel Menéndez Quiroga*.
[9] See document 122 EX/21 PRIV., paras. 150-160 (*supra*, pp. 697-701), communication No. 276/80 concerning *El Salvador*, case of *Leonel Menéndez Quiroga*.
[10] See document 124 EX/3 PRIV., paras. 143-152 (*supra*, pp. 701-704), communication No. 276/80 concerning *El Salvador*, case of *Leonel Menéndez Quiroga*.
[11] See document 125 EX/3 PRIV., paras. 168-179 (*supra*, pp. 704-709), communication No. 276/80 concerning *El Salvador*, case of *Leonel Menéndez Quiroga*.
[12] See document 126 EX/3 PRIV., paras. 196-203 (*supra*, pp. 710-712), communication No. 276/80 concerning *El Salvador*, case of *Leonel Menéndez Quiroga and others*.

El Salvador **No. 390/81**

Autumn 1987 session of the Committee on Conventions and Recommendations (127th session of the Executive Board)[13]

Spring 1988 session of the Committee on Conventions and Recommendations (129th session of the Executive Board)[14]

Autumn 1988 session of the Committee on Conventions and Recommendations (130th session of the Executive Board)[15]

Spring 1989 session of the Committee on Conventions and Recommendations (131st session of the Executive Board)[16]

Autumn 1989 session of the Committee on Conventions and Recommendations (132nd session of the Executive Board)[17]

Spring 1990 session of the Committee on Conventions and Recommendations (134th session of the Executive Board)[18]

---

[13] See document 127 EX/3 PRIV., paras. 136-145 (*supra*, pp. 712-714), communication No. 276/80 concerning *El Salvador*, case of *Leonel Menéndez Quiroga and others*.
[14] See document 129 EX/3 PRIV., paras. 132-139 (*supra*, pp. 714-716), communication No. 276/80 concerning *El Salvador*, case of *Leonel Menéndez Quiroga and others*.
[15] See document 130 EX/3 PRIV., paras. 152-166 (*supra*, pp. 717-720), communication No. 276/80 concerning *El Salvador*, case of *Leonel Menéndez Quiroga and others*.
[16] See document 131 EX/3 PRIV., paras. 186-195 (*supra*, pp. 720-722), communication No. 276/80 concerning *El Salvador*, case of *Leonel Menéndez Quiroga and others*.
[17] See document 132 EX/3 PRIV., paras. 148-156 (*supra*, pp. 722-723), communication No. 276/80 concerning *El Salvador*, case of *Leonel Menéndez Quiroga and others*.
[18] See document 134 EX/3 PRIV., paras. 173-181 (*supra*, pp. 724-725), communication No. 276/80 concerning *El Salvador*, case of *Leonel Menéndez Quiroga and others*.

No. 392/81

Concerning *Yugoslavia*
Case of *Milovan Djilas**

Communication of 16 July 1981 submitted by
Amy Young-Anawaty and Charles E. M. Kolb

Spring 1982 session of the Committee on Conventions and Recommendations (114th session of the Executive Board)[1]

274. This communication was submitted by Mrs Amy Young-Anawaty and Mr Charles E. M. Kolb (of the International Human Rights Law Group and Covington Burling), acting as representatives of the alleged victim.

275. Mr Milovan Djilas, aged 70 years and an author, translator and essayist, is stated to be a former prominent figure in the Yugoslav Government and Communist Party. He is reported to have fallen from power (as Vice-President of Yugoslavia) for political reasons in 1954. His many works and writings have apparently been published in various countries, and some in several languages, but it is stated that since 1954 none of his works have been published in Yugoslavia. This ban on publication of his writings in his own country has thus allegedly been effective for some 26 years. The government is further reported to have refused to issue him with a passport and so to have prevented his travelling abroad. Yet because of the fame of his publications, he is stated to have been frequently invited by foreign universities and other organizations. In June 1980, for instance, he was apparently invited to take part with several foreign journalists in a Spanish television programme which was to discuss developments in post-Tito Yugoslavia. He was reportedly forced to decline the invitation because his passport had been confiscated by the competent authorities in 1970. The refusal to issue a passport was reportedly dictated by considerations of state security.

* At the Committee's autumn 1982 and spring 1983 sessions, this communication was being referred to as case of *Milovan Djilas, Vlado Gotovac, Sabedin Haljiti, Sabit Rustemi, Franjo Tudjman and Marko Veselica.*

[1] See document 114 EX/38 PRIV., paras. 274-292; see also document 114 EX/CR/HR/3.

No. 392/81 **Yugoslavia**

276. Mr Djilas was allegedly imprisoned from 1962 to 1966 and subjected to various concomitant penalties - including a ban on writing in the press, appearing on radio or television, and forming associations or engaging in publishing activities - for publishing "Conversations with Stalin" (abroad) in 1962. He is stated to have been accused of engaging in hostile propaganda and revealing state secrets. A legislative measure aimed especially at his activities was allegedly adopted, the law being known as the "Djilas Code".

277. In 1972, when the accessory penalties had lapsed, Mr Djilas reportedly attempted in vain to publish a number of writings, namely "Gugavac", "Njegoš" and "Izgubljenebitke". He is stated to have been told, in particular, that the workers had refused to print his writings. He is also claimed to have been prevented from publishing his translation of a work by Milton. His activities in starting a cultural review "Casovnik" are said to have drawn bitter attacks from the official organs.

278. The authors of the communication consider that the ban on publication imposed on Mr Djilas, his imprisonment for attempting to express his political and non-political views abroad and the refusal to issue a passport constitute a violation of human rights within Unesco's sphere of competence since what is concerned is his freedom to express his ideas, to lecture, to travel in order to do so, and to take part in cultural activities in his own country and abroad.

279. Mrs Young-Anawaty and Mr Kolb also state that this violation of human rights falls within the purview of the Organization's concern with communication problems (MacBride Commission) and the free flow of information. According to the authors of the communication, other persons are in the same situation as Mr Djilas.

280. They affirm that while the judicial ban on publication is no longer in force, it remains effective in practice and no remedy has been possible. With regard to his passport, Mr Djilas is stated to have made two requests for its return, but to no avail. The matter has apparently not been submitted to any other international authority.

281. As to the purpose and aim of the communication, the authors request that the violated rights be restored and, in particular, that the Yugoslav Government return Mr Djilas's passport and guarantee his safety and freedom and the right to publish his works in his country. They further request that Yugoslavia amend its internal code and practice in a manner consistent with its international human rights obligations. Their final request is that the communication be submitted also to the Executive Board for consideration.

282. The representative of the Yugoslav Government explained that, contrary to what was said in the communication, there was no moratorium in Yugoslavia on the

works of Mr Djilas. Furthermore, this case had been examined at the Committee's [autumn 1979] session and it had at that session been found to be inadmissible.[2] As for the question of the passport, the Yugoslav representative pointed out that [104 EX/Decision 3.3] required that an attempt be made to exhaust domestic remedies and that since this had not been done the case was inadmissible.

283. A Committee member pointed out that since 1970 when Mr Djilas's passport had been confiscated, he had several times requested that his freedom to travel be restored. So it appeared that domestic remedies had indeed been attempted. While he felt that the purpose and aim of the Committee did go a bit beyond the Committee's competence, the Committee member felt that once the extreme requests concerning the revision of Yugoslav legislation were deleted from the communication, it would qualify for consideration by the Committee.

284. The representative of the Director-General confirmed that the case of Mr Djilas had indeed been examined by the Committee at its [autumn 1979] session but he pointed out that at that session the presentation had not been as detailed as it was here.

285. A Committee member stated that while national laws were not for the Committee to review it would have been more helpful if the Yugoslav representative had given some details concerning the two principal questions of the case. The question of a moratorium, or more correctly "ban" on the publication was said to be in the hands of the publishing houses. However, the Committee member pointed out that in many countries a government could influence what is or is not published, through its influence if not by a specific law or decree. It would be surprising that Mr Djilas's works were considered not of interest to the public since he was a famous writer, the Committee member said. A question also arose as to what domestic. remedies existed. The restriction on travel was disturbing also, even though it was true that Yugoslavia had a better record than many other countries with regard to freedom to travel. The Committee member felt that it would be a welcome act of great clemency to allow Mr Djilas to leave Yugoslavia. He further felt it would not be appropriate to be too strict in requiring "relevant evidence" as stated in paragraph [14 (*a*)] (v) of [104 EX/Decision 3.3].

286. Another Committee member agreed with this view and mentioned a decision of the European Court of Justice concerning human rights which held that a ban on a writer's works could only cover political works, not non-political works.

---

[2] See document 108 EX/38 PRIV., para. 233 (*supra*, p. 246), communication No. 92/79 concerning *Yugoslavia*, case of *Milovan Djilas*.

287. Still another Committee member endorsed this view. While he felt that it was worth noting that a former government official who split with the regime did not disappear from the scene, he still felt that his situation was one of concern for Unesco. He pointed out that the documentation submitted along with the communication form contained great detail and matters worth pursuing by the Committee.

288. Another Committee member wondered whether the Committee should raise the question of whether Mr Djilas's works ought to be published in Yugoslavia. It was a question of great significance which could lead the Committee far astray, since such subjective views of Committee members should not and could not be imposed on a government.

289. A lengthy debate ensued in which certain Committee members expressed the view that the Committee should not take decisions as to whether or not an author's works should be published in a country and other Committee members stressed the fact that it was not a question of suggesting an imperative publication but rather of ensuring that there were no obstacles being imposed on Mr Djilas's freedom to be able to publish. Several Committee members felt that obstacles probably existed for Mr Djilas since his works were such that they would be in great demand. A Committee member pointed to the fact that two publishing houses had expressed an interest in publishing Mr Djilas's works until something made them mysteriously and suddenly decide not to. Several Committee members hoped that the Yugoslav Government could clearly and publicly signal that it was not opposed to anyone publishing Mr Djilas's works.

290. The Yugoslav representative explained that as concerned Mr Djilas's works there was no official ban on them and Mr Djilas was free to receive foreign journalists. He went on to explain that the thousands of publishing houses in Yugoslavia decided what to publish on the basis of decisions of the self-management committees. Why there was no interest in his works was not known, the Yugoslav representative said. As concerned the passport, not all the remedies had been exhausted. Mr Djilas could still appeal to higher authorities for permission to travel abroad.

291. Several Committee members wondered if it might be possible to have the exact details concerning the procedures of the domestic remedies and appeals possibilities referred to by the Yugoslav representative.

292. After further debate the Committee *decided*:

> (i) to postpone until its next session the decision concerning the admissibility of this case;

(ii) to inform the author that there were still domestic remedies available to Mr Djilas as far as his right to travel was concerned;

(iii) to request the Executive Board to invite the Director-General to explore in pursuance of paragraph 14 (*k*) of [104 EX/Decision 3.3] with the Yugoslav authorities the ways at settling in various aspects of the present communication, to the extent that they concern the fields of competence of Unesco.

Autumn 1982 session of the Committee on Conventions and Recommendations (115th session of the Executive Board)[3]

398. The first communication[4] concerns the case of Mr Milovan Djilas, who is described as an author, translator and essayist and who, it is alleged, has not been able to publish his works in his own country and has not been allowed to travel abroad.

[398a.] The second communication concerns the case of Mr Vlado Gotovac, described as a writer, poet and philospher, who is said to have been sentenced, in June 1981, to two years' imprisonment and banned from the public expression of his views for four years for activities hostile to the population and peoples of Yugoslavia and its institutions.

399. The third communication concerns, in addition to the preceding case, the cases of:

Mr Sabedin Haljiti and Mr Sabit Rustemi. Mr Haljiti is stated to be the editor of a journal, and Mr Rustemi the author of a short story. They are alleged to have been sentenced in August 1981 to periods of imprisonment of, respectively, three years and four years for hostile propaganda;

Mr Franjo Tudjman, who is described as a historian and former army general, and is said to have been sentenced in February 1981 to three years' imprisonment and to a five-year ban on the public expression of his views for hostile propaganda;

Mr Marko Veselica, who is described as a former teacher and author, and is said to have been sentenced in August 1981 to 11 years' imprisonment and to

[3] See document 115 EX/28 PRIV., paras. 398-402; see also documents 115 EX/CR/HR/2 and Add. and Add.2.

[4] Communications No. 392/81 concerning *Yugoslavia*, case of *Milovan Djilas*, No. 421/81 concerning *Yugoslavia*, case of *Vlado Gotovac*, and No. 425/81 concerning *Yugoslavia*, case of *Sabedin Haljiti* et al., were being considered together.

a four-year ban on the public expression of his views for hostile propaganda, incitement to national hatred and participation in hostile activities.

400. According to the authors of these communications, the real reason why these people have suffered restrictions on their activities or deprivation of liberty is that they exercised their right to freedom of expression and opinion. These allegations have been rejected as unfounded by the representative of the Yugoslav Government.

401. At the spring 1982 session, the Committee decided to defer consideration of the admissibility of these communications until the present session, while awaiting:

the result of the action taken by the Director-General *vis-à-vis* the Yugoslav authorities, under paragraph 14 (*k*) of 104 EX/Decision 3.3 of the Executive Board (attempt to find a friendly solution) [the first communication];[5]

the final decision of the Federal Supreme Court in Belgrade [the second communication];[6]

additional information from the government concerned [the second and third communications] and also from the author of the communication [the third communication].[7]

402. At the autumn 1982 session, having been informed by the Secretariat of the Yugoslav Government's request that the examination of these communications should be postponed on account of the late arrival of the additional documents, which were submitted by their authors at a date close to that of the Committee's meeting, the Committee *decided* to postpone this examination until the next session.

Spring 1983 session of the Committee on Conventions and Recommendations (116th session of the Executive Board)[8]

238. The first communication[9] concerns the case of Mr Milovan Djilas, who is described as an author, translator and essayist and who, it is alleged, has not been able

[5] See document 114 EX/38 PRIV., para. 292 (i) and (iii) (*supra*, pp. 974-975).
[6] *Ibidem*, para. 300 (*infra*, p. 1046).
[7] *Ibidem*, paras. 300 (*infra*, p. 1046) and 327 [i] (*infra*, p. 1056), respectively.
[8] See document 116 EX/48 PRIV., paras. 238-261; see also documents 116 EX/CR/HR/2 and 116 EX/CR/HR/3.
[9] Communications No. 392/81 concerning *Yugoslavia*, case of *Milovan Djilas*, No. 421/81 concerning *Yugoslavia*, case of *Vlado Gotovac*, No. 425/81 concerning *Yugoslavia*, case of (*continued*)

to publish his works in his own country and has not been allowed to travel abroad. The second communication concerns the case of Mr Vlado Gotovac, described as a writer, poet and philosopher, who is said to have been sentenced, in June 1981, to two years' imprisonment and banned from the public expression of his views for four years for activities hostile to the population and peoples of Yugoslavia and its institutions.

239. The third communication concerns, in addition to the preceding case, the cases of:

> Mr Sabedin Haljiti and Mr Sabit Rustemi. Mr Haljiti is stated to be the editor of a journal, and Mr Rustemi the author of a short story. They are alleged to have been sentenced in August 1981 to periods of imprisonment of, respectively, three years and four years for hostile propaganda;
>
> Mr Franjo Tudjman, who is described as a historian and former army general, and is said to have been sentenced in February 1981 to three years' imprisonment and to a five-year ban on the public expression of his views for hostile propaganda;
>
> Mr Marko Veselica, who is described as a former teacher and author, and is said to have been sentenced in August 1981 to 11 years' imprisonment and to a four-year ban on the public expression of his views for hostile propaganda, incitement to national hatred and participation in hostile activities.

240. According to the authors of these communications, the real reason why these people have suffered restrictions on their activities or deprivation of liberty is that they exercised their right to freedom of expression and opinion. These allegations have been rejected as unfounded by the representative of the Yugoslav Government.

241. At the spring 1982 session, the Committee decided to defer consideration of the admissibility of these communications until the present session, while awaiting:

> the result of the action taken by the Director-General *vis-à-vis* the Yugoslav authorities, under paragraph 14 (*k*) of 104 EX/Decision 3.3 of the Executive Board (attempt to find a friendly solution) [the first communication];[10] or
>
> the final decision of the Federal Supreme Court in Belgrade [the second communication];[11] or

---

Sabedin Haljiti et al., No. 478/82 concerning *Yugoslavia*, case of *Franjo Tudjman*, and No. 511/82 concerning *Yugoslavia*, case of *Marko Veselica*, were being considered together.

[10] See document 114 EX/38 PRIV., para. 292 (i) and (iii) (*supra*, pp. 974-975).

additional information from the government concerned [the second and third communications] and also from the author of the communication [the third communication].[12]

242. At the autumn 1982 session, having been informed by the Secretariat of the Yugoslav Government's request that the examination of these communications should be postponed on account of the late arrival of the additional documents, which were submitted by their authors at a date close to that of the Committee's meeting, the Committee decided to postpone this examination until the next session.[13]

243. The fourth and fifth communications, which were received after the autumn 1982 session, concerned Mr Tudjman and Mr Veselica. They were submitted, respectively, by the International Human Rights Law Group (represented by Mrs Amy Young-Anawaty and Mr Steven J. Rosenbaum) in its capacity as a non-governmental organization having reliable knowledge of the alleged violation, and by Mr Hans Hulin, a lawyer. The facts alleged in those communications were practically the same as those set forth in [the third communication].

244. On 28 March 1983, the Secretariat received a letter from Mrs Vlasta Gotovac, author of [the second communication]. In that letter she declared that she was very concerned about her husband's health. She hoped that an appeal would be made at once to the President of the Socialist Republic of Croatia and to the President of the Socialist Federal Republic of Yugoslavia.

245. Mrs Gotovac added to the file a copy of a letter addressed to the Union of Yugoslav Writers in Belgrade and a copy of a letter addressed to the Association of Croatian Writers in Zagreb, requesting their assistance, and a copy of a plea submitted by Mr Gotovac to the Supreme Court requesting that his sentence be commuted in the light of exceptional circumstances.

246. At the present session of the Committee, the representative of the Yugoslav Government made a lengthy preliminary statement in which he reminded those present that his country still had reservations regarding the procedure established by 104 EX/Decision 3.3 of the Executive Board; however, in agreeing to be represented before the Committee, his government wished to demonstrate its open-mindedness, good faith and desire to co-operate with Unesco, particularly in the field of human rights.

---

[11] *Ibidem*, para. 300 (*infra*, p. 1046).
[12] *Ibidem*, paras. 300 (*infra*, p. 1046) and 327 [i] (*infra*, p. 1056), respectively.
[13] See document 115 EX/28 PRIV., para. 402 (*supra*, p. 976).

Yugoslavia **No. 392/81**

247. As regards the case of Mr Tudjman [the fourth communication], the representative pointed out that, while the right to freedom of expression was recognized and protected, it was limited by the need to maintain public order and national security. In the case in hand, the incitement to racial hatred and violence, the activities hostile to the nation and the subversive propaganda of which the alleged victim was guilty constituted violations of criminal law which the state was obliged to curb, particularly in view of the fact that Yugoslavia was a country whose population was made up of several nationalities.

248. Several members of the Committee found the facts and arguments presented by the representative of the Yugoslav Government convincing. Others thought that speech or writing did not necessarily constitute a danger to a state.

249. Addressing himself to the humanitarian concerns of the Committee members, the representative of the Yugoslav Government said that Mr Tudjman had not yet served his full sentence, but that he had been authorized to return home to be cared for by his family.

250. After thorough discussion, the Committee,

> Considering that there were serious problems regarding the admissibility of the communication, particularly since doubts remained as to whether the alleged violations fell within the fields of competence of Unesco,
>
> (i) *decides*, accordingly, to declare the communication inadmissible;
>
> (ii) notwithstanding this, and in accordance with the humanitarian spirit motivating the Committee, *requests* the government concerned, bearing in mind the action that it has already taken in favour of Mr Franjo Tudjman in view of his state of health, to re-examine, on the same grounds and in a spirit of clemency, the case of the alleged victim;
>
> (iii) should the government in question or the author of the communication provide the Director-General with relevant information concerning this case, *requests* the Director-General, through the Executive Board, to transmit such information to the Committee so that it may take due note of it.

251. As regards the case of Mr Veselica [the third and fifth communications], the representative of the Yugoslav Government objected that [the fifth communication] not only contained no specific information but also had been drafted in improper terms. He referred specifically to one of the items stating the purposes and aims of the communication, which read: "to bring awareness about an organized crime per-

formed by the Party in Yugoslavia". He added that even if [the third communication] had been more courteously and adroitly worded, it was nevertheless unfounded. He said that Mr Veselica had been found guilty of incitement to racial intolerance and participation in activities inimical to Yugoslavia. His right to defence had been respected before the court, and the Federal Supreme Court had even commuted his prison sentence to seven years. To criticize the government was not a crime, but it became one when it constituted an abuse of the right to freedom of expression and when it was used as a means towards acts of violence against the community.

252. Several members of the Committee considered [the fifth communication] inadmissible under paragraph 14 (*a*) (vi) of 104 EX/Decision 3.3 of the Executive Board (regarding offensive communications).

253. Other members of the Committee thought that [the third communication] might also be inadmissible; but, since the alleged victim could not be regarded as a terrorist, they hoped that a humanitarian appeal would be made to the government concerned.

254. The two communications were finally *declared* inadmissible by the Committee, which, at the same time, was at pains to express its humanitarian concern over this affair.

255. As regards the case of Mr Haljiti and Mr Rustemi [the third communication], the representative of the government concerned informed the Committee that the appeals courts had revoked the sentence passed by the lower court judges and that the two alleged victims had been released a long time ago and were at present going about their daily work and leading normal lives.

256. After a brief exchange of views, the Committee *deemed* the cases of Mr Haljiti and Mr Rustemi settled in accordance with paragraph 14 (*a*) (x) of 104 EX/Decision 3.3 of the Executive Board.

257. Regarding the case of Mr Gotovac [the second and third communications], the representative of the Yugoslav Government informed the Committee that the same reasons cited in the preceding cases applied to Mr Gotovac; he had been sentenced to prison because he had abused his right to freedom of expression and because the actions with which he had been charged constituted violations of the penal code.

258. The representative of the Yugoslav Government added that, moreover, the alleged victim had requested a special review of his case, and that the competent authorities to which the appeal had been made were in the process of examining it.

Yugoslavia **No. 392/81**

259. Following an exchange of views, the Committee *decided* to declare the communications inadmissible and, in accordance with the Committee's practice, to request the representative of the government concerned to in-form his government of the humanitarian concern expressed by members of the Committee.

260. Regarding the case of Mr Djilas [the first communication], the representative of the Yugoslav Government maintained that the conditions of admissibility of that communication, particularly those specified in paragraph 14 (*a*) (iii), (v), (vi) and (ix) of 104 EX/Decision 3.3 of the Executive Board (relevance to the fields of competence of Unesco, provision of relevant evidence, absence of abuse of the right to submit communications, indication that domestic remedies have been exhausted), had not been met in this particular case. He noted, more particularly, that while the author of the communication claimed to have acted on behalf of the alleged victim, the documents submitted had not been drawn up in accordance with Yugoslav law. As for the substance of the communication, he informed the Committee that in Yugoslavia the government did not intervene in decisions regarding the publication of a work, such decisions being entirely the responsibility of the boards of management of publishing firms. Referring to the problem of issuing Mr Djilas with a passport, he said that the matter was covered by the internal regulations of the country, which made provision for appeal in the event of refusal. Replying to a request for greater detail, he said that only a few of Mr Djilas's works were on the official list of banned books in Yugoslavia. He concluded that the communication had been politically motivated.

261. Following lengthy discussion and noting that only a few of Mr Djilas's works had been banned (from being imported, since it was understood that he could have his other works published wherever he wished if he could not do so in his own country), and that it was still possible for Mr Djilas to renew his request for a passport so that he could express his opinions through courses and lectures abroad, the Committee *decided*:

(i) to keep this communication on its agenda, and

(ii) to request the Executive Board to ask the Director-General to continue to use his good offices pursuant to the decision taken by the Committee at the spring 1982 session [...], viz. to examine with the Yugoslav authorities, in pursuance of paragraph 14 (*k*) of 104 EX/Decision 3.3, ways and means of reaching a settlement on those aspects of the present communication, provided that they fell within Unesco's fields of competence.

No. 392/81 **Yugoslavia**

Autumn 1983 session of the Committee on Conventions and Recommendations (117th session of the Executive Board)[14]

197. Mr Milovan Djilas, aged 70 years and an author, translator and essayist, is stated to be a former prominent figure in the Yugoslav Government and Communist Party. He is reported to have fallen from power (as Vice-President of Yugoslavia) for political reasons in 1954. His many works and writings have apparently been published in various countries, and some in several languages, but it is stated that since 1954 none of his works have been published in Yugoslavia. The government is further reported to have refused to issue him with a passport and so to have prevented him from travelling abroad.

198. The authors of the communication consider that the ban on publication imposed on Mr Djilas, his imprisonment for attempting to express his political and non-political views abroad and the refusal to issue a passport constitute a violation of human rights within Unesco's sphere of competence since what is concerned is his freedom to express his ideas, to lecture, to travel in order to do so, and to take part in cultural activities in his own country and abroad.

199. Several members of the Committee expressed regret over the absence of a representative of the government concerned. They suggested that in the circumstances, the communication should not be declared admissible or inadmissible.

200. At the end of this brief discussion, the Committee *decided*:

(i) to postpone to its spring 1984 session the examination of the admissibility of the communication;

(ii) to recommend to the Executive Board to invite the Director-General to explain in an appropriate manner to the Yugoslav authorities, perhaps during the forthcoming twenty-second session of the General Conference, the fact that the Committee is not a tribunal applying an accusatory procedure but rather an organ motivated by purely humanitarian concerns; at the same time, it should be explained to these authorities that the Committee attached considerable importance to the co-operation they could provide the Committee in its consideration of the communication.

---

[14] See document 117 EX/18 PRIV., paras. 197-200; see also document 117 EX/CR/HR/2.

Yugoslavia **No. 392/81**

Spring 1984 session of the Committee on Conventions and Recommendations (119th session of the Executive Board)[15]

197. Mr Milovan Djilas is described as an author, translator and essayist, formerly a prominent Yugoslav figure, aged over 70. It is alleged that from 1954 onwards his writings could not be published in Yugoslavia. He is said to have been unable to obtain a passport. The authors of the communication consider that Mr Djilas has thus been prevented from exressing his ideas, travelling outside his country to state his views or give lectures, and hence from participating in cultural life in his own country and abroad.

198. This communication was examined initially at the Committee's spring 1982 session. At the autumn 1982 session, at the request of the Yugoslav Government its examination was deferred until the following session.[16] At the spring 1983 session, the representative of the Yugoslav Government maintained that the communication was inadmissible, on the basis of 104 EX/Decision 3.3, paragraphs 14 (*a*) (iii), (v),. (vi) and (ix) (absence of any connection with Unesco's spheres of competence, absence of relevant evidence, abuse of the right to submit a communication, non-exhaustion of the domestic means of redress).

199. At this spring 1984 session, as at the autumn 1983 session, the government concerned has not been represented.

200. The Committee members who spoke expressed regret at the absence of any representative of the Yugoslav Government. Some members considered that the Committee should express its deep concern at this case and that merely appealing to the government to resume its co-operation with the Committee was not enough. One member expressed surprise at the fact that a country which played a very important role in the United Nations system and in Unesco in particular should not have seen fit to provide at least some information on the case; this could not but be considered as a lack of respect for the Committee and for Unesco in general.

201. One Committee member was of the opinion that, generally speaking, there was no legal means of taking any sanctions against the government of a state concerned that did not send a representative to the Committee, but that the Committee could exercise its moral authority by putting such a case as that before the Executive Board. The Board, in turn, could bring it to the notice of the General Conference, which could adopt an appropriate resolution if it thought fit. Such a resolution might

---

[15] See document 119 EX/35 PRIV., paras. 197-206; see also document 119 EX/CR/HR/2.

[16] See document 115 EX/28 PRIV., para. 402 (*supra*, p. 976).

take the form of moral condemnation by the Organization's Member States as a whole.

202. One Committee member said that for an author to be unable to be read was equivalent to intellectual death. He expressed the wish that, should the government concerned be unable to permit publication of Mr Djilas's works in the country, Mr Djilas should be allowed to publish them abroad.

203. One Committee member expressed the view that if Yugoslavia had not sent a representative, it was perhaps because it thought that everything that could be said concerning the case had already been said. In his view, it should be recognized that Mr Djilas, who was a politician, had in some measure acted somewhat brutally *vis-à-vis* his country. One member of the Committee noted that almost all the cases submitted to the Committee for its consideration concerned persons who had not shown themselves unduly well disposed towards their governments.

204. Two Committee members endorsed this view. They nevertheless considered that the Executive Board should be requested to ask the Director-General to make humanitarian approaches with a view to finding some acceptable solution consistent with international standards relating to human rights.

205. Other Committee members were of the opinion that tact and courtesy were called for in this affair; given the significance of the case and the fact that Mr Djilas was not merely an author but also a politician who at a particular time had fallen out with the authorities of his country.

206. After discussion, the Committee *decided*:

> (i) to request the Executive Board to ask the Director-General to urge the government concerned to resume its co-operation with the Committee, which is all the more vital in this case as the communication is not only important as regards the principles of human rights but presents several complex and intricate aspects as well;
>
> (ii) to resume consideration of the admissibility of the communication at its autumn 1984 session.

Yugoslavia **No. 392/81**

Autumn 1984 session of the Committee on Conventions and Recommendations (120th session of the Executive Board)[17]

193. Mr Milovan Djilas is described as an author, translator and essayist, formerly a prominent Yugoslav figure, aged over 70. It is alleged that from 1954 onwards his writings could not be published in Yugoslavia. He is said to have been unable to obtain a passport. The authors of the communication consider that Mr Djilas has thus been prevented from expressing his ideas, travelling outside his country to state his views or give lectures, and hence from participating in cultural life in his country and abroad.

194. This communication was examined initially at the Committee's spring 1982 session. At the autumn 1982 session, at the request of the Yugoslav Government its examination was deferred until the following session.[18] At the spring 1983 session, the representative of the Yugoslav Government maintained that the communication was inadmissible, on the basis of 104 EX/Decision 3.3, paragraphs 14 (*a*) (iii), (v), (vi) and (ix) (absence of any connection with Unesco's spheres of competence, absence of relevant evidence, abuse of the right to submit a communication, non-exhaustion of the domestic means of redress). Since then, the government concerned has not been represented at any of the Committee's sessions.

195. At its present session, the Committee was informed of the contents of a letter of 8 August 1984 [...][19] by which the authors had provided additional information concerning their communication especially as regards the alleged arrest of Mr Djilas in April 1984. On the other hand, the Secretariat brought to the attention of the Committee a letter of 12 September 1984 [...][20] which it had received from the Permanent Delegate of Yugoslavia. In this letter, the Permanent Delegate referred *inter alia* to the view expressed by the representative of his government before the Committee's spring [1983 session] who had contended in particular that, on the basis of the applicable criteria, the communication was inadmissible. The Permanent Delegate indicated also in his letter that since no new element worthy of the attention of the members of the Committee had come to light in the meantime, the competent authorities of his country had nothing to add, at the present session of the Committee, to what had already been said by its representative. He added further that since the reasons for the inadmissibility of the communication in question were still valid, they con-

[17] See document 120 EX/15 PRIV., paras. 193-197; see also documents 120 EX/CR/HR/2 and Add.2 and 5.
[18] See document 115 EX/28 PRIV., para. 402 (*supra*, p. 976).
[19] See document 120 EX/CR/HR/2 Add.2.
[20] See document 120 EX/CR/HR/2 Add.5.

sidered it unnecessary for their representative to attend the present session of the Committee.

196. While thanking the government concerned for its letter referred to above, several members of the Committee none the less expressed their regret over the fact that the government had not sent a representative to the present session to co-operate with the Committee in its examination of the communication. One member stated his concern over allegations that workers of certain individual printing plants had refused to print the works of the alleged victim. The member said that this situation was more or less tantamount to these workers exercising veto power over what was or was not to be printed. Another member, however, declared that in his opinion, if the competent writers' trade union took the view that the works of the alleged victim should not be printed, the Committee should refrain from interfering with that appreciation. In this connection, the Legal Adviser stated that such restrictions on the freedom of expression as might be authorized by virtue of paragraph 3 of Article 19 of the International Covenant on Civil and Political Rights could normally be imposed only by a competent public authority. In answer to a question from a member of the Committee, he stated also that the alleged victim, who was said to have been arrested in April 1984, was currently not in detention.

197. After an exchange of views among its members, the Committee *decided*:

(i) to thank the government concerned for the letter dated 12 September 1984 that the Permanent Delegate of Yugoslavia to Unesco had sent the Secretariat on his government's behalf;

(ii) to express its regret at the absence of a representative of the government concerned and to make clear the importance attached by the Committee to the presence of a representative during its consideration of the communication;

(iii) to ask the Executive Board to request the Director-General to renew his appeal to the government concerned to resume its co-operation with the Committee, as the complex and sensitive nature of the matters raised makes such co-operation essential;

(iv) to resume consideration of this communication at its spring 1985 session.

Yugoslavia **No. 392/81**

Spring 1985 session of the Committee on Conventions and Recommendations (121st session of the Executive Board)[21]

193. Mr Milovan Djilas is described as an author, translator and essayist, formerly a prominent Yugoslav figure, aged over 70. It is alleged that from 1954 onwards his writings could not be published in Yugoslavia. He is said to have been unable to obtain a passport. The authors of the communication consider that Mr Djilas has thus been prevented from expressing his ideas, travelling outside his country to state his views or give lectures, and hence from participating in cultural life in his country and abroad.

194. The examination of the admissibility of this communication began at the Committee's spring 1982 session. At the spring 1983 session, the representative of the Yugoslav Government maintained that the communication was inadmissible, on the basis of 104 EX/Decision 3.3, paragraphs 14 (*a*) (iii), (v), (vi) and (ix) (absence of any connection with Unesco's spheres of competence, absence of relevant evidence, abuse of the right to submit a communication, non-exhaustion of the domestic means of redress). Since then, the government concerned has not been represented at any of the Committee's sessions. At the Committee's [autumn 1984] session, the Secretariat brought to its attention a letter of 12 September 1984 [...] which had been received from the Permanent Delegate of Yugoslavia. In this letter, the Permanent Delegate referred *inter alia* to the view expressed by the representative of his government before the Committee's spring [1983 session] who had contended in particular that on the basis of the applicable criteria, the communication was inadmissible. The Permanent Delegate indicated also in his letter that since no new element worthy of the attention of the members of the Committee had come to light in the meantime, the competent authorities of his country had nothing to add, at that session of the Committee, to what had already been said by its representative. He added further that since the reasons for the inadmissibility of the communication in question were still valid, they considered it unnecessary for their representative to attend that session of the Committee.

195. When discussion of this communication was resumed at the Committee's present session, the representative of the Director-General, who is also the Legal Adviser, informed the Committee that the Permanent Delegation of the Member State concerned had informed the Secretariat by telephone that the Government did not deem it necessary to be represented before the Committee at its present session since the position of the government as regards the communication in question had been

[21] See document 121 EX/46 PRIV., paras. 193-198; see also document 121 EX/CR/HR/2.

stated in clear and unequivocal terms. Reference was made in this respect to the Permanent Delegation's letter of 12 September 1984 [...].

196. A number of members of the Committee expressed their regret over the absence of a representative of the government concerned, more so since the government's reasons for its position that the communication was not admissible were not necessarily shared by all the members of the Committee.

197. A member of the Committee, on the other hand, declared that the government concerned had already shown humanitarian concern since the alleged victim was at liberty and not in prison. He added that, in the final analysis, it was the collective interest of the whole Yugoslav people that had to be given priority because, according to him, the non-publication of the so-called non-political Milton's "Paradise Lost" could, at worse, adversely affect the personal interest of the alleged victim above while the publication of the work could be detrimental to the legitimate interest of the whole of the Yugoslav people. Another member stated that Mr Djilas was a political dissident in Yugoslavia and not just any alleged victim and that accordingly it was advisable for the Committee to proceed with care in the examination of the communication. He declared that, in any event, the Committee lacked up-to-date relevant information about the current situation of the alleged victim.

198. At the end of its discussion, the Committee *decided*:

(i) to express once again its regret .at the absence of a representative of the government concerned and to emphasize once more the importance attached by the Committee to the presence of a representative during its consideration of the communication;

(ii) to ask the Executive Board to request the Director-General to renew again his appeal to the government concerned to resume its co-operation with the Committee more so, since the complex and sensitive nature of the matters raised makes such co-operation essential;

(iii) to resume consideration of this communication at its autumn 1985 session.

Yugoslavia **No. 392/81**

Autumn 1985 session of the Committee on Conventions and Recommendations (122nd session of the Executive Board)[22]

130. Mr Milovan Djilas is described as an author, translator and essayist, formerly a prominent Yugoslav figure, aged over 70. It is said that it has not been possible to publish his writings in Yugoslavia since 1954. He is said to have been unable to obtain a passport or to travel abroad to participate in cultural activities.

131. In a letter dated 14 August 1985, [...],[23] the International Human Rights Law Group states that there have been no developments in Mr Djilas's situation, since he is still denied a passport and he is still unable to publish his writings.

132. In a letter dated 16 August 1985, the Permanent Delegation of Yugoslavia to Unesco, referring to its letter [dated 12 September 1984],[24] stated that nothing new had come to light that could make it useful for a representative of the Yugoslav Government to attend the meeting of the Committee and that the declarations made by their representative at previous sessions, particularly [the spring 1983 session], were still valid [...].

133. One member of the Committee considered that, since there had been no developments in the affair, the Committee could only take the same decision as it had at the [spring 1985] session.

134. Another member of the Committee said that since Mr Djilas was an eminent person active in political life, his activities did not fall within Unesco's field of competence. He said that the government concerned had already stated its case clearly and the communication could only be deferred until a later date without comment.

135. After an exchange of views, the Committee *decided* to reiterate the decision they had taken at the spring 1985 session, which was as follows:

> (i) to express once again its regret at the absence of a representative of the government concerned and to emphasize once more the importance attached by the Committee to the presence of a representative during its consideration of the communication;

---

[22] See document 122 EX/21 PRIV., paras. 130-135; see also documents 122 EX/CR/HR/2 and Add.2.
[23] See document 122 EX/CR/HR/2 Add.2.
[24] See document 120 EX/CR/HR/2 Add.5.

(ii) to ask the Executive Board to request the Director-General to renew his appeal to the government concerned to resume its co-operation to the Committee, the more so as the complex and sensitive nature of the matters raised made such co-operation essential;

(iii) to resume consideration of this communication at its spring 1986 session.

Spring 1986 session of the Committee on Conventions and Recommendations (124th session of the Executive Board)[25]

105. Mr Milovan Djilas - author, translator, essayist and formerly a prominent Yugoslav figure - is said by the authors of the communication to have been unable to publish his writings in Yugoslavia since 1954. He is also said to have been unable to obtain a passport and hence to travel abroad to participate in cultural activities.

106. The government concerned has not sent a representative to the Committee. Nevertheless, in a letter dated 28 April 1986 [...],[26] it conveyed to the Organization its observations and comments concerning the allegations which are the subject of the communication.

107. After briefly outlining the alleged facts, the Chairperson read out the relevant part of this letter. In it, the Permanent Delegate of Yugoslavia to Unesco had made the following points: a representative of the Yugoslav Government had already explained to the Committee in 1983 the reasons why his government considered the communication inadmissible; there had never been any official or unofficial ban on the printing of Mr Djilas's books if he found a publisher; the printing of all types of books and publications was subject to the law on the elimination of abuses of the freedom of the press and of other forms of information; no book by Mr Djilas had to date been banned under that law; as far as the non-issue of a passport was concerned, Mr Djilas had not exhausted domestic remedies although he had been advised to do so; since there had been no new developments, the Yugoslav authorities continued to regard the communication as inadmissible.

108. After an exchange of views, the Committee *decided*:

(i) to take note of the information provided by the government concerned;

[25] See document 124 EX/3 PRIV., paras. 105-108; see also documents 124 EX/CR/HR/2 and Add.3.

[26] See document 124 EX/CR/HR/2 Add.3.

(ii) to ask the Secretariat to communicate it to the authors of the communication;

(iii) to resume consideration of this communication at its autumn 1986 session.

Autumn 1986 session of the Committee on Conventions and Recommendations (125th session of the Executive Board)[27]

131. Mr Milovan Djilas - author, translator, essayist and formerly a prominent Yugoslav figure - is said by the authors of the communication to have been unable to publish his writings in Yugoslavia since 1954. He is also said to have been unable to obtain a passport and hence to travel abroad to participate in cultural events.

132. The representative of the government concerned recalled that the case had already been examined by the Committee in 1979 and declared inadmissible [...].[28] When it had again been included in the Committee's agenda, his government had, [at the spring 1983 session], provided a very detailed explanation [...] as to Mr Djilas's position and why it considered the communication to be inadmissible:

> Mr Djilas had applied for a passport; he had not obtained satisfaction from the municipal authorities in his place of residence but he had made no application to the higher competent authorities at the level of the Republic or the Federal State, in spite of having been advised to do so; neither had he made any other application, which showed that he did not really seem to wish to obtain a passport; in the circumstances it could not be said that there was any ban on his travelling;
>
> with regard to his writings, only a legal decision could ban their publication or distribution; no such decision had been made; in Yugoslavia there was no censorship before publication; on the other hand, however, the Public Prosecutor could prohibit the distribution of a book which had already been published and have it withdrawn from the market, but only in restricted cases prescribed by law; that might occur, for example, if a publication contained documents or details concerning state secrets or of importance for the state, if it contained false or alarming information or statements that threatened public order, were harmful for the education of children and young people or hampered the investigations of certain state organs; Mr Djilas had been unable to

[27] See document 125 EX/3 PRIV., paras. 131-137; see also document 125 EX/CR/HR/2.
[28] See document 108 EX/38 PRIV., para. 233 (*supra*, p. 246), communication No. 92/79 concerning *Yugoslavia*, case of *Milovan Djilas*.

find publishers in the country for various reasons; one of them might be the understandable fear of publishing houses - whether public or private - of losing money if the Public Prosecutor believed it necessary to prohibit the distribution of a book by this author; in fact, although a writer, Mr Djilas appeared above all as a politician and his writings were often of a political nature; in any event, up to the present, none of his books had been banned and the Public Prosecutor had not even envisaged prohibiting the distribution of any of his works; in addition, Mr Djilas had found publishers abroad and he received his royalties regularly without the slightest difficulty.

133. In response to requests for clarification from certain members of the Committee, the representative of the government concerned explained that, should Mr Djilas manage to have his works published, subject to the possibility that the Public Prosecutor might decide to ban them in the instances provided for under the law, his publisher would have no difficulty in distributing them through the normal channels available to all publishing houses. The representative stated that no pressure had been brought to bear on Mr Djilas's potential publishers and that action would be taken against publishers only if they committed an offence but not merely for having published one of the writer's books. He added that there was no ban on the import of works by Mr Djilas published abroad, importing being an activity which concerned trade channels alone. He went on to say that a ban on the distribution of an imported book could, of course, be imposed by the Public Prosecutor in instances provided for by law. That would be the case, for example, if a book attacked Yugoslavia's worker self-management socialist order, if it contained propaganda defending aggression against humanity, international law and the objectives of the United Nations, if it disrupted the maintenance and development of friendly relations between Yugoslavia and other countries, if it attacked the honour of the Yugoslav people and the country's main institutions or respect for them, if it contained false or alarming information likely to disturb public order and arouse public anxiety, if it seriously offended morality, if it were harmful for the education of children and young people or if it contained documents or details that might jeopardize the inquiries carried out by the police in the context of criminal proceedings.

134. With regard to Mr Djilas's current cultural and intellectual activities, the representative of the Yugoslav Government stated that they were neither controlled nor restricted. The writer was in fact in receipt of a very large pension from the government, on a par with that of a member of the Presidency of the Republic, as well as the allowances to which he was entitled as an ex-serviceman.

135. It was the view of two members of the Committee that, in the light of the detailed information provided by the representative of the Government concerned, there appeared to be no ban on the publication of Mr Djilas's books and that, as re-

gards his application for a passport, he had not exhausted available internal procedures. They considered that the communication should be declared inadmissible.

136. Some members of the Committee considered that Mr Djilas should be informed of the available procedures which he might use in applying for a passport. In that respect, other members of the Committee pointed out that the Secretariat could communicate only with the authors of the communication.

137. Following an exchange of views, the Committee *decided*:

(i) to thank the government concerned for having sent a representative to the present session;

(ii) to take note of the statements made by the representative of that government and to instruct the Secretariat to transmit their substance to the authors of the communication;

(iii) to request the latter to furnish, in the light of the information they would accordingly have been provided with, relevant and detailed information on the facts alleged in the communication, in the absence of which the Committee would *ipso facto* strike the communication from its list at its next session;

(iv) to resume consideration of the communication at its spring 1987 session.

Spring 1987 session of the Committee on Conventions and Recommendations (126th session of the Executive Board)[29]

180. Mr Milovan Djilas, author, translator, essayist and formerly a prominent Yugoslav figure, is said by the authors of the communication to have been unable to publish his writings in Yugoslavia since 1954. He is also said to have been unable to obtain a passport and, hence, unable to travel abroad to participate in cultural events.

181. At the autumn 1986 session, the representative of the Yugoslav Government informed the Committee that Mr Djilas had not availed himself of existing procedures to obtain a passport nor had he made any new applications to obtain one. He also explained that the writer's works had not been banned, that the publication of his writings was a problem that concerned relations between the author and his publishers

[29] See document 126 EX/3 PRIV., paras. 180-188; see also documents 126 EX/CR/HR/2 and Add.2.

and that as far as his works published abroad were concerned, their import into Yugoslavia was a matter for normal commercial channels.

182. In a letter dated 5 February 1987 [...],[30] the Permanent Delegation of Yugoslavia to Unesco stated that the authorities of its country had, on 19 January 1987, issued a passport to Mr Djilas, authorizing him to travel abroad, as he had requested.

183. In a letter dated 31 March 1987 [...],[31] the authors of the communication confirmed this information. However, they requested the Committee to continue to look into the matter of the publication of Mr Djilas's works in Yugoslavia.

184. Taking the floor, the representative of the government concerned recalled that at the Committee's [autumn 1986] session, the representative of the Yugoslav Government had provided complete and satisfactory information and it had even been agreed that the Committee would, *ipso facto*, strike this communication from its list at the present session if relevant and detailed information on the allegations had not been received from the authors of the communication. In fact, their letter of 31 March 1987 provided no such information. The representative of the government concerned stressed that he did not therefore see any valid reason for the Committee to take into consideration the allegation that the writer had sent manuscripts to Yugoslav publishers last December and that none of them had been published. He pointed out that Mr Djilas himself had confirmed the lack of interest on the part of publishing houses in his works in an interview given to an Italian newspaper (*Domenica dello Corriere*, 12 April 1987 issue). As these publishing houses were autonomous undertakings, he concluded that the Yugoslav Government could not go against the law by ordering them to publish this writer's works.

185. The members of the Committee who took the floor held the view that it was inconceivable to put pressure on Yugoslav publishers to publish Mr Djilas's writings or to call for an amendment to Yugoslav legislation on the subject. According to them, the Committee should base its decision on facts and not on assumptions or rumours. In this case, there was no proof that this author's writings had been formally banned and as the passport problem had already been settled, these members considered that the communication should be struck from the list.

186. While endorsing this view, one Committee member wondered whether there was not some means of giving wide publicity to the fact that Mr Djilas's works had not been banned and that he had received his passport, which would make publish-

---

[30] See document 126 EX/CR/HR/2, annex.
[31] See document 126 EX/CR/HR/2 Add.2.

ing houses feel psychologically free in case they were interested in publishing certain of the writer's works.

187. On this point, the representative of the government concerned indicated that it had already been widely covered by the mass media.

188. Following an exchange of views, the Committee *decided*:

(i) to thank the representative of the government concerned for his presence and for his co-operation;

(ii) to take note of the fact that the problem concerning Mr Milovan Djilas's passport had been settled, and of the statements of the representative of the government concerned to the effect that this writer's works had not been banned;

(iii) to consider this communication as being no longer relevant and to strike it from its list.

No. 396/81

Concerning *Chile*
Case of *Jaime Fernando Rovira Soto*

Communication of 9 July 1981 submitted by
Jaime Fernando Rovira Soto

Spring 1982 session of the Committee on Conventions and Recommendations (114th session of the Executive Board)[1]

37. The author of the communication, Mr Jaime Fernando Rovira Soto, 21 years, a student in agronomy and a Chilean national, states that he is the victim of the alleged violations.

38. In April 1981, he was allegedly arrested by agents of the National Information Agency (FNI) and beaten; he allegedly had his hands bound and was kept blindfold in solitary confinement for six days between 25 April and 1 May 1981. During that time he claims to have been tortured by the application of electric current to his testicles, chest and temples. On his return to the university, the Dean, teaching staff and students on his course reportedly expressed their solidarity with him.

39. He states that he was again arrested on 25 June 1981 on his way to the university, but this time by *carabiñeros*, and was exiled from Chile on 27 June 1981 by a decree issued by the President of the Republic, and then expelled from the university without any accusation being brought against him.

40. He states that his parents are also in exile and refused the right to return to Chile; he adds that in Chile he was an active member of the Committee for the return of exiled persons, an organization which urges the government to repeal laws preventing thousands of Chileans from returning to their country.

41. The lawyers of the Vicaría de la Solidaridad in Santiago filed an application for *amparo* on two occasions: 27 April and 26 June 1981. The Court of Appeal alleg-

---

[1] See document 114 EX/38 PRIV., paras. 37-49; see also document 114 EX/CR/HR/3.

edly delivered no verdict on either of these applications. The author has also submitted his case to the United Nations [...] Commission on Human Rights in July 1981.

42. The purpose of the communication is to request the Chilean Government to rescind this arbitrary sentence and enable Mr Jaime Fernando Rovira Soto to return promptly to Chile so that he may complete his studies in agronomy.

43. The representative of the government concerned first of all stated that the two applications for *amparo* submitted by the lawyers of the Vicaría de la Solidaridad had been rejected because of lack of sufficient evidence; as regards Mr Rovira Soto's exclusion from the university and exile from the country, he had not had time to obtain the detailed information that he would have liked, since the communication had reached him late.

44. In reply to a question raised by a member of the Committee, he pointed out that the first application for *amparo* had been rejected since its purpose was to obtain the release of the person in question who had already been freed when the case came up. The second application alleged ill-treatment for which no evidence had been provided, whereas Mr Rovira Soto had been at liberty to supply this by having a detailed medical report made on his physical condition, for he spent only three days in prison then. In reply to another question, the representative of the Chilean Government explained that exile from the country by decree of the President of the Republic was a procedure used in exceptional cases and that the reasons for the decree did not have to be stated. If the person concerned wished to ascertain these reasons and/or contest the merits of the decision, he could either submit an appeal to the author of the decree, that was to say, the President of the Republic, or bring an action before the courts. However, he did not seem to have made use of either of these possibilities.

45. In rejecting the suggestion put forward by one of the members of the Committee that there might be a link between the case of Mr Jaime Castillo, exiled from Chile when he was Chairman of the Commission on Human Rights in Chile and that of Mr Roviro Soto who was reportedly an active member of the Committee for the return of exiled persons, the representative of the Chilean Government stated that the measures taken in respect of the alleged victim were in no way connected with his activities as a member of the Committee. Finally, he requested that the interested party should be asked to provide information with regard to the identity of his parents and concerning his testimony before the United Nations [...] Commission on Human Rights, including, more especially, the date on which this testimony was given and its content.

46. One member of the Committee stated that his country's concern for the human rights situation in Chile had been allayed in recent years but that if the allegations

contained in this communication were to be substantiated, it would mean, then, a return to a lamentable situation. He added that he had been disappointed by the inadequate information provided by the representative of the Chilean Government; in his view it was essential that, at the next meeting, the representative should have more detailed information available that would enable the Committee to continue consideration of this communication.

47. All the subsequent speakers associated themselves with the last part of the preceding statement, indicating that they would like to know why the author of the communication had been excluded from the university and exiled from his country.

48. So that the Committee might be better informed regarding the time taken in transmitting communications, it was suggested by the Chairman that the Secretariat should in future indicate on the communication form the date on which the form reached the Organization, as well as the date of dispatch shown by the author.

49. The Committee therefore *decided:*

(i) to postpone consideration of the admissibility of the communication to the next session;

(ii) to request the government concerned to take note of the concern expressed by the Committee and to be good enough to provide additional information for the next session;

(iii) to request the Secretariat to write to the author advising him of the remedies available to him and ask him to supply precise information in support of his allegations, as requested by the representative of the government concerned.

Autumn 1982 session of the Committee on Conventions and Recommendations (115th session of the Executive Board)[2]

37. This communication concerns the case of Mr Jaime Fernando Rovira Soto, who describes himself as a student in agronomy and an active member of the Committee for the return of exiled persons. He was allegedly arrested for the first time in April 1981 and tortured by the agents of the National Information Agency (FNI), arrested a second time in June of the same year, expelled from the university where he was studying and subsequently exiled from Chile.

---

[2] See document 115 EX/28 PRIV., paras. 37-46; see also document 115 EX/CR/HR/2.

38. Two applications for *amparo* had allegedly been filed in April and June 1981 by the lawyers of the Vicaría de la Solidaridad.

39. At the spring 1982 session, the representative of the Chilean Government, while informing the Committee that he did not have sufficient information at his disposal to provide the Committee with the necessary explanations, had pointed out that the alleged victim could either submit an appeal to the President of the Republic, requesting that the decree of exile should be rescinded, or transmit an application to the courts for the same purpose.

40. At the Autumn 1982 session, the representative of the Chilean Government stated that he did not have any fresh information, for it would seem that Mr Rovira Soto had not submitted an appeal concerning his return to Chile and that in that respect it might be useful to inform the author concerning this remedy by transmitting to him the note which he had drafted on that subject [...];[3] he recalled that the two appeals submitted by the lawyers of the Vicaría de la Solidaridad concerning the appellant's alleged torture had been rejected on grounds of insufficient evidence. Lastly he stated that it would be possible for him to speed up an administrative or legal decision but only provided the appellant himself put forward a request.

41. Many members of the Committee wished to have additional information on the torture to which the appellant had been subjected and on the circumstances in which he had been excluded from the university. Some speakers proposed that the above-mentioned note should be communicated to him and that he should be given sufficient time to make use of the domestic remedies at his disposal.

42. The representative of the government concerned suggested that the author should be requested to submit an appeal covering three points: the allegation of torture, concerning which he should give details on the time, the place and the persons allegedly responsible; his exclusion from the university; his return to Chile. It would also be essential for him to indicate in the appeal the name of his parents whom he claimed, without specifying their identity, had been refused the right to return to Chile.

43. One member of the Committee considered that the examination of the communication should be postponed because of the lack of adequate information. He was more concerned with the future of the student than with his past and therefore considered that the question of torture had now been superseded and that the main question was to know whether the author could resume his studies. Another member stressed the need to act rapidly, so the student would not be completely out of touch

---

[3] *Ibidem*, para. 27 (*supra*, pp. 798-799), communication No. 321/81 concerning *Chile*, case of *Victor Xavier Tiznado Rosas*.

with his university studies; a third member expressed the view that Mr Rovira Soto had been excluded from the university and exiled from his country for political reasons and that humanitarian measures should be taken to enable him to return to the university.

44. The representative of the Chilean Government concerned took the floor again, pointing out that he was not in a position to solve the problem personally, for the solution depended on the University Council; if, however, the additional information which he might obtain concerning the case led him to conclude that it deserved humanitarian treatment, he was prepared to employ his good offices to that effect.

45. One member pointed out that the case was of importance on account of the author's youth and proposed that, in addition to the action which the representative of the government concerned was prepared to make, the Director-General himself should be requested to take action on humanitarian grounds.

46. The Committee therefore *decided*:

(i) to transmit to the author the note concerning means of redress prepared by the representative of the Chilean Government and all the statements and recommendations made by that representative;

(ii) to request the author to keep the Committee informed of the results of his action;

(iii) to take note of the offer to use his good offices made by the representative of the Chilean Government;

(iv) to request the Executive Board to invite the Director-General to take any steps of a humanitarian nature that he might deem useful in order to enable Mr Rovira Soto to resume his studies in Chile.

Spring 1983 session of the Committee on Conventions and Recommendations (116th session of the Executive Board)[4]

26. This communication concerns the case of Mr Jaime Fernando Rovira Soto, who describes himself as a student in agronomy and an active member of the Committee for the return of exiled persons. He was allegedly arrested for the first time in April 1981 and tortured by the agents of the National Information Agency (FNI), arrested

[4] See document 116 EX/48 PRIV., paras. 26-30; see also document 116 EX/CR/HR/2.

a second time in June of the same year, expelled from the university where he was studying and subsequently exiled from Chile. Two applications for *amparo* had allegedly been filed in April and June 1981 by the lawyers of the Vicaría de la Solidaridad.

27. The Committee first examined this communication at its spring 1982 session. At its [autumn 1982] session, it decided to inform the author of the means of redress available to him.[5] In addition, the representative of the Chilean Government had offered his good offices, stating that it would be possible for him to speed up an administrative or legal decision but only provided the appellant himself put forward a request.

28. At the present session, the representative of the government concerned noted that, as in most of the cases before the Committee, Mr Rovira Soto had not filed an application, thus ignoring the advice he had been given. Furthermore, he found it regrettable that the person concerned had not seen fit to inform the Committee of the reasons for his failure to take action along the lines recommended.

29. One member of the Committee suggested that the communication should be dealt with in the same way as that of Mrs Cereceda Parra [...] at the [autumn 1982] session.[6] All the other members who took the floor endorsed that suggestion, especially, as one of them pointed out, in view of the fact that the representative of the Chilean Government had offered to intervene in his favour if the person concerned took the necessary action. One member of the Committee inquired whether Mr Rovira Soto would be able to resume his studies if he were authorized to return to Chile. The representative of the Chilean Government pointed out that any intervention on his part would be in two stages, the second of which, namely permission for the author to resume his studies, would be pointless until the first stage had been completed.

30. As a result the Committee *decided*:

(i) to defer consideration of the admissibility of this communication until the next session,

(ii) to request the Secretariat to pass on to the author the information provided by the Chilean Government and to inform him that unless he sought administrative or legal redress in Chile, the Committee would *ipso facto* strike his communication from its list at the next session.

---

[5] See document 115 EX/28 PRIV., para. 46 (i) (*supra*, p. 1001).
[6] *Ibidem*, para. 36 (i) (*supra*, p. 912), communication No. 356/81 concerning *Chile*, case of *Violeta Isabel Cereceda Parra*.

Chile **No. 396/81**

Autumn 1983 session of the Committee on Conventions and Recommendations (117th session of the Executive Board)[7]

12. The author of this communication describes himself as a student of agronomy and an active member of the Committee for the return of exiled persons. He was allegedly arrested for the first time in April 1981 and tortured by agents of the National Information Agency (FNI), arrested a second time in June of the same year, expelled from the university where he was studying and subsequently exiled from Chile. Two applications for *amparo* had allegedly been filed in April and June 1981 by the lawyers of the Vicaría de la Solidaridad.

13. The Committee first examined this communication at its spring 1982 session. At its [autumn 1982] session, it decided to inform the author of the means of redress available to him.[8] In addition, the representative of the Chilean Government had offered his good offices, stating that it would be possible for him to speed up an administrative or legal decision but only provided the appellant himself put forward a request.

14. At its [spring 1983] session, the Committe decided:[9]

(i) to defer consideration of the admissibility of this communication until the present session;

(ii) to request the Secretariat to pass on to the author the information provided by the Chilean Government and to inform him that unless he sought administrative or legal redress in Chile, the Committee would *ipso facto* strike his communication [from] its list at the present session.

15. At the present session, the representative of the government concerned said that the author of the communication had shown no interest in the proceedings that he had initiated with Unesco and had not availed himself of any of the remedies of which he had been informed. The representative of the government told the Committee that he had nevertheless continued to intervene on behalf of Mr J. F. Rovira Soto in view of his status as a student and in deference to the Committee, and that Mr J. F. Rovira Soto might be authorized to return to Chile if he applied as soon as possible to the appropriate Chilean Consulate for his case to be reconsidered. Accordingly, at the Committee's request, the Secretariat has already informed the author of the communication of the foregoing.

---

[7] See document 117 EX/18 PRIV., paras. 12-16; see also document 117 EX/CR/HR/2.
[8] See document 115 EX/28 PRIV., para. 46 (i) (*supra*, p. 1001).
[9] See document 116 EX/48 PRIV., para. 30 (*supra*, p. 1002).

No. 396/81 **Chile**

16. At the close of its discussions, the Committee *decided*:

(i) in view of the decision taken at the [spring 1983] session, to declare this communication inadmissible in accordance with paragraph 14 (*a*) (ix) of 104 EX/Decision 3.3, since the person concerned had not availed himself of the remedies of which he had been informed;

(ii) to inform the author of the communication, nevertheless, of what had been said by the representative of the government concerned and of the possibility open to him to submit a new communication if he could report new facts.

No. 397/81

Concerning *Bolivia*
Case of *Violation of human rights in Bolivia* *

Communication of 19 July 1981 submitted by
Joe Nordmann

Autumn 1981 session of the Committee on Conventions and Recommendations (113th session of the Executive Board)[1]

Spring 1982 session of the Committee on Conventions and Recommendations (114th session of the Executive Board)[2]

Autumn 1982 session of the Committee on Conventions and Recommendations (115th session of the Executive Board)[3]

Spring 1983 session of the Committee on Conventions and Recommendations (116th session of the Executive Board)[4]

---

* From the Committee's spring 1982 session, this communication was being referred to as case of *Violations of human rights in Bolivia* and at its spring 1983 session as case of *Alleged violations of human rights in Bolivia*.

[1] See document 113 EX/38 PRIV., paras. 72-107 (*supra*, pp. 805-812), communication No. 322/81 concerning *Bolivia*, case of *Violations of human rights in Bolivia following the events of 17 July 1980*.

[2] See document 114 EX/38 PRIV., paras. 347-399 (*supra*, pp. 812-824), communication No. 322/81 concerning *Bolivia*, case of *Violations of human rights in Bolivia*.

[3] See document 115 EX/28 PRIV., paras. 410-411 (*supra*, p. 824), communication No. 322/81 concerning *Bolivia*, case of *Violations of human rights in Bolivia*.

[4] See document 116 EX/48 PRIV., paras. 273-277 (*supra*, pp. 825-826), communication No. 322/81 concerning *Bolivia*, case of *Alleged violations of human rights in Bolivia*.

No. 398/81

Concerning *Cuba*
Case of *Armando Valladares*

Communication of 20 July 1981 submitted by
John Richardson

Spring 1982 session of the Committee on Conventions and Recommendations (114th session of the Executive Board)[1]

94. This communication has been submitted by Mr John Richardson, Jnr., President of "Freedom House", acting in his capacity as a person with reliable knowledge of the alleged violations.

95. Mr Armando Valladares is described as being an author, poet and painter. The facts of his case are given as follows:

> In 1958, when he was 21 years old, he is reported to have been employed in the Havana Police Department, as a civilian and not as a policeman. In the 1950s, he was allegedly a leader of a student movement allied with Mr Fidel Castro's revolutionary movement. He is reported to have later broken with Mr Castro, and consequently was arrested on 27 December 1960. On 17 January 1961 he is said to have been sentenced to 30 years' imprisonment by a military court as a counter-revolutionary acting against state security. It is said that he did not participate in any terrorist activities and that no munitions, arms or explosives were ever found in his possession or in his home. The alleged reason for his imprisonment is that he did not share the government's ideology. On his refusal to submit to the government's rehabilitation programmes, in August 1974, he is stated to have been deprived of food. This punishment reportedly left him an invalid, since which time he has been confined to a wheelchair. A wheelchair and various types of equipment sent by the Netherlands Red Cross were apparently not given to him.

[1] See document 114 EX/38 PRIV., paras. 94-109; see also document 114 EX/CR/HR/3.

At the time of his arrest (at the age of 23), he is reported to have been already writing poetry, and painting, but his works had not then been published. After his incarceration he is reported to have continued to write and draw whenever possible. It is stated that his poetry has been published in several languages ("From my wheelchair", "The heart with which I live"), and that his book, "Prisoner of Castro" has been published in Spanish and French. In recognition of his talent and ability, the French PEN Club is reported to have invited him in 1979, to become a member, and to have awarded him the "Liberty Prize" in 1980. It is claimed that he was deprived of all his possessions, including his books and Bible, and that the members of his family were told that they would receive permission to emigrate only if he agreed to write a letter to the foreign press denouncing the publication of his work abroad. This he apparently refused to do.

Mr Valladares is reported to be now suffering from partial paralysis, high blood pressure and malnutrition.

96. The author hopes that the communication will be brought to the attention of Member States and that steps will be taken to hasten Mr Valladares's release to enable him to resume his work as an author, poet and artist.

97. The case of Mr Valladares has already been brought to the notice of the Committee. The first time was in 1976, in accordance with the procedure laid down in 77 EX/Decision 8.3 adopted by the Executive Board and the second [at the spring 1981 session], in accordance with the [procedure laid down in 104 EX/Decision 3.3].[2]

98. During the [spring] 1981 session, the representative of the Cuban Government stated that before his arrest and detention, Mr Armando Valladares was neither a poet nor a painter, that, together with other persons, he had instigated terrorist activities in preparation for a revolt to overthrow the established order, and that arms, munitions and explosives had been discovered in his possession. The representative of the Cuban Government further pointed out that Valladares had been sentenced to 25 years' imprisonment not as an intellectual and author of literary and artistic works, but as a terrorist who had given up all professional activity to engage solely in counterrevolutionary activities. He also informed the Committee that the alleged victim was subjected to normal prison treatment, had been given a private room in the prison hospital and was receiving adequate health care. He stated that Mr Valladares had shown an unwillingness to co-operate, refusing to accept any treatment except medicines, and persisting in a negative attitude despite the existence of a rehabilitation programme which in no way required him to renounce his convictions. He specified

[2] Communication No. 290/80 concerning *Cuba*, case of *Armando Valladares Pérez*.

that once he had completed his sentence, Mr Valladares would not remain in prison and that Cuban legislation provides that any person may emigrate if he so wishes.

99. After thorough discussion, the Committee decided:[3]

> (i) to declare the communication submitted by Mrs Valladares inadmisssible in accordance with paragraph 14 (*a*) (iii) of 104 EX/Decision 3.3, since the alleged facts did not come within Unesco's fields of competence as there had been no violation of the human rights of either an author or an artist, Mr Valladares having been sentenced for ordinary criminal offences;
>
> (ii) to inform the author of the communication that, as the Cuban Government had demonstrated, Mr Valladares had been provided with satisfactory health care, but that it was he himself who had been uncooperative.

100. At the current session, the representative of the Cuban Government felt that there was practically nothing left to discuss in this matter. Recalling the general terms of a letter sent by his government to Unesco, dated 19 April 1982, he made the following points:

> Scarcely a year had passed since the decision to declare the communication submitted by Mrs Valladares inadmissible and no changes had occurred in the meantime.
>
> An intensive campaign of lies and distortion had been compounded by a certain kind of press coverage which depicted Mr Valladares as an intellectual martyr and handicapped poet.
>
> An attentive observer could easily pick out the contradictions inherent in the communication. It was claimed, for instance, that Mr Valladares was a civil servant and had not taken part in terrorist acts, but nothing could be further from the truth. He had, in fact, been an agent in the repressive police force of the Batista regime and had been involved in the activities of the most monstrous of its torturers. He had been arrested shortly after the victory of the revolutionary forces and found guilty of active terrorism on the basis of irrefutable evidence.
>
> The renewed presentation of the case was merely a repetition of the previous allegations in a new style intended to exert a psychological impact.

---

[3] See document 112 EX/30 PRIV., paras. 111-112 (*supra*, p. 747).

No. 398/81 **Cuba**

101. The representative of the Cuban Government considered that it would not be fitting for the Committee to give the communication further consideration.

102. One member of the Committee felt that Mr Valladares was receiving very humane treatment at the hands of the Cuban Government. He was in favour of confirming the decision of inadmissibility taken at [the spring 1981] session.

103. Some members of the Committee noted that Mr Valladares had been convicted many years ago and it was not the Committee's business to revert to those circumstances. However, while the alleged victim may not have been a poet before his arrest, he had become one subsequently, and the matter now under discussion was not terrorist acts but whether or not the poet had been subjected to repressive actions by the authorities on account of his writings.

104. Without questioning the threat that the prisoner represented for the Cuban state or referring to the causes of his conviction, one member of the Committee wondered whether the government concerned might not be prepared to make some gesture in favour of a man who had acquired a new talent during his imprisonment and had redeemed his personality by becoming a writer.

105. Several members of the Committee expressed the view that the Cuban Government could only solve the problem by humanitarian means, since there were no grounds for declaring the communication admissible.

106. In support of this conclusion, two members of the Committee pointed out that the communication submitted by Mrs Valladares, the person who seemed best qualified to take action, had been declared inadmissible by the Committee [at the spring 1981 session], pursuant to paragraph 14 (*a*) (iii) of 104 EX/Decision 3.3. The new communication by a different person contained no radically new evidence that might warrant a change in the previous decision. Until he had served his sentence, Mr Valladares was still a prisoner convicted of terrorism. For the sake of its credibility, the Committee should abide by what it had already decided.

107. To dispel all doubt from the minds of Committee members in their appraisal of the facts, the representative of the Cuban Government gave the following additional details:

> There had been reference to reprisals but nothing of the kind had occurred. At the presumed time of the allegations Mr Valladares had been in hospital where no effort had been spared in caring for his health.

Mr Valladares's case had been reconsidered by the competent legal authorities and his sentence had been reduced from 30 to 25 years.

It has been claimed in connection with the humanitarian aspects of the case [that] Mr Valladares had not received certain medical equipment, whereas he had received everything that had been sent to him. He had attempted to escape but the authorities had not retaliated, as a gesture of leniency.

There had been calls for Mr Valladares's release, but the latter was not even prepared to obey the rehabilitation rules currently in force, which on no account required prisoners to change their convictions or ideology. Mr Valladares was still in contact with terrorist groups and the Cuban authorities were therefore at a loss to know how his situation might be improved.

108. The Chairman of the Committee noted that no members had suggested that the communication be declared admissible or that it be kept on the agenda until the next session. On the other hand, while the members as a whole were not opposed to a decision of inadmissibility, some of them wished that their concern over the humanitarian aspects of the case be reflected in the formulation of that decision.

109. After a lengthy exchange of views, the Committee adopted the following *decision*:

(i) The Committee declared the communication inadmissible because the facts did not, in the form in which they were presented, alter the basis on which the Committee had declared the previous communication submitted by Mrs Valladares inadmissible, pursuant to paragraph 14 (*a*) (iii) of 104 EX/ Decision 3.3, because it did not fall within Unesco's fields of competence.

(ii) On the other hand, bearing in mind the measures already taken by the Cuban Government in this connection, the Committee requested the representative of that government to inform the authorities of his country of the humanitarian concern expressed by several members of the Committee during the examination of the communication.

No. 399/81

Concerning *Czechoslovakia*
Case of *Rudolf Battěk*

Communication of 20 July 1981 submitted by
John Richardson

Spring 1982 session of the Committee on Conventions and Recommendations (114th session of the Executive Board)[1]

172. This communication is submitted by Mr John Richardson Jnr., President of "Freedom House", acting as a person with reliable knowledge of the alleged violations.

173. Mr Rudolf Battěk, aged 57 years, is presented as a sociologist. It is stated that on 14 June 1980 he went to a police station to report the theft of his car. He was allegedly arrested there for assaulting a policeman, a charge claimed to be groundless. He has apparently been held since that time and it is said that a fresh charge has been made against him: subversion of the Republic (Article 98 of the Criminal Code). This charge, according to the author of the communication, has to do with Mr Battěk's activities as spokesman for Charter 77. Mr Battěk is stated to have sought to exert his rights to communicate with signatories of the Helsinki Agreements in the West. During his detention he has allegedly been unable to see his lawyer. It is reported that his wife has been unable to send him medicine and that his state of health requires specific medical treatment. Present conditions are said to be aggravating his state. It is alleged that towards the end of July 1981 he was sentenced to a prison term of seven and a half years, to be followed by police supervision for three years.

174. Mr Battěk's lawyer reportedly made various approaches to the judicial authorities, in vain. Mrs Battěk is stated to have done likewise, without drawing any response. She is even reported to have written to President Husák (a photocopy of a document is attached to the communication as evidence). A number of persons, members of Charter 77 and non-members, are reported to have staged hunger strikes

[1] See document 114 EX/38 PRIV., paras. 172-187; see also document 114 EX/CR/HR/3.

over a period of months and issued appeals on behalf of the alleged victim both to the Czechoslovak authorities and to the West. Mr Jiří Ruml, a Charter 77 member, allegedly now in prison, is claimed to have launched an appeal on 8 February 1981 to the Human Rights Committee of the United Nations. A copy of this appeal has apparently also been sent to the Prosecutor-General of the Republic. Amnesty International is reported to have adopted Mr Battěk as a prisoner of conscience (a photocopy of a document on this subject is attached to the communication). Other non-governmental organizations in Europe and the United States are said to have also attempted to secure his release.

175. With regard to the purpose and aim of the communication, the author requests that the case be brought to the attention of Member States and that measures be taken to hasten the release of Mr Battěk and enable him to resume his work as a sociologist.

176. The representative of the Czechoslovak Government informed the Committee that he had had discussions with the Prosecutor-General of the Republic, and that it was the view of his government that the communication was unfounded. No one in Czechoslovakia was imprisoned for an expression of his views, he said. In this case there had been an imprisonment for activities against the state and subversion of the Republic, and this had not been reprisal for the signing of the Charter 77. The Czechoslovak representative stated that Mr Battěk had in fact been a member of an illegal organization, the VONS, or the Committee for the protection of unjustly prosecuted persons. This group was not in fact registered with the authorities and was thus illegal. It collected information about policemen and government officials, and this information was distributed among the populace and passed on to Radio Free Europe and the enemy. This group had also supported a plane and school bus hijacking and conspirational activities and has received funds from abroad.

177. For such subversive activities, Mr Battěk had been tried and sentenced in accordance with Article 98 of the Czechoslovak Criminal Code. Furthermore, the Czechoslovak representative said, Mr Battěk had also been found guilty of a physical attack on a policeman for which he was sentenced to five and a half years. Contrary to what the communication stated, the lawyer of Mr Battěk had been allowed to visit him several times. Only on 9 December could he not visit due to an administrative problem, which was solved a few days later. It was explained that Mr Battěk's wife was allowed to visit him and he could receive mail. As concerned Mr Battěk's health, it appeared that he suffered from bronchitis, for which he received treatment. Since November 1981 no further health complaint had been received, the Czechoslovak representative stated.

Czechoslovakia **No. 399/81**

178. A member of the Committee wondered whether the judgement in 1981 was based merely on the fact that Mr Battěk merely belonged to the VONS organization, or whether he himself committed the acts which were attributed to this organization.

179. The Czechoslovak representative explained that Mr Battěk had been an active member of this group, had formulated subversive documents, had made contacts with foreign hostile groups and had received money for such subversive activities. It was not a crime to belong to the Charter 77 the Czechoslovak representative explained.

180. Another member of the Committee stated that it was his understanding that Mr Battěk was not in fact involved in acts of violence. It appeared that Mr Battěk was being punished for acts of communication, as member of Charter 77, for trying to inform people about Czechoslovakia's not respecting certain parts of the Helsinki Agreements. The case was clearly within Unesco's competence he said, because it involved a sociologist who was being punished for having tried to exercise his freedom to communicate.

181. Another Committee member felt that the Czechoslovak representative had clearly explained that his country did not punish persons merely for belonging to groups. Since this case was clearly parallel to others in which persons had been convicted for criminal activities it should likewise be deemed inadmissible as being manifestly ill-founded.

182. It was the view of another Committee member that it was important for the Committee to have before it the document outlining the specific charges which had been brought against Mr Battěk. These could be sent on to the author for comment and further information could be requested for the Committee.

183. The view was expressed by another Committee member that the authors were not reliable sources and that it would be inappropriate to in any way cast doubt on the sufficiency of the information provided by the Czechoslovak representative. The allegations concerning the communication had been shown to be ill-founded by the official information provided by the Czechoslovak Government, which had been based on a thorough and lengthy investigation.

184. Another Committee member stated that this case was different from another case that the Committee had examined earlier in the present session, in which a sentence had not yet been handed down, since in the present case a final sentence had indeed been handed down, and this for activities which had been of a terrorist nature. The Committee had received the information based on the court investigation

and had no reason to doubt it since it was presented by a representative of the government involved.

185. It was felt by another Committee member that it was important to have the record clearly show that the Czechoslovak representative had stated his government's position that the Charter 77 organization and membership in it was not illegal. The question thus arose why the accepting of money from abroad for a legal organization and the sending of information abroad through this organization could be deemed to be illegal.

186. A lengthy debate ensued over the procedural question as to how to best request additional information from the authors of the communication in the light of the information which had been provided by the Czechoslovak Government.

187. The Committee finally *decided*:

(i) to declare the communication inadmissible as not coming within the fields of competence of Unesco; and

(ii) to inform the author of all information which had been presented to the Committee by the representative of the government concerned.

No. 403/81

Concerning *Chile*
Case of *Gloria Pinto de Manríquez*

Communication of 25 August 1981 submitted by
Gloria Pinto de Manríquez

Spring 1982 session of the Committee on Conventions and Recommendations (114th session of the Executive Board)[1]

50. The author of the communication, Mrs Gloria Pinto de Manríquez, of Chilean nationality, claims to be the victim of the alleged violations. In her first letter of 25 August 1981, Mrs Pinto de Manríquez termed herself a student but in the communication form she gives her occupation as "telex operator".

51. Mrs Manríquez left Chile in 1973 with her daughter Carole, then aged one year, to follow her husband. They took refuge in France, where she gave birth to a second daughter, Tamara. This life as an exile in a society she describes in her letters as "alien and hostile" apparently aggravated the differences between her and her husband and led to their separation in February 1980. Early in 1981, Mr Manríquez is stated to have criticized his wife for not taking proper care of the children owing to the studies she was engaged in, and for this reason, reportedly requested their custody. Following her refusal, he is alleged to have taken advantage of a weekend during which the children were with him to send them to Chile, where they still apparently are today.

52. Tamara, who is aged two and a half years, is reportedly living with her maternal grandparents and Carole, who is eight years old, with her paternal grandparents. The latter are stated to have recently initiated a court case to obtain legal custody of Tamara on the grounds that their more substantial financial means and their better accommodation made them more suitable people to bring up Tamara. A hearing was scheduled for 29 September 1981.

[1] See document 114 EX/38 PRIV., paras. 50-62; see also document 114 EX/CR/HR/3.

53. In view of the pathetic and urgent situation of Mrs Manríquez, the Director-General has, for humanitarian reasons, appealed to the benevolence of the Government of Chile with emphasis on his attachment to the principle of family unity.

54. The right allegedly violated is the right to live in one's country (Article 13 of the Universal Declaration of Human Rights).

55. Her first application to return to Chile, made in 1978 to the Embassy of Chile, was reportedly rejected for "security reasons". The application for *amparo* (which is the usual remedy in such cases) made by her parents in Chile was apparently not successful because, according to her lawyer, she was stigmatized as the wife of an extreme left-wing militant.

56. The purpose and aim of the communication is to secure permission for Mrs Pinto de Manríquez to return permanently to Chile or, at least, temporarily for one month in order to fetch her daughters, who are refused permission by their father to leave Chile.

57. The representative of the Director-General informed the members of the Committee that the Permanent Delegate of Chile had replied to the Director-General's appeal by a letter whose main points were as follows: while pointing out that the affair was not one which came within the competence of Unesco, since Mrs Pinto de Manríquez's problem was of a family nature concerning a dispute between the parents over the custody of the children, the signatory to the letter stated that he had requested the competent authorities in his country to take steps to examine this case in the light of the humanitarian intervention by the Director-General. He added that, although Mrs Pinto de Mauríquez strictly speaking could not return to Chile, which she had left as a refugee, it seemed to him to be only fair to attempt to overcome this obstacle by allowing her to appear in person before the Chilean courts in order to assert her family rights.

58. The representative of the government concerned observed that Mrs Pinto de Manríquez's profession as a telex operator had nothing to do with Unesco's fields of competence. He added that he had, however, taken in an individual capacity certain steps of a humanitarian nature, not within the context of the communication as such, but as a result of the intervention by the Director-General. He was of the opinion that the measures he had taken had already achieved some progress and should result in the court delaying any decision until the administrative difficulties experienced by the author of the communication could be overcome. He pointed out nevertheless that if the matter were to be dealt with as a communication, his task would be much more difficult.

59. The Director-General's representative then recalled that in her first letter, Mrs Pinto de Manríquez had described herself as a student and that the fact that she was a student in Chile and in France had not in fact been disputed; at first sight, then, it had been possible to think that she had a link with Unesco's fields of competence and it was for this reason, the rule in such an affair being that the alleged victim should be given the benefit of the doubt, that her case had become the subject of the present communication.

60. Several members of the Committee expressed their satisfaction at the measures taken by the Director-General for humanitarian reasons. Some of them however emphasized that this broad interpretation of Unesco's competence, which in the present case had had praiseworthy results, should not be extended too far. One member also observed that Mrs Pinto de Manríquez herself was not in fact a refugee, but had left her country for sentimental reasons, i.e. to follow her husband, and that in any case she was asking to return to her country principally in order to resume her studies. As a result he was of the opinion that there were good reasons for the Committee to examine her case from a humanitarian point of view.

61. The Chairman of the Committee remarked that, since certain measures were now under way, it would be reasonable not to pursue discussions further and to consider this communication at the next session, by which time the Committee might have at its disposal additional information on the progress of the representations made to the Chilean authorities as a result of the Director General's intervention.

62. The members of the Committee supported the Chairman's proposal and the Committee therefore *decided* to postpone consideration of the admissibility of this communication until its next session in the hope of receiving additional information on the progress of the humanitarian measures taken on behalf of the alleged victim.

Autumn 1982 session of the Committee on Conventions and Recommendations (115th session of the Executive Board)[2]

47. The author of the communication, Mrs Gloria Pinto de Manríquez, of Chilean nationality, described herself in the first letter which she addressed to the Director-General as a student, and subsequently gives her occupation as telex operator. She states that she left Chile in 1973 with her daughter Carol, then aged one year, to follow her husband. They took refuge in France where she gave birth to a second daughter, Tamara. She and her husband separated in 1980 and her husband is al-

---

[2] See document 115 EX/28 PRIV., paras. 47-54; see also document 115 EX/CR/HR/2.

leged to have taken advantage of a weekend during which the children were with him to send them to Chile, where they still apparently are today.

48. The paternal grandparents of the children are said to have initiated a court case to obtain legal custody of the second daughter, Tamara, on the grounds that their more substantial means and their better accommodation made them more suitable people to bring her up. A hearing had been scheduled for 29 September 1981.

49. In view of the pathetic and urgent situation of Mrs Manríquez, the Director-General had, for humanitarian reasons, appealed to the benevolence of the Government of Chile with emphasis on his attachment to the principle of family unity.

50. At the spring 1982 session, the representative of the government concerned had pointed out that the profession of telex operator had nothing to do with Unesco's fields of competence. He had, however, taken in an individual capacity certain steps of a humanitarian nature, not within the context of the communication as such but as a result of the intervention by the Director-General. He was of the opinion that the measures he had taken had already achieved some progress and should result in the court delaying any decision until the administrative difficulties experienced by the author of the communication could be overcome.

51. The Committee had therefore decided to postpone consideration of the admissibility of the communication until the present session, in the hope of receiving additional information on the progress of the humanitarian measures taken on behalf of the alleged victim.[3]

52. At the autumn 1982 session, the representative of the Chilean Government stressed that it was doubtful whether the case came within the competence of Unesco, that political factors were involved and that certain claims by the author of the communication could be contested. He added, however, that despite the complex problems involved, the Chilean Government had decided, as an exceptional measure, to grant Mrs Pinto de Manríquez unconditional and definitive authorization to return to Chile. He considered therefore that the case might be regarded as settled.

53. All the members who took the floor shared that view and thanked the Director-General for his intervention as well as the representative of the Chilean Government for the efforts which he had made to settle the case.

---

[3] See document 114 EX/38 PRIV., para. 62 *(supra*, p. 1019).

Chile **No. 403/81**

54. The Committee therefore *decided* that the communication should be deleted from its list as having been settled in accordance with paragraph 14 (*a*) (x) of 104 EX/Decision 3.3.

No. 404/81

Concerning *Chile*
Case of *Hugo Muñoz*

Communication of 25 August 1981 submitted by
Hugo Muñoz

Spring 1982 session of the Committee on Conventions and Recommendations (114th session of the Executive Board)[1]

63. The author of the communication, Mr Hugo Muñoz, a Chilean, left his country in January 1974 and settled in France where he received a diploma in accounting and now works as an accountant. Since October 1978, he has twice requested permission to return to Chile, but without success. More recently, he requested permission to return to Chile for a month's stay in order to see his children (Mabel, 10 years old and Rogelio, nine years old) who live with his mother in Chile; he received no answer to his request.

64. No attempt has been made to exhaust domestic or international remedies. Mr Muñoz indicates that the purpose and aim of his communication is to obtain authorization to return to Chile or, at least, to return for a period of one month to enable him to see his children.

65. On 7 April the Permanent Delegate of Chile sent a letter to the Secretariat expressing the reasons for his view that this communication was inadmissible as not falling within Unesco's fields of competence, on account of the fact that Mr Hugo Muñoz's profession bore no relation to these fields.

66. The representative of the Chilean Government confirmed the contents of this letter and added that the success achieved by the steps which he had taken up to the present time in several cases were partly due to the fact that he had been able to stress the serious nature of the Committee and show that it was a body which was careful to operate in accordance with its established procedures. If that were no longer to be the case, his task would be made more difficult.

---

[1] See document 114 EX/38 PRIV., paras. 63-70; see also document 114 EX/CR/HR/3.

No. 404/81 **Chile**

67. Several members of the Committee were of the opinion that this case clearly fell outside Unesco's fields of competence. One of them suggested furthermore that the author should be informed of the existence of domestic means of redress.

68. In response to one member of the Committee who had inquired on what basis this communication had been included in the agenda, the representative of the Director-General recalled that, in accordance with the Committee's procedure it was not for the Secretariat, but for the Committee itself, to decide on the admissibility of a communication. He added that the Committee had encountered several cases in which the author requested permission to return to Chile, but that this was the first time that the representative of the Chilean Government had brought forward the argument referring to Unesco's fields of competence; he had previously always done his utmost to solve the problem, even when there was some doubt as to whether the matter fell within Unesco's competence.

69. The representative of the Chilean Government acknowledged this, but explained that he could not extend the area of his action indefinitely without endangering its success.

70. The committee therefore *decided*:

(i) to declare the communication inadmissible, as not falling within Unesco's fields of competence in accordance with the provisions of 104 EX/Decision 3.3, paragraph 14 (*a*) (iii);

(ii) to inform the author of this decision and also of the existence of the domestic means of redress available to him.

No. 406/81

Concerning *Italy*
Case of *Luciano Ferrari Bravo*

Communication of 27 August 1981 submitted by
Giuliano Ferrari Bravo

Spring 1982 session of the Committee on Conventions and Recommendations (114th session of the Executive Board)[1]

113. The author of this communication, Mr Giuliano Ferrari Bravo, is the brother of the alleged victim.

114. Mr Luciano Ferrari Bravo, a teacher, is alleged to have been arrested on 7 April 1979, together with other colleagues at Padua University, on the charge of being a member of the "Strategic Direction of the Red Brigades". Having being transferred to Rome, he is said to have been finally charged with "armed insurrection".

115. Apart from his public, political writings, no evidence is said to have been produced in support of such an accusation.

116. It is reported that he has not been brought before a judicial officer since 18 July 1979.

117. It is alleged that Mr Luciano Ferrari Bravo's lawyers have used all the ordinary means of redress provided by the Rome courts to no avail.

118. The author of the communication asked Unesco to examine the case and to help find a solution in accordance with its competence in the field of human rights and its role in the promotion of universal respect for justice, the rule of law and fundamental human freedoms.

---

[1] See document 114 EX/38 PRIV., paras. 113-128; see also documents 114 EX/CR/HR/3 and Add.3.

No. 406/81 **Italy**

119. Recalling the content of a note she had sent to the Secretariat on 22 April 1982 [...],[2] the representative of the Italian Government stressed the following points:

(i) the only possible connection between the communication and Unesco's fields of competence was the fact that Mr Luciano Ferrari Bravo was a teacher;

(ii) the accusations made against him were, however, in no way connected with his professional activities; the charges against him were of "having, in conjunction with numerous other persons, promoted, organized and directed an armed political association known as 'potere operaio', and other similar, interrelated associations, aimed at the violent subversion of state order, civil war and armed insurrection against the authority of the state through the action of a series of armed groups operating under various acronyms. Taken as a whole, these associations constitute a single organization which, in, tactical and operational concert with the Red Brigades and other armed groups, is pursuing the strategy of insurrection". Detailed proof could be found in the document concerning committal of the case for trial before the Criminal Court in Rome;

(iii) while it was true that Mr Ferrari Bravo had been in detention since 1979, the preliminary investigation had begun immediately; it had just ended and the public hearing before the court would take place on 7 June 1982; the legal procedure provided every possible safeguard;

(iv) the preliminary investigation might seem long, but the facts were complex and there were a large number of accused persons.

120. Several members of the Committee considered that the alleged facts did not concern acts committed in the exercise of his functions as a teacher but terrorist activities, and that such activities could not by any means be included within Unesco's fields of competence. They noted that the communication had been submitted while the legal procedure was still taking its course: in their opinion, the author should have waited for all domestic remedies to be exhausted. They concluded that the communication was inadmissible.

121. One member of the Committee, although in agreement with adopting such a decision, wanted to know what, in practical terms, the accused could have done to exhaust the domestic remedies.

---

[2] See document 114 EX/CR/HR/3 Add.3.

Italy **No. 406/81**

122. The representative of the Italian Government said:

> that if Mr Ferrari Bravo intended to challenge the competence of the Criminal Court in Rome he could do so;
>
> that Mr Ferrari Bravo and his lawyers could have requested provisional release;
>
> that in the Italian judiciary system there was a Higher Court of Appeal between the Criminal Court and the Supreme Court.

123. While not hostile to a decision of inadmissibility of the communication under the terms of paragraph 14 (*a*) (iii) of [104 EX/Decision 3.3], two members of the Committee considered that the Committee was in duty bound to be logical and consistent with itself by adjourning consideration of that communication's admissibility, the Committee having in other cases decided to await the verdict of the competent national court of law.

124. In reply to this observation, one member of the Committee said that, if an allegation was made within the framework of Unesco's competence, suspension of the consideration of the communication would be justified; since, however, terrorist activities in no way came within that framwork, it was not for the Committee to decide in the matter.

125. With a view to dispelling any doubts, the representative of the Italian Government said that in her country there was no provision in the penal code that allowed conviction and sentencing for writings or expressions of opinion.

126. The representative of the Director-General recalled that the fact that a case was *sub judice* in no way prevented the Committee from taking a decision of inadmissibility.

127. A number of members of the Committee considered that, whether Mr Ferrari Bravo was guilty or not, there was no alternative to declaring inadmissibility when there was no connection between the alleged facts and the fields of Unesco's competence.

128. After a long exchange of views, the Committee *decided* to declare the communication inadmissible on the grounds that it did not fall within the competence of Unesco, under the terms of paragraph 14 (*a*) (iii) of [104 EX/Decision 3.3].

No. 407/81

Concerning *Bolivia*
Case of *Jorge Baldibieso* et al.*

Communication of 31 Augusti 1981 submitted by
Ruth Navarro

Spring 1982 session of the Committee on Conventions and Recommendations (114th session of the Executive Board)[1]

36. The Committee *decided* to combine consideration of this communication with [three other communications] which covered virtually the same events.[2]

Autumn 1982 session of the Committee on Conventions and Recommendations (115th session of the Executive Board)[3]

Spring 1983 session of the Committee on Conventions and Recommendations (116th session of the Executive Board)[4]

---

* Case of *Jorge Baldibieso, José Luis Suárez, Gonzalo Barrón, Ricardo Navarro, Ramiro Velasco, Marcelo Quiroga Santa Cruz and Centro de Información y de Documentación sobre Bolivia (CIDOB)*. At the Committee's spring 1982 session, this communication was also being referred to as case of *Violations of human rights in Bolivia*, at its autumn 1982 session as case of *Violations of human rights in Bolivia* and at its spring 1983 session as case of *Alleged violations of human rights in Bolivia*.

[1] See document 114 EX/38 PRIV., paras. 36 and 347-399 (*supra*, pp. 812-824), communication No. 322/81 concerning *Bolivia*, case of *Violations of human rights in Bolivia*.

[2] Communications No. 322/81 concerning *Bolivia*, case of *Violations of human rights in Bolivia*, No. 359/81 concerning *Bolivia*, case of *Violations of human rights in Bolivia*, and No. 397/81 concerning *Bolivia*, case of *Violations of human rights in Bolivia*.

[3] See document 115 EX/28 PRIV., paras. 410-411 (*supra*, p. 824), communication No. 322/81 concerning *Bolivia*, case of *Violations of human rights in Bolivia*.

[4] See document 116 EX/48 PRIV., paras. 273-277 (*supra*, pp. 825-826), communication No. 322/81 concerning *Bolivia*, case of *Alleged violations of human rights in Bolivia*.

No. 409/81

Concerning *Union of Soviet Socialist Republics*
Case of *Anatoly Shcharansky*

Communication of 14 September 1981 submitted by
Patrick Bombal-Acampora

Spring 1982 session of the Committee on Conventions and Recommendations (114th session of the Executive Board)[1]

219. This communication is submitted by Mr Patrick Bombal-Acampora, who describes himself as a person with reliable knowledge of the alleged violations.

220. Mr Anatoly Shcharansky, a mathematician, is alleged to have been arrested on 15 March 1977 and to be currently imprisoned in Chistopol. The reasons for his arrest are said to be his Jewish cultural identity, his being the founder of the Group to monitor the application of the Helsinki Agreements and his desire to go to Israel to join his wife (his marriage has reportedly not been recognized by the Soviet authorities). He is alleged to have been deprived of employment and to have forfeited his rights following the rejection of his application to emigrate. He is stated to have been refused any possibility of continuing his scientific work.

221. In answer to the question concerning the means of redress used the author simply states that Mr Daniel Jacoby, a French lawyer, has concerned himself with the case of Mr Shcharansky and that representations have been made on his behalf by the French Communist Party and the Archbishop of Rheims. The case has reportedly been referred to the United Nations.

222. As regards the purpose and aim of the communication, the author asks that the mathematician be released and at the same time denounces the reprisals allegedly suffered by Soviet Jews.

223. In a letter dated 7 December 1981, addressed to the Secretariat, Mr Bombal-Acampora draws attention to the worrying state of health of Mr Shcharansky in pris-

[1] See document 114 EX/38 PRIV., paras. 219-235; see also document 114 EX/CR/HR/3.

on and to the various representations (by letter) he has made to various Soviet authorities. He appends a list of "prisoners of conscience" and reports on the religious persecutions that have allegedly taken place in the Soviet Union during the last few months.

224. In a letter of acknowledgement, the Secretariat pointed out to him that, for clarity's sake, it did not appear appropriate to include in the file on this communication other facts relating to other persons in a different situation.

225. The representative of the Soviet Government stated that in relation to this case he would raise a question which he had never raised before, and he was doing so as a matter of principle. The present communication was grossly offensive, he said, and ran counter to the many standard-setting decisions of Unesco. It was therefore inadmissible. The author in an official letter to Unesco had stated that the sole reason for the sentencing of Mr Shcharansky was that he was a Jew and that the legal proceedings had been a farce and a sham trial. Furthermore the author spoke of the striking persecution of minorities and other subgroups in the Soviet Union. The author further stated that the purpose of the communication was to denounce the reprisals against Soviet Jewry, to denounce the shameful and inhuman character of the living conditions prevailing in the Gulags and to secure Mr Shcharansky's release. The Soviet representative emphasized that such offensive assertions made impossible any form of dialogue and any serious consideration of the case. The import of this matter went far beyond that of this communication, he said.

226. A Committee member stated that while the language of the communication was slightly less dispassionate than that of other communications, he did not feel it was really offensive.

227. The Soviet representative re-emphasized his position that as a matter of principle he could not address the substance of this case as long as the starting point was the purpose and aim the author had put forth.

228. At the request of the Chairman, the representative of the Director-General explained that there were three ways in which the Committee could approach the communication. Paragraph 14 (*a*) (vi) of 104 EX/Decision 3.3 stated that a communication must not be offensive. The Committee was reminded that it was the practice of the Committee to write to the authors of offensive communications to request them to exclude the offensive or abusive parts, as was possible under the aforementioned paragraph 14 (*a*) (vi). Another provision, [paragraph 14 (*a*) (ii)], defined who could submit a communication. The question could be raised whether the author here was a person having reliable knowledge of the alleged violations. Finally, it was pointed out, there had been a case in which it had been deemed that the language of a com-

munication had been such as to disqualify it as a communication *per se*. In such a case it would be paragraph 10 of 104 EX/Decision 3.3 which would apply.

229. A Committee member felt that while in the present case some language might well in fact be inappropriate, other language which just stated the case was not.

230. A Committee member raised the question as to whether the author could really have been said to have "disseminated" the letter containing the offensive passages.

231. The Soviet representative said that he did not wish to further complicate the situation in view of the clarification which had been provided by the representative of the Director-General. It would do no good, he said, to split hairs about the term "dissemination"; what was meant was that these documents could not serve as the basis for international co-operation.

232. The only way to proceed was to send the communication back to the author and ask him to bring it into line with the Committee's requirements. It would be inappropriate to ask him to edit the communication and thus become a co-editor with the author, the Soviet representative went on to say.

233. The representative of the Director-General reminded the Committee that there had been several previous communications in which the language had been found to be offensive. The authors had been asked to revise them without specific indications as to which parts were deemed offensive. Most authors resubmitted their communication in a revised form. One had refused to change it and this led to its inadmissibility.

234. The Committee thereupon *decided* to resume consideration of the admissibility of the communication at its next meeting, and meanwhile to send the communication back to the author, to inform him that it contained offensive language and that the Committee was willing to re-examine it if he excluded the offensive language.

235. Two Committee members endorsed this decision while emphasizing that they in fact did not endorse all of the Soviet representative's objections.

No. 409/81 **Union of Soviet Socialist Republics**

Autumn 1982 session of the Committee on Conventions and Recommendations (115th session of the Executive Board)[2]

308. This communication concerns Mr Anatoly Shcharansky, a Soviet mathematician, who is alleged to have been arrested in March 1977 and to be currently imprisoned. As is explained below, the presentation of the facts of this case has been revised by the author.

309. At the spring 1982 session the representative of the Soviet Government stated that this communication contained offensive assertions running counter to many standard-setting decisions adopted by Unesco. He let it be known that he could not address the substance of this case as long as its starting-point remained the purpose and aim put forward by the author, which was to obtain the release of Shcharansky and to denounce the persecution of Soviet Jews.

310. After an exchange of views, the Committee decided:[3]

> (i) to resume consideration of the admissibility of the communication at its next meeting; and
>
> (ii) meanwhile to send the communication back to its author, informing him that it contained offensive language, on deletion of which the Committee would be willing to re-examine it.

311. Two members had endorsed this decision while indicating that they in fact did not endorse all of the Soviet representative's objections.[4]

312. On 4 June 1982, the Secretariat received from Mr Bombal-Acampora a letter dated 26 May 1982 in which he presented his "sincere apologies" to the Soviet Government for the offensive language, acknowledging that he had allowed himself to be "carried away" in formulating his communication and explaining that he had had no malicious intent. He has filled in a new form [...].

313. In his presentation of the facts, Mr Bombal-Acampora states merely that Mr Shcharansky has been arrested on charges on spying, anti-Soviet activities and agitation, under Articles 64A and 70/1 of the Soviet Penal Code.

---

[2] See document 115 EX/28 PRIV., paras. 308-320; see also document 115 EX/CR/HR/2.
[3] See document 114 EX/38 PRIV., para. 234 (*supra*, p. 1033).
[4] *Ibidem*, para. 235 (*supra*, p. 1033).

Union of Soviet Socialist Republics **No. 409/81**

314. The purpose and aim of the communication have been reformulated. The author asks:

(i) that Mr Shcharansky may enjoy more humane treatment and appropriate medical care in view of the state of his health;

(ii) that this mathematician may recover his freedom.

315. At the autumn 1982 session, the representative of the Soviet Union explained that Mr Shcharansky had been sentenced for a serious crime against the Soviet Union under the penal code; he had collected restricted information with the intention of distributing it abroad, which was a form of espionage. The Committee was not competent to review the decisions of a Soviet tribunal, the Soviet representative said.

316. As for the first part of the aims of the communication, the Committee could not concern itself with Mr Shcharansky's liberation. As for the second part of the aims of the communication, the Soviet representative said that he had contacted the appropriate medical authorities and had requested that they give Mr Shcharansky a complete medical examination. This had then been done during the June-August 1982 period.

317. The examining specialists had informed him that Mr Shcharansky's health was normal; he had made no complaints about his health. For these various reasons the Soviet representative considered the case to be inadmissible.

318. A Committee member stated that his own concern in this matter had been related to the medical problem of Mr Shcharansky and that in the light of the Soviet representative's information, he was in favour of considering this case inadmissible.

319. Another Committee member, while agreeing that the role of the Committee was not that of reviewing court sentences, stated that the Committee could and should examine cases in the light of internationally established standards. He noted that this was a well-known case of suppression of dissent. It would appear in this case that the Committee might be able to look at certain aspects which were of interest to Unesco, but it also appeared that the communication contained certain procedural shortcomings, which made it difficult to declare the case admissible.

320. The Committee *decided* to declare this communication inadmissible for reasons of lack of Unesco competence as far as the sentencing of Mr Shcharansky was concerned and because it was manifestly ill-founded as far as the allegations concerning his health were concerned.

No. 417/81

Concerning *Argentina*
Case of *Eduardo Federico Llosa*

Communication of 21 October 1981 submitted by
International Commission of Jurists

Spring 1982 session of the Committee on Conventions and Recommendations (114th session of the Executive Board)[1]

9. The author of this communication, the International Commission of Jurists (represented by its Secretary-General, Mr MacDermot) is acting in its capacity as a non-governmental organization having reliable knowledge of the alleged violations of which Mr Eduardo Federico Llosa is said to have been the victim.

10. According to the author of the communication, Mr Eduardo Federico Llosa, a doctor, psychiatrist, philosopher, professor of psychopathology at the University of San Luis and a member of the Regional Committee of Peronis Youth, is a leading figure in the educational, scientific and cultural world, whose work is well known in his native country.

11. It is alleged that he was arrested on 8 May 1975, tortured and taken to the prison in Rawson (Province of Chubut) more than 2,000 kilometres from his normal place of residence. He was reportedly sentenced to three years' imprisonment and irrevocable administrative sanctions for illegal association (Article 213 of the Argentine Penal Code) and to three and a half years' imprisonment for breaking Law No. 20840 concerning national security. On 2 April 1981, the two sentences were apparently combined and converted into six years' imprisonment. As a result, he should have completed his sentence on 8 May 1981, but it would seem that he has not been released and is still in the custody of the National Executive Power (PEN) on account of the state of siege which apparently allows PEN to detain individuals without trial.

[1] See document 114 EX/38 PRIV., paras. 9-27; see also documents 114 EX/CR/HR/3 and Add.2.

12. It is alleged that Dr Llosa was detained in the prison in Caseros (Province of Buenos Aires) where, it is said, the purpose of the system is to bring about the prisoners' physical and mental destruction, and, according to recent information communicated by the author in a letter dated 9 February 1982, was transferred, on 27 January 1982, to the prison in Rawson, 2,000 kilometres from the federal capital, and thus a considerable distance from his family and his lawyer. This prison is stated to be notorious for the severity of its system which, according to the Inter-American Commission on Human Rights, would appear to be even worse than that of the prison in Caseros.

13. On account of the ill-treatment which he has received, Dr Llosa is alleged to be in poor health: he is said to be suffering from vesicular defficiency of traumatic origin, chronic bronchitis, high blood pressure and a weak heart. It is said that he has not been given the necessary medical attention by the authorities. The author's fear for Dr Llosa's life has increased since his recent transfer to the prison in Rawson.

14. The information available to the author of the communication leads it to believe that the true "crime" committed by Dr Llosa lies in his research work in psychiatry, philosophy and theology, for which he makes use of bibliographic material covering all currents of thought, including Marxist thought. As a result, the author is of the opinion that Dr Llosa's freedom of opinion, thought and expression has been violated.

15. Furthermore, the author considers that Dr Liosa's continued detention violates the principle whereby a person may not be convicted twice for the same offence, a situation which is aggravated by the fact that the present period of imprisonment is of indefinite duration and that, as he has not been accused of any crime, Dr Llosa cannot put forward any defence.

16. Dr Llosa has reportedly asked to be granted his constitutional right to leave the country (Article 23 of the Argentine Constitution), but has been refused permission to do so. An application for *habeas corpus* submitted by the Centre of Legal and Social Studies would also appear to have been unsuccessful. In the opinion of the International Commission of Jurists there would not appear to be, at the present time, any further means of domestic redress which could put an end to the alleged violations or remedy their effects.

17. The purpose and aim of the comunication is to obtain the rapid release of Dr Llosa or, at least, enable him to take advantage of his right to leave Argentina for Switzerland, where his wife is now residing and for which he has a visa.

Argentina **No. 417/81**

18. On 6 April 1982, the Permanent Delegate of Argentina to Unesco had sent a letter to the Secretariat, [...].[2] He had stated in that letter that Professor Llosa had been taken into the custody of the Executive Power by virtue of Decree No. 1647, on 13 June 1975, i.e. under the government of Mrs Isabel Perón; that he had been a militant of the Montoneros extremist movement, and had taken part in acts of aggression against the institutions and property of the nation; that he had been sentenced on various charges to six years' imprisonment, which he had completed on 8 May 1981; that he had been refused permission to leave the country for reasons of security, and had remained in the custody of the Executive Power. He further recalled that the Executive was accorded power of arrest under Article 23 of the National Constitution, which had been in force since 1853; and that it was a political power designed to preserve social peace and the security of the nation, and was hence not subject to judicial review save in cases of manifest arbitrariness.

19. During his oral statement, the representative of the government concerned emphasized that the communication contained a number of inaccuracies: Dr Llosa had been arrested not for activities relating to his role as a professor, philosopher or psychiatrist, but for his acts of subversion; if he had been a member of the Regional Committee of Peronis Youth, it was hard to understand why he had been sentenced by the Peronis government; the Caseros prison was perhaps old and that in Rawson overcrowded, but to say that their purpose was to bring about the prisoners' physical and moral destruction was unacceptable; lastly, to claim that Dr Llosa's arrest was due to the fact that he had studied Marxism during his research was nonsense, since while the Argentine Government combated a tendentious presentation of Marxism, it certainly did not oppose the teaching of and research into Marxism providing they were done with the necessary scientific rigour. Consequently, the representative of the government concerned considered that the communication did not fall within Unesco's fields of competence. He added that Dr Llosa had, furthermore, received all necessary medical assistance and had access to a library in which he could continue his research. Lastly, he recalled that other prisoners held in custody by the Executive Power had obtained permission to leave the country because they had not represented a potential danger abroad; an instance was the case of Mr Roque Victoriano Galva.

20. One member expressed concern over the fact that the alleged victim had completed his sentence but was none the less still in detention without trial for an indefinite period; he then wondered whether Dr Llosa's plight did not stem from a conflict between two constitutional rules: one conferring on prisoners the right to leave the country and the other empowering the Executive Power to keep them in custody;

---

[2] See document 114 EX/CR/HR/3 Add.2.

lastly, he suggested that the Argentine authorities be asked to consider the possibility of allowing Dr Llosa to exercise his right to leave the country.

21. Another member observed that the issue did not involve a conflict of constitutional law, but the priority attaching to certain measures in force because of the state of siege; that additionally, Article 4 of the International Covenant on Civil and Political Rights authorized states to derogate from their obligations under that Covenant in certain circumstances; and that consequently, there were no grounds for considering the communication admissible.

22. While he did not disagree with the legal analysis provided by the previous speaker, another member of the Committee considered the essential question to be whether an individual could be kept in custody after he had completed his sentence.

23. At the request of the Chairman, the representative of the Director-General recalled that the Committee's role was clearly not to ascertain whether or not the Constitution of any state was respected, but whether international instruments were applied; 104 EX/Decision 3.3 referred, in its paragraph 14 (*a*) (iv), to various international instruments including the International Covenant on Civil and Political Rights. In the case at issue, the conditions specified in Article 4 of the Covenant appeared to have been fulfilled; moreover, the Committee had previously accepted in other cases that it should take account of exceptional situations.

24. A member pointed out that it had emerged during the debate that the Argentine Government had found it possible to free certain individuals or to alleviate certain situations; the representative of the Argentine Government might therefore be asked to draw his government's attention to the concern that had been expressed in the Committee over Dr Llosa to whom, as a man of culture, Unesco was not indifferent.

25. All subseguent speakers were in favour of such a solution.

26. The representative of the government concerned took the floor again, pointing out that the cases of persons held in custody by the Executive Power were studied each month by an ad hoc committee, which authorized some of them to be released as internal peace was gradually established in Argentina; however, the Argentine authorities were obliged to remain circumspect, since those concerned had been known to resume activism in the countries that accepted them. In the case in point, it should not be forgotten that Dr Llosa had been a terrorist, and that, with his future conduct to be in doubt, the Argentine Government could not show excessive leniency in order to protect both the Argentine state itself and any country that might accept him.

27. Consequently, the Committee *decided*:

(i) to request the Argentine Government to take note of the concern and disquiet expressed for humanitarian reasons by the members of the Committee;

(ii) to declare the communication inadmissible as manifestly ill-founded under the terms of paragraph 14 (*a*) (v) of 104 EX/Decision 3.3.

No. 418/81

Concerning *Union of Soviet Socialist Republics*
Case of *Victor Brailovski* *

Communication of 5 November 1981 submitted by
Kay O. Curry and Amy Young-Anawaty

Spring 1982 session of the Committee on Conventions and Recommendations (114th session of the Executive Board)[1]

236. In view of the fact that a communication concerning Mr Brailovski was already before the Committee,[2] the Committee *decided* to consider this communication at the same time as it considered the communication already pending [...].

Autumn 1982 session of the Committee on Conventions and Recommendations (115th session of the Executive Board)[3]

* At the spring 1982 session, this communication was also being referred to as case of *Irina and Victor Brailovski, Vladimir Kislik, Alexandre Lerner and Nahum Meinam* and at the autumn 1982 session as case of *Irina and Victor Brailovski, Vladimir Kislik, Alexandre Lerner and Nahum Meinam*.

[1] See document 114 EX/38 PRIV., paras. 236 and 580-618 (*supra*, pp. 611-625), communication No. 242/80 concerning *Union of Soviet Socialist Republics*, case of *Victor Brailovski* et al.

[2] See communication No. 346/81 concerning *Union of Soviet Socialist Republics*, case of *Victor Brailovski*.

[3] See document 115 EX/28 PRIV., paras. 232-262 (*supra*, pp. 625-630), communication No. 242/80 concerning *Union of Soviet Socialist Republics*, case of *Victor Brailovski* et al.

No. 421/81

Concerning *Yugoslavia*
Case of *Vlado Gotovac**

Communication of 17 November 1981 submitted by
Vlasta Gotovac

Spring 1982 session of the Committee on Conventions and Recommendations (114th session of the Executive Board)[1]

293. This communication is submitted by Mrs Vlasta Gotovac, wife of the alleged victim.

294. Mr Vlado Gotovac, aged 52, is described as a writer, poet and philosopher. He was reportedly the editor of a Croatian weekly, "Hrvatski tjednik". It is alleged that he has, in the space of 10 years, twice been sentenced:

(i) the first time, in 1971, to four years' imprisonment and to three years' administrative debarment from all public activity, for "counter-revolutionary activity"; it is said to have been impossible for him to publish anything whatsoever until 1979. However, even when the period of his punishment had ended, it is stated that he was not able either to publish anything or to find employment. Since release from prison (in 1976) he has reportedly been in contact with foreign journalists; the conversations he is alleged to have had with them are said to have been published in the form of interviews in the French, Italian, Swedish, Netherlands, Swiss, English and American press;

(ii) the second time, in June 1981, for these interviews, to two years' imprisonment and to four years' administrative debarment from all public activity.

---

* From the Committee's autumn 1982 session, this communication was being referred to as case of *Milovan Djilas, Vlado Gotovac, Sabedin Haljiti, Sabit Rustemi, Franjo Tudjman and Marko Veselica*.

[1] See document 114 EX/38 PRIV., paras. 293-300; see also document 114 EX/CR/HR/3.

No. 421/81 **Yugoslavia**

295. Mr Vlado Gotovac's lawyer reportedly appealed against the sentence of the court of first instance. But the higher court is said to have confirmed the sentence, on 2 December 1981. It is stated that the case has been referred to International PEN, Amnesty International and the International Human Rights Law Group. No result has been reported.

296. As regards the purpose and aim of the communication, Mrs Gotovac requests Unesco to intercede on behalf of her husband whom she considers to be innocent, having been sentenced purely on account of his convictions and his involvement in the defence of civil liberties and for having expressed his opinions in conversations with foreign journalists.

297. The representative of the Yugoslav Government explained that Mr Gotovac had been convicted and sentenced for hostile activity against the people and peoples of Yugoslavia and its institutions. Furthermore, he had been spreading national intolerance and advocating hatred and hostility among the peoples of the Republic. Thus the communication was outside of Unesco's competence and should be deemed to be inadmissible.

298. Certain Committee members felt that Yugoslavia had a legitimate concern with preventing strife among its various nationalistic groups, that this was a purely domestic affair and that the communication should be deemed outside of Unesco's competence.

299. Other Committee members felt that while Yugoslavia had legitimate concerns with preserving national unity, there was nevertheless the right of non-violent expression which needed to be looked at in this case, and that more information concerning the charges, evidence, and appeals possibilities in Mr Gotovac's case should be requested from Yugoslav authorities.

300. After a brief debate the Committee *decided* to postpone its examination of the admissibility of the case given that the affair is currently pending before the Supreme Federal Court of Belgrade, and to ask the representative of the Yugoslav Government any future information regarding this matter.

Yugoslavia **No. 421/81**

Autumn 1982 session of the Committee on Conventions and Recommendations (115th session of the Executive Board)[2]

Spring 1983 session of the Committee on Conventions and Recommendations (116th session of the Executive Board)[3]

[2] See document 115 EX/28 PRIV., paras. 398-402 (*supra*, pp. 975-976), communication No. 392/81 concerning *Yugoslavia*, case of *Milovan Djilas* et al.

[3] See document 116 EX/48 PRIV., paras. 238-261 (*supra*, pp. 976-981), communication No. 392/81 concerning *Yugoslavia*, case of *Milovan Djilas* et al.

No. 422/81

Concerning *Argentina*
Case of *Mario Jaime Zaraceansky*

Communication of 23 November 1981 submitted by
James Schwebel

Spring 1982 session of the Committee on Conventions and Recommendations (114th session of the Executive Board)[1]

28. The author of the communication, Mr James Schwebel, a college administrator in the United States of America, states that Mr Mario Jaime Zaraceansky is a lawyer, a specialist in labour law and a professor of social law. He is reported in particular to have taught at the School of Social Services, University of Córdoba; this school, according to the statement made by his wife, annexed to the form by the author of the communication, has been sharply criticized and a large number of its faculty members have allegedly been forced to emigrate. Mrs Zaraceansky expresses her conviction that her husband is being held in prison on account of the role he has played as a lawyer in defending the rights of workers, and as a teacher.

29. Professor Zaraceansky and his wife are alleged to have been arrested at their home in Córdoba on 27 July 1977 and taken without warrant or charge to La Perla, a clandestine torture centre where they are said to have been held for 15 months. Mrs Zaraceansky reportedly secured her own release by availing herself of her right of option to emigrate in October 1978 and is stated to be living at present in Spain with her six-year-old son. Her husband is alleged to have been transferred to La Plata prison No. 9. According to one of his cellmates, Professor Zaraceansky is taken out of his cell from time to time, for a period of a week or more, in order to be tortured.

30. The author of the communication explains that persons detained by the National Executive Power (PEN) have, under the Argentine Constitution, the guaranteed right to opt to leave the country instead of remaining in prison. It is alleged that Professor Zaraceansky has applied for this right on five occasions but that all his applications have been to no avail, even though he has a "certificate of acceptability" from the

---

[1] See document 114 EX/38 PRIV., paras. 28-35; see also document 114 EX/CR/HR/3.

United States of America, the Federal Republic of Germany, Spain and Israel and the necessary sponsorship.

31. The purpose and aim of this communication is to draw attention to the plight of Professor Zaraceansky who has spent five years in prison where he has been subjected to torture, without charge or trial, and also to obtain authorization for him to exercise his right of option so that he can be reunited with his family and resume his teaching.

32. The representative of the government concerned stated that if Mr Zaraceansky was a teacher, he was also a member of a wing of "the people's revolutionary army", a subversive organization against which his government had had to take measures. His country had, he said, been brought to the brink of disintegration as a result of the activities of such movements and Professor Zaraceansky's arrest was in conformity with the Constitution. The allegation that Professor Zaraceansky had been tortured was false; he had been visited by a representative of the [Inter-American] Commission on Human Rights of the Organization of American States, and Mr Pérez Esquivel, the Nobel Peace Prize winner, had also taken an interest in his case.

33. The representative of the Argentine Government stated, however, that the cases of persons detained by the National Executive Power were examined each month by an interministerial commission which he had informed of the concern for Professor Zaraceansky expressed within the Committee. Having regard to the interest thus displayed by the Committee, that ad hoc commission had brought forward the date of its meeting so as to give its ruling before the end of the Committee's session and had decided to free Professor M. J. Zaraceansky, with some restrictions on his movements. The relevant order was about to be signed. Once freed, Professor Zaraceansky would either be able to take steps to leave the country and join his family, or he could be reunited with them on Argentine territory.

34. All the members who took the floor expressed their satisfaction with the result obtained; they expressed their thanks to the representative of the Argentine Government and the Permanent Delegate of Argentina to Unesco for interceding with their government; they welcomed the spirit of co-operation of the Argentine Government, which, notwithstanding its current difficulties, had been willing to take the time to respond to the concern expressed by the Committee.

35. Consequently, the Committee *decided*, by virtue of [paragraph] 14 (*a*) (x) of [104 EX/Decision 3.3], to remove the communication from its list, considering the matter to have been settled.

No. 425/81

Concerning *Yugoslavia*
Case of *Sabedin Haljiti* et al.*

Communication of 4 December 1981 submitted by
Amnesty International

Spring 1982 session of the Committee on Conventions and Recommendations (114th session of the Executive Board)[1]

301. This communication is submitted by Amnesty International (International Secretariat), acting as a non-governmental organization with reliable knowledge of the alleged violations.

A. *Case of Sabedin Haljiti and Sabit Rustemi*

302. Sabedin Haljiti is described as the editor of an Albanian-language literary journal, "Fjalja"; Sabit Rustemi as the author of a short story, "Under the mask of guests", published in an issue of that journal, placed on sale on 4 April 1981, just after several days of nationalist demonstrations by the Albanian ethnic minority in Kosovo in support of demand that that province be granted republic status within the Yugoslav Federation.

303. Arrested and charged with hostile propaganda, with the intention of sowing national hatred and with depicting the situation in the country maliciously and untruthfully, Messrs Haljiti and Rustemi were reportedly sentenced by a Priština court to three and four years' imprisonment respectively. The defence is alleged to have demonstrated to the court that the story did not mention either the date or the place of the events (which might have corresponded to the aforementioned demonstrations, during which there were said to be violent clashes with the security forces).

* Case of *Sabedin Haljiti, Sabit Rustemi, Adem Demaçi,, Vjenceslav Čižek, Franjo Tudjman and Marko Veselica*. From the Committee's autumn 1982 session, this communication was being referred to as case of *Milovan Djilas, Vlado Gotovac, Sabedin Haljiti, Sabit Rustemi, Franjo Tudjman and Marko Veselica*.
[1] See document 114 EX/38 PRIV., paras. 301-327; see also document 114 EX/CR/HR/3.

No. 425/81 **Yugoslavia**

304. Amnesty International notes that, according to the 20 November 1981 issue of the Belgrade weekly *NIN*, the story in question is said to have already been published the previous year in a collection of literary works about the Partisan resistance in Yugoslavia during the Second World War, that is to say, well before the demonstrations of March and April 1981 in Kosovo: consequently the story could not have referred to those events. The author does not know whether the alleged victims have availed themselves of domestic means of redress.

B. *Case of Adem Demaçi*

305. The alleged victim is described as a writer. He is said to be known for his short stories published in the Albanian-language literary journal "Jeta e Re". This journal is said to have subsequently serialized his historical novel about Kosovo, entitled "Serpents of blood".

306. He is alleged to have been imprisoned:

(i) the first time, in 1958, for nationalist agitation;

(ii) the second time, from 1964 to 1974, for crimes against the people and the state;

(iii) the third time (15 years' imprisonment), in 1976, for hostile propaganda, association against the people and the state, and for endangering the territorial integrity and independence of Yugoslavia.

307. It is reported that the reason for this third term of imprisonment was that Demaçi and a number of Kosovo Albanians had attempted to circulate a petition asking for a referendum to be held in order to determine whether Kosovo Province, which is inhabited mainly by Albanians, should remain an integral part of Yugoslavia or be attached to Albania. Demaçi is alleged to have so far spent a total of 17 years in prison. He is said to be in poor health and to be having problems with his eyesight. The author of the communication does not know whether the alleged victim has availed himself of domestic means of redress.

C. *Case of Vjenceslav Čižek*

308. The alleged victim is described as a teacher and cultural adviser. He is reported to have been imprisoned for the first time, from 1955 to 1957, for having written a satirical poem. He is said to have left Yugoslavia in 1971 and to have taken asylum in the Federal Republic of Germany. It is alleged that, in that country, he joined an émigré political party and contributed to its journals satirical articles and caricatures

criticizing and ridiculing Yugoslavia's political system and leaders. It is stated that in 1977 an acquaintance offered to drive him to Milan (Italy), after which he disappeared, reportedly kidnapped by agents of the Yugoslav security service. He is said to have reappeared in August 1978 when he was reportedly tried by a Sarajevo court and sentenced to 15 years' imprisonment - said to have been reduced subsequently to 13 years - for counter-revolutionary and subversive activities conducted in collaboration with Croatian émigrés.

309. Mr Čižek's state of health is said to give grounds for concern at the present time. Amnesty International fears that conditions in Zenica prison where he is being held will reactivate the tuberculosis which he contracted in 1974 in the Federal Republic of Germany and will cause him to lose his sight completely, since he reportedly suffers from glaucoma in the right eye, said to be the only one with vision since he lost the sight in his left eye as a child. It is alleged that in 1980 the prison authorities did not allow him to receive medicine for his affected eye and rejected a medical recommendation that he undergo an urgent operation.

310. It is alleged that there has been a violation of Article 19 of the Universal Declaration of Human Rights (freedom of opinion and expression) and Articles 9, paragraph 1 (right to liberty and security), 10, paragraph 1 (right of persons deprived of their liberty to be treated with humanity), and 19 (freedom of opinion) of the International Covenant on Civil and Political Rights.

311. On appeal, his sentence was reportedly reduced merely from 15 to 13 years' imprisonment.

D. *Case of Franjo Tudjman*

312. The alleged victim is described as a historian and former general in the Yugoslav army. He is said to have held important posts in higher education and in the political apparatus. His main works are reported to be: *War against War* (1957), *The Formation of Socialist Yugoslavia* (1960), *Occupation and Revolution* (1963), *Introduction to the History of Socialist Yugoslavia* (1964), *The Yugoslav Committee and the Formation of the State of Southern Slavs* (1966), *Big Ideas and Small Nations* (1969) and *Nationalism in Contemporary Europe* [1981].

313. Mr Tudjman is alleged to have been expelled from the Croatian League of Communists in 1967 for nationalistic deviation. He is reported to have also lost his academic posts. In 1972, following nationalist unrest in Croatia, he is said to have been sentenced to two years' imprisonment of which he reportedly served only nine months, his sentence having been reduced. In February 1981 he is stated to have been again sentenced by a Zagreb court to three years' imprisonment, and a five-

year ban on public expression for hostile propaganda and for maliciously and untruthfully representing the situation in the country with assistance from abroad. This charge is alleged to have been based on the interviews reportedly given by Mr Tudjman to three foreign journalists - Bengt Göransson of Swedish television, Peter Miroschnikoff, Federal Republic of Germany, and Michel Barthélémy of "Radio France internationale". It is reported that in these interviews he spoke in particular of the repression of the Croatian nationalist movement in 1971 and 1972 and stated that there were deep contradictions between the principles of the League of Communists of Yugoslavia and the constitutional principles regarding the right of each nation of the Federation to self-determination; he is alleged to have complained also that the fact of speaking about the Croatian problem was too hastily regarded as evidence of nationalism and separatism.

314. Mr Tudjman is reportedly being held in Lepoglava prison. He is said to be in poor health and to be suffering from several diseases: high blood pressure, arteriosclerosis, diabetes etc.

315. With regard to the domestic means of redress used, Amnesty International states that the sentence was confirmed on appeal in November 1981.

E. *Case of Mariko Veselica*

316. The alleged victim is described as an author and former professor. Prior to his expulsion from the Croatian League of Communists and his dismissal in late 1971 from all the posts he held, he was reportedly a senior party official, a teacher in the Faculty of Economic Sciences, Zagreb, a member of the presidency of the Croatian Confederation of Trade Unions and deputy in the Federal Assembly. A member of the Croatian cultural organization "Matica Hrvatska", he is said to have contributed to the weekly publication "Hrvatski tjednik". He is reportedly the co-author of a work entitled "The Political Economy of Yugoslavia" with Mrs Savka Dabčević-Kučar.

317. In 1972, arrested together with several members of a so-called Croatian national movement, Mr Veselica is alleged to have been sentenced to seven years' imprisonment for conspiracy to overthrow Yugoslavia's social and political system. He was reportedly released at the end of 1977. He is alleged to have been arrested again in April 1981. Charged with hostile propaganda, incitement to national hatred and participation in hostile activity, he was reportedly sentenced to 11 years' imprisonment and a four-year ban on public expression. The first two charges were said to be based on an interview he is alleged to have given to a journalist from the Federal Republic of Germany in September 1980. Extracts from this interview were reportedly reprinted in various Croatian émigrés publications. According to Amnesty Interna-

tional, Mr Veselica stated that Croatia was politically, economically, and culturally discriminated against within the Yugoslav Federation; he did not, however, advocate violence. The third charge is said to have been based on documents that Mr Veselica was alleged to have sent abroad for publication in émigré newspapers. These documents were stated to have maliciously and untruthfully depicted the situation in Yugoslavia. Mr Veselica is said to have been also accused of having agreed to send to Croatian émigrés information regarding violations of human rights in Yugoslavia for submission to the Conference on Security and Co-operation in Europe, held in Madrid in 1980. He is reported to have acknowledged that he had given the interview in question but to have rejected the charges against him: the prosecution is said not to have succeeded in demonstrating the untruthfulness of his statements. Furthermore, Mr Veselica is reported to have denied having any contact with émigrés. He is alleged, in addition, to have informed the court that he was against any extremist organization, whether at home or abroad, and against violence and hatred.

318. The author of the communication does not know whether the alleged victim has availed himself of any domestic means of redress.

319. The cases of the seven alleged victims have reportedly not been referred to any other international authority.

320. With regard to the purpose and aim of the communication, Amnesty International requests that the victims be immediately released.

321. The representative of the Yugoslav Government stated to the Committee that as far as concerned Messrs Veselica, Tudjman and Čižek this communication neither came within Unesco's competence nor did it contain relevant evidence, and furthermore it was based exclusively on press information. It was thus inadmissible under [104 EX/Decision 3.3], paragraph 14 [*a*] (iii), (v) and (vii). He added that Mr Čižek had been tried and sentenced in conformity with the Yugoslav criminal code for subversive activities with an illegal Fascist group. As far as the other alleged victims were concerned they were tried and sentenced in accordance with Yugoslav law for hostile propaganda, inciting national hatred, and other subversive activities. The communication was based on press information and contained no relevant evidence with regard to these cases either, the representative said and they were thus inadmissible.

322. A Committee member pointed out that every international instrument limited the extent to which matters could be deemed to be within the sole interest of a state and he cited the apartheid situation in South Africa as an example. In the present case, he was aware of the problems caused in Yugoslavia by nationalistic terrorist groups, whose actions he did not condone, but he felt that such cases should be dis-

tinguished from those in which people were condemned for non-violent verbal expressions, which appeared to be the case here. He cited a report which indicated that 90 per cent of the political crimes in Yugoslavia were simple verbal expressions.

323. Another Committee member concurred with this view, pointed out that the concept of internal jurisdiction had changed, and that certain matters had been taken out of the jurisdiction of countries. The Committee's existence would have no sense if this were not true, he added.

324. Other Committee members felt that the problem was a purely domestic affair and that the communication should be deemed inadmissible. One Committee member pointed out that the Unesco Constitution prohibited the interference into the domestic affairs of Member States and he felt that it was not wise to commence a theoretical discussion on the question.

325. The Yugoslav representative categorically rejected the notion that his country was not respecting international law.

326. At the request of the Chairman, the representative of the Director-General clarified a matter which had come up during the discussion. He explained that while it was true that both the Unesco Constitution and [104 EX/Decision 3.3] prohibited the intervention in affairs which were essentially within the domestic competence of Member States, the key words were "intervention" and "essentially". He explained that an examination by the Committee was not considered to be an intervention but rather a co-operation. It was also an established fact, he added, that the area of human rights was no longer either an exclusive or essentially domestic affair of states. The main point to bear in mind however was the concept of a "co-operation".

327. After a prolonged debate on procedural and substantive questions the Committee *decided* that:

> [i] with respect to the case of Messrs Haljiti, Rustemi, Tudjman and Veselica, it would postpone until its next session the question of the admissibility of these cases and it would request further information from both the authors and the Yugoslav Government;

> [ii] with respect to the case of Mr Demaçi, it was inadmissible as not having been presented within a reasonable amount of time (paragraph 14 (*a*) (vii) of [104 EX/Decision 3.3]);

[iii] with respect to the Čižek case it was inadmissible as not being within Unesco's fields of competence (paragraph 14 (*a*) (iii) of [104 EX/Decision 3.3]).

Autumn 1982 session of the Committee on Conventions and Recommendations (115th session of the Executive Board)[2]

Spring 1983 session of the Committee on Conventions and Recommendations (116th session of the Executive Board)[3]

[2] See document 115 EX/28 PRIV., paras. 398-402 (*supra*, pp. 975-976), communication No. 392/81 concerning *Yugoslavia*, case of *Milovan Djilas* et al.
[3] See document 116 EX/48 PRIV., paras. 238-261 (*supra*, pp. 976-981), communication No. 392/81 concerning *Yugoslavia*, case of *Milovan Djilas* et al.

No. 426/81

Concerning *Union of Soviet Socialist Republics*
Case of *Vladimir Borisov*

Communication of 7 December 1981 submitted by
Michel A. Calvo

Spring 1982 session of the Committee on Conventions and Recommendations (114th session of the Executive Board)[1]

237. This communication is submitted by [Mr] Michel A. Calvo, legal representative of Mr Vladimir Borisov, described as the victim of the alleged violations.

238. Mr Borisov is said to be one of the founders of the free union SMOT (Free Interprofessional Workers' Union) and member of the Human Rights Defence Group in the Soviet Union. After several years of detention both in prison and in psychiatric hospitals, he was reportedly exiled from his country in June 1980 and invited shortly afterwards to France by the French Socialist Party. He now resides in France as a political refugee. His wife, Irina Kaplun, who died at the age of 30 in a traffic accident, was said to be an active member of the Working Group against psychiatric repression (a committee of the Helsinki Group). From the marriage, which lasted only five years, a child, Genia Kaplun Borisova, was born on 9 August 1979. She is now living with her grandmother, her two great-aunts and Mr Korostylev Alexei Yurevich. These persons have allegedly requested authorization to emigrate to France, without success.

239. [Mr] Calvo stresses that education is principally the responsibility of the parents, that it can only be provided adequately in the care and under the responsibility of the parents, in an atmosphere of affection and moral and material security, that the child should not be separated either from the mother or from the father, save in exceptional circumstances, that a child's education in its early years is mainly provided by the parents and that only the parents are in a position to provide certain information of a personal or family nature. The fact of preventing Genia Kaplun Bori-

[1] See document 114 EX/38 PRIV., paras. 237-245; see also document 114 EX/CR/HR/3.

sova from joining Mr Borisov in France and the fact of preventing the father from living with his child constitute a clear violation of human rights.

240. With reference to the question of what means of redress have already been used, the legal representative indicates that the applications for emigration in respect of the grandmother and great-aunts of Genia Kaplun Borisova as well as for the child herself, although supported by a certificate from Mr Borisov undertaking to provide accommodation for them were rejected.

241. With regard to the purpose and aim of the communication, the legal representative requests that Genia Kaplun Borisova may be allowed to join her father in France.

242. The representative of the Soviet Government stated that there were a number of reasons for finding this communication inadmissible. Mr Calvo had not filled out the standard form but rather submitted his own document. Furthermore Mr Borisov's profession had no links with Unesco's fields of competence, the representative said. He also explained that the daughter of Mr Borisov, her grandmother, and the sister of the grandmother had recently been given permission to leave the USSR. The Soviet representative said that he had an official document dated 3 March 1982, from the Moscow Council of Deputies which stated that these three persons were free to leave the USSR.

243. The representative of the Director-General explained to the Committee that Mr Calvo had without malice recopied the standard form in its entirety on to his own paper and that the Secretariat felt it would have been needlessly bureaucratic to insist on a second recopying back on to the form.

244. A Committee member expressed happiness over the events which had been announced, and expressed the hope that future cases might also be the subject of such an enlightened and humane attitude.

245. The Committee *decided* to strike the communication from its list as having been settled.

No. 429/81

Concerning *Portugal*
Case of *Mário Jorge da Graça Estêvão*

Communication of 9 December 1981 submitted by
Mário Jorge da Graça Estêvão

Spring 1982 session of the Committee on Conventions and Recommendations (114th session of the Executive Board)[1]

132. The author of this communication, Mr Mário Jorge da Graça Estêvão, a blind teacher of music of Portuguese nationality, complained that the Portuguese Ministry of Education had closed the Higher School of Music of the Lisbon National Conservatory, established pursuant to the decrees of 9 May 1919 and 25 September 1930, and cancelled the advanced piano courses and courses in musical composition formerly provided there. It was said that the effect had been to invalidate the diplomas which Mr Graça Estêvão had obtained in those subjects at the school in July 1950 and 1951, and to damage his position as a teacher, *inter alia*, by entailing a reduction in his salary from scale "g" to scale "j", a reduction which he claimed had caused him serious financial loss and which he feared would affect his pension.

133. The purpose and aim of the communication were to obtain the re-establishment of the advanced music courses and aforesaid diplomas, and the restitution of Mr Graça Estêvão's acquired rights, more particularly as concerned his salary.

134. On 25 March 1982, the Secretariat received a letter from the author of the communication, dated 18 March 1982, stating that, on 12 February 1982, the Portuguese Government had taken favourable action to solve his situation and that of other Portuguese music teachers holding higher educational diplomas, by restoring their legitimately acquired rights; he therefore considered that his complaint no longer applied.

135. The case having been settled to the complete satisfaction of the author of the communication, the Committee *decided* to accede to his request that his communica-

[1] See document 114 EX/38 PRIV., paras. 132-135; see also document 114 EX/CR/HR/3 Add.

tion be withdrawn, and therefore considers the matter settled. In accordance with its usual practice [...],[2] the Committee pointed out that it was not obliged to accept such requests, and that it reserved the right to reject them whenever it considered that the author or authors were acting under duress, that the complaint was of particular interest, or that there were other appropriate grounds for refusing withdrawal.

[2] See communications No. 37/78 concerning *United Kingdom*, case of *Children of nomadic Gypsies*, and No. 149/79 concerning *Union of Soviet Socialist Republics*, case of *Mstislav Rostropovich and Galina Vishnevskaya*.

ANNEX I

104 EX/DECISION 3.3

Study of the procedures which should be followed in the examination of cases and questions which might be submitted to Unesco concerning the exercise of human rights in the spheres of its competence, in order to make its action more effective: Report of the Working Party of the Executive Board (104 EX/3)*

The Executive Board,

1. Mindful that the competence and role of Unesco in the field of human rights derive primarily from Article I.1 of the Constitution of Unesco, which states: "The purpose of the Organization is to contribute to peace and security by promoting collaboration among the nations through education, science and culture in order to further universal respect for justice, for the rule of law and for the human rights and fundamental freedoms which are affirmed for the peoples of the world, without distinction of race, sex, language or religion, by the Charter of the United Nations", and from the Charter of the United Nations,

2. *Recalling* the Universal Declaration of Human Rights, the international covenants on human rights and the various conventions and recommendations adopted by Unesco,

3. *Recalling* 19 C/Resolution 6.113 concerning Unesco's responsibilities in the field of human rights,

4. *Recalling* also 19 C/Resolution 12.1: "Unesco's contribution to peace and its tasks with respect to the promotion of human rights and the elimination of colonialism and racialism - long-term programme of measures whereby Unesco can contribute to the strengthening of peace"; and in particular paragraph 10 of the resolution, which invites the Executive Board and the Director-General:

> "(*a*) to examine with particular attention the general situation with regard to respect for human rights throughout the world in Unesco's fields of competence,

* The Working Party was set up in pursuance of 102 EX/Decision 5.6.2. It drew up a draft decision of the Executive Board that was approved by the Board on 26 April 1978.

Annex I

(*b*) to study the procedures which should be followed in the examination of cases and questions which might be submitted to Unesco concerning the exercise of human rights in the spheres to which its competence extends, in order to make its action more effective,

(*c*) to continue to establish, with a view to the implementation of subparagraphs (*a*) and (*b*), close co-operation and co-ordination with the relevant United Nations organs so as to take advantage of their work and the lessons that can be learned from them in this field",

5. *Having considered* the report of a working group of the Board set up by virtue of 102 EX/Decision 5.6.2 to carry out an in-depth study of document 102 EX/19, the analytical summary of discussions that took place at the 102nd session of the Board, and additional written comments provided by members of the Board,

6. Mindful of Article I.3 of the Constitution of Unesco, which states: "With a view to preserving the independence, integrity and fruitful diversity of the cultures and educational systems of the States members of the Organization, the Organization is prohibited from intervening in matters which are essentially within their domestic jurisdiction",

7. *Considering* that, in matters concerning human rights within its fields of competence, Unesco, basing its efforts on moral considerations and its specific competence, should act in a spirit of international co-operation, conciliation and mutual understanding; and *recalling* that Unesco should not play the role of an international judicial body,

8. *Recognizing* the important role of the Director-General, in:

(*a*) seeking, continually to strengthen the action of Unesco in the promotion of human rights, both through the settlement of cases and the elimination of massive, systematic or flagrant violations of human rights and fundamental freedoms, and

(*b*) initiating consultations, in conditions of mutual respect, confidence and confidentiality, to help reach solutions to particular problems concerning human rights,

9. *Invites* the Director-General to pursue this role;

10. *Considering* that, in the exercise of its competence in the field of human rights, Unesco is called upon to examine:

(*a*) cases concerning violations of human rights which are individual and specific,

(*b*) questions of massive, systematic or flagrant violations of human rights which result either from a policy contrary to human rights applied *de jure* or *de facto* by a State or from an accumulation of individual cases forming a consistent pattern,

11. *Considering* the terms of reference of the Committee on Conventions and Recommendations in Education,

12. *Taking into account* the tasks already entrusted to the Committee concerning human rights matters within the Organization's fields of competence,

13. *Decides* that the Committee will henceforth be designated "the Committee on Conventions and Recommendations";

14. *Decides* that the Committee will continue to carry out its functions with respect to conventions and recommendations and will consider communications received by the Organization concerning cases and questions of violations of human rights within Unesco's fields of competence in accordance with the following conditions and procedures:

Conditions

(*a*) Communications shall be deemed admissible if they meet the following conditions:

(i) the communication must not be anonymous;

(ii) the communication must originate from a person or a group of persons who, it can be reasonably presumed, are victims of an alleged violation of any of the human rights referred to in paragraph (iii) below. It may also originate from any person, group of persons or non-governmental organization having reliable knowledge of those violations;

(iii) the communication must concern violations of human rights falling within Unesco's competence in the fields of education, science, culture and information and must not be motivated exclusively by other considerations;

(iv) the communication must be compatible with the principles of the Organization, the Charter of the United Nations, the Universal Declaration of Human Rights, the international covenants on human rights and other international instruments in the field of human rights;

(v) the communication must not be manifestly ill-founded and must appear to contain relevant evidence;

(vi) the communication must be neither offensive nor an abuse of the right to submit communications. However, such a communication may be considered if it meets all other criteria or admissibility, after the exclusion of the offensive or abusive parts;

(vii) the communication must not be based exclusively on information disseminated through the mass media;

(viii) the communication must be submitted within a reasonable time-limit following the facts which constitute its subject-matter or within a reasonable time-limit after the facts have become known;

(ix) the communication must indicate whether an attempt has been made to exhaust available domestic remedies with regard to the facts which constitute the subject-matter of the communication and the result of such an attempt, if any;

(x) communications relating to matters already settled by the States concerned in accordance with the human rights principles set forth in the Universal Declaration of Human Rights and the international covenants on human rights shall not be considered;

Procedures

(*b*) The Director-General shall:

(i) acknowledge receipt of communications and inform the authors thereof of the above-mentioned conditions governing admissibility;

(ii) ascertain that the author of the communication has no objection to his communication, after having been communicated to the government concerned, being brought to the notice of the Committee, and to his name being divulged;

(iii) upon receipt of an affirmative answer from the author of the communication, transmit the communication to the government concerned, informing it that the communication will be brought to the notice of the Committee, together with any reply the government may wish to make;

(iv) transmit the communication to the Committee, together with the reply, if any, of the government concerned and additional relevant information from the author, taking into account the need to proceed without undue delay;

(*c*) the Committee shall examine in private session the communications transmitted to it by the Director-General;

(*d*) the Committee shall decide on the admissibility of communications in accordance with the above-mentioned conditions;

(*e*) representatives of the governments concerned may attend meetings of the Committee in order to provide additional information or to answer questions from members of the Committee on either admissibility or the merits of the communication;

(*f*) the Committee may avail itself of the relevant information at the disposal of the Director-General;

(*g*) in consideration of a communication, the Committee may, in exceptional circumstances, request the Executive Board to authorize it under Rule 29 of the Rules of Procedure to take appropriate action;

(*h*) the Committee may keep a communication submitted to it on its agenda while seeking additional information it may consider necessary for the disposition of the matter;

(*i*) the Director-General shall notify the author of the communication and the government concerned of the Committee's decision on the admissibility of the communication;

(*j*) the Committee shall dismiss any communication which, having been found admissible, does not, upon examination of the merits, appear to warrant further action. The author of the communication and the government concerned shall be notified accordingly;

(*k*) communications which warrant further consideration shall be acted upon by the Committee with a view to helping to bring about a friendly solution designed to advance the promotion of the human rights falling within Unesco's fields of competence;

Annex I

15. *Decides further* that the Committee shall submit confidential reports to the Executive Board at each session on the carrying out of its mandate under the present decision. These reports shall contain appropriate information arising from its examination of the communications which the Committee considers it useful to bring to the notice of the Executive Board. The reports shall also contain recommendations which the Committee may wish to make either generally or regarding the disposition of a communication under consideration;

16. *Decides* to consider confidential reports of the Committee in private session and to take further action as necessary in accordance with Rule 28 of the Rules of Procedure;

17. *Decides also* that communications transmitted to it by the Committee which testify to the existence of a question shall be dealt with in accordance with paragraph 18 below;

18. *Considers* that questions of massive, systematic or flagrant violations of human rights and fundamental freedoms - including, for example, those perpetrated as a result of policies of aggression, interference in the internal affairs of States, occupation of foreign territory and implementation of a policy of colonialism, genocide, apartheid, racialism, or national and social oppression - falling within Unesco's fields of competence should be considered by the Executive Board and the General Conference in public meetings;

19. *Decides* to consider at its 105th session the report to be made by the Executive Board and the Director-General to the General Conference, at its twentieth session, on the implementation of Part II of 19 C/Resolution 12.1.

ANNEX II

STANDARD LETTER

Standard letter sent by the Director of the Office of International Standards and Legal Affairs to the authors of communications examined under 104 EX/ Decision 3.3*

CONFIDENTIAL

On behalf of the Director-General, I acknowledge receipt of your letter of ... alleging violations of human rights. In so far as your communication concerns human rights falling within UNESCO's competence in the fields of education, science, culture or communication, it can be examined under the procedure approved by the Executive Board of UNESCO on 26 April 1978 in 104 EX/Decision 3.3, a copy of which is attached for your information.

It must be stressed that in no case is UNESCO an international court nor can it become one. The rights falling within UNESCO's spheres of competence are essentially the following:

- the right to education (Article 26 of the Universal Declaration of Human Rights);
- the right to share in scientific advancement (Article 27);
- the right to participate freely in cultural life (Article 27);
- the right to information, including freedom of opinion and expression (Article 19).

These rights may imply the exercise of others, the most noteworthy of which are set out below:

- the right to freedom of thought, conscience and religion (Article 18);
- the right to seek, receive and impart information and ideas through any media and regardless of frontiers (Article 19);
- the right to the protection of the moral and material interests resulting from any scientific, literary or artistic production (Article 27);
- the right to freedom of assembly and association (Article 20) for the purposes of activities connected with education, science, culture and information.

* See document 179 EX/CR/2, annex III.

Annex II

In accordance with 104 EX/Decision 3.3, I wish to draw your attention to the conditions governing admissibility, which must be met before UNESCO can take action on your communication. They are listed in paragraph 14 (*a*) of 104 EX/Decision 3.3. In order to enable the Director-General to complete the file on your communication, you are invited to fill in the enclosed form and to return it to UNESCO, duly signed by yourself, as soon as possible.

The allegations should be set out in a concise statement, specifying which of the human rights is/are considered to have been violated and which of UNESCO's fields of competence is/are concerned. The date of the decisions complained of and the authority which took them should be clearly indicated, including, in particular, whatever legal remedies have been used (for instance, recourse to the courts in the country concerned) and the results of such action. There should also be an indication as to whether another international procedure has been used and, if so, before what body, the date on which the matter was referred to it and any results of this procedure.

You will notice that you are asked whether you have any objection to your name being divulged and to your communication being brought to the notice of the UNESCO Executive Board Committee on Conventions and Recommendations, after it has been transmitted to the government concerned. Failing an affirmative answer from you on this point, no action on your communication can be taken by UNESCO under the aforementioned decision.

Yours faithfully,

Director
Office of International Standards
and Legal Affairs

ANNEX III

FORM FOR COMMUNICATIONS

CONFIDENTIAL

UNESCO

FORM FOR COMMUNICATIONS CONCERNING HUMAN RIGHTS TO BE SUBMITTED TO UNESCO*

For UNESCO use only:

Number of communication: [ ]

Date of communication:
Date of dispatch of this form:

To be filled in by the author of the communication:

I. INFORMATION CONCERNING THE AUTHOR

Name: First name(s):
Nationality: Profession:
Date and place of birth:
Present address:

Address to be used for correspondence (if other than the present address):

* See document 179 EX/CR/2, annex IV.

Annex III

Indicate, by ticking the appropriate box, in what capacity you are acting:

☐ victim of the violation or violations described below

☐ representative of the victim or victims of the violations described below

☐ person, group of persons or non-governmental organization with reliable knowledge of the violations described below

☐ In another capacity. Specify

II. INFORMATION CONCERNING THE VICTIM OR VICTIMS OF THE ALLEGED VIOLATIONS°

☐ If the author is the victim, tick here and pass directly to Part III.

Give the following particulars for each victim, adding as many pages as necessary.

Name:	First name(s):
Nationality:	Profession:
Date and place of birth:	
Present address or whereabouts:	

III. INFORMATION CONCERNING THE ALLEGED FACTS

Name of the country considered by the author to be responsible for the alleged violation.

Human rights allegedly violated (refer, if possible, to the Universal Declaration of Human Rights, the International Covenant on Economic, Social and Cultural Rights and the International Covenant on Civil and Political Rights).

° N.B. This information is essential in cases where the communication concerns one or more individuals and specific cases of violation of human rights.

Connection between the alleged violation and education, science, culture or information.

Facts of the claim.

IV. INFORMATION CONCERNING MEANS OF REDRESS USED

What steps have been taken to exhaust domestic remedies (recourse to the courts or other public authorities), by whom, when and with what results?

Has the matter been submitted to another international authority concerned with protection of human rights? If so, when and with what results?

V. PURPOSE AND AIM OF THIS COMMUNICATION

VI. DECLARATION BY THE AUTHOR

Does the author agree to his communication being examined in accordance with the procedure approved by the Executive Board of UNESCO in 104 EX/Decision 3.3 and, in particular, is he willing for his name to be divulged and for the communication to be transmitted to the government concerned and brought to the notice of the UNESCO Executive Board Committee on Conventions and Recommendations?

☐ Yes ☐ No

Date:
Name, first name:
Signature of author:

ANNEX IV

PROCEDURAL PRACTICE

Procedural Practice of the Committee on Conventions and Recommendations*

1. *The Committee is not a judicial or quasi-judicial body*
[para. 7]

This principle is constantly recalled by the Committee when a government asserts that the Committee cannot set itself up as a supreme international court with the power to review the final judgments passed by the competent courts of Member States. The Committee has stated that its sole object is, for purely humanitarian reasons, to establish dialogue with the governments concerned in order to consider with them what might be done on behalf of alleged victims in the event of their having suffered from violations of human rights in UNESCO's fields of competence. The Committee's aim is to promote those rights by seeking a friendly solution to human problems. Its work consists in seeking information and facilitating conciliation.

I. CONDITIONS OF ADMISSIBILITY OF COMMUNICATIONS

2. *The concept of "reliable knowledge"*
[para. 14 (*a*) (ii)]

A communication may originate from the presumed victims of an alleged violation of human rights and from any person or group of persons or non-governmental organizations having reliable knowledge of those violations. On the matter of "reliable knowledge", it has been noted that in all legal systems good faith is presumed. It has been considered that this rule should also apply in respect of the condition of admissibility provided for in paragraph 14 (*a*) (ii).

* See document 179 EX/CR/2, annex II. References between square brackets are to the relevant provisions of 104 EX/Decision 3.3.

Annex IV

3. *When the profession of the alleged victim comes within UNESCO's fields of competence, there is a presumption at the stage of examination as to admissibility that there exists a link between the alleged violation and UNESCO's fields of competence*
[para. 14 (*a*) (iii)]

Such is the practice of the Committee, which has made it clear that this presumption cannot be considered to be a decisive factor justifying UNESCO's intervention. It counts only for the admissibility of the communication. UNESCO's competence is then determined *rationae personae*, according to the status of the alleged victim. Whenever there has been uncertainty as to that status, the alleged victim has always been given the benefit of the doubt.

4. *The activity of which the alleged victim is accused, and not necessarily his or her profession, is decisive in determining whether or not a communication is admissible*
[para. 14 (*a*) (iii)]

The Committee laid down this principle when considering a communication concerning an alleged victim whose profession did not, on the face of it, have any link with UNESCO's fields of competence (the case, for example, of a manual worker who had published articles). It is by virtue of this principle that the Committee asks the government concerned for further information about the grounds on which the alleged victim has been convicted or in order to establish whether the activities of which he or she was accused included incitement to violence.

5. *Rights that do not* per se *come within UNESCO's fields of competence*
[para. 14 (*a*) (iii)]

(*a*) Right of movement: Though this right, which is a fundamental human right, does not *per se* come within UNESCO's fields of competence, it might nevertheless do so when its exercise is linked to activities that do come within those fields, as for example going abroad in order to study, teach or engage in research. With regard to problems affecting the movement of scientists and other categories of persons within its fields of competence, the Committee considered at [the] 155th session [of the Executive Board] that, while it could not remain indifferent to such problems, UNESCO was not the appropriate forum for examining communications concerning the granting of visas by a government to citizens of a foreign country which was a matter pertaining to national sovereignty.

(*b*) Right to emigrate: The Committee has decided that this right does not *per se* come within UNESCO's fields of competence. The admissibility of a communication concerning this right should be determined on the basis of other criteria, i.e. the profession of the alleged victim, and in the light of additional information provided by the government concerned and by the author of the communication.

(*c*) Right to freedom of association: On one occasion, the Committee decided that a communication that had been submitted to it did not come within its competence because it hinged on the exercise of the right to freedom of association *per se* and should consequently be declared inadmissible. It nevertheless requested the representative of the government concerned to inform the relevant authorities in his country of the humanitarian concerns voiced by some of its members.

(*d*) The problem of compensation for an alleged victim does not fall within UNESCO's competence.

6. *Prior selection of communications by the Secretariat*
[para. 14 (*a*) (iii)]

In principle, the Secretariat is not authorized to weed out communications except in cases specified by the Committee, namely:

(*a*) Allegations manifestly not within UNESCO's competence. At the 105th session [of the Executive Board], the Committee decided to allow the Director-General to "proceed with a preliminary analysis of communications in order to exclude those which manifestly do not relate to the competence of UNESCO".

[para. 14 (*a*) (v)]

(*b*) Allegations manifestly ill-founded or whose authors are mentally unbalanced. The Committee decided to authorize the Secretariat "not to deal with communications whose authors are mentally unbalanced or which are manifestly ill-founded". However, in 1996 the Committee reasserted the principle that, when in doubt, the Secretariat must inform the Chairperson of the Committee, who decides whether the communication should be transmitted to the Committee.

In addition, some communications submitted to the Committee for consideration contain, in part, material not concerning UNESCO's fields of competence. Since it is "free to judge certain parts of a communication inadmissible while accepting other parts", the Committee has had occasion to ask the Secretariat to review such communications in order to eliminate from them allegations not concerning human rights within the Organization's competence.

Annex IV

7. *Emergency: derogation from certain human rights in accordance with Article 4 of the International Covenant on Civil and Political Rights*
[para. 14 (*a*) (iv)]

The Committee has recognized that, in accordance with Article 4 of the International Covenant on Civil and Political Rights, a state may, in time of public emergency, derogate from certain human rights to the extent strictly required by the exigencies of the situation. Consequently, it is not required to consider communications relating to such situations.

8. *When there is doubt within the Committee regarding the condition laid down in paragraph 14 (a) (v) of 104 EX/Decision 3.3 (a communication must not be manifestly ill-founded and must contain relevant evidence), the Committee asks the Secretariat to transmit the information provided by the government concerned to the author*
[para. 14 (*a*) (v)]

It should be made clear in this connection that the information supplied by the government concerned is transmitted to the author in summary form only after the Committee has taken cognizance of it. The Secretariat is thus not empowered to transmit that information upon receiving it. The Committee has also had occasion to ask the Secretariat to transmit to the author a record of its discussions concerning the communication in extenso, as contained in its report.

9. *When a communication contains material calling into question the foundations of a Member State it is declared inadmissible*
[para. 14 (*a*) (vi)]

This concerns cases where, for example, the communication contains slanderous and offensive attacks against the social structure, constitution and legislation of a state. As submitted, the communication cannot be considered, it being understood that the author of the communication might subsequently submit an amended communication not calling into question the foundations of a Member State.

10. *The Committee concerns itself only with actual and not potential violations of human rights*
[para. 14 (*a*) (vi)]

A communication that concerns only a potential violation of human rights and not an actual violation is declared inadmissible. The Committee cannot presume in advance that a human rights violation might occur (e.g. case of a person living abroad who wanted to go back to his country but feared that criminal proceedings would be instituted against him on his return, when it could not be known whether the authorities concerned would indeed prosecute him if he returned).

11. *It is the allegations contained in the communication form that must not be based exclusively on media reports*
[para. 14 (*a*) (viii)]

12. *A communication must be submitted within a reasonable time limit following the facts which constitute its subject-matter or within a reasonable time limit after the facts have become known*
[para. 14 (*a*) (viii)]

A communication that has not been submitted within a reasonable time limit following the facts which constitute its subject-matter or after the facts have become known is declared inadmissible.

13. *The author of a communication must indicate whether steps have been taken to exhaust all possible domestic remedies and what their outcome has been*
[para. 14 (*a*) (ix)]

Since the Committee is not a court of law, the author of a communication is not obliged to have exhausted domestic remedies, but to indicate whether steps have been taken to obtain them. The Committee has agreed that it should be flexible in this regard. Consequently, and contrary to the procedure applied by other authorities, a communication could therefore be admissible under the procedure established in 104 EX/Decision 3.3, even if domestic remedies have not been exhausted.

14. *Submission of a communication to the [Committee] or to another body in the United Nations system*
[para. 14 (*a*) (ix)]

At the 156th session of the Executive Board, most members of the Committee stressed the special character of UNESCO's procedure as compared with similar United Nations procedures, observing that those procedures were not incompatible but, rather, complementary. They did not wish to change the Committee's practice. The Committee specified that when a communication submitted to it for examination was being or had already been examined by another body in the United Nations system, the Secretariat would check with that other body that there was no unnecessary duplication or incompatibility, having due regard, in particular, for the Committee's humanitarian aims. Should there be any doubt, the Secretariat would submit the question to the Committee.

Annex IV

At the 171st session of the Executive Board, the Committee decided that contact would be made with other international organizations, in particular when they were dealing with the same cases, so as to obtain additional information.

15. *A communication considered to be settled may be struck by the Committee from its list, subject to the Secretariat receiving confirmation of the reason why the communication has been considered to be settled (e.g. confirmation that the alleged victim has indeed been authorized to return to his or her country)*
[para. 14 (*a*) (x)]

The Committee stated when adopting this decision that if such confirmation did not reach the Secretariat by the next session, the communication would then be placed on the agenda of the next session of the Committee.

16. *Communication struck from the list* ipso facto *in the event of there being no reply from its author*
[para. 14 (*a*) (x)]

In cases where the author of the communication does not reply to requests for further information made by the Committee, the practice of the Committee is to grant a period of grace and to strike the communication from its list only if the author still fails to reply. This rule is valid even in cases where the government concerned has never produced any comments. The Committee has also had occasion to request the Secretariat to notify the author of a communication that, should he fail to seek administrative or judicial redress in the country concerned, notwithstanding having been informed of this by the Committee, it would strike the communication from its list *ipso facto* at its next session.

II. PROCEDURES

17. *Time limits for the transmission of an additional communication or additional information to the governments concerned*
[para. 14 (*b*) (iii)]

The Committee has taken the view that any further communication or additional information transmitted by the author of a communication to the Secretariat should reach the government concerned at least one month before the Committee's session. Otherwise, the representative of the government concerned should be able to ask for the communication not to be considered until the following session, to enable the relevant authorities in his or her country to determine their position in the light of this new or additional information. At the 156th session of the Executive Board, the Committee having decided that any government concerned would in future be required to make its position known within a time limit of three months after the Secretariat had transmitted a new communication to it, the time limit for transmission of the communication is modified.

18. *Agreement of the Committee to a request to consider a communication submitted urgently on account of the seriousness of the matter*
[para. 14 (*b*) (iv)]

The Committee has made it clear in this connection that prior submission of the form is by no means a condition of admissibility. The sole purpose of the form is to make it easier for the author of the communication to set out his or her complaints and for the Committee to examine the communication.

19. *Need to preserve the confidential character of communications*
[para. 14 (*c*)]

Confidentiality is considered to be essential for the success of the Committee's action. In cases where this principle is not observed by the author of the communication, it is up to the Committee to decide whether such indiscretion constitutes an abuse of the right to submit communications under the terms of paragraph 14 (*a*) (vi) of 104 EX/Decision 3.3 and then to strike the communication from its list, as a kind of penalty. In practice, communications whose authors had clearly breached the confidential character of the procedure have been declared inadmissible (the Committee has sometimes instructed the Secretariat to remind the author of the need to preserve the confidential character of the Committee's work).

20. *A communication can only be declared admissible by express decision of the Committee*
[para. 14 (*d*)]

It is important to distinguish decisions on the "admissibility" of a communication, which are entirely the responsibility of the Committee, from those on the "transmissibility" of a complaint which, at the request of the Committee, are left to the discretion of the Secretariat. (See No. 6 above.)

21. *Decision on the admissibility of a communication*

At the 156th session of the Executive Board, the Committee stressed that *in declaring a communication admissible it was in no way implying any condemnation of the government concerned.* It was simply recognizing that the communication met the admissibility criteria set out in 104 EX/Decision 3.3 and that it might be examined as to its substance.

Annex IV

The Committee also agreed that, in order to speed up its decision-making on the admissibility of communications:

> any government concerned by a communication was required to make its position known within a time limit of three months after the Secretariat had transmitted a new communication to it, failing which the Committee would proceed without further delay to examine the admissibility of the communication;
>
> if the government concerned did not contest the admissibility of a communication, the [Committee] would decide on such admissibility at the first meeting devoted to the examination of the communication in question. If on the other hand the government concerned did contest admissibility, the Committee would obviously examine the arguments put forward by the government concerned and would endeavour to take a decision at the first meeting.

At the 171st session of the Executive Board, the Committee decided that more attention should be paid to the application of the criteria of admissibility of communications so as to ensure greater clarity and improve the work of the Committee in that field. To that end, when a communication is declared admissible, the Committee should specify, in the light of 104 EX/Decision 3.3, the criteria and conditions underlying the decision of admissibility.

22. *The Committee may express its concern regarding a particularly serious case and still declare the communication inadmissible*
[para. 14 (*d*)]

A communication may be struck from the Committee's list on the grounds that it does not satisfy the conditions for admissibility provided for in paragraph 14 (*a*) of the decision (for instance, it does not come within one of UNESCO's fields of competence). However, the Committee can declare a communication inadmissible and at the same time express its strong concern about the seriousness of the human rights violation it refers to.

23. *Cooperation of the government concerned*
[para. 14 (*e*)]

It is a constant rule of the Committee to invite the governments concerned to send representatives to the Committee, and they are always allowed to speak so that they can provide all the clarifications they consider appropriate. Even though the presence of a representative is not obligatory, the Committee has always considered it desirable that "solutions to human rights problems be sought through dialogue with the governments concerned". The Committee has therefore constantly drawn the attention of the governments concerned to the importance it attached to the presence of a representative.

Lack of cooperation from the government concerned has often prompted the Committee to request the Chairperson of the Committee or the Director-General to take steps to obtain the attendance of a government representative or at least a letter.

On one occasion, having noted for the third time that the government concerned by a communication had not replied or sent a representative, the Committee declared the communication to be admissible, after stressing that the procedure did not expressly require that government's attendance. It stated, however, that it should not be inferred from this that, in future, other communications would be automatically admitted when the government concerned did not send a representative. There has also been a case of the Committee considering submitting an individual report to the Executive Board so as to obtain the cooperation of the government concerned. At the 157th session, given the silence of the authorities, which on two occasions had not seen fit to reply to the letters which, at the Committee's request, the Director-General had addressed to the President of the Republic and to the Ambassador, Permanent Delegate of a country concerned, and failing any additional information supplied at the session by the representatives of the government concerned, the Executive Board, on the Committee's proposal, examined the communication in question at a private meeting, inviting the representative of the government concerned, in accordance with Rule 30, paragraph 3, of its Rules of Procedure.

24. *Members of the Committee who represent the states concerned by a communication should not be present during the private discussions leading to a decision or to recommendations concerning that communication*
[para. 14 (*e*)]

This principle was clearly established at the 140th session. The concern is to "ensure equal treatment of all states, recognizing the principle that states cannot be both judges and judged at the same time, assisting decision-making by consensus and maintaining confidentiality".

25. *The Committee may defer consideration of a communication until it receives additional information regarding it*
[para. 14 (*h*)]

A communication may be kept on the Committee's agenda and consideration of it suspended until such time as a national court reaches a decision.

Annex IV

The Committee may request information on a communication from other United Nations bodies, and from bodies such as the International Committee of the Red Cross or the Inter-American Commission on Human Rights.

On various occasions the Committee has found itself unable to continue consideration of a communication because it has not obtained sufficient information. In such cases, the Committee has decided to put the communication "on hold", that is, to suspend consideration of it whilst maintaining it on its list, it being understood that it would be put before the Committee again if new information were provided.

26. *Efforts to find a friendly solution*
[para. 14 (*k*)]

With the aim of seeking a humanitarian solution, on a friendly basis, to a case brought to its attention, the Committee has decided on several occasions to invite the Director-General, the Chairperson of the Committee or the Chairperson of the Executive Board to use their good offices, to consult or approach the governments concerned with appeals for clemency or to make contact with them with a view to achieving the desired result. The Committee has twice decided to send a mission of good offices, with the agreement of the governments concerned.

27. *The Committee is vested with discretionary powers for the examination of a communication*
[para. 14 (*k*)]

The Committee has had occasion to recall this basic principle. Accordingly, when acceding to the request of one government to postpone examination of a communication until its next session, the Committee specified that that decision did not constitute a precedent, reserving the right to examine communications whether or not the governments concerned were represented.

28. *Agreement of the Committee to the request to withdraw a communication made by its author*
[para. 14 (*k*)]

The Committee has had occasion to agree to withdraw a communication at the request of its author. It stressed, however, that this could not serve as a precedent for automatically granting such requests. The Committee reserves the right to check that the author has not come under any pressure. In such cases, the withdrawal must be regarded as a friendly solution within the meaning of paragraph 14 (*k*) of 104 EX/ Decision 3.3.

29. *Fresh allegations justify the re-examination of a communication declared inadmissible*

The Committee's decisions, in particular those declaring a communication inadmissible, are final. Nevertheless, the Committee does not refuse to re-examine a communication previously declared inadmissible if new facts relating to it are brought to its notice. In that event, the Secretariat must ask the author to fill out a new form.

30. *Changes in the circumstances under which a communication had been submitted*

If a number of circumstances that were relevant when the communication was submitted have changed in the meantime, the Committee has decided to suspend consideration of the communication in its present formulation.

31. *The Committee strikes from its list cases of alleged violations of human rights concerning persons whose death has been proved, in view of the fact that its intervention could have no result*

32. *A government is normally responsible for the safety of its citizens and of all those under its jurisdiction*

During the examination of communications relating to a period of disturbance in which the government concerned was not able to control a situation, the question has arisen of whether the alleged violations could be imputed to the government concerned. The Committee has not been unconcerned by such situations and has considered that, "without taking any decision having the force of a rule (...), a government is normally responsible for the safety of its citizens and of all those under its jurisdiction".

33. *The Committee is the only subsidiary body of the Executive Board empowered to take its own decisions (the others restricting themselves to making recommendations to the Board)*
[para. 16]

Although the Executive Board can modify neither the decisions nor the narrative part of the Committee's report, Members of the Board can nevertheless comment on the Committee's report and ensure that the position of the representatives of the governments concerned is reflected accurately in the minutes of the Board session. The Executive Board takes note and may or may not endorse the decisions contained in the Committee's report, regardless of whether or not they are intended to have effect. If it disagrees with a decision by the Committee it can request it to reconsider the case.

Annex IV

34. *Questions*
[paras. 10 (*b*), 17 and 18]

The Committee considered that:

(*a*) the sources of information for the purpose of deciding whether to describe a communication as a "question" would be the individual communications received by the Organization and such relevant information as the Director-General might provide, either at the request of the Committee or on his own initiative;

(*b*) the decision as to the designation of a communication as a "question" would be taken by the Committee only after a full examination of the substance of the communication, and then only if it was not possible to reach the friendly solution contemplated in paragraph 14 (*k*) of 104 EX/Decision 3.3;

(*c*) it was for the Executive Board to decide whether or not to examine in public meetings any "question" forwarded to it by the Committee, but that in any event the Committee should be extremely cautious before deciding to forward a matter as a "question" to the Board and should do so only as a last resort.

Consequently, the Committee has always stressed the need to submit communications referring by name to individual cases.

35. *Statistics on the procedure*

At the 171st session of the Executive Board, the Committee decided, while recalling the principle of confidentiality which dominated the entire 104 EX/Decision 3.3 procedure, that the private documents of the Committee should be published or made accessible to the public after a period of 20 years, as provided for by Rule 29, paragraph 4, of the Rules of Procedure of the Executive Board, in order to give a higher profile to the Committee's achievements.

ANNEX V

TABLES OF COMMUNICATIONS

(*a*) Communications examined under the 104 EX/Decision 3.3 Procedure of the Executive Board filed 1978-1981 (States concerned)

Argentina	No. 11/78	*Maria Ernestina Giachetti*	Inadmissible
	No. 26/78	*Elsa Alicia Nocent*	Disappearance
	No. 31/78	*César Antonio Minué*	Inadmissible
	No. 33/78	*Manuel Alberto Santamaria*	Suspended
	No. 49/78	*Ricardo Rodriguez Anido*	
		Ricardo Manuel Rodriguez Anido	Suspended
	No. 50/78	*Juan Carlos Aguirre*	Inadmissible
	No. 51/78	*Fernando de Hallgarten*	Inadmissible
	No. 53/78	*Abel Héctor Mateu*	Inadmissible
	No. 60/78	*Mario César Clar and*	
		Sergio Andrés Clar	Inadmissible
	No. 63/78	*Alejandro Enrique Gutiérrez Penette*	Disappearance
	No. 68/78	*Luis Alberto Verdú Espinosa*	Inadmissible
	No. 69/78	*Néstor Hugo Cherry*	Inadmissible
	No. 71/78	*Daniel Gorosito*	Struck off
	No. 74/78	*Perla Elizabeth Schneider*	Disappearance
	No. 75/78	*José Carlos Prat-Salvucci*	Disappearance
	No. 79/78	*Julia Natividad Huarque*	Disappearance
	No. 80/78	*Juan José Laso*	Inadmissible
	No. 81/78	*Guillermo Horacio White*	Inadmissible
	No. 82/78	*Maria Cristina Mattioli de Totterau*	Inadmissible
	No. 83/78	*Rodolfo Omar Rodriguez Echavarria*	Inadmissible
	No. 84/78	*Oscar Rubén Manzur*	Inadmissible
	No. 96/79	*Maria Inés Muchiutti*	Disappearance
	No. 97/79	*Analia Egle Maria Minetti*	Disappearance
	No. 98/79	*Mariano Alejandro Ramiro Martinez*	Inadmissible
	No. 104/79	*Violation of human rights in the sectors of education, science, culture and information*	
		Violations of human rights in the sectors of education, science, culture and information	
		Violation of human rights in the sectors of education, science, culture and information	Inadmissible/ Disappearance/ Dismissed

Annex V

Argentina	No. 105/79	*Julia Angélica Brocca de Herrero*	Suspended
	No. 106/79	*Gustavo Marcelo Juárez and María Gabriela Juárez*	Disappearance
	No. 111/79	*Héctor Alberto González*	Inadmissible
	No. 112/79	*Marcelo E. Vensentini and Rosalba Vensentini*	Inadmissible
	No. 113/79	*Federico Eduardo Álvarez Rojas*	Disappearance
	No. 125/79	*Juan Carlos Suárez*	Disappearance
	No. 127/79	*María Cristina García Suárez*	Inadmissible
	No. 129/79	*Oscar Ernesto Cocca Astrada*	Struck off
	No. 137/79	*Jorge Víctor Sznaider*	Disappearance
	No. 143/79	*Jacinto Rubén Montenegro*	Inadmissible
	No. 154/79	*Anatole Boris Julien Grisona and Eva Lucia Julien Grisona*	Inadmissible
	No. 176/79	*Klaus Zieschank*	Inadmissible
	No. 177/79	*Juan Ángel Nughes*	Disappearance
	No. 178/79	*Norberto Rey Ortalda*	Suspended
	No. 179/79	*Betina Tarnopolsky*	Disappearance
	No. 180/79	*Fausto Augusto Carillo Rodríguez*	Inadmissible
	No. 181/79	*Hugo Tarnopolsky*	Disappearance
	No. 182/79	*Blanca Edith Edelberg de Tarnopolsky*	Disappearance
	No. 190/80	*Sara Elba Grande*	Disappearance
	No. 211/80	*Carlos Alberto Pérez and Mirta Silber de Pérez*	Inadmissible
	No. 220/80	*Disappearance of scientists and doctors in Argentina*	Disappearance
	No. 224/80	*Graciela Esther Arabaolasa*	Inadmissible
	No. 241/80	*Antonio Satutto and María Cristina Ortiz*	Inadmissible
	No. 266/80	*Elba Aurora Martínez de Larrea*	Inadmissible
	No. 270/80	*Juan Carlos Higa*	Disappearance
	No. 289/80	*Juan Takara*	Disappearance
	No. 291/80	*Claudio Nicolás Grandi* et al.	Disappearance
	No. 293/80	*Isabel Hernando de Pelloli*	Inadmissible
	No. 319/81	*Antonio Maidana*	Struck off
	No. 369/81	*Alberto Horacio Giusti*	Disappearance
	No. 372/81	*Antonio Satutto*	Disappearance
	No. 417/81	*Eduardo Federico Llosa*	Inadmissible
	No. 422/81	*Mario Jaime Zaraceansky*	Settled
Bolivia	No. 322/81	*Violations of human rights in Bolivia following the events of 17 July 1980 Violations of human rights in Bolivia Alleged violations of human rights in Bolivia*	Dismissed
	No. 359/81	*Jorge Baldibieso* et al. *Violations of human rights in Bolivia*	

Annex V

Bolivia		*Alleged violations of human rights in Bolivia*	Dismissed
	No. 397/81	*Violation of human rights in Bolivia*	
		Violations of human rights in Bolivia	
		Alleged violations of human rights in Bolivia	Dismissed
	No. 407/81	*Jorge Baldibieso* et al.	
		Violations of human rights in Bolivia	
		Alleged violations of human rights in Bolivia	Dismissed
Chile	No. 25/78	*The situation of human rights in Chile in the fields of education, science, culture and information*	
		Situation of human rights in Chile in the fields of education, science, culture and information	
		Situation of human rights in Chile in the spheres of education, science, culture and communication	Dismissed
	No. 54/78	*Arturo Montes Larrain*	Settled
	No. 56/78	*Jorge Triviño Puelpan*	Settled
	No. 57/78	*Luis Pueller*	Settled
	No. 59/78	*Gustavo Adolfo Quintana Muñoz*	Settled
	No. 64/78	*Juan Patricio Cleary Zambón*	Settled
	No. 66/78	*Olga Victoria Morris Barrios*	Inadmissible
	No. 67/78	*Jorge Orlando Inostrosa Béjares and Rodrigo Mellado*	Inadmissible
	No. 72/78	*Elwin Ayamante*	
		Elwin Ayamante Bórquez	Settled
	No. 134/79	*Abelardo Castro Hidalgo*	Settled
	No. 154/79	*Anatole Boris Julien Grisona and Eva Lucia Julien Grisona*	Inadmissible
	No. 197/80	*Ernesto Ottone Fernández*	Inadmissible
	No. 267/80	*Pedro Segundo Ahumada Pizarro*	Inadmissible
	No. 273/80	*Eduardo Novoa Monreal*	Inadmissible
	No. 321/81	*Víctor Xavier Tiznado Rosas*	Settled
	No. 323/81	*Gracia Barrios Rivadeneira*	Settled
	No. 324/81	*José Balmes Parramón*	Settled
	No. 325/81	*Marco Antonio Peña Pérez*	Settled
	No. 327/81	*Concepción Balmes*	Settled
	No. 348/81	*Jorge Domingo Martínez Quezada and Irma del Carmen Flores Fajardo*	Inadmissible
	No. 356/81	*Violeta Isabel Cereceda Parra*	Struck off
	No. 396/81	*Jaime Fernando Rovira Soto*	Inadmissible

Annex V

Chile	No. 403/81	*Gloria Pinto de Manriquez*	Settled
	No. 404/81	*Hugo Muñoz*	Inadmissible
Colombia	No. 218/80	*Alba Nelda González Sousa*	Inadmissible
Cuba	No. 290/80	*Armando Valladares Pérez*	Inadmissible
	No. 398/81	*Armando Valladares*	Inadmissible
Czechoslovakia	No. 150/79	*Václav Havel and Otta Bednářová*	
		Václav Havel	Settled
	No. 354/81	*Karel Soukup*	Inadmissible
	No. 399/81	*Rudolf Battěk*	Inadmissible
Denmark	No. 144/79	*Kai Mogens H. Lång*	Inadmissible
	No. 196/80	*Kai Mogens H. Lång*	Inadmissible
Egypt	No. 371/81	*Ahmed Fouad Negm*	Inadmissible
	No. 386/81	*Ahmed Fouad Negm*	Inadmissible
El Salvador	No. 184/79	*Jaime Bairés*	Struck off
	No. 276/80	*Miguel Ángel García* et al.	
		Leonel Menéndez Quiroga	
		Leonel Menéndez Quiroga and others	Struck off
	No. 283/80	*Arrest and persecution of teachers in El Salvador*	Struck off
	No. 306/80	*Arrest and persecution of teachers in El Salvador*	Struck off
	No. 390/81	*Edgar Mauricio Vellejo*	Struck off
France	No. 175/79	*Lorella Sini*	Settled
	No. 264/80	*Zien Al Smail*	Inadmissible
	No. 274/80	*Simon Malley*	Inadmissible
German Democratic Republic	No. 205/80	*Michael Haugk*	Inadmissible
Germany, Federal Republic of	No. 65/78	*Karl Wilhelm Ströder*	Inadmissible
Guatemala	No. 193/80	*Teachers and students in Guatemala*	Inadmissible
	No. 317/81	*Alaíde Foppa*	Struck off
	No. 347/81	*Alaíde Foppa*	Struck off
Guinea	No. 314/80	*Barry Abdoulaye* et al.	Inadmissible
Guyana	No. 173/79	*Janet Jagan*	Dismissed

India	No. 305/80	*Govind Prasad*	Inadmissible
Indonesia	No. 155/79	*Irzadi Mirwan*	Settled
Israel	No. 12/78	*Abdul Jawad Saleh - Palestinian Human Rights Committee for the Defence of War and Political Prisoners Violations of human rights in the fields of education, science, culture and information in the Arab territories occupied by Israel Violations of human rights in the fields of education, science, culture and information in the occupied territories*	Suspended
	No. 233/80	*Ziad Abu Eain*	Inadmissible
	No. 316/80	*Tareq Ya'qoub Ashomali*	Settled
Italy	No. 406/81	*Luciano Ferrari Bravo*	Inadmissible
Korea, Republic of	No. 269/80	*Mong Yong Lee*	Inadmissible
	No. 279/80	*Kim Chi ha* et al.	Inadmissible
Lao People's Dem. Republic	No. 145/79	*Khamkhing Souvanlasy*	Settled
Morocco	No. 126/79	*Eddimaoui Lahbib*	Inadmissible
Nicaragua	No. 133/79	*Vilma Núñez de Escorcia*	Settled
Paraguay	No. 109/79	*Carmen Lara Castro*	Inadmissible
	No. 110/79	*Virgilio Barreiro*	Settled
	No. 319/81	*Antonio Maidana*	Struck off
	No. 361/81	*Andrés Centurión* et al.	Inadmissible
Poland	No. 124/79	*Zygmunt Elbiński*	Inadmissible
	No. 189/80	*Deaf-mute children in Poland*	Inadmissible
Portugal	No. 429/81	*Mário Jorge de Graça Estêvão*	Settled
Romania	No. 2/78	*Transylvanian populations in Romania*	Inadmissible
	No. 117/79	*A. Dan Vilcu*	Inadmissible
	No. 123/79	*Djoka Stojanović*	Inadmissible
	No. 221/80	*Remus Radina*	Settled
	No. 223/80	*The violation of human rights of the Hungarian minority in Romania*	Inadmissible
	No. 247/80	*Gheorghe Calciu-Dumitreasa*	Inadmissible
	No. 375/81	*Constantin Munteanu*	Settled

Annex V

Romania	No. 378/81	*Religious persecution in Romania*	Inadmissible/ Settled
Senegal	No. 312/80	*Repression against teachers, active members of the Syndicat unique et démocratique des enseignants du Sénégal*	Settled
Spain	No. 41/78	*José Candeas Garcia*	Inadmissible
	No. 200/80	*Emilio Mansera Conde*	Inadmissible
Switzerland	No. 38/78	*Ved Kalra*	Inadmissible
Ukrainian SSR	No. 21/78	*Yuri Orlov* et al.	Inadmissible
	No. 90/79	*Vadime Delaunay* et al.	Inadmissible
Union of Soviet Socialist Republics	No. 21/78	*Yuri Orlov* et al.	Inadmissible
	No. 90/79	*Vadime Delaunay* et al.	Inadmissible
	No. 132/79	*Georgi Mikhailov*	Inadmissible
	No. 149/79	*Mstislav Rostropovich and Galina Vishnevskaya*	Withdrawn
	No. 191/80	*Situation of religious activities in the USSR*	Inadmissible
	No. 195/80	*Andrei Sakharov*	Suspended
	No. 209/80	*Yosif Z. Begun*	Settled
	No. 242/80	*Victor Brailovski* et al.	Suspended
	No. 303/80	*Vladimir Feltsman and Victor Suslin*	Inadmissible/
		Victor Suslin	Struck off
	No. 328/81	*Georgij Danilovich Parkhomenko*	Inadmissible
	No. 334/81	*Mykola Danilovich Rudenko*	Inadmissible
	No. 342/81	*Iosef Samsonovich Irlin*	Inadmissible
	No. 345/81	*Yosif Ziselevich Begun*	Inadmissible
	No. 346/81	*Victor Brailovski* *Victor Brailovski* et al. *Victor Brailovski*	Settled
	No. 352/81	*Vasyl Semenovich Stus*	Suspended
	No. 353/81	*Yuli Kosharovsky*	Inadmissible
	No. 379/81	*Vladimir Feltsman*	Inadmissible
	No. 385/81	*Anatoly Koryagin*	Transferred
	No. 409/81	*Anatoly Shcharansky*	Inadmissible
	No. 418/81	*Victor Brailovski* *Victor Brailovski* et al.	Suspended
	No. 426/81	*Vladimir Borisov*	Settled
United Kingdom	No. 37/78	*Children of nomadic Gypsies*	Settled
	No. 309/80	*Dominic de Graft Aidoo*	Inadmissible

Annex V

United States of America	No. 115/79	*Vachel Lindsay*	Inadmissible
	No. 233/80	*Ziad Abu Eain*	Inadmissible
Uruguay	No. 10/78	*Armando Germinal González Ferrando*	Inadmissible
	No. 47/78	*Eduardo Anselmo Viera*	
		The newspaper "El Popular"	Inadmissible
	No. 103/79	*José Luis Massera*	Settled
	No. 108/79	*Hiber Conteris*	Struck off
	No. 146/79	*Alfonso Avelino Fernández Cabrelli*	Settled
	No. 154/79	*Anatole Boris Julien Grisona and*	
		Eva Lucia Julien Grisona	Inadmissible
	No. 169/79	*Missing children*	Inadmissible
	No. 218/80	*Alba Nelda González Sousa*	Inadmissible
	No. 222/80	*Elena Beatriz Vasilskis Castro*	Inadmissible
	No. 281/80	*Julio Castro*	Struck off
	No. 370/81	*José Luis Massera*	Settled
	No. 381/81	*Raúl Noel Martínez Machado*	Inadmissible
Yugoslavia	No. 92/79	*Milovan Djilas*	Inadmissible
	No. 94/79	*Mihajlo Mihajlov*	Inadmissible
	No. 95/79	*Nikola Novaković*	Inadmissible
	No. 123/79	*Djoka Stojanović*	Inadmissible
	No. 203/80	*Vladimir Bonačić* et al.	Inadmissible
	No. 210/80	*Kadri Osmani*	Inadmissible
	No. 238/80	*Mihajlo Mihajlov*	Inadmissible
	No. 261/80	*Zlatko Matković*	Inadmissible
	No. 277/80	*Vladimir Bonačić* et al.	Inadmissible
	No. 307/80	*Tomislav Krsmanović*	Inadmissible
	No. 392/81	*Milovan Djilas*	
		Milovan Djilas et al.	
		Milovan Djilas	Settled
	No. 421/81	*Vlado Gotovac*	
		Milovan Djilas et al.	Inadmissible
	No. 425/81	*Sabedin Haljiti* et al.	Settled/
		Milovan Djilas et al.	Inadmissible
Zaire	No. 271/80	*Taba and Kifuema*	Inadmissible

Annex V

(*b*) Communications examined under the 104 EX/Decision 3.3 Procedure of the Executive Board filed 1978-1981 (Cases)

Abdul Jawad Saleh - Palestinian Human Rights Committee for the Defence of War and Political Prisoners	*Israel*	No. 12/78
Abelardo Castro Hidalgo	*Chile*	No. 134/79
Abel Héctor Mateu	*Argentina*	No. 53/78
A. Dan Vilcu	*Romania*	No. 117/79
Adem Demaçi	*Yugoslavia*	No. 425/81
Ahmed Fouad Negm	*Egypt*	No. 371/81
Ahmed Fouad Negm	*Egypt*	No. 386/81
Alaíde Foppa	*Guatemala*	No. 317/81
Alaíde Foppa	*Guatemala*	No. 347/81
Alba Nelda González Sousa	*Colombia and Uruguay*	No. 218/80
Alberto Horacio Giusti	*Argentina*	No. 369/81
Alejandro Enrique Gutiérrez Penette	*Argentina*	No. 63/78
Alexander Ginsburg	*Union of Soviet Socialist Republics and Ukrainian SSR*	No. 21/78
Alexandre Lerner	*Union of Soviet Socialist Republics*	No. 242/80
Alexis Tikhy	*Union of Soviet Socialist Republics and Ukrainian SSR*	No. 21/78
Alfonso Avelino Fernández Cabrelli	*Uruguay*	No. 146/79
Alleged violations of human rights in Bolivia	*Bolivia*	No. 322/81
Alleged violations of human rights in Bolivia	*Bolivia*	No. 359/81
Alleged violations of human rights in Bolivia	*Bolivia*	No. 397/81
Alleged violations of human rights in Bolivia	*Bolivia*	No. 407/81
Analía Egle María Minetti	*Argentina*	No. 97/79
Anatole Boris Julien Grisona	*Argentina, Chile and Uruguay*	No. 154/79
Anatoly Koryagin	*Union of Soviet Socialist Republics*	No. 385/81
Anatoly Shcharansky	*Union of Soviet Socialist Republics*	No. 409/81
Andrei Sakharov	*Union of Soviet Socialist Republics*	No. 195/80
Andrés Centurión	*Paraguay*	No. 361/81
Ángel Erasmo Figueroa	*El Salvador*	No. 276/80
Antonio Maidana	*Argentina and Paraguay Paraguay*	No. 319/81
Antonio Satutto	*Argentina*	No. 241/80
Antonio Satutto	*Argentina*	No. 372/81
Armando Germinal González Ferrando	*Uruguay*	No. 10/78
Armando Valladares	*Cuba*	No. 398/81
Armando Valladares Pérez	*Cuba*	No. 290/80

Annex V

Arrest and persecution of teachers in El Salvador	*El Salvador*	No. 283/80
Arrest and persecution of teachers in El Salvador	*El Salvador*	No. 306/80
Arturo Montes Larrain	*Chile*	No. 54/78
Barry Abdoulaye	*Guinea*	No. 314/80
Barry Baba	*Guinea*	No. 314/80
Betina Tarnopolsky	*Argentina*	No. 179/79
Blanca Edith Edelberg de Tarnopolsky	*Argentina*	No. 182/79
Camara Balla	*Guinea*	No. 314/80
Carlos Alberto Pérez	*Argentina*	No. 211/80
Carlos Ernesto Alfaro Rodríguez	*El Salvador*	No. 276/80
Carmen Lara Castro	*Paraguay*	No. 109/79
Centro de Información y de Documentación sobre Bolivia	*Bolivia*	No. 407/81
César Antonio Minué	*Argentina*	No. 31/78
Chang Ki pyo	*Republic of Korea*	No. 279/80
Children of nomadic Gypsies	*United Kingdom*	No. 37/78
Claudio Nicolás Grandi	*Argentina*	No. 291/80
Concepción Balmes	*Chile*	No. 327/81
Constantin Munteanu	*Romania*	No. 375/81
Daniel Gorosito	*Argentina*	No. 71/78
Deaf-mute children in Poland	*Poland*	No. 189/80
Disappearance of scientists and doctors in Argentina	*Argentina*	No. 220/80
Djoka Stojanović	*Romania and Yugoslavia*	No. 123/79
Dominic de Graft Aidoo	*United Kingdom*	No. 309/80
Dunja Donassy	*Yugoslavia*	No. 203/80
Dunja Donassy	*Yugoslavia*	No. 277/80
Eddimaoui Lahbib	*Morocco*	No. 126/79
Edgar Mauricio Vellejo	*El Salvador*	No. 390/81
Eduardo Anselmo Viera	*Uruguay*	No. 47/78
Eduardo Federico Llosa	*Argentina*	No. 417/81
Eduardo Novoa Monreal	*Chile*	No. 273/80
Elba Aurora Martínez de Larrea	*Argentina*	No. 266/80
Elba Eva Acuña de Sáez	*Argentina*	No. 291/80
Elena Beatriz Vasilskis Castro	*Uruguay*	No. 222/80
Elías Rafael Flores	*Bolivia*	No. 359/81
Elsa Alicia Nocent	*Argentina*	No. 26/78
Elwin Ayamante	*Chile*	No. 72/78
Elwin Ayamante Bórquez	*Chile*	No. 72/78
Emilio Mansera Conde	*Spain*	No. 200/80
Enrique Daniel Guillen	*Argentina*	No. 291/80
Ernesto Ottone Fernández	*Chile*	No. 197/80
Eva Lucia Julien Grisona	*Argentina, Chile and Uruguay*	No. 154/79
Fausto Augusto Carillo Rodríguez	*Argentina*	No. 180/79
Federico Eduardo Álvarez Rojas	*Argentina*	No. 113/79

Annex V

Fernando de Hallgarten	*Argentina*	No. 51/78
Franjo Tudjman	*Yugoslavia*	No. 425/81
Galina Vishnevskaya	*Union of Soviet Socialist Republics*	No. 149/79
Georgij Danilovich Parkhomenko	*Union of Soviet Socialist Republics*	No. 328/81
Georgi Mikhailov	*Union of Soviet Socialist Republics*	No. 132/79
Gheorghe Calciu-Dumitreasa	*Romania*	No. 247/80
Gloria Pinto de Manríquez	*Chile*	No. 403/81
Gonzalo Barrón	*Bolivia*	No. 359/81
Gonzalo Barrón	*Bolivia*	No. 407/81
Govind Prasad	*India*	No. 305/80
Gracia Barrios Rivadeneira	*Chile*	No. 323/81
Graciela Esther Arabaolasa	*Argentina*	No. 224/80
Guillermo Horacio White	*Argentina*	No. 81/78
Gustavo Adolfo Quintana Muñoz	*Chile*	No. 59/78
Gustavo Marcelo Juárez	*Argentina*	No. 106/79
Ham suk hun	*Republic of Korea*	No. 279/80
Héctor Alberto González	*Argentina*	No. 111/79
Héctor Lemus Rosa	*El Salvador*	No. 276/80
Hiber Conteris	*Uruguay*	No. 108/79
Hugo Muñoz	*Chile*	No. 404/81
Hugo Tarnopolsky	*Argentina*	No. 181/79
Iosef Samsonovich Irlin	*Union of Soviet Socialist Republics*	No. 342/81
Irina Brailovski	*Union of Soviet Socialist Republics*	No. 242/80
Irma del Carmen Flores Fajardo	*Chile*	No. 348/81
Irzadi Mirwan	*Indonesia*	No. 155/79
Isabel Hernando de Pelloli	*Argentina*	No. 293/80
Jacinto Rubén Montenegro	*Argentina*	No. 143/79
Jaime Bairés	*El Salvador*	No. 184/79
Jaime Fernando Rovira Soto	*Chile*	No. 396/81
Janet Jagan	*Guyana*	No. 173/79
Jorge Baldibieso	*Bolivia*	No. 359/81
Jorge Baldibieso	*Bolivia*	No. 407/81
Jorge Domingo Martínez Quezada	*Chile*	No. 348/81
Jorge Orlando Inostrosa Béjares	*Chile*	No. 67/78
Jorge Triviño Puelpan	*Chile*	No. 56/78
Jorge Víctor Sznaider	*Argentina*	No. 137/79
José Balmes Parramón	*Chile*	No. 324/81
José Candeas García	*Spain*	No. 41/78
José Carlos Prat-Salvucci	*Argentina*	No. 75/78
José Luis Massera	*Uruguay*	No. 103/79
José Luis Massera	*Uruguay*	No. 370/81
José Luis Suárez	*Bolivia*	No. 359/81
José Luis Suárez	*Bolivia*	No. 407/81
Juan Ángel Nughes	*Argentina*	No. 177/79
Juan Carlos Aguirre	*Argentina*	No. 50/78
Juan Carlos Higa	*Argentina*	No. 270/80
Juan Carlos Suárez	*Argentina*	No. 125/79

Juan José Laso	*Argentina*	No. 80/78
Juan Patricio Cleary Zambón	*Chile*	No. 64/78
Juan Takara	*Argentina*	No. 289/80
Julia Angélica Brocca de Herrero	*Argentina*	No. 105/79
Julia Natividad Huarque	*Argentina*	No. 79/78
Julio Castro	*Uruguay*	No. 281/80
Julio Jorge Gudiño	*Argentina*	No. 291/80
Kadri Osmani	*Yugoslavia*	No. 210/80
Kai Mogens H. Lång	*Denmark*	No. 144/79
Kai Mogens H. Lång	*Denmark*	No. 196/80
Karel Soukup	*Czechoslovakia*	No. 354/81
Karl Wilhelm Ströder	*Federal Republic of Germany*	No. 65/78
Keita Kémoko	*Guinea*	No. 314/80
Keita Noumandian	*Guinea*	No. 314/80
Khamkhing Souvanlasy	*Lao People's Democratic Republic*	No. 145/79
Kifuema	*Zaire*	No. 271/80
Kim Chi ha	*Republic of Korea*	No. 279/80
Kim Dae Joong	*Republic of Korea*	No. 279/80
Klaus Zieschank	*Argentina*	No. 176/79
Lee Young hee	*Republic of Korea*	No. 279/80
Leonel Menéndez Quiroga	*El Salvador*	No. 276/80
Lorella Sini	*France*	No. 175/79
Luciano Centurión	*Paraguay*	No. 361/81
Luciano Ferrari Bravo	*Italy*	No. 406/81
Luis Alberto Verdú Espinosa	*Argentina*	No. 68/78
Luis Pueller	*Chile*	No. 57/78
Manuel Alberto Santamaria	*Argentina*	No. 33/78
Marcelo E. Vensentini	*Argentina*	No. 112/79
Marcelo Quiroga Santa Cruz	*Bolivia*	No. 359/81
Marcelo Quiroga Santa Cruz	*Bolivia*	No. 407/81
Marco Antonio Peña Pérez	*Chile*	No. 325/81
Margarita Erlich	*Argentina*	No. 291/80
Maria Claudia Falcone Méndez	*Argentina*	No. 291/80
Maria Cristina García Suárez	*Argentina*	No. 127/79
Maria Cristina Mattioli de Totterau	*Argentina*	No. 82/78
Maria Cristina Ortiz	*Argentina*	No. 241/80
Maria Ernestina Giachetti	*Argentina*	No. 11/78
Maria Gabriela Juárez	*Argentina*	No. 106/79
Maria Inés Muchiutti	*Argentina*	No. 96/79
Mariano Alejandro Ramiro Martinez	*Argentina*	No. 98/79
Mario César Clar	*Argentina*	No. 60/78
Mario Jaime Zaraceansky	*Argentina*	No. 422/81
Mário Jorge de Graça Estêvão	*Portugal*	No. 429/81
Marko Veselica	*Yugoslavia*	No. 425/81
Marof Achaar	*Guinea*	No. 314/80
Michael Haugk	*German Democratic Republic*	No. 205/80
Miguel Ángel Garcia	*El Salvador*	No. 276/80

Mihajlo Mihajlov	*Yugoslavia*	No. 94/79
Mihajlo Mihajlov	*Yugoslavia*	No. 238/80
Milovan Djilas	*Yugoslavia*	No. 92/79
Milovan Djilas	*Yugoslavia*	No. 392/81
Miroljub Cimerman	*Yugoslavia*	No. 203/80
Miroljub Cimerman	*Yugoslavia*	No. 277/80
Mirta Silber de Pérez	*Argentina*	No. 211/80
Missing children	*Uruguay*	No. 169/79
Mong Yong Lee	*Republic of Korea*	No. 269/80
Moon Ik hwan	*Republic of Korea*	No. 279/80
Mstislav Rostropovich	*Union of Soviet Socialist Republics*	No. 149/79
Mykola Danilovich Rudenko	*Union of Soviet Socialist Republics*	No. 334/81
Mykola Rudenko	*Union of Soviet Socialist Republics and Ukrainian SSR*	No. 21/78
Nahum Meinam	*Union of Soviet Socialist Republics*	No. 242/80
Néstor Hugo Cherry	*Argentina*	No. 69/78
Nikola Novaković	*Yugoslavia*	No. 95/79
Norberto Rey Ortalda	*Argentina*	No. 178/79
Olga Victoria Morris Barrios	*Chile*	No. 66/78
Oscar Ernesto Cocca Astrada	*Argentina*	No. 129/79
Oscar Rabine	*Union of Soviet Socialist Republics and Ukrainian SSR*	No. 90/79
Oscar Rubén Manzur	*Argentina*	No. 84/78
Otta Bednářová	*Czechoslovakia*	No. 150/79
Palestinian Human Rights Committee for the Defence of War and Political Prisoners	*Israel*	No. 12/78
Pedro Segundo Ahumada Pizarro	*Chile*	No. 267/80
Perla Elizabeth Schneider	*Argentina*	No. 74/78
Ramiro Velasco	*Bolivia*	No. 407/81
Raúl Noel Martínez Machado	*Uruguay*	No. 381/81
Religious persecution in Romania	*Romania*	No. 378/81
Remus Radina	*Romania*	No. 221/80
Repression against teachers, active members of the Syndicat unique et démocratique des enseignants du Sénégal	*Senegal*	No. 312/80
Ricardo Manuel Rodríguez Anido	*Argentina*	No. 49/78
Ricardo Navarro	*Bolivia*	No. 359/81
Ricardo Navarro	*Bolivia*	No. 407/81
Ricardo Rodríguez Anido	*Argentina*	No. 49/78
Rodolfo Omar Rodríguez Echavarría	*Argentina*	No. 83/78
Rodrigo Mellado	*Chile*	No. 67/78
Rosa Dalia Herrera	*Argentina*	No. 291/80
Rosalba Vensentini	*Argentina*	No. 112/79
Rudolf Battěk	*Czechoslovakia*	No. 399/81
Sabedin Haljiti	*Yugoslavia*	No. 425/81

Annex V

Sabit Rustemi	*Yugoslavia*	No. 425/81
Sara Elba Grande	*Argentina*	No. 190/80
Sergey Kovalev	*Union of Soviet Socialist Republics and Ukrainian SSR*	No. 21/78
Sergio Andrés Clar	*Argentina*	No. 60/78
Silvia Natalia Rivera	*Bolivia*	No. 359/81
Simon Malley	*France*	No. 274/80
Situation of human rights in Chile in the fields of education, science, culture and information	*Chile*	No. 25/78
Situation of human rights in Chile in the spheres of education, science, culture and communication	*Chile*	No. 25/78
Situation of religious activities in the USSR	*Union of Soviet Socialist Republics*	No. 191/80
Song Ki Sook	*Republic of Korea*	No. 279/80
Soumah Théodore	*Guinea*	No. 314/80
Sylla Fodé Saliou	*Guinea*	No. 314/80
Taba	*Zaire*	No. 271/80
Tareq Ya'qoub Ashomali	*Israel*	No. 316/80
Teachers and students in Guatemala	*Guatemala*	No. 193/80
The newspaper "El Popular"	*Uruguay*	No. 47/78
The situation of human rights in Chile in the fields of education, science, culture and information	*Chile*	No. 25/78
The violation of human rights of the Hungarian minority in Romania	*Romania*	No. 223/80
Tomislav Krsmanović	*Yugoslavia*	No. 307/80
Transylvanian populations in Romania	*Romania*	No. 2/78
Vachel Lindsay	*United States of America*	No. 115/79
Václav Havel	*Czechoslovakia*	No. 150/79
Vadime Delaunay	*Union of Soviet Socialist Republics and Ukrainian SSR*	No. 90/79
Vadime Netchaev	*Union of Soviet Socialist Republics and Ukrainian SSR*	No. 90/79
Vasyl Semenovich Stus	*Union of Soviet Socialist Republics*	No. 352/81
Ved Kalra	*Switzerland*	No. 38/78
Victoras Piatkus	*Union of Soviet Socialist Republics and Ukrainian SSR*	No. 21/78
Victor Brailovski	*Union of Soviet Socialist Republics*	No. 242/80
Victor Brailovski	*Union of Soviet Socialist Republics*	No. 346/81
Victor Brailovski	*Union of Soviet Socialist Republics*	No. 418/81
Victor Suslin	*Union of Soviet Socialist Republics*	No. 303/80
Víctor Xavier Tiznado Rosas	*Chile*	No. 321/81
Vidal Martínez	*Paraguay*	No. 361/81
Vilma Núñez de Escorcia	*Nicaragua*	No. 133/79
Violation of human rights in Bolivia	*Bolivia*	No. 397/81

Annex V

Violation of human rights in the sectors of education, science, culture and information	*Argentina*	No. 104/79
Violations of human rights in Bolivia	*Bolivia*	No. 322/81
Violations of human rights in Bolivia	*Bolivia*	No. 359/81
Violations of human rights in Bolivia	*Bolivia*	No. 397/81
Violations of human rights in Bolivia	*Bolivia*	No. 407/81
Violations of human rights in Bolivia following the events of 17 July 1980	*Bolivia*	No. 322/81
Violations of human rights in the fields of education, science, culture and information in the Arab territories occupied by Israel	*Israel*	No. 12/78
Violations of human rights in the fields of education, science, culture and information in the occupied territories	*Israel*	No. 12/78
Violations of human rights in the sectors of education, science, culture and information	*Argentina*	No. 104/79
Violeta Isabel Cereceda Parra	*Chile*	No. 356/81
Virgilio Barreiro	*Paraguay*	No. 110/79
Vjenceslav Čižek	*Yugoslavia*	No. 425/81
Vladimir Bonačič	*Yugoslavia*	No. 203/80
Vladimir Bonačič	*Yugoslavia*	No. 277/80
Vladimir Borisov	*Union of Soviet Socialist Republics*	No. 426/81
Vladimir Feltsman	*Union of Soviet Socialist Republics*	No. 303/80
Vladimir Feltsman	*Union of Soviet Socialist Republics*	No. 379/81
Vladimir Kislik	*Union of Soviet Socialist Republics*	No. 242/80
Vladimir Maximov	*Union of Soviet Socialist Republics and Ukrainian SSR*	No. 90/79
Vlado Gotovac	*Yugoslavia*	No. 421/81
Ziad Abu Eain	*United States of America and Israel*	No. 233/80
Zien Al Smail	*France*	No. 264/80
Zlatko Matkovič	*Yugoslavia*	No. 261/80
Zygmunt Elbiński	*Poland*	No. 124/79
Yang Song U	*Republic of Korea*	No. 279/80
Yoon po-sn	*Republic of Korea*	No. 279/80
Yosif Z. Begun	*Union of Soviet Socialist Republics*	No. 209/80
Yosif Ziselevich Begun	*Union of Soviet Socialist Republics*	No. 345/81
Yuli Kosharovsky	*Union of Soviet Socialist Republics*	No. 353/81
Yuri Orlov	*Union of Soviet Socialist Republics and Ukrainian SSR*	No. 21/78

Annex V

(*c*) Communications submitted under the 77 EX/Decision 8.3 Procedure of the Executive Board finally examined under the 104 EX/Decision 3.3 Procedure (States concerned)

Argentina	*María Seoane Toimil*	Disappearance[1]
	Eduardo Suárez	Inadmissible[2]
	Raúl Mateo Molina Luján	Disappearance[3]
	María Virginia Aurora Allende Calace	Disappearance[4]
	Eduardo Luis Ricci	Disappearance[5]
Chile	*Fernando Ortiz*	
	Fernando Ortiz Letelier	
	Fernando Ortiz Letelier et al.	Disappearance[6]
	A number of teachers and students who have disappeared in Chile	
	Fernando Ortiz Letelier et al.	Disappearance[7]
Nigeria	*Gustave Kpade Loko*	Inadmissible[8]
Uruguay	*Miguel Ángel Estrella*	Settled[9]
	Julio Castro	Setlled[10]

[1] See document 108 EX/38 PRIV., paras. 245-248; see also document 108 EX/CR/PRIV.1.
[2] *Ibidem*, paras. 249-253; see also document 108 EX/CR/PRIV.1.
[3] *Ibidem*, paras. 254-257; see also documents 108 EX/CR/PRIV.1 and Add.2.
[4] *Ibidem*, paras. 258-261; see also document 108 EX/CR/PRIV.1.
[5] *Ibidem*, paras. 262-264; see also document 108 EX/CR/PRIV.1.
[6] See document 134 EX/3 PRIV., paras. 163-172; see also document 134 EX/CR/HR/CHI.
[7] *Idem*.
[8] See document 108 EX/38 PRIV., paras. 276-278; see also documents 108 EX/CR/PRIV.1 and Add.4.
[9] See document 109 EX/52 PRIV., paras. 170-172; see also documents 109 EX/CR/HR/2 and Add.3.
[10] See document 108 EX/38 PRIV., paras. 284-287; see also document 108 EX/CR/PRIV.1.

The Raoul Wallenberg Institute Series of Intergovernmental Human Rights Documentation

VOLUME 5

The titles published in this series are listed at *brill.com/raou*

Cases of the UNESCO Committee on Conventions and Recommendations

Cases of the UNESCO Committee on Conventions and Recommendations

Communications examined under the 104 EX/Decision 3.3 Procedure of the Executive Board (1978–1988)

VOLUME 2

Communications filed 1982–1988

Edited by

Leif Holmström

With an Introduction by

Abdulqawi A. Yusuf and Béatrice Dupuy

In cooperation with

UNESCO Office International Standards and Legal Affairs

TUTA SUB AEGIDE PALLAS · 1683 ·

BRILL
NIJHOFF

LEIDEN | BOSTON

ISBN 978-90-04-39029-4 ((hardback, volume 2)
ISBN 978-90-04-16878-7 (hardback, set)
ISBN 978-90-04-35403-6 (e-book)

This book is printed on acid-free paper and produced in a sustainable manner.

Printed by Printforce, the Netherlands

CONTENTS

FOREWORD
By Audrey Azoulay
Director-General of UNESCO

INTRODUCTION
By Abdulqawi A. Yusuf and Beatrice Dupuy

ACKNOWLEDGEMENT
By Leif Holmstrom

A. PRELUDE	xxvii
B. HISTORICAL BACKGROUND	xxviii
C. THE DISTINCTIVE FEATURES OF THE "104 PROCEDURE"	xxx
1. Cooperation, dialogue and conciliation	xxx
2. The quest for a satisfactory solution	xxxi
3. Voluntary cooperation of the states concerned	xxxii
4. Confidentiality of the procedure	xxxiii
5. A non-confrontational procedure	xxxiii
D. ACHIEVEMENTS	xxxiv
1. A wide spectrum of cases considered and resolved	xxxv
2. An effective delivery of results over the years	xxxv
E. ATTEMPTS AT REFORM	xxxviii
F. CONCLUSION	xxxviii

UNESCO COMMITTEE ON CONVENTIONS AND RECOMMENDATIONS
Communications Examined under the 104 EX/Decision 3.3
Procedure of the Executive Board filed 1982–1988 1

No. 431/82	*Poland*					
	Krzysztof Sliwinski					3
	Spring 1982 session	3	Autumn 1982 session	3		
	Spring 1983 session	9				
No. 433/82	*Chile*					
	Enrique Ropert Gallet					11
	Spring 1982 session	11	Autumn 1982 session	13		
	Spring 1983 session	14	Autumn 1982 session	15		

No. 434/82	*Socialist Republic of Viet Nam*					
	Duyen Ahn					17
	Spring 1982 session	17	Autumn 1982 session	19		
No. 437/82	*Colomhia*					
	Leaders of the Colombian Federation of Teachers					21
	Spring 1982 session	21				
No. 439/82	*Chile*					
	Victor Ulices Sandoval Álvarez					25
	Spring 1983 session	25	Autumn 1983 session	26		
No. 440/82	*Peru*					
	Victor Rapray Robles					29
	Autumn 1982 session	29	Spring 1983 session	30		
	Autumn 1983 session	31	Spring 1984 session	32		
	Autumn 1984 session	33				
No. 441/82	*Union of Soviet Socialist Republics*					
	Vladimir Raiz and Grigory Rozenshtein					35
	Spring 1983 session	35	Autumn 1983 session	35		
	Spring 1984 session	37	Autumn 1984 session	40		
	Spring 1985 session	42	Autumn 1985 session	45		
	Spring 1986 session	48	Autumn 1986 session	49		
	Spring 1987 session	52				
No. 442/82	*Union of Soviet Socialist Republics*					55
	Aleksondr Paritsky					
	Autumn 1982 session	55	Spring 1983 session	58		
	Autumn 1983 session	61	Spring 1984 session	63		
	Autumn 1984 session	64				
No. 443/82	*Czechoslovakia*					
	Karel Kyncl					67
	Spring 1982 session	67	Autumn 1982 session	69		
	Spring 1983 session	74	Autumn 1983 session	75		
No. 444/82	*Union of Soviet Socialist Republics*					
	Kishore Dehadrai					77
	Autumn 1982 session	77				
No. 446/82	*Honduras*					
	Carlos Ramirez					
	Autumn 1982 session	79	Spring 1983 session	81		
	Autumn 1983 session	84	Spring 1988 session	85		
	Autumn 1988 session	86	Autumn 1989 session	88		
	Autumn 1989 session	90	Spring 1990 session	92		
	Autumn 1990 session	94	Spring 1991 session	96		

No. 447/82	*Chile*					
	Germán Molina Valdivieso					99
	Autumn 1982 session	99	Spring 1983 session	101		
No. 449/82	*Union of Soviet Socialist Republics*					
	Filip Moyseyevich Gershkovich					103
	Spring 1982 session	103	Autumn 1982 session	106		
No. 450/82	*Czechoslovakia*					
	Jozef Jablonicky					111
	Spring 1983 session	111	Autumn 1983 session	112		
No. 451/82	*Czechoslovakia*					
	František Lizna					113
	Spring 1983 session	113	Autumn 1983 session	114		
No. 460/82	*Uruguay*					
	Yolanda Catalina Ibarra Chávez de Chassale					115
	Autumn 1982 session	115				
No. 461/82	*Union of Soviet Socialist Republics*					
	Lev Blitshtein					119
	Spring 1982 session	119	Autumn 1982 session	119		
No. 462/82	*Union of Soviet Socialist Republics*					
	Victor Yelistratov and Basheva Hait Yelistratov					123
	Spring 1982 session	123	Autumn 1982 session	123		
No. 465/82	*Argentina*					
	Julio Juan Piumato					127
	Autumn 1982 session	127				
No. 468/82	*Uruguay*					
	Raúl Cariboni da Silva					129
	Autumn 1982 session	129				
No. 470/82	*Union of Soviet Socialist Republics*					
	Arseny Borisovich Roginsky					131
	Autumn 1982 session	131				
No. 472/82	*Zaire*					
	Ernest Wamba-dia-Wamba					133
	Autumn 1982 session	133	Spring 1983 session	134		
No. 473/82	*Ivory Coast*					
	Syndicat national de la recherche et de l'enseignement supérieur					135
	Autumn 1981 session	135				
No. 475/82	*Chile*					
	José Hugo Pueller Bravo					137
	Spring 1983 session	137	Autumn 1983 session	138		
	Spring 1984 session	138				

No. 477/82	*El Salvador*					
	Violation of human rights in El Salvador					141
	Autumn 1982 session	141	Spring 1983 session	141		
	Autumn 1983 session	141	Spring 1984 session	141		
	Autumn 1984 session	141	Spring 1985 session	142		
	Autumn 1985 session	142	Spring 1986 session	142		
	Autumn 1986 session	142	Spring 1987 session	142		
	Autumn 1987 session	142	Spring 1988 session	142		
	Autumn 1988 session	143	Spring 1989 session	143		
	Autumn 1989 session	143	Spring 1990 session	143		
No. 478/82	*Yugoslavia*					
	Franjo Tudjman					145
	Spring 1983 session	145				
No. 479/82	*Romania*					
	Ion Caraion					147
	Autumn 1982 session	147				
No. 480/82	*Lao People's Democratic Republic*					
	Khamkhing Souvanlasy					149
	Autumn 1982 session	149	Spring 1983 session	149		
	Autumn 1983 session	149	Spring 1984 session	149		
	Autumn 1984 session	149	Spring 1985 session	150		
	Autumn 1984 session	150	Spring 1986 session	150		
	Autumn 1986 session	150				
No. 481/82	*Union of Soviet Socialist Republics*					
	Alexander Temkin					151
	Autumn 1982 session	151				
No. 482/82	*Union of Soviet Socialist Republics*					
	Andrei Sakharov					153
	Spring 1983 session	153	Autumn 1983 session	157		
	Spring 1984 session	159	Autumn 1984 session	162		
	Spring 1985 session	163	Autumn 1985 session	163		
	Spring 1986 session	163	Spring 1987 session	168		
No. 483/82	*Union of Soviet Socialist Republics*					
	Discrimination in respect of admission to higher education courses in Moscow at the Faculty of Mechanics and Mathematics of the State University, the Institute of Physical Engineering, and the Physical-Technical Institute					171
	Autumn 1986 session	171	Spring 1983 session	173		
	Autumn 1983 session	176	Spring 1984 session	178		
	Autumn 1984 session	178				

No. 484/82 *Chile*
Sergio Spoerer 181
Autumn 1982 session 181 Spring 1983 session 182
No. 487/82 *Indonesia*
Tengku Muhammad Usman Lampoh Awé 185
Spring 1983 session 185
No. 489/82 *Zambia*
Students expelled or suspended from the University of Zambia 189
Spring 1983 session 189
No. 491/82 *Israel*
Violations of human rights committed by Israel against the Lebanese and Palestinian peoples 193
Autumn 1982 session 193 Extraordinary 1982 session 202
Spring 1983 session 207 Autumn 1983 session 209
Spring 1984 session 211 Autumn 1984 session 212
No. 494/82 *Romania*
Victoria Dragomir and Anca Dragomir 215
Spring 1983 session 215
No. 495/82 *Morocco*
Mohamed Elyazghi 217
Spring 1983 session 217
No. 500/82 *Union of Soviet Socialist Republics*
Vladimir Raiz 221
Spring 1983 session 221 Autumn 1983 session 221
Spring 1984 session 221 Autumn 1984 session 221
Spring 1985 session 222 Autumn 1985 session 222
Spring 1986 session 222 Autumn 1986 session 222
Spring 1987 session 222
No. 503/82 *Romania*
Radu Dinculescu 223
Spring 1983 session 223
No. 511/82 *Yugoslavia*
Marko Veselica 225
Spring 1983 session 225
No. 516/83 *Chile*
Vladimir Lenin Cháves Rodríguez 227
Spring 1983 session 227 Autumn 1983 session 228
Spring 1984 session 229

No. 517/83	*Uruguay*					
	Raúl Cariboni da Silva					231
	Spring 1983 session	231				
No. 518/83	*Chile*					
	Jorge Montes					235
	Spring 1983 session	235	Autumn 1983 session	237		
	Spring 1984 session	239				
No. 519/83	*Union of Soviet Socialist Republics*					
	Withdrawal of academic diplomas					241
	Spring 1983 session	241	Autumn 1983 session	241		
	Spring 1984 session	243	Autumn 1984 session	245		
	Spring 1985 session	247				
No. 525/83	*Iran*					
	Abolfazl Ghassemi					249
	Spring 1983 session	249	Autumn 1983 session	249		
	Spring 1984 session	251	Autumn 1984 session	252		
	Spring 1985 session	253	Autumn 1985 session	254		
	Spring 1986 session	255	Autumn 1986 session	257		
	Spring 1987 session	258				
No. 527/83	*Union of Soviet Socialist Republics*					
	Yuri Fedorovich Orlov					261
	Autumn 1983 session	261	Spring 1984 session	262		
	Autumn 1984 session	262	Spring 1985 session	264		
No. 528/83	*Morocco*					
	Right of civil servants to lifelong education					267
	Spring 1983 session	267	Autumn 1983 session	269		
No. 529/83	*Federal Republic of Germany*					
	Gudrun Melchior-Dollinger et al.					271
	Spring 1983 session	271				
No. 530/83	*Chile*					
	Luis Guillermo Deisler González					275
	Spring 1985 session	275	Autumn 1985 session	276		
	Spring 1986 session	278	Autumn 1986 session	279		
	Spring 1987 session	281				
No. 535/83	*Pakistan*					
	Jamil Omar					283
	Autumn 1984 session	283				
No. 536/83	*Union of Soviet Socialist Republics*					
	Yosif Z. Begun					285
	Spring 1983 session	285	Autumn 1983 session	285		

	Spring 1984 session	287	Autumn 1984 session	288	
	Spring 1985 session	290	Autumn 1985 session	291	
	Spring 1986 session	294	Autumn 1986 session	294	
	Spring 1987 session	296			
No. 539/83	*Pakistan*				
	Tariq Ahsan				301
	Spring 1984 session	301			
No. 540/83	*Federal Republic of Germany*				
	Helios Gürkov				303
	Spring 1983 session	303	Spring 1984 session	312	
	Autumn 1984 session	313	Spring 1985 session	314	
	Autumn 1985 session	316	Spring 1986 session	317	
No. 544/83	*Socialist Republic of Viet Nam*				
	Bui Hoang Câm				319
	Autumn 1983 session	319	Spring 1984 session	320	
No. 546/83	*Kenya*				
	Al-Amin Muhamed Kassim Mazrui				323
	Autumn 1983 session	323	Spring 1984 session	324	
No. 559/83	*Chile*				
	Delfin Guillermo Quiñones et al.				325
	Autumn 1983 session	325	Spring 1984 session	328	
	Autumn 1984 session	332	Spring 1985 session	334	
	Autumn 1985 session	336	Spring 1986 session	339	
No. 560/83	*Union of Soviet Socialist Republics*				
	Anatoli Raben				341
	Autumn 1983 session	341	Spring 1984 session	343	
	Autumn 1984 session	343			
No. 561/83	*Union of Soviet Socialist Republics*				
	Anatoli Khazanov				345
	Autumn 1983 session	345	Spring 1984 session	346	
	Autumn 1984 session	346	Spring 1985 session	347	
No. 564/83	*Union of Soviet Socialist Republics*				
	Igor Guberman				349
	Autumn 1983 session	349	Spring 1984 session	351	
	Autumn 1984 session	351			
No. 565/83	*Union of Soviet Socialist Republics*				
	Novosibirisk Association for the Promotion of Friendship between the Peoples of the USSR and Israel				353
	Autumn 1983 session	353	Spring 1984 session	355	
	Autumn 1984 session	355			

No. 577/83	*Chile*				
	Victor Hugo de la Fuente				357
	Autumn 1983 session	357	Spring 1984 session	358	
	Autumn 1984 session	359	Spring 1985 session	360	
	Autumn 1985 session	361	Spring 1986 session	362	
	Autumn 1986 session	364	Spring 1987 session	364	
No. 581/83	*Islamic Republic of Iran*				
	Arrest of leading figures in Iranian cultural life				367
	Autumn 1983 session	367	Spring 1984 session	368	
	Autumn 1984 session	368	Spring 1985 session	368	
	Autumn 1985 session	368	Spring 1986 session	369	
	Autumn 1986 session	369	Spring 1987 session	369	
	Autumn 1987 session	370	Spring 1988 session	371	
	Autumn 1988 session	373	Spring 1989 session	374	
	Autumn 1989 session	376	Spring 1990 session	377	
	Autumn 1990 session	379	Spring 1991 session	382	
	Autumn 1991 session	385			
No. 582/83	*Paraguay*				
	Enrique Goossen Martens et al.				389
	Autumn 1983 session	389	Spring 1984 session	390	
	Autumn 1984 session	391	Spring 1985 session	392	
No. 583/83	*Chile*				
	Mirna Donoso Garcia				395
	Spring 1984 session	395	Autumn 1984 session	396	
	Spring 1985 session	397	Autumn 1985 session	399	
	Spring 1986 session	400	Autumn 1986 session	401	
	Spring 1987 session	403			
No. 590/83	*Chile*				
	Carlos Lira Moscoso				405
	Spring 1984 session	405			
No. 595/83	*Czechoslovakia*				
	Ladislav Lis				407
	Spring 1984 session	407			
No. 601/84	*Chile*				
	Ulises Gómez				409
	Spring 1984 session	409	Autumn 1984 session	411	
	Spring 1985 session	412	Autumn 1985 session	414	
	Spring 1986 session	416	Autumn 1986 session	417	

No. 602/84	*New Zealand*					
	Alleged discriminatory tuition fees imposed on foreign students under the New Zealand Education Amendment Act 1979					419
	Spring 1984 session	419	Autumn 1984 session	420		
	Spring 1985 session	420	Autumn 1985 session	422		
No. 603/84	*Union of Soviet Socialist Republics*					
	Andrei Sakharov					425
	Spring 1984 session	425	Autumn 1984 session	425		
	Spring 1985 session	425	Autumn 1985 session	425		
	Spring 1986 session	425	Autumn 1986 session	426		
	Spring 1987 session	426				
No. 605/84	*Chile*					
	Luis Eduardo Labarca Goddard					427
	Spring 1984 session	427	Autumn 1984 session	428		
	Spring 1985 session	429	Autumn 1985 session	430		
	Spring 1986 session	431	Autumn 1986 session	432		
	Spring 1987 session	433				
No. 606/84	*Turkey*					
	Mahmut Dikerdem et al.					435
	Spring 1985 session	435				
No. 608/84	*Chile*					
	José Miguel Varas Morel					437
	Spring 1983 session	437	Autumn 1985 session	438		
	Spring 1986 session	439				
No. 610/84	*Turkey*					
	Sadun Aren					441
	Spring 1984 session	441				
No. 613/84	*United State of America*					
	Alleged discrimination in education against the black American minority					
	Spring 1984 session	443				
No. 610/84	*Denmark*					
	Kai Mogens H. Lång					447
	Spring 1984 session	447				
No. 616/84	*Czechoslovakia*					
	Jaromir Šavrda					449
	Spring 1984 session	449	Autumn 1984 session	450		

No. 618/84	*Chile*					
	Luis José Godoy González					451
	Autumn 1984 session	451	Spring 1985 session	452		
	Autumn 1985 session	454	Spring 1986 session	455		
No. 622/84	*France*					
	Mohamed Benrahhlate					457
	Spring 1984 session	457				
No. 623/84	*Malta*					
	Alleged discriminatory measures					459
	Spring 1984 session	459				
No. 624/84	*Czechoslovakia*					
	Marek Benda					461
	Autumn 1984 session	461				
No. 626/84	*Socialist Republic of Viet Nam*					
	Nguyên Hai Chi					463
	Spring 1984 session	463	Autumn 1984 session	464		
	Spring 1985 session	464	Autumn 1985 session	465		
No. 627/84	*Uruguay*					
	Mario Alberto Teti Izquierdo					467
	Spring 1984 session	467	Autumn 1984 session	468		
	Spring 1985 session	470				
No. 628/84	*Union of Soviet Socialist Republics*					
	Alexandre Broussilovski					473
	Spring 1984 session	473	Autumn 1984 session	474		
	Spring 1985 session	475				
No. 630/84	*Afghanistan*					
	Osman Taraki Rustar et al.					477
	Autumn 1984 session	477	Spring 1985 session	478		
	Autumn 1985 session	479	Spring 1986 session	482		
	Autumn 1986 session	484	Spring 1987 session	486		
	Autumn 1987 session	488				
No. 631/84	*Poland*					
	Marek Nowakowski					489
	Autumn 1984 session	489				
No. 632/84	*Chile*					
	Raúl Manriquez					491
	Autumn 1984 session	491				
No. 637/84	*France*					
	Léone Guyot					493
	Autumn 1984 session	493				

No. 638/84	*Czechoslovakia*					
	Jiří Wolf					495
	Spring 1985 session	495				
No. 639/84	*Federal Republic of Germany*					
	Christian Schmidt					497
	Spring 1985 session	497				
No. 640/84	*German Democratic Republic*					
	Ulrike Poppe and Bärbel Bohley					499
	Spring 1985 session	499				
No. 641/84	*Hungary*					
	Twenty female activists for peace					501
	Spring 1985 session	501				
No. 642/84	*Norway*					
	Ikkevold Magazine					503
	Spring 1985 session	503				
No. 643/84	*Union of Soviet Socialist Republics*					
	Victor Blik et al.					505
	Spring 1985 session	505				
No. 645/84	*Union of Soviet Socialist Republics*					
	Soviet scientists of Jewish origin who have filed applications to emigrate					507
	Autumn 1984 session	507	Spring 1985 session	507		
No. 647/84	*Uruguay*					
	Cinco Días					511
	Autumn 1984 session	511				
No. 648/84	*Uruguay*					
	Tribune Amplia					513
	Autumn 1984 session	513				
No. 649/84	*Uruguay*					
	Somos Idea					515
	Autumn 1984 session	515				
No. 650/84	*Uruguay*					
	Convicción					517
	Autumn 1984 session	517				
No. 651184	*Union of Soviet Socialist Republics*					
	Alleged discrimination with respect to education					
	Autumn 1984 session	519	Spring 1985 session	519		
	Autumn 1985 session	519	Spring 1986 session	523		
	Autumn 1986 session	523	Spring 1987 session	524		

No. 652/84	*Nigeria*					
	Tai Solarin					531
	Autumn 1984 session	531	Spring 1985 session	531		
	Autumn 1985 session	533				
No. 653/84	*Chile*					
	Carlos Mario Lira Moscoso					535
	Spring 1985 session	535				
No. 655/84	*Yugoslavia*					
	Jozo Gospodin Zovko et al					537
	Autumn 1986 session	537				
No. 656/84	*United States of America*					
	Alleged medical tyranny as practised in the United States of America					541
	Autumn 1984 session	541	Spring 1985 session	542		
No. 669/85	*Paraguay*					
	Radio Nanduti					545
	Spring 1985 session	545				
No. 671/85	*Czechoslovakia*					
	Jan Hájek					547
	Spring 1985 session	547	Autumn 1985 session	548		
	Spring 1986 session	550	Autumn 1986 session	553		
No. 674/85	*Paraguay*					
	Aldo Zuccolillo and ABC Color					555
	Spring 1986 session	555	Autumn 1986 session	557		
	Spring 1987 session	559	Autumn 1987 session	562		
	Spring 1988 session	565	Autumn 1988 session	566		
	Spring 1989 session	569				
No. 676/85	*Yugoslavia*					
	Jovan R. Gucič					571
	Autumn 1985 session	571	Spring 1986 session	572		
No. 677/85	*Italy*					
	Alberto Tessore					573
	Autumn 1986 session	573				
No. 684/85	*Yugoslavia*					
	Radomir Veljkovič					575
	Autumn 1985 session	575	Spring 1986 session	575		
	Autumn 1986 session	577				
No. 685/85	*Yugoslavia*					
	Vladimir Markovič					579
	Autumn 1985 session	579	Spring 1986 session	580		
	Autumn 1986 session	581				

No. 686/85 *Yugoslavia*
Božidar Todorović 585
Autumn 1985 session 585 Spring 1986 session 586
Autumn 1986 session 587
No. 687/85 *Yugoslavia*
Slobodan Živković et al. 589
Spring 1986 session 589
No. 690/85 *El Salvador*
Filomena Claros de Majano 591
Spring 1986 session 591 Autumn 1986 session 592
Spring 1987 session 593 Autumn 1987 session 594
Spring 1988 session 595 Autumn 1988 session 595
Spring 1989 session 595 Autumn 1989 session 595
Spring 1990 session 595
No. 691/85 *Union of Soviet Socialist Republics*
Hanna Vasylivna Mykhaylenko 597
Spring 1986 session 597 Autumn 1986 session 597
No. 692/85 *Union of Soviet Socialist Republics*
Vladimir Yurevkh Poresh 601
Spring 1986 session 601 Autumn 1986 session 601
No. 693/85 *People's Republic of China*
Liu Liping 603
Spring 1986 session 603
No. 694/85 *Union of Soviet Socialist Republics*
Aleksander Nicolaevich Bogoslovsky 605
Spring 1986 session 605 Autumn 1986 session 605
Spring 1987 session 606
No. 695/85 *Chile*
Leonardo Cáceres Castro 609
Spring 1986 session 609 Autumn 1986 session 610
No. 705/86 *Chile*
María Ximena Mora Pozo 611
Spring 1986 session 611 Autumn 1986 session 612
Spring 1987 session 613
No. 706/86 *Chile*
Adriana Susana Rondón González 615
Spring 1986 session 615
No. 712/86 *Romania*
Lacrima Cofaru 617
Autumn 1986 session 617 Spring 1987 session 618
Autumn 1987 session 620 Spring 1988 session 621

No. 719/86	*Italy*				
	Giulia Arena				623
	Autumn 1986 session	623			
No. 720/86	*Union of Soviet Socialist Republics*				
	Yosif Z. Begun				625
	Autumn 1986 session	625	Spring 1987 session	625	
No. 721/86	*Union of Soviet Socialist Republics*				
	Roald Zelichonok				627
	Autumn 1986 session	627	Spring 1987 session	627	
No. 722/86	*Chile*				
	José Luis Rojas Valencia				629
	Autumn 1986 session	629	Spring 1987 session	630	
No. 725/86	*Union of Soviet Socialist Republics*				
	Leonid Volvovski				631
	Autumn 1986 session	631	Spring 1987 session	631	
No. 726/86	*Union of Soviet Socialist Republics*				
	Vladimir Lifshits				633
	Autumn 1986 session	633	Spring 1987 session	633	
No. 728/86	*Union of Soviet Socialist Republics*				
	Yuli Edelshtein				635
	Spring 1987 session	635			
No. 729/86	*Union of Soviet Socialist Republics*				
	Alexis Magarik				639
	Spring 1987 session	639	Autumn 1987 session	640	
No. 730/86	*Republic of Korea*				
	Song Ki Won et al.				643
	Spring 1987 session	643	Autumn 1987 session	644	
	Spring 1988 session	646	Autumn 1988 session		
No. 731/86	*Chile*				
	Francisco Javier Andrés Peña Torres				649
	Spring 1987 session	649			
No. 734/86	*Indonesia*				
	Oesmany al Hamidy				651
	Spring 1987 session	651	Autumn 1987 session	653	
	Spring 1988 session	654	Autumn 1988 session	656	
	Spring 1989 session	658	Autumn 1989 session	660	
	Spring 1990 session	661	Autumn 1990 session	663	
	Spring 1991 session	665	Autumn 1991 session	667	

No. 736/86	*Somalia*					
	Abdulle Rage Taraweh					669
	Spring 1987 session	669	Autumn 1987 session	670		
	Spring 1988 session	671				
No. 737/86	*Union of Soviet Socialist Republics*					
	Mart Niklus					673
	Spring 1988 session	673	Autumn 1988 session	674		
No. 739/86	*Chile*					
	Fernando Ramón Azula Ponce					677
	Spring 1987 session	677				
No. 743/87	*Chile*					
	Francisco Javier Lira Bianchi					679
	Spring 1987 session	679				
No. 744/87	*Greece*					
	Ignace Philippoussis					681
	Autumn 1987 session	681	Spring 1988 session	682		
No. 745/87	*Somalia*					
	Abdi Ismail Younis					685
	Autumn 1987 session	685	Spring 1988 session	686		
	Autumn 1988 session	686	Spring 1989 session	687		
No. 746/87	*Greece*					
	Margarita Fréri and Rose Fréri					689
	Autumn 1987 session	689	Spring 1988 session	691		
No. 748/87	*Bulgaria*					
	Omer Mustafov Kochandzhiev et al.					693
	Autumn 1987 session	693				
No. 749/87	*Chile*					
	Luis Ibacache Silva					695
	Autumn 1987 session	695	Spring 1988 session	697		
No. 750/87	*Indonesia*					
	Achmad Zaini and Margono Bin Syafei					699
	Spring 1987 session	699	Autumn 1987 session	699		
	Spring 1988 session	701	Autumn 1988 session	703		
	Spring 1989 session	704				
No. 751/87	*Yugoslavia*					
	Ismet Kasumagic					707
	Spring 1987 session	707	Autumn 1987 session	707		
	Spring 1988 session	709				

No. 752/87	*Bulgaria*	
	Halim Pasadzhov	711
	Spring 1987 session 711 Autumn 1987 session 712	
No. 753/87	*Bulgaria*	
	Rasim Rezhebov et al.	715
	Spring 1987 session 715 Autumn 1987 session 715	
No. 754/87	*Union of Soviet Socialist Republics*	
	Alleged discriminations against access to Jewish history, culture and art	717
	Spring 1987 session 717	
No. 755/87	*France*	
	Lyudmila Pavlovna Varigin	719
	Autumn 1987 session 719	
No. 758/87	*Union of Soviet Socialist Republics*	
	History books and textbooks for pupils in the Soviet Union	723
	Autumn 1987 session 723	
No. 759/87	*Union of Soviet Socialist Republics*	
	Various works by contemporary Soviet authors	727
	Autumn 1987 session 727	
No. 760/87	*People's Republic of China*	
	Liu De	729
	Spring 1988 session 729 Autumn 1988 session 730	
No. 761/87	*People's Republic of Benin*	
	Baro Orou Mora	733
	Spring 1988 session 733 Autumn 1988 session 734	
	Spring 1989 session 736	
No. 762/87	*Turkey*	
	Recep Marasli	737
	Spring 1988 session 737 Autumn 1988 session 739	
	Spring 1989 session 742 Autumn 1989 session 744	
	Spring 1990 session 746 Autumn 1990 session 748	
	Spring 1991 session 752	
No. 763/87	*Socialist Republic of Viet Nam*	
	Nguyên Dan Que	755
	Spring 1988 session 755	
No. 764/87	*Socialist Republic of Viet Nam*	
	Truong Van Quynh	757
	Spring 1988 session 757	

No. 765/87	*Socialist Republic of Viet Nam*					
	Doan Quôc Sy					759
	Spring 1988 session	759	Autumn 1988 session	760		
	Spring 1989 session	761	Autumn 1989 session	763		
	Spring 1990 session	765	Autumn 1990 session	767		
	Spring 1991 session	769	Autumn 1991 session	771		
	Spring 1992 session	773				
No. 766/87	*Socialist Republic of Viet Nam*					
	Nguyên Chi Thien					777
	Spring 1988 session	777	Autumn 1988 session	778		
	Spring 1989 session	779	Autumn 1989 session	780		
	Spring 1990 session	781	Autumn 1990 session	783		
	Spring 1991 session	785	Autumn 1991 session	787		
	Spring 1992 session	788				
No. 768/87	*Côte d'Ivoire*					
	Teachers belonging to the National Union of Secondary School Teachers of Côte d'Ivoire					791
	Spring 1988 session	791				
No. 772/87	*Yugoslavia*					
	Uros Bukumira					793
	Spring 1988 session	793				
No. 773/88	*Chile*					
	Ledy del Carmen Castro Urra					795
	Spring 1988 session	795	Autumn 1988 session	797		
	Spring 1989 session	799	Autumn 1989 session	801		
	Spring 1990 session	802				
No. 776/88	*Bulgaria*					
	Omer Mustafov Kochandzhiev and Burhan Nedzhibov Hayrulov					805
	Spring 1988 session	805				
No. 778/88	*Nepal*					
	Sushil Chandra Amatya					807
	Spring 1988 session	807	Autumn 1988 session	808		
	Spring 1989 session	809				
No. 779/88	*Yugoslavia*					
	Bogdan Antić					811
	Autumn 1988 session	811				
No. 780/88	*Republic of Korea*					
	Lee Tae-Bok					813
	Spring 1988 session	813	Autumn 1988 session	814		

No. 781/88	*Malawi*					
	Jack Mapanje					817
		Spring 1988 session	817	Autumn 1988 session	818	
		Spring 1989 session	819	Autumn 1989 session	821	
		Spring 1990 session	822			
		Autumn 1990 session	824			
		Spring 1991 session	826			
No. 784/88	*Turkey*					
	Günay Avcı et al.					829
		Autumn 1988 session	829	Spring 1989 session	830	
No. 787/88	*Czechoslovakia*					
	Evžen Freimann					833
		Spring 1989 session	833			
No. 788/88	*Cuba*					
	Natividad González Freire et al.					835
		Spring 1988 session	835	Autumn 1988 session	836	
No. 789/88	*Morocco*					
	Mohamed Jaaidi					839
		Spring 1989 session	839	Autumn 1989 session	841	
		Spring 1990 session	844	Autumn 1990 session	846	
		Spring 1991 session	849	Autumn 1991 session	853	
No. 790/88	*Union of Soviet Socialist Republics*					
	Gintautas Iesmantas					855
		Spring 1989 session	855			
No. 791/88	*Turkey*					
	Bektaş Erdoğan					857
		Spring 1989 session	857	Autumn 1989 session	859	

ANNEXES 861

TABLES OF COMMUNICATIONS 861

(*a*) Communications examined under the 104 EX/Decision 3.3 Procedure of the Executive Board filed 1982–1988 (States concerned) 861

(*b*) Communications examined under the 104 EX/Decision 3.3 Procedure of the Executive Board filed 1982–1988 (Cases) 869

I. **104 EX/DECISION 3.3**
Study of the procedures which should be followed in the examination of cases and questions which might be submitted to UNESCO concerning the exercise of human rights in the spheres of its competence, in order to make its action more effective: report of the working party of the executive board (104 EX/3) 30

II **PROCEDURAL PRACTICE OF THE COMMITTEE ON CONVENTIONS AND RECOMMENDATIONS** 37

III **STANDARD LETTER SENT BY THE OFFICE OF INTERNATIONAL STANDARDS AND LEGAL AFFAIRS TO THE AUTHORS OF COMMUNICATIONS EXAMINED UNDER 104 EX/DECISION 3.3** 57

IV **UNESCO**
Form for communications concerning human rights to be submitted to UNESCO 59

V **THEMATIC LIST OF WORDING USED IN THE DECISIONS OF THE COMMITTEE ON CONVENTIONS AND RECOMMENDATIONS** 62

UNESCO
COMMITTEE ON CONVENTIONS AND RECOMMENDATIONS

Communications

Examined under the 104 EX/Decision 3.3
Procedure of the Executive Board
filed 1982-1988

No. 431/82

Concerning *Poland*
Case of *Krzysztof Śliwiński*

Communication of 13 January 1982 submitted by
Pax Romana

Spring 1982 session of the Committee on Conventions and Recommendations (114th session of the Executive Board)[1]

129. This communication, submitted by Pax Romana - International Movement of Catholic Jurists - concerns the case of a university professor said to have been arrested and interned as soon as the state of siege was proclaimed.

130. In a letter dated 21 April 1982, the Permanent Delegate of Poland to Unesco stated that the communication had reached him very shortly before the date of the Committee's session (26 March 1982), and that his government had been unable to consider it.

131. In accordance with its usual practice, the Committee *decided* to defer consideration of the admissibility of the communication until its next session.

Autumn 1982 session of the Committee on Conventions and Recommendations (115th session of the Executive Board)[2]

165. This communication was submitted by Pax Romana - International Movement of Catholic Jurists, a non-governmental organization in consultative relationship with Unesco, acting as an organization having reliable knowledge of the alleged violation.

166. Mr Krzysztof Śliwiński is described as a university professor of biochemistry and as one of the leaders of the Club of Catholic Intellectuals in Poland. He was al-

[1] See document 114 EX/38 PRIV., paras. 129-131; see also document 114 EX/CR/HR/3 Add.
[2] See document 115 EX/28 PRIV., paras. 165-197; see also document 115 EX/CR/HR/2.

legedly interned as soon as the state of siege was proclaimed, and deprived of all opportunities to exercise his profession, communicate with others or disseminate his works and ideas. The author of the communication emphasizes that the surveillance and subsequent internment of Mr Śliwiński with the purpose of suppressing the activities of a committee in support of unjustly arrested persons constitute a violation of the rights to freedom of expression and to disseminate works and ideas.

167. This is claimed to be a violation of Articles 18 and 19 of the Universal Declaration of Human Rights. It is said that there were no possible means of redress, and that the case has not been submitted to any other international authority.

168. As regards the purpose and aim of the communication, the author seeks the restoration of the alleged victim's civic rights and human rights as defined by international conventions.

169. The dossier includes various press articles and an excerpt from a report dealing with the complaints submitted to ILO by the World Confederation of Labour (WCL) and the International Confederation of Free Trade Unions (ICFTU). These documents may be consulted by members of the Committee at the Secretariat.

170. The Committee was unable to examine this communication at the previous session owing to its late receipt by the Polish Government. On 30 June 1982, the Secretariat received from the author of the communication a letter in which he indicates that Mr Śliwiński is still in detention.

171. At the [autumn 1982] session, the representative of the Polish Government stated that his government was of the opinion that this communication was inadmissible. He reminded the Committee that nine months ago Poland had been on the brink of an abyss, the state had virtually ceased to function. Chaotic and terrorist situations had become commonplace. Certain persons worked to destroy the state machinery and formed alliances with foreign circles towards this end. Crime became rampant. The worst threat, that of civil war loomed ever nearer. Under such circumstances not to act would have been a crime against the nation, the Polish representative said. It became necessary to choose the lesser of two evils; a state of siege was proclaimed in accordance with the Constitution.

172. Preventive internment of extremists and anti-state agitators was carried out. It was thus that Mr Śliwiński came to be interned.

173. The internment decree allowed the internment of all persons whose activities give rise to suspicion and who if free would undertake activities threatening or harmful to the state.

174. The decree in question was a preventive measure and was applied cautiously, he said. The authorities carefully considered to what extent activities in question were a threat to the state. Internment was lifted in certain individual cases if the situation developed favourably or if humanitarian reasons called for it. The Polish representative went on to say that most states had provisions allowing internment measures, in fact the [International] Covenant on Civil and Political Rights allowed the Parties to it to suspend certain rights under certain conditions.

> Article 4, paragraph 1, of the Covenant stated that:
>
> In time of public emergency which threatens the life of the nation and the existence of which is officially proclaimed, the States Parties to the present Covenant may take measures derogating from their obligations under the present Covenant to the extent strictly required by the exigencies of the situation, provided that such measures are not inconsistent with their other obligations under international law and do not involve discrimination solely on the ground of race, colour, sex, language, religion or social origin.
>
> And article 4, paragraph 3, stated that:
>
> Any State Party to the present Covenant availing itself of the right of derogation shall immediately inform the other States Parties to the present Covenant, through the intermediary of the Secretary-General of the United Nations, of the provisions from which it has derogated and of the reasons by which it was actuated. A further communication shall be made, through the same intermediary, on the date on which it terminates such derogation.

The state of siege in Poland had been promulgated in conformity with the Covenant, he emphasized.

175. He added that many observers felt that this action by the Polish authorities had helped Poland to avoid a civil war.

176. This matter was one coming within the purely domestic competence of Poland, he said, and the Committee could not concern itself with such an internal affair since Article I (3) of Unesco's Constitution prohibited it from intervening in matters which are essentially within the domestic jurisdiction of Member States.

177. Furthermore, the representative said, a careful reading of the communication revealed that it was not in Unesco's competence. Mr Śliwiński was not in fact a professor. Having abandoned teaching during all of 1981, he acted as a permanent salaried official of "Solidarity", responsible for the foreign affairs section thereof.

178. Thus the allegation that Mr Śliwiński had been deprived of the opportunity to exercise his profession was very misleading, since he had abandoned teaching for full-time work as an official of "Solidarity". Furthermore, as such he could not have been doing any scientific research. Thus, for several reasons the communication could not be deemed admissible by the Committee, the Polish representative said.

179. The authors also alleged that Mr Śliwiński was interned under bad conditions, since he was put with workers and in unhygienic surroundings. Such a statement showed contempt for the working classes, the Polish representative said. Given that communications must not be offensive, the Secretariat should have rejected the communication in its present form the representative said. He went on to say that the internment camps had been visited by the delegates of the International Committee of the Red Cross and the authors could have gone down the street to consult the ICRC on this question.

180. It also appeared that the authors had not complied with the rule that communications must not be based exclusively on information disseminated through the mass media.

181. The Polish representative said that all internees had the possibility of recourse to the Minister of Internal Affairs.

182. The authors' assertion that there were no remedies available was thus clearly false and showed that the communication was manifestly ill-founded, he said. He stated that for that reason the Secretariat should have refused to accept this communication.

183. The representative of the Director-General by way of clarification pointed out that international law and the preparatory work for 104 EX/Decision 3.3 clearly indicated that what was meant by domestic remedies were judicial remedies, not administrative appeals.

184. On the question as to what was offensive in a communication, this was a question which only the Committee could decide and the Secretariat was not in a position to reject communications for this reason. The Director-General's representative further pointed out that the reports of the International Committee of the Red Cross were strictly confidential and were only communicated to governments; neither the authors of the communication nor the Secretariat could thus have been able to read the reports of the ICRC concerning Poland.

185. A Committee member raised the question as to what specific illegal activity on the part of Mr Śliwiński had caused him to be interned. The Committee member also

pointed out that there was an objective and subjective aspect to the question of what was offensive, and he felt that the Secretariat has acted properly in leaving this question for the Committee to decide. He himself did not find it offensive. He wondered if the authors had not mentioned the means of redress available because their letter pre-dated the decree concerning the administrative remedies. He also wondered whether the administrative remedies were indeed adequate.

186. It was the view of another Committee member that it would be difficult to dissociate this case from its underlying political and economic root factors, that a state had the right to maintain order, and that the case could not be declared admissible.

187. Yet another Committee member disagreed with the interpretation that the communication was offensive to workers. What was in fact offensive in this case was the use of massive force to violate human rights in Poland, and to force workers to renounce their allegiance to "Solidarity".

188. To listen without reply to a statement which was so much at odds with the reality in Poland would be an acquiescence to the violation of human rights in that country, the Committee member said.

189. In other cases where the information of the author and the Covenant did not concord it was the practice of the Committee to inform the author of the communication and the government concerned and to ask for new information. In this case it might in addition be possible to bring the communication to the attention of the United Nations special rapporteur.

190. Certain other Committee members felt that Article 4 of the [International] Covenant on Civil and Political Rights allowed the suspension of certain rights in exceptional circumstances, and such circumstances did exist in Poland, they said. Thus the measures taken by the Polish authorities could not be described as violations of human rights, they added, and because of the legal context of this case the Committee should not therefore consider it.

191. Another Committee member stated that Unesco could not effectively deal with a state of war, a war which had been declared by the Polish Government on its own citizens. The Polish state had constructed a clever legal apparatus for carrying out its suppression of dissent, but what was legal was not always legitimate, the Committee member said.

192. Furthermore, the question arose as to whether Mr Śliwiński was not in fact still a teacher even if he did not possess the formal title of full professor and whether it

was not possible that he had merely been on loan or leave from his university to work with the union. The Committee member also expressed the view that the Polish representative had unwisely belaboured the question of offensiveness of the communication and that the domestic remedies cited were not true remedies.

193. Yet another Committee member felt this communication might have been of interest to Unesco under normal circumstances, but that it was not of interest under these special circumstances. Mr Śliwiński, had deliberately chosen to leave his teaching post to engage in agitation, the Committee member said.

194. Another Committee member felt that the Committee should proceed as it had in other similar cases by asking for further information from the Polish Government.

195. The representative of the Director-General then explained that while 104 EX/ Decision 3.3 did not foresee exceptional situations, the Committee had addressed the question of such situations at its [autumn 1979] session:

> Recognizing the principle that "necessity determines the law" and the consequent possibility of derogating from the enforcement of certain rules when an exceptional situation arises, the Committee decided to apply 104 EX/Decision 3.3 "with due regard to the spirit of the provisions of Article 4 of the International Covenant on Civil and Political Rights".[3]

196. Several Committee members were of the opinion that the Committee was perfectly competent to look at this case to see whether the measures taken by the Polish authorities had been proportional to the situation as far as matters in Unesco's competence were concerned.

197. The Committee then *decided* to suspend its consideration of the question of admissibility of this case, to request the Polish Government to provide it with information whether and to what extent the five (5) conditions mentioned in Article 4 of the [International] Covenant on Civil and Political Rights existed in Poland, and to follow its usual procedure in informing the authors of the information provided by the government concerned.

[3] See document 108 EX/38 PRIV., paras. 20-24.

Poland **No. 431/82**

Spring 1983 session of the Committee on Conventions and Recommendations (116th session of the Executive Board)[4]

117. This communication concerns the case of a university professor, one of the leaders of the Club of Catholic Intellectuals in Poland and a member of the "Solidarity" movement, who was arrested as soon as martial law was proclaimed. It has been on the Committee's agenda since its spring 1982 session.

118. At the spring 1983 session, the representative of the Director-General informed the Committee that the Permanent Delegation of Poland to Unesco had notified the Secretariat that the alleged victim had been freed on 12 December 1982. He also read out a letter dated 11 May 1983 from the author of the communication conveying the latter's thanks and expressing the hope that Mr Śliwiński would be able to take part in a Pax Romana Assembly due to be held in London from 14 to 21 September 1983.

119. Having noted this information, the Committee *decided* to consider the case as having been settled in accordance with paragraph 14 (*a*) (x) of 104 EX/Decision 3.3 and to transmit the above-mentioned letter to the government concerned.

---

[4] See document 116 EX/48 PRIV., paras. 117-119; see also documents 116 EX/CR/HR/2 and Add.

No. 433/82

Concerning *Chile*
Case of *Enrique Ropert Gallet*

Communication of 30 December 1981 submitted by
Enrique Ropert Gallet

Spring 1982 session of the Committee on Conventions and Recommendations (114th session of the Executive Board)[1]

71. The author of this communication, Mr Enrique Ropert Gallet, an engineer of Chilean nationality and former professor at the Catholic University of Chile, aged 70, describes himself as the victim of the alleged violations.

72. Arrested on 20 September 1973 in his office at the Ministry of Public Works, he claims to have been tried on 16 July 1974 by a court martial which sentenced him to 300 days' imprisonment and six months' banishment. The first sentence came to an end on 21 July 1974, since Mr Ropert Gallet had been in prison since his arrest, and the second expired on 30 January 1975. From that date onwards, the author claims to have applied to the Chilean authorities repeatedly for the papers he needed to return to Chile. In October 1976 he was given a passport marked with the letter "L", which did not entitle him to return to his country. He accordingly applied again repeatedly to the Chilean authorities in Paris and in Chile either personally, in writing or through the intermediary of a lawyer - this is corroborated by a large number of letters in the dossier - with a view to obtaining an unmarked passport and an explanation of the legal reasons for which he is prevented from returning to Chile.

73. Mr Enrique Ropert Gallet points out that this enforced situation results in an arbitrary prolongation, without any basis in law, of the duration of his exile in France. He thinks that he was issued an "L" passport due to a misinterpretation of the Decree-Law No. 81, which applies to those sentenced to exile and not to those in his case, who have completed their term of banishment.

[1] See document 114 EX/38 PRIV., paras. 71-82; see also document 114 EX/CR/HR/3 Add.

No. 433/82 **Chile**

74. In April 1982, the Consul-General of Chile in Paris allegedly informed Mr Enrique Ropert Gallet that under Decree No. 31 issued by the Ministry of the Interior on 23 January 1980 he would be forbidden to return to Chile. Mr Ropert Gallet states that to date, neither the text of the decree, whose publication in the Official Gazette is apparently not mandatory, nor the reasons for this decision have been communicated to him.

75. Under the heading "Human rights allegedly violated", Mr Ropert Gallet includes the fact of being kept indefinitely in exile, without justification, seven years after the completion of his sentence. He considers the connection between the alleged violation and Unesco's fields of competence to reside in the fact that he is prevented from discharging his duties as a university professor, from participating in his country's cultural life and from contributing through his experience to scientific and technological progress.

76. The author of the communication gives no information as to attempts to exhaust domestic remedies or submission to other international authorities.

77. The purpose and aim of this communication are to obtain documents from the Chilean authorities authorizing Mr Ropert Gallet to return to Chile under normal legal conditions that would enable him to resume his cultural and academic activities.

78. This communication was transmitted to the government concerned on 18 March 1982.

79. The representative of the government concerned stated that the extensive dossier accompanying the communication had not reached him in sufficient time for him to gather the necessary information, but that he was ready to inform the Committee as soon as he could do so.

80. The Chairman recalled that it was the Committee's practice in such cases to postpone consideration of the communication pending the availability of such information.

81. Two members stated that they supported such a decision, at the same time adding that the Committee might take advantage of the delay to request the Secretariat to draw the author's attention to the fact he had available to him means of redress which he had not used.

82. The Committee therefore *decided*:

(i) to postpone consideration of the admissibility of this communication until its next session;

(ii) to draw the attention of the author of the communication to the fact that he had available to him means of redress which he had not used.

Autumn 1982 session of the Committee on Conventions and Recommendations (115th session of the Executive Board)[2]

55. The author of this communication, Mr Enrique Ropert Gallet, an engineer of Chilean nationality and former professor at the Catholic University of Chile, aged 70, alleges that he was arrested on 20 September 1973 and tried on 16 July 1974 by a court martial which sentenced him to 300 days' imprisonment and six months' banishment. The first sentence came to an end on 21 July 1974 and the second expired on 20 January 1975. From that date onwards, the author claims to have applied to the Chilean authorities repeatedly for the papers he needed to return to Chile. In October 1976 he was given a passport marked with the letter "L", which did not entitle him to return to his country.

56. Mr Enrique Ropert Gallet points out that this enforced situation has resulted in an arbitrary prolongation, without any basis in law, of the duration of his exile in France and wishes to obtain authorization to return to Chile under normal legal conditions that would enable him to resume his cultural and academic activities.

57. At its spring 1982 session, the Committee had decided to comply with the request for postponement of consideration of the communication, put forward by the representative of the government concerned, who considered that he had received the file too late, and to postpone its consideration of the admissibility of the communication until the present session. The Committee had also decided to draw the attention of the author of the communication to the fact that he had remedies available to him which he had not used.[3]

58. On 21 July 1982 the Secretariat received from Mr Ropert Gallet a letter in which he explained that he had used all existing administrative means of redress; as for legal remedies he had found no one in Chile who could appeal on his behalf. He therefore reiterated his request to the Chilean authorities for authorization to return to Chile so as to be able to take steps himself.

---

[2] See document 115 EX/28 PRIV., paras. 55-60; see also document 115 EX/CR/HR/2.

[3] See document 114 EX/38 PRIV., para. 82 (*supra*, pp. 12-13).

No. 433/82 **Chile**

59. At the Committee's autumn 1982 session, the representative of the government concerned stressed that the letter of July 1982 showed clearly that the author had not exhausted all existing domestic legal remedies but only the administrative means of redress; he wished to point out however that an application for *amparo* could be filed in Chile, on behalf of the alleged victim, by any person prepared to do so, even though that person was not in possession of an authorization or a lawyer. There was therefore no objection to institutions such as the Vicaría de la Solidaridad filing such applications. He added that in view of the age of the author of the communication, he had intervened personally, on humanitarian grounds, but it was essential that Mr Ropert Gallet should submit a legal appeal through the normal channels, which did not mean that he himself would not pursue the matter. He concluded by recalling that he had drafted a note on existing remedies in Chile in such cases, which could be usefully transmitted to the author.

60. After a short debate during which one member of the Committee proposed that the Director-General should be requested to intervene, the Committee *decided*:

(i) to take note of the statement of the representative of the Chilean Government, in particular of his offer to intervene personally on behalf of Mr Ropert Gallet;

(ii) to request the Executive Board to invite the Director-General to take humanitarian measures in order to find a solution to the case;

(iii) to postpone consideration of the admissibility of the communication until the next session, pending the results of the above-mentioned measures.

Spring 1983 session of the Committee on Conventions and Recommendations (116th session of the Executive Board)[4]

31. The author of this communication, Mr Enrique Ropert Gallet, an engineer of Chilean nationality and former professor at the Catholic University of Chile, aged 70, alleges that he was arrested on 20 September 1973 and tried on 16 July 1974 by a court martial which sentenced him to 300 days' imprisonment and six months' banishment. The first sentence came to an end on 21 July 1974 and the second expired on 20 January 1975. From that date onwards, the author claims to have applied to the Chilean authorities repeatedly for the papers he needed to return to Chile. In October 1976 he was given a passport marked with the letter "L", which did not entitle him to return to his country.

[4] See document 116 EX/48 PRIV., paras. 31-34; see also document 116 EX/CR/HR/2.

Chile **No. 433/82**

32. On 11 May 1983, the Secretariat received a letter from the author of the communication enclosing numerous documents intended to prove that he had, in his own opinion, made every possible effort to exhaust all domestic means of redress, both administrative and legal.

33. The representative of the government concerned stated that in accordance with his offer, made at the [autumn 1982] session, to intervene personally on behalf of Mr Ropert Gallet, he had requested the appropriate authorities to examine the case of the person concerned as a matter of priority in view of the person's age. He trusted that his intervention would prove successful, and he would inform the Committee of the outcome at the next session.

34. Consequently, the Committee *decided* to defer consideration of the admissibility of this communication until the next session, in anticipation of the additional information which the representative of the Chilean Government proposed to provide.

Autumn 1983 session of the Committee on Conventions and Recommendations (117th session of the Executive Board)[5]

17. The author of this communication, an engineer of Chilean nationality and former professor at the Catholic University of Chile, aged 70, alleges that he was arrested on 20 September 1973 and tried on 16 July 1974 by a court martial which sentenced him to 300 days' imprisonment and six months' banishment. The first sentence came to an end on 21 July 1974 and the second expired on 20 January 1975. From that date onwards, the author claims to have applied to the Chilean authorities repeatedly for the papers he needed to return to Chile. In October 1976 he was given a passport marked with the letter "L", which did not entitle him to return to his country.

18. The representative of the government concerned informed the Committee that he had intervened for humanitarian reasons on behalf of Mr Enrique Ropert Gallet and that Mr Gallet had been authorized to return to Chile.

19. One member thanked the representative of the government concerned for the steps that he had taken.

20. At the proposal of two members of the Committee, the Committee *decided* by consensus to declare this communication settled in accordance with paragraph 14 (*a*) (x) of 104 EX/Decision 3.3.

---

[5] See document 117 EX/18 PRIV., paras. 17-20; see also document 117 EX/CR/HR/2.

No. 434/82

Concerning *Socialist Republic of Viet Nam*
Case of *Duyen Ahn*

Communication of 22 December 1981 by
Zygmunt Elbiński

Spring 1982 session of the Committee on Conventions and Recommendations (114th session of the Executive Board)[1]

136. This communication is submitted by Mr Zygmunt Elbiński, a retired physicist of Polish nationality, acting as a person with reliable knowledge of the alleged victim.

137. Mr Duyen Ahn is described as a writer and former editor of two weekly papers. He is apparently a very well-known author and a member of a national writers' association constituting a branch of International PEN. He has written some thirty novels and stories, dealing largely with themes of childhood and family life. It appears that, after the re-evaluation of Vietnamese literature, his writing was considered to be decadent. He is reported to have been arrested in April 1976 and to be held at present in a "re-education camp" in the Ham Tan region.

138. It is said that Amnesty International has succeeded in persuading the Vietnamese Government to release a number of persons whose names appear on a list submitted by that organization. However, Duyen Ahn and Pham Van Tam are still in detention. The case has not been referred to any other international authority.

139. Mr Elbiński requests the Vietnamese Government to reconsider the writer's present situation, and seeks to obtain the establishment of normal conditions enabling him to produce literary works.

140. Pointing out that he had received the communication in question only very recently and had therefore no relevant information available, the representative of the Vietnamese Government provided the Committee with some general information.

[1] See document 114 EX/38 PRIV., paras. 136-150; see also document 114 EX/CR/HR/3 Add.

141. The name of Duyen Ahn was completely unknown to him. In his country, no one was detained except for a serious crime against the people. No former servants or collaborators of the old regime, he said, had been executed; many of those placed in re-education camps had already regained their freedom; and many former writers, journalists and teachers had agreed to work for the Administration currently established. The Vietnamese Government, he went on to say, had adopted a very humanitarian policy towards those involved in the old society; several had been allowed to leave the country. Those who violated the people's right, he said, thereby debarred themselves from human rights, and the communication should consequently be ruled inadmissible.

142. Most of the Committee's members considered the measures taken by the Vietnamese authorities to be legitimate and in keeping with their country's interests. They further felt that Viet Nam had undergone several years of upheaval, that it was unnecessary to recall all the sufferings the Vietnamese people had sustained in fighting for its freedom, and that consideration of the case submitted [by] Mr Elbiński would be tantamount to interference in a state's affairs.

143. One member of the Committee was surprised that it should be said that criminals or offenders had no human rights.

144. In reply to that comment, a member pointed out that the representative of the Vietnamese Government had never said that human rights had been abolished. In his view, the problem lay in the reliability of the sources on which the communication drew, and it was his opinion that the information supplied by Mr Elbiński was not sufficient to substantiate the allegations.

145. Several Committee members pointed out that the representative of the Vietnamese Government had stated that he had just received the communication. They felt it appropriate for the government concerned to provide the Committee with fuller information, without in any way wishing to prejudge the Committee's decision or to imply any affront to that government.

146. Some members expressed surprise that the government concerned should be asked for additional information, since they considered that it was for the author of the communication to provide proof of his allegations.

147. The Committee discussed at length the advisability of asking for further information from both the Vietnamese Government and the author of the communication (the latter being asked more specifically to provide information about domestic remedies, since in his communication he had mentioned only the representations made

by Amnesty International), in view of the fact that it was the Committee's practice to give the author a second chance.

148. Acting in the spirit of 104 EX/Decision 3.3 adopted by the Executive Board, which recommends that communications be examined with a view to bringing about a friendly solution, and in view of the Committee's desire to obtain further information, the Committee adopted the following *decision*:

> In the absence of adequate information, the Committee decides to resume consideration of the admissibility of the communication at its next session, in the light of the information that the government concerned may supply.

149. The Committee did not feel it necessary to stipulate in this decision that the author of the communication would be advised of its discussions. As the Chairman mentioned, it is for the Secretariat to inform the author of the outcome of the Committee's deliberations. Whether or not the author should provide additional information would be a matter for him to decide.

150. The representative of the Vietnamese Government promised to comply with the Committee's request for the next session.

Autumn 1982 session of the Committee on Conventions and Recommendations (115th session of the Executive Board)[2]

198. This communication concerns the case of Mr Duyen Ahn, who is described as a writer and former editor of two weekly papers, whose writings was allegedly considered to be decadent, after the re-evaluation of Vietnamese literature. He is reported to have been held in a "re-education camp" since April 1976.

199. Having recalled that his predecessor had already described, at the [spring 1982] session, the main outlines of the policy adopted by his country's authorities towards those who had been involved in the former regime, which was a very humanitarian policy, the representative of the Vietnamese Government provided detailed information on the personal and family situation of Mr Duyen Ahn. He described his activities between 1956 and 1976: Mr Duyen Ahn had served the previous regime of Saigon; from 1975 to 1976 - after the establishment of the new administration in Ho Chi Minh City - he had incited writers and journalists to take counter-revolutionary action, to act against the people's interests and against national independence. On account of those activities he had been arrested on 8 April 1976 and had been sent to

[2] See document 115 EX/28 PRIV., paras. 198-201; see also document 115 EX/CR/HR/2.

a re-education camp. He had respected the regime of the centre, had obeyed its discipline and been freed on 11 September 1981, following a decision by the Ministry of the Interior dated 28 August - a date previous to that of the communication - 22 December 1981.

200. The representative of the Vietnamese Government concluded that the communication must be declared inadmissible as it was no longer justifiable.

201. After a brief discussion, the Committee *decided* to delete the communication from its list.

No. 437/82

Concerning *Colombia*
Case of *Leaders of the Colombian Federation of Teachers*

Communication of 12 January 1982 submitted by
Justine Ranivosoa

Spring 1982 session of the Committee on Conventions and Recommendations (114th session of the Executive Board)[1]

83. This communication is submitted by Mrs Justine Ranivosoa, Secretary-General of the Syndicats des Enseignants de Madagascar (SMM-FISEMA) (Madagascar Teachers' Unions) on behalf of that group.

84. Leaders of the Colombian Federation of Teachers (FECODE) were allegedly arrested and imprisoned a few days before the "civic strike" of 21 October 1981, along with other trade union leaders.

85. In a letter dated 12 January 1982 addressed to the President of the Republic of Colombia, a copy of which is attached to the letter accompanying the communication, the author states that the strike was called by the United National Trade Union Committee in support of the demands submitted by the Committee to the Colombian Government in September 1981.

86. Mrs Ranivosoa cites three names of arrested FECODE leaders: the two Dusán brothers and Cecilia de Castro Blanca. FECODE and a number of trade union organizations which took part in the strike have also allegedly been deprived of their legal status.

87. As to the purpose and aim of the communication, the author requests:

(i) the release of the imprisoned trade unionists;

---

[1] See document 114 EX/38 PRIV., paras. 83-93; see also document 114 EX/CR/HR/3 Add.

(ii) the rescindment of the decision to deprive trade union organizations of their legal status;

(iii) the cessation of the illegal occupation of trade union premises;

(iv) respect for Conventions 87 and 98[2] and other international conventions on trade union freedom and the rights of assembly and association, including the Unesco/ILO Recommendation of 1966 concerning the Status of Teachers.

88. The representative of the government concerned said that the Colombian people were very proud of their country's respect for human rights since independence, a record that it intended to maintain in the future. Colombia's legal system, he continued, was very well structured, indeed one of the most progressive in the world today; its Constitution, for instance, had been described as the "angels' Constitution".

89. Refuting the allegations made by the author of the communication to the effect that Article 20 of the Universal Declaration of Human Rights had been violated, the representative of the Colombian Government said that the statement did not correspond to reality, since Colombian labour legislation was highly revolutionary, allowing the trade unions to play a major role in the country. He pointed out that while the right to strike was respected, the law could not tolerate violence and prohibited all acts that ran counter to or were designed to overthrow the existing order established by a clear mandate of the people. He went on to say that his country, just as the rest of Latin America, was going through a difficult period at present, chiefly on account of the economic crisis. Subversive groups had committed acts of violence, even murdering teachers while carrying out their professional duties. In order to control this movement which threatened to destabilize the country, the government had been obliged to take appropriate legislative action, within the framework of the Constitution.

90. With regard to the strike of October 1981, the representative of the Colombian Government noted that only a small number of groups had supported it and that in order to avoid playing into the terrorists' hands and to protect the national interest, the authorities had been compelled to take the administrative steps that the situation required.

91. Reviewing the conditions governing admissibility of the communication as laid down in paragraph 14 (*a*) of 104 EX/Decision 3.3 of the Executive Board, he made the following points:

---

[2] ILO Conventions No. 87 concerning Freedom of Association and Protection of the Right to Organise and No. 98 concerning the Application of the Principles of the Right to Organise and to Bargain Collectively, respectively.

(*a*) The author of the communication referred to the two Dusán brothers and to Blanca Cecilia de Castro; these were not the precise names of the alleged victims, but very common names that might correspond to several different people. It had been established that at the time of the events in question, no Malagasy national had been in Colombia, and Mrs Ranivosoa did not know the true state of affairs in that country, which explained why such inaccurate information had been placed before the Committee. It could not be said that the author had, as required under paragraph 14 (*a*) (ii), a reliable knowledge of the alleged violation;

(*b*) Mrs Ranivosoa's allegations, the purpose and aim of her communication, related exclusively to trade union problems; they were therefore in no way connected with the fields of competence of Unesco and failed to conform to the requirements of paragraph 14 (*a*) (iii).

(*c*) The communication contained no solid proof and consisted only of fragmentary information: it did not therefore fulfil the condition laid down in paragraph 14 (*a*) (v).

(*d*) A letter to the President of the Republic of Colombia could not be considered as an effort to exhaust domestic remedies; recourse should have been had to the courts. The provisions of paragraph 14 (*a*) (ix) had not therefore been complied with.

(*e*) No trade union leader who took part in the strike of October 1981 was now in prison: under the terms of paragraph 14 (*a*) (x), the communication could not therefore be considered.

92. Several members of the Committee were of the opinion that the communication was clearly inadmissible and that it was only a matter of choosing which reasons to adduce in support of that decision.

93. After an exchange of views, the Committee *decided* to declare the communication inadmissible, not only because the alleged facts did not fall within Unesco's fields of competence but also because, given the lack of solid proof, the communication was manifestly ill-founded and in any case the matter had already been settled by the state concerned (paragraph 14 (*a*) (iii), (v) and (x) of 104 EX/Decision 3.3).

No. 439/82

Concerning *Chile*
Case of *Víctor Ulices Sandoval Álvarez*

Communication of 21 January 1982 submitted by
Mr Víctor Ulices Sandoval Álvarez

Spring 1983 session of the Committee on Conventions and Recommendations (116th session of the Executive Board)[1]

35. The author of this communication, Mr Víctor Ulices Sandoval Álvarez, an economics lecturer of Chilean and (since 1978) French nationality, states that he was a lecturer at the State Technical University of Santiago until October 1973, when his contract was terminated for reasons unknown to him, and that since November 1974 he has lived in France, where he has worked as a lecturer at the University of Paris XI. Although he holds an unrestricted passport, he was seemingly refused entry to Chile on 17 December 1980 at Santiago airport because his name appeared on a list of persons designated as international "terrorists" by Decree No. 55, of 1 February 1980, concerning exiles. This apparently debars him from returning to Chile for a period of seven years. His Chilean passport is said to have been renewed in 1981 but with a ban on entering Chilean territory.

36. Mr Sandoval states that he has not instituted legal proceedings because he considers that his name was included in the decree of 1 February 1980 simply by mistake.

37. The representative of the government concerned emphasized that once again it was a question of a person who had not had recourse to legal proceedings and who consequently had to be informed of the procedures that were available to him.

38. A discussion was then held among the members of the Committee on the respective values of the right to leave one's country and the right to return to it: one member observed that Article 13 (2) of the Universal Declaration of Human Rights treats these two rights as being strictly equal; the representative of the Director-General

[1] See document 116 EX/48 PRIV., paras. 35-41; see also document 116 EX/CR/HR/3.

drew the attention of members of the Committee to the wording of Article 12 of the International Covenant on Civil and Political Rights, which stipulates that the right to leave one's country can be subject to restrictions as specified in paragraph 3 of the article, whereas on the right of entry to one's country paragraph 4 of the same article says: "No one shall be arbitrarily deprived of the right to enter his own country".

39. One member of the Committee said that in his view the Committee should concern itself with problems that involved the crossing of a border only if they were connected with Unesco's fields of competence, adding that the Committee had taken that decision in cases concerning other countries and that it was essential for the rules to be applied in the same way for everyone. In the same vein, two members stressed how important they thought it that persons whose cases were submitted to the Committee should be able to exercise in their own countries those human rights that fell within Unesco's fields of competence they considered that the Committee should see to it that such was the case, no matter which country was concerned.

40. All members who in the course of their remarks made suggestions as to how the given problem should be solved were of the opinion that the right thing to do would be to suspend consideration of this communication and inform the author that a new accelerated procedure had been introduced.

41. Consequently, the Committee *decided*:

(i) to defer consideration of the admissibility of this communication to the next session, and meanwhile;

(ii) to inform the author of the existing remedies available to him in the light of the statements by the representative of the Chilean Government.

Autumn 1983 session of the Committee on Conventions and Recommendations (117th session of the Executive Board)[2]

21. The author of this communication, an economics lecturer of Chilean and (since 1978) French nationality, states that he was a lecturer at the State Technical University of Santiago until October 1973, when his contract was terminated for reasons unknown to him, and that since November 1974 he has lived in France, where he has worked as a lecturer at the University of Paris XI. Although he holds an unrestricted passport, he was apparently refused entry to Chile on 17 December 1980 at

[2] See document 117 EX/18 PRIV., paras. 21-23; see also document 117 EX/CR/HR/2.

Santiago airport because his name appeared on a list of persons designated as international "terrorists" by Decree No. 55, of 1 February 1980, concerning exiles. This debars him from returning to Chile for a period of seven years. His Chilean passport is said to have been renewed in 1981 but with a ban on entering Chilean territory.

22. At the present session, the representative of the government concerned informed the Committee that, in response to a request made by Mr V. U. Sandoval Álvarez, permission to return to Chile had been granted to him, since his name was on a list published in the Chilean official gazette and transmitted to all Chilean Consulates. He was not, however, certain that Mr Álvarez had been informed of this. At the Committee's request, the Secretariat has informed Mr V. U. Sandoval Álvarez of this authorization.

23. Accordingly, the Committee *decided* to declare the communication settled in accordance with paragraph 14 (*a*) (x) of 104 EX/Decision 3.3.

No. 440/82

Concerning *Peru*
Case of *Víctor Rapray Robles*

Communication of 3 February 1982 submitted by
Daniel Rétureau

Autumn 1982 session of the Committee on Conventions and Recommendations (115th session of the Executive Board)[1]

160. The author of this communication, Mr Daniel Rétureau, Secretary-General of the World Federation of Teachers' Unions, states that Mr Víctor Rapray Robles, a teacher, was arrested by police 17 months ago in Huacho, Peru. He is reportedly accused of acts of terrorism, although no proof of these acts has been offered; he seems nevertheless to have been held in prison and to have been subjected to repeated physical and mental ill-treatment amounting to torture.

161. In so far as Mr V. Rapray Robles is a teacher and a leader of the Peruvian National Teachers' Organization FENTEP, the author considers the repressive measures taken with regard to the alleged victim to constitute a violation of the professional, individual and trade union rights of teachers in Peru. The purpose of the communication is to free Mr Rapray Robles and to end the persecution to which other teachers in Peru are allegedly subject. The Secretariat has received several letters protesting against the alleged treatment of Mr Víctor Rapray Robles and his colleagues and asking that they be set free.

162. At the [autumn] 1982 session, the representative of the government concerned began by drawing attention to the fact that it was the first time that a communication concerning his country had appeared on the agenda of the Committee. He then explained that he had not received any detailed information from his government on the case of Mr V. Rapray Robles but that the communication seemed to him to be clearly inadmissible on formal grounds, as being both imprecise and incomplete; incomplete in that it did not state which rights had been violated and provided no proof of the alleged tortures, as required by paragraph 14 (*a*) (v) of 104 EX/Decision

---

[1] See document 115 EX/28 PRIV., paras. 160-164; see also document 115 EX/CR/HR/3.

3.3; imprecise in that it did not indicate the dates on which the events were supposed to have taken place, the authorities alleged to be responsible or the names of the other persons in the same situation as Mr Rapray Robles. Lastly, he expressed surprise that the teachers' unions, which were very powerful in Peru and well able to act on behalf of their members, had not secured the liberation of Mr Rapray Robles. As evidence of his government's good faith, however, the representative of the Peruvian Government stated that he was willing for consideration of the communication to be postponed until the next session, in order to enable his government and the author of the communication to provide additional information.

163. All the members who took the floor thanked the representative of the government concerned for his co-operative attitude and suggested that the Committee should adopt his proposal to postpone consideration of the communication until the following session.

164. The Committee therefore *decided*:

(i) to postpone consideration of the admissibility of the communication until the following session; and meanwhile

(ii) to request the government concerned and the author of the communication to provide additional information.

Spring 1983 session of the Committee on Conventions and Recommendations (116th session of the Executive Board)[2]

113. This communication concerns Mr Víctor Rapray Robles, a teacher and leading member of the Peruvian National Teachers' Organization FENTEP, who has been allegedly arrested and tortured, and is still reportedly in prison.

114. This communication was included for the first time on the Committee's agenda at its autumn 1982 session. Consideration thereof had at that time been deferred to the present session pending the receipt of further information.[3]

115. By letter dated 18 March 1983, the Permanent Delegation of Peru to Unesco informed the Committee that [...] the Permanent Delegate was absent from Paris and could not therefore attend the Committee's session. He accordingly asked that consideration of the communication be postponed until the next session.

[2] See document 116 EX/48 PRIV., paras. 113-116; see also document 116 EX/CR/HR/2.
[3] See document 115 EX/28 PRIV., para. 164 (*supra*, p. 30).

Peru **No. 440/82**

116. In accordance with the usual practice, the Committee agreed to the request of the representative of the government concerned and accordingly *decided* to postpone consideration of the admissibility of the communication until the next session.

Autumn 1983 session of the Committee on Conventions and Recommendations (117th session of the Executive Board)[4]

109. A teacher and leading member of the Peruvian National Teachers' Organization (FENTEP), Mr Víctor Rapray Robles was allegedly arrested in late 1980 and tortured, and is still reportedly in prison.

110. The Permanent Delegation of the government concerned had already twice requested that examination of the case of this teacher be postponed (autumn 1982 session and spring 1983 session). At the present [...] session, it again requested, by letter dated 15 September 1983, that examination of the case be deferred until the next session of the Committee, on the grounds that it had still not received any relevant information from the competent Peruvian authorities.

111. Some members of the Committee pointed out that the alleged victim was apparently in prison without having been tried. The question was whether in this case the international human rights instruments had been respected.

112. Given the situation, some other members of the Committee expressed their concern about the repeated request that examination of the communication be postponed and emphasized their feeling of dissatisfaction in this respect.

113. After discussion, the Committee *decided*:

(i) to inform the government of its concern about respect for the standards set by international instruments, particularly concerning the trial and treatment of an arrested person;

(ii) to request the Executive Board to ask the Director-General to take humanitarian action on behalf of Mr Rapray Robles by any means he deems effective, in particular by contacting the Peruvian Delegation on the occasion of the forthcoming session of the General Conference in Paris;

(iii) to request the author of the communication to provide further information in order to bring it up to date;

---

[4] See document 117 EX/18 PRIV., paras. 109-113; see also document 117 EX/CR/HR/2.

(iv) to resume its examination of this case at the spring 1984 session.

Spring 1984 session of the Committee on Conventions and Recommendations (119th session of the Executive Board)[5]

132. A teacher and a leading official of the Peruvian National Teachers' Organization (FENTEP) Mr Víctor Rapray Robles was allegedly arrested in late 1980, tortured and imprisoned. He is apparently still in prison without having been tried.

133. Ever since this communication has been on the Committee's agenda the government concerned has requested postponement of the examination of this case, at the [autumn 1982] session through its representative and at the [spring and autumn 1983] sessions in a letter sent to.the Secretariat. At its [autumn 1983] session, the Committee decided:[6]

(i) to inform the government of its concern about respect for the standards set by international instruments, particularly concerning the trial and treatment of an arrested person;

(ii) to request the Executive Board to ask the Director-General to take humanitarian action on behalf of Mr Rapray Robles by any means he deems effective, in particular by contacting the Peruvian Delegation on the occasion of the next session of the General Conference in Paris;

(iii) to request the author of the communication to provide further information in order to bring it up to date;

(iv) to resume its examination of this case at the spring 1984 session.

134. At its current session, the Committee once again noted the absence of the representative of the Peruvian Government, and after an exchange of views, took the following *decision*:

The Committee:

(i) draws the attention of the Executive Board to the fact that it is impossible for the Committee to establish a dialogue on the subject of the communica-

[5] See document 119 EX/35 PRIV., paras. 132-134; see also document 119 EX/CR/HR/2.
[6] See document 117 EX/18 PRIV., para. 113 (*supra*, pp. 31-32).

tion on account of the continued absence of the representative of the government concerned;

(ii) requests the Executive Board to invite the Director-General to emphasize to the Peruvian Minister of Foreign Affairs that it is not in his country's interest for a communication to be examined in the absence of its representative;

(iii) decides that, in the absence of effective participation by the representative of the government concerned at the [autumn 1984] session, it will be bound to consider as established the facts alleged in the communication and consequently to submit to the Executive Board a specific report on the case in question.

Autumn 1984 session of the Committee on Conventions and Recommendations (120th session of the Executive Board)[7]

95. A teacher and a leading official of the Peruvian National Teachers' Organization (FENTEP), Mr Víctor Rapray Robles was allegedly arrested in late 1980, tortured and imprisoned.

96. By letter dated 17 May 1984 [...][8] the Permanent Delegation of Peru to Unesco asked the Secretariat to inform the Committee that after having been sentenced to three years' imprisonment for terrorist acts, Mr Rapray Robles was released on 3 January 1983 by order of the Correctional Court of Lima, which considered that the sentence had been duly served.

97. The representative of the Peruvian Government confirmed orally the content of this letter pointing out, moreover, that Mr Rapray Robles had been released 10 months before his sentence expired

98. All the members of the Committee who spoke regarded this case as settled.

99. The Committee *decided* to take note of the release of Mr Víctor Rapray Robles and to regard this case as settled under the provisions of paragraph 14 (*a*) (x) of 104 EX/Decision 3.3 of the Executive Board.

[7] See document 120 EX/15 PRIV., paras. 95-99; see also documents 120 EX/CR/HR/2 and Add.3.
[8] See document 120 EX/CR/HR/2 Add.3.

No. 441/82

Concerning *Union of Soviet Socialist Republics*
Case of *Vladimir Raiz and Grigory Rozenshtein* *

Communication of 11 February 1982 submitted by
Alfred Kastler°

Spring 1983 session of the Committee on Conventions and Recommendations (116th session of the Executive Board)[1]

178. At the request of the representative of the Soviet Government, and in accordance with procedural practice, the Committee *decided* to postpone consideration of these communications[2] until the autumn 1983 session.

Autumn 1983 session of the Committee on Conventions and Recommendations (117th session of the Executive Board)[3]

136. The Committee decided to consider these two communications together.[4]

137. Mr Vladimir Raiz and Mr Grigory Rozenshtein aged about 41 and 44 respectively are both said to be Soviet scientists of Jewish origin. Mr Raiz is claimed to have sought permission to emigrate and left his job in the same year. Mr Rozen-

---

* From the Committee's spring 1986 session, this communication was being referred to as case of *Vladimir Raiz*.

° On behalf of the French National Council for the protection of the rights of the Jews of the USSR. From the Committee's autumn 1984 session, the French National Council for the protection of the rights of the Jews of the USSR was being stated as author.

1 See document 116 EX/48 PRIV., para. 178; see also documents 116 EX/CR/HR/3 and Add.

2 Communications No. 441/82 concerning *Union of Soviet Socialist Republics*, case of *Vladimir Raiz and Grigory Rozenshtein*, and No. 500/82 concerning *Union of Soviet Socialist Republics*, case of *Vladimir Raiz*.

3 See document 117 EX/18 PRIV., paras. 136-141; see also document 117 EX/CR/HR/2.

4 Communications No. 441/82 concerning *Union of Soviet Socialist Republics*, case of *Vladimir Raiz and Grigory Rozenshtein*, and No. 500/82 concerning *Union of Soviet Socialist Republics*, case of *Vladimir Raiz*.

shtein did the same in 1973. Since these dates, the two alleged victims are said to have been unable to obtain work in their specialized fields. They are also alleged to have been refused access to facilities to pursue their professional activities. It is claimed further that they are banned from travelling abroad and that this has made it impossible for them to attend international scientific congresses. It is also claimed that the two scientists who have been organizing scientific seminars in their respective apartments, have been subjected to harassment by the Soviet authorities and that Mr Rozenshtein has been warned that he would be prosecuted for anti-Soviet activities if he continued to hold such seminars.

138. The examination of the admissibility of these two communications was postponed by the Committee to its present [...] session.[5] When this examination resumed, the representative of the Government of the USSR who is also a member of the Committee explained that the two alleged victims had not been dismissed from the post they previously held. He informed the Committee that, as a matter of fact, the two scientists concerned had voluntarily decided to resign from their posts at about the same time that they applied for authorization to emigrate. The representative of the government concerned added that, if as it is alleged, the two scientists were dismissed, they should have taken appropriate action to exhaust available remedies. He submitted that since this appears not have been done, the communications should be declared inadmissible. For the information of the Committee, he stated that there are no restrictions on the right of Messrs Raiz and Rozenshtein to work in areas of their specialization and that if they had so far not found appropriate employment it might be that they had not been doing serious job-hunting. He pointed out in this connection that vacancy notices appear very often in newspapers and journals as well as at certain public places.

139. Noting that the case of these two scientists were, in their material particular similar to some other cases the Committee has had to deal with concerning the USSR, some members said that the two communications confirm what they considered to be a certain unfortunate pattern of victimization following unsuccessful application for authorization to emigrate. They expressed their concern that such highly qualified scientists as the two alleged victims should be unable for so long to find employment commensurate with their qualifications and experience. They added that it would be useful for the representative of the government concerned to indicate the practical steps which should be taken by Messrs Raiz and Rozenshtein in order to find suitable employment.

140. Some other members expressed the view that it would be wrong to generalize these otherwise two specific cases and thereby discover patterns which did not in

[5] See document 116 EX/48 PRIV., para. 178 (*supra*, p. 35).

fact exist. One member added in this connection that, in his opinion, even about 10 cases similar to that of Messrs Raiz and Rozenshtein could not properly be considered as elements leading to a conclusion that a pattern of victimization exists and more so if one took into consideration the fact that many thousands of people of Jewish origin have been authorized in the past to emigrate from the USSR.

141. After this exchange of views, the Committee *decided*:

(i) to take note of the explanations given by the representative of the government concerned and to request him to take into consideration the wish of the Committee to see the situation of Messrs Raiz and Rozenshtein improved;

(ii) to keep the examination of the admissibility of the communications in abeyance until its spring 1984 session.

Spring 1984 session of the Committee on Conventions and Recommendations (119th session of the Executive Board)[6]

160. Mr Vladimir Raiz and Mr Grigory Rozenshtein aged about 41 and 44 respectively are both said to be Soviet scientists of Jewish origin. Mr Raiz is claimed to have sought permission to emigrate in 1972 and left his job in the same year. Mr Rozenshtein did the same in 1973. Since these dates, the two alleged victims are said to have been unable to obtain work in their specialized fields. It is claimed further that they are banned from travelling abroad and that this has made it impossible for them to attend international scientific congresses.

161. The Committee resumed at its present session the examination of the admissibility of the two communications.[7] The representative of the Government of the USSR who is also a member of the Committee remarked that the two alleged victims had not been dismissed from the posts they previously occupied. According to him, they had decided on their own to resign from their posts just about the time they were going to submit their respective applications for authorization to emigrate. In this connection, the representative of the government concerned explained that in his country authorization to emigrate is not accorded automatically upon a request by a person desirous of emigrating. He said that there were formalities provided in this respect by Soviet law which naturally had to be complied with and that, in evaluating any given application for authorization to emigrate, it was quite legitimate for

[6] See document 119 EX/35 PRIV., paras. 160-166; see also document 119 EX/CR/HR/2.

[7] Communications No. 441/82 concerning *Union of Soviet Socialist Republics*, case of *Vladimir Raiz and Grigory Rozenshtein*, and No. 500/82 concerning *Union of Soviet Socialist Republics*, case of *Vladimir Raiz*, were being considered together.

the competent authorities of the USSR to take into account considerations of State security as well as the interests of countries friendly to the USSR especially where the prospective receiving country of the applicants happened to be in state of war with such friendly countries. He remarked in this connection that in the West restrictions are imposed on the travel of certain scientists to the USSR and on the exportation of computer technology to that country. In answer to a question posed by a member of the Committee, the representative of the government concerned stated that his country was not in a state of war with Israel. He added that Israel with which the USSR had no diplomatic relations was an aggressive country and that his government did not want to do anything that would help that country in its aggression.

162. One member of the Committee said that in a number of countries it was not only possible but also quite normal for one to leave his country without any special authorization. Declaring that he saw no relationship between Soviet State security and the respective fields of specialization of the two alleged victims, he added that in any event since a period more than 10 years had elapsed since the persons concerned lost their jobs, they could hardly with any justification be considered as constituting a security risk at the present time. Several members of the Committee agreed with him on this point. A number of members of the Committee emphasized what they considered the human aspect of the situation of the two scientists concerned who, according to these members, could neither emigrate nor obtain employment commensurate with their qualifications and experience. These members expressed the hope that, on humanitarian grounds, the competent authorities of the USSR would allow the two alleged victims to emigrate to the country of their choice.

163. A number of members of the Committee as well as the Legal Adviser referred to Article 12 (2) of the International Covenant on Civil and Political Rights which provides that "Everyone shall be free to leave any country, including his own". The Legal Adviser said that in the past the Committee had taken the view that the right to emigrate *per se* was not of concern to it. To come within the terms of reference of the Committee, the right to emigrate must have some connection with activities within the fields of competence of the Organization. The representative of the Government of the USSR pointed out that under Article 12 (3) of the aforementioned Covenant, each State party had the right to restrict the right to emigrate any given case in which it considered such a restriction necessary to protect its national security or public order. Some members of the Committee agreed with him that it was up to each State party to decide what it considered "necessary" in that context. Some other members however took the view that the test of what was necessary was rather objective and that irrespective of the opinion of the government concerned, an international human rights body could make its own appreciation of that issue in any given case.

164. Some members of the Committee insisted that, in their opinion, the State security argument put forward by the government concerned was thin and unconvincing. A member declared that if authorization to emigrate were accorded or withheld from emigration applicants depending on whether the prospective receiving country was friendly or not, international free circulation of persons would be seriously hampered. One other member queried why the alleged victims had been refused the right to hold seminars in their respective apartments. Another member declared that since the applications of emigration submitted by the two scientists concerned had been examined and rejected on the basis of the national laws of the USSR, the Committee was not competent to question the decision to reject them. One member expressed his disagreement with this point of view adding that if it were sustained all international control of the application of human rights instruments would be rendered meaningless.

165. In answer to a question from a member of the Committee who wanted to know what offences, if any, the two scientists concerned were alleged to have committed, the representative of the government concerned informed the Committee that the two alleged victims might have committed minor administrative offences. He added, however, that no action had been taken against them in that respect. He also informed the Committee that some countries friendly to the USSR had questioned the idea of brain drain from that country into Israel. The representative of the government concerned, however, added that the decision of the competent authorities of the USSR not to authorize the two alleged victims to emigrate to Israel was motivated by considerations of Soviet State security. In this connection, he recalled that the authorities of his country had so far allowed about 250,000 Soviet Jews to emigrate to Israel. On the question of whether or not the state of the knowledge of the two scientists concerned constituted or did not constitute at present a security risk for the USSR, he submitted that it was for the competent specialists of his country to make an appropriate evaluation in that respect. He declared that that issue fell beyond the scope of the Committee's terms of reference. With respect to the prospects for the two scientists concerned to obtain suitable employment, he stated that it was for them to apply for vacant posts they considered appropriate in the light of their respective qualifications and experience. With respect to the country to which the two alleged victims had manifested their wish to emigrate, the representative of the Government of the USSR stated that the prospective receiving country concerned was an aggressive one. He also said that contrary to what had been suggested, the alleged victims were not using their apartments for the organization of seminars but rather for the purpose of disseminating subversive documents.

166. At the end of its discussion of the two communications concerned, the Committee *decided*:

(i) to take note, on the one hand, of the information supplied to it by the representative of the government concerned and, on the other hand, of his generous offer to provide such additional information as would assist the Committee in examining these communications;

(ii) to make another appeal to the authorities of the USSR in the hope that they would find a purely humanitarian solution to the case of the two scientists concerned;

(iii) to keep in abeyance until its autumn 1984 session the examination of the admissibility of the communications.

Autumn 1984 session of the Committee on Conventions and Recommendations (120th session of the Executive Board)[8]

121. Mr Vladimir Raiz and Mr Grigory Rozenshtein, described by the authors of these communications[9] as being, respectively, a Soviet biophysicist and a Soviet biocybernetician, both of Jewish origin, are said to have sought permission to emigrate, the first in 1972 and the second in 1973. Since these dates, it is claimed that they have been unable to obtain work in their specialized fields. It is further claimed that they are banned from travelling abroad and that this has made it impossible for them to attend international scientific congresses.

122. The representative of the Government of the USSR, who is also a member of the Committee, stated that the two scientists did not appear desirous of seeking work in keeping with their skills, whereas people in the USSR had every opportunity of finding employment appropriate to their experience and qualifications. According to him, the persons concerned had not applied to scientific undertakings or institutes that had advertised vacancies, nor had they applied to sit for examinations, which was the normal procedure for appointment to scientific posts. Referring more particularly to [the second communication] (which concerned the case of Mr Raiz alone), he observed that the authors were endeavouring to show that the alleged victim had to be allowed at all costs to emigrate to Israel, taking it upon themselves to judge and define the requirements of Soviet State security, which constituted an inadmissible interference in the domestic affairs of the USSR. Without wishing to dwell at length on the problem of the brain drain, he added that, in the present circumstances, when the international situation was extremely complex, i.e. when missiles aimed at

[8] See document 120 EX/15 PRIV., paras. 121-127; see also document 120 EX/CR/HR/2.

[9] Communications No. 441/82 concerning *Union of Soviet Socialist Republics*, case of *Vladimir Raiz and Grigory Rozenshtein*, and No. 500/82 concerning *Union of Soviet Socialist Republics*, case of *Vladimir Raiz*, were being considered together.

his country were within five to six minutes' reach of its capital, it would be highly hypocritical to demand that specialists in cybernetics be urged to leave for the Western countries.

123. In reply to a question concerning the scientific seminars organized by Mr Raiz and Mr Rozenshtein, he explained that, if they had been prohibited, it was because the meetings were in fact being held for the purpose of collecting and spreading slanderous, anti-Soviet material. The position of the representative of the Soviet Government was supported by some members of the Committee, who stated that both persons had violated the Soviet law and had not taken any action in order to obtain suitable jobs. The representative of the government concerned explained that the case of Mr Rozenshtein and Mr Raiz was absolutely an internal affair of the Soviet State and since they were not persecuted in any way and their rights were by no means limited, they deserved no attention from the Committee. He considered that the case was inadmissible and that no international agreement had been violated here.

124. One member of the Committee remarked that the impression he had gained from the information contained in the two communications was that Mr Raiz and Mr Rozenshtein had worked as biologists, which consequently seemed to rule out the possibility of their being concerned by national security problems. Another member of the Committee refuted the allegation that the rights in question were subject to limitations due to domestic legislation and that the procedures of the Committee constituted an interference in internal affairs of that State. In this connection, he referred to Article 29 of the Universal Declaration of Human Rights and to Article 12, paragraph 2, of the International Covenant on Civil and Political Rights. He was supported by several other members of the Committee.

125. Some other members of the Committee who spoke, taking note of the reasons of State that were at present preventing Mr Raiz and Mr Rozenshtein from emigrating, wondered whether it might not be possible to have an assurance that the cases of these scientists would be reconsidered once the national security problems concerning them no longer applied.

126. In the opinion of other members of the Committee, a humanitarian solution should be sought, with a view to enabling the two alleged victims to continue their scientific work. In that connection, the representative of the Government concerned stated that unlike the situation in Western countries where unemployment was rampant, there was no unemployment in the USSR and that if the two persons concerned did want to find work it could be very easily achieved. Therefore no humanitarian measures should be applied here. One member of the Committee said that the right to work was a right recognized by the entire international community and one

to which her country unreservedly subscribed; however, she considered that the right to work had two faces, and the other side of the coin was the freedom to choose one's employment and place of work. She did not wish to dwell on this matter which she felt lay rather within the competence of the ILO.

127. Following an exchange of views, the Committee *decided*:

(i) to take note with interest of the fresh information supplied to it by the representative of the government concerned in regard to the opportunities open to Mr Raiz and Mr Rozenshtein for continuing their scientific activities in fields not involving the requirements of national security;

(ii) to request the authors of the communications to provide the Committee with any relevant information concerning the foregoing;

(iii) to ask the representative of the government concerned to inform the competent authorities of his country of the humanitarian concerns expressed by some members of the Committee;

(iv) to suspend consideration of these communications until its next session.

Spring 1985 session of the Committee on Conventions and Recommendations (121st session of the Executive Board)[10]

146. Mr Vladimir Raiz and Mr Grigory Rozenshtein, described by the authors of the two communications[11] as being, respectively, a Soviet biophysicist and a Soviet biocybernetician, both of Jewish origin, are said to have been unable, after having applied unsuccessfully for authorization to emigrate, to obtain work in their specialized fields, or to take part in other scientific activities, including international scientific congresses organized abroad.

147. In its letter dated 11 April 1985 [...],[12] the International Human Rights Law Group pointed out that it had not specially asked for its communication to be considered from the point of view of Mr Raiz's application to emigrate, but rather from that of the repeated and continuous violations of his scientific, religious, cultural and

---

[10] See document 121 EX/46 PRIV., paras. 146-151; see also documents 121 EX/CR/HR/2 and Add.2.

[11] Communications No. 441/82 concerning *Union of Soviet Socialist Republics*, case of *Vladimir Raiz and Grigory Rozenshtein*, and No. 500/82 concerning *Union of Soviet Socialist Republics*, case of *Vladimir Raiz*, were being considered together.

[12] See document 121 EX/CR/HR/2 Add.2.

professional rights within the Soviet Union. It indicated that, according to a close relative of the scientist, he was still denied the opportunity to pursue his research, he had tried in vain to obtain employment appropriate to his qualifications, he was no longer even permitted to make application and he now had a job delivering letters. The author of the communication had transmitted, as an appendix to her letter, an affidavit by a person who had met Mr Raiz at his home the previous January. According to that person, the Soviet authorities had not only refused Mr Raiz employment in line with his competence, but had also denied him the right to participate in cultural and religious practices in accordance with his beliefs; his mail and telephone conversations were said to be continually intercepted and the possibilities of his receiving visitors restricted; he was even alleged to have been ill-treated by plain-clothes policemen.

148. The representative of the government concerned pointed out first of all that Mr Rozenshtein's case seemed to have become less interesting, in view of the silence of the authors of the communication concerning him. So far as Mr Raiz's case was concerned, he reminded the Committee that Mr Raiz had left his former employment of his own free will, that he had refused the post of chief engineer in the telecommunications service of Lithuania, and that the reason why he had not been authorized to emigrate was that, during his previous employment, he had been acquainted with secret information relating to national security which had not yet become outdated. In this connection, the representative of the government concerned recalled what had been said by him with regard to the emigration of the persons involved at earlier sessions of the Committee. With regard to the letter from the International Human Rights Law Group outlined above, he stated that he had only just received it and would have the allegations checked by the competent authorities of his country, but he already had a very definite impression that the letter constituted an abuse of the right to submit a communication, since it contained crude attacks on the Soviet Union and its government. In fact, according to the representative of the government concerned, it was incorrect to say that Mr Raiz could be obliged to work as a postman; if he had chosen that job, it was possibly because he wished to avoid holding any post which might be classified by the competent authority as defence-related and thus prolong the period which would have to elapse before he would get security clearance permitting him to emigrate if he so wished. Moreover, it was inconceivable that a firm should be forced to accept someone who had not made an application; furthermore, in the USSR, synagogues were open to all those who wanted to go to them; it was unlikely that any authority could have prevented Mr Raiz from going there, especially as he had neither been arrested nor detained. The representative of the government concerned stressed that, in his opinion, the authors of the communication were trying a manoeuvre designed to compel the Soviet authorities to let Mr Raiz leave immediately, before the end of the time-limitation for the State secrets applying to him, the period of which could only be fixed by the competent Soviet

authorities. Referring to the United Nations Declaration of the Inadmissibility of Intervention and Interference in the Internal Affairs of States of 9 December 1981, he declared that it was not sound practice to use human rights as a means of interference and pressure. With respect to the affidavit submitted by the International Human Rights Law Group, he stated that its submission constituted a violation of the Committee's procedure since the Committee was not a tribunal.

149. Some of the Committee members who spoke were surprised that, after a lapse of more than 10 years or so, any secrets relating to national security of which Mr Raiz could have knowledge could still be of topical interest, given the rapid development of technology; others regretted that two high-level scientists should be deprived of a number of rights on account of their past activities, and hoped that the representative of the government concerned would be good enough to provide the Committee, at its next session, with additional information concerning the specific allegations contained in the letter of 11 April 1985 from the International Human Rights Law Group, in respect of which the explanations given by the representative of the government concerned were merely, in their opinion, an initial reaction, the accuracy of which had not yet been verified by the competent Soviet authorities. One member of the Committee felt that the situation was quite clear: in Vilnius, where Mr Raiz lived, he had, with his own eyes, seen that Jews were able to practise their faith and engage in their cultural activities unhampered; at the emigration department, he had been informed that about 98 per cent of Soviet Jews who had applied for authorization to emigrate from the USSR had obtained it and that a very few persons had been only temporarily refused authorization to leave because they had held positions or followed an occupation with a bearing on national security; this member of the Committee felt that it would be more appropriate to ask Mr Raiz why he had chosen to work as a postman, a job which was usually done by young women.

150. The representative of the government concerned stated that all the necessary information on the cases in question had already been transmitted to the Committee and that, as regards Mr Rozenshtein, his case could not, for procedural reasons, be maintained on the agenda of the Committee since for a long time the authors of the communication concerned had not been transmitting fresh information. With respect to the case of Raiz, he declared that there was full clarity on it. For these reasons, the representative of the government concerned considered that there was no point in keeping the communications on the agenda of the Committee. This point of view was supported by a number of members of the Committee.

151. After discussion, the Committee *decided*:

(i) on the one hand, to take note of the information provided by the representative of the government concerned, and on the other, to request the latter to make all the relevant information available to the Committee at its next session;

(ii) to request the authors of the two communications to provide concrete information about the efforts made by Mr. Raiz to find employment other than that of a postman;

(iii) to suspend consideration of these communications until its next session.

Autumn 1985 session of the Committee on Conventions and Recommendations (122nd session of the Executive Board)[13]

103. Mr Vladimir Raiz and Mr Grigory Rozenshtein, described by the authors of the two communications[14] as being, respectively, a Soviet biophysicist and a Soviet biocybernetician, both of Jewish origin, are said to have been unable, after having applied unsuccessfully for authorization to emigrate, to obtain work in their specialized fields, or to take part in other scientific activities, including international scientific congresses organized abroad.

104. At its present session, the Committee was informed by the representative of the Director-General, who is also the Legal Adviser, that by a letter dated 28 August 1985 the International Human Rights Law Group had reiterated its allegation that Mr Raiz was summarily dismissed from his employment in 1972 in a period of time following his request for a visa to emigrate and that in the intervening years he had repeatedly applied for employment in a scientific field but has been permitted only to work at such non-skilled jobs as telephone mechanic or mail-carrier. The Group alleged also that in early 1985 Mr Raiz renewed his application in an official letter to the Soviet Academy of Sciences urgently requesting employment in his field, and that when no action was taken he was told upon inquiries made by him that he would in no event be permitted to work in any scientific field.

105. It was generally agreed within the Committee that since no fresh information had been received for a very long time concerning Mr Rozenshtein, there was no need for the examination of his case to be continued.

---

[13] See document 122 EX/21 PRIV., paras. 103-111; see also document 122 EX/CR/HR/2.

[14] Communications No. 441/82 concerning *Union of Soviet Socialist Republics*, case of *Vladimir Raiz and Grigory Rozenshtein*, and No. 500/82 concerning *Union of Soviet Socialist Republics*, case of *Vladimir Raiz*, were being considered together.

106. With respect to the case of Mr Raiz, the representative of the government concerned who is also a member of the Committee remarked that in accordance with 104 EX/Decision 3.3 the case was utterly out of the competence of the Committee and should thus be dismissed. He added that originally the authors of the communication had presented the case as one concerning emigration and that they were changing their claim by alleging that the case concerned the difficulty Mr Raiz is meeting in his search for a suitable scientific work. On the facts of the case as he saw them, he reiterated that Mr Raiz had not been dismissed from the post he previously occupied as a senior computer engineer but rather he had decided on his own to give up that post, rather long after he had submitted an application for authorization to emigrate to Israel. The representative of the government concerned added that Mr Raiz had resigned his post because he thought that would enhance the chances of his obtaining a permit to emigrate. It was stated further that thereafter the alleged victim, on the advice of certain foreign organizations, refused for a long time to look for a new job for the same reasons. The representative of the government concerned pointed out the necessity to avoid interference in the internal affairs of his State and recalled that thousands of Soviet citizens of Jewish origin who did not constitute a risk for State security had been allowed to emigrate from the USSR and declared that so long as the emigration of Mr Raiz was considered by the competent authorities as involving a potential risk for State security he would not be allowed to leave the USSR, and that this would be strictly in accordance with the International Covenant on Civil and Political Rights and 104 EX/Decision 3.3. The representative of the USSR stated in this connection that on the territory of a number of Western countries foreign missiles are located and they are aimed against his country and can reach his country in five or six minutes, and in such conditions it would be rather strange to ask that specialists on defence technology should be allowed to leave the USSR.

107. Observing that the alleged victim found himself in an unfortunate impasse since he could neither emigrate nor find an appropriate scientific employment, one member of the Committee pleaded with the government concerned to take steps with the view to obtaining a purely humanitarian solution to the case. Several of the members supported this plea. A member queried if resignation of Mr Raiz from his post of senior computer engineer was in fact voluntary since the alleged victim had been made to understand that unless he gave up his post there was absolutely no chance for his application for authorization to emigrate to be considered favourable.

108. The representative of the government concerned declared on his part that to the extent that the communications concerned employment avenues which might be open to Mr Raiz they were outside the competence of the Committee and consequently not admissible. He added that his government's co-operation with the Committee in no way implied a change of opinion in this connection. He informed the Commit-

tee that Mr Raiz had in recent times been applying for scientific posts but he had so far not been successful because he had applied for posts which required qualifications and a level of experience that the alleged victim lacked. It was stated that, in any event, it was difficult to understand why the Committee should concern itself with the situation of Mr Raiz when in many other countries, including those of the West, there were many scientists who could not find appropriate employment.

109. Some members of the Committee agreed that employment issues were not within the fields of competence of the Organization. While also concurring with this view, some other members stated that the case in issue related not to employment or unemployment matters as such but rather to allegations that a scientist was being prevented from exercising his scientific skills in an appropriate manner. In this connection, a number of members expressed the hope that, at its next session, the Committee would have at its disposal additional information on the case from the authors of the communications as well as from the government concerned.

110. In answer to a question from a member of the Committee, the representative of the government denied allegations to the effect that Mr Raiz had been subjected either to repeated beatings by plain-clothes policemen or to any other harassment on the part of the Soviet authorities. He and some other members of the Committee reiterated their reservations regarding the admissibility of the communications.

111. After this exchange of views, the Committee *decided*:

(i) to take note of the information provided by the representative of the government concerned;

(ii) to delete the case of Mr Grigory Rozenshtein from its list since no new information concerning him had been received by the Committee for a long time;

(iii) to request the authors of the two communications to provide concrete and detailed information on the efforts made by Mr Raiz to find employment other than that of postman;

(iv) to defer consideration of these communications until the next session.

No. 441/82 **Union of Soviet Socialist Republics**

Spring 1986 session of the Committee on Conventions and Recommendations (124th session of the Executive Board)[15]

101. The Chairperson informed the Committee that a member of the Permanent Delegation of the Union of Soviet Socialist Republics had informed her that the person to be elected to replace the late Mr Ermolenko (USSR) on the Executive Board and on the Committee would be the one who was to be the spokesman of his government during the Committee's examination of the above-mentioned communications concerning the USSR[16] and that since this new member of the Executive Board would not be elected by the Board until after the Committee had terminated the part of its work relating to the examination of the communications in question, his government wanted the Committee to defer to its autumn 1986 session the consideration of the said communications. The Chairperson declared in this connection that in her opinion, a Member State did not necessarily have to have its representative serving as a member of the Executive Board or of the Committee in order to be able to put a spokesman at the disposal of the Committee during its examination of communications concerning that State.

102. Some members of the Committee agreed with the Chairperson's view and proposed that the Committee should examine the communications concerned in the absence of any representative of the Government of the USSR. They stated that, if for the reasons invoked by the Permanent Delegation of the USSR, the Committee adjourned the examination of the communications in question to its autumn 1986 session, that could create an unfortunate precedent. A member of the Committee recalled that the examination of one of the communications concerned had been deferred during several preceding sessions of the Committee and expressed reservations with regard to the request formulated by the Permanent Delegation of the Member State concerned.

---

[15] See document 124 EX/3 PRIV., paras. 101-104; see also documents 124 EX/CR/HR/2 and Add. and Add.2 and 124 EX/CR/HR/3.

[16] Communications No. 441/82 concerning *Union of Soviet Socialist Republics*, case of *Vladimir Raiz*, No. 500/82 concerning *Union of Soviet Socialist Republics*, case of *Vladimir Raiz*, No. 482/82 concerning *Union of Soviet Socialist Republics*, case of *Andrei Sacharov*, No. 603/84 concerning *Union of Soviet Socialist Republics*, case of *Andrei Sacharov*, No. 536/83 concerning *Union of Soviet Socialist Republics*, case of *Yosif Z. Begun*, No. 651/84 concerning *Union of Soviet Socialist Republics*, case of *Alleged violation with respect to education*, No. 691/85 concerning *Union of Soviet Socialist Republics*, case of *Hanna Vasylivna Mykhaylenko*, No. 692/85 concerning *Union of Soviet Socialist Republics*, case of *Vladimir Yurevich Poresh*, and No. 694/85 concerning *Union of Soviet Socialist Republics*, case of *Aleksander Nicolaevich Bogoslovsky*, were being considered together.

Union of Soviet Socialist Republics **No. 441/82**

103. While also agreeing that the Chairperson's point of view in the matter was right from a strictly legal standpoint, some other members of the Committee recalled that dialogue was an essential tool in the work of the Committee and that it would not be prudent for the Committee to examine the communications in question without a representative of the Government of the USSR, even more so since the government concerned, far from withholding its co-operation from the Committee, was in fact asking for the deferral of the examination of the communications in order to make it possible for it to make such co-operation forthcoming. They emphasized in particular the fact that in the past the Government of the USSR had always manifested its willingness to engage in a dialogue with the Committee within the framework of the latter's examination of communications concerning that country. These members of the Committee recalled also that the constant practice of the Committee in the past had been to react favourably to demands from Member States for the adjournment of the examination of communications concerning them.

104. At the end of its discussion, the Committee *decided* to accept the request of the competent authorities of the USSR that the examination of the communications concerned be deferred to the Committee's autumn 1986 session, it being understood that this decision in no way constituted a precedent limiting the discretionary authority of the Committee, in cases it considered appropriate, to examine communications even where the governments concerned did not send representatives to meetings of the Committee at which the communications were to be discussed.

Autumn 1986 session of the Committee on Conventions and Recommendations (125th session of the Executive Board)[17]

77. Mr Vladimir Raiz described by the authors of the two communications[18] as being a Soviet biophysicist of Jewish origin, is said to have been summarily dismissed from his employment in 1972 following his request for a visa to emigrate and that this application having been unsuccessful, he had been unable to obtain work in his specialized fields or to take part in other scientific activities, including international scientific congresses organized abroad.

78. At the Committee's present session, it was recalled that at its spring 1986 session, it had accepted the USSR Government's request to defer consideration of all communications concerning the USSR submitted to that session pending the appointment by the Executive Board of a person to replace the member of the Board

[17] See document 125 EX/3 PRIV., paras. 77-83; see also document 125 EX/CR/HR/2.

[18] Communications No. 441/82 concerning *Union of Soviet Socialist Republics*, case of *Vladimir Raiz*, and No. 500/82 concerning *Union of Soviet Socialist Republics*, case of *Vladimir Raiz*, were being considered together.

and of the Committee who, at previous sessions of the Committee, had also represented his government for the purposes of the Committee's examination of communication concerning that government.[19]

79. In his initial declaration, the representative of the government concerned recalled that the case of Mr Raiz had been before the Committee for a number of years now and that the position of his government regarding the allegations that constituted the subject-matter of the communications concerned had been made known to the Committee at several of the Committee's previous sessions. However, in order to facilitate the Committee's examination of the two communications concerned at the present session of the Committee, he reiterated that Mr Raiz had not been dismissed from the post he previously occupied as a senior computer engineer but rather had decided on his own to resign from that post. The representative of the government concerned informed the Committee that for a period of time after Mr Raiz resigned, the latter chose not to work. Subsequently he competed for a scientific post with the Soviet Academy of Sciences but was unsuccessful. It was also stated that if Mr Raiz had become a telephone mechanic or postman, it was of his own volition. The representative of the government concerned submitted that, for the foregoing reasons, the communications did not evoke any case of alleged violation of human rights falling within the Organization's fields of competence and that accordingly they should be declared inadmissible.

80. A number of members of the Committee concurred in this submission of inadmissibility noting in particular that the authors had failed to react to the Committee's request made at its autumn 1985 session by asking them to provide concrete and detailed information on the efforts made by Mr Raiz to find employment other than that of a postman. Some other members, however, stated that the authors should be given a last opportunity to provide the Committee with the detailed information requested, failing which the communications concerned could be struck off the Committee's list of communications. Another member expressed her regret that a highly trained scientist like the alleged victim should be forced by circumstances to work on unskilled jobs. One other member asked whether Mr Raiz could again work as a computer engineer. Another member of the Committee asked whether the competent authorities of the USSR would permit Mr Raiz to emigrate, since it appeared that he had lost his job as a result of his application for authorization to emigrate.

81. In reply, the representative of the government concerned stated that the alleged victim had applied in 1973 for authorization to emigrate and that his resignation took place in 1979, so there did not appear to be any direct relationship between the two questions. He stated further that no competent authority in the USSR had direct-

[19] See document 124 EX/3 PRIV., para. 104 (*supra*, p. 49).

ed or declared that Mr Raiz could not work in the computer science field or that he should work only on unskilled jobs such as those of a telephone mechanic or a postman. He added that in order to obtain a job as a computer engineer it was necessary to apply for one but that according to information at his disposal the alleged victim had submitted no application for any such post. The representative of the government concerned declared that while one might find it regrettable that a scientist with a high degree in the USSR or in any other Member State of the Organization should work on unskilled assignments, that might be a political or philosophical issue but not a human rights one.

82. A number of members of the Committee emphasized that the information provided by the representative of the government concerned to the effect that Mr Raiz was in no way banned from seeking employment in the scientific field, especially in the area of computer science, was very important and should be brought to the attention of the authors of the communications concerned and that in that case, unless a relevant reaction were forthcoming from the authors, the Committee would *ipso facto*, at its spring 1987 session, strike the two communications concerned from its list of communications.

83. After an exchange of views and subject to the reservation expressed by one of its members, the Committee *decided*:

(i) to thank the government concerned for sending a representative;

(ii) to take note of the statement of the representative of the government concerned that Mr Raiz was not dismissed but rather resigned his post voluntarily as a senior computer engineer and that there was no ban on the alleged victim's seeking employment in the scientific field, including the area of computer science;

(iii) to ask the Secretariat to communicate the information provided by the representative of the government concerned to the authors of the two communications in question, it being understood that, at its spring 1987 session, the Committee would *ipso facto* declare the communications inadmissible if by that time no pertinent reaction had been received from the authors.

(iv) to defer consideration of these communications until the spring 1987 session.

No. 441/82 **Union of Soviet Socialist Republics**

Spring 1987 session of the Committee on Conventions and Recommendations (126th session of the Executive Board)[20]

96. Mr Vladimir Raiz described by the authors of the two communications[21] as being a Soviet biophysicist of Jewish origin, is said to have been summarily dismissed from his employment in 1972 following his request for a visa to emigrate and that this application having been unsuccessful, he had been unable to obtain work in his specialized fields or to take part in other scientific activities, including international scientific congresses organized abroad.

97. At the Committee's autumn 1986 session, the representative of the government concerned recalled that the case of Mr Raiz had been before the Committee for a number of years now and that the position of his government regarding the allegations that constituted the subject-matter of the communications concerned had been made known to the Committee at several of the Committee's previous sessions. However, in order to facilitate the Committee's examination of the two communications concerned he reiterated that Mr Raiz had not been dismissed from the post he previously occupied as a senior computer engineer but rather had decided on his own to resign from that post. The representative of the government concerned informed the Committee that for a period of time after Mr Raiz resigned, the latter chose not to work. Subsequently he competed for a scientific post with the Soviet Academy of Sciences but was unsuccessful. It was also stated that if Mr Raiz had become a telephone mechanic or postman, it was of his own volition. The representative of the government concerned submitted that, for the foregoing reasons, the communications did not evoke any case of alleged violation of human rights falling within the Organization's fields of competence and that accordingly they should be declared inadmissible.

98. After an exchange of views and subject to the reservation expressed by one of its members, the Committee decided at that autumn 1986 session to ask the Secretariat to communicate the information provided by the representative of the government concerned to the authors of the two communications, it being understood that, at its spring 1987 session, the Committee would *ipso facto* declare the communications inadmissible if by that time no pertinent reaction had been received from the authors.[22]

---

[20] See document 126 EX/3 PRIV., paras. 96-100; see also document 126 EX/CR/HR/2.

[21] Communications No. 441/82 concerning *Union of Soviet Socialist Republics*, case of *Vladimir Raiz*, and No. 500/82 concerning *Union of Soviet Socialist Republics*, case of *Vladimir Raiz*, were being considered together.

[22] See document 125 EX/3 PRIV., para. 83 (iii) (*supra*, p. 51).

Union of Soviet Socialist Republics **No. 441/82**

99. At the Committee's present session, the representative of the Director-General informed the Committee that the decision taken by it at its [autumn 1986] session had been communicated to the authors and to the government concerned on 31 October 1986 and 13 November 1986 respectively and that no pertinent reaction had been received from the authors.

100. The Committee *decided*:

(i) to thank the representative of the government concerned for his presence and his co-operation;

(ii) to declare the communicatons inadmissible, in conformity with the third paragraph of the decision taken by it at its [autumn 1986] session.

No. 442/82

Concerning *Union of Soviet Socialist Republics*
Case of *Aleksandr Paritsky*

Communication of 10 February 1982 submitted by
Joel L. Lebowitz

Autumn 1982 session of the Committee on Conventions and Recommendations (115th session of the Executive Board)[1]

321. This communication is submitted by Mr Joel L. Lebowitz, a professor, on behalf of the New York Academy of Sciences, acting as an organization with reliable knowledge of the alleged violation.

322. Mr Aleksandr Paritsky is described as a highly qualified scientist, aged 44, previously employed as an electronics engineer. He is said to have published some 30 articles.

[322a.] A Soviet Jew, he apparently applied for permission to emigrate in 1976. This application, like many others he made subsequently, is said to have been turned down on grounds of national security despite the fact that, before seeking permission to emigrate, he had resigned from his post at the Kharkov Institute of Metrology where he studied ocean waves and designed testing apparatus.

[322b.] Since 1977, Mr Paritsky has allegedly found it impossible to work in his field of specialization and has had to do menial jobs. It is claimed that his wife has suffered harassment at her place of work - causing her to resign from her post - and that his two daughters have experienced the same treatment at school.

[322c.] According to the author of the communication, Mr Paritsky's degree of "Candidate of Technical Sciences" - the equivalent of a Ph.D - was rescinded in 1981 by the high authority concerned, thereby preventing Mr Paritsky from finding a job in the future in the Soviet Union comparable to that which he held previously. The new regulations governing the awarding of advanced degrees to scientists are

---

[1] See document 115 EX/28 PRIV., paras. 321-330; see also document 115 EX/CR/HR/3.

said to require of scientists not only a thorough knowledge of their professional field but also mastery of Marxist-Leninist theory combined with the convictions of an active constructor of Communist society.

[322d.] Arrested in August 1981, he was reportedly sentenced on 13 November of that year by a Kharkov court to three years' imprisonment for slandering the Soviet Union. The Prosecutor's Department is said to have adduced in support of the accusation a school essay written three years earlier by Dorina, one of Paritsky's daughters, in which she explained that she felt herself divided between the country of her birth, the Soviet Union, and Israel, the homeland of the Jewish people where she would like to live. Mr Paritsky is stated to have lodged an appeal with the Supreme Court of the Ukraine on 6 January 1982.

323. The representative of the Soviet Government stated that Mr Paritsky had started his work in 1965 at the Kharkov Institute of Metrology, that he had obtained a Ph.D equivalent degree in 1973, and that he had become the head of a sector at the Institute. His research work had concerned defence matters and much confidence had been placed in him. In 1976 Mr Paritsky left the Institute of his own free will and made an application to leave the country. The Soviet representative stated that Mr Paritsky should not have been surprised that his application was refused, since his work had been important in security matters. Thereafter, Mr Paritsky had taken up work in various technical areas concerning tractors and agricultural machines at an agricultural institute. His visa application had not prevented him from continuing to work in his field until the end of 1979. However, Mr Paritsky stopped working in the sector of the Ministry of Agriculture and started preparing and spreading material alleging racial discrimination in the USSR. He was assisted in these actions, the Soviet representative said, by people who visited him from abroad, apparently even a citizen from the United States. Mr Paritsky was warned by the authorities but he continued his activities and was eventually sentenced to three years for preparing materials slandering the Soviet Union. Furthermore, the Council which was competent in such matters decided by unanimous decision to deprive Paritsky of his degree. Evidence was submitted that Mr Paritsky had not been particularly proud of his degree and had brought dishonour upon it. The Soviet representative emphasized that Mr Paritsky never protested the revocation of his degree, even though he could have had recourse in that matter.

324. The Soviet representative was of the view that it must have been for personal reasons that Mr Paritsky had given up such a fruitful career and had become involved in illegal activities. The case was clearly inadmissible.

325. A member of the Committee pointed out that there were two issues in this case which clearly came within Unesco's fields of competence. Firstly, there was the

question of the academic degree. A degree was not something which was awarded as an honour, it was something which one earned through work and rigorous testing. There had been no allegation of fraud in this case, so it was clear that the revocation of the degree had been a political sanction. Secondly, as to the imprisonment for slander, the right of a person to free expression under international law was quite clear, and this included the right to say things about one's country, whether they be right or wrong. In the present case Mr Paritsky had been imprisoned for nothing more than expressing his views. The case was clearly admissible for these two reasons.

326. There ensued a lengthy debate on the two points raised. Certain Committee members felt that the action taken against Mr Paritsky could be seen as a legitimate restricting by the state of a person's professional activity, that the title in question was more in the nature of a revocable "titre" rather than a diploma, and that a state could justifiably punish a person for slanderous activities such as those carried out by Mr Paritsky. Other Committee members felt that the actions taken by the Soviet authorities violated international standards because Mr Paritsky was being punished in his professional field for activities unrelated to that profession, and because he had been sentenced to several years of prison merely for expressing a critical opinion of the Soviet Union in an exercise of his freedom of expression, a freedom which the international instruments allowed states to restrict only a limited extent.

327. In reply to questions, the Soviet representative explained that Mr Paritsky had received a degree along the lines of a French "titre", and that it was perfectly possible for the Council concerned to revoke this degree. The Council, though a state institution, had a certain autonomy, and it was inappropriate to suggest that state political sanctions could be exercised through such an institution, the representative said. He went on to say that the revocation of the degree did not contravene any international standards, and this question should not be examined by the Committee.

328. As for the matter of the essay of the thirteen-year-old daughter of Mr Paritsky, the Soviet representative explained that it was that essay which had drawn the attention of his daughter's teacher to Mr Paritsky's indoctrination of his daughter with the view that her homeland was not the Soviet Union but Israel. Further investigation had shown that Mr Paritsky had distributed passages of the essay abroad, asserting that the view of his daughter was typical of Jewish children in the Soviet Union, an assertion which was false and slanderous.

329. Another long debate followed during which certain Committee members stated their views that the communication was inadmissible because Mr Paritsky had been punished for anti-social attitudes and not for the exercise of rights in Unesco's fields of competence; other Committee members expressed their view that the case was

admissible because Mr Paritsky's educational rights had been violated as a result of his request to emigrate and that even if Mr Paritsky had in fact circulated assertions concerning his daughter's essay, his imprisonment for three years for this act was a violation of his right to freedom of expression, and still other Committee members expressed the view that more information would be needed before the question of admissibility could be decided.

330. After an exchange of views, the Committee *considered* that:

(i) the communication did not appear prima facie to be manifestly ill-founded inasmuch as it concerned the question of the revocation of the degree on grounds of an apparently discriminatory nature and inasmuch as it concerned the question of the access of Mr Paritsky's child to higher education and the legal consequences for Paritsky himself of his activities as a teacher of Hebrew and Jewish history;

(ii) the communication was inadmissible in its other respects;

(iii) the government concerned should be requested to provide additional information on those aspects referred to under (i);

(iv) the author of the communication should be entitled to supplement the data relating to the case.

Spring 1983 session of the Committee on Conventions and Recommendations (116th session of the Executive Board)[2]

179. This communication is submitted by Mr Joel L. Lebowitz, a professor, on behalf of the New York Academy of Sciences, acting as an organization with reliable knowledge of the alleged violation.

180. Mr Aleksandr Paritsky is described as a highly qualified scientist, aged 44, previously employed as an electronics engineer. He is said to have published some 30 articles.

181. A Soviet Jew, he apparently applied for permission to emigrate in 1976. This application, like many others he made subsequently, is said to have been turned down on grounds of national security despite the fact that, before seeking permission

[2] See document 116 EX/48 PRIV., paras. 179-195; see also documents 116 EX/CR/HR/2 and Add.

to emigrate, he had resigned from his post at the Kharkov Institute of Metrology where he studied ocean waves and designed testing apparatus.

182. Since 1977, Mr Paritsky has allegedly found it impossible to work in his field of specialization and has had to do menial jobs. It is claimed that his wife has suffered harassment at her place of work - causing her to resign from her post - and that his two daughters have experienced the same treatment at school.

183. According to the author of the communication, Mr Paritsky's degree of "Candidat of Technical Sciences" - the equivalent of a Ph.D - was rescinded in 1981 by the high authority concerned, thereby preventing Mr Paritsky from finding a job in the future in the Soviet Union comparable to that which he held previously. The new regulations governing the awarding of advanced degrees to scientists are said to require of scientists not only a thorough knowledge of their professional field but also mastery of Marxist-Leninist theory combined with the convictions of an active constructor of Communist society.

184. Arrested in August 1981, he was reportedly sentenced on 13 November of that year by a Kharkov court to three years' imprisonment for slandering the Soviet Union. The Prosecutor's Department is said to have adduced in support of the accusation a school essay written three years earlier by Dorina, one of Mr Paritsky's daughters, in which she explained that she felt herself divided between the country of her birth, the Soviet Union, and Israel, the homeland of the Jewish people where she would like to live.

185. Mr Paritsky is stated to have lodged an appeal with the Supreme Court of the Ukraine on 6 January 1982.

186. At the autumn 1982 session, the representative of the Soviet Government stated that Mr Paritsky should not have been surprised that his application to emigrate had been rejected, since his work had been important in security matters. He made it clear that the engineer had left the Kharkov Institute of Metrology of his own free will, that he had subsequently worked at an agricultural institute, and that he had later given up a fruitful career, doubtless for personal reasons, to become involved in illegal activities, drawing up documents slandering the Soviet Union.

187. With regard to his degree of "Candidate of Technical Sciences", the representative of the Soviet Government said that this was a "titre" or title more than a diploma, and that it was perfectly possible for the appropriate Council to revoke such a degree without contravening any international standards. He pointed out the Mr Paritsky had not been particularly proud of this degree and had not protested against its revocation, even though he could have appealed.

188. With regard to the essay written by Mr Paritsky's daughter, who considered that her homeland was not the Soviet Union but Israel, the representative of the Soviet Government explained that it had been established that the engineer had distributed extracts from the essay abroad, asserting that this opinion was typical of Jewish children in the Soviet Union, an assertion both false and slanderous.

189. After a lengthy exchange of views, the Committee:[3]

(i) considering that the communication did not appear prima facie to be manifestly ill-founded inasmuch as it concerned the question of the revocation of the degree on grounds of an apparently discriminatory nature and inasmuch as it concerned the question of the access of Mr Paritsky's child to higher education and the legal consequences for Mr Paritsky himself of his activities as a teacher of Hebrew and Jewish history, decided to request the government concerned to provide additional information on the above-mentioned points,

(ii) declared the communication to be inadmissible in other respects,

(iii) granted the author of the communication the option of supplementing the data relating to the case.

190. On 3 January 1983, the Secretariat received from the author of the communication a copy of a letter that a brother of Mr Paritsky had sent to the International Red Cross in Geneva, to which was attached a letter (doubtless a translation) thought to be from Mr Paritsky himself.

191. According to his brother, Mr Paritsky's health is giving cause for concern, and does not appear to be compatible with the nature of the work which he is required to undertake at the camp where he is interned (he is obliged in particular to lift heavy loads).

192. At this session, the representative of the Soviet Government informed the Committee that of the three penitentiary systems existing in the Soviet Union, the system under which Mr Paritsky was imprisoned was the lightest. He added that the scientist's daughters had not been denied access to education, and that, once they had attained the age required, they could enter higher education in a perfectly normal fashion. Concerning an allegation in the communication to the effect that warm clothing was not delivered to the prisoner, the representative stated that there must have been a misunderstanding, and that he had not had sufficient time to look into this matter. So far as the revocation of the academic degree was concerned, he informed the

[3] See document 115 EX/28 PRIV., para. 330 (*supra*, p. 58).

Committee that for the time being he did not have specific information to submit to the Committee.

193. One member of the Committee expressed disappointment that the representative of the Soviet Government was not yet in possession of the information that the Committee had hoped to receive at this session. Another member of the Committee was of the opinion that the Committee should express its concern with regard to Soviet citizens of Jewish origin who, after having requested permission to emigrate, had their diplomas or academic titles suddenly revoked, which in turn had serious consequences on their professional career.

194. Other members of the Committee wondered what the grounds were for Mr Paritsky's imprisonment, but at the same time suggested that the Committee gratefully accept the good offices of the representative of the Soviet Government, who offered to see what could be done to improve the conditions of Mr Paritsky's imprisonment.

195. After an exchange of views, the Committee *decided* to:

(i) take note of the offer of the good offices of the representative of the government concerned, and to thank him for this,

(ii) postpone consideration of the admissibility of this communication until its next session, pending the provision of additional information by the government concerned.

Autumn 1983 session of the Committee on Conventions and Recommendations (117th session of the Executive Board)[4]

142. Mr Aleksandr Paritsky is described as a highly qualified scientist, aged 44, previously employed as an electronics engineer. A Soviet Jew, he apparently applied for permission to emigrate in 1976. This application, like many others he made subsequently, is said to have been turned down on grounds of national security despite the fact that, before seeking permission to emigrate, he had resigned from his post at the Kharkov Institute of Metrology where he studied ocean waves and designed testing apparatus.

143. According to the author of the communication, Mr Paritsky's degree of "Candidate of Technical Science" was rescinded in 1981 by the high authority concerned, thereby preventing Mr Paritsky from finding a job in the Soviet Union comparable

[4] See document 117 EX/18 PRIV., paras. 142-148; see also document 117 EX/CR/HR/2.

to that which he held previously. Arrested in August 1981, he was reportedly sentenced on 13 November of that year by a Kharkov court to three years' imprisonment for slandering the Soviet Union.

144. It was recalled that the consideration of the admissibility of this communication was postponed by the Committee from its spring 1983 session to its present session, pending the provision of additional information by the Government of the USSR.[5]

145. In this connection, the representative of the government concerned, who is also a member of the Committee, informed the Committee that Mr Paritsky would finish serving his prison sentence in May 1984. In the meantime, measures to improve the conditions of his detention were being taken within the framework of the existing prison regulations. Members of the Committee were reminded however that imprisonment was a form of punishment. In reply to a member of the Committee who wanted to know the kind of work Mr Paritsky was required to do in prison, the representative of the government concerned stated that the alleged victim's prison regime was one of the mildest in the USSR. This representative indicated also that he did not know the outcome of the appeal which Mr Paritsky was said to have submitted in January 1982 to the Supreme Court. However, he assured members of the Committee that, in his country, there was a policy on the remission of prison sentences which was based on the good behaviour of each prisoner. He hinted in this connection that, in the case of Mr Paritsky, something might be in the offing, but he could not say more than that. The Committee was assured that the alleged victim had been receiving normally his parcels and letters and that, subject to the usual applicable rules, these would continue to be received by him until his release.

146. With respect to the allegation that Mr Paritsky's degree had been revoked, the representative of the Government of the USSR explained that the degree concerned which was "Candidate of Technical Sciences" was not just an ordinary academic degree but rather one that was perhaps akin to a professional qualification in the sense that the holder was required to possess not only a thorough knowledge of the chosen academic field but also a mastery of Marxism-Leninism and a firm commitment to place his knowledge at the service of Soviet society. It was pointed out that the alleged victim's purely academic diplomas remained valid and therefore he could continue to use them to work in areas of his scientific competence.

[146a.] One member of the Committee said he would like to be assured that Mr Paritsky would be able to obtain employment at a level comparable with that at which

[5] See documents 115 EX/28 PRIV., para. 330 (i) and (iii) (*supra*, p. 58) and 116 EX/48 PRIV., para. 195 (ii) (*supra*, p. 61), respectively.

he had previously worked, given that his professional qualifications had been revoked.

147. One member of the Committee expressed the hope that Mr Paritsky's children would not be victimized, especially as regards their education. The representative of the government concerned informed the Committee in this connection that a son of the alleged victim was already enrolled in an institute of higher education and gave the assurance that, subject to their passing the necessary examinations, the latter's two daughters should at the appropriate time find places in institutes of a similar level.

148. At the end of this exchange of views, the Committee *decided*:

(i) to note with satisfaction the information provided by the representative of the government concerned;

(ii) to keep the communication on its list, it being understood that it would be put before the Committee again only if new information were provided either by the author of the communication or the government concerned.

Spring 1984 session of the Committee on Conventions and Recommendations (119th session of the Executive Board)[6]

167. Mr Aleksandr Paritsky is described as a highly qualified scientist, previously employed at the Kharkov Institute of Metrology. His is alleged to have been sentenced to three years' imprisonment for slandering the Soviet Union.

168. This communication was first examined by the Committee at its autumn 1982 session. At the present [...] session, after recalling that Mr Paritsky had prepared and circulated slanderous information about the Soviet Union and had been sentenced accordingly, the representative of the Soviet Union, who is also a member of the Committee, informed the Committee that the person concerned would be released by the end of May 1984 at the latest. He added that Mr Paritsky could resume work in his speciality if he so desired, and that he would be completely free to submit a further application for permission to emigrate, it being understood that the competent authorities would examine it with due regard for all relevant factors, including national security. As regards the rescindment of Mr Paritsky's degree of "Candidate of Technical Science", the representative of the Soviet Government, recalling what his

[6] See document 119 EX/35 PRIV., paras. 167-169; see also documents 119 EX/CR/HR/2 and Add.2 and 3.

predecessor had said at the autumn 1983 session, explained the difference between that qualification and a university degree which, according to him, had never been taken away from anyone. He stated that, under the law, redress existed for the withdrawal of a qualification, but that Mr Paritsky had never availed himself of that possibility. He went on to say that in any case this problem of the rescindment of a degree would be expounded at greater length when the Committee came to examine another communication dealing more generally with the question [...].[7] In response to a question concerning the period at the end of which a secret regarding national seurity could be considered to have ceased to be a secret, he pointed out hat each counry had its own standards and laws in this matter and that it would be wrong to asume that it was five years.

169. After an exchange of views, the Committee *decided*:

(i) to take note of the statements of the representative of the government conerned;

(ii) to resume its examination of this communication at its autumn 1984 session.

Autumn 1984 session of the Committee on Conventions and Recommendations (120th session of the Executive Board)[8]

128. Mr Aleksandr Paritsky, a highly-qualified scientist, previously employed at the Kharkov Institute of Metrology, was sentenced to three years' imprisonment in November 1981 for slandering the Soviet Union.

129. The representative of the government concerned, who is also a member of the Committee, informed the Committee that Mr Paritsky had committed a crime and was therefore prosecuted according to the law. The verdict was three years of imprisonment, which was extremely mild for the crime he had committed. Nevertheless, the competent authorities had been preparing to release Mr Paritsky the previous May but, owing to his reprehensible conduct towards the authorities, at his place of detention, it had not then been possible to allow him that concession. He added, however, that the authorities had decided, on humanitarian grounds, to release him on 13 August 1984 without instituting further proceedings against him.

---

[7] See communication No. 519/83 concerning *Union of Soviet Socialist Republics*, case of *Withdrawal of academic diplomas and degrees*.

[8] See document 120 EX/15 PRIV., paras. 128-130; see also documents 120 EX/CR/HR/2 and Add. and Add.2.

Union of Soviet Socialist Republics **No. 442/82**

130. After an exchange of views, the Committee *decided* to consider the case in question settled and to strike the communication from its list.

No. 443/82

Concerning *Czechoslovakia*
Case of *Karel Kyncl* *

Communication of 2 February 1982 submitted by
Czechoslovak National Council of America

Spring 1982 session of the Committee on Conventions and Recommendations (114th session of the Executive Board)[1]

188. This communication is submitted by the Czechoslovak National Council of America acting as a non-governmental organization with reliable knowledge of the alleged violations.

189. Mr Karel Kyncl is described as a journalist who has written articles for a number of newspapers and magazines and for the Czechoslovak radio. He was permanent correspondent in the United States and later correspondent for South-East Asia. In 1968 it is claimed that he concentrated his attention on domestic issues and thus began to work for Czechoslovak television. He is alleged to have been deprived of his job and excluded from the Central Committee of the Communist Party and the Association of Czech Journalists for having participated in direct television coverage of the funeral of Jan Palach, the Czechoslovak student who set fire to himself in protest against the Soviet invasion of Czechoslovakia. Since then, he has apparently been the victim of "systematic persecution": difficulty in finding work, loss of his disability pension (he underwent stomach surgery in 1974, and suffers from an ulcer and inflammation of the kidneys), withdrawal of his driving licence, identity card and passport; his telephone has been cut off and he has been frequently interrogated and detained, and his house searched. It is stated that in January 1972 he was sentenced to 20 months' imprisonment for "subversion" for having signed a leaflet reminding citizens of their right to abstain from voting. He eventually decided to emi-

* At the Committee's autumn 1982 session, this communication was being referred to as case of *Ladislav Hejdánek and Václav Benda* and case of *Karel Kyncl*, respectively, at its spring 1983 session as case of *Karel Kyncl, Václav Benda and Ladislav Hejdánek* and at its autumn 1983 session as case of *Ladislav Hejdánek*.

[1] See document 114 EX/38 PRIV., paras. 188-195; see also document 114 EX/CR/HR/3 Add.

grate; but was unable to do so. In May 1981 he was arrested on a charge of subversion in collusion with a foreign power, in connection with the interrogation a short time previously of the French nationals, Françoise Anise and Gilles Thonon, at the Czechoslovak-Austrian border.

190. The author requests that:

(i) Mr Kyncl should be released so as to be able to receive appropriate medical treatment;

(ii) he should be given a regular trial so as to be able to defend himself properly;

(iii) an end should be put to the violation of his human and civic rights, including the right to receive and impart information regardless of frontiers;

(iv) he should be given permission to emigrate should he so desire.

191. The representative of the Czechoslovak Government stated that the case of Mr Karel Kyncl had still not been settled in court and that since the alleged victim had now been released, he was consequently presumed to be innocent.

192. Some members of the Committee considered that the only solution was to postpone consideration of the admissibility of this communication since legal proceedings were still pending.

193. In reply to a question by a member of the Committee, the representative of the government concerned said that, since Mr Kyncl had been released, he was free to participate in the activities of Czechoslovak society.

194. One member of the Committee wondered whether it would not be advisable to ask for the legal proceedings to be speeded up.

195. After an exchange of views, the Committee, considering that it was unable to come to any conclusion for the time being, *decided* to postpone consideration of the admissibility of this communication until the next session, by which time an official verdict might have been given.

Czechoslovakia **No. 443/82**

Autumn 1982 session of the Committee on Conventions and Recommendations (115th session of the Executive Board)[2]

213. The cases of Messrs Ladislav Hejdánek and Václav Benda form part of [the present communication] in which the Czechoslovak National Council of America announces its intention to place before Unesco facts relating to violations of the human rights of five Czechoslovak citizens

A. *Case of Mr Ladislav Hejdánek*

214. He is described as a professor and philosopher, aged 55. A graduate of the Philosophy Faculty of the Charles University in Prague, he is said to have been a disciple of the late Professor Jan Patočka, one of the founders of Charter 77. He is reported to have published a number of articles on philosophy in various journals and to have delivered several lectures.

[214a.] During 1968-1969 he became the founding member of the Society for Human Rights and was the Secretary of the Preparatory Committee for the Students' Ecumenical Movement. He was also on the editorial staff of several publications.

[214b.] In 1971 he is stated to have been expelled from his employment at the Philosophical Institute because his views did not conform with the official standpoint. It is alleged that he was subsequently arrested and imprisoned for nine months. Since his release from prison he has worked as night watchman, guard and stoker.

[214c.] In 1977 he signed Charter 77. He became spokesman for this organization in 1978, and was co-author of several Charter 77 documents and appeals. Since April 1980 he has organized in his apartment philosophy seminars to which lecturers from abroad have been invited.

[214d.] The harassment to which he was allegedly subjected by the police is said to have reached a peak on 14 December 1981, when his apartment was entered and most of the participants in the seminar were detained by the police for 48 hours. Two weeks later, Mr Jacques Derrida, a French professor and lecturer, was arrested and was released only after representations by the French Government.

[2] See document 115 EX/28 PRIV., paras. 213-231; see also documents 115 EX/CR/HR/2 and 3.

B. *Case of Václav Benda*

215. He is described as a mathematician and philosopher, aged 36.

[215a.] A graduate of the same university as Mr Hejdánek, Mr Benda taught philosophy but was allegedly dismissed for his political and religious views. He then began to study mathematics and became a mathematician and computer programmer at the Research Institute for Computer Science (VUMS). He published a number of articles in the field of automation and applied logic.

[215b.] A signatory of Charter 77, he was allegedly dismissed once again from his post, and was subsequently obliged to take a job as a stoker.

[215c.] It is claimed that Mr Benda, with his wife and five children, has been subject to constant harassment by the police. His apartment is said to have been searched on numerous occasions. Having been detained several times for brief periods, he was finally arrested in May 1979 and charged with subversion. In October of the same year he was sentenced to four years' imprisonment.

[215d.] It is claimed that in prison he is not entitled to receive more than two food parcels a year, that visits from his family depend on the permission of the prison authorities and that mail delivery is not regular.

[215e.] On 25 March 1982 the police allegedly subjected his wife to an apartment search and confiscated 130 harmless notes together with the passports of both husband and wife, though these were out of date.

216. In the case of Mr Hejdánek as in that of Mr Benda, the author of the communication states that there is no legal remedy in Czechoslovakia for citizens arrested or detained for civic or political reasons. The author considers that the lawyers appointed by the state work in the interests of the state rather than in the interests of their clients.

217. In neither case has the matter been submitted to any other international authority.

[217a.] The National Academy of Sciences of the United States of America [has] apparently sent several letters to the Czechoslovak authorities on Mr Benda's behalf.

218. The representative of the Czechoslovak Government explained to the Committee that his government had never refused to take a humanistic attitude towards communications, and had always shown a high regard for the Committee on Conven-

tions and Recommendations. In the case of Mr Benda, the Prosecutor had established that Mr Benda was a founder of the "Committee for the Defense of Unjustly Accused Persons" and had thus violated law 68 of 1952 and law 74 of 1963. This Committee had collected information on police and judicial organs, had distorted this information and distributed it.

219. Mr Benda had therefore been sentenced to prison, the Czechoslovak representative said; the humanistic attitude of the Czechoslovak Government towards him had been reflected by a sentence of 4 years instead of the possible maximum of 10. Mr Benda in fact did receive letters, parcels and visits. His state of health was good, the Czechoslovak representative said, and he received regular medical examinations.

220. As concerned Mr Hejdánek, he was presently at liberty, circulating freely in society.

221. A Committee member stated that it was clear that this case involved a very serious violation of Articles 18 and 19 of the Universal Declaration of Human Rights. Mr Benda had been convicted for the act of distributing information on the violation of human rights, and the case was clearly one for the Committee. As for Mr Hejdánek, if in fact the legal process had not yet reached an end in his case, it would be appropriate to postpone the consideration of the case, the Committee member said.

222. Another Committee member stated his agreement with the previous speaker as concerned Mr Benda, and went on to point out that Mr Hejdánek though free was suffering from constant police surveillance, harassment, and deprivation of his liberty to exercise a profession in Unesco's fields of competence.

223. Another Committee member wondered why it was not clear that this was a case which should be treated as were other cases concerning persons working subversively against their governments. The case should be rejected as being ill-founded, he said.

224. In the view of another Committee member, Mr Hejdánek had regained his freedom; he wondered, however, what sort of freedom he was enjoying, since his activities were under constant surveillance and were rendered difficult in certain respects. With regard to Mr Benda, the same Committee member went on to say that such relative freedom did not appear to have been granted to him, and that despite a certain degree of clemency in the judges' sentence, the state seemed to have overreacted somewhat towards a man who had merely expressed his opinions. The Committee member expressed himself in favour of postponing examination of the communication.

225. A lengthy debate ensued. Some Committee members considered that the communication was inadmissible, firstly, because the "normality" of Mr Hejdánek's activities needed to be assessed within the context of the country concerned, an assessment that did not lie within Unesco's competence, and, secondly, because, in Mr Benda's case, determining the subversive nature of his activities lay wholly within the sovereign powers of the Czechoslovak courts, which, in the case at issue, had handed down a virtually minimal sentence. In the view of some other Committee members, the case under review involved neither terrorist activity nor the transportation of arms, nor acts of violence but simply intellectual activities. Freedom of opinion and expression should be defended; the decision of a country's judicial or administrative authorities should not escape analysis or criticism.

226. Finally, the Committee *decided*:

(*a*) in the case of Mr Benda, noting that he had been sentenced in 1979 to four years' imprisonment and that he had therefore already served over two-thirds of his sentence;

(i) to appeal to the Czechoslovak authorities for clemency to be shown forthwith to Mr Václav Benda;

(ii) to suspend consideration of the admissibility of the communication until the next session;

(*b*) in the case of Mr Hejdánek, noting that the allegation concerning violation of the right to education did not, in the case in point, appear to be manifestly ill-founded, to ask the government concerned for further precise information on the seminars organized by Mr Hejdánek and on their status in relation to the Czechoslovak laws applicable and the international human rights instruments.

[C. *Case of Karel Kyncl*]

227. Mr Karel Kyncl is described as a journalist who has written articles for a number of newspapers and magazines and for the Czechoslovak radio. He was permanent correspondent in the United States and later correspondent for South-East Asia. In 1968 it is claimed that he concentrated his attention on domestic issues and thus began to work for Czechoslovak television. He is alleged to have been deprived of his job and excluded from the Central Committee of the Communist Party and the Association of Czech Journalists for having participated in direct television coverage of the funeral of Jan Palach, the Czechoslovak student who set fire to himself in protest against the Soviet invasion of Czechoslovakia. Since then, he has apparently

been the victim of "systematic persecution": difficulty in finding work, loss of his disability pension (he underwent stomach surgery in 1974, and suffers from an ulcer and inflammation of the kidneys), withdrawal of his driving licence, identity card and passport; his telephone has been cut off and he has been frequently interrogated and detained, and his house searched. It is stated that in January 1982 he was sentenced to 20 months' imprisonment for "subversion" for having signed a leaflet reminding citizens of their right to abstain from voting. He eventually decided to emigrate, but was unable to do so; in May 1981 he was arrested on a charge of subversion in collusion with a foreign power, in connection with the interrogation a short time previously of the French nationals, Françoise Anise and Gilles Thonon, at the Czechoslovak-Austrian border.

228. Spring 1982 session: The representative of the Czechoslovak Government stated that the case of Mr Karel Kyncl had still not been settled in court and that, as he had been released, he was free to participate in the activities of Czechoslovak society.

[228a.] After an exchange of views, the Committee, pending a verdict by the competent judicial authorities, decided to postpone consideration of the admissibility of this communication until its present session.[3]

229. At the autumn 1982 session, the representative of the Czechoslovak Government informed the Committee that Mr Kyncl still remained at liberty, that he had not been formally charged and that, as a result, it would at present be premature to reply to the allegations contained in the communication.

230. Certain Committee members, while joining the consensus to postpone consideration of the case, felt that it should nevertheless be pointed out that despite the lack of formal accusations, Mr Kyncl was apparently suffering from informal harassment by the authorities. One of these Committee members also wanted to point out that if the Czechoslovak authorities ever felt able to allow Mr Kyncl to leave Czechoslovakia, his own country would allow Mr Kyncl to immigrate.

231. The Committee thereupon *decided* to postpone its consideration of this case until its next session.

[3] See document 114 EX/38 PRIV., para. 195 (*supra*, p. 68).

No. 443/82 **Czechoslovakia**

Spring 1983 session of the Committee on Conventions and Recommendations (116th session of the Executive Board)[4]

A. *Case of Karel Kyncl*

155. This case concerns a journalist who had allegedly been the subject of harassment by the Czechoslovak authorities and who wished to emigrate, but who had been unable to do so after having been questioned by the police in May 1981, following the arrest, a short time beforehand, of two French citizens.

156. The representative of the government concerned informed the Committee that the person concerned was no longer a Czechoslovak citizen and that he had already left the country.

157. The Committee *decided* to consider this case as having been settled within the terms of paragraph 14 (*a*) (x) of 104 EX/Decision 3.3 of the Executive Board.

B. *Case of Václav Benda*

158. This case concerns a mathematician and philosopher accused of subversion and sententenced to four years' imprisonment.

159. The representative of the Czechoslovak Government announced that Mr Benda would have completed his sentence in a few days' time.

160. Noting the information just given, one member of the Committee, in order to mark his disapproval of the conviction of the alleged victim, stressed the fact that, while it was true that he had almost completed his sentence, that sentence had been passed on a man who had had the courage to exercise his human rights.

161. As this report was being approved, the Committee received confirmation of the release of Mr Václav Benda and *decided* to consider the case as settled in accordance with paragraph 14 (*a*) (x) of 104 EX/Decision 3.3.

C. *Case of Ladislav Hejdánek*

162. This case concerns a teacher and philosopher who was alleged to have been the subject of harassment by the authorities. At the autumn 1982 session, the Committee had requested the government concerned to provide further information concerning

[4] See document 116 EX/48 PRIV., paras. 155-165; see also document 116 EX/CR/HR/2.

the seminars Mr Hejdánek had organized and their status in relation to Czechoslovak legislation and the international instruments relating to human rights.[5]

163. The representative of the Czechoslovak Government stated that the alleged victim had not been accused of any offence, that he still remained at liberty, that the authorities had no intention of restricting his cultural activities and that given the Committee's concern, the competent Czechoslovak authorities were in the process of collecting the information sought by the Committee.

164. Several members of the Committee expressed their gratitude to the representative of the government concerned for his willingness to co-operate.

165. After a brief discussion, the Committee *decided* to postpone consideration of the admissibility of the case until its autumn 1983 session, while awaiting additional information.

Autumn 1983 session of the Committee on Conventions and Recommendations (117th session of the Executive Board)[6]

119. Mr Hejdánek, a teacher and philosopher, is alleged to have been the subject of harassment by the Czechoslovak authorities (constant police surveillance, frequent interrogations, house searched numerous times, seizure of some of his publications, private seminars disrupted).

120. At the autumn 1982 session and the spring 1983 session [...], the Committee had requested the government concerned to provide further information particularly concerning the subject-matter of the seminars conducted by Mr Hejdánek.[7]

121. At the present [...] session, the representative of the Czechoslovak Government informed the Committee that the alleged victim had engaged in activities which were harmful to the domestic and foreign policy of the State, and that under the pretext of so-called "seminars", he had conducted anti-governmental activities; this all however, belonged to the past, although the alleged victim continued, none the less, to engage in similar activities at the present time, at a level which was still within the limits of legality. He added that Mr Hejdánek was not detained at the present time, and that he could, within the framework of the Constitution and current legislation in his country, continue his philosophical pursuits.

---

[5] See document 115 EX/28 PRIV., para. 226 (*b*) (*supra*, p. 72).
[6] See document 117 EX/18 PRIV., paras. 119-124; see also document 117 EX/CR/HR/2.
[7] See documents 115 EX/28 PRIV., para. 226 (*b*) (*supra*, p. 72), and 116 EX/48 PRIV., para. 165 (*supra*, p. 75), respectively.

No. 443/82 **Czechoslovakia**

122. Some members of the Committee pointed out that while it appeared that the philosopher was free and that there existed no charge against him, he nevertheless did not seem at liberty to express himself. They also wondered if he could henceforth receive and disseminate information across national frontiers, and if he could find employment corresponding to his qualifications. Other members of the Committee felt that to demand guarantees with regard to Mr Hejdánek's future would be asking too much.

123. Taking the floor once again, the representative of the government concerned made it clear that Mr Hejdánek, having recovered all his rights as a Czechoslovak citizen, was free to engage in any activities that did not contravene the law; as far as his employment in an academy was concerned, the question was of a contractual nature between the academy and the applicant for the position, and was not the concern of the police or the government.

124. After a lengthy exchange of views, the Committee *decided* to:

(i) take note of the information furnished by the representative of the government concerned;

(ii) declare that the communication was inadmissible, on the grounds that it lacked relevant evidence of the alleged violation of human rights, in compliance with paragraph 14 (*a*) (v) of 104 EX/Decision 3.3;

(iii) ask the Secretariat, in accordance with the practice of the Committee, to inform the author of the communication of this decision, it being understood that the latter would be able to submit a new communication if new developments arose.

No. 444/82

Concerning *Union of Soviet Socialist Republics*
Case of *Kishore Dehadrai*

Communication of 14 January 1982 submitted by
Kishore Dehadrai

Autumn 1982 session of the Committee on Conventions and Recommendations (115th session of the Executive Board)[1]

331. This communication concerns the case of a father, Mr Kishore Dehadrai (of Indian nationality) who wishes to obtain custody of his son, currently living with his mother (of Soviet nationality) in Zhdanov, in the Soviet Union.

332. The representative of the government concerned stated that the affair related to a dispute in private law between a husband and wife, that, as indeed had been pointed out by the author of the communication himself, the Indian Consulate in Odessa had advised him, and rightly so, to take the matter to a Soviet court of civil law, and that in no way did it come within Unesco's spheres of competence.

333. After an exchange of views the Committee *decided* to declare the communication inadmissible on the grounds that it did not fall within the Organization's competence, in pursuance of 104 EX/Decision 3.3, paragraph 14 (*a*) (iii), of the Executive Board.

[1] See document 115 EX/28 PRIV., paras. 331-333; see also document 115 EX/CR/HR/3.

No. 446/82

Concerning *Honduras*
Case of *Carlos Ramírez*

Communication of 30 December 1981 submitted by
Matilde de Ramírez

Spring 1982 session of the Committee on Conventions and Recommendations (114th session of the Executive Board)[1]

111. On 20 April 1982, the Permanent Delegate of Honduras to Unesco sent a letter to the Secretariat to the effect that she had forwarded the communication in question to her government on 4 March 1982, and that she had received a letter dated 31 March from her country's Secretariat for External Affairs, informing her that the communication had been transmitted to the appropriate government body. However, since the Permanent Delegate of Honduras was not in possession of any further information, she asked the Committee to be kind enough to take into account the short time which her government had had at its disposal.

112. On the Chairman's suggestion, the Committee *decided* to postpone consideration of this communication for its next session.

Autumn 1982 session of the Committee on Conventions and Recommendations (115th session of the Executive Board)[2]

117. The author of this communication, Mrs Matilde de Ramírez, a Guatemalan student, alleges that Mr Carlos Ramírez, a student and leader of the University Students' Association of Guatemala, was arrested on 27 April 1981 at the "El Guasaule" frontier post between Honduras and Nicaragua, by a lieutenant from the Choluteca military base in charge of the frontier post, while on his way back to Guatemala after an international tour of solidarity with his people.

---

[1] See document 114 EX/38 PRIV., paras. 111-112; see also document 114 EX/CR/HR/3 Add.
[2] See document 115 EX/28 PRIV., paras. 117-124; see also document 115 EX/CR/HR/2.

No. 446/82 **Honduras**

118. At the spring 1982 session, the Committee had decided to postpone consideration of this communication to the present session,[3] the Permanent Delegate of Honduras having advised the Committee that her government had not had time to gather the necessary information.

119. At the autumn 1982 session, the representative of the government concerned told the Committee that her government had instituted the necessary investigations and inquiries, that these had not yet been completed and were accordingly being actively pursued. She was therefore unable for the time being to make any statement regarding the fate of Mr C. Ramírez, as she did not even know whether he had crossed the border. She added that in her country, which had a democratic system and a government freely elected by the people, human rights had always been respected.

120. One Committee member urged that the communication be deemed admissible, considering that, since Mr C. Ramírez's life might be in danger, the time factor was vital, and that simply to postpone consideration of the communication would in fact be a negative response in this respect. Many other members also stressed the urgency of the situation, and expressed the wish that an appeal be made to the Honduran Government to act swiftly and to provide the Committee with the most detailed information possible, at the latest in time for its next session. They nevertheless considered that examination of the admissibility of the communication should be postponed to the next session in view of their lack of adequate information. Sharing the concern expressed by several of their colleagues regarding the urgency of the situation, some members proposed that, in view of the importance which the Committee attached to obtaining the necessary information rapidly, the Executive Board be invited to request the Director-General to make such approaches to the Honduran Government as he might deem necessary to expedite the process of finding a solution to the problem raised by the communication. Some members expressed their astonishment that since March 1982, the date on which the case had been referred to it, the Honduran Government had still not verified the accuracy of facts that had been quite clearly set out in the communication. Several members suggested that, while keeping the communication on its agenda, the Committee should instruct the Secretariat to transmit the case to the Working Group on [Enforced or Involuntary Disappearances] of the United Nations Commission on Human Rights.

121. The Director-General's representative reminded the Committee that transmission of a communication to that Working Group did not have the effect of causing it to be withdrawn from the Committee's own agenda.

---

[3] See document 114 EX/38 PRIV., para. 112 (*supra*, p. 79).

122. Lastly, one member pointed out that it might be useful to refer the case to the International Committee of the Red Cross and to ask it if it could take any action in such situations.

123. The representative of the government concerned then took the floor again to say that, as a woman and a mother, she was keenly aware of the human problem posed by the communication, and that she would do her utmost to ensure that her government responded quickly.

124. The Committee therefore *decided*:

(i) to postpone consideration of the admissibility of the communication to its next session;

(ii) to request the representative of the Honduran Government to inform her government of the serious concern voiced within the Committee and to appeal to it to take urgent steps to shed all possible light on the case and to supply the Committee as rapidly as possible with the most detailed possible information;

(iii) to instruct the Secretariat to transmit the case to the Working Group of the United Nations Commission on Human Rights which deals with cases of enforced or involuntary disappearance of persons and to explore the possibility of improving co-operation with the said Working Group and more particularly with its Chairman;

(iv) to contact the International Committee of the Red Cross in order to ascertain what it might be able to do in the present case and similar cases.

Spring 1983 session of the Committee on Conventions and Recommendations (116th session of the Executive Board)[4]

72. The author of this communication, Mrs Matilde de Ramírez, a Guatemalan student, alleges that her husband, Mr Carlos Ramírez, a student and leader of the University Students' Association of Guatemala, was arrested on 27 April 1981 at the "El Guasaule" frontier post between Honduras and Nicaragua, by a lieutenant from the Choluteca military base in charge of the frontier post, while on his way back to Guatemala after an international tour of solidarity with his people.

---

[4] See document 116 EX/48 PRIV., paras. 72-81; see also document 116 EX/CR/HR/2.

No. 446/82 **Honduras**

73, At the spring 1982 session, the Committee decided to postpone consideration of this communication to the [autumn 1982] session,[5] the Permanent Delegate of Honduras having advised the Committee that her government had not had time to gather the necessary information.

74. At the autumn 1982 session, the representative of the Honduran Government stated that the investigations instituted by the authorities of her country had not yet been completed, and that she was therefore not in a position to indicate the whereabouts of Mr Carlos Ramírez.

75. After a debate during which the urgency of the situation had been emphasized, the Committee decided:[6]

(i) to postpone consideration of the admissibility of the communication to the present session,

(ii) to request the representative of the Honduran Government to inform her government of the serious concern voiced within the Committee and to appeal to it to take urgent steps to shed all possible light on the case and to supply the Committee as rapidly as possible with the most detailed possible information;

(iii) to instruct the Secretariat to transmit the case to the Working Group of the United Nations Commission on Human Rights which deals with cases of enforced or involuntary disappearance of persons and to explore the possibility of improving co-operation with the said Working Group and more particularly with its Chairman;

(iv) to contact the International Committee of the Red Cross in order to ascertain what it might be able to do in the present case and similar cases.

76. At the present session, the representative of the Honduran Government stated that his government had taken the case of Mr Carlos Ramírez very seriously, which was why the previous representative of his country had assured the Committee that she would endeavour to provide it with further information. A very thorough investigation had therefore been conducted by the Government of Honduras, at the end of which it had been established that Mr Carlos Ramírez had never officially entered, the territory of Honduras, that he had never passed through the "El Guasaule" frontier post, and that he had never been detained. It was reported that the Nicaraguan

---

[5] See document 114 EX/38 PRIV., para. 112 (*supra*, p. 79).
[6] See document 115 EX/28 PRIV., para. 124 (*supra*, p. 81).

authorities had likewise no record of Mr C. Ramírez leaving their country. It was difficult to say with certainty that there were no clandestine border crossings in that area. The representative of the government concerned stated that he personally could vouch for the thoroughness with which the investigations had been conducted. He was convinced that Mr C. Ramírez had not been arrested by any police force, but he would nevertheless do all he could to try to shed some light on the case.

77. One member of the Committee said that the case continued to give cause for concern since the situation was not progressing in the way desired by the Committee and the tenor of the statements made by the representative of the government concerned was the same as at the previous sessions. If Mr Carlos Ramírez had indeed been arrested, as the information supplied by his wife seemed to indicate [...],[7] only the authorities responsible for his arrest could indicate his whereabouts.

78. Another member of the Committee asked why, if the government concerned was really taking the matter seriously, it did not collaborate with the International Committee of the Red Cross which, according to the letter it had sent to the Secretariat on 8 April 1982 [...][8] did not seem to have been able to establish itself in Honduras.

79. The representative of the Director-General explained that even though the ICRC did not have a delegation in Honduras, it had certainly appointed a general delegate for Central America. Although the Red Cross was acting at the request of the family concerned, the Committee could, through the Secretariat, ask it whether it could undertake an investigation at the Committee's request through its delegate for Central America.

80. All the members of the Committee who then took the floor declared themselves in favour of that solution, especially since, as one of them said, other Central American countries bordering on Honduras might have information regarding the case.

81. The Committee therefore *decided*:

(i) to suspend consideration of the admissibility of the communication until the next session;

(ii) to instruct the Secretariat to re-establish contact with the International Committee of the Red Cross to ask it whether, at the Committee's request, it could investigate through its regional delegate in Central America the disappearance of Mr Carlos Ramírez.

---

[7] See document 116 EX/CR/HR/2.

[8] *Ibidem*.

No. 446/82 **Honduras**

Autumn 1983 session of the Committee on Conventions and Recommendations (117th session of the Executive Board)[9]

84. The author of this communication alleges that her husband, Mr Carlos Ramírez, a student and leader of the University Students' Association of Guatemala, was arrested on 27 April 1981 at the "El Guasaule" frontier post between Honduras and Nicaragua, by a lieutenant from the Choluteca military base in charge of the frontier post, while on his way back to Guatemala after an international tour of solidarity with his people.

85. This communication has been on the agenda of the Committee since its spring 1982 session.

86. At the spring 1983 session, the representative of the Honduran Government stated that his government had conducted a very thorough investigation at the end of which it had been established that Mr Carlos Ramírez had certainly not entered the territory of Honduras officially and that, consequently, his country could not be held responsible for him.

87. At the present session, the representative of the government concerned stated that the relevant authorities in his country had continued their investigation, but still to no avail; they would, however, not fail to carry on with their investigations in an attempt to trace Mr C. Ramírez.

88. On the proposal of those of its members who had spoken, the Committee *decided* to take note of the offer by the government concerned to arrange for the investigations to be continued and to defer consideration of this communication pending further information either from the author of the communication or from the Honduran Government.

Autumn 1987 session of the Committee on Conventions and Recommendations (127th session of the Executive Board)[10]

189. The communication concerned is [...] submitted by Mrs Matilde de Ramírez, the wife of the alleged victim, Mr Carlos Ramírez, a Guatemalan student. He was reportedly arrested on 27 April 1981, at the "El Guasaule" frontier post between Hon-

[9] See document 117 EX/18 PRIV., paras. 84-88; see also document 117 EX/CR/HR/2.
[10] See document 127 EX/3 PRIV., paras. 189-193; see also document 127 EX/CR/HR/2, annex V.

duras and Nicaragua, by a lieutenant from the Choluteca military base, while on his way back to Guatemala after an international tour of solidarity.

190. The representative of the Director-General informed the Committee that owing to a change of Ambassador, the Permanent Delegation of Honduras was unable to send a representative.

191. According to information received from the specialized Working Group of the Commission on Human Rights, the government had informed the Group in a letter dated 31 August 1983 that there was no trace of Mr Carlos Ramírez having entered Honduran territory.

192. This information therefore differed little from the information already in the Committee's possession.

193. After an exchange of views, the Committee *decided*:

(i) to express its regret that the government concerned had not sent a representative;

(ii) to ask both the government concerned and the author of the communication for additional information;

(iii) to resume consideration of this communication at its spring 1988 session.

Spring 1988 session of the Committee on Conventions and Recommendations (129th session of the Executive Board)[11]

166. Mr Carlos Ramírez, a Guatemalan student, was reportedly arrested on 27 April 1981, at the "El Guasaule" frontier post between Honduras and Nicaragua, by a Honduran lieutenant from the Cheluteca military base, on his return to his country after an international tour of solidarity.

167. The government concerned had informed the Committee that very intensive efforts had been made to trace Mr Carlos Ramírez and that it had been established that he had never officially entered Honduran territory.

168. The information received from the specialized Working Group of the Commission on Human Rights did not differ from that in the Committee's possession.

[11] See document 129 EX/3 PRIV., paras. 166-170; see also document 129 EX/CR/HR/2.

No. 446/82 **Honduras**

169. As occurred at the [autumn 1987] session, the government concerned did not send a representative to the present session.

170. After an exchange of views, the Committee *decided*:

(i) to express once again its regret regarding the absence of a representative of the government concerned;

(ii) to request its Chairman to contact the Honduran authorities to inform them of the importance that the Committee attached to the attendance of a government representative, and to reiterate its request for additional information;

(iii) to resume consideration of this communication at [its autumn 1988 session].

Autumn 1988 session of the Committee on Conventions and Recommendations (130th session of the Executive Board)[12]

44. This communication concerns the case of a person alleged to be missing. It is still at the stage of being considered as to its admissibility.

45. A Guatemalan student, Mr Carlos Ramírez was reportedly arrested on 27 April 1981, at the "El Guasaule" frontier post between Honduras and Nicaragua, by a Honduran lieutenant from the Cheluteca military base, while on his way back to his country after an international tour of solidarity.

46. In 1982, at the Committee's request, the Secretariat contacted the International Committee of the Red Cross, requesting it to make representations to the Government of Honduras. The ICRC had replied at the time that it could not do anything as it had been unable to establish a delegation in Honduras.

47. The government concerned had for its part informed the Committee that very extensive investigations had been undertaken in order to trace Mr Carlos Ramírez and that it has been established that he had never officially entered the territory of Honduras.

[12] See document 130 EX/3 PRIV., paras. 44-53; see also document 130 EX/CR/HR - Honduras.

Honduras **No. 446/82**

48. As at its previous two sessions, the government concerned was not represented at the present session.

49. The Chairman told the Committee that, in response to its request, he had made representations to the Honduran authorities to draw their attention to the importance attached by the Committee to the attendance of a government representative, but that he had not obtained an answer.

50. In reply to a question, the representative of the Director-General stated that the Secretariat had been in touch with the specialized Working Group of the United Nations Commission on Human Rights, but that the information obtained concerning this case differed very little from that made available to the Committee.

51. Several members of the Committee expressed the wish that the Secretariat recontact the ICRC and that the Director-General consider the possibility of sending a delegation to Honduras since, according to the communication, the person responsible for the arrest of Mr Carlos Ramírez was a Honduran lieutenant from the Cheluteca military base. Some members of the Committee suggested that investigations also be carried out in Nicaragua and Guatemala, the country of origin of the alleged victim. The ICRC might perhaps obtain information from those countries.

52. One member of the Committee noted that Honduras had promised to co-operate with the United Nations Commission on Human Rights. Action should consequently be taken to ensure that Mr Carlos Ramírez's case was dealt with by that Commission.

53. After an exchange of views, the Committee *decided*:

(i) to express its regret at the continued failure of any representative of the government concerned to attend its meetings, despite the representations made to that end by its Chairman at its request, to which there had been no response from the government;

(ii) to request its Chairman to recontact the Honduran authorities in order to reiterate the importance attached by the Committee to the attendance of a government representative and to repeat its request for information regarding this case;

(iii) to invite the Secretariat once more to ask the International Committee of the Red Cross to make representations through its delegations in Honduras, Nicaragua and Guatemala in an attempt to retrace Mr Carlos Ramírez's itinerary in those countries prior to his disappearance;

(iv) to take note with satisfaction of the information according to which the Government of Honduras had notified the United Nations Commission on Human Rights that it was prepared to collaborate with that Commission, whose Working Group on [Enforced or Involuntary] Disappearances had already had Mr Carlos Ramírez's case referred to it;

(v) to resume consideration of this communication at its [spring 1989 session].

Spring 1989 session of the Committee on Conventions and Recommendations (131st session of the Executive Board)[13]

35. This communication, which has been on the Committee's agenda since the [spring 1982 session], is still at the stage of being considered as to its admissibility.

36. Mr Carlos Ramírez, a Guatemalan student aged 27 at the time, was reportedly arrested by a Honduran lieutenant from the Choluteca military base at the "El Guasaule" frontier post between Honduras and Nicaragua on 27 April 1981 while he was on his way back to his country after an international tour of solidarity.

37. This case was transmitted to the specialized Working Group of the United Nations Commission on Human Rights following a decision taken by the Committee at the [autumn 1982 session].[14]

38. At previous sessions, the Committee was informed by the government concerned that very extensive investigations had been undertaken by the Honduran authorities in order to trace Mr Carlos Ramírez and that it had been established that he had never officially re-entered the territory of Honduras.

39. In 1982, the International Committee of the Red Cross (ICRC) stated, in response to the Secretariat's representations, that it was unable to intervene in this case as it had not been able to establish a delegation in Honduras.

40. At the [autumn 1988] session, the Committee requested its Chairman to recontact the Honduran authorities in order to reiterate the importance attached by the Committee to the attendance of a representative of the government concerned and to repeat its request for information regarding this case. It took note of the information that the Government of Honduras had stated its readiness to collaborate with the

[13] See document 131 EX/3 PRIV., paras. 35-46; see also document 131 EX/CR/HR/HON.

[14] See document 115 EX/28 PRIV., para. 124 (iii) (*supra*, p. 81).

United Nations Commission on Human Rights, under which the specialized Working Group responsible for studying cases of enforced or involuntary disappearances comes. In addition, the Committee requested the Secretariat once more to ask the ICRC to take steps, through its delegations in Honduras, Nicaragua and Guatemala, to attempt to retrace the student's itinerary in those countries prior to his disappearance.[15]

41. The case was referred to the ICRC once more. By a letter dated 11 January 1989, it informed the Secretariat that in view of the negative information already communicated to the Committee by the Honduran Government, and considering the date of Mr Carlos Ramírez's disappearance, which dated back to 1981, it doubted whether any move on its part could provide further information on the case. It said that it was nevertheless ready to attempt to make representations to that government through its office in Honduras if, in accordance with established principle, Mr Carlos Ramírez's wife were to request it to do so.

42. The Secretariat wrote to Mrs Matilde Ramírez on 14 January 1989 to inform her of the ICRC's reply. It has not yet received any answer.

43. In its annual report to the Commission on Human Rights [...],[16] the Working Group on Enforced or Involuntary Disappearances made no allusion to the existence of fresh information about this case.

44. At this session, as at the three previous sessions, the government concerned was not represented.

45. In the opinion of several members of the Committee, the ICRC was in the best position to act in this case. It was therefore advisable to wait and see whether it had received authorization from the alleged victim's wife to approach the Honduran authorities. The ICRC should also be urged to attempt to retrace Mr Carlos Ramírez's itinerary in Guatemala and Nicaragua. It would even be desirable to suggest to Mrs Matilde Ramírez that she should make a request to the ICRC to that effect. The Committee could approach the three States concerned in support of her request.

46. After an exchange of views, the Committee *decided*:

(i) to express once again its regret at the continued failure of any representative of the government concerned to attend its meetings, despite the representations made by its Chairman;

---

[15] See document 130 EX/3 PRIV., para. 53 (*supra*, pp. 87-88).
[16] See document E/CN.4/1989/18, paras. 131-148.

No. 446/82 **Honduras**

(ii) to request its Chairman to continue his representations in order to persuade the Honduran authorities of the value of co-operating with the Committee;

(iii) to invite the Secretariat to recontact Mrs Matilde Ramírez in order to suggest to her that she should write to the International Committee of the Red Cross (ICRC) requesting it to attempt to retrace the itinerary of her husband, not only in Honduras but also in Guatemala and Nicaragua;

(iv) to resume consideration of this communication at its [autumn 1989 session].

Autumn 1989 session of the Committee on Conventions and Recommendations (132nd session of the Executive Board)[17]

45. This communication, which was submitted by Mrs Matilde de Ramírez, wife of the alleged victim, is still at the stage of being considered as to its admissibility. It has been on the Committee's agenda since the [spring 1982 session].

46. Mr Carlos Ramírez, a Guatemalan student aged 27 at the time of the alleged incident, had been on an international tour of solidarity outside his own country. Returning by bus, he was reportedly arrested on 27 April 1981 by a Honduran lieutenant from the Choluteca military base at the "El Guasaule" frontier post between Honduras and Nicaragua.

47. At previous sessions, the Committee was informed by the government concerned that very extensive investigations had been undertaken by the Honduran authorities with a view to tracing Mr Carlos Ramírez, and that it had been established that he had never officially entered the territory of Honduras.

48. The information provided by the specialized Working Group of the United Nations Commission on Human Rights on Enforced or Involuntary Disappearances was virtually identical with that already brought to the Committee's attention.

49. At the Committee's invitation, the Secretariat wrote to Mrs Matilde de Ramírez to inform her that the International Committee of the Red Cross (ICRC) was willing to attempt to make representations to the Government of Honduras if, in accordance with established principle, she were to request it to do so. The Secretariat had not received a reply to its letter.

[17] See document 132 EX/3 PRIV., paras. 45-56; see also document 132 EX/CR/HR/HON.

Honduras **No. 446/82**

50. At its [spring 1989] session, the Committee requested the Secretariat to contact Mrs Matilde de Ramirez once again with the suggestion that she write to the ICRC requesting it to attempt to retrace her husband's itinerary, not only in Honduras but also in Guatemala and Nicaragua.[18]

51. The Secretariat therefore wrote to Mrs Matilde de Ramírez and referred the matter once more to the ICRC. Mrs Matilde de Ramirez has still not replied.

52. By a letter dated 24 July 1989, the section head of the Central Tracing Agency of the ICRC reported that it was difficult "to take up a case dating back to 1981" about which the ICRC had never received a request from the family of the alleged victim. He stated, however, that as an exceptional measure he had forwarded the file on the case to the ICRC delegations in Costa Rica and Honduras in an attempt both to get in touch with Mrs de Ramírez and to "learn a little more about the matter", leaving it to the discretion of the delegation in Honduras to decide whether it was advisable to include Mr Carlos Ramírez's case with others.

53. At this session, as at the four previous sessions, the government concerned was not represented.

54. A member of the Committee wondered whether the time had not come to declare the communication admissible, in view of the persistent refusal of the government concerned to co-opetate.

55. Regarding the silence of Mrs Matilde de Ramírez, some members of the Committee said they felt certain that she had not received the letters sent to her by the Secretariat.

56. After an exchange of views, the Committee *decided*:

(i) to express once again its regrets that the government concerned had not sent a representative, despite the repeated representations made by its Chairman;

(ii) to request its Chairman to contact the delegation of Honduras at the forthcoming session of the General Conference in order to convey to the Honduran authorities the importance that the Committee attached to the attendance of a representative of the government concerned by a communication;

[18] See document 131 EX/3 PRIV., para. 46 (iii) (*supra*, p. 90).

(iii) to take note of the letter of 24 July 1989 from the International Committee of the Red Cross (ICRC);

(iv) to invite the Secretariat to request the ICRC to use the means at its disposal in order to find out whether Mrs Matilde de Ramírez had received the letters sent by Unesco;

(v) to resume consideration of this communication at its [spring 1990 session].

Spring 1990 session of the Committee on Conventions and Recommendations (134th session of the Executive Board)[19]

65. This communication is at the stage of examination as to its admissibility. It has been on the Committee's agenda since the [spring 1982 session].

66. A student of Guatemalan nationality, Mr Carlos Ramírez, aged 27 at the time, had been on an international tour of solidarity outside his own country. Returning by bus, he was reportedly arrested on 27 April 1981, at the "El Guasaule" frontier post between Honduras and Nicaragua, by a Honduran lieutenant from the Choluteca military base.

67. At previous sessions, the Committee was informed by the government concerned that very extensive investigations had been undertaken by the Honduran authorities in order to trace Mr Carlos Ramírez and that it had been established that he had never officially entered the territory of Honduras.

68. The information provided by the specialized Working Group of the United Nations Commission on Human Rights on Enforced or Involuntary Disappearances was virtually identical with that already brought to the Committee's attention.

69. At the Committee's invitation, the Secretariat wrote to Mrs Matilde de Ramírez to inform her that the International Committee of the Red Cross (ICRC) was willing to attempt to make representations to the Government of Honduras if she were to request it to do so. The Secretariat received no reply to its letter.

70. By a letter dated 24 July 1989, the section head of the Central Tracing Agency of the ICRC reported that it was difficult "to take up a case dating back to 1981" about which the ICRC had never received a request from the family of the alleged victim.

[19] See document 134 EX/3 PRIV., paras. 65-75; see also document 134 EX/CR/HR/HON.

He stated, however, that as an exceptional measure he had forwarded the file on the case to the ICRC delegations in Costa Rica and Honduras in an attempt both to get in touch with Mrs de Ramírez and to "learn a little more about the matter", leaving it to the discretion of the delegation in Honduras to decide whether it was advisable to include Mr Carlos Ramírez's case with others.

71. At its [spring and autumn 1989 sessions], the Committee requested the Secretariat to contact Mrs Matilde de Ramírez once again with the suggestion that she write to the ICRC requesting it to attempt to retrace her husband's itinerary, and to request the ICRC to use the means at its disposal in order to find out whether Mrs Matilde de Ramírez had received the letters sent by Unesco.[20]

72. The Secretariat therefore wrote once again to Mrs Matilde de Ramírez, who has still not replied, and to the ICRC which stated, in a letter dated 15 November 1989, that its delegation in San José had made several attempts to communicate with Mrs Matilde de Ramírez but had received no reply from her. The ICRC indicated that its delegation in Honduras considered that "in the absence of a direct request from the family, it would not be appropriate to take up the matter with the national authorities".

73. As at the five previous sessions, the government concerned was not represented at this session despite the repeated representations made by the Chairman of the Committee.

74. In the view of several members of the Committee, the lack of interest on the part of the author of the communication and of the government concerned could not justify striking this communication from its list. The Honduran authorities should be urged to agree to co-operate with the Committee.

75. After an exchange of views, the Committee *decided*:

(i) to express once again its regrets that the government concerned had not sent a representative, despite the repeated representations made by its Chairman;

(ii) to request its Chairman to pursue his efforts with the delegation of Honduras in order to convey to the Honduran authorities the importance attached by the Committee to the attendance of a representative of the government concerned by a communication;

[20] See documents 131 EX/3 PRIV., para. 46 (iii) (*supra*, p. 90), and 132 EX/3 PRIV., para. 56 (iv) (*supra*, p. 92), respectively.

(iii) to resume consideration of this communication at its [autumn 1990 session].

Autumn 1990 session of the Committee on Conventions and Recommendations (135th session of the Executive Board)[21]

32. This communication is at the stage of examination as to its admissibility. It has been on the Committee's agenda since the [spring 1982 session].

33. A student of Guatemalan nationality, Mr Carlos Ramírez, aged 27 at the time, had been on an international tour of solidarity outside his own country. Returning by bus, he was reportedly arrested on 27 April 1981, at the "El Guasaule" frontier post between Honduras and Nicaragua, by a Honduran lieutenant from the Choluteca military base.

34. At previous sessions, the Committee was informed by the government concerned that very extensive investigations had been undertaken by the Honduran authorities in order to trace Mr Carlos Ramírez and that it had been established that he had never officially entered the territory of Honduras.

35. The information provided by the specialized Working Group of the United Nations Commission on Human Rights on Enforced or Involuntary Disappearances was virtually identical with that already brought to the Committee's attention.

36. At the Committee's invitation, the Secretariat wrote to Mrs Matilde de Ramírez to inform her that the International Committee of the Red Cross (ICRC) was willing to attempt to make representations to the Government of Honduras if she were to request it to do so. The Secretariat received no reply to its letter.

37. By a letter dated 24 July 1989, the section head of the Central Tracing Agency of ICRC reported that it was difficult "to take up a case dating back to 1981" about which ICRC had never received a request from the family of the alleged victim. He stated, however, that as an exceptional measure he had forwarded the file on the case to ICRC delegations in Costa Rica and Honduras in an attempt both to get in touch with Mrs de Ramírez and to "learn a little more about the matter", leaving it to the discretion of the delegation in Honduras to decide whether it was advisable to include Mr Carlos Ramírez's case with others.

---

[21] See document 135 EX/3 PRIV., paras. 32-41; see also document 135 EX/CR/HR/HON.

Honduras **No. 446/82**

38. At the [spring and autumn 1989 sessions], the Committee requested the Secretariat to contact Mrs Matilde de Ramírez once again with the suggestion that she write to ICRC requesting it to attempt to retrace her husband's itinerary, and to request ICRC to use the means at its disposal in order to find out whether Mrs Matilde de Ramírez had received the letters sent by Unesco.[22]

39. The Secretariat therefore wrote once again to Mrs Matilde de Ramírez, who has still not replied, and to ICRC, which stated, in a letter dated 15 November 1989, that its delegation in San José had made several attempts to communicate with Mrs Matilde de Ramírez but had received no reply from her. ICRC indicated that its delegation in Honduras considered that "in the absence of a direct request from the family, it would not be appropriate to take up the matter with the national authorities".

40. At the [spring 1990] session, the Committee once again expressed regret that the Government of Honduras had not sent a representative (to any of the past six sessions), despite the repeated representations made by its Chairman to the Honduran authorities. The Committee made a point of reaffirming the importance that it attached to the attendance of a representative of the government concerned by a communication.[23]

41. Following an exchange of views, the Committee *decided*:

(i) to deplore the persistent lack of interest shown by the Government of Honduras in this communication, whereas, even if that government could not be held responsible for the disappearance of the alleged victim, the latter had nevertheless, according to the author of the communication, disappeared on that country's border and as a result of action by a Honduran serviceman;

(ii) to request the Honduran authorities to check the address of Mrs Matilde de Ramírez, author of the communication, and to inform the Secretariat of any change;

(iii) to invite its Secretariat to make one last attempt to contact the wife of the alleged victim, author of the communication, who had remained silent since February 1983 despite various promptings by the Committee, and to inform her that, failing some response on her part, the Committee would be compelled to strike the communication from its list;

---

[22] See documents 131 EX/3 PRIV., para. 46 (iii) (*supra*, p. 90), and 132 EX/3 PRIV., para. 56 (iv) (*supra*, p. 92), respectively.
[23] See document 134 EX/3 PRIV., para. 75 (i) and (ii) (*supra*, p. 93).

(iv) to resume consideration of this communication at its [spring 1991 session].

Spring 1991 session of the Committee on Conventions and Recommendations (136th session of the Executive Board)[24]

30. This communication is at the stage of examination as to its admissibility. It has been on the Committee's agenda since the [spring 1982 session]. The author of the communication alleges the following:

31. A student of Guatemalan nationality, Mr Carlos Ramírez, aged 27 at the time, had been on an international tour of solidarity outside his own country. Returning by bus, he was arrested on 27 April 1981, at the "El Guasaule" frontier post between Honduras and Nicaragua, by a Honduran lieutenant from the Choluteca military base.

32. At previous sessions, the Committee was informed by the government concerned that very extensive investigations had been undertaken by the Honduran authorities in order to trace Mr Carlos Ramírez and that it had been established that he had never officially entered the territory of Honduras.

33. Notwithstanding the information gathered over a period of several years now by the specialized Working Group of the United Nations Commission on Human Rights on Enforced or Involuntary Disappearances, the steps taken by the International Committee of the Red Cross (ICRC) in seeking to retrace the itinerary of the alleged victim, the Secretariat's repeated attempts to contact the author of the communication, and the efforts of the Chairman of the Committee to obtain the co-operation of the Honduran authorities, the situation in regard to this communication has been at a standstill for a considerable number of sessions - six, to be precise.

34. At the [autumn 1990] session, the Committee had deplored the persistent lack of interest shown by the Government of Honduras in this communication, whereas, even if that government could not be held responsible for the disappearance of the alleged victim, the latter had nevertheless, according to the author of the communication, disappeared on that country's border and as a result of action by a Honduran serviceman. It requested the Honduran authorities to check the address of Mrs Matilde de Ramírez, the author of the communication, and to inform the Secretariat of any change. In addition, the Committee invited its Secretariat to make one last attempt to contact the wife of the alleged victim, author of the communication, who

---

[24] See document 136 EX/3 PRIV., paras. 30-35; see also document 136 EX/CR/HR/HON.

Honduras **No. 446/82**

had remained silent since February 1983 despite various promptings by the Committee, and to inform her that, failing some response on her part, the Committee would be compelled to strike the communication from its list.[25] The Secretariat had received no response.

35. After an exchange of views, the Committee *decided*:

(i) to deplore once again the persistent lack of interest shown by the government concerned in this communication;

(ii) to keep this communication on its list, but to resume consideration of it only when it had received information enabling it to pursue its task.

[25] See document 135 EX/3 PRIV., para. 41 (i), (ii) and (iii) (*supra*, p. 95).

No. 447/82

Concerning *Chile*
Case of *Germán Molina Valdivieso*

Communication of 12 February 1982 submitted by
International Council for Adult Education

Autumn 1982 session of the Committee on Conventions and Recommendations (115th session of the Executive Board)[1]

61. The author of the communication, the International Council for Adult Education (ICAE), represented by its Secretary-General Mr Budd L. Hall, stated that Mr Valdivieso, a lawyer, a teacher of human rights and ICAE nominee for the Unesco prize in his field and Secretary of the Chilean Human Rights Commission, was apparently arrested on 10 December 1981 as he was leaving the headquarters of the Human Rights Commission, where he had just delivered a speech commemorating the thirty-fifth anniversary of the Universal Declaration of Human Rights. Other members of the Commission were reportedly also arrested on the same occasion and taken away blindfold to the headquarters of the Secret Police (CNJ), where they were detained for four days. It is alleged that some of them were given electric shocks.

62. A letter received on 27 April from the Permanent Representative of Chile to Unesco informed the Secretariat of the following facts: on 18 December 1981 the Chilean Ministry of the Interior instituted proceedings against Mr Germán Molina Valdivieso and others, charging them with illegal activities; the Court of Appeal recognized the admissibility of the proceedings and appointed an examining magistrate, who ordered the detention of the defendants on the grounds that there was sufficient presumption of their involvement in the activities that were the subject of the investigation; the lawyers for the defendants appealed against the decision on admissibility and asked for their conditional release; the Court of Appeal rejected both requests; on 6 April 1982 the Supreme Court overruled the decision of the Court of Appeal against conditional release, resulting in the release of all the defendants;

[1] See document 115 EX/28 PRIV., paras. 61-70; see also documents 115 EX/CR/HR/3 and Add.5.

however, as it has not yet come to a decision on the second request, the appeal against the decision on admissibility is still pending.

63. At the autumn 1982 session, the representative of the government concerned reported that Mr Valdivieso's case was still *sub judice*, the Court of Appeal not yet having ruled on the decision of the first judges sentencing him to 541 days' banishment. The Chilean representative promised to inform the Committee of the final sentence handed down by the judicial authorities.

64. Two members wondered whether Mr Valdivieso and his co-defendants had been sentenced for defending human rights. If so, they considered that the Committee should take the case very seriously. Two other members feared that a sentence of 541 days' banishment might in practice amount to exile for life.

65. Replying, the representative of the government concerned stressed the fact that, so far, only the lower court had reached a decision and that the case was still *sub judice* because the defendants were also charged with possessing firearms and explosives. He protested that there was no connection between the charges and activities in defence of human rights, which were legitimate in his country. He also pointed out that trials in Chile were held in public.

66. Some members expressed surprise at the fact that the representative of the Chilean Government should bring up at this stage the charge of possessing weapons, which had not previously been mentioned in the file, particularly the written reply from the Chilean Government. One member reminded the meeting that the Committee had laid down the principle that credence should always be given to statements by government representatives. Several Committee members spoke in favour of declaring the communication admissible, on the grounds that the case fell squarely within Unesco's competence. A larger number of members considered that before taking any stand they required further information, particularly in view of the fact that the case was still *sub judice* and that domestic remedies were still available.

67. In reply to a question raised during the discussion, regarding the allegation that Mr Valdivieso and his co-defendants had been tortured, the representative of the government concerned stated that, after his release, Mr Valdivieso had apparently been invited to inform the competent authorities whether he had undergone torture and had not done so. He went on to say that he was willing to contact the authorities of his country to find out whether the Court of Appeal had already handed down its decision, as one member of the Committee believed, and to inform the Committee on this matter before the end of the session. Furthermore, he would make a point of obtaining the documents relating to the case: the charge, the defence case and the final verdict.

Chile **No. 447/82**

68. On 2 September 1982 the Permanent Delegation of Denmark had sent a letter [...][2] to the Secretariat which had been communicated to the Committee in conformity with paragraph 14 (*f*) of 104 EX/Decision 3.3. It supplied the three following items of information: Mr Valdivieso had in fact been sentenced by the lower court to 541 days' banishment for unlawful association and membership of an unauthorized political party; the Court of Appeal would not announce its decision until after 20 September, the Chilean national day; and Mr Valdivieso did not appear to have been charged with possessing weapons.

69. When the Committee took up the case again, at its eleventh working meeting (on the afternoon of 6 September 1982), the representative of the government concerned stated that this letter contained no new information; it merely confirmed that the case was still *sub judice*. For his part, he had learnt that the defence had raised a procedural issue that was holding up the Court of Appeal's decision and that it was not Mr Valdivieso but only one of his co-defendants who had been charged with possessing weapons. After the Court of Appeal, Mr Valdivieso could still have recourse to the Supreme Court, whose task it was to correct abuses or errors committed by lower courts.

70. After discussion the Committee *decided*:

(i) to inform the author of the statements made by the representative of the Chilean Government;

(ii) to invite the government concerned to keep the Committee informed of how the case was proceeding;

(iii) to defer consideration of the admissibility of this communication to its next session.

Spring 1983 session of the Committee on Conventions and Recommendations (116th session of the Executive Board)[3]

42. The author of the communication, the International Council for Adult Education (ICAE), represented by its Secretary-General Mr Budd L. Hall, stated that Mr Valdivieso, a lawyer, a teacher of human rights and ICAE nominee for the Unesco prize in his field and Secretary of the Chilean Human Rights Commission, was apparently arrested on 10 December 1981 as he was leaving the headquarters of the Human

[2] See document 115 EX/CR/HR/3 Add.5.

[3] See document 116 EX/48 PRIV., paras. 42-45; see also document 116 EX/CR/HR/2.

Rights Commission, where he had just delivered a speech on the occasion of the thirty-fifth anniversary of the Universal Declaration of Human Rights. Other members of the Commission were reportedly also arrested on the same occasion and taken away blindfold to the headquarters of the Secret Police (CNJ), where they were detained for four days. It is alleged that some of them were given electric shocks.

43. At the autumn 1982 session, the representative of the Chilean Government informed the Committee that Mr Valdivieso's case was *sub judice*, and that he would notify the Committee without fail of the decisions taken by the judicial authorities of his country.

44. At the present session, the representative of the Chilean Government stated that the case of Mr Valdivieso had reached its final stage, his lawyers having submitted two applications. One of them, an appeal for annulment, had been favourably received. By a judgement handed down by the Supreme Court, the decisions taken by the lower courts had been quashed and the immediate and unconditional release of Mr Valdivieso ordered. Mr Valdivieso was now free and had resumed work.

45. At the suggestion of the members, who all spoke in the same vein, the Committee *decided* to declare this communication settled, in accordance with paragraph 14 (*a*) (x) of 104 EX/Decision 3.3.

No. 449/82

Concerning *Union of Soviet Socialist Republics*
Case of *Filip Moyseyevich Gershkovich*

Communication of 26 February 1982 submitted by
Yves Haguenauer

Spring 1982 session of the Committee on Conventions and Recommendations (114th session of the Executive Board)[1]

246. This communication is submitted by Mr Yves Haguenauer, acting as a person having a reliable knowledge of the alleged violations.

247. Filip Moyseyevich Gershkovich is described as a 75-year old composer of music.

248. Born in Romania, he is said to be of the Jewish faith. As a young man, he apparently studied under Alban Berg and Webern in Vienna. In 1939 he fled from Nazism and took refuge in the Soviet Union. Having settled in Central Asia, he is said to have been a member of the Union of Soviet Composers until 1948, when he was expelled on grounds of "cosmopolitanism". His musical career is said to have suffered considerably. It is claimed that Mr Gershkovich gave free training to all the modern Soviet composers. The "Neue Zeitschrift für Musik" of March-April 1981 is said to have paid tribute to him as the "father of contemporary music in the USSR". Being prevented from the normal exercise of his profession as a result of his expulsion from the Union of Composers, Mr Gershkovich is said to have requested permission to emigrate with his wife, but to no avail.

249. With respect to the means of redress used, the author of the communication states that following Mr Gershkovich's request for permission to emigrate to Austria in 1979 (which remained unanswered) he was immediately expelled from the "Musicians' Fund" for "inadequate professional work". In February 1981, Mr Gershkovich is said to have sent a long letter to Mr Leonid Brezhnev, but to date has re-

[1] See document 114 EX/38 PRIV., paras. 246-258; see also document 114 EX/CR/HR/3 Add.

ceived no reply. The Union of Composers has reportedly refused to help him. The matter has not been referred to any other international authority

250. As regards the purpose and aim of the communication, Mr Haguenauer requests that the alleged victim be authorized to leave the Soviet Union for a country of his choice, so as to renew contacts with the musical institutions from which he has reportedly been cut off for over 40 years.

251. The representative of the Soviet Government stated that this case, which dealt wholly with an emigration matter, was submitted by Mr Yves Haguenauer. It would appear that Mr Haguenauer had made a second occupation of the seeking of the release of Soviet musicians. This probably accounted for the emotional excesses and oversimplifications of the presentation, the representative said. While it was true that Mr Gershkovich had trained a certain number of Soviet composers, the great number of the most famous Soviet composers had not been trained by him. It was not true furthermore that his request for emigration had received no reply. It had in fact been refused for the following reason: Mr Gershkovich had married a woman 40 years younger than himself and the two of them submitted a joint application for emigration; the wife's parents filed an official objection because they did not want their daughter to leave. The refusal was thus in perfect conformity with national legislation and international standards. Had Mr Gershkovich submitted a request for himself only the reply might have been different, but he had not done so. In view of these facts, the Soviet representative said, the communication could clearly be seen as being inadmissible.

252. A Committee member pointed out that Mr Gershkovich was definitely a well-known musician and was without doubt a person working within Unesco's fields of competence. The main question was whether this case was a simple emigration matter or whether emigration was linked to the search for the possibility of continuing one's artistic work. It seemed clear here that Mr Gershkovich was requesting the right to participate fully in artistic matters and though the wording of the communication was not as well drafted technically as might be preferred, it was still quite clear in presenting a case of interest to Unesco.

253. It was the view of another Committee member that the Committee should not examine the nature of domestic legislation, and he felt that international legislation should not supervene national legislation. Furthermore, he went on to say, the Committee's procedures required that local remedies be exhausted, and since that had not been done in this case the communication was inadmissible.

254. Another Committee member wondered how parents could block the emigration request of a child who had reached the age of majority.

Union of Soviet Socialist Republics **No. 449/82**

255. The Soviet representative explained that the author of the communication himself had characterized the case as being one concerning emigration, and he explained that the parents were not blocking the request but were merely expressing their wishes to the competent authorities, who in turn took those wishes into consideration among other factors before blocking the request. The Soviet representative went on to say that Mr Gershkovich was perfectly free to compose music in the Soviet Union. The fact that he was excluded from the Composers' Union was a matter for the Union, since it was a sort of private club, and that one did not need to belong to the Union to compose music.

256. A Committee member and the Soviet representative then expressed their view that the communication was not admissible for the further reason that it had not been presented within a reasonable period, the author having complained of action taken in 1948.

257. Several Committee members then pointed out that in most countries membership of a professional organization was a prerequisite for doing business in certain professions and they expressed concern that the fact of Mr Gershkovich being barred from the Composers' Union may have been due to government interference, may prevent him from getting his works published, or may have other adverse effects on his career. It was also pointed out that the Committee's procedures did not require the exhaustion of domestic remedies but only that an attempt be made to use them, and that the question of submission within a reasonable period of time was not applicable in a case where a continuing wrong was alleged. The point was further made that one of the specific purposes of international norms was to provide a standard by which national legislation could be judged.

258. After much discussion the Committee adopted the following *position*: It

(i) observes that, to the extent that it concerns the exercise of an artistic profession and to that extent only, the communication seems prima facie to fall within Unesco's competence, it being understood that the right to emigrate does not as such fall within the fields of competence of Unesco;

(ii) considers, however, that it is necessary, before it decides on the admissibility of the communication, to ask the author for supplementary information after the details supplied by the representative of the government concerned have been transmitted to him.

No. 449/82 **Union of Soviet Socialist Republics**

Autumn 1982 session of the Committee on Conventions and Recommendations (115th session of the Executive Board)[2]

334. This communication is submitted by Mr Yves Haguenauer, acting as a person having a reliable knowledge of the alleged violations. Mr Filip Moyseyevich Gershkovich is described as a 75-year old composer of music.

335. Born in Romania, he is said to be of the Jewish faith. As a young man, he apparently studied under Alban Berg and Webern in Vienna. In 1939 he fled from Nazism and took refuge in the Soviet Union. Having settled in Central Asia, he is said to have been a member of the Union of Soviet Composers until 1948, when he was expelled on grounds of "cosmopolitanism". His musical career is said to have suffered considerably. It is claimed that Mr Gershkovich gave free training to all the modern Soviet composers. The "Neue Zeitschrift für Musik" of March-April 1981 is said to have paid tribute to him as the "father of contemporary music in the USSR". Being prevented from the normal exercise of his profession as a result of his expulsion from the Union of Composers, Mr Gershkovich is said to have requested permission to emigrate with his wife, but to no avail.

336. With respect to the means of redress used, the author of the communication states that following Mr Gershkovich's request for permission to emigrate to Austria in 1979 - which remained unanswered - he was immediately expelled from the "Musicians' Fund" for "inadequate professional work". In February 1981, Mr Gershkovich is said to have sent a long letter to Mr Leonid Brezhnev, but to date has received no reply. The Union of Composers has reportedly refused to help him. The matter has not been referred to any other international authority.

337. At the spring 1982 session the representative of the Soviet Government stated that this case, which dealt wholly with an emigration matter, was submitted by Mr Yves Haguenauer. It would appear that Mr Haguenauer had made a second occupation of the seeking of the release of Soviet musicians. This probably accounted for the emotional excesses and oversimplifications of the presentation, the representative said. While it was true that Mr Gershkovich had trained a certain number of Soviet composers, the great number of the most famous Soviet composers had not been trained by him. It was not true furthermore that his request for emigration had received no reply. It had in fact been refused for the following reason: Mr Gershkovich had married a woman 40 years younger than himself and the two of them submitted a joint application for emigration; the wife's parents filed an official objec-

[2] See document 115 EX/28 PRIV., paras. 334-350; see also documents 115 EX/CR/HR/2 and Add.3.

fect conformity with national legislation and international standards. Had Mr Gershkovich submitted a request for himself alone the reply might have been different, but he had not done so. In view of these facts, the Soviet representative said, the communication could clearly be seen as being inadmissible.

338. A Committee member pointed out that Mr Gershkovich was definitely a well-known musician and was without doubt a person working within Unesco's fields of competence. The main question was whether this case was a simple emigration matter or whether emigration was linked to the search for the possibility of continuing one's artistic work. It seemed clear here that Mr Gershkovich was requesting the right to participate fully in artistic matters and though the wording of the communication was not as well drafted technically as might be preferred, it was still quite clear in presenting a case of interest to Unesco.

339. It was the view of another Committee member that the Committee should not examine the nature of domestic legislation, and he felt that international legislation should not supervene national legislation. Furthermore, he went on to say, the Committee's procedures required that local remedies be exhausted, and since that had not been done in this case the communication was inadmissible.

340. After much discussion the Committee adopted the following position:[3] it

(i) observes that, to the extent that it concerns the exercise of an artistic profession and to that extent only, the communication seems prima facie to fall within Unesco's competence, it being understood that the right to emigrate does not as such fall within the fields of competence of Unesco;

(ii) considers, however, that it is necessary, before it decides on the admissibility of the communication, to ask the author for supplementary information after the details supplied by the representative of the government concerned have been transmitted to him.

341. The Secretariat received two letters from the author of the communication, on 13 and 17 August 1982 respectively, in which he put the following arguments before the Committee:

(i) the difference in age of the spouses, who are legally married, cannot be put forward as grounds for refusing an emigration visa;

[3] See document 114 EX/38 PRIV., para. 258 (*supra*, p. 105).

(ii) the parents of Mrs Gershkovich have merely expressed disapproval of their daughter's departure; they are not in financial difficulties; they receive a pension from the government; they also have a son who looks after them; so there is no "material hardship", such as might alone be put forward as grounds for opposing the emigration of Mr and Mrs Gershkovich;

(iii) the Soviet Government would be guilty of "forcibly breaking up a family" if it authorized Mr Gershkovich alone to leave the country;

(iv) almost all Soviet composers in their forties or fifties have been trained by Mr Gershkovich; today they are famous in their own country and abroad, particularly in France, the Federal Republic of Germany, Poland and the United States;

(v) the exclusion of Mr Gershkovich from the Composers' Union in 1951 and from the "Muzfond" in 1979 constituted an "offence against humanity". The consequences of those exclusions have been that:

the composer's work are no longer performed or published;

he can no longer find work in radio, television or the cinema, nor can he receive royalties;

his recordings have been withdrawn from record libraries and his published music withdrawn from libraries;

he can no longer earn a living by practising his profession.

342. Enclosed with these letters are a number of documents, including two articles and a piece of music by Mr Gershkovich, together with various reviews paying him tribute. Among these documents there is also one concerning the exclusion of Mr Victor Suslin from the Composers' Union following his application to emigrate to Israel, and a document showing that this composer, changing his occupation, worked for some time as a street-sweeper in the Sverdlov quarter of Moscow (Mr Victor Suslin's case was the subject of [another communication] but was struck off the list of communications at the request of its author at the time of the [autumn 1981 session], since permission to emigrate had been granted to the alleged victim).[4]

[4] See document 113 EX/38 PRIV., para. 306 (vol. I, p. 754), communication No. 303/80 concerning *Union of Soviet Socialist Republics*, case of *Victor Suslin*.

Union of Soviet Socialist Republics **No. 449/82**

343. At the autumn 1982 session, the representative of the Soviet Government explained that Mr Gershkovich's recordings could not have been withdrawn from the market for the simple reason that he had made none; Mr Gershkovich was a teacher and a theoretician. It furthermore appeared that the [author was] trying to pad this case by adding elements from the case concerning Mr Suslin, the Soviet representative said.

344. The Soviet representative also stated that his words had been distorted by the [author] since he had never asserted that the difference of age of Mr Gershkovich and his wife could be used as grounds for refusing permission to emigrate.

345. The Soviet representative then showed to the Committee documents proving that Mr Gershkovich was not only free to compose works but was also free to have them published. Mr Gershkovich was in fact a top expert in a little-known kind of a-tonal music called dodecaphony.

346. A Committee member pointed out that the Committee had decided at its [spring 1982] session that the case did not solely concern emigration matters and that the communication seemed prima facie to fall within Unesco's competence to the extent that it concerned the exercise of an artistic profession.

347. The Committee member thought that the most reasonable approach would be to inform the Soviet authorities of the importance that the Committee attached to intellectual and cultural freedom.

348. Another Committee member lent his support to this proposal.

349. The Soviet representative thanked the Committee members for their understanding of his position and he assured them again that Mr Gershkovich was absolutely free to pursue his professional activities. The Soviet representative was not sure why the examples of Mr Gerschkovich's works put forth by the author of the communication had not been published in the Soviet Union. Nor was he sure as to whom in the Soviet Union he should transmit the concern of the Committee. He presumed it would have to be the professional association for musicians, and he promised to do so.

350. The Committee *took note* of the information supplied, on the one hand, by the government concerned and, on the other, by the author of the communication;

deemed the communication to be inadmissible;

notwithstanding this decision, *requested* the representative of the government concerned to take every step to help the alleged victim to find employment and to report to it thereon at its next session, without this formality giving rise to further discussion as to the substance of the communication on the basis of the information it contained at present.

No. 450/82

Concerning *Czechoslovakia*
Case of *Jozef Jablonicky*

Communication of 3 February 1982 submitted by
Emil Jacob Zseleczky*

Spring 1983 session of the Committee on Conventions and Recommendations (116th session of the Executive Board)[1]

166. This communication alleges the violation of the human rights of a historian who is reported to have been subjected to various forms of harassment. He is said to have been charged by the authorities with harming the interests of the Republic abroad.

167. The representative of the Czechoslovak Government informed the Committee that the alleged victim was not in custody and enjoyed all the rights of a Czechoslovak citizen, and that, owing to the interest expressed by the Committee in this case, the competent authorities of his country, in a spirit of co-operation, were in the process of giving serious consideration to the details of this matter.

168. Some members of the Committee asked if Mr Jablonicky had been acquitted of all charges, and if his writings, alleged to have been confiscated, had been restored to him.

169. A member of the Committee pointed out that by stating in part IV of the communication form that there were no domestic remedies available in Czechoslovakia, the author had committed an offence against a sovereign state. He added that, as the alleged victim was already free, no guarantee in his favour could be obtained with regard to his future activities.

170. After an exchange of views, the Committee *decided* to:

* On behalf of the National Republican Heritage Groups Council.
[1] See document 116 EX/48 PRIV., paras. 166-170; see also document 116 EX/CR/HR/3.

(i) take note of the statements of the representative of the Czechoslovak Government,

(ii) to ask that government to provide additional information concerning this communication at the autumn 1983 session, and accordingly,

(iii) to keep the communication pending.

Autumn 1983 session of the Committee on Conventions and Recommendations (117th session of the Executive Board)[2]

125. Mr Jozef Jablonicky, a historian, is reported to have been subjected to various forms of harassment on the part of the Czechoslovak authorities (interrogations, house searches, confiscation of various writings, suspension of his research pass, etc.). The authorities are alleged to have charged him with harming the interest of the Republic abroad.

126. In response to the request for additional information made by the Committee at its spring 1983 session,[3] the representative of the government concerned declared at the present [...] session that, on the basis of information furnished by the competent authorities of his country, Mr Jablonicky was currently free to carry out his work in Bratislava. He added that in 1981, in the course of an investigation, the police simply asked the alleged victim to explain his relationship with an émigré who was known to the police for his connections with a foreign secret service.

127. After having noted that no specific charge had been brought against Mr Jablonicky, the Committee *decided* to:

(i) declare the communication inadmissible, on the grounds that it lacked relevant evidence of the alleged violation of human rights, in compliance with paragraph 14 (*a*) (v) of 104 EX/Decision 3.3;

(ii) ask the Secretariat, in accordance with the practice of the Committee, to inform the author of the communication of this decision, it being understood that the latter would be able to submit a new communication if new developments arose.

---

[2] See document 117 EX/18 PRIV., paras. 125-127; see also document 117 EX/CR/HR/2.

[3] See document 116 EX/48 PRIV., para. 170 (ii) (*supra*. p. 112).

No. 451/82

Concerning *Czechoslovakia*
Case of *František Lízna*

Communication of 3 February 1982 submitted by
Emil Jacob Zseleczky[*]

Spring 1983 session of the Committee on Conventions and Recommendations (116th session of the Executive Board)[1]

171. This communication alleges the violation of the human rights of a priest who, it is said, has not been authorized to carry out his pastoral duties and who was allegedly sentenced in September 1981 to 20 months' imprisonment on a charge of illegal trading for having distributed religious literature, and in January 1982 to seven months' imprisonment for having reportedly committed acts contrary to the interests of the state abroad.

172. The representative of the Czechoslovak Government stated that in all countries trade was subject to regulations, and that the case of Mr Lízna could not be considered as a violation of human rights as it involved the violation of the trading, customs and tax regulations of the country. He added that the alleged victim would complete his sentence in June.

173. Some members of the Committee considered that it did not appear from the communication that there had been trading in holy books, but simply the distribution of religious literature.

174. A member of the Committee pointed out that Mr Lízna was not a priest, but worked as a hospital orderly, and that his case came within the jurisdiction of the criminal law, and that there was, in fact, no link with the fields of competence of Unesco.

---

[*] On behalf of the National Republican Heritage Groups Council.

[1] See document 116 EX/48 PRIV., paras. 171-177; see also document 116 EX/CR/HR/3.

No. 451/82 **Czechoslovakia**

175. In this connection, some members of the Committee pointed out that the individual concerned had been ordained as a priest in 1974, but had been banned by the state from carrying out his duties.

176. Other Committee members declared that the problem at hand was not so much that of priesthood or ordination, but of the distribution of religious literature which had no profit-making motive. In their opinion, this was a case of the violation of the freedom of thought, conscience, opinion, expression and the right to receive and impart information and ideas, regardless of frontiers.

177. After a brief discussion, the Committee *decided* to postpone consideration of the admissibility of this communication until its autumn 1983 session, pending the provision of fuller information by the government concerned.

Autumn 1983 session of the Committee on Conventions and Recommendations (117th session of the Executive Board)[2]

128. Mr František Lízna, said to be a priest, is reported to have been prevented from carrying out his pastoral duties, and to have been obliged to work as a hospital orderly and ambulance driver. He is said to have been charged with illegal trading, and was allegedly sentenced in September 1981 to 20 months' imprisonment according to the author of the communication, for having distributed religious literature.

129. Endorsing what had been said by his predecessor at the spring 1983 session of the Committee, the representative of the government concerned declared at the present [...] session that Mr Lízna had been released on 27 June 1983 and that his conviction for tax fraud had involved a large sum of money.

130. After a brief discussion, and after having determined that the objective of the communication had been effectively achieved by the release of Mr Lízna, the Committee *decided* to consider the matter settled and to strike the case from its list, in compliance with paragraph 14 (*a*) (x) of 104 EX/Decision 3.3.

---

[2] See document 117 EX/18 PRIV., paras. 128-130; see also document 117 EX/CR/HR/2.

No. 460/82

Concerning *Uruguay*
Case of *Yolanda Catalina Ibarra Chávez de Chassale*

Communication of 27 February 1982 submitted by
Eliane Guiery

Autumn 1982 session of the Committee on Conventions and Recommendations (115th session of the Executive Board)[1]

387. The author of this communication, Mrs Eliane Guiery, of the French Section of Amnesty International - Group 242, alleges that Mrs Yolanda Catalina Ibarra Chávez de Chassale, a teacher and bookseller, was arrested in 1978 and has been tortured. She states that she does not know the exact nature of the charges against Mrs de Chassale but that her indictment may be based on "evidence of a conspiracy to subvert" or of assisting such a conspiracy. It is alleged that all visits to Mrs de Chassale are forbidden and that she can communicate with members of her family only by letter.

388. It is stated that the purpose and aim of the communication are to ensure that Mrs de Chassale be released or, at least, that information be provided on her legal position and the conditions under which she is being detained. Mrs Guiery would also like to know the address of Mrs de Chassale's parents in order to be able to contact them.

389. The representative of the government concerned stated that Mrs Chávez de Chassale had engaged in subversive activities within the paramilitary apparatus of a seditious group which had been banned in November 1973 and which had gone underground. Arrested on 13 November 1978, she had been sentenced on 23 March 1980 to seven years' imprisonment on a charge of conspiracy to subvert and of endangering the security of the state, and the prison sentence had been confirmed on 28 May 1981. Both her arrest and her trial had been in conformity with the law; she had not been tortured, as claimed, without proof, by the author of the communication. The representative of the Government of Uruguay considered that this un-

[1] See document 115 EX/28 PRIV., paras. 387-391; see also document 115 EX/CR/HR/3.

founded accusation was part of a systematic campaign against his country, designed to make it appear guilty of the practice of torture. He added that Mrs Chávez de Chassale was currently being held in women's prison No. 2 where she could receive correspondence and visits from members of her immediate family. He stated, lastly, that this prison had been visited by representatives of the Red Cross and other national and international organizations and by prominent figures including Mr Pérez de Cuellar, at the time the envoy of Mr Waldheim, the Secretary-General of the United Nations.

390. One member pointed out that, while the communication could not immediately be declared admissible, it was, however, not inadmissible: he felt that, if the communication contained gaps, this was due to the fact that, as made clear by the author in the form, the Uruguayan Government had for a while denied that the alleged victim was being held and that, furthermore, she had been held in secret; in addition, he considered that the Uruguayan Government's reply on the question of torture was inadequate because it was too general and did not make it clear whether or not, in this particular case, Mrs Chávez de Chassale had in fact been subjected to torture. Some members, while not necessarily sharing this speaker's view concerning the possible admissibility of the communication, also stated that they were not satisfied by the statement of the representative of the government concerned on the question of torture. All the other members declared themselves in favour of the communication being declared inadmissible, some considering it to be ill-founded and others feeling that, owing to the nature of the acts for which Mrs Chávez de Chassale had been convicted, there was no connection between the charges made and Unesco's spheres of competence. Another member stressed that the communication was not compatible with the Universal Declaration of Human Rights, Article 20, paragraph 1, of which protected only the right to freedom of peaceful assembly and association. Most of the members also expressed the wish that the author be informed of the statements made by the representative of the Uruguayan Government and that she be asked whether, in the light of those statements, she desired to add anything to her communication. Lastly, one member asked whether, on humanitarian grounds, the government concerned might not agree to provide the author of the communication with fuller information, in particular by letting her know the address of the alleged victim's parents.

391. The Committee accordingly *decided*:

(i) to request the representative of the government concerned kindly to take note of the misgivings expressed by the members of the Committee;

(ii) to declare the communication inadmissible on the grounds that it did not fall within Unesco's competence and was manifestly ill-founded, in pursuance of 104 EX/Decision 3.3, paragraph 14 (*a*) (iii), (iv) and (v);

(iii) to make known to the author the content of the statements made by the representative of the government concerned and to ask her whether, in the light of those statements, she wished to submit a further communication.

No. 461/82

Concerning *Union of Soviet Socialist Republics*
Case of *Lev Blitshtein*

Communication of 8 March 1982 submitted by
Michel A. Calvo

Spring 1982 session of the Committee on Conventions and Recommendations (114th session of the Executive Board)[1]

259. This communication submitted by [Mr] Michel A. Calvo acting as counsel for the alleged victim, concerns a Soviet engineer whose rights to education and science are alleged to have been violated.

260. In view of the request of the Soviet Government to have the consideration of this case postponed until the Committee's next session, due to the fact that it had been received only very recently, the Committee *decided* so to postpone the case.

Autumn 1982 session of the Committee on Conventions and Recommendations (115th session of the Executive Board)[2]

351. This communication is submitted by [Mr] Michel A. Calvo, acting as counsel for the alleged victim. Mr Lev Blitshtein is described as an engineer, of Jewish origin. He is said to have worked for over 20 years at the Meat Research Institute of the Ministry of the Meat and Dairy Industry, where he was employed as chief engineer. It is said that on 9 June 1974, he asked permission to emigrate to Israel with his wife and two children; he was immediately dismissed, and exit visas were refused. The reason said to have been given him "verbally" was that he was "too well informed about the time processed meat spends in the warehouse" and that he knew "how to make sausage meat". [Mr] Calvo stresses that this is really what he was told, and is not a joke in bad taste. Mr Blitshtein was allegedly advised to seek a divorce if he wished his family to receive permission to emigrate, and is said to have done so in

[1] See document 114 EX/38 PRIV., paras. 259-260; see also document 114 EX/CR/HR/3 Add.
[2] See document 115 EX/28 PRIV., paras. 351-358; see also document 115 EX/CR/HR/2.

July 1975. His wife and son are said to have left the Soviet Union accordingly in October 1975, and his daughter in January 1976. He himself was apparently advised to wait another year. Since 1975, he has been working as a labourer in a pork butchery.

352. With regard to the connection between the alleged violations and Unesco's fields of competence, [Mr] Calvo maintains that:

> (i) Mr Blitshtein's separation from his wife and children constitutes a clear violation of the children's and father's educational rights, since education is primarily the responsibility of the parents, and can be provided only in an atmosphere of affection and of moral and material security;
>
> (ii) Mr Blitshtein's particular knowledge of sausage-meat production does not appear to be a scientific advance amounting to a "state secret"; on the principle that scientific knowledge should circulate and be shared by all for the good of mankind, the refusal of an exit visa to Mr Blitshtein constitutes a continuing violation of the human right to scientific knowledge; Mr Blitshtein's relegation to a labourer's job constitutes a violation of his right to accede to science through his work; and as regards his knowledge of "the warehouse storage time of processed meat", technical progress since 1974 has probably reduced his knowledge to a great extent, the more so in that stripped of his post of chief engineer, he is now employed only as a labourer.

[Mr] Calvo adds that this case also involves violation by the Soviet authorities of the right to culture (as transmitted by the parents) and to information (whether information in general or information of a personal and family nature which can only be imparted by parents)

353. The representative of the Soviet Government stated that this was a pure emigration case, as was clearly reflected in the "purpose and aim" section of the communication. He said that the author had incorrectly informed the Committee about the family situation of Mr Blitshtein; his marriage had been dissolved voluntarily and the family had not in any way been separated by force.

354. The knowledge Mr Blitshtein possessed concerning the conservation of meat and long-term storage was in fact of national security interest.

355. He was not a mere sausage-maker, the Soviet representative said, but had in fact been a vice-director of a department of the Meat Ministry.

Union of Soviet Socialist Republics **No. 461/82**

356. The fact that Mr Blitshtein lost this post after he declared his preference for a different nationality was not surprising in the opinion of the Soviet representative. In light of these circumstances the Soviet representative considered the case to be inadmissible.

357. A Committee member felt that this was not a pure emigration case since it involved aspects of the right to work. Unesco needed to examine to what extent the profession of Mr Blitshtein came within its competence.

358. After several Committee members had expressed the opinion that this communication was not admissible, the Committee *decided* to declare it inadmissible on the grounds that it did not come within Unesco's fields of competence.

No. 462/82

Concerning *Union of Soviet Socialist Republics*
Case of *Victor Yelistratov and Basheva Hait Yelistratov*

Communication of 8 March 1982 submitted by
Michel A. Calvo

Spring 1982 session of the Committee on Conventions and Recommendations (114th session of the Executive Board)[1]

261. This communication, submitted to Unesco by [Mr] Michel A. Calvo acting as counsel for the alleged victims, concerns a former translator whose rights to education, science and culture are alleged to have been violated.

262. In view of the request of the Soviet Government to have the consideration of this case postponed until the Committee's next session, due to the fact that it had been received only very recently, the Committee *decided* so to postpone the case.

Autumn 1982 session of the Committee on Conventions and Recommendations (115th session of the Executive Board)[2]

359. This communication is submitted by [Mr] Michel A. Calvo, acting as counsel for the alleged victims. Mr Victor Yelistratov is described as a film projectionist. He is said to have worked between 1962 and 1969 as a translator in various electronics and telecommunications enterprises, and to have requested permission to emigrate with his wife in 1972. It is alleged that he immediately lost his job on grounds of "staff reductions". Since then he has been unable to find another post as a translator, such employment being considered too specialized. He was thus forced to take work as a tailor's cutter (1972-1977) and as a furnace-man in a block of flats (1977-1978). He is now (1978-1982) working part-time as a film projectionist in a secondary school, earning about 38 roubles a month. Mr Yelistratov's wife is said to be unem-

[1] See document 114 EX/38 PRIV., paras. 261-262; see also document 114 EX/CR/HR/3 Add.
[2] See document 115 EX/28 PRIV., paras. 359-367; see also document 115 EX/CR/HR/2.

ployed, and to have a son by a previous marriage who was allowed to emigrate to Israel in 1977.

360. With regard to the connection between the alleged facts and Unesco's fields of competence, [Mr] Calvo maintains that:

(i) depriving Mr Yelistratov of his post as a translator in the circumstances outlined above constitutes a violation of his right to education and science, both because work is considered to be a form of education, and because a translator can improve his knowledge of languages and of experiments and work carried out abroad;

(ii) the case also involves a violation of the right to culture (through his work as a translator, Mr Yelistratov could learn about the development of science abroad and the cultural options and models underlying research and marketing topics) and to information (both information as a factor making for understanding between men and peoples, and information between members of the same family: the family of the Yelistratov couple is now said to be in the United States of America).

361. The Committee was unable to consider this communication at the spring 1982 session owing to its having been received late by the Soviet Government.[3]

362. At the autumn 1982 session, the representative of the Soviet Government stated that this was a case involving only emigration questions. Mr Yelistratov's application for an emigration visa had been rejected for national security reasons; this had been explained to Mr Yelistratov, the Soviet representative said. He further stated that as recently as six months ago the application for emigration had been reviewed again, and the grounds for refusing it were still considered to be valid. Since the case concerned only emigration questions, the Committee should consider it to be inadmissible. He added that the author's request that Unesco review the extent to which Mr Yelistratov's knowledge was a threat to national security was inappropriate, since that question was one for the Soviet authorities to decide.

363. Certain Committee members pointed to the author's stated aim of the communication and expressed the view that the requests did not come within Unesco's competence, that Mr Yelistratov's profession had no links with Unesco, and that the case was therefore inadmissible

[3] See document 114 EX/38 PRIV., para. 262 (*supra*, p. 123).

Union of Soviet Socialist Republics **No. 462/82**

364. Another Committee member agreed that the question of emigration *per se* was not within Unesco's competence, but he indicated that the question of the right to work in fields concerning Unesco were within its competence. He went on to say that as concerned part V of the form, it asked for the aims of the communication only to give additional information to the Committee and not to satisfy any conditions of admissibility of 104 EX/Decision 3.3. The Committee member further emphasized that in this case the main question concerned the violation of the right to work of a professional in electronic sciences. This was the question the Committee should examine, not the question of emigration or national security.

365. It was the view of another Committee member that although there did appear to be a disquieting pattern in the Soviet Union of persons suffering professional consequences because of their requests for emigration visas, and although the previous speaker's analysis of the issues was basically correct, the profession of Mr Yelistratov, that of a scientific translator, was not a profession coming within Unesco's fields of competence and it thus made the case inadmissible.

366. The Soviet representative stated to the Committee that 250,000 Jews had emigrated to Israel and had not been denied the right to work, it would be wrong to generalize from a single case, he said. The fact that a person did not work in his special field did not mean that it was because he was not allowed to do so; some persons chose not to work in the field they had studied.

367. The Committee then *decided* that the case was inadmissible under paragraph [14] (*a*) (iii) of 104 EX/Decision 3.3 since it did not come within Unesco's fields of competence.

No. 465/82

Concerning *Argentina*
Case of *Julio Juan Piumato*

Communication of 18 March 1982 submitted by
Hilda Teresa Saltarello de Piumato

Autumn 1982 session of the Committee on Conventions and Recommendations (115th session of the Executive Board)[1]

15. Hilda Teresa Saltarello de Piumato's complaint concerns the arrest of her son on 1 June 1976 and the sentence of seven years' imprisonment passed on him by the Court Martial for possession of firearms, an offence which would not appear to have been proved. She maintains that the real reason for his conviction was his trade union activity while he was court official in a Buenos Aires law court. Mr Julio Juan Piumato is a lawyer of French descent and Argentine by birth.

16. The representative of the Argentine Government stated that the case of Mr Julio Juan Piumato was well known to the authorities of his country, since the Piumato family had already made representations about Mr Piumato to the Director-General, as had the French Consulate in Buenos Aires on account of the dual nationality which he possessed. He explained that Mr Piumato had been convicted not on account of his trade union activities, which were in fact not extensive, but because he was in possession of firearms. He stated that this offence was severely punished because of the state of siege which existed, and that it fell within the jurisdiction of the military court, which had reached its decision in full conformity with the law. Finally, he added that provision for conditional release when two-thirds of the sentence had been served did not exist in the case of offences tried by military courts.

17. All but two of the members who spoke were clearly in favour of this communication being declared inadmissible on the grounds that neither the professional activity of the alleged victim nor the acts of which he had been accused lay within Unesco's field of competence. One of them suggested that the Committee's decision

[1] See document 115 EX/28 PRIV., paras. 15-22; see also document 115 EX/CR/HR/3.

might also be based on [paragraph] 14 (*a*) (viii) of 104 EX/Decision 3.3, as the communication had not been presented within a reasonable period.

18. Two members said they were concerned by the contradiction existing between the position of the author and the position of the Argentine Government as to the reasons which were alleged to be behind Mr Piumato's conviction. They inquired whether it might not be possible to intervene on humanitarian grounds, given the fact that two-thirds of the sentence had already been served, and whether in military law there existed the possibility of granting a judicial pardon.

19. The representative of the Argentine Government pointed out that in military law there were no precedents for conditional release, and that while such a possibility could not be totally excluded, it would be an innovation which could only be adopted for an important reason. As for a pardon, that was a decision for the higher military authorities or for the President of the Republic.

20. One member pointed out that it was difficult to consider a communication to be inadmissible and at the same time to make representations to the government for humanitarian reasons. However, the Committee could hope that the representative of the Argentine Government would report to his government the concerns and the wishes expressed by the members of the Committee.

21. The representative of the Argentine Government declared that he would certainly pass on those views.

22. The Committee consequently *decided* to declare this communication inadmissible as not coming within the fields of competence of Unesco, in accordance with [paragraph] 14 (*a*) (iii) of 104 EX/Decision 3.3.

No. 468/82

Concerning *Uruguay*
Case of *Raúl Cariboni da Silva*

Communication of 16 April 1982 submitted by
Patrick Bombal Acampora

Autumn 1982 session of the Committee on Conventions and Recommendations (115th session of the Executive Board)[1]

392. The author of this communication, Mr Patrick Bombal Acampora, states that Mr Raúl Cariboni da Silva, a history teacher, who is 51 years old and a founder member of the Montevideo Union of Teachers and of the National Federation of Teachers in Uruguay, was arrested in March 1973 and tortured. In 1977, he is said to have been condemned to 15 years' imprisonment for subversive association and for conspiracy to undermine the Constitution. He is said to be in poor health.

393. Mr Bombal Acampora asks that there should be no further torture of Mr Raúl Cariboni da Silva; that he should be allowed to undergo the surgical operation recommended by a group of doctors from the National Institute of Cardiology in Montevideo; that the Uruguayan authorities should recognize the Union of Teachers and the National Federation of Teachers founded by Mr Raúl Cariboni da Silva, and that the alleged victim should be set free.

394. The representative of the government concerned stated that in his opinion, that communication was not admissible since it did not come within the fields of competence of Unesco and that, in fact, Mr Raúl Cariboni da Silva had not been convicted in his capacity as a teacher and founder member of a union of teachers, but because he belonged to the group OPR 33, an organization which had come into being as a result of a split within the Tupamaros anarchist movement. That terrorist organization, which was broken up in 1973, engaged in acts of violence, including the kidnapping of both Uruguayan and foreign dignataries. Mr Cariboni da Silva was arrested and tried in accordance with the law of his country which severely punished the type of operations fomented by the group to which he belonged. In addition, the

[1] See document 115 EX/28 PRIV., paras. 392-397: see also document 115 EX/CR/HR/3.

allegation that he had been tortured was unsubstantiated since Uruguayan law prohibited physical constraints and torture and severely punished those responsible for such deeds. Finally, the communication did not fulfil the conditions of admissibility laid down by [paragraph] 14 (*a*) (viii) of 104 EX/Decision 3.3, since it had not been submitted within a reasonable period, Mr Raúl Cariboni da Silva having been sentenced by the court of first instance in 1975, and that decision having been upheld on appeal in 1977.

395. All those who spoke took the view that several factors made the communication inadmissible, particularly the fact that the alleged victim had been convicted for subversive activities, which did not come within the fields of competence of Unesco, and also the fact that the communication had not been submitted within a reasonable period. While agreeing that the communication should be considered inadmissible, one member nevertheless pointed out that Mr Raúl Cariboni da Silva had problems with his health and he wondered whether it might not be possible to intervene on humanitarian grounds so that the alleged victim could have the operation mentioned by the author of the communication. Another member shared that concern, but considered that it would be difficult for the Committee to intervene.

396. The representative of the Uruguayan Government then intervened to say that he would personally undertake to pass on the feelings of anxiety and concern expressed by the members of the Committee to his government and that he was certain that the government would not prove insensitive to them.

397. Consequently, the Committee *decided*:

(i) to take note of the declarations of the government concerned with regard to the humanitarian concern shown by the members of the Committee;

(ii) to declare the communication inadmissible as not coming within the fields of competence of Unesco and as not having been submitted within a reasonable period, as required in [paragraph 14 (*a*) (iii) and (viii)] of 104 EX/ Decision 3.3.

No. 470/82

Concerning *Union of Soviet Socialist Republics*
Case of *Arseny Borisovich Roginsky*

Communication of 15 April 1982 submitted by
Richard E. Neff and Amy Young-Anawaty

Autumn 1982 session of the Committee on Conventions and Recommendations (115th session of the Executive Board)[1]

368. This communication concerns the case of Mr Arseny Borisovich Roginsky, described as a historian arrested on a charge of falsifying official documents granting him certain rights or exempting him from certain duties and who was sentenced, in December 1981, to four years in labour camps.

369. The representative of the Soviet Government stated that, leaving out of account the tendentious assertions contained in the communication, the affair was of a purely criminal character, in no way relating to a case of violation of human rights falling within Unesco's competence. He stated:

(i) that Mr Roginsky had violated the legislation on archives, particularly with regard to their use and publication and the communication of their contents;

(ii) that he had forged documents granting access to archive holdings and had made use of them;

(iii) that in the course of the judicial inquiry he had acknowledged his guilt.

370. As regards the purpose and aim of the communication, the representative of the Soviet Government stated that Mr Roginsky would be released when he had served his sentence under ordinary law; that any person living in Leningrad could have access to the city's libraries in the normal way; and that it was premature at this stage

[1] See document 115 EX/28 PRIV., paras. 368-373; see also document 115 EX/CR/HR/3.

to bring up the problem of emigration since the person actually concerned had not yet raised the question.

371. Those members of the Committee who spoke were of the opinion that the communication was manifestly ill-founded; all the Committee could do was to request the representative of the Soviet Government to have the authorities of his country consider the possibility of alleviating Mr Roginsky's sentence on grounds of health.

372. One member of the Committee, while sharing this opinion, expressed his regrets at the limitations on access to archives, which should not be regarded as being in any way confidential.

373. After an exchange of views the Committee *decided*:

> (i) to declare the communication inadmissible on the grounds that it was manifestly ill-founded under the terms of 104 EX/Decision 3.3, paragraph 14 (*a*) (v);
>
> (ii) to request the representative of the government concerned kindly to take note of the humanitarian concerns expressed by the Committee regarding Mr Roginsky's situation.

No. 472/82

Concerning *Zaire*
Case of *Ernest Wamba-dia-Wamba*

Communication of 2 April 1982 submitted by
University of Dar es Salaam Academic Staff Assembly

Autumn 1982 session of the Committee on Conventions and Recommendations (115th session of the Executive Board)[1]

403. This communication concerns the case of Mr Ernest Wamba-dia-Wamba, who is described as a lecturer in history at the University of Dar es Salaam (Tanzania) and of Zairian nationality.

404. It is alleged that he was arrested and then detained from 18 December 1981 to 22 January 1982 by the Zairian authorities when he was returning to his country in order to spend his holidays with his family. It would seem that he is not at present allowed to leave Zaire and has therefore not been able to resume his work in Tanzania or rejoin his wife and his children.

405. As he had not yet received any relevant information which might enable him to enlighten the Committee, the representative of the government concerned requested that consideration of this communication should be deferred until the next session.

406. In view of the fact that a period of approximately six months will elapse between the present session and the spring 1983 session, one member of the Committee expressed the wish that a solution might be reached before the next session.

407. Another member of the Committee expressed the view that the Committee should indicate to the representative of the Zairian Government that at the session in question, no further postponement could be granted and that by that date all relevant information should be provided in order to allow this case to be settled.

---

[1] See document 115 EX/28 PRIV., paras. 403-408; see also document 115 EX/CR/HR/3 Add.

No. 472/82 **Zaire**

408. After an exchange of views and after requesting the representative of the government concerned to take note of the wishes expressed, the Committee, in accordance with its usual practice, *agreed* to the request for a postponement.

Spring 1983 session of the Committee on Conventions and Recommendations (116th session of the Executive Board)[2]

262. This communication concerns the case of Mr Ernest Wamba-dia-Wamba, of Zairian nationality, a professor of history at the University of Dar es Salaam (Tanzania), who was arrested, held, and subsequently released, and was then served with an injunction not to leave Zaire.

263. Confirming the substance of a letter dated 6 May 1983 from his country's Permanent Delegation to Unesco, the representative of the government concerned informed the Committee that the alleged victim had been authorized to leave Kinshasa on 3 November 1982 and that in addition, when he had been apprehended at Ndjili airport, subversive documents had been found in his case.

264. After a brief discussion, the Committee *decided* to consider this case as having been settled in accordance with paragraph 14 (*a*) (x) of 104 EX/Decision 3.3.

[2] See document 116 EX/48 PRIV., paras. 262-264; see also document 116 EX/CR/HR/2.

No. 473/82

Concerning *Ivory Coast*
Case of *Syndicat national de la recherche et de l'enseignement supérieur*

Communication of 30 March 1982 submitted by
Daniel Rétureau

Autumn 1982 session of the Committee on Conventions and Recommendations (115th session of the Executive Board)[1]

78. This communication, submitted by Mr Daniel Rétureau on behalf of the World Federation of Teachers' Unions [WFTU], reports the following:

(*a*) "acts of brutality" allegedly committed by police officers against militants of the Syndicat national de la recherche et de l'enseignement supérieur, SYNARES (National Union for Research and Higher Education), attending a general meeting on the premises of the University of Abidjan;

(*b*) the dissolution of SYNARES;

(*c*) the closure of the University of Abidjan and Ivory Coast institutions of higher education.

79. The representative of the Ivory Coast Government informed the Committee that the authorities of his country were studying with the utmost attention the communication transmitted to them. He stated that the reported occurrences took place in the context of a crisis, social tension and a confrontation between students supporting the government and students opposed to the government, following a strike which had been called by teachers without prior notice, for an indefinite period. He added that the government had been forced to react very swiftly and to take various indispensable temporary measures to prevent the destabilization of the country's institutions; that, since July 1982, the government had been in contact with various groups, that it had carried out a series of consultations and launched an information cam-

[1] See document 115 EX/28 PRIV., paras. 78-83; see also document 115 EX/CR/HR/3 Add.

paign in order to ease social tension and that an undoubtedly positive solution would soon be found.

80. The representative of the Ivory Coast Government assured the Committee that all institutions of education had been reopened since March 1982, at the end of the strike. He stated that while, for the time being, SYNARES remained dissolved, this did not mean that teachers could no longer form unions.

81. Referring to the purpose and aim of the communication, several members of the Committee were of the opinion that, in view of the reopening of institutions of education, the problem as regards Unesco's spheres of competence was settled since trade union matters did not concern the Organization.

82. One member of the Committee expressed reservations regarding the last point in the argument put forward, feeling that Unesco nevertheless had the duty to concern itself with a trade union seeking to play an active part in the protection of teachers' rights.

83. Following an exchange of views, the Committee *decided*:

(i) to take note of the assurance given by the representative of the government concerned regarding the reopening of institutions of education;

(ii) to strike the communication from its list in pursuance of 104 EX/Decision 3.3, paragraph 14 (*a*) (x), of the Executive Board, the main problem falling within Unesco's fields of competence having already been settled through the reopening of institutions of education;

(iii) to request the representative of the government concerned to keep the Committee informed of the situation of SYNARES.

No. 475/82

Concerning *Chile*
Case of *José Hugo Pueller Bravo*

Communication of 26 March 1982 submitted by
José Hugo Pueller Bravo

Spring 1983 session of the Committee on Conventions and Recommendations (116th session of the Executive Board)[1]

46. The author of the communication, Mr José Hugo Pueller Bravo, reporter-photographer, of Chilean nationality, states that after the change of government in 1973 he was forced to resign from his job of reporter-photographer at the State Technical University. Subsequently, he was reportedly imprisoned by the Chilean authorities for 13 months without trial. Finally, he was reportedly expelled from Chile in February 1975 without the right to return.

47. The representative of the Chilean Government stated that the person concerned was the brother of the first person to have received permission to return to Chile thanks to intervention by Unesco; once again he had to stress that Mr J. H. Pueller Bravo had made no attempt to use the remedies available to him and that therefore it seemed to be necessary to communicate to him the information to which the representative had referred in his preliminary statement.

48. A member of the Committee endorsed that solution.

49. By consensus, the Committee *decided*:

(i) to defer consideration of the admissibility of this communication to the next session, and meanwhile;

(ii) to inform the author of the existing remedies available to him in the light of the statements made by the representative of the Chilean Government.

---

[1] See document 116 EX/48 PRIV., paras. 46-49; see also document 116 EX/CR/HR/3.

No. 475/82 **Chile**

Autumn 1983 session of the Committee on Conventions and Recommendations (117th session of the Executive Board)[2]

24. The author of the communication, a reporter-photographer, of Chilean nationality, states that after the change of government in 1973 he was forced to resign from his job of reporter-photographer at the State Technical University. Subsequently, he claims to have been imprisoned by the Chilean authorities for 13 months without trial. Finally, he was reportedly expelled from Chile in February 1975 without the right to return.

25. The representative of the government concerned stated that, to the best of his knowledge, Mr J. H. Pueller Bravo had not filed any petition and that nothing could therefore be done on his behalf.

26. All the members of the Committee who spoke during the brief discussion considered that the author should be informed once again of the remedies available to him and should be told that, if he failed to act along the lines suggested, the Committee would strike the communication from its list.

27. Accordingly, the Committee *decided*:

(i) to defer consideration of the admissibility of this communication to its spring 1984 session;

(ii) to request the Secretariat to inform the author of what had been said by the representative of the government concerned and to tell him that, should he fail to avail himself of the administrative and legal remedies of which the Secretariat had already informed him, the Committee would *ipso facto* strike his communication from its list at its spring 1984 session.

Spring 1984 session of the Committee on Conventions and Recommendations (119th session of the Executive Board)[3]

9. The author of the communication, a reporter-photographer, of Chilean nationality, states that after the change of government in Chile in 1973 he was forced to resign from his job of reporter-photographer at the State Technical University. Subsequent-

---

[2] See document 117 EX/18 PRIV., paras. 24-27; see also document 117 EX/CR/HR/2.
[3] See document 119 EX/35 PRIV., paras. 9-14; see also document 119 EX/CR/HR/2.

ly, he claims to have been imprisoned for 13 months without trial. He was reportedly expelled from Chile in February 1975.

10. At the autumn [1983 session] the Committee decided:[4]

> to request the Secretariat to inform the author of what had been said by the representative of the government concerned and to tell him that, should he fail to avail himself of the administrative and legal remedies of which the Secretariat had already informed him, the Committee would *ipso facto* strike his communication from its list at its spring 1984 session.

11. At the present session the Committee had before it a letter from Mr José Hugo Pueller Bravo dated 18 January 1984 in which he explained that the lung operation which he had had to undergo in July 1983 had been the cause of his delay in replying to the Committee. He recalled the various steps which he had taken since 1979, the last of them in September 1983.

12. The representative of the Chilean Government repeated the explanations which he had already given the Committee on the existence of two possible means of redress which could be used in his country by Chileans who wished to return to their country: one through administrative channels, which was simplified in 1983 to emphasize the humanitarian aspect; the other legal - the "recurso de amparo". He added that in cases where it had been possible for him to give personal support through administrative channels he had never failed to do so, as for example in the case of the brother of Mr José Hugo Pueller, who had been authorized to return to Chile.[5] In the present case, however; as the author of the communication was a member of a terrorist movement responsible for several criminal attempts and murders, he was not prepared to intervene on his behalf. Nevertheless "recurso de amparo" was still open to him and he should avail himself of that possibility. Replying to questions raised by members of the Committee, the representative of the government concerned then stated that in Chile the fact of belonging to a terrorist group was a criminal offence in itself. He added in that respect that if Mr Pueller Bravo were to submit to the appropriate legal procedure, the court in charge of his case could then establish whether he had had any personal responsibility as regards the criminal acts of which the terrorist movement had been accused.

13.Two members of the Committee expressed the hope that the author would be given another chance, and suggested that the communication should not be struck from the Committee's list before the following session; other members considered that, as

---

[4] See document 117 EX/18 PRIV., para. 27 (ii) (*supra*, p. 138).

[5] See document 112 EX/30 PRIV., para. 59 (vol. I, p. 193), communication No. 57/78 concerning *Chile*, case of *Luis Pueller*.

the author had [not] tried to exhaust the domestic remedies which had been indicated to him, the communication should be declared inadmissible, in accordance with the decision taken by the Committee at its previous session; some speakers hoped however that the author would be notified again of the means of redress at his disposal and the possibility of his case being submitted once again to the Committee.

14. After discussion, the Committee *decided*:

(i) in view of its previous decision and the persistent lack of response from the author, to declare the communication inadmissible under the terms of paragraph 14 (*a*) (ix) of 104 EX/Decision 3.3 of the Executive Board;

(ii) to notify the author, nevertheless, of the means of redress available to him and the possibility open to him of submitting a fresh communication which would fulfil the conditions of admissibility laid down in the above-mentioned decision of the Executive Board.

No. 477/82

Concerning *El Salvador*
Case of *Violation of human rights in El Salvador**

Communication of 3 May 1982 submitted by
World Federation of Teachers' Unions

Autumn 1982 session of the Committee on Conventions and Recommendations (115th session of the Executive Board)[1]

Spring 1983 session of the Committee on Conventions and Recommendations (116th session of the Executive Board)[2]

Autumn 1983 session of the Committee on Conventions and Recommendations (117th session of the Executive Board)[3]

Spring 1984 session of the Committee on Conventions and Recommendations (119th session of the Executive Board)[4]

Autumn 1984 session of the Committee on Conventions and Recommendations (120th session of the Executive Board)[5]

---

* At the Committee's autumn 1988 session, this communication was being referred to as case of *Violations of human rights in El Salvador* and from the spring 1989 session as case of *Alleged violations of human rights in El Salvador*.

[1] See document 115 EX/28 PRIV., paras. 84-116 (vol. I, pp. 678-687), communication No. 276/80 concerning *El Salvador*, case of *Miguel Ángel García* et al.

[2] See document 116 EX/48 PRIV., paras. 66-71 (vol. I, pp. 687-688), communication No. 276/80 concerning *El Salvador*, case of *Leonel Menéndez Quiroga*.

[3] See document 117 EX/18 PRIV., paras. 80-83 (vol. I, pp. 688-689), communication No. 276/80 concerning *El Salvador*, case of *Leonel Menéndez Quiroga*.

[4] See document 119 EX/35 PRIV., paras. 88-93 (vol. I, pp. 690-691), communication No. 276/80 concerning *El Salvador*, case of *Leonel Menéndez Quiroga*.

No. 477/82 **El Salvador**

Spring 1985 session of the Committee on Conventions and Recommendations (121st session of the Executive Board)[6]

Autumn 1985 session of the Committee on Conventions and Recommendations (122nd session of the Executive Board)[7]

Spring 1986 session of the Committee on Conventions and Recommendations (124th session of the Executive Board)[8]

Autumn 1986 session of the Committee on Conventions and Recommendations (125th session of the Executive Board)[9]

Spring 1987 session of the Committee on Conventions and Recommendations (126th session of the Executive Board)[10]

Autumn 1987 session of the Committee on Conventions and Recommendations (127th session of the Executive Board)[11]

Spring 1988 session of the Committee on Conventions and Recommendations (129th session of the Executive Board)[12]

---

[5] See document 120 EX/15 PRIV., paras. 62-69 (vol. I, pp. 691-694), communication No. 276/80 concerning *El Salvador*, case of *Leonel Menéndez Quiroga*.
[6] See document 121 EX/46 PRIV., paras. 200-209 (vol. I, pp. 694-697), communication No. 276/80 concerning *El Salvador*, case of *Leonel Menéndez Quiroga*.
[7] See document 122 EX/21 PRIV., paras. 150-160 (vol. I, pp. 697-701), communication No. 276/80 concerning *El Salvador*, case of *Leonel Menéndez Quiroga*.
[8] See document 124 EX/3 PRIV., paras. 143-152 (vol. I, pp. 701-704), communication No. 276/80 concerning *El Salvador*, case of *Leonel Menéndez Quiroga*.
[9] See document 125 EX/3 PRIV., paras. 168-179 (vol. I, pp. 704-709), communication No. 276/80 concerning *El Salvador*, case of *Leonel Menéndez Quiroga*.
[10] See document 126 EX/3 PRIV., paras. 196-203 (vol. I, pp. 710-712), communication No. 276/80 concerning *El Salvador*, case of *Leonel Menéndez Quiroga and others*.
[11] See document 127 EX/3 PRIV., paras. 136-145 (vol. I, pp. 712-714), communication No. 276/80 concerning *El Salvador*, case of *Leonel Menéndez Quiroga and others*.
[12] See document 129 EX/3 PRIV., paras. 132-139 (vol. I, pp. 714-716), communication No. 276/80 concerning *El Salvador*, case of *Leonel Menéndez Quiroga and others*.

El Salvador **No. 477/82**

Autumn 1988 session of the Committee on Conventions and Recommendations (130th session of the Executive Board)[13]

Spring 1989 session of the Committee on Conventions and Recommendations (131st session of the Executive Board)[14]

Autumn 1989 session of the Committee on Conventions and Recommendations (132nd session of the Executive Board)[15]

Spring 1990 session of the Committee on Conventions and Recommendations (134th session of the Executive Board)[16]

[13] See document 130 EX/3 PRIV., paras. 152-166 (vol, I pp. 717-720), communication No. 276/80 concerning *El Salvador*, case of *Leonel Menéndez Quiroga and others*.
[14] See document 131 EX/3 PRIV., paras. 186-195 (vol. I, pp. 720-722), communication No. 276/80 concerning *El Salvador*, case of *Leonel Menéndez Quiroga and others*.
[15] See document 132 EX/3 PRIV., paras. 148-156 (vol. I, pp. 722-723), communication No. 276/80 concerning *El Salvador*, case of *Leonel Menéndez Quiroga and others*.
[16] See document 134 EX/3 PRIV., paras. 173-181 (vol. I, pp. 724-725), communication No. 276/80 concerning *El Salvador*, case of *Leonel Menéndez Quiroga and others*.

No. 478/82

Concerning *Yugoslavia*
Case of *Franjo Tudjman**

Communication of 11 May 1982 submitted by
The International Human Rights Law Group

Spring 1983 session of the Committee on Conventions and Recommendations (116th session of the Executive Board)[1]

* At the Committee's spring 1983 session, this communication was being referred to as case of *Milovan Djilas, Vlado Gotovac, Sabedin Haljiti, Sabit Rustemi, Franjo Tudjman and Marko Veselica*.

[1] See document 116 EX/48 PRIV., paras. 238-261 (vol. I, pp. 976-981), communication No. 392/81 concerning *Yugoslavia*, case of *Milovan Djilas* et al.

No. 479/82

Concerning *Romania*
Case of *Ion Caraion*

Communication of 14 May 1982 submitted by
Ion Caraion

Autumn 1982 session of the Committee on Conventions and Recommendations (115th session of the Executive Board)[1]

207. This communication concerns Mr Ion Caraion, who describes himself as a writer. He had left Romania in August 1981 in accordance with the legal regulations and had settled in Switzerland with his family.

208. The author had not filled in part V of the regulation form relating to the purpose and aim of the communication. He seemed to be alleging:

(i) the confiscation of a number of his manuscripts;

(ii) the ban in Romania imposed on the publication of the second volume of his journal and of any other works bearing his signature;

(iii) attacks and threats directed against him by the periodical *Sâptamana.*

209. Confirming the content of the letter dated 18 August 1982 addressed to the Director-General by the Permanent Delegation of Romania to Unesco [...][2] the representative of the government concerned stated:

that Mr Caraion's manuscripts had never been confiscated;

that Mr Caraion had been at liberty to publish his works in Romania: a long list of his works published between 1970 and 1981 was produced; the amount

---

[1] See document 115 EX/28 PRIV., paras. 207-212; see also documents 115 EX/CR/HR/3 and Add.2.
[2] See document 115 EX/CR/HR/3 Add.2.

of royalties paid to him (1,469,579 lei) was also indicated; it was even pointed out that after he had left Romania, the publishing house "Cartea Românească" had issued a new edition of one of his works; it was also stated that if the second volume of his journal had remained unpublished it was because it had been rejected by the publisher concerned, a purely contractual problem between author and publisher;

that with regard to item (iii) of Mr Caraion's claim, the problem was of another order and did not come within the fields of competence of Unesco.

210. The representative of the Romanian Government considered that the communication which contained malicious propaganda against his country, was abusive and should be declared inadmissible in accordance with paragraph 14 (*a*) (vi) of 104 EX/Decision 3.3 of the Executive Board.

211. The members of the Committee who spoke in the debate stressed the vagueness of the communication. They noted that there was no tangible proof that Mr Caraion had been unable to publish his works. They considered that if a weekly publication criticized him, this amounted to an expression of the views of the publication and it was not for Unesco to intervene. They pointed out that as Mr Caraion was already in Switzerland, the communication was no longer justifiable.

212. After an exchange of views, the Committee *decided* to declare the communication inadmissible as being manifestly ill-founded in accordance with paragraph 14 (*a*) (v) of 104 EX/Decision 3.3 of the Executive Board.

No. 480/82

Concerning *Lao People's Democratic Republic*
Case of *Khamkhing Souvanlasy*

Communication on 17 May 1982 submitted by
Amnesty International

Autumn 1982 session of the Committee on Conventions and Recommendations (115th session of the Executive Board)[1]

Spring 1983 session of the Committee on Conventions and Recommendations (116th session of the Executive Board)[2]

Autumn 1983 session of the Committee on Conventions and Recommendations (117th session of the Executive Board)[3]

Spring 1984 session of the Committee on Conventions and Recommendations (119th session of the Executive Board)[4]

Autumn 1984 session of the Committee on Conventions and Recommendations (120th session of the Executive Board)[5]

---

[1] See document 115 EX/28 PRIV., paras. 460-461 (vol. I, pp. 383-384), communication No. 145/79 concerning *Lao People's Democratic Republic*, case of *Khamkhing Souvanlasy*.
[2] See document 116 EX/48 PRIV., paras. 316-318 (vol. I, p. 384), communication No. 145/79 concerning *Lao People's Democratic Republic*, case of *Khamkhing Souvanlasy*.
[3] See document 117 EX/18 PRIV., paras. 223-227 (vol. I, pp. 385-386), communication No. 145/79 concerning *Lao People's Democratic Republic*, case of *Khamkhing Souvanlasy*.
[4] See document 119 EX/35 PRIV., paras. 228-231 (vol. I, p. 386), communication No. 145/79 concerning *Lao People's Democratic Republic*, case of *Khamkhing Souvanlasy*.
[5] See document 120 EX/15 PRIV., paras. 216-221 (vol. I, pp. 387-388), communication No. 145/79 concerning *Lao People's Democratic Republic*, case of *Khamkhing Souvanlasy*.

No. 480/82 **Lao People's Democratic Republic**

Spring 1985 session of the Committee on Conventions and Recommendations (121st session of the Executive Board)[6]

Autumn 1985 session of the Committee on Conventions and Recommendations (122nd session of the Executive Board)[7]

Spring 1986 session of the Committee on Conventions and Recommendations (124th session of the Executive Board)[8]

Autumn 1986 session of the Committee on Conventions and Recommendations (125th session of the Executive Board)[9]

---

[6] See document 121 EX/46 PRIV., paras. 218-224 (vol. I, pp. 388-390), communication No. 145/79 concerning *Lao People's Democratic Republic*, case of *Khamkhing Souvanlasy*.
[7] See document 122 EX/21 PRIV., paras. 164-169 (vol. I, pp. 390-391), communication No. 145/79 concerning *Lao People's Democratic Republic*, case of *Khamkhing Souvanlasy*.
[8] See document 124 EX/3 PRIV., paras. 158-168 (vol. I, pp. 392-393), communication No. 145/79 concerning *Lao People's Democratic Republic*, case of *Khamkhing Souvanlasy*.
[9] See document 125 EX/3 PRIV., paras. 185-189 (vol. I, pp. 394-395), communication No. 145/79 concerning *Lao People's Democratic Republic*, case of *Khamkhing Souvanlasy*.

No. 481/82

Concerning *Union of Soviet Socialist Republics*
Case of *Alexander Temkin*

Communication of 14 June 1982 submitted by
Michel A. Calvo

Autumn 1982 session of the Committee on Conventions and Recommendations (115th session of the Executive Board)[1]

374. This communication concerns the case of a professor, Mr Alexander Temkin, who has lived in Israel since October 1973, after receiving permission to emigrate from the Soviet Union, and who wishes to see his daughter again, now aged 23, and to have news of her.

375. The representative of the Soviet Government stated that the matter was a purely private one, in no way falling within Unesco's spheres of competence.

376. He let it be known, out of humanitarian considerations, that Mr Temkin's daughter had completed her studies, that she had married and that she was now leading, in Moscow, a life in keeping with her wishes.

377. The representative of the Soviet Government deemed it inappropriate on his part to add anything else regarding the private life of the person concerned who, if she so wished, could freely correspond with her father.

378. After an exchange of views the Committee *decided* to declare the communication inadmissible on the grounds that it did not fall within Unesco's competence, in pursuance of 104 EX/Decision 3.3, paragraph 14 (*a*) (iii).

---

[1] See document 115 EX/28 PRIV., paras. 374-378; see also document 115 EX/CR/HR/3.

No. 482/82

Concerning *Union of Soviet Socialist Republics*
Case of *Andrei Sakharov*

Communication of 9 June 1982 submitted by
The Lawyers Committee for International Human Rights

Spring 1983 session of the Committee on Conventions and Recommendations (116th session of the Executive Board)[1]

196. This communication is submitted by the Lawyers Committee for International Human Rights, which describes itself as a non-governmental organization with reliable knowledge of the alleged violations.

197. Dr Andrei Sakharov, a world-famous physicist, has been in enforced residence in Gorky since January 1980. His case was dealt with in [another communication],[2] submitted by the same organization and considered by the Committee at four successive sessions. At its spring 1982 session, the Committee noted the information provided by the representative of the government concerned on the recent scientific work of the great physicist and the opportunities available to him to make contact with scientists in order to continue his scientific research, and decided:[3]

(i) to suspend consideration of the communication in question in view of the fact that a number of circumstances had changed since the date of its submission;

(ii) to ask the Director-General to continue his efforts to obtain additional information about the possibilities for Dr Sakharov to pursue his scientific work in accordance with the Unesco Recommendation on the Status of Scientific Researchers of 20 November 1974.

---

[1] See document 116 EX/48 PRIV., paras. 196-211; see also documents 116 EX/CR/HR/3 and Add.2.
[2] Communication No. 195/80 concerning *Union of Soviet Socialist Republics*, case of *Andrei Sakharov*.
[3] See document 114 EX/38 PRIV., para. 579 (ii) and (iii) (vol. I, p. 545).

No. 482/82 **Union of Soviet Socialist Republics**

198. In the present communication, the author recalls that Dr Sakharov has been in exile in Gorky for over three years now. The author asserts that Dr Sakharov has been cut off from all contact with scientific colleagues, both Soviet and foreign, that he is deprived of professional literature, that consequently he cannot keep abreast of current developments in his field, and that he is still subjected to harassment and intimidation by the authorities. The Lawyers Committee for International Human Rights mentions a note sent by Dr Sakharov to Mr Alexandrov, President of the USSR Academy of Sciences, in which the scientist complained of his isolation by unlawful exile within the country and of repeated thefts of his scientific writings and other manuscripts. As a result of these thefts, he has had to devote a great deal of time and effort to reconstructing the stolen material.

199. The author refers to two incidents in particular. On 11 October 1982, Dr Sakharov is said to have been attacked in his car and to have been immediately overcome by an incapacitating agent. While he was unconscious, his attackers are said to have stolen an attaché case containing various scientific and personal documents. On 4 November 1982, Dr Sakharov is said to have been summoned to the Office of the Procurator of the City of Gorky, where he was allegedly placed under an injunction to stop making public statements.

200. The author of the communication adds to the file a statement purportedly by Dr Sakharov, asking the authorities of countries that are signatories of the Helsinki Final Act and his colleagues abroad to defend him, and giving details of the incidents referred to above. It alleges that the persons who stole his attaché case were not common criminals but KGB agents. It alleges that the Deputy Procurator of Gorky condemned as libellous his statements about the theft in question, which were distributed to foreign correspondents, and warned Dr Sakharov that he had contravened the terms of his isolation as decreed by the Presidium of the Supreme Soviet. Dr Sakharov is said to have asked the Deputy Procurator to show him the Presidium's decision, but to no avail.

201. In addition, on 7 December 1982, the KGB allegedly confiscated from Mrs Sakharov 300 manuscript pages which Dr Sakharov had reconstructed after the 11 October theft.

202. Dr Sakharov is described as having been deprived of rest, the right to leave the city where he resides, virtually deprived of the right to think or write, the right to free scientific and human contacts, and the right to correspond and to talk over the telephone. The scientist is said to have been permitted only six visits from his scientific colleagues during the past three years. These brief encounters are alleged not to have been sufficient to enable him to keep abreast of recent developments in physics, and in particular he has been unable to discuss his own scientific theories with

other competent scientists. In addition, he is said to be unable to receive proper medical attention in Gorky. This additional information is said to have been provided by Mrs Sakharov in a letter dated 16 November 1982, which is submitted by the author of the communication in support of [the] allegations.

203. With respect to domestic remedies, the author of the communication indicates that there are none available to Dr Sakharov. Inasmuch as he has never been charged with any offence, all he has been able to do has been to appeal to the Soviet authorities to put an end to the violation of his rights, but these appeals have gone unheeded.

204. In conclusion, the Lawyers Committee for International Human Rights states that not only have these violations continued unabated, but that they have become more severe, and are even a threat to Dr Sakharov's very life. It requests:

> that the Director-General should continue his efforts to obtain additional information about the opportunities for Dr Sakharov to pursue his scientific work;
>
> that the Committee should resume its inquiry;
>
> that it should verify the true conditions of Dr Sakharov's exile, if necessary by setting up a commission of inquiry;
>
> that Dr Sakharov should be allowed to communicate directly with the Committee;
>
> that the Committee should take all necessary steps to obtain redress for the alleged violations.

205. On 22 April 1983, the Secretariat received from the author of the communication a letter in which [the author] requested permission to be heard by the Committee under the provisions of paragraph 14 (*g*) of 104 EX/Decision 3.3.

206. The representative of the Soviet Union said that the major part of the communication in question had already been examined in the context of the first communication, that Dr Sakharov was still at liberty, that his removal to Gorki was on grounds of national security and that as an academician he was still in a position to pursue his scientific work - less so admittedly than in the 1950s and 1960s, but that this was quite understandable. With regard to the request by the author of the communication

to be allowed to appear before the Committee [...],[4] he considered that it was an attempt by circles hostile to his country to draw greater attention to the communication under consideration and that it should be rejected. Concerning the letter purportedly originating from Mrs Sakharov and produced by the author of the communication in support of [the] allegations, he pointed out that it contained remarks extremely insulting to the Soviet Government and requested that the document in question should be removed from the file.

207. The representative of the government concerned stated in conclusion that the communication contained false allegations and that it should be considered inadmissible by the Committee.

208. A member of the Committee expressed disquiet at the fact that Dr Sakharov had been punished without having been previously tried by a court of law. Other members of the Committee stressed that Dr Sakharov was one of the greatest men of science of the century and a person of whom the Soviet Union could be proud. The intellectual community throughout the world, the Third World included, was concerned at the situation of this great scientist and his case should not therefore be looked at from the standpoint of an East-West confrontation. To the extent that Dr Sakharov found himself unable to carry out his research, the loss was that of the world as a whole. Several members of the Committee were in favour of exploring the possibility of sending a representative of the Director-General to the Soviet Union to enter discreetly into contact with the competent authorities on the situation of Dr Sakharov.

209. A member of the Committee pointed out that Dr Sakharov, while a man of science, was above all a Soviet citizen and that he was viewed in the Ukraine as a traitor of whom one could not be proud.

210. Following a lengthy exchange of views, the members of the Committee agreed that Unesco could not cease to concern itself with the case of this man who had made and continued to make a great contribution to mankind, and that an equitable solution to this case must be sought.

211. The Committee finally *decided*:

> (i) to suspend its consideration of the admissibility of this communication and not to take account of Mrs Sakharov's letter in its discussions,

[4] See document 116 EX/HR/3 Add.2.

(ii) to request the Executive Board to invite the Director-General to continue his efforts along the lines of the decision taken by the Committee at its spring 1982 session (obtaining additional information about the possibilities for Dr Sakharov to pursue his scientific work in accordance with the Recommendation on the Status of Scientific Researchers of 20 November 1974, keeping in mind the concern expressed by members of the Committee with regard to this matter).

Autumn 1983 session of the Committee on Conventions and Recommendations (117th session of the Executive Board)[5]

149. Dr Andrei Sakharov, a world famous physicist, has been in enforced residence in Gorky since January 1980. The Committee had considered his case at four successive sessions, in connection with [another communication].[6]

150. At its spring 1982 session [...], the Committee had decided, *inter alia*, to suspend further consideration of the communication as formulated in view of the fact that it was submitted as long ago as 1980 and that a number of circumstances then relevant had in the interim changed.[7]

151. The Committee had been called upon to consider this new communication [...] for the first time at its spring 1983 session. According to the facts of the claim as set out in this communication, Dr Sakharov is still cut off from all contact with his colleagues, both Soviet and foreign; it is also alleged that he is unable to keep his knowledge up to date and is constantly subjected to harassment and intimidation by the Soviet authorities.

152. At the spring 1983 session, the Committee had decided to suspend its consideration of the admissibility of this new communication, not to take account in its discussions of a letter supposedly emanating from Mrs Sakharov (a document supplied by the author of the communication in support of [the] allegations, the tenor of which, the representative of the Soviet Government had pointed out, appeared to be extremely offensive towards that government) and to request the Executive Board to invite the Director-General to continue his efforts with a view to obtaining additional information about the possibilities for Dr Sakharov to pursue his scientific work in accordance with the Recommendation on the Status of Scientific Researchers of

[5] See document 117 EX/18 PRIV., paras. 149-155 ; see also documents 117 EX/CR/HR/2 and Add.3.

[6] Communication No. 195/80 concerning *Union of Soviet Socialist Republics*, case of *Andrei Sakharov*.

[7] See document 114 EX/38 PRIV., para. 579 (ii) (vol. I, p. 545).

20 November 1974, keeping in mind the concern expressed by members of the Committee with regard to this matter.[8]

153. At the present [...] session, the representative of the Soviet Government, who is also a member of the Committee, stated that despite his having been removed to Gorky, Dr Sakharov still maintained noxious contacts with foreign circles, mainly through his wife. He added that by presenting himself as the spiritual father of the anti-Soviet elements, the physicist was behaving as a self-declared enemy of the regime. Referring to the letter dated 5 September 1983 from Mr Efrem Yankelevich, Dr Sakharov's son-in-law [...],[9] he indicated that Dr Sakharov was continuing to receive the most assiduous medical care in keeping with his professional status. He pointed out that although much was made of the Sakharov affair in the Western press, things were otherwise in the Soviet Union; according to him, many Soviet citizens, and particularly the physicist's colleagues, regarded the latter's activities as being in fact of a highly political rather than scientific nature, with the result that Dr Sakharov was even looked upon in the Soviet Union as a traitor to his country.

154. In the view of one Committee member, it was always difficult to distinguish an academic's scientific activities from his thought as a whole. Accordingly, in view of the absence of any truly new elements, the Committee's decision could in his opinion only be identical to the one previously taken. Another Committee member expressed the view that the Committee was in duty bound to continue to express its concern regarding this case, for it was clear that Dr Sakharov could not pursue his scientific work in a normal manner. Moreover, in the same member's view, the position of the physicist, the symbol of the spirit of opposition, was, in the event, perfectly legitimate.

155. After an exchange of views, the Committee *decided*:

(i) to request the Executive Board to invite the Director-General to continue to use his good offices on behalf of Dr Sakharov;

(ii) to appeal on humanitarian grounds to the government concerned to ensure that everything be done to safeguard Dr Sakharov's health.

---

[8] See document 116 EX/48 PRIV., para. 211 (*supra*, pp. 156-157).
[9] See document 117 EX/CR/HR/2 Add.3.

Union of Soviet Socialist Republics **No. 482/82**

Spring 1984 session of the Committee on Conventions and Recommendations (119th session of the Executive Board)[10]

170. The Committee examined these two communications together.[11] It was at its spring 1983 session that the Committee was first seized with [the first communication]. [The second communication] on the other hand is a new one.

171. Dr Andrei Sakharov, a physicist, is alleged to have been sent, without any indictment or trial, into internal exile at Gorky in January 1980 for an indefinite period. He is reported to have been subjected to constant harassment, anonymous threats and to have had his manuscripts stolen. He is alleged to be unable to communicate or receive scientific and cultural information, to work freely, to receive the medical attention to which he is entitled as an academician, to respond to invitations from various foreign university institutions or to accept the offer to live in Norway made to him by the Government of that country.

172. The representative of the USSR, who is also a member of the Committee, stated that in accordance with the relevant provisions of this International Covenant the case raised by the communications concerned fell within the international affairs of the USSR and that the consideration of the communications constituted interference in his country's internal affairs, but in the interest of international co-operation he is prepared to co-operate with the Committee and give information on some facts. He also stated that while it was true that the movements of Dr Sakharov had been limited, he was not in exile. He explained that the academician has been subjected to enforced residence in Gorky for Soviet State security reasons. The Committee was further informed by the representative of the government concerned that Gorky is a large city and that appropriate facilities exist there to enable Dr Sakharov, if he so desires, to pursue his scientific activities. The representative noted the contribution which the academician has made to science and added that this partly explains why the authorities of the USSR had taken a humanitarian approach to his case and had merely subjected him to enforced residence in Gorky. In this connection, the representative pointed out that the International Covenant on Civil and Political Rights permitted restrictions on certain civil liberties if the protection of national security justified it.

[10] See document 119 EX/35 PRIV., paras. 170-179; see also documents 119 EX/CR/HR/2 and Add.4 and 119 EX/CR/HR/3 Add. and Add.5.
[11] Communications No. 482/82 concerning *Union of Soviet Socialist Republics*, case of *Andrei Sakharov*, and No. 603/84 concerning *Union of Soviet Socialist Republics*, case of *Andrei Sakharov*.

173. Several members of the Committee queried whether the action in restricting the alleged victim's movements could be considered humanitarian to the extent that the person concerned did not consider it to be in his interest. These members indicated that, in their view, the reason of State security which had been evoked to justify the enforced residence imposed on Dr Sakharov, as well as his ban from talking to or making contacts with foreigners, was not convincing because the academician has not, for the past four years, worked on anything that would be of interest to Soviet State security. One member asked that if the restrictions on the movements of the alleged victim did not amount to placing him in exile, what else could that be. Another member remarked that while it appeared that Soviet public opinion and Dr Sakharov himself preferred the latter to be tried publicly, the Soviet authorities through what these authorities referred to as a humanitarian gesture, continue to keep him in Gorky without trial. This member asked what would happen if the academician were to renounce this humanitarian gesture of the Soviet authorities. It was also asked if special procedures were gone through before the alleged victim was subjected to enforced residence in Gorky.

174. The representative of the government concerned repeated that the academician was not in exile which was a more stringent regime of restriction than the one to which the latter is subjected to. It was indicated in this connection that but for the humanitarian view which the Soviet authorities had taken of the academician's case, the latter might very well have been prosecuted under Soviet penal law for activities that were prejudicial to the security of the USSR. The representative of the government informed the Committee that the decision to restrict Dr Sakharov to Gorky was taken by the competent authorities of the USSR and that this decision was taken in accordance with pertinent Soviet laws. He added that if the alleged victim were to leave Gorky contrary to the decision, the normal legal consequences would result and that the person concerned would probably be tried. He counselled the Committee against a comparison of the Soviet legal system with others and pointed out that such a comparison would not help the Committee in its work. The representative of the USSR stated that it was for Soviet competent experts to decide when the academician would cease to be a depositary of sensitive Soviet State secrets and consequently no longer potentially dangerous to Soviet security. On the professional work of Dr Sakharov, the representative of the government reiterated that the academician has at his disposal in Gorky appropriate facilities for pursuing his scientific activities and that as a matter of fact the alleged victim was in constant touch with a number of his scientific colleagues. Another member of the Committee stated that he had no doubt that Dr Sakharov was being treated properly by the Soviet authorities. He added that the academician had knowledge which, if he were to misuse it or if he were to have it misused, could have consequences which would be indeed very dangerous.

Union of Soviet Socialist Republics **No. 482/82**

175. While admitting that the alleged victim may have been treated less harshly than otherwise might have been the case, one other member stated that, in his opinion, the Soviet authorities had overreacted in the academician's case and expressed the hope that the authorities concerned would adopt a much more humanitarian approach to it. Another member of the Committee remarked that even if the alleged victim had the possibility of pursuing his scientific activities at Gorky, the facilities available there would be necessarily limited. He therefore suggested that, in accordance with the pertinent provisions of relevant international standard-setting human rights instruments, especially the Recommendation on the Status of Scientific Researchers, the competent authorities of the USSR should take appropriate action to ensure that Dr Sakharov was able to undertake his scientific activities without let or hindrance. This member suggested also that if the offer of the Norwegian Government to receive the academician were confirmed, the competent authorities of the USSR should take a compassionate view of his situation and should let him go and live in Norway if he so wished.

176. One other member counselled the Committee to purge the communications concerned of their ideological implications. In this way, the Committee could limit itself to the situation and condition of Dr Sakharov as a renowned scientist of international dimension. He proposed that the Director-General should be requested to make, in favour of the academician, whatever humanitarian intervention he deemed appropriate. Another member remarked that it was not disputed that the alleged victim had in fact been subjected to restrictions on his movements and that this factual situation was more important than the technical designation given to it. In his view, Dr Sakharov had been subjected to enforced residence at Gorky not because he was really a threat to Soviet State security but because he belonged to a group monitoring the application by the USSR of various texts, constitutional and international, relating to civil liberties. He urged the Committee to try and find an amicable solution to the problem; a solution which could be achieved only if the academician were allowed to regain his liberty.

177. Another member of the Committee stated that, in his view, the alleged victim had become an enemy of his own country. He declared that it was the sovereign right of every State to decide what was or was not a State secret and that consequently it was for the USSR to determine when the academician might be considered as having ceased to be a threat to Soviet State security. For the information of the Committee, the representative of the Government of the USSR provided details of steps which the competent authorities of his country had taken, in some cases as recently as in April 1984, with the view to safeguarding the health of Dr Sakharov.

178. The Committee confirmed the conclusion reached at one of its previous sessions to the effect that it would not take into account exhibit E attached to [the first

communication].[12] A similar conclusion was arrived at in respect of passages contained in [the second communication] and which the representative of the Government of the USSR considered offensive to his country. Consequently, it was agreed that the exhibit and the passages concerned would be expunged from the respective communications.

179. At the end of its discussion of the communications concerned, the Committee *decided*:

(i) to request the Executive Board to ask the Director-General to use his good offices to settle the case in question, in the light, particularly, of the relevant provisions of the Unesco Recommendation on the Status of Scientific Researchers;

(ii) to expunge from the communications the terms considered insulting or offensive by the representative of the Soviet Government;

(iii) to note with interest the information provided by the representative of the Soviet Government concerning all the measures taken by the Soviet authorities to protect Mr Sakharov's health.

Autumn 1984 session of the Committee on Conventions and Recommendations (120th session of the Executive Board)[13]

131. The Committee examined these two communications together.[14] It was at its spring 1983 [...] and spring 1984 [...] sessions that the Committee was first seized with [the two communications respectively].

132. At its present session, the Committee had before it additional information transmitted by the authors of the communications by two letters dated 12 September and 14 September 1984 respectively [...].[15]

133. After an exchange of views, the Committee *decided* to defer consideration of the two communications until its spring 1985 session, pending the receipt of further

[12] See document 116 EX/48 PRIV., para. 211 (i) (*supra*, p. 156).
[13] See document 120 EX/15 PRIV., paras. 131-133; see also documents 120 EX/CR/HR/2 and Add.2 and 4.
[14] Communications No. 482/82 concerning *Union of Soviet Socialist Republics*, case of *Andrei Sakharov*, and No. 603/84 concerning *Union of Soviet Socialist Republics*, case of *Andrei Sakharov*.
[15] See documents 120 EX/CR/HR/2 Add.2 and 4.

information from the government concerned with regard to the allegations contained in the letters dated 12 and 14 September 1984, which had been sent by the authors to the Secretariat and received by that government only very recently.

Spring 1985 session of the Committee on Conventions and Recommendations (121st session of the Executive Board)[16]

152. The Committee *decided* to defer consideration of these communications[17] until its autumn 1985 session.

Autumn 1985 session of the Committee on Conventions and Recommendations (122nd session of the Executive Board)[18]

112. The discussion of these communications[19] was resumed but, noting that new information had been received by the Secretariat from the authors of one of the communications too late for it to be made available to it in its working languages, the Committee *decided* to adjourn it to its spring 1986 session, it being understood that the debate of the present session will be reflected in the document of presentation of communications to be submitted to the next session.

Spring 1986 session of the Committee on Conventions and Recommendations (124th session of the Executive Board)[20]

[16] See document 121 EX/46 PRIV., para. 152; see also document 121 EX/CR/HR/2.

[17] Communications No. 482/82 concerning *Union of Soviet Socialist Republics*, case of *Andrei Sakharov*, and No. 603/84 concerning *Union of Soviet Socialist Republics*, case of *Andrei Sakharov*.

[18] See document 122 EX/21 PRIV., para. 112; see also document 122 EX/CR/HR/2.

[19] Communications No. 482/82 concerning *Union of Soviet Socialist Republics*, case of *Andrei Sakharov*, and No. 603/84 concerning *Union of Soviet Socialist Republics*, case of *Andrei Sakharov*, were being considered together.

[20] See document 124 EX/3 PRIV., paras. 101-104 (*supra*, pp. 48-49), communication No. 441/82 concerning *Union of Soviet Socialist Republics*, case of *Vladimir Raiz*.

No. 482/82 **Union of Soviet Socialist Republics**

Autumn 1986 session of the Committee on Conventions and Recommendations (125th session of the Executive Board)[21]

84. According to the authors of the communications[22] Dr Andrei Sakharov, physicist, who was banished to Gorky in January 1980, has been subjected to constant harassment. He is reported to be unable to communicate or receive scientific and cultural information, to work freely, to receive proper medical care, to reply to invitations from foreign university institutions or to accept the proposal made to him that he go and live in Norway.

85. At the spring 1986 session these two communications, like all the other communications concerning the Soviet Union, could not be considered.[23] However, in a letter dated 30 August 1985, [...],[24] the author of [the first communication] transmitted fresh information about Dr Sakharov's state of health and isolation and about the trial of Dr Elena Bonner, regarding which the representative of the government concerned declared at the autumn 1985 session, while stressing that the case of Mrs Bonner had no connection with Unesco's fields of competence, that she had been sentenced to only five years' internal exile whereas she could have been more severely punished for sending abroad information defaming the Soviet Union and that in any case she was serving that sentence quite simply in the company of her husband.

86. By a letter dated 19 August 1986, [...],[25] the author of the same communication set out to bring up to date the allegations made by [the author], reporting on the treatment undergone by Academician Sakharov during his hunger strike in 1984 and 1985 and the various forms of unpleasantness said to have been met with by the Sakharovs in their private life.

87. At the present session the representative of the government concerned pointed out that the case of Mr Sakharov had already been discussed at length within the Committee, that the authors had relied largely on the mass media and that consequently there arose the question of violation of the rule of confidentiality provided

---

[21] See document 125 EX/3 PRIV., paras. 84-98; see also documents 125 EX/CR/HR/2 and Add.2.

[22] Communications No. 482/82 concerning *Union of Soviet Socialist Republics*, case of *Andrei Sakharov*, and No. 603/84 concerning *Union of Soviet Socialist Republics*, case of *Andrei Sakharov*, were being considered together.

[23] See document 124 EX/3 PRIV., para. 104 (*supra*, p. 49), communication No. 441/82 concerning *Union of Soviet Socialist Republics*, case of *Vladimir Raiz*.

[24] See document 124 EX/CR/HR/2, annex II.

[25] See document 125 EX/CR/HR/2 Add.2.

for by 104 EX/Decision 3.3. He went on to observe that Mr Sakharov worked at the Lebedev Institute of the USSR Academy of Sciences - not at the Steklov Institute as had been stated by the authors of [the second communication]. He said that the physicist had been banished to Gorky by decree of the Presidium of the Supreme Soviet to prevent leaks of secret information, as Academician Sakharov was in possession of secrets relating to national defence. The representative of the government concerned emphasized that such situations also existed in other countries, each State having the right to take appropriate measures to guarantee its security. In Gorky, he asserted, Mr Sakharov had freedom of movement; he met other citzens; he continued to concern himself with scientific matters; he saw his work colleagues; he had published some of his work through the Academy of Sciences, and it was even issued abroad; he also, as usual, received science journals. He was provided with qualified medical assistance by a renowned hospital in the city. In the opinion of the doctors who had recently examined him, his state of health was satisfactory. His children, who lived in Moscow, visited him normally. Referring to the letter dated 19 August 1986 from the author of [the first communication], the representative of the government concerned stated that, as he had only recently received it, he could not immediately check on the allegations contained therein, although, from a rapid perusal, they already appeared to be ill-founded. He added that, in any event, both communications, as had been repeated over and over again to the Committee, dealt with a case that related to the purely domestic affairs of the USSR.

88. In response to the requests for further information, the representative of the government concerned replied that, as the question of the duration of Dr Sakharov's assignation to a forced residence in Gorky was a legal matter and as he did not have a copy of the relevant document at his disposal, he did not intend to give an interpretation of it. As for the possibility of appealing against the decision of the Presidium of the Supreme Soviet, he went on to say that the physicist, like every Soviet citizen, had the right to seek redress from the Supreme Court and from other competent bodies. In addition, the private lives of individuals were protected, he said, both by the Constitution and by a whole series of legal provisions in the USSR.

89. Some members of the Committee wished to know whether Dr Sakharov could continue his research work in Gorky, receive material from abroad and exchange scientific information with foreign scientists and whether a member of the Executive Board could visit him.

90. The representative of the government concerned observed in this connection that it should not be overlooked that the very reason for assigning Dr Sakharov to forced residence in Gorky was to guard against leaks of information that might be prejudicial to State security and to national defence. No activity could be envisaged for the physicist that was not subject to this limitation. The representative of the govern-

ment concerned further assured the Committee that Gorky, the fourth largest city in the Soviet Union, possessed all that was necessary for the academician to be able to continue his scientific activities.

91. One member of the Committee, basing his remarks on an observation by another member that, since the adoption of the United Nations Charter in 1945, the question of human rights had become a matter of international responsibility, raised the question whether the Soviet Union could provide precise details, both for Dr Sakharov and in order to allay the concerns of the international community, about the conditions in which he would in future be authorized to work and live.

92. Taking the floor again, the representative of the government concerned said that his feeling was that there was often a tendency to give a political overtone to this case. He stated that, in the light of humanitarian considerations and Dr Sakharov's work record, the latter, in spite of his activities jeopardizing national security, had been simply assigned to forced residence in Gorky, for he could have been more severely penalized if he had been prosecuted; this preventive measure against the leaking of military secrets was by no means contrary to international human rights instruments, which authorized certain restrictions of freedom if they were justified by considerations regarding national security. The representative of the government concerned explained once again that in Gorky Dr Sakharov led a normal life like many other scientists who also lived in that city.

93. Certain members of the Committee felt that the statements of the representative of the government concerned made it appear that the case in question did not come within the Committee's purview since, being a political case - a case concerning the security of the Soviet Union - it was a matter of State sovereignty. As for the references made by the author of [the first communication] to information taken from the mass circulation press, particularly certain video-cassettes, and as for the interpretations that had been given of it, the members in question thought that the Committee should not discuss them, especially since, in their opinion, it was plain that the authors of the communications had been strongly influenced by propaganda put out by the media. Moreover, the search for a humanitarian solution, they said, was a problem of another kind. They were satisfied that the government concerned had furnished ample explanations that could not be challenged. According to those members of the Committee, a great deal had been read and heard about this case, and it was known that Dr Sakharov could work normally, that he had meetings with his scientific colleagues and that a regular check was kept on his state of health. They therefore felt that, in pursuance of 104 EX/Decision 3.3, paragraph 14 (*a*) (iii) and (vii), the communications should be declared inadmissible.

94. Other members of the Committee, while thanking the representative of the government concerned for the information he had been good enough to provide, considered that there still remained some unexplained points, particularly in respect of the details of the decision of the Presidium of the Supreme Soviet concerning Dr Sakharov's assignation to a forced residence, the legal basis for that decision, the duration of the measure taken by virtue of it and the exact nature of the remedies that could be sought in this case. Those members pointed out that the information contained in the two communications had been obtained not from the mass media but from the physicist's wife and from witnesses.

95. In response to a request for information concerning the humanitarian action of the Director-General pursuant to 104 EX/Decision 3.3, paragraph 8 (*b*), the representative of the Director-General stated that whenever the Director-General's good offices were requested by the Executive Board on the recommendation of the Committee he took the utmost account of such requests and that this kind of action was always confidential.

96. The discussion then centred on the desirability of including in the Committee's decision the questions that had been raised by some members of the Committee for the attention of the government concerned.

97. In that connection, some members of the Committee felt that, for the sake of clarity, it would be desirable to mention them. According to one member of the Committee, it would be more advisable to leave it to the government concerned to judge the relevance of any further information it might wish to provide. The representative of the Director-General reminded the Committee that up to now its practice had been to request the government concerned to reply to the questions raised during the discussion.

98. Following an exchange of views, the Committee *decided*:

(i) to thank the government concerned for sending a representative;

(ii) to take note of the information provided by the representative of that government;

(iii) to ask the government concerned for further information concerning the questions raised during the discussion, particularly in respect of the Soviet legislation on which the decision of the Presidium of the Supreme Soviet to assign Dr Sakharov to forced residence in Gorky was based, the duration of that measure, available means of redress that the physicist did not so far seem to have used, his activities as a researcher, his recent publications, his state of health and the protection of his private life;

(iv) to ask the Executive Board to request the Director-General to continue to use his good offices on behalf of Dr Sakharov;

(v) to resume consideration of these two communications at its spring 1987 session.

Spring 1987 session of the Committee on Conventions and Recommendations (126th session of the Executive Board)[26]

101. According to the authors of the communications[27] Dr Andrei Sakharov, physicist, who was banished to Gorky in January 1980, has been subjected to constant harassment. He is reported to be unable to communicate or receive scientific and cultural information, to work freely, to receive proper medical care, to reply to invitations from foreign university institutions.

102. At the present session of the Committee, the representative of the government concerned stated that the Presidium of the Supreme Soviet, in December 1986, had issued a decision which annulled the decision of January 1980 assigning Mr Sakharov to the city of Gorky.

103. A decision of 17 December 1986 pardoned Ms Elena Bonner; thus all questions concerning Mr Sakharov and Ms Bonner were now outdated and overtaken by events the representative of the government concerned said. The representative further informed the Committee that in recent years Mr Sakharov had written five works in his field of study. These works had appeared in the publications of the Moscow Academy of Sciences and also in the United States of America. This proved, the representative said, that Mr Sakharov had been free to pursue his scientific work in Gorky.

104. The Chairperson thanked the representative for the information he had provided to the Committee and expressed satisfaction that the recent decision of the Presidium had resolved matters concerning these communications.

105. The Committee *decided*:

---

[26] See document 126 EX/3 PRIV., paras. 101-105; see also document 126 EX/CR/HR/2.

[27] Communications No. 482/82 concerning *Union of Soviet Socialist Republics*, case of *Andrei Sakharov*, and No. 603/84 concerning *Union of Soviet Socialist Republics*, case of *Andrei Sakharov*, were being considered together.

Union of Soviet Socialist Republics **No. 482/82**

(i) to thank the representative of the government concerned for his presence and his co-operation;

(ii) to strike the communications from its list as settled in conformity with paragraph 14 (*a*) (x) of [104 EX/Decision 3.3].

No. 483/82

Concerning *Union of Soviet Socialist Republics*
Case of *Discrimination in respect of admission to higher education courses in Moscow at the Faculty of Mechanics and Mathematics of the State University, the Institute of Physical Engineering, and the Physical-Technical Institute**

Communication of 25 June 1982 submitted by
Michel A. Calvo

Autumn 1982 session of the Committee on Conventions and Recommendations (115th session of the Executive Board)[1]

379. This communication is submitted by [Mr] Michel A. Calvo, a Paris barrister, acting on behalf of Mr Laurent Schwartz, Professor of Mathematics at the Université de Paris VIII, and Mr David Ruzié, Professor of International Law at the Université de Paris V, both of whom allege that in the Soviet Union discrimination has been practised in respect of admission to higher education courses in Moscow at the Faculty of Mechanics and Mathematics of the State University, at the Institute of Physical Engineering and at the Physical-Technical Institute.

380. In 1981, the 64 school-leavers from the same schools who were authorized to sit the entrance examination for the Faculty of Mechanics and Mathematics were allegedly subjected to a selective classification:

> 49 were classed as having neither Jewish nationality nor Jewish parents or grandparents;
>
> 15 were classed either as having Jewish nationality, or as having a Jew among their close forebears.

---

* From the Committee's spring 1984 session, this communication was being referred to as case of *Alleged discrimination in respect of admission to higher education courses in Moscow at the Faculty of Mechanics and Mathematics of the State University, the Institute of Physical Engineering, and the Physical-Technical Institute*.

1 See document 115 EX/28 PRIV., paras. 379-386; see also document 115 EX/CR/HR/3.

381. The successful candidates - whose names were announced on 26 July 1981 - included 41 belonging to the first group and only two belonging to the second group (one being the daughter of a member of the teaching staff of the Faculty and the other the son of a renowned theoretical physicist who is a corresponding member of the Academy of Sciences of the Soviet Union; it appears that the latter candidate, although a medallist of the 43rd Mathematics Olympiad, was admitted only after the authorities had received many representations and complaints).

382. The authors of the communication give a list of the candidates, together with numerous observations and an analysis of the marks obtained. They give prominence to the discrepancies between the entrance examination results of the two groups and stress that such discrepancies cannot be accounted for "except by coming to the conclusion that a policy of deliberate and/or non-fortuitous discrimination was practised". They provide, in addition, a statistical chart with full explanatory notes (apparently based on a computerized data processing operation) which is designed to show the importance of the "ethnic group" as a factor determining success in the entrance examinations for the aforementioned Faculty.

383. In order to give a "general picture" of the situation as regards the existence of the alleged policy of discrimination, the authors of the communication also supply the figures for the year 1979. The figures for 1980 could not be used as the basis for a comprehensive assessment, since, in that year, the entrance examination to the Moscow institutes of higher education were being held at the same time.

384. The same kind of discrimination is also alleged to have occurred at the Moscow Institute of Physical Engineering (MIFI) and at the Moscow Physical-Technical Institute (MFTI).

385. The representative of the Soviet Government explained to the Committee that the arrival of this communication during the school summer break had made it impossible for him to locate any school officials with whom to discuss this matter. He stated that in the event that the Committee did not decide to declare this communication inadmissible, he would request that the consideration of its admissibility be postponed until the Committee's next session.

386. A lengthy discussion ensued, during which several members of the Committee expressed their concern about some of the methods used to present the data on which the communication in question was based and drew attention to the danger inherent in such communications from the point of view of respect for the independence of teachers and educational examining bodies. Other members emphasized that the data on which the communication was based seemed sufficiently precise for it not to be possible to declare the communication inadmissible at the present stage

and the representative of the government concerned, while stating that the communication was as of now clearly inadmissible on which point he was supported by some members of the Committee, declared that he was ready to submit further information at the following session. The Committee then *decided*, in the spirit of consensus that has always guided its work, to suspend consideration of the communication until its next session pending receipt of the information to be provided by the representative of the government concerned regarding the data, including statistical data, set out by the authors of the communication.

Spring 1983 session of the Committee on Conventions and Recommendations (116th session of the Executive Board)[2]

212. This communication is submitted by [Mr] Michel A. Calvo, a Paris barrister, acting on behalf of Mr Laurent Schwartz, Professor of Mathematics at the Université de Paris VIII, and Mr David Ruzié, Professor of International Law at the Université de Paris V, both of whom allege that in the Soviet Union discrimination has been practised in respect of admission to higher education courses in Moscow at the Faculty of Mechanics and Mathematics of the State University, at the Institute of Physical Engineering and at the Physical-Technical Institute.

213. In 1981, the 64 school-leavers from the same schools who were authorized to sit the entrance examination for the Faculty of Mechanics and Mathematics were allegedly subjected to a selective classification:

> 49 were classed as having neither Jewish nationality nor Jewish parents or grandparents;
>
> 15 were classed either as having Jewish nationality, or as having a Jew among their close forebears.

214. The successful candidates - whose names were announced on 26 July 1981 - included 41 belonging to the first group and only two belonging to the second group (one being the daughter of a member of the teaching staff of the Faculty and the other the son of a renowned theoretical physicist who is a corresponding member of the Academy of Sciences of the Soviet Union; it appears that the latter candidate, although a medallist of the 43rd Mathematics Olympiad, was admitted only after the authorities had received many representations and complaints) .

---

[2] See document 116 EX/48 PRIV., paras. 212-226; see also documents 116 EX/CR/HR/2 and Add.

No. 483/82 **Union of Soviet Socialist Republics**

215. The authors of the communication give a list of the candidates, together with numerous observations and an analysis of the marks obtained. They give prominence to the discrepancies between the entrance examination results of the two groups and stress that such discrepancies cannot be accounted for "except by coming to the conclusion that a policy of deliberate and/or non-fortuitous discrimination was practised". They provide, in addition, a statistical chart with full explanatory notes (apparently based on a computerized data-processing operation) which is designed to show the importance of the "ethnic group" as a factor determining success in the entrance examinations for the aforementioned Faculty.

216. In order to give a "general picture" of the situation as regards the existence of the alleged policy of discrimination, the authors of the communication also supply the figures for the year 1979. The figures for 1980 could not be used as the basis for a comprehensive assessment, since, in that year, the entrance examination to the Moscow institutes of higher education were being held at the same time.

217. The same kind of discrimination is also alleged to have occurred at the Moscow Institute of Physical Engineering (MIFI) and at the Moscow Physical-Technical Institute (MFTI).

218. The representative of the Soviet Government explained to the Committee that the arrival of this communication during the school summer break had made it impossible for him to locate any school officials with whom to discuss this matter. He stated that in the event that the Committee did not decide to declare this communication inadmissible, he would request that the consideration of its admissibility be postponed until the Committee's next session.

219. A lengthy discussion ensued, during which several members of the Committee expressed their concern about some of the methods used to present the data on which the communication in question was based and drew attention to the danger inherent in such communications from the point of view of respect for the independence of teachers and educational examining bodies. Other members emphasized that the data on which the communication was based seemed sufficiently precise for it not to be possible to declare the communication inadmissible at the present stage and the representative of the government concerned, while stating that the communication was as of now clearly inadmissible on which point he was supported by some members of the Committee, declared that he was ready to submit further information at the following session. The Committee then decided, in the spirit of consensus that has always guided its work, to suspend consideration of the communication until its next session pending receipt of the information to be provided by the representative

of the government concerned regarding the data, including statistical data, set out by the authors of the communication.[3]

220. On 25 January, 1 April and 2 May 1983, the Secretariat received from [Mr] Calvo letters and annexes giving further particulars concerning this case.

221. At the Committee's present session, the representative of the Soviet Government explained that in the Soviet Union any person could apply for admission to institutions of higher education. There existed, he said, a large quota, roughly 50 per cent of the slots for graduates of secondary schools. There was a 25 per cent quota for applicants from factory schools and also for army veterans. Entrance examinations were held in staggered fashion so that a person could apply to other schools if he did not succeed at his first choice.

222. Of the 64 students mentioned in the communication, 45 were presently studying in institutions of higher learning. Of these 45, seven were in Moscow State University and the others were in various institutions such as the Forestry Institute, Radio Institute, institutes for civil engineering and technical institutes.

223. The Soviet representative explained that Moscow State University simply did not have enough places for everyone who wanted to attend. The alleged victims in this communication may simply not have fallen within the allocated quotas mentioned above, or various of the subjective admissions committees, such as the Parents' Committee, might not have supported their candidatures. Or perhaps they were simply not enthusiastic enough; this was also a factor which was taken into consideration, the Soviet representative explained. He pointed out that there were an enormous number of Jews in the Soviet Academy of Sciences, and that if one applied the authors' statistical methods to Tartars or Moldavians one would get a similarly misleading impression of percentages. The Soviet representative felt that Zionist organizations were probably behind the submission of this communication. He said that the data was in fact incorrect and falsified, and he wanted the Committee to be informed of the fact that three persons had been convicted for disseminating the false information underlying these statistics and had been sentenced.

224. Certain Committee members felt very strongly that Unesco should not review university admission procedures and consequently should not review this case. One Committee member explained that he had a long experience in admission procedures and pointed out that in his experience only the students' names were known to the admissions committees. He felt that the figures were falsified. Other Committee members felt that allegations of discrimination in education were of direct interest to

[3] See document 115 EX/28 PRIV., para. 386 (*supra*, pp. 172-173).

Unesco and that the matter should not be dismissed without careful consideration. It was felt that the principle of admission on the basis of merit, and not other factors, was an important one to defend, and the point was made that a standard system for ensuring objectivity in the admission process in certain other countries was that of not even providing the students names to the admissions committee.

225. Certain Committee members felt that the presentation of highly complex theoretical calculations was of little use to the Committee and was in somewhat bad taste. Other Committee members felt that simple mathematics showed that the admission data in the communication could well be a cause for concern, if in fact the sample was sufficiently large and representative. These Committee members felt that certain questions needed to be answered before further discussion could take place: was the admission process in question similar to that in other Soviet universities or was it an exceptional procedure? Exactly which parts of the data were deemed to be falsified and why? How would an admissions committee know about the ethnic origin of an applicant or his ancestors? On the basis of what information did the authors establish their statistical breakdown regarding nationality as shown in the nationality column of their chart?

226. After an involved debate, the Committee *decided* to suspend its examination of the admissibility of this communication until the autumn 1983 session and to request further information from the government concerned and from the author concerning the questions raised.

Autumn 1983 session of the Committee on Conventions and Recommendations (117th session of the Executive Board)[4]

156. This communication alleges that the conditions for admission to higher education courses in Moscow at the Faculty of Mechanics and Mathematics of the State University, the Institute of Physical Engineering and the Physical-Technical Institute, are not identical for all candidates regardless of their ethnic origin.

157. This communication has appeared on the Committee's agenda since its autumn 1982 session. At the present session, the representative of the Soviet Government, who is also a member of the Committee, emphasized that the word "discrimination" which appeared in the communication prejudged, in his opinion, the reality of the facts; he then explained that admission to these institutions was by competitive examination, and that it was to be expected that some applicants would be unsuccess-

---

[4] See document 117 EX/18 PRIV., paras. 156-159; see also documents 117 EX/CR/HR/2 and Add.2.

ful; this was not because of their nationality or Jewish background, and they could apply to other institutions of higher education. In that connection, he stated that most of the persons concerned were already enrolled at such institutions. He also challenged the validity and/or the relevance of some of the data given in the communication, as well as the testimonies that had been added to the file by the authors of the communication for the present session [...],[5] in some instances because they were anonymous, in others because the authors of the communication made use of them to insinuate that the problem raised in connection with these three institutions in Moscow was one found throughout the USSR.

158. Three members of the Committee supported some aspects of this statement: one said that in his view the presentation of the communication was in fact somewhat slanted and that the Committee should be vigilant to make sure that such was not the case, in this instance or in others; another member said that in his opinion the Committee should not accept anonymous testimony inasmuch as under paragraph 14 (*a*) (i) it did not accept communications from anonymous authors; lastly, a third speaker emphasized that the Committee should not accept testimony concerned with matters other than those dealt with in the communication, which in the present instance originally referred only to institutions of higher education that were located in Moscow and identified by name. Two members of the Committee said that they would like the authors to place additional material at their disposal, so that they would be in a better position to determine whether this communication might be regarded as constituting a question within the meaning of 104 EX/Decision 3.3.

159. After a brief discussion, the Committee *decided*:

(i) to take note of the statements of the government concerned;

(ii) to eliminate from its discussion on this communication any anonymous testimony or other document, in view of the provisions of paragraph 14 (*a*) (i) of 104 EX/Decision 3.3; and not to retain on file any item of evidence that was not clearly relevant to the communication, in accordance with paragraph 14 (*a*) (v) of that decision;

(iii) to inform the authors of the communication of the statements of the representative of the government concerned and to advise them that they were free to submit further information in the form of specific instances of discrimination in respect of admission to institutions of higher education; and

[5] See document 117 EX/CR/HR/2 Add.2.

(iv) to resume consideration of the admissibility of this communication at its spring 1984 session.

Spring 1984 session of the Committee on Conventions and Recommendations (119th session of the Executive Board)[6]

180. The Committee *decided* to defer consideration of these communications[7] until the autumn [1984 session].

Autumn 1984 session of the Committee on Conventions and Recommendations (120th session of the Executive Board)[8]

134. This communication alleges that the conditions for admission to higher education courses in Moscow at the Faculty of Mechanics and Mathematics of the State University, the Institute of Physical Engineering and the Physical-Technical Institute, are not identical for all candidates regardless of their ethnic origin. This communication has appeared on the Committee's agenda since its autumn 1982 session. At its spring 1984 session, the Committee decided to defer consideration of the communication to its present session[9] at which effectively the examination of the communication resumed.

135. When the Committee took up again at its present session the examination of the communication, the representative of the government concerned, who is also a member of the Committee, stated that, with a view to providing the Committee with information about the allegations contained in the communication, he paid a visit to the Moscow State University which was alleged to be practising discriminatory admission policy against students of Jewish origin wishing to enter its Mechanics and

[6] See document 119 EX/35 PRIV., para. 180; see also documents 119 EX/CR/HR/2 and Add. and Add.2.

[7] Communications No. 483/82 concerning *Union of Soviet Socialist Republics*, case of *Alleged discrimination in respect of admission to higher education courses in Moscow at the Faculty of Mechanics and Mathematics of the State University, the Institute of Physical Engineering, and the Physical-Technical Institute*, No. 527/83 concerning *Union of Soviet Socialist Republics*, case of *Yuri Fedorovich Orlov*, No. 560/83 concerning *Union of Soviet Socialist Republics*, case of *Anatoli Raben*, No. 561/83 concerning *Union of Soviet Socialist Republics*, case of *Anatoli Khazarov*, No. 564/83 concerning *Union of Soviet Socialist Republics*, case of *Igor Guberman*, and No. 565/83 concerning *Union of Soviet Socialist Republics*, case of *Novosibirsk Association for the Promotion of Friendship between the Peoples of the USSR and Israel*.

[8] See document 120 EX/15 PRIV., para. 134-137; see also document 120 EX/CR/HR/2.

[9] See document 119 EX/35 PRIV., para. 180 (*supra*, p. 178).

Mathematics Faculty. On that occasion, the member concerned declared that he met the Pro-Rector of the Faculty. He suggested that the letter referred to in the communication be excluded from the file as derogatory and calumnious, explaining that the person who had allegedly informed of the discriminatory admission policy had categorically denied it. This member of the Committee indicated also that he had cross-checked the information obtained by him from those associated directly with the Faculty concerned with other sources who confirmed that the allegation of discriminatory admission practice at the Faculty was a blatant lie. Declaring that the percentage of senior scientific workers of Jewish origin in the USSR was higher than the corresponding percentage of citizens of Jewish origin *vis-à-vis* the USSR population as a whole, he gave concrete data about the students of Jewish origin at the Mechanics and Mathematics Department as well as about the professors and lecturers; he contended that the allegations contained in the communication before the Committee were offensive to his country and proposed that the communication should be struck off the Committee's roll of communications.

136. One member of the Committee suggested that the Committee should take note of the information provided by the representative of the government concerned according to which there were in the USSR many eminent scientists and students of science of Jewish origin, including those at the Mechanics and Mathematics [Faculty]. This member proposed equally that note should also be taken of the representative's categorical denial that admissions to the Faculty of Mechanics and Mathematics of the Moscow State University was effected on the basis of one separate examination for applicants of Jewish origin and another separate one for other applicants. In this connection, the representative of the government concerned stated that, as a matter of fact, some of the senior officials responsible for organizing entrance examinations to the Faculty in question were of Jewish descent and that, at least for this reason alone, it would be absurd for anybody to claim that they would co-operate in the execution of any scheme calculated to bar or limit Jewish students to that Faculty.

137. The Committee, having heard the explanations of the representative of the government concerned, seeking to show that the communication did not contain relevant evidence, *decided* that the communication could not, accordingly, be deemed admissible under the terms of paragraph 14 (*a*) (v) of 104 EX/Decision 3.3, it being understood that the Committee on Conventions and Recommendations could always be asked to consider a new communication containing evidence which was prima facie admissible.

No. 484/82

Concerning *Chile*
Case of *Sergio Spoerer*

Communication of 25 June 1982 submitted by
Sergio Spoerer

Autumn 1982 session of the Committee on Conventions and Recommendations (115th session of the Executive Board)[1]

71. Mr Sergio Spoerer, a sociologist and writer of Chilean nationality, complains that on arrival at Santiago airport on 28 June 1980 he was refused admission by the Chilean authorities although in possession of a valid Chilean passport. The representations made by Mr Spoerer's counsel and by Don Felipe Herrera, former Executive Secretary of [United Nations Economic Commission for Latin America (ECLA)] and a former minister, had been to no avail.

72. At the autumn 1982 session, the representative of the Chilean Government stated that he had made inquiries with a view to obtaining information on Mr Spoerer's case, but without result. He believed that a solution to this case might be found if he could obtain further details, and for this purpose he would like to know the name of Mr Spoerer's counsel. At the request of certain members he explained that this was a purely practical matter, not a prior condition.

73. As a result, the Committee decided to entrust the Secretariat with the task of contacting Mr Spoerer on this matter before the end of the session.

74. Mr Spoerer had replied to the Secretariat in a letter dated 1 September 1982 [...].[2] After recapitulating the circumstances in which he had been detained at the airport and the representations he had made, Mr Spoerer supplied his counsel's name, adding that the explanation the latter had received from the Ministry of the Interior had been given orally.

---

[1] See document 115 EX/28 PRIV., paras. 71-77; see also documents 115 EX/CR/HR/3 and Add.4.
[2] See document 115 EX/CR/HR/3 Add.4.

No. 484/82 **Chile**

75. The representative of the government concerned affirmed that Mr Jorge Molina Valdivieso, Mr Spoerer's counsel, had not made all the necessary representations and that, in particular, after his interview at the Ministry, he could have immediately requested a review of the case; this was why the Chilean Government representative had found no trace of the matter. He stated that, as soon as he returned to Chile, he would get in touch with Don Felipe Herrera and Mr Spoerer's counsel to give them fuller information on the procedures to be followed.

76. A member of the Committee thanked the representative of the Chilean Government for his helpful attitude.

77. In conclusion, the Committee *decided*:

(i) to note the offer by the representative of the government concerned to undertake the necessary steps to find a solution to this case;

(ii) to defer consideration of the admissibility of this communication to the next session.

Spring 1983 session of the Committee on Conventions and Recommendations (116th session of the Executive Board)[3]

50. Mr Sergio Spoerer, a sociologist and writer of Chilean nationality, complains that on arrival at Santiago airport on 28 June 1980 he was refused admission by the Chilean authorities although in possession of a valid Chilean passport. The representations made by Mr Spoerer's counsel and by Don Felipe Herrera, former Executive Secretary of [United Nations Economic Commission for Latin America (ECLA)] and a former minister, have been to no avail.

51. In a letter dated 16 May 1983, the Permanent Delegation of Chile to Unesco informed the Committee that its petition on humanitarian grounds on behalf of Mr Sergio Spoerer had been favourably received and that he had received immediate and unconditional authorization to return to Chile.

52. A member of the Committee expressed his satisfaction.

[3] See document 116 EX/48 PRIV., paras. 50-53; see also documents 116 EX/CR/HR/2 and Add.2.

Chile **No. 484/82**

53. By consensus, the Committee *decided* to delete this communication from its list as having been settled, in accordance with paragraph 14 (*a*) (x) of 104 EX/Decision 3.3.

No. 487/82

Concerning *Indonesia*
Case of *Tengku Muhammad Usman Lampoh Awé*

Communication of 6 August 1982 submitted by
Husaini Mohammad Hasan

Spring 1983 session of the Committee on Conventions and Recommendations (116th session of the Executive Board)[1]

82. This communication alleges the violation of the rights of a person, described as a businessman from Acheh Sumatra, who is said to have been sentenced to 20 years' hard labour for defending himself before an Indonesian court in his mother tongue.

83. The representative of the Indonesian Government communicated the following information to the Committee:

> Mr Usman Lampoh Awé had been arrested for subversive activities within an illegal political movement, the NLFAS (National Liberation Front of Acheh Sumatra). The Prosecutor had demanded life imprisonment but the court had delivered a sentence of only 20 years' imprisonment. The hearing had been public. The judgement had been delivered in accordance with the penal legislation in force.
>
> Mr Usman Lampoh Awé had refused to speak in Indonesian during the trial and had spoken in Acheh (Atjeh), but that was not the point at issue since the Indonesian judicial system provided for the services of an interpreter to ensure that the proceedings could be conducted normally. The court had not suddenly stopped the proceedings and had not summarily sentenced the defendant. Since the latter was capable of expressing himself in Indonesian, the court had considered that attitude to be a refusal to reply to the questions asked and had applied Article 270 of the Revised Internal Act (Herziend Inlands Reglement) which stipulated that "In case the accused does not or re-

[1] See document 116 EX/48 PRIV., paras. 82-90; see also documents 116 EX/CR/HR/3 and Add.2.

fuses to answer questions addressed to him/her by the judge, the judge will remind him/her of his/her obligation to response and then proceed with the trial of the case".

The Constitution of the Republic of Indonesia declared Indonesian to be the official national language, but the government provided for the development of local languages as integral parts of the living cultures of Indonesia. Those languages were taught in primary and secondary schools.

Under the Indonesian judicial system, a defendant could appeal against a court's decision if he considered it unfair. Mr Usman Lampoh Awé had not availed himself of that right. In his communication, the author stated that no means of redress existed in the judicial system, which was alleged to be "based on corruption and repression". That was an insult to the Republic of Indonesia.

The independence and unity of Indonesia were recognized by the United Nations The NLFAS was not a political and educational movement. It was a separatist movement employing means such as terrorism, sabotage, intimidation, kidnapping, assassination, the burning down of factories, and so on, that ran counter to the principles of democracy. The author of the communication and the alleged victim even claimed to be ministers of the government of that movement.

84. The acts committed by the NLFAS were violations of the Universal Declaration of Human Rights (Article 29), the International Covenant on Economic, Social and Cultural Rights (Article 8) and the International Covenant on Civil and Political Rights (Articles 12, 19 and 22) because they gave rise to social disturbances prejudicial to public order, imperilling national security and integrity and impairing the exercise of individual rights and freedoms.

85. The communication appeared to be based essentially on second-hand and third-hand information or on information put out by certain publications, including those issued by the NLFAS itself, and "Tapol", an anti-Indonesian bulletin. For those reasons, it could not be said to be from a person with reliable knowledge of the alleged violations.

86. Considering that the communication did not meet the conditions for admissibility laid down in 104 EX/Decision 3.3 of the Executive Board, paragraph 14 (*a*) (ii), (iii), (v), (vii), (ix) and (x), the representative of the Indonesian Government requested that it should be declared inadmissible.

Indonesia **No. 487/82**

87. Several members of the Committee felt that the information supplied by the government concerned was exhaustive and satisfactory.

88. One member of the Committee asked whether the NLFAS had existed before Indonesia's independence.

89. The representative of the Indonesian Government said that the movement had come into being well after the date of independence.

90. After discussing the matter, the Committee *declared* the communication inadmissible as not falling within Unesco's fields of competence, especially since no effort had been made to exhaust available domestic remedies (104 EX/Decision 3.3 of the Executive Board, paragraph 14 (*a*) (iii) and (ix)).

No. 489/82

Concerning *Zambia*
Case of *Students expelled or suspended from the University of Zambia*

Communication of 18 August 1982 submitted by
John Tox Japhet Ngwata Phiri

Spring 1983 session of the Committee on Conventions and Recommendations (116th session of the Executive Board)[1]

265. This communication alleges violation of the rights of a number of students, 18 of whom are named, who are said to have been expelled or suspended from the University of Zambia without valid reasons, apparently just because they were leaders of the Students Union or had an influence on their fellow students, and because of the fear of the University authorities of being criticized by them on account of possible administrative shortcomings.

266. In a long statement supported by a very detailed written report, and corroborated by a series of appended documents, among them various writings and publications of the students concerned, the representative of the Zambian Government refuted point by point the allegations made by the author of the communication. He gave the chronology of the events which had begun towards the end of November 1981 and had led up to the expulsion or suspension of the students, notified in letters dated 29 March 1982. He showed how the agitation and disturbances provoked by the students and incited by their leaders, among them the author of the communication, Mr Phiri, had escalated. Great East Road had been blocked for several hours. A provisional Union Executive was installed on 3 December 1981, and then on 26 January 1982 a new Executive replaced the former Executive of the Students Union, which was accused of cowardice for having observed discipline and complied with the regulations. Classes were boycotted several times in a row; dishes on which meals were served in the refectory were broken and damage was done to refectory furniture on 14 February 1982; communiqués and publications were distributed containing insulting remarks about the Party and the government, particularly in one

[1] See document 116 EX/48 PRIV., paras. 265-271; see also document 116 EX/CR/HR/3.

document distributed at the ceremony to inaugurate the Institute of Human Relations (23 February 1982), which was attended by many foreign diplomats; the new Executive of the Students Union refused to withdraw that document and to apologize for the gross lack of tact that had been displayed; there was a succession of student gatherings and violent statements were made against the authorities; the student leaders displayed a persistently aggressive attitude in spite of considerable concessions by the University authorities aimed at moderating the atmosphere of disorder and indiscipline; etc.

267. Referring to an allegation by the author of the communication that the letters giving notice of expulsion or suspension were signed by an official who did not have the authority to do so, the representative of the Zambian Government said that the decision concerned had been taken by the Principal, and his subordinate, the Registrar, had merely carried it out. Concerning a further allegation that the students disciplined had not been given a hearing, he pointed out that on various occasions the University authorities had invited them to discuss a compromise which might restore calm and order, and several warnings had been given before the disciplinary measures were taken, but to no avail. As for the claim that the motives for the decision had been vague, he said that, as the facts which he had set out proved, the students concerned were perfectly well aware of them, being unable to deny their own roles in the disturbances which they had fomented. He informed the Committee that most of the students who had been expelled or suspended from the University had subsequently expressed their regrets and been readmitted. In addition, he maintained that the communication did not meet the conditions of admissibility stipulated in paragraph 14 (*a*) of 104 EX/Decision 3.3, since it did not refer to a violation of human rights within Unesco's fields of competence, the measures taken against the students being disciplinary measures which were neither arbitrary nor unjustified and which were within the jurisdiction of the University of Zambia. He noted, in conclusion, that the right to freedom of expression and opinion did not recognize the right to insult others, and that the right to freedom of assembly did not authorize abuses, since the law was able to impose limitations to ensure recognition of and respect for the rights of others.

268. Several members of the Committee were of the opinion that the students concerned had acted illegally, that the University administrators had used all means available to try to solve the problem, and that there had not been any violation of human rights as the author of the communication had claimed. Some members, referring to Article 29 (2) of the Universal Declaration of Human Rights, were anxious to stress that in the exercise of their rights and the enjoyment of their freedoms everyone was required to give due recognition and respect to the rights and freedoms of others and to meet "the just requirements of morality, public order and the general welfare in a democratic society". Other members supported that view and stressed

that the decision which the University authorities had felt obliged to take resulted from the actions of the students who had provoked disturbances that prevented the University from functioning normally.

269. In answer to a question from a Committee member who wanted to know if a similar case had ever arisen when communications were being considered at previous sessions, the representative of the Director-General said that the Committee had considered the case of a student of a Latin American country who had been barred from his faculty by a disciplinary measure.[2] He added that at the time, the representative of the government concerned had maintained that the matter was entirely within the competence of the university itself but had, at the Committee's request, offered his good offices to try to get the student reinstated. His efforts had been unsuccessful, however, because of the attitude of the person concerned. The student had in fact carried on distributing pamphlets, and against the new rector whom he had asked only a few days beforehand to reconsider his position.[3]

270. Later speakers acknowledged that the information provided by the representative of the Zambian Government had been very well presented and that there did not seem to have been a refusal of the right to education, to the detriment of the students. However, they felt that interruption of studies was a very serious matter for the students and that an appeal for clemency should therefore be made to the authorities, and particularly to the Chancellor of the University who was the President of the Republic, in order to obtain a reduction of the sanctions imposed and enable the students to go back to their respective faculties.

271. After an extensive exchange of views, the Committee *decided* to declare the communication inadmissible, since human rights had not been violated in this instance, and, in accordance with the Committee's practice, to ask the representative of the government concerned to note the views expressed by Committee members, especially their appeal for clemency.

---

[2] Communication No. 267/80 concerning *Chile*, case of *Pedro Segundo Ahumada Pizarro.*

[3] See document 114 EX/38 PRIV., para. 413 (vol. I, p. 645).

No. 491/82

Concerning *Israel*
Case of *Violations of human rights committed by Israel against the Lebanese and Palestinian peoples**

Communication of 24 August 1982 submitted by
International Commission of Enquiry into Israeli Crimes
Against Lebanese and Palestinian Peoples

Autumn 1982 session of the Committee on Conventions and Recommendations (115th session of the Executive Board)[1]

125. By a telex dated 24 August 1982, Mr John Platts-Mills, Secretary-General of the International Commission of Enquiry into Israeli Crimes Against Lebanese and Palestinian Peoples submitted to Unesco a communication, requesting an urgent examination of the question of violation of human rights allegedly committed by Israel against the Lebanese and Palestinian peoples falling within Unesco's fields of competence. The telex reads as follows:

> Urgent
>
> H.E. Mr Amadou-Mahtar M'Bow
> Director-General
> Unesco
> Paris
>
> International Commission of Enquiry into Israeli Crimes Against Lebanese and Palestinian Peoples requests Your Excellency to submit to extraordinary hearing of Committee on Conventions and Recommendations of Unesco Ex-

---

* From the Committee's spring 1984 session, this communication was being referred to as case of *Alleged violations of human rights committed by Israel against the Lebanese and Palestinian peoples*

[1] See document 115 EX/28 PRIV., paras. 125-159; see also documents 115 EX/CR/HR/3 Add.3 and 5.

ecutive Council at its 115th session due to begin on 30 August 1982 the issue of brutal and mass scale violations of human rights by Israel against Lebanese and Palestinian peoples, of aggressive military actions and particularly of the violations of the right to education, information and other violations subject to Unesco authority.

As Israeli actions violate binding laws we kindly request Your Excellency submit these violations to extraordinary Committee hearing.

We are sending you by urgent post results and conclusions of first session of International Commission of Enquiry into Israeli Crimes Against Lebanese and Palestinian Peoples on 15 and 16 August in Nicosia, Cyprus. Findings are based on evidence presented by witnesses.

Highest regards,
Sincerely
John Platts-Mills
Queen's Counsellor
Secretary-General
International Commission of Enquiry into Israeli
Crimes Against Lebanese and Palestinian Peoples

126. The telex was supplemented by a 16-page document received by Unesco on 3 September 1982 which set forth in detail the allegations of the Commission. The allegations are as follows:

> On 6 June 1982, the regular Israeli troops invaded Lebanon and committed aggression against the Lebanese and Palestinian peoples. The goal of this invasion was to liquidate the Palestine Liberation Organization primarily by killing as many Palestinians as possible. The aggressors killed, wounded and mained dozens of thousands of the Lebanese and Palestinians, predominantly women, children and old people; thousands upon thousands of people are missing, while close to a million people have been left homeless or have been forced to flee from their native cities and villages. It was in cold blood that the invaders destroyed 14 Palestinian refugee camps, three major cities in southern Lebanon, and 32 villages...
>
> ... The Commission is an independent body responsible for its own activities and decisions. Its members took part in the Commission as individuals, not as representatives of organizations or states. The functions of the Commission are to collect, hear and evaluate evidence of facts and events within the scope

of the inquiry for which it is constituted and come to its conclusion on the evidence...

... The State of Israel and its Zionist rulers are accused of the following criminal actions:

(i) crimes against peace,

(ii) crimes against humanity,

(iii) war crimes, and

(iv) actions aimed at denying the right of self-determination to the Palestinian people.

127. After presenting the communication, the representative of the Director-General read to the Committee the written reply the Secretariat had received from the Permanent Delegation of Israel to Unesco. In it, the Permanent Delegate of Israel pointed out to the Committee that her government had been co-operating with the Committee since 1978. The Permanent Delegate further informed the Committee that

> ... With regard to the telegram attached to your above-mentioned letter, it is in contradiction with the procedures established in Executive Board [104 EX/ Decision 3.3] and with procedural practices of the Committee on Conventions and Recommendations and therefore cannot be brought before the Committee.
>
> Thus not only has no form been presented and the time-limit of one month respected, but the very title of the so-called Commission of Enquiry headed by Mr Platts-Mills, to inquire into "Israeli crimes against the Lebanese and Palestinian peoples" indicates, from the outset, its blatant prejudicial character, as a Commission which reached its conclusions before commencing its work.
>
> The submission of the cable to the Committee on Conventions and Recommendations would thus be inconsistent with Unesco's procedures and would question the credibility of both the Committee on Conventions and Recommendations and Unesco.

128. Thereupon the Chairman explained to the Committee that the first question before it which needed to be decided was whether the Committee would grant the author's request for immediate examination of the communication.

No. 491/82 **Israel**

[128a.] One member of the Committee said that in his view there was no valid reason to defer examination of the communication.

129. He argued as follows:

(i) The communication, although submitted in the form of a telegram, was not in contradiction with the conditions laid down in 104 EX/Decision 3.3, for an exceptional procedure was involved: the acts committed by Israel in Lebanon had been a matter of concern to international opinion as a whole and shocked the conscience of all mankind.

(ii) The communication, although submitted without a form, was not irregular: the form simply enabled a methodical approach to be adopted to the work involved; it was not an absolute necessity.

(iii) The name "International Commission of Enquiry into Israeli Crimes Against the Lebanese and Palestinian Peoples" did not "indicate its prejudicial character" as alleged by the Permanent Delegate of Israel. The Commission could not call itself by any other name. Israel had committed manifest crimes against the two peoples.

(iv) The communication was quite consistent with the procedure established by Unesco.

(v) The credibility of the Committee would be at stake if it did not examine the communication.

(vi) The Commission which had submitted the communication was made up of persons of different nationalities and it had submitted a coherent, descriptive and well-documented case (the speaker cited by way of illustration a passage in the Commission's report: paragraph 10 - destruction of cultural and scientific monuments and institutions).

130. Another member of the Committee said that he had been very impressed by the arguments of the preceding speaker. He wished merely to make some further points.

(i) With regard to the urgency of the communication: the circumstances were exceptional as a result of the Israeli military action in Lebanon. The attitude of the Permanent Delegate of Israel to Unesco, who pleaded the one-month interval between receipt of the communication and the date of the Committee's meeting, was showing a lack of respect for the Committee. What interval and what procedures had the Israeli army observed when it attacked Lebanon?

(ii) With regard to the membership of the Commission: it comprised many eminent figures, whose impartiality could not be questioned; good many Israeli citizens had been shocked by the actions of their own government.

(iii) With regard to the admissibility of the communication: the documents submitted in support of it clearly indicated which matters involved Unesco's spheres of competence (the speaker referred to the passage in the Commission's report concerning the destruction of monuments, the destruction of educational institutions and the destruction of the Exhibition Hall for the works of Palestinian artists. He also referred to an article in the newspaper, "Le Monde", in which it was reported that the French school, St. Joseph's, had been destroyed). The communication thus seemed to be admissible.

131. This Committee member added that it was difficult to restrict attention solely to what fell within Unesco's purview, for there were not only children who were unable to continue their education, but also children whom fragmentation bombs and indiscriminate bombing had deprived of the right to life.

132. Another member of the Committee endorsed the two preceding statements.

133. He observed that it was apparent from the attitude of the Director-General's representative that the government concerned did not wish to respond to the communication.

134. After saying that he considered the communication admissible, he asked whether the Committee could not submit it direct to the Executive Board, in view of the fact that it manifestly involved war crimes.

135. One Committee member stated that an exceptional situation called for exceptional procedures: an emergency procedure was imperative, for the acts of violence committed by Israel in Lebanon had been flung in the face of mankind.

[135a.] Another member of the Committee said that since the communication referred to exceptional occurrences which were the result of Israel's universally condemned military intervention in Lebanon and which manifestly called for urgent humanitarian measures, it should benefit from exceptional treatment and could not possibly be rejected for narrow procedural reasons. It was therefore important that the Committee decide in favour of an urgent examination of the case concerned, which would nevertheless be without prejudice to the actual substance of the question, and in which recourse would be had to additional information regarding aspects within Unesco's competence and to humanitarian action by the Director-General. The Committee's objective should be to set in train measures for the urgent safeguarding of human rights in Lebanon, which rights fell within Unesco's spheres of competence, and to do so regardless of purely political considerations which could be examined more fruitfully in other forms.

136. Another member of the Committee expressed the view that the Committee had not been set up to condemn one state or another. In support of this opinion he cited 104 EX/Decision 3.3, paragraph 7:

> ... in matters concerning human rights within its fields of competence, Unesco, basing its efforts on moral considerations and its specific competence, should act in a spirit of international co-operation, conciliation and mutual understanding; and ... should not play the role of an international judicial body.

137. He considered that the Committee should give the government concerned time to reply. Referring to [...] "Procedural Practice of the Executive Board's Committee on Conventions and Recommendations in Applying 104 EX/Decision 3.3",[2] which document had been adopted by the Committee as a working tool, he pointed out that the interval of one month had been strictly observed by the Committee in the past. He therefore proposed deferring the discussion to the next session.

138. Another member of the Committee expressed the view that the Committee ought to think of what it could do in a practical way, however sad and bitter the allegations were. Allowing an interval of one month to elapse would also enable Committee members to examine the communication with the requisite attention and discuss it objectively.

139. Another member of the Committee considered that given the unprecedented acts of brutality committed by Israel in Lebanon, given the importance and urgency of the question, the idea of one month's interval could not be entertained: the representative of the Israeli Government could not be unaware of the aggression perpetrated by her country against Lebanon, which was an incontrovertible fact.

140. The speaker shared the opinion of those members of the Committee who spoke in favour of declaring the communication to be admissible.

---

[2] See document 112 EX/CR/HR/5.

141. Another member of the Committee was of the view that paragraph 18 of 104 EX/Decision 3.3 established that the Committee was quite competent to examine questions of massive, systematic or flagrant violations of human rights and fundamental freedoms, in particular, those perpetrated as a result of policies of aggression, occupation of foreign territory and genocide.

142. Another member of the Committee stated that he strongly dissented from the discussion that had just taken place and shared the view of those members of the Committee who thought that the Committee should not depart from its usual practice and should defer the discussion to the next session. He noted the importance of strictly adhering to the Committee's established practice of a one-month interval.

143. The representative of the Director-General pointed out in connection with the one-month interval that it was the Committee itself which had established it and not the Director-General.

144. One member of the Committee was of the view that the Committee should try as far as possible not to exceed its brief, that practical results were to be preferred to the expression of feelings and that it was unwise to depart from procedure.

145. Another member of the Committee stated that the Committee was set up to find amicable solutions: it had to be admitted that 90 per cent of the contents of the communication did not come within the competence of Unesco; other international bodies could deal with it; when referring to paragraph 18 of 104 EX/Decision 3.3, it should be stressed that the Committee's brief was limited to Unesco's sphere of activity; furthermore, the Committee ought not examine accounts published in the press and it was not for the Committee to denounce anyone.

146. Answering an inquiry from the Chairman of the Committee, the representative of the Director-General, the Legal Adviser, explained that the communication had been submitted to the Committee in accordance with the procedure laid down in 104 EX/Decision 3.3 and that it could be placed before the Executive Board in accordance with the same procedure: examination of admissibility, examination of the substance. It was when it was impossible to reach an amicable agreement that a special report had to be prepared for the Executive Board.

147. The representative of the Director-General added that there was a different procedure which could be followed to have a question included on the Executive Board's agenda.

148. One member of the Committee proposed two alternative courses of action:

(i) declare the communication admissible; defer examination of the substance of the communication to the next session; or

(ii) transmit the communication to the Executive Board, as proposed by some members, making no attempt to examine it in the Committee.

149. One member of the Committee observed that the discussion had been distorted in three respects:

(i) The "urgency" of the question had deliberately been separated from its "substance", when in fact only an examination of the substance would have made it clear whether or not the matter was "urgent".

(ii) The one-month interval had been invoked. That interval applied only in ordinary cases in normal times; whereas the case under discussion was urgent.

(iii) It had been insinuated that there might be some sanction against Israel if the Committee examined the communication, whereas there had never been any question of any sort of sanction.

150. One member of the Committee expressed the wish that the Secretariat inform the author of the communication of the Committee's discussions and, at the same time, ask him to provide the Committee with various statistics concerning the destruction referred to and all the details of violations of human rights falling within Unesco's spheres of competence.

151. After summing up the discussion that had taken place, the Chairman of the Committee asked the representative of the Director-General to read out a draft version of the Committee's decision.

152. One member of the Committee informed the Committee that he could not approve the draft because the Committee had only discussed the urgency of the communication and not its admissibility.

153. After another member of the Committee had asked for the addition of a specific invitation to Israel to co-operate with the Committee and, in the event of an impasse, for the Committee simply to report to the Executive Board, he stated that he was in favour of declaring the case admissible and was willing to approve the draft decision.

Israel **No. 491/82**

154. One member of the Committee informed the Committee that if the wording of the decision was to stand as it was, he would be compelled to ask for a vote. He quoted a precedent in the Committee in this respect.

155. The representative of the Director-General explained to the Committee that the precedent alluded to was not a true precedent for it involved a vote of a purely indicative nature asked for at the time by the Chairman of the Committee to ascertain the current of opinion in the Committee. After the vote the Committee had adopted a decision by consensus.

156. Another member of the Committee proposed that the Committee decide by consensus, and that it be indicated in the report that one member had expressed a reservation with regard to paragraph 2 of the decision.

157. After a suspension of the meeting, a vote was taken by show of hands. The result of the vote was 15 in favour, and one against, with one abstention.

158. The text of the *decision* as adopted by the Committee is as follows:

The Committee,

(i) Taking cognizance of the request for urgent examination of the communication, decides to comply with it, noting that preliminary submission of a form is in no way a condition of admissibility and that the said form is designed solely to facilitate the setting forth of the complaint by the author of the communication and its examination by the Committee;

(ii) Decides to declare the communication admissible in so far as it falls within Unesco's spheres of competence, namely: education, science, culture and communication;

(iii) Noting that the documents submitted in support of the communication contain some elements which fall within Unesco's spheres of competence and some elements which do not, instructs the Secretariat to go through the communication, in co-operation with its author, in order to eliminate any element that does not come within Unesco's sphere of competence;

(iv) Emphasizing the importance it attaches to the co-operation of the governments concerned by communications, urges the government concerned to co-operate with the Committee in the examination of this communication;

(v) Considers that in order to continue examination of the communication it must have supplementary information which should be requested of both the author of the communication and the government concerned;

(vi) Requests the Executive Board to ask the Director-General to make available to the Committee, in accordance with 104 EX/Decision 3.3, paragraph 14 (*f*), any information which might be available to him and which he might deem relevant to the present communication, and also to take any action he may consider possible, in accordance with 104 EX/Decision 3.3, paragraph 8;

(vii) Decides to resume examination of the communication at its next session as the first item on its agenda, owing to the urgency and gravity of the whole affair.

159. Two members explained their votes: one Committee member said that he had voted against the text because the Committee could play an effective role only with the co-operation of the governments concerned, which could only be obtained if the Committee's practices were strictly adhered to, and the government concerned were given adequate time to reply, that the communication was defective in several respects and that the Committee had not actually examined the question of the admissibility of the communication; another Committee member said that his vote in favour of adopting the decision declaring the communication admissible did not imply any attitude of approval or disapproval as regards either the substance of the question or the language actually used in the original communication, in view of the fact that in several places the language gave rise to reservations; he added that he had voted in favour of the text for reasons that were well known to the members of the Committee and that his government would have had reservations with regard to the text if Israel, and, of course, the author of the communication as well, had not been asked to provide additional information for the examination of the substance of the communication.

Extraordinary 1982 session of the Committee on Conventions and Recommendations[3]

6. This communication, sent by telex dated 24 August 1982, was submitted by Mr John Platts-Mills, Secretary-General of the "International Commission of Inquiry into Israeli Crimes Against the Lebanese and Palestinian Peoples", crimes alleged to have been committed since the Israeli troops' entry into Lebanon; it was the subject

[3] See document 116 EX/48 PRIV., annex I, paras. 6-21; see also documents 3 X/EX/CR/HR/1 and Add.1 and 2, 116 EX/48 PRIV., paras. 332-333, and 116 EX/CR/HR/4.

of an urgent examination by the Committee at its autumn 1982 session and was declared admissible on 7 September 1982.[4]

7. By a letter dated 25 October 1982, the Secretariat, in compliance with the Committee's instructions, informed the author of the communication that the alleged facts which seemed at first sight to fall within Unesco's spheres of competence were the following:

> (*a*) the destruction of monuments and cultural and scientific institutions, including the Arab University, the Stadium and the Centre for the exhibition of works of Palestinian artists; the destruction of extensive parts of Beirut, Tyre, Nabatia and Sidon, and of various other towns; and the violation of the provisions of the Hague Convention of 14 May 1954 and Article 54 of the Supplementary Protocol, concerning the protection of cultural property in the event of armed conflict;
>
> (*b*) the use of a school in Sidon as a prison [...].[5]

8. On 29 November 1982 the author of the communication transmitted to the Secretariat two letters and one document providing further particulars regarding the extent of the damage caused to education, culture, science and information. He illustrated his remarks with examples. He emphasized the disorganization of the education system and of its administration in Lebanon. He particularly stressed:

> (i) the fact that he could not agree to a narrow approach to Unesco's fields of competence, particularly in regard to the right to education - which, according to him, presupposes each child's right to life and to physical, intellectual, moral, spiritual and social development in conditions of freedom and dignity - and the violation of that right by Israel in Lebanese territory;
>
> (ii) the fact that the acts perpetrated by Israel in Lebanon should be described as massive, systematic or flagrant violations of human rights within the meaning of 104 EX/Decision 3.3, paragraph 18.

9. He considered that only the immediate withdrawal of the Israeli troops would enable a normal situation to be restored in Lebanon.

10. The following elements put forward by him appeared to be new ones, not having been included in the original communication:

[4] See document 115 EX/28 PRIV., para. 158 (ii) (*supra*, p. 201).
[5] See document 3 X/EX/CR/HR/1, para. 4.

(i) contempt of religious feelings and religious and cultural traditions;

(ii) the disorganization of the network of news services;

(iii) the use by Israel of scientific-technical means for anti-humanitarian purposes [...].[6]

11. In her letter dated 29 November 1982, received by the Secretariat the following day, the Permanent Delegate of Israel to Unesco stated that she had not been informed what part of the communication had been declared admissible by the Committee. She felt that her government could not be expected to co-operate in the same way as before since she did not know what accusation would be discussed by the Committee and especially since, in her view, none of the accusations was founded. She drew the Committee's attention to the fact that the communication submitted to it for examination was almost a word-for-word copy of the press release of 18 August 1982 issued by the PLO office in New York [...],[7] and she therefore considered that, without raising other procedural and substantive questions, the communication should be rejected pursuant to 104 EX/Decision 3.3, paragraph 14 (*a*) (vii).

12. At this extraordinary session of the Committee the discussions began with an exchange of views concerning the procedure adopted for examining the communication at the autumn 1982 session and that to be adopted on this occasion.

13. Some members of the Committee felt that at the [autumn 1982] session the Committee had not complied with the usual procedure in agreeing to examine the communication, submitted without the endorsement of the prescribed form, on 7 September 1982, following an extension of the session, initially scheduled to last from 30 August to 3 September, at a time when some members, not previously informed, had already left the Organization's Headquarters. According to them, the Committee had consequently not been able to make a proper study of the problems raised and had been somewhat hasty in taking a decision as to admissibility, not having granted the government concerned the customary month's notice to present its observations.

14. One member of the Committee stated that his government was deeply concerned over the aforesaid serious procedural deficiencies in the case, and delivered a prepared statement setting forth that government's views on the subject. The statement noted that the case had not been on the Committee's agenda at the outset, that only a brief telegram on the subject had been circulated during the Committee's regularly

---

[6] See document 3 X/EX/CR/HR/1 Add.1, paras. 17-19.
[7] See document 3 X/EX/CR/HR/1 Add.2.

scheduled session and that the communication itself was presented to the Committee belatedly, not in the form normally required, and allowing only one day for study and analysis. The statement faulted the Secretariat for its failure to apply in this case the procedures generally followed by the Committee. The member emphasized that his government was opposed to a system under which there was no single set of rules which would apply to all cases, a system which would apply different rules to different countries. He added that it may be necessary to adopt formal procedures to be applied uniformly in all cases, irrespective of which country may be involved.

15. Some members of the Committee regretted that this official statement had been read out; they considered that it might well give a political tone to the discussions. They were of the opinion that the Committee had not violated any procedural rule. They confirmed, in passing, the words of the representative of the Director-General to the effect that the Committee's attention had, at various times during meetings preceding that of 7 September 1982, been drawn to a communication transmitted by the Director-General in accordance with 104 EX/Decision 3.3 for which the supporting documents could not be available until around the end of the session as initially scheduled. The examination of this communication had been requested by its authors as a matter of urgency and the Committee should appreciate that fact, as well as the manner in which it had been presented. According to them, the present case was indisputably an urgent one; the adoption of an emergency procedure in keeping with the events was consequently reasonable and fair; it was true that the Committee was not a court of law, but the decision taken at the [autumn 1982] session was irrevocable and remained valid.

16. In response to the request of some members of the Committee, the representative of the Director-General said that the Secretariat had been instructed to go through the communication in co-operation with its author; but as the latter had not sent his reply to the Secretariat until 29 November 1982, stating in addition that he could not agree to a narrow approach to Unesco's spheres of competence, that reply had been communicated without delay, that is to say on 29 November 1982, to the Permanent Delegation of Israel to the Organization.

17. Some members of the Committee then considered that the Secretariat had already made an effort to eliminate any element extraneous to the alleged facts, but that those facts had not yet been fully identified; that, in regard to the violation of the Hague Convention, for instance, there existed a specific procedure for dealing with it; that the state concerned should be allowed to investigate the alleged facts; that the Committee should, in particular, raise the question of whether it had proof of the alleged violations of human rights, whether those violations came within Unesco's fields of competence, and what practical action the Organization could take since it did not lie within its functions to condemn or denounce a state. Those

members also said that they did not wish to minimize the gravity of the events that had occurred in the Middle East and that they were not insensitive to the human suffering that those events had caused. They emphasized, however, that the Committee's role should not be placed in jeopardy through its concerning itself with problems that were not within its competence.

18. Some members of the Committee, alluding to the argument put forward by the government concerned regarding the inadmissibility of the communication (last sentence of paragraph 11 above), pointed out that the press release of 18 August 1982 issued by the PLO office in New York was not exactly the same as the communication submitted at the autumn 1982 session [...][8] and that, above all, that press release contained no mention of the lodging of a complaint with the Committee, and therefore did not violate the rule of confidentiality.

19. Some other members of the Committee stated that the alleged violations of human rights were but the consequences of a war. War was, first and foremost, a violation of a fundamental right, the right to life.

20. A number of Committee members pointed out that to adopt this line of reasoning would be tantamount to recognizing Unesco's powerlessness; there would then be a risk of opening the way to the justification of other violations of human rights in more or less similar situations, for instance during a state of emergency or martial law. Those members were of the opinion that Unesco should react firmly so as to restore normal life in Lebanon. They felt that the facts alleged by the author of the communication, backed up by his letter dated 29 November 1982, afforded in themselves serious grounds, in the absence of refutation, for:

> considering that, in this particular case, massive, systematic violations of human rights had occurred, within the scope of 104 EX/Decision 3.3, paragraph 18;
>
> preparing accordingly a specific report on the affair to the Executive Board.

21. After thorough discussion, the Committee adopted by consensus and without any reservation the following *decision*:

> The Committee,
>
> Recalling its decision by which it declared [this communication] admissible,

---

[8] See document 115 EX/CR/HR/3 Add.5.

Considering that the alleged facts, which are extremely serious, are consequently still a matter of urgency,

Noting that fresh information was submitted by the author of the communication on 29 November 1982 and conveyed to the government concerned on the same day, and that that government has not, as of 3 December 1982, made any reply,

Decides:

1. To keep the communication on its agenda and to continue to examine its substance at its next session as the first item on its agenda;

2. To confine that examination to those facts which lie within Unesco's competence, namely,

(i) paragraph 4, subparagraphs (*a*) and (*b*), of document 3 X/EX/CR/HR/1;

(ii) the points put forward in the statement of the facts on 29 November 1982, on the understanding that the Secretariat shall be responsible for reviewing that statement in co-operation with the author of the communication and after informing the government concerned, in order to remove from it any material which clearly does not lie within Unesco's competence;

3. To urge the government concerned to co-operate with the Committee in establishing the above-mentioned specific facts by supplying all relevant information for the purpose;

4. To request the Director-General to continue his action in the spirit of paragraph 14 (*k*) of 104 EX/Decision 3.3 with a view to the friendly settlement of the individual and specific cases included in the communication.

Spring 1983 session of the Committee on Conventions and Recommendations (116th session of the Executive Board)[9]

307. This communication alleges violations of human rights committed by the State of Israel against the Lebanese and Palestinian peoples within the fields of competence of Unesco, following the entry of Israeli troops into Lebanon in June 1982.

[9] See document 116 EX/48 PRIV., paras. 307-315; see also documents 116 EX/CR/HR/1 and Add.2.

No. 491/82 **Israel**

308. As the communication was declared admissible at the Committee's [autumn 1982 session],[10] the Committee examined its substance following the extraordinary session of 3 December 1982.

309. The government concerned was not represented at the two previous sessions, neither was it represented at this spring 1983 session. In the letter dated 9 May 1983 [...],[11] which the representative of the Director-General read out, the Permanent Delegation of Israel to Unesco maintained that the alleged events were caused by considerations of a political nature which had no connection with Unesco's fields of competence. The Permanent Delegation noted that the author of the communication had not replied to the letter sent by the Secretariat in pursuance of the decision taken by the Committee at its extraordinary session of 3 December 1982, and that this was further proof of the manifestly ill-founded nature of the communication.

310. At the request of some Committee members, copies of that letter were distributed as well as copies of the letter sent by the Secretariat to the government concerned.

311. Speaking on behalf of the Committee, the Chairman acknowledged that the Secretariat had carried out its task with care and diligence.

312. Some Committee members felt that Unesco ought to take practical action on behalf of the Palestinian people, and especially its children, by building schools, rebuilding the Arab University and the stadium, safeguarding cultural monuments, etc. Most of them were also of the opinion that the time had come to set up a Committee of Experts to estimate the damage caused in the areas relating to the Organization's activities. One member proposed that the communication should be put before the Executive Board and before the international community as a whole. In his opinion, the facts forming the basis of the communication shocked the conscience of mankind, especially since the government's refusal to co-operate was preventing examination of the communication.

313. Some other members said that although on the humanitarian level all members shared the same sentiments, one should nevertheless not lose sight of the requirements of 104 EX/Decision 3.3. In their opinion, given the vagueness of the allegations and the context of military conflict in which the events had occurred, one had to apply to this communication paragraphs 14 (*a*) (v) and 14 (*j*) of the above-mentioned decision. Relevant evidence had not been adduced by the author of the communication, and although it had been declared admissible it did not merit any decision being taken.

---

[10] See document 115 EX/28 PRIV., para. 158 (ii) (*supra*, p. 201).

[11] See document 116 EX/CR/HR/1 Add.2.

314. Other members made the point that the Committee did not have the same powers as the Security Council, and that although it was possible to envisage helping the Palestinian people, for example, to set up schools, that was not something that seemed to come within the Committee's sphere of competence. One member pointed out that the events had occurred in Lebanon and that, through its specialized bodies, Unesco had already taken what action it could.

315. After an extensive exchange of views, the Committee, stressing the common elements in the views of its members, *decided*:

(i) to keep the communication on its agenda; and

(ii) to ask the Executive Board to inform the Director-General of its anxieties, to request him to continue his representations in keeping with paragraph 14 (*k*) of 104 EX/Decision 3.3, and to impress upon the government concerned the importance which the Committee attached to obtaining its co-operation.

Autumn 1983 session of the Committee on Conventions and Recommendations (117th session of the Executive Board)[12]

215. This communication alleges violations of human rights committed by the State of Israel against the Lebanese and Palestinian peoples within the fields of competence of Unesco, following the entry of Israeli troops into Lebanon in June 1982. As the communication was declared admissible by the Committee at its [autumn 1982 session],[13] the Committee subsequently examined its substance following its extraordinary session of 3 December 1982 and also at the spring 1983 session.

216. The government concerned has not been represented at any of the three previous sessions at which the communication has been examined by the Committee.

217. After an exchange of views on this communication by members at the Committee's spring 1983 session, the Committee decided to keep the communication on its agenda, and to ask the Executive Board to inform the Director-General of its anxieties, to request him to continue his representations in keeping with paragraph 14 (*k*) of 104 EX/Decision 3.3, and to impress upon the government concerned the importance which the Committee attached to obtaining its co-operation.[14]

---

[12] See document 117 EX/18 PRIV., paras. 215-222; see also documents 117 EX/CR/HR/1 and Add.3.

[13] See document 115 EX/28 PRIV., para. 158 (ii) (*supra*, p. 201).

[14] See document 116 EX/48 PRIV., para. 315 (*supra*, p. 209).

No. 491/82 **Israel**

218. At the current autumn 1983 session, when it was announced that the Committee was going to resume consideration of this communication, the Permanent Delegate of Israel who had represented his government before the Committee in connection with another communication informed the Committee that he was leaving the meeting room. However, before he left the Chairman asked him if his decision to quit the room implied that his government was not prepared to co-operate with the Committee in the examination of [this communication]. The representative of the government concerned stated that his government was prepared to co-operate with Unesco but that in a case like this one where the very title of the body which submitted the communication prejudged the allegations and the issues raised by that body, his firm instructions were that he should not participate in the proceedings of the Committee during the examination of the communication concerned. After having made this statement he left the meeting room and the Committee resumed discussion of the communication. Remarking that this was the first time that, as far as he was aware, this had happened, a member of the Committee expressed his regret that the representative of the government concerned had left the room before the communication concerning his country was discussed.

219. The Secretariat read out a letter dated 12 September 1983 by which, in reply to a request from the Secretariat and without prejudice to the position of the Israeli Government regarding the communication, the Permanent Delegate of Israel provided the Committee with information on a number of specific cases invoked in the communication. In his letter, the Permanent Delegate indicated in this connection that the Israeli authorities had investigated the alleged arrest of Abbas Baidum, Hikmat Amin and Ahmad Murad and that their names did not appear in any of the lists of detainees held by Israel - neither the Israeli list, nor the list maintained by the [International Committee of the Red Cross (ICRC)]. He stated also that no person had been detained merely for his being an intellectual, a teacher or a student. In the event that a person was detained, this was solely on the grounds of suspicion of terrorist or other hostile activity, or rendering assistance to such activity. He added that in this context, the competent authorities of his country were unable to respond to the allegation regarding 120 scientists in view of its generality and lack of any detail or particulars. The Permanent Delegate also affirmed in his letter that similarly no school equipment, works of art or cultural objects and library funds had been confiscated.

220. A member of the Committee said that he found some of the allegations contained in the communication too general to permit them to be examined properly while others lay beyond the scope of Unesco's fields of competence. He proposed that, without prejudice to the humanitarian approach that might be adopted in deserving cases, the communication should be dismissed in pursuance of paragraph 14 (*j*) of 104 EX/Decision 3.3. Some members of the Committee, however, took the view that the communication contained sufficient factual details such as names and

dates to permit its examination in a normal way. A member stated that the title of the body submitting the communication was offensive and accordingly he asked whether paragraph 14 (*a*) (vi) of 104 EX/Decision 3.3 could not be invoked to dismiss the communication.

221. The representative of the Director-General explained that, since the communication had already been declared admissible by the Committee, it might be too late to apply that provision. He suggested that the Committee could indicate in an unambiguous manner that the name of the authors in no way raised any presumption in favour of the allegations contained in their communication. He added that, in the light of the practice of certain regional human rights organs, the Committee could also reopen the question of admissibility and indicate to the authors of the communication the feeling of the Committee on their title. On this issue, a member queried if the Committee had not acted rather hastily in declaring the communication admissible at its autumn 1982 session. Another member explained that if the decision were put in its proper historical context of conflict, war, destruction and massacres, it would be understood why, at that time, the Committee had perhaps not given too much weight to certain technicalities. Several members suggested that the Executive Board should request the Director-General to pursue his humanitarian action to help in specific individual or identifiable cases.

222. At the end of its discussion, the Committee *decided*:

(i) to keep the communication on its agenda;

(ii) that the author of the communication should be asked to provide, for the consideration of the Committee at a subsequent session, such relevant additional information as it might have on the allegations contained in the communication.

Spring 1984 session of the Committee on Conventions and Recommendations (119th session of the Executive Board)[15]

226. This communication alleges violations of human rights said to have been committed by the State of Israel against the Lebanese and Palestinian peoples within the fields of competence of Unesco, following the entry of Israeli troops into Lebanon in June 1982.

---

[15] See document 119 EX/35 PRIV., paras. 226-227; see also document 119 EX/CR/HR/1.

No. 491/82 **Israel**

227. After noting that the government concerned had not sent any representative and that the author of the communication had still not been heard from since the spring 1983 session, the Committee *decided* to postpone examination of the communication until its autumn 1984 session.

Autumn 1984 session of the Committee on Conventions and Recommendations (120th session of the Executive Board)[16]

209. This communication alleges violations of human rights said to have been committed by the State of Israel against the Lebanese and Palestinian peoples within the fields of competence of Unesco, following the entry of Israeli troops into Lebanon in June 1982.

210. The Legal Adviser provided the Committee with the historical antecedents of the communication noting in particular that since the Committee's spring 1983 session the authors of the communication had neither submitted any new information nor otherwise manifested their continued interest in the examination of the communication concerned.

211. Several members of the Committee proposed that the "double silence" rule should be applied and that accordingly the communication should be struck off the Committee's list of communications. One member contested the existence of any such rule. He stated that the rules to be followed by the Committee have been spelt out by the Executive Board in [104 EX/Decision 3.3]. He stressed that to the extent that the double silence rule is not provided for in that decision, it could not be said to be a rule the Committee was required to follow. He therefore proposed that the Committee should continue to examine the communication. In this connection the Legal Adviser recalled that while the double silence rule was not expressly provided for in [104 EX/Decision 3.3], the Committee had, since the early stages of the implementation of that decision, always applied that rule in appropriate cases. The Chairman ad hoc stated that the Committee would do well to stick to the rule concerned because it was, in his view, a practical and useful rule even if not expressly stated. Several members of the Committee expressed their agreement with this view. One of them added that, in his opinion, the Committee had an inherent right *ex proprio motu* to devise rules of practice which would enable it to discharge with efficiency the responsibilities entrusted to it within the framework of [104 EX/Decision 3.3].

---

[16] See document 120 EX/15 PRIV., paras. 209-215; see also document 120 EX/CR/HR/1.

Israel **No. 491/82**

212. Many members of the Committee expressed their regret that the Member State concerned had not sent a representative to the Committee. One of them stated that if the communication were simply rejected out of hand, that would be tantamount to recording, without firmly contesting it, the opinion of the Member State concerned which denied in a written communication, the utility of its co-operation with the Committee which, in its opinion, would have treated the affair in violation of the rules governing its operation. He and some other members proposed that the communication should continue to be examined because it evoked alleged violations in the occupied Arab territories of human rights in Unesco's fields of competence such as the harassment of teachers and students, the destruction of schools, other academic institutions and cultural monuments.

213. Other members of the Committee insisted that the communication should be dismissed through the application of the double silence rule. One of them remarked that an indispensable input of the Committee work was information. He contended in this connection that, given the fact that the authors of the communication had, since the spring [1983 session], provided no new information that could usefully be considered by the Committee at its present session, the communication appeared to him to warrant no further action on the part of the Committee.

214. In answer to a question posed by a member of the Committee, the Legal Adviser stated that when a Member State failed to react to a communication concerning it, it was the usual practice of the Committee to ask the Executive Board to request the Director-General to indicate to the government concerned the importance that the Committee attaches to the government's co-operation in the examination of the communication in question.

215. At the end of its discussion of the communication, the Committee adopted the following *decision*:

> The Committee,
>
> Regretting the attitude of the government concerned, which has always refused to send a representative to it,
>
> Mindful, however, of the fact that the authors of the communication, although invited by registered letter to enter into contact with the Committee at four of its sessions, have never done so,
>
> Considers that, under these circumstances, it is not possible for it to continue to consider this communication, which should consequently be struck off its list, on the understanding, however, that:

(i) this decision shall have no bearing on the merits or demerits of the allegations advanced,

(ii) those same allegations may be referred to the Committee again at any time, either by the same authors or by any other person or organization.

No. 494/82

Concerning *Romania*
Case of *Victoria Dragomir and Anca Dragomir*

Communication of 30 August 1982 submitted by
Constantin Dragomir

Spring 1983 session of the Committee on Conventions and Recommendations (116th session of the Executive Board)[1]

141. The author of the communication, Mr Constantin Dragomir, a political refugee of Romanian nationality residing in France, explains that his wife, Mrs Victoria Dragomir, an engineer of Romanian nationality, submitted an emigration application on 4 April 1982 for herself and their daughter, Anca, aged four years, in the name of the principle of family reunion, and that she has seemingly obtained no satisfaction from the Romanian authorities.

142. Even before the representative of the government concerned had spoken, a member of the Committee stated that in his opinion, and in accordance with the practice followed by the Committee in such matters, the question raised by this communication did not come within the fields of competence of Unesco.

143. The representative of the government said that that was precisely the point he had been about to make.

144. Without further discussion, the Committee *decided* to declare this communication inadmissible as not coming within the fields of competence of Unesco in pursuance of paragraph 14 (*a*) (iii) of 104 EX/Decision 3.3.

---

[1] See document 116 EX/48 PRIV., paras. 141-144; see also document 116 EX/CR/HR/3.

No. 495/82

Concerning *Morocco*
Case of *Mohamed Elyazghi*

Communication of 27 August 1982 submitted by
Mohamed Elyazghi

Spring 1983 session of the Committee on Conventions and Recommendations (116th session of the Executive Board)[1]

94. This communication concerns the prevention by the police of access to the head office of two newspapers - the daily, *Al Mouharir*, and the weekly *Libération*, which could therefore not be published, and the arrest of Mr Mustapha El Karchaoui, the editor of the daily.

95. The representative of the Moroccan Government stated that the communication contained no relevant evidence constituting grounds for assertion that the decisions taken by the government were arbitrary and that it did not fulfil the conditions of admissibility laid down in paragraph 14 (*a*) of 104 EX/Decision 3.3 of the Executive Board, as the questions raised did not come within the fields of competence of Unesco and the allegations were based exclusively on press reports, i.e., on "information disseminated through the mass media".

96. Informing the Committee of the reasons which had led to the suspension of the two newspapers in question and the arrest of the editor of one of them, the representative of the Moroccan Government described the events leading up to Sunday, 21 June 1981, as follows:

97. At the suggestion of the International Monetary Fund (IMF), the government had envisaged correcting the prices of basic food products which were well below their proper level. The question was to be put before Parliament before adoption and, moreover, had finally not been adopted. Strikes and demonstrations had taken place, but these had not been forbidden. On Saturday, 20 June 1981, however, at the instigation of the two newspapers, which had called for a massive and violent demon-

[1] See document 116 EX/48 PRIV., paras. 94-103; see also document 116 EX/CR/HR/3.

stration, rioting and bloodshed had taken place at Casablanca. In accordance with the press code and the legislation in force, the Minister of the Interior had had to take steps to maintain public order: the two newspapers, having been recognized responsible, were sentenced to suspension and the editor of *Al Mouharir* was brought before the courts. Mr Elyazghi, the author of the communication (acting as an alleged victim), who was a member of parliament and managing editor of the newspaper in question, had not been the subject of any policy measures; he was entirely free and could express himself as he wished.

98. The representative of the Moroccan Government pointed out that the measures taken did not constitute a violation of freedom of opinion, nor of the freedom of the press, nor of the right to information. As was explained in a document entitled "La presse marocaine d'aujourd'hui - Pluralité et [éclectisme]" (The Moroccan press today - plurality and eclecticism) which he had submitted to the Committee, those freedoms were fully respected in Morocco, the formalities for publishing a newspaper were very simple and the author of the communication was at liberty to publish a new newspaper.

99. One member of the Committee expressed surprise that a newspaper could be held responsible for events which took place during a demonstration.

100. The representative of the Moroccan Government then stated that in his country the people had the right to demonstrate freely if they felt victimized by any government measure and that the political parties, unions and various national and regional institutions were there to see that that right was observed. However, the exercise of that right should not go so far as to violate public order. By inciting the demonstrators to riot, the two newspapers had infringed the law. Replying to a request for clarification, he said that the newspapers in question were still suspended for the moment and that Mr Mustapha El Karchaoui had already been sentenced. He read out a provision of the law which had been applied in the case.

101. One member of the Committee considered that although the communication did come within Unesco's fields of competence, it should be recognized that the international instruments authorized certain restrictions on the exercise of the right to freedom of information.

102. Several members of the Committee, endorsing that view, noted that, in the communication, a problem of public order was involved. Some quoted in support of their arguments the provisions of Article 19, paragraphs 2 and 3, of the International Covenant on Civil and Political Rights (the exercise of the right to freedom of expression and of the right to seek, receive and impart information and ideas of all kinds carries with it special duties and responsibilities; it may therefore be subject to

certain restrictions provided by law). Other speakers noted that the communication was formulated in a laconic and imprecise fashion, particularly the author's reply to item V on the official form (he had described the purpose and aim of the communication simply as "consideration of this case of violation of human rights, in accordance with 104 EX/Decision 3.3"). They raised the question whether the Committee was in a position to assess an incident which had taken place two years previously. One member considered that the communication seemed to have a more political purpose than simply to ensure the observance of human rights by the Moroccan Government.

103. After an extensive discussion, the Committee considered that violations of human rights had not in fact taken place, as the state concerned had intervened only in order to maintain public order, for which it was responsible. It therefore *decided* to declare the communication inadmissible on the grounds that it was manifestly ill-founded and did not contain relevant evidence, in pursuance of paragraph 14 (*a*) (v) of 104 EX/Decision 3.3 of the Executive Board, and, in accordance with the Committee's constant practice, to request the representative of the government concerned to transmit to his government the Committee's concern that freedom of the press should be maintained in Morocco.

No. 500/82

Concerning *Union of Soviet Socialist Republics*
Case of *Vladimir Raiz* [*]

Communication of 22 October 1982 submitted by
Amy Young-Anawaty and Ian E. Davidson [°]

Spring 1983 session of the Committee on Conventions and Recommendations (116th session of the Executive Board) [1]

Autumn 1983 session of the Committee on Conventions and Recommendations (117th session of the Executive Board) [2]

Spring 1984 session of the Committee on Conventions and Recommendations (119th session of the Executive Board) [3]

Autumn 1984 session of the Committee on Conventions and Recommendations (120th session of the Executive Board) [4]

---

[*] At the Committee's spring 1983 session, this communication was being referred to as case of *Vladimir Raiz and Grigory Rozenshtein*.

[°] On behalf of the International Human Rights Law Group.

[1] See document 116 EX/48 PRIV., para. 178 (*supra*, p. 35), communication No. 441/82 concerning *Union of Soviet Socialist Republics*, case of *Vladimir Raiz and Grigory Rozenshtein*.

[2] See document 117 EX/18 PRIV., paras. 136-141 (*supra*, pp. 35-37), communication No. 441/82 concerning *Union of Soviet Socialist Republics*, case of *Vladimir Raiz and Grigory Rozenshtein*.

[3] See document 119 EX/35 PRIV., paras. 160-166 (*supra*, pp. 37-40), communication No. 441/82 concerning *Union of Soviet Socialist Republics*, case of *Vladimir Raiz and Grigory Rozenshtein*.

[4] See document 120 EX/15 PRIV., paras. 121-127 (*supra*, pp. 40-42), communication No. 441/82 concerning *Union of Soviet Socialist Republics*, case of *Vladimir Raiz and Grigory Rozenshtein*.

No. 500/82 **Union of Soviet Socialist Republics**

Spring 1985 session of the Committee on Conventions and Recommendations (121st session of the Executive Board)[5]

Autumn 1985 session of the Committee on Conventions and Recommendations (122nd session of the Executive Board)[6]

Spring 1986 session of the Committee on Conventions and Recommendations (124th session of the Executive Board)[7]

Autumn 1986 session of the Committee on Conventions and Recommendations (125th session of the Executive Board)[8]

Spring 1987 session of the Committee on Conventions and Recommendations (126th session of the Executive Board)[9]

---

[5] See document 121 EX/46 PRIV., paras. 146-151 (*supra*, pp. 42-45), communication No. 441/82 concerning *Union of Soviet Socialist Republics*, case of *Vladimir Raiz and Grigory Rozenshtein*.

[6] See document 122 EX/21 PRIV., paras. 102-111 (*supra*, pp. 45-47), communication No. 441/82 concerning *Union of Soviet Socialist Republics*, case of *Vladimir Raiz and Grigory Rozenshtein*.

[7] See document 124 EX/3 PRIV., paras. 101-104 (*supra*, pp. 48-49), communication No. 441/82 concerning *Union of Soviet Socialist Republics*, case of *Vladimir Raiz*.

[8] See document 125 EX/3 PRIV., paras. 77-83 (*supra*, pp. 49-51), communication No. 441/82 concerning *Union of Soviet Socialist Republics*, case of *Vladimir Raiz*.

[9] See document 126 EX/3 PRIV., paras. 96-100 (*supra*, pp. 52-53), communication No. 441/82 concerning *Union of Soviet Socialist Republics*, case of *Vladimir Raiz*.

No. 503/82

Concerning *Romania*
Case of *Radu Dinculescu*

Communication of 28 October 1982 submitted by
Ligue pour la défense des droits de l'homme
en Roumanie

Spring 1983 session of the Committee on Conventions and Recommendations (116th session of the Executive Board)[1]

145. This communication concerns the case of a general practitioner of medicine who wishes to continue his studies in France at Nice, in order to specialize in gynaecology and obstetrics, but who has been unable to obtain permission to leave his country.

146. The representative of the Romanian Government stated that [the] communication was clearly ill-founded, since the case involved no violation of the right to education. He pointed out that it was thanks to the education which he had received in Romania that the alleged victim had become a general practitioner and that that country possessed adequate facilities which would enable him to train to become a specialist in the field which interested him. He added that the right to education established a link between the state and its citizens, that this right could be invoked only within the territory of the state concerned and within the limit of the latter's resources and that, with regard to the issue of a passport, that was a matter subject to clearly defined regulations.

147. Some members of the Committee observed that it was not within the competence of the Committee to intervene in order to obtain an exit visa for an individual and that account should also be taken of the problem of the brain drain in the developing countries.

148. Other members of the Committee pointed out that, even if a request to emigrate as such did not come within the competence of Unesco, when it concerned a right

[1] See document 116 EX/48 PRIV., paras. 145-154; see also document 116 EX/CR/HR/3.

which did come within Unesco's fields of competence, such as the right to education - as, for example, when someone wished to go abroad either to study or to teach - that competence could then always be invoked.

149. Referring to Article 13 (2) of the Universal Declaration of Human Rights, one member of the Committee expressed the view that the Committee should adopt a uniform approach in its decisions concerning the right of a person to leave his country and his right to return there.

150. Replying to a request for further information on the sentence of a year's "hard labour" passed on Mr Dinculescu in July 1982, the representative of the Romanian Government stated that the offences with which Mr Dinculescu had been charged had nothing to do with the subject of the communication, i.e. the issue of a passport.

151. Recalling the practice of the Committee in such matters, the representative of the Director-General pointed out that the Committee had always been reluctant to accept as a matter of course any element in a communication about which the author himself was not complaining.

152. One member of the Committee stated that he considered this a wise principle to follow.

153. Another member of the Committee observed that the case before the Committee formed an exception to this principle, since the representative of the government concerned had stated that a person who had been convicted could have his passport withdrawn.

154. After detailed discussions, the Committee *decided*:

(i) to take note of the assurances given by the representative of the government concerned regarding the existence in Romania of facilities which would enable Mr Dinculescu to pursue his studies to become a specialist and regarding the opportunities which existed for him to gain access to this specialization on the same basis as all other Romanian citizens,

(ii) to declare the communication inadmissible,

(iii) notwithstanding this, and in accordance with the practice of the Committee to request the government concerned to keep the Committee informed of any further developments which might occur in this case.

No. 511/82

Concerning *Yugoslavia*
Case of *Marko Veselica*[*]

Communication of 29 October 1982 submitted by
Hans Hulin

Spring 1983 session of the Committee on Conventions and Recommendations
(116th session of the Executive Board)[1]

[*] At the Committee's spring 1983 session, this communication was being referred to as case of *Milovan Djilas, Vlado Gotovac, Sabedin Haljiti, Sabit Rustemi, Franjo Tudjman and Marko Veselica.*

[1] See document 116 EX/48 PRIV., paras. 238-261 (vol. I, pp. 976-981), communication No. 392/81 concerning *Yugoslavia*, case of *Milovan Djilas* et al.

No. 516/83

Concerning *Chile*
Case of *Vladimir Lenin Cháves Rodríguez*

Communication of 15 December 1982 submitted by
Vladimir Lenin Chávez Rodríguez

Spring 1983 session of the Committee on Conventions and Recommendations (116th session of the Executive Board)[1]

54. The author of the communication, Mr Vladimir Lenin Chávez Rodríguez, a secondary-school teacher, a former member of parliament and a Chilean national, alleges that, following the 1973 coup d'état, his home was forcibly entered and his wife, also a secondary-school teacher, was taken hostage. To force Mr Chávez Rodríguez to report to the military authorities, the latter allegedly put pressure on his wife and on his father, an elderly man, who purportedly became deaf as a result of the tortures to which he was subjected. Mr Chávez Rodríguez says he took refuge in the Embassy of the Federal Republic of Germany in November 1973 and left Chile with his wife in August 1974. He states that he did not violate either the Constitution or the laws in force in Chile up to 11 September 1973, and wishes to be authorized to return to his country.

55. The representative of the Chilean Government stated that he lacked precise information on this case, since the communication had arrived after his departure from Santiago, but that it appeared that Mr Chávez's case was the same as the preceding ones.

56. As regards this and the preceding cases, a member of the Committee asked the representative of the government concerned whether the persons in question should first go to the Consulate and subsequently submit a *recurso de amparo*, or vice versa, and whether it was not necessary to be on the spot to submit a *recurso de amparo*. Another member was concerned that the Committee had to wait for a legal decision, which might take some time, thus constituting a kind of denial of justice.

---

[1] See document 116 EX/48 PRIV., paras. 54-59; see also document 116 EX/CR/HR/3 Add.

No. 516/83 **Chile**

57. The representative of the Chilean Government explained that both the administrative and legal channels were open to petitioners but that, in his own professional opinion, it was advisable to start by submitting a request for re-examination to the Consulate, which would transmit it to Santiago; and that after a reasonable period of time, about 30 days, a legal appeal could be made. For the latter it was in fact necessary to establish residence in Santiago. In reply to a question by one of the members of the Committee, the representative of the government concerned specified that alleged victims were not required to exhaust all domestic remedies, but that they should at least attempt to use them.

58. Another member hoped that the Committee would appeal to the Chilean authorities to speed up the examination of the appeals submitted, on the humanitarian grounds advanced in the Committee.

59. The Committee therefore *decided*:

(i) to request the representative of the Chilean Government to inform that government of the Committee's wish to see the appeals submitted by the authors of communications examined as speedily as possible,

(ii) to postpone examination of the admissibility of this communication until the next session, and in the meantime

(iii) to inform the author of the existing remedies available to him in the light of the statements by the representative of the Chilean Government.

Autumn 1983 session of the Committee on Conventions and Recommendations (117th session of the Executive Board)[2]

28. The author of the communication, a secondary-school teacher, a former member of parliament and a Chilean national, alleges that, following the 1973 coup d'état, his home was forcibly entered and his wife, also a secondary-school teacher, was taken hostage. Mr Chávez Rodríguez says he took refuge in the Embassy of the Federal Republic of Germany in November 1973 and left Chile with his wife in August 1974. He wishes to be authorized to return to his country.

29. The representative of the Chilean Government said that he had no further information to add to the information which he had given the Committee at its [spring

[2] See document 117 EX/18 PRIV., paras. 28-30; see also document 117 EX/CR/HR/2.

1983] session, namely that the author of the communication did not appear to have filed an appeal, which was a failure that in his view was without justification.

30. The Committee *decided* by consensus:

(i) to defer consideration of the admissibility of this communication until its [spring 1984 session];

(ii) to request the Secretariat to inform the author of what the representative of the government concerned had said, and to tell him that, should he fail to avail himself of the administrative and legal remedies of which he had been informed at the [spring 1983] session, the Committee would *ispo facto* strike his communication from its list at its spring 1984 session.

Spring 1984 session of the Committee on Conventions and Recommendations (119th session of the Executive Board)[3]

15. The author of the communication, a secondary-school teacher, a former member of parliament and a Chilean national, alleges that, following the 1973 coup d'état, his home was forcibly entered and his wife, also a secondary-school teacher, was taken hostage, Mr Chávez Rodríguez says he took refuge in the Embassy of the Federal Republic of Germany in November 1973 and left Chile with his wife in August 1974. He wishes to be authorized to return to his country.

16. At its [autumn 1983] session the Committee had requested the Secretariat to inform the author of what the representative of the government concerned had said, and to tell him that, should he fail to avail himself of the administrative and legal remedies of which he had been informed at the [spring 1983] session, the Committee would *ipso facto* strike his communication from its list at its spring 1984 session.[4]

17. At its present session the Committee had before it a letter from the author dated 23 January 1984 indicating that he had submitted several requests to return to his country to the Consulates of Chile in Paris and Berlin and that the most recent, dated 30 November 1983 and submitted to the Consulate in Berlin, had not been answered.

18. The representative of the government concerned explained to the Committee that a lawyer representing Mr Vladimir Lenin Chávez Rodríguez had contacted him by

---

[3] See document 119 EX/35 PRIV., paras. 15-20; see also document 119 EX/CR/HR/2.

[4] See document 117 EX/18 PRIV., para. 30 (ii) (*supra*, p. 229).

telephone in Santiago in January 1984, asking for further information on the *recurso de amparo* and requesting an appointment; he said that this person had failed to appear at either of the appointments that had been arranged for him and that no *recurso de amparo* had been submitted on behalf of Mr Vladimir Lenin Chávez Rodríguez. He therefore considered that the author did not really wish to solve his problem and that there were probably other reasons for his communication, since he had not availed himself of the remedies of which he was now fully aware. In reply to a question by a member of the Committee, the representative of the government concerned pointed out that the *recurso de amparo* was available to any person wishing to return to Chile, who could avail himself of it either directly or following a negative reply to a request made through administrative channels.

19. Two members of the Committee were in favour of maintaining the communication on the Committee's agenda; all the other members of the Committee considered that the communication was inadmissible; some of them nevertheless wished the author to be informed once again of the remedies available to him and of the possibility open to him of sending a further communication to the Committee.

20. After discussion, the Committee *decided*:

(i) taking into account its previous decision and the author's persistent inaction, to declare this communication inadmissible in in accordance with paragraph 14 (*a*) (ix) of 104 EX/Decision 3.3;

(ii) nevertheless to inform the author of the communication once again of the remedies available to him and of the possibility still open to him of submitting a new communication should his representations fail to bring about the solution he desired.

No. 517/83

Concerning *Uruguay*
Case of *Raúl Cariboni da Silva*

Communication of 7 January 1983 submitted by
Marc-Alain Berberat

Spring 1983 session of the Committee on Conventions and Recommendations (116th session of the Executive Board)[1]

229. Professor Raúl Cariboni da Silva, who has Uruguayan and Italian nationality and was born in 1930, was arrested on 24 March 1973 when attending a gathering of members of a far-left opposition movement, OPR 33. Allegedly, Professor Cariboni's role within the group was purely intellectual and at no time did his judges accuse him of taking part in any violent action. Furthermore, many of the reasons on which the accusation rests are said to be statements extracted from Professor Cariboni under torture.

230. It is claimed that the torture to which he was subjected has left him with a heart condition that could cause sudden death.

231. A Military Court of First Instance is said to have sentenced Professor Cariboni in 1977 to 13 years' imprisonment, although the prosecutor had demanded only nine. His lawyer is reported to have submitted an appeal in 1979, following which the military judges apparently sentenced Professor Cariboni to 15 years' imprisonment, despite the fact that no fresh charges had been brought against him.

232. At the autumn 1982 session a first communication concerning the Professor was submitted to the Committee, which decided to inform the government concerned of its humanitarian concern, and declared the communication inadmissible.[2]

---

[1] See document 116 EX/48 PRIV., paras. 229-237; see also document 116 EX/CR/HR/3.
[2] See document 115 EX/28 PRIV., para. 397 (*supra*, p. 130), communication No. 468/82 concerning *Uruguay*, case of *Raúl Cariboni da Silva*.

No. 517/83 **Uruguay**

233. The present communication, apart from the fact that it comes from a different author, contains fresh information concerning, in particular, the type of activities in which Professor Cariboni is said to have engaged within the OPR 33 group, details of his trials and the date of his second sentence (1979), and it is supported by evidence which was not available to the Committee at the [autumn 1982] session: summary of the indictment, medical reports, etc.

234. The representative of the Uruguayan Government said that he could only confirm what he had told the Committee during its examination of the previous communication concerning the OPR 33 group, of which Professor R. Cariboni da Silva was a member. That terrorist organization, born of a split in the Tupamaros anarchist movement, engaged in acts of violence such as kidnapping, of which he cited several examples. The alleged victim had not been detained arbitrarily, and his prison sentence, which was passed because he had committed illegal actions, had nothing to do with his being a teacher or a trade unionist.

235. Some members of the Committee promptly stated that they were in favour of declaring the communication inadmissible, but two other members thought that the communication contained fresh information, including more specifically, the contention that Mr R. Cariboni da Silva's activities within the OPR 33 movement had been solely ideological and theoretical. They felt that mere membership of an organization, even a terrorist organization, was not, in itself, sufficient proof that an individual had himself committed criminal acts. Three other members recalled that, while declaring the communication inadmissible at its [autumn 1982] session, the Committee had also decided to make a humanitarian appeal to the government concerned.

236. The representative of the Uruguayan Government declared that the activities of Professor Cariboni da Silva had not been exclusively theoretical; he had also taken part in actions falling within the purview of criminal law. Responding to a question raised during the discussion, he added that Professor R. Cariboni da Silva's prison sentence had been extended in 1979 because the Court had at that time taken cognizance of aggravating circumstances. Lastly, he wished to point out that one of the reasons motivating the author of the communication had to do with the state of the alleged victim's health; however, medical examinations had been administered in prison, a fact which proved that Mr Cariboni da Silva had been closely attended and well cared for.

237. Following a brief discussion, during which one member suggested that the government concerned be asked to show clemency towards Professor R. Cariboni da Silva once he had served the major part of his sentence, the Committee *decided*:

(i) to appeal to the goodwill of the government concerned, requesting it to consider how far it might be able to show clemency towards Professor R. Cariboni da Silva;

(ii) to declare the communication inadmissible on the grounds that it had not been submitted within the reasonable time-limit specified in paragraph 14 (*a*) (viii) of 104 EX/Decision 3.3.

No. 518/83

Concerning *Chile*
Case of *Jorge Montes*

Communication of 24 December 1982 submitted by
Jorge Montes

Spring 1983 session of the Committee on Conventions and Recommendations (116th session of the Executive Board)[1]

60. The author of the communication, Mr Jorge Montes, a schoolteacher and former senator and a Chilean national, was allegedly arrested in July 1974 and, with his wife and two daughters, taken to the "Academia de Guerra Aérea", a "torture centre"; four months later, he was purportedly sent to a "concentration camp" where he was kept prisoner for three years without being brought to trial until June 1977, when he was deported to the German Democratic Republic. He says that he cannot return to Chile, because the letter "L" is entered on his passport.

61. The representative of the Chilean Government explained to the Committee that the information provided by the author of the communication was incomplete. Mr Jorge Montes had in fact been prosecuted, tried and sentenced, under a 1972 law on the control of weapons and explosives, for acts committed after 1973; the sentence had become final in 1975; in 1977 the International Red Cross had asked the Chilean Government to accept Mr Montes's freedom on humanitarian grounds in exchange for that of 11 political prisoners in the German Democratic Republic. Although it was not the Chilean Government's policy to resort to such measures, it had agreed to be party to them in view of their humanitarian purpose. The Chilean authorities had accordingly noted the liberation of the 11 political prisoners and commuted Mr Montes's prison sentence to one of exile; these facts incidentally indicated Mr Montes's political importance at that time.

62. Asked whether Mr Montes would be free if he returned to Chile, the representative of the Chilean Government said that Mr Montes was at liberty to invoke the amnesty law if he had not already done so; he also said that Mr Montes had not at-

---

[1] See document 116 EX/48 PRIV., paras. 60-65; see also document 116 EX/CR/HR/3 Add.

tempted to use domestic remedies to obtain authorization to return to Chile, and that in his opinion it was not a case involving authorization to return. Finally, he emphasized the fact that Mr Montes continued to receive both his teacher's pension and his former senator's pension; not many governments would necessarily act in a similar way. All the members of the Committee who spoke felt that the author of the communication should be informed of the existence of the domestic remedies available to him, with regard to both the authorization to return to Chile and the possibility of amnesty. One member, however, regretted that the communication was incomplete, while another stressed the fact that Mr Montes was more of a politician than a teacher.

63. In reply to a question from a member of the Committee regarding the letter "L", the representative of the government concerned said that it was no longer entered on passports; he added that in the same spirit of co-operation which had led him to answer all the questions asked, he had provided the Committee with information which he considered essential for an understanding of the situation, but that he did not think that the case fell within Unesco's fields of competence. It was in fact a long time since Mr Montes had been a teacher; he was an important political figure and a member of the Central Committee of the Communist Party; moreover, he was not an exile but a person who had been freed as the result of an exchange.

64. Several members then expressed the view that the communication was inadmissible, though some hoped that the information provided above would be conveyed to the author. Other members pointed out that before deciding on the admissibility of the communication, it would be preferable to ask the author himself what was his purpose in wishing to return to Chile.

65. After discussion, the Committee *decided*:

(i) to postpone examination of the admissibility of this communication until the next session,

(ii) to inform the author of the existence of the amnesty law and the remedies available to him with regard to an authorization to return to Chile,

(iii) to ask the author to state to the Committee what his purpose was in wishing to return to Chile.

Chile **No. 518/83**

Autumn 1983 session of the Committee on Conventions and Recommendations (117th session of the Executive Board)[2]

31. The author of the communication, a schoolteacher and former senator and a Chilean national, was allegedly arrested in July 1974 and, with his wife and two daughters, taken to the "Academia de Guerra Aérea", a "torture centre". Four months later, he claims to have been sent to a "concentration camp" where he was kept prisoner for three years, without being brought to trial, until June 1977 when he was deported to the German Democratic Republic. He says that he cannot return to Chile because the letter "L" is entered on his passport.

32. At the [spring 1983] session, the representative of the government concerned had explained that Mr J. Montes had been convicted and that, following representations by the Red Cross, he had been given his freedom in exchange for the freeing of political prisoners held in another country. He had added that Mr Montes was at liberty to invoke the amnesty law if he had not already done so and that he could also avail himself of domestic remedies to obtain permission to return to Chile, but that, in his opinion, it was not a case involving permission to return.

33. After discussion, the Committee had decdided:[3]

(i) to postpone examination of the admissibility of this communication until the present session;

(ii) to inform the author of the existence of the amnesty law and the remedies available to him with regard to an authorization to return to Chile;

(iii) to ask the author to state to the Committee what his purpose was in wishing to return to Chile.

34. On 30 August 1983 the Secretariat received a letter from Mr J. Montes in which he disputed some of the statements made by the representative of the Chilean Government at the [spring 1983] session and supplied further information about the events in which he had been involved. He then said that, while he was no longer a teacher, he was writing and was consequently engaged in an activity within Unesco's spheres of competence. Lastly, in reply to the Committee's question, he stated that his purpose in wishing to return to Chile was "to live there ... with all that that implies".

---

[2] See document 117 EX/18 PRIV., paras. 31-39; see also documents 117 EX/CR/HR/2 and Add.

[3] See document 116 EX/48 PRIV., para. 65 (*supra*, p. 236).

No. 518/83 **Chile**

35. The representative of the Chilean Government stated that he did not consider this letter to be relevant. Mr J. Montes was entitled to cast doubt on what he had said but his main concern should be to institute legal proceedings in support of his assertions, for it was only by that means that he could have access to all the information concerning him and that he could refute it. The representative of the Chilean Government then added that he considered the communication to be inadmissible since what was involved was not a case of exile. As he had explained at the [spring 1983] session, Mr J. Montes had been the object of an exchange which had been arranged with his full and complete agreement.

36. Several members of the Committee also said that in their view it was not really a case of exile, but that Mr J. Montes could nevertheless be given a last chance by being asked to act as the Committee had suggested after hearing the information provided by the representative of the Chilean Government.

37. In reply to questions from members of the Committee, the representative of the government concerned stated that the penalty of withdrawal of nationality did not apply to any of the cases examined by the Committee and that banishment did not exist as a punishment in Chile. The government nevertheless remained free to suspend the right of individuals to return to their country, in conformity with the provisions of Article 4 of the International Covenant on Civil and Political Rights, and that this represented an administrative measure against which those concerned had the remedies indicated to them. With regard more specifically to the case of Mr J. Montes, he pointed out that he had been sentenced by a court of first instance, that nothing had ever been done against his will, that he had not lodged an appeal against that sentence and had agreed to the exchange arrangement involving him. If that had not been the case, the proceedings would have followed their course, that is, all the way to the Supreme Court.

38. Questioned then about the opportunities for Mr J. Montes to return to Chile and the length of the sentence remaining for him to serve, the representative of the government concerned said that Mr Montes's return depended on the legal or administrative action that he might institute and on the decisions of the courts, but that if he were authorized to return, he would not go to prison as he would be considered to have served his sentence.

39. The Committee consequently *decided*:

(i) to postpone examination of the admissibility of this communication until its next sesion;

(ii) to request the Secretariat to inform the author of what had been said by the representative of the government concerned and to indicate to him that, should he fail to avail himself of the administrative or legal remedies of which he had been informed at the [spring 1983] session, the Committee would *ipso facto* strike his communication from its list at its next session.

Spring 1984 session of the Committee on Conventions and Recommendations (119th session of the Executive Board)[4]

21. The author of the communication, a schoolteacher and former senator and a Chilean national, was allegedly arrested in July 1974 and, with his wife and two daughters, taken to the "Academia de Guerra Aérea", a "torture centre". Four months later, he claims to have been sent to a "concentration camp" where he was kept prisoner for three years, without being brought to trial, until June 1977 when he was deported to the German Democratic Republic. He says that he cannot return to Chile because the letter "L" is entered on his passport.

22. At its [autumn 1983] session the Committee had decided to request the Secretariat to inform the author of what had been said by the representative of the government concerned and to indicate to him that, should he fail to avail himself of the administrative or legal remedies of which he had been informed at the [spring 1983] session, the Committee would, *ipso facto* strike his communication from its list at the present session.[5]

23. At the present session the Secretariat informed the Committee that in a letter dated 10 March 1984 Mr Montes had explained that he had asked his lawyer (from the Vicaría de la Solidaridad) in Chile to seek "information on his situation" from the courts, but that, January and February being holidays for the judiciary in Chile, he had still not received a reply; he also claimed to have presented a further request to return to his country to the Consul of Chile in West Berlin.

24. The representative of the Government of Chile pointed out that since the end of the holidays two months had elapsed during which no "amparo" appeal had been entered despite the ease and rapidity of the procedure involved; he then noted that Mr Montes had not given a clear answer to the Committee's question concerning his purpose in wishing to return to Chile, and said that it seemed highly unlikely that he wished to return there as a teacher, since he had not exercised that profession for over 30 years. In reply to a question raised by a member of the Committee, the rep-

---

[4] See document 119 EX/35 PRIV., paras. 21-26; see also document 119 EX/CR/HR/2.

[5] See document 117 EX/18 PRIV., para. 39 (ii) (*supra*, p. 239).

resentative of the Chilean Government stated that, contrary to what Mr Montes claimed in his communication, he had in fact been brought to trial under circumstances that had already been explained at previous sessions; otherwise, he could not have been included in an exchange for prisoners held by certain foreign countries, as had been the case.

25. Several members of the Committee were in favour of postponing examination of the communication to allow Mr Montes a further respite; other members of the Committee took the view that the communication should be struck from the list, since the author had not followed the Committee's advice that he avail himself of the remedies of which he had been informed several times.

26. After discussion and in the light of its previous decision and the persistent inaction of the author, the Committee *decided*:

(i) to declare this communication inadmissible in accordance with paragraph 14 (*a*) (ix) of 104 EX/Decision 3.3;

(ii) nevertheless to inform the author once again of the remedies available to him and of the possibility open to him to submit a new communication should these remedies not produce a satisfactory solution.

No. 519/83

Concerning *Union of Soviet Socialist Republics*
Case of *Withdrawal of academic diplomas**

Communication of 28 December 1982 submitted by
Laurent Schwartz *et al.*°

Spring 1983 session of the Committee on Conventions and Recommendations (116th session of the Executive Board)[1]

227. At the request of the representative of the Soviet Government, and in accordance with procedural practice, the Committee *decided* to postpone its consideration of this communication until the autumn 1983 session.

Autumn 1983 session of the Committee on Conventions and Recommendations (117th session of the Executive Board)[2]

160. The victims are stated to be holders of degrees in higher education, teaching or working at universities or other institutions or laboratories, who were reportedly deprived of their academic diplomas and degrees because of having applied for emigration visas. The authors drew up a list of 11 similar cases which, in their opinion, revealed the existence of a deliberate and premeditated policy. The examination of the admissibility of this communication was carried over by the Committee to its present session from its [spring 1983] session.[3]

161. The representative of the government concerned, who is also a member of the Committee, referred to the title of the case and said that it was misleading to the ex-

* As from the Committee's autumn 1983 session, this communication was being referred to as case of *Withdrawal of academic diplomas and degrees*.

° Laurant Schwartz, David Ruzié, Alfred Kastler, Paul Kessler and André Lwoff.

[1] See document 116 EX/48 PRIV., para. 227; see also document 116 EX/CR/HR/3.

[2] See document 117 EX/18 PRIV., paras. 160-165; see also document 117 EX/CR/HR/2.

[3] See document 116 EX/48 PRIV., para. 227 (*supra*, p. 241).

tent that the allegations contained in the communication did not concern the withdrawal of academic diplomas and degrees properly so-called.

162. Several members of the Committee expressed the view that an academic diploma or degree represented the fruits of one's academic endeavours and that once awarded should not be withdrawn from a person for the sole reason that he happened either to want to emigrate from the USSR or not to profess a given ideology.

163. The representative of the government concerned explained the difference in kind between ordinary academic diplomas and the "candidate" degree. He informed the Committee that academic diplomas were not revocable on ideological grounds and not a single one had been so withdrawn. The "candidate" degree however attested to a different type of academic and professional attainment. He explained that for one to obtain that degree which is more or less akin to a professional qualification or title, the person concerned should not only possess a high level of academic knowledge in his chosen field, but must also possess a mastery of Marxism-Leninism coupled with a solid commitment to place his knowledge at the service of the Soviet society. The "candidate" degree was therefore something like a special encouragement which could logically be withdrawn from a holder who ceased to display the required moral rigour. The representative of the government concerned pointed out in this connection that a Soviet citizen who applied for authorization to emigrate to Israel in fact wished to break with Marxism-Leninism. He added that the withdrawal of degrees was effected at the request of the scientific community.

164. The Committee was assured that the withdrawal of "candidate" degrees was subject to an established procedure which permitted a person aggrieved by a withdrawal decision to appeal against it. The Committee was also assured that a person who had his "candidate" degree withdrawn could continue to use any purely academic degrees and diplomas he might possess in his field of specialization. In conclusion, the representative of the government concerned stated that, according to information at his disposal, there had been only seven cases involving the withdrawal of "candidate" degrees and that, in any event, such cases had not occurred recently.

165. At the end of its discussion, the Committee *decided*:

(i) to take note of the statement of the representative of the Government of the USSR to the effect that cases of withdrawal of "candidate" degrees had not occurred recently.

(ii) to ask the government concerned, through its representative on the Committee, as well as the authors, to provide additional information on the communication;

Union of Soviet Socialist Republics **No. 519/83**

(iii) to defer the examination of the admissibility of the communication to its spring 1984 session.

Spring 1984 session of the Committee on Conventions and Recommendations (119th session of the Executive Board)[4]

181. The victims are stated to be holders of degrees in higher education, teaching or working at universities or other institutions or laboratories, who were reportedly deprived of their academic diplomas and degrees because of having applied for emigration visas. The authors drew up a list of 11 alleged specific cases of this nature. At its present session the Committee resumed the examination of the admissibility of the communication with which it has been seized since its spring 1983 session.

182. The representative of the government concerned, who is also a member of the Committee, referred to the title of the case and said that it was misleading to the extent that the allegations contained in the communication did not concern the withdrawal of academic diplomas and degrees properly so-called. He explained the difference of substance that existed between ordinary academic degrees and diplomas on the one hand and academic titles on the other hand, informing the Committee that such academic degrees and diplomas were not revocable on ideological grounds and not a single one had been so withdrawn. The academic title which in reality is the subject of the communication concerned attested to a different type of academic and professional attainment. He further explained that for one to obtain that title, one had to possess not only a high level of academic knowledge in his chosen field, but also a thorough mastery of Marxist-Leninist theory coupled with a solid commitment to be guided by Soviet patriotism and by the spirit of internationalism. The representative of the government concerned added that if the holder of a title ceased to possess this commitment or manifested a clear intention to repudiate some of the important principles which underline the granting of the title, the competent scientific council might be seized with the question whether or not the title should be withdrawn from its holder. The scientific council's recommendation, which is taken by secret ballot, is subsequently transmitted to the Attestation Commission which decides if the title deserves to be withdrawn or not. He informed the Committee that internal remedies exist for any person aggrieved by a decision of the Commission and that, in any case, there had been of late very few cases involving revocation of titles. Noting the difficulty in finding in other countries the exact equivalent of the Soviet title in question, the representative of the Government of the USSR expressed the hope that, in order to avoid similar difficulties in the future, appropriate bilateral agreements

[4] See document 119 EX/35 PRIV., paras. 181-185; see also documents 119 EX/CR/HR/2 and Add.

could be reached between his country and others, if possible within the framework of the Convention on the Recognition of Studies, Diplomas and Degrees concerning Higher Education in the States belonging to the Europe Region adopted under the auspices of Unesco in 1979. A member of the Committee remarked in this connection that while the USSR and several European socialist countries were parties to this Convention an important number of the Western European countries were not.

183. Noting that the qualifications for the title concerned contained both ideological as well as academic components, some members of the Committee asked if it could be withdrawn for failure of its holder to maintain the level of his academic standard. These members insisted that the fact that the procedure for the revocation of a title was claimed to be in strict conformity with Soviet law would not by itself prevent the Committee from examining the question whether the very idea of withdrawing titles was or was not in conformity with international standards laid down in the field of human rights protection. One member counselled that, in the examination of the communication, it would be useful for all concerned to avoid ideological value-judgements. Expressing his appreciation for the thoroughness of the representative of the government concerned in providing information to the Committee, another member stated that usually, holders of special honorific titles were the first who had to be aware that if they ceased to maintain the high standards which had earned them their titles, they risked losing them. Some members expressed regret that there appeared to be a direct causal relationship between application for authorization to emigrate to Israel and the revocation of the titles. Another member stated that since a title enabled its holder to enjoy certain privileges and facilities, its withdrawal could adversely change the whole life-style of the person concerned. One other member queried why people holding high academic qualifications should be punished for their opinion.

184. The representative of the Government of the USSR denied that there was any causal relationship between application for authorization to emigrate to Israel and withdrawal of the titles of the alleged victims. He recalled in this connection that about 250,000 Soviet Jews had emigrated to Israel. Reiterating that the titles concerned are awarded outside the framework of the programmes of Soviet institutions of higher learning, the representative of the Government of the USSR stated that while persons living outside the Soviet system might like or dislike the conditions under which the titles in question might be granted or revoked, there was according to him, no doubt that the granting and revocation of titles were effected in full conformity with applicable Soviet laws and international human rights instruments.

185. After a discussion, the Committee adopted the following *decision*:

Union of Soviet Socialist Republics **No. 519/83**

The Committee:

(i) Notes with interest the very detailed information provided by the representative of the government concerned, and the very full replies he gave to the many questions raised by members of the Committee;

(ii) Considers it necessary, in order to have an overall view of the problems raised in the communication, to ask its author to provide additional information bearing in mind all the points raised in the Committee's discussion;

(iii) Takes note of the statement by the representative of the government concerned according to which there is no procedure for the withdrawal of academic diplomas, and that in any event the cases of the withdrawal of titles mentioned in the communication are very few in number and are not on the increase;

(iv) Considers that given the extreme complexity of the problems raised, it is essential that consideration of the communication should be resumed at its next session, in particular in the light of the Convention on the Recognition of Studies, Diplomas and Degrees in Higher Education in the States belonging to the Europe Region.

Autumn 1984 session of the Committee on Conventions and Recommendations (120th session of the Executive Board)[5]

138. The victims are stated to be holders of degrees in higher education, teaching or working at universities or other institutions or laboratories, who were reportedly deprived of their academic diplomas and degrees because of having applied for emigration visas. The authors drew up a list of 11 alleged specific cases of this nature. At its present session the Committee resumed the examination of the admissibility of the communication with which it has been seized since its spring 1983 session.

139. The Legal Adviser recalled that at its spring 1984 session, the Committee had decided *inter alia* that it considered it necessary, in order to have an overall view of the problems raised in the communication, to ask its author to provide additional information having in mind all the points raised in the Committee's discussion.[6] He added that in conformity with this decision, the authors of the communication had

---

[5] See document 120 EX/15 PRIV., paras. 138-142; see also documents 120 EX/CR/HR/2 and Add.

[6] See document 119 EX/35 PRIV., para. 185 (ii) (*supra*, p. 245).

addressed a letter dated 24 July 1984 [...][7] by which they communicated additional information to the Secretariat for onward transmission to the Committee.

140. The representative of the government concerned, who is also a member of the Committee, recalled the fact that he had previously provided detailed information concerning the allegations contained in the communication. He pointed out that the attempts at making the Committee consider this case are a gross interference within the internal affairs of his country, which strictly follows the norms of the international human rights law and respectively established the procedure of awarding as well as annulling these high academic degrees. He stated that the key question raised by the communication was whether or not the competent authorities or bodies in the USSR could legitimately withdraw an academic title (as opposed to an academic diploma) when the holder ceased to possess the indispensable qualifications for it. He stated that there are certain laws and regulations adopted in his country which allow the withdrawal of high academic status in the case of a person who loses the necessary qualifications for it. It is done by strictly lawful procedure and there is no reason to doubt its legality. The member concerned suggested that some of the complex matters raised by the communication could perhaps be better handled within the framework of the Convention on the Recognition of Studies, Diplomas and Degrees concerning Higher Education in the States belonging to the European Region which was adopted in 1979 under the auspices of Unesco. He noted, however, that a number of European States were yet to become parties to this Convention and therefore a question arises whether the Committee can have any legal right whatsoever to discuss the communication; and proposed that this communication be declared inadmissible.

141. One other member of the Committee declared that the communication raised, in his view, a practically non-existent problem for the Committee's discussion. In this connection he stated that since the end of the last World War, only two cases involving the withdrawal of the academic title in question had arisen in the Ukrainian Soviet Socialist Republic. Another member referred to the authors' letter of 24 July 1984 and the differentiation it made between different types of academic degrees, diplomas and titles. This member also drew the Committee's attention to the fact that the representative of the government concerned had stated in the past that there were now virtually no new cases involving the withdrawal of academic titles concerned. She accordingly proposed that the Committee adjourn *sine die* its examination of the communication.

142. At the end of its discussion, the Committee *decided* to defer to its spring 1985 session the examination of this communication.

---

[7] See document 120 EX/CR/HR/2 Add.

Union of Soviet Socialist Republics **No. 519/83**

Spring 1985 session of the Committee on Conventions and Recommendations (121st session of the Executive Board)[8]

153. The authors of the communication allege that Soviet citizens teaching or working in universities, institutions or laboratories have been deprived of their academic diplomas or degrees in consequence of having applied for emigration visas. A list of 11 specific individual cases said to be of this nature is produced by way of evidence.

154. The representative of the government concerned reminded the meeting that no university diplomas or degrees had ever been withdrawn in the Soviet Union but only academic titles or distinctions conferred in respect of a particular type of qualification, and that he and his predecessors had already furnished lengthy explanations on this case at previous sessions. In any event, he added, decisions on the withdrawal of academic titles or distinctions, which in practice occurred very rarely, were taken by the Scientific Council by secret ballot in conformity with the legislation in force and after careful consideration of each individual case; such decisions were, moreover, founded on precise criteria, including insufficient scientific merit of the work of the person concerned, plagiarism, a falling away from the high ethical standard required of such persons under the Soviet system, and certain and other judicial convictions.

155. One member of the Committee stated that, in his country, there was little difference between university degrees and titles and, while he could understand that a person might have been deprived of his title in consequence of failing to perform his duties, he found it difficult to understand how that could apply to someone who merely wished to emigrate. The representative of the government concerned pointed out in reply that there was no direct connection between the withdrawal of an academic title or distinction and a scientist's application to emigrate. He emphasized the fact that until now a number of European States had not yet become parties to the Convention on the Recognition of Studies, Diplomas and Degrees concerning Higher Education in the States belonging to the European Region which was adopted in 1979 under the auspices of Unesco and for this reason he queried whether it was appropriate for the Committee to examine the type of allegations made in the communication. This view was supported by some other members.

156. Other members of the Committee who spoke recognized that the Soviet Union had its own system, even if it was unlike others, and that it was not for the Committee to judge it.

---

[8] See document 121 EX/46 PRIV., paras. 153-157; see also document 121 EX/CR/HR/2.

No. 519/83 **Union of Soviet Socialist Republics**

157. After an exchange of views, the Committee *decided* to declare the communication inadmissible on the ground that it did not fall within Unesco's fields of competence, and to strike it from its list.

No. 525/83

Concerning *Iran**
Case of *Abolfazl Ghassemi*

Communication of 12 February 1983 submitted by
Farhang Ghassemi

Spring 1983 session of the Committee on Conventions and Recommendations (116th session of the Executive Board)[1]

91. This communication concerns the case of Mr Abolfazl Ghassemi, aged 63, a writer and historian who is alleged to have been sentenced to life imprisonment for having sought to overthrow the Islamic Republic of Iran.

92. In its letter dated 24 May 1983, the Permanent Delegation of Iran to Unesco requested postponement of the examination of this communication pending receipt of instructions from its government.

93. After a brief discussion, the Committee approved that request and, in the meantime, in view of the recommendation of Imam Khomeiny, referred to by the author of the communication, one of whose eight points concerned the release of prisoners over the age of 60, *decided* to appeal to the government concerned, on humanitarian grounds.

Autumn 1983 session of the Committee on Conventions and Recommendations (117th session of the Executive Board)[2]

89. Mr Abolfazl Ghassemi, a 63-year-old historian and writer, is alleged to have been sentenced to life imprisonment for having sought to overthrow the Islamic Republic of Iran.

---

* From the Committee's autumn 1983 session, this communication was being referred to as concerning *Islamic Republic of Iran*.
[1] See document 116 EX/48 PRIV., paras. 91-93; see also document 116 EX/CR/HR/3 Add.
[2] See document 117 EX/18 PRIV., paras. 89-92; see also documents 117 EX/CR/HR/2 and Add.4.

No. 525/83 **Iran**

90. In his letter dated 14 September 1983 addressed to the Secretariat [...],[3] the Permanent Delegate of that country to Unesco stated that the judicial authorities possessed a sufficient number of documents concerning him, and in many instances actually signed by him, justifying his sentence.

91. Several members of the Committee felt that the terms of this letter were vague. Some remarked that the representatives of the government concerned had repeated on various occasions that their country always respected the International Covenants on Human Rights previously ratified. Others took the view that this letter clearly showed the belief of the government concerned in the ideals of Unesco, that accordingly it was not unreasonable to hope to obtain the co-operation of that government and that consequently the goal pursued by the Committee in the spirit of 104 EX/Decision 3.3 should be explained to it. Furthermore, they considered that, given the force of law of the recommendations of the Imam Khomeini concerning the Constitution of the Islamic Republic of Iran, it would be appropriate to appeal to the Iranian authorities for clemency on the basis of his recommendation regarding the release of prisoners over 60 years old.

92. After discussion, the Committee *decided*:

(i) to request the Secretariat to call the attention of the Iranian authorities to the importance attached by the Committee to the presence of a representative of the government concerned by a communication at the meeting at which that communication would be examined so that, in accordance with 104 EX/Decision 3.3, paragraph 14 (*e*), an open dialogue might be established with a view to achieving a friendly solution designed to advance the promotion of human rights;

(ii) to inform the government its intense concern about respect for the International Covenants on Human Rights, and to ask that government whether, in view of the Imam Khomeini's recommendation regarding the release of prisoners over 60 years old, this measure of clemency might not be applied in the case of Mr Abolfazl Ghassemi;

(iii) to request the government concerned to provide the Committee with the text of the sentence passed on that historian;

(iv) to resume its examination of the communication at its spring 1984 session.

---

[3] See document 117 EX/CR/HR/2 Add.4.

Iran **No. 525/83**

Spring 1984 session of the Committee on Conventions and Recommendations (119th session of the Executive Board)[4]

106. The first communication[5] concerns the case of a historian and writer, aged 63, Mr Abolfazl Ghassemi, who has allegedly been sentenced to life imprisonment for attempting to overthrow the Islamic Republic of Iran.

107. The second communication concerns the case of arrests of a number of personalities whom the author describes as belonging to the world of Iranian culture.

108. As at the autumn session in 1983, the government concerned has not sent a representative to this [spring 1984] session of the Committee. Its one and only official reaction has been a letter dated 14 September 1983 from the Permanent Delegate of the Islamic Republic of Iran to Unesco [...] in which the latter stated that according to his government the sentence passed against Mr Ghassemi was justified by the documented evidence of his guilt possessed by the judicial authorities; and that as regards the other persons arrested, described as "eminent" intellectuals and men of culture, some of them were involved in purely political activities.

109. The members of the Committee who spoke expressed their disappointment at the absence of a representative of the government concerned. Considering that it would be desirable to resume examination of these communications in the presence of a representative of the Iranian Government, the Committee *decided*:

(i) to reiterate the terms of its decision concerning these communications at its autumn [1983 session];

(ii) again to stress the humanitarian nature of these communications and to request the Executive Board to invite the Director-General again to inform the competent Iranian authorities to that effect;

(iii) to resume examination of the admissibility of the communications at its autumn 1984 session.

---

[4] See document 119 EX/35 PRIV., paras. 106-109; see also document 119 EX/CR/HR/2.

[5] Communications No. 525/83 concerning *Islamic Republic of Iran*, case of *Abolfazl Ghassemi*, and No. 581/83 concerning *Islamic Republic of Iran*, case of *Alleged arrests of eminent personalities in the world of Iranian culture*, were being considered together.

No. 525/83 **Iran**

Autumn 1984 session of the Committee on Conventions and Recommendations (120th session of the Executive Board)[6]

106. The first of the two communications[7] concerns the case of a historian and writer aged 63, Mr Abolfazl Ghassemi, who has allegedly been sentenced to life imprisonment for attempting to overthrow the Islamic Republic of Iran, and the second concerns the arrest of a number of personalities whom the author describes as belonging to the world of Iranian culture.

107. No representative of the government concerned attended the [autumn 1983 and spring and autumn 1984 sessions of the Committee]. Nevertheless, the Permanent Delegate of the Islamic Republic of Iran to Unesco had submitted to the Secretariat a letter, dated 24 september 1984, in which he stressed the inadmissibility of the two communications, by virtue of paragraph 14 (*a*) (iii) of 104 EX/Decision 3.3 of the Executive Board (in order to be admissible the communication "must concern violations of human rights falling within Unesco's competence ... and must not be motivated exclusively by other considerations"). In his opinion, the individuals mentioned in these communications had committed extremely serious offences, verging on espionage and crime in certain cases; to disregard this aspect of the matter and to declare that these individuals belonged to the world of culture while omitting to draw attention to the acts for which they had been sentenced was an attempt to distort the truth. The Permanent Delegate hoped that "this was not a way of taking advantage of the Organization with a view to manipulating it". He repeated his country's attachment to the ideals and noble objectives of Unesco, stressing that the Iranian legal system, inspired by Islamic principles, "made it possible to act with justice and clemency in the most difficult cases".

108. The members of the Committee who spoke regretted the absence of a representative of the government concerned, but drew attention to the willingness of that government to co-operate with the Committee, as shown by the letter of the Permanent Delegate, and considered it appropriate to renew the Committee's humanitarian appeal.

109. After discussion, the Committee *decided*:

---

[6] See document 120 EX/15 PRIV., paras. 106-109; see also document 120 EX/CR/HR/2.

[7] Communications No. 525/83 concerning *Islamic Republic of Iran*, case of *Abolfazl Ghassemi*, and No. 581/83 concerning *Islamic Republic of Iran*, case of *Alleged arrests of eminent personalities in the world of Iranian culture*, were being considered together.

(i) to express its thanks to the government concerned for the letter dated 24 September 1984 from the Permanent Delegate of the Islamic Republic of Iran to Unesco;

(ii) nevertheless, to express its regret that no representative of that government had been able to attend its meeting, for that would have helped to initiate a fruitful dialogue;

(iii) to launch a further humanitarian appeal to the government concerned in order to obtain clemency for Mr Abolfazl Ghassemi and the other persons detained;

(iv) to resume examination of the admissibility of the two communications at its spring [1985 session].

Spring 1985 session of the Committee on Conventions and Recommendations (121st session of the Executive Board)[8]

94. The first of the two communications[9] concerns the case of an historian and writer over 63 years of age, Mr Abolfazl Ghassemi, who has allegedly been sentenced to life imprisonment for attempting to overthrow the Islamic Republic of Iran; the second concerns the arrest of a number of personalities whom the author of the communication describes as belonging to the world of Iranian culture.

95. The government concerned did not send a representative because it felt that it had already explained its point of view on these communications. As the Committee was informed, by a letter dated 24 September 1984, at its autumn 1984 session, the Permanent Delegate of the Islamic Republic of Iran to Unesco had announced that his government refuted all the allegations put forward, maintaining that the persons mentioned in the communications had committed extremely serious offences, in some cases verging on espionage and crime. The members of the Committee who spoke regretted the absence of a representative of the government concerned. They again expressed their concern on humanitarian grounds and made particular reference to the recommendation of Imam Khomeiny concerning measures of clemency for the benefit of prisoners over 60 years of age.

96. Following an exchange of views, the Committee *decided*:

---

[8] See document 121 EX/46 PRIV., paras. 94-96; see also document 121 EX/CR/HR/2.

[9] Communications No. 525/83 concerning *Islamic Republic of Iran*, case of *Abolfazl Ghassemi*, and No. 581/83 concerning *Islamic Republic of Iran*, case of *Alleged arrests of eminent personalities in the world of Iranian culture*, were being considered together.

(i) to repeat its regret that no representative of the government concerned had been able to be present when the two communications were being examined;

(ii) to renew its appeal to the government concerned for clemency for the persons detained;

(iii) to resume examination of the admissibility of the communications at its next session.

Autumn 1985 session of the Committee on Conventions and Recommendations (122nd session of the Executive Board)[10]

78. The first of the two communications[11] concerns the case of an historian and writer over 63 years of age, Mr Abolfazl Ghassemi, who had been sentenced to life imprisonment for attempting to overthrow the Islamic Republic of Iran; the second concerns the arrest of a number of personalities whom the author of the communication describes as belonging to the world of Iranian culture.

79. The government concerned did not send a representative.

80. One member of the Committee was of the opinion that these communications should be declared admissible. Other Committee members considered than an effort should be made to establish contact with the government concerned and that the appeal for clemency made to it by the Committee should be renewed. Some of those members also took the view that in the absence of any reaction from the government concerned by the next session of the Committee, the latter should then decide upon the admissibility of the communications.

81. Following an exchange of views, the Committee took the following *decision*:

The Committee:

(i) repeats its regret at the attitude of the government concerned, which, once more, did not send a representative;

(ii) also expresses its regret at not having received any information regarding the outcome of the humanitarian appeal it made to that government;

[10] See document 122 EX/21 PRIV., paras. 78-82; see also document 122 EX/CR/HR/2.
[11] Communications No. 525/83 concerning *Islamic Republic of Iran*, case of *Abolfazl Ghassemi*, and No. 581/83 concerning *Islamic Republic of Iran*, case of *Alleged arrests of eminent personalities in the world of Iranian culture*, were being considered together.

(iii) invites the Executive Board to request the Director-General to use his good offices to reconvey that humanitarian appeal to the government concerned;

(iv) decides to rule upon the admissibility of these communications at its next session.

82. One member of the Committee requested to be placed on record as having abstained on the matter referred to in subparagraph (iii) above.

Spring 1986 session of the Committee on Conventions and Recommendations (124th session of the Executive Board)[12]

85. The first of the two communications[13] concerns the case of an historian and writer over 63 years of age, Mr Abolfazl Ghassemi, who was sentenced in 1981 to life imprisonment for attempting to overthrow the Islamic Republic of Iran; the second concerns the arrest in Iran in 1982 and 1983 of 28 personalities whom the author of the communication describes as belonging to the world of Iranian culture.

86. Having thanked the government concerned for having sent a representative to the Committee at this spring 1986 session, for the Iranian authorities had previously contacted the Committee only by correspondence and through the Secretariat, the Chairman made a brief statement on the alleged violations of human rights with which the communications were concerned.

87. In his statement, the representative of the government concerned paid tribute to the efforts made by the Committee in defence of human rights and in the search for dialogue and reiterated his country's attachment to the ideals and lofty aims of Unesco. Recalling the terms of a letter dated 24 September 1984 addressed to the Secretariat by the Permanent Delegation of the Islamic Republic of Iran to Unesco [...], he upheld the inadmissibility of the two communications by virtue of paragraph 14 (*a*) (iii) of the 104 EX/Decision 3.3 of the Executive Board in order to be admissible, a communication "must concern violations of human rights falling within Unesco's competence ... and must not be motivated exclusively by other considerations". He added that the offences committed by the persons to which these communications referred were extremely serious acts verging in certain cases on espionage and treason and that to disregard that aspect of the matter and to declare that those

[12] See document 124 EX/3 PRIV., paras. 85-92; see also document 124 EX/CR/HR/2.

[13] Communications No. 525/83 concerning *Islamic Republic of Iran*, case of *Abolfazl Ghassemi*, and No. 581/83 concerning *Islamic Republic of Iran*, case of *Alleged arrests of eminent personalities in the world of Iranian culture*, were being considered together.

persons belonged to the world of culture, while omitting to mention the acts for which they had been convicted appeared as an attempt to distort the truth. In his view the communications were motivated by considerations of a political nature. Moreover he stated that in the case of Mr Abolfazl Ghassemi, the legal authorities had relevant proof in their possession, including some documents signed by the person concerned, and that a certain number of the 28 other personalities concerned by [the second communication] had been convicted of high treason for the benefit of a foreign power. He pointed out that at the time the government had had to expel 18 foreign diplomats. He then informed the Committee that the trial of these 29 persons had taken place according to the legal provisions of a sovereign country. Lastly, emphasizing the fact that the accused had not been tried for their cultural and intellectual activities but for serious crimes, and referring to Article 1 of Unesco's Constitution (the principle of non-interference by the Organization in the internal affairs of a Member State) and to the provision established by 104 EX/Decision 3.3 to the effect that Unesco should not play the role of an international judicial body, he concluded by reiterating that the two communications were inadmissible.

88. Replying to requests for clarification, the representative of the government concerned said that the 29 personalities alleged to be victims had been given sentences by the Revolutionary Court which differed according to the nature of their respective crimes and that none of them had been executed.

89. Some members of the Committee asked to be provided with further information concerning the concrete facts upon which the charges against the alleged victims were based and concerning their trial proceedings. Several members also asked to be informed of the respective ages of the persons concerned, as there had been a recommendation by Imam Khomeiny concerning the release of prisoners aged over 60.

90. Other members, referring more specifically to the terms of the letter of 24 September 1984 from the Permanent Delegation of the Islamic Republic of Iran mentioned by the representative of the government concerned, according to which the Iranian legal system, based on Islamic principles, "made it possible to act with justice and clemency even in the most difficult cases", renewed the appeal for clemency on behalf of all the alleged victims which the Committee had addressed at previous sessions to the government concerned.

91. Referring to the recommendation of Imam Khomeiny and to the import of the Committee's previous humanitarian appeals, the representative of the Iranian Government stated that his government took considerable interest in the Committee's humanitarian action, not only on behalf of Mr Ghassemi, but also on behalf of the other personalities whose names were listed in [the second communication]. He also

promised to transmit the Committee's message to the competent authorities of his country.

92. After discussion, the Committee *decided*:

(i) to express its thanks to the government concerned for having for the first time sent a representative to this spring 1986 session, which had enabled a fruitful dialogue to take place;

(ii) to request the government concerned for more detailed information on those who had been sentenced, particularly in regard to their age, the circumstances surrounding their trial, their conviction and the conditions in which they were serving their sentences;

(iii) to make an urgent request to the government concerned for information on the response made to the humanitarian appeal which it had launched at its previous session and, at the same time, to renew that appeal;

(vi) to resume examination of these two communications at its autumn 1986 session.

Autumn 1986 session of the Committee on Conventions and Recommendations (125th session of the Executive Board)[14]

64. The first of the two communications[15] concerns the case of an historian and writer over 63 years of age, Mr Abolfazl Ghassemi, who was sentenced in 1981 to life imprisonment for attempting to overthrow the Islamic Republic of Iran. The second concerns the arrest in Iran, in 1982 and 1983, of 28 personalities whom the author of the communication describes as belonging to the world of Iranian culture.

65. The representative of the government concerned stated that, with regard to [the first communication], he was in a position to announce the good news that a positive outcome, although not yet confirmed officially, was practically certain. Mr Abolfazl Ghassemi had been released for some time now on account of his age and in accordance with the spirit of clemency which characterized Islamic justice. In connection with [the second communication], the representative of the government concerned recalled that the Islamic Republic of Iran had always expressed admiration

[14] See document 125 EX/3 PRIV., paras. 64-66; see also document 124 EX/CR/HR/2.

[15] Communications No. 525/83 concerning *Islamic Republic of Iran*, case of *Abolfazl Ghassemi*, and No. 581/83 concerning *Islamic Republic of Iran*, case of *Alleged arrests of eminent personalities in the world of Iranian culture*, were being considered together.

and encouragement for Unesco's work in the field of culture. He regretted, however, that certain persons made use of that work as a pretext to pursue aims which were not those of the Organization. In reply to questions raised by a number of members of the Committee, he pointed out that the 28 persons concerned by the communication had been convicted not for their cultural and intellectual activities but for espionage on behalf of a foreign power and for the preparation of a coup d'état. With regard to the further information requested by the Committee at its [spring 1986] session and reiterated by members of the Committee who had spoken at the present session (information concerning the age of those convicted, the circumstances of their trial, the conditions under which they were serving their sentences and the response to the Committee's humanitarian appeal), the representative of the Iranian Government said that he had not yet received that information from the competent authorities of his country.

66. After discussion, the Committee *decided*:

(i) to thank the government concerned for having sent a representative;

(ii) to take note of the information provided by the representative of that government concerning the release of Mr Abolfazl Ghassemi;

(iii) consequently, to strike [the first communication] from its list, on the understanding that if official confirmation had not reached the Secretariat before the next session, the examination of that communication would be resumed by the Committee;

(iv) to reiterate its request for further information addressed to the government concerned on the subject of the [the second communication] relating to the age of those convicted, the circumstances of their trial, the terms of their sentences and the conditions under which they were serving their sentences; to renew once again its appeal for clemancy on behalf of those concerned and to resume examination of the communication at its spring 1987 session.

Spring 1987 session of the Committee on Conventions and Recommendations (126th session of the Executive Board)[16]

63. This communication concerns the case of a historian and writer over 63 years of age, Mr Abolfazl Ghassemi, who was sentenced in 1981 to life imprisonment for attempting to overthrow the Islamic Republic of Iran.

[16] See document 126 EX/3 PRIV., paras. 63-65; see also document 126 EX/CR/HR/2.

Iran **No. 525/83**

64. The government concerned did not send a representative to this session. However, in a letter dated 13 May 1987, the Permanent Delegate of the Islamic Republic of Iran to Unesco informed the Secretariat that Mr Abolfazl Ghassemi had been granted an amnesty and had been released on 26 May 1986.

65. After an exchange of views, the Committee *decided*:

(i) to take note of the information provided by the government concerned regarding the release of Mr Abolfazl Ghassemi;

(ii) consequently, to strike this communication from its list, the case having been settled in accordance with paragraph 14 (*a*) (x) of 104 EX/Decision 3.3.

No. 527/83

Concerning *Union of Soviet Socialist Republics*
Case of *Yuri Fedorovich Orlov*

Communication of 17 February 1983 submitted by
American Physical Society

Autumn 1983 session of the Committee on Conventions and Recommendations (117th session of the Executive Board)[1]

166. By this communication, it is alleged that Mr Yuri F. Orlov, described as a physicist, was arrested in February 1977, tried and sentenced in May 1978 to seven years' confinement in a labour camp to be followed by five years' internal exile for anti-Soviet agitation and propaganda on account of his role in organizing the first of the groups set up to monitor the implementation of the Helsinki accords. He is alleged to have been mistreated in prison. His personal and scientific papers are reported to have been confiscated. It is further claimed by the author of the communication that Mr Orlov's incarceration for publishing information on human rights violations in the Soviet Union prevents him from working as a scientist and making a contribution to science.

167. Some members of the Committee stated that the communication was, in their view, admissible because according to the communication Mr Orlov had been tried, convicted and sentenced by reason only of the fact that he was the chairman of a watch group monitoring the implementation in the USSR of the Helsinki accords and issuing reports on them. For this reason, it was claimed by these members of the Committee that Mr Orlov's right to information, including freedom of opinion and expression, had been violated.

168. The representative of the Government of the USSR, who is also a member of the Committee, stated that Mr Orlov was tried and sentenced by a Moscow court not for monitoring the Helsinki accords but for certain activities which were criminal under the laws of the USSR. The Committee was informed that the alleged victim had criminal ties with certain representatives of Western circles to whom he trans-

[1] See document 117 EX/18 PRIV., paras. 166-169; see also document 117 EX/CR/HR/3.

mitted anti-state or anti-Soviet information and material, some of which had been falsified by him and his associates. He stated that on account of the foregoing and also because a period of more than five years had elapsed since Mr Orlov was sentenced, the communication was inadmissible. One member of the Committee, however, expressed the view that the delay of about five years was reasonable in the particular circumstances of the case, all the more so since Mr Orlov's seven-year prison term was to be followed by five years of internal exile. Another member contended that, since Mr Orlov was still in detention, the violation of the latter's human rights was a continuing wrong and for that reason the question of delay was, in his opinion, not quite pertinent.

169. At the conclusion of the discussion, the Committee *decided*, by consensus:

(i) to appeal on humanitarian grounds to the Government of the USSR for clemency in favour of Mr Orlov so that he might be accorded some form of remission of his sentence;

(ii) to keep in abeyance until its spring 1984 session the examination of the admissibility of the communication.

Spring 1984 session of the Committee on Conventions and Recommendations (119th session of the Executive Board)[2]

Autumn 1984 session of the Committee on Conventions and Recommendations (120th session of the Executive Board)[3]

143. Mr Yuri F. Orlov, described as a physicist by the authors of the communication, is alleged to have been arrested in February 1977 and sentenced in May 1978 to seven years' confinement in a labour camp, to be followed by five years' internal exile, for anti-Soviet agitation and propaganda. According to the most recent information communicated by the American Physical Society (letter dated 16 August 1984

---

[2] See document 119 EX/35 PRIV., para. 180 (*supra*, p. 178), communication No. 483/82 concerning *Union of Soviet Socialist Republics*, case of *Alleged discrimination in respect of admission to higher education courses in Moscow at the Faculty of Mechanics and Mathematics of the State University, the Institute of Physical Engineering, and the Physical-Technical Institute*.

[3] See document 120 EX/15 PRIV., paras. 143-149; see also documents 120 EX/CR/HR/2 and Add.2.

[...]),[4] Mr Orlov is not in good health and is at present working as a night watchman on a construction site at his place of exile (region of Siberia).

144. The representative of the Soviet Government, who is also a member of the Committee, stated that the case had been presented in detail by his predecessor at the autumn 1983 session of the Committee [...]. He pointed out that Mr Orlov had slandered the Soviet Union, that his activities against the State constituted criminal offences, and that it was under Section 70 of the Penal Code punishing anti-Soviet agitation and propaganda that Mr Orlov had been sentenced in 1978 to seven years' imprisonment and five years of internal exile. He stressed that that sentence was, moreover, entirely in keeping with Article 29 of the Universal Declaration of Human Rights, and with international agreements relating to human rights which provide that limitations upon the exercise of rights and freedoms may be determined by national law. He informed the Committee that Mr Orlov had already served his principal sentence, and that he was at present at his place of exile, where he was housed, in accordance with Soviet law, and where he was working in an industrial gas undertaking. The representative of the Soviet Government stated that Mr Orlov's wife had been able to visit him and that Mr Orlov himself had made no complaint to the responsible administration in regard either to his previous situation in prison or to his present situation. He considered that the case should accordingly be regarded as closed and inadmissible.

145. One member of the Committee expressed the view that Mr Orlov's situation had been alleviated by the completion of his principal sentence, and that, in view of the fact that he himself had made no complaint, the examination of his case should be terminated.

146. Other Committee members considered that the case had not been settled and still gave cause for concern, since the sentence of internal exile remained in force. Without wishing to dwell upon the facts that had led to Mr Orlov's sentencing under a law that they had difficulty in comprehending, they considered it essential, in the light of the recent information supplied by the authors of the communication, to issue an appeal to the Soviet authorities to re-examine the physicist's situation, with a view to lightening what remained to be served of his sentence and making it possible for him to work in his fields of competence and to receive appropriate medical attention. In the view of one of these Committee members, Mr Orlov had, admittedly, been declared guilty according to the national law; but the Committee nevertheless remained competent to consider the case, since account had also to be taken of international agreements and the commitments entered into by the USSR in regard to the standard-setting instruments relating to human rights. He went on to say that in man-

[4] See document 120 EX/CR/HR/2 Add.2.

y communications there had been no complaints by the alleged victims - as was indeed so in the case of Mr Orlov - but the Committee was nevertheless in duty bound to examine cases in which such alleged victims were unable to communicate directly with it.

147. One member wondered whether the Committee still remained competent to consider Mr Orlov's case when the United Nations Commission on Human Rights also had the case before it.

148. In reply, the Legal Adviser explained that, under the terms of the Executive Board's 104 EX/Decision 3.3, the fact that a case was pending before another international authority did not rule out the Committee's remaining competent. He stated that, in any event, the procedure of the United Nations Commission on Human Rights, as laid down by resolution 1503 (XLVIII) of the Economic and Social Council, dated 27 May 1970, concerned the examination not of an individual case but of a situation that appeared to reveal a consistent pattern of gross and reliably attested violations of human rights and fundamental freedoms.

149. At the end of its discussion, the Committee *decided* to suspend consideration of the admissibility of the communication and to request the representative of the government concerned to provide additional information concerning the alleged facts.

Spring 1985 session of the Committee on Conventions and Recommendations (121st session of the Executive Board)[5]

158. The authors of the communication allege that Mr Yuri Fedorovich Orlov, a physicist, was arrested in February 1977 and sentenced in May 1978 to seven years' confinement in a labour camp, followed by five years' internal exile, for anti-Soviet agitation and propaganda. He is said not to be in good health and to be working as a night watchman on a construction site in a region of Siberia

159. Reminding the meeting of the information he had given the Committee at its [autumn 1984] session, the representative of the government concerned stated that he had provided full explanations about that case: Mr Orlov had been sentenced under the Penal Code for having slandered the Soviet Union; he had already served his principal sentence and had been sent to his place of internal exile, where he was leading a normal life; he was already retired and regularly drew his retirement pension; his present wife, whom he had recently married, was able to live with him; so far as his health was concerned, he had had dental problems but had been properly

[5] See document 121 EX/46 PRIV., paras. 158-161; see also document 121 EX/CR/HR/2.

treated in an appropriate medical centre. In any case, the representative of the government concerned pointed out, Mr Orlov had made no complaints.

160. One member of the Committee expressed the view that, while Mr Orlov's present situation was admittedly less serious, it was identical to that in which he had been at the time of the Committee's autumn 1984 session. As he saw it, there were therefore grounds for making a humanitarian appeal to the government concerned. Another member of the Committee pointed out, however, that, in accordance with the decision taken by the Committee at that session, the government concerned had provided additional information showing that the person in question was leading a normal life and was drawing a regularly established retirement pension. In his view, the case should be considered closed.

161. After an exchange of views, the Committee, while expressing its humanitarian concern for Mr Orlov who, after all, had not yet served his full sentence, *decided* to declare the communication inadmissible on the ground that it was unfounded.

No. 528/83

Concerning *Morocco*
Case of *Right of civil servants to lifelong education*

Communication of 25 February 1983 by
World Conference of Organizations of the Teaching Profession

Spring 1983 session of the Committee on Conventions and Recommendations (116th session of the Executive Board)[1]

104. By this communication, the World [Conference] of Organizations of the Teaching Profession (WCOTP), acting on behalf of the Moroccan National Union of Teachers (SNE), alleges that, on 18 March 1982, the Moroccan Prime Minister sent a circular (504/d) to the ministers in his government, informing them that, in order to alleviate the inconvenience caused by the large number of enrolments in courses of higher studies by public servants, it had been decided "that no civil servant shall be allowed to enrol in courses of higher studies unless he presents an authorization signed by the Minister or the Secretary-General of the Ministry to which he is attached". It is claimed that several requests for the cancellation of the circular have been made in the Moroccan Parliament, that the press has taken up the matter and that the problem has become a national issue. On 7 December 1982, replying to a question in Parliament, the Minister of Education reportedly stated that the provisions of circular 504/d were still operative.

105. The representative of the Moroccan Government explained that the purpose of the measures adopted was not to limit access to higher education but rather to put an end to the abuse by civil servants of the right to attend university courses. It frequently happened, in fact, that primary-school teachers in particular deserted their classes, notably when university examinations were drawing close, presenting medical certificates in justification. The Moroccan Government considered however that teacher training should take place outside school hours, and should not result in teachers being prevented from performing the tasks for which they were paid. It was therefore a beneficial measure, taken for the common good.

---

[1] See document 116 EX/48 PRIV., paras. 104-112; see also document 116 EX/CR/HR/3.

106. Two Committee members pointed out that the circular in question did no more than clarify the working conditions of civil servants and did not accordingly infringe a recognized human right. The communication was therefore, in their view, ill-founded. One Committee member expressed concern at the fact that the circular had the effect of restricting access to university education not on the basis of merit but at the discretion of the supervisor of the civil servant concerned.

107. Another Committee member was of the view that there could not be considered to be a surplus of teachers in the world, and that any regulation whose effect was to restrict access to higher education represented an infringement of human rights.

108. Many members who subsequently took the floor were reluctant to reach any conclusion before knowing whether the courses attended by civil servants took place during their working hours or outside them, and whether opportunities for lifelong education were available to civil servants.

109. The representative of the government concerned stated that university education was open to all those who met the entrance requirements, and that a distinction should be made in the case of civil servants between those working in ministries, and teachers. The former were able to attend courses, with the authorization of the minister to whom they were responsible, by staggering their hours of work, provided that there was no contradiction between their continuing education and their public service duties. In the case of the latter, such freedom to adapt their timetable of courses was not a practical possibility in view of teachers' obligations towards their own pupils. On the other hand, everyone had the opportunity to follow radio, television and correspondence courses. Finally, he suggested that the Committee would understand the Moroccan Government's motives better if it had the full text of the circular.

110. Many members were of the view that civil servants frequently found themselves subject to specific restrictions and that, in any case, civil servants could not be paid for not working. Accordingly, it was particularly important that the limitations prescribed by an administrative measure should not be arbitrary or unreasonable. One member made it clear in this connection that all depended upon the way in which the circular was applied, and expressed his personal wish that it be applied in a liberal manner. Several members asked that further information, in particular the text of the circular, should be made available, particularly since, as one member pointed out, the question had been raised in Parliament and the press had taken up the matter. The Committee should therefore refrain from reaching a conclusion too rapidly.

Morocco **No. 528/83**

111. The representative of the Moroccan Government stated that teachers were clearly free to attend university courses outside their hours of work, but that the right to primary education had been rendered inoperative by a group of individuals influenced by the National Union of Teachers (SNE). The question had been brought to the attention of the Moroccan Parliament, which knew the facts better than anyone, and which had upheld the decision taken by the Minister. In conclusion, he was pleased to be able to report that, since the circular's entry into force, not a single authorization had been refused, civil servants pledging in all cases to perform their duties.

112. The Committee therefore *decided* to postpone consideration of the admissibility of the communication until the next session pending receipt of the information, including in particular the full text of circular 504/d mentioned in the communication, to be provided by the representative of the government concerned.

Autumn 1983 session of the Committee on Conventions and Recommendations (117th session of the Executive Board)[2]

100. By this communication, the World Conference of Organizations of the Teaching Profession (WCOTP) acting on behalf of the Moroccan National Union of Teachers (SNE), alleges that, on 18 March 1982, the Moroccan Prime Minister sent a circular (504/d) to the ministers in his government, informing them that, in order to alleviate the inconvenience caused by the large number of enrolments in courses of higher studies by civil servants, it had been decided "that no civil servant shall be allowed to enrol in courses of higher studies unless he presents an authorization signed by the Minister or the Secretary-General of the ministry to which he is attached".

101. At the [spring 1983] session, the Committee had decided, after detailed discussions, to postpone examination of the admissibility of the communication until the current session pending receipt of information, including in particular the full text of circular 504/d mentioned in the communication, to be provided by the representative of the government concerned.[3]

102. At the current session, the representative of the government concerned read out the full text of circular 504/d and stressed that it was not a regulation for general application, but simply an administrative instruction asking ministers to adopt measures designed to ensure the smooth running of the administration. This circular was

---

[2] See document 117 EX/18 PRIV., paras. 100-105; see also document 117 EX/CR/HR/2.

[3] See document 116 EX/48 PRIV., para. 112 (*supra*, p. 269).

motivated by two considerations: first, the limited intake possibility of universities which made it impossible for all students wanting to enrol to do so; secondly, the fact that a drop in administrative productivity had been observed each year at examination time. There was, then, no intention on the part of the government to prevent civil servants completing their studies, but merely the desire to facilitate access by students to university and to control a rising rate of absenteeism in the administrations. Furthermore, when the civil servants were teachers who deserted their classes in order to pursue their studies, it was the education of the children in their charge which suffered, and this circular was also intended to protect such children.

103. The representative of the Moroccan Government then added, in response to the concern which had been expressed in the Committee at the [spring 1983] session, that possibilities for lifelong education, particularly in the ministries themselves, existed in his country.

104. The Committee members who took the floor considered that the communication should be declared inadmissible, some being of the view that civil service regulations were wholly and solely a matter of internal administration which should not be the subject of international discussion; in the opinion of others, it seemed normal that priority be given to the performance of the tasks for which the teachers in question were paid. Some speakers, however, emphasized the importance they attached to the existence of possibilities for lifelong education.

105. At the close of its discussions the Committee *decided* to declare the communication inadmissible as under the provisions of paragraph 14 (*a*) (v) of 104 EX/Decision 3.3, it was manifestly ill-founded; none the less it asked the representative of the Moroccan Government to take note of the importance that the Committee attached to the continued efforts by his government to promote the lifelong education of civil servants.

No. 529/83

Concerning *Federal Republic of Germany*
Case of *Gudrun Melchior-Dollinger* et al.*

Communication of 23 February 1983 submitted by
Patrick Bombal Acampora

Spring 1983 session of the Committee on Conventions and Recommendations (116th session of the Executive Board)[1]

120. This communication is submitted by Mr Patrick Bombal Acampora, a factory worker, acting as a person with reliable knowledge of the alleged violations. Mrs Melchior-Dollinger and Mr Heinrich Häberlein, Mr Manfred Lehner-Wendt and Mr Edward Hertel are described as teachers.

121. Owing to their membership of the German Communist Party or of a union (Mr Bombal Acampora does not say which union), or because of their activities on behalf of movements for peace and disarmament, they are alleged to have been "professionally disqualified" (Mr Bombal Acampora gives no precise indication of the nature of this measure).

122. In his letter presenting the communication, the author seems to wish to take into consideration in the first instance only the case of Mrs Gudrun Melchior-Dollinger, since he gives specific details only of the latter's situation: Mrs Melchior-Dollinger is alleged to have taken a first state examination in the field of education sciences in 1979; the authorities are alleged not to have allowed her to finish her training for the following reasons:

her candidature in trade union elections;

the publication of a tract concerning the election of a committee of students;

---

* Gudrun Melchior-Dollinger, Heinrich Häberlein, Manfred Lehner-Wendt and Edward Hertel.

[1] See document 116 EX/48 PRIV., paras. 120-129; see also document 116 EX/CR/HR/3.

the announcement of her engagement in a publication of the German Communist Party.

In the communication form, the author states:

that Mr Manfred Lehner-Wendt has been re-employed as "a probationary civil servant";

that the suspension of Mr Heinrich Häberlein has been lifted but that, owing to his membership of any association for peace, the accusation brought against him of "non-allegiance to the Constitution" still stands;

that Mr Edward Hertel has been appointed to the Bavarian Council for the Environment.

123. The representative of the Federal Republic of Germany pointed out to the Committee that the author of the communication did not mention that two of the alleged victims, Mr Häberlein and Mr Lehner-Wendt were mentioned in the circular letter as having been reinstated on a provisional basis in their positions. The representative went on to say that the author did not appear to have reliable information and that he had taken only selected excerpts from the circular letter to include in his communication.

124. The representative reminded the Committee that it was normal for a person to be admitted first on a probationary basis to the civil service before being accepted as a lifetime employee therein. It could thus be seen that the only alleged victims whose cases called for examination were Mrs Gudrun Melchior-Dollinger and Mr Edward Hertel, he said. He went on to explain that during recent years the difference between an employee under contract with the government and a civil servant had diminished in his country, and that in many cases the contract employees enjoyed better conditions in terms of job security, social security and other benefits.

125. The representative of the Federal Republic of Germany also explained to the Committee that the Constitutional Court of Karlsruhe had ruled that it was not the party membership or affiliation of a person which by itself could be seen as determinant of a person's loyalty to the Constitution but that these factors had to be examined in conjunction with the person's activities to see if he was in fact engaged in activities against the state. The cases of Mrs Melchior-Dollinger and Mr Hertel were still *sub judice* and the domestic remedies were thus not exhausted. Both cases were consequently inadmissible, the representative said. He further wished to point out that the practice which was misleadingly referred to as "Berufsverbot" was widely misunderstood. It was not a practice of preventing someone from preparing for or

practising a trade or profession, but was simply a policy of excluding only from government employment those persons who were clearly acting to undermine the constitutional system.

126. In response to questions, the representative of the Federal Republic of Germany explained that neither participation in the peace movement nor membership in the Communist Party *per se* would constitute a bar to employment with the government. However the latter might give rise to the question as to whether the person was involved in activities aimed at undermining the constitutional system. If an investigation showed that such was the case, then the person could be barred from employment with the government on the basis of those activities.

127. During the discussion which followed, views were expressed to the effect that the cases were inadmissible because domestic remedies had not been exhausted, and that a government had the right to exclude from its employ persons working to overthrow it.

128. Other Committee members felt it would be wiser to suspend the examination of admissibility until the outcome of the court proceedings could be known. One member of the Committee felt that the case was particularly worthy of the Committee's attention because there was great public interest in such cases.

129. After having debated the matter the Committee *decided* to:

(i) declare the cases of Mr Häberlein and Mr Lehner-Wendt as having been settled, and

(ii) suspend the examination of the other two cases until further information on those cases was received.

No. 530/83

Concerning *Chile*
Case of *Luis Guillermo Deisler González*

Communication of 14 February 1983 submitted by
Luis Guillermo Deisler González

Spring 1985 session of the Committee on Conventions and Recommendations (121st session of the Executive Board)[1]

20. The author of the communication, a graphic artist of Chilean nationality, alleges that while he was an art teacher in Antofagasta (University of Chile) he was arrested following the coup d'état of 11 September 1973. He claims that the charge against him was dismissed on 24 October 1973 and that in December 1973 he was expelled from the University of Chile. He says that in January 1974 he came to France at the invitation of the French Embassy, and in March he went to the German Democratic Republic, where he worked as a theatre producer; in July, he settled in Plovdiv with his wife and four children, and since then has been working there as an independent artist.

21. He claims that he requested authorization to return to Chile in 1980 and 1983, but without success, and submitted a fresh request to the Chilean Consulate in Paris on 21 November 1984. He has not, however, sought any other remedy.

22. After pointing out that he had had little time before leaving Chile to study this case, the representative of the Chilean Government drew attention to the fact that the author of the communication had made use of no administrative or legal means of redress, and suggested that he should be told what he ought to do: he should first lodge an appeal for reconsideration of his case directly with the Ministry of the Interior in Santiago and should notify the Unesco Secretariat of the date on which he did so, so that the Secretariat might transmit the information to the representative of the Chilean Government in order that he might intervene personally on behalf of Mr González. If his appeal were to be rejected, he should then file an application for

[1] See document 121 EX/46 PRIV., paras. 20-25; see also document 121 EX/CR/HR/3.

amparo with the the competent judicial authority, preferably the Court of Appeal in Santiago.

23. One member of the Committee proposed, that the course suggested by the representative of the government concerned should be followed. While approving that solution, another member of the Committee voiced his disquiet regarding the series of events that Mr Deisler González had experienced: he had been arrested, the charge against him had been dismissed, and despite that he had been expelled from Chile. Now that he was seeking to return to Chile, he was unable to obtain the necessary authorization. In such circumstances, in that same Committee member's view, there were grounds for expressing humanitarian concerns about his case.

24. The representative of the government concerned pointed out, on his side, that the statements contained in the communication represented the author's own personal assessment of the situation, and should be regarded as allegations rather than as established facts.

25. Following an exchange of views, the Committee *decided*:

(i) to inform the author of the communication of the administrative and legal remedies available to him in the light of the statements made by the representative of the Chilean Government, and to invite him to avail himself thereon;

(ii) to resume consideration of the admissibility of the communication at its autumn 1985 session.

Autumn 1985 session of the Committee on Conventions and Recommendations (122nd session of the Executive Board)[2]

18. The author of the communication, a graphic artist of Chilean nationality, alleges that while he was an art teacher in Antofagasta (University of Chile) he was arrested following the coup d'état of 11 September 1973. He claims that the charge against him was dismissed on 24 October 1973 and that in December 1973 he was expelled from the University of Chile. He says that in January 1974 he came to France at the invitation of the French Embassy, and in March he went to the German Democratic Republic, where he worked as a theatre producer; in July, he settled in Plovdiv with his wife and four children, and since then has been working there as an independent artist. He claims that he requested authorization to return to Chile in 1980 and 1983,

[2] See document 122 EX/21 PRIV., paras. 18-23; see also document 122 EX/CR/HR/2.

but without success, and submitted a fresh request to the Chilean Consulate in Paris on 21 November 1984, he has not, however, sought any other remedy.

19. At its [spring 1985] session, the Committee had decided to instruct the Secretariat to inform the author of the administrative and legal remedies available to him and to resume consideration of the admissibility of this communication at the present session.[3]

20. On 31 July 1985, the Secretariat received from Mr Luis Guillermo Deisler González a letter dated 17 July in which he stated that he had noted the information communicated to him and was prepared to take the steps suggested.

21. At the present session, the representative of the Chilean Government explained that the procedure for obtaining authorization to return to Chile had been improved, in particular by setting the authorities concerned a time limit of 120 days within which they had to reply to an application, and requiring them to provide grounds for any refusal to grant an application. He added that this procedure was operating effectively. Of 400 requests submitted in recent months, 392 had been granted; a list of 262 persons authorized to return had been published in August and a further list of over 350 names was expected to be issued shortly. Turning to the case of Mr Luis Guillermo Deisler González, the representative of the government concerned stated that Mr González had still not lodged an appeal which met the conditions notified to him. It was important, he stressed, that Mr González should submit an appeal that complied with the prescribed norms, since priority was given to consideration of such appeals. He accordingly considered it necessary to remind Mr Deisler González of the new procedure and of the adjustments that had been made, using as a basis the note that he had just transmitted to the Secretariat.

22. The members of the Committee who took the floor supported this proposal.

23. At the end of its discussions, the Committee *decided*:

(i) to inform the author of the communication once again of the measures which he should take;

(ii) to resume examination of the admissibility of the communication at its spring 1986 session.

[3] See document 121 EX/46 PRIV., para. 25 (*supra*, p. 276).

No. 530/83 **Chile**

Spring 1986 session of the Committee on Conventions and Recommendations (124th session of the Executive Board)[4]

17. The author of the communication, a graphic artist of Chilean nationality, alleges that while he was an art teacher in Antofagasta (University of Chile) he was arrested following the coup d'état of 11 September 1973. He claims that the charge against him was dismissed on 24 October 1973 and that in December 1973 he was expelled from the University of Chile. He says that in January 1974 he came to France at the invitation of the French Embassy, and in March he went to the German Democratic Republic, where he worked as a theatre producer; in July, he settled in Plovdiv with his wife and four children, and since then has been working there as an independent artist. He claims that he requested authorization to return to Chile in 1980 and 1983, but without success, and submitted a fresh request to the Chilean Consulate in Paris on 21 November 1984, he has not, however, sought any other remedy.

18. At its [autumn 1985] session, the Committee had decided to instruct the Secretariat to inform the author of the measures he should take and to resume consideration of this communication at the present session.[5] The Committee was subsequently informed by a letter dated 9 September 1985 from the Permanent Delegation of Chile to Unesco that Mr Luis Guillermo Deisler González had obtained a renewable temporary authorization to return to Chile for 60 days.

19. By letter dated 18 November 1985 the author of the communication informed Unesco that, on 12 August 1985, his parents had submitted on his behalf a request for authorization to return or for a temporary authorization on humanitarian grounds to the Minister of the Interior and that, on 5 September 1985, the lawyer of the Vicaría de la Solidaridad had taken his file in order to make the necessary representations in accordance with the indications given by Unesco in its letter of 2 July 1985. Finally, he expressed his gratitude to the Organization for its help and stated that he was very happy to be able to use his temporary authorization and as stated in a letter dated 19 January 1986, he had done so as from 31 January 1986.

20. At the present session, the representative of the government concerned declared that, for his part, he had no further information regarding Mr Luis Guillermo Deisler González; the latter did not appear to have lodged an appeal or even to have made use of his temporary authorization to return. He accordingly considered it desirable to ask Mr Deisler González what steps he had taken. In reply to the questions raised by several members of the Committee, the representative of the government con-

---

[4] See document 124 EX/3 PRIV., paras. 17-22; see also document 124 EX/CR/HR/2.

[5] See document 122 EX/21 PRIV., para. 23 (*supra*, p. 277).

cerned stated that the person in question could make use of the temporary authorization to return whenever he so desired, and that the issue of a permanent authorization depended on what steps were taken subsequently.

21. While expressing his gratitude to the representative of the Chilean Government for his efforts, one member of the Committee said that a situation could hardly be regarded as satisfactory where individuals had to make repeated appeals and go to the country on a temporary basis in order to take action in the hope of being granted authorization to return to their homeland. Observing that nearly 13 years had elapsed since the events of September 1973, he expressed the hope that it would now be possible to act generously towards all Chileans currently in exile, and directed an appeal to that effect to the representative of the Chilean Government.

22. After an exchange of views, the Committee *decided* to ask the author of the communication for information concerning the steps he had taken since receiving his temporary authorization to return and to resume examination of the admissibility of the communication at its autumn 1986 session.

Autumn 1986 session of the Committee on Conventions and Recommendations (125th session of the Executive Board)[6]

17. Mr Luis Guillermo Deisler González, a graphic artist of Chilean nationality, alleges that while he was an art teacher in Antofagasta (University of Chile) he was arrested following the coup d'état of 11 September 1973. He claims that the charge against him was dismissed on 24 October 1973 and that in December 1973 he was expelled from the University of Chile. He says that in January 1974 he came to France at the invitation of the French Embassy, and in March he went to the German Democratic Republic, where he worked as a theatre producer; in July, he settled in Plovdiv, Bulgaria, with his wife and four children, and since then has been working there as an independent artist. He claims that he requested authorization to return to Chile on several occasions, but without success.

18. At its autumn 1985 session the Committee instructed the Secretariat to inform the author of the communication of the representations he should make;[7] the Secretariat complied with these instructions.

19. In response to the request for information made by the Committee at its spring 1986 session concerning these representations,[8] and after a temporary authorization

---

[6] See document 125 EX/3 PRIV., paras. 17-22; see also documents 125 EX/CR/HR/2 and Add.

[7] See document 122 EX/21 PRIV., para. 23 (i) (*supra*, p. 277).

No. 530/83 **Chile**

to return to Chile had been granted to him, Mr Deisler González describes [...][9] the difficulties he encountered, especially with the police authorities at Santiago Airport, who detained him for more than 10 hours. In addition, he claims that it was suggested that he change his nationality. He states that he applied once again on 6 March 1986 to the Ministry of the Interior for authorization to return permanently to Chile, and that he sought the support of the United Nations representative in the country, the official in charge of the Unesco Office, the Chairman of the Chilean Human Rights Commission, the Society of Writers and the Chilean Association of Painters and Sculptors.

20. The representative of the government concerned informed the Committee that Mr Deisler González had met one of his colleagues in Chile but had not returned to see him, and had taken other unofficial steps. He added that if the claimant had strictly followed the advice given him, he would undoubtedly have obtained satisfaction. In reply to requests for clarification concerning the difficulties encountered by the alleged victim, he stated that he would call for an inquiry to be made on the matter and that in any event he intended to intervene on behalf of the claimant with his country's authorities.

21. One member of the Committee pointed out that, according to the information available, Mr Deisler González was in despair at not being able to return to Chile, and was preparing to leave the country in which he was living at present for an unspecified destination.

22. After an exchange of views, the Committee *decided*:

(i) to thank the government concerned for sending a representative;

(ii) to take note of the proposal by the representative of that government to use his good offices on behalf of Mr Deisler González and of the fact that he intended to inquire into the allegations concerning the lengthy detention of Mr Deisler González at the airport and the alleged suggestion that he change his nationality;

(iii) to resume consideration of this communication at its spring 1987 session.

---

[8] See document 124 EX/3 PRIV., para. 22 (*supra*, p. 279).
[9] See also documents 125 EX/CR/HR/2, annex II, and Add.

Chile **No. 530/83**

Spring 1987 session of the Committee on Conventions and Recommendations (126th session of the Executive Board)[10]

20. Mr Luis Guillermo Deisler González, a graphic artist of Chilean nationality, claims that he has requested authorization to return to Chile on several occasions, but without success.

21. Confirming the terms of the letter dated 11 February 1987 from the Permanent Delegation of Chile to Unesco [...],[11] the representative of the government concerned stated that the person concerned had been authorized to return to his country unconditionally and on a permanent basis. He added that persons in this situation who encountered problems of an administrative nature could apply to an interministerial commission over which he presided, which would give them all the necessary help in overcoming such problems.

22. After an exchange of views, the Committee *decided*:

(i) to thank the representative of the government concerned for his presence and for his co-operation;

(ii) to strike the communication from its list as having been settled, in conformity with paragraph 14 (*a*) (x) of 104 EX/Decision 3.3.

---

[10] See document 126 EX/3 PRIV., paras. 20-22; see also documents 126 EX/CR/HR/2 and 126 EX/CR/HR/1, annex.

[11] See document 126 EX/CR/HR/1, annex.

No. 535/83

Concerning *Pakistan*
Case of *Jamil Omar*

Communication of 16 March 1983 submitted by
Amy Young-Anawaty*

Autumn 1984 session of the Committee on Conventions and Recommendations (120th session of the Executive Board)[1]

86. It is alleged in this communication that a lecturer in computer science at Quaid-e-Azam University was arrested in November 1981, accused of having distributed subversive pamphlets and sentenced by a special military court to seven years of criminal detention and a fine of 50,000 rupees.

87. By letter dated 10 September 1984 [...],[2] the Permanent Delegation of Pakistan to Unesco informed the Secretariat that the President of the Islamic Republic of Pakistan had granted the person concerned a conditional release on 30 July 1984.

88. The Committee took note of this release with satisfaction and *decided* to strike the communication from its list on the grounds that the case had been settled.

* On behalf of the International Human Rights Law Group.

[1] See document 120 EX/15 PRIV., paras. 86-88; see also documents 120 EX/CR/HR/3 Add. and Add.3.

[2] See document 120 EX/CR/HR/3 Add.3.

No. 536/83

Concerning *Union of Soviet Socialist Republics*
Case of *Yosif Z. Begun*

Communication of 16 March 1983 submitted by
American Association for the Advancement of Science and
American Jewish Committee

Spring 1983 session of the Committee on Conventions and Recommendations (116th session of the Executive Board)[1]

228. At the request of the representative of the Soviet Government, and in accordance with procedural practice, the Committee *decided* to postpone its consideration of this communication until the autumn 1983 session.

Autumn 1983 session of the Committee on Conventions and Recommendations (117th session of the Executive Board)[2]

170. Mr Yosif Z. Begun is described as a mathematician and Hebrew teacher. It is alleged that, in 1971, he lost his job as a mathematician when he applied for an exit visa for Israel. Unable to find work as a mathematician or in a related field, it is said that he gave Hebrew lessons to earn a living. Despite repeated efforts to register as a Hebrew teacher with the tax authorities, he was, it is claimed, denied permission to do so. Allegedly, no official regulations existed to justify such a refusal. However, subsequent to this refusal, he was, it is said, convicted of "parasitism" and sentenced to two years' exile in Siberia after a trial at which he was allegedly not allowed to present witnesses on his behalf. On his release, in 1978, he reportedly attempted to rejoin his family in Moscow, his wife, it is stated, having agreed to have him registered at her address. He was, it appears, given official assurance that he could remain in Moscow while his administrative appeals were pending. However, the authorities having refused to issue him a residence permit for Moscow, he was allegedly sen-

[1] See document 116 EX/48 PRIV., para. 228; see also document 116 EX/CR/HR/3 Add.
[2] See document 117 EX/18 PRIV., paras. 170-175; see also documents 117 EX/CR/HR/2 and Add.

tenced to a three-year term of exile in Siberia. Since his release in 1980, he is said to have been subjected to all kinds of harassment at the hands of the Soviet authorities culminating in his arrest in November 1982 for alleged anti-Soviet agitation and propaganda. It is claimed that Mr Begun is currently being held in a Moscow prison pending his trial in respect of this accusation which, if proved, is said to carry a maximum prison term of 15 years and exile.

171. Before the discussion of this communication was started, the representative of the Director-General informed the Committee that it had received letters and cables from many sources supporting the objective of that communication [...].

172. In a brief opening statement, the representative of the government concerned, who is also a member of the Committee, informed members of the Committee that pre-trial action and investigations were still continuing and that, according to indications he had obtained from the competent authorities in his country, the case against Mr Begun had nothing to do with the alleged victim's teaching of Hebrew. He pointed out that as is the practice in a number of countries, it was not unusual for pre-trial investigations to take some time. A member of the Committee having remarked that a provision of Soviet Penal Code restricts the period of such pre-trial investigation to nine months which in Mr Begun's case expired in August 1983, the representative of the Government of the USSR stated that he had been advised that in special cases the nine months' time-limit could be exceeded.

173. One member of the Committee queried why Mr Begun had not so far been formally charged and urged that, if the prosecuting authorities had not sufficient elements to proceed to trial, the alleged victim should be released from detention instead of being held incommunicado. He also asked if Mr Begun had the help of counsel. Other members insisted that the alleged victim was entitled to a fair trial which in turn implied trial within a reasonable time. In this connection, several members of the Committee expressed concern at the situation of Mr Begun and urged that the competent authorities of the USSR should, in the case of the alleged victim, ensure the respect of the relevant provisions of the International Covenant on Civil and Political Rights concerning the rights of persons held on suspicion of having committed criminal offences. In this respect, references were made in particular to Articles 9 (2), (3) and (4) and 14 (3) of that Covenant.

174. In his concluding remarks, the representative of the government concerned reiterated that the case concerning Mr Begun was a complicated one and before it went on trial the competent authorities had to have a thoroughly clear view of it. He added this probably explained the long pre-trial investigation. He queried if the Committee could properly discuss the communication without relevant detailed information

which he admitted not to be in possession of so far and therefore could not put at the Committee's disposal at its present [...] session.

175. At the end of this exchange of views, the Committee *decided*:

(i) to postpone until its spring 1984 session the examination of the admissibility of the communication;

(ii) to ask, through the representative of the Government of the USSR, the competent authorities of that country to take the Committee's concern into consideration and to take more speedy and appropriate action to ensure that Mr Begun was treated in a manner that would be in conformity with the international standards indicated in the International Covenant on Civil and Political Rights (Articles 9 and 14).

Spring 1984 session of the Committee on Conventions and Recommendations (119th session of the Executive Board)[3]

186. This communication concerns the case of a mathematician who is also described as a teacher of Hebrew. According to the authors, Mr Begun has been subjected to interference of various kinds on the part of the Soviet authorities and was arrested on 6 November 1982 because he was allegedly guilty of anti-Soviet agitation and propaganda.

187. The communication was placed on the agenda of the spring 1983 session of the Committee.

188. At the autumn 1983 session, the representative of the Soviet Government informed the Committee that the case was being prepared for a hearing.

189. In a letter dated 6 April 1984, accompanied by an addendum to the communication [...],[4] the authors reported that Mr Begun had been sentenced in October 1983 to seven years' imprisonment under strict regime and to five years' internal exile. His appeal against the sentence was said to have been rejected.

190. At the present [...] session, the Committee was informed by the Secretariat that humanitarian representations were being made on behalf of the person concerned

---

[3] See document 119 EX/35 PRIV., paras. 186-190; see also documents 119 EX/CR/HR/2 and Add.2.

[4] See document 119 EX/CR/HR/2 Add.2.

and therefore *decided* to defer consideration of the acceptability of this communication until its autumn 1984 session.

Autumn 1984 session of the Committee on Conventions and Recommendations (120th session of the Executive Board)[5]

150. Mr Yosif Z. Begun is described by the authors of the communication as a mathematician and private teacher of Hebrew who was sentenced in October 1983 to seven years' imprisonment and five years' internal exile for anti-Soviet agitation and propaganda.

151. In a letter dated 8 August 1984 [...],[6] the authors of the communication reported that Mr Begun's situation had worsened, with harsher conditions of confinement, no opportunity for the members of his family to visit him, and hospitalization as a result of his hunger strike.

152. The representative of the Soviet Government, who is also a member of the Committee, stated that Mr Begun had been employed in a concern engaged in work connected with national defence and state security, that he had applied for permission to emigrate, and that he had given up his job. In that connection, he said that while the Soviet Union was meticulous about respect for the right to employment of every individual, it could not prevent people from giving up their jobs. He said that Mr Begun had declined a position as an engineer and had begun to aspire to teach Hebrew and Yiddish, even though in the first place he was not a qualified teacher, as he did not possess the appropriate degree, and in the second place there were no private schools in the USSR.

153. The representative of the Soviet Government asserted that he could understand perfectly well that people might wish to leave the USSR and go to another country, but that it was also necessary to recognize that the Soviet State, for entirely justifiable reasons, was entitled in accordance with the international agreements relating to human rights to refuse to allow some of them to leave. Mr Begun fell into that category, not because of his Jewish background, but because the Soviet State had the right to protect its national security.

154. Concerning Mr Begun's sentence, the representative of the Soviet Government stated that since the matter had been brought before the Committee (since its autumn 1983 session) the judicial process had been accelerated and had resulted in the sen-

[5] See document 120 EX/15 PRIV., paras. 150-[157a]; see also documents 120 EX/CR/HR/2 and Add.2.
[6] See document 120 EX/CR/HR/2 Add.2.

tencing of the person concerned, in October 1983, to seven years' imprisonment and five years' internal exile. He added that in engaging in propaganda hostile to the State and defaming the Soviet Union, Mr Begun had deliberately courted the risk of a sentence as his acts constituted an offence. While expressing doubt about the truth of the allegations made by the authors of the communication in their letter of 8 August 1984, referred to above, he asked to be allowed enough time to carry out any necessary checks. Mr Begun himself wrote that "the attention of the Western press heated up his ambitious mood". The punishment to which he was subjected was not accepted by him as being justified for violation of laws, but as a retorsive measure for his speeches. Instead of recognizing the rule of law, he took it as a persecution directed against him personally.

155. In reply to questions about the factual basis for the charge brought against Mr Begun and the conduct of his trial, which had reportedly been held *in camera*, the representative of the Soviet Government replied that in the Soviet Union it was not an offence to criticize government policy, but that in this instance they were dealing with a person who had denounced the Soviet socialist order and had distorted and falsified the facts of the case. He asserted that Mr Begun could have been given a heavier sentence if his trial had not been held *in camera*. Furthermore, it had been held *in camera* only in the sense that public access to the courtroom had been restricted to some extent.

156. With reference to the decisions taken by the Committee at its autumn 1983 and spring 1984 sessions concerning the humanitarian aspect of this case,[7] the Director-General's representative informed the Committee that the Director-General, was already making representations.

157. The Committee discussed the advisability of including in its decision a provision recommending that the Executive Board should ask the Director-General to continue his humanitarian representations, and discussed the need for discretion in order to leave all possibilities open. At the end of its discussion, the Committee *decided*:

> (i) to take note of the humanitarian representations being made on Mr Begun's behalf; and
>
> (ii) to defer examination of the admissibility of this communication until its spring 1985 session.

[7] See documents 117 EX/18 PRIV., para. 175 (ii) (*supra*, p. 287), and 119 EX/35 PRIV., para. 190 (*supra*, pp. 287-288), respectively.

No. 536/83 **Union of Soviet Socialist Republics**

[157a.] A number of members of the Committee stated, however, that Mr Begun was a prisoner who had committed crimes against his State and people and therefore did not deserve any humanitarian steps. They therefore did not deem it necessary to take note of any such steps in his favour.

Spring 1985 session of the Committee on Conventions and Recommendations (121st session of the Executive Board)[8]

162. Mr Yosif Z. Begun, a mathematician, is described by the authors of the communication as being also a private teacher of Hebrew. He was sentenced in October 1983 to seven years' imprisonment and five years' internal exile for anti-Soviet agitation and propaganda.

163. On 5 April 1985, the Secretariat received from the authors of the communication a letter accompanied by a document [...] entitled "Statement concerning Unesco communication on behalf of Yosif Z. Begun".[9] According to that document, Mr Begun's state of health is giving particularly serious cause for concern, as he is said to have contracted a serious heart disease. It is alleged that his family has been unable to visit him since April 1984 or to exchange any correspondence with him since October-November 1984. His wife and son are reported to have gone on hunger strike in support of their written protests on the subject. Mr Begun is alleged furthermore to have been punished while in prison for having observed minimal Jewish religious practices. The Committee is requested to explore the possibilities of securing the alleged victim's release on medical grounds.

164. On 10 April 1985, the authors conveyed to the Secretariat another letter transmitting a notification from the International Federation for Human Rights stating that that Federation wished formally to endorse the communication.

165. The representative of the government concerned stated that Mr Begun's case had long since been clarified. The alleged victim had worked in an area related to national defence; he had not been dismissed from his post as a mathematician, but had resigned from that post for personal reasons; his emigration visa had been refused for reasons of State security; on the pretext of teaching Hebrew, he had engaged in anti-Soviet activities, which included collecting material intended to slander the Soviet Union and even receiving assistance from foreign circles to that end, as his legal record showed; his conviction was consequently justified. So far as his conditions in prison were concerned, he had recently been transferred, by a decision

---

[8] See document 121 EX/46 PRIV., paras. 162-168; see also documents 121 EX/CR/HR/2 and Add.

[9] See document 121 EX/CR/HR/2 Add.

of the competent court, from the strict-regime prison camp to a prison where he was no longer required to do physical labour; his state of health was normal for a man of his age, though affected to some extent by a hunger strike which had recently caused him to be hospitalized. Replying to questions concerning the possibility of Mr Begun's having his sentence reduced, the representative of the government concerned stated that for the time being there were no grounds for such a step, since the person concerned had shown no signs of repenting. He reminded the Committee in that connection that, at its [autumn 1984] session, some of its members had expressed the very firm view that there could be no question of humanitarian measures on behalf of Mr Begun. In reply to a request for further information about the teaching of Hebrew at home, he said that that kind of teaching was not prohibited, but that outside State educational establishments, certain registration formalities were required for fiscal purposes.

166. Some members of the Committee, while noting with interest the explanations given by the representative of the government concerned, felt that they were still not clear in their minds about the nature of the charges brought against Mr Begun. There seemed to them to be a considerable discrepancy between the information he had provided and the allegations made by the authors of the communication.

167. Some of the other members were of the opinion that it would be more appropriate to consider Mr Begun's case from the humanitarian standpoint, since the Committee's constant concern was to find a practical way of assisting alleged victims. In that context, they reiterated their humanitarian concerns about Mr Begun. Other members maintained that such an appeal was not necessary, since in their view Mr Begun did not deserve humanitarian measures.

168. After an exchange of views, the Committee *decided* to keep the communication on its list and to resume consideration thereof at its next session.

Autumn 1985 session of the Committee on Conventions and Recommendations (122nd session of the Executive Board)[10]

113. Mr Yosif Z. Begun, a mathematician, was described as also being a private teacher of Hebrew. In October 1983 he had been condemned to seven years' imprisonment and five years of internal exile for anti-Soviet agitation and propaganda.

---

[10] See document 122 EX/21 PRIV., paras. 113-120; see also documents 122 EX/CR/HR/2 and Add.

No. 536/83 **Union of Soviet Socialist Republics**

114. In a letter dated 1 August 1985 [...],[11] the authors of the communication informed the Committee that Mr Begun had been transferred from his workcamp to the prison of Tchistopol. Conditions in this penal institution were said to be harsher and the state of health of the person involved to be giving cause for concern.

115. The representative of the government concerned, also a member of the Committee, pointed out that the Committee faced an undoubted legal difficulty: the fact was that although the case had been submitted to the Committee for confidential consideration in accordance with the procedure laid down by 104 EX/Decision 3.3 it had been widely discussed in the press, with the result that one might well wonder whether it represented an attempt at direct interference in the internal affairs of the USSR. He also expressed astonishment at the author's threat no longer to keep this communication confidential. He then recalled that on completing his studies Mr Begun had of his own free will chosen a job in a field related to national defence and that in 1973, after breaching the discipline of the undertaking for which he was working by adopting an attitude which deviated increasingly from rational norms, he had wished to make use of his knowledge abroad, submitting an application to emigrate which was rejected for reasons of State security but which could have been accorded had he agreed to change his job and to await the declassification of the secrets in his possession. The representative of the government added that Mr Begun, finding that irksome over a period of time, had ostentatiously submitted his resignation and had since that time engaged in anti-Soviet activities, in particular circulating material slandering the USSR and its political system and even getting in touch with an agent of a foreign secret service, a matter which was formally recognized by that agent. He stated that it was these criminal actions which had brought Mr Begun before the judicial authorities. Turning to the present situation of the prisoner, the representative of the government concerned assured the Committee that humanitarian efforts had been made on his behalf, that in his prison, not far from Moscow, he had been exempted from all physical work, that his wife had been able to visit him normally but that he did not appear to wish to solicit a reprieve on his own initiative and that legally no other person was able to act in his place.

116. Certain members of the Committee considered that the few references made to the case in the press did not violate the rule of confidentiality as this case had for some years been a symbol for a great many people and that as the person in question was ill and serving what they regarded as an excessively heavy sentence, even heavier than that laid down for crimes of bloodshed, it would be appropriate to ask that clemency be shown towards him.

[11] See document 122 EX/CR/HR/2 Add.

Union of Soviet Socialist Republics **No. 536/83**

117. Certain other members of the Committee observed that Mr Begun, as a teacher of Hebrew, was also an expert on the Judaic religion. Accordingly, in their view, less attention should be paid to the problem of his emigration than to the fact that the accusations against him and the confiscation of the teaching and religious materials belonging to him were connected with his activities to preserve Jewish culture, which undoubtedly came within Unesco's fields of competence.

118. Another member of the Committee recalled that the case of Mr Begun had been considered by the Committee on various occasions and had even been declared inadmissible in 1980, following his liberation.[12] He maintained that Mr Begun had in point of fact been condemned not on account of his religious persuasion but for his anti-Soviet activities, which had been encouraged by certain foreign sources. He added that to question the decision of a Soviet tribunal constituted an attack on the sovereignty of the USSR. It was for this general reason that, while expressing his surprise at the threatening and inappropriate tone of the letter from the authors of the communication, he considered that the only possibility that could be examined was that of obtaining a measure of clemency or a reprieve, though in that case Mr Begun would have to agree to submit a request to that end.

119. In reply to a question, the representative of the government concerned indicated that there were no private schools in the USSR. He emphasized that, in any case, Mr Begun had not been sentenced for teaching Hebrew without the appropriate diploma required by Soviet legislation, an offence punished at the most by a fine, but for a crime against the State, for his political agitation and not for his cultural activities.

120. At the end of the discussion, and after reservations had been expressed by certain members who considered that the communication was inadmissible, the Committee *decided*:

(i) to take note of the statements of the representative of the government concerned;

(ii) to ask the Secretariat to transmit to the authors of the communication the record of the Committee's deliberations as given in the report of the Committee;

(iii) to defer consideration of this communication until its next session.

---

[12] See document 110 EX/40 PRIV., para. 211 (vol. I, p. 567), communication No. 209/80 concerning *Union of Soviet Socialist Republics*, case of *Yosif Z. Begun*.

No. 536/83 **Union of Soviet Socialist Republics**

Spring 1986 session of the Committee on Conventions and Recommendations (124th session of the Executive Board)[13]

Autumn 1986 session of the Committee on Conventions and Recommendations (125th session of the Executive Board)[14]

99. Mr Yosif Z. Begun, a mathematician, is described as also being a private teacher of Hebrew. In October 1983 he was condemned to seven years' imprisonment and five years of internal exile for anti-Soviet agitation and propaganda.

100. At the [autumn 1985] session the representative of the government concerned informed the Committee that on completing his studies Mr Begun had of his own free will chosen a job in a field related to national defence and that in 1973, after breaching the discipline of the undertaking for which he was working by adopting an attitude which deviated increasingly from rational norms, he had wished to make use of his knowledge abroad, submitting an application to emigrate which was rejected for reasons of State security. The representative of the government added that Mr Begun, finding that irksome, had after a period of time ostentatiously submitted his resignation and had since that time engaged in anti-Soviet activities, in particular circulating material slandering the USSR and its political system and even getting in touch with an agent of a foreign secret service, a matter which had been formally recognized by that agent. He stated that it was these criminal actions which had brought Mr Begun before the judicial authorities. Turning to the present situation of the prisoner, the representative of the government concerned assured the Committee that humanitarian efforts had been made on his behalf, that in his prison he had been exempted from all physical work, that his wife had been able to visit him normally but that he did not appear to wish to solicit a reprieve on his own initiative and that legally no other person was able to act in his place.

101. At the spring 1986 session, this communication, along with all the other communications concerning the Soviet Union, was not examined by the Committee.[15] However, in a letter dated 28 March 1986 [...][16] the authors of the communication allege that Mr Begun's state of health is continuing to deteriorate and that his wife and son have been permitted no visits since August 1985. They reiterate that Mr Be-

---

[13] See document 124 EX/3 PRIV., paras. 101-104 (*supra*, pp. 48-49), communication No. 441/82 concerning *Union of Soviet Socialist Republics*, case of *Vladimir Raiz*.

[14] See document 125 EX/3 PRIV., paras. 99-107; see also document 125 EX/CR/HR/2.

[15] See document 124 EX/3 PRIV., para. 104 (*supra*, p. 49), communication No. 441/82 concerning *Union of Soviet Socialist Republics*, case of *Vladimir Raiz*.

[16] See document 124 EX/CR/HR/2 Add.2.

gun had not slandered the Soviet State or engaged in political agitation and that his activities were confined solely to the fields of the culture, religion and language of the Jewish people. They request once again that a humanitarian solution be found to his case.

102. At the present session, the representative of the government concerned stated that the discussion of the case at previous sessions showed clearly that the communication was ill-founded, that the confidential debates within the Committee had spilled over into public debates in the press, that there had obviously been an attempt at direct interference in the domestic affiars of the Soviet Union and that, therefore, the communication should be declared inadmissible on the grounds of being politically motivated. In any event, the judicial decisions concerning Mr Begun, including the most recent concerning anti-Soviet agitation and propaganda, had been made in full accordance with Soviet law, and all means of redress had been made available to him.

103. In reply to requests for further details, the representative of the government concerned said that, contrary to the allegations of those submitting the communication, Mr Begun did not possess a doctor's degree but was a "candidate" in technical science. Moreover, he was not a teacher holding a proper teaching qualification as required by Soviet law. Speaking of the reasons for which the authorities had refused him an emigration visa, he said that the scientist had previously worked in a post connected with national security.

104. Some members of the Committee considered that it was inappropriate to ask the representative of the government concerned for details when he had already supplied a great deal of information from which it was clear that Mr Begun, a recidivist, had been condemned not for his cultural and educational activities but for criminal acts, and that in addition the authors of the communication had made use of the information in the press. These members considered that, under the conditions set out in paragraph 14 (*a*) 104 EX/Decision 3.3, the Committee was bound to declare the communication inadmissible.

105. Other members of the Committee considered that the sentence passed on Mr Begun was excessively heavy for the acts allegedly committed since he had not committed a crime of violence. They considered that, on humanitarian grounds and in the hope that there would be new developments in the matter, consideration of the communication should be deferred until the next session, particularly since all means of redress did not yet seem to have been exhausted and that the reasons of State security which had prevented Mr Begun from obtaining an exit visa in the past might no longer exist.

No. 536/83 **Union of Soviet Socialist Republics**

106. One member of the Committee stated that the Committee, whatever its decision, must, at its next session, reconsider the case of Mr Begun, who was also the subject of another communication [...].[17]

107. At the close of the discussion, and after reservations had been expressed by one of its members, the Committee *decided*:

(i) to thank the government concerned for sending a representative;

(ii) to request the Secretariat to inform the authors of the communication that, according to the clarification provided by the representative of the government concerned, Mr Yosif Z. Begun had not yet exhausted all available remedies in Soviet law;

(iii) to resume consideration of the communication at its spring 1987 session in the hope that, from the humanitarian angle, new factors would come to the fore, particularly with regard to the means of redress not yet exhausted and the fact that the reasons of State security which had prevented Mr Yosif Z. Begun from obtaining permission to emigrate might no longer exist.

Spring 1987 session of the Committee on Conventions and Recommendations (126th session of the Executive Board)[18]

106. Mr Yosif Z. Begun, a mathematician, is described as also being a private teacher of Hebrew. In October 1983 he was condemned to seven years' imprisonment and five years of internal exile for anti-Soviet agitation and propaganda.

107. At the [autumn 1985] session the representative of the government concerned informed the Committee that on completing his studies Mr Begun had of his own free will chosen a job in a field related to national defence and that in 1973, after breaching the discipline of the undertaking for which he was working by adopting an attitude which deviated increasingly from rational norms, he had wished to make use of his knowledge abroad, submitting an application to emigrate which was rejected for reasons of State security. The representative of the government added that Mr Begun, finding that irksome, had after a period of time ostentatiously submitted his resignation and had since that time engaged in anti-Soviet activities, in particular circulating material slandering the USSR and its political system and even getting in

[17] Communication No. 720/86 concerning *Union of Soviet Socialist Republics*, case of *Yosif Z. Begun*.

[18] See document 126 EX/3 PRIV., paras. 106-116; see also documents 126 EX/CR/HR/2 and Add.2.

touch with an agent of a foreign secret service, a matter which had been formally recognized by that agent. He stated that it was these criminal actions which had brought Mr Begun before the judicial authorities. Turning to the present situation of the prisoner, the representative of the government concerned assured the Committee that humanitarian efforts had been made on his behalf, that in his prison he had been exempted from all physical work, that his wife had been able to visit him normally but that he did not appear to wish to solicit a reprieve on his own initiative and that legally no other person was able to act in his place.

108. At its autumn 1986 session, the Committee decided, after reservations had been expressed by one of its members, to request the Secretariat to inform the authors of the communication that, according to the clarification provided by the representative of the government concerned, Mr Yosif Z. Begun had not yet exhausted all available remedies in Soviet law, and to resume consideration of the communication at its spring 1987 session in the hope that, from the humanitarian angle, new factors would come to the fore, particularly with regard to the means of redress not yet exhausted and the fact that the reasons of State security which had prevented Mr Yosif Z. Begun from obtaining permission to emigrate might no longer exist.[19]

109. At the Committee's present session the representative of the government concerned informed the Committee that Mr Begun had archived and distributed anti-Soviet literature, had conducted subversive activities against the Soviet State and made appeals for struggle against the Soviet system. Mr Begun was sentenced to seven years' imprisonment, on the basis of considerable amounts of evidence and the testimony of witnesses, in conformity with Soviet law. He had finished over half his sentence, and on 17 February 1987, at the request of his wife, he had been pardoned, his remaining sentence having been cancelled. Concerning the question of emigration, the representative pointed out that a person could not leave the Soviet Union if he had not served his prison sentence. Now that Mr Begun had been pardoned he could reapply for an exit visa and his case could appropriately be re-examined. The representative stated that the case should consequently be struck from the Committee's list.

110. A member of the Committee indicated that it seemed clear that this case had been settled since Mr Begun had been pardoned and released. The other question concerning a possible emigration was one which depended on Mr Begun's personal decision on whether or not he wanted to apply for permission to emigrate. The matter was beyond the competence of the Committee and the case should be considered as closed.

[19] See document 125 EX/3 PRIV., para. 107 (ii) and (iii) (*supra*, p. 296).

111. Another member of the Committee emphasized that the Committee had not been told anything about whether Mr Begun could work as he wished in a field of his choice, such as natural history or Hebrew studies. The important question was not the question of a theoretical emigration, but rather whether Mr Begun was able to work as a scientist. The Committee member wondered whether the representative of the government concerned could assure the Committee that Mr Begun was not only freed from prison but also from limitations imposed on his freedom to work.

112. In reply, the representative stated that in the Soviet Union there was no unemployment. There were no restrictions in general on the right to choose a field of work. The representative added that he did not know how Mr Begun intended to rebuild his life after coming out of prison. In principle there were no restrictions, he said, on Mr Begun's choice of work.

113. Certain Committee members expressed their concern that only one of the three points raised by the communication, namely the question of imprisonment, had been resolved and that the other two problems, i.e. Mr Begun's right to emigrate and his right to work in the fields of his choice, still needed to be examined in depth.

114. Other Committee members emphasized that the Committee could not speculate on what decisions Mr Begun might make concerning emigration or his choice of work. For the moment, there were no specific allegations before the Committee that Mr Begun had been restricted in any way in making such choices. If in the future specific allegations were made to the Committee in this regard, the Committee could examine them at that time, but at the present time, there was not even any indication before the Committee as to what Mr Begun himself had decided to do. In any event, the representative of the government concerned had given the Committee certain information and assurances, and it would be inappropriate for the Committee to raise further questions in this regard.

115. The representative of the Director-General recalled that at its [spring 1981] session the Committee had made the distinction between actual and potential violations of human rights and had decided that it would deal only with cases alleging actual violations and not potential violations. The question which the Committee needed to decide now was whether the facts before it pointed to actual violations or only potential violations of Mr Begun's rights. Once the Committee had decided on that issue it could then decide on what action it wished to take.

116. After a further lengthy debate on the issues and after reservations had been expressed by two of its members, the Committee *decided*:

(i) to thank the representative of the government concerned for his presence and his co-operation;

(ii) to note with satisfaction that Mr Begun had been released from prison;

(iii) to take note of the assurances of the representative of the government concerned that no restrictions would be imposed on Mr Begun's choice of livelihood, as was the case with any Soviet citizen;

(iv) to strike this case[20] from its list as settled in conformity with paragraph 14 (*a*) (x) of [104 EX/Decision 3.3].

[20] Communications No. 536/83 concerning *Union of Soviet Socialist Republics*, case of *Yosif Z. Begun*, and No. 720/86 concerning *Union of Soviet Socialist Republics*, case of *Yosif Z. Begun*, were being considered together.

No. 539/83

Concerning *Pakistan*
Case of *Tariq Ahsan*

Communication of 16 March 1983 submitted by
The International Human Rights Law Group

Spring 1984 session of the Committee on Conventions and Recommendations (119th session of the Executive Board)[1]

124. Mr Tariq Ahsan, a lecturer at Quaid-i-Azam University (Pakistan) was allegedly arrested in November 1981 and charged with conspiracy and publishing and distributing subversive literature, which are crimes punishable by a maximum sentence of 25 years' imprisonment or even the death penalty. He was allegedly tried in February 1983.

125. In its letter dated 29 March 1984 [...],[2] the Permanent Delegation of Pakistan to Unesco informed the Secretariat that Mr Ahsan had been found guilty of the clandestine distribution of subversive literature, that he had been sentenced to two years' imprisonment and a fine of 10,000 rupees, but that he had already been released.

126. The Committee noted this release, and considering that the case of this teacher is thus closed, has *decided* to strike the communication from its list.

---

[1] See document 119 EX/35 PRIV., paras. 124-126; see also documents 119 EX/CR/HR/3 and Add.2.

[2] See document 119 EX/CR/HR/3 Add.2.

No. 540/83

Concerning *Federal Republic of Germany*
Case of *Helios Gürkov*

Communication of 23 June 1983 submitted by
Helios Gürkov

Spring 1983 session of the Committee on Conventions and Recommendations (116th session of the Executive Board)[1]

130. This communication is submitted by Mr Helios Gürkov, who describes himself as an agronomist and as victim of the alleged violation. Mr Gürkov studied agronomy at the G. Dimitrov University for Agriculture in Sofia, Bulgaria, from 1955 to 1960. He alleges that the diploma he was awarded has not been fully recognized by the Bavarian Ministry of Education. According to him, at the time he was a student the admission requirements to the university were very stringent and the subjects studied during the five-year course far outnumbered those required in similar institutions in Germany, where the study programme lasts for only three years. The author has filed various documents which, in his opinion, bear out his assertion, including a letter, dated 17 February 1983, from the International Association of Universities attesting to the high academic level of the G. Dimitrov University for Agriculture.

131. Mr Gürkov considers that his right to work in his profession has been violated. He refers to the Universal Declaration of Human Rights, the International Covenant on Economic, Social and Cultural Rights and the Convention on the Recognition of Studies, Diplomas and Degrees in Higher Education in the States belonging to the Europe Region.

132. On the grounds that agronomic studies in G. Dimitrov University were not at exactly the same level as such studies in similar institutions in the Federal Republic of Germany, the Bavarian Ministry of Education allegedly dismissed Mr Gürkov's demands in July 1977. The court before which he tried to bring an action reportedly nonsuited him in 1982.

---

[1] See document 116 EX/48 PRIV., paras. 130-140; see also document 116 EX/CR/HR/3 Add.

133. As for the purpose and aim of the communication, the author requests that his Sofia diploma be recognized in the Federal Republic of Germany and that he be allowed to work as an agronomist.

134. The representative of the Federal Republic of Germany informed the Committee that an administrative court in Munich had reviewed the matter and had rejected it on the merits. Furthermore an attempt had been made to obtain information on the matter from the Bulgarian authorities but they never responded.

135. The representative went on to explain that the regional court was still examining the case and had asked for an expert opinion. Thus the domestic remedies had not yet been exhausted. The question also arose, he said, as to which human right was allegedly being violated. Mr Gürkov was in fact working in Germany in the field of agronomy. The authorities were willing to let him be recognized as a technical agrarian engineer, but he was insisting on receiving a special recognition, the equivalent of a diploma. The representative wondered aloud whether there was a human right to recognition of an academic title acquired in another country. As concerned the Unesco-sponsored Convention on the Recognition of Studies, Diplomas and Degrees in Higher Education in the States belonging to the Europe Region, the representative pointed out that the Federal Republic of Germany had made a reservation upon signing it and had in fact not ratified it yet; thus the question of his country's obligations under that Convention could not validly be raised.

136. For these reasons the representative of the Federal Republic of Germany felt that the communication was clearly inadmissible.

137. Many Committee members quickly agreed that, while the subject-matter was within the competence of Unesco, no violation of a human right was involved in this case, that a state had the right to set its own standards for the recognition of foreign academic qualifications, and that the communication was clearly inadmissible.

138. One Committee member felt that because the subject-matter fell within Unesco's competence the case was admissible. He asked the representative whether Mr Gürkov's competence had been tested in Germany by way of examinations or whether one had just looked at his academic transcript to judge his abilities.

139. The representative of the Federal Republic of Germany explained that it was the experts called by the competent court which had made the evaluation, and that, in any event, it was evident from Mr Gürkov's own documentation that he did not have the requisite training in animal husbandry since the Bulgarian school he attended was only oriented towards the study of plants.

Federal Republic of Germany **No. 540/83**

140. The Committee *decided* that the communication was inadmissible, since there was no indication of any violation of human rights within Unesco's fields of competence (paragraph 14 (*a*) (iii) of 104 EX/Decision 3.3).

No. 543/83

Concerning *Chile*
Case of *Héctor Hernán Bravo Zamora* et al.*

Communication of 12 April 1983 submitted by
Héctor Hernán Bravo Zamora *et al.*°

Autumn 1983 session of the Committee on Conventions and Recommendations (117th session of the Executive Board)[1]

40. The representative of the government concerned said that, at the [spring 1983] session, he had given the Committee very full information about the new procedure introduced by his government to help Chilean nationals who were having to contend with temporary difficulties in returning to their country. He added that that procedure was still in force and that, in addition, it was now being given speeded effect in that, since that time, 3,090 authorizations to return had been granted, including 860 following requests for re-examination.

Case of Héctor Hernán Bravo Zamora

41. The author of the communication, Mr Héctor Hernán Bravo Zamora, a sports coach of Chilean nationality, apparently acknowledged by the Chilean Fencing Federation to be one of the most highly qualified Chilean fencing instructors, states that, after being imprisoned and tortured by the Chilean police, he was forced to leave his

* Case of *Héctor Hernán Bravo Zamora, Rafael and Maria Marta Rivas de Gumucio, Juan Guillermo López Carmona, Jorge Segundo Insunza Becker and Osvaldo Hernán Rodrigues Musso.* At the Committee's spring 1984 session, this communication was being referred to as case of *Héctor Hernán Bravo Zamora, Juan Guillermo López Carmona, Osvaldo Hernán Rodrigues Musso and Jorge Segundo Insunza Becker*, at the autumn 1984 session as case of *Jorge Segundo Insunza Becker* and from the spring 1985 session as case of *Severo Augusto Samaniego Mesias*.

° Héctor Hernán Bravo Zamora, Rafael and María Marta Rivas de Gumucio, Juan Guillermo López Carmona, Jorge Segundo Insunza Becker, Osvaldo Hernán Rodrígues Musso and Severo Augusto Samaniego Mesias, respectively.

[1] See document 117 EX/18 PRIV., paras. 40-62; see also document 117 EX/CR/HR/3.

country in December 1973. Although he had never been involved with the law in his country, it seems that he was unsuccessful in his attempt to return to Chile following the first amnesty announced by the Chilean Government.

42. The representative of the government concerned said that, in conformity with current procedures, further authorizations were on the point of being granted and that he was in a position to state that Mr H. H. Bravo Zamora's name would be on one of the forthcoming lists of those who were being granted authorization. As soon as that list became official, he would communicate it to the Committee and to the Chilean Consulate in Paris in order to alleviate any possible administrative difficulties.

43. Some members suggested that note should be taken of what had been said by the representative of the Chilean Government and that examination of the communication should be postponed until the next session.

44. The representative of the government concerned then explained that two remedies were available to Chilean nationals wishing to return to Chile: an administrative remedy, the "request for re-examination", and a judicial remedy which could be used either in the event of the administrative appeal being rejected or directly. In the case of the judicial remedy, the government was obliged to hand over to the court all the information that it had on its files. One member had asked whether the events currently taking place in Chile were affecting the procedures established but the representative of the government concerned stated that they were not. He then added that, as he had said at the [spring 1983] session, the letter "L" no longer appeared on passports issued by the authorities and that the aforementioned remedies were available to those whose passports still bore that letter. Lastly, he confirmed that the state of emergency, previously in force in his country, had not been prolonged.

45. The Committee consequently *decided*:

(i) to take note of the statements made by the representative of the Chilean Government to the effect that Mr H. H. Bravo Zamora was on the point of being authorized to return to Chile;

(ii) pending confirmation of this information, to postpone examination of the admissibility of this case until its next session.

Case of Rafael and Maria Marta Rivas de Gumucio

46. Following the events of September 1973, Mr and Mrs Gumucio, both university teachers, were allegedly forced to relinquish their teaching posts.

Chile **No. 543/83**

47. They are said to have taken refuge in the Embassy of Venezuela from where it is claimed that they left for France. The applications for authorization to return, which Mrs Gumucio is said to have submitted to the Chilean Consulate in Paris, were apparently without effect.

48. The representative of the government concerned stated that, following the representations made by the Director-General on humanitarian grounds, Mr and Mrs Gumucio had been authorized in July 1983 to return to Chile, without any conditions being laid down, and that they had arrived in Santiago last August.

49. After a brief discussion, the Committee *decided* to strike the cases of Mr and Mrs Gumucio from its list, considering them to have been settled separately, in accordance with 104 EX/Decision 3.3, paragraph 14 (*a*) (x).

Case of Juan Guillermo López Carmona

50. The author of the communication, Mr Juan Guillermo López Carmona, a teacher of philosophy of Chilean nationality, asserts that in December 1973 he was compelled to seek asylum in the French Embassy after being warned by his students that he was wanted by the military authorities. Around the same time he was dismissed from his position at the University of Valparaíso, where he taught in the philosophy, history and arts departments. He regards his situation as serious in view of the fact that his exile has prevented him from practising his profession as a teacher of philosophy, and has caused him to lose all contact with his colleagues and with national research centres. Moreover, from his position abroad he is able to carry out very little research relating to his own country.

51. During the Committee's examination of the communication, the representative of the government concerned said that the name of Mr J. G. López Carmona was going to be included on one of the lists of persons authorized to return to Chile which were about to be issued.

52. One member asked whether, as a result of being included on such a list, the person concerned would be given a passport which made no reference to the letter "L". Several other members said they were satisfied to learn that Mr J. G. López Carmona was going to be authorized to return, but asked whether he would be reinstated in his post at the university. One of them said that this question, being linked to the exercise of a right falling within Unesco's spheres of competence, was a matter of concern to the Committee and that examination of the communication should consequently be postponed until the Committee had received information in that connection.

53. The representative of the government concerned explained that any person authorized to return to Chile was *ipso jure* delivered a normal passport without any reference to the previous passport. Furthermore, what was considered essential by the Chilean Government was that the person concerned should be allowed to return to Chile in order to enjoy his full rights there, but it was difficult for him to say that the person concerned would indeed recover his post at the university and exercise his former activities. There was, however, no doubt that he would enjoy the same rights as any other Chilean citizen.

54. The Committee consequently *decided*:

(i) to take note of what had been said by the representative of the government concerned; and, pending further information, particularly in regard to the possibilities afforded to Mr J. G. López Carmona for exercising his profession;

(ii) to postpone examination of the admissibility of this case until the next session.

Case of Jorge Segundo Insunza Becker

55. The author of the communication, Mr Jorge Segundo Insunza Becker, a civil engineer of Chilean nationality, describes himself as the victim of the alleged violations, which also concern his wife and two children. He states that, after living in hiding for two and a half years, he was forced to leave his country in the early part of 1976. Under Decree-Law No. 81, he is therefore unable to return without the prior permission of the Ministry of the Interior. He has apparently been unsuccessful in his attempts to obtain such permission, except for 1979 when he was allowed to attend his father's funeral.

56. The representative of the government concerned suggested that Mr J. S. Insunza Becker be invited to use the means of redress available to him, since it appeared that he had not yet done so.

57. One member of the Committee agreed that this should be done for humanitarian reasons, but he noted that the communication concerned a civil engineer and was aimed solely at securing respect for his right to return to his country. Another member pointed out that the person concerned had already submitted applications to the Consulate in West Berlin for permission to return.

58. The representative of the Chilean Government stated that since Mr J. S. Insunza Becker had submitted his applications the procedure had been modified and that consequently he should make a further request. On that occasion he could mention

on his own behalf that he had already been provisionally authorized to return; in addition, legal means were also available to him.

59. The Committee consequently *decided*:

(i) to inform the author of the existence of new procedures and accordingly to invite him to submit an application for authorization to return;

(ii) to postpone examination of the admissibility of this case until the next session.

Case of Osvaldo Hernán Rodríguez Musso

60. The author of the communication, Osvaldo Hernán Rodríguez Musso, a musician and writer of Chilean nationality, claims that in 1981 he submitted to the Chilean Consulate in Paris an application for permission to return to his country but that his application was rejected.

61. The representative of the Chilean Government stated that if Mr O. H. Rodríguez Musso were to submit a request for re-examination of his case to the Chilean Consulate in Bonn it would very probably be favourably received; he even considered it advisable that Mr Musso make his request as soon as possible in order to have his name appear on a forthcoming list and hasten his return. At the request of the Committee, the Secretariat informed the person concerned of the foregoing.

62. After a brief discussion, the Committee *decided*:

(i) to request the Secretariat to send a telegram to the author of the communication to inform him of the statements made by the representative of the Chilean Government;

(ii) to postpone examination of the admissibility of this case until the next session.

No. 543/83 **Chile**

Spring 1984 session of the Committee on Conventions and Recommendations (119th session of the Executive Board)[2]

Case of Héctor Hernán Bravo Zamora, Juan Guillermo López Carmona and Osvaldo Hernán Rodríguez Musso

27. Mr Héctor Hernán Bravo Zamora, a sports coach, Mr Juan Guillermo López Carmona, a teacher of philosophy, and Mr Osvaldo Hernán Rodríguez Musso, a musician and writer, are three Chilean citizens who wish to return to Chile and who state that their requests to do so have been unsuccessful.

28. When the communication was examined at the present session of the Committee, the representative of the Chilean Government assured Committee members that the requests of these persons would be favourably received provided they took the necessary steps but that up to now none of them had done so.

29. Consequently, the Committee *decided*:

(i) to inform the authors of the communication of the statements made by the representative of the government concerned;

(ii) to consider the cases of these persons as settled, in accordance with paragraph 14 (*a*) (x) .of 104 EX/Decision 3.3.

Case of Jorge Segundo Insunza Becker

30. The author of the communication, Mr Jorge Segundo Insunza Becker, a civil engineer, states that after living in hiding for two and a half years he was forced to leave his country in the early part of 1976. Under Decree-Law No. 81, he is, allegedly, unable to return without the prior permission of the Ministry of the Interior. He has apparently been unsuccessful in his attempts to obtain such permission except in 1979, when he was allowed to attend his father's funeral.

31. At its autumn 1983 session the Committee decided to inform the author of the communication of the existence of new procedures under which he might submit an application for authorization to return.[3]

---

[2] See document 119 EX/35 PRIV., paras. 27-34; see also document 119 EX/CR/HR/2.
[3] See document 117 EX/18 PRIV., para. 59 (i) (*supra*, p. 311).

Chile **No. 543/83**

32. At the present session, the representative of the Chilean Government told the Committee that investigations he had carried out in Santiago had shown that Mr Jorge Segundo Insunza Becker had not availed himself of any of the remedies that had been indicated to him.

33. After expressing doubt as to whether the case of this civil engineer really fell within Unesco's fields of competence, a member of the Committee said he considered that the communication should in any case be deemed inadmissible on the grounds that its author had not made an attempt to exhaust domestic remedies. Without disagreeing with what that Committee member had said, the other members who spoke felt that the author of the communication should be given one last chance.

34. The Committee therefore *decided*:

(i) to postpone examination of the admissibility of this communication until its autumn 1984 session;

(ii) to ask the Secretariat to inform the author again of the administrative and legal remedies at his disposal and point out to him that if he failed to avail himself of them the Committee would *ipso facto* strike his communication from its list at its autumn 1984 session.

Autumn 1984 session of the Committee on Conventions and Recommendations (120th session of the Executive Board)[4]

15. The author of the communication, a civil engineer, states that after living in hiding for two and a half years he was forced to leave his country in the early part of 1976. Under Decree-Law No. 81, he is, allegedly, unable to return without the prior permission of the Ministry of the Interior. He has apparently been unsuccessful in his attempts to obtain such permission except in 1979, when he was allowed to attend his father's funeral.

16. At its [spring 1984] session, the Committee had decided to ask the Secretariat to inform the author again of the administrative and legal remedies at his disposal and point out to him that if he failed to avail himself of them the Committee would *ipso facto* strike his communication from its list at its autumn 1984 session.[5]

---

[4] See document 120 EX/15 PRIV., paras. 15-17; see also document 120 EX/CR/HR/2.
[5] See document 119 EX/35 PRIV., para. 34 (ii) (*supra*, p. 313).

17. After an exchange of views the Committee *decided*, in view of its previous decision and the author's persistent inaction, to declare this communication inadmissible under the terms of paragraph 14 (*a*) (ix) of 104 EX/Decision 3.3 of the Executive Board.

Spring 1985 session of the Committee on Conventions and Recommendations (121st session of the Executive Board)[6]

26. The author of the communication, a history teacher of Chilean nationality, alleges that he was arrested on 12 September 1973 at his place of work, the State Technical University of Santiago, and detained for 11 months, at the end of which he was released without any charge having been brought against him. Despite the various steps he has taken, he is reportedly still debarred from returning to Chile.

27. He claims that during the period between 1978 and 1983 he was orally informed by the Chilean Consulate in Paris that he was not authorized to return to Chile. His wife, Mrs Gloria C. Salinas, was authorized to return in August 1983 and since then has been living in Santiago with their two children. For Mr Samaniego, the fact that he is separated from his family makes his request for reconsideration all the more urgent. The further request for reconsideration that he reportedly submitted in 1984 is also said to have elicited an unfavourable oral reply.

28. The representative of the Chilean Government pointed out that Mr Samaniego had sought none of the appropriate remedies available to him but that, for humanitarian reasons due in particular to the fact that he had been separated from his family, he could avail himself of the exceptional procedure for temporary return outlined in connection with [another communication].[7] Once in Chile, he could explain his situation and the reasons why he had not made use of the remedies available.

29. Some members of the Committee said they were worried about that way of dealing with the problem, as it had the effect of obliging those concerned to travel, in some cases first to Paris, and then to Santiago, thereby incurring expenses without any certainty that their representations would produce satisfactory results. These members accordingly wondered whether the persons concerned could not complete the appropriate formalities from the place where they were living. One member of the Committee thought it deplorable that returning to one's country should give rise to so many difficulties, and urged that as many cases as possible should be settled

---

[6] See document 121 EX/46 PRIV., paras. 26-33; see also document 121 EX/CR/HR/3.

[7] *Ibidem*, para. 39 (*infra*, pp. 335-336), communication No. 559/83 concerning *Chile*, case of *Carlos Alfredo Andrade Vera and Guillermo Vera Paulo*.

before people travelled at all, and that the procedure contemplated should remain exceptional.

30. The representative of the government concerned stated that the procedure was indeed exceptional, and that it had been introduced for humanitarian reasons, in order to help people whose situation was more complex than it at first appeared because they were, among other things, at a distance and whose presence would make it possible to clear up certain difficulties more easily and more speedily. It was quite obvious that the normal procedure to be employed was the one that he had outlined on several occasions to the Committee and that he had formalized in a memorandum transmitted to the Secretariat which was periodically updated and which described the appeal for review to be submitted to the Ministry of the Interior in Santiago, and the remedy of *amparo*. When those concerned did not follow that normal procedure, they complicated their own situation, which was why an exceptional procedure had been regarded as necessary. It was possible, however, that it might subsequently cease to be used.

31. On the question of travel costs, the representative of the Chilean Government said that the Office of the High Commissioner for Refugees in Santiago might help some people, particularly if Unesco showed that it was concerned about their fate. Moreover, there was a ministerial office in Santiago, of which he was the coordinator, which was helping to deal with university and other medical problems. In reply to a member of the Committee who had expressed surprise at the number of cases in which those concerned had not done what they should have done, and had wondered whether, in order to lighten the Committee's task, the Chilean authorities could not make arrangements to see that the requisite information was more explicit and more widely available, the representative of the Chilean Government said that he would convey the Committee's anxieties in that regard to his government, although such information was in principle available to everyone in all Chilean consulates.

32. All the members of the Committee who spoke thought that the communication should be kept on the Committee's agenda.

33. At the conclusion of its discussion, the Committee *decided*:

(i) to take note of the statements made by the representative of the Chilean Government and to instruct the Secretariat to inform the author of the communication accordingly;

(ii) to resume its examination of the admissibility of this communication at its autumn [1985 session].

No. 543/83 **Chile**

Autumn 1985 session of the Committee on Conventions and Recommendations (122nd session of the Executive Board)[8]

24. The author of the communication, a history teacher of Chilean nationality, alleges that he was arrested on 12 September 1973 at his place of work, the State Technical University of Santiago, and detained for 11 months, at the end of which he was released without any charge having been brought against him. Despite the various steps he has taken, he is reportedly still debarred from returning to Chile.

25. He claims that during the period between 1978 and 1983 he was orally informed by the Chilean Consulate in Paris that he was not authorized to return to Chile. His wife, Mrs Gloria C. Salinas, was authorized to return in August 1983 and since then has been living in Santiago with their two children. For Mr Samaniego, the fact that he is separated from his family makes his request for reconsideration all the more urgent. The further request for reconsideration that he reportedly submitted in 1984 is also said to have elicited an unfavourable oral reply.

26. At the [spring 1985] session, the Committee had decided to inform the author that he might be granted an exceptional authorization to return temporarily, which would enable him to clarify his situation on the spot.[9]

27. On 19 July 1985 the Secretariat received from the author of the communication a letter dated 12 July 1985 in which he expressed his great happiness to be in Chile since 2 July, reunited with his wife, his children and all his family, and to note that the interest taken by Unesco in his case had been well received by the Chilean authorities. He expressed his heartfelt gratitude to the Organization and said that he would keep it informed of further developments without fail.

28. At the present session, the representative of the Chilean Government explained that it would not be long before a favourable final solution was achieved, as he had taken steps to ensure that the temporary authorization granted to Mr Severo Augusto Samaniego Mesias would be extended for an indefinite period. In his view, this case made it quite clear that when those concerned complied with the instructions given them, they could obtain satisfaction. Accordingly, he considered that the case could be regarded as settled.

29. One member of the Committee proposed that consideration of the communication be deferred until the next session, pending confirmation that Mr Severo Augus-

---

[8] See document 122 EX/21 PRIV., paras. 24-30; see also document 122 EX/CR/HR/2.
[9] See document 121 EX/46 PRIV., para. 33 (i) (*supra*, p. 315).

to Samaniego Mesias had indeed been granted definitive authorization. Other Committee members suggested that the Committee should decide here and now to strike the communication from its list, subject to receiving such information, as it had done previously in similar situations. Two members expressed reservations regarding a decision that would result in a communication being struck off the list before it was certain that the problem which it raised had been solved, and urged that the author of the communication be requested to keep the Committee informed of the action taken in response to his appeal.

30. Following a discussion, the Committee *decided*:

(i) to ask the author of the communication to provide full information on the results of the steps he had taken;

(ii) to strike the communication from its list once the Secretariat had received confirmation that Mr Severo Augusto Samaniego Mesias had indeed been authorized to return to Chile for good, on the clear understanding that should such confirmation not have reached the Secretariat by the spring 1986 [session] the Committee would resume its examination of the communication.

Spring 1986 session of the Committee on Conventions and Recommendations (124th session of the Executive Board)[10]

23. The author of the communication, a history teacher of Chilean nationality, alleges that he was arrested on 12 September 1973 at his place of work, the State Technical University of Santiago, and detained for 11 months, at the end of which he was released without any charge having been brought against him. Despite the various steps he has taken, he is reportedly still debarred from returning to Chile.

24. He claims that during the period between 1978 and 1983 he was orally informed by the Chilean Consulate in Paris that he was not authorized to return to Chile. His wife, Mrs Gloria C. Salinas, was authorized to return in August 1983 and since then has been living in Santiago with their two children. For Mr Samaniego, the fact that he is separated from his family makes his request for reconsideration all the more urgent. The further request for reconsideration that he reportedly submitted in 1984 is also said to have elicited an unfavourable oral reply.

25. At the [autumn 1985] session, the representative of the Chilean Government had explained that it would not be long before a favourable final solution was achieved,

---

[10] See document 124 EX/3 PRIV., paras. 23-27; see also document 124 EX/CR/HR/2.

as he had secured approval of an indefinite extension of the temporary authorization granted to Mr Severo Augusto Samaniego Mesias, of which the latter had made use in July 1985. After discussion, the Committee had decided to strike the communication from its list once the Secretariat had received confirmation that the person concerned had indeed been authorized to return to Chile for good, on the clear understanding that should such confirmation not have reached the Secretariat by the present session the Committee would resume its examination of the communication.[11]

26. At the present session, the representative of the government concerned explained that the request for reconsideration submitted by Mr Severo Augusto Samaniego Mesias had been approved and that in December 1985 he had received an unconditional authorization to return to Chile and to make that country his permanent home if he so desired.

27. After an exchange of views, the Committee *decided* to declare the case settled under the terms of 104 EX/Decision 3.3, paragraph 14 (*a*) (x).

[11] See document 122 EX/21 PRIV., para. 30 (ii) (*supra*, p. 317).

No. 544/83

Concerning *Socialist Republic of Viet Nam*
Case of *Bui Hoang Câm*

Communication of 13 April 1983 submitted by
Amnesty International

Autumn 1983 session of the Committee on Conventions and Recommendations (117th session of the Executive Board)[1]

114. Mr Bui Hoang Câm, a 62-year-old poet, was allegedly arrested on 20 August 1982 following the seizure of a collection of his poems in the possession of a Vietnamese émigré visiting Hanoi. He was reportedly accused of having cultural relations with foreigners.

115. The representative of the government concerned informed the Committee that in 1956-1957 Mr Câm had carried out subversive activities against the Socialist Republic of Viet Nam and against the Vietnamese people, and that at the time, through a measure of clemency, he had not been arrested, but only excluded from the writers' association. The representative claimed that Mr Câm had been arrested for the following reasons:

(i) he had organized an opium den at the back of a refreshment shop which he had been running since his retirement from the cultural service of Hanoi;

(ii) his poems were notoriously subversive political writings.

116. The representative of the Vietnamese Government stated, lastly, that Mr Câm could easily be released once there were signs of a change in his behaviour at the reeducation centre where he was now detained.

117. Several members of the Committee raised the problem of the right of an arrested person to a fair trial without undue delay, referring to Articles 9 and 14 of the International Covenant on Civil and political Rights. In their view, Mr Câm was im-

[1] See document 117 EX/18 PRIV., paras.114-118; see also document 117 EX/CR/HR/3.

prisoned without charge, without trial and for an indeterminate period. Some of them wondered whether there was any domestic means of redress available to a man undergoing re-education, and also raised the question whether the poet would be allowed to write and publish his works. Other members of the Committee felt that Vietnamese law should be considered to be very humane since it allowed the authorities simply to prescribe re-education for delinquents instead of giving them a prison sentence.

118. After a lengthy discussion and taking into account Mr Câm's age, the Committee *decided*:

(i) to appeal to the government concerned for clemency towards Mr Bui Hoang Câm; and

(ii) to postpone examination of the communication until the spring 1984 session pending further information from the government concerned, especially as regards the domestic means of redress available in such cases.

Spring 1984 session of the Committee on Conventions and Recommendations (119th session of the Executive Board)[2]

136. Mr Bui Hoang Câm, a 63-year old poet, was allegedly arrested in August 1982 following the seizure of a collection of his poems in the possession of a Vietnamese émigré visiting Hanoi. He was reportedly accused of having cultural relations with foreigners.

137. According to the information provided by the representative of the Vietnamese Government at the autumn 1983 session of the Committee, Mr Câm's arrest was due to the fact that he had organized an opium den at the back of a refreshment shop and that his poems were notoriously subversive writings. At the conclusion of the discussions on this case, the Committee had decided, *inter alia*, to make an appeal for clemency to the goverment concerned.[3]

138. In its letter dated 11 April 1984 [...],[4] the Permanent Delegation of the Socialist Republic of Viet Nam to Unesco informed the Director-General that by virtue of its government's policy of clemency Mr Bui Hoang Câm had been released on 15 Janu-

---

[2] See document 119 EX/35 PRIV., paras. 136-139; see also documents 119 EX/CR/HR/2 and Add. and Add.2.
[3] See document 117 EX/18 PRIV., para. 118 (i) (*supra*, p. 320).
[4] See document 119 EX/CR/HR/2 Add.2.

ary 1984 and had therefore been able to celebrate the traditional Têt new year with his family.

139. The Committee took note of his release and, considering that the poet's case had thus been settled, *decided* to strike the communication from its list.

No. 546/83

Concerning *Kenya*
Case of *Al-Amin Muhamed Kassim Mazrui*

Communication of 6 April 1983 submitted by
Amnesty International

Autumn 1983 session of the Committee on Conventions and Recommendations (117th session of the Executive Board)[1]

96. This communication alleges the violation of the rights of a teacher at Kenyatta University College, Mr Al-Amin Muhamed Kassim Mazrui, who is said to have been detained under an administrative order since 7 June 1982.

97. After having summarized the facts of the case, the representative of the Director-General told the Committee that in his letter dated 12 September 1983 the Permanent Delegate wished to inform the Committee that information from his government on the communication had not yet reached him. He therefore requested that consideration of the communication be postponed until the next session, pending receipt of the information.

98. Several members of the Committee agreed to this request. However, in view of the information contained in the communication which gave cause for concern as regards Mr Mazrui's health and the conditions of his detention, they considered that it would seem appropriate for a humanitarian appeal to be made without delay to the government concerned.

99. After an exchange of views, the Committee *dedcided*:

(i) to accede to the request of the Permanent Delegate of Kenya that consideration of the admissibility of the communication should be postponed until the spring [1984 session];

[1] See document 117 EX/18 PRIV., paras. 96-99; see also documents 117 EX/CR/HR/3 and Add.2.

(ii) to ask the Secretariat to draw the attention of the Permanent Delegate of Kenya to the importance the Committee attached to the presence of a representative of the government concerned by a communication at the meeting during which it would be considered;

(iii) to ask the Executive Board to request the Director-General to make such representations as he might deem appropriate, having regard to the concern expressed by the members of the Committee as regards the health and conditions of detention of Mr Mazrui.

Spring 1984 session of the Committee on Conventions and Recommendations (119th session of the Executive Board)[2]

110. This communication alleges the violation of the rights of a teacher at Kenyatta University College, Mr Al-Amin Muhamed Kassim Mazrui, who is said to have been detained under an administrative order since 7 June 1982.

111. In a letter dated 21 October 1983 [...], the Permanent Delegation of Kenya to Unesco requested the Secretariat to inform the Committee that Mr Al-Amin Muhamed Kassim Mazrui had been released on 12 October 1983.

112. The Committee noted this release and, considering that the case of this teacher was thus closed, *decided* to strike the communication from its list.

---

[2] See document 119 EX/35 PRIV., paras. 110-112; see also document 119 EX/CR/HR/2.

No. 559/83

Concerning *Chile*
Case of *Delfín Guillermo Quiñones* et al.*

Communication of 2 June 1983 submitted by
Delfín Guillermo Quiñones *et al.*°

Autumn 1983 session of the Committee on Conventions and Recommendations (117th session of the Executive Board)[1]

Case of Delfín Guillermo Quiñones

63. The author of this communication, Mr Delfín Guillermo Quiñones, a teacher of Chilean nationality, claims that in September 1973, he was obliged by the Vice-Rector of the University of Chile to resign his post as lecturer in this establishment because of his political ideas, which were considered to be contrary to those of the government. He allegedly left his country in 1974 as a political exile, and was followed shortly afterwards by his wife and four children. He went to reside in the German Democratic Republic. In 1978, he is said to have requested recognition of his right to live and work in Chile through the Chilean Consulate in West Berlin. The Consulate is said to have stamped his passport with the letter "L", thereby indicating that his name appeared on a list of persons prohibited from returning to the country.

64. The representative of the government concerned stated that in his opinion the case of Mr D. G. Quiñones was settled as his name appeared on a list of persons au-

---

* Case of *Delfín Guillermo Quiñones, Luis Ramón Contreras Parada and Carlos Alfredo Andrade Vera*. At the Committee's spring 1984 session, this communication was being referred to as case of *Delfín Guillermo Quiñones, Carlos Alfredo Andrade Vera, Rosaura Mendoza Careaga and Guillermo Vera Paulo*, at the autumn 1984 session as case of *Carlos Alfredo Andrade Vera, Rosaura Mendoza Careaga and Guillermo Vera Paulo*, from the spring 1985 session as case of *Carlos Alfredo Andrade Vera and Guillermo Vera Paulo* and at the spring 1986 session as case of *Carlos Alfredo Andrade Vera*.

° Delfín Guillermo Quiñones, Luis Ramón Contreras Parada, Carlos Alfredo Andrade Vera, Rosaura Mendoza Careaga and Guillermo Vera Paulo, respectively.

[1] See document 117 EX/18 PRIV., paras. 63-74; see also document 117 EX/CR/HR/3.

thorized to return to Chile and the Consulate responsible for him would issue him a normal passport enabling him to return at will. At the request of the Committee, the Secretariat informed the person concerned of the foregoing.

65. The members of the Committee taking part in the discussion wondered about the professional prospects that would be open to Mr D. G. Quiñones upon his return to Chile. The representative of the Director-General drew the attention of the members of the Committee to the provisions of Article 25 (*c*) of the International Covenant on Civil and Political Rights, which provides for every citizen to have access, on general terms of equality and without discrimination, to public service in his country, but does not establish an unconditional right to be a civil servant.

66. After a brief discussion, and in order to take into account the concerns expressed by the members of the Committee regarding the professional prospects of the person concerned, the Committee *decided* to postpone examination of the admissibility of this case until the next session pending further information.

Case of Luis Ramón Contreras Parada

67. The author of this communication, Mr Luis Ramón Contreras Parada, a teacher of Chilean nationality, claims that in August 1973, on business connected with his profession, he left Chile for the German Democratic Republic. On 23 November 1982, the Chilean Consulate in West Berlin stamped the letter "L" on his passport without telling him why he was not to be allowed to return to his country.

68. The representative of the government concerned stated that, as with regard to Mr O. H. Rodríguez Musso,[2] if Mr L. R. Contreras Parada were very rapidly to submit a request for re-examination of his case to the Consulate responsible for him, it would very probably be favourably received. At the request of the Committee, the Secretariat informed the person concerned of the foregoing.

69. Some time after this case had been considered, the representative of the Chilean Government informed the Secretariat that the person concerned had been authorized to return to Chile. The Committee therefore *decided* to consider the case as settled and to strike it from the list of communications.

---

[2] *Ibidem*, para. 61 (*supra*, p. 311), communication No. 543/83 concerning *Chile*, case of *Héctor Hernán Bravo Zamora* et al.

Chile **No. 559/83**

Case of Carlos Alfredo Andrade Vera

70. The author of the communication, Mr Carlos Alfredo Andrade Vera, is a primary-school teacher of Chilean nationality. He states that he was the victim of political persecution, for which reason he had to leave Chile on 9 June 1974 after taking refuge at the Finnish Embassy in Santiago de Chile, where it is said he stayed seven months.

71. It is stated that Mr C. A. Andrade Vera, who is nearly 70 years old, was a teacher for 35 years, including 23 as head of a large school in the city of Valparaíso. He is said to have then been, on two occasions, a member of the Valparaíso City Council and to have been twice elected to the national Parliament as Deputy for the Province of Valparaíso. Since he is not allowed to return to Chile, his wife, Mrs Irma Hernández Alvarado, who is nearly 70 and was a teacher for 42 years, is also in exile.

72. The representative of the Chilean Government noted that since the communication was recent, he had no information concerning this case. However, in view of the age of the person concerned (70), the representative promised to take humanitarian action on his behalf and also on behalf of his wife in order for them to be authorized to return to Chile although they had not made a request to that effect.

73. In reply to a question from one member of the Committee, the representative of the concerned government stated that the retirement rights of persons authorized to return to Chile were not affected by their present situation.

74. The Committee consequently *decided*:

(i) to inform the author of the communication of the statements made by the representative of the government concerned;

(ii) to postpone examination of the admissibility of this case until the next session.

No. 559/83 **Chile**

Spring 1984 session of the Committee on Conventions and Recommendations (119th session of the Executive Board)[3]

Case of Delfin Guillermo Quiñones

35. The author of this communication, Mr Delfin Guillermo Quiñones, a teacher of Chilean nationality, states that in September 1973 he was obliged by the Vice-Rector of the University of Chile to resign his post as lecturer in that establishment because of his political ideas, which were considered to be contrary to those of the government. He allegedly left his country in 1974 as a political exile and was followed shortly afterwards by his wife and children. He went to reside in the German Democratic Republic. He says that in 1978 he requested, through the Chilean Consulate in West Berlin, recognition of his right to live and work in Chile, but to no avail.

36. At its [autumn 1983] session, after a brief discussion and in order to take into account the concern expressed by members of the Committee regarding Mr Quiñones's professional prospects, the Committee decid to postpone examination of the admissibility of this case until the present session in the hope of receiving further information.[4]

37. At its present session the Committee had before it a letter from Mr Delfin Guillermo Quiñones, dated 7 November 1983 [...],[5] alleging that he had no prospects of employment in Chile and, moreover, would be denied his pension rights.

38. The representative of the Chilean Government informed the Committee that a decision by the Chilean Ministry of the Interior of November 1983 authorized Mr Delfin Guillermo Quiñones to return permanently and unconditionally to Chile, that he could claim his pension rights on his return to Chile and, lastly, that as far as his employment situation was concerned, the representative was not competent to give guarantees in that respect.

39. After discussing the matter, the Committee *decided* to consider the case settled, in accordance with paragraph 14 (*a*) (x) of 104 EX/Decision 3.3.

---

[3] See document 119 EX/35 PRIV., paras. 35-53; see also documents 119 EX/CR/HR/2 and 119 EX/CR/HR/3 Add.
[4] See document 117 EX/18 PRIV., para. 66 (*supra*, p. 326).
[5] See document 119 EX/CR/HR/2.

Chile **No. 559/83**

Case of Carlos Alfredo Andrade Vera

40. The author of the communication, Mr Carlos Alfredo Andrade Vera, who is nearly 70 years old, was, it is stated, a teacher for 35 years, including 23 as head of a large school in the city of Valparaíso. He is said to have been subsequently, on two occasions, a member of the Valparaíso City Council and to have been elected twice to the national Parliament as Deputy for the Province of Valparaíso. He alleges that because he has not been allowed to return to Chile his wife, Mrs Irma Hernández Alvarado, who is also nearly 70 and was apparently a teacher for 42 years, is also in exile.

41. At the Committee's [autumn 1983] session the representative of the Chilean Government stated that he was prepared to make humanitarian representations on behalf of Mr Andrade Vera and his wife. The Committee decided to inform the author about this and to re-examine the communication at its present session.[6]

42. At the present session the representative of the government concerned again stated that he thought a solution could be found to this case provided that he could obtain some additional information and offered to contact the Secretariat for that purpose.

43. The Committee accordingly *decided*:

(i) to instruct the Secretariat to take steps to obtain from the author of the communication the information needed by the representative of the Chilean Government;

(ii) to postpone examination of the admissibility of this case until the autumn 1984 session.

Case of Rosaura Mendoza Careaga

44. The author of the communication, Mrs Rosaura Mendoza Careaga, teacher of Spanish, of Chilean nationality, states that following the military coup d'état on 11 September 1973 she was dismissed from the teaching posts which she held at the Catholic University in Frontera and at the University of Chile in Temuco. After taking refuge in the Embassy of the Federal Republic of Germany in November 1973, she was allegedly forced to leave her country on 15 December of that year, together with her family. Her husband., Mr Mario Torres, is said to have also been dismissed from his post as Principal of the "Padre Las Casas" High School in Temuco.

---

[6] See document 117 EX/18 PRIV., para. 74 (*supra*, p. 327).

No. 559/83 **Chile**

45. It is stated that there has been no reply to an application for authorization to return which the author submitted in September 1978 to the Ministry of the Interior in Chile, through the Chilean Consulate in West Berlin. The application for *amparo* submitted on 5 September 1980 to the Court of Appeal at Concepción is said to have been rejected.

46. The representative of the Chilean Government reminded the [Committee] that Chilean citizens wishing to return to Chile had two means of recourse open to them: an administrative recourse which, since the introduction of the new procedures brought to the notice of the [Committee] at preceding sessions, had made it possible to grant 4,217 applications to return, i.e. about 80 per cent of those submitted, and a judicial recourse, the "recurso de amparo" in which connection he wished to draw attention to a ruling of the Supreme Court of Santiago of 30 January 1984 which was very favourable to petitioners whose "recurso de amparo" had been rejected by the Court of Appeal. Since the steps taken by Mrs Rosaura Mendoza Careaga dated back to 1978 and 1980 respectively, the representative of the government concerned considered that they could be taken up once again. Answering a question as to the existence of a prescribed period after which recourse to the High Court would be precluded, he explained that another "recurso de amparo" could be submitted in the event of new circumstances changing the legal status of the person concerned and, should it be rejected, the petitioner could then apply to the Supreme Court. When asked which of the two procedures was to be preferred, he replied that the legal procedure offered the advantage of procuring a legal decision, but that the administrative procedure was probably quicker and was the only one in connection with which he could propose his good offices on humanitarian grounds. Then again, should the administrative recourse fail, the legal procedure was still open. He also said that he was not in a position to give an opinion as to the employment opportunities that would be open to Mrs Rosaura Mendoza Careaga.

47. The Legal Adviser, answering a question put by one of the Committee members, said that the problem of the possible return of Mrs Rosaura Mendoza Careaga's husband was not expressly referred to in the communication. One Committee member was in favour of admitting the communication, whereas other members were of the opinion that its examination should be deferred and its author informed of the means of recourse at her disposal.

48. After an exchange of views the Committee *decided*:

(i) to inform the author of the communication of the forms of administrative and judicial recourse available to her for applying for authorization to return;

(ii) to defer examination of the admissibility of this communication to its autumn 1984 session.

Case of Guillermo Vera Paulo

49. Mr Guillermo Vera Paulo, inspector and teacher of natural sciences at the Polytechnical Institute of Cauquenes alleges that after his arrest in September 1973 he was sentenced to 10 years' imprisonment and debarred for life from holding public office. Subsequently his sentence was commuted to exile. Mr Vera Paulo says that although he had worked for more than 28 years, he had been refused his right to a retirement pension.

50. The representative of the Chilean Government explained that all Chilean citizens, even those resident abroad, enjoyed their right to a retirement pension in the normal way. Although Mr Guillermo Vera Paulo had contributed for only 28 of the 30 years required in order to be granted a retirement pension, he had been informed several years ago by the Fund to which he had contributed that by making a voluntary contribution to cover the missing period he would be able to exercise his rights in the normal way. He did not, however, seem to have taken the necessary action. As he could be assumed to have been prevented from doing so by circumstances beyond his control, the representative of the government concerned said that the a bove-mentioned opportunity of making a voluntary contribution, which Mr Guillermo Vera Paulo ought to have taken earlier, within the prescribed time-limit, might again be made available to him on condition that he applied in writing to the Fund, detailing the circumstances beyond his control which had prevented him from doing so earlier. It was imperative, however, that his application be submitted within one month of receipt of the letter from the Secretariat informing him of this condition. The representative of the government concerned added that he personally would take the necessary steps *vis-à-vis* the Fund concerned.

51. One Committee member was of the opinion that the author of the communication also wished to return to his country.

52. The representative of the Chilean Government said that that was neither the subject nor the purpose of the communication, but that if it was the wish of the person concerned he should make an official application to the appropriate Chilean authorities.

53. The Committee accordingly *decided* to inform the author of the statements made by the representative of the Chilean Government and to defer examination of the admissibility of this communication to its autumn 1984 session.

No. 559/83 **Chile**

Autumn 1984 session of the Committee on Conventions and Recommendations (120th session of the Executive Board)[7]

Case of Carlos Alfredo Andrade Vera

18. The author of the communication, Mr Carlos Alfredo Andrade Vera, who is nearly 70 years old, was, it is stated, a teacher for 35 years, including 23 as head of a large school in the city of Valparaíso. He is said to have been subsequently, on two occasions, a member of the Valparaíso City Council and to have been elected twice to the national Parliament as Deputy for the Province of Valparaíso. He alleges that because he has not been allowed to return to Chile his wife, Mrs Irma Hernández Alvarado, who is also nearly 70 and was apparently a teacher for 42 years, is also in exile.

19. By a letter dated 14 July 1984 [...],[8] the author of the communication had replied to the questions which the Committee had instructed the Secretariat to ask him at its [spring 1984] session. Furthermore, by a telex of 17 September 1984, Mr C. A. Andrade Vera had stated that he had submitted a fresh application to the Chilean Ministry of the Interior by a special-delivery letter on 15 September 1984.

20. The representative of the Chilean Government stated that this case was eminently worthy of the humanitarian concern of the Committee in view of the background and age of the person concerned. Accordingly, he had looked into the matter, but his efforts had been hampered by the fact that Mr C. A. Andrade Vera had placed his name on a list of Members of Parliament in exile, although his exile was voluntary, while the situation had been further complicated by a similarity of names; that was why it had taken some time to clarify the situation. This being the case, and in view of the additional information provided by Mr C. A. Andrade Vera, he was convinced that a solution satisfactory to Mr Andrade Vera would be reached some time in October 1984.

21. After an exchange of views, the Committee *decided* to regard this communication as settled and to strike it from its list, subject to confirmation that Mr C. A. Andrade Vera had in fact been allowed to return to Chile; in the event that such confirmation had not reached the Secretariat before its next session, this communication would be included on the agenda at the Committee's spring 1985 session.

---

[7] See document 120 EX/15 PRIV., paras. 18-31; see also documents 120 EX/CR/HR/2 and Add.

[8] See document 120 EX/CR/HR/2 Add.

Chile **No. 559/83**

Case of Rosaura Mendoza Careaga

22. The author of the communication, Mrs Rosaura Mendoza Careaga, teacher of Spanish, of Chilean nationality, states that following the military coup d'état on 11 September 1973 she was dismissed from the teaching posts which she held at the Catholic University in Frontera and at the University of Chile in Temuco. After taking refuge in the Embassy of the Federal Republic of Germany in November 1973, she was allegedly forced to leave her country on 15 December of that year, together with her family. Her husband, Mr Mario Torres, is said to have also been dismissed from his post as Principal of the "Padre Las Casas" High School in Temuco.

23. It is stated that there has been no reply to an application for authorization to return which the author submitted in September 1978 to the Ministry of the Interior in Chile, through the Chilean Consulate in West Berlin. The application for *amparo* submitted on 5 September 1980 to the Court of Appeal at Concepción is said to have been rejected.

24. The representative of the Chilean Government reiterated the offer to use his good offices which, as he reminded the Committee, he had made at the [spring 1984] session. However, he emphasized that it was essential for Mrs R. Mendoza Careaga to act quickly in submitting an application for reconsideration, referring to the procedure established by the Chilean authorities in August 1983; in that connection, he pointed out that the applications submitted by the person concerned dated back some considerable time and hence had not been covered by the new regulations. For his own part, he was certain that if Mrs Mendoza Careaga were to do that the case could be resolved quickly.

25. After discussion, the Committee *decided* to regard this communication as settled and to strike it from its list, subject to confirmation that Mrs R. Mendoza Careaga had in fact been allowed to return to Chile; in the event that such confirmation had not reached the Secretariat before the next session, this communication would be included on the agenda at the Committee's spring 1985 session.

26. As the report was being adopted, the Secretariat confirmed to the Committee that the alleged victim had been authorized to return to Chile unconditionally and definitively.

Case of Guillermo Vera Paulo

27. Mr Guillermo Vera Paulo, inspector and teacher of natural sciences at the Polytechnical Institute of Cauquenes alleges that after his arrest in September 1973 he was sentenced to 10 years' imprisonment and debarred for life from holding public

office. Subsequently his sentence was commuted to exile. Mr Vera Paulo says that although he had worked for more than 28 years, he had been refused his right to a retirement pension.

28. At its [spring 1984] session, the Committee had asked the Secretariat to inform Mr G. Vera Paulo that the competent Chilean authorities were prepared to offer him an opportunity to become eligible for a pension on condition that he fulfilled certain financial conditions; on 17 June 1984 the author of the communication had written to the Secretariat to state that taking advantage of the offer that had been made to him, he had got in touch with the Pension Fund to which he belonged and had agreed to meet the conditions enabling him to enjoy his pension rights; in the same letter he had stated that he was deeply grateful to Unesco.

29. At the present session, the representative of the Chilean Government stated that without prejudice to Mr G. Vera Paulo's decision in the matter of his pension, he had included him in the initiatives he was undertaking on behalf of persons wishing to return to Chile; in that connection, he considered that Mr Vera Paulo's case should not present any problems provided only that he made use of the appropriate procedures, concerning which he should be informed.

30. The Legal Adviser noted that the communication did not formally raise the issue of the author's return to his country.

31. Accordingly, the Committee *decided* to inform the author of the communication of the statements made by the representative of the Chilean Government, and to regard the communication as settled and to strike it from its list, subject to receiving confirmation that Mr Vera Paulo was indeed able to enjoy his pension rights, it being understood that if information to that effect had not reached the Secretariat before the next session, the communication would be included in the Committee's agenda for its spring 1985 session.

Spring 1985 session of the Committee on Conventions and Recommendations (121st session of the Executive Board)[9]

34. One of the authors of this communication, Mr Carlos Alfredo Andrade Vera, who is nearly 70 years old, is stated to have been a teacher for 35 years, including 23 as head of a large school in the city of Valparaíso. He is said to have been subsequently, on two occasions, a member of the Valparaíso City Council and to have been elected twice to the national Parliament as Deputy for the Province of Valparai-

[9] See document 121 EX/46 PRIV., paras. 34-42; see also document 121 EX/CR/HR/2.

so. He alleges that because he was not allowed to return to Chile with his wife, Mrs Irma Hernández Alvarado, she - who is also nearly 70 and was apparently a teacher for 42 years - is also in exile.

35. The other person concerned by this communication, Mr Guillermo Vera Paulo, inspector and teacher of natural sciences at the Polytechnical Institute of Cauquenes, alleges that after his arrest in September 1973 he was sentenced to 10 years' imprisonment and debarred for life from holding public office. Subsequently his sentence was commuted to exile. Mr Vera Paulo says that, although he had worked for more than 28 years, he had been refused his right to a retirement pension.

36. At the [autumn 1984] session, the representative of the Chilean Government had said that he was convinced that a solution satisfactory to Mr C. A. Andrade Vera would be reached some time in October 1984. For his part, Mr G. Vera Paulo had informed the Committee that he had got into touch with the Pension Fund to which he belonged in accordance with the instructions given to him.. The representative of the government concerned had added that, although Mr Vera Paulo had not explicitly made any such request, he had included him in the representations he was making on behalf of persons wishing to return to Chile, and that his case should not present any problem.

37. The Committee had accordingly decided to consider the communication as settled and to strike it from its list, subject to receiving confirmation that Mr C. A. Andrade Vera had indeed been authorized to return to Chile, and that Mr Vera Paulo was indeed able to enjoy his pension rights, it being understood that if information to that effect had not reached the Secretariat before the Committee's current session, the communication would then be included in its agenda.[10]

38. On 4 February 1985, the Secretariat received from Mr G. Vera Paulo a letter [...][11] in which he explained that he had taken steps to return to Chile, and that the problem of his pension rights was still awaiting solution.

39. The Secretariat has received nothing concerning Mr C. A. Andrade Vera. At the current session, the representative of the Chilean Government said that he had secured, for Mr C. A. Andrade Vera and for others, the introduction of an exceptional procedure designed to enable them to return to Chile for a period of 60 days in order to have their situation reviewed on the spot in Santiago. If those concerned wished then to get into touch with him at the Ministry of External Relations, he proposed to help them in taking the appropriate steps. He added that, in order to obtain such au-

[10] See document 120 EX/15 PRIV., paras. 21 and 31 (*supra*, pp. 332 and 334), respectively.
[11] See document 121 EX/CR/HR/2, annex I.

thorization, the persons concerned should submit a request to that effect to the Chilean Consulate in Paris any time after 15 May 1985. That Consulate would be empowered to issue passports to them and the necessary documents authorizing them temporarily but unconditionally to travel at whatever dates suited them.

40. So far as Mr G. Vera Paulo was concerned, the representative of the government concerned stated that, contrary to what he had been led to expect, the problem of his pension rights had not been solved, but that he, too, could obtain the abovementioned temporary authorization and settle the question on the spot.

41. One member of the Committee regretted that these cases, which had been presented as virtually settled at the [autumn 1984] session, were in fact not settled. Other Committee members expressed their appreciation of the efforts made by the representative of the government concerned while at the same time urging that the communication be kept on the Committee's agenda in the hope that these cases would shortly be satisfactorily settled.

42. After discussion, the Committee *decided*:

(i) to take note of the statements made by the representative of the government concerned and to instruct the Secretariat to inform the authors of the communication accordingly;

(ii) to resume its examination of the admissibility of this communication at its autumn 1985 session.

Autumn 1985 session of the Committee on Conventions and Recommendations (122nd session of the Executive Board)[12]

Case of Carlos Alfredo Andrade Vera

31. One of the authors of this communication, Mr Carlos Alfredo Andrade Vera, who is over 70 years old, is stated to have been a teacher for 35 years, including 23 as head of a large school in the city of Valparaíso. He is said to have been subsequently, on two occasions, a member of the Valparaíso City Council and to have been elected twice to the national Parliament as Deputy for the Province of Valparaíso. He alleges that because he was not allowed to return to Chile with his wife,

[12] See document 122 EX/21 PRIV., paras. 31-41; see also documents 122 EX/CR/HR/2 and Add.

Mrs Irma Hernández Alvarado, she - who is herself nearly 70 and was apparently a teacher for 42 years - is also in exile.

32. At its [spring 1985] session, the Committee had decided to inform Mr Carlos Alfredo Andrade Vera that the Chilean authorities had made available to him an exceptional procedure enabling him to return temporarily and clarify his situation on the spot.[13]

33. On 31 May and 3 September 1985 the Secretariat received from the author of the communication two letters dated respectively 18 May [...][14] and 19 August. From these, it emerges that, following two operations undergone by him early in 1985, Mr Carlos Alfredo Andrade Vera's state of health is very precarious. As a result, he cannot contemplate making the return journey to Chile from the German Democratic Republic and then, in the event of a favourable response, back to Chile again with his wife and belongings. Furthermore, he has no assurance that he will not meet with a refusal. He therefore feels able to travel only once in order to return for good and thinks that the Chilean Government might authorize him to do so out of consideration for his age, his state of health and the fact that he has been away from his country and his family for more than 11 years. While thanking Unesco for obtaining a 60-day authorization, he requests it to press for a permanent authorization. Lastly, he expresses the hope that any formalities that he might be required to comply with can be seen to at the Consulate in West Berlin.

34. At the present session, the representative of the government regretted that Mr Carlos Alfredo Andrade Vera could not use the temporary authorization granted to him. He emphasized that, in any event, the authorization had not ceased to be valid and that the person concerned could avail himself of it when he was in better health. However, the representative of the government concerned stated that he was willing to use his good offices on humanitarian grounds and suggested that Mr Carlos Alfredo Andrade Vera should, as soon as possible, send a medical certificate to the Unesco Secretariat, describing precisely his present state of health. The Secretariat would pass the certificate on to him and with its help, he would try to arrange for an authorization to return permanently to be granted to Mr Carlos Alfredo Andrade Vera. He then confirmed that Mr Carlos Alfredo Andrade Vera could apply to the Consulate in West Berlin rather than to the one in Paris, if he so wished.

35. The members of the Committee who took the floor expressed the wish that, on humanitarian grounds, an authorization to return permanently should be granted to

---

[13] See document 121 EX/46 PRIV., para. 42 (i) (*supra*, p. 336).
[14] See document 122 EX/CR/HR/2.

Mr Carlos Alfredo Andrade Vera in view of his state of health, which could be duly attested by a medical certificate.

36. After an exchange of views, the Committee *decided*:

(i) to instruct the Secretariat to transmit to the author of the communication the statements made by the representative of the government concerned;

(ii) to resume its examination of the admissibility of this communication at its spring 1986 session.

Case of Guillermo Vera Paulo

37. The other person concerned by this communication, Mr Guillermo Vera Paulo, inspector and teacher of natural sciences at the Polytechnical Institute of Cauquenes, alleges that after his arrest in September 1973 he was sentenced to 10 years' imprisonment and debarred for life from holding public office. Subsequently his sentence was commuted to exile. Mr Vera Paulo says that, although he had worked for more than 28 years, he had been refused his right to a retirement pension.

38. After receiving from the author of the communication, on 13 August 1985, a letter dated 1 July [...][15] in which Mr Guillermo Vera Paulo explained that he had still not obtained satisfaction, the Secretariat received on 21 August another letter dated 13 August 1985 stating that the Pension Fund to which Mr Guillermo Vera Paulo belonged had finally allowed him to contribute voluntarily to make up the 30 years' service needed to entitle him to a pension. Mr Guillermo Vera Paulo expresses his profound gratitude to Unesco, considering that such a result could not have been obtained without the Organization's support. He consequently feels that there is no point in his case continuing to be examined.

39. At the present session, the representative of the Government of Chile explained that there had been some delay in solving this problem because questions relating to pension rights were complex. He stated that the authorization to return temporarily which had been granted to the person concerned (and of which he had notified the Committee at its [spring 1985] session) remained valid. Mr Guillermo Vera Paulo could avail himself of it at any time, but the sooner he did so the sooner he would be able to receive an authorization to return permanently.

40. The members of the Committee who took the floor said that they were satisfied to see this case settled.

[15] See document 122 EX/CR/HR/2 Add.

Chile **No. 559/83**

41. The Committee consequently *decided* to consider that this communication was a matter settled under 104 EX/Decision 3.3, paragraph 14 (*a*) (x), and to strike it from its list.

Spring 1986 session of the Committee on Conventions and Recommendations (124th session of the Executive Board)[16]

28. The author of this communication, who is over 70 years old, is stated to have been a teacher for 35 years, including 23 as head of a large school in the city of Valparaíso. He is said to have been subsequently, on two occasions, a member of the Valparaíso City Council and to have been elected twice to the national Parliament as Deputy for the Province of Valparaíso. He alleges that because he was not allowed to return to Chile with his wife, Mrs Irma Hernández Alvarado, she - who is herself nearly 70 and was apparently a teacher for 42 years - is also in exile.

29. When this communication was examined at the present session of the Committee, the Committee was informed that on 11 February 1986 the Secretariat had received from the author of the communication a letter dated 3 February 1986 stating that on 21 December 1985 he had been authorized to return to Chile and thanking Unesco for its good offices.

30. The representative of the government concerned for his part, confirmed that Mr Carlos Alfredo Andrade Vera had indeed received permanent unconditional authorization to return to Chile.

31. In consequence, the Committee *decided* to declare the case raised by the communication settled under the terms of 104 EX/Decision 3.3, paragraph 14 (*a*) (x).

---

[16] See document 124 EX/3 PRIV., paras. 28-31; see also document 124 EX/CR/HR/2.

No. 560/83

Concerning *Union of Soviet Socialist Republics*
Case of *Anatoli Raben*

Communication of 20 June 1983 submitted by
Michel A. Calvo*

Autumn 1983 session of the Committee on Conventions and Recommendations (117th session of the Executive Board)[1]

176. The communication describes the alleged victim, Mr Anatoli Raben as a professor of medicine, of Jewish origin and aged 60. Arrested in 1950 and charged among other things with anti-sovietism, spreading pro-American propaganda and belonging to a counter-revolutionary organization, Mr Raben was apparently sentenced to 10 years in a labour camp. He was reportedly released in August 1954 and cleared some months later. It is claimed that, having been compelled to give up his work at the Academy of Medical Sciences of the USSR as soon as he submitted his application to emigrate, Mr Raben who is said to be a highly qualified professor of oncology is at present allegedly unable to find work in any branch of his field of specialization or to consult scientific libraries.

177. The representative of the government concerned who is also a member of the Committee stated that there had been no violation of the human rights of Mr Raben. The representative informed the Committee that the facts presented in the communication were not accurate. In this connection, he explained that there was no prohibition against Mr Raben working as oncologist, publishing scientific works or otherwise pursuing intellectual and scientific activities in the fields of his qualification and experience. He added that the problem with Mr Raben was that he was insisting on his being given back the same post which he had voluntarily relinquished at the time he made his unsuccessful application for authorization to emigrate.

* On behalf of Laurent Schwartz, Alfred Kastler, Paul Kessler, André Lwoff, David Ruzié and Léon Schwartzenberg.

[1] See document 117 EX/18 PRIV., paras. 176-179; see also document 117 EX/CR/HR/3.

[177a]. A member of the Committee remarked in this connection that the stated purpose and aim of the communication was not to have Mr Raben given back his former post but rather to enable him to teach, publish, pursue his research, have contact with his Soviet and foreign colleagues and participate in scientific meetings. Another member specifically asked if Mr Raben had the liberty to have contacts with his Soviet and foreign colleagues and to participate in scientific meetings. A member also queried if Mr Raben was in fact requested to resign as an indispensable pre-condition for a fair consideration of his application to emigrate. One other member indicated that it would be useful for the Committee to be informed of what Mr Raben has been doing professionally since his resignation in 1979. Another member of the Committee, on his part, stated that he would like to know what remedies were available to the alleged victim.

178. In answer to some members of the Committee who wanted to know if the alleged victim could obtain alternative employment which would be commensurate with his qualifications and experience, the representative of the government stated that, in the USSR, there were dozens of medical centres of high standing at which Mr Raben could endeavour to obtain employment. In reply to the question whether Mr Raben could travel to attend international scientific meetings outside the USSR, the representative of the government concerned said that there were rules governing travel abroad. He added that he could not give detailed information on these rules. He drew attention, however, to the relationship that existed between travel abroad and emigration. On whether Mr Raben risked being labelled a parasite, he stated that the alleged victim was an eminent scientist and, far from such a situation arising, he hoped Mr Raben would be able to continue to make a contribution in the field of research on cancer.

179. At the end of the discussion concerning this communication, the Committee *decided*:

(i) to take note of the information provided by the representative of the government concerned;

(ii) that, at its next session, it would welcome from the government concerned additional information, especially in respect of the following;

(iii) that this decision should also be communicated to the authors concerned on the understanding that they may also provide the Committee with additional information;

(iv) to suspend until its spring 1984 session the examination of the admissibility of the communication.

Union of Soviet Socialist Republics **No. 560/83**

Spring 1984 session of the Committee on Conventions and Recommendations (119th session of the Executive Board)[2]

Autumn 1984 session of the Committee on Conventions and Recommendations (120th session of the Executive Board)[3]

158. Mr Anatoli Raben, a professor of oncology, is alleged to have been compelled to give up his employment as a result of his application to emigrate and is said to be unable to find work in any branch of his special field, use scientific libraries, or attend international conferences.

159. After recalling what his predecessor had said at the Committee's autumn 1983 session on this case, the representative of the Soviet Government, who is also a member of the Committee, stated that Mr Raben was at liberty, that he had reached the age of retirement, that he was receiving a normal pension in quite a normal way and that he had made no request to continue his research activities.

160. In reply to requests from several members of the Committee, the representative of the government concerned explained that the age of retirement in the Soviet Union was ordinarily 55 in the case of women and 60 in the case of men, and that retired persons were free to work subject to certain restrictions, particularly with regard to earnings in view of the fact that they received pensions, but that in any event Mr Raben could not be reappointed to the last position he had held before his retirement.

161. After an exchange of views, the Committee adopted the following *decision*:

> The Committee,
>
> Noting that the alleged victim is now retired, and that, accordingly, the allegations made no longer appear to present themselves in the same human rights context,
>
> Decides, in consequence, to strike the communication from its list.

---

[2] See document 119 EX/35 PRIV., para. 180 (*supra*, p. 178), communication No. 483/82 concerning *Union of Soviet Socialist Republics*, case of *Alleged discrimination in respect of admission to higher education courses in Moscow at the Faculty of Mechanics and Mathematics of the State University, the Institute of Physical Engineering, and the Physical-Technical Institute*.

[3] See document 120 EX/15 PRIV., paras. 158-161; see also document 120 EX/CR/HR/2.

No. 561/83

Concerning *Union of Soviet Socialist Republics*
Case of *Anatoli Khazanov*

Communication of 20 June 1983 submitted by
Michel A. Calvo[*]

Autumn 1983 session of the Committee on Conventions and Recommendations (117th session of the Executive Board)[1]

180. The alleged victim, Mr Anatoli Khazanov is described in the communication as a scientific researcher in ethnography and anthropology, of Jewish origin and aged 46. He is said to have worked from 1960 to 1980 at the Institute of Ethnography of the Academy of Sciences of the USSR. Immediately after his application to emigrate he was reportedly dismissed and was no longer permitted to carry out research or to publish books or papers. It is claimed that Mr Khazanov can no longer teach, publish, pursue scientific research, travel abroad or take part in international conferences and that these restrictions constitute a violation of his human rights falling within Unesco's fields of competence.

181. The representative of the Government of the USSR who is also a member of the Committee indicated that Mr Khazanov had not been dismissed from his post. He said it was a case of voluntary resignation by the alleged victim. It was explained in this connection that many individuals in the USSR who wished to emigrate chose normally to resign voluntarily from their posts either before they submitted their applications for the necessary authorization, or at about the same time. By so doing, they believed they would enhance the chances of having their applications approved especially where a given would-be applicant was subject to certain clearance procedures because of the access he might have to secret or confidential information. It was pointed out that although Mr Khazanov was not in the category of people subject to particular clearance procedures, he had none the less chosen to resign from his post before submitting his application for authorization to emigrate. The representative of the government informed the Committee that while possibilities for finding an alternative post or employment existed, Mr Khazanov might encounter

---

[*] On behalf of Laurent Schwartz, Alfred Kastler, Paul Kessler, André Lwoff and David Ruzié.
[1] See document 117 EX/18 PRIV., paras. 180-182; see also document 117 EX/CR/HR/3.

some difficulties because of the area of his specialization. In his conclusion, the representative of the government concerned formally submitted that the communication be declared inadmissible on the grounds that it contained no information on whether or not an attempt had been made to exhaust available domestic remedies.

182. Considering that, in many material particulars, this case concerning Mr Khazanov was similar to Mr Raben's case [...], the Committee *decided* that the decision it took in the latter case [...][2] should apply *mutatis mutandis* to the present case.

Spring 1984 session of the Committee on Conventions and Recommendations (119th session of the Executive Board)[3]

Autumn 1984 session of the Committee on Conventions and Recommendations (120th session of the Executive Board)[4]

162. Mr Anatoli Khazanov, who is described by the authors of the communication as an ethnographer and anthropologist, is said to have been dismissed from his employment immediately after applying for permission to emigrate. He has allegedly been unable to teach, publish, continue his scientific research or attend international conferences.

163. According to the representative of the Soviet Government, who is also a member of the Committee, this communication contained inaccuracies, as had been pointed out by his predecessor at the Committee's autumn 1983 session. He stated that Mr Khazanov enjoyed all the rights to which scientists of a particular grade were entitled. He had been denied an emigration visa because in the first place he had an elderly father living in the Soviet Union, for whom he must be regarded as responsible, and in the second place he had no family in Israel. The representative of the Soviet Government emphasized that the restriction in question was entirely in accordance with the Soviet Union's national legislation and the international obligations to which it had subscribed. He maintained that it was not true that Mr Khazanov had been relieved of his duties immediately after his application for permission

---

[2] *Ibidem*, para. 179 (*supra*, p. 342), communication No. 560/83 concerning *Union of Soviet Socialist Republics*, case of *Anatoli Raben*.

[3] See document 119 EX/35 PRIV., para. 180 (*supra*, p. 178), communication No. 483/82 concerning *Union of Soviet Socialist Republics*, case of *Alleged discrimination in respect of admission to higher education courses in Moscow at the Faculty of Mechanics and Mathematics of the State University, the Institute of Physical Engineering, and the Physical-Technical Institute*.

[4] See document 120 EX/15 PRIV., paras. 162-165; see also document 120 EX/CR/HR/2.

to emigrate. That application had been submitted in January 1980. Over a year later, in April 1981, Mr Khazanov had been required, in accordance with the usual Soviet practice of making appointments by means of examinations, to submit to an examination based on his scientific colleagues' assessment of his work and the results of his research over the previous five years. The Scientific Council, in a decision reached by secret ballot, had not re-elected him to his post. He had thus been unsuccessful, but despite this, the director of the institute concerned had, for humanitarian reasons, nevertheless kept him on at the establishment in a different post at a lower level than the one he had previously held. The representative of the Soviet Government added that the person concerned could enter for other examinations and that every opportunity was open to him to work in the Soviet Union, except at the abovementioned Institute. In this connection, he indicated that the case should be considered inadmissible.

164. Of the members of the Committee who spoke, some pointed out that the authors of the communication had not provided any additional information, in particular on efforts to exhaust domestic remedies. Others expressed astonishment that Mr Khazanov should have lost his job, his right to meet foreign colleagues and his right to attend international scientific meetings as a result of a vote. Others again emphasized that the problem of emigration was not within Unesco's fields of competence, that Mr Khazanov was still working as a scientist and that it was curious to refer to his right to teach inasmuch as he had no training as a teacher.

165. After discussion, the Committee adopted the following *decision*:

> The Committee decides, with a view to enabling the authors of the communication to take note of the information provided by the representative of the government concerned, to suspend examination of this communication until its spring 1985 session.

Spring 1985 session of the Committee on Conventions and Recommendations (121st session of the Executive Board)[5]

169. Mr Anatoli Khazanov, an ethnographer and anthropologist, is said to have been dismissed from his employment immediately after applying for permission to emigrate. He has allegedly been unable to teach, publish, continue his scientific research or attend international conferences.

---

[5] See document 121 EX/46 PRIV., paras. 169-172; see also document 121 EX/CR/HR/2.

No. 561/83 **Union of Soviet Socialist Republics**

170. Reminding the Committee of the information he had provided at its autumn 1984 session, the representative of the government concerned stated that Mr Khazanov's situation was perfectly clear: he had not been dismissed because of his application to emigrate; in accordance with the usual Soviet practice of appointing scientists on the results of examinations, he was required to sit a periodic examination in order to remain in his post; although he had failed that test, he had, on humanitarian grounds, been kept on at the Institute where he was working in a different post at a lower grade, on the understanding that he had every opportunity to enter for other examinations. In regard to the allegations that he was unable to teach, it was pointed out that he was not a teacher; if he wished to become one, he could take all the necessary steps to do so; in any event, nobody had any intention of humiliating him in any way. The refusal of an emigration visa was due to family considerations. In reply to a question concerning opportunities for the anthropologist to publish his work, the representative of the government concerned said that Mr Khazanov participated in the normal way in scientific research work and reviews.

171. Some of the members of the Committee who spoke remarked that the authors of the communication had provided no additional information, that the explanations given by the representative of the government concerned were adequate and reassuring, and that consideration of the communication should therefore be terminated; others, noting that the communication was submitted by a group of renowned professors, including three Nobel Prize-winners, and that it concerned a scientist who was highly regarded in international anthropological circles, who seemed to have lost his high-level post solely because he had requested permission to emigrate, wished to express their concern; they felt that the case of that scientist was not the only one of its kind but was similar to those of other scientists in the same position. That was symptomatic of a prevailing situation which gave them serious cause for concern; some argued that the fact of taking part in scientific research work and reviews did not mean that Mr Khazanov's writings were published, and expressed their concern in that respect as well. Other members, while noting that the government concerned could do no more for Mr Khazanov and that the problem of emigration did not fall within Unesco's sphere of competence, were reluctant to agree to the communication's being struck from the Committee's list.

172. After an exchange of views, the Committee *decided* to strike the communication concerned from its list, it being understood that the authors might, if they had fresh relevant information, submit a new communication to the Committee should they so desire.

No. 564/83

Concerning *Unoin of Soviet Socialist Republics*
Case of *Igor Guberman*

Communication of 28 June 1983 submitted by
Michel A. Calvo*

Autumn 1983 session of the Committee on Conventions and Recommendations (117th session of the Executive Board)[1]

183. Mr Igor Guberman, aged 47, is described in the communication as a poet and writer of Jewish origin. In December 1978, he is said to have submitted an application to emigrate, which was turned down. In May 1979, persons claiming to belong to the KGB reportedly asked him for information about the editors of the samizdat journal "The Jew in the Soviet Union" and told him to stop writing poems and political anecdotes. He apparently refused. On 13 August 1979, he is said to have been arrested for having purchased stolen icons and, in March 1980, he was sentenced to five years' hard labour and his property confiscated. Mr Guberman's human rights are alleged to have been violated because by his imprisonment it is claimed that he is prevented from expressing himself in his own language, that is to say poetry, from writing, from having his works published and from participating in cultural life.

184. In giving his government's version of the case, the member of the Committee who represented the USSR said that Mr Guberman had been charged, tried and convicted for dishonestly purchasing icons stolen by third parties from churches. The representative of the government concerned explained that it was usual for persons intending to emigrate from the USSR to try to turn the wealth they might have in that country into items of value, such as icons, to smuggle them out of the country. He added that icons were such items. Pointing out that Mr Guberman had been imprisoned for an act which constituted an ordinary crime under the penal legislation of the USSR, the representative of the government concerned invited the Committee to declare inadmissible the communication under consideration.

---

* On behalf of Bernard Dupuy, Alfred Kastler, Paul Kessler, André Lwoff, David Ruzié, Laurent Schwartz and Pierre Emmanuel.

[1] See document 117 EX/18 PRIV., paras. 183-189; see also document 117 EX/CR/HR/3.

No. 564/83 **Union of Soviet Socialist Republics**

185. Several members of the Committee expressed concern over the punishment meted out to Mr Guberman. In this connection, they pointed out that the alleged victim was sentenced to five years' hard labour and his property confiscated while the two persons prosecuted for theft and whose declarations had provided the basis for Mr Guberman's prosecution had been sentenced to three years' imprisonment only.

186. The representative of the government stated however that the sentence imposed on Mr Guberman was in conformity with applicable laws of the USSR. All the same, one member of the Committee queried if what this member considered to be excessively severe punishment inflicted on the alleged victim had not been influenced by the latter's prior demand for authorization to emigrate. Another member suggested in this connection that, perhaps the relatively light sentences received by the two persons said to have been prosecuted for theft was to be explained by the help they had provided the prosecuting authorities in securing the conviction of Mr Guberman. On this point, it was pointed out that on the basis of the contents of the communication, one could not conclude that what the two persons concerned had been accused of stealing were necessarily the icons allegedly purchased by Mr Guberman, and not something else. It was suggested that the authors of the communication should provide additional information on this point.

187. A member of the Committee proposed that the authors of the communication should be asked to provide further information also on the issue of whether remedies were available for Mr Guberman after his conviction by the lower court and by the appeal court.

188. On the claim that Mr Guberman was a poet and a writer, the representative of the government expressed doubt and said that the alleged victim's writing had been limited to a samizdat journal. Other members of the Committee however took the view that the information at the Committee's disposal indicated clearly that Mr Guberman was a writer and a poet who belonged to the International PEN which is a well-known international literary organization.

189. At the end of its discussion, the Committee *decided* to postpone to its spring 1984 session consideration of the admissibility or otherwise of this communication pending the provision of additional information by the authors concerned.

Union of Soviet Socialist Republics **No. 564/83**

Spring 1984 session of the Committee on Conventions and Recommendations (119th session of the Executive Board)[2]

Autumn 1984 session of the Committee on Conventions and Recommendations (120th session of the Executive Board)[3]

166. Mr Igor Guberman is described by the authors of the communication as a poet and writer. He reportedly applied for authorization to emigrate in December 1978. In May 1979, persons claiming to act on the authority of the KGB allegedly requested him to stop writing anti-Soviet poems and anecdotes. He is said to have refused. He was reportedly arrested in August 1979 and sentenced in March 1980 to five years' hard labour for having bought stolen icons.

167. Recalling the statements made by his predecessor during the autumn 1983 session of the Committee, the representative of the Soviet Government, also a member of the Committee, stated that Mr Guberman had not been recognized as a writer, that he had taken part in the writing of anti-Soviet literature, but that he had not been troubled on that score, the authorities showing indulgence and merely making observations to him. In this connection he referred to a decision of the Executive Board at its 118th session against political interference of the PEN Club which was now interfering in the internal affairs of the USSR regarding Mr Guberman. If he had been sentenced, the representative of the Soviet Government added, it was because he had contravened the Penal Code in regard to the offences of theft and receiving, by purchasing and selling stolen goods. With regard to the sentence served, the representative of the Soviet Government specified that the person in question had been sent to take part in work of service to the community and that he had not had a hard time. He disclosed, lastly, that Mr Guberman had been released on 13 August 1984.

168. After an exchange of views, the Committee *decided* as follows:

The Committee,

(i) Having been informed of the release of the alleged victim on 13 August 1984,

---

[2] See document 119 EX/35 PRIV., para. 180 (*supra*, p. 178), communication No. 483/82 concerning *Union of Soviet Socialist Republics*, case of *Alleged discrimination in respect of admission to higher education courses in Moscow at the Faculty of Mechanics and Mathematics of the State University, the Institute of Physical Engineering, and the Physical-Technical Institute.*

[3] See document 120 EX/15 PRIV., paras. 166-168; see also document 120 EX/CR/HR/2.

(ii) Considers that the communication should therefore be regarded as settled,

(iii) Decides, accordingly, to strike it from its list.

No. 565/83

Concerning *Union of Soviet Socialist Republics*
Case of *Novosibirisk Association for the Promotion of Friendship between the Peoples of the USSR and Israel*[*]

Communication of 28 June 1983 submitted by
Michel A. Calvo[°]

Autumn 1983 session of the Committee on Conventions and Recommendations (117th session of the Executive Board)[1]

190. It is alleged that Mr Kochubievsky established on 17 November 1979 an association entitled "Novosibirsk Association for the Promotion of Friendship between the Peoples of the Union of Soviet Socialist Republics and Israel". The normal registration procedure is reported to have been followed.

191. The aim of the Association are said to be *inter alia* to study the history and everyday life of Israel, to study Hebrew in order to gain a closer understanding of original documents, to organize lectures and discussions on the history and everyday life of Israel and to exchange information about culture, ways of life, ideas and knowledge in various fields.

192. The Soviet authorities are alleged to have considered the Association to be not in conformity with the legislation in force and declared it an illegal organization. In January 1982 criminal proceedings relating to the steps taken by Mr Kochubievsky to found the Association are said to have been instituted against him. Arrested in September 1982, he was reportedly sentenced, in December 1982, to two and a half years in a labour camp.

---

[*] The complete title of the case was *Novosibirsk Association for the Promotion of Friendship between the Peoples of the USSR and Israel, Mssrs F. Kochubievsky, Gorbman, Perkis, Friedling, Altshul and Land, and Mrs Kochubievskaya.*

[°] On behalf of Henri Paul Cartan, Gérard Cohen-Jonathan, Bernard Dupuy, Alfred Kastler, Paul Kessler, André Lwoff, David Ruzié and Laurant Schwartz.

[1] See document 117 EX/18 PRIV., paras. 190-196; see also document 117 EX/CR/HR/3.

No. 565/83 **Union of Soviet Socialist Republics**

193. In an opening remark, the representative of the Government of the USSR who is also a member of the Committee stated that the legislation in his country permitted the formation of varied associations and societies and that, in fact, many of such associations and societies currently existed and functioned normally. He pointed out however that, as is the practice in many countries, the agreement of the competent authorities is required before an association or society is legally constituted. The representative of the government concerned informed the Committee that the activities of associations and societies constituted in the USSR should contribute to the positive development of the Soviet society. In this connection, he stated that Mr Kochubievsky had praised Mr Begin's policy, which was contrary to the policy of the USSR towards Israel. On relations between the Soviet and Israeli peoples, the government representative informed the Committee that within the Union of Soviet Association for the Promotion of Friendship and Cultural Relations with Foreign Countries, there existed a branch, in fact, that dealt with cultural ties with Israel. He remarked that political realities such as lack of diplomatic relations between the USSR and Israel made cultural contacts between the two countries more difficult than would otherwise be the case.

194. One member of the Committee asked if the interdiction of the Novosibirsk Association was effected at the time registration inquiries were being made or after registration, when it became evident to the Soviet authorities that the activities of the Association were anti-state in character. Another member of the Committee asked why this Association was refused authorization to operate in the USSR while an anti-Zionism committee was functioning normally in the country. Another member stated that a pro-Soviet association existed in Israel and queried why the Novosibirsk Association could not be authorized to operate in the USSR. On this point, another member of the Committee said that, in his view, there were still some obscure elements about the case. He asked what remedy existed when the request for the registration of the Association concerned was rejected. He added that it would also be useful to know if Mr Kochubievsky had been convinced because he tried to form the friendly association in question and, if not, the particulars of the offence he was said to have committed.

195. Remarking that no state tolerated hostile associations, another member of the Committee said the Novosibirsk Association was a hostile organization which under the pretext of friendship between the Soviet and Israeli peoples undertook activities which were not in conformity with the Association's proclaimed objective.

196. After this exchange of views, the Committee *decided*:

(i) to request the Executive Board to invite the Director-General to enter into consultation with the Soviet authorities to determine the conditions in which, having regard to the legislation in force, the association in question might be authorized to function;

(ii) to launch a humanitarian appeal to the government concerned on behalf of Mr Kochubievsky and to suspend consideration of this communication until the spring 1984 session pending receipt of additional information.

Spring 1984 session of the Committee on Conventions and Recommendations (119th session of the Executive Board)[2]

Autumn 1984 session of the Committee on Conventions and Recommendations (120th session of the Executive Board)[3]

169. The Novosibirsk Association for the Promotion of Friendship between the Peoples of the USSR and Israel was reportedly set up in November 1979 by Mr Kochubievsky; it is said that it did not receive authorization to operate for it was declared to be illegal by the Soviet authorities. According to the authors of the communication, because of the steps he had taken in setting up this association, Mr Kochubievsky was allegedly sentenced in December 1982 to two-and-a-half years' internment in a work camp.

170. The representative of the Soviet Government, also a member of the Committee, stated that this communication should be rejected, since it was entirely at variance with the terms of paragraph 14 (*a*) (iv) of 104 EX/Decision 3.3 of the Executive Board according to which a communication, to be admissible "must be compatible with the principles of the Organization, the Charter of the United Nations, the Universal Declaration of Human Rights, the International Covenants on Human Rights and other international instruments in the field of human rights". In his view, the communication sought to influence the Committee in order to exert pressure on a State, arouse mistrust within a State and even between States. In this connection, he referred to the fact that this communication is in radical contradiction with the United Nations Declaration on the Inadmissibility of Intervention and Interference in the Internal Affairs of States adopted in 1981. The representative of the Soviet Government pointed out that the establishment of the association in question infringed leg-

---

[2] See document 119 EX/35 PRIV., para. 180 (*supra*, p. 178), communication No. 483/82 concerning *Union of Soviet Socialist Republics*, case of *Alleged discrimination in respect of admission to higher education courses in Moscow at the Faculty of Mechanics and Mathematics of the State University, the Institute of Physical Engineering, and the Physical-Technical Institute*.

[3] See document 120 EX/15 PRIV., paras. 169-173; see also document 120 EX/CR/HR/2.

islation in force and that what it was setting out to do was not to serve the building of communism as specified in the Constitution of the country, but rather, to justify the acts of a State which was conducting a war of aggression against States friendly to the Soviet Union. He added that the authorities had shown indulgence towards Mr Kochubievsky, the promoter of this association, by giving him a light sentence which would terminate soon. Lastly, he pointed out that Mr Kochubievsky had not applied for the remission of his sentence.

171. Certain members of the Committee, without wishing to dwell at length on the purpose, goal and activities of the association in question, which they did not regard as reprehensible, or on Mr Kochubievsky's sentence, which they found hard to understand since he had acted openly and apparently had intended to comply with the basic principles of the Soviet Union, laid particular stress on the humanitarian aspect of the matter. They did not contest the view that the establishment of an association lay outside Unesco's fields of competence.

172. Some members of the Committee considered that the wisest course would be simply to take a decision of inadmissibility without adding other considerations, since it was not possible to question the laws of a country or interfere in its internal affairs.

173. At the end of its discussions, the Committee adopted the following *decision*:

The Committee,

(i) Notes that the communication submitted to it does not lie within its competence, since it raises the question of the exercise of the right to freedom of association as such, and should therefore be declared inadmissible;

(ii) Requests, nevertheless, the representative of the government concerned to inform the competent authorities of his country of the humanitarian concerns expressed by some of its members.

No. 577/83

Concerning *Chile*
Case of *Víctor Hugo de la Fuente*

Communication of 4 July 1983 submitted by
Víctor Hugo de la Fuente

Autumn 1983 session of the Committee on Conventions and Recommendations (117th session of the Executive Board)[1]

75. The author of this communication is a journalist of Chilean nationality. It is alleged that he first requested permission from the Chilean Consulate in Paris to return to Chile in 1978. He apparently made the same request in 1979 and in 1980, but to no avail. He claims that he submitted a further request to the same Consulate on 1 July 1983.

76. The representative of the government concerned stated that if Mr Víctor Hugo de la Fuente were to submit a request for his case to be re-examined, it would be favourably received.

77. One member of the Committee observed that the last request made by the person concerned dated from 1 July 1983, a time when the new procedure had, some thought, already been established.

78. The representative of the Chilean Government replied that if such were indeed the case, it was sufficient for Mr V. Hugo de la Fuente to indicate on his new request the date on which he had submitted his previous one. At the Committee's request the Secretariat informed the person concerned of the foregoing.

79. Following this short discussion, the Committee *decided* to postpone consideration of the admissibility of this case until the next session.

---

[1] See document 117 EX/18 PRIV., paras. 75-79; see also document 117 EX/CR/HR/3.

No. 577/83 **Chile**

Spring 1984 session of the Committee on Conventions and Recommendations (119th session of the Executive Board)[2]

54. The author of this communication, a journalist of Chilean nationality, is alleged to have first requested permission from the Chilean Consulate in Paris to return to Chile in 1978. He apparently made the same request in 1979 and in 1980, but to no avail. He claims that he submitted a further request to the same Consulate on 1 July 1983.

55. At its [autumn 1983] session, the Committee decided to postpone consideration of the admissibility of the case until the present session,[3] after learning from the representative of the government concerned that if Mr Víctor Hugo de la Fuente were to submit a request for his case to be re-examined it would be favourably received.

56. At the present session, the Committee had before it a letter from the author dated 25 April 1984 explaining that, while he had indeed been authorized to return to Chile temporarily for 30 days in September last, he was still not authorized to return there definitively.

57. The representative of the Chilean Government informed the Committee that, contrary to what the person concerned claimed, the temporary authorization to return to Chile that had been granted to him had been secured not thanks to the intervention of any third party but rather as a result of the steps that he himself had taken at the Committee's request. He expressed his astonishment that the alleged victim had not taken advantage of his stay in Santiago to settle his problem in circumstances that would have been manifestly more favourable than those prevailing abroad. He nevertheless observed that the case did not appear to present major difficulties, but that it might be necessary for the Secretariat to explain once again to Mr Víctor Hugo de la Fuente what steps he should take.

58. After discussion, the Committee *decided*:

(i) to request the Secretariat to contact the person concerned in order to make clear to him what steps he should take;

(ii) to resume consideration of this communication at its autumn 1984 session.

---

[2] See document 119 EX/35 PRIV., paras. 54-58; see also document 119 EX/CR/HR/2.

[3] See document 117 EX/18 PRIV., para. 79 (*supra*, p. 357).

Chile **No. 577/83**

Autumn 1984 session of the Committee on Conventions and Recommendations (120th session of the Executive Board)[4]

32. The author of this communication, a journalist of Chilean nationality, is alleged to have first requested permission from the Chilean Consulate in Paris to return to Chile in 1978. He apparently made the same request in 1979 and in 1980, but to no avail. He claims that he submitted a further request to the same Consulate on 1 July 1983.

33. At the beginning of July 1984, the Secretariat contacted the person concerned in order to explain the steps which he should take, as the Committee had requested it to do at its [spring 1984] session.

34. The representative of the Chilean Government recalled that Mr Víctor Hugo de la Fuente had already been authorized in the past to return temporarily to Chile to settle his problems and to secure authorization for his definitive return once there, but he had not taken any steps. The mother of the person concerned stated that this inertia was due to a family problem; the representative of the government concerned therefore stated that he was prepared to do his utmost to secure a new temporary authorization for Mr de la Fuente to return to Chile, but he insisted that the Secretariat explain to him this time that he should not fail to take the necessary steps to settle his situation.

35. One of the members of the Committee expressed the view that the excuse made by the mother of the author of the communication was somewhat flimsy and wondered whether this situation would not be repeated if another temporary authorization were granted him; he therefore suggested that the person concerned be invited to file an application from France in accordance with the new procedures. Another member of the Committee endorsed this suggestion.

36. The representative of the Chilean Government confirmed that Mr de la Fuente was in fact free to file for an authorization to return and that personally, he would welcome this since it would be likely to help him in his own endeavours.

37. Consequently, the Committee *decided*:

(i) to request the Secretariat to inform the author of the communication of the statements made by the representative of the government concerned, if necessary, by contacting him;

---

[4] See document 120 EX/15 PRIV., paras. 32-37; see also document 120 EX/CR/HR/2.

(ii) to resume consideration of the admissibility of this communication at its [spring 1985] session.

Spring 1985 session of the Committee on Conventions and Recommendations (121st session of the Executive Board)[5]

43. The author of this communication, a journalist of Chilean nationality, is alleged to have first requested permission to return to Chile from the Chilean Consulate in Paris in 1978. He apparently made the same request in 1979 and in 1980, but to no avail. He claims that he submitted a further request to the same Consulate on 1 July 1983.

44. At its [autumn 1984] session, the Committee decided to request the Secretariat to inform the author of the remedies available to him, and to resume consideration of this communication at its present session.[6]

45. At the present session, the representative of the Chilean Government remarked that this case highlighted the difficulties with which he had to contend: not content with providing the necessary information, he took the trouble, in certain circumstances involving humanitarian considerations, to intervene personally on behalf of the persons concerned; but they themselves did not then complete the appropriate formalities, or did not do so correctly. He reminded the Committee that Mr Víctor Hugo de la Fuente had already been granted a temporary authorization to return of which he had not taken advantage as he should have done. The representative of the government concerned added that he had nevertheless again managed to ensure that such an opportunity was offered to Mr Víctor Hugo de la Fuente on the same conditions as he had outlined in connection with [another communication];[7] this time, however, it was imperative that Mr Víctor Hugo de la Fuente should avail himself of this opportunity to clear up his position.

46. Two members of the Committee spoke in favour of keeping the communication on the Committee's agenda. Several Committee members, in the light of the statements made by the representative of the Chilean Government, felt that the communication should be struck off its list, pointing in particular to the scant efforts made by the person concerned himself despite the fact that the Committee had been examining his case for many sessions. One member suggested that the Committee should make it clear to the author of the communication that he would be granted no further

---

[5] See document 121 EX/46 PRIV., paras. 43-47; see also document 121 EX/CR/HR/2.
[6] See document 120 EX/15 PRIV., para. 37 (*supra*, pp. 359-360).
[7] See document 121 EX/46 PRIV., para. 39 (*supra*, pp. 335-336), communication No. 559/83 concerning *Chile*, case of *Carlos Alfredo Andrade Vera and Guillermo Vera Paulo*.

opportunity, and that if he did not take advantage of this one, the Committee would automatically strike his communication from its list at its next session. Most of the Committee members who spoke subsequently endorsed this proposal.

47. The Committee accordingly *decided*:

(i) to suspend examination of the admissibility of this communication until its autumn 1985 session;

(ii) to inform the author of the communication that, should he fail to make use of the exceptional procedure once again made available to him by applying to the Chilean Consulate in Paris, the Committee would *ipso facto* strike his communication from its list at its [autumn 1985 session].

Autumn 1985 session of the Committee on Conventions and Recommendations (122nd session of the Executive Board)[8]

42. The author of this communication, a journalist of Chilean nationality, is said to have first requested the Chilean Consulate in Paris for permission to return to Chile in 1978. He repeated his request in 1979 and in 1980, but to no avail. He claims that he submitted a further request to the same Consulate on 1 July 1983.

43. At the [spring 1985] session, the Committee decided to inform the author of the communication of the new exceptional procedure for obtaining temporary authorization to return, made available to him by the Chilean authorities, and to strike the communication off its list if he had not availed himself of the opportunity.[9]

44. On 2, 26 and 29 August 1985, the Secretariat received from Mr Víctor Hugo de la Fuente three letters dated respectively 30 July and 13 and 21 August 1985, from which it is apparent that he took the necessary steps to go to Chile, where he contacted the appropriate office in the Ministry of the Interior. The text of this application, dated 19 August 1985, was attached to his most recent letter.

45. At this session, the representative of the Chilean Government noted that, in contrast with what had happened before, the person concerned had this time taken the necessary steps to solve his problem. The Chilean representative had in fact met him on several occasions and had helped him to draft his application. He added that he had requested for him an extension of the 60-day limit on his permission to stay and

[8] See document 122 EX/21 PRIV., paras. 42-47; see also document 122 EX/CR/HR/2.
[9] See document 121 EX/46 PRIV., para. 47 (ii) (*supra*, p. 361).

hoped that there would be a favourable outcome before the end of 1985. He felt nevertheless that Mr Víctor Hugo de la Fuente was acting rather slowly.

46. One member said that he was pleased that the author of the communication had availed himself of this further opportunity given to him, since he had not done so previously. Another member said that it was understandable that the author was acting slowly because, in addition to the problem of his return, he was likely to come up against an employment problem in his special field in Chile. The Committee members who spoke were of the opinion that the communication should be kept on the Committee's agenda.

47. At the close of its deliberations, the Committee *decided* to resume examination of the admissibility of this communication at its spring 1986 session in the hope that a favourable solution would be found in the meantime.

Spring 1986 session of the Committee on Conventions and Recommendations (124th session of the Executive Board)[10]

32. The author of this communication, a journalist of Chilean nationality, is said to have first requested the Chilean Consulate in Paris for permission to return to Chile in 1978. He repeated his request in 1979 and in 1980, but to no avail. He claims that he submitted a further request to the same Consulate on 1 July 1983.

33. At the [autumn 1985] session, the Committee, having been informed by the representative of the government concerned that the person in question had taken the necessary steps to solve his problem during his temporary stay in Santiago, that an extension of the 60-day limit on his permission to stay had been requested for him and that there should be a favourable outcome before the end of 1985, had decided to resume examination of the admissibility of the communication at the present session, in the hope that a favourable solution would have been found in the meantime.[11]

34. On 3 April 1986, the Secretariat received from the author of the communication a letter dated 28 March 1986 [...][12] in which he explained that he had been granted a further authorization for temporary entry to Chile for 60 days and that on 30 December 1985 he had gone to Chile, where he had again taken appropriate action; having received no reply, on 4 February he had again written to the Ministry of the Interior

---

[10] See document 124 EX/3 PRIV., paras. 32-37; see also documents 124 EX/CR/HR/2 and Add.2.

[11] See document 122 EX/21 PRIV., para. 47 (*supra*, p. 362).

[12] See document 124 EX/CR/HR/2 Add.2.

stressing the fact that his father was seriously ill and that he wished to stay with him. He had received a reply dated 14 February indicating that the prohibition on his return to Chile was still in force. He thanked the Committee for its assistance and hoped that it would be able to obtain the final withdrawal of the ban on his return to Chile.

35. At the present session, the representative of the government concerned explained that the last negative reply was probably due to the fact that Mr de la Fuente's request had not been submitted in the appropriate form laid down by the procedure in force; that was why he had again requested and obtained for him a provisional authorization to return for 90 days, during which time the person concerned could come and see him at the Ministry of Foreign Affairs; it would also be most useful if Mr de la Fuente or his lawyer requested the Ministry of the Interior to indicate the reasons why permission had been refused. Lastly, he pointed out that he had always shown himself willing to assist the person concerned and was still prepared to use his good offices. In reply to questions from the Chairman and other members of the Committee, the representative of the Chilean Government stated that whatever might be the case in certain other countries, under Chilean law there was no reason why the administrative authority responsibile for a decision should not be requested to provide in writing its reasons for that decision; whether the authority replied or did not reply within a reasonable time, that procedure had in any case the effect of facilitating recourse to the courts, even if it did not constitute an essential precondition of such recourse. In this particular case, moreover, his action would be facilitated if Mr de la Fuente could provide him with a copy of the letter to be written in due course by himself or his lawyer to the Ministry of the Interior, inquiring why permission had been refused.

36. Several members of the Committee considered that it would be desirable to inform the author, to avail the results of his subsequent endeavours, and to resume examination of the admissibility of the communication at the next session, in the hope that there would have been a favourable outcome in the meantime. One member expressed regret that possible errors of form affecting applications could not be corrected in Paris, and that a further visit - which he would like to be certain would yield tangible results - was necessary; supported by many other members of the Committee, he considered that the communication should be regarded as admissible. In that connection, it was pointed out that the fact of declaring a communication admissible did not necessarily have the effect of facilitating a friendly solution.

37. At the close of its deliberations, the Committee *decided*:

(i) to inform the author of the communication of the statements made by the representative of the Chilean Government;

(ii) to declare the communication admissible and to resume examination of it at the Committee's autumn 1986 session.

Autumn 1986 session of the Committee on Conventions and Recommendations (125th session of the Executive Board)[13]

160. Mr Víctor Hugo de la Fuente, a journalist of Chilean nationality, is said to have been unable to obtain permission to return to Chile after submitting several requests to do so.

161. This communication was declared admissible at the Committee's spring 1986 session.[14]

162. At the present session, the representative of the government concerned informed the Committee that Mr de la Fuente had, in Chile, given power of attorney to his own brother. He added that, during an interview, he had provided the latter, with all the relevant explanations and that the situation had been clarified. According to him, the journalist was at present in Chile taking appropriate action. The representative of the Chilean Government expressed his confidence in a satisfactory outcome.

163. After an exchange of views, the Committee *decided*:

(i) to thank the government concerned for having sent a representative;

(ii) to maintain the communication on its list pending the envisaged solution referred to by the representative of that government and to resume consideration of the communication at its spring 1987 session.

Spring 1987 session of the Committee on Conventions and Recommendations (126th session of the Executive Board)[15]

193. Mr Víctor Hugo de la Fuente, a journalist of Chilean nationality, is said to have been unable to obtain permission to return to Chile after submitting several requests to do so.

194. Confirming the substance of the letter dated 11 February 1987 from the Permanent Delegation of Chile to Unesco [...],[16] the representative of the government con-

[13] See document 125 EX/3 PRIV., paras. 160-163; see also document 125 EX/CR/HR/1.
[14] See document 124 EX/3 PRIV., para. 37 (ii) (*supra*, p. 364).
[15] See document 126 EX/3 PRIV., paras. 193-195; see also document 126 EX/CR/HR/1.

cerned stated that Mr de la Fuente had been authorized to return to his country unconditionally and on a permanent basis. He added that persons in that situation who encountered administrative problems could take them up with an interministerial commission which he presided over and which would provide them with all the assistance required to solve them.

195. After an exchange of views, the Committee *decided*:

(i) to thank the representative of the government concerned for his presence and for his co-operation;

(ii) to strike the communication from its list, considering it as settled, in accordance with paragraph 14 (*j*) of 104 EX/Decision 3.3.

[16] See document 126 EX/CR/HR/1, annex.

No. 581/83

Concerning *Islamic Republic of Iran*
Case of *Arrest of leading figures in Iranian cultural life* [*]

Communication of 1 August 1983 submitted by
David Nashtat [°]

Autumn 1983 session of the Committee on Conventions and Recommendations (117th session of the Executive Board)[1]

93. A total of 28 leading figures in Iranian cultural life are said to have been arrested, one in June 1982, and the others in February, April and May 1983. Most of them were over 60 years old. It is alleged that no information can be obtained concerning the charges brought against them.

94. In a letter dated 14 September 1983 which was addressed to the Secretariat [...],[2] the Permanent Delegate of the Islamic Republic of Iran mentioned the slander levelled at his country according to which the Iranian authorities are said to have "sold off", "destroyed" or "offered for sale" the cultural property of his country. In this connection, he drew attention to the conclusions of a mission which the Director-General had sent to Iran and which had invalidated these allegations. The Permanent Delegate added that among those imprisoned who were said to be eminent intellectuals and men of culture were people whose activities were purely political.

---

[*] From the Committee's spring 1984 session, this communication was being referred to as case of *Alleged arrests of eminent personalities in the world of Iranian culture*, at the spring 1988 session as case of *Twenty-eight personalities in the world of culture* and from the autumn 1988 session as case of *Alleged arrests of personalities in the world of Iranian culture*.

[°] On behalf of the International Association of Democratic Lawyers.

[1] See document 117 EX/18 PRIV., paras. 93-95; see also documents 117 EX/CR/HR/3 Add. and 117 EX/CR/HR/2 Add.4.

[2] See document 117 EX/CR/HR/2 Add.4.

No. 581/83 **Islamic Republic of Iran**

95. After an exchange of views and in the light of the examination of [another communication],[3] of the solidarity declared by the government concerned with the objectives of Unesco and its faith in the impartiality of the Director-General, the Committee *decided*:

(i) to suspend examination of the admissibility of this communication until the spring [1984 session];

(ii) to ask the Executive Board to request the Director-General to communicate to the government concerned the appeal for clemency made by the Committee, emphasizing, on the one hand, its concern as regards respect for articles 9 and 14 of the International Covenant on Civil and Political Rights concerning the fair trial of a person who is arrested and, on the other, the recommendation of Imam Khomeiny concerning the release of persons over 60 years of age.

Spring 1984 session of the Committee on Conventions and Recommendations (119th session of the Executive Board)[4]

Autumn 1984 session of the Committee on Conventions and Recommendations (120th session of the Executive Board)[5]

Spring 1985 session of the Committee on Conventions and Recommendations (121st session of the Executive Board)[6]

Autumn 1985 session of the Committee on Conventions and Recommendations (122nd session of the Executive Board)[7]

---

[3] See document 117 EX/18 PRIV., paras. 89-92 (*supra*, pp. 249-250), communication No. 525/83 concerning *Islamic Republic of Iran*, case of *Abolfazl Ghassemi*.
[4] See document 119 EX/35 PRIV., paras. 106-109 (*supra*, p. 251), communication No. 525/83 concerning *Islamic Republic of Iran*, case of *Abolfazl Ghassemi*.
[5] See document 120 EX/15 PRIV., paras. 106-109 (*supra*, pp. 252-253), communication No. 525/83 concerning *Islamic Republic of Iran*, case of *Abolfazl Ghassemi*.
[6] See document 121 EX/46 PRIV., paras. 94-96 (*supra*, pp. 253-254), communication No. 525/83 concerning *Islamic Republic of Iran*, case of *Abolfazl Ghassemi*.
[7] See document 122 EX/21 PRIV., paras. 78-82 (*supra*, pp. 254-255), communication No. 525/83 concerning *Islamic Republic of Iran*, case of *Abolfazl Ghassemi*.

Islamic Republic of Iran **No. 581/83**

Spring 1986 session of the Committee on Conventions and Recommendations (124th session of the Executive Board)[8]

Autumn 1986 session of the Committee on Conventions and Recommendations (125th session of the Executive Board)[9]

Spring 1987 session of the Committee on Conventions and Recommendations (126th session of the Executive Board)[10]

66. This communication alleges that in Iran, in 1982 and 1983, 28 persons eminent in the world of Iranian culture, whose names are listed [...],[11] were arrested and imprisoned without their families being able to see them or obtain information about their fate or the charges brought against them.

67. At the Committee's [autumn 1986] session, the representative of the government concerned stated that the 28 persons had been convicted not for their cultural and intellectual activities but for espionage on behalf of a foreign power and for preparing a coup d'état. In its decision, the Committee, *inter alia*, reiterated its request for further information relating to the age of those convicted, the circumstances of their trial, the terms of their sentences and the conditions under which they were serving their sentences.[12]

68. The government concerned did not send a representative to this session. The Permanent Delegate of the Islamic Republic of Iran sent a letter to the Secretariat containing information concerning [another communication] only.[13]

69. The members of the Committee who took the floor said that, while it was gratifying to note the favourable outcome of [that communication], they could only express their regret at the inadequacy and vagueness of the information provided about

---

[8] See document 124 EX/3 PRIV., paras. 85-92 (*supra*, pp. 255-257), communication No. 525/83 concerning *Islamic Republic of Iran*, case of *Abolfazl Ghassemi*.
[9] See document 125 EX/3 PRIV., paras. 64-66 (*supra*, pp. 257-258), communication No. 525/83 concerning *Islamic Republic of Iran*, case of *Abolfazl Ghassemi*.
[10] See document 126 EX/3 PRIV., paras. 66-70; see also document 126 EX/CR/HR/2.
[11] See document 117 EX/CR/HR/3 Add.
[12] See document 125 EX/3 PRIV., para. 66 (iv) (*supra*, p. 258).
[13] Communication No. 525/83 concerning *Islamic Republic of Iran*, case of *Abolfazl Ghassemi*.

the present communication, by the government concerned, despite repeated requests by the Committee.

70. After an exchange of views, the Committee *decided*:

(i) to reiterate its regret that the government concerned had not sent a representative;

(ii) also to express its regret that it had received no information about the sequel to its humanitarian appeal to that government;

(iii) to request the Executive Board to ask the Director-General to use his good offices to transmit this humanitarian appeal once more to the government concerned;

(iv) to take a decision on the admissibility of this communication at its autumn 1987 session.

Autumn 1987 session of the Committee on Conventions and Recommendations (127th session of the Executive Board)[14]

90. This communication alleges that in Iran, in 1982 and 1983, 28 persons eminent in the world of Iranian culture, whose names are listed [...],[15] were arrested and imprisoned without their families being able to see them or obtain information about their fate or the charges brought against them.

91. The government concerned did not send a representative to the Committee's session. However, in a letter dated 15 September 1987, the Permanent Delegate of the Islamic Republic of Iran stated that, pending a reply promised by the competent authorities of his country, he wished to remind the Committee of the terms of his letter of September 1984 [...][16] in which he had raised the question of the inadmissibility of the communication on the grounds that it contravened the provisions of paragraph 14 (*a*) (iii) of 104 EX/Decision 3.3 (a communication must not be motivated exclusively by other considerations than those falling within Unesco's competence). According to him, the offences committed by the persons in question had nothing to do with education, science, culture and information, and the fact of claiming that those persons were writers or intellectuals was not sufficient to clear them of the their

[14] See document 127 EX/3 PRIV., paras. 90-93; see also document 127 EX/CR/HR/2.
[15] See document 117 EX/CR/HR/3 Add.
[16] See document 120 EX/15 PRIV., para. 107 (*supra*, p. 252), communication No. 525/83 concerning *Islamic Republic of Iran*, case of *Abolfazl Ghassemi*.

crimes and spare them the need to stand trial in their country. The Permanent Delegate added that, since it was a trial and judgement in accordance with the prevailing legislation in the Islamic Republic of Iran, it would be desirable to apply paragraph 6 of the aforesaid decision (the Organization is prohibited from intervening in matters which are essentially within the domestic jurisdiction of a Member State). He concluded with an assurance that his country appreciated and at all times encouraged the noble objective of Unesco and the Committee but desired that it should not be exploited by certain persons or bodies pursuing other unavowed aims.

92. One member of the Committee observed that, owing to the personality of the alleged victims, who belonged to the world of culture, and given the lack of relevant information from the government concerned and, consequently, its lack of co-operation, the communication should be declared admissible.

93. After an exchange of views, the Committee *decided*:

(i) to express its regret that the government concerned had not sent a representative;

(ii) to take note of the content of the letter dated 15 September 1987 from the Permanent Delegate of the Islamic Republic of Iran to Unesco;

(iii) to declare the communication admissible;

(iv) once more to request the Executive Board to ask the Director-General to continue to use his good offices for the sake of a humanitarian approach on behalf of the persons detained;

(v) to consider the substance of this communication at its spring 1988 session.

Spring 1988 session of the Committee on Conventions and Recommendations (129th session of the Executive Board)[17]

140. According to the author of the communication, 28 persons eminent in the world of Iranian culture, whose names were listed [...],[18] had been imprisoned without their families being able to see them or obtain information about their fate or the charges brought against them.

[17] See document 129 EX/3 PRIV., paras. 140-145; see also document 129 EX/CR/HR/1.
[18] See document 117 EX/CR/HR/3 Add.

No. 581/83 **Islamic Republic of Iran**

141. At its previous sessions, the government concerned had informed the Committee by letter or through its representatives that those persons had been sentenced by the Revolutionary Tribunal to various terms of imprisonment, not for their cultural or intellectual activities, but for spying for a foreign power and preparing a coup d'état. It had stated that none of them had been executed.

142. That communication had been declared admissible by the Committee at its [autumn 1987] session in the course of which it had also requested the Executive Board to ask the Director-General to continue to use his good offices on behalf of the persons in detention.[19]

143. At the present session, the representatives of the government concerned informed the Committee that they were appearing before it out of respect for it and for the lofty ideals of Unesco. They recalled the reasons for which the persons involved had been convicted, namely common law offences, a matter involving national sovereignty alone and in no way coming within the competence of the Committee. They nevertheless informed the Committee of the release of four of the 28 people detained, and gave their names.

144. Several Committee members questioned the representatives of the government concerned on the state of health of the prisoners, the conditions of their detention, the internal remedies which they might possibly have recourse to, the clemency which the Islamic Republic might exercise on behalf of the elderly, and the precise activities which formed the basis of the charges brought against them.

145. Following an exchange of views, the Committee *decided*:

(i) to thank the representatives of the government concerned for their attendance and co-operation;

(ii) to take note with satisfaction of the release of four of the persons detained (Mr Chahbazi Abdollah, Mr Djafari Mohammed Ali, Mr Kasrai Siavash and Mr Tabari Eshan) and to strike those four cases from its list as being settled in accordance with paragraph 14 (*a*) (x) of 104 EX/Decision 3.3;

(iii) to reiterate its request to the government concerned for additional information on the cases of the other 24 persons detained;

(iv) to renew its appeal for clemency towards those persons, especially the ill and the elderly;

[19] See document 127 EX/3 PRIV., para. 93 (iii) and (iv) (*supra*, p. 371).

(v) to request the Executive Board once again to ask the Director-General to continue to use his good offices in that affair;

(vi) to resume consideration of the communication at [its autumn 1988 session].

Autumn 1988 session of the Committee on Conventions and Recommendations (130th session of the Executive Board)[20]

167. This communication has been on the Committee's agenda since [its autumn 1983 session]. It is at the stage of examination of its substance, having been declared admissible by the Committee at [its autumn 1987 session].[21]

168. According to the author of the communication 28 persons eminent in the world of Iranian culture have been arrested and imprisoned without their families being able to see them or obtain information about their fate.

169. At previous sessions, the government concerned informed the Committee that the accused had been sentenced by the Revolutionary Tribunal to various terms of imprisonment, not for their cultural or intellectual activities, but for spying for a foreign power and preparing a coup d'état.

170. Four of the alleged victims had been released.

171. The government did not send a representative to the present session, but, in a letter dated 10 October 1988, the Permanent Delegation of the Islamic Republic of Iran had reiterated the position taken by its countrys' authorities, who considered that the matter came exclusively under national jurisdiction and was not within Unesco's purview.

172. After an exchange of views, the Committee *decided*:

(i) to express its regret that no representative of the government concerned had been present;

(ii) to request the Director-General to continue to use his good offices on behalf of the persons who were the subject of the present communication;

[20] See document 130 EX/3 PRIV., paras. 167-172; see also document 130 EX/CR/HR - Islamic Republic of Iran.
[21] See document 127 EX/3 PRIV., para. 93 (iii) (*supra*, p. 371).

(iii) to urge the government to allow the families of the alleged victims to obtain information about their fate and to visit them;

(iv) to invite the author of the communication to bring up to date the information contained in it, to the extent that the situation of certain alleged victims seems to have changed;

(v) to appeal once more for clemency towards those persons, especially the ill and the elderly;

(vi) to resume consideration of this communication at its [spring 1989 session].

Spring 1989 session of the Committee on Conventions and Recommendations (131st session of the Executive Board)[22]

196. This communication has been on the Committee's agenda since [its autumn 1983 session]. It is at the stage of examination of its substance, having been declared admissible by the Committee at [its autumn 1987 session].[23]

197. According to the author of the communication 28 persons eminent in the world of Iranian culture have been arrested and imprisoned without their families being able to see them or obtain information about their fate.

198. At previous sessions, the government concerned informed the Committee that the accused had been sentenced by the Revolutionary Tribunal to various terms of imprisonment, not for their cultural or intellectual activities, but for spying for a foreign power and preparing a coup d'état. Four of them had been released.

199. At its [autumn 1988] session, after expressing its regret that no representative of the government concerned had been present, the Committee had urged the government to allow the families of the alleged victims to obtain information about their fate and to visit them. It invited the author of the communication to bring up to date the information contained in it, to the extent that the situation of the alleged victims seemed to have changed. While requesting the Director-General to continue to use his good offices, it appealed once more for clemency, especially for the ill and the elderly.[24]

---

[22] See document 131 EX/3 PRIV., paras. 196-204; see also document 131 EX/CR/HR - Islamic Republic of Iran.

[23] See document 127 EX/3 PRIV., para. 93 (iii) (*supra*, p. 371).

[24] See document 130 EX/3 PRIV., para. 172 (*supra*, pp. 373-374).

Islamic Republic of Iran **No. 581/83**

200. Once again the government concerned did not send a representative. The Committee was informed that the government was unable to understand why the Committee persisted in making inquiries when it had already clearly displayed its willingness to co-operate in the matter. The Chairman said that he was prepared to write to the government concerned to explain that its inquiries were in no way intended to be inquisitorial but were motivated solely by humanitarian concern and a wish for further dialogue.

201. One member of the Committee wondered whether some of the persons concerned had been executed. Another member wished to know whether some of them had been amnestied.

202. Another member of the Committee commented that a large proportion of the 24 alleged victims belonged to the Tudeh Party, many of whose members had been executed. He regretted that the author of the communication, which had access to the relevant information, had not seen fit to reply to the Committee's request for additional information at its [autumn 1988] session. He also urged the Committee to repeat that request.

203. Another member of the Committee suggested that the Director-General should again be requested to continue the representations that he was making on humanitarian grounds.

204. After an exchange of views, the Committee *decided*:

(i) to express deep regret that no representative of the government concerned had been present;

(ii) once more to request the Director-General to continue his representations on behalf of the persons referred to in the communication;

(iii) to make an earnest appeal to the government concerned to allow the families of the alleged victims to obtain information about their fate and to visit them;

(iv) to remind the author of the communication of the Committee's invitation to bring the information contained in it up to date, as the situation of certain alleged victims seemed to have changed and some were said to have been released;

(v) to appeal once more for clemency, especially towards the ill and the elderly;

(vi) to resume consideration of this communication at the [autumn 1989 session].

Autumn 1989 session of the Committee on Conventions and Recommendations (132nd session of the Executive Board)[25]

157. This communication has been on the Committee's agenda since [its autumn 1983 session]. It is at the stage of examination of substance, having been declared admissible in 1987.[26]

158. According to the author of the communication, the alleged victims were initially 28 persons belonging to the world of Iranian culture, who were said to have been arrested and imprisoned without their families being able to obtain any informatin about what had happened to them.

159. According to the government concerned, these persons had been sentenced by the Revolutionary Tribunal to various terms of imprisonment, not for their cultural or intellectual activities, but for spying for a foreign power and preparing a coup d'état. At the [spring 1988 session], the Committee was informed that four of them had been released.

160. The 24 persons remaining are listed [...].[27]

161. At its [spring 1989] session, the Committee made an earnest appeal to the government concerned to allow the families of the alleged victims to obtain information about them and to visit them. It also appealed once more for clemency, especially towards the sick and the elderly. It again requested the Director-General to continue the representations he was making on humanitarian grounds and it reminded the author of the communication of the Committee's invitation to bring the information contained in it up to date, as the situation of certain alleged victims seemed, in fact, to have changed and some had possibly been released.[28]

162. In a letter to the Iranian authorities, the Chairman of the Committee explained the reasons why the Committee was continuing to keep the communication on its agenda and the importance that the Committee attached to dialogue with the government.

---

[25] See document 132 EX/3 PRIV., paras. 157-163; see also document 132 EX/CR/HR/IRA.
[26] See document 127 EX/3 PRIV., para. 93 (iii) (*supra*, p. 371).
[27] See document 130 EX/CR/HR - Islamic Republic of Iran.
[28] See document 131 EX/3 PRIV., para. 204 (*supra*, pp. 375-376).

Islamic Republic of Iran **No. 581/83**

163. After an exchange of views, the Committee *decided*:

(i) to deplore once again the absence of any representative of the government concerned;

(ii) to recall the decision it had taken at its [spring 1989] session, especially its earnest appeal for clemency;

(iii) to invite the author of the communication once again to bring it up to date and to inform the Committee if he maintained it;

(iv) to request its Chairman to continue to make representations to the Iranian authorities on the occasion of the twenty-fifth session of the General Conference;

(v) to resume consideration of this communication at [its spring 1990 session].

Spring 1990 session of the Committee on Conventions and Recommendations (134th session of the Executive Board)[29]

182. This communication has been on the Committee's agenda since [its autumn 1983 session]. It is at the stage of being examined as to its substance.

183. The alleged victims initially numbered 28 persons belonging to the world of Iranian culture, who were said to have been arrested and imprisoned without their families being able to obtain any information about what had happened to them.

184. According to the information provided by the Government of the Islamic Republic of Iran at previous sessions, these persons had been sentenced by the Revolutionary Tribunal not for their cultural or intellectual activities, but for spying for a foreign power and preparing a coup d'état. At the [spring 1988 session] the Committee was informed that four of them had been released.

185. The 24 persons whose fate has not yet been clarified are listed [...].[30]

---

[29] See document 134 EX/3 PRIV., paras. 182-190; see also document 134 EX/CR/HR/IRA.
[30] See document 134 EX/CR/HR/IRA.

No. 581/83 **Islamic Republic of Iran**

186. On 13 February 1990 the Secretariat received a visit from [the] Director-General for International Relations at the Ministry of Foreign Affairs of the Islamic Republic of Iran, who had come to explain the position of his country's authorities.

187. At the present session the representative of the Iranian Government declared that much erroneous information had been spread about Iran. Mr Reynaldo Galindo Pohl, the Special Representative of the United Nations Commission on Human Rights, in his report to the Commission of 12 February 1990 [...] on the situation concerning human rights in the Islamic Republic of Iran,[31] had noted, for example, that persons included on a list of people brought to [his] attention as having been executed were in fact still alive; indeed, he had been able to speak to some of them. He had also noted the devastating effects of the armed conflict Iran had suffered and of terrorism. He had been fully informed and had thanked the Iranian Government for its full co-operation.

188. With regard to the persons who are the subject of the communication, the representative of the Iranian Government stated that they were members of the People's Party and had carried out acts of espionage on behalf of a foreign power. During the particularly turbulent period of the Revolution - and above all in time of war - citizens betraying the nation had to be punished. 10 of these persons had thus been executed; they were Keyhan Mehdi, Pourhormozan Mohammad, Fathi Mehdi, Ghaempanah Gholam-Hossein, Mahboub Asghar, Mohammadzadeh Rafat, Ebtehadj Houchang, Bagherzadeh Aboutorab, Behzadi Manoutchehr and Danesh Ahmad. Four persons were still serving their sentences; they were: Etemadzadeh (Behazine) Mahmoud and three women: Farmanfarmaian (Firouw) Maryam, Ghaeni Zohreh and Mohammadi Malek-Tadj. One person (Agahi Abdol-Hossein) had been killed at the time of his arrest. Another (Chaltouki Reza) had died of cancer. As to the other eight persons on the above-mentioned list, the names were incorrect; in any event, they did not correspond to any known person, either deceased or still in prison.

189. In response to requests for further clarification, the representative of the Iranian Government stated that in his country no one had been persecuted for having expressed his or her ideas and that political prisoners had no difficulty in receiving visits. However, he did not have more detailed information on the sentences passed on the four persons still in detention, nor on their situation in prison. In view of the information provided, which, in his opinion, showed that the alleged facts did not come within Unesco's competence, he requested that the examination of the communication be brought to a conclusion. He assured the Committee that the Iranian authorities attached very great importance to human rights and that the period of disturbance was over and had given way to a new era of reconstruction.

---

[31] See document E/CN.4/1990/24.

Islamic Republic of Iran **No. 581/83**

190. After an exchange of views the Committee *decided*:

(i) to thank the representatives of the Iranian Government for having attended the meeting and for their co-operation;

(ii) to affirm its competence *rationae personae* with regard to this communication, since the 24 persons concerned belong to the world of Islamic culture;

(iii) to express its profound dismay at learning that 10 of the persons had been executed;

(iv) to request the Secretariat to inform the author of the communication that, according to the representative of the Iranian Government, eight of the names were entirely incorrect and did not correspond to any known person;

(v) to launch an appeal for clemency on behalf of the four persons still in detention, bearing in mind that the state of emergency applying in time of war had come to an end: Mr Etemadzadeh (Behazine) Mahmoud, Ms Ghaeni Zohreh, Ms Mohammadi Malek-Tadj and Ms Farmanfarmaian (Firouw) Maryam, who was over 80 years old;

(vi) to resume examination of this communciation at its [autumn 1990 session].

Autumn 1990 session of the Committee on Conventions and Recommendations (135th session of the Executive Board)[32]

128. [The first communication][33] had been on the Committee's agenda since [its autumn 1983 session]. It was at the stage of being examined as to its substance. [The other communication] was appearing on the Committee's agenda for the first time.

129. Ms Mariam Firouz and Ms Maryam Farmanfarmaian (Firouw) whose names appear among the alleged victims in [the first communication] were one and the same person. As the facts alleged regarding her were the same in both communications, the Committee *decided* to examine them together.

---

[32] See document 135 EX/3 PRIV., paras. 128-139; see also documents 135 EX/CR/HR/IRA and Add.

[33] Communications No. 581/83 concerning *Islamic Republic of Iran*, case of *Alleged arrests of personalities in the world of Iranian culture*, and No. 835/90 concerning *Islamic Republic of Iran*, case of *Mariam Firouz*, were being considered together.

No. 581/83 **Islamic Republic of Iran**

130. The persons referred to in [the first communication] initially numbered 28. They were persons belonging to the world of Iranian culture who, according to the author of the communication, had been arrested and imprisoned without their families being able to obtain any information about them. According to the author of [the second communication, Amnesty International], Ms Mariam Firouz, a writer and translator aged about 75, was arrested on 6 April 1983 with several other members of the Tudeh Party. She was kept for over three years in preventive detention, often incommunicado, and was tried by an Islamic Revolutionary Court and sentenced to death in 1986. During her trial she had no defence representation and the precise charges against her were not known. The death sentence was later commuted, but Amnesty International had no information on the date of the commutation. The alleged victim was still detained in Evin Prison in Tehran; she was suffering from rheumatism and heart disease. It was also reported that on several occasions she had been denied medical treatment.

131. According to the information provided at previous sessions by the government concerned, these persons had been sentenced by the Revolutionary Tribunal not for their cultural or intellectual activities, but for spying for a foreign power and preparing a coup d'état. At the [spring 1988 session] the Committee was informed that four of them had been released.

132. The 24 persons whose fate has not yet been clarified are listed [...].[34]

133. At the [the spring 1990] session, the representative of the Iranian Government had stated that the alleged victims were members of the People's Party and had carried out acts of espionage on behalf of a foreign power. During the particularly turbulent period of the Revolution - and above all in time of war - citizens betraying the nation had to be punished. 10 of these persons had thus been executed; four persons were still serving their sentences; they were: Etemadzadeh (Behazine) Mahmoud and three women: Farmanfarmaian (Firouw) Maryam, Ghaeni Zohreh and Mohammadi Malek-Tadj. One person (Agahi Abdol-Hossein) had been killed at the time of his arrest. Another (Chaltoukl Reza) had died of cancer. As to the other eight persons on the above-mentioned list, the names were incorrect; in any event, they did not correspond to any known person, either deceased or still in prison.

134. In reply to questions, the representative of the government said that he did not have more detailed information on the sentences passed on the four persons still in detention or on their situation in prison.

---

[34] See document 134 EX/CR/HR/IRA.

Islamic Republic of Iran **No. 581/83**

135. After an exchange of views, the Committee had decided to affirm its competence *rationae personae* with regard to that communication, since the 24 persons concerned belonged to the world of Islamic culture, to express its profound dismay at learning that 10 of the persons had been executed, and to appeal for clemency on behalf of the four persons still in detention.[35]

136. At the present session, the representative of the government concerned reminded the Committee that the Iranian authorities attached very great importance to human rights and that the troubled period had ended and had given way to an era of reconstruction. The general climate in Iran had changed and the President of the Republic had said that the situation of prisoners should be normalized in the near future. The representative of Iran said that if he obtained further information before the Committee's next session, he would certainly communicate it to Committee members by letter. He went on to recall that much erroneous information had been spread about Iran. Mr Reynaldo Galindo Pohl, the Special Representative of the United Nations [Commission on Human Rights], in his report to the Commission of 12 February 1990 [...] on the situation concerning human rights in the Islamic Republic of Iran,[36] had noted, for example, that persons included on a list of people brought to his attention as having been executed were in fact still alive; indeed, he had been able to speak to some of them. He had also noted that devasting effects of the armed conflict Iran had suffered and of terrorism. He had been fully informed and had thanked the Iranian Government for its full co-operation. The representative of the government concerned felt that it would be desirable to ask Mr Reynaldo Galindo Pohl to inquire about the four alleged victims during his next mission to Iran, which he would be carrying out very soon. He said that Ms Mariam Firouz was in good health and that, in accordance with the legislation in force, she was being visited by her husband, who was himself in prison.

137. In reply to questions, the representative of the government concerned said that the authority empowered to show clemency was the Head of State or the Department of Justice.

138. The members of the Committee welcomed the spirit of co-operation of the Iranian authorities.

139. After an exchange of views, the Committee *decided*:

(i) to thank the representatives of the government concerned for their presence and their co-operation;

---

[35] See document 134 EX/3 PRIV., para. 190 (*supra*, p. 379).
[36] See document E/CN.4/1990/24.

(ii) to ask the Secretariat to contact Mr Reynaldo Galindo Pohl, Special Representative of the United Nations [Commission on Human Rights], asking him, during his next mission to Iran, to visit the four alleged victims and intercede on their behalf;

(iii) to reiterate its appeal for clemency on behalf of the four persons still in detention, i.e. Mr Etemadzadeh (Behazine) Mahmoud, Ms Ghaeni Zohreh, Ms Mohammadi Malek-Tadj and Ms Farmanfarmaian (Firouw) Maryam, especially the last named, who was a person of particularly advanced age;

(iv) to resume examination of [these communications] at its [spring 1991 session].

Spring 1991 session of the Committee on Conventions and Recommendations (136th session of the Executive Board)[37]

162. [The first communication][38] has been on the Committee's agenda since [its autumn 1983 session]. It is at the stage of examinination of substance. [The other communication] has been on the Committee's agenda since [its autumn 1990 session]. It is at the stage of examination of substance.

163. Ms Mariam Firouz and Ms Maryam Farmanfarmaian (Firouw) whose name appears among the alleged victims in [the first communication] are one and the same person. As the facts alleged regarding her are the same in both communications, the Committee decided to examine them together.

164. The alleged victims referred to in [the first communication] initially numbered 28. They were persons belonging to the world of Iranian culture who, according to the author of the communication, had been arrested and imprisoned without their families being able to obtain any information about them. According to the author of [the other communication, Amnesty International], Ms Mariam Firouz, a writer and translator, founder of the Democratic Organization of Iranian Women, aged about 75, was arrested on 6 April 1983 with several other members of the Tudeh Party. She was kept for over three years in preventive detention, often incommunicado, was tried by an Islamic Revolutionary Court and sentenced to death in 1986. During her trial she had no defence representation and the precise charges against her were not known. The death sentence was later commuted. The alleged victim is still de-

---

[37] See document 136 EX/3 PRIV., paras. 162-174; see also document 136 EX/CR/HR/IRA.

[38] Communications No. 581/83 concerning *Islamic Republic of Iran*, case of *Alleged arrests of personalities in the world of Iranian culture*, and No. 835/90 concerning *Islamic Republic of Iran*, case of *Mariam Firouz*, were being considered together.

tained in Evin Prison in Tehran; she is suffering from rheumatism and heart disease. She has been denied medical treatment on several occasions.

165. According to the information provided at previous sessions by the government concerned, these persons, all members of the People's Party, had been sentenced by the Revolutionary Tribunal not for their cultural or intellectual activities, but for spying for a foreign power and preparing a coup d'état. At the [spring 1988 session] the Committee was informed that four of them had been released.

166. At the [spring 1990] session, the representative of the Iranian Government stated that the alleged victims were members of the People's Party and had carried out acts of espionage on behalf of a foreign power. During the particularly turbulent period of the Revolution - and above all in time of war - citizens betraying the nation had to be punished. 10 of these persons had thus been executed; four persons were still serving their sentences; they were: Etemadzadeh (Behazine) Mahmoud and three women: Farmanfarmaian (Firouw) Maryam, Ghaeni Zohreh and Mohammadi Malek-Tadj. In response to questions, the representative of the government concerned indicated that he lacked more detailed information on the sentences of the four persons still in prison, and on the conditions of their detention. One person (Agahi Abdol-Hossein) had been killed at the time of his arrest. Another (Chaltouki Reza) had died of cancer. As to the other eight persons on the above-mentioned list, the names were incorrect; in any event, they did not correspond to any known person, either deceased or still in prison.

167. The Committee had decided to affirm its competence *rationae personae* with regard to that communication, since the 24 persons concerned belonged to the world of culture, to express its profound dismay at learning that 10 of the persons had been executed, and to appeal for clemency on behalf of the four persons still in detention.[39]

168. At the [autumn 1990] session, the representative of the government concerned reminded the Committee that the Iranian authorities attached very great importance to human rights and that the troubled period had ended and had given way to an era of reconstruction. The general climate in Iran had changed and the President of the Republic had said that the situation of prisoners should be normalized in the near future. The representative of Iran said that if he obtained further information before the Committee's next session, he would certainly transmit it. The representative of the government concerned felt that it would be desirable to ask Mr Reynaldo Galindo Pohl, Special Representative of the United Nations Commission on Human Rights, to inquire about the four alleged victims during his next mission to Iran. He said that

---

[39] See document 134 EX/3 PRIV., para. 190 (ii), (iii) and (v) (*supra*, p. 379).

Ms Mariam Firouz was in good health and that, in accordance with the legislation in force, was allowed visits by her husband, former First Secretary of the Tudeh Party, who was himself in prison.

169. The Committee reiterated its appeal for clemency on behalf of the four persons still in detention, i.e. Mr Etemadzadeh (Behazine) Mahmoud, Ms Ghaeni Zohreh, Ms Mohammadi Malek-Tadj and Ms Farmanfarmaian (Firouw) Maryam, especially the last named, on account of her advanced age. It also asked the Secretariat to contact Mr Reynaldo Galindo Pohl, with the request that during his next mission to Iran, he visit the four alleged victims and intercede on their behalf.[40]

170. As regards the present session, in response to its request, the Secretariat has received from the Chief of the Special Procedures Section of the United Nations Centre for Human Rights a letter dated 29 January 1991 [...].[41] Relevant extracts from the interim report by the Special Representative, Mr Galindo Pohl, and a letter from the Iranian Government were attached to this letter. The extracts from the report indicated, among other things, that Ms Mariam Firouz had suffered reprisals subsequent to the Special Representative's first visit, and that various types of torture inflicted upon her at the beginning of her detention had, among other things, resulted in her loss of hearing. The letter from the Iranian Government stated that Ms Zohren Ghaeni and Ms Malek-Tadj Mohammadi had been released. None of those who met the Special Representative had been subjected to intimidation or mistreatment by Iranian officials. Ms Mariam Firouz was under the special supervision of the prison health authorities because of her age, and her state of health was checked regularly by doctors.

171. On 16 April 1991, the Secretariat received additional information from the author of [the second communication], recapitulating that contained in the Special Representative's report.

172. In a statement made to the Committee, the representative of the government concerned announced the release of Ms Mariam Firouz who was now in a nursing home. There was nothing to stop her from receiving visitors, including those from international humanitarian organizations. She was no longer subject to any restrictive conditions.

173. The Committee noted with satisfaction that according to this information, three of the four imprisoned persons had been released; doubt still remained concerning Mr Etamadzadeh (Behazine) Mahmoud, due to the fact that, according to the letter

---

[40] See document 135 EX/3 PRIV., para. 139 (iii) and (ii) (*supra*, p. 382), respectively.
[41] See document 136 EX/CR/HR/IRA.

of 29 January 1991 from the United Nations Centre for Human Rights, the names of the persons in question had been spelt very differently in the various communications and that it could not be ruled out that the case of Mr Etemadzadeh (Behazihe) Mahmoud figured in Mr Galindo Pohl's report under another name.

174. After an exchange of views, the Committee *decided*:

(i) to thank the representatives of the government concerned for their attendance and co-operation;

(ii) to note with satisfaction the release of Ms Mariam Firouz, Ms Ghaeni Zoreh and Ms Mohammadi Malek-Tadj, and to strike these cases from its list, regarding them as settled in accordance with paragraph 14 (*a*) (x) of 104 EX/ Decision 3.3;

(iii) to request the government concerned to provide additional information concerning Mr Etemadzadeh (Behazine) Mahmoud, whose situation had not been clarified;

(iv) to appeal for clemency for Mr Etemadzadeh (Behazine) Mahmoud if he was still in detention;

(v) to request that the Secretariat re-establish contact with Mr Reynaldo Galindo Pohl, Special Representative of the United Nations Commission on Human Rights, in order to obtain additional information concerning Mr Etemadzadeh (Behazine) Mahmoud;

(vi) to resume examination of this communication at the [autumn 1991 session].

Autumn 1991 session of the Committee on Conventions and Recommendations (137th session of the Executive Board)[42]

137. This communication has been on the Committee's agenda since [its autumn 1983 session], and it is at the stage of examinination of substance.

138. The persons referred to in this communication initially numbered 28. They were persons belonging to the world of Iranian culture who, according to the author of the communication, had been arrested and imprisoned without their families be-

[42] See document 137 EX/3 PRIV., paras. 137-143; see also document 137 EX/CR/HR/IRA.

ing able to obtain any information about their fate. At subsequent sessions, the fate of 27 of these persons was clarified. One of them was still serving his sentence in Evin Prison in Tehran. The facts as reported are as follows: Mr Mahmoud Etemadzadeh, a well-known writer, translator of several masterpieces of French literature, Secretary of the National Council for Peace, editor-in-chief of the weekly publication *Ettehad-e-Mardom*, and Secretary of the Democratic Union of the Iranian People, was said to have been arrested on 6 February 1983 by the revolutionary guards and placed in solitary confinement. He was said to be suffering from severe heart disease and stomach disorders and is disabled in one arm.

139. The government concerned stated that the alleged victim, like the other persons involved, all members of the People's Party, had been sentenced by the Revolutionary Court to various periods of imprisonment, not because of his cultural or intellectual activities but because of acts of espionage on behalf of a foreign power and preparations for a coup d'état.

140. At the [spring 1991] session, the Committee had noted with satisfaction that, according to the information it had been given, three of the remaining four imprisoned persons had been released; doubt still existed concerning Mr Etemadzadeh (Behazine) Mahmoud, due to the fact that, according to the letter of 29 January 1991 from the United Nations Centre for Human Rights, the names of the persons in question had been spelt very differently in the various communications and that it could not be ruled out that the case of Mr Etemadzadeh (Behazine) Mahmoud figured under another name in the report of the Special Representative of the United Nations Commission on Human Rights, Mr Galindo Pohl.

141. The Committee decided to request the government concerned to provide additional information concerning Mr Etemadzadeh (Behazine) Mahmoud, whose situation had not been clarified and to appeal for clemency for him if he was still in detention. It also requested that the Secretariat re-establish contact with Mr Reynaldo Galindo Pohl, in order to obtain additional information concerning this case.[43]

142. At this session of the Committee, the Permanent Delegation of the Islamic Republic of Iran to UNESCO informed the Committee, in a letter dated 24 September 1991, that Mr Etemadzadeh (Behazine) Mahmoud had been released.

143. After an exchange of views, the Committee *decided*:

(i) to thank the representative of the government concerned for his letter of 24 September 1991;

[43] See document 136 EX/3 PRIV., para. 174 (iii), (iv) and (v) (*supra*, p. 385).

Islamic Republic of Iran **No. 581/83**

(ii) to take note with satisfaction of the release of Mr Etemadzadeh (Behazine) Mahmoud;

(iii) to strike this communication from its list, considering it settled in accordance with paragraph 14 (*a*) (x) of 104 EX/Decision 3.3.

No. 582/83

Concerning *Paraguay*
Case of *Enrique Goossen Martens* et al.*

Communication of 2 August 1983 submitted by
Amnesty International

Autumn 1983 session of the Committee on Conventions and Recommendations (117th session of the Executive Board)[1]

106. Mr Enrique Goossen Martens, along with nine other employees of the Banco Paraguayo de Datos (BPD), which published monthly analyses of the trade union, political, social and economic situation in Paraguay, and two employees of the Estudio Gráfico, a printing company which produced the BPD's material, were allegedly arrested by the police in May 1983; it is claimed that some of them were tortured; they are described as having been charged under Law 209/70 entitled "Defence of Public Peace and Liberty of the Individual" because according to the author of the communication, they participated in the production of the said material.

107. The representative of the government concerned stated that according to the information provided by his country's authorities, Law 209/70 was a preventive and not a repressive law and that it had been promulgated in 1979, during an upsurge of revolutionary activity in neighbouring countries, for the purpose of preserving domestic stability, but that its provisions were less harsh than those of the Penal Code. He pointed out that approximately 80 per cent of the 110 persons arrested under that law since 1979 had already been released. However, he did not have at his disposal any relevant information enabling him to answer the questions asked concerning the names of the persons still detained, the exact charges against them, when they would be tried, and the provisional limitations imposed by the said law on the freedoms guaranteed by international human rights instruments.

---

* Case of *Enrique Goossen Martens and eleven employees of the Banco Paraguayo de Datos and Estudio Gráfico.*

[1] See document 117 EX/18 PRIV., paras. 106-108; see also documents 117 EX/CR/HR/3 Add. and Add.3.

No. 582/83 **Paraguay**

108. After an exchange of views and taking into account the concern expressed by several members with respect to the cases of torture alleged in the communication, the Committee *decided*:

(i) to request further information from both the government concerned and the author of the communication;

(ii) to request the representative of the government concerned to inform the relevant authorities of his country of the Committee's concern about the allegations made in respect of a number of persons arrested;

(iii) to resume its examination of this communication at its spring 1984 session.

Spring 1984 session of the Committee on Conventions and Recommendations (119th session of the Executive Board)[2]

127. The alleged victims were 10 employees of the Banco Paraguayo de Datos, a body which, according to the author of the communication, published monthly analyses of the trade union, political, social and economic situation in Paraguay, and two employees of the Estudio Gráfico, a firm which was allegedly responsible for the printing of these analyses. It is claimed that the victims were arrested by the police in May 1983 and charged under Law 209/70 on the defence of law and order and of the freedom of the individual.

128. This communication was first examined at the [autumn 1983] session of the Committee.

129. At this [...] session the Committee noted the information supplied by Amnesty International [...][3] to the effect that all the alleged victims had been released, but that the charges against a number of them had not yet been dropped and that the documents seized were still in government custody.

130. The Permanent Delegate of Paraguay to Unesco, representing his government, was however unable from the information available to him to provide further details, particularly in response to the questions raised during the meeting by members of the Committee concerning the nature of the proceedings initiated against these individuals for crimes of opinion or for common law crimes, the confiscation of the ar-

---

[2] See document 119 EX/35 PRIV., paras. 127-131; see also documents 119 EX/CR/HR/2 and Add.

[3] See document 119 EX/CR/HR/2 Add.

chives of the Banco Paraguyo de Datos and the acts of torture alleged by the author of the communication.

131. After an exchange of views the Committee *decided*:

(i) to note that there were the beginnings of a settlement of this case;

(ii) to resume examination of the admissibility of the communication at the [autumn 1984] session pending additional information from the government concerned, in particular concerning the nature of the crimes allegedly imputed to the accused.

Autumn 1984 session of the Committee on Conventions and Recommendations (120th session of the Executive Board)[4]

89. This communication concerns the case of 10 employees of the Banco Paraguayo de Datos, a body which is said to have published monthly analyses of the trade union, political, social and economic situation in Paraguay, and two employees of Estudio Gráfico, a firm said to be responsible for the printing of these analyses. It is claimed that these 12 persons were arrested by the police in May 1983 and brought before the courts under the law on the defence of law and order, and of the freedom of the individual.

90. At the [spring 1984] session of the Committee, the representative of the government concerned reported that all the alleged victims had been released. According to the author of the communication, the charges brought against them had not yet been dropped and the equipment and documents confiscated had not yet been returned to their rightful owners.

91. Confirming the letter dated 21 September 1984 addressed to the Secretariat by the Permanent Delegation of Paraguay to Unesco, the representative of the government of Paraguay maintained that the matter concerned solely the legal authorities. In answer to requests for details, he stated that while crimes of opinion did not exist under Paraguayan law, there were crimes of subversion for which agitators and armed insurgents could be charged. He also said that it had not been established that the alleged victims had been tortured, and that they were now free.

92. Some members of the Committee wished to know what actions considered to be reprehensible by the authorities had led to the arrest of these persons.

---

[4] See document 120 EX/15 PRIV., paras. 89-94; see also document 120 EX/CR/HR/2.

No. 582/83 **Paraguay**

93. Other members wondered if, after their release, proceedings would still be brought against them; they wished to obtain more complete information on the charges held against these persons.

94. After an exchange of views the Committee *decided*:

(i) to ransmit to the author of the communication the information provided by the representative of the government concerned, so that the author would be in a position to make any necessary comments;

(ii) to ask the government concerned to inform the Committee on Conventions and Recommendations at its next session whether legal proceedings were still being taken against the alleged victims after their release and, in the case of an affirmative answer, what had been the results, and under what specific legislation such proceedings had been taken;

(iii) to resume the examination of this communication at its next session, while reiterating its humanitarian concern in this case.

Spring 1985 session of the Committee on Conventions and Recommendations (121st session of the Executive Board)[5]

112. This communication concerns the case of 10 employees of the Banco Paraguayo de Datos, a body which is said to have published monthly analyses of the trade union, political, social and economic situation in Paraguay, and two employees of Estudio Gráfico, a firm said to be responsible for the printing of those analyses. It is claimed that these 12 persons were arrested by the police in May 1983 and brought before the courts under the law on the defence of law and order and of the freedom of the individual.

113. At the spring 1984 session of the Committee, the representative of the government concerned had reported that all the alleged victims had been released but, according to the author of the communication, the charges brought against them had not yet been dropped and the equipment and documents confiscated had not yet been returned to their rightful owners.

114. At its [autumn 1984] session, the Committee had decided, *inter alia*, to request the government concerned to provide further information about the allegations made by the author of the communication.[6]

---

[5] See document 121 EX/46 PRIV., paras. 112-118; see also document 121 EX/CR/HR/2.

Paraguay **No. 582/83**

115. The representative of the Government of Paraguay reported that a letter had been sent by the permanent delegation of his country to the Secretariat on 26 April 1985, informing it that his government considered that the case was closed, since the Paraguayan courts had passed judgement in the matter in strict conformity with the laws in force, and that, moreover, all the persons concerned were entirely free and had been so for some time, as he had already had occasion to inform the Committee.

116. In answer to requests for clarification, the representative of the government concerned stated that no legal proceedings were any longer being taken against the persons concerned; that, contrary to the allegations made by the author of the communication, the property of the Banco Paraguayo de Datos could not have been confiscated since those responsible for the publication were not the owners; and that, lastly, the allegations that the persons arrested had been maltreated were totally incorrect and that those persons had been treated as intellectuals and in a proper manner.

117. One member of the Committee was in favour of keeping this communication on the Committee's agenda, taking the view that it was necessary to convey the information received to its author and to await his reply; other members of the Committee considered that all the questions raised by the communication had now been settled and that it should be struck from the Committee's list; in support of the latter view, one member pointed out that the Committee had known since the [spring 1984 session] that the alleged victims had been released, and that it had since received all the additional information it needed to conclude its examination.

118. At the conclusion of its deliberations, the Committee *decided* to declare this communication settled under the terms of 104 EX/Decision 3.3, paragraph 14 (*a*) (x).

[6] See document 120 EX/15 PRIV., para. 94 (ii) (*supra*, p. 392).

No. 583/83

Concerning *Chile*
Case of *Mirna Donoso García*

Communication of 4 August 1983 submitted by
Mirna Donoso García

Spring 1984 session of the Committee on Conventions and Recommendations (119th session of the Executive Board)[1]

59. Mrs Mirna Donoso García, a Chilean teacher, states that she was arrested by the Military Intelligence Service, then sentenced by the Internal Security Area Command, Southern Military Region, (War-time court case No. 30/74) to three years and one day plus 61 days' imprisonment. While serving this sentence she was allegedly dismissed from her post as headmistress of School No. 9 in Onaisin-Magallanes in Chile. She is stated to have left Chile on 18 January 1977 for Switzerland where she is now living and working as a social worker. After reportedly sending two letters on 24 January and 24 july 1983 to the Chilean Consulate in Zurich (Switzerland), she is said to have been informed that she was on the list of persons who are not authorized to return to Chile.

60. The representative of the Chilean Government wished first of all to correct and clarify certain particulars: while Mrs Mirna Donoso García had indeed been arrested by the Military Intelligence Service, she had subsequently been tried and sentenced by a tribunal, otherwise it would not have been possible for her to have her sentence commuted. He then indicated that once the period of exile, which was of the same length as the prison sentence, had expired, the means of recourse to which he had referred in connection with [another communication][2] had been open to Mrs Mirna Donosa García, but that she did not appear to have availed herself of them.

61. One member of the Committee wished to know whether the person concerned had been apprised of the means of recourse available to her. Another Committee

[1] See document 119 EX/35 PRIV., paras. 59-64; see also document 119 EX/CR/HR/3.
[2] *Ibidem*, para. 46 (*supra*, p. 330), communication No. 559/83 concerning *Chile*, case of *Delfin Guillermo Quiñones* et al.

member asked whether, on returning to Chile, Mrs Donoso García was liable to serve more time in prison, while a third member expressed concern regarding her future professional career in Chile.

62. The representative of the government concerned explained that on the occasion of the recent amendment of the administrative procedures governing return, the matter had been extensively publicized and all consulates had received detailed information. He pointed out that Mrs Mirna Danoso García did not appear to have called at the consulate competent to deal with her case in order to make inquiries. He then emphasized that none of the 4,217 Chileans who had been authorized to return since the new procedure had been instituted had been harassed, despite the fact that some of them were former political leaders and had resumed their activities. In any case, Mrs Mirna Donoso García had served her sentence. Finally, he stated that the problem of the reinstatement of the alleged victim in her original work as a schoolteacher must be dealt with under the regulations governing the teaching profession, and that it was not in his power to make certain that she was reappointed to her post.

63. Several Committee members expressed the wish that the author of the communication be informed of the remedies available to her, and that she be requested to let the Committee know the results of the action she had taken in time for the next session. Other members of the Committee supported this position.

64. The Committee accordingly *decided*:

(i) to inform the author of the communication of the administrative and legal means of recourse available to her and to invite her to avail herself of them and to communicate to the Committee the result of the steps she had taken.

(ii) to resume its consideration of the admissibility of this case at its autumn 1984 session.

Autumn 1984 session of the Committee on Conventions and Recommendations (120th session of the Executive Board)[3]

38. Mrs Mirna Donoso García, a Chilean teacher, states that she was arrested by the Military Intelligence Service, then sentenced by the Internal Security Area Command, Southern Military Region (War-time court case No. 30/74) to three years and one day plus 61 days' imprisonment. While serving this sentence she was allegedly dismissed from her post as headmistress of School No. 9 in Onaisin-Magallanes in

[3] See document 120 EX/15 PRIV., paras. 38-40; see also document 120 EX/CR/HR/2.

Chile. She is stated to have left Chile on 18 January 1977 for Switzerland where she is now living and working as a social worker. After reportedly sending two letters on 24 January and 24 July 1983 to the Chilean Consulate in Zurich (Switzerland), she is said to have been informed that she was on the list of persons who are not authorized to return to Chile.

39. The representative of the Chilean Government declared that, in his view, the case was similar to that of Mrs R. Mendoza Careaga and that for the present case, he could only repeat what he had said then,[4] that is, that it was essential that Mrs Mirna Donoso García should file an appeal for reconsideration as soon as possible, referring to the procedure instituted by the Chilean authorities in August 1983; he declared that the previous applications had been submitted by the person concerned prior to that date and had not been subject to the new regulations. He was certain that if the alleged victim were to take such action, her case could be solved quickly.

40. Consequently, the Committee *decided*:

(i) to inform the author of the communication of the statements made by the representative of the Chilean Government, namely those inviting her to make an administrative appeal based on the new procedure in force since August 1983;

(ii) to consider this communication as settled and to strike it from its list subject to receipt of confirmation that Mrs M. Donoso García has been in fact authorized to return to Chile, it being understood that if this information did not reach the Secretariat before the next session, this communication would then be included on the agenda of the spring 1985 session of the Committee.

Spring 1985 session of the Committee on Conventions and Recommendations (121st session of the Executive Board)[5]

48. Mrs Mirna Donoso García, a Chilean teacher, states that she was dismissed from her post as a school headmistress while serving a sentence of three years and one day plus 61 days' imprisonment imposed by a military tribunal. She is stated thereafter to have left Chile on 18 January 1977 for Switzerland, where she is now living and working as a social welfare officer. After reportedly sending two letters on 24 January and 24 July 1983 to the Chilean Consulate in Zurich (Switzerland), she is

[4] *Ibidem*, para. 24 (*supra*, p. 333), communication No. 559/83 concerning *Chile*, case of *Carlos Alfredo Andrade Vera* et al.

[5] See document 121 EX/46 PRIV., paras. 48-53; see also document 121 EX/CR/HR/2.

said to have been informed that she was on a list of persons who are not authorized to return to Chile.

49. At its [autumn 1984] session, the Committee decided to inform the author of the communication of the statements made by the representative of the Chilean Government, namely those inviting her to file an appeal on the basis of a new procedure in force since August 1983, to consider the communication as settled and to strike it from its list, subject to receipt of confirmation that Mrs Donoso García had in fact been authorized to return to Chile, it being understood that, in the absence of such information, this communication would be included in the agenda of the present session.[6]

50. On 10 December 1984 the Secretariat received from Mrs Denoso García a letter, dated 28 November 1984, in which she states that, with her agreement, the Vicaría de la Solidaridad of the town of Punta Arenas has filed an appeal to the courts against the Chilean Government's decisions rejecting four requests for authorization for her to return to her country (three submitted by herself to the Chilean Consulate in Zurich and one submitted locally by the Vicaría de la Solidaridad to the competent authorities in Chile). She asserts that all these applications were made with due regard for the procedures instituted by the Chilean Government.

51. Mrs Mirna Donoso García also states that she found, to her dismay, that her name was on a list of 4,800 persons banned from returning to Chile, which was given to the press by the Chilean Government in September 1984. The said list was also reportedly transmitted to the airline companies of various countries with a recommendation that they refuse to sell tickets for Chile-bound flights to persons whose names were on the list.

52. At the present session, the representative of the Chilean Government stated that the list of 4,800 names mentioned by the author of the communication was a list not of persons banned from returning but of persons required to request authorization. Whereas in November 1983, it had comprised 11,000 names, today it contained no more than 4,800; all the other cases had been settled. He added that he was not aware of the application for *amparo* filed by Mrs Donoso García, but that, in any case, he had secured for her the same opportunity as for Mr Carlos Alfredo Andrade Vera [...].[7] One member of the Committee suggested that the Committee should accordingly, take a similar decision

53. After an exchange of views, the Committee *decided*:

---

[6] See document 120 EX/15 PRIV., para. 40 (*supra*, p. 397).

[7] See document 121 EX/46 PRIV., para. 39 (*supra*, pp. 335-336), communication No. 559/83 concerning *Chile*, case of *Carlos Alfredo Andrade Vera and Guillermo Vera Paulo*.

(i) to take note of the statements made by the representative of the government concerned and to request the Secretariat to inform the author of the communication accordingly;

(ii) to resume examination of the admissibility of this communication at its autumn 1985 session.

Autumn 1985 session of the Committee on Conventions and Recommendations (122nd session of the Executive Board)[8]

48. Mrs Mirna Donoso García, a Chilean teacher, states that she was dismissed from her post as a headmistress while serving a sentence of three years and one day plus 60 days' imprisonment imposed by a military tribunal. She is stated thereafter to have left Chile on 18 January 1977 for Switzerland, where she is now living and working as a social welfare officer. After reportedly sending two letters on 24 January and 24 July to the Chilean Consulate in Zurich (Switzerland), she is said to have been informed that she was on a list of persons who are not authorized to return to Chile. At its [spring 1985] session, the Committee decided to inform the author of the communication of the statements made by the representative of the Chilean Government, in particular those inviting her to avail herself of an exceptional procedure for obtaining temporary authorization to return, which would allow her to clarify her situation on the spot.[9]

49. On 25 July 1985, the Secretariat received from the author of the communication a letter dated 20 July [...][10] in which Mrs Mirna Donoso García states that she is bitterly disappointed by the offer of a temporary return that has been made to her. She considers this procedure illogical and in her case inadequate, for she does not see how her presence in Santiago would enable her to obtain in two months a result which she was unable to obtain through approaches made over a period of two years from her place of exile. What is more, she is afraid that if she goes to Chile in these circumstances she may lose her status as a political refugee. Finally, her financial situation does not enable her to meet the cost of travel and of staying in Santiago.

50. At the present session, the representative of the Chilean Government said that he was sorry that Mrs Mirna Donoso García did not wish to avail herself of the opportunity given to her, because it had not been easy to obtain that opportunity and because her case was rather complex. He reminded the Committee that she had never

[8] See document 122 EX/21 PRIV., paras. 48-51; see also documents 122 EX/CR/HR/2 and Add.
[9] See document 121 EX/46 PRIV., para. 53 (i) (*supra*, p. 399).
[10] See document 122 EX/CR/HR/2 Add.

submitted an application for authorization to return under the new procedure. He nevertheless made the following suggestions. First of all, he felt that Mrs Mirna Donoso García should ask for help from the Office of the United Nations High Commissioner for Refugees, which could help her finance her journey. The representative of the Office in Santiago was Mr Hugo Idoyaga. He then thought it advisable for her to apply personally to the Ministry of the Interior for reconsideration of her application under the new procedure, applications submitted in that form being given prior consideration, and to inform the Unesco Secretariat of the date on which she made her application so that it could inform him and he could keep the case under review.

51. On the proposal of one of its members, the Committee *decided*:

(i) to transmit to the author of the communication the information provided by the representative of the government concerned;

(ii) to resume examination of the admissibility of this communication at its spring 1986 session.

Spring 1986 session of the Committee on Conventions and Recommendations (124th session of the Executive Board)[11]

38. Mrs Mirna Donoso García, a Chilean teacher, states that she was dismissed from her post as a headmistress while serving a sentence of three years and one day plus 60 days' imprisonment imposed by a military tribunal. She is stated thereafter to have left Chile on 18 January 1977 for Switzerland, where she is now living and working as a social welfare officer. After reportedly sending two letters on 24 January and 24 July to the Chilean Consulate in Zurich (Switzerland), she is said to have been informed that she was on a list of persons who are not authorized to return to Chile.

39. At its [autumn 1985] session, the Committee had been informed that Mrs Donoso García did not wish to avail herself of the temporary authorization to return which had been granted to her, in particular on account of her financial situation and of her fear of losing her status as a political refugee; the Committee had then decided to resume examination of the communication at the present session, while transmitting to the author the information provided by the representative of the government concerned, which included the suggestion that the person concerned should ask for help

[11] See document 124 EX/3 PRIV., paras. 38-41; see also document 124 EX/CR/HR/2.

from the Office of the United Nations High Commissioner for Refugees, and should also submit an application for reconsideration of her case.[12]

40. At the present session the representative of the Chilean Government said that he was still prepared to help Mrs Donoso García but that to the best of his knowledge she still had not submitted an application for reconsideration. Replying to questions from members of the Committee, he stated that in his view the use of a temporary authorization to return should not affect a person's right to asylum, but that that was a question of Swiss law.

41. At the end of its discussion, the Committee *decided*:

(i) to request the Secretariat to ask the Office of the United Nations High Commissioner for Refugees for information on the conditions under which the right to asylum could be forfeited in Switzerland;

(ii) to inform the author of the communication of the statements made by the representative of the government concerned;

(iii) to resume examination of the admissibility of this communication at its autumn 1986 session.

Autumn 1986 session of the Committee on Conventions and Recommendations (125th session of the Executive Board)[13]

23. Mrs Mirna Donoso García, a Chilean teacher, states that she was dismissed from her post as a headmistress while serving a sentence of imprisonment imposed by a military tribunal. She is stated to have left Chile on 18 January 1977 for Switzerland, where she is now living and working as a social welfare officer. It is said that she is named on a list of persons who are not authorized to return to Chile.

24. At its last two sessions the Committee was informed (i) that Mrs Donoso García did not wish to avail herself of the temporary authorization to return which had been granted to her, in particular on account of her financial situation and of her fear of losing her political refugee status, and (ii) that the representative of the government concerned was prepared to help her if she personally submitted an application for reconsideration of her case to the Ministry of the Interior, in accordance with the appropriate procedure.

---

[12] See document 122 EX/21 PRIV., para. 51 (*supra*, p. 400).

[13] See document 125 EX/3 PRIV., paras. 23-29; see also documents 124 EX/CR/HR/2 and Add.

No. 583/83 **Chile**

25. As regards the conditions which might lead to the loss of the right of asylum in Switzerland, the Secretariat informed the Committee on 25 August 1986 that the Office of the United Nations High Commission for Refugees had notified the Organization as follows:

> the normal practice of the Swiss authorities is to withdraw refugee status from a person who returns, even temporarily, to his or her country of origin;
>
> nevertheless, if the refugee is also the holder of residence permit "C", return to Switzerland is authorized if it takes place within six months following the departure of the person concerned, and if he or she wishes to re-obtain refugee status a fresh application must be made.

26. The representative of the government concerned informed the Committee that his country's authorities had just renewed Mrs Donoso García's temporary authorization to return. He pointed out that Mrs Donoso García had said in her letter that representations had been made to the military authorities of the Magallanes region; however, those authorities were not competent to act in the matter.

27.In this regard, the Chairperson pointed out that the representations had been made by the parents of the alleged victim, but that in any event it appeared from the communication that the alleged victim had previously submitted five requests through the Chilean Consulate in Zurich.

28. In order to avoid any risk of Mrs Donoso García's losing her refugee status in taking advantage of the temporary authorization to return to her country, the representative of the government concerned agreed to intervene on her behalf with the competent Chilean authorities. To this end, he suggested that the Secretariat obtain and transmit to him an official confirmation from the Swiss authorities of the information provided by the Office of the United Nations High Commissioner for Refugees.

29. At the end of its discussion, the Committee *decided*:

(i) to thank the government concerned for sending a representative;

(ii) to take note of the proposal by the representative of that government to use his good offices on Mrs Donoso García's behalf;

(iii) to request the Secretariat to ask the Permanent Delegation of Switzerland to Unesco for a written confirmation of the circumstances which might result in the loss of refugee status in Switzerland, and to communicate it with the information provided by the Office of the United Nations High Commissioner for Refugees to the representative of the government concerned;

(iv) to resume examination of this communication at its spring 1987 session.

Spring 1987 session of the Committee on Conventions and Recommendations (126th session of the Executive Board)[14]

23. Mrs Mirna Donoso García, a teacher, states that she was dismissed from her post as a headmistress while serving a sentence of imprisonment imposed by a military tribunal. She is stated to have left Chile on 18 January 1977 for Switzerland, where she is now living and working as a social welfare officer. It is claimed that her name is on a list of persons who are prohibited from returning to Chile.

24. At previous sessions, the Committee was informed that she did not wish to avail herself of the temporary authorization to return which had been granted to her, in particular on account of her financial situation and of her fear of losing her political refugee status.

25. In accordance with the request of the Committee at its autumn 1986 session, the Secretariat asked the Permanent Delegation of Switzerland to Unesco to provide written confirmation of the circumstances which might result in the loss of refugee status in that country. In a letter dated 27 November 1986 [...],[15] this Delegation provided the following information: Swiss practice has always been based on the principle that refugees who place themselves, even temporarily, under the responsibility of the authorities of the State from which they had previously fled thereby furnish proof that the main reason, i.e., the fear of persecution, no longer exists; in the case in point, if the person concerned returned to her country, she would forfeit her refugee status; however, the withdrawal of political asylum in no way affected the way in which the ordinary stay of a foreigner in Switzerland is controlled; thus, if such a foreigner has obtained, at the end of five years' stay in Switzerland, a residence permit, such permission will be withdrawn only if the person remains outside Switzerland for a period exceeding six months (if a request is made in advance, that period may be extended to a maximum of two years); in other words, during that period the foreigner may return to Switzerland without hindrance, regardless of whether refugee status has previously been granted.

---

[14] See document 126 EX/3 PRIV., paras. 23-27; see also document 126 EX/CR/HR/2.

[15] See document 126 EX/CR/HR/2, annex II.

No. 583/83 **Chile**

26. In his statement, the representative of the government concerned thanked the Permanent Delegation of Switzerland for the clarifications which it had been kind enough to provide and assured the Committee that if Mrs Donoso García were to take advantage of the temporary authorization to return to Chile for two months, she would be able to obtain a permanent solution to her problem. He personally undertook to do everything within his power to help her and to settle this affair, once she was in Chile. However, he stressed that the presence of Mrs Donoso García in Chile was essential.

27. After an exchange of views, the Committee *decided*:

(i) to thank the representative of the government concerned for his presence and for his co-operation;

(ii) to take note of the assurances which he had given on the prospects of a satisfactory outcome to this affair should Mrs Mirna Donoso García avail herself of the temporary authorization to return to Chile;

(iii) to invite Mrs Mirna Donoso García to avail herself of this authorization;

(iv) to resume consideration of the communication at its autumn 1987 session.

No. 590/83

Concerning *Chile*
Case of *Carlos Lira Moscoso*

Communication of 10 October 1983 submitted by
Carlos Lira Moscoso

Spring 1984 session of the Committee on Conventions and Recommendations (119th session of the Executive Board)[1]

65. The author of the communication, Mr Carlos Lira Moscoso, a journalist and writer of Chilean nationality, states that he was arrested on 12 September 1973, accused of carrying a firearm and brought before a court-martial. He explains that he was indeed in possession of firearm because, as a prison governor, he was legally required to hold one. He says he was sentenced to six years' imprisonment and has already served 26 months of the term, the remainder of his sentence having been commuted to exile of unspecified duration.

66. He says he has repeatedly been refused authorization for himself and his family to return to Chile. The Supreme Court of Chile is also said to have turned down his request.

67. The representative of the Chilean Government contended that the information given by the author in his communication was not complete: the weapons for the possession of which Mr Moscoso had been sentenced to six years' imprisonment were of the sort that could be used in support of terrorist activities; he had been sentenced to a further three-year prison term for the ill-treatment he had inflicted upon prisoners. Furthermore, the representative considered that the status of author claimed by Mr Moscoso was fraudulent because he had written nothing but political tracts against the Chilean Government. This communication therefore did not fall within the sphere of competence of Unesco and, in any case, did not justify the taking of humanitarian measures on behalf of its author. The representative of the government also reminded the Committee that the Supreme Court of Chile had twice rejected appeals submitted by the author of the communication.

---

[1] See document 119 EX/35 PRIV., paras. 65-70; see also document 119 EX/CR/HR/3.

No. 590/83 **Chile**

68. Several members of the Committee said that they considered the communication to be inadmissible on the grounds that it did not fall within the fields of competence of Unesco. One member said that whatever the offence committed by an individual, a date for permission to return to his country should be given.

69. The Legal Adviser said that the right of return was not in itself a right protected by Unesco unless it was claimed by a person whose professional activities fell within the fields of competence of the Organization. He added that Article 12, paragraph 4, of the International Covenant on Civil and Political Rights provided that "No one shall be arbitrarily deprived of the right to enter his own country" and that the term "arbitrarily" indicated that this right was not absolute. A member of the Committee took the floor once again to propose that the communication be declared inadmissible but that the author be informed that he might submit a new communication provided that he could prove that it fulfilled the conditions of admissibility provided by 104 EX/Decision 3.3, particularly by making good his claim to the status of author.

70. After considering the matter, the Committee *decided*:

> (i) to declare the communication inadmissible, on the grounds that it did not fall within the fields of competence of Unesco, in accordance with paragraph 14 (*a*) (iii) of 104 EX/Decision 3.3 of the Executive Board;
>
> (ii) to inform its author that he was entitled to submit a new communication provided that he could demonstrate that the conditions of admissibility stipulated in [104 EX/Decision 3.3] had been satisfied.

No. 595/83

Concerning *Czechoslovakia*
Case of *Ladislav Lis*

Communication of 30 August 1983 submitted by
Zygmunt Elbiński

Spring 1984 session of the Committee on Conventions and Recommendations (119th session of the Executive Board)[1]

143. According to the author of the communication, Mr Ladislav Lis, a lathe operator, was arrested in January 1983 and sentenced in July 1983 to 14 months' imprisonment followed by three years' protective surveillance for distributing documents hostile to the Czechoslovak Socialist Republic.

144. The representative of the Czechoslovak Government informed the Committee that Mr Lis had been released in March 1984 and that he now enjoyed all the recognized rights of Czechoslovak citizens.

145. The members of the Committee who took the floor were of the opinion that Mr Lis's occupational activities did not fall within Unesco's fields of competence and that since he was in any case now at liberty the case should be considered as settled.

146. At the close of its debate, the Committee *decided* to declare the communication inadmissible on the grounds of falling outside Unesco's fields of competence, pursuant to paragraph 14 (*a*) (iii) of 104 EX/Decision 3.3 of the Executive Board.

---

[1] See document 119 EX/35 PRIV., paras. 143-146; see also document 119 EX/CR/HR/3.

No. 601/84

Concerning *Chile*
Case of *Ulises Gómez*

Communication of 19 December 1983 submitted by
Cecilia Gómez

Spring 1984 session of the Committee on Conventions and Recommendations (119th session of the Executive Board)[1]

71. Mr Ulises Gómez, a Chilean journalist aged 37, is said to have been arrested in October 1979, when he was editor-in-chief of the underground newspaper "El Rebelde", the information organ of the Revolutionary Left Movement. He had reportedly worked, under the previous government, in the Information Bureau of the Presidency and for Radio Nacional. He is said to have been on hunger strike twice since his arrest to secure the status of political prisoner and to protest against the conditions under which prisoners were being detained. During his imprisonment, he allegedly caught typhus and still suffers from its after-effects. He is said to have been sentenced to 11 years' imprisonment in February 1982 for offences under the Internal Security of the State Act and transferred to the Temuco Prison, 1,000 km to the south of the capital, which, it is stated, prevents his family from visiting him. The Chilean authorities are said to have refused to apply the provisions of Decree No. 504, whereby political prisoners can have their prison sentences commuted to exile.

72. Several appeals for the release of Mr Gómez or the commutation of his sentence have reportedly been submitted to the Chilean courts to no avail. It was stated that the French and the Swedish Governments have both granted visas to the alleged victim.

73. The representative of the Chilean Government explained that the procedure for the commutation of prison sentences to exile, which was designed to alleviate the plight of persons deprived of their liberty, had been simplified and speeded up in the period 1974-1976 at the request of Unesco; however, such commutation was an act of grace, and petitioners should address their requests not to the courts, as the al-

[1] See document 119 EX/35 PRIV., paras. 71-77; see also document 119 EX/CR/HR/3.

leged victim or his representative seemed to have done, but to an ad hoc commission responsible for submitting recommendations on the matter to the Ministry of Justice, which had the sole authority to take the appropriate judicial decision. In any case, the alleged victim should provide proof that a foreign country was willing to receive him. The representative of the government concerned added that even though Mr Ulises Gómez had been sentenced for an offence under criminal law because of his terrorist activities and not for a "political offence" he could still apply to have his sentence commuted.

74. After explaining, in response to a question asked by a member of the Committee, that in principle only prison terms of under five years and one day could be commuted, the representative of the Chilean Government said that he was ready to do all that he could to have an ad hoc commission give this matter priority consideration as soon as the matter was referred to it. A member of the Committee said that, in his view, this communication raised two issues: that of the commutation of the sentence, concerning which he could confirm that the French Government had in fact granted Mr Ulises Gómez an entry and long-term residence visa in February 1982, and that of the terms of Mr Gómez's detention, which seemed to him to be severe and to merit the attention of the Committee.

75. On the second issue, the representative of the government concerned informed the Committee that Temuco Prison, where Mr Ulises Gómez was detained, was visited regularly by the International Red Cross, which systematically drew the attention of the Chilean Ministry of Justice to the irregularities it observed; the name of Mr Ulises Gómez had never been mentioned by that body. He also said that at the end of his period of exile Mr Ulises Gómez could apply through the usual channels for authorization to return to Chile.

76. Some members of the Committee.considered the communication admissible on the grounds that it related to a journalist imprisoned for his ideas. A member of the Committee noted that Mr Ulises Gómez had been tried as a terrorist and not as a journalist; he agreed with certain other members of the Committee that a decision on admissibility was premature and that it would be preferable to await the receipt of new facts on the situation of Mr Ulises Gómez.

77. After considering the matter, the Committee *decided*:

(i) to inform the author of the statements made by the representative of the government concerned, mainly as regards the procedure he should follow in submitting his application for commutation of his sentence;

(ii) to take note of the offer made by the representative of the Chilean Government to use his good offices on behalf of the alleged victim;

(iii) to reconsider the admissibility of this communication at its autumn 1984 session in the light of the results of the above-mentioned action.

Autumn 1984 session of the Committee on Conventions and Recommendations (120th session of the Executive Board)[2]

41. Mr Ulises Gómez, a Chilean journalist aged 37, is said to have been arrested in October 1979, when he was editor-in-chief of the underground newspaper "El Rebelde", the information organ of the Revolutionary Left Movement. He had reportedly worked, under the previous government, in the Information Bureau of [the] Presidency and for Radio Nacional. He is said to have been on hunger strike twice since his arrest to secure the status of political prisoner and to protest against the conditions under which prisoners were being detained. During his imprisonment, he allegedly caught typhus and still suffers from its after-effects. He is said to have been sentenced to 11 years' imprisonment in February 1982 for offences under the Internal Security of the State Act and transferred to the Temuco Prison, 1,000 km to the south of the capital, which, it is stated, prevents his family from visiting him. The Chilean authorities are said to have refused to apply the provisions of Decree No. 504, whereby political prisoners can have their prison sentences commuted to exile.

42. Several appeals for the release of Mr Gómez or the commutation of his sentence have reportedly been submitted to the Chilean courts to no avail. It was stated that the French and the Swedish Governments have both granted visas to the alleged victim.

43. At the [spring 1984] session, the Committee decided:[3]

(i) to inform the author of the statements made by the representative of the government concerned, mainly as regards the procedure she should follow in submitting an application for commutation of the sentence;

(ii) to take note of the offer made by the representative of the Chilean Government to use his good offices on behalf of the alleged victim;

---

[2] See document 120 EX/15 PRIV., paras. 41-46; see also documents 120 EX/CR/HR/2 and Add.2.

[3] See document 119 EX/35 PRIV., para. 77 (*supra*, pp. 410-411).

(iii) to reconsider the admissibility of this communication at the present session in the light of the results of the above-mentioned action.

44. At the present session, the Committee was informed that on 3 September 1984, the Secretariat had received a letter from the author of the communication giving details of the applications which her brother's lawyer had filed to date and on action which had been taken on behalf of Mr Ulises Gómez [...].[4]

45. The representative of the Chilean Government informed the Committee that, in principle, the commutation of a prison sentence to exile could not be granted before at least one-third of the prison sentence had been served, which would not be the case for Mr Ulises Gómez before March 1985; exceptionally, however, and in order to take into account the interest shown by the Committee in this matter, the competent authorities were prepared to examine favourably, as of October 1984, an application for the commutation of the sentence on behalf of the person concerned.

46. At the end of its discussions, the Committee *decided* to note the information provided by the representative of the Chilean Government and to resume consideration of the admissibility of this communication at the spring 1985 session.

Spring 1985 session of the Committee on Conventions and Recommendations (121st session of the Executive Board)[5]

54. Mr Ulises Gómez, a Chilean journalist aged 37, is said to have been arrested in October 1979, when he was editor-in-chief of the underground newspaper "El Rebelde", the information organ of the Revolutionary Left Movement. He had reportedly worked, under the previous government, in the Information Bureau of the Presidency and for Radio Nacional. He is said to have been on hunger strike twice since his arrest to secure the status of political prisoner and to protest against the conditions in which prisoners were being detained. During his imprisonment, he allegedly caught typhus and still suffers from its after-effects. He is said to have been sentenced to 11 years' imprisonment in February 1982 for offences under the Internal Security of the State Act and transferred to the Temuco Prison, 1,000 km to the south of the capital, which, it is stated, prevents his family from visiting him. The Chilean authorities are said to have refused to apply the provisions of Decree No. 504, whereby political prisoners can have their prison sentences commuted to exile.

[4] See document 120 EX/CR/HR/2 Add.2.

[5] See document 121 EX/46 PRIV., paras. 54-60; see also document 121 EX/CR/HR/2.

55. Several appeals for the release of Mr Gómez or the commutation of his sentence have reportedly been submitted to the Chilean courts to no avail. It was stated that the French and the Swedish Governments have both granted visas to the alleged victim.

56. At the autumn 1984 session of the Committee, as the representative of the government concerned had informed the Committee that, from October 1984, his country's authorities were prepared to give favourable consideration to an application for commutation of Mr Gómez's sentence, the Committee decided to take note thereof and to resume consideration of this communication at the present session.[6]

57. On 12 December 1984 the Secretariat received a letter from the author of the communication, Mrs Cecilia Gómez, in which she drew the Committee's attention to the fact that Mr Ulises Gómez had already served not one-third but indeed nearly half of his prison sentence (he had been arrested in October 1979 and sentenced in February 1982 to 11 years' imprisonment); that, although the Chilean Government had stated that it was prepared to examine the case favourably, at the time of her letter (10 December 1984), Mrs Gómez had received no reply to that effect; that, on the contrary, her brother had allegedly been transferred further south, to a corrective training prison known as Victoria disciplinary prison; finally, that, before the transfer, Mr Gómez had allegedly been maltreated, had suffered a cranial traumatism, and that he was not allowed visits by relatives, doctors or lawyers at the place where he was being held.

58. At the present session, the representative of the Chilean Government stated that, although the problem was a purely judicial one, he had not hesitated, on humanitarian grounds, to use his good offices on behalf of Mr Ulises Gómez. On the basis of the information in his possession, he was able to say that Mr Ulises Gómez, like all prisoners in Chile, was entitled to receive visits from his family and from his lawyer; that, moreover, all Chilean prisons were regularly visited by the Red Cross, which recorded any anomalies or cases of maltreatment of detainees. The representative of the Chilean Government went on to say he was convinced that Mr Ulises Gómez's judicial problem would be solved; he made it clear, however, that he could not insist on speedier solutions from bodies that were responsible to the Ministry of Justice, although he had nevertheless urged upon them the need for finding a rapid solution on humanitarian grounds without delay.

59. All the members of the Committee who spoke said they would like to have favourable news as soon as possible regarding the commutation of Mr U. Gómez's sentence to exile. Most of them also voiced their concern regarding the facts report-

---

[6] See document 120 EX/15 PRIV., para. 46 (*supra*, p. 412).

ed in Mrs Gómez's letter, and felt it necessary to obtain further particulars about them.

60. Pending receipt of the additional information requested, the Committee *decided* to defer examination of the admissibility of this communication to its autumn 1985 session.

Autumn 1985 session of the Committee on Conventions and Recommendations (122nd session of the Executive Board)[7]

52. Mr Ulises Gómez, a Chilean journalist aged 37, is said to have been arrested in October 1979, when he was editor-in-chief of the underground newspaper "El Rebelde", the information organ of the Revolutionary Left Movement. He had reportedly worked, under the previous government, in the Information Bureau of the Presidency and for Radio Nacional. He is said to have been on hunger strike twice since his arrest to secure the status of political prisoner and to protest against the conditions in which prisoners were being detained. During his imprisonment, he allegedly caught typhus and still suffers from its after-effects. He is said to have been sentenced to 11 years' imprisonment in February 1982 for offences under the Internal Security of the State Act and transferred to the Temuco Prison, 1,000 km to the south of the capital, which, it is stated, prevents his family from visiting him. The Chilean authorities are said to have refused to apply the provisions of Decree No. 504, whereby political prisoners can have their prison sentences commuted to exile.

53. Several appeals for the release of Mr Gómez or the commutation of his sentence have reportedly been submitted to the Chilean courts to no avail. It was stated that the French and Swedish Governments have both granted visas to the alleged victim.

54. At its autumn 1984 session, the Committee had been informed that the matter might be settled by October 1984 or thereabouts. At its spring 1985 session, having considered additional information submitted by the author of the communication, the Committee requested further details from the government concerned; it accordingly deferred examination of this communication to the present session.[8]

55. At the present session, the representative of the Chilean Government stated that although the problem was a judicial one and outside his field of competence, he had intervened on behalf of the person concerned; however, the case was fairly complicated and the offences more serious than first appeared. Moreover, the initial ad-

[7] See document 122 EX/21 PRIV., paras. 52-59; see also document 122 EX/CR/HR/2.
[8] See document 121 EX/46 PRIV., para. 60 (*supra*, p. 414).

ministrative stage of commutation of sentence was followed by a judicial stage during which the Court of Appeal that had pronounced the original sentence was required to take a decision; as far as he knew, the affair was now in the hands of the Court of Appeal and a judicial decision could be expected shortly.

56. One Committee member said he found the case very worrying: the fact that Mr Ulises Gómez had been editor-in-chief of an opposition newspaper and had been accused of possessing arms and of jeopardizing State security indicated that the offence in question was a political one; but the provisions of Decree No. 504 gave political prisoners the option of converting their sentence into exile; he therefore considered that Mr Ulises Gómez should be allowed to take advantage of this provision, especially since France and Sweden were willing to receive him, he had already served half his sentence and he was in poor health, particularly since his transfer to a prison operating a stricter regime; in his view, therefore, the communication was clearly admissible and the Chilean Government should be asked to ensure that the person concerned was given humanitarian treatment.

57. Other members of the Committee also found the case admissible. They noted that the case had been pending for some time and that there had been no favourable developments, contrary to the hopes raised at the autumn 1984 session. One member of the Committee suggested that a humanitarian appeal be made to the Chilean Government and this proposal received widespread support.

58. The representative of the Chilean Government pointed out that Mr Ulises Gómez had been given a proper trial and sentenced for common law offences that had always been considered as such and had been proscribed by legislation adopted by previous governments in 1958 and 1962. One member of the Committee expressed reservations in regard to the description of the offences of the alleged victim as common law offences. He also expressed doubts as to the legal validity of the established procedure; the representative of the government concerned made no reply.

59. At the end of its discusssion, the Committee *decided*:

(i) to declare the communication admissible;

(ii) to make a humanitarian appeal to the government concerned to alleviate the situation of Mr Ulises Gómez, for instance, by commuting his sentence to one of exile, if need be, in accordance with the provisions of Decree No. 504;

(iii) to resume its examination of this communication at its spring 1986 session.

No. 601/84 **Chile**

Spring 1986 session of the Committee on Conventions and Recommendations (124th session of the Executive Board)[9]

138. Mr Ulises Gómez, a Chilean journalist aged 37, is said to have been arrested in October 1979. when he was editor-in-chief of the underground newspaper "El Rebelde", the information organ of the Revolutionary Left Movement. He had reportedly worked, under the previous government, in the Information Bureau of the Presidency and for Radio Nacional. He is said to have been on hunger strike twice since his arrest to secure the status of political prisoner and to protest against the conditions in which prisoners were being detained. During his imprisonment, he allegedly caught typhus and still suffers from its after-effects. He is said to have been sentenced to 11 years' imprisonment in February 1982 for offences under the Internal Security of the State Act and transferred to the Temuco Prison, 1,000 km to the south of the capital, which, it is stated, prevents his family from visiting him. The Chilean authorities are said to have refused to apply the provisions of Decree No. 504, whereby political prisoners can have their prison sentences commuted to exile.

139. Several appeals for the release of Mr Gómez or the commutation of his sentence have reportedly been submitted to the Chilean courts to no avail. It was stated that the French and the Swedish Governments have both granted visas to the alleged victim.

140. At its autumn 1984 session, the Committee had been informed that the matter might be settled by October 1984 or thereabouts. At its spring 1985 session, having considered additional information submitted by the author of the communication, the Committee requested further details from the government concerned.[10] At the autumn 1985 session, the representative of the Chilean Government had stated that the matter was more serious than had at first appeared but that the Court of Appeal would soon take a decision. The Committee had decided to declare the communication admissible and to make a humanitarian appeal to the Chilean authorities.[11]

141. At the present session, the representative of the government concerned explained that many efforts to secure the commutation of Mr Ulises Gómez's sentence had been made both by the Chancellery of his country and by the French Government, which was willing to grant him the right to asylum, and that a solution had been on the point of being found. However, in December 1985, Mr Ulises Gómez had taken part in an attempted riot during which the director of the prison had been injured; it should be said that one of the conditions for the granting of a commuta-

---

[9] See document 124 EX/3 PRIV., paras. 138-142; see also document 124 EX/CR/HR/1.
[10] See document 121 EX/46 PRIV., para. 60 (*supra*, p. 414).
[11] See document 122 EX/21 PRIV., para. 59 (*supra*, p. 415).

tion of a sentence was good conduct. The representative of the Chilean Government added that in spite of Mr Ulises Gómez's attitude, he had approached the Ministry of Justice to ask that no formal charge be brought against Mr Gómez, and he was expecting an imminent decision on the part of that Ministry. If, however, no further charge was indeed filed against the person concerned and the commutation of his sentence was approved. he greatly hoped that the Ambassador of France in Chile and the Committee itself would make Mr Gómez understand that he had to behave in a more dignified manner.

142. After discussing the matter, the Committee *decided*:

(i) to express its concern that a positive solution had not yet been found;

(ii) to take note of the statements of the representative of the Chilean Government to the effect that there was hope that a favourable issue would be found very shortly;

(iii) to make an urgent humanitarian appeal to the Chilean Government to commute Mr Ulises Gómez's sentence to one of exile;

(iv) to defer its consideration of the communication to its autumn 1986 session.

Autumn 1986 session of the Committee on Conventions and Recommendations (125th session of the Executive Board)[12]

164. Mr Ulises Gómez, a Chilean journalist arrested in October 1979, was editor-in-chief of the underground newspaper "El Rebelde", the organ of information of the Revolutionary Left Movement. In February 1982, he was said to have been sentenced to 11 years of imprisonment for offences under the Internal Security of the State Act and transferred to the Temuco Prison, 1,000 km to the south of the capital. He was said to have been unable to obtain the commutation of his prison sentence to exile by virtue of the legal provisions in force (Decree No. 504).

165. During the spring 1986 session, the representative of the government concerned informed the Committee that, in response to its humanitarian concern, he had approached the Ministry of Justice on behalf of Mr Ulises Gómez. He had asked that no charge should be brought against the prisoner - who had, in December 1985, tak-

[12] See document 125 EX/3 PRIV., paras. 164-167; see also document 125 EX/CR/HR/1.

en part in an attempted riot during which the governor of the prison had been injured - so that he could receive commutation of his sentence.

166. At its present session, the representative of the government concerned confirmed the news given to the Committee by the Chairwoman regarding the freeing of the journalist and his arrival in France, stating that Mr Gómez had left Chile about two weeks previously. The Committee expressed its gratification at this solution.

167. After an exchange of views, the Committee *decided*:

(i) to thank the government concerned for having sent a representative;

(ii) to declare the communication settled and to strike it from its list in application of 104 EX/Decision 3.3, paragraph 14 (*j*), since the communication did not appear to merit further consideration as to its substance as the alleged victim had been freed.

No. 602/84

Concerning *New Zealand*
Case of *Alleged discriminatory tuition fees imposed on foreign students under the New Zealand Education Amendment Act 1979*

Communication of 15 December 1983 submitted by
Jerome Bernard Elkind*

Spring 1984 session of the Committee on Conventions and Recommendations (119th session of the Executive Board)[1]

121. This communication alleges that the tuition fees imposed on a certain category of foreign students by the New Zealand Education Amendment Act 1979 is discriminatory in nature.

122. In a letter dated 30 April 1984 [...] addressed to the Secretariat,[2] the Permanent Delegate of New Zealand to Unesco stated that the authorities of his country would co-operate fully with the Committee, that they were preparing their response to the allegations made in the communication and that they therefore requested that its examination be deferred.

123. The Committee agreed to this request and *decided* to defer examination of the admissibility of the communication to its [autumn 1984] session.

---

* On behalf of the New Zealand University Students' Association.
[1] See document 119 EX/35 PRIV., paras. 121-123; see also documents 119 EX/CR/HR/3 Add. and Add.4.
[2] See document 119 EX/CR/HR/3 Add.4.

No. 602/84 **New Zealand**

Autumn 1984 session of the Committee on Conventions and Recommendations (120th session of the Executive Board)[3]

83. This communication alleges that the tuition fees imposed on a certain category of foreign students by the New Zealand Education Amendment Act 1979 are discriminatory in nature.

84. Confirming the tenor of the letter dated 10 September 1984 sent by the Permanent Delegation of New Zealand to Unesco [...],[4] the representative of the government concerned said that the question of the tuition fees payable by overseas students would be examined thoroughly by the new government formed after the recent elections which had taken place in the country. Without prejudging any future decision of the competent authorities, he believed that the problem raised in the communication would then find a satisfactory solution. Accordingly, he requested that the examination of this communication be deferred to a later session.

85. After an exchange of views, the Committee *decided* to resume examination of the communication at its [spring 1985] session, in the hope that a solution would have been found by that date.

Spring 1985 session of the Committee on Conventions and Recommendations (121st session of the Executive Board)[5]

107. This communication alleges that the tuition fees imposed on a certain category of foreign students by the New Zealand Education Amendment Act 1979 are discriminatory in nature.

108. At its [autumn 1984] session, the Committee was informed by the representative of the government concerned that the question of the tuition fees payable by overseas students would be examined thoroughly by the new government formed after the elections which had taken place in the country. Without prejudging any future decision of the competent authorities, he believed that the problem raised in the communication would then find a satisfactory solution. Accordingly, he requested that the examination of this communication be deferred to a later session.

---

[3] See document 120 EX/15 PRIV., paras. 83-85; see also documents 120 EX/CR/HR/2 and Add.2.

[4] See document 120 EX/CR/HR/2 Add.2.

[5] See document 121 EX/46 PRIV., paras. 107-111; see also document 121 EX/CR/HR/2.

New Zealand **No. 602/84**

109. In introducing this communication to the Committee at its present session, the representative of the Director-General, who is also the Legal Adviser, informed the Committee that in a letter to the Secretariat dated 30 January 1985, the permanent delegate of the Member State concerned had transmitted information according to which his government remained committed to the principle of abolishing the tuition fees imposed on foreign students. This information, confirmed by another letter to the Secretariat dated 19 April 1985, indicated that in the 1985 academic year, the government of New Zealand had reduced from approximately US $700 to about US $450 the fees payable by foreign students. In order to await further developments in this direction on the part of his government, the representative of the government of New Zealand asked that further examination of the admissibility of the communication be postponed to the Committee's autumn 1985 session.

110. Some members of the Committee pointed out that in their respective countries education was free and that foreign students, a good number of whom were from developing countries, admitted to various education institutions in these countries also enjoyed this facility. Some other members stated however that, in their view, foreign students could be asked to pay higher tuition fees than their non-foreign counterparts to the extent that the parents of such foreign students do not pay some of the taxes which go into the running of the educational institutions concerned. These members nevertheless added that any tuition fees differential between foreign and local students should be reasonable rather than dissuasive. A number of members took note of the fact that the declared policy of the government concerned was the complete abolition of the special tuition fees imposed on foreign students and expressed the hope that this policy commitment would be implemented without too much delay.

111. At the end of its discussion, the Committee *decided*:

(i) to take note of the government concerned's commitment to abolish the special tuition fees imposed on foreign students studying in New Zealand;

(ii) to urge the government to implement this commitment as soon as possible;

(iii) to defer to its autumn 1985 session its examination of the admissibility of the communication.

No. 602/84 **New Zealand**

Autumn 1985 session of the Committee on Conventions and Recommendations (122nd session of the Executive Board)[6]

86. This communication alleges that the tuition fees imposed on a certain category of foreign students by the New Zealand Education Amendment Act 1979 are discriminatory in nature.

87. At its [spring 1985] session, the representative of the government concerned informed the Committee that his government remained committed to the principle of abolishing the tuition fees imposed on foreign students and that for the 1985 academic year, the Government of New Zealand had reduced from approximately US $700 to about US $450 the fees payable by foreign students. In order to await further developments in this direction on the part of his government, the representative of the Government of New Zealand asked that further examination of the admissibility of the communication be postponed to the Committee's autumn 1985 session.

88. At its present session, the Committee was informed by the representative of the government concerned that her government still remained committed to the principle of abolishing tuition fees imposed on foreign students. She added that a new decision by her government might be taken later this year for 1986 and asked that in the meantime the examination of the communication be deferred to the spring 1986 session of the Committee. In answer to questions posed by some members of the Committee, she stated that the fees were imposed on all foreign students on a non-discriminatory basis adding that foreign students who went to study in New Zealand on bilateral aid programmes were however awarded scholarships or fellowships.

89. Some members of the Committee stated in this connection that, in their opinion, to the extent that all foreign students were treated alike, there was no discrimination and consequently the communication was not admissible because it was not within the competence of the Committee to question the particular policy of the government concerned which related in effect to a decision not to grant aid to foreign students. These members added that they did not consider the policy in question to be wrong because education had to be paid for from the resources of the country to which the parents of foreign students made no contribution. One member declared that it was pertinent to recall that Article 1 of the International Convention on the Elimination of All Forms of Racial Discrimination permitted distinctions, exclusions, restrictions or preferences made by a State Party to the Convention between citizens and non-citizens.

---

[6] See document 122 EX/21 PRIV., paras. 86-91; see also document 122 EX/CR/HR/2.

New Zealand **No. 602/84**

90. A member of the Committee stated that in his view the issue raised by the communication was not to be considered in terms of the privileges of those who paid taxes in New Zealand as opposed to those students whose parents were foreigners and thus paid no taxes in that country but rather in the context of the duty of a developed country to help a developing one. Another member expressed his satisfaction at the action taken by the authorities of the State concerned to reduce the fees payable for the 1985 academic year by foreign students and added that his satisfaction would be greater if the government concerned were to abolish the fees altogether.

91. At the end of its discussion, the Committee concluded that there had been no discrimination and accordingly *decided* to strike out the communication from its list.

No. 603/84

Concerning *Union of Soviet Socialist Republics*
Case of *Andrei Sakharov*

Communication of 14 December 1983 submitted by
José Féron

Spring 1984 session of the Committee on Conventions and Recommendations (119th session of the Executive Board)[1]

Autumn 1984 session of the Committee on Conventions and Recommendations (120th session of the Executive Board)[2]

Spring 1985 session of the Committee on Conventions and Recommendations (121st session of the Executive Board)[3]

Autumn 1985 session of the Committee on Conventions and Recommendations (122nd session of the Executive Board)[4]

Spring 1986 session of the Committee on Conventions and Recommendations (124th session of the Executive Board)[5]

---

[1] See document 119 EX/35 PRIV., paras. 170-179 (*supra*, pp. 159-162), communication No. 482/82 concerning *Union of Soviet Socialist Republics*, case of *Andrei Sakharov*.
[2] See document 120 EX/15 PRIV., paras. 131-133 (*supra*, pp. 162-163), communication No. 482/ 82 concerning *Union of Soviet Socialist Republics*, case of *Andrei Sakharov*.
[3] See document 121 EX/46 PRIV., para. 152 (*supra*, p. 163), communication No. 482/82 concerning *Union of Soviet Socialist Republics*, case of *Andrei Sakharov*.
[4] See document 122 EX/21 PRIV., para. 112 (*supra*, p. 163), communication No. 482/82 concerning *Union of Soviet Socialist Republics*, case of *Andrei Sakharov*.
[5] See document 124 EX/3 PRIV., paras. 101-104 (*supra*, pp. 48-49), communication No. 441/ 82 concerning *Union of Soviet Socialist Republics*, case of *Vladimir Raiz*.

No. 603/84 **Union of Soviet Socialist Republics**

Autumn 1986 session of the Committee on Conventions and Recommendations (125th session of the Executive Board)[6]

Spring 1987 session of the Committee on Conventions and Recommendations (126th session of the Executive Board)[7]

[6] See document 125 EX/3 PRIV., paras. 84-98 (*supra*, pp. 164-168), communication No. 482/82 concerning *Union of Soviet Socialist Republics*, case of *Andrei Sakharov*.
[7] See document 126 EX/3 PRIV., paras. 101-105 (*supra*, pp. 168-169), communication No. 482/82 concerning *Union of Soviet Socialist Republics*, case of *Andrei Sakharov*.

No. 605/84

Concerning *Chile*
Case of *Luis Eduardo Labarca Goddard*

Communication of 31 December 1983 submitted by
Luis Eduardo Labarca Goddard

Spring 1984 session of the Committee on Conventions and Recommendations (119th session of the Executive Board)[1]

78. The author of the communication, Mr Luis Eduardo Labarca Goddard, a lawyer, journalist, writer and film-maker of Chilean nationality, explains that after being arrested on 11 September 1973 and freed several days later he left Chile on 24 February 1974 and is at present residing as a political refugee in France, where he is continuing his intellectual activity.

79. Two requests for permission to return to Chile, which he says he lodged with the Chilean Consulate in Paris in April 1980 and December 1983, have apparently not been acknowledged.

80. The representative of the Chilean Government stated that, although he had not had time to obtain further details on the subject, the case did not seem to him *a priori* to present overwhelming difficulties; on the other hand, it appeared necessary to inform the person concerned of the procedures recently established by his government, of which he had informed the Committee at previous sessions.

81. In reply to a question from a member of the Committee, the representative of the Chilean Government stated that consulates were informed of these procedures but that letters sent by individuals involved were not always in the form required for applications for permission to return.

82. A member of the Committee suggested that the Secretariat should be authorized to contact the person concerned, who was living in Paris, in order to inform him of

---

[1] See document 119 EX/35 PRIV., paras. 78-83; see also document 119 EX/CR/HR/3 Add.2.

the procedure to be followed; all the members of the Committee who spoke subsequently were in favour of suspending the examination of the communication.

83. Consequently, the Committee *decided*:

(i) to authorize the Secretariat to contact the person concerned to inform him of the procedures open to him as explained by the representative of the Chilean Government;

(ii) to suspend examination of the admissibility of this communication until the autumn [1984 session].

Autumn 1984 session of the Committee on Conventions and Recommendations (120th session of the Executive Board)[2]

47. The author of the communication, Mr Luis Eduardo Labarca Goddard, a lawyer, journalist, writer and film-maker of Chilean nationality, explains that after being arrested on 11 September 1973 and freed several days later he left Chile on 24 February 1974 and is at present residing as a political refugee in France, where he is continuing his intellectual activity.

48. Two requests for permission to return to Chile, which he says he lodged with the Chilean Consulate in Paris in April 1980 and December 1983, have apparently not been acknowledged.

49. At the [spring 1984] session, the Committee decided to authorize the Secretariat to contact the person involved to inform him of the procedures open to him.[3] Mr Labarca Goddard replied to the Secretariat's letter informing him of the decision of the Committee by a letter dated 27 June 1984 stating that his appeal for reconsideration had been rejected in January 1984 and that he had not filed an application for *amparo*, mainly because he felt it was difficult to do so from France, as it involved contacting a lawyer in Santiago, etc.

50. At the present session, the representative of the Chilean Government declared that the communication was incomplete since the author did not give the reasons for which his application for reconsideration had been rejected; moreover, the reasons presented by Mr Labarca Goddard for not having filed an application for *amparo* were not valid; in fact, such an application could be filed on his behalf by a third

---

[2] See document 120 EX/15 PRIV., paras. 47-52; see also document 120 EX/CR/HR/2.
[3] See document 119 EX/35 PRIV., para. 83 (i) (*supra*, p. 428).

party, and he could even contact the Vicaría de la Solidaridad, which had a free legal assistance service specializing in this type of affair. The representative of the government concerned reminded the Committee that at the [spring 1984] session he had referred to a Supreme Court ruling, dated 30 January 1984, which had upheld the requests submitted by 25 persons whose application for *amparo* had been rejected by the Court of Appeal. When Mr Labarca Goddard had filed this application he could be considered to have met the conditions set in paragraph 14 (*a*) (ix) of 104 EX/Decision 3.3 on efforts to be made to exhaust all internal remedies; if such recourse failed there would then be reason to take humanitarian steps on his behalf. In reply to a member of the Committee who had wondered why the application for reconsideration made by the person concerned had been rejected, the representative of the Chilean Government stated that the administrative authority taking the decision to reject an application for *amparo* was required to give reasons for its decision.

51. Another member of the Committee inquired into the circumstances under which Mr Labarca Goddard had left Chile, since he was a political refugee in France. The Legal Adviser explained that the status of political refugee did not imply that the person concerned had been obliged to leave his country, since it was possible to become a refugee when already in the country of residence abroad. Two members of the Committee spoke in favour of maintaining this communication on the agenda of the Committee, one of them stressing that the information received should be passed on to the author and the other expressing the hope that this case would have a favourable outcome.

52. Consequently, the Committee *decided*:

(i) to transmit to the author of the communication the additional information provided by the representative of the Chilean Government;

(ii) to resume consideration of the admissibility of this communication at its spring 1985 session.

Spring 1985 session of the Committee on Conventions and Recommendations (121st session of the Executive Board)[4]

61. The author of the communication, Mr Luis Eduardo Labarca Goddard, a lawyer, journalist, writer and film-maker of Chilean nationality, explains that, after being arrested on 11 September 1973 and freed a few days later, he left Chile on 24 Febru-

[4] See document 121 EX/46 PRIV., paras. 61-65; see also document 121 EX/CR/HR/2.

ary 1974 and is at present residing as a political refugee in France, where he is continuing his intellectual activity.

62. At the [autumn 1984] session, the Committee decided to resume consideration of the admissibility of this communication once the information supplied by the representative of the Chilean Government regarding the remedies available to the author, and particularly the remedy of *amparo*, had been transmitted to him.[5]

63. Mr Luis Eduardo Labarca Goddard replied to the Secretariat's letter on 8 April 1985, confirming his intention to take all the necessary steps in order to be authorized to return to Chile. He expressed his readiness to file an application for *amparo*, as he had been advised to do, and this will be lodged on his behalf by his wife, who will be visiting Chile next June. He accordingly asked that the examination of his case be held over until the results of this application were known.

64. At the present session, the representative of the Chilean Government stated that, since, as he had indicated to the Committee, the author was going to file an application with the courts, the only course was to await the latter's decision.

65. The Committee consequently *decided* to accede to the request made by the author of the communication and to resume its examination of the admissibility of the communication at its autumn 1985 session.

Autumn 1985 session of the Committee on Conventions and Recommendations (122nd session of the Executive Board)[6]

60. The author of the communication, Mr Luis Eduardo Labarca Goddard, a lawyer, journalist, writer and film-maker of Chilean nationality, explains that, after being arrested on 11 September 1973 and freed a few days later, he left Chile on 24 February 1974 and is at present residing as a political refugee in France, where he is continuing his intellectual activity.

61. At the [spring 1985] session, the Committee decided to accede to the request made by the author of the communication, who was awaiting the outcome of the steps he had taken, and to defer consideration of this communication to the present session.[7]

---

[5] See document 120 EX/15 PRIV., para. 52 (*supra*, p. 429).
[6] See document 122 EX/21 PRIV., paras. 60-65; see also document 122 EX/CR/HR/2.
[7] See document 121 EX/46 PRIV., para. 65 (*supra*, p. 430).

Chile **No. 605/84**

62. On 27 August 1985, the Secretariat received a letter dated 22 August 1985 from the author of the communication stating that, in accordance with the information he had been given by officials of the Ministry of the Interior and Ministry of External Relations of Chile, he had filed a plea for reconsideration on 19 August 1985, together with an application for provisional authorization to return for 60 days. A copy of the text of the plea was enclosed with his letter.

63. At the present session, the representative of the Chilean Government confirmed that he had indeed received a visit from Mr Labarca Goddard's wife and had helped her to draw up the plea; he noted that after contemplating an application for *amparo* the person concerned had opted for a plea for administrative reconsideration, which took less time; he said that he would follow up the case on returning to Santiago and that he did not expect any problems, at least as far as the temporary authorization was concerned.

64. Some members of the Committee proposed that the communication be deleted from the list as soon as the Secretariat had received confirmation that Mr Labarca Goddard had been authorized to return for good; others wished to keep the communication on the Committee's agenda until a final solution had been found.

65. At the end of the discussion, the Committee *decided*, pending further information, to resume consideration of the admissibility of this communication at its spring 1986 session.

Spring 1986 session of the Committee on Conventions and Recommendations (124th session of the Executive Board)[8]

42. The author of communication, Mr Luis Eduardo Labarca Goddard, a lawyer, journalist, writer and film-maker of Chilean nationality, explains that, after being arrested on 11 September 1973 and freed a few days later, he left Chile on 24 February 1974 and is at present residing as a political refugee in France, where he is continuing his intellectual activity.

43. At the [autumn 1985] session, the Committee had been informed by the representative of the Chilean Government that the person concerned had filed a plea for reconsideration in accordance with the information given to him by officials of the Ministries concerned and that he should not have any problem in obtaining at least a temporary authorization; it had accordingly been decided, pending further informa-

[8] See document 124 EX/3 PRIV., paras. 42-46; see also documents 124 EX/CR/HR/2 and Add.2.

tion, to defer consideration of the admissibility of the communication until the present session.[9]

44. At the present session, the Secretariat informed the Committee that, on 16 April 1986, the Organization had received a letter dated 14 April 1986 from the author of the communication describing the steps recently taken by his son, by the Colegio de Abogados de Chile and by the Colegio de Periodistas - two bodies of which he is a member - and stating that despite these efforts he had still not received an answer to the plea for reconsideration he had submitted in August 1985. In that plea he had requested permanent authorization to return, or failing that, provisional authorization to return for 60 days.

45. The representative of the Chilean Government stated that a provisional authorization for 60 days would very shortly be granted to Mr Labarca Goddard and that the latter, as a lawyer sponsored by the Colegio de Abogados, would not fail, once in Chile, to take the necessary steps to obtain permanent authorization, which he was confident would be accorded.

46. After an exchange of views, the Committee *decided* to take note of the statements by the representative of the Chilean Government, to communicate them to the person concerned and to resume its examination of the admissibility of the communication at its autumn 1986 session.

Autumn 1986 session of the Committee on Conventions and Recommendations (125th session of the Executive Board)[10]

30. Mr Luis Eduardo Labarco Goddard, a lawyer, journalist, writer and film-maker of Chilean nationality, after being arrested on 11 September 1973 and freed a few days later, is said to. have left Chile on 24 February 1974. He is currently residing in France and has reportedly filed two applications for authorization to return to Chile at the Chilean Consulate in Paris, but has received no reply.

31. At the [autumn 1985 and spring 1986] sessions the representative of the government concerned informed the Committee that the person in question had lodged an appeal for reconsideration of his case in accordance with the information given to him by officials of the Ministries concerned, and that there should be no problem in his obtaining at least temporary authorization.

---

[9] See document 122 EX/21 PRIV., para. 65 (*supra*, p. 431).
[10] See document 125 EX/3 PRIV., paras. 30-34; see also document 125 EX/CR/HR/2.

32. In a letter dated 11 August 1986, Mr Labarca Goddard stated that he had just learned from the Chilean Consulate in Vienna that he was still prohibited from returning to his country.

33. At the present session, the representative of the government concerned informed the Committee that the person in question had recently sent a long letter to the Chilean authorities, that his case was still under consideration but that he had every reason to suppose that a favourable decision would be taken. He pointed out that the author of the communication had to all intents and purposes accused him (in the letter dated 14 April 1986 [...])[11] by stating that his proposal of good offices was a delaying tactic aimed at reassuring the Committee. On the advice of the Chairperson and the Committee members who took the floor, he agreed to take the view that this was simply an expression of discouragement by someone who was worn out by waiting.

34. After an exchange of views, the Committee *decided*:

(i) to thank the government concerned for sending a representative;

(ii) to take note of the clarifications and observations made by that government's representative and to request him to continue to make use of his good offices with the competent authorities of his country, in the hope that a positive solution would be found before the next session;

(iii) to resume consideration of this communication at its spring 1987 session.

Spring 1987 session of the Committee on Conventions and Recommendations (126th session of the Executive Board)[12]

28. Mr Luis Eduardo Labarca Goddard, a lawyer, journalist, writer and film-maker, is alleged to have been arrested on 11 September 1973 and then released a few days later and is said to have left Chile on 24 February 1974. It is claimed that his applications for authorization to return there have received no reply.

29. In a letter dated 14 April 1987, he stated that, in spite of what the representative of the Chilean Government declared at the [autumn 1986] session of the Committee, he was still prohibited from returning to his country.

[11] See document 124 EX/CR/HR/2 Add.2.

[12] See document 126 EX/3 PRIV., paras. 28-31; see also document 126 EX/CR/HR/2.

No. 605/84 **Chile**

30. Taking the floor, the representative of the government concerned informed the Committee that he had just learned officially that the person concerned would be authorized to return permanently to Chile during May. He stated that, in accordance with normal procedures, the Permanent Delegation of Chile to Unesco would not fail to confirm this in writing as soon as possible. He added that he was in contact with Mr Labarca Goddard's lawyer in Santiago and that the date of the authorization in question would also be communicated.

31. After an exchange of views, the Committee *decided*:

(i) to thank the representative of the government concerned for his presence and for his co-operation;

(ii) to strike *ipso facto* this communication from its list, as soon as the Secretariat has received confirmation of the authorization granted to Mr Luis Eduardo Labarca Goddard to return to Chile, on the understanding that the Secretariat will inform the Committee if the communication is struck off, but that if the confirmation does not reach the Secretariat before the autumn 1987 session, consideration of this communication will be resumed by the Committee.

No. 606/84

Concerning *Turkey*
Case of *Mahmut Dikerdem* et al.*

Communication of 2 January 1984 submitted by
Zygmunt Elbiński

Spring 1985 session of the Committee on Conventions and Recommendations (121st session of the Executive Board)[1]

142. It is alleged in this communication that, under martial law, 23 members of the Turkish Peace Association were sentenced, in November 1983, to up to eight years' imprisonment, wrongly accused of running a communist front organization and of slandering the State abroad, just because they exchanged information and ideas with Greek peace activists on questions relating to peaceful settlement of the conflict of Cyprus. It is said that among them, there were Mr Mahmut Dikerdem, a former Turkish Ambassador, who, according to the author of the communication, is seriously ill and in need of intensive medical care, Mr Erdal Atabek, Chairman of the Turkish Medical Association, and Mr Orhan Apaydın, Chairman of the Turkish Bar Association.

143. In his submission to the Committee, the representative of the government concerned declared that the allegations put forward by the author of the communication were outside the fields of competence of Unesco. He stated further that, in the case submitted to the Committee, no attempt had been made by the alleged victims to exhaust the internal remedies available to them. He added that, in any case, the communication submitted to Unesco was premature to the extent that the examination of the allegations contained in the communication was still pending before the Court of Cassation and that until and unless there was a definitive pronouncement by this Court in that respect, all of the alleged victims were, and remained, free.

144. A number of members of the Committee pointed out that legal proceedings relating to the alleged victims were still continuing in the courts of the Member State

* Case of *Mahmut Dikerdem, Erdal Atabek and Orhan Apaydın.*
[1] See document 121 EX/46 PRIV., paras. 142-145; see also document 121 EX/CR/HR/3 Add.

concerned. They declared that, for this reason and also on account of the nature of the alleged victims' activities, the communication should be declared inadmissible. A member of the Committee however disagreed with this suggestion and counter-proposed that the communication should not be disposed of by the Committee until the conclusion of the pending legal proceedings. Pointing out that the accusations against the alleged victims were highly criminal in character, another member counselled that the Committee should not do anything which could be construed as interference with the judicial system of the Member State concerned. In this connection, another member expressed the hope that the Committee, in its examination of communications, would show consistency with respect to the sovereign right of States to regulate by law their internal affairs, especially as regards State security matters. Another member supported the proposal to suspend the examination of the admissibility of the communication. He pointed out that the case against the alleged victims was pending not on their initiative but rather on the initiative of the competent authorities of the Member State concerned.

145. After an exchange of views among its members, the Committee *decided* to declare the communication inadmissible as it fell outside the Organization's fields of competence.

No. 608/84

Concerning *Chile*
Case of *José Miguel Varas Morel*

Communication of 19 January 1984 submitted by
José Miguel Varas Morel

Spring 1985 session of the Committee on Conventions and Recommendations (121st session of the Executive Board)[1]

66. The author of the communication, Mr José Miguel Varas Morel, a journalist and writer of Chilean nationality, complains that he is not authorized to return to Chile. He explains that, as an active member of the Communist Party and head of the news department of the national television corporation from 1970 to 1973, he felt it preferable, during the events of September 1973, to ask the Embassy of the Federal Republic of Germany for political asylum, and subsequently to leave Chile in December 1973. Since 7 January 1974 he has been residing in Moscow, where he is a Radio Moscow commentator working on programmes intended for Chile.

67. He allegedly requested permission to return to Chile in 1978 and in 1983, to no avail. He was also refused permission in 1981 to return temporarily to see his mother who was ill, and subsequently to attend her funeral. His sister, Ines Varas Morel, reportedly applied to the special office of the Chilean Ministry of the Interior responsible for exiles, and on 24 May 1984 received a negative reply, giving no grounds. The Chilean Colegio de Periodistas reportedly supports his request.

68. The representative of the Chilean Government stated that he felt it necessary for Mr Varas Morel to be informed of the administrative and legal remedies available to him, and that he would for that purpose transmit to the Secretariat, as he had previously done, an updated memorandum on the procedures to be followed in order to obtain authorization to return to Chile. He wished, moreover, to know what representations the Chilean Colegio de Periodistas had made on behalf of Mr Varas Morel, since he for his part had had no knowledge thereof. Finally, in reply to a question regarding the failure to provide grounds for the negative reply received by the

[1] See document 121 EX/46 PRIV., paras. 66-69; see also document 121 EX/CR/HR/3.

sister of Mr Varas Morel following the steps she had taken, the representative of the government concerned explained that it was precisely in such a case that it became necessary to apply to a higher authority, in the event the Court of Appeal, by filing an application for *amparo*, which was the only means whereby Mr Varas Morel could ascertain the grounds for the refusal.

69. Following an exchange of views, the Committee *decided*:

(i) to inform the author of the communication of the administrative and legal remedies available to him in the light of the statements made by the representative of the Chilean Government;

(ii) to suspend examination of the admissibility of this communication until its autumn 1985 session.

Autumn 1985 session of the Committee on Conventions and Recommendations (122nd session of the Executive Board)[2]

66. The author of the communication, Mr José Miguel Varas Morel, a journalist and writer of Chilean nationality, complains that he is not authorized to return to Chile. He explains that, as an active member of the Communist Party and head of the news department of the national television corporation from 1970 to 1973, he felt it preferable, during the events of September 1973, to ask the Embassy of the Federal Republic of Germany for political asylum, and subsequently to leave Chile in December 1973. Since 7 January 1974 he has been residing in Moscow, where he is a Radio Moscow commentator working on programmes intended for Chile.

67. He allegedly requested permission to return to Chile in 1978 and in 1983, to no avail. He was also refused permission in 1981 to return temporarily to see his mother who was ill, and subsequently to attend her funeral. His sister, Ines Varas Morel, reportedly applied to the special office of the Chilean Ministry of the Interior responsible for exiles, and on 24 May 1984 received a negative reply, giving no grounds. The Chilean Colegio de Periodistas reportedly supports his request.

68. At the [spring 1985] session the Committee had decided to inform the person concerned of the remedies available to him and to resume consideration of this communication at the present session.[3]

---

[2] See document 122 EX/21 PRIV., paras. 66-71; see also document 122 EX/CR/HR/2.
[3] See document 121 EX/46 PRIV., para. 69 (*supra*, p. 438).

Chile **No. 608/84**

69. At this session, the representative of the Chilean Government informed the Committee that Mr J. M. Varas Morel had taken no steps to seek any administrative or legal remedy.

70. Some members of the Committee suggested that additional time be granted to the author of the communication, it being understood that no further extension would be granted if, in the meantime, the person concerned did not take action on his own behalf.

71. Following its discussions, the Committee *decided*:

(i) to request the Secretariat to inform the author of the communication once more of the administrative and legal remedies available to him and to indicate to him that, should he not make use of them, the Committee would *ipso facto* strike his communication off its list at its spring 1986 session;

(ii) to postpone consideration of the admissibility of this communication until its next session.

Spring 1986 session of the Committee on Conventions and Recommendations (124th session of the Executive Board)[4]

47. The author of the communication, Mr José Miguel Varas Morel, a journalist and writer of Chilean nationality, complains that he is not authorized to return to Chile. He explains that, as an active member of the Communist Party and head of the news department of the national television corporation from 1970 to 1973, he felt it preferable, during the events of September 1973, to ask the Embassy of the Federal Republic of Germany for political asylum, and subsequently to leave Chile in December 1973. Since 7 January 1974 he has been residing in Moscow, where he is a Radio Moscow commentator working on programmes intended for Chile.

48. He allegedly requested permission to return to Chile in 1978 and in 1983, to no avail. He was also refused permission in 1981 to return temporarily to see his mother who was ill, and subsequently to attend her funeral. His sister, Ines Varas Morel, reportedly applied to the special office of the Chilean Ministry of the Interior responsible for exiles, and on 24 May 1984 received a negative reply, giving no grounds. The Chilean Colegio de Periodistas reportedly supports his request.

[4] See document 124 EX/3 PRIV., paras. 47-53; see also document 124 EX/CR/HR/2.

No. 608/84 **Chile**

49. At the [autumn 1985] session the Committee, having been informed that Mr Varas Morel had taken no action to seek remedies about which he had previously been advised, had decided to inform the author of the communication once more of the administrative and legal remedies available to him and to indicate to him that, should he not make use of them, the Committee would *ipso facto* strike his communication off its list at its present session.[5]

50. On 9 September 1985, a few days after the Committee's autumn 1985 session, the Secretariat received from the author of the communication a letter in which he explains that, on 20 August 1985, the Chairman of the Chilean Commission on Human Rights submitted a collective application for *amparo* for all Chilean citizens whom the Chilean Government refuses to allow to live in their country. He is included in the list of those covered by the application and considers that he has therefore complied with the Committee's recommendation that he avail himself of the legal remedies existing in Chile.

51. At the present session, the representative of the government concerned explained that such collective action could not, in Chile, be regarded as valid and that in such matters it was essential to file an individual plea; he therefore considered that Mr Varas Morel ought to have submitted an application for *amparo* on his own behalf. He stressed that, in addition, the case was not without its political aspects and it would be prudent to leave a decision to the courts.

52. Several members of the Committee considered that Mr José Miguel Varas Morel had not made use of the remedies available to him, as had been suggested to him on several occasions, in particular through the decision taken by the Committee at its [autumn 1985] session.

53. The Committee accordingly *decided*, bearing in mind its previous decision, to declare the communication not admissible under the terms of paragraph 14 (*a*) (ix) of 104 EX/Decision 3.3.

---

[5] See document 122 EX/21 PRIV., para. 71 (i) (*supra*, p. 439).

No. 610/84

Concerning *Turkey*
Case of *Sadun Aren*

Communication of 24 January 1984 submitted by
Christine Aren

Spring 1984 session of the Committee on Conventions and Recommendations (119th session of the Executive Board)[1]

150. Mr Sadun Aren, a teacher, is alleged, by Mrs Christine Aren, to have been arrested in November 1982 for his activities in managing the Research Centre of the Union DISK.

151. Confirming the substance of his letter to the Secretariat, dated 3 May 1984, the representative of the Turkish Government made known that in her letter of 24 January 1984 Mrs Christine Aren, while pointing out that her intention was not to interfere in the course of justice, had asked that Mr Aren be freed on bail. Having stated that in accordance with the principle of the separation of powers his government was not able to take action in matters relating to justice, he told the Committee that the investigating magistrate concerned had just granted the accused bail for humanitarian reasons, in view of his age and delicate state of health.

152. A member of the Committee asked whether as a general rule it was possible for the Committee to go a little further than the author requested in its consideration of a communication.

153. The Legal Adviser said that on the basis of the Committee's past practice the answer to that question could only be in the negative. This view was supported by a Committee member, who said that for the moment it was not for the Committee to concern itself with the charges brought against the alleged victim.

154. One member felt that even so the Committee should reflect a degree of hope in its decision, in view of the positive reaction of the Turkish authorities.

---

[1] See document 119 EX/35 PRIV., paras. 150-155; see also document 119 EX/CR/HR/3 Add.

No. 610/84 **Turkey**

155. Following an exchange of views, the Committee, considering that since the aim of the communication had been to secure the release of Mr Aren, it no longer had any point, *decided*:

(i) to strike it from its list; and

(ii) to express the hope that the person concerned would, after his trial, be able to enjoy on a permanent basis the freedom recently accorded to him.

No. 613/84

Concerning *United States of America*
Case of *Alleged discrimination in education against the black American minority*

Communication of 31 January 1984 submitted by
Charles Knox *et al.*[*]

Spring 1984 session of the Committee on Conventions and Recommendations (119th session of the Executive Board)[1]

94. According to the authors of the communication, there is in the United States of America discrimination in education against the black American minority. They allege that the decision of 28 June 1978 rendered by the United States Supreme Court in the *Allan Bakke* case denies members of the black American minority the right to special measures or affirmative action which aimed at establishing equal access to higher education by alleviating damage caused by past and continuing discrimination. In that case (*Regents of the University of California* v. *Bakke*), the United States Supreme Court invalidated a special admissions programme which the Medical School of the University of Califernia at Davis had established in favour of applicants who were economically and/or educationally disadvantaged and members of a minority group (blacks, Chicanos, Asians, American Indians). The authors of the communication point out however that under international human rights law, governments undertake to provide special measures in order to ensure for their ethnic minorities educational, social and economic equality as well as the maintenance of their ethnic identities and cultural development.

95. The representative of the Government of the United States of America, who is a member of the Committee, stated that in his opinion, the communication failed to establish that there had been a violation of any internationally recognized human rights. He stated that the *Bakke* case arose out of a challenge to a separate admis-

[*] Charles Knox, Yussuf Khy and Yvonne King on behalf of the National Leadership Council for African-Americans and the National Conference of Black Lawyers Community College of Law and International Diplomacy.
[1] See document 119 EX/35 PRIV., paras. 94-100; see also document 119 EX/CR/HR/3 Add.

sions system that was intended to help disadvantaged applicants to the University concerned. It was explained that in practice however, this system benefited only applicants who fell into four racial categories, namely, blacks, Chicanos, Asians and American Indians.

96. The representative of the government concerned explained further that individual applicants who fell into any of these four categories were considered apart from all other candidates and were treated as competing against one another and not against all the other applicants. It was pointed out that it was in this context that Mr Bakke had applied unsuccessfully twice to gain admission to the University in question even though on both occasions his score in the entrance test was higher than the entrance score for the admission of the disadvantaged; also on both occasions, some of the places reserved for those in the four categories concerned were left unfilled. On the scope of the United States Supreme Court judgement in question, the representative of the Government of the United States of America stated that, contrary to what the authors of the communication claimed, the Court did not rule against the principle of affirmative action in favour of university applicants belonging to the four racial categories in question. He said that the Supreme Court, acting on the premise that all racial classification was inherently suspect, had scrutinized the particular admissions system which was in force at the University of California and had concluded that that system violated the 14th Amendment to the United States Constitution which provided for equal protection of the laws because in the application of that specific system, race was a determining factor. He remarked that even if the United States of America were party to the International Convention on the Elimination of All Forms of Racial Discrimination, it would have respected fully the provisions of Article 1 (4) of that Convention because the Supreme Court decision concerned precisely sought to avoid the application of admissions system that led to the maintenance of separate rights for different racial groups. The representative submitted that it was the position of his government that the communication was not admissible.

97. One member of the Committee stated that the communication raised an important question of principle. He added that personally and from the standpoint of his political convictions, he was in favour of affirmative action and accordingly regretted the United States Supreme court decision. He pointed out that the issue for the consideration of the Committee was however whether the United States of America had an international obligation to take affirmative action. He submitted that Article 1 (4) of the International Convention on the Elimination of All Forms of Racial Discrimination did not impose an obligation but rather it provided authorization for States Parties to take affirmative action if they so wished. Several members of the Committee concurred on this viewpoint. The Legal Advisor also agreed with the interpretation given in Article 1 (4) of the aforementioned Convention. He added in this connection that the 1960 Unesco Convention against Discrimination in Educa-

tion on the other hand appeared to him to prohibit affirmative action in the field of education. He suggested that perhaps in the near future the competent authorities of the Organization would take appropriate action to ensure that this Convention were aligned in this respect to the International Convention on the Elimination of All Forms of Racial Discrimination.

98. A member of the Committee stated that in his opinion, the communication submitted to the Committee raised a general question rather than individual cases. In this connection, he referred to paragraph 10 (*b*) of 104 EX/Decision 3.3 and pointed out that the authors of the communication had not provided any evidence of massive, systematic or flagrant violations of human rights. He queried whether in the form submitted to the Committee the communication was admissible. Another member said that the Committee had no jurisdiction to review the decision of the United States Supreme Court and proposed that the Committee should declare itself not competent to examine the communication in the form in which it had been submitted. In supporting this proposal, one other member remarked that if affirmative action was important, the methods and strategies for achieving it were equally important.

99. A member of the Committee stated that the communication concerned about 25 million blacks as well as other racial minority groups in the United States of America. He pointed out that the communication raised issues coming within the field of education and hence within Unesco's competence and suggested that the authors should be asked to provide more detailed information about the specific cases of four individuals mentioned in the communication in order to enable the Committee to examine them. In supporting this suggestion, one other member said that the authors may not be lawyers and might have not known the technicalities involved in submitting a communication to the Committee. He added that the human rights of thousands of black Americans are violated in the United States of America. He expressed regret that the United States of America is a party to neither the International Convention on the Elimination of All Forms of Racial Discrimination nor to any of the two United Nations Human Rights Covenants. Another member of the Committee remarked that the case is based on the abrogation of a training programme that was necessary for training black Americans needed for their community and for the United States of America as a whole. He counselled the Committee against allowing legal technicalities to cloud the substance of the complaint submitted to it. He suggested that the authors should be asked to reformulate their communication in a form that would be acceptable to the Committee. The representative of the government concerned declared that he was against the idea of reformulating the communication which was before the Committee. He added however that he had no objection against the submission of a new communication by the authors.

No. 613/84 **United States of America**

100. At the end of the discussion, the Committee *decided*:

(i) to declare the communication inadmissible as at present drawn up;

(ii) to inform its authors that they were entitled to redraft it in the form of individual cases with all the necessary items of information.

No. 614/84

Concerning *Denmark*
Case of *Kai Mogens H. Lång*

Communication of 4 February 1984 submitted by
Kai Mogens H. Lång

Spring 1984 session of the Committee on Conventions and Recommendations (119th session of the Executive Board)[1]

84. The author of the communication describes himself as a student and victim of discrimination on the part of the administration of the Institute of Comparative Literature of the University of Copenhagen, which, because of his political convictions (he is a member of Moderate Studenter - a minority student group), his religious convictions (he belongs to a religious group) and his ethnic origin (he is of Swedish origin), has allegedly not respected the regulations relating to studies and examinations. He also complains about the decision of the Supreme Court, which, by not condemning this discrimination, he considers to have exceeded the limits of its competence and "thus legalized" the discrimination.

85. The representative of the Danish Government explained that Mr Lång had exhausted all the available administrative and legal remedies and that an examination of the records of the proceedings instituted by Mr Lång in the different courts to which the case had been submitted had shown that everything was in order and that there had been no discrimination of any sort against him.

86. From the exchanges of views which followed, it emerged that the alleged grounds for the alleged discrimination (political and religious convictions and ethnic origin) were the same as those alleged in the previous two communications submitted by Mr Lång [...],[2] which was in itself sufficient reason to declare the present communication inadmissible; moreover, with reference to the alleged irregularities

[1] See document 119 EX/35 PRIV., paras. 84-87; see also document 119 EX/CR/HR/3 Add.
[2] Communications No. 144/79 concerning *Denmark*, case of *Kai Mogens H. Lång*, and No. 196/80 concerning *Denmark*, case of *Kai Mogens H. Lång*.

in the examination procedure objected to by this student, no tangible proof had been advanced of the alleged discrimination or, particularly, of its purpose.

87. The Committee *decided* to declare this communication inadmissible as being clearly without foundation and lacking relevant evidence, under paragraph 14 (*a*) (v) of 104 EX/Decision 3.3.

No. 616/84

Concerning *Czechoslovakia*
Case of *Jaromir Šavrda*

Communication of 2 February 1984 submitted by
Zygmunt Elbiński

Spring 1984 session of the Committee on Conventions and Recommendations (119th session of the Executive Board)[1]

147. Mr Jaromir Šavrda is presented as a writer and signatory of Charter 77. He was reportedly arrested in March 1983 and sentenced to 25 months' imprisonment, according to the author of the communication for reproducing and distributing Charter 77 documents. He is apparently not in good health.

148. The representative of the Czechoslovak Government requested that consideration of this communication be deferred until the autumn 1984 session of the Committee, as he had been unable to obtain the relevant information in time for the present session. As far as Mr Šavrda's health was concerned, he assured the Committee that in Czechoslovakia all citizens including prisoners received the necessary medical attention free of charge.

149. Following an exchange of views, the Committee *decided*:

(i) to accede to the request by the representative of the government concerned for deferral of the examination of the communication's admissibility until its [autumn 1984] session;

(ii) to express its humanitarian concern on behalf of Mr Šavrda to the government concerned.

[1] See document 119 EX/35 PRIV., paras. 147-149; see also document 119 EX/CR/HR/3 Add. 2.

No. 616/84 **Czechoslovakia**

Autumn 1984 session of the Committee on Conventions and Recommendations (120th session of the Executive Board)[2]

113. Mr Jaromir Šavrda is presented by the author of the communication as a writer and signatory of Charter 77. He was reportedly arrested in March 1983 and sentenced to 25 months' imprisonment for reproducing and distributing Charter 77 documents.

114. The representative of the government concerned stated that the actions of which Mr Šavrda was accused had been proven and that he had been sentenced in accordance with the provisions of the Penal Code for inciting the population against the Czechoslovak Republic. He then informed the Committee that the judicial authorities had decided to show clemency to the prisoner and to release him on 25 October next, before the end of his sentence, as a humanitarian measure and taking account of his conduct.

115. The members of the Committee who spoke considered that the purpose and aims of the communication had been achieved but that if there were any new developments concerning Mr Šavrda they could be the subject of a new communication.

116. Following an exchange of views, the Committee *decided* to consider the case as settled and to strike the communication from its list.

[2] See document 120 EX/15 PRIV., paras. 113-116; see also document 120 EX/CR/HR/2.

No. 618/84

Concerning *Chile*
Case of *Luis José Godoy González*

Communication of 6 February 1984 submitted by
Luis José Godoy González

Autumn 1984 session of the Committee on Conventions and Recommendations (120th session of the Executive Board)[1]

53. The author of the communication, a doctor of Chilean nationality, currently studying to be a specialist, alleges that after obtaining his medical degree at the University of Chile, in June 1978, he left that country in July of the same year and is now debarred from returning there. He mentions three of the reasons that prompted him at the time to leave Chile, namely, lack of career prospects, the possibility of specializing abroad and the fact that his parents and brothers lived in Europe. He is said to have applied for grants offered in Sweden, Spain and Hungary, and reportedly it was this last country that offered him the opportunity of specializing in internal medicine and gastro-enterology. It is claimed that in 1978 he left Chile with a "regular" passport which he renewed in 1980 at the Chilean Consultate in Belgrade. In 1982, the Chilean Consultate in Vienna allegedly renewed his passport for only six months (instead of the usual two years), at the end of which it is said that the passport returned to him was marked with the letter "L".

54. Relatives of Mr Godoy González living in Santiago are said to have submitted an appeal on his behalf to the Ministry of the Interior in accordance with the new provisions in force concerning exiles; that appeal was reportedly rejected by the Ministry on 28 December 1983.

55. The representative of the Chilean Government said that he had already taken up the case and had got in touch with the Ministry of the Interior in that connection, but the circumstances in which Mr L. J. Godoy González had left Chile had not yet been clarified and the appeal on his behalf submitted by relatives had not shed any light on the subject. In particular, it was necessary to make sure that there had been no

---

[1] See document 120 EX/15 PRIV., paras. 53-57; see also document 120 EX/CR/HR/3.

problem of a criminal nature. He hoped that the person concerned would provide detailed indications of the motives for and circumstances surrounding his departure from Chile and would be requested to submit a copy of the appeal made by his relatives to the Secretariat. The representative of the government concerned added that, on the face of it, the case should not pose any major problems; then, in reply to a member of the Committee who had pointed out that Mr Godoy González would have to leave Hungary before the end of 1984, he said that he was aware of that circumstance and would expedite his representations as soon as he had received the desired information. Finally, at the request of another member of the Committee, he confirmed that the procedure of marking passports with the letter "L" had been abandoned and had since been replaced by a list of citizens not authorized to return to Chile; this list could be consulted in Chilean Consulates by everybody concerned, but the number of names shown on it was gradually diminishing as solutions were found.

56. The members who then took the floor expressed the view that the necessary information should be requested from the individual concerned by whatever means the Secretariat deemed appropriate and that the communication should be kept on the Committee's agenda.

57. The Committee therefore *decided*:

(i) to inform the author of the communication of the statement of the representative of the Chilean Government and to request him to furnish the information and document demanded by the latter;

(ii) to resume consideration of the admissibility of the communication at the spring 1985 session of the Committee.

Spring 1985 session of the Committee on Conventions and Recommendations (121st session of the Executive Board)[2]

70. The author of the communication, a doctor of Chilean nationality, currently studying to be a specialist, alleges that after obtaining his medical degree at the University of Chile, in June 1978, he left that country in July of the same year and is now debarred from returning there. He mentions three of the reasons that prompted him at the time to leave Chile, namely, lack of career prospects, the possibility of specializing abroad, and the fact that his parents and brothers were living in Europe. He is said to have applied for grants offered in Sweden, Spain and Hungary, and report-

[2] See document 121 EX/46 PRIV., paras. 70-75; see also document 121 EX/CR/HR/2.

edly it was this last country that offered him the opportunity of specializing in internal medicine and gastro-enterology. It is claimed that in 1978 he left Chile with a "regular" passport which he renewed in 1980 at the Chilean Consulate in Belgrade. In 1982, the Chilean Consulate in Vienna allegedly renewed his passport for only six months (instead of the usual two years), at the end of which it is said that the passport returned to him was marked with the letter "L".

71. Relatives of Mr Godoy González living.in Santiago are said to have submitted an appeal on his behalf to the Ministry of the Interior in accordance with the new provisions in force concerning exiles; that appeal was reportedly rejected by the Ministry on 28 December 1983.

72. At the [autumn 1984] session, the Committee decided, among other things, to ask the author of the communication to supply the information, and a copy of the abovementioned application for *amparo*, which had been requested by the representative of the Chilean Government, and to resume its consideration of the admissibility of this communication at its present session.[3]

73. On 22 November 1984, the Secretariat received from Mr L. J. Godoy González a letter [...][4] in which he indicated that his departure from Chile had taken place under normal circumstances, that he had not sought political asylum in any country, and that he had gone to Hungary primarily for family reasons (his two brothers were living there) and because of the need to specialize in his profession; that he had been convicted of no offence in any country; that his relatives had not submitted a written application to the Ministry of the Interior but had merely inquired orally about his position; that his name was on a list of Chilean citizens prohibited from returning to Chile; and, finally, that he was taking steps to secure an extension of his sojourn in Hungary, without prejudice to any other diplomatic representations he might make.

74. At the present session, the representative of the Chilean Government pointed out that an application for reconsideration could only be submitted in writing, which was possibly why he had been unable to find any trace of the case. He suggested that Mr Godoy González should also make use of the exceptional procedure to which he had referred in connection with [another communication][5] in order to go to Chile to clarify his situation on the spot.

75. The Committee consequently *decided*:

---

[3] See document 120 EX/15 PRIV., para. 57 (*supra*, p. 452).

[4] See document 121 EX/CR/HR/2, annex II.

[5] See document 121 EX/46 PRIV., para. 39 (*supra*, pp. 335-336), communication No. 559/83 concerning *Chile*, case of *Carlos Alfredo Andrade Vera and Guillermo Vera Paulo*.

(i) to take note of the statements made by the representative of the Chilean Government and to request the Secretariat to inform the author of the communication accordingly;

(ii) to resume consideration of the admissibility of this communication at its autumn 1985 session.

Autumn 1985 session of the Committee on Conventions and Recommendations (122nd session of the Executive Board)[6]

72. The author of the communication, a doctor of Chilean nationality, currently studying to be a specialist, alleges that after obtaining his medical degree at the University of Chile, in June 1978, he left that country in July of the same year and is now debarred from returning there. He mentions three of the reasons that prompted him at the time to leave Chile, namely, lack of career prospects, the possibility of specializing abroad, and the fact that his parents and brothers were living in Europe. He is said to have applied for grants offered in Sweden, Spain and Hungary, and reportedly it was this last country that offered him the opportunity of specializing in internal medicine and gastro-enterology. It is claimed that in 1978 he left Chile with a "regular" passport which he renewed in 1980 at the Chilean Consulate in Belgrade. In 1982, the Chilean Consulate in Vienna allegedly renewed his passport for only six months (instead of the usual two years), at the end of which it is said that the passport returned to him was marked with the letter "L".

73. Relatives of Mr Godoy González living in Santiago are said to have submitted an appeal on his behalf to the Ministry of the Interior in accordance with the new provisions in force concerning exiles; that appeal was reportedly rejected by the Ministry on 28 December 1983.

74. At the [spring 1985] session, the Committee had decided to inform the author of the communication that the Chilean authorities had granted him special permission to return on a temporary basis in order to clarify his situation in Chile itself.[7]

75. On 30 August 1985 the Secretariat received from the author of the communication a letter dated 26 August 1985, in which he thanked Unesco for the temporary authorization obtained on his behalf, but stated that for family reasons he would not be able to take advantage of this opportunity before the end of October or the begin-

[6] See document 122 EX/21 PRIV., paras. 72-77; see also document 122 EX/CR/HR/2.
[7] See document 121 EX/46 PRIV., para. 75 (i) (*supra*, p. 454).

ning of November; however, he would contact the Chilean Consulate in Paris in the very near future.

76. At the present session the representative of the Chilean Government explained that the fact that Mr Godoy González could not for the moment take up the offer to return on a temporary basis did not mean that it would automatically lapse. However, he expressed regret that the person concerned had not yet submitted an application for reconsideration to the Ministry of the Interior and pointed out that not only might he do so before returning to Chile, but that in addition such a step would facilitate his task, once there, and speed up the course of events.

77. At the suggestion of one of its members, the Committee *decided*:

(i) to inform the author of the communication of the statements made by the representatives of the government concerned;

(ii) to resume consideration of the admissibility of this communication at its spring 1985 session.

Spring 1986 session of the Committee on Conventions and Recommendations (124th session of the Executive Board)[8]

54. The author of the communication, a doctor of Chilean nationality, currently studying to be a specialist, alleges that after obtaining his medical degree at the University of Chile, in June 1978, he left that country in July of the same year and is now debarred from returning there. He mentions three of the reasons that prompted him at the time to leave Chile, namely, lack of career prospects, the possibility of specializing abroad, and the fact that his parents and brothers were living in Europe. He is said to have applied for grants offered in Sweden, Spain and Hungary, and reportedly it was this last country that offered him the opportunity of specializing in internal medicine and gastro-enterology. It is claimed that in 1978 he left Chile with a "regular" passport which he renewed in 1980 at the Chilean Consulate in Belgrade. In 1982, the Chilean Consulate in Vienna allegedly renewed his passport for only six months (instead of the usual two years), at the end of which it is said that the passport returned to him was marked with the letter "L".

55. Relatives of Mr Godoy González living in Santiago are said to have submitted an appeal on his behalf to the Ministry of the Interior in accordance with the new

[8] See document 124 EX/3 PRIV., paras. 54-59; see also document 124 EX/CR/HR/2.

provisions in force concerning exiles; that appeal was reportedly rejected by the Ministry on 28 December 1983.

56. At the [autumn 1985] session, the Committee had decided to inform the author of the communication of the statements made by the representative of the government concerned to the effect that the offer to return on a temporary basis previously made to him remained valid even though he was unable to take it up immediately, but that it would be desirable for him to submit an application for reconsideration; the Committee had accordingly deferred examination of the communication to the present session.[9]

57. On 29 November 1985, the Secretariat had received from the author of the communication a letter dated 25 November 1985 which brought up to date the information previously made available to the Committee.

58. At the present session, the representative of the Chilean Government stated that he had just been informed by telex that Mr Luis Jose Godoy González had been given permanent and unconditional authorization to return to Chile.

59. In consequence, the Committee *decided* to declare the case raised by this communication settled under the terms of paragraph 14 (*a*) (x) of 104 EX/Decision 3.3.

[9] See document 122 EX/21 PRIV., para. 77 (*supra*, p. 455).

No. 622/84

Concerning *France*
Case of *Mohamed Benrahhlate*

Communication of 16 February 1984 submitted by
Mohamed Benrahhlate

Spring 1984 session of the Committee on Conventions and Recommendations (119th session of the Executive Board)[1]

101. The author describes himself as a Moroccan student, the victim of an irregularity in the marking of a written examination for the *licence* at the Université de Sciences in Nice which he claims was coloured by racism.

102. According to the representative of the French Government, who is also a member of the Committee, there are two aspects to this communication:

(1) The academic aspect: Judging from his university record Mr Benrahhlate was not an outstanding student; he had frequently failed in the first and second year examinations and in the third year, 1981, he had failed the written examination. He had been given a second chance oral examination but had failed. He had then entered a protest against the mark on his written examination paper, and had given up taking the other tests. He had been granted a second correction and exceptionally a third correction, which was done in Paris. The Administrative Tribunal of Nice, to which he referred the matter, had recently rejected his request on grounds of time bar.

(2) The breach of the peace aspect: Mr Benrahhlate had threatened to kill one of his professors; the matter had even been referred to the Nice public prosecutor; Mr Benrahhlate had been forced to apologize, and his case had then been considered closed. He and his father had undertaken a hunger strike on the university premises; according to the police report, the two hunger strik-

[1] See document 119 EX/35 PRIV., paras. 101-105; see also document 119 EX/CR/HR/3 Add. 2.

ers had been evacuated without trouble and after routine identity checks at the police station had been set free.

103. The representative of the French Government concluded by stating that Mr Benrahhlate had been accorded the benefit of all possible guarantees, that he had not been the victim of any discriminatory measure whatsoever, and that if he and his father believed they had been victims of acts of violence on the occasion of their attempted hunger strike, the normal means of redress in French justice were available to them in this respect.

104. In reply to the question as to whether Mr Benrahhlate could continue his studies in France, the representative of the French Government said that to his knowledge there was nothing to prevent him from doing so, especially since his resident's papers had just been renewed.

105. Following an exchange of views; the Committee *decided* to declare the communication inadmissible, in as being manifestly ill-founded in the terms of paragraph 14 (*a*) (v) of 104 EX/Decision 3.3 of the Executive Board.

No. 623/84

Concerning *Malta*
Case of *Alleged discriminatory measures concerning university admissions*

Communication of 17 January 1984 submitted by
Christian Democratic World Union

Spring 1984 session of the Committee on Conventions and Recommendations (119th session of the Executive Board)[1]

113. It is claimed that in 1978, the Maltese Government introduced certain reforms to the university system. One of these new changes was the student-worker scheme which in practice signifies that a student must alternate six months of study with another six months of work.

114. It is further alleged that, in August 1982, the Education Ministry instructed the Chairman of the Student's Selection Board for University, to allocate a bonus of 20 points to those student-workers who attend public schools, if the former had finished their course or were still student-workers at the time of their application for admission to university. Thus in practice, a student who attends a private school has, according to the authors, no possibility of, or is seriously handicapped in, continuing his studies at university. The authors contend that since 20 points out of a maximum of 30 are awarded to students merely because they attend a public school, private-school students (who receive no bonus points) in spite of their intellectual capacity, are thus put at an unjust disadvantage in university selection.

115. The representative of the Government of Malta who is also the Permanent Delegate referred to his letter of 25 April 1984 by which he had transmitted to the Secretariat his government's written comments on the communication. This letter is reproduced [...].[2] He stated that the communication in question did not evoke any specific case of alleged violation of human rights. He contended that the submission of

[1] See document 119 EX/35 PRIV., paras. 113-120; see also documents 119 EX/CR/HR/3 Add. and Add.4.
[2] See document 119 EX/CR/HR/3 Add.4.

the communication by the authors concerned was an unfortunate attempt to extend into the forum of Unesco a purely political debate taking place in Malta about ongoing educational reforms in that country. The representative of the government concerned referred to Article 46 (i) of the Maltese Constitution which provides that "no law shall make any provision that is discriminatory either of itself or in its effect". He contended that, if in the light of this categorical constitutional prohibition of discrimination, the authors claim that no legal remedies existed against the governmental measures complained of, then it was an admission on their part that those measures are not discriminatory. He declared that, in his opinion, the communication was motivated by pure political considerations and that it constituted an attempt to misuse or abuse the good offices of the Committee. On the university selection procedures, the representative of the government explained that since November 1983 the bonus points awarded for work-study experience had been reduced from 20 to 10 out of a maximum of 75-84 points for admission depending on the type of course to be followed at the university. The Committee was informed that, contrary to what is alleged in the communication, students from private schools continue to be admitted to the university and that there were about 50 such students among the last university intake. The representative of the government informed the Committee that it was his government's declared policy to ensure that all schools in Malta at the appropriate level applied the work-study system. For this reason any private school which presented an acceptable work-study programme would be permitted to take part in the scheme. In conclusion, he submitted that the communication was not admissible and should be so declared by the Committee.

116. A member of the Committee remarked that the Maltese Government had stated that any private school which produced an "acceptable" work-study programme would be allowed to join the work-study scheme. He asked what the criterion for acceptability was and wondered why it was that so far no private school seemed to have been able to produce any programme the government had found acceptable. This member observed that according to the authors of the communication maximum points awarded in the university selection was 30 while the government put it at between 75 and 84. The representative of the government confirmed that the maximum points were as indicated by him. He added that the figure 30 given by the authors of the communication was due to either bad faith or bad preparation on their part. He also explained that by "acceptable" work-study programme, his government had in mind an annual programme that devoted six months to work and the other six months to study. He informed the Committee that the work-study scheme was new and that his government was doing all it could to persuade private schools join it.

117. Several members of the Committee agreed that, as a component part of the educational policy of the Maltese Government, the work-study scheme could not be reviewed by the Committee. They however expressed the view that the manner in

which the scheme was carried out could not escape the scrutiny of the Committee which needed to be assured that no discrimination was involved in the implementation of the scheme. One member remarked that the question before the Committee was political and that the bonus-points issue appeared to be only a small element of an ongoing political argument in Malta. He and several other members suggested that the Committee's role should be limited to satisfying itself that the scheme was not implemented in a discriminatory manner. In this connection, one member of the Committee stated that since public schools were already operating work-study programmes when the bonus-points policy was introduced, there appeared to him to have been a de facto discrimination against private schools since they needed time to organize themselves with the view to adopting similar programmes. A number of the Committee's members expressed the hope that in the implementation of its contested educational policy, the competent authorities of Malta would ensure the full respect of relevant international standard-setting human rights instruments, especially those adopted by Unesco in the field of education.

118. Several members of the Committee praised the work-study scheme as a step in the right direction towards democratization of education since it made it possible for people to study and work at the same time. One member recalled that his own country was already familiar with the Maltese work-study scheme which, in his view, contributed to instil in the students the respect for the dignity of labour. Another member, on his part, urged that, in the application of its work-study policy, the government concerned would not violate or compromise the right of parents to have their children educated at private schools.

119. The representative of the Government of Malta informed the Committee that neither the work-study policy nor the manner of its implementation was in any way discriminatory. He stated that if the private schools wanted to adopt appropriate work-study programmes, they could already have done so because far from obstructing them in that respect, the government was in fact pleading with them to adopt such programmes. Declaring that his country had not violated any of the relevant international standard-setting human rights instruments, he asked that the Committee should rule out the communication as inadmissible.

120. Upon completing its discussion of the communication, the Committee *decided* to declare the communication inadmissible as being manifestly ill-founded in the terms of 104 EX/Decision 3.3, paragraph 14 (*a*) (v) of the Executive Board.

No. 624/84

Concerning *Czechoslovakia*
Case of *Marek Benda*

Communication of 17 February 1984 submitted by
František A. Janouch

Autumn 1984 session of the Committee on Conventions and Recommendations
(120th session of the Executive Board)[1]

117. The young Marek Benda, presented as a brilliant pupil, was allegedly refused admission to the middle school at Sladkovského náměstí (Prague 3) although, according to the author of the communication, he had fulfilled the legal conditions for admission to an establishment of that type (a "gymnasium" - middle school).

118. According to the representative of the government concerned, the author of the communication had attempted to politicize the incident, which had taken place in a period of confusion, a transitional period during the restructuring of the educational system in Czechoslovakia: in fact, both primary and secondary education were now compulsory. Formerly, he explained, a limited number of deserving pupils were able to enrol in a secondary establishment at the end of the eighth year of primary education; but, as this system had been criticized, the Ministry of National Education had decided to abolish it by adopting the system of nine years primary and four years secondary education for all pupils. With reference to the case of Marek Benda, he continued, his father had now enrolled the youth in a technical middle school on the completion of his ninth year of primary education: after completion of this secondary level, he would be able to continue his higher studies in the normal manner.

119. In reply to the questions posed by several members of the Committee, the representative of the Czechoslovak Government stated that in Czechoslovakia technical middle schools were valued more highly than ordinary middle schools in that the education given there was specialized and they provided the pupils with a better preparation for working life. In order to reassure certain members of the Committee in relation to the alleged discrimination against Marek Benda, he pointed out that all of

[1] See document 120 EX/15 PRIV., paras. 117-120; see also document 120 EX/CR/HR/3.

the pupils in the eighth year had been treated in the same manner; a technical middle school was not a second class middle school; at the end of the secondary level, the pupil could seek access to higher studies; he could also, if he wished, be admitted to an ordinary middle school.

120. After an exchange of views, during which some members of the Committee stressed the very advanced nature of the reform of the educational system in Czechoslovakia and recalled that it was not possible to make valid comparisons between the educational systems in different countries, the Committee *decided* to consider the case in question as settled; to communicate the information provided to the author of the communication and to strike the communication from its list, with the provison that any new developments could form the subject of a new communcation.

No. 626/84

Concerning *Socialist Republic of Viet Nam*
Case of *Nguyên Hai Chi*

Communication of 19 March 1984 submitted by
Amnesty International

Spring 1984 session of the Committee on Conventions and Recommendations (119th session of the Executive Board)[1]

140. Mr Nguyên Bai Chi is presented as a satirical.cartoonist living in southern Viet Nam. He was reportedly arrested in April 1976 and is said to be detained at present in a re-education camp in Gia Trung, without charge or trial

141. In a letter dated 2 May 1984 [...], the Permanent Delegation of the Socialist Republic of Viet Nam to Unesco, requesting that consideration of this communication be deferred, informed the Secretariat that Mr Nguyên Bai Chi's name was not known to it and that it would try to obtain information from the competent authorities of its country.

142. After an exchange of views, the Committee *decided*:

(i) to accede to the request for postponement of the examination of the communication's admissibility until the autumn 1984 session;

(ii) to ask the Executive Board to request the Director-General to make a humanitarian appeal on behalf of Mr Nguyên Bai Chi.

---

[1] See document 119 EX/35 PRIV., paras. 140-142; see also document 119 EX/CR/HR/3 Add.

No. 626/84 **Socialist Republic of Viet Nam**

Autumn 1984 session of the Committee on Conventions and Recommendations (120th session of the Executive Board)[2]

110. Mr Nguyên Hai Chi is presented by the author of the communication as a satirical cartoonist living in southern Viet Nam. He was reportedly arrested in April 1975 and is said to be detained at present in a re-education camp at Gia Trung, without charge or trial.

111. In a letter dated 12 September 1984, the Permanent Delegation of the Socialist Republic of Viet Nam to Unesco stated that it had not yet received the relevant information from its government.

112. After an exchange of views, the Committee *decided*:

(i) to postpone the examination of this communication until its spring [1985 session];

(ii) to reiterate its humanitarian concern for Mr Nguyên Hai Chi;

(iii) to ask the author of the communication for any further information on this case.

Spring 1985 session of the Committee on Conventions and Recommendations (121st session of the Executive Board)[3]

129. Mr Nguyên Hai Chi, presented by the author of the communication as a satirical cartoonist living in southern Viet Nam, was reportedly arrested in April 1976 and is said to be detained at present in a re-education camp, apparently without charge or trial.

130. The government concerned did not send a representative to the current session.

131. Some members of the Committee said how very much they regretted this fact. They reminded the meeting that the Permanent Delegation of the Socialist Republic of Viet Nam to Unesco had informed the Committee, by letter, at its spring 1984 session, that the name of Nguyên Hai Chi was unknown to it but that it would take steps to obtain information from the competent authorities of its country. In their

[2] See document 120 EX/15 PRIV., paras. 110-112; see also document 120 EX/CR/HR/2.
[3] See document 121 EX/46 PRIV., paras. 129-132; see also document 121 EX/CR/HR/2.

view, the case in question appeared to fall, prima facie, within Unesco's fields of competence and should be declared admissible. Other members of the Committee pointed out that the author of the communication had made no further move or adduced any additional information, and that the Committee should therefore drop the matter, particularly since it dated back to 1976. They pointed out that, in the past, when considering a very important communication, the Committee had taken the author's silence as an argument for rejecting it, despite the continuing failure of the government concerned to send a representative. In the present instance, they added, the government concerned had not made itself unavailable to seek the relevant information and therefore, if the Committee was not prepared to strike the communication from its list, it should at least postpone consideration of its admissibility rather than declare it admissible. One member of the Committee considered that the author of the communication had remained silent because he had nothing to add to his allegations, particularly since nothing had been received from the government concerned which would enable him to reply. Another member of the Committee considered that it would be advisable to declare the communication admissible, while yet another argued that, at the stage reached and in the absence of additional information from the government concerned, it would be premature to decide on its admissibility. Several members of the Committee having considered it opportune that the Committee's humanitarian preoccupations in favour of Mr Nguyên Hai Chi be reiterated, some members expressed their reservations in this connection.

132. After an exchange of views, the Committee *decided*:

(i) to postpone examination of the admissibility of the communication until its next session;

(ii) to reiterate its humanitarian concerns about Mr Nguyên Hai Chi;

(iii) to request supplementary information both from the government concerned and from the author of the communication.

Autumn 1985 session of the Committee on Conventions and Recommendations (122nd session of the Executive Board)[4]

93. Mr Nguyên Hai Chi, described by the author of the communication as a satirical cartoonist living in southern Viet Nam, was reportedly arrested in April 1976 and was said to be detained in a re-education camp, apparently without having been charged or tried.

[4] See document 122 EX/21 PRIV., paras. 93-96; see also document 122 EX/CR/HR/2.

No. 626/84 **Socialist Republic of Viet Nam**

94. In a letter dated 23 August 1985, Amnesty International reported that the person concerned had been freed in January or February 1985.

95. Some members of the Committee expressed their satisfaction with this positive outcome. Some other members stated that, in their view, the alleged victim had not necessarily been released because of the humanitarian intervention of the Committee. Subject to this reservation, they associated themselves with the feeling of relief at the liberation of Mr Nguyên Hai Chi.

96. After an exchange of views, the Committee *decided*:

(i) to note the information provided by the authors of the communication concerning the release of the alleged victim;

(ii) to consider the case as settled under the terms of paragraph 14 (*a*) (x) of 104 EX/Decision 3.3.

No. 627/84

Concerning *Uruguay*
Case of *Mario Alberto Teti Izquierdo*

Communication of 10 January 1984 submitted by
Yves Haguenauer *et al.*[*]

Spring 1984 session of the Committee on Conventions and Recommendations (119th session of the Executive Board)[1]

194. Mr Mario A. Teti Izquierdo, of Uruguayan and Italian nationality, a medical student when he was arrested on 7 December, was sentenced in 1972 to nine years' imprisonment, in 1976 to eight years' imprisonment and in September 1983 to nine years and six months' imprisonment and from one to four years of "precautionary detention". The authors note that Mr Teti Izquierdo is now both physically and morally exhausted and they wish to obtain his release.

195. By a letter dated 2 May 1984 [...],[2] the Permanent Delegation of Uruguay to Unesco informed the Secretariat that it had not yet received the relevant information from its government and that it therefore requested consideration of the case to be deferred until the next session of the Committee.

196. After an exchange of views, the Committee *decided*:

(i) to agree to the request made by the representative of the government concerned and to defer examination of the admissibility of this communication until its autumn 1984 session;

(ii) to request the Executive Board to ask the Director-General to make a humanitarian appeal to the appropriate authorities, asking them to alleviate the lot of Mr Mario Alberto Teti Izquierdo.

---

[*] Yves Haguenauer, the "Mario Teti" Committee and Ana Caetano Teti.
[1] See document 119 EX/35 PRIV., paras. 194-196; see also documents 119 EX/CR/HR/3 Add.3 and 4.
[2] See document 119 EX/CR/HR/3 Add.4.

No. 627/84 **Uruguay**

Autumn 1984 session of the Committee on Conventions and Recommendations (120th session of the Executive Board)[3]

181. According to the original communication, Mr Mario A. Teti Izquierdo, of Uruguyan and Italian nationality, a medical student when he was arrested on 7 December 1970, was sentenced successively in 1972 to nine years' imprisonment, in 1976 to eight years' imprisonment and in September 1983 to nine years and six months' imprisonment and from one to four years of "precautionary detention"'. The authors note that Mr Teti Izquierdo is now both physically and morally exhausted and they wish to obtain his release.

182. At the [the spring 1984] session, the Committee decided to agree to the request for a deferral made by the representative of the Uruguayan Government, who had not yet received the relevant information from the Uruguayan authorities, and to request the Executive Board to invite the Director-General to make a humanitarian appeal to the appropriate authorities, asking them to alleviate the lot of Mr Mario Alberto Teti Izquierdo.[4]

183. On 27 July 1984 the Secretariat received from the authors of the communication a letter indicating that they wished to withdraw from their communication any reference to an alleged trial of Mr Teti Izquierdo in September 1983, since, according to that letter, the Ambassador of Uruguay in Paris had denied that information [...].[5]

184. The representative of the Uruguayan Government said that the communication was inadmissible under paragraph 14 (*a*) (iii), (iv) and (vi) of 104 EX/Decision 3.3; Mr Teti Izquierdo had in fact been sentenced for criminal conspiracy against the Constitution because he had directly participated in subversive activities within the Tupamaros group, which wished to seize power by force; he had subsequently been an accomplice in an attempt to revive that movement. The fact that he was a medical student in no way changed the nature of the offences he had committed, and did not place him above the law. Finally, she felt that the authors of the communication could be accused of abusing the right to submit communications, since theirs contained paragraphs which she considered offensive in that they appeared to cast doubt on the regularity of the judicial procedures followed in the case of Mr Teti Izquierdo, and she regarded this as interference in Uruguay's internal affairs.

---

[3] See document 120 EX/15 PRIV., paras. 181-187; see also documents 120 EX/CR/HR/2 and Add.

[4] See document 119 EX/35 PRIV., para. 196 (*supra*, p. 467).

[5] See document 120 EX/CR/HR/2 Add.

Uruguay **No. 627/84**

185. Certain members pointed out that, without wishing to contest the nature of such offences as had been committed by the accused, in their view his case fell within Unesco's fields of competence. Several members wished to receive details on the sentences that Mr Teti Izquierdo was now serving, and some wished to know whether the sentences passed were concurrent or otherwise. Some members commented that certain sentences seemed to have been passed for offences committed while the alleged victim was in prison, and wondered whether the accused had been provided with legal assistance at his trials. Several members of the Committee emphasized that, over and above the legal problems, they were particularly concerned with the humanitarian aspect of the case, since Mr Teti Izquierdo had already undergone nearly 14 years' detention, in what seemed to be extremely rigorous conditions; inspired by purely humanitarian considerations, they therefore hoped that an appeal would be made to the clemency of the Uruguayan authorities. One member of the Committee suggested that the Director-General be invited to intervene to this end with the government concerned.

186. The representative of the Uruguayan Government took the floor again to provide details on points raised by members of the Committee during the discussion. She explained that Mr Teti Izquierdo had not committed offences in the context of a student movement which might have had ideological differences with the government at the time, but had been involved in thefts and acts of violence which had sometimes led to fatal casualties. She added that the fact that he had been imprisoned, even in a high-security penitentiary, did not preclude his responsibility for illegal actions; and she assured the Committee that Mr Izquierdo's state of health was as good as any detainee's could be and that he was well looked after. Lastly, she said that she shared the Committee's concerns and would try to see whether a solution could be found, since in view of the elections due to take place on 25 November 1984, the military courts were currently examining the situation of convicted persons who were still detained. She expressed the hope that Mr Teti Izquierdo's case would be one of those with a favourable outcome.

187. After an exchange of views, the Committee *decided*:

(i) to ask the government concerned to provide it with detailed information on how the different sentences had been passed on the alleged victim, at successive dates and with non-concurrent effect;

(ii) to ask the Executive Board to request the Director-General to make humanitarian representations on behalf of Mr A. Teti Izquierdo, who had now been in prison for nearly 14 years, adopting any method that the Director-General deemed most likely to bring about a rapid solution to the case;

(iii) to resume consideration of the admissibility of the communication at its [spring 1985] session.

Spring 1985 session of the Committee on Conventions and Recommendations (121st session of the Executive Board)[6]

187. According to the original communication, Mr Mario A. Teti Izquierdo, of Uruguayan and Italian nationality, a medical student when he was arrested on 7 December 1970, was sentenced successively in 1972 to nine years' imprisonment, in 1976 to eight years' imprisonment and in September 1983 to nine years and six months' imprisonment and from one to four years of "precautionary detention".

188. At the [autumn 1984] session of the Committee, the representative of the Uruguayan Government said that the communication was inadmissible under paragraph 14 (*a*) (iii), (iv) and (vi) of 104 EX/Decision 3.3; Mr Teti Izquierdo had in fact been sentenced for criminal conspiracy against the Constitution because he had directly participated in subversive activities within the Tupamaros group, which wished to seize power by force; he had subsequently been an accomplice in an attempt to revive that movement. The fact that he was a medical student in no way changed the nature of the offences he had committed, and did not place him above the law.

189. At the Committee's present session, the representative of the Director-General, who is also the Legal Adviser, informed the Committee that by a letter dated 14 March 1985, one of the authors of the communication had informed the Secretariat that the alleged victim had been released from prison; she added that this information had subsequently been corroborated by a letter dated 22 April 1985 received by the Secretariat from the Permanent Delegate of the Member State concerned.

190. The representative of the government concerned confirmed to the Committee the liberation of the imprisoned alleged victim. In this connection, she emphasized to the Committee the solid attachment of the new government of her country to the protection and promotion of human rights.

191. A number of members of the Committee expressed their thanks to the government of the Member State concerned as well as their satisfaction for the positive and humanitarian solution found to the rather painful case evoked by the communication.

192. On concluding its debate, the Committee *decided* to:

[6] See document 121 EX/46 PRIV., paras. 187-192; see also document 121 EX/CR/HR/2.

(i) take note of the release of the alleged victim;

(ii) thank the government concerned for its co-operation in finding a humanitarian and friendly solution to the problem raised by the communication;

(iii) declare as solved the problem raised by the communication and to strike it off the Committee's list of communications.

No. 628/84

Concerning *Union of Soviet Socialist Republics*
Case of *Alexandre Broussilovski*

Communication of 10 January 1984 submitted by
Yves Haguenauer

Spring 1984 session of the Committee on Conventions and Recommendations (119th session of the Executive Board)[1]

191. This communication concerns a violinist who, according to the author, has not been able to pursue his career in the Soviet Union in a normal way and has requested authorization to emigrate to Israel, which is said to have been refused.

192. Having received the communication only very shortly before leaving Moscow (although it had been transmitted by the Secretariat to the Permanent Delegation of the Soviet Union to Unesco within the time-limit), the representative of the Soviet Government, while assuring the Committee that he had already taken the necessary steps to obtain the relevant information, requested that consideration of this communication should be deferred to the autumn 1984 session. The representative, however, expressed his doubts about the allegations contained in the communication.

193. Following an exchange of views, during which a Committee member expressed the hope that the problem raised in the communication would be solved at the autumn 1984 session, the Committee *decided* to comply with the request that had been made.

---

[1] See document 119 EX/35 PRIV., paras. 191-193; see also document 119 EX/CR/HR/3 Add. 2.

No. 628/84 **Union of Soviet Socialist Republics**

Autumn 1984 session of the Committee on Conventions and Recommendations (120th session of the Executive Board)[2]

174. According to the author of the communication, Mr Alexandre Broussilovski, a violinist, has been unable to pursue his musical career in the Soviet Union in a normal way and has been refused authorization to emigrate to exercise his musical activities in the country of his choice.

175. The representative of the Soviet Government, also a member of the Committee, said that he had had the opportunity to talk with several musicians and also with the late Mr Leonid Kogan, the great violinist, mentioned by the author as having taught Mr Broussilovski, but he had never heard the case described as presented in the communication. He said that Mr Broussilovski was not yet widely known in the Soviet Union as an eminent violinist and that Mr Kogan himself had not only played in major cities but had also performed in small towns. The representative of the Soviet Government added that according to official information supplied by the governing body of the Moscow Philharmonic, Mr Broussilovski had not been the victim of any discrimination or ban; he could actively pursue his musical career, even giving concerts as a soloist. He mentioned by way of example a number of major cities where the violinist had performed, namely Kiev, Tallin, Kharkov, Rostov, Novosibirsk and Kazan. If the musician had not played in some cities, specifically Moscow and Leningrad, it might have been because he had not been invited to do so and because GosKonzert had to plan and run its activities in such a way as to ensure that its concerts were financially viable. To give an idea of the scale of Mr Broussilovski's activities, he informed the Committee that he had played at 70 concerts in 1983 and at 45 in 1984 (from the beginning of the year up to 21 August 1984).

176. In reply to a question, the representative of the Soviet Government said that Mr Broussilovski had not been forbidden to make records, that this depended on a variety of factors, particularly on the performers, and that it would be a strange state of affairs if people were allowed to appeal to Unesco whenever they were unable to make recordings.

177. With regard to the refusal to authorize the violinist to emigrate, the representative of the Soviet Government said that it had been based on impediments of a family nature, a matter regulated by national legislation.

178. Among the Committee members who took the floor, some expressed the opinion that Mr Broussilovski had not been the victim of any discrimination, that he had

[2] See document 120 EX/15 PRIV., paras. 174-179; see also document 120 EX/CR/HR/2.

every opportunity for artistic creativity and that his case was basically a problem of emigration and thus lay outside Unesco's fields of competence. Others wondered whether the violinist's earnings could be considered normal and expressed concern about the allegation that the musician's wife was unable to find employment. The representative of the Soviet Government said that in relation to the standard of living in the Soviet Union Mr Broussilovski was well off, earning about 500 roubles a month, practically as much as the salary of eminent musicians. He pointed out, moreover, that there was no unemployment in the USSR, that there were plenty of vacancies and that one could not give credence to a mere statement by the author of the communication regarding Mrs Broussilovski's situation. The Committee should therefore consider this case as absolutely inadmissible.

179. After an exchange of views, the Committee *decided* to request the Secretariat to communicate the information thus provided to the author of the communication and to resume consideration of the case at its spring 1985 session.

Spring 1985 session of the Committee on Conventions and Recommendations (121st session of the Executive Board)[3]

173. According to the author of the communication, Mr Alexandre Broussilovski, a violinist, has been unable to pursue his musical career in the Soviet Union in a normal way and has been refused authorization to emigrate to exercise his musical activities in a country of his choice.

174. On 27 March 1985, the Secretariat received a letter from Mr Haguenauer in which he stated that, because of the difficulties of communicating with persons who had filed an application to emigrate, he had been unable to obtain additional information, as the Committee had requested him to do at its autumn 1984 session. Mr Haguenauer added that he hoped that the representative of the government concerned would facilitate his contacts with Mr Broussilovski.

175. The representative of the government concerned stated that, at the Committee's [autumn 1984] session, he had given it ample information about the opportunities and facilities for self-expression available to the violinist, that there had been no impediment to his artistic creativity, that he enjoyed the same rights as all his colleagues, and that the matter was merely a problem of emigration which did not fall within the Organization's competence.

---

[3] See document 121 EX/46 PRIV., paras. 173-176; see also document 121 EX/CR/HR/2.

No. 628/84 **Union of Soviet Socialist Republics**

176. At the conclusion of its deliberations, the Committee *decided* to declare the communication inadmissible on the ground that it did not fall within Unesco's fields of competence.

No. 630/84

Concerning *Afghanistan*
Case of *Osman Taraki Rustar* et al.*

Communication of 24 April 1984 submitted by
Amnesty International

Autumn 1984 session of the Committee on Conventions and Recommendations (120th session of the Executive Board)[1]

11. Mr Osman Taraki Rustar, Mr Hassan Kakar and Mr Shukrullah Kohgadai are stated by the author of the communication to be lecturers at the University of Kabul. They are alleged to have founded an association aimed *inter alia* at reforming the educational and administrative system of the University in such a way that the apparent causes of dissent and factionalism on the campus could be peacefully eradicated. They are said to have been arrested in 1982 and sentenced in July 1983 to 10, eight and seven years' imprisonment respectively for counter-revolutionary offences and having constituted an unlawful association.

12. The representative of the Government of Afghanistan stated that as yet he did not have at his disposal information that would clarify the matter for the Committee, and promised to take measures to secure such information. In the meantime, he wished to point out that Afghanistan respected the rule of law and human rights and complied meticulously with international standards relating to those rights. He directed the Committee's attention to the difficult situation currently obtaining in his country, involving a situation of undeclared war which was being waged against his country, and to the fact that the competent authorities had to take measures to protect the civilian population.

13. Of the Committee members who took the floor, some emphasized the urgency of the matter and the desirability of arriving at a solution without delay in view of the

---

* Case of *Osman Taraki Rustar, Hassan Kakar and Shukrullah Kohgadai*. At the Committee's autumn 1987 session, this communication was being referred to as case of *Osman Taraki Rustar and Shukrullah Kohgadai*.
[1] See document 120 EX/15 PRIV., paras. 11-14; see also document 120 EX/CR/HR/3.

fact that the alleged victims were in prison and that one of them was said to be in poor health. Other speakers pointed out that the persons in question had been sentenced in accordance with the law of the land for counter-revolutionary activities, which were serious offences, committed in a period of unrest. Still other speakers stressed the desirability of avoiding any form of political statement and the importance of concentrating on the actual facts, which had not yet been clarified by the representative of the Government of Afghanistan, and on the humanitarian aspects of the case. One member of the Committee said that this was a crime and no humanitarian steps should be taken.

14. After an exchange of views, the Committee *decided*:

(i) to suspend the examination of this communication until its spring 1985 session, pending the information promised by the representative of the government concerned;

(ii) to request the representative of the government concerned kindly to convey to that government the concern of the Committee on humanitarian grounds as to the situation of Mr Osman Taraki Rustar, Mr Hassan Kakar and Mr Shukrullah Kohgadai.

Spring 1985 session of the Committee on Conventions and Recommendations (121st session of the Executive Board)[2]

17. Mr Osman Taraki Rustar, Mr Hassan Kakar and Mr Sukrullah Kohgadai, lecturers at the University of Kabul, are alleged to have founded an association with the purpose, among others, of reforming the educational and administrative system of the University with a view to removing any causes of dissent and factionalism which might exist on the campus in a peaceful way. They are said to have been arrested in 1982 and sentenced in July 1983 to 10, eight and seven years' imprisonment respectively for counter-revolutionary offences and for having constituted an unlawful association.

18. Of the Committee members who spoke, some, regretting that no representative of the government concerned was present, took the view that it would be appropriate to remind that government of the undertaking given by its representative at the Committee's [autumn 1984] session that the relevant information would be supplied to the Committee, and to express once more the concerns that the Committee felt on humanitarian grounds for the three teachers; others pointed out that the chargé d'af-

[2] See document 121 EX/46 PRIV., paras. 17-19; see also document 121 EX/CR/HR/2.

faires of the Embassy of Afghanistan in Paris had been unable to appear before the Committee because of his very many obligations, which entailed frequent absences from the French capital for him. These members also stressed that the government concerned had always shown great regard for the Committee.

19. After an exchange of views and subject to reservations expressed by two members regarding (ii) below, the Committee *decided*:

(i) again to request the government concerned to be good enough to provide the relevant information promised by its representative at the Committee's autumn 1984 session;

(ii) to renew its appeal for clemency to that governmemt, in view of the Committee's concern on humanitarian grounds about the situation of Mr Osman Taraki Rustar, Mr Hassan Kakar and Mr Sukrullah Kohgadai;

(iii) to resume consideration of this communication at its next session.

Autumn 1985 session of the Committee on Conventions and Recommendations (122nd session of the Executive Board)[3]

9. Mr Osman Taraki Rustar, Mr Hassan Kakar and Mr Shukrullah Kohgadai are described by the author of the communication as being lecturers at the University of Kabul. They are said to have founded an association, one of whose purposes was the reform of the educational and administrative system of the University with a view to eliminating in a peaceful way any causes of dissent and factionalism which might exist on the campus. They are said to have been arrested in 1982 and sentenced in July 1983 to 10, eight and seven years' imprisonment respectively for counter-revolutionary offences and for having set up an unlawful association.

10. In a letter dated 16 August 1985 [...],[4] Amnesty International stated that no further information on the circumstances of Mr Osman Taraki Rustar had been received. Mr Hassan Kakar was reportedly now being held in a cell containing about 170 detainees, he was permitted family visits every three weeks and was authorized to receive parcels of food and medicine from his family. It was said that he was suffering from varicose veins and that his eyesight had deteriorated.

---

[3] See document 122 EX/21 PRIV., paras. 9-17; see also documents 122 EX/CR/HR/2 and Add.2.
[4] See document 122 EX/CR/HR/2 Add.2.

11. The author of the communication indicated that Mr Shukrullah Kohgadai was also said to have been authorized to receive family visits but that his health appeared to have deteriorated considerably.

12. The representative of the Afghan Government, taking the floor, stated that his presence before the Committee bore witness once again to the spirit of co-operation shown by his country. Quoting a number of relevant provisions from the Afghan Constitution, he stated that despite the situation of undeclared war in Afghanistan, his government was applying the law strictly and was scrupulously respecting human rights and the fundamental freedoms of citizens. In his view, the allegations made in the communication were surprising. The author described Mr Osman Taraki Rustar, Mr Hassan Kakar and Mr Shukrullah Kohgadai as wishing to form a cultural association. Now, the Constitution was in favour of such activities. No one could therefore possibly think that the authorities would have wished to prevent such initiatives. In fact, if those persons had been sentenced it was not because they had made normal use of the right of association, meeting, expression and opinion. It was because they had formed an unlawful association which aimed, particularly through the publication and circulation of various documents inciting young people to disobedience and refusal to defend their country, at propagating ideas which were closely linked with the foreign-based armed organizations which were acting against Afghanistan. These organizations had already caused immense destruction in his country, affecting many schools and hospitals, had murdered thousands of schoolteachers and had ruined the national economy. The representative of the government concerned also indicated that, contrary to the assertions of Amnesty International, the trial of these three teachers had been conducted not *in camera* but in public, that the right to defence had been honoured but that those concerned had themselves refused legal assistance. He added that in prison, their right to receive visits and books had been observed, they had been given normal medical care and were in good health.

13. Some members of the Committee observed that the special situation of Afghanistan should not become the subject of a discussion within the Committee and that the Committee should confine itself to examining just the individual and specific cases put before it. In their view, it did not appear that the alleged victims had engaged in terrorist activities. They pointed out that all universities throughout the world always constituted an environment for questioning and the challenging of ideas. In their view it was excessive to sanction the right to discussion and expression of ideas in so severe a fashion. They considered that the Committee ought to renew an appeal for clemency to the government concerned, with a view to obtaining reconsideration of the cases in question. Other members of the Committee pointed out that the representative of the Afghan Government had shown great regard for the Committee and that he had approached a by no means simple problem in a frank manner, providing detailed information. In any case it was not possible to ignore the

situation of undeclared war in Afghanistan, all the more so because the party responsible for the aggression was not only violating human rights but also the rules of war. In their view, to throw doubt on the right of the Afghan courts to pass sentences would amount to challenging the sovereignty of Afghanistan and interfering in its internal affairs.

14. Replying to questions raised by several members of the Committee on means of redress still available to Mr Osman Taraki Rustar, Mr Hassan Kakar and Mr Shukrullah Kohgadai, the representative of the Afghan Government stated that as the verdict had acquired the force of a final judgement now that two years had elapsed, it could hardly be said that other remedies were available.

15. One member of the Committee said that as the possibility of other remedies was thus no longer available owing to the time that had elapsed, only a pardon could be envisaged.

16. Another member of the Committee said that as the Committee was supposed to try to achieve a practical result any attitude of conflict should be avoided and no decision should be taken which might give the impression that pressure was being brought to bear on the government concerned, especially as in his view there was still some hope of obtaining a reduction of the sentence. A number of members of the Committee stressed the absolute inadmissibility of the case and asked for it to be deleted on the ground that it was inacceptable under the procedure laid down by [104 EX/Decision 3.3].

17. After the discussion, during which reservations were expressed by a number of members of the Committee regarding subparagraph (ii) below, the Committee *decided*:

(i) to note the information provided by the representative of the government concerned;

(ii) to renew its appeal for clemency to that government, in view of the Committee's concern on humanitarian grounds about the situation of Mr Osman Taraki Rustar, Mr Hassan Kakar and Mr Shukrullah Kohgadai;

(iii) to resume consideration of this communication at its next session.

No. 630/84 **Afghanistan**

Spring 1986 session of the Committee on Conventions and Recommendations (124th session of the Executive Board)[5]

10. Mr Osman Taraki Rustar, Mr Hassan Kakar and Mr Shukrullah Kohgadai, lecturers at the University of Kabul, are said to have founded an association, one of whose purposes was the reform of the educational and administrative system of the University with a view to eliminating in a peaceful way any causes of dissent and factionalism which might exist on the campus. After being arrested in 1982, they are said to have been sentenced in July 1983 to 10, eight and seven years' imprisonment respectively for counter-revolutionary offences and for having set up an unlawful association. The health of Mr Hassan Kakar and Mr Shukrullah Kohgadai is said to be giving cause for concern.

11. At the Committee's [autumn 1985] session, the representative of the government concerned had maintained that the allegations made by the author of the communication were unfounded and that the three lecturers had been sentenced not because they had made normal use of the right of association, meeting, expression and opinion, but because of the unlawful nature of their association, which aimed at propagating ideas that were closely linked with the foreign-based armed organizations currently acting against Afghanistan. He had also indicated that, contrary to the assertions of Amnesty International, their trial had not been conducted *in camera* but in public, and their right to defence fully honoured. He had also informed the Committee that as the verdict had acquired the force of a final judgement, no other remedies were available. He had added that the prisoners were being given normal medical care and were in good health.

12. Taking the floor, the representative of the government concerned said that, regarding this communication, his predecessor had explained at length that the association formed by the three lecturers was a counter-revolutionary association engaged in terrorist activities. It was only because of their status as teachers that the alleged victims had not been given heavier sentences.

13. Some members of the Committee pointed out that even the sentences that had been imposed were very severe and expressed surprise at the lack of precision in the charges against the three teachers, because as far as they could see, the persons in question had not committed any acts of terrorism. They asked to be supplied with a copy of the statutes of the offending association and a copy of tbe court's ruling in the case, so as to be in a position to form an opinion on the real nature of the actions of which the alleged victims were accused. Those members considered that in any e-

[5] See document 124 EX/3 PRIV., paras. 10-16; see also document 124 EX/CR/HR/2.

vent it was necessary at least to renew the Committee's appeal for clemency with a view to obtaining a pardon for the accused.

14. One member of the Committee said that since the parties concerned had been sentenced for counter-revolutionary activities, the Committee was not competent to deal with their case. Other members of the Committee felt that additional information should be sought from the author of the communication rather than from the government concerned, since in their opinion the explanations already provided by that government were adequate. At the same time, it was in their view doubtful whether the association in question was involved in purely cultural activities and it was for Amnesty International to fill in the gaps by producing, in particular, the statutes of that association and other evidence to support its allegations.

15. In this connection, the Chairperson pointed out that in practice it was difficult for alleged victims or their spokesmen to produce certain written documents, whereas the governments concerned were very well placed to do so.

16. Following an exchange of views, the Committee *decided*:

(i) to thank the government concerned for the spirit of co-operation it had shown by sending a representative to continue the dialogue before the Committee;

(ii) to ask both the author of the communication and the government concerned for the additional information requested by the members of the Committee, particularly regarding the statutes and the activities of the association formed by Mr Osman Taraki Rustar, Mr Hassan Kakar and Mr Shukrullah Kohgadai, the text of the sentence handed down in their case and their situation in prison;

(iii) to reiterate once again its appeal for clemency to the government concerned, since not only had two of the three prisoners apparently already served more than half of their sentences, but also because their state of health was giving cause for concern;

(iv) to resume consideration of this communication at its autumn 1986 session.

No. 630/84 **Afghanistan**

Autumn 1986 session of the Committee on Conventions and Recommendations (125th session of the Executive Board)[6]

10. Mr Osman Taraki Rustar, Mr Hassan Kakar and Mr Shukrullah Kohgadai, lecturers at the University of Kabul, are said to have founded an association, one of whose purposes was the reform of the educational and administrative system of the University with a view to eliminating in a peaceful way any causes of dissent and factionalism which might exist on the campus. After being arrested in 1982, they are said to have been sentenced in July 1983 to 10, eight and seven years' imprisonment respectively for counter-revolutionary offences and for having set up an unlawful association. The health of Mr Hassan Kakar and Mr Shukrullah Kohgadai is said to be giving cause for concern.

11. Taking the floor at the Committee's present [...] session, the representative of the government concerned confirmed once more his government's refutation of the alleged violation of human rights that are complained of in the communication. He stated that freedom of association was protected by law in his country and that many private associations operate in fields which fall within the competence of Unesco. He reiterated in this connection that the three lecturers had been prosecuted not because they had made normal use of the right of association or of freedom of opinion and expression, but because they had formed an association that was involved in a number of terrorist activities. He said that before the three lecturers were arrested in 1982, they had been advised by some of their colleagues to consider mending their ways but they had paid no heed to the advice. On the contrary, they had continued their illegal activities which had resulted in the loss of the life of three students all of whom were victims of a terrorist bomb explosion. In answer to questions posed by the Chairperson and some other members of the Committee, the representative of the government concerned informed the Committee that conditions in general and, in particular, health-care facilities obtaining in prisons in his country were reasonable and satisfactory. He added that the three lecturers had been allowed visits by members of their families as well as by his own predecessor in office who, on the basis of what he had observed and of audio-cassette recordings of statements made in prison by the three alleged victims, had formed the impression that they had been well treated in their detention. Asked by some members of the Committee if he could make these audio-cassette recordings available to the Committee, the representative of the government concerned stated that he would look into what, if anything, he could do in that respect.

[6] See document 125 EX/3 PRIV., paras. 10-16; see also document 125 EX/CR/HR/2.

12. Some members of the Committee took the position that to the extent that the three lecturers concerned had been regularly tried, convicted and sentenced for terrorist activities, their case did not come within the Organization's fields of competence and that the communication in question should consequently be considered inadmissible. One other member said that it would be useful for the Committee to be given the particulars of the terrorist activities for which the three lecturers had allegedly been responsible. She asked that information be also provided by the government concerned on the period of time the alleged illegal association had organized meetings attended by the imprisoned lecturers and some of their academic colleagues and students before the three of them were arrested in 1982. Several members reiterated the Committee's previous demand that it be supplied with a copy of the statutes of the association accused by the government as being responsible for terrorist activities as well as transcripts of the trial of the three lecturers concerned, including a copy of the judgement rendered at the end of the trial. One member proposed that a written statement concerning the state of the health of the three detainees as well as the conditions of their imprisonment should be provided by the government concerned. Another member however stated that all these elements of information had been requested at its [spring 1986] session adding that the information so demanded had not been forthcoming from the government.

13. However, some other members of the Committee queried the necessity for this information to be requested from the government concerned adding that the nature of the information being requested could give the impression that the proceedings of the Committee were judicial or quasi-judicial in character. One of them declared that in his view, it would not be right for the Committee to ask the government concerned to provide proofs in order to refute mere allegations unsubstantiated by the author of the communication. For this reason, he proposed that the communication should be declared inadmissible.

14. The Chairperson explained in this connection that the Committee would be asking the government concerned for information and not proofs or counterproofs. She pointed out that the nature of the information being requested was such that it was the government concerned, and not the author of the communication, which was in a better position to provide most of it. Taking note of the statement of the representative of the government concerned according to which the laws of his country provided the possibility for convicts who have served half of their sentences to benefit from reductions in the remaining part of the sentences, several members of the Committee expressed the hope that the three lecturers concerned, two of whom have already served more than half of their sentences, would be given the benefit of the pertinent laws and that they would be set free without delay. One member stated that it would perhaps be useful for the text of the relevant laws concerning the possibility of a partial remission of sentences to be made available to the Committee.

No. 630/84 **Afghanistan**

15. Following an exchange of views, the Committee *decided*:

(i) to thank the government concerned for its spirit of co-operation in sending a representative to the Committee to enter into a dialogue;

(ii) to ask both the author of the communication and the government concerned to provide the Committee with pertinent information they may respectively have in their possession concerning the allegations contained in the communication, especially regarding the statutes and the particulars of the activities of the association formed by Mr Osman Taraki Rustar, Mr Hassan Kakar and Mr Shukrullah Kohgadai, transcripts of their trial together with a copy of the judgement delivered in their case and their situation in prison, including the state of their health;

(iii) to appeal urgently to the government concerned for a flexible application of the pertinent clemency laws in favour of the three detained lecturers so that, for purely humanitarian considerations, they may be released without delay, especially taking into account that two of them have already served more than half of their sentences;

(iv) to resume consideration of the communication at its spring 1987 session.

16. Several members of the Committee expressed reservations concerning subparagraph (ii) of this decision.

Spring 1987 session of the Committee on Conventions and Recommendations (126th session of the Executive Board)[7]

11. Mr Osman Taraki Rustar, Mr Hassan Kakar and Mr Shukrullah Kohgadai, lecturers at the University of Kabul, are said to have been sentenced in July 1983 to 10, eight and seven years' imprisonment respectively for counter-revolutionary offences and for having set up an unlawful association.

12. At the previous sessions, the representatives of the government concerned explained that if these persons had been sentenced, it was not because they had made normal use of the right of association and assembly or of freedom of opinion and expression, but because they had formed an association that was involved in a number of terrorist activities.

[7] See document 126 EX/3 PRIV., paras. 11-15; see also documents 126 EX/CR/HR/2 and Add.2.

Afghanistan **No. 630/84**

13. In a letter dated 7 April 1987 [...],[8] the author of the communication stated that, according to as yet unconfirmed reports, Mr Hassan Kakar had been released on 2 March 1987.

14. Taking the floor, the representative of the Afghan Government recalled that, the previous year, he had reassured the Committee regarding the state of health of the three lecturers, who were receiving the best possible treatment. He stated that he was at present in a position to announce that Mr Hassan Kakar had been set free on 2 March 1987. He added that he had even received from Amnesty International a letter of thanks in that connection, as well as other letters warmly welcoming the new policy of the Afghan Government. Since the ceasefire decreed in January 1987, a general amnesty had in fact been proclaimed. Some 4,000 persons might benefit therefrom. The names of Mr Osman Taraki Rustar and Mr Shukrullah Kohgadai were included in the list of the National Reconciliation Commission among the 1,500 persons to be released by the end of April 1987. The representative of the Government concerned considered that they must, accordingly, now be free. In response to a request from the Chairperson, he stated that he would take the necessary steps to secure confirmation of the release of these two lecturers. He pointed out, finally, that, in pursuance of its policy of leniency, the Afghan Government had furthermore instituted a law enabling prisoners thus released to recover their full rights, and in particular to be re-instated in their employment, and refugees to recover possession of their property confiscated by the State, if they returned to the country.

15. Following an exchange of views, the Committee *decided*:

(i) to thank the representative of the government concerned for attending the meeting and for his co-operation;

(ii) to take note of the information which he had supplied, particularly in connection with the release of Mr Hassan Kakar, and to strike out this case in accordance with paragraph 14 (*a*) (x) of 104 EX/Decision 3.3;

(iii) to strike this communication *ipso facto* from its list as soon as the Secretariat received confirmation of the release of Mr Osman Taraki Rustar and Mr Shukrullah Kohgadai, on the understanding that should such confirmation not reach the Secretariat before the autumn 1987 session, the Committee would resume consideration of the communication.

---

[8] See document 126 EX/CR/HR/2 Add.2.

No. 630/84 **Afghanistan**

Autumn 1987 session of the Committee on Conventions and Recommendations (127th session of the Executive Board)[9]

10. Mr Osman Taraki Rustar and Mr Shukrullah Kohgadai, lecturers at the University of Kabul, are said to have been sentenced in July 1983 to 10 and seven years' imprisonment respectively for counter-revolutionary offences and for having set up an unlawful association.

11. At the spring 1987 session, the representative of the government concerned informed the Committee that the names of these two teachers were included in a National Reconciliation Commission list among the 1,500 persons to be released by the end of April, following the ceasefire proclaimed in January 1987, and that they must accordingly now be free.

12. On the basis of this information, the Committee had decided to strike the communication *ipso facto* from its list as soon as the Secretariat received confirmation of the release of the two lecturers.[10]

13. At the present session, the Permanent Delegation of the Democratic Republic of Afghanistan apologized to Unesco for being unable to send a representative to appear before the Committee owing to a change of staff.

14. In a letter dated 10 August 1987 [...][11] and a telegram dated 14 September 1987, the author of the communication reported that Mr Shukrullah Kohgadai and Mr Osman Taraki Rustar had indeed been released, the former under the general amnesty proclaimed after the ceasefire and the latter on 31 August 1987.

15. Following an exchange of views, in the light of the decision taken at its [spring 1987] session, the Committee *decided*:

(i) to take note with satisfaction of the release of Mr Osman Taraki Rustar and Mr Shukrullah Kohgadai;

(ii) to strike the communication from its list, considering it as finally settled.

---

[9] See document 127 EX/3 PRIV., paras. 10-15; see also documents 127 EX/CR/HR/2 and Add.

[10] See document 126 EX/3 PRIV., para. 15 (iii) (*supra*, p. 487).

[11] See document 127 EX/CR/HR/2 Add.

No. 631/84

Concerning *Poland*
Case of *Marek Nowakowski*

Communication of 30 May 1984 submitted by
Marie-Pierre Bay

Autumn 1984 session of the Committee on Conventions and Recommendations (120th session of the Executive Board)[1]

100. Mr Marek Nowakowski, a writer of Polish nationality, was allegedly arrested on 7 March 1984. According to the author of the communication, the reason for his arrest was that one of his books, a collection of texts on the life of "Polish civilians during the state of war", had been translated and published abroad while it had not been published in Poland.

101. The author of the communication informed Unesco by letter dated 5 July 1984, that Mr Marek Nowakowski was to be released provisionally and stated by letter of 31 July 1984 that, in view of the amnesty which had just been declared in Poland, she preferred to withdraw her communication.

102. The Legal Adviser noted that according to well-established practice, the Committee was not necessarily bound to accept the author's request, since the withdrawal of the communication should be considered as constituting a friendly solution designed, as stated in paragraph 14 (*k*) of 104 EX/Decision 3.3, "to advance the promotion of the human rights falling within Unesco's fields of competence".

103. All members of the Committee who spoke noted that the problem raised by the communication was now solved; they thought that the author could be relied on to submit a new communication if there was a need to do so.

104. The Committee therefore *decided* to accede to the author's request to withdraw the communication and to inform her that she was entitled to submit a new communication if new developments took place.

---

[1] See document 120 EX/15 PRIV., paras. 100-104; see also document 120 EX/CR/HR/3.

No. 632/84

Concerning *Chile*
Case of *Raúl Manríquez*

Communication of 29 May 1984 submitted by
World Federation of Teachers' Unions

Autumn 1984 session of the Committee on Conventions and Recommendations (120th session of the Executive Board)[1]

58. Professor Raúl Manríquez, a teacher and leader of AGECH (Asociación Gremial Educadores Chile - Chilean Teachers' Union), was reportedly arrested for no reason while walking along a street watching a demonstration pass by in which he was not taking part; it is claimed by the author of the communication that he has been held since 11 May last in a prison in Santiago and that there he has suffered maltreatment.

59. The representative of the Chilean Government explained to the Committee that the case was a simple police incident: Mr R. Manríquez had indeed been arrested by the police during a street demonstration but had been released without legal proceedings as soon as his identity had been checked. He added that the local press had reported on the arrest of the individual concerned and on his release the following day or two days later.

60. Most of the Committee members who took the floor considered that the matter had been settled and that the communication should be struck off its list; two other members wondered whether it might not be preferable to resume consideration of the communication at the Committee's next session because on 29 June 1984, the date on which the form had been filled in by the author of the communication, the latter had asserted that the alleged victim was still in prison. According to another member of the Committee, [WFTU's] attention should be drawn to the fact that it was important to check its information before referring cases that had been settled to the Committee. One member of the Committee said he was opposed to any such procedure.

---

[1] See document 120 EX/15 PRIV., paras. 58-61; see also document 120 EX/CR/HR/3.

No. 632/84 **Chile**

61. Following discussion, the Committee *decided* to strike this communication from its list since the case it presented had been settled.

No. 637/84

Concerning *France*
Case of *Léone Guyot*

Communication of 29 May 1984 submitted by
Léone Guyot

Autumn 1984 session of the Committee on Conventions and Recommendations (120th session of the Executive Board)[1]

75. Mrs Léone Guyot, a primary-school teacher, complains that following on health problems which have prevented her from working in classes in contact with children, she has been unable to obtain an administrative post. She also alleges that she has been subjected to various forms of moral and financial pressure, and claims to have had no income since 31 July 1983.

76. The representative of the French Government said in her speech that she had obtained the following information from the competent authorities:

> Mrs Guyot had refused to undergo the examinations required by the medical committee. She had been suspended from duty for health reasons for periods of three months from 1 September 1981. Everything had been done to enable her to draw health insurance benefits without delay during that period. Following the medical committee's decision of 27 May 1982, which declared that she was fit to resume work in an administrative post, she had been informed that that possibility would be open to her only if she changed her job or was successful in a competitive administrative examination. Finally, in June 1984, the medical committee had supported her suspension from duty for health reasons for the period from 1 August 1983 to 31 July 1984, and had decided that she would be reinstated in an ordinary class from 1 August 1984. Although she had been duly informed of that decision, she had not contacted the competent department. Nor had she complied with the administration's request that she produce a certificate signed by an officially approved general practitioner specifying the nature of her illness and the degree of her

[1] See document 120 EX/15 PRIV., paras. 75-79; see also document 120 EX/CR/HR/3 Add.

disability, so as to enable the Commission de Réferme to determine the amount of temporary disability benefits to which she was eligible.

77. The representative of the French Government suggested that Mrs Guyot should forthwith contact the appropriate services in order to settle the matter, and that in particular she should reply to the letter dated 20 June 1984 from the Inspection Académique to which she was responsible.

78. The members of the Committee who spoke were unanimous in their view that this was a very sad human case, but that there had not actually been any violation of human rights detrimental to Mrs Guyot.

79. After an exchange of views, the Committee *declared* the communication inadmissible in application of paragraph 14 (*a*) (v) of 104 EX/Decision 3.3 of the Executive Board and, requesting the Secretariat to transmit the information provided by the representative of the government concerned to Mrs Guyot, *expressed* the hope that she would be given appropriate advice in order to help her settle her situation in respect of the competent administration.

No. 638/84

Concerning *Czechoslovakia*
Case of *Jiří Wolf*

Communication of 11 June 1984 submitted by
Zygmunt Elbiński

Spring 1985 session of the Committee on Conventions and Recommendations (121st session of the Executive Board)[1]

133. This communication alleges that Mr Jiří Wolf, a Charter 77's signatory, was sentenced, in December 1983, to six years' imprisonment for criticizing the deployment of the Soviet SS-20 missiles in Czechoslovakia. The author of the communication claims that there was, in this case, a violation by the Czechoslovak Government of Mr Wolf's right to freedom of opinion and expression and to freedom to seek, receive and impart information and ideas.

134. When discussion on the admissibility of the communication was opened, the representative of the government concerned stated that, as it had done in the past, his government was prepared to co-operate with the Committee in the examination of the communication. He added however that his government had received the communication only about a month earlier. For this reason and in order to permit his government to collect and provide relevant information concerning the communication, he proposed that the examination of the admissibility of the communication should be deferred to the autumn 1985 session of the Committee.

135. While noting and expressing appreciation for the willingness of the government concerned to co-operate with the Committee in the latter's examination of the communication, several members of the Committee stated that, in their view, the communication raised matters which were outside Unesco's fields of competence. Another member declared that, in his opinion, not only was the communication manifestly ill-founded but also it constituted an abuse, by its author, of the right to submit communications to the Committee.

---

[1] See document 121 EX/46 PRIV., paras. 133-136; see also document 121 EX/CR/HR/3 Add.

No. 638/84 **Czechoslovakia**

136. After an exchange of views, the Committee:

(i) *Concluded* that the alleged violations of human rights did not fall within any of Unesco's fields of competence and that the communication was manifestly ill-founded;

(ii) *Decided* accordingly to declare the communication inadmissible.

No. 639/84

Concerning *Federal Republic of Germany*
Case of *Christian Schmidt*

Communication of 11 June 1984 submitted by
Zygmunt Elbiński

Spring 1985 session of the Committee on Conventions and Recommendations (121st session of the Executive Board)[1]

10. Mr Christian Schmidt is stated by the author of the communication to be a member of the section of the War Resisters' International in the Federal Republic of Germany. He is alleged to have been charged, together with two other persons, Angelika Strobl and Walter Strobl, with disparaging the State and with "inciting to crime" merely because they produced and distributed pacifist leaflets calling upon the population to refuse military service.

11. The representative of the government concerned stated that the communication in question did not satisfy the conditions for admissibility stipulated by 104 EX/Decision 3.3. It did not contain relevant evidence, in particular regarding the identity and profession of the persons concerned. The author himself had acknowledged that the information he had collected was derived from periodicals produced by peace movements, and that he had endeavoured in vain to gather further particulars, a fact which attested that he did not have reliable knowledge of the alleged facts.

12. The representative or the government concerned then informed the Committee that two of the persons concerned were students aged between 25 and 27 and the third was a natural health care trainee, all three of whom already had police records, for acts of violence and breaches of the laws governing associations, and indeed, in the case of two of them, for theft. He added that the facts that had led to their being sentenced to pay fines ranging from 400 to 900 Deutschmarks were criminal acts having no connection with their student status or with the dissemination of pacifist ideas.

---

[1] See document 121 EX/46 PRIV., paras. 10-16; see also document 121 EX/CR/HR/3 Add.

13. He went on to say that, as the competent courts had noted, while their ideas and convictions might be regarded as estimable, the ways in which they had expressed them constituted offences under the terms of the penal code. Not only had they called upon soldiers to desert and to disobey the orders given them; they had also urged civilians called up for national service not to enrol as conscientious objectors and to refuse to undertake the civilian service specially organized for such objectors, for example in hospitals and in various social institutions. They had, moreover, defamed the State in their leaflets and desecrated the national symbol by presenting the Eagle in a supremely ridiculous guise. The representative of the government concerned pointed out that, in the account of the facts of the claim (part III of the form), the quotation given by the author was simply an excerpt from those leaflets, and that in any case the sentence passed on the three persons concerned was not yet enforceable, since they had lodged an appeal with the Supreme Court. In conclusion, he considered that, since no human rights falling within Unesco's fields of competence had been violated, the communication should be declared inadmissible.

14. The members of the Committee who spoke thanked the representative of the government concerned for the explanations that he had supplied and acknowledged that nothing in the communication could be seriously taken into consideration.

15. In reply to a question, the representative of the government concerned stated that there was no legislation against those who declared themselves in favour of peace in the Federal Republic of Germany.

16. Following an exchange of views, the Committee *decided* to declare the communication inadmissible as not meeting the requirements stipulated in that respect in paragraph 14 (*a*) of 104 EX/Decision 3.3.

No. 640/84

Concerning *German Democratic Republic*
Case of *Ulrike Poppe and Bärbel Bohley*

Communication of 11 June 1984 submitted by
Zygmunt Elbiński

Spring 1985 session of the Committee on Conventions and Recommendations (121st session of the Executive Board)[1]

124. Ulrike Poppe and Bärbel Bohley, whose professions are not indicated, are presented as members of a peace movement in the German Democratic Republic. It is alleged that they were arrested in December 1983 and charged with treason against the State simply for having described their peace activities to a woman peace campaigner from New Zealand. According to the author of the communication, the maximum penalty for treason in the German Democratic Republic is 12 years' imprisonment.

125. The representative of the Government of the German Democratic Republic confirmed the substance of the letter addressed to the Director-General on 19 April 1985 by the Permanent Delegate of that State to Unesco, reporting that the two persons mentioned in the communication had been freed on 24 January 1984; consequently, in the opinion of the writer of the letter, the communication was neither well founded nor admissible. On being asked to clarify certain points, the representative of the government concerned said that no further proceedings were being taken against the alleged victims; he confirmed that judicial inquiries had indeed been started on 13 December 1983 but he did not know why the persons concerned had been remanded in custody until 24 January 1984. He had no more idea of the profession of the persons concerned by the communication than its author had.

126. All the members of the Committee who spoke in the debate took the view that the communication had been settled, since Mrs Ulrike Poppe and Mrs Bärbel Bohley had been released. Some of them also noted that the communication gave so few de-

[1] See document 121 EX/46 PRIV., paras. 124-127; see also document 121 EX/CR/HR/3 Add.

tails that it was even doubtful whether it fell within Unesco's spheres of competence.

127. At the close of the discussion, the Committee *decided* that, since the two alleged victims had been freed, the communication should be considered as a matter settled, under the terms of paragraph 14 (*a*) (x) of 104 EX/Decision 3.3.

No. 641/84

Concerning *Hungary*
Case of *Twenty female activists for peace*

Communication of 11 June 1984 submitted by
Zygmunt Elbiński

Spring 1985 session of the Committee on Conventions and Recommendations (121st session of the Executive Board)[1]

90. It is alleged that, in July 1983, while they were discussing questions about Eastern Europe and non-violence with a group of Hungarians, 20 members of the women's peace movement from the United Kingdom, other European countries and America, were forced by the Hungarian police to leave Hungary.

91. The government concerned was not represented (letter of 29 April 1985 from the Permanent Delegation of Hungary to Unesco, read out by the representative of the Director-General).

92. Some members of the Committee, while regretting the absence of any representative of the government concerned, recognized that the communication was clearly inadmissible: on the one hand, it appeared that the author had drawn his information solely from the press and that he therefore had no reliable knowledge of the alleged violations, not even knowing whether the 20 peace campaigners concerned had lodged complaints with the competent Hungarian authorities; on the other hand, although freedom of opinion, association and assembly should be guaranteed, such freedom was not only limited by each country's own requirements with regard to the maintenance of order but did not, as such, fall within Unesco's fields of competence. In the case in point, the problem raised concerned purely and simply a question of political propaganda and not a question relating to education for peace. In that connection, one member of the Committee said that if, in fact, the problem raised concerned peace and disarmament, it would then fall within the Organization's fields of activities as provided for under Major Programme XIII ("Peace, international understanding, human rights and the rights of peoples"), but such was not the case. With

[1] See document 121 EX/46 PRIV., paras. 90-93; see also document 121 EX/CR/HR/3 Add.

regard to the absence of a representative of the government concerned, he noted that, under the terms of 104 EX/Decision 3.3 (paragraph 14 (*e*)), the presence of such a representative was not compulsory and that, in any case, the communication was quite unfounded.

93. Following an exchange of views, the Committee *decided* to declare the communication inadmissible as not falling within Unesco's fields of competence.

No. 642/84

Concerning *Norway*
Case of Ikkevold Magazine

Communication of 11 June 1984 submitted by
Zygmunt Elbiński

Spring 1985 session of the Committee on Conventions and Recommendations (121st session of the Executive Board)[1]

103. The author of the communication alleges that, in October 1983, Norwegian police searched the offices of the Norwegian section of the War Resisters' International "Folkereisning Mot Krig" (FMK) and the houses of 12 persons associated with the latter and with *Ikkevold Magazine*, because, in three of its issues, this magazine had published lists of NATO installations in Norway. The author of the communication adds that those responsible for the said magazine face the possibility of serious charges of threatening State security.

104. The representative of the government concerned informed the Committee that the *Ikkevold Magazine* which is an organ of the Norwegian section of the War Resisters' International, had published in three issues in 1983 articles about secret Norwegian military constructions and installations. Because of these articles, the Chief of the Defence Staff asked the Director of the Public Prosecutions for investigation. She added that consequent upon this investigation, members of the editorial staff of the magazine were formally charged with, on the one hand, disclosure of information which should have been kept secret for the safety of the State and, on the other hand, placing themselves or others in possession of such secrets. She stated that in accordance with judicial authorization, search and seizure were carried out in the residence of the members of the editorial staff. She indicated further that the trial of the accused was scheduled to begin at the City Court on 29 April 1985 and was expected to last approximately two weeks. The representative of the government concerned contended that the communication was inadmissible on the grounds that, lacking first-hand information on the case, the author concerned had based his allegations only on the information obtained directly or indirectly from the mass media

[1] See document 121 EX/46 PRIV., paras. 103-106; see also document 121 EX/CR/HR/3 Add.

and that the process of exhausting available internal remedies had not even been initiated by the alleged victims. She also submitted that the communication was manifestly ill-founded and thus inadmissible. In this connection, she declared that regulations limiting the freedom of expression when national security was at stake were permitted under international law, especially under Article 29 (2) of the Universal Declaration of Human Rights, Article 19 (3) of the International Covenant on Civil and Political Rights and Article 10 (2) of the European Convention on Human Rights.

105. Several members of the Committee concurred with the contention that the communication was inadmissible. Several members also observed in this respect that the acts complained of by the author had been accomplished in conformity with due process of law and for legitimate reasons. While expressing his regret that the accused peace activists had not, according to him been tried expeditiously enough after charges were instituted against them, another member stated that the objective of the communication was contrary to the purposes of the Committee. Some other members of the Committee agreed with this point of view. These members emphasized that the purpose and aim of the communication as specified by the author himself in part V of the questionnaire attached to it, were clearly outside the competence of the Committee.

106. On concluding its discussion, the Committee *decided* that the communication fell outside the fields of competence of the Organization and was accordingly inadmissible.

No. 643/84

Concerning *Union of Soviet Socialist Republics*
Case of *Victor Blik* et al.*

Communication of 12 June 1984 submitted by
Zygmunt Elbiński

Spring 1985 session of the Committee on Conventions and Recommendations (121st session of the Executive Board)[1]

177. The author of the communication alleges that 10 Soviet citizens, belonging to an organization called "Group for Establishing Trust between the United States of America and the Union of Soviet Socialist Republics", founded in June 1982, have been subjected to harassment and persecution by the authorities of their country.

178. The representative of the government concerned stated that it emerged from an examination of this communication that the information contained in it was derived entirely from newspapers and, in particular, related to facts dating back some time, and gave no details about domestic means of redress used or any adequate indication of the status of the alleged victims. In his view, this was a case of abuse of the right to submit a communication and, in view of the conditions for admissibility laid down in paragraph 14 (*a*) of 104 EX/Decision 3.3, the communication should be declared inadmissible.

179. The members of the Committee who spoke recognized that the communication comprised a rather flimsy assemblage of facts, from which it was quite clear that the author did not have reliable knowledge of the alleged violations of human rights. Moreover, they found that the purpose and aim of the communication, which called upon the Committee to put questions of a political nature to a government, was not within the Committee's terms of reference.

---

* Case of *Victor Blik, Vladimir Brodsky, Lev Dudkin, Valery Godyak, Gennady Krochik, Yuri Hronopulo, Olga Lusnikova, Yuri Medvedkov, Olga Medvedkova and Oleg Radzinsky*.

[1] See document 121 EX/46 PRIV., paras. 177-181; see also document 121 EX/CR/HR/3 Add.

No. 643/84 **Union of Soviet Socialist Republics**

180. For information, the representative of the government concerned indicated that the events took place at a time when the President of the United States of America had declared a crusade against the Soviet Union. He said that the stated desire of the Group in question to establish trust between the United States of America and the Soviet Union might be considered laudable if the situation were actually so, that the Soviet authorities had not prevented the members of the Group from meeting and that most of the alleged self-styled victims and their families had even been authorized to emigrate. Replying to a request for information from some of the members of the Committee concerning the situation of a linguist, Oleg Radzinsky, who was said to have been condemned to one year's imprisonment and five years' internal exile, he stated that the sentence had no connection with the activities of the Group in question and that it had been based on the provision of the Penal Code relating to slanderous propaganda undermining the Soviet regime, an offence which the person concerned had himself admitted, not only in court but also in two open letters, one of them addressed to the President of the United States of America.

181. After an exchange of views, the Committee *declared* the communication inadmissible on the grounds that it was clearly ill-founded and did not fall within Unesco's fields of competence.

No. 645/84

Concerning *Union of Soviet Socialist Republics*
Case of *Soviet scientists of Jewish origin who have filed applications to emigrate*

Communication of 2 July 1984 submitted by
Michel A. Calvo*

Autumn 1984 session of the Committee on Conventions and Recommendations (120th session of the Executive Board)[1]

180. The Committee *decided* to defer consideration of these communications[2] to its spring 1985 session.

Spring 1985 session of the Committee on Conventions and Recommendations (121st session of the Executive Board)[3]

182. The authors of this communication allege that a considerable number of high-level Soviet scientists of Jewish origin have been opliged to leave their posts and have subsequently been unable to find employment appropriate to their qualifications, on account of their having filed applications to emigrate to Israel. Two lists comprising 127 names of alleged victims are submitted in support of these allegations.

---

* On behalf of Henri Cartan, André Lwoff, David Ruzié, Laurent Schwartz and Bernard Dupuy.

1 See document 120 EX/15 PRIV., para. 180; see also documents 120 EX/CR/HR/3 Add. and Add.4.

2 Communications No. 645/84 concerning *Union of Soviet Socialist Republics*, case of *Soviet scientists of Jewish origin who have filed applications to emigrate*, and No. 651/84 concerning *Union of Soviet Socialist Republics*, case of *Alleged discrimination with respect to education*.

3 See document 121 EX/46 PRIV., paras. 182-185; see also document 121 EX/CR/HR/2.

No. 645/84 **Union of Soviet Socialist Republics**

183. The representative of the government concerned stated that the case in point was a typical example of abuse of the right to submit a communication: the individual cases presented went back several years; the information concerning each of the cases was extremely brief; the authors were even unaware of whether the persons concerned had had recourse to means of redress; they were using a miscellaneous assortment of vague pieces of information to make a whole series of statements that were insulting to the Soviet Union and, moreover, were attempting to put them across as a communication that might be classified as a "question". Referring to resolution 32/130 adopted by the United Nations General Assembly on 16 December 1977, entitled "Alternative approaches and ways and means within the United Nations system for improving the effective enjoyment of human rights and fundamental freedoms", the representative of the government concerned said that human rights issues should not be turned into instruments of tension among States. In his view, the communication did not satisfy the conditions for admisssibility laid down by 104 EX/Decision 3.3 and was totally at variance with the spirit of Article 1 of Unesco's Constitution, since it was, in his view, an attempt to interfere in the domestic affairs of the Soviet Union. Referring to the problem of emigration as a whole, he stated that some 250,000 Soviet Jews had been able to emigrate, that no particular obstacle had been placed in the way of persons wishing to join their families abroad, and that, while there were admittedly cases in which visas had been refused, those restrictions - which affected a number of scientists - were due to the fact that the persons concerned either had had access to State secrets that had not yet ceased to be of importance, or had family problems that had not yet been settled in the Soviet Union, or again had no close relatives in the receiving country. With regard to the purpose and aim of the communication, the representative of the government concerned specified that those who applied for emigration visas were not automatically dismissed from their posts; most of them had even refused promotion for fear of being obliged to take on responsibilities that would give them knowledge of secrets concerning State security, which might preclude their obtaining permission to emigrate. That was the case, for example, of Mr Alexandre Ioffe (No. 5 on the list of alleged victims); others had been dismissed for having committed offences under the ordinary law, as in the case, for example, of Nadezhda Fradkova, Mark Nashpitz and Samuel Rombe (Nos. 48, 94 and 103 on the list). So far as the problem of the *kharakteristika* was concerned, that document was not needed for an application to emigrate. In regard to the question concerning access to libraries, everyone had the right to frequent them; and in regard to participation in scientific conferences, it was for the competent scientific authorities to designate those who should attend them. The representative of the government concluded that, in view of the unreasonable and indeed offensive nature of the requests made in the communication, it should be declared inadmissible.

Union of Soviet Socialist Republics **No. 645/84**

184. Some of the members of the Committee who spoke considered the explanations given by the representative of the government concerned to be satisfactory; it was pointed out, moreover, that of the three alleged victims who seemed to be of Ukrainian origin (Nos. 99, 117 and 122 on the list), one of the mathematicians, Leonid Varvak, had just been offered a post in the suburbs of Kiev, while the construction engineer, Yakov Tohar, was still working as an engineer and not as a caretaker, as stated in the communication; furthermore, it was pointed out that the reason why, as statistics showed, the number of Soviet Jews wishing to emigrate was falling was not that there had been a change in the Soviet Union's policy on the subject, but that Jews did not wish to emigrate, the younger ones because they did not want to go off to war in the receiving country, and the older ones because they were afraid that they would not find work there. The other members of the Committee who spoke noted that the alleged victims represented a wide range of professions, and that most of those professions could have no connection with State secrets; they were therefore inclined to think that dismissals, the dates of which often corresponded with the dates of applications for permission to emigrate, were frequent in the case of those who wished to emigrate. They therefore felt that. there was cause for concern, particularly as the Committee, following its usual humanitarian approach, was in duty bound to look more thoroughly into the individual cases presented, bearing in mind, among other things, Unesco's Recommendation on the status of scientific researchers. Other members regretted that so much talent was being left unused, and shared that concern, but acknowledged that the information concerning the 127 alleged victims was too succinct for the Committee to be able to make good use of it, particularly as it could not take the place of either the authors or the alleged victims.

185. After discussing the matter, the Committee *declared* the communication inadmissible in its present form.

No. 647/84

Concerning *Uruguay*
Case of *"Cinco Días"*

Communication of 8 June 1984 submitted by
Committee to protect journalists

Autumn 1984 session of the Committee on Conventions and Recommendations (120th session of the Executive Board)[1]

188. The four newspapers in question,[2] the first a daily and the others weeklies, were allegedly all banned in March, April or May 1984, following their publication of articles which, according to the Uruguayan authorities, violated certain administrative provisions, including Decree No. 251/983 of 3 [August] 1983.

189. The representative of the Uruguayan Government said that on 8 August 1984 Decree No. 311 had annulled Decree No. 251 of 3 August 1983, which had served as the legal basis for the decisions to ban the newspapers and periodicals in question. Decree No. 251 had been passed as a temporary measure to make it possible to suspend all publications referring to political activities, on account of the exceptional situation which had existed in Uruguay for some time. The representative of the government concerned expressed the view that as this situation no longer existed, and Decree No. 251 was no longer in force, the problems posed by these communications had been solved.

190. In reply to questions raised by members of the Committee, the representative of the Uruguayan Government stated that since the promulgation of Decree No. 311 on 8 August 1984, many new publications had appeared, in particular in connection with the preparatory process for the elections to be held shortly in the country; these included publications which reflected political trends opposed to those of the gov-

[1] See document 120 EX/15 PRIV., paras. 188-192; see also document 120 EX/CR/HR/3 Add.
[2] Communications No. 647/84 concerning *Uruguay*, case of *"Cinco Días"*, No. 648/84 concerning *Uruguay*, case of *"Tribune Amplia"*, No. 649/84 concerning *Uruguay*, case of *"Somos Idea"*, and No. 650/84 concerning *Uruguay*, case of *"Convicción"*, were being considered together.

ernment, but the representative of the government concerned could not confirm that the publications covered by the present communications had in fact reappeared. She added that there were internal remedies against publication bans, and even the possibility of compensation if such bans resulted in financial loss.

191. The members of the Committee who spoke considered that there no longer seemed to be any legal obstacle to the publication of the newspapers mentioned in the communications, and that the communications could therefore be struck from the Committee's list.

192. The Committee therefore *decided* as follows:

> The Committee,
>
> Noting that the legal basis for the measures taken to suspend and ban the publication of the four newspapers in question no longer exists, since Decree No. 251/983 of 3 August 1983 has been annulled by Decree No. 311 of 8 August 1984;
>
> Considers that the four cases should therefore be deemed settled.

No. 648/84

Concerning *Uruguay*
Case of *"Tribune Amplia"*

Communication of 8 June 1984 submitted by
Committee to protect journalists

Autumn 1984 session of the Committee on Conventions and Recommendations
(120th session of the Executive Board)[1]

[1] See document 120 EX/15 PRIV., paras. 188-192 (*supra*, pp. 511-512), communication No. 647/84 concerning *Uruguay*, case of *"Cinco Dias"*.

No. 649/84

Concerning *Uruguay*
Case of *"Somos Idea"*

Communication of 8 June 1984 submitted by
Committee to protect journalists

Autumn 1984 session of the Committee on Conventions and Recommendations (120th session of the Executive Board)[1]

[1] See document 120 EX/15 PRIV., paras. 188-192 (*supra*, pp. 511-512), communication No. 647/84 concerning *Uruguay*, case of *"Cinco Dias"*.

No. 650/84

Concerning *Uruguay*
Case of *"Convicción"*

Communication of 8 June 1984 submitted by
Committee to protect journalists

Autumn 1984 session of the Committee on Conventions and Recommendations (120th session of the Executive Board)[1]

[1] See document 120 EX/15 PRIV., paras. 188-192 (*supra*, pp. 511-512), communication No. 647/84 concerning *Uruguay*, case of *"Cinco Dias"*.

No. 651/84

Concerning *Union of Soviet Socialist Republics*
Case of *Alleged discrimination with respect to education*

Communication of 25 July 1984 submitted by
Michel A. Calvo*

Autumn 1984 session of the Committee on Conventions and Recommendations (120th session of the Executive Board)[1]

Spring 1985 session of the Committee on Conventions and Recommendations (121st session of the Executive Board)[2]

186. This communication was examined by the Committee but, for lack of time, it was unable to arrive at conclusions. The examination will be resumed at the next session, it being understood that the debate of the present session will be reflected in the document of presentation of communications submitted to the next session.

Autumn 1985 session of the Committee on Conventions and Recommendations (122nd session of the Executive Board)[3]

121. This communication alleges discrimination, in respect of education, to which Soviet citizens of Jewish origin are said to be subject.

122. The authors of the communication allege that there has been de facto exclusion first of Hebrew and then of Yiddish as the mother tongues or national languages of

---

* On behalf of André Lwoff, David Ruzié, Laurent Schwartz, Henri Cartan and Bernard Dupuy.

[1] See document 120 EX/15 PRIV., para. 180 (*supra*, p. 507), communication No. 645/84 concerning *Union of Soviet Socialist Republics*, case of *Soviet scientists of Jewish origin who have filed applications to emigrate*.

[2] See document 121 EX/46 PRIV., para. 186; see also documents 121 EX/CR/HR/2 and Add.

[3] See document 122 EX/21 PRIV., paras. 121-129; see also document 122 EX/CR/HR/2.

the Jews, and that no instruction is available in these two languages. The Soviet authorities are said not to tolerate any private lessons in these languages and to refuse to register persons to teach them; they are also said to have trained no teachers to teach them to persons who wish to study them and not to have allowed such persons to make use of the appropriate means and learning materials necessary for private study.

123. Recapitulating what he had said at the Committee's [spring 1985] session, the representative of the government concerned stated that [Mr] Calvo had sought, with the help of eminent scholars, to turn the Committee into an international court and that the communication in no way met the conditions for admissibility laid down in 104 EX/Decision 3.3, paragraph 14 (*a*): the allegations made were nothing other than a premeditated falsification of the facts calculated to arouse hatred between national communities and to aggravate international tension by attempting to give a false picture of the Soviet Union's policy and to distract the international community's attention from the crimes perpetrated by the State of Israel against the Arab peoples; with regard to certain persons of Jewish origin mentioned in the communication and against whom judicial proceedings had been instituted, those persons were guilty of having committed criminal acts - in that they had engaged in anti-Soviet propaganda and activities - and not of having taught Hebrew or Yiddish; consequently, the authors did not have reliable knowledge of the alleged facts, not even knowing whether any domestic means of redress had been used by the persons concerned; as for the statistics tending to prove the fall in the number of Soviet citizens of Jewish origin who had declared Yiddish as their mother tongue when each census was taken, it should be noted that those statistics covered the period of the Second World War, during which many Soviet Jews had been killed by the Fascists; it was an untruth to say that Soviet citizens of Jewish origin did not enjoy the same rights as other Soviet citizens and were not allowed to express themselves in their language; in the USSR many prominent personalities, in the Supreme Soviet and elsewhere, and many eminent scientists, talented writers and Heroes of Socialist Labour were Jews, which proved that they had received proper education; as compared with the national average, the Jewish population in the USSR aged 10 and over had received a suitable education more than any other ethnic group; in relative percentage terms, moreover, there were among the Jews four times as many people who had received a higher education and five times as many who had received a secondary education than there were in the population as a whole; there was no discrimination in regard either to education or to work; of the peoples of the USSR the Jews occupied the first place; about 10 per cent of those had been awarded the Lenin prize and more than 200 Heroes of the Soviet Union were Jews. Speaking of the development of Jewish culture, with particular reference to knowledge of Yiddish and/or Hebrew, the representative of the government concerned pointed out that the problem was much more complex than the authors of the communication thought, since the selec-

tion of either one of those languages depended quite often on a choice freely made by the parents concerned; it was indeed an inalienable right of all individuals to express themselves in the language they regarded as their own, depending on the region where they lived; it should be recognized that, in comparison with certain Western countries, a large percentage of Jews in the USSR spoke their mother tongue: more than 14.2 per cent in the USSR as against 10 to 12 per cent in England and France. By way of illustration, he mentioned an exchange between one of his predecessors, Professor Zivs, and his American colleague at the time, who, although of Jewish origin, was not familiar with the Hebrew language and who therefore, unlike Professor Zivs, was unable to read the titles of two works published in the USSR in that language. He added that the example in question tended to prove, were it necessary, that neither Yiddish nor Hebrew was forbidden in the USSR, that there were schools to teach those two languages, especially as some people had seen for themselves that there were Jewish theatres, artistic groups, synagogues, books, dictionaries of a high standard and newspapers. He informed the Committee that certain television serials shown in France with Jewish actors had also been shown in the USSR, that the works of a major Jewish writer had been translated into several languages, running to 540 editions totalling about nine-and-a-half million copies, and that a leading publishing house in the USSR had published hundreds of books in Yiddish with translations into Russian, many books translated into Yiddish and large numbers of books for children translated into Hebrew and Yiddish, totalling about 41 million copies for the period since 1961. As an example, he showed the Committee a textbook in Hebrew published in 1982. One of the purposes of the communication in question, he said, was to secure the importing and distributing of material from Israel, whose Zionist policies had been vigorously condemned by the United Nations.

[123a.] Considering that it contained not only manifestly false and slanderous information but also made unacceptable demands with a view to having a series of Soviet laws repealed, he concluded that it constituted a gross violation of 104 EX/ Decision 3.3 and an attempt to interfere in the domestic affairs of the USSR and that consequently the communication was inadmissible.

124. Asked whether certain persons had been prevented from teaching Hebrew or Yiddish, the representative of the government concerned replied in the negative, provided those persons had fulfilled the necessary conditions. He explained that in the Soviet system anyone wishing to teach a particular subject had to apply for registration, submitting proof of the required level of knowledge, principally in the form of an appropriate diploma; otherwise authorization could not be given.

125. Some members of the Committee, while thanking the representative of the government concerned for his detailed statement, observed that the information provid-

ed related more to questions of a general nature. In their view, as Judaism was both a culture and a religion, parents had a responsibility to bring up their children in that religion by teaching them the language of their ancestors. One might therefore wonder what standards were set with regard to the knowledge needed for authorization to teach that language. They felt that the communication raised in specific terms the question of the right to speak one's own language and have one's own cultural life, which was a cultural right guaranteed both by the Universal Declaration of Human Rights and by the two International Covenants on Human Rights and one which fell within Unescos' fields of competence. As for the statistics placed at the Committee's disposal by the authors, one Committee member noted that they derived from official Soviet statistics, which had, incidentally, been communicated by the Soviet authorities to the Committee on the Elimination of Racial Discrimination. Referring to information according to which various persons had been arrested and interrogated and had had Hebrew books and cassettes, bibles and religious objects confiscated, these members asked on what grounds this material had been confiscated, given that the persons concerned were said to have been arrested and sentenced for common law offences unconnected with their religious beliefs. In that connection the representative of the Soviet Government explained that the material had been confiscated in accordance with paragraph 12 (3) of the International Covenant on Civil and Political Rights because it contained defamatory expressions with regard to the Soviet and Arab peoples.

126. Certain other members of the Committee were amazed that the Soviet Union could be accused of racial discrimination or anti-Semitism. In their view, the allegations made were political and aimed at imposing the teaching of Hebrew throughout the territory of the USSR. The facts presented had been set out in a tendentious and unacceptable manner so as to create the false impression that there had been massive and systematic violations of the rights of Soviet Jews and the communication, which was defamatory to the government concerned, should therefore be rejected.

127. Other members also expressed their concern about the opportunities for Soviet citizens of Jewish origin to learn Yiddish or Hebrew. Yet others felt that there was a need for additional information.

128. At the end of the discussion, the Committee *decided*:

(i) to take note of the statements of the representative of the government concerned and ask the Secretariat to transmit the content to the authors of the communication;

(ii) to ask the authors of the communication, in the light of the information thus transmitted to them, to provide relevant and detailed particulars on the facts alleged in the communication, failing the reception of which the Committee would *ipso facto* strike the communication from its list at the next session;

(iii) to resume consideration of this communication at its spring 1986 session.

129. Following the adoption of this decision, a member of the Committee stated that he himself and a number of other members regarded the communication as inadmissible.

Spring 1986 session of the Committee on Conventions and Recommendations (124th session of the Executive Board)[4]

Autumn 1986 session of the Committee on Conventions and Recommendations (125th session of the Executive Board)[5]

108. This communication alleges discrimination, in respect of education, to which Soviet citizens of Jewish origin are said to be subject.

109. The authors of the communication allege that there has been de facto exclusion first of Hebrew and then of Yiddish as the mother tongues or national languages of the Jews, and that no instruction is available in these two languages. The Soviet authorities are said not to tolerate any private lessons in these languages and to refuse to register persons to teach them; they are also said to have trained no teachers to teach them to persons who wish to study them and not to have allowed such persons to make use of the appropriate means and learning materials necessary for private study.

110. In view of the scope of these allegations and the bulk of documentation, the Committee *decided* to resume examination of this communication at its spring 1987 session, in order to devote as much time to it as was necessary.

[4] See document 124 EX/3 PRIV., paras. 101-104 (*supra*, pp. 48-49), communication No. 441/82 concerning *Union of Soviet Socialist Republics*, case of *Vladimir Raiz*.
[5] See document 125 EX/3 PRIV., paras. 108-110; see also document 125 EX/CR/HR/2.

No. 651/84 **Union of Soviet Socialist Republics**

Spring 1987 session of the Committee on Conventions and Recommendations (126th session of the Executive Board)[6]

117. This communication alleges discrimination, in respect of education, to which Soviet citizens of Jewish origin are said to be subject. The authors of the communication allege that there has been de facto exclusion first of Hebrew and then of Yiddish as the mother tongues or national languages of the Jews, and that no instruction is available in these two languages. The Soviet authorities are said not to tolerate any private lessons in these languages and to refuse to register persons to teach them; they are also said to have trained no teachers to teach them to persons who wish to study them and not to have allowed such persons to make use of the appropriate means and learning materials necessary for private study.

118. The Committee examined this communication at the Committee's [spring and autumn 1985] sessions. The representative of the government concerned stated that the author of the communication had sought to turn the Committee into an international court and that the communication in no way met the conditions for admissibility laid down in 104 EX/Decision 3.3, paragraph 14 (*a*): the allegations made were nothing other than a premeditated falsification of the facts calculated to arouse hatred between national communities and to aggravate international tension by attempting to give a false picture of the Soviet Union's policy and to distract the international community's attention from the crimes perpetrated by the State of Israel against the Arab peoples; it was an untruth to say that Soviet citizens of Jewish origin did not enjoy the same rights as other Soviet citizens and were not allowed to express themselves in their language; in the USSR many prominent personalities, in the Supreme Soviet and elsewhere, and many eminent scientists, talented writers and Heroes of Socialist Labour were Jews, which proved that they had received proper education; as compared with the national average, the Jewish population in the USSR aged 10 and over had received a suitable education more than any other ethnic group; in relative percentage terms, moreover, there were among the Jews four times as many people who had received a higher education and five times as many who had received a secondary education than there were in the population as a whole. He added that neither Yiddish nor Hebrew was forbidden in the USSR, that there were schools to teach those two languages, especially as some people had seen for themselves that there were Jewish theatres, artistic groups, synagogues, books, dictionaries of a high standard and newspapers. He informed the Committee that certain television serials with Jewish actors had also been shown in the USSR, that the works of a major Jewish writer had been translated into several languages, running to 540 editions totalling about nine-and-a-half million copies, and that a leading

[6] See document 126 EX/3 PRIV., paras. 117-141; see also document 126 EX/CR/HR/2.

publishing house in the USSR had published hundreds of books in Yiddish with translations into Russian, many books translated into Yiddish and large numbers of books for children translated into Hebrew and Yiddish, totalling about 41 million copies for the period since 1961. One of the purposes of the communication in question, he said, was to secure the importing and distributing of material from Israel, whose Zionist policies had been vigorously condemned by the United Nations.

[118a.] Considering that it contained not only manifestly false and slanderous information but also made unacceptable demands with a view to having a series of Soviet laws repealed, he concluded that it constituted a gross violation of 104 EX/Decision 3.3 and an attempt to interfere in the domestic affairs of the USSR and that consequently the communication was inadmissible.

119. At the end of the discussion, the Committee, at its autumn 1985 session decided to ask the authors of the communication, in the light of the statements of the representative of the government concerned to provide relevant and detailed particulars on the facts alleged in the communication, failing the reception of which the Committee would *ipso facto* strike the communication from its list at the next session [...].[7]

120. At the Committee's present session, the Committee resumed its examination of the case. The representative of the government concerned stated that the communication was not about a violation of human rights but rather about the teaching of the Hebrew and Yiddish languages in the Soviet Union. It did not appear to be indispensable to dwell on the arguments and counter-arguments which had already been expressed, he said. The representative reminded the Committee that it had decided that the communication would be struck from its list *ipso facto* if the authors did not provide relevant and detailed particulars on the facts alleged.

121. Had the authors in fact provided such information? The document submitted by the authors was quite disappointing, the representative said. Instead of providing information pertaining to the facts, the authors went into polemics concerning the remarks made by the representative of the government. Such polemics constituted an abuse of the right to submit communications and were totally unacceptable. Even though the Secretariat was not allowed to make value judgments on communications, it should nevertheless ensure that the Committee's decisions were respected. If in the present instance the Committee had decided to ask the authors to provide additional information, the representatives of the Secretariat were obliged to see to it that the documents submitted contained such information and did not engage in polemics with the representative of the government. In that connection, the representa-

[7] See document 122 EX/21 PRIV., para. 128 (ii) (*supra*, pp. 522-523).

tive of the Director-General pointed out that it was for the Committee, not the Secretariat, to make a value judgment on a communication. The Secretariat could not, therefore, withhold a communication from the Committee.

122. There was an unbalanced approach here, the representative pointed out. The representatives of governments were bound by established procedures, whereas no such restrictions applied to the authors of communications. That led, as could be seen in the present instance, to abuses. As was obvious from the case under consideration, and from a series of other communications, the authors overstepped the limits of what was acceptable, making use of the Committee to disseminate their propaganda, as international Zionist centres in particular were doing by resorting to propaganda for Zionism.

123. Referring to the facts mentioned by the authors of the communication, the representative went on to explain that the letter addressed to Mr Abramovitch by the Finance Section of the Moscow City Council did not mean that Hebrew could not be taught; it simply dealt with certain administrative formalities. Hebrew and Yiddish were included on the curriculum of a number of universities. It was clearly false that they were not taught in the Soviet Union.

124. Mr Abramovitch ran into problems because he was not licensed to teach, the representative explained. The State authorities in establishing licensing requirements were merely verifying that a person had the necessary professional qualifications or training. The State could not simply give licences to any person who wished to teach French, Geography, or other subjects. Certain minimum qualifications had to be established.

125. On a different point, the representative indicated that the correspondence put forth in this communication had spanned a seven-year period. The letter addressed to Mr Platonov by Mr Abramovitch proved that the latter had taught Hebrew during a six-year period though he had no license. Thus it can be taken as proof that the authors were wrong in their assertions that one could not teach Hebrew without a license.

126. The representative of the government concerned also pointed out that it was a condition of the Committee's procedure that a communication must be submitted within a reasonable time period. That was not the case here since it contained elements almost 20 years old, dating back to 1969.

127. The representative also stated that there was no evidence whatever in the correspondence cited by the authors that teaching of the languages was prohibited. The authors contradicted themselves. On the one hand they stated that Yiddish and He-

brew could not be taught, while on the other they themselves acknowledged that these languages were studied in a number of Soviet VUZy, in the Birobidzhan teacher-training college, in the general education schools of the city of Birobidzhan, etc. Literature was published in Yiddish in the USSR and there were Yiddish theatre groups. In 1984 a Russian-Hebrew dictionary had been published, while in 1982 a Yiddish primer had come out. The Yiddish monthly "Sovietish Heimland" regularly produced materials to help teachers of Yiddish. Starting with the tenth issue of 1985, the magazine was publishing a teach-yourself-Yiddish manual.

128. The representative informed the Committee that he was in a position to state officially and frankly that there was no restriction on teaching or learning these languages. He went on to explain that there were of course certain problems which sometimes arose. These problems consisted in the fact that Soviet public opinion reacted unfavourably when, on the pretext of teaching Hebrew, "international Zionist centres" engaged in propaganda on behalf of "Zionist chauvinism". In accordance with the United Nations General Assembly resolution, Soviet public opinion regarded "Zionism" as a form of racism and reacted unfavourably to the basic proposition of "Zionism" which claimed that Jews from different countries formed a single people, whose native land, it was said, was Israel. Soviet Jews, in their overwhelming majority, regarded themselves as an organic and inseparable part of the Soviet people in general. In that context, Soviet public opinion reacted unfavourably when "international Zionist centres" attempted to infiltrate Zionist ideology among a certain section of the Jewish population of the USSR, when "Zionism" counted on the use of independent Hebrew study circles as a sort of clandestine base for propagating the ideas of "Zionism", which directly contradicted the provisions of the [International] Covenant on Civil and Political Rights. The representative agreed with the assertions by the authors of the communication that the number of persons using the Yiddish language was declining in Soviet Union. This was not, however, as a result of any restrictions, but the consequence of the abolition of the restrictions of all kinds that had existed before the October revolution, when Jews had lived in a social and psychological ghetto. They had been confined to small towns and villages of the infamous "Pale" and Yiddish had remained the basic vehicle of national communication. After the October revolution had put an end to discrimination against Jews and they had become citizens with equal rights of a multinational Soviet land, real opportunities had opened up for them to use their talents, capabilities and knowledge in all manner of social, economic, cultural and State activities, and the role of Yiddish had declined. For the Jews, as for other large or small peoples of the Soviet Union, the basic vehicle of communication between nations had become the Russian language. Such was the objective process that had resulted from the spiritual and economic drawing together of socialist nations and nationalities.

129. After the revolution there was an end to the discrimination against minorities, and Jews became citizens with equal rights and privileges. There was a growing together of the nationalities as a natural consequence. As a result the use of the Jewish languages diminished on its own. There were in fact measures adopted by the Soviet authorities to assist persons wishing to learn the Jewish languages. A Yiddish-Russian dictionary had been published, there were publications in Yiddish, and Yiddish language theatre groups. However, the Jewish population of the Soviet Union constituted only 0.69 per cent of the total Soviet population. Thus, in every community there were only a small number of Jews. It would not be possible to set up in every community a school for every minority, whether Jews, Armenians, or other. There was in fact, no necessity to isolate minority children and put them in special schools, the representative said. The authors themselves admitted that interest in the languages was diminishing even among the Jews. There were many minorities in the Soviet Union but no minority should have the right to exclusive and special treatment.

130. The representative concluded by stating that the communication should be *ipso facto* struck from the Committee's list because the authors had not supplied pertinent documentation.

131. A member of the Committee wondered why the representative of the government concerned had asserted that the case concerned only a broad question of educational policy and thus did not come within the Committee's competence. The Committee member read out Article 27 of the [International] Convenant on Civil and Political Rights, which provided that:

> In those States in which ethnic, religious or linguistic minorities exist, persons belonging to such minorities shall not be denied the right, in community with the other members of their group, to enjoy their own culture, to profess and practise their own religion, or to use their own language.

132. This was a modest provision, he said, and it did not create a group right but rather a right of individuals to enjoy their own culture within a group. The right did not apply to immigrants or to guest workers but only to existing minorities, which the Jews clearly were in the Soviet Union. The total figure of 0.69 per cent was a misleading one because the Jews were in fact concentrated in the cities. There were apparently 250,000 Jews in Moscow, the Committee member indicated. It was true, however, that the use of Jewish languages was diminishing everywhere, even in Israel.

133. Did Article 27 require that the State should provide facilities? The answer would seem to be yes, though one could not say that special schools could be de-

manded. Those schools where the languages in question were presently taught in the Soviet Union were not accessible to the public; for example, the school for diplomats offered access to diplomatic trainees only. It should be possible for the Soviet Union to at least allow members of minorities to obtain the necessary licenses. At present, this appeared to be the case only for a few teachers in the specialized schools the Committee member said.

134. The example of the teaching and learning possibilities in Birobidzhan was not really relevant because this autonomous region was thousands of miles from the main Jewish communities. Only 0.5 per cent of the Jewish population lived there. The Committee member concluded by stating that this communication did make a valid case, a somewhat weak one but nevertheless a legitimate one.

135. In reply to the points raised by the Committee member, the representative of the government concerned explained that he had not said that it was a question of educational policy, he had simply stated that there was not a violation of human rights involved. It was more a question of cultural identity. This was an interesting question and one worth discussing, but it did not come within the procedure of [104 EX/Decision 3.3] he said.

136. He went on to explain that in Moscow students attended local schools. Moscow was a large and extended city. Even if five out of every 100 students were Jewish, it still would not be practical to set up special schools for them. Such schools would be possible if the Jews were concentrated in one place, but the fact was that the Jews did not want to live in separate communities; they wanted to live like everyone else. They were much more interested in learning English and French than in learning the Jewish languages. The government did try to provide facilities. But in the Soviet Union as in other countries assimilation of the Jews into the society was occuring. That was a not deliberate process of discrimination, it was a result of the Jews' own preferences. As concerned the access to teaching and learning facilities, it was a fact that major Soviet universities, Moscow, Odessa, Tbilisi, etc. offered courses. These were accessible facilities open to all. Possibilities also existed in the synagogues. The fact remained, however, that demand determines supply, and the demand was simply not very high. In any event Hebrew had never been a widespread language in the first place. It was Yiddish which had been more prevalent among the Jews. All these factors had to be kept in mind, the representative said.

137. Several Committee members found the information offered by the representative of the government concerned to be very convincing and felt that the communication should be struck from the Committee's list. The view was expressed that it would be inappropriate for special privileges to be accorded to a minority within a country just because a certain group of chauvinistic persons were making com-

plaints. A member stated that while there were indeed certain minimum rights one could expect a State to provide in the field of education, the authors of the communication were demanding privileges which went far beyond the reasonable minimum. The Committee could not pontificate to a Member State on how to run its educational policies. The Committee member went on to suggest that it might be useful to have the Secretariat prepare for the Committee a study as to exactly what constituted the minimum rights in the field of education. Other Committee members agreed that such a study might be useful.

138. The representative of the Director-General explained that while the Secretariat stood ready to carry out a study for the Committee, it was necessary to point out that such a study would necessarily consist of a compiling of pertinent texts of relevant international instruments and not an interpretation of those texts, since the Secretariat had no competence to pass judgement on the substance of international standard-setting instruments.

139. A Committee member, while supporting the striking of the communication, expressed the view that the new openness in the Soviet Union represented a great hope for many people and the member wondered whether it might not be possible within that context to allow those persons who were viewed as attempting to improperly impose their culture to emigrate from the Soviet Union.

140. In response to questions the representative of the government concerned stated that there were no limitations or restrictions on teaching or learning the Jewish languages in the Soviet Union. Concerning the question raised as to whether a person could teach these languages privately with or without a license as long as the appropriate taxes were paid, the representative indicated that in order to obtain a license in conformity with the law it was necessary to have certain training, which could usually be proved by showing the possession of a diploma. In the case of Mr Abramovitch this had not been problematic because he had in fact demonstrated that he could teach by simply doing so for several years.

141. At the end of the discussion the Committee *decided*:

(i) to thank the representative of the government concerned for his presence and his co-operation;

(ii) to strike this communication from its list as inadmissible, under paragraph 14 (*a*) (v) of [104 EX/Decision 3.3];

(iii) to request the Secretariat to present to it at its next session a document listing the texts concerning the right to education.

No. 652/84

Concerning *Nigeria*
Case of *Tai Solarin*

Communication of 21 July 1984 submitted by
Amnesty International

Autumn 1984 session of the Committee on Conventions and Recommendations (120th session of the Executive Board)[1]

80. The authors of the communication allege that Mr Solarin, a newspaper columnist and educator, is currently detained in Maiduguri prison, in Borno State, that the members of his family have not been allowed to see him and that there are fears for his health since he is suffering from chronic asthma.

81. The representative of the Nigerian Government said that she had received the communication one month to the date of the meeting of the Committee and immediately transmitted the file to her government but that she had not received a reply. She therefore asked the Committee to be so kind as to give her an extension during which time she hoped to receive her government's response to the communication.

82. The Committee *decided* to accede to the request of the government concerned and, consequently, to defer examination of the admissibility of the communication until the next session.

Spring 1985 session of the Committee on Conventions and Recommendations (121st session of the Executive Board)[2]

97. The authors of the communication allege that Mr Solarin, a newspaper columnist and educator, is currently detained in prison, that the members of his family have not been allowed to see him and that there are fears for his health since he is suffering from chronic asthma.

---

[1] See document 120 EX/15 PRIV., paras. 80-82; see also document 120 EX/CR/HR/3 Add.
[2] See document 121 EX/46 PRIV., paras. 97-102; see also document 121 EX/CR/HR/2.

No. 652/84 **Nigeria**

98. At the Committee's autumn 1984 session, the representative of the Nigerian Government said that she had received the communication only one month to the date of the meeting of the Committee and requested that the examination of the admissibility of the communication be deferred until the spring 1985 session so as to give her government sufficient time to collect and provide appropriate information concerning the communication. In accordance with this request, the Committee decided to postpone the examination of the communication.[3]

99. When the Committee took up the consideration of the admissibility of the communication, one of the representatives of the government concerned informed the Committee that, in the view of her government, the communication was inadmissible because it did not fulfil the conditions of admissibility laid down in paragraph 14 (*a*) of 104 EX/Decision 3.3 of the Executive Board, more particularly in subparagraphs (ii), (iii), (iv), (v), (vii) and (ix). She contended that the detention of the alleged victim had no connection with any of the Organization's fields of competence because he was neither a journalist by profession nor an active teacher. She stated that the alleged victim was arrested and detained not because of what he wrote as a journalist, a writer or a teacher as alleged in the communication, but because he was involved in acts prejudicial to State security.

100. It was further contended on behalf of the government concerned:

(i) that the communication was incompatible with the principles enshrined in the Constitution of Unesco, the Charter of the United Nations, the Universal Declaration of Human Rights, the International Covenant on Civil and Political Rights as well as other international instruments in the field of human rights;

(ii) that the communication was manifestly ill-founded because it was based on press reports;

(iii) that the communication contained alleged falsehoods and that its author did not appear to have reliable information of the alleged violation of human rights;

(iv) that no attempt had been made to exhaust the domestic remedies open to the alleged victim;

---

[3] See document 120 EX/15 PRIV., para. 82 (*supra*, p. 531).

(v) that, in any event, the enactment and the enforcement of State Security (Detention of Persons) Decree of 9 February 1984 were permitted under relevent international human rights instruments.

101. Some members of the Committee expressed concern over the fact that, on the one hand, the alleged victim was re-arrested after he had been set free following an application for a writ of *habeas corpus* had successfully been filed in his case and, on the other hand, he had not been tried on the charge of committing "acts prejudicial to the security of the State". In this connection, it was explained that the alleged victim had been re-arrested because he had been set free merely on the basis of a technicality. Another representative of the government concerned who also represented her country on the Committee emphasized that the alleged victim had been detained solely and exclusively for acts prejudicial to the security of the State. The Committee was informed by her in this connection that the alleged victim's detention was subject to a review at three months' intervals which could result in his being set free or tried on specific charges. She stated however that she had no information about the exact nature of the acts for which the alleged victim had been detained.

102. At the end of its discussion, the Committee concluded that it did not have sufficient information to enable it to form an opinion on the admissibility or otherwise of the communication and accordingly *decided*:

(i) that the information provided by the government concerned should be communicated to the authors of the communication, who should be asked to provide additional information;

(ii) that the government concerned should also be requested to provide additional information;

(iii) to postpone to its autumn 1985 session the examination of the communication.

Autumn 1985 session of the Committee on Conventions and Recommendations (122nd session of the Executive Board)[4]

83. The authors of the communication allege that Dr Tai Solarin, a newspaper columnist and educator, is currently detained in prison, that the members of his family have not been allowed to see him and that there are fears for his health since he is

[4] See document 122 EX/21 PRIV., paras. 83-85; see also document 122 EX/CR/HR/2.

suffering from chronic asthma. In introducing this communication to the Committee at its present session, the representative of the Director-General who is also the Legal Adviser stated that by a letter dated 29 August 1985, the Permanent Delegate of the State concerned had informed the Organization that Dr Tai Solarin was among 85 detainees released on 6 August 1985 by the Federal Military Government of her country and that the alleged victim had since returned to his home town.

84. The representative of the government concerned who also represented his country on the Committee confirmed the release of the alleged victim from detention. Some members expressed their thanks to the government concerned. While expressing their satisfaction at the release of Dr Solarin, some other members stated that in their view the reason for which he had been detained, namely the commission of "acts prejudicial to State security" was questionable to the extent that the accusation was as vague as it was lacking in details. In this connection, one member stated that, in her opinion, the fact that a given governmental action was taken in conformity with national law did not necessarily mean that the action was not contrary to international and objective human rights standards. In reply, the representative of the government concerned recalled that at the spring 1985 session of the Committee, the representative of his government had explained that it was for the competent authorities of the State concerned to decide what acts were or were not prejudicial to the security of the State.

85. At the close of the discussion, the Committee *decided* that, since the alleged victim had been released from detention, the case raised by the communication was to be considered as settled under the terms of paragraph 14 (*a*) (x) of 104 EX/Decision 3.3.

No. 653/84

Concerning *Chile*
Case of *Carlos Mario Lira Moscoso*

Communication of 19 July 1984 submitted by
Carlos Mario Lira Moscoso

Spring 1985 session of the Committee on Conventions and Recommendations (121st session of the Executive Board)[1]

76. The author of the communication, a journalist and writer of Chilean nationality, says that he was arrested in September 1973 because he was carrying a firearm; and that he was then brought before a court martial, which sentenced him to six years' imprisonment. He explains that, as Chief Prison Officer and as Head of the Press, Radio and Public Relations Service of the Gendarmerie, he was authorized to be in possession of a firearm. The sentence of six years' imprisonment was reportedly reduced to three years, of which the author is said to have served 26 months. Subsequently, the remainder of the sentence was commuted to exile. Since then, he is said to have been living in Hamburg (Federal Republic of Germany) with his family as a political exile.

77. Mr Carlos Mario Lira Moscoso says that he requested authorization to return to Chile on several occasions, but that none of these requests produced any result. There has been no reply to the latest request, submitted to the Chilean Consulate in Hamburg on 21 February 1983.

78. At the [Committee's spring 1984 session], Mr Lira Moscoso's case was referred to the Committee by [another communication]. The Committee declared the request inadmissible on the grounds it did not come within Unesco's field of competence, since Mr Moscoso's occupation as a writer had been challenged; but the author still had the possibility of submitting a fresh communication.[2] Under the present communication, Mr Lira Moscoso considers that he adds certain new facts, in particular re-

[1] See document 121 EX/46 PRIV., paras. 76-80; see also document 121 EX/CR/HR/3.
[2] See document 119 EX/35 PRIV., para. 70 (*supra*, p. 406), communication No. 590/83 concerning *Chile*, case of *Carlos Lira Moscoso*.

garding his status as a writer. He explains that the books that he has writen, both in German and in Spanish, describe the reality of the situation in which he had been living since 11 September 1973, but that they are not hostile to the present Chilean Government. As an author, he cannot be held responsible for the way in which they are interpreted.

79. The representative of the Chilean Government stated that Mr Lira Moscoso had been sentenced for offences which he had committed under the ordinary law and not for activities he had engaged in as a journalist or writer. He added that, if the person concerned wished to know the reasons why he had not been authorized to return to Chile, he should seek a remedy at law (application for *amparo*) upon completion of which those reasons would be communicated to him.

80. At the end of its discussions, the Committee *decided* to declare the communication inadmissible as not falling within Unesco's fields of competence.

No. 655/84

Concerning *Yugoslavia*
Case of *Jozo Gospodin Zovko* et al.*

Communication of 24 July 1984 submitted by
John Matthews

Autumn 1986 session of the Committee on Conventions and Recommendations (125th session of the Executive Board)[1]

138. It is alleged that, in June 1981, six children from the village of Medjugorje, Ivanka Ivanković, Mirjana Dragićević, Vicka Ivanković, Ivan Dragićević, Jakov Colo and Marija Pavlović, had seen what they claimed to be a vision of the Madonna and that a large number of people had, at the site of the apparitions, watched the children go into a trance. It is alleged also that these events were considered, according to government-controlled press, as a political plot with religious cover. The six children were summoned twice to undergo psychiatric examinations, but they were found sane, sound and healthy. The children were also allegedly subjected to police harassment. It is claimed that, on 16 August 1981, the police gave orders to Father Jozo Zovko that no more religious assemblies could take place outside the church and that shortly afterwards Father Zovko and two nuns were taken into custody. Files and documents from the presbytery are alleged to have been confiscated. According to Mr Matthews, the nuns were later released, but Father Zovko is said to have been charged and sentenced in October 1981 to two and a half years' imprisonment for sedition. The author of the communication indicates further that, for having published articles on the apparitions from October 1981 to April 1982, two other priests, Father Tomislav Ferdo Vlasich and Father Jozo Krizich were also, it is alleged, arrested and sentenced respectively to eight and two and a half years' imprisonment. It is also claimed that, in December 1983, the Yugoslav authorities detained and interrogated some of the six children about some diaries believed to have been kept by them, and that, after serving his sentence, Father Zovko was exiled.

* Case of *Jozo Gospodin Zovko, Tomislav Ferdo Vlasich, Jozo Krizich, Jakov Colo, Ivan Dragićević, Marija Pavlović, Mirjana Dragićević, Ivanka Ivanoković, Vicka Ivanoković.*

[1] See document 125 EX/3 PRIV., paras. 138-[142a]; see also document 125 EX/CR/HR/3.

No. 655/84 **Yugoslavia**

139. The representative of the government concerned stated first of all that the communication was inadmissible, having regard to the provisions of [paragraph] 14 (*a*) of 104 EX/Decision 3.3. On the one hand it was ill-founded, containing no relevant evidence and, on the other, it was offensive to the government, particularly in referring to the press as being State-controlled (which was not the case in Yugoslavia) and in going so far as to call for greater tolerance from the government towards its citizens and especially those living in Medjugorje, when all the allegations made were absolutely false. As regards the apparition of the Madonna at Medjugorje, the government had never refused the right to such a belief. The judicial authorities of the region had examined the events. Of the 2,506 village people, the only persons who had been called to order were a taxi driver who had drawn his gun to fire at a policeman on point duty and five young people who had disturbed public order and were singing Fascist songs. As for the children, some of them had simply been questioned. In no case, under Yugoslav law, could they have been sentenced by a court. As regards the religious gatherings, no ban had been imposed on them by State organs. In fact, up to the present, Medjugorje had become a place of pilgrimage to some extent for people from other regions of the country and also from abroad. The village had even experienced considerable economic growth. The allegation that human rights in Unesco's fields of competence had been violated on the occasion of the events in Medjugorje, added the representative of the government concerned, was tendentious. As for the facts relating to the three priests, Jozo Gospodin Zovko, Tomislav Ferdo Vlasich and Jozo Krizich, they were as follows:

> Father Zovko had received a sentence of three and a half years, reduced to 18 months by the Federal Tribunal, for violating Article 133 of the Penal Code: he had exploited religious feelings for political ends by attacking the State and the political system of the country, especially by preaching that believers were afraid to go to church, although the church was full, that the State had prevented baptisms, confessions and marriages from being celebrated in the church because of the threat that the church-goers would lose their jobs, and that blood must be shed for the Catholic Church; furthermore, the Yugoslav authorities had not replaced the priest, that procedure being the exclusive responsibility of the religious hierarchy; after serving his sentence, Father Zovko had long since resumed his functions as priest.
>
> The brothers Vlasich and Krizich had been sentenced, also in breach of Article 133 of the Penal Code in proceedings having no connection with the events at Medjugorje, to eight and five years' imprisonment respectively and those sentences had been reduced to five and a half years and four and a half years by the Federal Tribunal; since 1977 they had maintained links with émigré terrorist organizations which had stirred up activities hostile to Yugoslavia for the purpose of overthrowing the established order; these were, then,

reprehensible activities having no relationship with the apparition of the Madonna; Father Vlasich had in fact already been sentenced once, in 1952, to eight years' imprisonment; after serving their sentences, the two priests had also returned to their duties.

140. Of the members of the Committee who took part in the debate, some were of the opinion that the communication did not fall into Unesco's competence and that the author had tried in vain to bring everything he could to bear on the case by referring to untrue situations; others believed that the allegations made lacked precision and reliability, Mr Matthews not even knowing the addresses of the people he put forward as victims.

141. One member of the Committee, recalling the preparatory work done in drawing up 104 EX/Decision 3.3, said that the right to freedom of religion had not been accepted by the working group concerned at that time as a right which could be included among the human rights in Unesco's fields of competence. In addition, when that decision came into force, contacts had been made between the United Nations Human Rights Committee and Unesco to find out which parts of the reports established by the States Parties to the International [Covenant] on Civil and Political Rights should be communicated to the Organization for information. On that occasion, reference had been made to religious instruction alone and not to the question of religion as such. That member of the Committee concluded that, in his view, the communication should be declared inadmissible.

142. Several members of the Committee supported that point of view.

[142a.] At the close of the discussion, the Committee *decided*:

(i) to thank the government concerned for sending a representative;

(ii) to declare the communication inadmissible on the grounds that it did not fall within Unesco's fields of competence under [paragraph] 14 (*a*) (iii) of 104 EX/Decision 3.3.

No. 656/84

Concerning *United States of America*
Case of *Alleged medical tyranny as practised in the United States of America**

Communication of 12 June 1984 submitted by
Robert W. Bradford°

Autumn 1984 session of the Committee on Conventions and Recommendations (120th session of the Executive Board)[1]

70. A 70-page document entitled "A complaint against medical tyranny as practised in the United States of America: American Medical Genocide" indicates that the complaints which are the subject of the communication are directed against the United States Food and Drug Administration, the American Medical Association, the American Cancer Society, the United States National Cancer Institute and "all divisions, State and local affiliates and similar or parallel organizations, public or private, of the above".

71. The facts alleged in this complaint are supported by examples of persecution of doctors, pharmacists, researchers, clinic administrators and other practitioners of "alternative medicine" and of persons who have had recourse to such forms of treatment. The complaint also denounces the suppression of certain treatments useful in the case of cancer or cardiovascular diseases, and collusion between the United States health services and pharmaceutical laboratories. In conclusion the authors of the communication claim that the United States medical monopoly is leading to the spread of degenerative diseases and an increase in United States health costs.

72. The representative of the United States Government remarked that the voluminous file concerning the communication had reached him only two and a half weeks previously and that, given the number and variety of the allegations contained there-

* At the Committee's spring 1985 session, this communication was being referred to as *Alleged medical tyranny in the United States of America*.

° On behalf of the Committee for Freedom of Choice in Medicine.

[1] See document 120 EX/15 PRIV., paras. 70-74; see also document 120 EX/CR/HR/3 Add.2.

in, he was not in a position to provide the necessary answers. He added that, in any event, the communication seemed to him at first sight to be inadmissible, firstly because the accusations it contained were directed against private groups and not against authorities responsible to the United States Government and, secondly, because it raised questions that were extremely controversial both in the United States and in other countries, but nothing that could be regarded as a violation of human rights. The representative of the government concerned said, however, that he was prepared to participate in a more detailed examination of the communication at the next session, if the Committee deemed it necessary.

73. Most members of the Committee considered the communication inadmissible, since it did not fall within Unesco's fields of competence. One of them felt that in the interest of the authors of the communication, it would be advisable to inform them of this fact now, during the present session, so that they could seek a more suitable channel through which to settle the question. Other members of the Committee preferred examination of the communication to be deferred to the next session. Two members of the Committee noted that the Government concerned had not yet ratified the 1948 Convention on the Prevention and Punishment of the Crime of Genocide, or the two 1966 International [Covenants] on Human Rights.

74. After an exchange of views, the Committee *decided* to resume the examination of the admissibility of this communication at the [spring 1985] session.

Spring 1985 session of the Committee on Conventions and Recommendations (121st session of the Executive Board)[2]

81. A 70-page document entitled "A complaint against medical tyranny as practised in the United States of America: American Medical Genocide" indicates that the complaints which are the subject of the communication are directed against the United States Food and Drug Administration, the American Medical Association, the American Cancer Society, the United States National Cancer Institute and "all divisions, State and local affiliates and similar or parallel organizations, public or private, of the above".

82. The facts alleged in this complaint are supported by examples of persecution of doctors, pharmacists, researchers, clinic administrators and other practitioners of "alternative medicine" and of persons who have had recourse to such forms of treatment. The complaint also denounces the suppression of certain treatments useful in the case of cancer or cardiovascular diseases, and collusion between the United

[2] See document 121 EX/46 PRIV., paras. 81-89; see also document 121 EX/CR/HR/2.

States health services and pharmaceutical laboratories. In conclusion the authors of the communication claim that the United States medical monopoly is leading to the spread of degenerative diseases and an increase in United States health costs.

83. In accordance with the decision it had taken at its previous session,[3] the Committee resumed the examination of this communication at the current session.

84. Before doing so, however, the Committee considered whether it was competent to examine this communication, which concerned a State that was no longer a Member of the Organization, and whether that State could, if necessary, be represented before the Committee when the communication was being examined. Noting that the procedure laid down in 104 EX/Decision 3.3 was not confined to Member States, the Committee replied to these two questions in the affirmative.

85. The representative of the United States Government remarked that, as his country was no longer a Member of Unesco, it was legitimate for the Committee to have raised the question whether the communication should not be simply struck from its agenda. Without prejudice to that preliminary question, he felt that the communication was, in any event, inadmissible, firstly because it was directed essentially against private groups and, secondly, because it was clearly up to each government to define legal medical practices on the basis of the most advanced techniques; the federal, State and local authorities were, at their respective levels, responsible for ensuring compliance with the rules in force constituting the specific domestic legislation of the United States. In order for a new medical treatment to be authorized, it had to be proved, in accordance with strictly scientific standards, that it was harmless, effective and reliable. It was true that the authors of the communication had the right to disagree with the medical practices approved by the competent authorities, but nothing in the communication proved that that right had been denied them; on the contrary, the sole purpose of having a medical code was to ensure the general welfare, as was provided for under Article 29 (2) of the Universal Declaration of Human Rights. In the case in point, as the authors of the communication had not established that there had been any violation of human rights, and still less of human rights within Unesco's fields of competence, the Committee should, in the opinion of the representative of the government concerned, declare the communication inadmissible.

86. After explaining the reasons for his being personally very knowledgeable about the questions raised by the communication, one member of the Committee pointed out that each State was responsible for defining its own rules and standards in the medical field. He explained that, before authorization for marketing a product was

[3] See document 120 EX/15 PRIV., para. 74 (*supra*, p. 542).

granted, three types of research or studies were undertaken (toxicological research, molecular research and clinical tests). He added that some medicines might, in the course of time, prove to be carcinogenic, mutagenic or teratogenic and that, despite the precautions thus taken, accidents such as those caused by thalidomide, for instance, still occurred. He stressed how useful it was for the major laboratories to collaborate with government services in that field and how important it was to ensure that the necessary safeguards were not called into question by individuals who wished to practise a simpler type of medicine; furthermore, it was common knowledge in international medical circles that the United States Food and Drug Administration was one of the strictest institutes and that it had drawn up a medical ethics code of a high standard; in any event, the formulation of rules concerning public health was a matter for the domestic law of a State and moreover, in the case in question, the matter raised involved an area of activity that did not come within Unesco's spheres of competence.

87. In reply to questions put by members of the Committee, the representative of the government concerned stated that the Food and Drug Administration was indeed a government department; he had not, incidentally, disputed that fact in his preliminary statement, when he had merely emphasized that the communication was also directed against private groups for which he could not answer; he added that the Convention on the Prevention and Punishment of the Crime of Genocide and the International Covenants on Economic, Social and Cultural Rights and on Civil and Political Rights had been submitted to the Senate for ratification but that, as in all States with a federal structure like the one he represented, ratification was a slow and difficult process; the provisions of those international instruments were, however, fully respected by his country.

88. One member of the Committee was in favour of keeping the communication on the Committee's agenda; several other members of the Committee considered for their part that the problem dealt with did not fall within Unesco's fields of competence; some of them wondered whether the authors of the communication would not have been better advised to make representations to another organization of the United Nations system, such as WHO.

89. At the close of its discussions the Committee *decided* to declare the communication inadmissible as not falling within Unesco's fields of competence under the terms of 104 EX/Decision 3.3, paragraph 14 (*a*) (iii).

No. 669/85

Concerning *Paraguay*
Case of *"Radio Nanduti"*

Communication of 18 December 1984 submitted by
Carlos Rivas and Lincoln Almada*

Spring 1985 session of the Committee on Conventions and Recommendations (121st session of the Executive Board)[1]

119. The authors state that the Government of Paraguay gave orders on 25 November 1984 that "Radio Nanduti", founded in 1962, should be closed down permanently, and that its director and owner, Mr Humberto Rubín, should be placed under house arrest, on the grounds that he had instituted a programme entitled "Political Fridays" and invited leaders of the Social Democratic and Christian Democratic Parties of Paraguay to participate in it.

120. The representative of the Government of Paraguay confirmed the substance of the letter addressed to the Secretariat on 26 April 1985 by the Permanent Delegation, stating that the Committee should not consider this communication since "Radio Nanduti" was operating normally and Mr Rubín was entirely free and was still acting as director. While it was true that "Radio Nanduti" had had administrative and legal problems to face, they had subsequently been cleared up. Moreover, the communication had defects as regarded both form and substance, being based, in particular, on information derived from the press, and should consequently be declared inadmissible.

121. In reply to questions raised by members of the Committee, the representative of the Government of Paraguay explained that "Radio Nanduti" had been closed down for one month only, that the closure had been effected in conformity with the laws in force in Paraguay, precluding any need to go back over the grounds for the closure, and that it had since regained total political, commercial and cultural freedom. His statement that the communication derived its information from the press was based

---

* On behalf of "PROMA" (Promusica y arte).

[1] See document 121 EX/46 PRIV., paras. 119-123; see also document 121 EX/CR/HR/3.

on the fact that, in their letter of 18 December 1984, the authors themselves had stated that they had learnt of the closure of "Radio Nanduti" from the issue of "El País" dated 16 November 1984; he accordingly considered the communication to be inadmissible under the terms of paragraph 14 (*a*) (vii) of 104 EX/Decision 3.3.

122. Two members of the Committee pointed out that the communication came fully within Unesco's areas of competence and that it was only partly, and not entirely, based on information obtained from the press; moreover, the reasons for which the radio station had been closed down were still not clear to them and they therefore wished the communication to be kept on the Committee's agenda; lastly, they deeply regretted that such events had taken place and would like to have guarantees that they would not occur again. Other members of the Committee considered that the matter had been settled, since the sanctions denounced by the communication had all been raised. They pointed out that, in any event, the authors of the communication could submit another communication if new facts should occur that were likely to be admissible under the terms of the aforementioned decision. All members of the Committee, however, stressed their strong commitment to respect for the freedom of the press and broadcasting, and their concern over any violation of such freedom.

123. The Committee consequently *decided* to declare this communication settled under the terms of paragraph 14 (*a*) (x) of 104 EX/Decision 3.3.

No. 671/85

Concerning *Czechoslovakia*
Case of *Jan Hájek*

Communication of 11 December 1984 submitted by
Jiří Hájek

Spring 1985 session of the Committee on Conventions and Recommendations (121st session of the Executive Board)[1]

137. The author of the communication, a retired professor and father of the alleged victim who is a Czechoslovak student, alleged that discriminatory practices have been applied against Jan Hájek for the only reason of being the son of the author whose political opinion is said to have led to his exclusion from the ruling party ranks after 1968. The author states that he was one of the signatories to the human rights manifesto "Charter 77".

138. The representative of the government concerned informed the Committee that the communication, which was received just about a month earlier by his country's Permanent Delegation to Unesco, had been transmitted to the competent authorities in Prague for information. He added that the allegations contained in the communication were still being examined by his government and therefore requested that the consideration of the admissibility of the communication should be postponed to the autumn 1985 session of the Committee in order to give the competent authorities of his country reasonable time to collect and provide relevant information relating to the alleged violations of human rights.

139. Several members of the Committee, while expressing their thanks to the government concerned for the goodwill manifested by sending a representative to cooperate with the Committee, indicated that the alleged violation of human rights related to a case that, on its face, fell squarely within Unesco competence. They agreed that, as requested by the representative of the government concerned, the examination of the admissibility of the communication should be deferred to the Committee's next session. These members however expressed their preoccupation over the

---

[1] See document 121 EX/46 PRIV., paras. 137-141; see also document 121 EX/CR/HR/3 Add.

situation of the alleged victim and expressed the hope that, without prejudice to the admissibility or otherwise of the communication, the Committee would receive at its next session good news to the effect that the problems of the alleged victim have found a satisfactory solution on the basis of humanitarian considerations which would permit him to pursue his academic career, without further loss of time, in an appropriate institution in or outside his country.

140. While supporting the request for the postponement of the examination of the communication, some other members counselled against any rush in making judgement about the allegations contained in the communication.

141. At the end of its discussion, the Committee:

(i) *Decided*, as requested, to postpone to its autumn 1985 session the examination of the admissibility of the communication;

(ii) *Requested*, nevertheless, the representative of the government concerned to inform the competent authorities of his country of the humanitarian concerns expressed by some of the members of the Committee.

Autumn 1985 session of the Committee on Conventions and Recommendations (122nd session of the Executive Board)[2]

97. The author of this communication, a retired professor and father of the student Jan Hájek, alleges that the latter has been the victim of discriminatory practices for the sole reason that he is the son of a man whose political opinions led to his exclusion from the ruling party in 1968 and who is also one of the signatories to the human rights manifesto known as "Charter 77".

98. Jan Hájek is said to have been accepted for admission to the Building Faculty of the Technical Institute in Prague on 5 Septemberr 1983, at the conclusion of his secondary education. This admission is said to have been cancelled two weeks later by the Minister of Education. It is further claimed that the student performed satisfactorily in the entrance examination for the academic year 1984-1985, but that his application was rejected on the grounds that his marks in the mathematics test were inadequate. His application for admission to the Faculty of Architecture is also said to have been rejected in March 1985, on the grounds of his not having proved "a necessary measure of talent pre-conditions". After once again taking the competitive

---

[2] See document 122 EX/21 PRIV., paras. 97-102; see also documents 122 EX/CR/HR/2 and Add.

examination for admission to the Building Faculty, in June 1985, he is said to have been rejected once again, this time on the grounds that his results in the written test in physics were unsatisfactory.

99. The representative of the government concerned explained that because of the limited number of places and the particularly large number of candidates seeking admission to the Building Faculty and the Faculty of Architecture, the selection process was naturally very rigorous. He pointed out that the rules of the competitive examinations were set out in regularly published and universally accessible legislative texts. Refuting the allegations made, he maintained that Jan Hájek had been the victim of no discrimination whatsoever; proof of that, he said, lay in the fact that the student had been able to complete his secondary studies without hindrance, although his father had been active in the opposition since 1968 and a leader of the "Charter 77" Group. He added that if the student had been denied admission to the two faculties of his choice, that was simply because there were other, more deserving students; it was ridiculous to try to make people believe that there had been manipulation by the police or other authorities, since the selection boards were composed of highly qualified persons. In the view of the representative of the Czechoslovak Government, the case involved no violation of human rights, and the communication should consequently be declared inadmissible.

100. Some members of the Committee were of the opinion that the case involved the right to education, and that an impartial observer would find it difficult to understand how such a brilliant student as Jan Hájek, who had already been admitted to the Building Faculty, could have been excluded therefrom shortly afterwards without any plausible explanation. They also asked why the competent authorities had not allowed the student to accept the invitations he had received to continue his studies in Norway or Austria. Some other members of the Committee, pointing out that it was difficult to pronounce on the claims that had been made, expressed the opinion that the problem should be approached in a strictly pragmatic and humanitarian fashion, through efforts to obtain authorization for Jan Hájek to travel to Oslo or Vienna, and that the case of the son should not be confused with that of the father. Other members of the Committee noted that that body was not competent to pronounce on decisions made by selection boards, and that it was invidious to attempt to compare different education systems, especially in view of the fact that certain European States were still not parties to the Convention on the Recognition of Studies, Diplomas and Degrees in Higher Education in the Europe Region, adopted under the aegis of Unesco in 1979. It was their view that if the student was authorized to leave his country, he would find little use for his foreign diploma or degree when he returned; furthermore, to accord more favourable treatment to one student than to others would be to contravene national regulations concerning study abroad. For

these members, there were no legal grounds for declaring the communication admissible.

101. In reply to questions, the representative of the government concerned pointed out that although Jan Hájek had been refused admission to the Building Faculty and the Faculty of Architecture because he had failed the "talent examinations", other options remained open to him: he could, for example, apply to other types of faculty better suited to his abilities, or attempt to follow a work-study programme. The representative went on to point out that there would be no point in obtaining a foreign diploma or degree which would not be valid in Czechoslovakia. He informed the Committee that the disciplines which could be studied abroad were determined by the Ministry of Education and formed the subject of a decree. As regards the cancellation of the initial admission of Jan Hájek to the Building Faculty, he explained that it had been due to the fact that the first decision had been taken too hastily; comparison with the findings of other selection boards had shown that other candidates than he were better qualified.

102. At the end of the discussion, bearing in mind the humanitarian aspect of the case, and after reservations had been expressed by a number of members of the Committee on (ii) below, especially on non-interference in the internal affairs of the State concerned, the Committee *decided*:

(i) to take note of the information provided by the representative of the government concerned;

(ii) to reiterate its appeal, on humanitarian grounds, to the Government of Czechoslovakia, for a solution to the case in question;

(iii) to resume consideration of the communication at its next session.

Spring 1986 session of the Committee on Conventions and Recommendations (124th session of the Executive Board)[3]

94. Mr Jiří Hájek alleges that his son Jan Hájek, a student, has been the victim of discriminatory practices for the sole reason that he is the son of a man who was excluded from the ruling party in 1968 because of his political views and who is also one of the signatories of the human rights manifesto known as "Charter 77". According to the communication, the alleged victim, although he did outstanding well

[3] See document 124 EX/3 PRIV., paras. 94-100; see also documents 124 EX/CR/HR/2 and Add.

at the end of his secondary education, was in 1983 refused admission to both the Building Faculty and the Faculty of Architecture. His applications for enrolment in the academic years 1984-1985 and 1985-1986 are also said to have been rejected. His request for a re-appraisal of his entrance examination scripts that were considered to have been unsatisfactory is said to have been turned down, and his request to be allowed to continue his studies abroad, in particular in Norway, is said not to have met with a favourable response.

95. In his letter dated 14 February 1986 [...],[4] the author of the communication states that Jan Hájek would be willing to renounce his nationality in order to obtain authorization to leave the country, since there would appear to be no other way out.

96. After the Chairperson's account of the alleged facts, the representative of the government concerned said that the complaint of Mr Jiří Hájek had been discussed at length at the Commission's [autumn 1985 session]. He then informed the Committee that, for the current academic year (1986-1987), Jan Hájek had not taken the proper steps to seek admission to an institution of higher education and that, for this reason and in accordance with the regulations in force, he could not expect to be granted an authorization for study abroad. He added that the student, on the other hand, had on 9 April 1986 submitted an application for emigration which had been officially acknowledged on 30 April. The relevant Czechoslovak authorities were at present considering the application since the applicant had to complete a number of administrative formalities regarding the renunciation of his nationality and the problem of moving house. The representative of the government concerned concluded that, since the present issue was one of emigration, the subject of the communication no longer fell within the competence of Unesco and should therefore be declared inadmissible. In reply to requests for clarification, the representative of the government concerned pointed out that the Ministry of Education, taking account of the specialist fields considered useful to the country, sent the best students abroad, selecting them mainly from those who were in the second year of their higher education. He said that for those who wanted to study abroad at their own expense, the only possibility was to leave the country for good, and that was precisely what was under consideration in the case of Jan Hájek. He said that invitations from abroad to Czechoslovak students could only be for short courses as exit permits for students were restricted especially as foreign diplomas were not automatically recognized in Czechoslovakia.

97. Some members of the Committee expressed regret that it was not possible for Jan Hájek to study abroad unless he renounced his nationality. They were disturbed that a problem of alleged discrimination in access to higher education was turning

[4] See document 124 EX/CR/HR/2 Add.

into a problem of emigration. In their view, it should not be considered in that light but as a problem closely related to the fact that it was impossible for the person concerned to pursue his university studies in his own country. In this connection, they referred to a number of relevant instruments such as the Convention against Discrimination in Education and the two International [Covenants] on Human Rights and the Helsinki Final Act which proclaimed freedom of movement.

98. Some other members stated that the representative of the country concerned had been very clear and very frank in explaining his country's situation, that Czechoslovakia had its own particular system of education which had to be accepted as such and that it should not be judged in comparison with other countries. They considered that as Jan Hájek had decided not to take entrance examinations for admission to a national institution of higher education and had chosen the procedure of emigration, it would be desirable for the Committee to await the outcome of the steps he had taken and defer examination of the communication until the next session.

99. While associating themselves with those views, some members of the Committee expressed their concern over the communication, which was for them a matter of conscience. One of them hoped that the dialogue with the foreign countries that had agreed to accept Jan Hájek could be pursued and that his application for emigration would be successful.

100. After an exchange of views, the Committee *decided*:

(i) to thank the representative of the government concerned for his contribution to the dialogue with the Committee and to ask him to provide at the next session the necessary information concerning the application for emigration submitted by Jan Hájek;

(ii) to reiterate its humanitarian appeal to the government concerned in the hope that the authorization to leave Czechoslovakia that might be granted the student would not rule out the possibility of his return;

(iii) to resume consideration of the communication at its autumn 1986 session.

Czechoslovakia **No. 671/85**

Autumn 1986 session of the Committee on Conventions and Recommendations (125th session of the Executive Board)[5]

72. Mr Jiři Hájek alleges that his son Jan Hájek, a student, has been the victim of discriminatory practices for the sole reason that he is the son of a man who was excluded from the ruling party in 1968 because of his political views and who is also one of the signatories of the human rights manifesto known as "Charter 77". According to the communication, the alleged victim, although he did outstandingly well at the end of his secondary education, was in 1983 refused admission to both the Building Faculty and the Faculty of Architecture. His applications for enrolment in the academic years 1984-1985 and 1985-1986 are also said to have been rejected. His request for a re-appraisal of his entrance examination scripts that were considered to have been unsatisfactory is said to have been turned down, and his request to be allowed to continue his studies abroad, in particular in Norway, is said not to have met with a favourable response.

73. In his letter dated 14 February 1986 [...], the author of the communication states that Jan Hájek would be willing to renounce his nationality in order to obtain authorization to leave the country, since there would appear to be no other way out.

74. The representative of the Director-General read out a letter [...] dated 28 August 1986 (received by the Secretariat on 1 September 1986) in which the Permanent Delegate of Czechoslovakia to Unesco informed the Committee that the competent authorities in his country had granted Jan Hájek's request to be released from the ties of Czechoslovak nationality, that the person concerned had collected his travel document on 10 August 1986 and that he had already left the country.

75. While noting that the case had developed in such a way that Jan Hájek had finally got access to academic studies, some members of the Committee said that the process leading up to this result had been a painful one. Jan Hájek had indeed been authorized to leave the country but he had had to give up his nationality, it being unacceptable that relinquishment of nationality should in any case, be a prerequisite for access to studies. The author of the communication had simply wanted his son to be able to pursue his studies in his own country. As a last resort and as it were through discouragement, he had envisaged the possibility of the son's doing so abroad by means of a temporary exit visa that would enable him to return to his family in Czechoslovakia. Several members of the Committee therefore expressed the hope that Jan Hájek would be able to return to his home country.

---

[5] See document 125 EX/3 PRIV., paras. 72-76; see also document 125 EX/CR/HR/2.

No. 671/85 **Czechoslovakia**

76. After an exchange of views, the Committee *decided*:

(i) to take note of the information provided by the government concerned;

(ii) to consider the communication as being settled and to strike it from its list.

No. 674/85

Concerning *Paraguay*
Case of *Aldo Zuccolillo and* ABC Color

Communication of 1 March 1985 submitted by
The International Human Rights Law Group

Spring 1986 session of the Committee on Conventions and Recommendations (124th session of the Executive Board)[1]

80. According to the authors of the communication, on 22 March 1984, the Paraguayan Ministry of the Interior ordered the suspension for an indefinite term of the printing and distribution of the daily newspaper *ABC Color*, accused of systematic violation of constitutional norms and the creation of social unrest. This paper, which had a large circulation, also published three separate weekly supplements: a grade school supplement, a cultural supplement and an agricultural supplement designed to provide information for peasants. Mr Aldo Zuccolillo, the paper's editor-in-chief, is alleged to have been subjected to harassment and threats in various forms. The authors of the communication also allege that the reason for the closing of *ABC Color* was that the newspaper had reported on the return to Paraguay in December 1983 of some 30 members of the exiled opposition party known as MOPOCO (Movimiento Popular Colorado) and had published some paid MOPOCO advertisements and open letters.

81. After a statement of the alleged facts by the Chairperson and in accordance with the written request of the authors, the representative of the Director-General explained to the Committee the reasons why it had not been possible to submit the communication, which bore the date 29 March 1985, to the Committee at its [autumn 1985 session]. She then read out a letter [...] which the Permanent Delegate of Paraguay to Unesco had handed to her on the morning of 5 May 1986. In that letter the Permanent Delegation rejected the allegations of violations of human rights of which its country was accused. It maintained that the administrative action against *ABC Color* had been taken in conformity with the legislation in force and that the

[1] See document 124 EX/3 PRIV., paras. 80-84; see also document 124 EX/CR/HR/3.

owner of the newspaper had had the opportunity to make use of all available means of redress.

82. The representative of the government concerned took the floor to state that *ABC Color* had not been closed, but that its publication had simply been suspended by a decision of the Ministry of the Interior, a decision that had been confirmed by the competent court of law. He added that the newspaper had criticized the constitutional norms, thereby endangering the peace which the government constantly endeavoured to maintain so as to preserve economic and social stability and enable true democracy and human rights to prevail, in the interests of all citizens. He referred in particular to the provisions of the Paraguayan Constitution relating to the freedom of the press and the prohibition of any incitement to hatred, violence, disobedience, or public unrest jeopardizing peace and security, and of the expression of seditious opinions. Replying to a request for clarification on the publication of the three *ABC Color* supplements, the representative of the government concerned stated that these were supplements annexed to the newspaper and not independent publications. In that connection, some members of the Committee expressed regret that the suspension also affected the supplements.

83. Several members of the Committee said that they would like to be given further information about the material facts that had led to the suspension of the newspaper, in particular the nature of the offending articles and the activities of the newspaper which the Paraguayan authorities had deemed harmful to the established order. They also said they would like to have further information on the procedure which had been followed before the judicial authorities and raised the question of whether it would be possible for the newspaper to appeal again to the Supreme Court for a review of the decision to suspend its publication. One member of the Committee asked whether it would be possible to obtain copies of the judicial decisions and a copy of the resolution of the Inter-American Commission on Human Rights recommending to the Government of Paraguay to cancel its decision ordering the closing of *ABC Color*.

84. After an exchange of views, the Committee *decided*:

(i) to thank the representative of the government concerned for his contribution to the dialogue and to ask him to provide the Committee at its next session with information about the nature of the offences for which *ABC Color*, its editor-in-chief and its journalists had been penalized, the legal procedure that had been followed in the case, and the length of time for which the publication of the newspaper had been suspended;

(ii) to request the Secretariat to collect all possible information from the Inter-American Commission on Human Rights, to which the case had also been submitted;

(iii) to resume examination of this communication at its autumn 1986 session.

Autumn 1986 session of the Committee on Conventions and Recommendations (125th session of the Executive Board)[2]

56. According to the authors of the communication, on 22 March 1984, the Paraguayan Ministry of the Interior ordered the suspension for an indefinite term of the printing and distribution of the daily newspaper *ABC Color*, accused of systematic violation of constitutional norms and the creation of social unrest. This paper, which had a large circulation, also published three separate weekly supplements: a supplement for primary schools, a cultural supplement and an agricultural supplement to provide information for peasants. Mr Aldo Zuccolillo, the paper's editor-in-chief, is alleged to have been subjected to harassment and threats in various forms. The authors of the communication also allege that the reason for the closing of *ABC Color* was that the newspaper had reported on the return to Paraguay in December 1983 of some 30 members of the exiled opposition party known as MOPOCO (Movimiento Popular Colorado) and had published some paid MOPOCO advertisements and open letters.

57. In introducing the communication for discussion at the Committee's present session, the Chairperson recalled that the responsibility of the Committee was to find out if by suspending the printing and distribution of the newspaper *ABC Color* and by the alleged arrest and harassment of its editor-in-chief, Mr Aldo Zuccolillo, the authorities of the Member State concerned had failed in their internationally recognized obligation to respect freedom of opinion and expression. She pointed out that the fact that the same allegations that are contained in the communication concerned had been brought before the Inter-American Commission on Human Rights did not constitute a bar to the competence of the Committee. She added that in any event the complaint did not appear to be currently pending before that Commission.

58. Taking the floor, the representative of the government concerned stated that the Committee should be assured that his government respected freedom of opinion and expression adding that the respect of those rights was evidenced by the fact that there were independent newspapers other than *ABC Color* that were functioning in

[2] See document 125 EX/3 PRIV., paras. 56-63; see also documents 125 EX/CR/HR/2 and Add. and Add.3.

his country and that opposition views were communicated in the columns of those papers as well as in parliament. He stated in this connection that the Minister of the Interior had, by Resolution No. 227 dated 22 March 1984, suspended the printing and distribution of *ABC Color* because, contrary to Article 71 of the National Constitution, the newspaper had been preaching hatred among the people of his country. He pointed out that this suspension had been effected by virtue of Article 50 of the National Constitution which provided that it was the fundamental duty of the State to protect the safety, honour and reputation of persons. The representative of the government concerned added that as for the case of the editor-in-chief of the newspaper in question, Mr Aldo Zuccolillo, it had been settled to the extent that he was now no longer under any form of detention. He declared that the case of *ABC Color* had been brought before the Supreme Court of his country and that the Court had held that the suspension order of the Minister of the Interior was valid in law. That showed that the competent authorities of his country had committed no infringement of the laws of that country.

59. One member of the Committee stated in this connection that the obligation of the government concerned was to be seen against international standards and that the fact that the suspension order had been recognized as legal under national law did not necessarily imply that the government concerned had respected fully its international obligation to respect freedom of opinion and expression. She declared that if *ABC Color* had committed some specific offences by the contents of its publication, she would have thought that those responsible would be given a normal trial for the specific offences instead of the newspaper being suspended purely and simply for a peiod of which now exceeded two years. Supported by some other members of the Committee, she suggested that the Committee should initiate a mission consisting of one or more of its members to visit the Member State concerned in order to have a diogue with the competent authorities concerned on the case of the suspended newspaper. A number of members of the Committee expressed the wish to have informaion regarding the particulars of the allegations on the basis of which *ABC Color* had been suspended. They also wanted to know if a decision had been taken by the government concerned to lift in the near future the suspension order and if so what conditions, if any, were to be attached to such an abrogation of the suspension order.

60. On the question of the procedure used against *ABC Color*, the representative of the government concerned stated that an administrative rather than a judicial one had been used because the latter was considered to be rather too cumbersome. He also informed the Committee that a mission of the United Nations [Commission on Human Rights] had recently visited his country in order to examine the human rights situation obtaining there and that it might be useful for the Committee to obtain a copy of that mission's report when it was ready. He also stated that if *ABC Color* and those responsible for it made it clear to his government that they were prepared

to resume publication in a way that would respect the laws of the country, then the government concerned was very likely to give serious consideration to lifting the suspension order against the newspaper.

61. One member of the Committee stated that information should be provided on whether or not *ABC Color* currently had open to it internal remedies against its suspension. She added that it would also be useful to know why the government concerned had not implemented Resolution No. 6/84 by which the Inter-American Commission on Human Rights had recommended to the government to cancel the suspension order against *ABC Color*. The representative of the government replied in that connection that even though the Commission was a respectable body, the resolution in question was not binding on his government.

62. In any case, he promised to convey to his government the concerns expressed by members of the Committee regarding the current situation of *ABC Color*.

63. At the end of the discussion, the Committee *decided*:

(i) to thank the government concerned for sending a representative;

(ii) to make an urgent appeal to the government concerned for the lifting of the suspension order issued against the printing and distribution of *ABC Color*;

(iii) to request the representative of the government concerned to provide the Committee at its next session with information about the gravity and particulars of the offences for which *ABC Color*, its editor-in-chief and its journalists had been penalized, the legal procedure that had been followed in the case, and the length of time for which the publication of the newspaper has been suspended;

(iv) to resume examination of this communication at its spring 1987 session.

Spring 1987 session of the Committee on Conventions and Recommendations (126th session of the Executive Board)[3]

71. According to the authors of the communication, on 22 March 1984, the Paraguayan Ministry of the Interior ordered the suspension for an indefinite term of the printing and distribution of the daily newspaper *ABC Color*, accused of systematic

[3] See document 126 EX/3 PRIV., paras. 71-77; see also document 126 EX/CR/HR/2.

No. 674/85 **Paraguay**

violation of constitutional norms and the creation of social unrest. This paper, which had a large circulation, also published three separate weekly supplements: a supplement for primary schools, a cultural supplement and an agricultural supplement to provide information for peasants. Mr Aldo Zuccolillo, the paper's editor-in-chief, is alleged to have been subjected to harassment and threats in various forms. The authors of the communication also allege that the reason for the closing of *ABC Color* was that the newspaper had reported on the return to Paraguay in December 1983 of some 30 members of the exiled opposition party known as MOPOCO (Movimiento Popular Colorado) and had published some paid MOPOCO advertisements and open letters.

72. The Chairperson recalled that at its [autumn 1986] session, the Committee had made an urgent appeal to the government concerned to lift the suspension order issued against the printing and distribution of *ABC Color* and had also requested that government to provide information about the gravity and particulars of the offences for which *ABC Color*, its editor-in-chief and its journalists had been penalized, the legal procedure that had been followed in the case and the length of time for which publication of the newspaper had been suspended.[4]

73. Taking the floor, the representative of the government concerned stated that detailed explanations had been given by the deputy Permanent Delegate, chargé d'affaires, at the Committee's autumn 1986 session. So far, the only information he had received from his country's authorities had been a very brief statement to the effect that the case was no longer within the jurisdiction of the Ministry of the Interior since it had been brought before the courts, Mr Aldo Zuccolillo being entirely free to defend his rights.

74. The members of the Committee who took the floor were unanimous in regretting that the situation regarding this communication was unchanged for want of precise information, with supporting evidence from the government concerned. Noting that reference had previously been made to an administrative procedure for the suspension of the newspaper and that there was now reference to a judicial procedure, they wondered whether there had been a definite sentence confirming the decision of the Ministry of the Interior and whether an appeal had been filed. They wished to have a copy of the sentences passed. Referring to the letter dated 28 July 1986 from the authors of the communication [...],[5] one of the members noted that not only had *ABC Color* been censored but the main independent radio station, "Radio Nanduti", had been censored, too, since it had been subjected to jamming and interference. It had subsequently been closed down. The same member of the Committee requested the

[4] See document 125 EX/3 PRIV., para. 63 (ii) and (iii) (*supra*, p. 559).
[5] See document 125 EX/CR/HR/2 Add.

representative of the government concerned to convey to his country's authorities the Committee's concerns about freedom of the press in Paraguay and the lack of relevant information that would enable the Committee to fulfil its task.

75. The representative of the government concerned informed the Committee that he had no objection to conveying the Committee's concerns and questions to the authorities. He wished to point out, however, that, as in any country, there was a law in Paraguay, Law No. 209/70, concerning the use of freedom of the press and freedom of information, which laid down rules about such freedom in order to ensure an atmosphere of peace, coexistence and tolerance. He added that, furthermore, in response to the wishes expressed by the international community, his government had just suspended the state of emergency and that the situation in his country was returning to normal.

76. With reference to the report of a mission by the United Nations [Commission on Human Rights], to which the representative of the government concerned had referred at the Committee's [autumn 1986] session, the representative of the Director-General stated that, according to information received by the Secretariat, it was a document prepared by a special rapporteur of the Sub-Commission on Prevention of Discrimination and Protection of Minorities. It was to have been submitted to that body at its 39th session (August/September 1986) but the Sub-Commission had been unable to meet, following a decision taken by the General Assembly, and should be meeting at about the same time in 1987.

77. After an exchange of views, the Committee *decided*:

(i) to thank the representative of the government concerned for his presence during the examination of this communication;

(ii) to express its regret that the government concerned had not provided it with further relevant information, written or oral, to enable it to continue its work;

(iii) to renew its appeal to the government concerned to rescind the suspension order against the printing and distribution of *ABC Color*;

(iv) to request the representative of the government concerned:

(*a*) to convey to the authorities of his country:

the Committee's concerns about freedom of the press in Paraguay;

the questions asked by the members of the Committee concerning the exact facts of the case and the charges brought against *ABC Color*, its editor-in-chief and its journalists, the duration of the suspension of the newspaper, the sentences imposed by the courts to which the case had been referred, the available means of redress which had been or could be used, and Law No. 209/70 on the use of freedom of the press and freedom of information;

(*b*) also to inform these authorities that, failing receipt of the relevant information requested, the Committee would be compelled at its next session to declare the communication admissible;

(v) to resume examination of this communication at its autumn 1987 session.

Autumn 1987 session of the Committee on Conventions and Recommendations (127th session of the Executive Board)[6]

75. According to the authors of the communication, on 22 March 1984, the Paraguayan Ministry of the Interior ordered the suspension for an indefinite term of the printing and distribution of the daily newspaper *ABC Color*, accused of systematic violation of constitutional norms and the creation of unrest. This paper, which had a large circulation, also published three separate weekly supplements: a supplement for primary schools, a cultural supplement and an agricultural supplement to provide information for peasants. Mr Aldo Zuccolillo, the paper's editor-in-chief, is alleged to have been subjected to harassment and threats in various forms. The authors of the communication also allege that the reason for the closing of *ABC Color* was that the newspaper had reported on the return to Paraguay in December 1983 of some 30 members of the exiled opposition party known as MOPOCO (Movimiento Popular Colorado) and had published some paid MOPOCO advertisements and open letters.

76. By a letter dated 4 September 1987 [...],[7] the International Human Rights Law Group provided the following further information:

resolution 227 of 22 March 1984 which suspended the printing and distribution of *ABC Color* accused the newspaper of preaching hatred among Paraguayans, a pretext, according to the author of the communication, for stifling the peaceful expression of dissent;

no court had ever ruled on the constitutionality of the banning of *ABC Color*;

---

[6] See document 127 EX/3 PRIV., paras. 75-83; see also documents 127 EX/CR/HR/2 and Add.3.

[7] See document 127 EX/CR/HR/2 Add.3.

the Supreme Court, to which the matter had been referred by the publisher of the newspaper, had twice refused to rule on the constitutionality of the ban;

the basic issue was not the constitutionality of resolution 227 but the violation of internationally recognized human rights, including the right to freedom of opinion and expression, the right to education and the right to freedom of information;

El Pueblo, another newspaper, is also said to have been indefinitely suspended on 28 August 1987, and "Radio Nanduti", the nation's leading independent radio station, temporarily forced off the air.

77. In conclusion, the letter asked that Mr Aldo Zuccolillo's safety, as well as his liberty and his right to publish *ABC Color*, be guaranteed.

78. The representative of the government concerned declared that the communication contained an allegation which was contrary to the facts. He asserted, quoting the opinion of an independent legal expert in support of his view, that the Supreme Court of Paraguay was competent to rule on the constitutionality of a governmental act or decision. In the case at issue, he said, the Court had on two occasions rejected the appeals lodged by the publisher of *ABC Color*, thereby demonstrating that resolution 227 was in accordance with the Constitution. Regarding the freedom of movement of those responsible for the newspaper, he said that it was total, Mr Aldo Zuccolillo for example, having been able to travel abroad, to take part in conferences, to make statements in Madrid against the government and to return to the country without any difficulty. Justifying the Paraguayan Government's decision to suspend *ABC Color*, he stressed that there was no question of the government's failing to fulfil its constitutional obligations, especially those of preserving peace in society from all forms of subversion and of ensuring the country's development. In his opinion, this suspension was not indefinite. The government hoped that Mr Zuccolillo would abide by the law and no longer wish to impose his own ideas on the Republic.

79. Several members of the Committee wondered what in fact were the terms of the Supreme Court's decision and whether there were other means of redress.

80. In that connection, the representative of the government concerned informed the Committee that the publisher of *ABC Color* could indeed refer the matter to the regular courts but that it had not done so.

81. Other members of the Committee considered that no precise answers had yet been given to the questions raised during the spring 1987 session and that the government concerned should be urged to supply further information, but that the author

of the communication shouid also be requested to provide a detailed account of the legal steps taken by those responsible for *ABC Color*.

82. To supplement the required information, the Secretariat was requested to obtain and to place in the file the document prepared by a special rapporteur of the Sub-Commission on Prevention of Discrimination and Protection of Minorities which dealt, *inter alia*, with the situation in Paraguay and which, according to the information supplied at the [spring 1987] session of the Committee by the representative of the Director-General, was to be submitted to that body at its 39th session, scheduled to be held in September 1987.

83. Following an exchange of views, the Committee *decided*:

(i) to thank the representative of the government concerned for his presence and co-operation;

(ii) to take note of his statements according to which:

(*a*) the Supreme Court's rejection of the appeal made by the publisher of *ABC Color* implies recognition by that body of the constitutionality and lawfulness of the decision to suspend the newspaper; and

(*b*) there are other legal means of redress that have not yet been used by *ABC Color*;

(iii) to transmit these statements to the author of the communication, requesting him to reciprocate by submitting a detailed account of the legal steps taken by those responsible for *ABC Color* to assert their rights;

(iv) to request the representative of the government concerned:

(*a*) to convey to the authorities of his country:

the Committee's concerns about freedom of the press in Paraguay;

the request for further information concerning the questions raised by the members of the Committee at its [spring 1987] session and at its present session, especially in respect of the terms of the relevant decision of the Supreme Court, and particulars regarding the body to which the publisher of *ABC Color* might now have recourse and the procedure whereby it might seek to have the decision to suspend the newspaper rescinded;

(*b*) also to inform those authorities that, failing receipt of the relevant information requested, the Committee would be compelled at its next session to declare the communication admissible;

(v) to resume examination of this communication at its spring 1988 session.

Spring 1988 session of the Committee on Conventions and Recommendations (129th session of the Executive Board)[8]

75. According to the author of the communication, on 22 March 1984 the Paraguayan Ministry of the Interior ordered the suspension for an indefinite term of the printing and distribution of the daily newspaper *ABC Color*. This decision reportedly applied likewise to this newspaper's three weekly supplements. Mr Aldo Zuccolillo, the paper's editor-in-chief is alleged to have been subjected to harassment and threats in various forms.

76. In a letter dated 5 April 1988, the author of the communication once more pointed out that the authorities' accusation that *ABC Color* had preached hatred among Paraguayans was a pretext for stifling the peaceful expression of dissent. As regards the decisions by various courts concerning the suspension of *ABC Color*, the author stated that neither the Supreme Court nor any other court had directly or indirectly ruled on the constitutionality of the banning of the newspaper. He also alleged that the Supreme Court had rejected the appeal lodged by the publisher of *ABC Color* on procedural grounds. He claimed that recently, following representations by the Inter-American Press Association, the Minister of the Interior had said that if *ABC Color* submitted a request accompanied by a declaration stating that its editor-in-chief would assume responsibility for any item published, the newspaper might be authorized to resume publication. The author of the communication added that Mr Zuccolillo had submitted a request along these lines to the Minister on 10 March 1988.

77. Denying the allegations made by the International Human Rights Law Group, the representatives of the government concerned reiterated to the Committee that the decision to ban the publication of *ABC Color* was in keeping with the Constitution. They informed the Committee that the Paraguayan authorities would like this matter to be cleared up and that talks between the Ministry of Interior and the *ABC Color* group were now in progress. They said that the government had no intention of depriving the newspaper of the right to freedom of expression, but that the newspaper should respect the rules of the Constitution. The newspaper had *inter alia* published unsigned articles that impugned the honour of certain individuals, and Mr Zuccolil-

[8] See document 129 EX/3 PRIV., paras. 75-79; see also document 129 EX/CR/HR/2.

lo, on the grounds that he was obliged to protect his sources of information, had refused to reveal the names of their authors, while at the same time refusing to assume responsibility himself. They added that Mr Zuccolillo had not been persecuted and enjoyed all his rightful freedoms.

78. Several members of the Committee said that they were puzzled by the reasons given by the government concerned for indefinitely suspending publication of *ABC Color*, since the editor-in-chief, the manager and the editor of a newspaper were normally responsible for unsigned articles. One of the members expressed surprise that the Supreme Court had, on procedural grounds, rejected the appeal lodged by the publisher of *ABC Color*, whose action was based on the rights and freedoms guaranteed by the Constitution.

79. Following an exchange of views, the Committee *decided*:

(i) to thank the representatives of the government concerned for their presence and co-operation;

(ii) to appeal to the government concerned, in the name of the freedom of the press enshrined in the relevant instruments of the United Nations and of Unesco, to authorize *ABC Color* to resume publication as soon as possible;

(iii) to resume examination of this communication at [its autumn 1988 session].

Autumn 1988 session of the Committee on Conventions and Recommendations (130th session of the Executive Board)[9]

82. This communication has been on the Committee's agenda since the [spring 1986 session]. It is still at the stage of examination of its admissibility.

83. According to the author of the communication, on 22 March 1984, the Paraguayan Government ordered the suspension for an indefinite term of the printing of the daily newspaper *ABC Color* and also of its three weekly supplements aimed at primary schools, and at promoting culture and information in rural areas. Mr Aldo Zuccolillo, the paper's editor-in-chief is alleged to have been subjected to harassment and threats in various forms. The closure of the newspaper is allegedly due to the fact that in December 1983 it reported the return to Paraguay of some 30 mem-

[9] See document 130 EX/3 PRIV., paras. 82-90; see also document 130 EX/CR/HR - Paraguay.

bers of the opposition party in exile, known as MOPOCO (Movimiento Popular Colorado) and published several paid communications and open letters from the party.

84. Neither the Supreme Court nor any other court is said to have directly or indirectly ruled on the constitutionality of the banning of the newspaper. All available means of redress are said to have been resorted to. Following an intervention by the Inter-American Press Association, the Minister of the Interior allegedly intimated that if *ABC Color* lodged a request accompanied by a statement to the effect that its editor-in-chief would assume responsibility for all texts published, publication of the newspaper might perhaps be authorized. Mr Zuccolillo reportedly made such a request to the Minister on 10 March 1988, but has apparently received no reply.

85. At the Committee's [spring 1988] session, the representative of the government concerned, refuting the allegations made by the author of the communication, reiterated that the decision to ban the newspaper *ABC Color* was in keeping with the Constitution. The newspaper had published unsigned articles impugning the honour of other individuals and Mr Zuccolillo, on the grounds that he was obliged to protect his sources of information, had refused to reveal the names of their authors, at the same time refusing to assume responsibility himself. Conversations were in progress between the Minister of the Interior and *ABC Color* with a view to finding a solution.

86. In the name of the freedom of the press enshrined in the relevant instruments of the United Nations and of Unesco, the Committee had appealed to the Paraguayan Government to authorize *ABC Color* to resume publication as soon as possible.[10]

87. On 5 September 1988, the Secretariat received a letter from the author of the communication expressing satisfaction at the appeal made by the Committee and concern over the fact that the government in question maintained that its decision to ban publication of the newspaper was in keeping with the Constitution and affirmed that Mr Zuccolillo had not been persecuted. He added a memorandum from Mr Zuccolillo's lawyer to the dossier which stated that Mr Zuccolillo had been arrested twice for refusing to reveal his sources of information, the first time in 1983 and the second time in March 1984. Attached to the memorandum was a translation of the two requests made by Mr Zuccolillo to the Minister of the Interior on 10 March and 21 July 1988 to have the decision to ban the newspaper revoked. The author of the communication stressed that the banning of *ABC Color* constituted a violation of internationally recognized human rights. He requested that Mr Zuccolillo's freedom and the freedom to publish *ABC Color* be ensured.

---

[10] See document 129 EX/3 PRIV., para. 79 (ii) (*supra*, p. 566).

No. 674/85 **Paraguay**

88. Confirming the terms of a *note verbale* from the Permanent Delegation of Paraguay to Unesco dated 10 October 1988, the representative of the government concerned stated that if this case had not yet been solved, it was not the fault of the authorities, but of Mr Zuccolillo and his group who had refused to submit a statement undertaking to abide by the law and the Constitution in the exercise of their press activities. The government whose duty it was to ensure law and order and keep subversive movements at bay, was receptive to dialogue but was awaiting a gesture of good will. However, Mr Zuccolillo and his group persisted in claiming that the decision of the Minister of the Interior to ban publication of *ABC Color* was unjustified. The representative of the government concerned added that subject to observance of the regulations on the subject, press freedom was guaranteed in Paraguay where there was no censorship or any other form of restriction.

89. Several members of the Committee were surprised that the representative of the government concerned could speak of its open approach as the case had been dragging on for four years. They wondered whether the conditions laid down by the government for the newspaper to resume publication were so demanding as to become unacceptable. It was, accordingly, their view that the communication should be declared admissible, its substance examined and the author asked what prior conditions had been laid down by the government for *ABC Color* to resume publication.

90. After an exchange of views, the Committee *decided*:

(i) to thank the representative of the government concerned for his presence and co-operation;

(ii) to express regret that negotiations between *ABC Color* and the government had still not been successful;

(iii) to declare the communication admissible in so far as the Committee had reason to consider that the banning of *ABC Color* was an act contrary to the freedom of the press;

(iv) to request the author of the communication to provide information on the conditions laid down by the government for authorizing the newspaper to resume publication;

(v) to resume examination of this communication at its [spring 1989 session].

Paraguay **No. 674/85**

Spring 1989 session of the Committee on Conventions and Recommendations (131st session of the Executive Board)[11]

216. This communication has been on the Committee's agenda since the [spring 1986 session]. It is being considered from the point of view of its substance, having been declared admissible by the Committee at its [autumn 1988] session.[12]

217. According to the author of the communication, the Paraguayan Government decided on 22 March 1984 to suspend indefinitely the daily newspaper *ABC Color* together with its three weekly supplements intended for primary schools and aimed at promoting culture and information in rural areas. Mr Aldo Zuccolillo, editor-in-chief, was reportedly subjected to harassment and threats in various forms.

218. The government's decision is allegedly due to the fact that in December 1983 the newspaper reported the return to Paraguay of some 30 members of the opposition party in exile, known as MOPOCO (Movimiento Popular Colorado) and published several paid communications and open letters from the party.

219. During the [spring 1988 session], in the name of the freedom of the press enshrined in the relevant instruments of the United Nations and of Unesco, the Committee appealed to the Paraguayan Government to authorize the newspaper to resume publication as soon as possible.[13]

220. On 26 April 1989, the Secretariat received a letter from the International Human Rights Law Group stating that *ABC Color* had been authorized to resume publication, the present Paraguayan Government having taken a number of positive measures regarding the freedom of expression and the freedom of the press. In addition to abrogating the decision to suspend the newspaper, it had authorized "Radio Nanduti", an independent radio station, to resume broadcasting and the weekly of a political party, *El Pueblo*, to resume publication.

221. The author of the communication expressed great satisfaction with the work done by the Committee which had helped to restore and ensure respect for fundamental human rights.

222. After an exchange of views, the Committee *decided*:

---

[11] See document 131 EX/3 PRIV., paras. 216-222; see also document 131 EX/CR/HR/PAR.
[12] See document 130 EX/3 PRIV., para. 90 (iii) (*supra*, p. 568).
[13] See document 129 EX/3 PRIV., para. 79 (ii) (*supra*, p. 566).

No. 674/85 **Paraguay**

(i) to note with satisfaction the information provided by the author of the communication;

(ii) to strike the communication from its list, considering it to have been settled in accordance with paragraph 14 (*a*) (x) of 104 EX/Decision 3.3.

No. 676/85

Concerning *Yugoslavia*
Case of *Jovan R. Gucič*

Communication of 17 January 1985 submitted by
Jovan R. Gucič

Autumn 1985 session of the Committee on Conventions and Recommendations (122nd session of the Executive Board)[1]

136. The author of the communication describes himself as a physicist. He complains that he is subjected to political persecution. He claims that he has been given a suspended sentence of one year's imprisonment, put on probation for a year and heavily fined.

137. In a letter dated 30 August 1985, received by the Secretariat on 3 September 1985, the Permanent Delegation of Yugoslavia to Unesco declared that since Mr Gucič's case was still before the courts it was unable to provide the relevant information before the conclusion of the case.

138. On the day this communication was considered, the Secretariat received a letter from the author providing information additional to his original allegations.

139. In view of what is stated in the above-mentioned letter from the Yugoslav Government and the late arrival of the letter from the author of the communication, which was not transmitted in time to the government concerned, the Committee *decided* to postpone consideration of the communication to its next session.

[1] See document 122 EX/21 PRIV., paras. 136-139; see also document 122 EX/CR/HR/3.

No. 676/85 **Yugoslavia**

Spring 1986 session of the Committee on Conventions and Recommendations (124th session of the Executive Board)[2]

109. Mr Gucič a physicist, complains that he is subjected to political persecution. Given a suspended prison sentence in March 1985 and fined, he is said to have been acquitted, finally, by the Supreme Court of Serbia. According to his latest letter of 18 April 1986 to the Secretariat, the "Tanjug" agency announced this acquittal on 23 January 1986. Of the documents said to have been seized during his questioning, his passport has apparently already been returned to him.

110. The government concerned has not sent a representative. Nevertheless, in a letter dated 28 April 1986 [...],[3] it conveyed to the Organization its observations and comments concerning the allegations which are the subject of the communication.

111. After summarizing the alleged facts, the Chairperson read out the relevant part of this letter. In it, the Permanent Delegate of Yugoslavia to Unesco pointed out that criminal proceedings had been lawfully initiated against Mr Gucič, who had been charged with revealing an official secret, but that they had terminated before the Supreme Court of Serbia with his acquittal. He added that the documents seized during the investigation were being returned to Mr Gucič and that on 23 January 1986 the daily newspaper *Politika* had published an article informing the public of the acquittal.

112. The members of the Committee who took the floor noted the reply by the government concerned, according to which Mr Gucič faced no further charges.

113. After an exchange of views, the Committee *decided* to strike this communication from its list as settled.

---

[2] See document 124 EX/3 PRIV., paras. 109-113; see also documents 124 EX/CR/HR/2 and Add.3.

[3] See document 124 EX/CR/HR/2 Add.3.

No. 677/85

Concerning *Italy*
Case of *Alberto Tessore*

Communication of 26 March 1985 submitted by
The International Human Rights Law Group and
Steptoe and Johnson

Autumn 1986 session of the Committee on Conventions and Recommendations (125th session of the Executive Board)[1]

48. Mr Alberto Tessore is described as a teacher and scholar who has published books and articles of historical, geographical and cultural content. Holding a post in the Italian Cultural Institute at Addis Ababa, in Ethiopia, he is said, in November 1982, to have participated as a private scholar in a symposium at Addis Ababa University, in the course of which he presented an article entitled "Different approaches to other cultures by foreign travellers". According to the authors of the communication, one of the travellers mentioned by Dr Tessore was Cardinal Massaja who had visited Ethiopia for more than 30 years in the nineteenth century. In his article, Dr Tessore was said to have been very critical of Cardinal Massaja who was alleged to have been critical of Ethiopian Muslims and mainly interested in converting people to his faith. The alleged victim is said to have also accused Cardinal Massaja as being incapable of any judgement which was strongly based on his intolerant Catholicism. It is alleged that because of this article and upon the denunciation, in June 1984, of Rev. Antonio Rosso, an Italian priest of Capuchin Convent of Padua, who accused him of having slandered the Italian missionary Massaja, Dr Tessore has lost his promotion to a position in Bombay (India) as the Director of a newly established Italian Cultural Institute and was afterwards forced to resign due to the reaction of the Italian authorities and to the intolerable conditions of his work under the circumstances.

49. The representative of the government concerned explained that contrary to the impression that one might get on reading the communication, the alleged victim, Mr Alberto Tessore, had not been, at all the relevant times, a Foreign Ministry official

[1] See document 125 EX/3 PRIV., paras. 48-51; see also document 125 EX/CR/HR/3.

of his country but rather a teacher who was on loan to that Ministry. He declared that Mr Tessore had no right to a transfer from Addis Ababa in Ethiopia to the office of the Italian Cultural Institute in Bombay, India, nor did he *a fortiori* have the right to be transferred with a promotion to the directorship of that Institute. For these reasons, the representative of the government concerned stated that in the opinion of his government, the communication did not involve any alleged violation of human rights coming within Unesco's fields of competence. He informed the Committee that Mr Tessore was only one of a number of people who had been sounded in respect of possible appointment to the post of Director of the Bombay Institute, and that no decision on his definite appointment to the post had ever been taken. The representative of the government concerned furthermore refuted the allegation that the alleged victim had been forced to resign from the post he held and explained that Mr Tessore's own resignation telex to the competent authorities in Rome indicated that he had resigned for health and family reasons.

50. The Chairperson pointed out that one of the author's allegations was that Mr Tessore had been victimized for the contents of some of his statements made at a symposium and not that he had a right to a promotion which had not been respected. Another member of the Committee declared that in his view, the professional position of the alleged victim necessarily imposed a certain degree of discretion on him as regards his public utterances and that respect for that obligation appeared to have been wanting in this case. He said further that he felt the case did not concern any alleged violation of human rights in the Organization's fields of competence. Several members of the Committee concurred with this view. In reply to a member of the Committee who wanted to know what internal remedies, if any, were available to Mr Tessore, the representative of the government concerned informed the Committee that not only were there appropriate internal remedies open to the alleged victim but that he had in fact, in December 1985, brought his complaint before the competent administrative tribunal and that the case was still pending. Furthermore, the alleged victim could take his case further to the Council of State if he was not satisfied with the decision that the administrative tribunal might render.

51. At the end of its examination of the communication, the Committee *decided* to declare it inadmissible on the ground that the allegations contained therein did not relate to the violation of any human rights coming within Unesco's fields of competence.

No. 684/85

Concerning *Yugoslavia*
Case of *Radomir Veljković*

Communication of 9 February 1985 submitted by
Dragan Veljković

Autumn 1985 session of the Committee on Conventions and Recommendations (122nd session of the Executive Board)[1]

140. Mr Radomir Veljković is described by his brother, the author of this communication, as a former teacher at the Military Academy of Sarajevo. He is said to have been detained in a psychiatric hospital since July 1973, following a court decision. He is alleged to have expressed political opinions considered to be at odds with those of the Yugoslav authorities.

141. In a letter dated 30 August 1985, the Permanent Delegation of Yugoslavia to Unesco stated that the papers relating to the communication (transmitted by the Secretariat to that delegation within the statutory time limit of one month before the session of the Committee) had not reached the relevant authorities in its country until mid-August 1985 and that, as a result, they had been unable to prepare a reply.

142. Considering that those authorities should be given time to gather relevant information, the Committee *decided* to defer consideration of the communication until its next session.

Spring 1986 session of the Committee on Conventions and Recommendations (124th session of the Executive Board)[2]

114. Described by the author of the communication as a former teacher at the Military Academy of Sarajevo, Mr Radomir Veljković is said to have been detained in a

[1] See document 122 EX/21 PRIV., paras. 140-142; see also document 119 EX/CR/HR/3 Add.
[2] See document 124 EX/3 PRIV., paras. 114-121; see also documents 124 EX/CR/HR/2 and Add.3.

psychiatric hospital since July 1973 because his political opinions were considered to be at odds with those of the Yugoslav authorities.

115. The government concerned has not sent a representative. Nevertheless, in a letter dated 28 April 1986 [...],[3] it conveyed to the Organization its observations and comments concerning the allegations which are the subject of the communication.

116. After summarizing the alleged facts, the Chairperson read out the relevant part of that letter. In it, the Permanent Delegate of Yugoslavia to Unesco pointed out that Mr Veljković, by decision of the Departmental Court of Sarajevo, had been placed under observation and given treatment at the psychiatric hospital of the central prison, on the basis of an expert opinion according to which he was highly dangerous to those around him. He went on to say that Mr Veljković had refused to be examined by the health services of the Yugoslav People's Army and that his complaints had been rejected as unfounded, in accordance with ordinary procedure, by both the Military Supreme Court and the Supreme Court of the Socialist Republic of Bosnia. He further stated that according to medical reports submitted to the Departmental Court of Sarajevo in 1980, 1981, 1983 and 1985, the conditions that would justify the termination of the measures taken with regard to Mr Veljković had not yet been met.

117. One member of the Committee stated that the communication contained no relevant evidence and should be declared inadmissible on the grounds of being unfounded.

118. In the view of another member of the Committee, the alleged facts were not unfounded since they had been reflected in the 1984 annual report of Amnesty International.

119. Other members of the Committee who took the floor noted that the medical certificates placed on record by the author of the communication were already very old and that more recent ones should be obtained and additional information collected.

120. In reply to a question concerning the Committee's competence, *ratione personae*, given the status of the alleged victim who had connections with a military institution, the Chairperson explained that, according to the file, Mr Veljković was a teacher, a scientist and even, in the opinion of the author of the communication, a scholar whose career had been interrupted because of his opinions.

121. After an exchange of views, the Committee *decided*:

---

[3] See document 124 EX/CR/HR/2 Add.3.

(i) to ask the government concerned and also the author of the communication for further information, in particular on the current clinical state of Mr Veljković;

(ii) to resume consideration of this communication at its autumn 1986 session.

Autumn 1986 session of the Committee on Conventions and Recommendations (125th session of the Executive Board)[4]

143. Described by the author of the communication as a former teacher at the Sarajevo Military Academy, Mr Radomir Veljković is said to have been detained in a psychiatric hospital since July 1973 because his political opinions are deemed to be at odds with those of the Yugoslav authorities.

144. As a follow-up to the information concerning the state of mental health of Mr Veljković that had been conveyed to the Committee at its [spring 1986] session in a letter dated 28 April 1986 from the Permanent Delegate of Yugoslavia to Unesco [...], the representative of the government concerned stated that the latest report by the psychiatric hospital claimed that the patient was suffering from a persecution complex and that he was bringing a variety of legal proceedings against his acquaintances. Following treatment, Mr Veljković's state had improved and he had for some time been taking an interest in the study of arithmetic, astronomy and physics. He no longer seemed to constitute a danger to people around him and the doctors had proposed on 27 June 1986, in accordance with Article 231 of the Criminal Code, that the Court of Sarajevo review the case of this patient, observing that he would be able to leave the present "closed" psychiatric hospital, provided, however, that he remained under the regular supervision of an "open" civilian psychiatric hospital. A court decision is expected shortly. Without prejudice to that decision, added the representative of the government concerned, the court of law to which the case was referred would, as a rule, follow the recommendations of the doctors.

145. After an exchange of views, the Committee *decided*:

(i) to thank the government concerned for sending a representative;

(ii) to strike the communication from its list as soon as the Secretariat had received confirmation of the decision of the competent court to release Mr Radomir Veljković, on the understanding that should such confirmation not

[4] See document 125 EX/3 PRIV., paras. 143-145; see also document 125 EX/CR/HR/2.

reach the Secretariat before the spring 1987 session of the Committee, it would resume consideration of the communication.

No. 685/85

Concerning *Yugoslavia*
Case of *Vladimir Marković*

Communication of 17 May 1985 submitted by
Vladimir Marković

Autumn 1985 session of the Committee on Conventions and Recommendations (122nd session of the Executive Board)[1]

143. The author of this communication describes himself as a journalist. He states that he was confined to a psychiatric hospital for approximately three years from May 1979 to April 1982 by virtue of a court decision for allegedly circulating an interview with Mr Franjo Tudjman, a historian and former army general. He states that he has been unable to find employment in his profession or to marry, since he was considered a former mental patient.

144. In a letter dated 30 August 1985, the Permanent Delegation of Yugoslavia to Unesco stated that the papers relating to the communication (transmitted by the Secretariat to that delegation within the statutory time limit of one month before the session of the Committee) had not reached the relevant authorities in its country until mid-August 1985 and that, as a result, they had been unable to prepare a reply.

145. Considering that those authorities should be given time to gather relevant information, the Committee *decided* to defer consideration of the communication until its next session.

[1] See document 122 EX/21 PRIV., paras. 143-145; see also document 122 EX/CR/HR/3.

No. 685/85 **Yugoslavia**

Spring 1986 session of the Committee on Conventions and Recommendations (124nd session of the Executive Board)[2]

122. The author of the communication describes himself as a journalist and alleged victim. He states that he was confined to a psychiatric hospital from May 1979 to April 1982 by virtue of a court decision for circulating an interview with Mr Franjo Tudjman, a historian and former army general. Thus stigmatized as a former mental patient, he states that he was unable to find employment in his profession or to marry.

123. The government concerned did not send a representative. However, by a letter dated 28 April 1986 [...],[3] it had informed the Organization of its comments and observations on the allegations made in the communication.

124. After presenting the alleged facts, the Chairperson read out the relevant portion of that letter. In it, the Permanent Delegate of Yugoslavia to Unesco had indicated that the medical experts concerned had considered that in view of his illness, Mr Marković was not responsible for the acts he had committed, and that in accordance with the regulations in force, it had been found necessary to prescribe a security measure in the form of compulsory treatment in an appropriate medical institution; the treatment had lasted from 1979 to 1982. The Permanent Delegate had added that Mr Marković had used all available means of redress. He had also indicated that Mr Marković's assertion that he had been prevented from getting married for health reasons was without foundation, as no provision of Yugoslav law required evidence of health as a necessary condition for contracting marriage.

125. Some members of the Committee considered that in view of the fact that Mr Marković had been released and was legally free to marry, the Committee should terminate its consideration of the communication. Other members wondered whether the Committee was competent to consider a psychiatric case.

126. Some members of the Committee noted that Mr Marković had also complained that he was unable to find employment in his profession or to study the subjects that interested him. Some other members were of the opinion that as a first step, the information provided by the government concerned should be forwarded to the author of the communication, and that consideration of the communication in question should be deferred to the next session.

---

[2] See document 124 EX/3 PRIV., paras. 122-127; see also documents 124 EX/CR/HR/2 and Add.3.
[3] See documents 124 EX/CR/HR/2 Add.3.

Yugoslavia **No. 685/85**

127. Following an exchange of views, the Committee *decided*:

(i) to request the Secretariat to communicate the reply from the government concerned to the author of the communication;

(ii) to request further information both from the government concerned and from the author of the communication about the reasons why the latter could not find employment as a journalist, and about his wishes;

(iii) to defer consideration of the communication to its autumn 1986 session.

Autumn 1986 session of the Committee on Conventions and Recommendations (125nd session of the Executive Board)[4]

146. The author of the communication describes himself as a journalist and the alleged victim. He states that he was confined to a psychiatric hospital from May 1979 to April 1982 by virtue of a court decision for circulating an interview with Mr Franjo Tudjman, a historian and former army general. Thus stigmatized as a former mental patient, he states that he was unable to find employment in his profession or to marry.

147. In response to the request for additional information made by the Committee at its [spring 1986] session, the author of the communication sent the Secretariat a letter dated 4 August 1986 in which, after recalling the alleged reasons for his confinement to a psychiatric hospital, he provides, *inter alia*, the following particulars:

according to him, the Commission of Experts that examined him, consisting of only two members, conversed with him for only about half an hour; the psychiatrists reportedly asked him utterly trivial questions;

in Yugoslavia there is said to be a law (Article 133 of the Penal Code) against crimes of opinion; the authorities reportedly tend to regard political criticism as a sort of non-conformism and hence a symptom of mental illness;

he states that following his confinement no periodical or newspaper has consented to publish anything written by him;

he states that he has already been employed for three and a half years as a mere manual worker; that he has had no dispute with those around him; that,

[4] See document 125 EX/3 PRIV., paras. 146-151; see also document 125 EX/CR/HR/2.

not expecting to be able to find work as a journalist, he would like to obtain office employment;

the Court and the psychiatrists allegedly told him that before marrying he would have to inform his wife to be that he was suffering from schizophrenia and that failure to do so would render him liable to a three-year prison sentence, and that his wife could demand an immediate annulment of the marriage.

148. The representative of the government concerned recalled that the case in question did not lie within the competence of the Committee and that the facts were already self-explanatory. Mr Marković had admittedly completed a six-month course in 1976 in journalism, but to profess to be a journalist after such a short period of training was an exaggeration. In fact he had not worked as a professional journalist. While he had succeeded in having a number of articles published in various periodicals over a period of time, this did not suffice to make him a journalist. In that connection, the representative of the Yugoslav Government stated that in his country there was a university course for prospective journalists, but that owing to the unemployment problem not all students ultimately entered the profession. In any case, at the time of his trouble with the law, Mr Marković had been merely a first-year student at the Higher School of Tourism in Belgrade. The offence of which he was accused had been an article in which he had made untrue assertions about events connected with the Second World War. He had also circulated the article to an organization abroad, which had published it in a periodical. Charged with spreading false information, he had been recognized irresponsible by the psychiatrists, who had pronounced him to be suffering from schizophrenia. Article 133 of the Penal Code referred to by Mr Marković did not punish crimes of opinion and was not directed against political opponents. It enumerated a number of acts punishable by law, concerned essentially with acts against the State, against the unity of the country and against national security and defence. They included incitement or support for the overthrow of the authority of the people of Yugoslavia; acts conducive to unconstitutional change in the socialist self-management system; incitement to acts detrimental to the fraternity and equality of the peoples and nationalities of Yugoslavia; popular incitement to defiance of legal governmental decisions essential to the protection of the country's security or defence; misrepresentation of the social and political conditions prevailing in the country, etc.

149. As to Mr Marković's allegations that a prospective husband must inform his future wife of his state of health, confirming the letter from the Permanent Delegate of Yugoslavia to Unesco dated 28 April 1986 [...], which the Committee had seen at its [spring 1986] session, the representative of the government concerned stated that, under Yugoslav law, future spouses were not obliged to make known their state of

physical or mental health before contracting marriage. Finally, he observed that the letter from the author of the communication dated 4 August 1986 was supported only by press articles, which contravened paragraph 14 (*a*) (vii) of [104 EX/Decision 3.3 of the Executive Board].

150. The members of the Committee who spoke expressed the view that in the light of the information supplied by the representative of the Yugoslav Government, Mr Marković had been a student at the Higher School of Tourism before becoming a manual worker, that he had not been a professional journalist and that his case, however distressing, did not fall within Unesco's competence. Furthermore, the person in question had been confined by virtue of a regular court decision, and mental health problems were not the concern of the Organization.

151. Following an exchange of views, the Committee *decided*:

(i) to thank the government concerned for sending a representative;

(ii) to declare the communication inadmissible as not falling within Unesco's fields of competence in accordance with the provisions of paragraph 14 (*a*) (iii) of 104 EX/Decision 3.3.

No. 686/85

Concerning *Yugoslavia*
Case of *Božidar Todorović* *

Communication of 13 February 1985 submitted by
Božidar Todorović°

Autumn 1985 session of the Committee on Conventions and Recommendations (122nd session of the Executive Board)[1]

146. The author of this communication describes himself as a teacher of history and sociology. He states that he has been subject to political persecution and has been dismissed from his employment as "morally and politically unfit". He has apparently been unable to find work suited to his skills for the same reason.

147. In a letter dated 30 August 1985, the Permanent Delegation of Yugoslavia to Unesco stated that the papers relating to the communication (transmitted by the Secretariat to that delegation within the statutory time limit of one month before the session of the Committee) had not reached the relevant authorities in its country until mid-August 1985 and that, as a result, they had been unable to prepare a reply.

148. Considering those authorities should be given time to gather relevant information, the Committee *decided* to defer consideration of the communication until its next session.

---

* From the Committee's spring 1986 session, this communication was being referred to as case of *Božidar Todorović and Milica Todorović*.

° From the Committee's spring 1986 session, Božidar Todorović and Milica Todorović were being stated as authors.

[1] See document 122 EX/21 PRIV., paras. 146-148; see also document 122 EX/CR/HR/3 Add.

No. 686/85 **Yugoslavia**

Spring 1986 session of the Committee on Conventions and Recommendations (124th session of the Executive Board)[2]

128. Mr Božidar Todorović, a teacher of history and sociology, complains that he has been the subject of political persecution, that he has been dismissed from his employment as "morally and politically unfit" and that he has been unable to find work suited to his skills.

129. Miss Milica Todorović, his sister, a teacher of Latin, was apparently dismissed from her post in 1981 and transferred to a librarian's post. She was allegedly suspended from the latter post in November 1983, on the grounds of mental illness. She asserts that that measure was a move to force her to retire, although according to the Belgrade Sickness and Retirement Insurance Department she was recognized as still capable of working. She was also allegedly the subject of disciplinary action following an inventory of the stock of the library where she was working, in the course of which it was apparently discovered, on 25 August 1985, that 115 books were missing.

130. The government concerned was not represented. However, by a letter dated 28 April 1986 [...],[3] it had informed the Organization of its comments and observations on the allegations made in the communication.

131. After presenting the alleged facts, the Chairperson read out the relevant part of that letter. In it, the Permanent Delegate of Yugoslavia to Unesco stated:

> by decision of the School Board, the authority empowered by the law to decide in such matters, Mr Božidar Todorović had been dismissed from his position as he exercised a harmful influence on the education of pupils through his work and behaviour; he had used all available legal remedies; his assertion that he was unable to find work because of his moral and political unsuitability was unfounded since, according to the Constitutional Court in Yugoslavia, moral and political suitability could not be cited as a justification for withdrawing or limiting the right to work guaranteed by the Constitution to all citizens; unemployment in Yugoslavia affected teachers as well; it was a problem which the government was attempting to resolve within the limits of the means at its disposal;

---

[2] See document 124 EX/3 PRIV., paras. 128-132; see also documents 124 EX/CR/HR/2 and Add.3 and 124 EX/CR/HR/3.

[3] See document 124 EX/CR/HR/2 Add.3.

Miss Milica Todorović was mentally ill, suffering from a third-category disability; should she so wish, she might use all the available means of redress.

132. Following an exchange of views, the Committee *decided*:

(i) to request the Secretariat to communicate the information provided by the government concerned to the authors of the communication;

(ii) to defer examination of the latter to its autumn 1986 session.

Autumn 1986 session of the Committee on Conventions and Recommendations (125th session of the Executive Board)[4]

152. Mr Božidar Todorović, a teacher of history and sociology, complains that he has been the subject of political persecution, that he has been dismissed from his employment as "morally and politically unfit" and that he has been unable to find work suited to his skills.

153. Miss Milica Todorović, his sister, a teacher of Latin, was apparently dismissed from her post in 1981 and transferred to a librarian's post. She was allegedly suspended from the latter post in November 1983, on the grounds of mental illness. She asserts that that measure was a move to force her to retire, although according to the Belgrade Sickness and Retirement Insurance Department she was recognized as still capable of working. She was also allegedly the subject of disciplinary action following an inventory of the stock of the library where she was working, in the course of which it was apparently discovered, on 25 August 1985, that 115 books were missing.

154. Recalling the information provided to the Committee at its [spring 1986] session by the Permanent Delegate of Yugoslavia to Unesco [...], the representative of the government concerned said that Mr Božidar Todorović had been dismissed from the school in which he taught following a decision by the School Board. By his behaviour, he had exerted an extremely bad influence on his pupils; he had no sense of responsibility, had insulted the other teachers, even in front of the Board, maliciously made offensive remarks about the work done by pupils, created disturbances in the school and used his position as a teacher to spread false information. The representative of the government concerned stated that in each of the Federal Republics, authority in educational matters, especially in matters relating to the recruitment or dismissal of teachers, lay entirely with the School Board. The decision taken con-

[4] See document 125 EX/3 PRIV., paras. 152-158; see also document 125 EX/CR/HR/2.

cerning Mr Božidar Todorović was therefore entirely legal and the government could not intervene. Mr Božidar Todorović had, moreover, exhausted all available legal remedies. His assertion that he was unable to find work because of his political opinions was unfounded since, according to a decision by the Constitutional Court of Yugoslavia, the text of which had been sent to the ILO and which had led to amendments to the law in the Federal Republics, moral and political convictions could not be cited as special grounds justifying prohibition or limitation of the exercise of the right to work. The representative of the government concerned pointed out that with the unemployment problem in Belgrade, it was understandable that, on account of his previous work record, Mr Božidar Todorović might have difficulty in finding a teaching post.

155. With regard to Miss Milica Todorović, the representative of the government concerned informed the Committee that she now seemed to be satisfied with her situation. The school no longer had any problems with her. The disciplinary action which had been taken against her had been stopped, and her colleagues had proved tolerant towards her despite her bouts of mental derangement.

156. One member of the Committee wondered whether it were possible to convey to the Yugoslav Government its wish that the case of Mr Božidar Todorović should be considered with leniency.

157. In that connection, the representative of the government concerned stated that it was within his power to transmit such a wish, but that the government could not return the person concerned to his former post against a decision by a competent school authority. This point of view was shared by other members of the Committee.

158. At the conclusion of the discussion, the Committee *decided*:

(i) to thank the government concerned for sending a representative;

(ii) to declare the case of Mr Božidar Todorović inadmissible on the grounds that it was unfounded, and that of Miss Milica Todorović settled by virtue of paragraph 14 (*a*) (v) and (x) of 104 EX/Decision 3.3.

No. 687/85

Concerning *Yugoslavia*
Case of *Slobodan Živković* et al.*

Communication of 9 February 1985 submitted by
Slobodan Živković *et al.*°

Spring 1986 session of the Committee on Conventions and Recommendations (124th session of the Executive Board)[1]

133. The Živković family are described as a family of manual workers and farmers. They complain of being persecuted by the Yugoslav authorities because they belong to the community of Jehovah's Witnesses.

134. The government concerned was not represented. However, by a letter dated 28 April 1986 [...],[2] it had informed the Organization of its comments and observations on the allegations made in the communication.

135. After presenting the alleged facts, the Chairperson read out the relevant part of that letter. In it, the Permanent Delegate of Yugoslavia to Unesco stated:

> The Constitution of the Socialist Federal Republic of Yugoslavia proclaimed the right to the free practice of religion, which was a personal matter for the individual. Churches and religious communities were separate from the State and were free to practise their religion as they saw fit. The community of Jehovah's Witnesses had a headquarters in Belgrade and was divided into seven provinces with 130 parishes. It published a monthly review in 36,000 copies. The members of the Živković family were suffering from mental illness and were frequently in conflict with their circle of acquaintances and the law (they had physically assaulted relatives and neighbours). Their occupations

* Case of *Slobodan Živković, Živojin Živković, Života Živković and Božidarka Živković.*
° Slobodan Živković, Živojin Živković, Života Živković and Božidarka Živković.
[1] See document 124 EX/3 PRIV., paras. 133-136; see also documents 124 EX/CR/HR/3 Add. and 124 EX/CR/HR/2 Add.3.
[2] See document 124 EX/CR/HR/2 Add.3.

(farmers and manual workers) and the subject of their communication did not come within the field of competence of Unesco.

136. Following an exchange of views, the Committee *decided* to declare the communication inadmissible as not coming within Unesco's field of competence.

No. 690/85

Concerning *El Salvador*
Case of *Filomena Claros de Majano*

Communication of 4 July 1985 submitted by
Thomas Hammarberg*

Spring 1986 session of the Committee on Conventions and Recommendations (124th session of the Executive Board)[1]

74. A secretary at the Ministry of Education, a third-year law student and a member of the Executive of the Law Students' Association, Mrs Filomena Claros de Majano, who, according to the author, was aged 34 at the time of the events, married and the mother of a one-year old child, is said to have been abducted on 3 January 1984 at 7.20 p.m. in front of the San Nicolas Pharmacy in Hula-Hula Park (San Salvador). A witness reportedly saw armed men in plain clothes push the alleged victim into a landrover with smoked-glass windows, licence plate No. P-17-157, and drive off pointing a gun at the witness. 18 days earlier, on 16 December, Mrs Claros de Majano had allegedly received an anonymous letter advising her to stop her "subversive studies".

75. The representative of the Salvadorian Government explained that immediately upon receipt of the communication, the Ministry of Education had undertaken an investigation and that the inquiry had been entrusted to the Public Prosecutor at the Supreme Court. From the results obtained to date, it appeared that Mrs Carlos de Majano was not being detained in any prison.

76. One member of the Committee suggested that this case should be added to those in connection with which a mission had been established by the Executive Board with instructions to visit El Salvador. Another member of the Committee then asked whether this would not require the communication to be declared admissible.

* On behalf of Amnesty International. From the Committee's spring 1987 session, Amnesty International was being stated as author.
[1] See document 124 EX/3 PRIV., paras. 74-79; see also document 124 EX/CR/HR/3.

No. 690/85 **El Salvador**

77. The representative of the government concerned pointed out that the conditions of admissibility as set forth in 104 EX/Decision 3.3 had not been met and that there was no evidence on the strength of which the communication could be declared admissible; furthermore, he emphasized, his country's current exceptional situation was a factor that should be taken into account. He added, however, that he had no objection to the Executive Board's mission collecting information on that case in El Salvador.

78. The representative of the Director-General pointed out that it was the Committee's practice to gather as much information as possible before deciding whether a communication was admissible or not; accordingly, there was nothing incompatible about entrusting the mission with the task of seeking additional information without having declared the communication admissible.

79. After the discussion, the Committee *decided*:

(i) to request the Executive Board to include the present communication in the mandate of the mission appointed by the Executive Board in connection with other communications concerning the same country;

(ii) to resume consideration of this communication, in the light of the information communicated to it by the above-mentioned mission, by the author of the communication and/or by the government concerned, at its autumn 1986 session.

Autumn 1986 session of the Committee on Conventions and Recommendations (125th session of the Executive Board)[2]

46. A secretary in the Directorate-General for Basic Education, a law student and a leading member of the Law Students' Association, Mrs Filomena Claros de Majano is said to have been abducted in San Salvador at about 7.20 p.m. on 3 January 1984, opposite the San Nicolas Pharmacy in Hula-Hula Park, by armed men in plain clothes driving a landrover.

47. The Committee considered this communication at the same time as [five other communications].[3]

---

[2] See document 125 EX/3 PRIV., paras. 46-47; see also documents 125 EX/CR/HR/2 and 125 EX/CR/HR/1 Add.2.

[3] *Ibidem*, paras. 168-179 (vol. I, pp. 704-705), communication No. 276/80 concerning *El Salvador*, case of *Leonel Menéndez Quiroga*.

El Salvador **No. 690/85**

Spring 1987 session of the Committee on Conventions and Recommendations (126th session of the Executive Board)[4]

49. A secretary in the Directorate-General for Basic Education, a law student and a leading member of the Law Students' Association, Mrs Filomena Claros de Majano is said to have been abducted in San Salvador at about 7.20 p.m. on 3 January 1984, opposite the San Nicolas Pharmacy in Hula-Hula Park, by armed men in plain clothes driving a landrover.

50. The government concerned did not send a representative to the present session of the Committee.

51. In [a letter] dated 5 May 1987, the Permanent Delegate of El Salvador to Unesco stated that despite the efforts made by the authorities in his country, it had not been possible to obtain any further information on this case. He reiterated, however, that the authorities were willing to receive, if necessary, a visit from a member of the Executive Board or of the Committee, so as to end this painful situation.

52. The discussion on the absence of a representative of the government concerned and on the situation in El Salvador, which took place during the examination of [five other communications], also applies to this communication.[5]

53. After an exchange of views, the Committee *decided*:

(i) to express its regret that a representative of the government concerned had not been present and to request the Chairperson to send a letter to that effect to the Permanent Delegation of El Salvador to Unesco;

(ii) to request the government concerned to provide information on progress made, as an inquiry had been entrusted to the Attorney-General of the Supreme Court and as the appointed representative of the Executive Board, during his mission to El Salvador in July 1986, had received assurances that the result of that inquiry would be communicated to Unesco;

(iii) to resume consideration of the communication at its autumn 1987 session.

---

[4] See document 126 EX/3 PRIV., paras. 49-53; see also document 126 EX/CR/HR/2.
[5] *Ibidem*, paras. 196-203 (vol. I, pp. 710-712), communication No. 276/80 concerning *El Salvador*, case of *Leonel Menéndez Quiroga and others*.

No. 690/85 **El Salvador**

Autumn 1987 session of the Committee on Conventions and Recommendations (127th session of the Executive Board)[6]

34. A secretary in the Directorate-General for Basic Education, a law student and leading member of the Law Students' Association, Mrs Filomena Claros de Majano is said to have been abducted in San Salvador on 3 January 1984 at about 7.20 p.m. opposite the San Nicolas Pharmacy in Hula-Hula Park by armed men in plain clothes driving a Land Rover-type vehicle.

35. In a letter dated 10 August 1987, the author of the communication stated that it did not have any additional information relating to this case.

36. Taking the floor, the representative of the Government of El Salvador informed the Committee that the conscientious inquiry carried out by the Attorney-General had yielded no evidence that Mrs Filomena Claros de Majano was detained in an establishment under the responsibility of the State authorities. He recalled that for a number of years now, El Salvador had been in a context of armed insurrection in which several factions used the same methods and it was therefore very difficult to identify the individuals responsible for the abduction of people.

37. Observations of a general nature relating in particular to assistance to the families of alleged victims and the request to close the matter which he had made during consideration of [five other communications] also applied to this communication.[7] This was also true of the opinions expressed by members of the Committee in this regard.

38. After an exchange of views, the Committee *decided*:

(i) to thank the representative of the government concerned for his attendance and co-operation;

(ii) while noting the efforts made by this government, to request it to be good enough to extend the inquiry already undertaken still further so as to obtain fuller information;

(iii) to resume consideration of this communication at its spring 1988 session.

---

[6] See document 127 EX/3 PRIV., paras. 34-38; see also document 127 EX/CR/HR/2.

[7] *Ibidem*, paras. 136-145 (vol. I, pp. 712-714), communication No. 276/80 concerning *El Salvador*, case of *Leonel Menéndez Quiroga and others*.

El Salvador **No. 690/85**

Spring 1988 session of the Committee on Conventions and Recommendations (129th session of the Executive Board)[8]

Autumn 1988 session of the Committee on Conventions and Recommendations (130th session of the Executive Board)[9]

Spring 1989 session of the Committee on Conventions and Recommendations (131st session of the Executive Board)[10]

Autumn 1989 session of the Committee on Conventions and Recommendations (132nd session of the Executive Board)[11]

Spring 1990 session of the Committee on Conventions and Recommendations (134th session of the Executive Board)[12]

[8] See document 129 EX/3 PRIV., paras. 132-139 (vol. I, pp. 714-716), communication No. 276/80 concerning *El Salvador*, case of *Leonel Menéndez Quiroga and others*.
[9] See document 130 EX/3 PRIV., paras. 152-166 (vol. I, pp. 717-720), communication No. 276/80 concerning *El Salvador*, case of *Leonel Menéndez Quiroga and others*.
[10] See document 131 EX/3 PRIV., paras. 186-195 (vol. I, pp. 720-722), communication No. 276/80 concerning *El Salvador*, case of *Leonel Menéndez Quiroga and others*.
[11] See document 132 EX/3 PRIV., paras. 148-156 (vol. I, pp. 722-723), communication No. 276/80 concerning *El Salvador*, case of *Leonel Menéndez Quiroga and others*.
[12] See document 134 EX/3 PRIV., paras. 173-181 (vol. I, pp. 724-725), communication No. 276/80 concerning *El Salvador*, case of *Leonel Menéndez Quiroga and others*.

No. 691/85

Concerning *Union of Soviet Socialist Republics*
Case of *Hanna Vasylivna Mykhaylenko*

Communication of 19 July 1985 submitted by
Philippe David*

Spring 1986 session of the Committee on Conventions and Recommendations (124th session of the Executive Board)[1]

Autumn 1986 session of the Committee on Conventions and Recommendations (125th session of the Executive Board)[2]

111. Mrs Hanna Vasylivna Mykhaylenko is described as a librarian at School No. 1 in Odessa. She is alleged to have been suspected of "Ukrainian nationalism". In 1977 legal proceedings were instituted against her but she was pardoned under an amnesty. However, she lost her job. In 1979 she was sentenced to a fine for hooliganism. In February 1980 she was arrested for anti-Soviet agitation and propaganda. She was found to be of unsound mind and sentenced by the court in November to be interned in a psychiatric clinic for an unspecified period.

112. In a letter of 27 July 1986 [...][3] the author of the communication claims that Mrs Mykhaylenko is still detained in conditions that are giving rise to serious concern.

113. The representative of the government concerned informed the Committee that in 1977 Mrs Mykhaylenko, in a fit of incomprehensible behaviour, had ill-treated the pupils at her school. A suit had been brought against her, at the parents' request,

---

* On behalf of the Association des bibliothécaires français.
[1] See document 124 EX/3 PRIV., paras. 101-104 (*supra*, pp. 48-49), communication No. 441/82 concerning *Union of Soviet Socialist Republics*, case of *Vladimir Raiz*.
[2] See document 125 EX/3 PRIV., paras. 111-117; see also documents 125 EX/CR/HR/2 and Add.
[3] See document 125 EX/CR/HR/2 Add.

for assault and battery, but while the proceedings were under way she had been pardoned under an amnesty. Also at the request of the parents and of all the teachers at the school, who were very concerned about Mrs Mykhaylenko's conduct, the Educational Council had decided to dismiss her. However, for humanitarian reasons she had been allowed to take voluntary leave. She had subsequently become a cleaner in a business firm in the town of Odessa. At her new place of work she had continued to behave oddly, insulting and assaulting her colleagues. It was for this reason that she had again been prosecuted: the competent court, in pursuance of Articles 125 and 126 of the Ukrainian Penal Code relating to offences of slander and abuse, had sentenced her to one year of corrective labour. Despite these two prosecutions, she had spread slander about the country's social and political regime by word of mouth and in writing, and it was this which had led to her being prosecuted once more, this time for anti-Soviet propaganda and agitation, an offence covered by Article 62 of the same Penal Code. During the preliminary inquiry, it was observed that she showed obvious signs of mental derangement. The Oblast Court had ordered a psychiatric examination, to be followed, moreover, by a second psychiatric opinion. Found to be of unsound mind, she had not been sentenced, and in December 1980 she had been sent for compulsory medical treatment to an institution providing the most modern forms of treatment. In reply to requests for details by some members of the Committee, the representative of the government concerned pointed out that, in any event, the prosecutions brought against Mrs Mykhaylenko had not been the result of her activities in defence of the Ukrainian language and culture. Such activities were in fact encouraged by the authorities. The representative of the government concerned assured the Committee that since detention in a psychiatric institution was a very sensitive and delicate matter, strict legal provisions existed to protect the individual against arbitrary internment. He added that Mrs Mykhaylenko had every opportunity to seek redress. Answering a question on the state of health of the interested party, he said that according to the latest information in his possession it was satisfactory, but that it was for the competent medical authorities to suggest whether it would be advisable to allow the patient to leave hospital.

114. Several members of the Committee expressed the view that the information provided by the representative of the government concerned was very detailed and that a reading of the communication gave the impression that the author's knowledge of the alleged events was not reliable. As far as they were concerned, this communication was inadmissible.

115. Two members of the Committee, while endorsing this conclusion, felt that it would be advisable to communicate the tenor of the declarations made by the representative of the government concerned to the author, before striking the communication from the Committee's list.

116. In this connection, the Chairperson explained that it would be communicated automatically to the author, together with the notification of the Committee's decision, and that if any new relevant facts came to light he could submit a new communication.

117. After an exchange of views, the Committee *decided* to declare the communication inadmissible, on the grounds that it was ill-founded, under paragraph 14 (*a*) (ii), (iii) and (v) of 104 EX/Decision 3.3.

No. 692/85

Concerning *Union of Soviet Socialist Republics*
Case of *Vladimir Yurevich Poresh*

Communication of 15 July 1985 submitted by
Philippe David*

Spring 1986 session of the Committee on Conventions and Recommendations (124th session of the Executive Board)[1]

Autumn 1986 session of the Committee on Conventions and Recommendations (125th session of the Executive Board)[2]

118. Mr Vladimir Yurevich Poresh is described by the author of the communication as a librarian at the Academy of Sciences in Leningrad. He was reportedly arrested on 1 August 1979 and sentenced on 25 April 1980 to five years' detention in a labour camp and three years' internal exile for the dissemination of false information criticizing the Soviet State and the socialist system and for anti-Soviet agitation and propaganda. On 31 July 1984, he was allegedly charged with "premeditated infringement of the detention regulations" and again sentenced to three years' detention in a labour camp.

119. In a letter dated 27 July 1985 [...],[3] the author of the communication stated that according to various items of "sometimes vague" and unconfirmed information from unofficial sources, the competent Supreme Court had quashed the second sentence. He called for compensation for Mr Poresh and for an inquiry to determine whether Mr Poresh had ben reinstated in his profession and was in a position to enjoy all his civil and political rights.

---

* On behalf of the Association des bibliothécaires français.

[1] See document 124 EX/3 PRIV., paras. 101-104 (*supra*, pp. 48-49), communication No. 441/82 concerning *Union of Soviet Socialist Republics*, case of *Vladimir Raiz*.

[2] See document 125 EX/3 PRIV., paras. 118-121; see also documents 125 EX/CR/HR/2 and Add.

[3] See document 125 EX/CR/HR/2 Add.

No. 692/85 **Union of Soviet Socialist Republics**

120. The representative of the government concerned offered to provide the Committee with detailed information on this case. The Committee members who spoke thanked him for his good will and spirit of co-operation, but considered it obvious that the communication did not meet the conditions of admissibility provided for in paragraph 14 (*a*) of 104 EX/Decision 3.3, and that it did not therefore appear indispensable for him to embark on lengthy explanations. As the author himself acknowledged, he did not have relevant first-hand information, and consequently he had no reliable knowledge of the alleged violations. Furthermore, it was not within the Committee's powers to decide on a matter of damages or to take inquisitorial measures against a government.

121. After an exchange of views, the Committee *decided*:

(i) to thank the government concerned for sending a representative;

(ii) to declare the communication inadmissible under paragraph 14 (*a*) (ii), (iii) and (v) of 104 EX/Decision 3.3.

No. 693/85

Concerning *People's Republic of China*
Case of *Liu Liping*

Communication of 15 July 1985 submitted by
Philippe David*

Spring 1986 session of the Committee on Conventions and Recommendations (124th session of the Executive Board)[1]

70. Mr Liu Liping, described by the author of the communication as a librarian at the Jichu University of Chansha and editor of a journal, is said to have signed a petition calling for the release of an editor of another journal and to have been arrested himself on 22 April 1981.

71. After a brief statement of the facts, the Chairperson read out a letter dated 27 January 1986 which the Permanent Delegate of the People's Republic of China to Unesco had sent to the Director-General [...].[2] In that letter, the Permanent Delegate said that Mr Liu Liping had been, in 1981, the subject of an inquiry and of re-education "on account of acts committed by him which were detrimental to public order", but had resumed his work more than four years before. In his opinion, since the matter had been closed for some considerable time, the communication was clearly without foundation and should be considered inadmissible.

72. In reply to a question, the representative of the government concerned stated that Mr Liu Liping had returned to the post he had previously occupied and was living at his usual place of residence.

73. Considering the case to be settled, the Committee *decided* to strike it from its list.

* On behalf of the Association des bibliothécaires français.
[1] See document 124 EX/3 PRIV., paras. 70-73; see also document 124 EX/CR/HR/3 Add.
[2] See document 124 EX/CR/HR/3 Add.

No. 694/85

Concerning *Union of Soviet Socialist Republics*
Case of *Aleksander Nicolaevich Bogoslovsky*

Communication of 15 July 1985 submitted by
Philippe David*

Spring 1986 session of the Committee on Conventions and Recommendations (124th session of the Executive Board)[1]

Autumn 1986 session of the Committee on Conventions and Recommendations (125th session of the Executive Board)[2]

122. Mr Aleksander Nicolaevich Bogoslovsky is described as a librarian, archivist and bibliographer who has specialized in modern Russian poetry.

123. During two searches carried out at his home, on 4 June and 27 October 1983, the police allegedly confiscated various books and documents. After being summoned on several occasions for questioning to the public prosecutor's office in the Dzerzhinsky district of Moscow, he was finally arrested on 31 May 1984 and prosecuted for the dissemination of wilfully untrue assertions slandering the Soviet State and its social system. He was sentenced in July 1984 to three years in a common regime camp. The Court apparently ordered the destruction of a confiscated bibliographical index which, according to the author of the communication, was the result of 15 years' research work by Mr Bogoslovsky, undertaken at the request of the "Literary Encyclopaedia" and "Literary Heritage Editions".

124. In a letter dated 27 July 1986 [...],[3] Mr Philippe David claims that Mr Bogoslovsky is still in detention and that his state of health is giving rise to concern.

---

* On behalf of the Association des bibliothécaires français.

[1] See document 124 EX/3 PRIV., paras. 101-104 (*supra*, pp. 48-49), communication No. 441/82 concerning *Union of Soviet Socialist Republics*, case of *Vladimir Raiz*.

[2] See document 125 EX/3 PRIV., paras. 122-129; see also documents 125 EX/CR/HR/2 and Add.

No. 694/85 **Union of Soviet Socialist Republics**

125. The representative of the government concerned explained that if Mr Bogoslovsky had been sentenced it was because he had infringed Article 190 of the Penal Code: he had collaborated with various anti-Soviet publishing houses abroad and had prepared and disseminated in the USSR calumnious material damaging to the honour of the country and to the established social order.

126. One Committee member expressed the view that, given the reasons for this sentence, the communication should be declared inadmissible as falling outside Unesco's competence.

127. Some other members of the Committee were of the opinion that not enough background data was yet at their disposal, and that, as the dissemination of written material was involved, there were grounds for supposing the offence to be the expression of opinions.

128. As Mr Bogoslovsky seemed to have served two-thirds of his sentence already, the Chairman wondered whether, on humanitarian grounds, the representative of the government concerned might not intercede with the authorities of his country on behalf of the Committee in order to secure the detainee's early release.

129. The representative of the country concerned having agreed to this request, after an exchange of views, the Committee *decided*:

(i) to thank the government concerned for sending a representative;

(ii) to make a humanitarian appeal to that government through its representative for Mr Aleksander Nicolaevich Bogoslovsky to be granted an early release, considering that he had apparently already served two-thirds of his sentence;

(iii) to resume consideration of this communication at its spring 1987 session.

Spring 1987 session of the Committee on Conventions and Recommendations (126th session of the Executive Board)[4]

142. Mr Aleksander Nicolaevich Bogoslovsky is described as a librarian, archivist and bibliographer who has specialized in modern Russian poetry. During two searches carried out at his home, on 4 June and 27 October 1983, the police alleged-

---

[3] See document 125 EX/CR/HR/2 Add.
[4] See document 126 EX/3 PRIV., paras. 142-147; see also document 126 EX/CR/HR/2.

ly confiscated various books and documents. After being summoned on several occasions for questioning to the public prosecutor' office in the Dzerzhinsky district of Moscow, he was finally arrested on 31 May 1984 and prosecuted for the dissemination of wilfully untrue assertions slandering the Soviet State and its social system. He was sentenced in July 1984 to three years in a common regime camp. The Court apparently ordered the destruction of a confiscated bibliographical index which, according to the author of the communication, was the result of 15 years' research work by Mr Bogoslovsky, undertaken at the request of the "Literary Encyclopaedia" and "Literary Heritage Editions".

143. At the Committee's autumn 1986 session the representative of the government concerned explained that if Mr Bogoslovsky had been sentenced it was because he had infringed Article 190 of the Penal Code: he had collaborated with various anti-Soviet publishing houses abroad and had prepared and disseminated in the USSR calumnious material damaging to the honour of the country and to the established social order.

144. After an exchange of views, the Committee decided to make a humanitarian appeal to the government concerned through its representative for Mr Aleksander Nicolaevich Bogoslovsky to be granted an early release, considering that he had apparently already served two-thirds of his sentence [...].[5]

145. At the Committee's present session, the representative of the government concerned informed the Committee that since its [autumn 1986] session Mr Bogoslovsky had appealed to the Presidium of the Supreme Soviet for a pardon, and in doing so agreed to commit no further crimes in the future. It appeared that his appeal had been given a favourable treatment, the representative said, and Mr Bogoslovsky was now free, though no official confirmation had yet been received.

146. At a subsequent meeting of the Committee the representative announced that he had received confirmation that Mr Bogoslovsky had been freed.

147. In light of this information the Committee *decided*:

(i) to thank the representative of the government concerned for his presence and his co-operation;

(ii) to strike the communication from its list as settled in conformity with paragraph 14 (*a*) (x) of [104 EX/Decision 3.3].

---

[5] See document 125 EX/3 PRIV., para. 129 (ii) (*supra*, p. 606).

No. 695/85

Concerning *Chile*
Case of *Leonardo Cáceres Castro*

Communication of 21 August 1985 submitted by
Leonardo Cáceres Castro

Spring 1986 session of the Committee on Conventions and Recommendations (124th session of the Executive Board)[1]

60. The author of the communication, a journalist of Chilean nationality, reports the following facts concerning himself: he was Director of Information of Radio Magallanes in Chile, the radio station from which President Salvador Allende broadcast his final message to the country shortly before his death. Although no charge was brought against him, a warrant was issued for his arrest and his home searched. He took advantage of the political asylum offered to him by the Argentine Embassy and subsequently left Chile in October 1973. Since 1978, he has repeatedly requested permission to return to his country without obtaining a positive reply. In September 1984 his name was included in a list of 4,942 people forbidden to return to the country. It is reported that on 7 August 1985 the daughter of Mr Leonardo Cáceres Castro submitted a request for a review of his case to the Head of the Confidential Public Order Affairs Department (Departamento Confidencial de Orden Público).

61. The representative of the Chilean Government explained that as soon as this communication was received in December 1985 he had contacted the Chilean Ministry of Interior in Santiago, and had been informed that Mr Leonardo Cáceres Castro was at that time taking the necessary steps to obtain authorization to reside permanently in Chile and that his request was very likely to be granted.

62. After an exchange of views, the Committee *decided*, pending further information, to resume consideration of the admissibility of this communication at its autumn 1986 session.

---

[1] See document 124 EX/3 PRIV., paras. 60-62; see also document 124 EX/CR/HR/3.

No. 695/85 **Chile**

Autumn 1986 session of the Committee on Conventions and Recommendations (125th session of the Executive Board)[2]

35. A journalist of Chilean nationality and former Director of Information of Radio Magallanes in Chile, Mr Cáceres Castro says that a warrant was issued for his arrest, although no charge was brought against him. Taking advantage of the political asylum offered him by the Argentine Embassy, he left Chile in October 1973. Since 1978, he has repeatedly requested authorization to return to his country without obtaining a positive reply. On 7 August 1985, his daughter reportedly submitted a request for a review of his case to the Head of the Confidential Public Order Affairs Department (Departamento Confidencial de Orden Público).

36. Confirming the favourable prospect that he had announced at the Committee's spring 1986 session, the representative of the government concerned declared that Mr Cáceres Castro had obtained satisfaction and was already in Chile.

37. In light of this information, the Committee *decided*:

(i) to thank the government concerned for sending a representative;

(ii) to take note of the information provided by that government's representative and to strike the communication from its list as settled.

[2] See document 125 EX/3 PRIV., paras. 35-37; see also document 125 EX/CR/HR/2.

No. 705/86

Concerning *Chile*
Case of *María Ximena Mora Pozo*

Communication of 24 January 1986 submitted by
María Pozo de Mora

Spring 1986 session of the Committee on Conventions and Recommendations (124th session of the Executive Board)[1]

63. The author of the communication states that her daughter, María Ximena Mora Pozo, of Chilean nationality, a medical auxiliary and psychologist, has not been authorized to return to Chile.

64. She says that in 1973 Mrs María Ximena Pozo, then in her twenties, was employed on completion of her university studies at the Santiago dental school; since her parents did not live in Santiago, she rented a flat and, for financial reasons, sublet two rooms to a couple who had contacts with extreme left-wing groups. The latter, taking advantage of her inexperience, reportedly left a large batch of documents in her care. These were discovered during the events of 1973. The couple had apparently disappeared. It is stated that Mrs María Ximena Mora Pozo was not prosecuted but that she took refuge in the Nicaraguan Embassy and left the country for Finland, where she found the cold climate hard to bear because of a serious congenital kidney ailment. She was pregnant and had a miscarriage there. When she became pregnant again, the doctors apparently advised her to move to a warm country for the safety of the unborn child, and only Cuba was willing to take her in. Her child, which was allegedly abandoned by the father at the age of two, is now eleven. The author of the communication, Mrs Pozo de Mora, says that she herself is 76, that she lost her husband, an airline pilot, in a plane crash, and that her younger son, a doctor, was killed in a road accident four years ago. She would like to end her days with her daughter, whose health is frail, cannot be considered a danger to her country and that she has been sufficiently punished by her 12 years of exile for what was merely a youthful error.

[1] See document 124 EX/3 PRIV., paras. 63-66; see also document 124 EX/CR/HR/3 Add.

No. 705/86 **Chile**

65. The representative of the Chilean Government pointed out that the communication (which had been transmitted to him on 27 March 1986) had reached Santiago when he was already abroad and that he had been unable to deal with the matter. However, while pointing out that the person concerned had waited 12 years before requesting authorization to return to Chile, he felt that the case deserved to be considered from a humanitarian point of view. He added that he would not fail to take the necessary measures as soon as he returned home.

66. Pending further information from the government concerned, the Committee *decided* to postpone consideration of this communication to its autumn 1986 session.

Autumn 1986 session of the Committee on Conventions and Recommendations (125th session of the Executive Board)[2]

38. María Ximena Mora Poza, of Chilean nationality, a medical auxiliary and psychologist, has allegedly not been authorized to return to Chile.

39. In 1973, then in her twenties, she is said to have been employed on completion of her university studies at the Santiago Dental School; since her parents did not live in Santiago, she rented a flat and, for financial reasons, sublet two rooms to a couple who had contacts with extreme left-wing groups. Taking advantage of her inexperience, the couple reportedly left a large batch of documents in her care which were allegedly discovered during the events of 1973. The couple are said to have disappeared. It is stated that María Ximena Mora Pozo was not prosecuted, but that she took refuge in the Nicaraguan Embassy and left the country for Finland. Mrs Pozo de Mora, the author of the communication and mother of the alleged victim, aged 76, says that she would like to end her days with her daughter and her grandson at her side.

40. At the [spring 1986] session, feeling that the case deserved to be considered from a humanitarian point of view, the representative of the government concerned proposed his good offices.

41. At the present session, he stated that a positive solution was in sight and that the Committee could rely on him to notify the Committee as soon as he was informed of it.

42. After an exchange of views, the Committee *decided*:

[2] See document 125 EX/3 PRIV., paras. 38-42; see also document 125 EX/CR/HR/2.

(i) to thank the government concerned for sending a representative;

(ii) to take note of the statement by that government's representative regarding the action he had taken on behalf of María Ximena Mora Pozo and the assurances given by him that a solution was in sight;

(iii) to resume consideration of this communication at its spring 1987 session, with the hope that before then a favourable solution would have been found.

Spring 1987 session of the Committee on Conventions and Recommendations (126th session of the Executive Board)[3]

32. Mrs María Ximena Mora Pozo, a medical auxiliary and psychologist of Chilean nationality, has allegedly been prohibited from returning to her country.

33. Confirming the terms of the letter dated 11 February 1987 from the Permanent Delegation of Chile to Unesco [...],[4] the representative of the government concerned stated that the person concerned had been authorized to return to her country unconditionally and on a permanent basis. He added that persons in this situation who might encounter problems of an administrative nature could apply to an interministerial commission over which he presided, which would give them all the necessary help in overcoming such problems.

34. After an exchange of views, the Committee *decided*:

(i) to thank the representative of the government concerned for his presence and for his co-operation;

(ii) to strike the communication from its list as having been settled, in conformity with paragraph 14 (*a*) (x) of 104 EX/Decision 3.3.

[3] See document 126 EX/3 PRIV., paras. 32-34; see also documents 126 EX/CR/HR/2 and 126 EX/CR/HR/1, annex.
[4] See document 126 EX/CR/HR/1, annex.

No. 706/86

Concerning *Chile*
Case of *Adriana Susana Rondón González*

Communication of 3 February 1986 submitted by
Adriana Susana Rondón González

Spring 1986 session of the Committee on Conventions and Recommendations (124th session of the Executive Board)[1]

67. The author of the communication, a visual arts teacher of Chilean nationality, reports that she was obliged to abandon the teaching post she had held for 14 years and leave Chile on 10 December 1976 with her children in order to accompany her husband, a history teacher, who was expelled on the same date. Since then, she has apparently lived in France as a refugee with her husband and children and is not allowed to return to Chile. On 3 February 1986, as an only daughter and because of the advanced age and failing health of her parents, she sent a letter to the Minister of the Interior asking him to review the ban on her returning to the country or, failing that, to grant her a temporary 90-day permit.

68. The representative of the Chilean Government said that he had been interested in this person's case and had interceded on her behalf with the Ministry of the Interior; he had just been informed by telex that Mrs Adriana Susana Rondón González had been granted authorization to return to Chile unconditionally and permanently and that the Chilean Consulate in Paris had been instructed to hand over her passport as soon as she applied in person; it would therefore be advisable to inform her of the situation.

69. After an exchange of views, the Committee *decided* to declare the case raised by this communication settled in accordance with the terms of paragraph 14 (*a*) (x) of 104 EX/Decision 3.3.

[1] See document 124 EX/3 PRIV., paras. 67-69; see also document 124 EX/CR/HR/3.

No. 712/86

Concerning *Romania*
Case of *Lacrima Cofaru*

Communication of 15 March 1986 submitted by
Yves Lenoir

Autumn 1986 session of the Committee on Conventions and Recommendations (125th session of the Executive Board)[1]

68. Miss Lacrima Cofaru is described as a piano teacher aged 37. She is said to have had a son by the author of the communication. Following the official application for permission to marry, made to the Council of State in Bucharest on 27 October 1982, she is said to have had various administrative sanctions inflicted on her, culminating in her dismissal in September 1985. She is said to have no means of subsistence at present and to be unable either to practice her art or to participate in the cultural life of her country.

69. In a letter dated 16 July 1986 [...],[2] the Permanent Delegate of Romania to Unesco stated that the competent authorities in his country had given their approval for Miss Lacrima Cofaru's marriage to Mr Yves Lenoir.

70. One member of the Committee wondered whether Miss Cofaru intended to leave Romania or to stay there. If she opted to stay, the problem was not settled because the Committee's main concern was not so much her marriage as her professional situation. He believed, however, that in marrying a foreigner she would lose her original nationality and could therefore emigrate. Another member of the Committee said that marriage did not fall within the Committee's field of competence. A third member said that he supported this point of view and considered that the case had been settled. He suggested asking the author of the communication about the professional prospects of the person concerned.

---

[1] See document 125 EX/3 PRIV., paras. 68-71; see also documents 125 EX/CR/HR/3 and Add.
[2] See document 125 EX/CR/HR/3 Add.

No. 712/86 **Romania**

71. At the end of the discussion, the Committee *decided*:

(i) to request additional information both from the government concerned and from the author of the communication;

(ii) to resume consideration of the matter at its spring 1987 session.

Spring 1987 session of the Committee on Conventions and Recommendations (126th session of the Executive Board)[3]

83. Mrs Lacrima Cofaru, a piano teacher, is said to have had various administrative sanctions inflicted on her, culminating in her dismissal in September 1985, following the application she made to the Council of State in Bucharest for permission to marry.

84. At the Committee's [autumn 1986] session the Romanian Government had told the Committee that it had given its approval for Miss Lacrima Cofaru's marriage to Mr Yves Lenoir.

85. In a letter dated 23 April 1987 Mr Lenoir stated that since his marriage he was finding it extremely difficult to obtain permission for his wife and son to join him in Brussels. He referred to threats against him and his wife. He also mentioned a letter from his wife informing him that she had withdrawn her request for a passport, which was incomprehensible to him. He hoped that if it was impossible for her and her son to leave Romania she could at least regain her position of piano teacher at the Cluj Conservatoire and exercise her profession freely in order to be able to support her son.

86. In a letter dated 5 May 1987 the Permanent Delegate to Unesco of Romania made it known that Mrs Cofaru, who was living at Cluj-Napoca, had not applied to leave the country and that she had explained to the Romanian authorities that she had had words with her husband in the autumn of 1986 about her child, who was of a previous marriage. He added that she had invited Mr Lenoir, in a succession of letters, to come to Romania to clarify the family situation. He also stated that once the couple had settled their personal problems and Mrs Cofaru had requested permission to join her husband abroad the Romanian authorities would immediately give her a passport. He stated that, in any case, for the moment Mrs Cofaru had expressed her preference that her husband join her in Romania and settle there.

[3] See document 126 EX/3 PRIV., paras. 83-90; see also document 126 EX/CR/HR/2.

Romania **No. 712/86**

87. Some members of the Committee considered that the doubts they had had concerning the Committee's competence in this matter had been strengthened by the letter from the author of the communication itself. In their opinion, it was in fact a private matter that should be solved through usual channels within the country concerned: the problems posed by children of a former marriage constituted a private matter for husband and wife, and the question of Mrs Cofaru's work fell under Romania's internal jurisdiction. These members were of the opinion that the Committee should confine its attention to the purpose and aim given in part V of the communication form: the author was requesting both the opportunity to be married to Mrs Cofaru and bring his family to France and, contradicting himself, that she be allowed to exercise her profession and to participate in the cultural life of her country. They thought that France and Romania should therefore be left to solve this problem at bilateral level and that the parties concerned should resort to remedies not yet used or exhausted.

88. Several other members of the Committee, while recognizing that the problem of marriage and of paternity of children was outside the competence of the Committee, considered that the question of Mrs Cofaru's employment, on the other hand was relevant, since it concerned the dismissal of a person exercising a profession that fell within Unesco's fields of competence. Most of these members wished without prejudicing the Committee's final decision, to obtain purely factual additional information from the government concerned, in particular to do with the information contained in the letter from the Permanent Delegate of Romania, Mrs Cofaru's employment possibilities, the domestic remedies to which she could have recourse should an administrative decision prevent her from exercising her profession, and the choice she wished to make, namely either leaving her country or staying there and being allowed to work as a musician.

89. In this respect a member remarked that the burden of proof should not be transposed and that it was for the author of the communication first to prove that it was because she had married a foreigner that Mrs Cofaru was not being allowed to work and, secondly, to specify his intentions and those of his wife.

90. Having discussed the communication the Committee *decided*:

(i) to take note of the information received from the author of the communication and the government concerned;

(ii) to transmit to the author of the communication the information provided by that government;

(iii) to ask the government concerned if it could supplement the information contained in the letter dated 5 May 1987 and, in particular, comment on the allegation by the author of the communication that Mrs Cofaru could not work in her profession because she was married to a Frenchman;

(iv) to request the author of the communication to state whether Mrs Cofaru wished to join him abroad or stay in her country;

(v) to request the author of the communication, should Mrs Cofaru wish to remain in her country and be unable to get her job back, to see that she take advantage of all available means of recourse in order to find work as a musician in the public or private sector;

(vi) to resume consideration of this communication at its autumn 1987 session.

Autumn 1987 session of the Committee on Conventions and Recommendations (127th session of the Executive Board)[4]

94. Mrs Lacrima Cofaru, a piano teacher, is said to have had various administrative sanctions inflicted on her, culminating in her dismissal in September 1985, following the application she made for permission to marry.

95. At previous sessions, the Government of Romania informed the Committee by letter that the marriage of Mrs Cofaru and Mr Lenoir had been authorized, that Mrs Cofaru had not applied to leave the country, that she had had words with her husband about a child of a previous marriage, that she had expressed the desire that her husband should join her in Romania and settle there, and that in any case when she requested permission to join Mr Lenoir abroad, once the personal problems had been settled, the Romanian authorities would immediately issue her a passport.

96. Under cover of a letter dated 6 September 1987, Mr Lenoir produced a copy of a declaration of paternity dated 29 July 1985 and a copy of a telegram from Mrs Cofaru, dated 6 November 1986, announcing that she had undertaken the necessary formalities with a view to obtaining a passport from the Romanian authorities. He also stated that he had proposed that his wife and son come to a Western country or to Hungary to meet him, but that he had received no reply. Referring to a question that the Committee had asked at its spring 1987 session, he indicated that to the best of his knowledge there was no artistic private sector in Romania. He further repeated

---

[4] See document 127 EX/3 PRIV., paras. 94-101; see also document 127 EX/CR/HR/2.

his request that Mrs Cofaru should regain her position at the Conservatoire where she worked and be compensated for the prejudice suffered.

97. Since this letter from the author of the communication was received only belatedly by the Secretariat, it could not be transmitted to the Permanent Delegation of Romania until 14 September 1987.

98. Some members of the Committee expressed their perplexity regarding the admissibility of the communication. In their view, it was a purely private matter between a man, a woman and a child and not an affair involving violation of human rights in Unesco's fields of competence.

99. Other members considered that the information so far available was inadequate for the Committee to reach a decision in full knowledge of the facts. They felt it preferable to defer examination of the communication until the next session.

100. In this respect, some members of the Committee observed that the interval between the receipt of Mr Lenoir's letter by the Permanent Delegation of Romania and the consideration of the communication by the Committee was too short to enable the government concerned to react in time.

101. After an exchange of views, the Committee *decided* to defer consideration of this communication until its spring 1988 session pending further information.

Spring 1988 session of the Committee on Conventions and Recommendations (129th session of the Executive Board)[5]

87. According to the author of the communication, Mrs Lacrima Cofaru, his wife, was dismissed from her post as piano teacher in 1985, following her application for permission to marry. He alleges that she was unable to travel with her child to join him in Brussels.

88. In a letter dated 16 May 1988, the Permanent Delegation of the Socialist Republic of Romania to Unesco informed the Committee that the Romanian authorities had approved Mrs Lacrima Cofaru's application to leave the country permanently in order to join her husband.

89. It was understood that if Mrs Lacrima Cofaru was in fact unable to rejoin her husband it would still be open to him to submit a new communication.

[5] See document 129 EX/3 PRIV., paras. 87-90; see also document 129 EX/CR/HR/2.

No. 712/86 **Romania**

90. Following an exchange of views, the Committee *decided*:

(i) to note with satisfaction the happy outcome of this case;

(ii) to strike this communication from its list as settled in conformity with paragraph 14 (*a*) (x) of 104 EX/Decision 3.3.

No. 719/86

Concerning *Italy*
Case of *Giulia Arena*

Communication of 19 September 1985 submitted by
Giulia Arena

Autumn 1986 session of the Committee on Conventions and Recommendations (125th session of the Executive Board)[1]

52. The author of the communication introduces herself as a music teacher. According to her, the Italian authorities excluded her from teaching in 1955, thus depriving her of her means of subsistence. The Council of State decided in her favour in 1959 in a court case which she brought against the government authorities, ruling that the authorities should reinstate her in the teaching service and also pay her the salary due to her since 1955. To date, this decision has apparently not been implemented by the administration in spite of various types of action she has ceaselessly taken to maintain her rights as regards negative prescription. Mrs Giulia Arena believes that in this case, the Italian authorities have violated her right to teach and to participate freely in the cultural life of her country, her right to freedom of thought and conscience and her right to defend the moral and cultural interests of Italy and of young people.

53. The Chairperson drew the attention of the Committee to the fact that, according to the author's own declaration, she had as far back as in 1959 obtained a ruling that the competent authorities should reinstate her in the teaching service and also pay her the salary due to her since 1955. The Chairperson added that this judicial decision had allegedly not been implemented by the competent authorities. She further underlined the fact that, still according to the alleged victim who is also the author of the communication, she had submitted her case to the United Nations Human Rights Committee in 1984 but that the Committee declared it inadmissible on the grounds that it did not raise legal questions coming under the International Convenant on Civil and Political Rights.

---

[1] See document 125 EX/3 PRIV., paras. 52-55; see also document 125 EX/CR/HR/3.

No. 719/86 **Italy**

54. In his statement before the Committee, the representative of the government concerned queried whether a complaint that had been declared inadmissible by the United Nations Human Rights Committee could be considered admissible by the Committee on Conventions and Recommendations in the absence of any new and important material facts. He contended that, in any event, the latter Committee should also declare the communication inadmissible since the allegations concerned matters which arose more than a quarter of a century ago. The Chairperson concurred with this point of view.

55. Taking note of the views expressed by the representative of the government concerned as well as those of the Chairperson, the Committee *decided*:

(i) to thank the government concerned for sending a representative;

(ii) to declare the communication inadmissible on the grounds that it was not submitted within a reasonable time-limit following the facts which constituted its subject matter or within a reasonable time after the facts had become known.

No. 720/86

Concerning *Union of Soviet Socialist Republics*
Case of *Yosif Z. Begun*

Communication of 4 June 1986 submitted by
Laurent Schwartz*

Autumn 1986 session of the Committee on Conventions and Recommendations (125th session of the Executive Board)[1]

130. In view of their late submission,[2] and at the request of the representative of the government concerned, who had not had the opportunity to examine them, the Committee *decided* to defer consideration of these communications to its spring 1987 session.

Spring 1987 session of the Committee on Conventions and Recommendations (126th session of the Executive Board)[3]

* On behalf of the Yosif Begun Committee.
[1] See document 125 EX/3 PRIV., para. 130; see also document 125 EX/CR/HR/3 Add.2.
[2] Communications No. 720/86 concerning *Union of Soviet Socialist Republics*, case of *Yosif Z. Begun*, No. 721/86 concerning *Union of Soviet Socialist Republics*, case of *Roald Zelichonok*, No. 725/86 concerning *Union of Soviet Socialist Republics*, case of *Leonid Volvovski*, and No. 726/86 concerning *Union of Soviet Socialist Republics*, case of *Vladimir Lifshits*.
[3] See document 126 EX/3 PRIV., paras. 106-116 (*supra*, pp. 296-299), communication No. 536/83 concerning *Union of Soviet Socialist Republics*, case of *Yosif Z. Begun*.

No. 721/86

Concerning *Union of Soviet Socialist Republics*
Case of *Roald Zelichonok*

Communication of 30 June 1986 submitted by
André Lwoff*

Autumn 1986 session of the Committee on Conventions and Recommendations (125th session of the Executive Board)[1]

Spring 1987 session of the Committee on Conventions and Recommendations (126th session of the Executive Board)[2]

148. Mr Roald Zelichonok, who is described as an informatics specialist and doctor of technology, reportedly worked at the Institute of Cytology of the USSR Academy of Sciences. It is said that he submitted an application to emigrate to Israel in 1978 but was refused an exit visa on the grounds that he was in possession of secrets. These grounds were later changed to "insufficient family ties". His apartment was subsequently searched, his salary frozen and his professional contacts with colleagues restricted. In 1980, he was prohibited by the police from teaching Hebrew, which he did on an unpaid basis. In April 1984, he was forced to resign from his post. In 1985, his mail was intercepted on several occasions; he was then arrested and sentenced in August to three years in a camp for "slandering the Soviet State".

149. The representative of the government concerned informed the Committee that Mr Zelichonok had been sentenced by a Leningrad court to three years' imprisonment in 1985. He was accused of a long list of criminal offences, of which the main offences had been proven on the basis of voluminous evidence. The representative went on to inform the Committee that on 12 March 1987, Mr Zelichonok had been pardoned and released. He was now out of prison and his activities were not re-

* Assisted by Michèle Valensi-Lubineau.
[1] See document 125 EX/3 PRIV., para. 130 (*supra*, p. 625), communication No. 720/86 concerning *Union of Soviet Socialist Republics*, case of *Yosif Z. Begun*.
[2] See document 126 EX/3 PRIV., paras. 148-152; see also document 126 EX/CR/HR/2.

stricted in any way. As a consequence, the representative said, it would be appropriate to strike the case from the Committee's list.

150. A member of the Committee indicated that Mr Zelichonok, according to the communication, had been prohibited from teaching Hebrew by the police in 1980. The Committee member raised the question as to whether this police prohibition of 1980 was still in force or whether it had been dropped.

151. The representative of the government concerned replied that there did not appear to be any practical issue raised by this question. It seemed unlikely that the police would make such a prohibition since it was not within their power to do so. In any event Mr Zelichonok was now free to undertake whatever activity he wished as long as it was not illegal. Mr Zelichonok in asking for his release had pledged not to undertake any further illegal activities.

152. The Committee thereupon *decided*:

(i) to thank the representative of the government concerned for his presence and his co-operation;

(ii) to strike the communication from its list as settled in conformity with paragraph 14 (*a*) (x) of [104 EX/Decision3.3].

No. 722/86

Concerning *Chile*
Case of *José Luis Rojas Valencia*

Communication of 14 June 1986 submitted by
Gloria Irma Miranda Torrejón

Autumn 1986 session of the Committee on Conventions and Recommendations (125th session of the Executive Board)[1]

43. Mr José Luis Rojas Valencia, a pediatrician, is said to have been in exile in Finland since 1973. In 1984 the Supreme Court of Chile, during *amparo* proceedings, is reported to have ordered the annulment of the decree prohibiting him from returning to the country; but the government is said to have issued a new decree which had the effect of maintaining the prohibition. It is said that Mr Rojas was subsequently authorized to return to Chile but that this authorization was withdrawn in April 1985. Following an operation, he is said to have become hemiplegic and aphasic and could no longer write. His doctors reportedly consider that his return to Chile could contribute to a relative improvement in his state of health.

44. The representative of the government concerned stated that this communication had only just come to his attention on his arrival in Paris. Considering that Mr Rojas's case deserved humanitarian treatment, he undertook to make the appropriate representations to authorities of his country.

45. After an exchange of views, the Committee *decided*:

(i) to thank the government concerned for sending a representative;

(ii) to defer consideration of this communication to its spring 1987 session, pending information from that government and to request the Secretariat to recommend to the author that he get in touch with that government's representative or its appropriate services.

---

[1] See document 125 EX/3 PRIV., paras. 43-45; see also document 125 EX/CR/HR/3 Add.2.

No. 722/86 **Chile**

Spring 1987 session of the Committee on Conventions and Recommendations (126th session of the Executive Board)[2]

35. Mr José Luis Rojas Valencia, a pediatrician of Chilean nationality, who is said now to be hemiplegic and aphasic, has allegedly been prohibited from returning to his country.

36. Confirming the terms of the letter dated 11 February 1987 from the Permanent Delegation of Chile to Unesco [...],[3] the representative of the government concerned stated that the person concerned had been authorized to return to his country unconditionally and on a permanent basis. He added that persons in this situation who encountered problems of an administrative nature could apply to an interministerial commission over which he presided which would give them all the necessary help in overcoming such problems.

37. After an exchange of views, the Committee *decided*:

(i) to thank the representative of the government concerned for his presence and for his co-operation;

(ii) to strike the communication from its list as having been settled, in conformity with paragraph 14 (*a*) (x) of 104 EX/Decision 3.3.

---

[2] See document 126 EX/3 PRIV., paras. 35-37; see also documents 126 EX/CR/HR/2 and Add.2 and 126 EX/CR/HR/1, annex.
[3] See document 126 EX/CR/HR/1, annex.

No. 725/86

Concerning *Union of Soviet Socialist Republics*
Case of *Leonid Volvovski*

Communication of 30 June 1986 submitted by
Henri Cartan*

Autumn 1986 session of the Committee on Conventions and Recommendations (125th session of the Executive Board)[1]

Spring 1987 session of the Committee on Conventions and Recommendations (126th session of the Executive Board)[2]

153. Mr Leonid Volvovski is described as a computer engineer. He is stated to have worked from 1965 to 1968 as a researcher at Gorki University, from 1968 to 1970 as a chief engineer in Krasnoyarsk, and subsequently as a researcher at the Gas and Petroleum Research Institute of Moscow. In 1973 he applied to emigrate to Israel. In 1974 he lost his employment, and worked as a lift attendant and as a refuse collector. In October 1976 he was sentenced to 15 days' imprisonment for attempting to submit a letter to the Presidium of the Supreme Soviet. In November 1976, as he was taking part in the preparation of a symposium on Jewish culture, his apartment was searched. In March 1978 the authorities forced him to stop giving Hebrew lessons. In September 1979 his books, cassettes and records of Hebrew disappeared after a house search. In February 1980 he was forced by the police to go back and live in Gorki against his will. In April 1980 he was imprisoned without any reason for three weeks. In June 1983, on the occasion of a new search, the authorities confiscated all his textbooks of Hebrew and religion. In May 1984 the police ordered him to stop giving Bible lessons at home. In June 1985, after a further search and seizure of Hebrew and religious material, he was arrested. He was finally sentenced in October 1985 to three years in a camp.

---

* Assisted by Michèle Valensi-Lubineau.

[1] See document 125 EX/3 PRIV., para. 130 (*supra*, p. 625), communication No. 720/86 concerning *Union of Soviet Socialist Republics*, case of *Yosif Z. Begun*.

[2] See document 126 EX/3 PRIV., paras. 153-156; see also document 126 EX/CR/HR/2.

No. 725/86 **Union of Soviet Socialist Republics**

154. The representative of the government concerned informed the Committee that Mr Volvovski had been tried and sentenced to a prison term of three years in 1985 and that he had recently requested a pardon, pledging himself at the same time to not commit further crimes.

155. The Presidium of the Supreme Soviet had pardoned Mr Volvovski on 12 March 1987 and he had been released.

156. The Committee consequently *decided*:

(i) to thank the representative of the government concerned for his presence and his co-operation;

(ii) to strike the communication from its list as settled in conformity with paragraph 14 (*a*) (x) of [104 EX/Decision 3.3].

No. 726/86

Concerning *Union of Soviet Socialist Republics*
Case of *Vladimir Lifshits*

Communication of 30 June 1986 submitted by
Henri Cartan*

Autumn 1986 session of the Committee on Conventions and Recommendations (125th session of the Executive Board)[1]

Spring 1987 session of the Committee on Conventions and Recommendations (126th session of the Executive Board)[2]

157. Mr Vladimir Lifshits is described as a mathematician/analyst. He is said to have made an application to emigrate to Israel in 1981, but was reportedly refused the exit visa on the grounds of "insufficient family ties". He was subsequently forced to leave his post as head of the Economic Forecast Department at the Soviet Jewellery Industry Research Institute and to become an industrial air-conditioning installer. In December 1982, following a second request to emigrate, he was forced to give up even that job. In order to earn a living he did translation work and gave private mathematics lessons. In June 1985 his house was searched and a large number of books confiscated. In July 1985 he was detained for 24 hours for having telephoned a foreign friend. Several registered letters addressed by him to acquaintances abroad were intercepted; some were read and handed over to the police. He was arrested on 8 January 1986 and sentenced on 19 March to three years in a camp for "slandering the Soviet State". During his trial he was not allowed to conduct his defence in accordance with the normal procedure.

158. The representative of the government concerned informed the Committee that, in order to save time he would not address the substance of the communication but

* Assisted by Michèle Valensi-Lubineau.

[1] See document 125 EX/3 PRIV., para. 130 (*supra*, p. 625), communication No. 720/86 concerning *Union of Soviet Socialist Republics*, case of *Yosif Z. Begun*.

[2] See document 126 EX/3 PRIV., paras. 157-160; see also document 126 EX/CR/HR/2.

that did not mean that the allegations therein were not denied. Mr Lifshits had requested a pardon, pledging not to undertake any further criminal activities and had been pardoned on 12 March 1987.

159. According to information available, the representative said, Mr Lifshits had not, since his release, requested permission to emigrate from the country.

160. The Committee *decided*:

(i) to thank the representative of the government concerned for his presence and his co-operation;

(ii) to strike the communication from its list as settled in conformity with paragraph 14 (*a*) (x) of [104 EX/Decision 3.3].

No. 728/86

Concerning *Union of Soviet Socialist Republics*
Case of *Yuli Edelshtein*

Communication of 21 July 1986 submitted by
Michel A. Calvo*

Spring 1987 session of the Committee on Conventions and Recommendations (126th session of the Executive Board)[1]

161. Mr Edelshtein is described as a teacher of English, aged 28, who is also said to have engaged in the teaching of Hebrew and Jewish history. The Soviet authorities are claimed to have requested him on several occasions to cease such teaching. On 24 August 1984, when a search was allegedly made of his home, during which all his Hebrew books are claimed to have been seized, the police reportedly discovered there 1,006 grams of marijuana and 8 grams of opium powder which, according to the alleged victim, had not been there before. According to the authors of the communication, the Soviet press states it to be impossible to obtain drugs in the USSR, since apparently no one feels the need for them. It is claimed that Mr Edelshtein himself has shown no sign of dependence on such substances. He was reportedly arrested on 3 September 1984. Although he protested his innocence, he is stated to have been sentenced to three years' imprisonment. A recording is said to have been made of his trial. A version reputed to be a transcript of the trial, translated into French, is included in the file. The Secretariat is holding it at the disposal of members of the Committee. According to that document, Mr Edelshtein's lawyer drew the attention of the court to several irregularities in the search operation and thus demonstrated that the investigator and the witnesses could not state with certainty where the seized drugs were alleged to have been found. At the Vydrino camp where he is said to be detained, Mr Edelshtein is reported to have been a victim of a very serious industrial injury, suffering multiple fractures and lesions; it is claimed that he is now an invalid and must even undergo a surgical operation on the urethra.

* On behalf of André Lwoff, Henri Cartan, Laurent Schwartz, David Ruzié and Paul Kessler.
[1] See document 126 EX/3 PRIV., paras. 161-169; see also document 126 EX/CR/HR/3.

No. 728/86 **Union of Soviet Socialist Republics**

162. The representative of the government concerned informed the Committee that Mr Edelshtein had been sentenced to prison by the Moscow Municipal Court. Narcotic substances had been found in Mr Edelshtein's apartment, substances which were proven by the police to be illegal. The authors' communication, he said, was inaccurate and not in accordance with the facts.

163. The representative went on to explain that the Deputy Attorney-General had contested the Court's sentence on the grounds that it was excessively severe. As a result the Court decided to lighten the sentence, taking into account Mr Edelshtein's youth and his lack of previous convictions. He was apparently released on 4 May 1987. Official confirmation would no doubt soon be received, the representative said.

164. A member of the Committee asked whether any information was available concerning Mr Edelshtein's medical condition and whether his problems were receiving proper treatment.

165. The representative replied that there were no indications to the effect that he was in particularly poor health. In any event, he said, now that Mr Edelshtein had been released he could seek any medical treatment he might want.

166. Another member of the Committee stated that it was a fact that police officers sometimes planted evidence to falsely incriminate a victim. Such abuses had occurred in the speaker's country and in many other countries and the possibility of such an act should not be excluded in this case. It seemed unlikely that Mr Edelshtein would keep drugs in his apartment, knowing that it was regularly searched by the police.

167. The representative of the government concerned agreed that abuses by the police, or even by other authorities, could sometimes occur, and that that possibility had been taken into account in this case. An investigation had been carried out by higher authorities and it had been found that no abuses of power had taken place.

168. At a subsequent meeting of the Committee the representative announced that he had received confirmation that Mr Edelshtein was now free.

169. The Committee then *decided*:

(i) to thank the representative of the government concerned for his presence and his co-operation;

(ii) to strike the communication from its list as settled in conformity with paragraph 14 (*a*) (x) of [104 EX/Decision 3.3].

No. 729/86

Concerning *Union of Soviet Socialist Republics*
Case of *Alexis Magarik*

Communication of 21 July 1986 submitted by
Michel A. Calvo*

Spring 1987 session of the Committee on Conventions and Recommendations (126th session of the Executive Board)[1]

170. Mr Alexis Magarik, a 28 year-old musician, is also said to have engaged in the teaching of Hebrew. It is reported that the Soviet authorities requested him to cease such teaching and his activities as a celloist in an orchestra specializing in the folk music of the Jews of Eastern Europe. Apparently, on 14 March 1986, in Tbilisi, when he was preparing to board the plane to return to Moscow in the company of a friend, an inspector discovered in one of his two travelling bags a cigarette packet full of drugs which, according to the authors of the communication, had not been there before. Again according to the authors of the communication, the Soviet press states it to be impossible to obtain drugs in the USSR and hence, so it would seem, the celloist would have been unable to purchase or sell drugs, since apparently no one feels the need for them. Reportedly, the alleged victim himself has shown no sign of dependence on the substance in question. It is alleged that an investigator suggested to him that he say that it was his friends who had placed it in his luggage, but that he refused to comply. Tried on 6 June 1986, Mr Magarik is said to have been sentenced to three years' detention in a camp, despite his protestations of innocence.

171. The representative of the government concerned informed the Committee that Mr Magarik had been sentenced on 9 June 1986 by a Tbilisi court to three years' imprisonment. On 10 July 1986 his sentence had been confirmed by a higher court. It had been shown that during a verification of Mr Magarik's luggage at the Tbilisi airport a cigarette packet full of drugs had been discovered.

---

* On behalf of André Lwoff, Henri Cartan, Laurent Schwartz, David Ruzié and Paul Kessler.

[1] See document 126 EX/3 PRIV., paras. 170-173; see also document 126 EX/CR/HR/3.

172. A further search was conducted at Mr Magarik's residence and other drugs were found. The representative pointed out that there had been numerous corroborating witnesses at the trial. At the airport Mr Magarik had told officials that the substance found in the cigarette packet was tobacco which he was taking to his wife. The fact that Mr Magarik made this comment suggested that he was trying to mislead the officials, the representative said. He went on to inform the Committee that the Deputy Attorney-General of the Soviet Union had protested the harshness of the sentence, especially in view of the fact that Mr Magarik was the father of a young child and had no previous criminal record. This protest had been heeded and Mr Magarik should shortly be released.

173. At the close of its discussion the Committee *decided*:

(i) to thank the representative of the government concerned for his presence and his co-operation;

(ii) to ask the Secretariat *ipso facto* to strike the communication from the Committee's list as settled in conformity with paragraph 14 (*a*) (x) of [104 EX/Decision 3.3] once the Secretariat had received official confirmation of Mr Magarik's pardon.

Autumn 1987 session of the Committee on Conventions and Recommendations (127th session of the Executive Board)[2]

111. Mr Alexis Magarik, a musician, is said to have been sentenced in June 1986 to three years' detention in a camp for drugs possession. He is reported to have protested his innocence.

112. At its spring 1987 session, the Committee was informed that Mr Magarik had been found guilty on the strength of evidence and corroborating testimonies, and that the sentence of the Tbilisi court had been confirmed by a higher court on 10 July 1986. It was also informed that a protest had been lodged with the competent court against the harshness of the sentence, in view of the fact that Mr Magarik had a young dependent child, and that he was a first offender.

113. At the present session, the representative of the government concerned stated that the above-mentioned protest had been taken into consideration and the Mr Magarik's sentence had been commuted to one of 18 months' imprisonment. Released on 14 September 1987, he had returned to his home.

---

[2] See document 127 EX/3 PRIV., paras. 111-114; see also document 127 EX/CR/HR/2.

Union of Soviet Socialist Republics **No. 729/86**

114. After an exchange of views, the Committee *decided*:

(i) to thank the representative of the government concerned for his presence and his co-operation;

(ii) to strike the communication from its list as settled in conformity with paragraph 14 (*a*) (x) of 104 EX/Decision 3.3.

No. 730/86

Concerning *Republic of Korea*
Case of *Song Ki Won* et al.*

Communication of 29 March 1986 submitted by
The International Human Rights Law Group

Spring 1987 session of the Committee on Conventions and Recommendations (126th session of the Executive Board)[1]

78. The Ministry of Education of the Republic of Korea is said to have ordered several public and private schools, on 5 August 1985, to dismiss 21 teachers who had allegedly either participated in a symposium on education or contributed articles for publication in the journal *MinJoong Education*. It accused them of wanting to bring about the violent destruction of the social system by their criticisms and of negating the values of liberal democracy and the national education system. According to the author of the communication, the articles in question merely discussed the limitations and flaws of that system with a view to improving it.

79. Allegedly, on 23 August 1985 the Shilchun Literary Company, a publishing firm that handled the above-mentioned journal among others, had its licence revoked.

80. Mr Song Ki Won, the editor of *MinJoong Education*, and two teachers, Mr Yoon Jae Chul and Mr Kim Jin Kyung, who were allegedly arrested on 11 August 1985 and detained for nine days, were said to have been sentenced on 8 February 1986, the first two to one year's imprisonment and the third to one and a half year's imprisonment.

81. Confirming the information contained in the letter dated 12 August 1986 from the International Human Rights Law Group, the representative of the government concerned informed the Committee that Mr Song Ki Won and Mr Yoon Jae Chul

---

* Case of *Song Ki Won, Yoon Jae Chul, Kim Jin Kyung and 16 other teachers*. From the Committee's autumn 1987 session, this communication was being referred to as case of *Dismissal of teachers and withdrawal of the Shilchun Literary Company's publishing licence*.

[1] See document 126 EX/3 PRIV., paras. 78-82; see also document 126 EX/CR/HR/3.

had been released in June 1986 and Mr Kim Jin Kyung in October 1986. He added that the author of the communication had obtained a complete report on this matter from the authorities of his country, that since then it had been considered closed and that the persons involved had infringed the law on national security and had received a fair trial. He did not, however, have any information concerning the dismissal of the teachers [and] the withdrawal of the Shilchun Literary Company's publishing licence. He promised to take the necessary steps to obtain details from his government for the next session of the Committee.

82. After an exchange of views the Committee *decided*:

(i) to thank the representative of the government concerned for attending the session and for his co-operation;

(ii) to take note of the release of Mr Song Ki Won, Mr Yoon Jae Chul and Mr Kim Jin Kyung and to delete those cases, in accordance with paragraph 14 (*a*) (x) of 104 EX/Decision 3.3;

(iii) to request the government concerned to provide additional information on the dismissal of the teachers and the withdrawal of the Shilchun Literary Company's publishing licence;

(iv) to resume consideration of this communication at its autumn 1987 session.

Autumn 1987 session of the Committee on Conventions and Recommendations (127th session of the Executive Board)[2]

84. According to the author of the communication, the Ministry of Education of the Republic of Korea is said to have ordered several public and private schools, on 5 August 1985, to dismiss 21 teachers who had allegedly either participated in a symposium on education or contributed articles for publication in the journal *MinJoong Education*. It accused them of wanting to bring about the violent destruction of the social system by their criticisms and of negating the values of liberal democracy and the national education system.

85. The Shilchun Literary Company, a publishing firm that handled the above-mentioned journal among others, allegedly had its licence revoked on 23 August 1985.

[2] See document 127 EX/3 PRIV., paras. 84-89; see also document 127 EX/CR/HR/2.

Republic of Korea **No. 730/86**

86. At its spring 1987 session, the Committee was informed of the release of the editor of the journal *MinJoong Education* and of two teachers who had been arrested and detained. Information was still required regarding the problem of the dismissal of the teachers and of the withdrawal of the Shilchun Literary Company's publishing licence.[3]

87. During the present session, the representative of the government concerned stated that the teachers could return to their schools in accordance with established procedure if they so wished. According to the information at his disposal, three of the 30 teachers dismissed (the list supplied by the International Human Rights Law Group contained only 19 names) were now teaching in the same school as before (including Mr Kim Jong Man, No. 19 on the list); two were working as teachers in private schools (Mr Hong Sun Woong and Mr Song Dae Hyun, Nos. 9 and 11 on the list), four were working as writers (Mr Yoon Jae Chul, Mr Kim Jin Kyung, Mr Goh Gwang Hyun and Mr Chao Jae Do, Nos. 1, 2, 8 and 10 on the list) and three were in business (Mr Lee Soon Gwan and Mr Lee Chul Guk, Nos. 4 and 6 on the list); the others were in other forms of employment.

88. Replying to requests for details, the representative of the government concerned explained that, under current legislation, the Shilchun Literary Company had infringed the law governing the registration of publishing companies. He added that this law was the subject of controversy at the present time and that discussions were being conducted in political circles with a view to its revision. With particular reference to the withdrawal of the publishing licence of the Shilchun Literary Company, he stated that the editor had taken legal action and that a decision was awaited. He also informed the Committee that, since 1 July 1987, the Government of the Republic of Korea had taken a number of measures aimed at democratizing all aspects of the country's life and at reforming controversial legislation including the Constitution itself. He was sure that all the cases which were the subject of complaints would be gradually settled and asked the Committee to bear this situation in mind when examining the communication.

89. After an exchange of views, the Committee *decided*:

(i) to thank the representative of the government concerned for attending the session and for his co-operation;

(ii) to take note of the information which he had provided;

---

[3] See document 126 EX/3 PRIV., para. 82 (iii) (*supra*, p. 644).

(iii) to request the government concerned to provide additional information on the position of the other teachers whose names appeared on the communication list and regarding whom he had not provided the information requested, and also on the state of the legal proceedings initiated by the publishing company;

(iv) to resume consideration of this communication at its spring 1988 session.

Spring 1988 session of the Committee on Conventions and Recommendations (129th session of the Executive Board)[4]

80. According to the author of the communication, the Ministry of Education of the Republic of Korea is said to have ordered several public and private schools, on 5 August 1985, to dismiss 21 teachers (the author's list attached to the communication contains only 19 names) on the grounds of their having allegedly criticized the social system of the country and the government's education policy, particularly in their articles published in the journal *MinJoong Education*. The Shilchun Literary Company which published this journal is reported to have had its licence withdrawn.

81. Taking the floor, the representative of the government concerned informed the Committee that the publishing firm in question had had its publishing licence restored on 23 March 1988. Adding to the information which he had supplied to the Committee at its [autumn 1987] session concerning the dismissed teachers, some of whom had resumed their posts or had found other jobs, he produced a list indicating that:

seven teachers had found employment in schools. These were: Mr Kim Jong-Man, Mr Hong Sun Woong, Mr Song Dae-Hyun, Mr Shim Im-Sup, Mr Shim Sung-Bo, Mr Goh Gwang-Hyun and Mr Lee Chul-Kook;

six teachers were completing the formalities required in order to be readmitted to the education system. These were: Mr Kang Byung-Chul, Mr Chun Moo-Woong, Mr Chun In-Soon, Mr Hwang Jae-Hak, Mr Yoo Do-Hyuk and Mr Cho Jae-Do;

two teachers had chosen to take up literary activities. These were Mr Yoon Jae-Chul and Mr Kim Jin-Kyung;

one teacher had opted for business, namely, Mr Lee Soon-Kwon.

---

[4] See document 129 EX/3 PRIV., paras. 80-82; see also document 129 EX/CR/HR/2.

Republic of Korea **No. 730/86**

82. Following an exchange of views, the Committee *decided*:

(i) to thank the representative of the government concerned for his presence and his co-operation, and to express its gratitude to the government concerned for the exemplary manner in which it had helped to settle the cases forming the subject of the communication;

(ii) to strike the communication from its list as settled and falling under paragraph 14 (*a*) (x) of 104 EX/Decision 3.3, with the exception (until it is settled) of the case of the six teachers who were at present completing the formalities for re-admission to the education system.

Autumn 1988 session of the Committee on Conventions and Recommendations (130th session of the Executive Board)[5]

91. This communication has been on the agenda of the Committee since the [spring 1987 session]. It is still at the stage of examination of its admissibility. It concerns the case of teachers who are said to have been dismissed by the Ministry of Education in August 1985 for having criticized the social system of the country and the government's education policy, particularly in their articles published in a journal, *MinJoong Education*.

92. The Shilchun Literary Company which published the journal was reported to have had its licence withdrawn.

93. At [the spring 1988] session, the representative of the government concerned had stated that the publishing firm had had its licence restored and the situation of the dismissed teachers had been settled. There remained only the case of the six who were to comply with the necessary formalities to be readmitted to the teaching profession.

94. At its [spring 1988] session, the Committee had decided to strike that communication from its list, except with regard to those six teachers.[6]

95. In that connection, the Secretariat had received a letter dated 7 September 1988 from the Permanent Delegation of the Republic of Korea informing the Committee that five of those teachers had effectively been readmitted to the teaching profession and that the sixth, not wishing to return to teaching, had found other employment.

[5] See document 130 EX/3 PRIV., paras. 91-96; see also documents 130 EX/CR/HR Add. - Republic of Korea 2 and Add.2.
[6] See document 129 EX/3 PRIV., para. 82 (ii) (*supra*, p. 647).

No. 730/86 **Republic of Korea**

96. That communication having been entirely settled, the Committee *decided* to strike it from its list, in pursuance of paragraph 14 (*a*) (x) of 104 EX/Decision 3.3.

No. 731/86

Concerning *Chile*
Case of *Francisco Javier Andrés Peña Torres*

Communication of 5 August 1986 submitted by
Francisco Javier Andrés Peña Torres

Spring 1987 session of the Committee on Conventions and Recommendations (126th session of the Executive Board)[1]

38. Mr Francisco Javier Andrés Peña Torres, a teacher of Chilean nationality, allegedly left Chile in February 1975 and has requested authorization to return there, without success.

39. Confirming the terms of the letter dated 11 February 1987 from the Permanent Delegation of Chile to Unesco [...],[2] the representative of the government concerned stated that the person concerned had been authorized to return to his country unconditionally and on a permanent basis. He added that persons in this situation who encountered problems of an administrative nature could apply to an interministerial commission over which he presided, which would give them all the necessary help in overcoming such problems.

40. After an exchange of views, the Committee *decided*:

(i) to thank the representative of the government concerned for his presence and for his co-operation;

(ii) to strike the communication from its list as having been settled, in conformity with paragraph 14 (*a*) (x) of 104 EX/Decision 3.3.

---

[1] See document 126 EX/3 PRIV., paras. 38-40; see also documents 126 EX/CR/HR/3, 126 EX/CR/HR/2 Add.2 and 126 EX/CR/HR/1, annex.
[2] See document 126 EX/CR/HR/1, annex.

No. 734/86

Concerning *Indonesia*
Case of *Oesmany al Hamidy*

Communication of 18 September 1986 submitted by
Amnesty International

Spring 1987 session of the Committee on Conventions and Recommendations (126th session of the Executive Board)[1]

54. Mr Oesmany al Hamidy, aged 72, a teacher in a religious institution, is said to have been arrested on 14 September 1984 for subversion and for having undermined the authority of the State and provoked unrest among the population. He was reportedly sentenced in March 1986 to eight years' imprisonment, although he had apparently simply criticized government policy and had at no time been accused of advocating the overthrow of the government.

55. In a letter dated 27 April 1987, the government concerned addressed to the Secretariat its reply to the allegations contained in the communication [...].[2] According to the government, Amnesty International had no reliable knowledge of the case. The tendentious and provocative sermons made by Mr Oesmany al Hamidy had caused social unrest. The basic issue was political in nature. The communication was not compatible with the principles of Unesco and contained no relevant evidence, being based merely on information put out by the mass media. As Mr Oesmany al Hamidy had been given a regular trial and sentenced, his case had therefore been settled in accordance with the principles of human rights. The Indonesian Government had considered that, in accordance with paragraphs 6 and 14 (*a*) (ii) and (x) of 104 EX/ Decision 3.3, the communication should be deemed inadmissible.

56. In his statement, the representative of the government concerned said that in the sermons which Mr Oesmany al Hamidy had given in various public places, sometimes even outside the religious establishments, he had incited the population to re-

---

[1] See document 126 EX/3 PRIV., paras. 54-59; see also documents 126 EX/CR/HR/3 and Add.2.
[2] See document 126 EX/CR/HR/3 Add.2.

sist established authority and use arms to assert the supremacy of religion. He added that this was how Indonesia had experienced a "Black September" in September 1984 in the form of an uprising which had led to serious public disorder and caused particularly heavy damage to the national heritage.

57. Having been asked on what grounds Mr Oesmany al Hamidy had been sentenced, the representative of the government concerned, referring to his government's reply [...],[3] replied that the person concerned had been sentenced under the provisions of Law No. 11 of 1963 relating to the struggle against subversive activities and under Articles 55 and 65 of the Penal Code. He was not, however, able to inform the [Committee] whether Mr Oesmany al Hamidy had been arrested during a demonstration, whether he had been tried alone or with other accused persons, whether the accusation against him concerned essentially his sermons and whether possible measures of clemency might be applied for a person of advanced age with such a heavy sentence.

58. One member of the Committee considered that as the problem was connected with religious issues, the Committee would not be able to decide between the government's opinion and that of Mr Oesmany al Hamidy. In his view, the Committee should confine itself to an appeal for clemency.

59. After an exchange of views, the Committee *decided*:

(i) to thank the government concerned for its co-operation in sending not only a representative to the Committee but also a written reply;

(ii) to request the representative of the government concerned to transmit to the appropriate Indonesian authorities the concern expressed by the Committee on humanitarian grounds and its appeal for clemency towards Mr Oesmany al Hamidy in view of his advanced age and the severity of his sentence;

(iii) to resume consideration of the communication at its autumn 1987 session.

---

[3] *Ibidem*, para. 2.

Indonesia **No. 734/86**

Autumn 1987 session of the Committee on Conventions and Recommendations (127th session of the Executive Board)[4]

59. Mr Oesmany al Hamidy, who is described by the author of the communication as a teacher in a religious institution, aged 72, is said to have been arrested on 14 September 1984 for subversion, for having undermined the authority of the State and provoked unrest. He was reportedly sentenced in March 1986 to eight years' imprisonment.

60. At the [spring 1987] session, the representative of the government concerned had informed the Committee that Mr Oesmany al Hamidy had incited the population to resist established authority and to use arms to assert the supremacy of religion and that he had been given a fair trial.

61. In a letter dated 10 August 1987 [...],[5] Amnesty International had stated that the communication had been prepared on the basis of information given by the alleged victim during his trial and that it did not seem to be established that he had either used or recommended violence.

62. Confirming the content of his letter dated 27 August 1987 [...],[6] the representative of the government concerned stressed that, while aware of the Committee's humanitarian concerns, his country's authorities considered that the case in question was strictly a matter within the domestic jurisdiction of Indonesia. With regard to the Committee's appeal for clemency, he said that under national legislation, an appeal to the President of the Republic for pardon was possible, but so far Mr Oesmany al Hamidy had submitted no such appeal. He then gave detailed information about the state of health of the alleged victim who was well cared for in a rest home south of Jarkarta where in particular he was following a diet to lose weight. He added that the individual concerned could read and receive visits from members of his family in the normal way.

63. Several members of the Committee wondered whether the Head of the Indonesian State could act *ex officio* and consider the possibility of granting the requested measure of clemency.

64. One member of the Committee wondered whether, on the contrary, the reply of the Indonesian Government did not imply that he could not so act. In that connec-

---

[4] See document 127 EX/3 PRIV., paras. 59-65; see also documents 127 EX/CR/HR/2 and Add.

[5] See document 127 EX/CR/HR/2 Add.

[6] See document 127 EX/CR/HR/2.

tion, the representative of the government concerned pointed out that an appeal for pardon made by the convicted person or by an authorized person would be taken into consideration and that consequently this procedure could not be neglected.

65. After an exchange of views, the Committee *decided*:

(i) to thank the government concerned for its co-operation in not only sending a representative to appear before the Committee, but in also forwarding a written reply;

(ii) to inform the author of the communication of the possibility of submitting an appeal for pardon to the President of the Republic, of which Mr Oesmany al Hamidy had not yet availed himself;

(iii) to request the representative of the government concerned to transmit once again to the appropriate Indonesian authorities its appeal for clemency towards Mr Oesmany al Hamidy, in view of his advanced age and state of health;

(iv) to resume consideration of the communication at its spring 1988 session.

Spring 1988 session of the Committee on Conventions and Recommendations (129th session of the Executive Board)[7]

52. A teacher of religious education, aged over 72, Mr Oesmany al Hamidy is reported to have been sentenced to eight years' imprisonment for subversion.

53. At previous sessions, the representative of the government concerned had informed the Committee that Mr Oesmany al Hamidy had incited the population to resist established authority and to use arms to assert the supremacy of religion. He had pointed out to the Committee that Mr Oesmany al Hamidy had been properly looked after at his place of detention. He had stated that under national legislation an appeal to the Head of State for pardon was possible, but that the person concerned had submitted no such appeal.

54. At its [autumn 1987] session, the Committee decided to inform the author of the communication of the possibility of an appeal for pardon to the President of the Republic and to request the representative of the government concerned to transmit

---

[7] See document 129 EX/3 PRIV., paras. 52-60; see also document 129 EX/CR/HR/2.

once again to the appropriate Indonesian authorities its appeal for clemency, in view of the advanced age and the state of health of the alleged victim.[8]

55. On 7 April 1988, the Secretariat received from the author of the communication a letter in which he wished to inform the Committee that although Mr Oesmany al Hamidy, the alleged victim, had been admitted to hospital in 1986, he was now detained in Cipinang Prison and not in a rest home and that his health was still giving cause for concern.

56. At the present session of the Committee, the representative of the government concerned informed the Committee that his government stood by the replies which it had given to the Committee at previous sessions, particularly at the spring 1987 session.

57. With regard to the humanitarian concerns of the Committee, the representative of the government concerned recalled that his government had already indicated at the [autumn 1987] session the possibility of an appeal for pardon. With regard to the state of health of the person in question, the representative of the government concerned also recalled the detailed medical information which he had already brought to the attention of the Committee, to the effect that Mr Oesmany al Hamidy had not had heart disease, a kidney infection or a lung ailment, but suffered from chronic polyarthritis contracted before his detention. Having been well looked after in a hospital located ouside the prison and after his recovery, he had returned to his place of detention.

58. In conclusion, the representative of the government concerned stated that as Mr Oesmany al Hamidy had been found guilty, in accordance with the laws in force, of having, by his tendentious sermons, caused a riot (which had occurred in the north of Jakarta in September 1984) and public disorder, the Indonesian Government was of the opinion that the communication should be declared inadmissible.

59. During the discussion, a Committee member pointed out that an eight-year prison sentence for a 72 year old man was the equivalent of a life sentence, and he wondered if the possibility for clemency could not be explored again.

60. After an exchange of views, the Committee *decided*:

> (i) to thank the government concerned for its co-operation in not only sending a representative to appear before the Committee, but in also forwarding a written reply;

[8] See document 127 EX/3 PRIV., para. 65 (ii) and (iii) (*supra*, p. 654).

(ii) to inform the author of the communication that the possibility existed for Mr Oesmany al Hamidy, or his attorneys, to submit to the President of the Republic an appeal for him to be pardoned;

(iii) to request the representative of the government concerned to transmit once again to the appropriate Indonesian authorities its appeal for clemency towards Mr Oesmany al Hamidy, in view of his advanced age and state of health;

(iv) to resume consideration of this communication at [its autumn 1988 session].

Autumn 1988 session of the Committee on Conventions and Recommendations (130th session of the Executive Board)[9]

54. This communication has been on the Committee's agenda since the [spring 1987 session]. It is still at the stage of examination of its admissibility.

55. According to Amnesty International, Mr Oesmany al Hamidy, a teacher of religious education, aged over 72, has been sentenced to eight years' imprisonment for subversion, although - it is said - he simply exercised in a non-violent way his right to freedom of opinion and expression.

56. At previous sessions, the representative of the government concerned informed the Committee that Mr Oesmany al Hamidy had incited the population to resist established authority and to use arms to achieve the supremacy of religion. He had been found guilty in accordance with the legislation in force, in particular of having by means of his tendentious sermons caused a riot. In such circumstances, the Indonesian Government considered that the communication should be declared inadmissible. Mr Oesmany al Hamidy was being properly treated and well cared for. An appeal for clemency to the Head of State was possible, but the person concerned had not submitted one.

57. On 5 September 1988, the Secretariat received from the Permanent Delegation of Indonesia a letter assuring the Committee that the Indonesian Government had given serious attention to the Committee's decision, particularly its appeal for clemency. The Permanent Delegation recalled that the case of Mr Oesmany al Hamidy was strictly within the country's national jurisdiction, and that national law gave

[9] See document 130 EX/3 PRIV., paras. 54-62; see also documents 130 EX/CR/HR - Indonesia and Add.2.

convicted persons the right to appeal for clemency to the President of the Republic, but that the person concerned had not to date made use of that right.

58. On 5 September 1988, the Secretariat also received from the author of the communication a letter drawing the Committee's attention to the fact that the presidential pardon was solely a matter of executive discretion and did not constitute a judicial or other independent review of the case. Amnesty International considered that since Mr Oesmany al Hamidy had done no more than exercise his right to freedom of opinion and expression in a non-violent manner, presidential pardon would not be an appropriate remedy.

59. The Indonesian member of the Committee drew attention to the information and explanations supplied by the government concerned both by letters and orally through its representative. The Committee had been fully informed of the events which had resulted in the arrest of Mr Oesmany al Hamidy. His sermons, even if they did not contain any direct incitement to violence, had contained the seeds thereof. He had aroused discontent, and identified the target. The riot had then broken out. His trial had been a fair trial. He had been sentenced in accordance with the law. He was well taken care of and in better health. His morale had improved. The humanitarian concerns of the Committee were also those of the authorities, and were the rule in Indonesia. They were even enshrined in the Constitution. Nevertheless, an appeal for clemency was necessary in order for the Head of State to be able to grant it in consultation with the Supreme Court, the Attorney General and the Minister of Justice. The case was strictly within the national jurisdiction of Indonesia, and the communication should be declared inadmissible.

60. One member of the Committee expressed his sympathy for the alleged victim, who was demanding justice, and who refused to appeal for clemency.

61. Some members of the Committee nevertheless wondered whether Mr Oesmany al Hamidy was fully aware of the possibility open to him to lodge an appeal for clemency, and whether it would not be proper to make sure that he was. The Indonesian member of the Committee drew attention to the fact that Mr Oesmany al Hamidy was assisted by two competent, well-known legal advisers and, while he was a learned man himself, it was obvious that he should be familiar with the provision in the Indonesian law to extend an appeal for clemency.

62. Following an exchange of views, the Committee *decided*:

(i) to take note of the information which the government concerned had kindly communicated by letter and to thank the Indonesian member of the Committee for his further clarifications;

(ii) to take note of the statement by Amnesty International, the author of the communication, to the effect that presidential pardon was not an appropriate remedy in the case under consideration;

(iii) to ask the government concerned to inform Mr Oesmany al Hamidy of the possibility available to him to lodge an appeal for clemency and to inform the Committee of Mr Oesmany al Hamidy's attitude in that regard;

(iv) to resume consideration of this communication at its [spring 1989 session].

Spring 1989 session of the Committee on Conventions and Recommendations (131st session of the Executive Board)[10]

47. This communication has been on the Committee's agenda since the [spring 1987 session]. It is still at the stage of examination as to its admissibility.

48. Mr Oesmany al Hamidy, a teacher of religious education, aged 75, is said to have been arrested on 14 September 1984 for subversion, and to have been sentenced on 26 March 1986 to eight years' imprisonment.

49. According to the government concerned, Mr Oesmany al Hamidy had been found guilty in accordance with the legislation in force of, among other things, causing a riot by tendentious sermons in which he incited the population to resist established authority and to resort to arms to further the supremacy of religion. He had been defended at his trial by two well-known legal advisers. He was being properly treated and well cared for at his place of detention. An appeal to the Head of State for pardon was possible, but Mr Oesmany al Hamidy had not thought it appropriate to make such an appeal.

50. The author of the communication agreed that presidential pardon, which was a matter of executive discretion, would not be an appropriate remedy in this case.

51. At its [autumn 1988] session, the Committee, while taking note of Amnesty International's point of view nevertheless decided to ask the government concerned to inform Mr Oesmany al Hamidy of the possibility available to him of lodging an appeal for pardon, and to inform the Committee of Mr Hamidy's position.[11]

---

[10] See document 131 EX/3 PRIV., paras. 47-56; see also document 131 EX/CR/HR/INS.

[11] See document 130 EX/3 PRIV., para. 62 (ii) and (iii) (*supra*, p. 658).

Indonesia **No. 734/86**

52. By letter dated 7 March 1989, Amnesty International pointed out that Mr Oesmany al Hamidy had been prosecuted not for committing acts of violence or for having advocated violence, but for subversion. No evidence had been produced which made it possible to think that he had engaged in such acts, or incited others to commit them. Moreover, numerous irregularities were alleged to have occurred during his trial: witnesses were said to have been accused of lying, and one of them beaten in a cell for having been unable to answer the questions put to him.

53. At the present session, the government concerned was not represented. However, by letter dated 27 April 1989, the Permanent Delegation of Indonesia to Unesco recalled that, in accordance with the law, Mr Oesmany al Hamidy was entitled to lodge an appeal for pardon. He had been informed of this possibility by his legal advisers, but had not submitted an appeal. This had been confirmed by the North Jakarta court, by the Supreme Court and more recently by the director of Cipinang prison, where he was being detained. He had not wished to avail himself of this remedy and could not be forced to do so. He had nevertheless had his sentence reduced by two months in 1987 and by three months in 1988. His general state of health was satisfactory. The rheumatism from which he had suffered before his imprisonment had improved. He was now able to walk around the premises of the penitentiary establishment without difficulty, whereas formerly he had been confined to a wheelchair. He engaged in various activities, in particular giving lectures and delivering sermons on Fridays. He also read a great deal. His fellow detainees and the warders found him jovial and good humoured.

54. Some members of the Committee considered that it was still not clear why Mr Oesmany al Hamidy had refused to appeal for pardon. In these circumstances, the Committee could appeal to the Indonesian authorities for clemency on his behalf, in view of his advanced age and the lengthy sentence which he still had to serve.

55. Other members pointed out that, in reply to the recommendation which the Committee had addressed to the government concerned at its [autumn 1988] session, the latter had indicated that Mr Hamidy had refused to appeal for presidential pardon because he considered himself to be innocent. Pardon could be appealed for only by the convicted person himself, or by a person whom he had duly empowered to do so. Although the Committee could not ask for his pardon, it could still appeal to the government concerned to show clemency towards the alleged victim.

56. Following an exchange of views, the Committee *decided*:

(i) to take note of the letter of 27 April 1989 from the Permanent Delegation of Indonesia to Unesco, and to thank the government concerned for the information provided therein, in particular regarding the state of health of Mr Oesmany al Hamidy;

(ii) to request the government concerned to show extreme clemency towards Mr Oesmany al Hamidy, in view of his advanced age and the many years of detention that he had already served;

(iii) to resume consideration of this communication at its [autumn 1989 session].

Autumn 1989 session of the Committee on Conventions and Recommendations (132nd session of the Executive Board)[12]

57. This communication has been on the Committee's agenda since the [spring 1987 session]. It is still at the stage of consideration as to its admissibility.

58. Mr Oesmany al Hamidy, a teacher of religious education, aged 75 at the time the communication was submitted, was arrested on 14 September 1984 for subversion and is said to have been sentenced on 26 March 1986 to eight years' imprisonment.

59. The government concerned informed the Committee at previous sessions that Mr Oesmany al Hamidy had been duly tried and found guilty of causing a riot by his tendentious sermons. He had been accused in particular of inciting the population to resist the established authority and to resort to arms to achieve the supremacy of religion. A plea for a pardon to the Head of State was possible but, to date, Mr Oesmany al Hamidy had not seen fit to make such a plea. Nevertheless, a two months' remission of sentence had been granted to him in 1987 and a three months' remission in 1988. His state of health was satisfactory.

60. In view of the fact that a plea for pardon could only be made by the convicted individual in person, the Committee decided at its [spring 1989] session to ask the government concerned to show the utmost clemency towards the alleged victim in view of his advanced age and the long years of detention that he had already endured.[13]

61. In a letter dated 14 August 1989, the author of the communication advised the Secretariat that it had no further information relating to the communication but that it was still extremely concerned about the fate of Mr Oesmany al Hamidy.

---

[12] See document 132 EX/3 PRIV., paras. 57-63; see also document 132 EX/CR/HR/INS.
[13] See document 131 EX/3 PRIV., para. 56 (ii) (*supra*, p. 660).

Indonesia **No. 734/86**

62. The government concerned was not represented at this session nor was it represented at the [spring 1989] session. Nevertheless, in a letter dated 13 September 1989, the Permenent Delegation of the Republic of Indonesia to Unesco reiterated the information given to the Committee at previous sessions and pointed out that Mr Oesmany al Hamidy had confirmed his refusal to appeal for pardon to the Head of State. He was in good health, jovial and in good humour. He read a lot, taught and preached on Fridays. The delegation also pointed out that the Indonesian Government had co-operated fully with the Committee. It expressed the view that the Committee should terminate its examination of the communication in a case which fell completely within the country's internal jurisdiction.

63. After an exchange of views, the Committee *decided*:

(i) to express its regret at the fact that the government concerned had not been represented at the session of the Committee and could thus not engage in dialogue with the Committee in spite of the fact that it had a representative on the Executive Board who was even a member of the Committee;

(ii) to express its regret at the fact that its appeal for clemency had not been heeded in spite of the advanced age of Mr Oesmany al Hamidy and the long years of detention that he had already endured;

(iii) urgently to renew that appeal for clemency;

(iv) to ask the government concerned to grant Mr Oesmany al Hamidy conditional release if such a procedure existed under Indonesian law;

(v) to resume its examination of the communication at its [spring 1990 session].

Spring 1990 session of the Committee on Conventions and Recommendations (134th session of the Executive Board)[14]

76. This communication is still at the stage of examination as to its admissibility. It has been on the Committee's agenda since the [spring 1987 session].

77. Mr Oesmany al Hamidy, a teacher of religious education, today aged nearly 80, was reportedly arrested on 14 September 1984 for subversion and sentenced on 26 March 1986 to eight years' imprisonment.

[14] See document 134 EX/3 PRIV., paras. 76-85; see also document 134 EX/CR/HR/INS.

No. 734/86 **Indonesia**

78. According to the information supplied at previous sessions by the government concerned, Mr Oesmany al Hamidy had been duly tried and found guilty of causing a riot by tendentious sermons. He had been accused in particular of inciting the population to resist the established authority and to resort to arms to achieve the supremacy of religion.

79. In response to the question as to whether all possible remedies had been exhausted, it was indicated that a plea for pardon to the Head of State still remained possible, but that Mr Oesmany al Hamidy had refused to make such a plea. His general state of health was satisfactory.

80. At its [autumn 1989] session, after expressing its regret at the fact that the government concerned had not been represented, and deploring that its appeal for clemency for Mr Oesmany al Hamidy had not been heeded, the Committee urgently renewed its humanitarian appeal. It asked the government concerned to grant Mr Oesmany al Hamidy conditional release if such a procedure existed under Indonesian law.[15]

81. Confirming his letter of 3 April 1990, the Permanent Delegate of Indonesia to Unesco recalled that, while understanding the Committee's humanitarian concerns, his government continued to consider that the case of Mr Oesmany al Hamidy fell strictly within the country's internal jurisdiction, his sentence having been passed in full conformity with Indonesian law. Moreover, although he had been informed of the possibilities of appealing for pardon to the President of the Republic, Mr Oesmany al Hamidy had never been willing to lodge such an appeal, and had confirmed his refusal in writing. With regard to his state of health, this was quite satisfactory since he was now able to walk and was no longer confined, as he had been prior to entering prison, to a wheel-chair. He had been granted a two months' remission of sentence in 1987, a three months' remission in 1988 and a four months' remission in 1989 (his sentence of eight years' imprisonment ran from 14 September 1984, the date of his arrest). The permanent delegate concluded by stating that his government, having co-operated fully with the Committee by providing all relevant information, wished that the examination of this communication be terminated.

82. On 25 April 1990, the Secretariat received from Amnesty International a letter in which that organization reiterated its concern regarding this case.

83. Some members of the Committee wondered whether, in view of Mr Oesmany al Hamidy's refusal to appeal for pardon because he considered himself innocent, the Committee might not itself appeal directly for clemency for the alleged victim.

---

[15] See document 132 EX/3 PRIV., para. 63 (ii), (iii) and (iv) (*supra*, p. 661).

Indonesia **No. 734/86**

84. Referring to the question of the admissibility of the communication, a number of Committee members pointed out that the right of freedom of religion was not a human right that fell within Unesco's fields of competence. Most members nevertheless considered that the activities for which Mr Oesmany al Hamidy had been sentenced consisted in the teaching of religion, and that consequently they fell within the Organization's fields of competence. Another member maintained that not only did the right to freedom of religion lie within Unesco's fields of competence but also that religion was itself an essential element of cultural identity.

85. After an exchange of views, the Committee *decided*:

(i) to thank the representative of the government concerned for his attendance and his co-operation;

(ii) to renew its appeal for clemency on behalf of Mr Oesmany al Hamidy;

(iii) to ask the government concerned to grant Mr Oesmany al Hamidy a remission of sentence in view of his advanced age and the many years he had already spent in detention;

(iv) to ask the author of the communication whether it could not attempt to persuade Mr Oesmany al Hamidy to lodge an appeal for pardon;

(v) to resume its examination of the communication at its [autumn 1990 session].

Autumn 1990 session of the Committee on Conventions and Recommendations (135th session of the Executive Board)[16]

43.This communication is still at the stage of examination as to its admissibility. It has been on the Committee's agenda since the [spring 1987 session].

44. Mr Oesmany al Hamidy, a teacher of religious education, today aged 76, was reportedly arrested on 14 September 1984 for subversion and sentenced on 26 March 1986 to eight years' imprisonment.

45. According to the information supplied at previous sessions by the government concerned, Mr Oesmany al Hamidy had been duly tried and found guilty of causing a riot by tendentious sermons. He had been accused in particular of inciting the pop-

[16] See document 135 EX/3 PRIV., paras. 43-50; see also document 135 EX/CR/HR/INS.

ulation to resist the established authority and to resort to arms to achieve the supremacy of religion. It was possible for him to submit a plea for pardon to the Head of State, but Mr Oesmany al Hamidy had declined to do so.

46. At the [autumn 1989] session, after expressing its regret at the fact that the government concerned had not been represented, and deploring that its appeal for clemency for Mr Oesmany al Hamidy had not been heeded, the Committee urgently renewed its humanitarian appeal. It asked the government concerned to grant Mr Oesmany al Hamidy conditional release if such a procedure existed under Indonesian law.[17]

47. At the [spring 1990] session, confirming his letter of 3 April 1990, the Permanent Delegate of Indonesia to Unesco recalled that, while understanding the Committee's humanitarian concerns, his government continued to consider that the case of Mr Oesmany al Hamidy fell strictly within the country's internal jurisdiction, his sentence having been passed in full conformity with Indonesian law. Moreover, although he had been informed of the possibilities of appealing for pardon to the President of the Republic, Mr Oesmany al Hamidy had never been willing to lodge such an appeal, and had confirmed his refusal in writing. He had nevertheless been granted a two months' remission of sentence in 1987, a three months' remission in 1988 and a four months' remission in 1989 (his sentence of eight years' imprisonment ran from 14 September 1984, the date of his arrest). With regard to his state of health, this was quite satisfactory since he was now able to walk and was no longer confined, as he had been prior to entering prison, to a wheel-chair.

48. In a letter dated 20 August 1990, the author of the communication, Amnesty International, reiterated its concern regarding this case, and stated that it had received no confirmation of the four months' remission of sentence that the victim was alleged to have been granted.

49. In a letter dated 2 October 1990, the Permanent Delegation of the Republic of Indonesia to Unesco informed the Committee that his government would continue to act in this case in accordance with the legislation in force in his country. He indicated that Mr Oesmany al Hamidy had not exercised, or did not wish to exercise, his right to appeal for pardon. Nevertheless, on 17 August 1990, he had been granted a further remission of five months, thereby bringing to a total of 14 months the periods of remission that he had been granted to date.

50. After an exchange of views, the Committee *decided*:

[17] See document 132 EX/3 PRIV., para. 63 (ii), (iii) and (iv) (*supra*, p. 661).

(i) to express its regret that the government concerned had not sent a representative;

(ii) to thank the government concerned for the information that it had supplied in its letter of 2 October 1990, in particular regarding the further five months' remission;

(iii) to request the government concerned to indicate to it the precise date on which Mr Oesmany al Hamidy would be released, taking account of the remissions that he had already been granted and of the time that he had spent in detention;

(iv) to renew its appeal for clemency in order that Mr Oesmany al Hamidy might be granted an early release in view of his advanced age, his exemplary conduct in detention and the fact that he had already served the greater part of his long sentence;

(v) to resume consideration of this communication at its [spring 1991 session].

Spring 1991 session of the Committee on Conventions and Recommendations (136th session of the Executive Board)[18]

36. This communication is still at the stage of examination as to its admissibility, It has been on the Committee's agenda since the [spring 1987 session]. The author of the communication alleges the following:

37. Mr Oesmany al Hamidy, a teacher of religious education, today aged 76 was arrested on 14 September 1984 for subversion and sentenced on 26 March 1986 to eight years' imprisonment.

38. According to the information supplied at previous sessions by the government concerned, Mr Oesmany al Hamidy had been duly tried and found guilty of causing a riot by tendentious sermons. He had been accused in particular of inciting the population to resist the established authority and to resort to arms to achieve the supremacy of religion. It was possible for him to submit a plea for pardon to the Head of State, but Mr Oesmany al Hamidy had declined to do so.

[18] See document 136 EX/3 PRIV., paras. 36-45; see also documents 136 EX/CR/HR/INS and Add.2.

39. At the [autumn 1989] session, after expressing its regret at the fact that the government concerned had not been represented, and deploring that its appeal for clemency for Mr Oesmany al Hamidy had not been heeded, the Committee urgently renewed its humanitarian appeal. It asked the government concerned to grant Mr Oesmany al Hamidy conditional release if such a procedure existed under Indonesian law.[19]

40. At the [spring 1990] session, the Permanent Delegate of Indonesia to UNESCO recalled that, while understanding the Committee's humanitarian concerns, his government continued to consider that the case of Mr Oesmany al Hamidy fell strictly within the country's internal jurisdiction, his sentence having been passed in full conormity with Indonesian law. Moreover, although he had been informed of the posibilities of appealing for pardon to the President of the Republic, Mr Oesmany al Hamidy had confirmed his refusal to do so in writing. He had nevertheless been granted a two months' remission of sentence in 1987, a three months' remission in 1988 and a four months' remission in 1989 (his sentence of eight years' imprisonment ran from 14 September 1984, the date of his arrest). With regard to his state of health, this was quite satisfactory since he was now able to walk and was no longer confined, as he had been prior to entering prison, to a wheel-chair.

41. At the [autumn 1990] session, the Permanent Delegation of the Republic of Inoesia to UNESCO informed the Committee that its government would continue to act in this case in accordance with the legislation in force in its country. It indicated that Mr Oesmany al Hamidy had not exercised or did not wish to exercise his right to appeal for pardon. Nevertheless, on 17 August 1990, he had been granted a further remission of five months, bringing to 14 months the total remission he has been granted to date.

42. In a letter dated 9 April 1991, the author of the communication reiterated its concern regarding this case, and stated that it had received no additional information.

43. Confirming his letter of 6 May 1991 [...],[20] the Permanent Delegate of Indonesia to UNESCO recalled that his government wished to reiterate its position in this matter as set forth in his letter of 2 October 1990. He stated that Mr Oesmany al Hamidy was scheduled to be released on 21 August 1991.

44. Several members of the Committee welcomed the co-operation of the government concerned, but felt that in view of the advanced age of the alleged victim, the

[19] See document 132 EX/3 PRIV., para. 63 (ii), (iii) and (iv) (*supra*, p. 661).
[20] See document 136 EX/CR/HR/INS Add.2.

Committee should renew once again its appeal for clemency so that Mr Oesmany al Hamidy might be granted a further reduction in his sentence.

45. After an exchange of views, the Committee *decided*:

(i) to thank the government concerned for its attendance and co-operation;

(ii) to note with satisfaction Mr Oesmany al Hamidy's release scheduled for 21 August 1991;

(iii) to renew its appeal for clemency in order that Mr Oesmany al Hamidy might be granted an early release in view of his advanced age, his exemplary conduct in detention and the fact that he had already served the greater part of his long sentence;

(iv) to retain this communication on its list until its [autumn 1991 session].

Autumn 1991 session of the Committee on Conventions and Recommendations (137th session of the Executive Board)[21]

36. This communication, which is still at the stage of examination as to its admissibility, has been on the Committee's agenda since the [spring 1987 session].

37. Mr Oesmany al Hamidy, a teacher of religious education, now over 76 years of age (1987), is alleged to have been arrested on 14 September 1984 for subversion and sentenced on 26 March 1986 to eight years' imprisonment.

38. According to the information supplied by the government concerned at earlier sessions, Mr Oesmany al Hamidy was sentenced for causing a riot by tendentious sermons and inciting the population to resist the established authority and to resort to arms to achieve the supremacy of religion. The government considered the case of Mr Oesmany al Hamidy as coming strictly within the bounds of national jurisdiction. He had been sentenced in full conformity with Indonesian law. Although he had been informed of the possibility of submitting an appeal for pardon to the President of the Republic, he had rejected that remedy in writing. He had nevertheless been granted remissions of sentence amounting to a total of 14 months. He was due to be released on 21 [August] 1991. His state of health was entirely satisfactory as he was now able to walk and was no longer confined to a wheelchair, as he had been before entering prison.

[21] See document 137 EX/3 PRIV., paras. 36-42; see also document 137 EX/CR/HR/INS.

No. 734/86 **Indonesia**

39. The Committee had continued to appeal for clemency to the authorities.[22]

40. At the present session, the author of the communication informed the Committee in a letter dated 30 August 1991 that Mr Oesmany al Hamidy had been released on 17 August 1991.

41. His release was confirmed in a letter sent by the Permanent Delegate of Indonesia to UNESCO, dated 5 September 1991, and by the Permanent Delegate himself speaking before the Committee.

42. After an exchange of views, the Committee *decided*:

(i) to thank the representatives of the government concerned for their attendance and co-operation;

(ii) to note with satisfaction the release of Mr Oesmany al Hamidy;

(iii) to strike the communication from its list and to consider that it had been settled in accordance with paragraph 14 (*a*) (x) of 104 EX/Decision 3.3.

[22] See document 136 EX/3 PRIV., para. 45 (iii) (*supra*, p. 667).

No. 736/86

Concerning *Somalia*
Case of *Abdulle Rage Taraweh*

Communication of 20 October 1986 submitted by
William Courson

Spring 1987 session of the Committee on Conventions and Recommendations (126th session of the Executive Board)[1]

91. Described by the author of the communication as a writer and poet, Mr Abdulle Rage Taraweh is said to have been arrested in 1982 and imprisoned since then under the provisions of a preventive detention law. He was reportedly accused of expressing anti-government opinions in his poems.

92. Refuting the allegations made, the representative of the government concerned stated that the accusation against his country by the author of the communication amounted to interference in a State's internal affairs. He informed the Committee that Mr Abdulle Rage Taraweh was not a writer but merely an official responsible for theatre co-ordination and that he had been guilty of offences against national sovereignty and unity, using poetry as a medium. He said that, contrary to Mr William Courson's assertions, Somali law did not allow any form of torture. In reply to a question, he said that there was no law authorizing detention without trial, either having gained the impression that the author of the communication did not have reliable knowledge of the alleged facts, he expressed the wish to get in touch with him to discuss the matter.

93. In this connection, the Chairperson pointed out that the communication transmitted to the government concerned on 3 December 1986 contained all the details of Mr Courson's identity and that if that government saw fit to get in touch with him it was quite free to do so, but that in any case such action did not fall within the framework of the Committee's procedures.

[1] See document 126 EX/3 PRIV., paras. 91-95; see also document 126 EX/CR/HR/3.

No. 736/86 **Somalia**

94. The members of the Committee who took the floor considered that the government concerned should be asked to provide further information, in particular with a view to establishing whether Mr Abdulle Rage Taraweh was still in prison, whether his trial had taken place and the exact nature of the offence with which he was charged.

95. Following an exchange of views, the Committee *decided*:

(i) to thank the representative of the government concerned for his presence and co-operation;

(ii) to request him to provide the next session of the Committee with information concerning the date of arrest of Mr Abdulle Rage Taraweh, the charges brought against him and any sentence passed;

(iii) further to request him to inform his government of the Committee's humanitarian concerns so that Mr Abdulle Rage Taraweh might be shown clemency;

(iv) to resume consideration of this communication at its autumn 1987 session.

Autumn 1987 session of the Committee on Conventions and Recommendations (127th session of the Executive Board)[2]

102. Described by the author of the communication as a writer and poet, Mr Abdulle Rage Taraweh is said to have been arrested in 1982 and imprisoned since that date. He was reportedly accused of expressing anti-government opinions in his poems.

103. At the spring 1987 session, the representative of the government concerned stated that Mr Rage Taraweh, an official responsible for theatre co-ordination, had been guilty of offences against national sovereignty and unity, using poetry as a medium. He possessed no other relevant information.

104. The government concerned had not sent a representative to the present session of the Committee.

---

[2] See document 127 EX/3 PRIV., paras. 102-106; see also document 127 EX/CR/HR/2.

Somalia **No. 736/86**

105. In this regard, the Secretariat informed the Committee that the Ambassador, Permanent Delegate of Somalia to Unesco, had been recalled to his country for consultation.

106. After an exchange of views, the Committee *decided*:

(i) to express its regret that a representative of the government concerned had not been present;

(ii) to reiterate its request to the government concerned for further information concerning in particular the date of arrest of Mr Abdulle Rage Taraweh, the charges brought against him and any sentence passed;

(iii) to renew its humanitarian appeal in order that Mr Abdulle Rage Taraweh might be shown clemency;

(iv) to resume consideration of this communication at its spring 1988 session.

Spring 1988 session of the Committee on Conventions and Recommendations (129th session of the Executive Board)[3]

91. Mr Abdulle Rage Taraweh, who is described by the author of the communication as a writer and poet, is alleged to have been arrested in 1982 and imprisoned since that date under a law relating to pre-trial detention. He was reportedly accused of expressing anti-government opinions in his poems.

92. Mr Abdi Ismail Younis,[4] who is described by the International Human Rights Law Group as a mathematician, is said to have been arrested in November 1982 and imprisoned since that date for belonging to an organization opposed to the government. He was allegedly sentenced in February 1988 to capital punishment. This was reportedly commuted by the President of the Republic to a 24-year prison sentence.

93. During the meeting at which this report was adopted the representative of the government concerned informed the Committee of the release of Mr Abdulle Rage Taraweh. As for Mr Abdi Ismail Younis, the representative of the government concerned confirmed that he had been sentenced by a court in accordance with the law.

---

[3] See document 129 EX/3 PRIV., paras. 91-95; see also document 129 EX/CR/HR/2.
[4] Communications No. 736/87 concerning *Somalia*, case of *Abdulle Rage Taraweh*, and No. 745/87 concerning *Somalia*, case of *Abdi Ismail Younis*, were being considered together.

No. 736/86 **Somalia**

94. By a *note verbale* dated 5 May 1988, the Permanent Delegation of Somalia to Unesco requested that consideration of the communications concerning Somalia be deferred pending receipt of relevant information from the Somalian authorities. The Committee held discussions on the basis of that note but also took account of the last-minute information provided by the representative of the government concerned at the time when this report was adopted.

95. After an exchange of views, the Committee *decided*:

(i) to reiterate its request to the government concerned for information concerning the case of Mr Abdi Ismail Younis;

(ii) to make a further appeal for clemency on behalf of Mr Abdi Ismail Younis, on humanitarian grounds;

(iii) to resume consideration of this case at [its autumn 1988 session].

No. 737/86

Concerning *Union of Soviet Socialist Republics*
Case of *Mart Niklus*

Communication of 20 September 1986 submitted by
Toomas Karmo

Spring 1988 session of the Committee on Conventions and Recommendations (129th session of the Executive Board)[1]

103. Mr Mart Niklus, a Soviet citizen, is described by the author of the communication as being a foreign language teacher, aged 54. He is reported to have been sentenced on 8 January 1981 to 10 years' detention in a hard labour camp and five years' internal exile for anti-Soviet agitation and propaganda. He is said to have been maltreated at his place of detention and to have had his mail intercepted. On 24 January 1987, his books and papers are alleged to have been confiscated and partly destroyed.

104. The representative of the Soviet Government explained to the Committee that Mr Niklus had been sentenced under the Penal Code of the Estonian SSR and that the case was under appeal to the Supreme Court. Mr Niklus had been informed that he could petition the Court for clemency, but to date he had not chosen to avail himself of this opportunity. The representative of the Soviet Government stated that according to the information available to him there was no evidence that Mr Niklus was in fact a language teacher. In any event, he said, it would be inappropriate for the Committee to examine this case since the internal domestic remedies had not yet been exhausted.

105. In response to a question, the representative of the Soviet Government explained that it was not possible to estimate how long the appeals process would take since the case was being handled with due care and the entire file needed to be translated from the original Estonian.

---

[1] See document 129 EX/3 PRIV., paras. 103-108; see also document 129 EX/CR/HR/3 Add.

No. 737/86 **Union of Soviet Socialist Republics**

106. Certain members of the Committee were of the view that the case should be deemed inadmissible since the Committee could not act as a tribunal and because the domestic remedies had not yet been exhausted.

107. Other Committee members felt that the examination of the case should be suspended until the Supreme Court had handed down its decision. It was pointed out that the Committee had a great number of precedents of keeping cases suspended on its agenda even though the cases in question had been pending before national courts.

108. After an exchange of views, the Committee *decided*:

(i) to thank the representative of the government concerned for his presence and co-operation;

(ii) to suspend its consideration of this communication, awaiting the pronouncement of the Supreme Court of the Soviet Union.

Autumn 1988 session of the Committee on Conventions and Recommendations (130th session of the Executive Board)[2]

125. This communication has been on the Committee's agenda for examination of its admissibility since the [spring 1988 session].

126. Mr Mart Niklus, described by the author of the communication as a foreign language teacher, is said to have been sentenced on 8 January 1981 to 10 years' detention in a labour camp and five years' internal exile for anti-Soviet agitation and propaganda. According to Mr Toomas Karmo, the alleged victim merely wished to promote public discussion of government policy and the free dissemination of information.

127. At the [spring 1988 session], the representative of the government concerned stated that according to the information available to him there was no evidence that Mr Niklus was a language teacher. Sentenced under the Penal Code of the Estonian SSR, Mr Niklus had appealed to the Supreme Court, but although he was aware that he could petition the Court for clemency, he had made no attempt to do so. As the case before that Court was pending, the Committee decided to suspend examination of the communication pending the final legal decision.[3]

---

[2] See document 130 EX/3 PRIV., paras. 125-129; see also document 130 EX/CR/HR - USSR.
[3] See document 129 EX/3 PRIV., para. 108 (ii) (*supra*, p. 674).

Union of Soviet Socialist Republics **No. 737/86**

128. At the present session, the representative of the government concerned communicated the following additional information to the Committee. Mr Mart Niklus, who had been first sentenced in the 1950s, and later released, committed a subsequent offence and was sentenced for the second time in 1981. He appealed to the Supreme Court. In May 1982, the Vice-President of the Supreme Court asked for the case to be reopened and the sentence reduced. The Collegium of the Supreme Court, considering that the sentence of the court of first instance had not been sufficiently well-founded, particularly in so far as it had described Mr Niklus as a dangerous recidivist, reduced his sentence to three years' imprisonment. As he had already spent three years in prison, Mr Mart Niklus was released.

129. Following an exchange of views, the Committee *decided*:

(i) to thank the representative of the government concerned for his attendance and his co-operation;

(ii) to express its satisfaction at the outcome of this case;

(iii) to strike the communication from its list.

No. 739/86

Concerning *Chile*
Case of *Fernando Ramón Azula Ponce*

Communication of 5 November 1986 submitted by
World Federation of Organizations of the Teaching Profession

Spring 1987 session of the Committee on Conventions and Recommendations (126th session of the Executive Board)[1]

41. Mr Fernando Ramón Azula Ponce, who is presented as a history and geography teacher and as one of the leaders of the Asociación Gremial de Educadores de Chile (AGECH), is alleged to have been detained for a while on 16 September 1986. During a visit to Spain, he is said to have given an interview on 25 August 1986 to a magazine on the situation in Chile. Subsequently, on 16 September 1986, it is alleged that he was dismissed from his post. According to the author of the communication, this dismissal was mainly connected with the trade union activities of the person concerned.

42. Taking the floor, the representative of the government concerned stated that Mr Ramón Azula Ponce had been dismissed from two private educational establishments, in 1983 and in 1984, for failing to respect the rules laid down by his employers and for contesting instructions given by his superiors. He was, however, regarded as a good and professional teacher. The Ministry of Education accordingly decided to employ him in an educational establishment within its jurisdiction. As the representative of the group of teachers of this establishment, he was often in communication with the Ministry in order to settle various problems and solutions were always found. Subsequently, he took part in demonstrations and he was seen to throw stones at members of the forces of law and order. He was arrested, but was freed thanks to the intervention of the Ministry of Education which stood bail for him. During a visit to Spain, he made some extremely harsh comments in an interview against the government and against the Ministry which had employed him. The representative of the government concerned emphasized in this connection that the text of the litigious publication was offensive. He explained that in this particular case it

[1] See document 126 EX/3 PRIV., paras. 41–45; see also document 126 EX/CR/HR/3.

was not a question of freedom of expression, since the person concerned could, in his capacity as an individual, freely express himself in Chile, but that the fact of taking advantage of an opportunity provided by his public office to criticize his own country abroad was inadmissible. No country would accept such an attitude. It was for this reason that the competent authorities had been led to terminate Mr Ramón Azula Ponce's contract. The representative of the government concerned added that the dispute between this teacher and the administration was now pending before the courts and that it would be only right, consequently, to await their final verdict, particularly as the Committee on Freedom of Association of the Governing Body of [the International Labour Office], to which the matter has been submitted, had apparently not yet given its decision. In his opinion, the communication should be declared inadmissible.

43. Several members of the Committee who took the floor considered that in view of the fact that the internal remedies had not yet been exhausted it was not clear whether Mr Ramón Azula Ponce had been dismissed for reasons coming within Unesco's competence or for other reasons and that as a consequence, the submission of this communication to the Committee was premature and, hence, inadmissible.

44. As to whether contacts had been made by the Secretariat with ILO in order to obtain relevant information, a member of the Committee observed that while it was necessary to develop co-operation with other international organizations, the Committee should not have to await their decisions, since it had its own appropriate procedure. Moreover, the representative of the Director-General explained that, in conformity with the decision taken by the Committee at its spring 1980 session, the Secretariat could only take action *vis-à-vis* official, public international organizations on the instructions of the Committee.[2]

45. After an exchange of views, the Committee *decided*:

(i) to thank the representative of the government concerned for his presence and for his co-operation;

(ii) to declare that under the present circumstances the communication was inadmissible, its submission to the Committee being premature, since the internal remedies now being pursued had reached a stage which did not enable it to determine whether or not this case came within Unesco's competence.

---

[2] See document 109 EX/52 PRIV., para. 41 (vol. I, p. 351), communication No. 125/79 concerning *Argentina*, case of *Juan Carlos Suárez*, and *ibidem*, annex I, para. 5.

No. 743/87

Concerning *Chile*
Case of *Francisco Javier Lira Bianchi*

Communication of 22 December 1986 submitted by
Javier Lira Merino

Spring 1987 session of the Committee on Conventions and Recommendations (126th session of the Executive Board)[1]

46. A commercial engineer of Chilean nationality, whose wife is said to be a teacher and one of whose children is of university age, Mr Francisco Javier Lira Bianchi is alleged to have been prohibited from returning to his country.

47. Confirming the terms of the letter dated 11 February 1987 from the Permanent Delegation of Chile to Unesco [...],[2] the representative of the government concerned stated that the person concerned had been authorized to return to his country unconditionally and on a permanent basis. He added that persons in this situation who encountered problems of an administrative nature could apply to an interministerial commission over which he presided, which would give them all the necessary help in overcoming such problems.

48. After an exchange of views, the Committee *decided*:

(i) to thank the representative of the government concerned for his presence and for his co-operation;

(ii) to strike the communication from its list as having been settled, in conformity with paragraph 14 (*a*) (x) of 104 EX/Decision 3.3.

[1] See document 126 EX/3 PRIV., paras. 46-48; see also document 126 EX/CR/HR/3 Add. and 126 EX/CR/HR/1, annex.
[2] See document 126 EX/CR/HR/1, annex.

No. 744/87

Concerning *Greece*
Case of *Ignace Philippoussis*

Communication of 30 January 1987 submitted by
François Papamanolis*

Autumn 1987 session of the Committee on Conventions and Recommendations (127th session of the Executive Board)[1]

47. Described by the author of the communication as a primary-school teacher, Mr Ignace Philippoussis, after studying at training college, is said to have applied for a post in the State education system. It is alleged that at the end of his military service, he received notification of the rejection of his application by the Ministry of Education on the grounds that he was not of the Orthodox faith.

48. By a letter dated 4 September 1987, the Permanent Delegate of Greece to Unesco stated that Mr Ignace Philipoussis had not yet exhausted available domestic remedies and that the court of appeal for administrative matters, to which the case had been referred, would give its ruling next October. On behalf of the Greek Government, the Delegation requested that consideration of the communication be postponed until the following session of the Committee.

49. In response to a request for further information about the possibilities of redress and the length of time involved, the representative of the government concerned stated that, following the decision of the court of appeal which, barring a postponement, would be known towards the end of October 1987, an appeal could be lodged with the Council of State and that the procedure could then last some time, in view of that body's work-load.

50. After an exchange of views and in view of the judicial proceedings still under way, the Committee *decided* to comply with the request made by the Greek Govern-

* The Catholic Bishop of Syros.
[1] See document 127 EX/3 PRIV., paras. 47-50; see also document 127 EX/CR/HR/3.

ment and to postpone consideration of the communication until its spring 1988 session.

Spring 1988 session of the Committee on Conventions and Recommendations (129th session of the Executive Board)[2]

47. In view of the similarity of the facts alleged, the Committee decided to examine these two communications together.[3]

48. Mr Ignace Philippoussis, Miss Margarita Fréri and Miss Rose Fréri, having duly qualified, are reported to have applied for posts in the State education system, but it is alleged that their applications were rejected by the Ministry of Education on the grounds that they were not of the Orthodox faith.

49. In a letter dated 12 April 1988, the Catholic Bishop of Syros stated that the "unjust and discriminatory situation" affecting the alleged victims had been ended by the action of the courts and by a law which had recently been passed. He expressed his intense satisfaction and deep gratitude to the Committee.

50. The representative of the government concerned informed the Committee that these two communications could therefore be regarded as settled. As far as the case of Mr Ignace Philippoussis was concerned, a law recently passed by the National Assembly with such speed that it was possible to report on it to the present session of the Committee would enable the person concerned to be appointed in the near future since he had kept his place on the list of applicants. With regard to the case of Miss Margarita Fréri and Miss Rose Fréri, the representative of the government concerned stated that the court hearing the case had declared in their favour by annulling the administrative decision which had penalized them. As they had also kept their places on the list of applicants, their appointments would soon become effective.

51. After an exchange of views, the Committee *decided*:

(i) to thank the representative of the government concerned for attending the meeting and for his co-operation;

(ii) to note with satisfaction the information which he had provided;

---

[2] See document 129 EX/3 PRIV., paras. 47-51; see also document 129 EX/CR/HR/2.

[3] Communications No. 744/87 concerning *Greece*, case of *Ignace Philippoussis*, and No. 746/87 concerning *Greece*, case of *Margarita Fréri and Rose Fréri*.

(iii) to strike these two communications from its list as having been settled in accordance with paragraph 14 (*a*) (x) of 104 EX/Decision 3.3.

No. 745/87

Concerning *Somalia*
Case of *Abdi Ismail Younis*

Communication of 11 February 1987 submitted by
The International Human Rights Law Group

Autumn 1987 session of the Committee on Conventions and Recommendations (127th session of the Executive Board)[1]

107. Mr Abdi Ismail Younis, described by the.author of the communication as a mathematician, is said to have been arrested on 12 November 1982 on the grounds of belonging to an organization opposed to the government. He was alledgedly tortured in the early stages of his interrogation. The conditions of his imprisonment are reported to be extremely harsh. He is said to have suffered greatly, and is in poor health (letter from the International Human Rights Law Group dated 4 August 1987).

108. The government concerned had not sent a representative to the present session of the Committee, for the same reason as that indicated in [another communication].[2]

109. The members of the Committee who took the floor, while considering that it was difficult for the Committee to form an opinion on this case in the absence of information from the government concerned, felt it important to express as of now to that government their humanitarian concern regarding Mr Abdi Ismail Younis.

110. After an exchange of views, the Committee *decided*:

(i) to express its regret that a representative of the government concerned had not been present;

[1] See document 127 EX/3 PRIV., paras. 107-110; see also document 127 EX/CR/HR/3.
[2] *Ibidem*, paras. 104-105 (*supra*, pp. 670-671), communication No. 736/86 concerning *Somalia*, case of *Abdulle Rage Taraweh*.

(ii) to express it humanitarian concern to that government and to appeal to it to show clemency in regard to Mr Abdi Ismail Younis;

(iii) to resume consideration of this communication at its spring 1988 session.

Spring 1988 session of the Committee on Conventions and Recommendations (129th session of the Executive Board)[3]

Autumn 1988 session of the Committee on Conventions and Recommendations (130th session of the Executive Board)[4]

103. This communication has been on the Committee's agenda since the [autumn 1987 session]. It is still at the stage of examination of its admissibility.

104. According to the International Human Rights Law Group, Mr Abdi Ismail Younis, a mathematician, has been imprisoned since November 1982 and was sentenced to death on 7 February 1988 for infringements of the National Security Act and, in particular, for having formed a subversive association together with eight other persons, for having formed an armed group and for having been in possession of seditious material. His sentence was reportedly commuted by the President of the Republic to a 24-year prison sentence. The alleged victim is said to have been denied a fair trial and to be detained in extremely harsh conditions.

105. On 21 September 1988 the Secretariat received a letter from the International Human Rights Law Group reporting a sharp deterioration in Mr Ismail Younis's health and requesting that an appeal be made to the Somali Government for the immediate release of the alleged victim on humanitarian grounds.

106. The government concerned did not send a representative.

107. Several members of the Committee expressed very deep concern about this case. They felt that the Chairman of the Committee should make personal representations to the Somali authorities at the highest level and that he should also approach the Somali member of the Executive Board.

108. Following an exchange of views, the Committee *decided*:

---

[3] See document 129 EX/3 PRIV., paras. 91-95 (*supra*, pp. 671-672), communication No. 736/86 concerning *Somalia*, case of *Abdulle Rage Taraweh*.

[4] See document 130 EX/3 PRIV., paras. 103-109; see also document 130 EX/CR/HR - Somalia.

(i) to express regret that the government concerned had sent no representative;

(ii) to issue an urgent appeal to the government concerned to ensure that Mr Abdi Ismail Younis was treated with the clemency warranted by his critical state of health;

(iii) to request its Chairman to make personal representations to the highest Somali authorities and to [...] the Somali member of the Executive Board;

(iv) to resume consideration of this communication at its [spring 1989 session].

109. When the Committee's report was being adopted, the Somali member of the Executive Board made the following statement: "Mr Abdi Ismail was granted every means and opportunity to ensure his defence and received a fair trial; he was found guilty according to the laws of his country. He is imprisoned in an ordinary prison and in normal conditions. He cannot be regarded as a victim as he has been found guilty of having committed offences punishable by law. As for his state of health, the required information will be supplied to the Committee at the next session, after contact has been made with the appropriate authorities."

Spring 1989 session of the Committee on Conventions and Recommendations (131st session of the Executive Board)[5]

105. This communication has been on the Committee's agenda since the [autumn 1987 session]. It is still at the stage of being considered as to its admissibility.

106. Mr Abdi Ismail Younis, a mathematician who apparently has no political past, is reported to have been arrested in November 1982 and sentenced to death on 7 February 1988 for infringements of the National Security Act. His sentence is said to have been subsequently commuted to a 24-year prison sentence.

107. At its [autumn 1988] session, the Committee issued an urgent appeal to the government concerned to ensure that Mr Abdi Ismail Younis was treated with the utmost clemency in view of his state of health, described as critical by the author of the communication. The Committee also requested its Chairman to make personal

---

[5] See document 131 EX/3 PRIV., paras. 105-110; see also document 131 EX/CR/HR/SOM.

representations on behalf of the mathematician to the highest Somali authorities and to the Somali member of the Executive Board.[6]

108. In response to the representations made, the Embassy of the Somali Democratic Republic in France reported, in a letter dated 21 March 1989, that Mr Abdi Ismail Younis had just been pardoned by the Head of State together with 20 other persons. This measure of clemency followed an amnesty granted in February to 200 political prisoners.

109. The author of the communication confirmed this release in a letter dated 30 March 1989. He also expressed his entire satisfaction at the happy outcome of this case

110. After an exchange of views, the Committe *decided*:

(i) to take note with satisfaction of the release of Mr Abdi Ismail Younis;

(ii) to strike the communication from its list, considering it to be settled in accordance with paragraph 14 (*a*) (x) of 104 EX/Decision 3.3.

[6] See document 130 EX/3 PRIV., para. 108 (ii) and (iii) (*supra*, p. 687).

No. 746/87

Concerning *Greece*
Case of *Margarita Fréri and Rose Fréri*

Communication of 24 February 1987 submitted by
Margarita Fréri and Rose Fréri

Autumn 1987 session of the Committee on Conventions and Recommendations (127th session of the Executive Board)[1]

51. Miss Margarita Fréri and Miss Rose Fréri, who are said to hold primary-school teaching diplomas, reportedly applied for posts in State education. It is alleged that in February 1987 their applications were rejected on the grounds that they were not of the Orthodox faith.

52. By the same letter dated 4 September 1987, reported on during consideration of [another communication],[2] the Greek Government also requested that consideration of this communication be postponed until the next session of the Committee as the alleged victims had not exhausted available domestic remedies.

53. In reply to the question whether under present-day Greek law a person's religious affiliation was taken into account when that person applied for a post in the public sector, the representative of the government concerned stated that he did not wish to broach the substance of the case under consideration as he had to respect the future decisions of the judicial authorities. He noted, however, that, generally speaking, under the Constitution the dominant religion in Greece was that of the Eastern Orthodox Church and it therefore had to be protected. He added that it was necessary in particular to protect the teaching of religion according to Greek Orthodox dogma in primary school and in nursery school. The teaching of a religion could not be entrusted to someone who did not believe in that religion nor could such a person be asked to educate the youth of a country in the spirit of the dominant religion.

[1] See document 127 EX/3 PRIV., paras. 51-58; see also document 127 EX/CR/HR/3.
[2] *Ibidem*, para. 48 (*supra*, p. 681), communication No. 744/87 concerning *Greece*, case of *Ignace Philippoussis*.

54. Several members of the Committee expressed their concern over the explanations put forward. In their view, there should not be any problem of conscience when a teacher was called on to teach subjects other than a religion that was not his own. They raised the following questions:

whether in Greece, in nursery schools and primary schools, teachers were responsible for providing religious instruction;

whether such instruction included other religions or only the Greek Orthodox religion;

whether Greek law contained provisions to the effect that teachers should believe in that religion and whether there were provisions governing this situation;

whether the Greek Constitution guaranteed freedom of religious belief;

whether a citizen could question the constitutionality of a measure whose purpose was to deny a person the possibility of employment on religious grounds;

whether other means of redress were available in this regard beside those offered by the administrative tribunals;

whether assurances could be given to the Committee regarding the prevailing climate in respect of the religious minority in Greece.

55. Referring to the 1830 Protocol signed by France, Great Britain and Russia, mentioned by the authors of the communication as being an instrument guaranteeing full equality among all Greek citizens, particularly in the matter of worship and employment, some of those members also wished to know whether this text was in force in Greece and whether the principles it contained had been included in the national legislation.

56. In this connection, one member of the Committee pointed out that as the instrument in connection had been imposed upon a country during the colonial period, it should not be taken into consideration. Subscribing to the view expressed by the Chairwoman, he was of the opinion that any reference made should relate to the Universal Declaration of Human Rights.

57. Other members of the Committee felt that the main issue was whether the alleged victims had an effective means of redress and that, in the absence of relevant

information, it would be desirable to accede to the request for a postponement made by the government concerned.

58. After an exchange of views, the Committee *decided*:

(i) to thank the representative of the government concerned for his presence and co-operation;

(ii) in view of the judicial proceedings still in progress, to comply with the request made by the Greek Government and to postpone consideration of the communication until its spring 1988 session;

(iii) to request further information from that government in the light of the discussions that had taken place and the questions that had been asked.

Spring 1988 session of the Committee on Conventions and Recommendations (129th session of the Executive Board)[3]

[3] See document 129 EX/3 PRIV., paras. 47-51 (*supra*, pp. 682-683), communication No. 744/87 concerning *Greece*, case of *Ignace Philippoussis*.

No. 748/87

Concerning *Bulgaria*
Case of *Omer Mustafov Kochandzhiev* et al.*

Communication of 20 March 1987 submitted by
The International Human Rights Law Group

Autumn 1987 session of the Committee on Conventions and Recommendations (127th session of the Executive Board)[1]

16. Mr Omer Mustafov Kochandzhiev, whose profession is not stated, was reportedly arrested and imprisoned in 1985 for having opposed a name-changing campaign.

17. Mr Burhan Nedzhibov Hayrulov, whose profession is similarly not stated, was reportedly arrested on 31 December 1984 after a demonstration against the aforementioned campaign. He is said to have been sentenced to 10 years' imprisonment.

18. Mr Gyursel Hasanov Saadettinov, a student, was allegedly arrested on 28 December 1984 following a gathering of students of Turkish origin who were protesting against the same campaign.

19. Confirming the preliminary statement by the representative of the government concerned at the beginning of the discussion on [two other communications],[2] which also applied to the present communication, one of the other two representatives of the Bulgarian Government accompanying him said that the International Human Rights Law Group had omitted certain vital information from its communication, relating, in particular, to the identity and addresses of the alleged victims of a human rights violation. This showed that the author did not have reliable knowledge of the alleged facts, particularly since Mr Kochandzhiev (an agricultural worker) and Mr Saadettinov (a student) had never been arrested or sentenced. Mr Hayrulov (a driver)

* Case of Omer Mustafov Kochandzhiev, Burhan Nedzhibov Hayrulov and Gyursel Hasanov Saadettinov.
[1] See document 127 EX/3 PRIV., paras. 16-24; see also document 127 EX/CR/HR/3.
[2] *Ibidem*, para. 26 (*infra*, p. 712), communications No. 752/87 concerning *Bulgaria*, case of *Halim Pasadzhov*, and No. 753/87 concerning *Bulgaria*, case of *Rasim Reshebov* et al.

had been sentenced on appeal to four years' imprisonment, and not to 10, for a common-law offence. There was therefore no connection with Unesco's fields of competence. The allegations were defamatory, based exclusively on information circulated by the media and politically motivated. No relevant proof had been provided and the communication had not been submitted within a reasonable time-limit. The representative of the Bulgarian Government concluded that, under these circumstances, the communication should be declared inadmissible inasmuch as it failed to fulfil the conditions laid down in paragraph 14 (*a*) of 104 EX/Decision 3.3.

20. In reply to a question, the representative said that the student Saadettinov was continuing his studies normally and that the offence of which Mr Hayrulov was accused - insulting policemen and three other persons - was covered by Article 54 of the Penal Code.

21. Some members of the Committee pointed out that the name-changing process could be a source of distress to some people, whatever their occupation, since it affected their cultural identity, one of Unesco's major concerns. Moreover, the problem had figured prominently in Amnesty International's report for the previous year.

22. One member of the Committee said that if the communication were inadmissible under 104 EX/Decision 3.3, there could be no discussion of the matter.

23. Several members of the Committee considered that, in the light of the explanations given by the representative of the government concerned, the communication was unfounded in the case of Mr Kochandzhiev and Mr Saadettinov, since they had not been arrested or sentenced and were still at liberty, and inadmissible in the case of Mr Hayrulov *ratione personae* and *ratione materiae*.

24. Following an exchange of views and subject to the reservation expressed by one of its members, the Committee *decided*:

(i) to thank the representatives of the government concerned for their attendance and co-operation;

(ii) to declare the communication inadmissible under the terms of paragraph 14 (*a*) (ii), (iii) and (v) of 104 EX/Decision 3.3 and to strike it from its list.

No. 749/87

Concerning *Chile*
Case of *Luis Ibacache Silva*

Communication of 13 March 1987 submitted by
International Union of Students

Autumn 1987 session of the Committee on Conventions and Recommendations (127th session of the Executive Board)[1]

30. Described by the author of the communication as a medical student at the University of Valparaíso and a student leader at that institution, Mr Luis Ibacache Silva was allegedly arrested on 2 April 1984 for an offence under the law on the control of weapons and explosives. Released provisionally in October 1984, he is said to have been re-arrested on 3 September 1986. On 10 November 1986 he was allegedly sentenced to a prison term of three years and one day. This sentence was reportedly reduced on appeal to the Military Appeal Court. He is said to have been released on parole, conditional upon remaining under the surveillance of a special service over a three-year period and reporting to it regularly.

31. In his statement, the representative of the government concerned said that the law on the control of weapons and explosives had been in force since 1972 and that the competent courts in that regard were the military courts. He explained that the sentence passed in the first instance on Mr Luis Ibacache Silva was reduced, on appeal, to 541 days which had enabled him to be released on parole. His further explanations were confirmed by the written communication dated 17 September 1987 from the Permanent Delegation of Chile to Unesco which sought to clarify the position of its government as follows:

> "... With regard to the case of Luis Ibacache Silva, it is obvious that this communication is inadmissible both from the standpoint of the background information itself and under the procedure of the [Committee]. Mr Ibacache is, in fact, free; his appeal has been received by the courts of justice; his sentence has been substantially reduced although his criminal responsibility has been

[1] See document 127 EX/3 PRIV., paras. 30-33; see also document 127 EX/CR/HR/3.

established and he has been granted 'freedom on parole'. If Mr Ibacache is still not satisfied with this outcome, he can have recourse to a legal appeal for review and a remedy of complaint, the latter application being lodged with the Supreme Court of Justice. This means that in accordance with the procedure of the [Committee], paragraph 14, subparagraph (ix), this communication is clearly inadmissible."

32. The members of the Committee who took the floor wondered whether Mr Luis Ibacache Silva, released on parole, was able fully to enjoy his right to education and to exercise his right of association given that he was a medical student and also a leader of the student movement of his university. In their view, neither the letter from the author of the communication dated 25 June 1987 [...][2] nor the note of the Permanent Delegation of Chile to Unesco mentioned above contained any precise information on this point. They hoped that if the student was not able to pursue his studies during the period of release on parole, the government concerned would authorize him to do so as of now.

33. After an exchange of views, the Committee *decided*:

(i) to thank the representative of the Government concerned for his attendance and co-operation;

(ii) to take the note of the written communication dated 17 September 1987 of the Permanent Delegation of Chile to Unesco;

(iii) to request the government concerned to be good enough to:

(*a*) provide additional information on the question of whether Mr Luis Ibacache Silva's release on parole permitted him to exercise his right to education and to continue his activities within the student movement of his university;

(*b*) in the event of a negative reply, to take all the necessary steps to ensure that the student might immediately enjoy those rights, and to indicate, if appropriate, whether any procedures existed that enabled him to recover them;

(iv) to resume consideration of this communication at its spring 1988 session.

---

[2] See document 127 EX/CR/HR/3.

Chile **No. 749/87**

Spring 1988 session of the Committee on Conventions and Recommendations (129th session of the Executive Board)[3]

19. Mr Luis Ibacache Silva, a medical student, was sentenced in November 1986 to a term of imprisonment lasting three years and one day. This sentence was reduced on appeal to 541 days which enabled him to be released on parole.

20. At its [autumn 1987] session, the Committee requested the government concerned to inform it whether Mr Ibacache Silva, on parole, was able to exercise his right to education and continue his activities within the student movement of his university.[4]

21. At the present session, the representative of the government concerned informed the Committee that Mr Ibacache Silva had completed his studies normally and had obtained his diploma in medicine and surgery. He added that the person concerned was now carrying on his profession in Valparaíso.

22. After an exchange of views, the Committee *decided*:

(i) to thank the representative of the government concerned for attending the meeting and for his co-operation;

(ii) to note with satisfaction the favourable outcome of this case and to strike this communication from its list, considering it as settled in accordance with paragraph 14 (*a*) (x) of 104 EX/Decision 3.3.

[3] See document 129 EX/3 PRIV., paras. 19-22; see also document 129 EX/CR/HR/2.
[4] See document 127 EX/3 PRIV., para. 33 (iii) (*a*) (*supra*, p. 696).

No. 750/87

Concerning *Indonesia*
Case of *Achmad Zaini and Margono Bin Syafei*

Communication of 16 March 1987 submitted by
Amnesty International

Spring 1987 session of the Committee on Conventions and Recommendations (126th session of the Executive Board)[1]

60. Mr Achmad Zaini and Mr Margono Bin Syafei were reportedly sentenced to imprisonment, the former for displaying notices containing criticism of the government, the latter for distributing copies of such documents.

61. Confirming the content of its letter dated 27 April 1987 [...],[2] the representative of the government concerned requested that consideration of the communication should be deferred until the next session of the Committee as he had not had time to obtain the relevant information.

62. After an exchange of views, the Committee *decided* to comply with that request and to defer examination of the communication until its autumn 1987 session.

Autumn 1987 session of the Committee on Conventions and Recommendations (127th session of the Executive Board)[3]

66. Mr Achmad Zaini and Mr Margono Bin Syafei were reportedly sentenced in January 1987, the former to two and a half years' imprisonment for having had his pupils post up on the notice board of the Tamanggyung Mosque documents that were

[1] See document 126 EX/3 PRIV., paras. 60-62; see also documents 126 EX/CR/HR/3 and Add.2.
[2] See document 126 EX/CR/HR/3 Add.2.
[3] See document 127 EX/3 PRIV., paras. 66-74; see also documents 127 EX/CR/HR/2 and Add.2.

considered to bring the government into disrepute, and the latter to three years' imprisonment for having distributed such documents.

67. Under cover of a letter dated 2 September 1987 [...],[4] the government concerned sent the Secretariat its reply to the allegations contained in the communication.

68. According to the government, Mr Achmad Zaini and Mr Margono Bin Syafei had been sentenced after a fair trial by the Tribunal of Magelang and that of Yogyakarta (Central Java) respectively, for having violated Articles 155 (1) and 55 (1), para. 1, of the Penal Code which state "that whoever diffuses, exhibits or sticks up notices or pictures in public, inciting hatred, animosity or insults towards the State and Government of the Republic of Indonesia, will be sentenced for a maximum of four years and six months". It was also stipulated that the sentences against those two persons also included the time spent during temporary detention.

69. The Indonesian Government considered that the author of the communication did not have reliable knowledge of the alleged facts and that as the cases in question had been settled in accordance with the principles set forth in the Universal Declaration of Human Rights, the communication should be deemed inadmissible in accordance with paragraph 14 (*a*) (ii) and (x), of 104 EX/Decision 3.3.

70. Replying to some members of the Committee, the representative of the government concerned explained that like every country and in accordance with its culture, Indonesia was seeking to develop a political system that would ensure peace within the country and reduce tensions that might destabilize the regime. In this case the contentious documents had been declared illegal and consequently they could not be disseminated. In his view the case came entirely within the jurisdiction of Indonesia and he referred in this connection to Article 1, paragraph 3, of the Constitution of Unesco according to which the Organization is prohibited from intervening in such matters.

71. One member of the Committee raised the question whether the opinions disseminated by Mr Achmad Zaini and Mr Margono Bin Syafei were of a peaceful nature or whether they contained incitements to violence with a view to overthrowing.the government.

72. Other members of the Committee pointed out that according to the information contained in the communication, all means of redress had apparently not been used or exhausted and it was not known what type of recourse was available to the two alleged victims.

---

[4] See document 127 EX/CR/HR/2 Add.2.

Indonesia **No. 750/87**

73. The representative of the government concerned replied that in any case it was a common practice in Asia to reduce the sentences of a number of convicted persons each year and that the sentences of Mr Achmad Zaini and Mr Margono Bin Syafei might consequently be shortened.

74. After an exchange of views, the Committee *decided*:

(i) to thank the government concerned for its co-operation in not only sending a representative to appear before the Committee but in also forwarding a written reply;

(ii) to request both the author of the communication and the government concerned for further information regarding the possible means of redress available to Mr Achmad Zaini and Mr Margono Bin Syafei and whether they had availed themselves of them;

(iii) to resume examination of the communication at its spring 1988 session.

Spring 1988 session of the Committee on Conventions and Recommendations (129th session of the Executive Board)[5]

61. These two alleged victims were reportedly sentenced respectively to two and a half and three years' imprisonment, the former for having had his pupils post up on the noticeboard of the Tamanggung Mosque documents that were considered to bring the governmnent into disrepute, and the latter for having distributed such documents.

62. At its [autumn 1987] session, the representative of the government concerned informed the Committee that these two persons had been sentenced in accordance with the penal law in force, which stated that whosoever dessiminated, exhibited or posted notices or pictures in public which incited hatred or animosity towards the State or the government or made insulting remarks about them was liable to a maximum of four years and six months in prison. He also stated that it was possible to reduce the sentences of a number of convicted persons each year and that the sentences of Mr Achmad Zaini and Mr Margono Bin Syafei might consequently be shortened. After an exchange of views, the Committee decided to request both the government concerned and the author of the communication for further information regarding

[5] See document 129 EX/3 PRIV., paras. 61-68; see also document 129 EX/CR/HR/2.

the possible means of redress available to the two alleged victims and whether they had availed themselves of them.[6]

63. On 7 April 1988, the Secretariat received from the author of the communication a letter in which he stated that he did not possess any further information. He wished, however, to point out that the two alleged victims had not advocated the use of violence and that, therefore, their sentences would appear to constitute a violation of their right to freedom of thought, conscience and religion and their right to freedom of opinion and expression.

64. At the present session, the representative of the government concerned informed the Committee that his government had provided, at the [autumn 1987] session, all the relevant information, which showed that Mr Achmad Zaini and Mr Margono Bin Syafei had been properly judged in accordance with the law and the principles of human rights. The representative of the government concerned emphasized that these two persons had not been sentenced solely on the basis of the charges made by the State Prosecutor's Office. In fact, after having heard the witnesses and the defence and examined the evidence, the court had only passed judgement on the offence relating to the dissemination, exhibition and posting of notices or pictures in public which incited hatred and animosity or insulted the State and the government.

65. In response to a question as to whether the alleged victims had expressed their views peacefully or whether they had advocated the use of violence, the government representative read out the terms of the law to the case and explained that the law had evolved out of the Dutch legal system.

66. It was the view of a Committee member that this law could conceivably be used to suppress even peaceful expression of opinions, and that questions remained as to what acts of the alleged victims had been the basis of their punishment.

67. Another Committee member expressed the view that in developing countries the parameters of national security were sometimes narrower than in developed countries and that special consideration had to be given to the particularities of certain situations.

68. After an exchange of views, the Committee *decided*:

(i) to thank the government concerned for its co-operation in not only sending a representative to appear before the Committee, but in also forwarding a written reply;

---

[6] See document 127 EX/3 PRIV., para. 74 (ii) (*supra*, p. 701).

(ii) to request the government concerned for information as to which specific acts performed by Mr Achmad Zaini and Mr Margono Bin Syafei were the basis for their prosecution and as to whether or not they had advocated the use of violence;

(iii) to resume consideration of this communication at [its autumn 1988 session].

Autumn 1988 session of the Committee on Conventions and Recommendations (130th session of the Executive Board)[7]

63. This conununication has been on the Committee's agenda since the [spring 1987 session]. It is still at the stage of examination of its admissibility.

64. According to Amnesty International, Mr Achmad Zaini and Mr Margono Bin Syafei were sentenced to two and a half and three years' imprisonment respectively, the former for having had his pupils post up on the notice-board of the Tamanggung Mosque documents that were considered to bring the government into disrepute, and the latter for having distributed such documents. They did not - it is said - advocate the use of violence. Their sentences are claimed to be a violation of their right to freedom of thought, conscience and religion and of their right to freedom of opinion and expression.

65. At previous sessions, the representative of the government concerned informed the Conunittee that these two persons had been sentenced in accordance with the Penal Code, which provided that whoever disseminated, exhibited or posted in public notices or pictures which incited hatred and animosity in regard to the State or government, or which formulated insulting remarks about them, would be sentenced to a maximum of four years and six months' imprisonment. The sentences which the court had imposed on them were less than those demanded by the Public Prosecutor. The period spent in custody had also been taken into account. Moreover, each year a number of convicted persons had their sentences reduced. It was possible that Mr Achmad Zaini and Mr Margono Bin Syafei might benefit from such reductions of sentence.

66. On 5 September 1988, the Secretariat received from the Permanent Delegation of Indonesia a letter recapitulating the information previously supplied by its government and its position as regards this case.

---

[7] See document 130 EX/3 PRIV., paras. 63-70; see also documents 130 EX/CR/HR - Indonesia and Add.2.

No. 750/87 **Indonesia**

67. On 5 September 1988, the Secretariat also received from the author of the communication a letter indicating that it had examined a number of issues of *Ar-Risalah* and *Al-Ikhwan*, the two contentious publications forbidden by the Indonesian authorities, but had found no incitement to violence therein.

68. Without referring in detail to the explanations already supplied by his government, the Indonesian member of the Committee pointed out, in reply to a question, that it was sometimes difficult to establish a direct link between the remarks made by an individual and the violence which ensued, but that it was clear that Mr Achmad Zaini and Mr Margono Bin Syafei had sown the seeds of such violence. As the persons concerned would in any case soon be released, having all but served their sentences, the communication should in his view be struck from the Committee's list.

69. Several Committee members expressed scepticism as regards the responsibility of Mr Achmad Zaini and Mr Margono Bin Syafei in the violence that had been reported. One member wondered whether, as the representative of the government concerned had hinted at the previous sessions, they might not have their sentences reduced, since they had only a few more months of imprisonment to serve.

70. Following an exchange of views, the Committee *decided*:

(i) to take note of the information which the government concerned had kindly supplied by letter and to thank the Indonesian member of the Committee for his further clarifications;

(ii) to request the government concerned to grant to Mr Achmad Zaini and Mr Margono Bin Syafei the reductions of sentence which its representative at previous sessions of the Committee had hinted might be possible;

(iii) to resume consideration of this communication at its [spring 1989 session].

Spring 1989 session of the Committee on Conventions and Recommendations (131st session of the Executive Board)[8]

57. Included on the Committee's agenda since the [spring 1987 session], this communication is still at the stage of examination as to its admissibility.

[8] See document 131 EX/3 PRIV., paras. 57-63; see also document 131 EX/CR/HR/INS.

Indonesia **No. 750/87**

58. Mr Margono Bin Syafei, a tailor, and Mr Achmad Zaini, a merchant and Quranic teacher, were reportedly arrested in December 1985 and in January 1987, and subsequently sentenced respectively to three and two and a half years' imprisonment, the former for having distributed documents considered defamatory towards the government and the latter for having had his pupils post such documents on the noticeboard of the Tamanggung Mosque.

59. According to the government concerned, these two persons were sentenced in accordance with the Penal Code, which provided for a sentence of up to four years and six months' imprisonment for anyone who disseminated, exhibited or posted in public notices or pictures which incited hatred or animosity towards the State or government or made insulting remarks about them. Although the public prosecutor had demanded a more severe sentence, the courts to which the cases had been referred had passed relatively moderate sentences.

60. At its [autumn 1988] session, the Committee had appealed to the government concerned to grant these two persons a reduction in their sentences, inasmuch as they had practically finished serving them.[9]

61. At the present session, by a letter dated 7 March 1989, Amnesty International informed the Committee that Mr Margono Bin Syafei and Mr Achmad Zaini had been prosecuted not for having committed acts of violence or for having advocated violence, but for subversion, for they had distributed copies of a banned newsletter entitled "Al-Ikhwan". Examination of a few issues of that newsletter and of another newsletter entitled "Ar-Risalah", also banned, had revealed no incitement to violence. This case involved a violation of Article 28 of the Indonesian Constitution, which guaranteed freedom of expression, as well as of Articles 18 and 19 of the Universal Declaration of Human Rights.

62. By letter dated 27 April 1989, the Permanent Delegation of Indonesia to Unesco let it be known that Mr Achmad Zaini, benefiting from the reductions in his sentence which had been granted to him in 1987 and 1988, had been freed on 17 September 1988. Mr Margono Bin Syafei, for his part, had been granted no reduction of his sentence. He had served it and had been freed on 25 April 1989.

63. Following an exchange of views, the Committee *decided*:

(i) to take note of the letter of 27 April 1989 from the Permanent Delegation of Indonesia to Unesco and to thank the government concerned for the information contained therein regarding the release of Mr Achmad Zaini and Mr

---

[9] See document 130 EX/3 PRIV., para. 70 (ii) (*supra*, p. 704).

Margono Bin Syafei, the latter after having served his sentence, the former as a result of the reduction of his sentence;

(ii) to declare that this communication had thus ceased to be relevant and to strike it from its list.

No. 751/87

Concerning *Yugoslavia*
Case of *Ismet Kasumagic*

Communication of 25 March 1987 submitted by Amnesty International

Spring 1987 session of the Committee on Conventions and Recommendations (126th session of the Executive Board)[1]

189. Mr Ismet Kasumagic, presented by the author of the communication as a metallurgical engineer and lecturer at the Faculty of Metallurgy, Sarajevo, is alleged to have been sentenced to 10 years' imprisonment for hostile propaganda. This sentence is said to have been reduced by the higher courts to seven years' imprisonment.

190. Given the relatively short interval between receipt of the communication and the holding of this session, the representative of the government concerned requested that its examination be deferred to the Committee's next session.

191. Following an exchange of views, the Committee *decided* to accede to this request and to defer examination of the communication to its autumn 1987 session.

Autumn 1987 session of the Committee on Conventions and Recommendations (127th session of the Executive Board)[2]

125. Described by the author of the communication as a metallurgical engineer and lecturer at the Metallurgical Faculty of Sarajevo, Mr Ismet Kasumagic is said to have been sentenced to seven years' imprisonment for hostile propaganda.

---

[1] See document 126 EX/3 PRIV., paras. 189-191; see also document 126 EX/CR/HR/3 Add.
[2] See document 127 EX/3 PRIV., paras. 125-134; see also documents 127 EX/CR/HR/2 and Add.

No. 751/87 **Yugoslavia**

126. In a letter dated 10 August 1987 [...],[3] Amnesty International reported that the sentence had been reduced by one and a half years and that Mr Ismet Kasumagic was therefore due for release on 24 September 1988.

127. The representative of the Yugoslav Government stated that there were at least three gounds on which this communication should be declared inadmissible.

128. In the first place, Mr Kasumagic was not a recognized university teacher or lecturer. The status of this category of teachers was governed by very precise regulations. In particular, it was necessary to be the holder of a State doctorate or a science doctorate, to have published scientific works and to comply with a whole series of admission procedures. In point of fact, the person concerned had simply delivered a number of lectures and merely held the title of metallurgical engineer.

129. Secondly, Mr Kasumagic had infringed Article 133 of the Penal Code which prohibited, among other things, the dissemination of ideas inciting racial hatred and hatred between peoples and between the country's ethnic groups. The author of the communication had himself mentioned that this engineer had put forward the idea of the establishment of an ethnically pure Muslim Republic in Bosnia-Hercegovina, which was contrary not only to national legislation but also to the International Convention on the Elimination of All Forms of Racial Discrimination, in particular Article 4. The case was not, therefore, one of the mere exercise of the right to freedom of opinion and expression.

130. Thirdly, Mr Kasumagic had received a public trial in accordance with the procedure laid down by the legislation in force and had been able to exercise all the available domestic remedies. As regards the reduction of his sentence mentioned in Amnesty International's letter of 10 August 1987, this was the result of an extraordinary appeal that he had made to the Presidency of the Socialist Federal Republic of Yugoslavia which is able, depending on the case concerned, to decree a pardon or a reduction of sentence, having particular regard to the behaviour of the prisoner while serving his sentence. This was the standpoint from which the Presidency of the Republic decided, on 1 July 1987, to reduce by a year and a half the sentence of Mr Kasumagic, who will therefore be released in September 1988 after serving five and a half years of imprisonment.

131. Some members of the Committee considered that, as an enginner by profession, Mr Kasumagic was a scientist and that Committee was therefore competent to consider his case.

---

[3] See document 127 EX/CR/HR/2 Add.

132. While opposing this viewpoint, the representative of the government concerned agreed not to contest the issue.

133. One member of the Committee observed that he had doubts in this instance about describing this engineer as a scientist. He maintained that, while in certain cases a metallurgical engineer could be a scientist, one could not generalize by terming everyone who had studied science a scientist. In any event, he concurred with the view of other Committee members who thought that the Committee should examine the humanitarian aspects of the case and he wondered whether there was a possibility under Yugoslav legislation of releasing on parole a prisoner who had served two thirds of his sentence.

134. After an exchange of views, the Committee *decided*:

(i) to thank the representative of the government concerned for his attendance and co~operation;

(ii) to take note of the information he had provided and to ask him to convey to the relevant authorities in his country the Committee's purely humanitarian appeal that Mr Ismet Kasumagic should be accorded the maximum clemency and should be released;

(iii) to reconsider this communication at its spring 1988 session.

Spring 1988 session of the Committee on Conventions and Recommendations (129th session of the Executive Board)[4]

124. According to the author of the communication Mr Ismet Kasumagic, a metallurgical engineer and lecturer at the Metallurgical Faculty of Sarajevo, was sentenced to 10 years' imprisonment in 1983 for hostile propaganda. The sentence was reportedly reduced on appeal to seven years' imprisonment and later reduced by 18 months following an extraordinary appeal to the Presidency of the Socialist Federal Republic of Yugoslavia.

125. In a letter dated 5 April 1988 Amnesty International informed the Committee that Mr Ismet Kasumagic, as the result of a pardon granted on the occasion of the anniversary of the Socialist Federal Republic of Yugoslavia on 29 November 1987, had been released.

---

[4] See document 129 EX/3 PRIV., paras. 124-126; see also document 129 EX/CR/HR/2.

No. 751/87 **Yugoslavia**

126. After an exchange of views, the Committee *decided*:

(i) to thank the representative of the government concerned for his attendance and his co-operation;

(ii) to take note with satisfaction of the release of Mr Ismet Kasumagic;

(iii) to strike the communication from their list as settled and falling under paragraph 14 (*a*) (x) of 104 EX/Decision 3.3.

No. 752/87

Concerning *Bulgaria*
Case of *Halim Pasadzhov*

Communication of 25 March 1987 submitted by
Amnesty International

Spring 1987 session of the Committee on Conventions and Recommendations (126th session of the Executive Board)[1]

16. Mr Halim Pasadzhov, who is presented as a journalist and reportedly opposed the official campaign to change the names of persons of Turkish origin, is said to have been arrested in May 1985 and accused of spying.

17. Mr Rasim Rezhebov, Mr Salim Salimov and Mr Ismet Abdulov,[2] who reportedly attempted to organize a protest meeting against the same campaign, are said to have been sentenced to terms of imprisonment early in 1985.

18. In a letter dated 30 April 1987, the Permanent Delegate of Bulgaria to Unesco assured the Committee that his government was assiduously gathering the relevant information. Nevertheless, in view of the relatively short interval between the receipt of these two communications and the holding of the present session, he requested that consideration of them be deferred to the next session of the Committee.

19. Following an exchange of views, the Committee *decided* to agree to the request so formulated and to defer consideration of these two communications to its autumn 1987 session.

[1] See document 126 EX/3 PRIV., paras. 16-19; see also document 126 EX/CR/HR/3 Add.
[2] Communications No. 752/87 concerning *Bulgaria*, case of *Halim Pasadzhov*, and No. 753/87 concerning *Bulgaria*, case of *Rasim Rezhebov* et al., were being considered together.

No. 752/87 **Bulgaria**

Autumn 1987 session of the Committee on Conventions and Recommendations (127th session of the Executive Board)[3]

25. According to the author of these communications,[4] Mr Halim Pasadzhov, described as a journalist, and Mr Rasim Reshebov, Mr Salim Salimov and Mr Ismet Abdulov, whose occupations were not stated, opposed the campaign to change the names of persons of Turkish origin. The former is said to have been arrested in May 1985 and accused of spying. The three others reportedly attempted to organize a protest meeting against the same campaign. They are said to have been sentenced to terms of imprisonment in early 1985.

26. In a preliminary statement, the representative of the Bulgarian Government stated that Amnesty International had omitted vital information from its communications, referring in particular to the identity of the four persons and their addresses, which indicated that the author did not possess reliable knowledge, especially since Mr Reshebov and Mr Salimov (manual workers) had already been freed. Mr Abdulov (a cook) had been sentenced to four years' imprisonment for a serious breach of the peace. Mr Pasadzhov (who had not worked as a journalist since 1966) had been sentenced to 11 years' imprisonment for terrorism and not for the reasons mentioned by the author. There was therefore no connection with Unesco's fields of competence. Moreover, none of them practised a profession related to the Organization's activities. The representative of the government concerned further stated that the allegations were false and defamatory and those relating to a name-changing campaign in Bulgaria were based exclusively on information circulated by the media. He also stressed that the communications had not been submitted within a reasonable time-limit, since they referred to events occurring in 1985. In any case, the problems raised had been settled by the competent authorities with due regard for human rights. He concluded that the communications should therefore be declared inadmissible. He then gave the floor to one of the other two representatives of the Bulgarian Government accompanying him.

27. The latter provided the necessary details.

28. The members of the Committee who took the floor recognized that the two communications did not contain reliable information and that they would have to be declared inadmissible in the light of Unesco's competence *ratione personae* and *ratione materiae*.

---

[3] See document 127 EX/3 PRIV., paras. 25-29; see also document 127 EX/CR/HR/2.

[4] Communications No. 752/87 concerning *Bulgaria*, case of *Halim Pasadzhov*, and No. 753/87 concerning *Bulgaria*, case of *Rasim Rezhebov* et al., were being considered together.

Bulgaria **No. 752/87**

29. Following an exchange of views, the Committee *decided*:

(i) to thank the representatives of the government concerned for their attendance and co-operation;

(ii) to declare the two communications inadmissible under the terms of paragraph 14 (*a*) (ii), (iii) and (v) of 104 EX/Decision 3.3 and to strike them from its list.

No. 753/87

Concerning *Bulgaria*
Case of *Rasim Rezhebov* et al.*

Communication of 25 March 1987 submitted by
Amnesty International

Spring 1987 session of the Committee on Conventions and Recommendations (126th session of the Executive Board)[1]

Autumn 1987 session of the Committee on Conventions and Recommendations (127th session of the Executive Board)[2]

---

* Case of *Rasim Rezhebov, Salim Salimov and Ismet Abdulov*.

[1] See document 126 EX/3 PRIV., paras. 16-19 (*supra*, p 711), communication No. 752/87 concerning *Bulgaria*, case of *Halim Pasadzhov*.

[2] See document 127 EX/3 PRIV., paras. 25-29 (*supra*, pp. 712-713), communication No. 752/87 concerning *Bulgaria*, case of *Halim Pasadzhov*.

No. 754/87

Concerning *Union of Soviet Socialist Republics*
Case of *Alleged discriminations against access to Jewish history, culture and art*

Communication of 27 March 1987 submitted by
Michel A. Calvo*

Spring 1987 session of the Committee on Conventions and Recommendations (126th session of the Executive Board)[1]

174. The alleged victims indicated are mainly Soviet citizens of Jewish origin or having an ancestor of Jewish origin, who wish to learn about Jewish history, culture and art. According to the authors of the communication, to date there is no Jewish museum in the Soviet Union dealing with these subjects. No Soviet museum contains a specialized section on the subject nor houses an exhibition in this field from foreign museums or collections. Works of Jewish art from various regions are said to have disappeared or to be stored in certain museums without being studied or put on public display. Furthermore, Soviet citizens of Jewish origin have allegedly been unable to leave the country to visit foreign museums devoted to these themes.

175. The representative of the government concerned stated that this communication was completely untrue and proved that "international Zionist centres" were using the Committee for their own ends by seeking baselessly to show that there was no way for Jews to have their own culture except by emigrating from the Soviet Union. Such claims could only be regarded as propaganda for "Zionist chauvinism", which was based on the principle that the native land of all Jews, regardless of the country where they lived, was Israel. It was highly regrettable, he said, that such propaganda could not be rejected automatically by the Unesco Secretariat. The communication was drafted in insulting language and those grounds alone sufficed to have it deemed inadmissible, he said. Even if one were to examine the substance of the communication one could see that it contained nothing but untruths. No supporting facts were offered for the allegations of this communication. The representative of

* On behalf of André Lwoff and David Ruzié.
[1] See document 126 EX/3 PRIV., paras. 174-179; see also document 126 EX/CR/HR/3.

the government concerned explained that there existed a number of Jewish museums and cultural institutions in the Soviet Union, just as such cultural institutions existed for other minorities. There were all sorts of nationalities in the Soviet Union and there was absolutely no cultural discrimination against any of them, the representative pointed out. The Committee should not allow itself to be influenced and should strike this communication from its list.

176. A Committee member stated that unlike the question of educational rights under Article 27 of the [International] Covenant on Civil and Political Rights, there was no question in this case that private initiatives were being prohibited. In this communication the authors were requesting action on behalf of the State for which no basis existed in the aforementioned Article 27.

177. Other Committee members agreed that the communication was ill-founded, and certain members, of the opinion that the communication was offensive as well as ill-founded, wondered whether it would not be possible for the Secretariat to prevent such abusive cases from coming before the Committee.

178. The Chairperson reminded the Committee that under the terms of its procedures it was for the Committee to decide whether the text of a communication was offensive or not; the Secretariat was obliged to forward all cases to the Committee without passing its own judgment on them. In any event, the Chairperson pointed out, the Committee's procedures provided that an abusive communication could be resubmitted to the Committee once the abusive parts had been deleted by the author.

179. After discussion the Committee *decided*:

(i) to thank the representative of the government concerned for his presence and his co-operation;

(ii) to declare the communication inadmissible, being ill-founded and offensive, under [paragraph 14 (*a*) (v) and (vi) of 104 EX/Decision 3.3].

No. 755/87

Concerning *France*
Case of *Lyudmila Pavlovna Varigin*

Communication of 27 April 1987 submitted by
Group of teachers and students from the Pedagogical Institute
of Yaroslavl (USSR)

Autumn 1987 session of the Committee on Conventions and Recommendations (127th session of the Executive Board)[1]

39. Mrs Lyudmila Pavlovna Varigin (married name: Verdier), described as a student of the Pedagogical Institute of Yaroslavl, is said to have been arrested unlawfully on 17 March 1987 at her marital home in Rouen, France. She is alleged to have been suspected of spying on behalf of a foreign power and to have been interrogated continuously for 12 hours without the benefit of an interpreter or the assistance of a lawyer. Reportedly, it was not until the following day that a lawyer was assigned to her, and one who did not speak Russian. It is claimed that she was brought before the examining magistrate in handcuffs. Apparently the diplomatic representatives of her country were not notified by the French authorities until 17 days after she had been questioned. Released on 3 April 1987, she is said to have been prevented from leaving Rouen or France and consequently from preparing or sitting for her examinations.

40. The representative of the government concerned stated that the case against Mrs Lyudmila Pavlovna Varigin had been dismissed on 5 June 1987 and that consequently all the charges had been dropped, that her passport had been returned to her, that she was now completely free to do as she pleased and that therefore the communication was no longer applicable. He added that in any case the communication did not meet the conditions for admissibility laid down in 104 EX/Decision 3.3. In particular, no evidence had been supplied in support of their allegations, no investigation had been made, and there was no document or correspondence originating from the alleged victim herself (para. 14 (*a*) (v) of 104 EX/Decision 3.3) which proved that the communication was based exclusively on information disseminated through

[1] See document 127 EX/3 PRIV., paras. 39-46; see also document 127 EX/CR/HR/3.

the mass media (para. 14 (*a*) (vii) of [104 EX/Decision 3.3]). He also stated that under French law a person who was able to produce relevant evidence and who considered himself to be the victim of an assault, in the event of ill-treatment, or to have suffered prejudice as a result of shortcomings in the public administration of justice was entitled to seek redress with a view to obtaining compensation. There was, however, no indication in the communication that any attempt had been made to seek such redress (para. 14 (*a*) (ix) of 104 EX/Decision 3.3). The communication should therefore be declared inadmissible.

41. In reply to a question from a member of the Committee, the representative of the government concerned stated that as the charges had been dropped against Mrs Lyudmila Pavlovna Varigin, the *status quo ante* had been re-established and that, as the wife of a French citizen, she would not encounter any difficulties in staying in France.

42. To the question whether the admissibility of the communication should first be considered even though that communication had ceased to be applicable, it was noted that, according to the constant practice of the Committee, the reply could only be in the negative.

43. Several members of the Committee considered that it would indeed be best not to enter into the finer points of the question of admissibility but rather to adopt a pragmatic solution in accordance with the practice always followed by the Committee, which was its strength. There were, for instance, no grounds for asserting that the authors of the communication had learned of the alleged facts exclusively through the mass media. It should therefore be noted simply that the purpose and aim of the communication had been achieved as the result of a judicial decision, that the case was therefore settled and that the communication no longer served any object. Moreover, in striking the communication from its list, the Committee was not adopting a position in favour of either party but was merely acknowledging that the case had been settled.

44. Other members of the Committee pointed out that, if such a decision could be taken, that did not mean that the Committee was in agreement with the French Government. The fact of the matter was that in this case certain legal norms had been violated as the alleged victim had been subjected to ill-treatment. Furthermore, while it was true that the situation had changed, it was not known whether Mrs Lyudmila Pavlovna Varigin's right to education was respected. One of those members considered that it would be advisable first to communicate the information provided by the government concerned to the authors of the communication and not to decide to strike it from its list until the next session.

France **No. 755/87**

45. In response to a request for further information from some members of the Committee, the Chairwoman explained that, as was customary, the decision of the Committee would be notified to the authors of the communication along with a summary of the statements made by the representative of the government concerned.

46. After an exchange of views the Committee *decided*:

(i) to thank the representative of the government concerned for his presence and co-operation;

(ii) to take note of his statements to the effect that since the charges against Mrs Lyudmila Pavlovna Varigin had been dropped on 5 June 1987 and since she was in possession of her passport, she was at present completely free to do as she pleased;

(iii) to declare the communication to be not applicable and to strike it from its list.

No. 758/87

Concerning *Union of Soviet Socialist Republics*
Case of *History books and textbooks for pupils in the Soviet Union*

Communication of 23 July 1987 submitted by
Michel A. Calvo*

Autumn 1987 session of the Committee on Conventions and Recommendations (127th session of the Executive Board)[1]

115. In [the first communication],[2] the authors allege that in the Soviet Union, various history textbooks for secondary-school pupils do not reflect the facts faithfully, and that there is a trend to develop in schoolchildren of Jewish origin a feeling of inferiority and frustration and to incite Soviet schoolchildren to hatred and/or racial and/or ethnic discrimination in respect of Jews throughout the world, and Soviet citizens of Jewish origin in particular.

116. In [the other communication], it is alleged that various works by contemporary Soviet authors contain the same incitements.

117. Following the detailed presentation of these two communications, the Chairwoman notified the Committee that by letter dated 14 September 1987, [Mr] Michel A. Calvo had informed the Secretariat that he was unable to communicate, in compliance with its request, the passages of the texts quoted and the bibliography provided therein in the original Russian before the present session of the Committee, and that he would do so within a few months, prior to the next session.

---

* On behalf of André Lwoff, David Ruzié, Laurent Schwartz, Henri Cartan and Bernard Dupuy.

[1] See document 127 EX/3 PRIV., paras. 115-124; see also document 127 EX/CR/HR/3 Add.

[2] Communications No. 758/87 concerning *Union of Soviet Socialist Republics*, case of *History books and textbooks for pupils in the Soviet Union*, and No. 759/87 concerning *Union of Soviet Socialist Republics*, case of *Various works by contemporary Soviet authors*, were being considered together.

118. In this connection, the representative of the Director-General explained that the excerpts from works written in Russian and the bibliography attached had been communicated to the Secretariat in French, translated from the original Russian version, and that the translation back into Russian might not coincide with the original text. This was why the Russian version of the documents available to Committee members contained the indication: "provisional translation undertaken by the Secretariat pending communication of the original Russian text requested from the authors of the communication".

119. Several members of the Committee recalled that, at its spring 1987 session, the Committee had examined [another communication], submitted by the same authors, which related to alleged discrimination in regard to access to Jewish history, culture and art in the Soviet Union. The Committee had declared it inadmissible.[3] These members stressed that the two communications currently under consideration contained terms that were wholly comparable with those of the above-mentioned communication. In particular, one of the founding Member States of the United Nations was accused of genocide, and of having used Nazi methods. The Committee had considered such statements to be offensive, which was one of:the reasons that had led to the decision to declare [the communication] inadmissible.

120. Secondly, the same members considered it improper on the part of the authors to continue to present communications of this kind, when virtually all those of the same nature submitted to previous sessions of the Committee had been declared inadmissible. They pointed out that in the course of 10 sessions of the Committee (from the autumn 1982 session to the present session) these authors had submitted some 15 communications most of which were intended to prove the same assertion, one that the Committee had consistently held to be unfounded.

121. The representative of the government concerned informed the Committee that the competent authorities of his country had received these two comunications in early September 1987 only, and without the original:Russian versions of the texts quoted. He stated that the allegations made were wholly unfounded and highly offensive; accordingly, he was fully in agreement with the above-mentioned opinion expressed by several Committee members. He asked that the two communications be declared inadmissible in conformity with paragraph 14 (*a*) (iii), (iv), (v) and (vi) of 104 EX/Decision 3.3.

122. The members of the Committee who subsequently took the floor made the point that, while history books and textbooks lay to some extent within Unesco's

---

[3] See document 126 EX/3 PRIV., para. 179 (ii) (*supra*, p. 718), communication No. 754/87 concerning *Union of Soviet Socialist Republics*, case of *Alleged discriminations against access to Jewish history, culture and art.*

competence, they should be assessed from another standpoint, for example in the context of an international meeting of historians, but not in connection with a communication. The Committee could not in fact ask a sovereign State to penalize particular persons responsible for the matter at issue, or call into question a country's policy, as had been requested *inter alia*, in the paragraphs dealing with the purpose and aim of the two communications.

123. One of these members stated moreover that such communications were contrary to the spirit of Unesco. He added that in recent years several States had formulated criticisms regarding an alleged politicization of Unesco's activities. In this context, however, a very different perception had emerged of the notion of politics and politicization. It had come to be realized that the diversity of and even the antagonism between political, ideological and religious positions should not create obstacles to cooperation for the purpose of attaining the Organization's aims and carrying out its functions. The Member States had approved a policy that fostered a climate of trust and constructive dialogue in the spirit of Unesco's intellectual role. The majority of these States had indeed rejected all attempts to undermine international co-operation founded on the principle of equality in the Organization's fields of competence by means of unjustified reproaches and slanderous charges aimed at Member States. If today certain circles were seeking, as it emerged from the present communications, to use Unesco in order to further their own interests, to politicize it in a destructive sense and to damage the climate of co-operation, it was incumbent on the Committee to be guided in its decisions not only by its formal rules of procedure but also by its spirit of shared responsibility for the future of Unesco.

124. Following a lengthy discussion, the Committee *decided*:

(i) to thank the representative of the government concerned for his presence and his co-operation;

(ii) to declare these two communications inadmissible as being incompatible with the Organization's principles, ill-founded and offensive, by virtue of paragraph 14 (*a*) (iv), (v) and (vi) of 104 EX/Decision 3.3;

(iii) to request the Secretariat to transmit the report on the Committee's discussions concerning these communications to their authors.

No. 759/87

Concerning *Union of Soviet Socialist Republics*
Case of *Various works by contemporary Soviet authors*

Communication of 28 July 1987 submitted by
Michel A. Calvo*

Autumn 1987 session of the Committee on Conventions and Recommendations (127th session of the Executive Board)[1]

* On behalf of André Lwoff, David Ruzié, Laurent Schwartz, Henri Cartan and Bernard Dupuy.

[1] See document 127 EX/3 PRIV., paras. 115-124 (*supra*, pp. 723-725), communication No. 758/87 concerning *Union of Soviet Socialist Republics*, case of *History books and textbooks for pupils in the Soviet Union*.

No. 760/87

Concerning *People's Republic of China*
Case of *Liu De*

Communication of 10 August 1987 submitted by
Amnesty International

Spring 1988 session of the Committee on Conventions and Recommendations (129th session of the Executive Board)[1]

28. According to the author of the communication, Mr Liu De, journalist, who had allegedly been charged with counter-revolutionary propaganda and incitement and sentenced to seven years' imprisonment with three years' deprivation of political rights, had been imprisoned solely for the non-violent exercise of his rights to freedom of thought, opinion and expression.

29. In a letter dated 3 May 1988, the Permanent Delegation of the People's Republic of China to Unesco informed the Committee that Mr Liu De, arrested on 29 August 1985, had been sentenced on 6 November of the same year to seven years' imprisonment and to three years' deprivation of political rights, for "political incitement and public disturbance with a view to overthrowing by force the power of the State". His appeal against this sentence had been rejected by the higher legal authority. According to the Permanent Delegation, the communication was based solely on a short article in the "China Legal News", of 5 February 1987, the object of which was not to present a full report on the crimes committed by Mr Liu De and his sentence, but to analyse the reasons why he had become a criminal and draw the appropriate conclusions, for the benefit of young people. The Permanent Delegation, taking the view that the allegations put forward by the author of the communication were purely subjective, considered that the communication was inadmissible under the terms of the provisions of paragraphs 6, 7 and 14 (*a*) (ii), (iii) and (vii) of 104 EX/Decision 3.3 of the Executive Board.

---

[1] See document 129 EX/3 PRIV., paras. 28-32; see also document 129 EX/CR/HR/3.

No. 760/87 **People's Republic of China**

30. Some members of the Committee considered that the information provided was not yet substantial enough to enable the Committee to come to a decision. In particular, it did not specify the nature of the public disturbances.

31. Other members of the Committee considered that the letter of the Permanent Delegation of the People's Republic of China indicated clearly that the acts of which Mr Liu De was accused were acts of a political nature aimed at overthrowing the government by force, and consequently that the communication did not come within Unesco's fields of competence. Moreover, the communication was based on information taken from a newspaper and was therefore inadmissible under the terms of paragraph 14 (*a*) (vii) of 104 EX/Decision 3.3.

32. After an exchange of views, the Committee *decided*:

(i) to express its regret that a representative of the government concerned had not been present;

(ii) to take note of the contents of the letter of 3 May 1988 from the Permanent Delegation of the People's Republic of China;

(iii) to request the government concerned, in view of the insufficient information concerning the communication, to be good enough to provide additional information on the factual and legal basis for Mr Liu De's sentence;

(iv) to resume examination of the communication at [its autumn 1988 session].

Autumn 1988 session of the Committee on Conventions and Recommendations (130th session of the Executive Board)[2]

23. Mr Liu De, described by the author of the communication as a journalist and member of the editorial board of a literary magazine in Mianyang City, was allegedly sentenced to seven years' imprisonment with three years' deprivation of political rights for "counter-revolutionary" propaganda and incitement.

24. On 5 September 1988 the Secretariat received a letter in which the author of the communication said that it possessed no additional information on the case, again

[2] See document 130 EX/3 PRIV., paras. 23-27; see also document 130 EX/CR/HR - People's Republic of China.

expressed its concern about the alleged victim's confined detention and reiterated its demand for his immediate and unconditional release.

25. At the present session, after recalling his government's position as expressed in a letter of 3 May 1988 which had been brought to the attention of the Committee at its [spring 1988] session, the representative of the People's Republic of China made the following observations:

(*a*) Mr Liu De had been arrested for inciting young people to violence and advocating the use of force to overthrow the government, which had led to public disturbances. These acts constituted a criminal offence. The question of the exercise of his right to freedom of thought, opinion and expression was not involved.

(*b*) Mr Liu De's case had been heard in a public trial which had been conducted in accordance with the provisions of the Penal Code and he had been sentenced in accordance with criminal law. This was a matter which lay within China's domestic jurisdiction.

(*c*) The author of the communication had made ill-founded accusations against a sovereign State, which was unacceptable. The accusations were based solely on a short article in the "China Legal News". However, 104 EX/ Decision 3.3 stated that communications must not be based exclusively on information disseminated through the mass media. Amnesty International had admitted, moreover, that it had no other sources of information. Consequently, the communication should be declared inadmissible.

(*d*) It was common knowledge that the Chinese authorities had undertaken an outward-looking policy of reform with a view to developing and modernizing the country. In that context, any attempt to undermine internal stability and national unity was harmful and should be sanctioned. However, the government was implementing a policy of education for prisoners. The "China Legal News" had simply pointed out the effectiveness of this policy as far as Mr Liu De was concerned. He would have his sentence reduced at the appropriate time.

26. Several members of the Committee had pointed out that the allegations contained in the communication were based exclusively on a newspaper article and were not supported by any other evidence.

27. After an exchange of views, the Committee *decided*:

(i) to thank the representative of the government concerned for his presence and co-operation;

(ii) to declare the communication inadmissible in accordance with 104 EX/ Decision 3.3, paragraph 14 (*a*) (vii), on the grounds that it was based exclusively on information published in the press.

No. 761/87

Concerning *People's Republic of Benin*
Case of *Baro Orou Mora*

Communication of 10 August 1987 submitted by
Amnesty International

Spring 1988 session of the Committee on Conventions and Recommendations (129th session of the Executive Board)[1]

8. According to the author of the communication Mr Baro Orou Mora, a trainee administrator at the Beninese National Commission for Unesco, was reportedly arrested on 31 January 1986 and held since then without charge or trial. It is alleged that his arrest was due either to his sympathy for student protests which were renewed in March 1985, or to his suspected membership of the Communist Party of Dahomey (PCD).

9. In view of the fact that Amnesty International had only submitted the case of Mr Baro Orou Mora, the Committee did not examine Appendix A, attached to the communication form, which listed a number of names.

10. Since he had not yet received any relevant information from the authorities in his country, the representative of the government concerned requested that examination of this communication be postponed until a later session.

11. After an exchange of views, the Committee *decided*:

(i) to thank the representative of the government concerned for attending the meeting and for his co-operation;

(ii) to request the government concerned to provide it with all relevant information on the substance of the facts alleged and on the state of progress of any proceedings which might be under way;

[1] See document 129 EX/3 PRIV., paras. 8-11; see also document 129 EX/CR/HR/3.

(iii) to request the representative of the government concerned to convey to the authorities of his country a humanitarian appeal from the Committee, having regard to the length of the period of detention to which Mr Baro Orou Mora is alleged to have been subjected;

(iv) to resume examination of this communication at [its autumn 1988 session].

Autumn 1988 session of the Committee on Conventions and Recommendations (130th session of the Executive Board)[2]

8. This communication has been on the Committee's agenda since the [spring 1988 session]. It is at the stage of being examined for its admissibility.

9. Mr Baro Orou Mora, described by the author of the communication as a trainee administrator at the Beninese National Commission for Unesco, is reported to have been arrested on 31 January 1986 and to have been held since then without charge or trial, either on account of his sympathetic attitude towards student protests, particularly the protest of March 1985, or because of his supposed membership of the Communist Party of Dahomey (PCD). It is claimed that he did no more than express his opinions without advocating the use of violence. Several representations on behalf of Mr Mora are reported to have been made without success. His case has also reportedly been submitted to the United Nations under the procedure set out in resolution 1503 (XLVIII) of 27 May 1970.

10. At its [spring 1988] session, the Committee acceded to the request of the representative of the government concerned that examination of this communication be postponed to the present session and requested the government to provide it with information on the substance of the allegations and on the progress of any proceedings which might be under way. It also made a humanitarian appeal on Mr Baro Orou Mora's behalf, having regard to the length of the period of detention to which he had been subjected.[3]

11. At the present session, the representative of the government concerned informed the Committee that a law of April 1988 had provided for the establishment of a special court to examine crimes and offences involving State security. This State security court had, in fact, just been set up and, between now and the end of the year, would be examining all the cases pending. In reply to questions, the representative

---

[2] See document 130 EX/3 PRIV., paras. 8-13; see also document 130 EX/CR/HR - Benin.
[3] See document 129 EX/3 PRIV., para. 11 (ii) and (iii) (*supra*, pp. 733-734).

of the government stated that the identification of crimes and offences coming under the new law did not depend on that law, but on the Penal Code. Thus, the principle of non-retroactivity had not been breached, since this was merely an implementing law. This State security court was an ordinary court of law established on a permanent basis. Consequently, it was not a special tribunal, as was clear from its powers, its jurisdiction and its procedures. Its judgements were subject to appeal (annulment or re-examination). With regard to Mr Baro Orou Mora, the preliminary inquiries into his case had not been completed. If the investigation revealed that there was insufficient evidence to bring charges against him, he would be released. Meanwhile, he was merely subject to an administrative regulation placing him under house arrest. He stood accused of having been a member or instigator of a movement which had seriously endangered State security. He would also appear to have been implicated in other affairs, but further information could not be divulged on account of the confidentiality of the inquiries.

12. Several members of the Committee expressed their regret that specific information had not been provided on the actions of which Mr Baro Orou Mora was accused or on the punishment laid down by the law for such actions. Some members expressed concern that matters relating to crimes and offences against the State should come within the jurisdiction of a special court. The time taken by the proceedings, which seemed to have awaited the establishment of the new State security court and during which the person concerned had remained under house arrest without trial, the nature of this administrative measure of house arrest, the nature of the law of April 1988 itself, which seemed to be an emergency law which could lead to a worsening of the position of the alleged victim, all of these considerations increased the speakers' concern and their fear that this was indeed a case of the violation of human rights.

13. After an exchange of views, the Committee *decided*:

(i) to thank the representative of the government concerned for attending the meeting and for his co-operation;

(ii) to express its concern regarding the length of the proceedings and their departure from the ordinary law of the land;

(iii) to request the government concerned to provide it with additional information on the allegations and the procedures involved and on the current state of proceedings;

(iv) to resume consideration of this communication at its [spring 1989 session].

No. 761/87 **People's Republic of Benin**

Spring 1989 session of the Committee on Conventions and Recommendations (131st session of the Executive Board)[4]

8. This conununication has been on the Conunittee's agenda since the [spring 1988 session]. It is still at the stage of being examined as to its admissibility.

9. Mr Baro Orou Mora, a trainee administrator at the Beninese National Conunission for Unesco, is reported to have been arrested on 31 January 1986 and to have been held since then without charge or trial, either on account of his sympathetic attitude towards student protests or because of his supposed membership of the Communist Party of Dahomey (PCD).

10. At its [auutmn 1988] session, the representative of the government concerned informed the Conunittee that a special court to examine crimes and offences involving State security had just been established under a law promulgated in April 1988, and that it would shortly be examining all the cases pending.

11. The Conunittee expressed its concern regarding the length of the proceedings and their departure from the ordinary law of the land. In addition, it requested the government concerned to provide it with additional information on the allegations against Mr Baro Orou Mora and on the current state of proceedings against him.[5]

12. At the current session, the Permanent Delegation of Benin to Unesco informed the Committee, in a letter dated 5 May 1989 sent to the Director-General, that Mr Baro Orou Mora had been released on 1 April 1989 on the instructions of the Head of State.

13. After an exchange of views, the Committee *decided*:

(i) to take note of this release with satisfaction;

(ii) to strike the conununication from its list, considering it to be settled in accordance with paragraph 14 (*a*) (x) of 104 EX/Decision 3.3.

---

[4] See document 131 EX/3 PRIV., paras. 8-13; see also document 131 EX/CR/HR/BEN.
[5] See document 130 EX/3 PRIV., para. 13 (ii) and (iii) (*supra*, p. 735).

No. 762/87

Concerning *Turkey*
Case of *Recep Marasli*

Communication of 10 August 1987 submitted by
Amnesty International

Spring 1988 session of the Committee on Conventions and Recommendations (129th session of the Executive Board)[1]

96. Mr Recep Marasli, described by Amnesty International as a publisher, aged 31, specializing in books on Kurdish history and culture and the situation of the Kurdish minority in Turkey, is alleged to have been sentenced by various military courts, following the imposition of martial law in 1980, to a total of 30 years' imprisonment on charges of insulting the memory of President Atatürk and attempting to establish an independent State or territory.

97. The representative of the government concerned stated before the Committee that the allegations of the author of the communication were completely unfounded. Their sole purpose was to slander the political regime in Turkey. Mr Recep Marasli had been convicted in seven different lawsuits, one of which was still the subject of an appeal, for acts described as crimes in the Turkish Penal Code, namely: insults, by means of publications, against the State, institutions and President Atatürk; incitement to separatism and anti-national propaganda motivated by racist considerations; falsification of identity card; and leadership of illegal organizations aimed at removing part of the national territory from the sovereignty of the State. The representative of the government concerned said that the sentence in the last-mentioned case had been quashed on the grounds that the leadership of those organizations was covered, not by the provisions of the Penal Code concerning the establishment of "secret alliances", but by those relating to the establishment of armed gangs. Consequently, what was at issue was not simply the non-violent exercise of the right to freedom of expression and association, as was claimed by the author of the communication. The representative of the government concerned considered that the communication should be deemed inadmissible on the grounds that it was prompted ex-

[1] See document 129 EX/3 PRIV., paras. 96-102; see also document 129 EX/CR/HR/3.

clusively by political motives, related to a case essentially falling within national jurisdiction, was contrary to the rule according to which the Organization cannot perform the role of an international judicial body impugning the decisions taken by national courts, was manifestly ill-founded and contained no relevant evidence, in particular, to support the allegations concerning the prohibition against the use of dialects, the existence of 48,000 political prisoners, the lack of independence of the courts and the use of torture. In that connection, the representative of Turkey pointed out that his country had signed the United Nations Convention against Torture and Other Cruel, Inhuman [or] Degrading Treatment or Punishment and the corresponding European Convention [for the Prevention of Torture and Inhuman or Degrading Treatment or Punishment] and that Turkey had recognized, in January 1987, the right of individual appeal to the European Commission [of] Human Rights provided for by the European Convention on Human Rights.

98. The representative of the government concerned replied to questions and general observations regarding the situation of the Kurdish community in Turkey, the use of the Kurdish language, which was authorized except in official documents, separatism, the transfer of prisoners from military prisons to civil prisons after the lifting of martial law, and the referral of cases to civil courts, which were at emergency courts, after the lifting of that law. With regard to the alleged victim, the representative of the government concerned repeated that the publications for which he had been charged were insulting and constituted an incitement to separatism, but that they had not given rise to detention without trial since they had been issued before the imposition of martial law. However, to this offence had been added other crimes, in particular the establishment of armed gangs, a matter still pending before the courts. The person concerned was in a civil prison and his state of health remained unchanged.

99. One member of the Committee, after making some general remarks about the human rights situation in Turkey, considered that the Committee should suspend consideration of the communication with regard to those aspects still *sub judice*, namely the establishment of the Rizgari and Alarizgari organizations, and keep the communication on its list with regard to the other facts for which the person concerned had been convicted, while requesting further information from the government concerned about what appeared to reflect a legitimate desire for the recognition of cultural identity, and possibly for the granting of a status of cultural autonomy, rather than a desire for separatism.

100. Other members of the Committee wished the Committee to request information from the government concerned regarding the state of health of the alleged victim, the precise reasons for his having been given such a heavy sentence and, in particular, whether he had been charged with acts of terrorism or merely with issuing ille-

gal publications. Some members also requested that the Committee make a humanitarian appeal for a reduced sentence.

101. One member of the Committee raised the question whether the Committee was not interfering in the domestic affairs of a State whose courts had considered the case and had reached a decision in accordance with the law and the national interest. That Committee member considered that the communication was manifestly prompted by exclusively political motives and hence was inadmissible.

102. After an exchange of views, the Committee *decided*:

(i) to thank the representative of the government concerned for his presence and his co-operation;

(ii) to request information from the government concerned regarding the precise reasons for Mr Recep Marasli's being convicted in six lawsuits, referred to by the representative of that government;

(iii) to suspend consideration of the communication in regard to those aspects which are the subject of a seventh lawsuit in progress, pending the judicial decision, and to resume consideration thereof at [its autumn 1988 session] in regard to its other aspects;

(iv) to appeal for clemency on behalf of Mr Recep Marasli on account of his state of health and the harshness of the sentences pronounced against him.

Autumn 1988 session of the Committee on Conventions and Recommendations (130th session of the Executive Board)[2]

110. This communication has been on the Committee's agenda since the [spring 1988 session]. It is at the stage of examination of its admissibility.

111. According to Amnesty International, the author of the communication, Mr Recep Marasli, a publisher specializing in books on Kurdish history and culture and the situation of the Kurdish minority in Turkey, has been sentenced by various military courts under martial law to a total of 36 years' imprisonment.

[2] See document 130 EX/3 PRIV., paras. 110-120; see also document 130 EX/CR/HR - Turkey.

No. 762/87 **Turkey**

112. Mr Recep Marasli is said to have gone on several hunger strikes and to be in poor health.

113. At the [spring 1988] session, the representative of the government concerned said that Mr Marasli had been convicted in seven different lawsuits, one of which was still the subject of an appeal. The crimes of which he was accused were as follows: insults, by means of publications, against the State, institutions and President Atatürk; incitement to separatism and anti-national propaganda motivated by racist considerations; falsification of identity card; and leadership of illegal organizations aimed at removing part of the national territory from the sovereignty of the State. The case concerning the last-mentioned offence was still in progress, the Court of Appeal having quashed the original sentence on the grounds that the facts related not to the "establishment of secret alliances", but to the "establishment of armed gangs", since it had been proved that the illegal organization to which Mr Marasli belonged was composed of persons who carried arms. The representative of the government concerned considered that the allegations made had no bearing on the right to freedom of expression and association and that, consequently, the communication was inadmissible as not being in conformity with the provisions of 104 EX/Decision 3.3. He pointed out that after the lifting of martial law, affairs pending before the military courts had been referred to civil courts. Likewise, the persons detained, including Mr Marasli, had been transferred from military prisons to civil prisons.

114. The Committee had requested information from the government concerned regarding the precise reasons for Mr Recep Marasli's conviction. It had appealed for clemency on his behalf on account of his state of health and the harshness of the sentences pronounced against him.[3]

115. In a letter dated 1 September 1988, the author of the communication furnished the Committee with the following additional information: the Rizgari organization, of which Mr Recep Marasli was a member, had not had recourse to violence, at any rate prior to 1982, the date of his arrest; nor did the publications held against him contain incitements to violence; the allegations regarding the prohibition against the use of the Kurdish language were true, and accordingly Mr Marasli had not been authorized to use that language for his defence; his trial, like that of thousands of others, was still pending before the military courts in spite of the lifting of martial law; State security courts had been operating since 1984, but they did not give political prisoners a fair trial; confessions obtained under torture were admitted as evidence.

116. On 29 September, 4 October and 13 October 1988, the Secretariat received letters from the Permanent Delegation of Turkey to Unesco informing the Committee

---

[3] See document 129 EX/3 PRIV., para. 102 (ii) and (iv) (*supra*, p. 739).

of additional observations by its government. Mr Marasli had not been convicted for his publishing activities but for acts proscribed by the Penal Code: use of force against the political, legal and social order; separatism based on racial criteria; offences against State security at home and abroad. None of these crimes bore any relation to Unesco's fields of competence or to freedom of peaceful expression and association. The fact that they had been perpetrated through publication was an aggravating circumstance. However, the publication was not the cause of his indictment. The sentence against the illegal organizations Rizgari and Alarizgari, which had been quashed, did not fall within Unesco's purview either, since it concerned the establishment of secret alliances or armed gangs. Mr Marasli had not been tried and convicted for crimes of conscience, a concept alien to Turkish legislation. Notwithstanding Amnesty International's allegations, the Rizgari organization practised and advocated violence. It had separatist aspirations and had never denied that fact. It was the State's right and duty to proceed against it. The official language in Turkey was Turkish and trials were conducted in that language. Those who did not understand it were entitled to the services of an interpreter. Rights of defence were respected and both the military courts established under martial law and the civil courts were independent. This was all guaranteed by the Constitution. The military courts were not special judicial bodies prohibited by the Constitution. The State security courts were ordinary civil courts. Judges could be impugned before any of those courts if there was the slightest doubt concerning their impartiality. Torture was severely punished. The United Nations Convention against Torture [and Other Cruel, Inhuman or Degrading Treatment or Punishment] formed part of the internal legal system, Turkey had recognized the right of individuals to have recourse to the United Nations Committee against Torture and the European Commission of Human Rights, which was competent to consider cases of torture. Confessions obtained under torture were not admitted as evidence. Mr Marasli had been well treated and was in good health.

117. Several members of the Committee expressed regret that they did not have sufficiently detailed information on the charges against Mr Marasli, in particular whether he had used violence or incitement to violence, or whether he had simply exercised his right to freedom of expression as a member of a minority anxious to affirm its cultural identity. The Committee had not been kept informed of developments in the proceedings against the Rizgari and Alarizgari organizations and did not even know whether, as announced by the representative of the government in May 1988, the case had been transferred to a civil court. Lastly, the Committee had had no response to its appeal for clemency on behalf of Mr Marasli.

118. One member of the Committee noted with satisfaction, however, that the Turkish Government's policy towards the Kurds seemed to be changing. The use of the

Kurdish language would soon be authorized and thousands of refugees had been given asylum.

119. One member of the Committee felt that striking the communication from the Committee's list would encourage the government to keep to this course. He pointed out that considerations of language or culture, which might have provided grounds for the Committee's competence, had little connection with a separatist case of this kind.

120. Following an exchange of views, the Committee *decided*:

(i) to thank the government concerned for the information it had provided by letter, while regretting that it had not sent a representative;

(ii) to repeat its request to the government for information regarding the precise reasons for Mr Recep Marasli's being convicted in six lawsuits, in particular whether he had been found guilty of violence or incitement to violence;

(iii) also to request information from the government regarding the stage reached in the lawsuit still in progress;

(iv) to appeal again for clemency on behalf of the person concerned;

(v) to resume consideration of this communication at its [spring 1989 session].

Spring 1989 session of the Committee on Conventions and Recommendations (131st session of the Executive Board)[4]

131. This communication is still at the stage of being considered as to its admissibility. It has been on the Committee's agenda since the [spring 1988 session].

132. Mr Recep Marasli, aged 33, a publisher specializing in books on Kurdish history and culture and the situation of the Kurdish minority in Turkey, is said to have been sentenced by various military courts under martial law to a total of 36 years' imprisonment. According to Amnesty International, the Rizgari organization, of which he was a member, did not have recourse to violence, at any rate prior to 1982, the date of his arrest. Nor, apparently, did the publications imputed to him advocate

[4] See document 131 EX/3 PRIV., paras. 131-137; see also document 131 EX/CR/HR/TUR.

violence. He is reported to have gone on several hunger strikes and to be in poor health.

133. At the [autumn 1988] session, the government concerned was not represented. However, in letters dated 29 September and 4 and 13 October 1988, the Permanent Delegation of Turkey to Unesco, supporting the statements made by the representative of his government at the [spring 1988] session, pointed out that Mr Marasli had not been convicted for his publishing activities but for acts prescribed by the Penal Code, including the use of force against the political, legal and social order, separatism based on racial criteria and offences against State security at home and abroad. None of these crimes bore any relation to Unesco's fields of competence or to freedom of peaceful expresssion and association. Furthermore, the fact that they had been perpetrated through publication was an aggravating circumstance. Notwithstanding Amnesty International's allegations, the illegal Rizgari organization practised and advocated violence. In Mr Marasli's lawsuits (there had been seven, six of which had already come to an end), the rights of the defendant had been respected. The alleged victim had been well treated in prison and was in good health.

134. The Committee decided *inter alia* to repeat its request to the government concerned for information regarding the precise reasons for Mr Marasli's being convicted in the first six lawsuits, in particular whether he had been found guilty of violence or incitement to violence, and the stage reached in the seventh lawsuit which was still in progress. It also appealed for clemency to be shown to the alleged victim.[5]

135. At the present session, the Permanent Delegate of Turkey to Unesco gave the Committee the following information. As he had already stated, six sentences passed on Mr Recep Marasli had been confirmed. A seventh trial had now ended. At this seventh trial, the Supreme Court had described as the "establishment of armed gangs" what had been referred to by the judges of the courts of first instance as the "establishment of secret alliances". Mr Recep Marasli had been sentenced in September 1988 to 13 years and four months' imprisonment and had been banned for life from employment in the civil service for "establishing an armed gang" (the Rizgari organization) with the aim of removing part of the territory from the sovereignty of the State (establishment of an independent Kurdish State) and for having been the chief of that armed gang whose members took part in terrorist actions to achieve their ends. There was therefore absolutely no justification for claiming that this gang had nothing to do with violence. The court's decision was subject to appeal. The Committee would be kept informed. As regards Mr Recep Marasli's health, he had received treatment and was in good health. Under Turkish law, a pardon could not

[5] See document 130 EX/3 PRIV., para. 120 (ii), (iii) and (iv) (*supra*, p. 742).

be considered until part of a prison sentence had been served. Amnesty International had a false idea of the Turkish judicial system and was unaware of the policy and practice of the authorities following ratification of the United Nations Convention against Torture and Other Cruel, Inhuman [or] Degrading Treatment or Punishment and recognition of the right of individuals to lodge complaints of human rights violations under various international procedures, including those established by the Convention against Torture and the European Convention for the Protection of Human Rights and Fundamental Freedoms. Referring to paragraphs 6, 7 and 14 (*a*) (iii), (iv) and (v) of 104 EX/Decision 3.3, the representative of the government concerned concluded by stating that this communication was motivated exclusively by political considerations, did not fall within Unesco's competence and should be regarded as inadmissible. In addition, it did not come within the normal scope of the procedure laid down in 104 EX/Decision 3.3 in that, on the basis of a particular case, it made unfounded allegations against the Republic of Turkey.

136. In reply to questions, the Permanent Delegate stated that the use of the Kurdish language was authorized in Turkey, but not in judicial procedures where, however, those who did not know Turkish were entitled to the services of an interpreter. He explained, lastly, that while the publication of writings was not an offence, it could constitute an aggravating circumstance under Turkish law when it was the means whereby an offence had been committed.

137. After an exchange of views, the Committee *decided*:

(i) to thank the representative of the government concerned for attending the meeting and for his co-operation;

(ii) to keep the communication on its list pending the final decision concerning the seventh case against Mr Recep Marasli;

(iii) to resume consideration of this communication at its [autumn 1989 session].

Autumn 1989 session of the Committee on Conventions and Recommendations (132nd session of the Executive Board)[6]

109. This communication has been on the Committee's agenda since the [spring 1988 session]. It is still at the stage of consideration as to its admissibility.

[6] See document 132 EX/3 PRIV., paras. 109-117; see also document 132 EX/CR/HR/TUR.

Turkey **No. 762/87**

110. Mr Recep Marasli, a publisher specializing in books on Kurdish history and culture and the situation of the Kurdish minority in Turkey, is said to have been sentenced to a total of 36 years' imprisonment by various military courts for action likely to weaken national sentiment, insulting the memory of President Kemal Atatürk, incitement to separatism and attempting to establish a State or independent territory.

111. At previous sessions, the Committee was informed by the representativ of the government concerned that Mr Marasli had been sentenced in seven different trials for the use of force against the political, legal and social order, separatism based on racial criteria and action endangering the internal and external security of the State. The sentences passed at the first six trials had already been confirmed. The seventh trial had resulted in a prison sentence of 13 years and four months and a lifetime ban on employment in the civil service. An appeal against this new sentence had been made to the Supreme Court. The "constitution of armed gangs", with which Mr Recep Marasli had been charged, referred to the illegal organization "Rizgari", which, according to the government, practised and incited to violence with a view to constituting an independent Kurdish State. The legal authorities had, in fact, established that members of that organization, led by Mr Marasli, had taken part in terrorist activities.

112. At the [spring 1989] session, the Committee decided to keep the communication on its list pending the final decision concerning the seventh trial.[7]

113. In a letter dated 6 June 1989, the Permanent Delegation of Turkey to Unesco stated that, in accordance with the Turkish Penal Code, Mr Marasli's release could not be considered before July 1992. That estimate would have to be reviewed in the light of the final decision concerning his appeal to the Supreme Court.

114. In a letter dated 14 August 1989, Amnesty International informed the Secretariat that it had no further information concerning this communication.

115. Finally, in a letter dated 19 September 1989, the Permanent Delegate of Turkey to Unesco repeated the information that his government had given the Committee at previous sessions. He assured the Committee that he would inform it of the Supreme Courts' decision but expressed the view that this waiting period could not warrant keeping the communication on the Committee's list inasmuch as the crimes on which the Court had to pass judgement did not fall within Unesco's competence and the communication should therefore be declared inadmissible.

---

[7] See document 131 EX/3 PRIV., paras. 137 (ii) (*supra*, p. 744).

No. 762/87 **Turkey**

116. At the present session, the representative of the government concerned read out this letter. In reply to questions, he said that he did not know whether his country's legal code included a provision for "concurrent offences" making it possible under certain circumstances to avoid cumulative sentences. It did, however, provide for remission of sentences. He confirmed the information already given to the Committee concerning the impossibility of a pardon, the good health of Mr Marasli and the civilian prison in which he was serving his sentence.

117. After an exchange of views, the Committee *decided*:

(i) to thank the representative of the government concerned for attending the meeting and for his co-operation;

(ii) to express regret at the slow pace of the continuing legal proceedings;

(iii) to resume consideration of this communication at its [spring 1990 session].

Spring 1990 session of the Committee on Conventions and Recommendations (134th session of the Executive Board)[8]

142. This communication is still at the stage of consideration as to its admissibility. It has been on the Committee's agenda since the [spring 1988 session].

143. Mr Recep Marasli, a publisher specializing in books on Kurdish history and culture and the situation of the Kurdish minority in Turkey, is said to have been sentenced to a total of 36 years' imprisonment by various military courts for action likely to weaken national sentiment, insulting the memory of President Kemal Atatürk, incitement to separatism and attempting to establish a State or independent territory.

144. At previous sessions, the Committee was informed by the representative of the Government of Turkey that Mr Marasli had been sentenced at seven different trials for the use of force against the political, legal and social order, separatism based on racial criteria and action endangering the internal and external security of the State. The sentences passed at the first six trials had already become *res judicata*. The seventh trial had resulted in a prison sentence of 13 years and four months and a lifetime ban on employment in the civil service. An appeal against this new sentence had been made to the Supreme Court. The "constitution. of armed gangs", with which Mr Recep Marasli had been charged, referred to the illegal organization "Riz-

[8] See document 134 EX/3 PRIV., paras. 142-151; see also document 134 EX/CR/HR/TUR.

gari", which, according to the government, practised and incited to violence with a view to constituting an independent Kurdish State. The legal authorities had, in fact, established that members of that organization, led by Mr Marasli, had taken part in terrorist activities.

145. At the [autumn 1989] session the Committee decided to keep the communication on its list and expressed regret at the slow pace of the legal proceedings then under way.[9]

146. In a letter dated 19 April 1990 the Permanent Delegate of Turkey to Unesco stated, that in the light of the final verdict concerning the appeal to the Supreme Court in respect of the last case, Mr Marasli had finally been sentenced to 29 years' imprisonment and that in accordance with the relevant articles of the Turkish Penal Code, he could be released on parole on 28 May 1993 at the earliest.

147. In a letter dated 23 April 1990, Amnesty International informed the Secretariat that the "Rizgari" organization, to which Mr Recep Marasli allegedly belonged, definitely did not at the time of his arrest in January 1982 advocate violence. No evidence had been provided to justify describing that organization as an "armed gang". Furthermore, the Turkish authorities had been unable to give any explanation for the fact that the charge against Mr Recep Marasli had been changed. Lastly, Mr Recep Marasli, who was currently at the prison at Ayden, was undergoing medical examinations.

148. At the present session the representative of the Government of Turkey stated that the necessary information had already been given to the members of the Committee by letter. He also repeated that the crimes committed by Mr Recep Marasli, which ranged from the formation of an armed gang to inciting the population to separatism with a view to creating an independent Kurdish State, did not in any way fall within Unesco's competence. For that reason, the communication should be considered inadmissible. The representative of the government pointed out that in January 1987 his country had recognized the right of individuals to submit petitions to the European Commission of Human Rights provided for by the European Convention on Human Rights.

149. In reply to questions, the representative of the government confirmed the information already given to the Committee concerning the impossibility of a pardon and concerning release on parole.

---

[9] See document 132 EX/3 PRIV., para. 117 (iii) and (ii), respectively (*supra*, p. 746).

No. 762/87 **Turkey**

150. Certain members of the [Committee] considered that the communication should be struck from the Committee's list. Others raised questions as to the basis on which Amnesty International claimed that the "Rizgari" organization definitely did not at the time of Mr Recep Marasli's arrest advocate violence. It was agreed that additional information would be requested on this matter from the author of the communication.

151. Afrer an exchange of views, the Committee *decided*:

(i) to thank the representative of the Government of Turkey for his attendance and co-operation;

(ii) to ask the author of the communication to provide more precise information and inform the Committee whether the "Rizgari" organization was a non-violent organization at the time of Mr Recep Marasli's detention;

(iii) to resume consideration of this communication at its [autumn 1990 session].

Autumn 1990 session of the Committee on Conventions and Recommendations (135th session of the Executive Board)[10]

106. This communication is still at the stage of consideration as to its admissibility. It has been on the Committee's agenda since the [spring 1988 session].

107. Mr Recep Marasli, a publisher specializing in books on Kurdish history and culture and the situation of the Kurdish minority in Turkey, is said to have been sentenced to a total of 36 years' imprisonment by various military courts for action likely to weaken national sentiment, insulting the memory of President Kemal Atatürk, incitement to separatism and attempting to establish a State or independent territory.

108. At previous sessions, the Committee was informed by the representative of the Government of Turkey that Mr Marasli had been sentenced at seven different trials for the use of force against the political, legal and social order, separatism based on racial criteria and action endangering the internal and external security of the State. The sentences passed at the first six trials had already become *res judicata*. The seventh trial had resulted in a prison sentence of 13 years and four months and a lifetime ban on employment in the civil service. An appeal against this new sentence

[10] See document 135 EX/3 PRIV., paras. 106-117; see also documents 135 EX/CR/HR/TUR and Add.

had been made to the Supreme Court. The Supreme Court had charged Mr Recep Marasli with a new offence in that it had described as the "constitution of armed gangs" what the court of first instance had deemed to be the "constitution of a secret alliance". The "constitution of armed gangs" referred to the illegal organization "Rizgari", which, according to the government, practised and incited to violence with a view to constituting an independent Kurdish State. The legal authorities had, in fact, established that members of that organization, led by Mr Marasli, had taken part in terrorist activities.

109. At the [autumn 1989] session, the Committee decided to keep the communication on its list and expressed regret at the slow pace of the legal proceedings then under way.[11]

110. In a letter dated 19 April 1990, the Permanent Delegate of Turkey to Unesco stated that, in the light of the final verdict concerning the appeal to the Supreme Court in respect of the last case, Mr Marasli had finally been sentenced to 29 years' imprisonment and that, in accordance with the relevant articles of the Turkish Penal Code, he could be released on parole on 28 May 1993 at the earliest.

111. In a letter dated 23 April 1990, the author of the communication indicated that the "Rizgari" organization, to which Mr Recep Marasli allegedly belonged, definitely did not at the time of his arrest in January 1982 advocate violence. No evidence had been provided to justify describing that organization as an "armed gang". Furthermore, the Turkish authorities had been unable to give any explanation for the alteration by the Supreme Court of the charge against Mr Recep Marasli. Lastly, Mr Recep Marasli was undergoing medical examinations.

112. At the [spring 1990] session, the representative of the government concerned repeated that the crimes committed by Mr Recep Marasli, which ranged from the formation of an armed gang to inciting the population to separatism with a view to creating an independent Kurdish State, did not in any way fall within Unesco's competence. He also confirmed the information already given to the Committee concerning the impossibility of a pardon and concerning release on parole. The representative of the government concerned pointed out that in January 1987, his country had recognized the right of individuals to submit petitions to the European Commission of Human Rights, set up by the European Convention on Human Rights.

113. On 3 August 1990, the author of the communication addressed to the Committee a letter to which were attached three documents in Turkish together with a sum-

[11] See document 132 EX/3 PRIV., para. 117 (iii) and (ii), respectively (*supra*, p. 746).

mary of them [...].[12] These were the indictment of 5 June 1981 against the organizations "Rizgari" and "Alarizgari", drawn up by the military prosecutor in Diyarbakir; the ruling given on 25 May 1984 by the Diyarbakir Military Court concerning Mr Recep Marasli, which contained a descripion of the organization "Rizgari"; and the ruling given on 25 October 1988 by the Diyarbakir Military Court, which contained personal details of 37 defendants, including Mr Recep Marasli, and general remarks about the organization "Rizgari". It emerged from these legal documents:

> that the aim of the organization "Rizgari" was to form an independent Kurdish Republic, based on Marxist-Leninist ideas, in the eastern and south-eastern part of the Turkish Republic. Like the organization "Rizgari", the activities of the organization "Alarizgari" were predominantly concerned with gaining supporters and were not based on violence. Members of "Alarizgari" had been involved in acts of violence as a result of a lack of internal discipline in the organization, but that had never occurred during the "Rizgari" period;
>
> that it was not a principle of the organization "Rizgari" to carry arms. This statement was not disputed by the judges in the ruling of 25 May 1984;
>
> that in the rulings of 25 May 1984 and 25 October 1988, Mr Recep Marasli had been sentenced for committing an offence as defined in Article 171 (1) of the Turkish Penal Code by "attempting to separate part of the State by special (personal) means in a secret alliance". The No. 4 Military Appeal Court had confirmed this ruling;
>
> that the Panel of Military Appeal Courts had decided that the defendant should be convicted under Article 168 (1) of the Penal Code for "membership of an armed gang".

114. The author of the communication pointed out that no explanation appeared to have been given for the change that had occurred between the rulings given by the court of first instance and by the appeal court in the assessment of the nature of the organization "Rizgari" and that had led to the alteration of the charge against Mr Recep Marasli to one of "membership of an armed gang". None of these documents showed that at the time of Mr Recep Marasli's arrest in January 1982 the organization had been armed or that acts of violence had been committed in its name. It did not know of any evidence that Mr Recep Marasli had committed or advocated violence, either in his capacity as owner of the Komal publishing house or as a member

[12] See document 135 EX/CR/HR/TUR Add.

of "Rizgari". Amnesty International continued therefore to appeal for the immediate and unconditional release of Mr Recep Marasli.

115. By a letter dated 25 September 1990, the Permanent Delegation of Turkey to Unesco pointed out that the Turkish authorities had never failed to co-operate with the Committee. It recalled the substance of its letters dated 25 November 1989 and 19 April 1990. The sentence passed on Mr Recep Marasli was now final and, all remedies having been exhausted, the Turkish Delegation was not empowered to reconsider the legal arguments or the sentences passed by the competent Turkish courts. Where the Committee was concerned, in pursuance of paragraphs 6 and 7 of 104 EX/Decision 3.3, it could not set itself up as an international supreme court with power to review final verdicts passed by the competent courts of Member States. If Mr Recep Marasli so desired, he could refer his case to the European Commission of Human Rights, Turkey having recognized the right of individuals to submit petitions to it. Finally, in view of the fact that all the necessary information had been communicated to the Committee, the Turkish Delegation to Unesco considered that this communication should be declared inadmissible and that the Delegation's participation in the work of the Committee would, in the absence of any new evidence, cease to be necessary.

116. As at the [spring 1990] session, some members of the Committee considered that the communication should be struck from its list. Others felt that the question of whether the organization "Rizgari" had or had not engaged in violence at the time of Mr Recep Marasli's arrest had not been fully clarified. Several members of the Committee pointed out that it was surprising that the government concerned had asserted that the alleged victim could refer his case to the European Commission of Human Rights when such recognition of the right of individuals to submit petitions to the Commission was not valid for acts antedating that recognition. They agreed to request further information on this matter from the government concerned.

117. Following an exchange of views, the Committee *decided*:

(i) to express its regret that no representative of the government concerned had been present;

(ii) nevertheless to thank the Ambassador, the Permanent Delegate of Turkey to Unesco, for his letter of 25 September 1990 in which he once again set forth his government's standpoint on this case;

(iii) to request the government concerned once again to inform the Committee whether the organization "Rizgari" was or was not, at the time of Mr Recep Marasli's arrest, an organization that practised or advocated violence;

(iv) to ask the government concerned whether the recognition by Turkey of the right of individual appeal in accordance with the provisions of the European Convention on Human Rights enabled Mr Recep Marasli to submit a petition to the European Commission [of Human Rights] in regard to the offences with which he had been charged, which dated back almost 10 years;

(v) to point out to the government concerned that the Committee did not claim in any way to set itself up as an international supreme court with power to review sentences passed by the competent courts of Member States, but sought solely, and for purely humanitarian reasons, to establish a dialogue with the governments concerned in order to examine with them what might be done on behalf of alleged victims in cases in which they might have suffered violations of their human rights in fields lying within Unesco's competence;

(vi) to resume consideration of this communication at its [spring 1991 session].

Spring 1991 session of the Committee on Conventions and Recommendations (136th session of the Executive Board)[13]

139. This communication is still at the stage of consideration as to its admissibility. It has been on the Committee's agenda since the [spring 1988 session].

140. Mr Recep Marasli, a publisher specializing in books on Kurdish history and culture and the situation of the Kurdish minority in Turkey, is said to have been sentenced to a total of 36 years' imprisonment by various military courts for action likely to weaken national sentiment, insulting the memory of President Kemal Atatürk, incitement to separatism and attempting to establish a State or independent territory.

141. At previous sessions the Committee was informed by the representative of the Government of Turkey that Mr Marasli had been sentenced at seven different trials for the use of force against the political, legal and social order, separatism based on racial criteria and action endangering the internal and external security of the State. The sentences passed at the first six trials had already become *res judicata*. The seventh trial had resulted in a prison sentence of 13 years and four months and a lifetime ban on employment in the civil service. An appeal against this new sentence had been made to the Supreme Court. The Supreme Court had charged Mr Marasli

[13] See document 136 EX/3 PRIV., paras. 139-151; see also documents 136 EX/CR/HR/TUR and Add. and Add.2.

with a new offence in that it had described as the "formation of armed gangs" what the court of first instance had deemed to be the "formation of a secret alliance". The "formation of armed gangs" referred to the illegal organization "Rizgari", which, according to the government, practised and incited to violence with a view to setting up an independent Kurdish State. The legal authorities had in fact established that members of that organization, led by Mr Marasli, had taken part in terrorist activities.

142. At the [autumn 1989] session the Permanent Delegate of Turkey to UNESCO stated in a letter that, further to the appeal to the Supreme Court in respect of the last case, Mr Marasli had finally been sentenced to 29 years' imprisonment and that, in accordance with the relevant articles of the Turkish Penal Code, he could be released on parole on 28 May 1993 at the earliest.

143. The author of the communication informed the Committee that the "Rizgari" organization, to which Mr Marasli allegedly belonged, definitely did not at the time of his arrest in January 1982 advocate violence. No evidence had been provided to justify describing that organization as an "armed' gang". Furthermore, the Turkish authorities had been unable to give any explanation for the alteration by the Supreme Court of the charge against Mr Marasli. Lastly, Mr Marasli was undergoing medical examinations.

144. At the [spring 1990] session the representative of the Government of Turkey repeated that the crimes committed by Mr Marasli, which ranged from the formation of an armed gang to inciting the population to separatism with a view to creating an independent Kurdish State, did not in any way fall within UNESCO's competence. He also confirmed the information already given to the Committee concerning the impossibility of a pardon and concerning release on parole. The representative of the Government of Turkey pointed out that in January 1987 his country had recognized the right of individuals to submit petitions to the European Commission of Human Rights set up by the European Convention on Human Rights.

145. During [the autumn 1990] session the author of the communication sent the Committee a letter to which were attached three documents in Turkish, together with a summary of them [...]. It pointed out that no explanation appeared to have been given for the change that had occurred between the rulings given by the court of first instance and the appeal court in the assessment of the nature of the organization "Rizgari", which had led to the alteration of the charge against Mr Marasli to one of "membership of an armed gang". None of these documents showed that at the time of Mr Marasli's arrest in January 1982 the organization had been armed or that acts of violence had been committed in its name. It did not know of any evidence that Mr Marasli had committed or advocated violence, either as owner of the Komal publish-

ing house or as a member of "Rizgari". The author continued therefore to appeal for Mr Marasli's immediate and unconditional release.

146. At around the same time the Permanent Delegation of Turkey to UNESCO pointed out in a letter that the Turkish authorities had never failed to co-operate with the Committee. It recapitulated the substance of its letters dated 25 November 1989 and 19 April 1990. The sentence passed on Mr Marasli was now final and, all remedies having been exhausted, the Turkish Delegation was not empowered to reconsider the legal arguments or the sentences passed by the competent Turkish courts.

147. At the present session, the author of the communication informed the Committee in a letter dated 11 April 1991 that it was unaware of any change in Mr Marasli's legal situation. His state of health was still very worrying.

148. In another letter, dated 29 April 1991, Amnesty International informed the Committee that the sentence on Mr Marasli had been suspended and that he had been conditionally released. However, Amnesty International was continuing to appeal for his release to be made unconditional.

149. In a letter dated 7 May 1991 the Permanent Delegate of Turkey to UNESCO informed the Committee that Mr Marasli had been released at the end of April, in accordance with the legal reforms adopted by the Turkish Grand National Assembly. A note concerning those reforms was attached to the letter [...].[14] The Permanent Delegate appeared before the Committee to confirm that information.

150. One member of the Committee noted that the release was conditional and expressed the view that it was too soon to strike the communication from the Committee's list.

151. After an exchange of views, the Committee *decided*:

(i) to thank the representative of the Government of Turkey for his attendance and co-operation;

(ii) to take note with satisfaction of Mr Recep Marasli's release;

(iii) to strike the communication from its list as settled, in conformity with paragraph 14 (*a*) (x) of 104 EX/Decision 3.3.

---

[14] See document 136 EX/CR/HR/TUR Add.2.

No. 763/87

Concerning *Socialist Republic of Viet Nam*
Case of *Nguyên Dan Que*

Communication of 10 August 1987 submitted by
Amnesty International

Spring 1988 session of the Committee on Conventions and Recommendations (129th session of the Executive Board)[1]

109. According to the author of the communication, Mr Nguyên Dan Que, a doctor, was arrested in February 1978. He is alleged to have openly expressed criticism of the government's medical policies.

110. In a letter dated 5 April 1988, Amnesty International informed the Committee that the alleged victim had been released in February 1988 following an amnesty proclaimed on the occasion of the New Year.

111. The release of the alleged victim was confirmed by the Permanent Delegation of the Socialist Republic of Viet Nam in a letter dated 16 May 1988.

112. Following an exchange of views, the Committee *decided*:

(i) to take note with satisfaction of the release of Mr Nguyên Dan Que;

(ii) to strike the communication from its list as settled in conformity with paragraph 14 (*a*) (x) of 104 EX/Decision 3.3.

[1] See document 129 EX/3 PRIV., paras. 109-112; see also document 129 EX/CR/HR/3.

No. 764/87

Concerning *Socialist Republic of Viet Nam*
Case of *Truong Van Quynh*

Communication of 10 August 1987 submitted by
Amnesty International

Spring 1988 session of the Committee on Conventions and Recommendations (129th session of the Executive Board)[1]

113. According to the author of the communication, Mr Truong Van Quynh, a doctor, was summoned on 15 June 1975 to undergo re-education and has been detained ever since without charge or trial.

114. By a letter dated 5 April 1988, Amnesty International informed the Committee that the alleged victim had been released in November 1987 following an amnesty proclaimed on the occasion of the national holiday.

115. The release of the alleged victim was confirmed by the Permanent Delegation of the Socialist Republic of Viet Nam in its letter of 16 May 1988.

116. Following an exchange of views, the Committee *decided*:

(i) to take note with satisfaction of the release of Mr Truong Van Quynh;

(ii) to strike the communication from its list as settled in conformity with paragraph 14 (*a*) (x) of 104 EX/Decision 3.3.

---

[1] See document 129 EX/3 PRIV., paras. 113-116; see also document 129 EX/CR/HR/3.

No. 765/87

Concerning *Socialist Republic of Viet Nam*
Case of *Doan Quôc Sy*

Communication of 10 August 1987 submitted by
Amnesty International

Spring 1988 session of the Committee on Conventions and Recommendations (129th session of the Executive Board)[1]

117. According to the author of the communication Mr Doan Quôc Sy, a teacher and writer, was detained in a re-education camp from 1976 to January 1984. He is alleged to have been arrested on 2 May 1984 with a number of other writers and to have been imprisoned since then without charge or trial. He is reportedly accused of having clandestinely sent writings abroad.

118. In a letter dated 16 May 1988 the Permanent Delegation of the Socialist Republic of Viet Nam informed the Committee that Mr Doan Quôc Sy had been sentenced to nine years' imprisonment by the People's Court of Ho Chi Minh City on 27 April 1988 for "breaking the law".

119. After an exchange of views, the Committee *decided*:

(i) to request the government concerned to provide further particulars concerning the case, and to express their humanitarian concern for Mr Doan Quôc Sy;

(ii) to resume consideration of this communication at [its autumn 1988 session].

---

[1] See document 129 EX/3 PRIV., paras. 117-119; see also document 129 EX/CR/HR/3.

No. 765/87 **Socialist Republic of Viet Nam**

Autumn 1988 session of the Committee on Conventions and Recommendations (130th session of the Executive Board)[2]

130. The communication has been on the Committee's agenda since the [spring 1988 session]. It is at the stage of examination of its admissibility.

131. Mr Doan Quôc Sy, a teacher and writer, the author of some 30 novels, stories and essays, who had reportedly already been detained from 1976 to January 1984 in a re-education camp, is alleged to have been arrested again, together with other writers, on 2 May 1984, and accused of having clandestinely sent writings abroad.

132. On 5 September 1988, the Secretariat received a letter from Amnesty International claiming that the alleged victim and the other writers arrested at the same time had been tried on 27 April 1988 by a people's court. Reportedly, no lawyer was present to defend them. The accused were allegedly permitted to speak in their own defence, but the sentence had been printed beforehand, and was read out and distributed immediately after it had been pronounced. The author of the communication believes that an appeal to the Court of Appeal would be possible, but is not well-informed about such matters. The author hopes that the Committee will be able to obtain fuller particulars concerning the trial, the charges upheld against the accused, and the possibility of lodging an appeal.

133. In a letter dated 5 October 1988, the Permanent Delegation of the Socialist Republic of Viet Nam to Unesco indicated, as it had previously done on the occasion of the Committee's [spring 1988] session, that Mr Doan Quôc Sy had been sentenced to nine years' imprisonment by the People's Court of Ho Chi Minh City for "breaking the law".

134. Several Committee members considered that this charge was too general and too vague, and provided no real information regarding the substance of the accusation against Mr Doan Quôc Sy. They expressed their grave concern at the severity of the sentence imposed, given that according to the author of the communication, Mr Doan Quôc Sy had been guilty only of having clandestinely sent writings abroad. The alleged victim having already been detained for almost 12 years, it was essential to request the government concerned once again to supply precise information regarding the substance of the charge against Mr Doan Quôc Sy, which had resulted in his receiving so harsh a sentence, and the legal basis of that sentence. They also laid particular emphasis on the humanitarian aspect of the case.

---

[2] See document 130 EX/3 PRIV., paras. 130-135; see also document 130 EX/CR/HR - Viet Nam 2.

Socialist Republic of Viet Nam **No. 765/87**

135. Following an exchange of views, the Committee *decided*:

(i) to express its regret that the government concerned had sent no representative;

(ii) to request the government concerned, in view of the extreme inadequacy of the information available on this case, to provide further particulars, firstly, regarding the precise grounds for the severe sentence passed on Mr Doan Quôc Sy and in particular as to whether he had simply made peaceful use of his right to freedom of expression or whether he had advocated violence, and, secondly, regarding the opportunities open to him to lodge an appeal;

(iii) to make a further appeal for clemency to be shown to Mr Doan Quôc Sy, who had already been in detention for almost 12 years;

(iv) to resume consideration of this communication at its [spring 1989 session].

Spring 1989 session of the Committee on Conventions and Recommendations (131st session of the Executive Board)[3]

158. This communication, which has been on the Committee's agenda since the [spring 1988 session], is still at the stage of being considered as to its admissibility.

159. Mr Doan Quôc Sy, aged 65, a teacher and writer, the author of some 30 novels, stories and essays, had reportedly been detained from 1976 to January 1984 in a re-education camp. He is alleged to have been arrested again on 2 May 1984, together with other writers, for having clandestinely sent writings abroad. He is said to have been tried on 27 April 1988 by a people's court.

160. According to the information provided at the time by the Permanent Delegation of the Socialist Republic of Viet Nam to Unesco, Mr Doan Quôc Sy had been sentenced to nine years' imprisonment by the People's Court of Ho Chi Minh City for "breaking the law".

161. In view of the extreme inadequacy of the information available on the case, the Committee had at its [autumn 1988] session requested the government concerned to provide further particulars, firstly regarding the precise grounds for the heavy sentence passed on Mr Doan Quôc Sy, and in particular as to whether he had simply

[3] See document 131 EX/3 PRIV., paras. 158-167; see also document 131 EX/CR/HR/VIE.

made peaceful use of his right to freedom of expression or whether he had advocated violence, and secondly, regarding the opportunities open to him to lodge an appeal. The Committee also reiterated its appeal for clemency, drawing the attention of the government concerned to the fact that the alleged victim had already been in detention for almost 12 years.[4]

162. At the present session, in a letter dated 7 March 1989, Amnesty International informed the Committee that Mr Doan Quôc Sy's prison sentence had been reduced on appeal to eight years. The author of the communication stated that according to the information available, the alleged victim and the other writers arrested at the same time had had no legal representation during the trial in the court of first instance. The sentence is said to have been printed, read [out] and distributed as soon as the accused, who had been defending themselves, had pleaded their case.

163. As at previous sessions, the government concerned did not send a representative, but in a letter dated 9 May 1989, the Permanent Delegation of the Socialist Republic of Viet Nam repeated the information which it had given previously, namely that Mr Doan Quôc Sy had been sentenced to nine years' imprisonment by the People's Court of Ho Chi Minh City on 27 April 1988.

164. Some members of the Committee drew attention to the imprecise nature of the information available at present, in particular concerning the date on which Mr Doan Quôc Sy had been detained, the sentence pronounced and the question of whether the first and second sentences had overlapped.

165. Other members of the Committee wondered if it might be helpful to request either the government concerned or the author of the communication for a copy of the court sentence passed on the writer.

166. On that point several members of the Committee felt it was important that the Committee should avoid giving the impression that it was setting itself up in a judgement over the national legal authorities and their decisions. The Committee could, however, request the State concerned for specific information relating to the procedures followed or to the relevant legal provisions. The examination of a communication mainly on the basis of dialogue with the government concerned had proved effective in the past, and it would be unwise to depart from that procedure.

167. After an exchange of views, the Committee *decided*:

[4] See document 130 EX/3 PRIV., para. 135 (ii) and (iii) (*supra*, p. 761).

(i) to express once again its regret that the government concerned had sent no representative;

(ii) to reiterate its request to the government concerned for information on the precise grounds for the heavy sentence passed on Mr Doan Quôc Sy, on the actual length of that sentence, and on the date on which he would be considered to have served it;

(iii) also to inform the government concerned that owing to the lack of adequate information, the Committee would be obliged at its next session to declare the communication admissible;

(iv) to launch a further appeal for clemency to be shown to Mr Doan Quôc Sy, who had been in detention for almost 13 years;

(v) to resume consideration of the communication at [its autumn 1989 session].

Autumn 1989 session of the Committee on Conventions and Recommendations (132nd session of the Executive Board)[5]

131. This communication had been on the Committee's agenda since the [spring 1988 session]. It was still at the stage of being considered as to its admissibility.

132. Mr Doan Quôc Sy, a teacher and writer, had reportedly been detained from 1976 to January 1984 in a re-education camp. He had allegedly been arrested again on 2 May 1984, together with other writers, for having clandestinely sent writings abroad. He was said to have been sentenced, on 27 April 1988, by a people's court, to nine years' imprisonment. The sentence had been commuted, on appeal, to eight years' imprisonment. It was claimed that he had not been defended by a lawyer during his trial. The sentence is alleged to have been printed, read out and distributed immediately after he had pleaded his own case.

133. At previous sessions, the Permanent Delegation of the Socialist Republic of Viet Nam to Unesco had informed the Committee that Mr Doan Quôc Sy had been sentenced on 27 April 1988 to nine years' imprisonment by the People's Court of Ho Chi Minh City for "breaking the law".

---

[5] See document 132 EX/3 PRIV., paras. 131-139; see also document 132 EX/CR/HR/VIE.

No. 765/87 **Socialist Republic of Viet Nam**

134. At its [spring 1989] session, the Committee decided that owing to the lack of adequate information from the government concerned, it would be obliged to declare the communication admissible.[6]

135. In a letter dated 14 August 1989, Amnesty International stated that it had no additional information concerning the communication.

136. As at the previous three sessions, the government concerned sent no representative.

137. Certain members of the Committee considered that the cause of this absence was probably the recent change of the Permanent Delegate to Unesco of the State concerned. In the search for a humanitarian solution and for reasons of efficiency, it was suggested that the Committee should renew its appeal for clemency to be shown to Mr Doan Quôc Sy, without yet declaring the communication admissible.

138. In view of the Vietnamese authorities' persistent failure to respond to the Committee's repeated requests for information, other members considered that the Committee had no choice but to be consistent and declare the communication admissible.

139. After an exchange of views, the Committee *decided*:

(i) to express once more its regret that no representative of the government concerned had attended its meeting;

(ii) to declare the communication admissible;

(iii) to urge the government concerned to provide it with information on the specific grounds for the heavy sentence passed on Mr Doan Quôc Sy, on the actual length of that sentence, and on the date on which he would be considered to have served it;

(iv) to appeal once more for clemency to be shown to the alleged victim, in view of the very long time already spent in detention;

(v) to ask its Chairman to approach the delegation of Viet Nam during the forthcoming General Conference in order to obtain that government's co-operation;

---

[6] See document 131 EX/3 PRIV., para. 167 (iii) (*supra*, p. 763).

(vi) to resume consideration of the communication at its [spring 1990 session].

Spring 1990 session of the Committee on Conventions and Recommendations (134th session of the Executive Board)[7]

208. This communication has been on the Committee's agenda since the [spring 1988 session]. It is at the stage of examination of substance.

209. Mr Doan Quôc Sy, aged 66, a teacher and writer, was reportedly detained from 1976 to January 1984 in a re-education camp. Arrested again on 2 May 1984, together with other writers, for having clandestinely sent writings abroad, he is alleged to have been sentenced on 27 April 1988 by a people's court to nine years' imprisonment, a sentence commuted on appeal to eight years' imprisonment. In the absence of any lawyer at his trial, he is reported to have had to plead his own case. The sentence is alleged to have been printed beforehand.

210. At the previous sessions, the Government of the Socialist Republic of Viet Nam was not represented. The Permanent Delegation of Viet Nam to Unesco had simply stated that Mr Doan Quôc Sy had been sentenced on 27 April 1988 to nine years' imprisonment by the People's Court of Ho Chi Minh City for "breaking the law".

211. On 25 April 1990 the Secretariat received from Amnesty International a letter in which that organization expressed its concern regarding this case.

212. At the present session the Permanent Delegate of Viet Nam to Unesco agreed to appear before the Committee. He stated that information had been requested from his country's authorities but that no reply had yet reached him. He undertook to communicate any reply to the Committee as soon as he received it. In response to requests for clarification he explained that the re-education camps had been established after the war in order to enable the former members of the armed forces of the deposed regime, who had committed serious crimes against the population, to escape capital punishment or reprisals by the victims and to learn to work and to understand the government's policy. With regard to the People's Court of Ho Chi Minh City, this was a regular court of law and not an emergency or summary court or tribunal. The Permanent Delegate expressed surprise at the allegation that there had been no lawyers to defend Mr Doan Quôc Sy. He thought the severity of the

[7] See document 134 EX/3 PRIV., paras. 208-214; see also document 134 EX/CR/HR/VIE.

sentence passed was due the fact that Mr Doan Quôc Sy had engaged in criminal activities other than those referred to in the communication.

213. Several members of the Committee expressed the wish to obtain full information concerning the grounds for Mr Doan Quôc Sy's arrest and sentence, the nature of the offence with which he had been charged, the judicial procedure followed in this case, whether he had advocated violence and what possibility he had of being shown clemency. One member of the Committee asked whether the offence for which he had been sentenced consisted in the clandestine sending of writings abroad or in the criminal nature of the writings themselves. Another Committee member pointed out that Viet Nam had ratified the International Covenant on Civil and Political Rights, and that freedom of opinion and expression were consequently guaranteed. He wished to know whether the Penal Code had been revised to bring it into conformity with that Covenant.

214. Following an exchange of views, the Committee *decided*:

(i) to thank the representative of the Government of the Socialist Republic of Viet Nam for his attendance and his co-operation;

(ii) to request that government to supply precise information on this case, particularly concerning the exact nature of the offences for which Mr Doan Quôc Sy had been sentenced, the definition of these offences in criminal law, the procedure followed during the trial, the length of the sentence passed, the date on which it would be considered to have been served, and Mr Doan Quôc Sy's situation in prison and state of health;

(iii) to make a further appeal for clemency to be shown to the alleged victim, in view of the already very lengthy period spent in detention;

(iv) to note the undertaking by the representative of the Government of the Socialist Republic of Viet Nam to endeavour to obtain the information requested;

(v) to resume consideration of the communciation at its [autumn 1990 session].

Socialist Republic of Viet Nam **No. 765/87**

Autumn 1990 session of the Committee on Conventions and Recommendations (135th session of the Executive Board)[8]

157. This communication has been on the Committee's agenda since the [spring 1988 session]. It is at the stage of examination of substance.

158. The author of the communication alleges the following. Mr Doan Quôc Sy, aged over 67, a teacher and writer, was detained from 1976 to January 1984 in a re-education camp. Arrested again on 2 May 1984, together with other writers, for having clandestinely sent writings abroad, he was sentenced on 27 April 1988 by a people's court to nine years' imprisonment, a sentence commuted on appeal to eight years' imprisonment. In the absence of any lawyer at his trial, he had to plead his own case. The sentence was printed beforehand.

159. At the previous sessions, the government concerned was not represented. The Permanent Delegation of Viet Nam to Unesco had simply stated that Mr Doan Quôc Sy had been sentenced on 27 April 1988 to nine years' imprisonment by the People's Court of Ho Chi Minh City for "breaking the law".

160. At the [spring 1990] session, the Permanent Delegate of Viet Nam to Unesco agreed to appear before the Committee. He stated that information had been requested from his country's authorities but that no reply had yet reached him. He undertook to communicate any reply to the Committee as soon as he received it. In response to requests for clarification he explained that the re-education camps had been established after the war in order to enable the former members of the armed forces of the deposed regime, who had committed serious crimes against the population, to escape capital punishment or reprisals by the victims and to learn to work and to understand the government's policy. With regard to the People's Court of Ho Chi Minh City, this was a regular court of law and not an emergency or summary court or tribunal. The Permanent Delegate expressed surprise at the allegation that there had been no lawyers to defend Mr Doan Quôc Sy. He thought the severity of the sentence passed was due to the fact that Mr Doan Quôc Sy had engaged in criminal activities other than those referred to in the communication.

161. At the close of the discussion, the Committee requested the Vietnamese authorities to supply it with precise information on the case, particularly concerning the charges against this writer, the definition of these offences in criminal law, the pro-

[8] See document 135 EX/3 PRIV., paras. 157-164; see also documents 135 EX/CR/HR/VIE and Add.

cedure followed during the trial, the date by which he would have served his sentence, and his state of health.[9]

162. In a letter dated 21 August 1990, the author of the communication expressed the view that Mr Doan Quôc Sy had been convicted under Article 82 of the Vietnamese Criminal Code, which prescribes the punishment for "spreading propaganda against the Socialist system with intent to oppose the people's government". The author of the communication considered that this article was in contravention of Article 19 of the International Covenant on Civil and Political Rights, which guarantees freedom of opinion and expression, and added that very little official information about the procedures under which Doan Quôc Sy had been tried were available. However, there had been no reports of his having been charged or convicted of any recognizably criminal offence.

163. The Permanent Delegation of the Socialist Republic of Viet Nam to Unesco confirmed, in a letter dated 10 September 1990, that Mr Doan Quôc Sy had been sentenced in the first instance on 27 April 1988 by the people's tribunal at Ho Chi Minh City to nine years' imprisonment for his activities against the Vietnamese State, in accordance with the governmental decree of 10 November 1967. The sentence had been commuted on appeal to eight years. As stipulated in the decree, he had had the right to choose his own lawyer. His health was normal and he was permitted to receive letters and gifts from his family.

164. After an exchange of views, the Committee *decided*:

(i) to express regret that no representative of the government concerned had been present;

(ii) to thank the Ambassador, Permanent Delegate of Viet Nam to Unesco, for his letter of 10 September 1990;

(iii) to renew its request to the government concerned to inform the Committee of the exact nature of the offences for which Mr Doan Quôc Sy had been sentenced, described in general terms as activities against the Vietnamese State, and also to communicate to the Committee the text of the sentences and of the relevant provisions of the national legislation;

(iv) to draw the attention of the government concerned to the international instruments relating to human rights to which Viet Nam was a party, in particular the International Covenant on Economic, Social and Cultural Rights and

---

[9] See document 134 EX/3 PRIV., para. 214 (ii) (*supra*, p. 766).

the International Covenant on Civil and Political Rights, and to the alleged incompatibility of Article 82 of the Vietnamese Criminal Code with those Covenants;

(v) to make a further appeal for clemency on behalf of Mr Doan Quôc Sy, who had spent many years in detention;

(vi) to resume consideration of the communication at its [spring 1991 session].

Spring 1991 session of the Committee on Conventions and Recommendations (136th session of the Executive Board)[10]

209. This communication has been on the Committee's agenda since the [spring 1988 session]. It is at the stage of examination as to its substance.

210. The author of the communication alleges the following. Mr Doan Quôc Sy, who is over 67 years of age and who is a teacher and writer, was detained from 1976 to January 1984 in a re-education camp. He was arrested again on 2 May 1984, together with other writers, for having clandestinely sent writings abroad and was sentenced on 27 April 1988 by a people's court to nine years' imprisonment, the sentence being commuted on appeal to eight years. In the absence of a defence counsel he had to plead his own case. The verdict had apparently been printed beforehand.

211. At previous sessions the representative of the Government of the Socialist Republic of Viet Nam stated that Mr Doan Quôc Sy had indeed been sentenced on 27 April 1988 to nine years' imprisonment by the People's Court of Ho Chi Minh City "for breaking the law". He informed the Committee that detailed information had been requested from his country's authorities but that no reply had yet reached him. He undertook to communicate any reply to the Committee as soon as he received it. On the question of re-education camps, he explained that they had been established after the war in order to enable the former members of the armed forces of the deposed regime, who had committed serious crimes against the population, to escape capital punishment or reprisals by the victims and to learn to work and to understand the government's policy. With regard to the People's Court of Ho Chi Minh City, this was a regular court of law and not an emergency or summary court or tribunal.

---

[10] See document 136 EX/3 PRIV., paras. 209-216; see also documents 136 EX/CR/HR/VIE and Add.

No. 765/87 **Socialist Republic of Viet Nam**

212. At the [autumn 1990] session the author of the communication informed the Committee in a letter that Mr Doan Quôc Sy had been convicted under Article 82 of the Vietnamese Criminal Code, which prescribes punishment for "spreading propaganda against the Socialist system with intent to oppose the people's government". The author of the communication considered that this article was in contravention of Article 19 of the International Covenant on Civil and Political Rights, which guarantees freedom of opinion and expression, and added that very little official information about the procedures under which Doan Quôc Sy had been tried was available. There was absolutely no proof, however, that he had been charged with or convicted of any recognizably criminal offence.

213. The Permanent Delegation of the Socialist Republic of Viet Nam to UNESCO confirmed by letter that Mr Doan Quôc Sy had been sentenced in the court of first instance on 27 April 1988 by the people's tribunal at Ho Chi Minh City to nine years' imprisonment for his activities against the Vietnamese State, in accordance with a governmental decree of 10 November 1967. The sentence had been commuted on appeal to eight years. As stipulated in the decree, he had had the right to choose his own defence counsel. His health was normal, and he was permitted to receive letters and gifts from his family.

214. At the current session, by a letter dated 9 April 1991, the author of the communication informed the Committee that it had no additional information concerning this communication but that it nevertheless remained most concerned about the fate of Mr Doan Quôc Sy, who was still in detention.

215. As at the previous sessions, the Government of the Socialist Republic of Viet Nam was not represented at the current session.

216. After an exchange of views, the Committee *decided*:

(i) to express its regret once again that it had been denied the presence of a representative of the Government of the Socialist Republic of Viet Nam and had not received any information from it;

(ii) to make a further appeal for clemency for Mr Doan Quôc Sy, who had spent many years in detention;

(iii) to renew its request to the Government of the Socialist Republic of Viet Nam that it inform the Committee of the specific illegal acts of which Mr Doan Quôc Sy had been accused and for which he had been sentenced (which had been described in general terms as "activities against the Vietnamese State") and also to communicate to the Committee the text of the sentences and the relevant provisions of the national legislation;

(iv) to draw the attention of the Government of the Socialist Republic of Viet Nam to the international instruments relating to human rights to which Viet Nam was a party, in particular the International Covenant on Economic, Social and Cultural Rights and the International Covenant on Civil and Political Rights, and to the alleged incompatibility of Article 82 of the Vietnamese Criminal Code with those Covenants;

(v) to request the Director-General to make humanitarian representations on behalf of the alleged victim and, pursuant to paragraph 14 (*k*) of 104 EX/Decision 3.3, to use his good offices to persuade the Government of the Socialist Republic of Viet Nam to co-operate better in this matter;

(vi) to resume consideration of the communication at its [autumn 1991 session].

Autumn 1991 session of the Committee on Conventions and Recommendations (137th session of the Executive Board)[11]

157. This communication has been on the Committee's agenda since the [spring 1988 session]. It is at the stage of examination as to its substance.

158. Mr Doan Quôc Sy, is a teacher and writer over 67 years of age. The author of the communication alleges the following: Mr Doan Quôc Sy was detained from 1976 to January 1984 in a re-education camp. He was arrested again on 2 May 1984, together with other writers, for having clandestinely sent writings abroad and was sentenced on 27 April 1988 by a people's court to nine years' imprisonment under Article 82 of the Vietnamese Criminal Code, which prescribes punishment for "spreading propaganda against the Socialist system with intent to oppose the people's government". The author of the communication considers that this article is in contravention of Article 19 of the International Covenant on Civil and Political Rights, which guarantees freedom of opinion and expression. There was no proof that Mr Doan Quôc Sy had been charged with or convicted of any recognizably criminal offence. His sentence had been commuted on appeal to eight years' imprisonment. During his trial he had had no lawyer and had been obliged to conduct his own defence. The sentence had been printed in advance.

[11] See document 137 EX/3 PRIV., paras. 157-163; see also document 137 EX/CR/HR/VIE.

No. 765/87 **Socialist Republic of Viet Nam**

159. The representative of the government concerned had confirmed the condemnation of Mr Doan Quôc Sy in 1988 to nine years' imprisonment by the People's Court of Ho Chi Minh City "for breaking the law", that is to say for his activities against the State, a sentence that had been reduced to eight years on appeal. Mr Doan Quôc Sy had been convicted by a regular court of law and not under any emergency procedures. He had had the right to choose defence counsel. His health was normal, and he was allowed to receive letters and parcels. On the subject of re-education camps, the representative of the government concerned had explained that they had been established after the war in order to enable former members of the armed forces of the deposed regime who had committed serious crimes against the population to escape capital punishment or reprisals by the victims and to learn to work and to understand the government's policy.

160. At its [spring 1991] session, the Committee had requested the Director-General to make humanitarian representations on behalf of the alleged victim and, pursuant to paragraph 14 (*k*) of 104 EX/Decision 3.3, to use his good offices to persuade the government concerned to collaborate more closely in this matter.[12]

[160a.] On 30 July 1991 the Director-General had met the Permanent Delegate of Viet Nam to UNESCO. At this meeting he had handed the Permanent Delegate a letter addressed to his country's Minister for Foreign Affairs.

161. At the current session, by letter dated 30 August 1991, the author of the communication informed the Committee that it had no additional information concerning this communication, but that it nevertheless continued to be most concerned about the fate of Mr Doan Quôc Sy, who was still in detention.

162. As at the [spring 1991] session, the government concerned was not represented.

163. After an exchange of views, the Committee *decided*:

(i) to express its regret once again that no representative of the government concerned had attended its meeting and that it had received no information from it;

(ii) to make a further appeal for clemency for Mr Doan Quôc Sy, who had spent many years in detention;

(iii) to repeat the requests for information it had addressed to the government and to which the government had not yet replied;

[12] See document 136 EX/3 PRIV., para. 216 (v) (*supra*, p. 771).

(iv) to request the government concerned for news concerning the state of health of the alleged victim;

(v) to draw the attention of the government concerned once again to the international instruments relating to human rights to which Viet Nam was a party, in particular the International Covenant on Economic, Social and Cultural Rights and the International Covenant on Civil and Political Rights, and to the alleged incompatibility of Article 82 of the Vietnamese Criminal Code with those Covenants;

(vi) to resume consideration of the communication at its [spring 1992 session].

Spring 1992 session of the Committee on Conventions and Recommendations (139th session of the Executive Board)[13]

181. This communication has been on the Committee's agenda since the [spring 1988 session]. It is at the stage of examination as to its substance.

182. Mr Doan Quôc Sy, is a teacher and writer over 67 years of age. The author of the communication alleges the following. Mr Doan Quôc Sy was detained from 1976 to January 1984 in a re-education camp. He was arrested again on 2 May 1984, together with other writers, for having clandestinely sent writings abroad and was sentenced on 27 April 1988 by a people's court to nine years' imprisonment under Article 82 of the Vietnamese Criminal Code, which prescribes punishment for "spreading propaganda against the Socialist system with intent to oppose the people's government". The author of the communication considers that this article is in contravention of Article 19 of the International Covenant on Civil and Political Rights. which guarantees freedom of opinion and expression. There was no proof that Mr Doan Quôc Sy had been charged with or convicted of any recognizably criminal offence. His sentence had been commuted on appeal to eight years' imprisonment. During his trial he had had no lawyer and had been obliged to conduct his own defence. The sentence had been printed in advance.

183. At previous sessions the representative of the government concerned had confirmed the condemnation of Mr Doan Quôc Sy in 1988 to nine years' imprisonment by the People's Court of Ho Chi Minh City "for breaking the law", that is to say for his activities against the State, a sentence that had been reduced to eight years on appeal. Mr Doan Quôc Sy had been convicted by a regular court of law and not under

---

[13] See document 139 EX/3 PRIV., paras. 181-186; see also document 139 EX/CR/HR/VIE.

any emergency procedures. He had had the right to choose defence counsel. His health was normal, and he was allowed to receive letters and parcels. On the subject of re-education camps, the representative of the government concerned had explained that they had been established after the war in order to enable former members of the armed forces of the deposed regime who had committed serious crimes against the population to escape capital punishment or reprisals by the victims and to learn to work and to understand the government's policy.

[183a.] The Committee had requested the Director-General to make humanitarian representations on behalf of the alleged victim and to use his good offices to persuade the government concerned to collaborate more closely in this matter.[14]

[183b.] On 30 July 1991 the Director-General had met the Permanent Delegate of Viet Nam to UNESCO. At this meeting he had handed the Permanent Delegate a letter addressed to his country's Minister for Foreign Affairs.

184. At the [autumn 1991] session, as at the preceding one, the government concerned had not been represented.

[184a.] The Committee had made a further appeal for clemency for Mr Doan Quôc Sy, who had spent many years in detention; it had repeated the requests for information it had addressed to the government and to which the government had not yet replied, and it had asked the government concerned for news concerning the state of health of the alleged victim. It had also decided to draw the attention of the government concerned once again to the international instruments relating to human rights to which Viet Nam was a party, in particular the International Covenant on Economic, Social and Cultural Rights and the International Covenant on Civil and Political Rights, and to the alleged incompatibility of Article 82 of the Vietnamese Criminal Code with those Covenants.[15]

185. At the present session, the author of the communication, in a letter dated 1 April 1992, informed the Committee that Mr Doan Quôc Sy had been released on 4 November 1991.

186. After an exchange of views, the Committee *decided*:

(i) to take note with satisfaction of the release of Mr Doan Quôc Sy;

[14] See document 136 EX/3 PRIV., para. 216 (v) (*supra*, p. 771).
[15] See document 137 EX/3 PRIV., para. 163 (ii), (iii), (iv) and (v) (*supra*, pp. 772-773).

Socialist Republic of Viet Nam **No. 765/87**

(ii) to strike the communication from its list as having been settled in accordance with paragraph 14 (*a*) (x) of 104 EX/Decision 3.3.

No. 766/87

Concerning *Socialist Republic of Viet Nam*
Case of *Nguyên Chi Thien*

Communication of 10 August 1987 submitted by
Amnesty International

Spring 1988 session of the Committee on Conventions and Recommendations (129th session of the Executive Board)[1]

120. According to the author of the communication Mr Nguyên Chi Thien, a poet, was first detained in 1958 for trying to discredit the regime through his writings and to publish a literary magazine. He was reportedly again arrested in 1979 and has been detained without charge or trial ever since.

121. On 7 April 1988 the Secretariat received from the author of the communication a letter stating that it had been reported at a conference in Stuttgart in January 1988 that Mr Nguyên Chi Thien had died at his place of detention in 1987.

122. In a letter dated 16 May 1988 the Permanent Delegation of the Socialist Republic of Viet Nam informed the Committee that Mr Nguyen Chi Thien was awaiting trial.

123. After an exchange of views, the Committee *decided*:

(i) to request the government concerned for further information on the case, and to express their humanitarian concern for Mr Nguyên Chi Thien;

(ii) to resume consideration of this communication at [its autumn 1988 session].

---

[1] See document 129 EX/3 PRIV., paras. 120-123; see also document 129 EX/CR/HR/3.

No. 766/87 **Socialist Republic of Viet Nam**

Autumn 1988 session of the Committee on Conventions and Recommendations (130th session of the Executive Board)[2]

136. The communication has been on the Committee's agenda since the [spring 1988 session]. It is at the stage of examination of its admissibility.

137. Mr Nguyên Chi Thien, a poet, first detained in 1958 for seeking to discredit the regime through his writings and for publishing an unauthorized literary magazine, was reportedly again arrested in 1979.

138. On 5 September 1988, the Secretariat received a letter from Amnesty International again expressing its disquiet as to the fate of Mr Nguyên Chi Thien.

139. In a letter dated 5 October 1988, the Permanent Delegation of the Socialist Republic of Viet Nam to Unesco stated, as it had already done at the time of the [spring 1988] session of the Committee, that Mr Nguyên Chi Thien was awaiting trial.

140. Several Committee members expressed their concern at the extreme slowness of the proceedings, Mr Nguyên Chi Thien having been detained for almost 10 years without any sentence having yet been passed. The Committee should declare the communication admissible and call for the release of the alleged victim, who had confined himself to expressing his ideas in poems without resorting to violence, a claim that the government concerned had not disputed.

141. Other Committee members considered it advisable to wait until fuller particulars had been supplied before the Committee decided on the admissibility of the communication.

142. Following an exchange of views, the Committee *decided*:

(i) to express its regret that the government concerned had not sent a representative;

(ii) to make known to the government concerned its concern at the extreme length of Mr Nguyên Chi Thien's detention without trial to date;

(iii) to request the government concerned to provide more precise information concerning the facts and the legal principles providing the basis for the

[2] See document 130 EX/3 PRIV., paras. 136-142; see also document 130 EX/CR/HR - Viet Nam.

arrest of Mr Nguyên Chi Thien, and further to inform that government that, in the absence of sufficient information, the Committee would be obliged, at its next session, to declare the communication admissible;

(iv) to appeal again for clemency to be shown to Mr Nguyên Chi Thien, in view of the extremely lengthy period of detention which he had already undergone;

(v) to resume examination of this communication at its [spring 1989 session].

Spring 1989 session of the Committee on Conventions and Recommendations (131st session of the Executive Board)[3]

168. This communication, which has been on the Committee's agenda since the [spring 1988 session], is still at the stage of being considered as to its admissibility.

169. Mr Nguyên Chi Thien, a poet aged 57, first detained in 1958 for seeking to discredit the regime in his writings and for publishing an unauthorized literary magazine, was reportedly arrested once again in 1979.

170. According to the information provided by the Permanent Delegation of the Socialist Republic of Viet Nam to Unesco at previous sessions, Mr Nguyên Chi Thien was awaiting trial.

171. At its [autumn 1988] session, the Committee had expressed concern at the extreme length of Mr Nguyên Chi Thien's detention without trial. It had requested the government concerned to provide precise information concerning the facts and legal principles providing the basis for the poet's arrest and decided that in the absence of sufficient information it would be obliged to declare the communication admissible at its next session. It also appealed again for clemency to be shown to the alleged victim, emphasizing the extremely lengthy period of detention which he had already undergone.[4]

172. In a letter dated 7 March 1989, Amnesty International informed the Secretariat that according to certain sources, Mr Nguyên Chi Thien had died in detention. According to other sources the poet, who was seriously ill, was still being held without charge or trial in an unknown place. The author of the communication expressed

[3] See document 131 EX/3 PRIV., paras. 168-174; see also document 131 EX/CR/HR/VIE.
[4] See document 130 EX/3 PRIV., para. 142 (ii), (iii) and (iv) (*supra*, pp. 778-779).

deep concern at such serious and contradictory reports, especially as in its view, nothing suggested that any trial was pending.

173. As at previous sessions, the government concerned did not send a representative. In a letter dated 9 May 1989, however, the Permanent Delegation of the [Socialist] Republic of Viet Nam repeated the information which it had provided, previously namely that Mr Nguyên Chi Thien was awaiting trial.

174. After an exchange of views, the Committee *decided*:

(i) to express once again its regret that the government concerned had not sent a representative;

(ii) to declare the communication admissible, as the letter from the Permanent Delegation of the Socialist Republic of Viet Nam of 9 May 1989 did not provide the information requested;

(iii) to express once again to the government in question its concern at the extreme length of Mr Nguyên Chi Thien's detention without trial;

(iv) to launch a further appeal for clemency to be shown to the poet, in view of his poor state of health;

(v) to resume examination of this communication at [its auutmn 1989 session].

Autumn 1989 session of the Committee on Conventions and Recommendations (132nd session of the Executive Board)[5]

178. This communication is at the stage of examination as to its substance, having been declared admissible by the Committee at its [spring 1989] session.[6]

179. Mr Nguyên Chi Thien, a poet, was allegedly first detained in 1958 on the charge of seeking to discredit the regime through his writings and of publishing an unauthorized literary magazine. He had reportedly been arrested once again in 1979.

---

[5] See document 132 EX/3 PRIV., paras. 178-184; see also document 132 EX/CR/HR/VIE.
[6] See document 131 EX/3 PRIV., para. 174 (ii) (*supra*, p. 780).

Socialist Republic of Viet Nam **No. 766/87**

180. The author of the communication states that, according to certain sources, Mr Nguyên Chi Thien is already dead. According to other sources, however, the poet is still alive, but seriously ill and still being held without charge or trial.

181. At previous sessions, the Permanent Delegation of the Socialist Republic of Viet Nam to Unesco informed the Committee that Mr Nguyên Chi Thien was awaiting trial.

182. By letter dated 14 August 1989, Amnesty International informed the Secretariat that it had no further information concerning this communication.

183. As at the three previous sessions, the government concerned was not represented at this session.

184. After an exchange of views, the Committee *decided*:

(i) to express once again its deep regret that a representative of the government concerned had not been present;

(ii) to convey once again to that government its grave concern at the extreme length of Mr Nguyên Chi Thien's detention without trial and at the particularly disquieting information regarding the poet's state of health;

(iii) to reiterate its appeal for clemency to be shown to the alleged victim, in view of the very lengthy period already spent by him in detention;

(iv) to request its Chairman to approach the delegation of Viet Nam during the next session of the General Conference in order to persuade the government of that country to co-operate with the Committee;

(v) to resume examination of this communication at its [spring 1990 session].

Spring 1990 session of the Committee on Conventions and Recommendations (134th session of the Executive Board)[7]

215. This communication is at the stage of examination as to its substance. It has been on the Committee's agenda since the [spring 1988 session].

[7] See document 134 EX/3 PRIV., paras. 215-221; see also document 134 EX/CR/HR/VIE.

No. 766/87 **Socialist Republic of Viet Nam**

216. Mr Nguyên Chi Thien, a poet, aged 57, was allegedly arrested in 1979 and imprisoned without charge or trial. He is alleged to have been detained previously, for several years, for seeking to discredit the regime in his poems and for publishing an unauthorized literary magazine.

217. The author of the communication expresses its grave concern about contradictory information it has received to the effect that the poet is already dead or seriously ill in his place of detention.

218. At previous sessions, the Government of the Socialist Republic of Viet Nam was not represented; the Permanent Delegation of Viet Nam to Unesco had merely stated that Mr Nguyên Chi Thien was awaiting trial.

219. On 25 April 1990 the Secretariat received from Amnesty International a letter in which that organization once more expressed its concern about this case.

220. The report on the discussion that took place at the present session, during examination of this communication, appears [in the report on another communication].[8] However, Mr Nguyên Chi Thien was still awaiting trial, and no one knew what the charges against him were. Members of the Committee expressed their concern at the uncertainty to which the poet's life was being subjected and at his state of health. They wondered how much longer his trial would remain pending. They stressed the need to obtain clemency for him.

221. After an exchange of views, the Committee *decided*:

(i) to thank the representative of the Government of the Socialist Republic of Viet Nam for his presence and co-operation;

(ii) to request that government to provide precise information on the case, particularly regarding the exact charges against Mr Nguyên Chi Thien, his situation in prison, whether his trial was still pending and his state of health;

(iii) to express once again to the government its grave concern about the extreme length of the poet's detention without trial and at the particularly disquieting information regarding his state of health;

(iv) to reiterate its appeal for clemency to be shown to the alleged victim, in view of the very lengthy period already spent by him in detention;

---

[8] *Ibidem*, paras. 212-213 (*supra*, pp. 765-766), communication No. 765/87 concerning *Socialist Republic of Viet Nam*, case of *Doan Quôc Sy*.

(v) to take note of the promise of the representative of the Government of the Socialist Republic of Viet Nam to obtain the information requested;

(vi) to resume examination of this communication at [its autumn 1990 session].

Autumn 1990 session of the Committee on Conventions and Recommendations (135th session of the Executive Board)[9]

165. This communication is at the stage of examination as to its substance. It has been on the Committee's agenda since the [spring 1988 session].

166. The author of the communication alleged that Mr Nguyên Chi Thien, a poet, aged 57, was arrested in 1979 and imprisoned without charge or trial. He had been detained previously, for several years, for seeking to discredit the regime in his poems and for publishing an unauthorized literary magazine. The author of the communication expressed grave concern about contradictory information received to the effect that the poet was already dead or seriously ill in his place of detention.

167. At previous sessions, the Government of the Socialist Republic of Viet Nam was not represented; the Permanent Delegation of Viet Nam to Unesco had merely stated that Mr Nguyên Chi Thien was awaiting trial.

168. At the [spring 1990] session, members of the Committee expressed their concern at the uncertainty to which the poet's life was being subjected and at his state of health. They wondered how much longer his trial would remain pending. They stressed the need to obtain clemency for him. The Committee again expressed concern about the extreme length of the poet's detention without trial and at the particularly disquieting information regarding his state of health. It requested the government concerned to provide it with more precise information on the case.[10]

169. In a letter dated 21 August 1990, the author of the communication stated that Mr Nguyên Chi Thien was suffering from tuberculosis and arthritis; that he was unable to walk and was losing his sight. He had reportedly been transferred to a different place of detention, but the author of the communication had no further information on that point.

---

[9] See document 135 EX/3 PRIV., paras. 165-172; see also documents 135 EX/CR/HR/VIE and Add.

[10] See document 134 EX/3 PRIV., para. 221 (iii) and (ii), respectively (*supra*, p. 782).

No. 766/87 **Socialist Republic of Viet Nam**

170. The Permanent Delegation of the Socialist Republic of Viet Nam to Unesco stated in a letter dated 10 September 1990 that it was still waiting for information on the case and would certainly inform the Committee as soon as it received news.

171. At the present session, some members of the Committee stressed grave concern over the situation of the alleged victim and over the fact that he had been kept in detention without a trial for nearly 12 years.

172. After an exchange of views, the Committee *decided*:

(i) to express regret that no representative of the government concerned had been present;

(ii) to thank the Ambassador, the Permanent Delegate of Viet Nam to Unesco, for his letter dated 10 September 1990;

(iii) to renew its request to the government concerned to provide precise information on the case, particularly regarding the exact charges against Mr Nguyên Chi Thien, his situation in prison, whether his trial was still pending and his state of health;

(iv) to express once more to the government its grave concern about the extreme length of the poet's detention, apparently without trial, and at the particularly disquieting information regarding his state of health;

(v) to reiterate its appeal for clemency on behalf of the alleged victim who has been held in detention for so many years;

(vi) to take note of the promise of the permanent delegate of the government concerned to obtain the information requested;

(vii) to resume consideration of the communication at [its spring 1991 session].

Socialist Republic of Viet Nam **No. 766/87**

Spring 1991 session of the Committee on Conventions and Recommendations (136th session of the Executive Board)[11]

217. This communication is at the stage of examination as to its substance. It has been on the Committee's agenda since the [spring 1988 session].

218. The author of the communication alleges that Mr Nguyên Chi Thien, a poet, aged 58, was arrested in 1979 and imprisoned without charge or trial. He had been detained previously, for several years, for seeking to discredit the regime in his poems and for publishing an unauthorized literary magazine. The author of the communication expressed grave concern about contradictory information received to the effect that the poet was already dead or seriously ill in his place of detention.

219. At previous sessions the Government of the Socialist Republic of Viet Nam merely stated that Mr Nguyên Chi Thien was awaiting trial.

220. At the [auutmn 1990] session members of the Committee expressed their concern at the uncertainty to which the poet's life was being subjected and at his state of health. They wondered how much longer his trial would remain pending. They stressed the need to obtain clemency for him. The Committee again expressed concern about the extreme length of the poet's detention without trial and at the particularly disquieting information regarding his state of health. It requested the Government of the Socialist Republic of Viet Nam to provide it with more precise information on the case.[12]

221. In a letter dated 21 August 1990 the author of the communication stated that Mr Nguyên Chi Thien was suffering from tuberculosis and arthritis, that he was unable to walk and was losing his sight. He had reportedly been transferred to a different place of detention, but the author of the communication had no further information on that point.

222. At the [auutmn 1990] session the Permanent Delegation of the Socialist Republic of Viet Nam to UNESCO stated by letter that it was still waiting for information on the case and would certainly inform the Committee as soon as it received news. Some members of the Committee expressed grave concern over the situation of the alleged victim and over the fact that he had been kept in detention without trial for nearly 12 years.

---

[11] See document 136 EX/3 PRIV., paras. 217-225; see also documents 136 EX/CR/HR/VIE and Add.

[12] See document 135 EX/3 PRIV., para. 172 (iv) and (iii), respectively (*supra*, p. 784).

No. 766/87 **Socialist Republic of Viet Nam**

223. At the current session, by a letter dated 9 April 1991, the author of the communication informed the Committee that it had no additional information concerning this communication but that it nevertheless remained most concerned about the fate of Mr Nguyên Chi Thien and about his state of health.

224. As at the previous sessions, the Government of the Socialist Republic of Viet Nam was not represented at the current session.

225. After an exchange of views, the Committee *decided*:

(i) to express its regret once again that it had been denied the presence of a representative of the Government of the Socialist Republic of Viet Nam and had not received the information that government had promised to send it;

(ii) to make a further appeal for clemency on behalf of Mr Nguyên Chi Thien, who has spent many years in detention;

(iii) to request the Government of the Socialist Republic of Viet Nam once again to provide it with detailed information on this case, especially on the specific acts Mr Nguyên Chi Thien was accused of having committed, on his situation in prison, on the question of whether he was still awaiting trial and on his state of health;

(iv) to inform the government again of its deep concern at the great length of time for which the poet had been detained, apparently without trial, and at the very alarming information received about his state of health;

(v) to request the Director-General to make humanitarian representations on behalf of the alleged victim and, pursuant to paragraph 14 (*k*) of 104 EX/Decision 3.3, to use his good offices to persuade the Government of the Socialist Republic of Viet Nam to co-operate better in this matter;

(vi) to resume consideration of the communication at its [autumn 1991 session].

Socialist Republic of Viet Nam **No. 766/87**

Autumn 1991 session of the Committee on Conventions and Recommendations (137th session of the Executive Board)[13]

164. This communication is at the stage of examination as to its substance. It has been on the Committee's agenda since the [spring 1988 session].

165. The author of the communication alleges that Mr Nguyên Chi Thien, a poet, aged 58, was arrested in 1979 and imprisoned without charge or trial. He had been detained previously, for several years, for seeking to discredit the regime in his poems and for publishing an unauthorized literary magazine. The author of the communication expressed grave concern about information received to the effect that the poet was seriously ill. He was said to be suffering from tuberculosis and arthritis, to be unable to walk and to be losing his sight. He had reportedly been transferred to another place of detention.

166. At previous sessions the government concerned merely stated that Mr Nguyên Chi Thien was awaiting trial.

167. Members of the Committee expressed their concern over the situation of the poet, who had been kept in detention without trial for so many years. They stressed the need to obtain clemency for him. The Committee endorsed this expression of concern. It requested the government concerned to provide it with more precise information on the case.[14]

168. At the [spring 1991] session, the Committee asked the Director-General to make humanitarian representations on behalf of Mr Nguyên Chi Thien and to use his good offices to obtain greater co-operation from the government concerned.[15]

[168a.] On 30 July 1991, the Director-General met the Permanent Delegate of Viet Nam to UNESCO and handed him a letter addressed to the Minister of Foreign Affairs of his country.

169. At the current session, the author of the communication informed the Committee by a letter dated 30 August 1991, that it had no additional information concerning this communication but that it nevertheless remained most concerned about the fate of Mr Nguyên Chi Thien.

[13] See document 137 EX/3 PRIV., paras. 164-170; see also document 137 EX/CR/HR/VIE.
[14] See document 136 EX/3 PRIV., para. 225 (iv) and (iii), respectively (*supra*, p. 786).
[15] *Ibidem*, para. 225 (v) (*supra*, p. 786).

No. 766/87 **Socialist Republic of Viet Nam**

[169a.] As at the previous sessions, the government concerned was not represented at the current session.

170. After an exchange of views, the Committee *decided*:

(i) to express its regret once again that it had been denied the presence of a representative of the government concerned and had not received any information from that government;

(ii) to make a further appeal on behalf of Mr Nguyên Chi Thien, who has spent many years in detention;

(iii) to urge the government concerned to provide it with detailed information on this case, especially on the specific acts Mr Nguyên Chi Thien was accused of having committed, on his situation in prison, on the question of whether he was still awaiting trial after so many years in detention, and on his state of health;

(iv) to resume consideration of the communication at its [spring 1992 session].

Spring 1992 session of the Committee on Conventions and Recommendations (139th session of the Executive Board)[16]

187. This communication is at the stage of examination as to its substance. It has been on the Committee's agenda since the [spring 1988 session].

188. The author of the communication alleges that Mr Nguyên Chi Thien, a poet. aged 58, was arrested in 1979 and imprisoned without charge or trial. He had been detained previously, for several years, for seeking to discredit the regime in his poems and for publishing an unauthorized literary magazine. The author of the communication expressed grave concern about information received to the effect that the poet was seriously ill. He was suffering from tuberculosis and arthritis, unable to walk and losing his sight. He had been transferred to another place of detention.

189. At previous sessions the government concerned had merely stated that Mr Nguyên Chi Thien was awaiting trial.

---

[16] See document 139 EX/3 PRIV., paras. 187-193; see also document 139 EX/CR/HR/VIE.

Socialist Republic of Viet Nam **No. 766/87**

[189a.] The Committee had asked the Director-General to make humanitarian representations on behalf of Mr Nguyên Chi Thien, and to use his good offices to obtain greater co-operation from the government concerned.[17]

[189b.] On 30 July 1991, the Director-General had met the Permanent Delegate of Viet Nam to UNESCO and handed him a letter addressed to the Minister of Foreign Affairs of his country.

190. At the [autumn 1991] session the Committee made a further appeal on behalf of Mr Nguyên Chi Thien, who had spent many years in detention. It had also requested the government concerned to provide it with detailed information on this case, especially on the specific acts Mr Nguyên Chi Thien was accused of having committed, on his situation in prison, on the question of whether he was still awaiting trial and on his state of health.[18]

191. At the present session, as at previous sessions, the government concerned was not represented.

192. In a letter dated 1 April 1992, the author of the communication informed the Committee that the alleged victim had been released on 22 October 1991.

193. After an exchange of views, the Committee *decided*:

(i) to take note with satisfaction of the release of Mr Nguyên Chi Thien;

(ii) to strike the communication from its list as having been settled in accordance with paragraph 14 (*a*) (x) of 104 EX/Decision 3.3.

[17] See document 136 EX/3 PRIV., para. 225 (v) (*supra*, p. 786).
[18] See document 137 EX/3 PRIV., para. 170 (ii) and (iii) (*supra*, p. 788).

No. 768/87

Concerning *Côte d'Ivoire*
Case of *Teachers belonging to the National Union of Secondary School Teachers of Côte d'Ivoire*

Communication of 1 September 1987 submitted by
World Federation of Teachers' Unions

Spring 1988 session of the Committee on Conventions and Recommendations (129th session of the Executive Board)[1]

39. According to the author of the communication, a group of individuals, most of whom were not members of the National Union of Secondary School Teachers of Côte d'Ivoire (SYNESCI), had sabotaged the 15th Congress of that Union with the agreement of the Minister of National Education and of the single party in power, making it necessary to suspend the proceedings of the Congress. These individuals had reportedly occupied the head office of the Union with the assistance of the police. The Union's property had reportedly been seized and its bank accounts frozen by order of the Minister. About 60 activists had been transferred to posts far away from their homes and a small group of leaders had been detained, most of them in a military camp, or their salary had been or was to be withheld. The Secretary-General of the Union, the Treasurer, and his assistant had reportedly been sentenced to four to six month prison terms.

40. In their introductory statement, the representatives of the government involved said that this case, which concerned the internal affairs of a union organization which had been taken to court and tried in accordance with national law, should not have been brought before the Committee. Replying to questions, they said that after the opening of the 15th Congress of SYNESCI and in the presence of the Minister of National Education, a disagreement had arisen between the participants on the application of a provision of the Union's statutes concerning the right to vote. When it was outvoted, the outgoing Bureau had suspended the proceedings. The participants had carried on with the meeting and elected a new Bureau, which filed a legal action against the members of the outgoing Bureau, alleging that it had drawn out the funds

[1] See document 129 EX/3 PRIV., paras. 39-42; see also document 129 EX/CR/HR/3.

from all the Union's accounts and seized its movable property. The trial resulted in the conviction of the former Secretary-General, the Treasurer, and the Treasurer's assistant. When released from prison, they and their friends had conducted a propaganda campaign against the President of the Republic and the government. The deferment from military service which some of them had enjoyed as teachers had then been lifted, and they had been conscripted into the army to do their national service. Disciplinary measures were being taken against others. The representatives of the government then pointed out that this communication had also been submitted to the ILO Committee on Freedom of Association and that this body would be considering it in the next few days.

41. All Committee members who spoke on this case felt that the matter related to the internal affairs of the union in question and was primarily the concern of ILO and that the Committee should either postpone consideration of this communication until it had been considered by ILO or strike it off its agenda, since all the legal guarantees had been provided in this case.

42. After an exchange of views, the Committee *decided*:

(i) to thank the representatives of the government concerned for their presence and co-operation;

(ii) to declare the communication inadmissible as it did not fall within the fields of competence of Unesco as defined in paragraph 14 (*a*) (iii) of 104 EX/Decision 3.3.

No. 772/87

Concerning *Yugoslavia*
Case of *Uros Bukumira*

Communication of 29 July 1987 submitted by
Uros Bukumira

Spring 1988 session of the Committee on Conventions and Recommendations (129th session of the Executive Board)[1]

127. Mr Uros Bukumira, a teacher of philosophy and Marxism in Ivangrad, complains of political persecution. He alleges that he was considered, or that attempts were made to have him branded, morally and politically unfit to teach. On 27 September 1984 he and his family are said to have been evicted from the apartment assigned to him. It is alleged that despite a decision delivered by the Bijelo Polje industrial tribunal - and confirmed by a higher court - ordering that he be allowed to reoccupy his accommodation, and despite a decision to the same effect by a commission of the Presidency of the Central Committee of the Montenegro Communist Party, the Ivangrad authorities refused to put those decisions into effect. He states that his wife, who was employed in government service, suffered various instances of harassment - until she could no longer bear them and was forced to resign. His children are also said to have suffered a great deal. Reportedly, in order to escape from the alleged persecution his entire family left Ivangrad for Belgrade, where his wife found employment as a shop assistant, earning barely enough to pay the rent of a room.

128. The representative of the Yugoslav Government explained to the Committee that the origins of the present case dated back to a series of transactions Mr Bukumira had entered into several years ago with other persons for the exchange of apartments which had been put at his disposal but which he had had no legal right to exchange. As a result of lengthy legal proceedings, which Mr Bukumira contested and appealed without success, Mr Bukumira was evicted from an apartment he had had no right to occupy. Another apartment had been put at his disposal, but he chose not to accept it. It was still at his disposal. Up until February of 1988 Mr Bukumira was

[1] See document 129 EX/3 PRIV., paras. 127-130; see also document 129 EX/CR/HR/3.

receiving his salary and medical benefits, but then, without giving any reason, Mr Bukumira of his own free will decided to move to Belgrade. The representative of the Yugoslav Government explained that he had not been expelled from the teaching profession and that the school board was holding his job open for him in case he wished to change his mind.

129. A member of the Committee was of the view that suffering such as that expressed by Mr Bukumira could grow out of feelings of alienation and solitude. He further pointed out that, while the Committee might be obliged to classify the communication as being inadmissible, this did not mean that the Committee could not express its compassion for the person involved. The representative of the government concerned indicated that the authorities of his country were also sympathetic to the difficulties faced by Mr Bukumira but that in society in general there were always cases of suffering or maladjustment which were outside the possibility or the realm of governments to solve.

130. During a lengthy exchange of views a consensus emerged that the nature of the existing problem was such that it did not come within the scope of the Committee's competence. The Committee therefore *decided*:

(i) to thank the representative of the government concerned for his presence and co-operation;

(ii) to declare the communication inadmissible under the terms of paragraph 14 (*a*) (iii) of 104 EX/Decision 3.3 and to strike it from its list, while at the same time expressing sympathy for Mr Bukumira's situation.

No. 773/88

Concerning *Chile*
Case of *Ledy del Carmen Castro Urra*

Communication of 17 December 1987 submitted by
World Federation of Teachers' Unions

Spring 1988 session of the Committee on Conventions and Recommendations (129th session of the Executive Board)[1]

23. According to the author of the communication, Mrs Ledy del Carmen Castro Urra, a teacher, was arrested on 19 October 1984 and convicted by a military tribunal of being in possession of firearms. She was allegedly detained without public trial for a whole year. Just as she was about to be granted a conditional release, towards the end of 1985, an examining magistrate in charge of a case concerning the abduction of a child, about which she knew nothing, is reported to have brought a series of charges against her. Apparently the child who had been kidnapped and subsequently found did not even recognize her. On 27 January 1986, she is said to have been accused of involvement in an armed robbery which took place in May 1984. It had in fact been established that she was conducting an English class at a private school, the Britannia School at that time.

24. The representative of the government concerned stated that the allegations contained in the communication were a gross distortion of the facts. Mrs Ledy del Carmen Castro Urra, in his view, was a member of a commando group of 11 people, the "Frente Patriótico Manuel Rodríguez", which had been responsible for numerous acts of terrorism. Four of those people, including Mrs Castro Urra, had been arrested after their leader had been shot and injured by a policeman and had fled abroad. The representative of the government concerned stated that between February 1983 and August 1984 the commando group had committed several ordinary criminal offences namely: unlawful association, armed robbery of three gunsmith's shops, attack on a taxi driver, storming of a radio broadcasting station, robbery at the headquarters of a newspaper, abduction and sequestration of a child. He pointed out that, during the inquiry, weapons and explosives had been found at the home of Mrs Cas-

[1] See document 129 EX/3 PRIV., paras. 23-27; see also document 129 EX/CR/HR/3 Add.

tro Urra, and that, contrary to the allegations in the communication, the child who had been kidnapped and returned after payment of ransom had recognized her and had also identified the place where he had been held. Of all the offences of which Mrs Castro Urra was accused, the most serious was that of kidnapping - an offence for which it was not possible to grant the accused a conditional release or even to envisage transforming the sentence into exile. The examining magistrate had been accused by the defence on three occasions before the Supreme Court but those accusations had been rejected. The representative of the government concerned also informed the Committee that the United Nations Special Rapporteur on the situation of human rights in Chile had decided not to examine the affair, which he considered came within the scope of ordinary law. The representative of the government concerned also rejected the allegations that Mrs Castro Urra had been tortured. He referred in this connection to the replies given by the accused herself before the tribunal.

25. Several members of the Committee expressed scepticism as to the credibility of the accusation of child abduction. According to one member, the "Frente Patriótico Manuel Rodríguez" was indeed an armed opposition group, but it was an offshoot of a party which had previously participated in the "People's Unity" government and he felt that it was unlikely that this Front has resorted to child abduction and demands for ransom.

26. Other members of the Committee considered that the information before them was insufficient. Some of them expressed concern over the allegations that Mrs Castro Urra had been tortured and over the slowness of the legal proceedings.

27. After an exchange of views, the Committee *decided*:

(i) to thank the representative of the government concerned for his presence and his co-operation;

(ii) to express concern at the length of time which had elapsed between Mrs Ledy del Carmen Castro Urra's arrest and her trial;

(iii) to resume examination of the communication at [its autumn 1988 session].

Chile **No. 773/88**

Autumn 1988 session of the Committee on Conventions and Recommendations (130th session of the Executive Board)[2]

14. This communication, which the Committee considered for the first time at its [spring 1988] session, is still at the stage of examination of its admissibility.

15. Mrs Ledy del Carmen Castro Urra, a teacher, was reportedly arrested on 19 October 1984 and charged by a military tribunal for possession of firearms. Just as she was about to be granted a conditional release, towards the end of 1985, an examining magistrate in charge of a case concerning the abduction of a child, brought a series of charges against her. On 27 January 1986 she was accused of being involved in an armed robbery which had taken place in May 1984; yet it is claimed that it was proved that at that time she had been conducting an English class at a private establishment, the Britannia School.

16. At the [spring 1988] session, the representative of the Chilean Government told the Committee that Mrs Ledy del Carmen Castro Urra was a member of a commando group connected with the Manuel Rodríguez Patriotic Front, which had been responsible for numerous acts of terrorism; that during the investigation, weapons and explosives had been found at her home and that, contrary to the allegations in the communication, the child who had been kidnapped and recovered had recognized her.

17. On 1 August 1988, the Secretariat received a letter from the Permanent Delegation of Chile to Unesco in which she noted that the decision taken by the Committee at [its spring 1988 session] concerning this communication was, in her view, marred by serious errors and omissions in respect of both the substance and the procedure followed. That letter was reproduced in an annex to the summary of the communication [...].[3]

18. On 29 September 1988 the Secretariat received from the author of the communication a letter containing additional information. Mrs Ledy del Carmen Castro Urra had still not been tried. She had admitted having received information of a political nature from persons accused of belonging to the Manuel Rodríguez Patriotic Front and having rented a room in her house to one of those persons, but nothing else. No court action had yet been taken on the charge brought against her for illegal possession of firearms, the file on which was reportedly made available to the defence lawyer only one year later. Yet if she had been tried within the statutory time-limit, any

---

[2] See document 130 EX/3 PRIV., paras. 14-22; see also document 130 EX/CR/HR - Chile.

[3] See document 130 EX/CR/HR.

sentence she might have received would not have been as long as the period for which she had already been held in detention.

19. As regards the case of the kidnapped child, the child who had been abducted and found had not recognized her. Moreover, she had never been officially charged with this crime. The one person who had been so charged had already been granted a conditional release six months earlier. As for the charge of armed robbery brought against her, the victim of that aggression had testified in a written statement that Mrs Castro Urro was not one of the assailants. Mrs Castro Urra's health has reportedly deteriorated. Lastly, it was claimed that the prison authorities had not transmitted to her letters sent by her son from England.

20. At the current session of the Committee, the representative of the Chilean Government said that the case was highly complex because it involved several charges and several accused persons. Since legal proceedings were continuing, this was not a matter for the government. Responding to the humanitarian concerns of the Committee, he had personally approached the magistrates in charge of the cases concerning Mrs Castro Urra. He had been able to gather the following information. As regards the charges of armed robbery, violating the privacy of the mail and illegal entry, Mrs Castro Urra would either be acquitted or would be liable to only minor sentences. As regards the charge of participating in the sequestration of a child, the accusation was that child had been sequestered in her house. If the defence succeeded in proving that this happened without her knowledge, she would not be implicated, but further examination would have to take place. As regards her membership of an illegal terrorist organization and the charge of the illegal possession of arms and explosives, the investigation was not yet completed. It seemed, however, that Mrs Castro Urra's guilt had been established. The magistrates believed that the investigation might be completed in December. In conclusion, the representative of the government concerned informed the Committee that, without prejudice to the verdict of the competent court, if Mrs Castro Urra were to be sentenced, and provided that it was not a prison sentence, a pardon might be envisaged.

21. Several members of the Committee expressed their grave concern and astonishment over this case. They thought that Mrs Castro Urra's four-year detention without judgement being passed was virtually a denial of justice. The indication given by the representative of the government concerned that the end of the case was near did however justify waiting for a legal decision but failing this, the Committee would be obliged to declare the communication admissible at its next session. Some Committee members noted that the charge of kidnapping a child brought against Mrs Castro Urra, which the Committee had not found convincing, had turned out to be less serious than the government had made out.

22. After an exchange of views, the Committee *decided*:

(i) to thank the representative of the government concerned for his presence and co-operation;

(ii) to express its regrets at the slow pace of the investigation of the case;

(iii) to request the government concerned to communicate information as soon as possible regarding any decisions taken by the legal authorities on the subject of Mrs Ledy del Castro Urra;

(iv) to resume examination of this communication at its [spring 1989 session].

Spring 1989 session of the Committee on Conventions and Recommendations (131st session of the Executive Board)[4]

15. This communication, which has been on the Committee's agenda since the [spring 1988 session], is still at the stage of being examined as to its admissibility.

16. According to [the author], Mrs Ledy del Carmen Castro Urra, a teacher, was arrested on 19 October 1984 and charged by a military tribunal for possession of firearms. Towards the end of 1985, an examining magistrate working on a case concerning the abduction of a child brought a series of other charges against her. According to the author of the communication, the child, who had been kidnapped and recovered, did not recognize her. In January 1986, Mrs Castro Urra was accused of being involved in an armed robbery which had taken place in May 1984. But it is said to have been established that she was giving an English lesson at the time.

17. At the [autumn 1988] session the representative of the government concerned had informed the Committee that according to the judges in charge of Mrs Castro Urra's files the investigation might be completed in December 1988. Without prejudging the verdict of the court, he had expressed the opinion that if Mrs Castro Urra were sentenced, and provided that it was not a prison sentence, a pardon might be envisaged.

18. After expressing its regrets at the slow pace of the investigation of the case, the Committee had decided to request the government concerned to communicate infor-

---

[4] See document 131 EX/3 PRIV., paras. 15-21; see also document 131 EX/CR/HR/CHI.

mation as soon as possible regarding any decisions taken by the legal authorities concerning the alleged victim.[5]

19. At the current session, the representative of the government concerned said that, as the Committee had already been told, the case was highly complex. The charges against Mrs Castro Urra came partly within the jurisdiction of military courts and partly within that of the civilian courts. The file with the civilian authorities alone contained several thousands of pages. She had been indicted on 14 counts involving 16 people. With regard to the accusation of child-kidnapping, the judge dealing with the case was personally convinced that Mrs Ledy del Carmen Castro Urra was involved, at least in keeping the child hidden away, but in the absence of tangible proof and in accordance with the principle that the accused is given the benefit of the doubt, the same judge thought that she would be cleared. A verdict was imminent in the case of armed robbery against the Associated Press Agency. The representative of the government concerned had formally asked the judge in charge of the case which came under the jurisdiction of the military whether it would be possible to dissociate the case of Mrs Ledy del Carmen Castro Urra from the others so that it would be tried separately. This request had been acceded to. The accused would therefore be tried with one other codefendant for the illegal possession of arms, ammunition and explosives and for belonging to an armed terrorist group. As she had already spent a number of years in preventive detention, the defence might, if it pressed its case, succeed in having this detention deducted in full from the sentence passed.

20. The representative of the government concerned said that the representations which he had made on humanitarian grounds could just as easily have been undertaken by Mrs Ledy del Carmen Castro Urra's lawyer.

21. After an exchange of views, the Committee *decided*:

(i) to thank the representative of the government concerned for his presence and co-operation;

(ii) to take note of the statements of this representative to the effect that the charge of child-kidnapping would no longer be pressed against Mrs Ledy del Carmen Castro Urra;

(iii) to request the government concerned to keep it informed of the final decisions taken by the military and civilian authorities with regard to this teacher;

---

[5] See document 130 EX/3 PRIV., para. 22 (iii) (*supra*, p. 799).

(iv) to resume examination of this communication at its [autumn 1989 session].

Autumn 1989 session of the Committee on Conventions and Recommendations (132nd session of the Executive Board)[6]

13. This communication, which has been on the Committee's agenda since the [spring 1988 session], is still at the stage of being considered as to its admissibility.

14. According to the author of the communication, Mrs Ledy del Carmen Castro Urra, a teacher, was arrested on 19 October 1984. She is said to have been charged in particular with possession of firearms, abducting a child and armed robbery.

15. According to the information provided at previous sessions by the representative of the government concerned, the charges against Mrs Ledy del Carmen Castro Urra came partly within the jurisdiction of civilian courts and partly within that of military courts. She was said to have been cleared of the charge of child abduction and a verdict was apparently imminent in the case of armed robbery. A verdict was also said to be imminent in the case of possession of firearms, ammunition and explosives, pending before the military courts. The defence would be entitled to request that the period she had spent in preventive detention should be deducted from the sentence passed.

16. At the present session, the representative of the government concerned reminded the Committee that Mrs Ledy del Carmen Urra belonged to an armed group that claimed responsibility for several terrorist attacks and had committed several criminal offences. Nevertheless, he had, as he had promised, made various representations in Chile on humanitarian grounds and in response to the Committee's concern that the case should be rapidly settled. Despite errors by the defence, he had succeeded in convincing the military judge that the sentence called for in the case against Mrs Castro Urra and her codefendant, a man by the name of Francisco Ismael Peña Riveros, was excessive. The verdict given on 16 September 1989, of which he had recently received a copy, thus sentenced them both to five years' imprisonment instead of the 25 years previously called for. It was false to claim, as the author of the communication had done, that the military legal authorities had advised the defence not to pass any more information to Unesco and that the trial was continually being postponed. It was now up to the defence to continue the procedure in the civilian courts, invoking the decision of the military court. If the defence did not make the mistake of attempting, for political reasons, to link the case of Mrs Castro Urra

---

[6] See document 132 EX/3 PRIV., paras. 13-18; see also document 132 EX/CR/HR/CHI.

with that of the other defendants, she could be released on 27 November 1989. In reply to a question, he stated that the period of time spent in preventive detention had been deducted from the sentence.

17. One member of the Committee said that this case illustrated the usefulness of the Committee's work. If the case had not been referred to Unesco, no doubt the sentence would not have been reduced to such an extent and the case would not have received the same attention.

18. After an exchange of views, the Committee *decided*:

(i) to thank the representative of the government concerned for his attendance and co-operation;

(ii) to request the Secretariat to inform the author of the communication that the defence would be well advised to bring the sentence passed by the military court rapidly to the attention of the civilian judicial authority in order to secure the release of Mrs Ledy del Carmen Castro Urra in November 1989;

(iii) to strike the communication from its list in the event of Mrs Ledy del Carmen Castro Urra being released on that date and, should she not then be released, to resume consideration of this communication at its [spring 1990 session].

Spring 1990 session of the Committee on Conventions and Recommendations (134th session of the Executive Board)[7]

9. This communication is still at the stage of examination as to its admissibility. It has been on the Committee's agenda since the [spring 1988 session].

10. Ms Ledy del Carmen Castro Urra, a teacher, was according to the author of the communication arrested on 19 October 1984 and charged with possession of firearms, the abduction of a child and armed robbery.

11. According to the information provided by the representative of the government concerned at previous sessions, the charges against Ms Ledy del Carmen Castro Urra came partly within the jurisdiction of civilian courts and partly within that of military courts. She was said to have been cleared of the charge of abduction of a child and would very shortly be tried for armed robbery. The case of illegal possession of

---

[7] See document 134 EX/3 PRIV., paras. 9-16; see also document 134 EX/CR/HR/CHI.

arms, ammunition and explosives was also pending before the military courts. Counsel for the defence would be entitled to request that the period she had spent in preventive detention be deducted from the sentence passed.

12. At the [autumn 1989] session, the Committee had been informed of the steps taken in Chile by the representative of the government concerned on humanitarian grounds and in response to the concern expressed by the Committee. The verdict delivered on 15 September 1989 sentenced Ms Ledy del Carmen Castro Urra to five years' imprisonment instead of the 25 years previously called for. It was for the defence to continue the procedure in the civilian courts, invoking the decision of the military court. If the defence did not make the mistake of attempting, for political reasons, to link the case of Ms Ledy del Carmen Castro Urra with that of the other defendants, she could be released on 27 November 1989, the period of time spent in preventive detention having been deducted from the sentence.

13. The Committee decided at the time to strike the communication from its list in the event of Ms Ledy del Carmen Castro Urra's being released in November 1989. Otherwise the Committee would resume consideration of the communication.[8]

14. As no information had reached the Secretariat, the communication was again placed on the Committee's agenda at its present session.

15. After reporting on the steps taken by the new government in Chile to guarantee the defence and promotion of human rights in his country, the representative of the government concerned informed the Committee that Ms Ledy del Carmen Castro Urra had been released in March 1990.

16. Following an exchange of views, the Committee *decided*:

(i) to thank the representatives of the government concerned for their attendance and co-operation;

(ii) to take note with satisfaction of Ms Ledy del Carmen Castro Urra's release;

(iii) to strike the communication from its list and consider it as settled in accordance with paragraph 14 (*a*) (x) of 104 EX/Decision 3.3.

---

[8] See document 132 EX/3 PRIV., para. 18 (iii) (*supra*, p. 802).

No. 776/88

Concerning *Bulgaria*
Case of *Omer Mustafov Kochandzhiev and Burhan Nedzhibov Hayrulov*

Communication of 17 February 1988 submitted by
The International Human Rights Law Group

Spring 1988 session of the Committee on Conventions and Recommendations (129th session of the Executive Board)[1]

12. The author of the communication states that, according to reports from reliable sources, the Bulgarian authorities have attempted to force ethnic Turks to change their names, which have Islamic connotations, to accept new identity cards bearing Bulgarian names and to give up their religious practices, language, customs and traditions. There have been reports of violence against those who resisted the measures and punitive action taken against them.

13. Mr Omer Mustafov Kochandzhiev, whose new name is reported to be Yuri Fidanor Kochandzhiev, is described as a teacher from Dolni Voden. He was reportedly arrested in 1985 for opposing the name-changing campaign. It is claimed that he is currently serving a three-year sentence of internal banishment in Beli Brod.

14. Mr Burhan Hayrulov, whose new name is reported to be Boyan Neykov Harakov, was also allegedly arrested, on 31 December 1984, following a demonstration against the name-changing campaign.

15. The representative of the Bulgarian Government reminded the Committee that the Committee at its autumn 1987 session had decided to declare inadmissible a communication dealing, *inter alia*, with the alleged victims in this case.[2] He pointed out that decisions of the Committee were final and without appeal. The purported new elements in the case were not in fact new, he said, since the question of the pro-

---

[1] See document 129 EX/3 PRIV., paras. 12-18; see also document 129 EX/CR/HR/3 Add.

[2] See document 127 EX/3 PRIV., para. 24 (ii) (*supra*, p. 694), communication No. 748/87 concerning *Bulgaria*, case of *Omer Mustafov Kochandzhiev* et al.

fessions of the two persons had been settled in previous discussions. The representative of the Bulgarian Government called upon the Committee to consider this case as being inadmissible.

16. Certain Committee members felt that there appeared to be new elements other than the question of professions which might make the case merit a re-examination. The point was made that the question of cultural identity was an important right within Unesco's fields of competence, regardless of a person's profession.

17. Several other Committee members shared the view of the representative of the Bulgarian Government and felt the case was clearly inadmissible.

18. After an exchange of views, and after four members of the Committee had expressed their reservations, the Committee *decided*:

> (i) to thank the representative of the government concerned for his presence and co-operation;
>
> (ii) to declare the communication inadmissible, a communication dealing with these two cases having been previously declared inadmissible by the Committee at its autumn 1987 session and no new elements would justify the re-examination thereof.

No. 778/88

Concerning *Nepal*
Case of *Sushil Chandra Amatya*

Communication of 5 April 1988 submitted by
Amnesty International

Spring 1988 session of the Committee on Conventions and Recommendations (129th session of the Executive Board)[1]

72. According to the author of the communication, Mr Sushil Chandra Amatya, a teacher, was arrested on 24 June 1987 under the provisions of the Public Security Act. In a telegram received by the Secretariat on 22 April 1988, Amnesty International stated that the alleged victim had apparently been released on 7 April 1988, but subsequently rearrested. His state of health was said to be giving cause for concern.

73. Confirming the tenor of a letter sent to the Secretariat on 2 May 1988, the representative of the government concerned stated that the authorities and the Permanent Delegation of his country were willing to co-operate with the Committee, but that, owing to the slowness of mail between Paris and Kathmandu, he had not yet received the relevant information. He asked the Committee to postpone examination of the communication to a later session.

74. After an exchange of views, the Committee *decided*:

(i) to thank the representative of the government concerned for his presence and co-operation;

(ii) to ask the government concerned to be kind enough to provide information on Mr Sushil Chandra Amatya's alleged offence and the sentence normally meted out for such an offence;

[1] See document 129 EX/3 PRIV., paras. 72-74; see also document 129 EX/CR/HR/3 Add.

(iii) to ask the representative of the government concerned to inform the appropriate authorities in his country of the Committee's concern about the accused's state of health;

(iv) to resume examination of this communication at [its autumn 1988 session].

Autumn 1988 session of the Committee on Conventions and Recommendations (130th session of the Executive Board)[2]

77. This communication has been on the agenda of the Committee since the [spring 1988 session]. It is at the stage of examination of its admissibility.

78. According to the author of the communication, Mr Sushil Chandra Amatya, a teacher and founder member of the Central Committee of the Nepal National Teachers' Association, which is not recognized by the Government, was arrested on 24 June 1987. He was apparently released on 7 April 1988, but subsequently rearrested. It is alleged that no authorization to visit him has been granted. His state of health is causing concern as he is said to suffer from a kidney ailment.

79. On 5 September 1988, the Secretariat received a letter from Amnesty International stating that Mr Sushil Chandra Amatya was still being held in Dilli Bazaar prison, in Kathmandu. He is said to have been hospitalized and to have received medical attention. Apparently he is now back in prison, but the author does not know whether he is allowed to follow the course of treatment prescribed for him.

80. The government concerned has not sent a representative, but by letter dated 3 October 1988 the Permanent Delegation of the Kingdom of Nepal to Unesco stated that Mr Sushil Chandra Amatya was involved in the activities of a teachers' association that had not been registered in conformity with the law governing the establishment and functioning of such bodies. The government had warned him several times about his activities. Detained in accordance with current legislation, Mr Amatya would not be held any longer than the legally prescribed period. Like other prisoners, he received proper medical treatment.

81. After an exchange of views, the Committee *decided*:

(i) to express its regret at not having benefited from the presence of a representative of the government concerned;

---

[2] See document 130 EX/3 PRIV., paras. 77-81; see also document 130 EX/CR/HR - Nepal.

(ii) to take note of the letter of 3 October 1988 from the Permanent Delegation of the Kingdom of Nepal to Unesco;

(iii) to request the government concerned to provide more detailed information on the alleged offence of Mr Sushil Chandra Amatya, the sentence normally meted out for this offence and the domestic remedies available;

(iv) to request the competent authorities to allow Mr Sushil Chandra Amatya to be visited by his family and lawyers;

(v) to make a fresh appeal for clemency on his behalf, particularly in view of his poor state of health;

(vi) to resume examination of this communication at its [spring 1989 session].

Spring 1989 session of the Committee on Conventions and Recommendations (131st session of the Executive Board)[3]

86. This communication has been on the agenda of the Committee since the [spring 1988 session]. It is still at the stage of examination as to its admissibility.

87. According to the author of the communication, Mr Sushil Chandra Amatya, a teacher, a founder member of the Nepal National Teachers' Association, an association which is not recognized by the government, was arrested on 24 June 1987. Released on 7 April 1988, he was subsequently rearrested. His state of health is said to be causing concern.

88. At the [autumn 1988] session, the Permanent Delegation of Nepal to Unesco informed the Committee by letter that Mr Sushil Chandra Amatya had been warned several times about the illegal activities of the said association, but he had not heeded that warning. Sentenced to a period of detention in accordance with the law he had, like other prisoners, received proper medical treatment.

89. While requesting the government concerned to provide more detailed information, the Committee had made an appeal for clemency on behalf of the alleged victim.[4]

---

[3] See document 131 EX/3 PRIV., paras. 86-91; see also document 131 EX/CR/HR/NEP.
[4] See document 130 EX/3 PRIV., para. 81 (iii) and (v) (*supra*, p. 809).

No. 778/88 **Nepal**

90. On 30 January 1989, the Secretariat received a letter from the Permanent Delegation of Nepal informing it that Mr Sushil Chandra Amatya had been released on 28 December 1988. The author of the communication confirmed this information in a letter dated 7 March 1989 and indicated that Mr Sushil Chandra Amatya had been released on the occasion of the birthday of His Majesty the King of Nepal. About 150 other prisoners had been similarly pardoned.

91. Following an exchange of views, the Committee *decided*:

(i) to note with satisfaction the release of Mr Sushil Chandra Amatya;

(ii) to strike the communication from its list as being settled in accordance with paragraph 14 (*a*) (x) of 104 EX/Decision 3.3.

No. 779/88

Concerning *Yugoslavia*
Case of *Bogdan Antić*

Communication of 22 March 1988 submitted by
Bogdan Antić

Autumn 1988 session of the Committee on Conventions and Recommendations (130th session of the Executive Board)[1]

143. This communication is submitted for the first time to the Committee by Mr Bogdan Antić, the alleged victim.

144. Mr Bogdan Antić describes himself as a doctor. He alleges that he has been accused of Serbian nationalism, hostile propaganda and impugning his country's prestige. He has reportedly been accused of refusing to treat Muslim patients, reading religious journals and being friendly with priests; his physical appearance, the way he dresses and his way of life are also said to be held against him. He reports that he was sentenced, on 3 November 1986, to four years' imprisonment by the Court of Tuzla, a sentence which was commuted to two years by the Supreme Court of Bosnia-Hercegovina. Following the request for amnesty that he sent to the President of the Republic, he was allegedly granted a suspended sentence. He claims to be out of work and to have been evicted from his apartment. His passport has reportedly been confiscated.

145. The representative of the government concerned stated that, since Mr Bogdan Antić was a doctor, his case did not fall within Unesco's fields of competence. He had been sentenced for infringement of the Penal Code according to the usual procedures. His four-year prison sentence had been commuted on appeal to two years. He had submitted a request for reconsideration of his sentence which had been rejected as not legally valid. Following a request that he had addressed to the President of the Republic, he had been released, in view of the time that he had already spent in detention. His problems of employment, accommodation, remuneration and passport

[1] See document 130 EX/3 PRIV., paras. 143-146; see also document 130 EX/CR/HR - Yugoslavia.

were the affair of the appropriate national authorities in accordance with the laws and regulations in force. He would not find a solution to those problems by having recourse to the Committee. However, to date he had not applied to those authorities, which had accordingly not yet rejected any application, or else had done so simply on a legal technicality. For example, Mr Bogdan Antić had applied for a passport in Belgrade, whereas he should have done so in Sarajevo, his city of residence, and he had taken no steps to find new employment.

146. Following an exchange of views, the Committee *decided*:

(i) to thank the representative of the government concerned for his presence and his co-operation;

(ii) to declare the communication inadmissible by virtue of paragraph 14 (*a*) (iii) and (v) of 104 EX/Decision 3.3 as being ill-founded and not falling within the fields of competence of Unesco.

No. 780/88

Concerning *Republic of Korea*
Case of *Lee Tae-Bok*

Communication of 5 April 1988 submitted by
Amnesty International

Spring 1988 session of the Committee on Conventions and Recommendations (129th session of the Executive Board)[1]

83. According to the author of the communication, Mr Lee Tae-Bok, a publisher, was reportedly arrested on 10 June 1981 and accused of being the leader of two underground anti-State groups. At his trial, he was allegedly accused of publishing books calling for class struggle, disseminating communist ideas and inciting students and workers to overthrow the government through demonstrations and strikes. His life sentence is said to have been commuted to 20 years' imprisonment and then reduced to 15 years.

84. Having referred to the recent radical reforms which had been introduced in the Republic of Korea with the aim of democratizing institutions and to the progress achieved in matters of freedom and the promotion of human rights, the representative of the government concerned went on to inform the Committee that an amnesty had been granted and clemency shown to many individuals, with the exception of a few extremists whose sole object was to overthrow the government and to change the political and social system by force. Mr Lee Tae-Bok was one such. He had founded two subversive organizations, the National Democratic Students' Federation and the National Democratic Workers' Federation, in whose members he had inculcated revolutionary theories. He had organized illegal meetings. He had published propaganda inciting readers to overthrow the government and to set up a different ideological system. He had in doing so violated the Penal Code, and was not a mere prisoner of conscience.

---

[1] See document 129 EX/3 PRIV., paras. 83-86; see also document 129 EX/CR/HR/3 Add.

No. 780/88 **Republic of Korea**

85. In reply to questions, the representative of the government concerned stated that Mr Lee Tae-Bok had been sentenced in the course of a properly conducted trial and had not undergone torture as was claimed by Amnesty International.

86. After an exchange of views, the Committee *decided*:

(i) to thank the representative of the government concerned for his presence and for his co-operation;

(ii) to express its concern regarding the fate of Mr Lee Tae-Bok;

(iii) to request the government concerned to provide more precise information, in particular as to whether Mr Lee Tae-Bok had been guilty of acts of violence or of incitement to armed violence, and whether the publication of the works mentioned in the communication constituted a criminal offence;

(iv) to ask the government concerned for information on the precise grounds on and reasons for which Mr Lee Tae-Bok had been given so heavy a sentence;

(v) to address to the government concerned an appeal for clemency, in view of the lengthy period that Mr Lee Tae-Bok had already spent in detention;

(vi) to resume consideration of this communication at its autumn 1988 session.

Autumn 1988 session of the Committee on Conventions and Recommendations (130th session of the Executive Board)[2]

97. This communication was examined for the first time by the Committee at the [spring 1988 session]. It is at the stage of examination of its admissibility.

98. Mr Lee Tae-Bok, a publisher, was alleged to have been arrested on 10 June 1981, and accused of being the leader of two underground anti-State groups. The accusation was apparently based on the fact that he had published books calling for class struggle, disseminating communist ideas and inciting students and workers to overthrow the government through demonstrations and strikes. His life sentence is

[2] See document 130 EX/3 PRIV., paras. 97-102; see also document 130 EX/CR/HR - Republic of Korea.

said to have been commuted to 20 years' imprisonment and then reduced to 15 years.

99. At the [spring 1988] session, the representative of the government concerned informed the Committee that Mr Lee Tae-Bok had founded two subversive organizations, the National Democratic Students' Federation and the National Democratic Workers' Federation, in whose members he had inculcated revolutionary theories, and that he had organized illegal meetings and published propaganda inciting readers to overthrow the government and to set up a different ideological system.

100. On 5 September 1988, the Secretariat received a letter from Amnesty International stating that no proof had been found that Mr Lee Tae-Bok had been guilty of advocating violence or that he had sought to change the political and social system of the country by force.

101. The government concerned had not sent a representative, but the Permanent Delegation of the Republic of Korea to Unesco informed the Committee by letter that Mr Lee Tae-Bok, benefiting from an amnesty granted by the President of the Republic on the occasion of the national festival, had been released on 3 October 1988.

102. After discussion, the Committe *decided*:

(i) to note with satisfaction the release of Mr Lee Tae-Bok;

(ii) to strike the communication from its list, considering it to be settled in accordance with paragraph 14 (*a*) (x) of 104 EX/Decision 3.3.

No. 781/88

Concerning *Malawi*
Case of *Jack Mapanje*

Communication of 5 April 1988 submitted by
Amnesty International

Spring 1988 session of the Committee on Conventions and Recommendations (129th session of the Executive Board)[1]

69. According to the author of the communication, Mr Jack Mapanje, a poet and head of the Department of Languages and Literature at the University of Malawi, was arrested on 25 September 1987 and taken to his office where copies of his book *Of Chameleons and Gods*, published in London in 1981, were seized. He was reportedly then detained without charge or trial under the Public Security Regulations

70. The government concerned had not sent a representative.

71. After an exchange of views, the Committee *decided*:

(i) to express its regret at the absence of a representative of the government concerned;

(ii) to request the government concerned to comment on the allegations contained in the communication, particularly regarding Mr Jack Mapanje's arrest, the reasons for his arrest and the legal basis for his detention;

(iii) likewise, to request the government concerned to have Mr Jack Mapanje's situation re-examined by the competent authorities in the event of his being held without trial;

(iv) to resume examination of this communication at [its autumn 1988 session].

---

[1] See document 129 EX/3 PRIV., paras. 69-71; see also document 129 EX/CR/HR/3 Add.

No. 781/88 **Malawi**

Autumn 1988 session of the Committee on Conventions and Recommendations (130th session of the Executive Board)[2]

71. This communication has been on the agenda of the Committee since the [spring 1988 session]. It is at the stage of examination of its admissibility.

72. Mr Jack Mapanje, described by the author of the communication as a poet and head of the Department of Language and Literature at the University of Malawi, is said to have been arrested on 25 September 1987. Copies of his book *Of Chameleons and Gods*, published in London in 1981, are reported to have been seized as the book had just been banned by a censorship committee. Yet he is stated not to have been politically active even though his poems had adopted increasingly political themes. It is said that he was not in contact with any opposition group. He is apparently detained under a detention order which the President of the Republic must review every six months.

73. On 5 September 1988, the Secretariat received a letter from Amnesty International indicating that that organization had received a communication last May from the High Commissioner of Malawi in Canada informing it that Mr Mapanje had been arrested for reasons of national security and that the matter was being investigated by the competent authorities.

74. As at the [spring 1988] session of the Committee, the government concerned was not represented but the Embassy of Malawi in France, in a note to Unesco, indicated that it would inform the Committee of its government's position as soon as it was communicated to it.

75. Several members of the Committee regretted the absence of dialogue with the government concerned. Some members expressed the wish that the Chairman of the Committee contact the representatives of Malawi in Paris. Others, stressing the humanitarian aspect of the case, requested that the Committee express its concern that Mr Jack Mapanje should receive a fair trial.

76. After an exchange of views, the Committee *decided*:

(i) to express once again its regret at being unable to benefit from the presence of a representative of the government concerned and at having received no information from it;

---

[2] See doument 130 EX/3 PRIV., paras. 71-76; see also document 130 EX/CR/HR - Malawi.

(ii) to launch a fresh appeal for clemency in favour of Mr Jack Mapanje, already held in administrative detention for over a year;

(iii) to resume examination of this communication at its [spring 1989 session].

Spring 1989 session of the Committee on Conventions and Recommendations (131st session of the Executive Board)[3]

64. This communication which has been on the agenda of the Committee since the [spring 1988 session], is still at the stage of examination as to its admissibility.

65. Mr Jack Mapanje, aged 44, a poet and head of the Department of Language and Literature at the University of Malawi, is said to have been arrested on 25 September 1987. Copies of his book *Of Chamelons and Gods*, published in London in 1981 and banned by a censorship committee, are reported to have been seized at his office. Even though he had adopted increasingly political themes in his poems, he is stated not to have been politically active or to have had links with any group opposed to the government.

66. The detention of the alleged victim was apparently ordered by the President of the Republic under the Public Security Regulations. It appears that there is no possibility of appeal to the courts. The President of the Republic is, however, reportedly required to review his decision every six months.

67. At the Committee's [autumn 1988] session, the government concerned was not represented but the Embassy of Malawi in France, in a *note verbale*, informed the Committee that it would convey to the Committee information from its country's authorities as soon as it was received.

68. The Committee expressed regret that no representative of the government concerned was present and that no information had been received from the government. It reiterated its appeal for clemency for Mr Jack Mapanje, stressing that he had already been held in administrative detention for over a year.[4]

69. At this session, the author of the communication, in a letter dated 7 March 1989, informed the Committee that it had no further information on this case but was still

---

[3] See doument 131 EX/3 PRIV., paras. 64-74; see also document 131 EX/CR/HR/Malawi.

[4] See doument 130 EX/3 PRIV., para. 76 (i) and (ii) (*supra*, pp. 818-819).

deeply concerned about the fate of the alleged victim, who was said to be still in detention.

70. One member of the Committee requested confirmation that the Chairman had, as requested at the Committee's [autumn 1988] session, made contact with the representatives of Malawi. This confirmation was given.

71. Another member of the Committee gave details about the case of Mr Jack Mapanje, taken from the latest reports by Amnesty International. He observed that Mr Mapanje was still being held in administrative detention and requested the Committee to ask the government concerned whether he would at last be brought before the courts.

72. Another member considered that the Committee should also inquire into the reasons for the arrest of Mr Jack Mapanje and those for which his book had been censored, and to ascertain whether the President of the Republic of Malawi had confirmed the administrative detention order against him.

73. The Members of the Committee agreed that they had no option but declare this communication admissible on which the government concerned, despite several requests by the Committee, had never provided any information whatsoever, showing total disregard for the Committee.

74. After an exchange of views, the Committee *decided*:

(i) to express once again its regret that a representative of the government concerned had not been present and that it had received no information whatsoever;

(ii) to declare the communication admissible;

(iii) to urge the government concerned to provide it with further information, particularly on the reasons why Mr Jack Mapanje had been arrested and why he had been kept in administrative detention since September 1987 without the President of the Republic terminating that detention or Mr Mapanje being brought before the courts, and on the reasons why his book had been seized;

(iv) to request the release of Mr Jack Mapanje for humanitarian reasons, which are the major concern of the Committee;

(v) to resume examination of this communication [at its autumn 1989 session].

Malawi **No. 781/88**

Autumn 1989 session of the Committee on Conventions and Recommendations (132nd session of the Executive Board)[5]

171. This communication is at the stage of examination as to its substance, having been declared admissible at the [spring 1989] session.[6] It has been on the agenda of the Committee since the [spring 1988 session].

172. Mr Jack Mapanje, a poet, working as head of the Department of Language and Literature of the University of Malawi, was allegedly arrested on 25 September 1987 and since then has been held in administrative detention for reasons of national security, on the orders of the Head of State. His arrest allegedly coincided with the banning of his book *Of Chameleons and Gods*, published in London 1981, a ban ordered by the national censorship committee. However, he is stated not to be politically active.

173. At the [spring 1989] session, the Committee urged the Government of Malawi to provide it with further information, particularly on the reasons why Mr Jack Mapanje had been arrested and why he had been kept in administrative detention for so long a period without the President of the Republic terminating that detention, or Mr Mapanje being brought before the courts, and on the reasons why his book had been seized. The Committee also requested the release of the alleged victim for humanitarian reasons.[7]

174. The government concerned had not been represented at three successive sessions.

175. By letter dated 14 August 1989, the author of the communication stated that he had no further information on this case, but that Mr Jack Mapanje was still in detention.

176. At the present session, the government concerned was still not represented, and communicated no further information.

177. Following an exchange of views, the Committee *decided*:

(i) deeply to deplore the persistent failure of the government concerned to be represented or to communicate any information, despite the fact that it was represented on the Executive Board;

---

[5] See doument 132 EX/3 PRIV., paras. 171-177; see also document 132 EX/CR/HR/MLW.

[6] See doument 131 EX/3 PRIV., para. 74 (ii) (*supra*, p. 820).

[7] *Ibidem*, para. 74 (iii) and (iv) (*supra*, p. 820).

(ii) to reiterate in the most urgent terms to the government concerned its request for information on this case;

(iii) to request its Chairman to contact the delegation of Malawi on this matter at the next session of the General Conference;

(iv) to resume consideration of this communication at its [spring 1990 session].

Spring 1990 session of the Committee on Conventions and Recommendations (134th session of the Executive Board)[8]

200. This communication is at the stage of examination as to its substance. It has been on the agenda of the Committee since the [spring 1988 session].

201. Mr Jack Mapanje, aged 45, a poet and head of the Department of Language and Literature of the University of Malawi, was allegedly arrested on 25 September 1987 and held in administrative detention for reasons of national security on the orders of the Head of State. His arrest reportedly coincided with the banning of his book *Of Chameleons and Gods*, published in London in 1981. Copies of this book are reported to have been seized at his office. Mr Jack Mapanje is stated not to be politically active or to have links with any group opposed to the government.

202. At its [autumn 1989] session, the Committee reiterated its request for information to the government concerned,[9] which had never been represented during the examination of this communication.

203. In a letter dated 17 April 1990, Amnesty International informed the Committee that Mr Jack Mapanje had now been authorized to receive visits from his wife and children.

204. At the present session, the member of the Executive Board representing the government concerned explained that during the previous sessions he had not been in Paris and had been unable to attend the Committee's meetings for this reason. He stated that he had requested information from his country's authorities through the Malawian Embassy in France, but had as yet received no reply.

---

[8] See doument 134 EX/3 PRIV., paras. 200-207; see also document 134 EX/CR/HR/MLW.

[9] See doument 132 EX/3 PRIV., para. 177 (ii) (*supra*, p. 822).

Malawi **No. 781/88**

205. The members of the Committee raised a number of questions concerning the exact grounds for the arrest and imprisonment of Mr Mapanje. They wondered whether he had advocated violence for political ends in his book *Of Chameleons and Gods*, or whether he had simply exercised his right to freedom of expression in a peaceful manner. They pointed out that under the terms of both the Universal Declaration of Human Rights and the African Charter on Human and Peoples' Rights any person arrested was entitled to receive a fair hearing within a reasonable period of time by an impartial court or tribunal, and that this had not happened in the case Mr Mapanje, who had been held in administrative detention "for reasons of national security" for three years already. This situation was incompatible with recognized international standards. Be that as it might, the Committee's sole concern was to achieve the settlement of a specific human case within the context of the promotion of human rights, following a strictly confidential procedure. Representations by the member of the Executive Board to the Government of Malawi would be greatly appreciated.

206. The latter undertook to transmit the Committee's wishes to his government.

207. Following an exchange of views, the Committee *decided*:

(i) to thank the representative of the government concerned for his attendance and co-operation;

(ii) urgently to request that government to provide it with all relevant information, in particular concerning the precise grounds for Mr Jack Mapanje's arrest and the question of whether the book *Of Chameleons and Gods* contained any incitement to violence or addressed questions relating to national security;

(iii) to recall that the Committee in no way set itself up as an international court of law but that its aim was to promote human rights relating to Unesco's fields of competence by seeking a friendly solution to specific human cases;

(iv) to resume consideration of this communication at its [autumn 1990] session].

No. 781/88 **Malawi**

Autumn 1990 session of the Committee on Conventions and Recommendations (135th session of the Executive Board)[10]

149. This communication is at the stage of examination of substance. It has been on the agenda of the Committee since the [spring 1988 session].

150. The author of the communication alleges the following. Mr Jack Mapanje, aged 45, a poet and head of the Department of Language and Literature of the University of Malawi, was arrested on 25 September 1987 and held in administrative detention for reasons of national security on the orders of the Head of State. His arrest coincided with the banning of his book *Of Chameleons and Gods*, published in London in 1981. Copies of this book were seized. Mr Jack Mapanje is not politically active and has no links with any group opposed to the government.

151. At its [spring 1990] session, the Committee reiterated its request for information to the government concerned,[11] which had never been represented during the examination of this communication.

152. In a letter dated 17 April 1990, Amnesty International informed the Committee that Mr Jack Mapanje had now been authorized to receive visits from his wife and children.

153. At the [spring 1990] session, the member of the Executive Board representing the government concerned explained that during the previous sessions he had not been in Paris and had been unable to attend the Committee's meetings for that reason. He stated that he had requested information from his country's authorities through the Malawian Embassy in France, but had as yet received no reply.

154. The members of the Committee raised a number of questions concerning the exact grounds for the arrest and imprisonment of Mr Mapanje. They wondered whether he had advocated violence for political ends in his book *Of Chameleons and Gods*, or whether he had simply exercised his right to freedom of expression in a peaceful manner. They pointed out that under the terms of both the Universal Declaration of Human Rights and the African Charter on Human and Peoples' Rights any person arrested was entitled to receive a fair hearing within a reasonable period of time by an impartial court or tribunal, and that this had not happened in the case of Mr Mapanje, who had been held in administrative detention "for reasons of national security" for three years already. The Committee said that its sole concern was to a-

[10] See doument 135 EX/3 PRIV., paras. 149-156; see also document 135 EX/CR/HR/MLW.
[11] See doument 134 EX/3 PRIV., para. 207 (ii) (*supra*, p. 823).

chieve the settlement of a specific human case within the context of the promotion of human rights, following a strictly confidential procedure. Representations to the Government of Malawi by the member of the Executive Board would therefore be greatly appreciated. The latter undertook to transmit the Committee's wishes to his government.

155. At the present session, the representative of the government concerned said that he had not received the additional information concerning this communication that he had requested from his country's authorities. He promised to convey it to the Committee as soon as he obtained it.

156. After an exchange of views, the Committee *decided*:

(i) to thank the representative of the government concerned for his attendance and co-operation;

(ii) to express regret that the government concerned had not yet provided the information requested;

(iii) again to request that government to provide all relevant information, particularly concerning the exact grounds for the arrest of Mr Jack Mapanje and in regard to whether the book *Of Chameleons and Gods* contained an incitement to violence and dealt with matters relating to national security;

(iv) to point out to the government concerned that the Committee was not in any way trying to set itself up as an international supreme court but was merely attempting, for purely humanitarian reasons, to establish a dialogue with the governments concerned in order to consider with them what might be done on behalf of alleged victims in the event of their having suffered violations of human rights in Unesco's fields of competence;

(v) to appeal to the President of the Republic of Malawi for clemency for Mr Jack Mapanje;

(vi) to resume consideration of this communication at its [spring 1991 session].

No. 781/88 **Malawi**

Spring 1991 session of the Committee on Conventions and Recommendations (136th session of the Executive Board)[12]

188. This communication is at the stage of examination of substance. It has been on the agenda of the Committee since the [spring 1988 session].

189. The author of the communication alleges the following. Mr Jack Mapanje, aged 45, a poet and head of the Department of Language and Literature of the University of Malawi, was arrested on 25 September 1987 and held in administrative detention for reasons of national security on the orders of the Head of State. His arrest coincided with the banning of his book *Of Chameleons and Gods*, published in London in 1981. Copies of this book were seized. Mr Jack Mapanje is not politically active and has no links with any group opposed to the government.

190. At its last sessions, the Committee reiterated its request for information to the government concerned, which had never been represented during the examination of this communication, except at the [spring 1990] session, when the member of the Executive Board representing the government concerned explained that he had not received the information he had requested from his country's authorities. The members of the Committee raised a number of questions concerning the exact grounds for the arrest and imprisonment of Mr Mapanje. They wondered whether he had advocated violence for political ends in his book *Of Chameleons and Gods*, or whether he had simply exercised his right to freedom of expression in a peaceful manner. They pointed out that under the terms of both the Universal Declaration of Human Rights and the African Charter on Human and Peoples' Rights any person arrested was entitled to receive a fair hearing within a reasonable period of time by an impartial court or tribunal, and that this had not happened in the case of Mr Mapanje, who had been held in administrative detention "for reasons of national security" for three years already. The Committee said that its sole concern was to achieve the settlement of a specific human case within the context of the promotion of human rights, following a strictly confidential procedure. Representations to the Government of Malawi by the member of the Executive Board would therefore be greatly appreciated. The latter undertook to transmit the Committee's wishes to his government.

191. At the [autumn 1990] session, the representative of the government concerned said that he had not received the additional information concerning this communication that he had requested from his country's authorities. He promised to convey it to the Committee as soon as he obtained it.

[12] See doument 136 EX/3 PRIV., paras. 188-195; see also documents 136 EX/CR/HR/MLW and Add. and Add.2.

Malawi **No. 781/88**

192. At its present session, the Committee took note of a letter dated 9 April 1991, in which the author of the communication informed it that it had no additional information concerning this case but remained deeply concerned about the fact that Mr Jack Mapanje was still in detention. Amnesty International noted with great interest, however, that the authorities of Malawi had recently released 98 detainees including political prisoners, a development which the author hoped the Committee might be able to take into account when it resumed its examination of this case with a view to securing the rapid release of Mr Jack Mapanje.

193. In a letter dated 3 May 1991, the Permanent Delegate of Malawi to UNESCO informed the Committee that Mr Jack Mapanje was being held for reasons that were strictly to do with national security and that there was therefore no connection between his detention and the publication of his book. In accordance with the law on the maintenance of public security, the Minister was required to re-examine detention orders every six months. The case of Mr Jack Mapanje was therefore regularly re-examined.

194. Finally, in a letter dated 13 May 1991, the representative of Malawi to UNESCO informed the Committee that Mr Jack Mapanje had been released.

195. After an exchange of views, the Committee *decided*:

(i) to take note with satisfaction of the release of Mr Jack Mapanje;

(ii) to strike this communication from its list, considering it settled in accordance with paragraph 14 (*a*) (x) of 104 EX/Decision 3.3.

No. 784/88

Concerning *Turkey*
Case of *Günay Avcı* et al.*

Communication of 29 June 1988 submitted by
Suphi Tuncer

Autumn 1988 session of the Committee on Conventions and Recommendations (130th session of the Executive Board)[1]

121. Mr Suphi Tuncer, the author of the communication, is said to have organized a debate in the context of the International Year of Peace in October 1986. The six alleged victims, all teachers, are reported to have been subjected to administrative harassment for having attended the debate and to have been transferred to other posts at a distance from their families.

122. This communication is before the Committee for the first time.

123. On 15 September 1988, the Secretariat received a letter from the Permanent Delegation of Turkey to Unesco stating that in view of the relatively short period between receipt of the communication and the Committee's session, his country's authorities found it necessary to request that consideration of the communication be postponed to a later session so that they could compile the information required by the Committee.

124. Following an exchange of views, the Committee *decided* to accede to this request and to resume consideration of this communication at its [spring 1989 session].

---

* Case of *Günay Avcı, Mithat Ünüvar, Hüseyin Kolkesen, Hüseyin Sungur, Hüseyin Sönmez and Hüsrev Erginöz.*

[1] See document 130 EX/3 PRIV., paras. 121-124; see also document 130 EX/CR/HR - Turkey 2.

No. 784/88 **Turkey**

Spring 1989 session of the Committee on Conventions and Recommendations (131st session of the Executive Board)[2]

138. This communication is still at the stage of being considered as to its admissibility. It has been on the Committee's agenda since the [autumn 1988 session].

139. Mr Tuncer is said to have organized a debate in October 1986 in the context of the International Year of Peace. The six alleged victims, all teachers, are reported to have been transferred to other posts at a distance from their families on account of their having attended the debate. Various representations are said to have been made to the mayor of Mügla and to the President of the Republic on behalf of these teachers, but to no avail.

140. Mr Tuncer requests that the teachers who have thus been penalized should be reinstated in their former posts, that it should be acknowledged that the holding of or attendance at a debate does not constitute a criminal offence and that human rights be respected.

141. At the [autumn 1988] session, the Committee acceded to the request made by the government concerned that consideration of the communication should be postponed to the present session in view of the fact that it had been received at a late date by the Turkish authorities.[3]

142. In a letter dated 31 January 1989, the author of the communication stated that the six teachers had been wrongly accused of participating in a political meeting.

143. At the present session, the Permanent Delegate of Turkey to Unesco gave the Committee the following information. Five of the six teachers had appealed to the administrative tribunals against the decision to transfer them. Four had had the decision quashed, the fifth had resigned before the end of the procedure. The sixth teacher had not appealed against the decision, preferring to take early retirement. In the opinion of the representative of the government concerned, the communication should therefore be declared inadmissible in accordance with paragraph 14 (*a*) (x) of 104 EX/Decision 3.3. The author of the communication had submitted it or maintained it at a time when the cases had already been settled, thus clearly taking improper advantage of Unesco's goodwill.

---

[2] See document 131 EX/3 PRIV., paras. 138-144; see also document 131 EX/CR/HR/TUR.

[3] See document 130 EX/3 PRIV., para. 124 (*supra*, p. 829).

Turkey **No. 784/88**

144. After an exchange of views, the Committee *decided*:

(i) to thank the representative of the government concerned for attending the meeting and for his co-operation;

(ii) to express satisfaction at the information received;

(iii) to strike the communication from its list, considering it to be settled in accordance with paragraph 14 (*a*) (x) of 104 EX/Decision 3.3.

No. 787/88

Concerning *Czechoslovakia*
Case of *Evžen Freimann*

Communication of 8 August 1988 submitted by
Evžen Freimann

Spring 1989 session of the Committee on Conventions and Recommendations (131st session of the Executive Board)[1]

111. Mr Evžen Freimann describes himself as a technician. He claims that for four years he applied for admission to a faculty of theology in his country, but that his applications were rejected by the authorities concerned. He was also allegedly unable to obtain a passport to go to Rome, where he claims to have been accepted by the Pontifico Collegio Nepomuceno. He nevertheless apparently succeeded in leaving Czechoslovakia secretly, on 20 September 1988. He claims that under Czechoslovak law he is liable to be sentenced to up to five years' imprisonment.

113. Mr Evžen Freimann states himself to be currently engaged in theological studies in Italy. He asks the Czechoslovak Government to acknowledge his right to study theology, to take note of his new place of residence and to issue him with a document permitting him to emigrate lawfully.

114. The representative of the government concerned informed the Committee that Mr Evžen Freimann, after completing his primary and secondary education with the equivalent of a technical secondary school diploma, had worked as an electrician in a coal mine. He had left this job after eight months, considering that the best use had not been made of his qualifications. His performance had not, however, been highly rated. He had subsequently been taken on as a technician in a small factory producing prams and trolleys. For eight years, he had been registered medically as a drug addict. He had become mentally unstable. He had, for that reason, been exempted from military service. In 1988, he had left the country without authorization.

[1] See document 131 EX/3 PRIV., paras. 111-119; see also document 131 EX/CR/HR/CZE.

No. 787/88 **Czechoslovakia**

115. The representative of the government concerned then stated that in Czechoslovakia, priests were trained in sufficient numbers by faculties of theology. The number of students was increasing regularly, and was in no way limited. Their selection was carried out, as in the other faculties, by a Faculty Board composed of lecturers in theology. Only one State observer attended the meetings. If the Board of the faculty to which Mr Evžen Freimann sought admission had not approved his application, this was doubtless because of his background and because the lecturers had perhaps felt that he lacked a vocation. In any case, the selection had been made in accordance with the regulations in force and current practice.

116. In reply to questions put to him, the representative of the government concerned stated that Mr Evžen Freimann's drug addiction was not irreversible. The issue of a passport was linked to measures of an economic nature restricting the allocation of foreign exchange. These measures were at present being relaxed. An exit visa could now be granted to an applicant on production of an invitation and an undertaking by the person issuing the invitation to defray the applicant's expenses. Although Mr Evžen Freimann had expressed his fear of being sentenced for leaving the country clandestinely, the representative of the government concerned assured the Committee that this offence had been the subject of an amnesty.

117. Several members of the Committee expressed their satisfaction at the exemplary spirit of co-operation shown by the representative of the government concerned, who had provided a wealth of information on the number of churches, their functioning, their maintenance and relations between Church and State, the State playing only a relatively limited role in religious matters.

118. Some members of the Committee voiced doubts about Mr Evžen Freimann's assertion that Cardinal Tomášek had given him his support, and that the Pontifico Collegio Nepomuceno in Rome had accepted a drug addict as a theology student.

119. Following an exchange of views, the Committee *decided*:

(i) to thank the representative of the government concerned for his attendance and his exemplary co-operation;

(ii) to declare the communication inadmissible as being manifestly ill-founded by virtue of paragraph 14 (*a*) (v) of 104 EX/Decision 3.3.

No. 788/88

Concerning *Cuba*
Case of *Natividad González Freire* et al.*

Communication of 17 February 1988 submitted by
César Eugenio Leante Magaloni

Spring 1988 session of the Committee on Conventions and Recommendations (129th session of the Executive Board)[1]

43. The author of the communication describes himself as a Cuban writer in disagreement with his country's regime. He states that he was granted political asylum in Spain in 1981 and was naturalized Spanish several years later. The members of his family are reported to have applied for permission to join him there, but to no avail. With regard to the purpose and aim of the communication, he requests that the violation of rights allegedly committed against the members of his family should cease, especially their right to depart freely from Cuba.

44. In addressing the Committee, the representative of the Cuban Government stated that he wished to request a postponement of the examination of this communication until the Committee's next session because his government had received the documentation only recently. He added that his country never put obstacles in the way of those citizens who wished to leave the country under normal circumstances and that discussions were now under way between the authorities of his country and those of other countries in order to facilitate the reunification of families; although this communication dealt with a case that had special features a deferment would enable his government to carry out a more detailed study of the case and prepare it better for presentation to the Committee.

---

* Case of *Natividad González Freire, César Eugenio Leante González, Laura Leante González, Luis Ricardo Cedeño Felipe and Alejandro Cedeño Leante*. At the autumn 1988 session, this communication was being referred to as case of *César Eugenio Leante Magaloni, Natividad González Freire, César Eugenio Leante González, Laura Leante González, Luis Ricardo Cedeño Felipe and Alejandro Cedeño Leante.*

[1] See document 129 EX/3 PRIV., paras. 43-45; see also document 129 EX/CR/HR/3 Add.

No. 788/88 **Cuba**

45. After a brief discussion, the Committee *decided*:

(i) to thank the representative of the government concerned for his presence and co-operation;

(ii) to postpone examination of this communication until the next session, in view of the fact that the documents concerning this case had been received late by the government concerned.

Autumn 1988 session of the Committee on Conventions and Recommendations (130th session of the Executive Board)[2]

36. This communication has been on the Committee's agenda for consideration of its admissibility since the [spring 1988 session].

37. Mr Leante Magaloni describes himself as a Cuban writer in disagreement with his countrys' regime. He states that he was granted political asylum in Spain in 1981 and became naturalized some years later. He requests that the members of his family be authorized to join him.

38. The case is also said to have been referred to the Inter-American Commission of Human Rights and the European Commission of Human Rights.

39. At its [spring 1988] session the Committee decided, at the request of the representative of the government concerned, to postpone examination of this communication until this session, in view of the fact that the documents concerning this case had been received late by that government.[3]

40. On 2 August 1988 the Secretariat received a letter from the author of the communication enclosing an open letter from his wife alerting international public opinion to the violation of human rights of which she claims to be a victim, along with extracts from a letter from his daughter describing the precarious and distressing character of her situation. He also submitted for inclusion in the file a copy of two letters from the immigration office of the Ministry of the Interior dated 7 January 1982 and 14 May 1988, refusing permission to emigrate to Mr Cedeño Felipe (son-in-law of the author of the communication), his wife and their son.

[2] See document 130 EX/3 PRIV., paras. 36-42; see also document 130 EX/CR/HR - Cuba.
[3] See document 129 EX/3 PRIV., para. 45 (ii) (*supra*, p. 836).

Cuba **No. 788/88**

41. At the present session the representative of the government concerned informed the Committee that Mr Leante's wife and children had left Cuba or were in the process of doing so. The case was therefore settled. The representative of the government nevertheless made some observations to the Committee, explaining that in reality those concerned were not apolitical or religious but former purportedly revolutionary militants and were rather extremist and dogmatic persons who, for some reason or other, had undergone a change of heart; furthermore, the assertion that it was not possible to give a religious education to children involved in such a situation was unfounded, since in Cuba there was complete religious freedom.

42. After an exchange of views, the Committee *decided*:

(i) to thank the representative of the government concerned for his attendance and co-operation;

(ii) to note with satisfaction the happy outcome ot this case;

(iii) to strike the communication from its list as being settled in accordance with paragraph 14 (*a*) (x) of 104 EX/Decision 3.3.

No. 789/88

Concerning *Morocco*
Case of *Mohamed Jaaidi*

Communication of 10 June 1988 submitted by
Denyse Piuz-Lavallé*

Spring 1989 session of the Committee on Conventions and Recommendations (131st session of the Executive Board)[1]

75. According to the author of the communication, Mr Mohamed Jaaidi, a psychiatrist, was arrested by the police on 7 November 1985, having been denounced by a prisoner in a statement obtained under torture. He was arrested mainly because of his desire to incorporate the latest medical research into practice without regard to any political considerations. He is said to have put forward a health plan for Morocco and to have refused to establish a prison unit for political prisoners in the "Mallorca" psychiatric hospital at Tétouan, of which he was director. He was also apparently accused of having distributed tracts, although there was no corroborative evidence to support that accusation. Before his transfer to the prison of Casablanca, he is said to have undergone torture. It appears that he was tried along with 25 other people and sentenced to 12 years' imprisonment for plotting against the State.

76. The author of the communication has included in the file a copy of the report of an observer mission by four barristers from the Hauts-de-Seine (France) during Mr Jaaidi's trial in February 1986. The report denounces irregularities in the application of the law as regards both procedure and substance. For example, Mr Jaaidi was apparently held in custody in a clandestine centre and the period of custody was extended illegally. The prisoners were said to have been tortured in order to obtain their confessions and to have been accused of having been part of the clandestine "ILAL AMAM" Organization, whose ultimate aim is to overthrow the monarchy and establish a people's socialist republic. Plotting against the State is apparently a sentence which enables the authorities to issue an indictment on the basis of mere intention, in the absence of any specific act. At the trial no witnesses were heard, the

* On behalf of the International Committee for the Defence of Dr Mohamed Jaaidi.
[1] See document 131 EX/3 PRIV., paras. 75-85; see also document 131 EX/CR/HR/MOR.

official seals enclosing the confiscated documents were not broken, the examinations were mere formal exercises and the composition of the court, the representation of the Public Ministry and the summons were described as irregular. The four French barristers considered that Mr Jaaidi had been sentenced without corroborative evidence.

77. Mr Jaaidi's appeal is said to have been rejected and his sentence confirmed on 4 November 1986 by the same court which had tried him in February 1986.

78. By way of a preliminary statement, the representative of the government concerned informed the Committee that, on the occasion of each religious feast, the King pardoned a large number of prisoners. Thus, to mark the end of Ramadan, the King had decided to grant an amnesty to 228 prisoners and it was possible that Mr Jaaidi might be among those so pardoned.

79. Explaining the reason why Mr Jaaidi had been sentenced to 12 years' imprisonment, the representative of the government concerned stated that Mr Jaaidi had been found guilty of incitement to disturb the public order and incitement to public violence, acts which had no relation to Unesco's fields of competence or to human rights. Moreover, since the individual concerned was a doctor, his case came rather within the field of competence of WHO. In any event, the court involved had arrived at its verdict quite independently and had shown scrupulous respect for procedure and the rights of the defendant.

80. In view of the above considerations, the representative of the government concerned considered that the case should be declared inadmissible. He noted that the author of the communication knew that to be since the communication attempted to present Mr Mohamed Jaaidi as a scientist rather than a doctor.

81. In response to questions, the representative of the government concerned said that Mr Jaaidi's appeal had been considered by the Supreme Court, which had confirmed the sentence. He added that, even if the prisoner was granted an amnesty, he had nevertheless committed very serious acts jeopardizing internal State security. He rejected the allegation that the doctor had been tortured. He explained that in Morocco medical provision existed in the form of both private and public medicine. Public medicine, which came under the Ministry of Health, was a truly "popular" medicine, providing free general health care and hospital treatment alike.

82. Some members of the Committee considered the communication to be inadmissible, as Mr Jaaidi was a practising doctor who had been sentenced not for scientific activities but for acts which did not come within Unesco's fields of competence.

83. In the view of other members of the Committee, the communication properly came within the Organization's field of competence inasmuch as it emerged from the alleged facts that the case at issue was one of scientific conscience, Mr Jaaidi having refused to establish a prison unit for political prisoners in the hospital where he worked. They also considered that the doctor had manifestly engaged in scientific activities by providing for the psychiatric and psychological protection of prisoners, and by seeking to put into practice the latest medical research.

84. Several members of the Committee considered that, whatever the case, the information currently at their disposal was insufficient for them to come to a decision on the admissibility of the communication.

85. When this report was being approved the Committee was informed that Mr Mohamed Jaaidi had not been among the beneficiaries of the King's amnesty at the end of Ramadan. After an exchange of views the Committee *decided*:

(i) to thank the representative of the government concerned for his attendance and co-operation;

(ii) to request the government concerned to provide it with more detailed information on the factual and legal bases for Mr Mohamed Jaaidi's conviction;

(iii) to make a humanitarian appeal on behalf of Mr Mohamed Jaaidi;

(iv) to resume examination of this communication at its [autumn 1989 session].

Autumn 1989 session of the Committee on Conventions and Recommendations (132nd session of the Executive Board)[2]

70. The first communication[3] has been on the Committee's agenda since the [spring 1989] session. The second communication is new. The facts alleged are the same.

71. According to the authors of these two communications, Mr Mohamed Jaaidi, a psychiatrist, was arrested by the police on 7 November 1985, having been denounced by a prisoner in a statement obtained under torture. He had been arrested mainly because of a stand he had taken on a matter of public health policy. He had

[2] See document 132 EX/3 PRIV., paras. 70-80; see also document 132 EX/CR/HR/MOR.

[3] Communications No. 789/88 concerning *Morocco*, case of *Mohamed Jaaidi*, and No. 799/89 concerning *Morocco*, case of *Mohamed Jaaidi*, were being considered together.

proposed a public health scheme for Morocco and had refused to establish a prison unit for political prisoners in the "Mallorca" psychiatric hospital in Tétouan, of which he was director. The authorities had also reportedly accused this psychiatrist of distributing pamphlets, although this accusation was not supported by any evidence. He was allegedly tortured before his transfer to the prison in Casablanca. He was tried with several others and was sentenced to 12 years' imprisonment for plotting against the State.

72. According to the report of an observer mission carried out by four members of the Bar of the Hauts-de-Seine (France), Mr Jaaidi's trial was vitiated by serious procedural and material irregularities.

73. Several letters of support written by various persons, particularly Spanish doctors, attesting to the humane and scientific qualities of Mr Jaaidi, were included in the file.

74. At the [spring 1989] session, the representative of the government concerned informed the Committee that Mr Mohamed Jaaidi had been found guilty by the courts of incitement to disturbances of the peace and to violence in public places, actions which bore no relationship to the fields of competence of Unesco or human rights. He said that proper procedure and the rights of the defence had been scrupulously observed during the psychiatrist's trial. He maintained that it was undoubtedly because Mrs Piuz-Lavallée knew that the communication was not admissible because of the alleged victim's profession that she had attempted to present him as a scientist and not just as a doctor.

75. By letter dated 14 August 1989, Mrs Piuz-Lavallée submitted further details, the most important of which are as follows:

(i) contrary to the information provided by the government, Mr Jaaidi had been sentenced for plotting against the State, an offence defined in and punishable in accordance with Articles 174 and 175 of the Penal Code;

(ii) Mr Jaaidi was not just a doctor. He had been recognized as a great scientist by a large number of medical and scientific authorities of international repute;

(iii) since taking up his duties, Mr Jaaidi had transformed the Mallorca hospital, which was a run-down establishment over-populated with inmates, many of whom had been summarily confined without medical advice, into a therapeutic institution where the most recent psychiatric techniques were applied;

(iv) as a scientist, he made no distinction between practice and research. He had also endeavoured to adapt to Arab culture models developed in Europe. He had published various articles on psychiatry, family planning and psychotherapy. He had given training courses and organized seminars. He had also been concerned with trainees and students;

(v) he was guilty only of having tried to apply the scientific ideas and therapeutic methods developed in his lectures and writings.

76. The government concerned was not represented at the present session.

77. In the opinion of some members of the Committee, Mr Jaaidi's activities, corroborated by many accounts from psychiatrists of international repute, indicated that this doctor was also a great scientist, a researcher, and a person who, in addition, took an interest in culture and the cultural policy of his country. He had made a choice which differed from that of the government and his intentions in so doing had been impugned for political reasons. His case consequently did indeed fall within Unesco's competence.

78. One Committee member noted that, according to the allegations in the communication, the charges against Mr Jaaidi were related to the suspicion of the authorities that this doctor belonged to a clandestine organization known as "ILAL AMAM" (whose aim was reportedly to overthrow the monarchy and to replace it with a people's socialist republic). In addition, as the framing of the public health policy came under the authority of the government, there was good reason for questioning Unesco's competence. The absence of a representative of the government concerned at the present session was not a refusal to co-operate but a matter of principle as the Moroccan authorities maintained that the matter fell exclusively within the domestic jurisdiction of the country.

79. Another Committee member maintained that the call by the authors of the two communications for the "unconditional release" of the alleged victim was completely out of place, as one could in no way tell a government what to do.

80. After an exchange of views, the Committee *decided*:

(i) to express its regrets that no representative of the government concerned had been present;

(ii) on the basis of the facts at its disposal, to assert its competence to examine these communications;

(iii) to renew its request to the government concerned to provide more specific information on the factual and legal evidence on which Mr Mohamed Jaaidi's conviction was based;

(iv) to renew its humanitarian appeal on behalf of Mr Mohamed Jaaidi, in view of the long period he had already served in detention;

(v) to examine these two communications once again at its [spring 1990 session].

Spring 1990 session of the Committee on Conventions and Recommendations (134st session of the Executive Board)[4]

92. These two communications[5] are at the stage of examination as to their admissibility. They have been on the Committee's agenda since the [spring and autumn 1989 sessions] respectively. As they make the same allegations the Committee examined them together.

93. Mr Mohamed Jaaidi, a psychiatrist aged 45, was reportedly arrested by the police on 7 November 1985, having been denounced by a prisoner in a statement obtained under torture. The psychiatrist is said to have attempted to put the latest medical research into practice in his work, without regard to any political considerations. He apparently put forward a health plan for Morocco and refused to establish a prison unit for political prisoners in the "Mallorca" hospital at Tétouan. The authorities allegedly accused him without evidence of having distributed tracts. According to the authors of the communications,. Mr Jaaidi was tortured before being transferred to the prison at Casablanca. It appears that he was tried with some other people and sentenced to 12 years' imprisonment for plotting against the State.

94. According to four French lawyers who went to Morocco on an observer mission, serious irregularities occurred during Mr Jaaidi's trial.

95. Ms Piuz-Lavallée and the International Human Rights Law Group stressed the fact that Mr Jaaidi is an eminent scientist. Ms Piuz-Lavallée stated her views on this subject in a long letter dated 14 August 1989, which was brought to the notice of the Committee at its [autumn 1989] session.

---

[4] See document 134 EX/3 PRIV., paras. 92-101; see also document 134 EX/CR/HR/MOR.

[5] Communications No. 789/88 concerning *Morocco*, case of *Mohamed Jaaidi*, and No. 799/89 concerning *Morocco*, case of *Mohamed Jaaidi*, were being considered together.

Morocco **No. 789/88**

96. In a letter dated 16 February 1990, the Ambassador of the Kingdom of Morocco to France restated the position of his country's authorities as presented to the Committee by the representative of his government at the [spring 1989 session]. Mr Jaaidi had been found guilty by the courts of incitement to lawless behaviour and to violence on the public highway, reprehensible acts that were in no way connected with Unesco's fields of competence or with human rights. The Ambassador stated that the communication contained unfounded claims and allegations and should therefore be declared inadmissible. He deplored its distribution to the members of the Committee, which was a serious affront to his country.

97. On 20 and 25 April 1990, the Secretariat received letters from the International Human Rights Law Group and Ms Piuz-Lavallée: the former urged that the communication be declared admissible; the latter pointed out that the Moroccan Government had not yet provided the Committee with specific information on Mr Jaaidi's sentence; she also requested that her communication be declared admissible.

98. Some members of the Committee expressed surprise at the tone of the letter from the Ambassador of the Kingdom of Morocco. They noted that it had furnished no additional information. They stressed the need for rigorous observance of the rule of confidentiality of the procedure for considering communications if the Committee's work were to continue to be effective, as it was well-known that the author's letter had given rise to indignation among the governmental authorities.

99. One member of the Committee took the view that the situation of hospitals in Morocco could on no account be considered as falling within Unesco's competence.

100. Other members felt that, judging by the information available to the Committee, Mr Jaaidi was a scientist who had been punished for refusing to perform acts that were incompatible with medical ethics. Some of them were in favour of declaring the communication admissible; others considered that it was still too early to do so and that efforts to achieve a humanitarian solution should take precedence over any other approach.

101. Following an exchange of views, the Committee *decided*:

(i) once again to express regret that no representative of the government concerned had been present;

(ii) on the basis of the information at its disposal to assert its competence to consider the two communications;

(iii) once more to request the government concerned to provide it with more specific information on the factual and legal grounds on which Mr Mohamed Jaaidi's conviction was based and on the allegations contained in the letter dated 14 August 1989 from the author of [the first communication];

(iv) to renew its appeal to the government concerned for clemency in the case of Mr Mohamed Jaaidi, in view of the long period he had already served in detention;

(v) to resume consideration of these two communications at its [autumn 1990 session].

Autumn 1990 session of the Committee on Conventions and Recommendations (135st session of the Executive Board)[6]

57. These two communications[7] are at the stage of examination as to their admissibilitv. They have been on the Committee's agenda since the [spring and autumn 1989 sessions] respectively. As they make the same allegations, the Committee considered them together.

58. The authors of the communications allege the following. Mr Mohamed Jaaidi, a psychiatrist aged 45 was arrested by the police on 7 November 1985, having been denounced by a prisoner in a statement obtained under torture. In his work, this psychiatrist had tried to incorporate the latest medical research into practice without regard to any political considerations. He had put forward a health plan for Morocco. He had refused to establish a prison unit for political prisoners in the "Mallorca" hospital at Tétouan. The authorities had accused him without evidence of having distributed tracts. Mr Jaaidi had been tortured before being transferred to the prison of Casablanca. He had been tried at the same time as other defendants and sentenced to 12 years' imprisonment for plotting against the State. According to four French barristers who had gone on an observer mission to Morocco, serious irregularities had occurred during Mr Jaaidi's trial. Ms Piuz-Lavallée and the International Human Rights Law Group stressed the fact that Mr Jaaidi was an eminent scientist. Ms Piuz-Lavallée had stated her views on this subject in a long letter dated 14 August 1989 which had been brought to the notice of the Committee at its [autumn 1989] session.

---

[6] See document 135 EX/3 PRIV., paras. 57-65; see also document 135 EX/CR/HR/MOR.

[7] Communications No. 789/88 concerning *Morocco*, case of *Mohamed Jaaidi*, and No. 799/89 concerning *Morocco*, case of *Mohamed Jaaidi*, were being considered together.

Morocco **No. 789/88**

59. In a letter dated 16 February 1990, the Ambassador of the Kingdom of Morocco to France restated the position of his country's authorities as presented to the Committee by the representative of his government at the [spring 1989 session]. Mr Jaaidi had been found guilty by the courts of incitement to lawless behaviour and to violence on the public highway, reprehensible acts that were in no way connected with Unesco's fields of competence or with human rights. The Ambassador stated that the communication contained unfounded claims and allegations and should therefore be declared inadmissible. He deplored its distribution to the members of the Committee, which was a serious affront to his country.

60. On 20 and 25 April 1990, the Secretariat received letters from the International Human Rights Law Group and Ms Piuz-Lavallée. The former urged that the communication be declared admissible; the latter pointed out that the Moroccan Government had not yet provided the Committee with specific information on Mr Jaaidi's sentence; she also requested that her communication be declared admissible.

61. At the [spring 1990] session some members of the Committee voiced misgivings about the letter from the Ambassador of the Kingdom of Morocco. One Committee member expressed the view that the situation of hospitals in Morocco did not in any way fall within Unesco's competence.

62. Other members were of the view that, judging by the information available to the Committee, Mr Jaaidi was a scientist, punished for having refused to perform acts that were incompatible with medical ethics. Some of them were in favour of declaring the communication admissible; others considered, however, that it was still too early to do so and that efforts to achieve a humanitarian solution should take precedence over any other approach. At the end of the discussion, the Committee asserted its competence to consider the two communications having regard to the information at its disposal. It renewed its appeal to the government concerned to provide it with more specific information on the factual and legal grounds on which Mr Mohamed Jaaidi's conviction was based. It also renewed its humanitarian appeal on behalf of Mr Mohamed Jaaidi.[8]

63. In a letter dated 16 August 1990, the International Human Rights Law Group disputed the account given of the facts by the Moroccan Government. It based its position on the report of an observer mission by four French barristers who had found that serious irregularities had been committed by the judicial authorities and the police in the application of the law as regards both procedure and substance. The actual terms of the indictment revealed a violation of international human rights law, for even if Mr Jaaidi had belonged to a political organization and distributed tracts,

[8] See document 134 EX/3 PRIV., para. 101 (ii), (iii) and (iv) (*supra*, pp. 845-846).

he would have done no more than exercise the universally recognized rights to freedom of association, opinion and expression. The author of the communication therefore asked the Committee to declare the communication admissible and requested that the authorities provide further information on the nature of the offences alleged to have been committed by the doctor and on the evidence against him. It also urged that an appeal be made for the immediate and unconditional release of Dr Mohamed Jaaidi on both legal and humanitarian grounds.

64. At the present session, the members of the Committee who spoke regretted the lack of dialogue with the government concerned. They noted that the government concerned had still not provided the Committee with the information that it had requested. They said that they were in favour of the communications being declared admissible. However, one member of the Committee considered that the Committee could have waited for its next session and for the new Ambassador of Morocco to take up his duties before reaching this decision.

65. After an exchange of views, the Committee *decided*:

(i) once again to express regret that no representative of the government concerned had been present and to urge the government to co-operate with the Committee, in particular by responding to the requests for information that the Committee had made to it at its [spring 1990] session regarding the factual and legal grounds on which Mr Mohamed Jaaidi's conviction was based and on the allegations contained in the letter dated 14 August 1989 from the author of [the first communication];

(ii) to declare the two communications admissible;

(iii) to request the government concerned also to provide information on Mr Mohamed Jaaidi's health and conditions of detention;

(iv) to renew its appeal for clemency for Mr Mohamed Jaaidi;

(v) to resume consideration of the communication at its [spring 1991 session].

Morocco **No. 789/88**

Spring 1991 session of the Committee on Conventions and Recommendations (136st session of the Executive Board)[9]

196. These two communications[10] are at the stage of examination as to their substance. They have been on the Committee's agenda since the [spring and autumn 1989 sessions] respectively. As they make the same allegations, the Committee considered them together.

197. The authors of the communications allege the following. Mr Mohamed Jaaidi, a psychiatrist aged 45, was arrested by the police on 7 November 1985, having been denounced by a prisoner in a statement obtained under torture. In his work, this psychiatrist had tried to incorporate the latest medical research into practice without regard to any political considerations. He had put forward a health plan for Morocco. He had refused to establish a prison unit for political prisoners in the "Mallorca" hospital at Tétouan. The authorities had accused him without evidence of having distributed tracts. Mr Jaaidi had been tortured before being transferred to the Casablanca prison. He had been tried at the same time as other defendants and sentenced to 12 years' imprisonment for plotting against the State. According to four French barristers who had gone on an observer mission to Morocco, serious irregularities had occurred during Mr Jaaidi's trial. Ms Piuz-Lavallée and the International Human Rights Law Group stressed the fact that Mr Jaaidi was an eminent scientist. Ms Piuz-Lavallee had stated her views on this subject in a long letter dated 14 August 1989 [...].[11]

198. At the [spring 1990] session the Committee took note of a letter from the Ambassador of the Kingdom of Morocco to France restating the position of his country's authorities presented to the Committee at the [spring 1989] session. Mr Jaaidi had been found guilty by the courts of incitement to lawless behaviour and to violence on the public highway, reprehensible acts that were in no way connected with UNESCO's fields of competence or with human rights. The Ambassador stated that the communication contained unfounded claims and allegations and should therefore be declared inadmissible. He deplored its distribution to the members of the Committee, which was a serious affront to his country.

199. The authors of the communications pointed out, in letters dated 20 and 25 April 1990, that the Moroccan Government had not yet provided the Committee with specific information on Mr Mohamed Jaaidi's sentence.

---

[9] See document 136 EX/3 PRIV., paras. 196-208; see also document 136 EX/CR/HR/MOR.
[10] Communications No. 789/88 concerning *Morocco*, case of *Mohamed Jaaidi*, and No. 799/89 concerning *Morocco*, case of *Mohamed Jaaidi*, were being considered together.
[11] See document 135 EX/CR/HR/MOR, paras. 6-11.

No. 789/88 **Morocco**

200. One Committee member expressed the view that the situation of hospitals in Morocco did not in any way fall within UNESCO's competence. Other members were of the view that, judging by the information available to the Committee, Mr Jaaidi was a scientist, punished for having refused to perform acts that were incompatible with medical ethics. Some members were in favour of declaring the communication admissible; others considered that it was still too early to do so and that efforts to achieve a humanitarian solution should take precedence over any other approach. At the end of the discussion, the Committee asserted its competence to consider the two communications having regard to the information at its disposal. It renewed its appeal to the government concerned to provide it with more specific information on the factual and legal grounds on which Mr Mohamed Jaaidi's conviction was based. It also renewed its humanitarian appeal on behalf of Mr Mohamed Jaaidi.[12]

201. At the [autumn 1990] session, the International Human Rights Law Group disputed by letter the account given of the facts by the Moroccan Government. It based its position on the report of an observer mission by four French barristers who had found that serious irregularities had been committed by the judicial authorities and the police in the application of the law as regards both procedure and substance. The actual terms of the indictment revealed a violation of international human rights law, for even if Mr Jaaidi had belonged to a political organization and distributed tracts, he would have done no more than exercise the universally recognized rights to freedom of association, opinion and expression. The author of the communication therefore asked the Committee to declare the communication admissible and requested that the authorities provide further information on the nature of the offences alleged to have been committed by the doctor and on the evidence against him. It also urged that an appeal be made for the immediate and unconditional release of Dr Mohamed Jaaidi on both legal and humanitarian grounds.

202. The members of the Committee who spoke regretted the lack of dialogue with the government concerned. They noted that the government concerned had still not provided the Committee with the information that it had requested. They said that they were in favour of the communications being declared admissible. However, one member of the Committee considered that the Committee should wait for its next session and for the new Ambassador of Morocco to take up his duties before reaching this decision.

203. At the present session, the Permanent Delegation of the Kingdom of Morocco to UNESCO transmitted the following information to the Committee in a letter dated 13 March 1991. The acts of which the prisoner was accused were considered under

---

[12] See document 134 EX/3 PRIV., para. 101 (ii), (iii) and (iv) (*supra*, pp. 845-846).

the Moroccan Penal Code as common-law public order offences. Furthermore, the person concerned had been tried in public by an ordinary rather than a special court. He had been assisted in his defence and had made use of the legally available remedies. The Kingdom of Morocco therefore restated its position, which consisted in challenging the competence of the Committee and the admissibility of the case. According to the government, if the Committee entered into discussions concerning the case, it would be arrogating to itself the authority to discuss and review a final verdict pronounced by a national court of law in a sovereign State. It would thus be assuming the authority of an international tribunal in violation of UNESCO's Constitution, the Charter of the United Nations and the principles of international law, since its action would amount to interference in a country's internal affairs. Lastly, the government concerned pointed out that the body authorized to deal with such complaints was the Consultative Council on Human Rights. It invited the author of the communication to refer the case to that body.

204. The author of [the second communication] sent a letter to the Secretariat dated 9 April 1991. The Law Group noted in that letter that the Moroccan authorities had again failed to send a representative to the Committee's [autumn 1990] session and that despite the Committee's repeated requests they had again refused to respond to the allegations contained in [the first communication] or to provide information concerning Dr Jaaidi's health and conditions of detention. The Law Group added that it had reliable information that Dr Jaaidi had been unjustly imprisoned since 1985 on unsubstantiated charges. Nevertheless, the government concerned had consistently refused to co-operate with the Committee. The Law Group requested the Committee to use its good offices to urge the Moroccan Government to release Dr Jaaidi immediately and unconditionally.

205. Some members of the Committee expressed regret at the absence of a representative of the government concerned. In their view, his letter did not contain the additional information they had hoped for. They wondered whether the government concerned was not being somewhat inconsistent when it stated that the alleged victim had made use of the legally available remedies but, on the other hand, asked the author of the communication whether it had referred the case to the Consultative Council on Human Rights, the body which it said was authorized to deal with such complaints.

206. Several members of the Committee thought that the Committee and the author could refer the case to this Council, set up in March 1990, in order to seek a humanitarian settlement in a spirit of dialogue, conciliation and mutual co-operation.

207. Some members of the Committee suggested that a good offices mission might be sent to the country concerned with the agreement of the Executive Board and the

authorities concerned. Others considered that the Chairman should continue to use his good offices with the Moroccan authorities.

208. After an exchange of views, the Committee *decided*:

(i) once again to express regret that no representative of the government concerned had been present and again to urge the government to co-operate with the Committee, in particular by responding to the requests for information that the Committee had made to it at its previous sessions regarding the factual and legal grounds on which Mr Mohamed Jaaidi's conviction was based and regarding the allegations contained in the letter dated 14 August 1989 from the author of [the first communication];

(ii) nevertheless to thank the Deputy Permanent Delegate of the Kingdom of Morocco to UNESCO for his letter dated 13 March 1991;

(iii) to reaffirm its competence with respect to the communications;

(iv) to point out that the principle of non-interference in the internal affairs of States did not absolve those States of the duties incumbent on them as a result of their accession to the international instruments relating to human rights;

(v) to invite its Secretariat to take up the case with the Moroccan Consultative Council on Human Rights, the body authorized by the government concerned to examine this type of case;

(vi) to remind the government concerned that the Committee had no ambition whatsoever to assume the authority of an international supreme court but was simply endeavouring for purely humanitarian reasons to initiate a dialogue with the governments concerned in order to discuss what might be done on behalf of alleged victims in cases in which their human rights might have been violated in UNESCO's fields of competence;

(vii) to renew its appeal for clemency for Mr Mohamed Jaaidi;

(viii) to resume consideration of the communications at its [autumn 1991 session].

Morocco **No. 789/88**

Autumn 1991 session of the Committee on Conventions and Recommendations (137st session of the Executive Board)[13]

151. These two communications[14] are at the stage of examination as to their substance. They have been on the Committee's agenda since the [spring and autumn 1989 sessions] respectively. As the alleged facts and victim are the same the Committee considered them together.

152. The authors of the communications allege the following. Mr Mohamed Jaaidi, a psychiatrist aged 45, was arrested by the police on 7 November 1985, having been denounced by a prisoner in a statement obtained under torture. In his work, this psychiatrist of renown had tried to incorporate the latest medical research into practice without regard to any political considerations. He had put forward a health plan for Morocco. He had refused to establish a prison unit for political prisoners in the "Mallorca" hospital at Tétouan. The authorities had accused him without evidence of having distributed tracts and of belonging to a political organization, which, even if it were true, would amount to no more than exercise of the fundamental freedoms of association, expression and opinion. According to the authors of the communications, Mr Jaaidi had been tortured before being transferred to the Casablanca prison. He had been tried at the same time as other defendants and sentenced to 12 years' imprisonment for plotting against the State. According to four French barristers who had gone on an observer mission to Morocco, serious irregularities had occurred during Mr Jaaidi's trial.

153. For the government concerned, Mr Jaaidi had been found guilty by the courts of incitement to lawless behaviour and to violence on the public highway, acts that were regarded as criminal offences under the Penal Code and in no way connected with UNESCO's fields of competence or with human rights, he had been sentenced by a court sitting in public which was not a special court, and provided with all the procedural guarantees. If the Committee took up the case it would be setting itself up as an international tribunal and interfering with a State's domestic affairs. Furthermore, the communication contained unfounded claims and allegations. For all these reasons, it should be declared inadmissible. He deplored its distribution to the members of the Committee, which was a serious affront to his country. The government invited the author of the communication to refer the case to the Consultative Council on Human Rights, the Moroccan body authorized to deal with such complaints.

---

[13] See document 137 EX/3 PRIV., paras. 151-156; see also documents 137 EX/CR/HR/MOR and Add.

[14] Communications No. 789/88 concerning *Morocco*, case of *Mohamed Jaaidi*, and No. 799/89 concerning *Morocco*, case of *Mohamed Jaaidi*, were being considered together.

No. 789/88 **Morocco**

154. The Committee had affirmed its competence to consider these two communications, having regard to the information at its disposal. It had no ambition whatsoever to assume the authority of an international supreme court but was simply endeavouring for purely humanitarian reasons to initiate a dialogue with the governments concerned in order to discuss what might be done on behalf of alleged victims. It had requested the government concerned to provide it with more detailed information on the factual and legal grounds on which Mr Mohamed Jaaidi's conviction was based. It had made repeated appeals for clemency on his behalf. Lastly, it had invited its Secretariat to contact the Moroccan Consultative Council on Human Rights.[15]

155. At the present session, the Committee had been informed of a letter dated 7 August 1991 in which the author of the communication had replied to the arguments of the government concerned.

[155a.] For its part, the Permanent Delegation of the Kingdom of Morocco to UNESCO informed the Committee, by a letter dated 13 September 1991, that Mr Mohamed Jaaidi had received a royal pardon on 16 August 1991 and had been freed.

156. After an exchange of views, the Committee *decided*:

(i) to thank the representative of the government concerned for his letter dated 13 September 1991;

(ii) to take note with satisfaction of the release of Mr Mohamed Jaaidi;

(iii) to strike the communications from its list, as having been settled in accordance with paragraph 14 (*a*) (x) of 104 EX/Decision 3.3.

---

[15] See document 136 EX/3 PRIV., para. 208 (iii), (vi), (i), (vii) and (v), respectively (*supra*, p. 852).

No. 790/88

Concerning *Union of Soviet Socialist Republics*
Case of *Gintautas Iesmantas*

Communication of 1 September 1988 submitted by
Amnesty International

Spring 1989 session of the Committee on Conventions and Recommendations (131st session of the Executive Board)[1]

153. This was the first submission of the communication to the Committee.

154. According to Amnesty International, Mr Gintautas Iesmantas, writer and journalist, was arrested on 5 March 1980 and accused with other persons of anti-Soviet propaganda and agitation, for the opinions expressed by him in his poems and philosophical essays published in *Perspektyvos*, an unofficial journal of liberal socialist orientation which appeared between 1978 and 1981. He is alleged to have been sentenced by the courts on 22 December 1980 to six years' imprisonment and five years' internal exile.

155. In a letter of 7 March 1989, the author of the communication reported that Mr Gintautas Iesmantas had been released on 31 October 1988.

156. The representative of the government concerned stated that Mr Gintautas Iesmantas had been a contributor to the *Komjaunimo Tiesa* newspaper and not a manager as Amnesty International had stated in its communication - and had indeed been pardoned. Having returned to Vilnius, he had requested that the grounds for his sentence be re-examined. After an appeal by the Procurator of Lithuania before the Presidium of the Supreme Soviet in March 1989, he had been fully rehabilitated.

157. After discussion, the Committee *decided*:

(i) to thank the representative of the government concerned for his presence and co-operation;

[1] See document 131 EX/3 PRIV., paras. 153-157; see also document 131 EX/CR/HR/USR.

(ii) to note with satisfaction the release and rehabilitation of Mr Gintautas Iesmantas;

(iii) to strike this communication from its list, considering it to have been settled in accordance with paragraph 14 (*a*) (x) of 104 EX/Decision 3.3.

No. 791/88

Concerning *Turkey*
Case of *Bektaş Erdoğan*

Communication of 1 September 1988 submitted by
Amnesty International

Spring 1989 session of the Committee on Conventions and Recommendations (131st session of the Executive Board)[1]

145. This communication appears on the Committee's agenda for the first time.

146. Mr Bektaş Erdoğan is described as an editor and journalist, aged 33. Apparently, he was, for a brief period, before the military coup in September 1980, editor-in-chief of the journal *Kitle*, a publication of the Turkish Socialist Workers' Party, several members of which were reportedly arrested and sentenced to various terms of imprisonment for having transformed that party into an illegal organization. The author of the communication states that it has no details of the trials in which Mr Erdoğan is said to have been involved but that, according to information at its disposal, the alleged victim, in prison since July 1980, received several sentences that were combined to make a total of 36 years' imprisonment on account of his many articles published in *Kitle*. Transferred from one military prison to another, he is reported to have been imprisoned finally in a civilian penal establishment for political prisoners.

147. The author considers that as long as Mr Erdoğan remains in prison merely on account of his having expressed his opinions through his articles, this represents a continuing violation of his human rights, since no evidence has been produced that the journal *Kitle* advocated violence. It would thus appear that in this case there have been violations of the right to freedom of thought and conscience and of the right to freedom of opinion and expression (Articles 18 and 19 of the Universal Declaration of Human Rights). Reportedly, the sentences pronounced against Mr Erdoğan have all been confirmed on appeal by military courts.

---

[1] See document 131 EX/3 PRIV., paras. 145-152; see also document 131 EX/CR/HR/TUR.

No. 791/88 **Turkey**

148. The author of this communication requests unconditional release of the alleged victim.

149. In a letter dated 7 March 1989, Amnesty International, the author of the communication, provided the following further information. According to government sources, Mr Bektaş Erdoğan had been sentenced to 20 years in prison for armed robbery, in addition to being convicted for communist and separatist propaganda and insulting the authorities. In fact, Amnesty International claims to have received confirmation from Mr Bektaş Erdoğan himself that he had indeed been convicted for robbery but that this conviction was based on a confession obtained from him under torture. Amnesty International did not know whether Mr Bektaş Erdoğan had lodged a judicial complaint in this connection but hoped to obtain further information on this matter and concerning whether an investigation had been carried out to establish the truth of the allegations that the confession had been obtained under torture. However, according to Amnesty International, there were many cases in which Turkish civil and military courts had based their decisions on statements obtained under torture and this gave grounds for thinking that Mr Bektaş Erdoğan's allegations should be taken seriously.

150. The Permanent Delegate of Turkey to Unesco gave the Committee the following information. Mr Bektaş Erdoğan, as editor-in-chief of a journal, had in various articles advocated revolutionary socialism, the supremacy of the working class and the revolt of the Kurdish people against the security forces. He had fomented feelings of hatred and animosity among the Kurds. He had advocated discrimination between Turks and Kurds. He had encouraged illegal demonstrations and had personally perpetrated an armed robbery. He had been convicted for his propaganda activities and for other activities aimed at destroying the socio-economic values of the State, democracy and the legal system, which guaranteed equal rights for all citizens, without discrimination of any kind, particularly discrimination based on Kurdish racism, for propaganda designed to weaken national feeling and for encouraging the holding of illegal demonstrations. He had also been convicted for armed robbery and for threatening a jeweller. Notwithstanding the allegations that the last conviction had been based on a confession obtained under torture, he had never made any statement to that effect during the proceedings and had not lodged a complaint in this connection. In fact, he had been recognized by the jeweller and the theft had been confirmed by his accomplices. He had confessed his crimes before the various courts during his trials and there was sufficient proof of his guilt. The decisions of the courts had been confirmed by the Supreme Court on appeal. Apart from the armed robbery, his other crimes had been judged without him being imprisoned. Mr Bektaş Erdoğan's criminal activities had no relationship with freedom of expression, conscience or opinion as was claimed by Amnesty International. He had not been convicted for his publishing activities as such but for propaganda and incitement to

revolt, racist separatism and civil war, with the aggravating circumstance, provided for by law, that this propaganda and these incitements had been engaged in through publications. The pardon and immediate release demanded by Amnesty International were not possible, according to the law, until January 1995. Of the 36 years' imprisonment to which he had been sentenced, 20 were for armed robbery. In conclusion, the communication not only distorted the facts but also did not come within the scope of the procedure set out in 104 EX/Decision 3.3, in particular paragraphs 6, 7, 14 (*a*) (iii), (iv) and (v) and should therefore be considered inadmissible.

151. In reply to questions, the Permanent Delegate explained that the expression "Kurdish racism" did not mean the mere fact of calling oneself a Kurd but referred to the desire to create a Kurdish State based on racial criteria. Mr Bektaş Erdoğan had continually advocated violence in his articles. He was in a civilian prison, in good health.

152. Following the discussions, the Committee, after thanking the representative of the government concerned for attending the meeting and for his co-operation, *considered* that it was unable to take a decision regarding the admissibility of the communication until it had additional information relating, in particular, to the armed robbery.

Autumn 1989 session of the Committee on Conventions and Recommendations (132nd session of the Executive Board)[2]

118. This communication has been on the Committee's agenda since the [spring 1989 session]. It is at the stage of consideration as to admissibility.

119. Mr Bektaş Erdoğan, an editor and journalist, is said to have been sentenced on account of his writings to a total of 16 years' imprisonment for communist propaganda and for offences against the authorities. He was also allegedly sentenced to 20 years' imprisonment for armed robbery. Mr Erdoğan apparently claimed in court that his confessions had been extracted from him under torture.

120. At the [spring 1989] session, the representative of the government concerned informed the Committee that Mr Bektaş Erdoğan had, in his various articles, advocated revolutionary socialism, the supremacy of the working class and the revolt of the Kurdish people against the security forces, fomenting among them feelings of hatred and animosity against the Turks. He had also carried out propaganda activi-

[2] See document 132 EX/3 PRIV., paras. 118-123; see also document 132 EX/CR/HR/TUR Add.

ties and other activities aimed at destroying the socio-economic values of the State, democracy and the legal and constitutional system of the country. Contrary to the allegations made by the author of the communication, Mr Bektaş Erdoğan had personally taken part in the armed robbery. The facts had been confirmed both by his accomplices and by the jeweller who was the victim of the robbery.

121. The Committee considered that it was not in a position to take a decision regarding the admissibility of the communication and decided to await additional information, in particular about the armed robbery.[3]

122. Under cover of a letter dated 27 July 1989, the Permanent Delegation of Turkey to Unesco sent to the Secretariat a summary translation of the verdict against Mr Bektaş Erdoğan in the armed robbery case. Following this, the author of the communication announced, in a letter dated 14 August 1989, that it was retracting its demand for the release of Mr Bektaş Erdoğan even though he had also been sentenced for writings that he had published.

123. After an exchange of views, the Committee *decided*:

(i) to thank the representative of the government concerned for attending the meeting and for his co-operation;

(ii) to declare the communication inadmissible as it did not fall within Unesco's fields of competence as defined in paragraph 14 (*a*) (iii) of 104 EX/ Decision 3.3.

---

[3] See document 131 EX/3 PRIV., para. 152 (*supra*, p. 859).

ANNEX

TABLES OF COMMUNICATIONS

(*a*) Communications examined under the 104 EX/Decision 3.3 Procedure of the Executive Board filed 1982-1988 (States concerned)

Afghanistan	No. 630/84	*Osman Taraki Rustar* et al. *Osman Taraki Rustar and Shukrullah Kohgadai*	Settled
Argentina	No. 465/82	*Julio Juan Piumato*	Inadmissible
Benin, People's Republic of	No. 761/87	*Baro Orou Mora*	Settled
Bulgaria	No. 748/87	*Omer Mustafov Kochandzhiev* et al.	Inadmissible
	No. 752/87	*Halim Pasadzhov*	Inadmissible
	No. 753/87	*Rasim Rezhebov* et al.	Inadmissible
	No. 776/88	*Omer Mustafov Kochandzhiev and Burhan Nedzhibov Hayrulov*	Inadmissible
Chile	No. 433/82	*Enrique Ropert Gallet*	Settled
	No. 439/82	*Victor Ulices Sandoval Alvarez*	Settled
	No. 447/82	*Germán Molina Valdivieso*	Settled
	No. 475/82	*José Hugo Pueller Bravo*	Inadmissible
	No. 484/82	*Sergio Spoerer*	Settled
	No. 516/83	*Vladimir Lenin Chávez Rodriguez*	Inadmissible
	No. 518/83	*Jorge Montes*	Inadmissible
	No. 530/83	*Luis Guillermo Deisler González*	Settled
	No. 543/83	*Hector Hernan Bravo Zamora* et al. *Jorge Segundo Insunza Becker* *Severo Augusto Samaniego Mesias*	Inadmissible/ Settled
	No. 559/83	*Delfin Guillermo Quinones* et al. *Carlos Alfredo Andrade Vera* et al. *Carlos Alfredo Andrade Vera and Guillermo Vera Paulo* *Carlos Alfredo Andrade Vera*	Settled
	No. 577/83	*Victor Hugo de la Fuente*	Settled
	No. 583/83	*Mirna Donoso Garcia*	Settled
	No. 590/83	*Carlos Lira Moscoso*	Inadmissible
	No. 601/84	*Ulises Gómez*	Settled

Annex

Chile	No. 605/84	*Luis Eduardo Labarca Goddard*	Settled
	No. 608/84	*José Miguel Varas Morel*	Inadmissible
	No. 618/84	*Luis José Godoy González*	Settled
	No. 632/84	*Raúl Manriquez*	Settled
	No. 653/84	*Carlos Mario Lira Moscoso*	Inadmissible
	No. 695/85	*Leonardo Càceres Castro*	Settled
	No. 705/86	*Maria Ximena Mora Pozo*	Settled
	No. 706/86	*Adriana Susana Rondón González*	Settled
	No. 722/86	*José Luis Rojas Valencia*	Settled
	No. 731/86	*Francisco Javier Andrés Peña Torres*	Settled
	No. 739/86	*Fernando Ramón Azula Ponce*	Inadmissible
	No. 743/87	*Francisco Javier Lira Bianchi*	Settled
	No. 749/87	*Luis Ibacache Silva*	Setlled
	No. 773/88	*Ledy del Carmen Castro Urra*	Settled
China, People's Republic of	No. 693/85	*Liu Liping*	Settled
	No. 760/87	*Liu De*	Inadmissible
Colombia	No. 437/82	*Leaders of the Colombian Federation of Teachers*	Inadmissible
Côte d'Ivoire	No. 768/87	*Teachers belonging to the National Union of Secondary School Teachers of Côte d'Ivoire*	Inadmissible
Cuba	No. 788/88	*Natividad González Freire* et al. *César Eugenio Leante Magaloni* et al.	Settled
Czechoslovakia	No. 443/82	*Karel Kyncl* *Ladislav Hejdánek and Václav Benda* *Karel Kyncl* *Ladislav Hejdánek*	Settled/ Inadmissible
	No. 450/82	*Jozef Jablonicky*	Inadmissible
	No. 451/82	*František Lizna*	Settled
	No. 595/83	*Ladislav Lis*	Inadmissible
	No. 616/84	*Jaromir Šavrda*	Settled
	No. 624/84	*Marek Benda*	Settled
	No. 638/84	*Jiři Wolf*	Inadmissible
	No. 671/85	*Jan Hájek*	Settled
	No. 787/88	*Evžen Freimann*	Inadmissible
Denmark	No. 614/84	*Kai Mogens H. Lång*	Inadmissible
El Salvador	No. 477/82	*Violation of human rights in El Salvador* *Violations of human rights in El Salvador*	

El Salvador		*Alleged violations of human rights in El Salvador*	Struck off
	No. 690/85	*Filomena Claros de Majano*	Struck off
France	No. 622/84	*Mohamed Benrahhlate*	Inadmissible
	No. 637/84	*Léone Guyot*	Inadmissible
	No. 755/87	*Lyudmila Pavlovna Varigin*	Settled
German Democratic Republic	No. 640/84	*Ulrike Poppe and Bärbel Bohley*	Settled
Germany, Federal Republic of	No. 529/83	*Gudrun Melchior-Dollinger* et al.	Settled/ Suspended
	No. 540/83	*Helios Gürkov*	Inadmissible
	No. 639/84	*Christian Schmidt*	Inadmissible
Greece	No. 744/87	*Ignace Philippoussis*	Settled
	No. 746/87	*Margarita Fréri and Rose Fréri*	Settled
Honduras	No. 446/82	*Carlos Ramírez*	Suspended
Hungary	No. 641/84	*Twenty female activists for peace*	Inadmissible
Indonesia	No. 487/82	*Tengku Muhammad Usman Lampoh Awé*	Inadmissible
	No. 734/86	*Oesmany al Hamidy*	Settled
	No. 750/87	*Achmad Zaini and Margono Bin Syafei*	Settled
Iran	No. 525/83	*Abolfazl Ghassemi*	Settled
Iran, Islamic Republic of	No. 581/83	*Arrest of leading figures in Iranian cultural life* *Alleged arrests of eminent personalities in the world of Iranian culture* *Twenty-eight personalities in the world of culture* *Alleged arrests of personalities in the world of Iranian culture*	Settled
Israel	No. 491/82	*Violations of human rights committed by Israel against the Lebanese and Palestinian peoples* *Alleged violations of human rights committed by Israel against the Lebanese and Palestinian peoples*	Struck off
Italy	No. 677/85	*Alberto Tessore*	Inadmissible
	No. 719/86	*Giulia Arena*	Inadmissible

Annex

Ivory Coast	No. 473/82	*Syndicat national de la recherche et de l'enseignement supérieur*	Settled
Kenya	No. 546/83	*Al-Amin Muhamed Kassim Mazrui*	Settled
Korea, Republic of	No. 730/86	*Song Ki Won* et al. *Dismissal of teachers and withdrawal of the Shilchun Literary Company's publishing licence*	Settled
	No. 780/88	*Lee Tae-Bok*	Settled
Lao People's Dem. Republic	No. 480/82	*Khamkhing Souvanlasy*	Settled
Malawi	No. 781/88	*Jack Mapanje*	Settled
Malta	No. 623/84	*Alleged discriminatory measures concerning university admissions*	Inadmissible
Morocco	No. 495/82	*Mohamed Elyazghi*	Inadmissible
	No. 528/83	*Right of civil servants to lifelong education*	Inadmissible
	No. 789/88	*Mohamed Jaaidi*	Settled
Nepal	No. 778/88	*Sushil Chandra Amatya*	Settled
New Zealand	No. 602/84	*Alleged discriminatory tuition fees imposed on foreign students under the New Zealand Education Amendment Act 1979*	Struck off
Nigeria	No. 652/84	*Tai Solarin*	Settled
Norway	No. 642/84	Ikkevold Magazine	Inadmissible
Pakistan	No. 535/83	*Jamil Omar*	Settled
	No. 539/83	*Tariq Ahsan*	Settled
Paraguay	No. 582/83	*Enrique Goossen Martens* et al.	Settled
	No. 669/85	*"Radio Nanduti"*	Settled
	No. 674/85	*Aldo Zuccolillo and* ABC Color	Settled
Peru	No. 440/82	*Victor Rapray Robles*	Settled
Poland	No. 431/82	*Krzysztof Śliwiński*	Settled
	No. 631/84	*Marek Nowakowski*	Withdrawn
Romania	No. 479/82	*Ion Caraion*	Inadmissible

Annex

Romania	No. 494/82	*Victoria Dragomir and Anca Dragomir*	Inadmissible
	No. 503/82	*Radu Dinculescu*	Inadmissible
	No. 712/86	*Lacrima Cofaru*	Settled
Somalia	No. 736/86	*Abdulle Rage Taraweh*	Settled
	No. 745/87	*Abdi Ismail Younis*	Settled
Turkey	No. 606/84	*Mahmut Dikerdem* et al.	Inadmissible
	No. 610/84	*Sadun Aren*	Settled
	No. 762/87	*Recep Marasli*	Settled
	No. 784/88	*Günay Avcı* et al.	Settled
	No. 791/88	*Bektaş Erdoğan*	Inadmissible
Union of Soviet Socialist Republics	No. 441/82	*Vladimir Raiz and Grigory Rozenshtein Vladimir Raiz*	Inadmissible
	No. 442/82	*Alexandr Paritsky*	Settled
	No. 444/82	*Kishore Dehadrai*	Inadmissible
	No. 449/82	*Filip Moyseyevich Gershkovich*	Inadmissible
	No. 461/82	*Lev Blitshtein*	Inadmissible
	No. 462/82	*Victor Yelistratov and Basheva Hait Yelistratov*	Inadmissible
	No. 470/82	*Arseny Borisovich Roginsky*	Inadmissible
	No. 481/82	*Alexander Temkin*	Inadmissible
	No. 482/82	*Andrei Sakharov*	Settled
	No. 483/82	*Discrimination in respect of admission to higher education courses in Moscow at the Faculty of Mechanics and Mathematics of the State University, the Institute of Physical Engineering, and the Physical-Technical Institute Alleged discrimination in respect of admission to higher education courses in Moscow at the Faculty of Mechanics and Mathematics of the State University, the Institute of Physical Engineering, and the Physical-Technical Institute*	Inadmissible
	No. 500/82	*Vladimir Raiz Vladimir Raiz and Grigory Rozenshtein Vladimir Raiz*	Inadmissible
	No. 519/83	*Withdrawal of academic diplomas Withdrawal of academic diplomas and degrees*	Inadmissible
	No. 527/83	*Yuri Fedorovich Orlov*	Inadmissible
	No. 536/83	*Yosif Z. Begun*	Settled
	No. 560/83	*Anatoli Raben*	Struck off

Annex

Union of Soviet Socialist Republics	No. 561/83	*Anatoli Khazanov*	Struck off
	No. 564/83	*Igor Guberman*	Settled
	No. 565/83	*Novosibirsk Association for the Promotion of Friendship between the Peoples of the USSR and Israel*	Inadmissible
	No. 603/84	*Andrei Sakharov*	Settled
	No. 628/84	*Alexandre Broussilovski*	Inadmissible
	No. 643/84	*Victor Blik* et al.	Inadmissible
	No. 645/84	*Soviet scientists of Jewish origin who have filed applications to emigrate*	Inadmissible
	No. 651/84	*Alleged discrimination with respect to education*	Inadmissible
	No. 691/85	*Hanna Vasylivna Mykhaylenko*	Inadmissible
	No. 692/85	*Vladimir Yurevich Poresh*	Inadmissible
	No. 694/85	*Aleksander Nicolaevich Bogoslovsky*	Settled
	No. 720/86	*Yosif Z. Begun*	Settled
	No. 721/86	*Roald Zelichonok*	Settled
	No. 725/86	*Leonid Volvovski*	Settled
	No. 726/86	*Vladimir Lifshits*	Settled
	No. 728/86	*Yuli Edelshtein*	Settled
	No. 729/86	*Alexis Magarik*	Settled
	No. 737/86	*Mart Niklus*	Settled
	No. 754/87	*Alleged discriminations against access to Jewish history, culture and art*	Inadmissible
	No. 758/87	*History books and textbooks for pupils in the Soviet Union*	Inadmissible
	No. 759/87	*Various works by contemporary Soviet authors*	Inadmissible
	No. 790/88	*Gintautas Iesmantas*	Settled
United States of America	No. 613/84	*Alleged discrimination in education against the black American minority*	Inadmissible
	No. 656/84	*Alleged medical tyranny as practised in the United States of America Alleged medical tyranny in the United States of America*	Inadmissible
Uruguay	No. 460/82	*Yolanda Catalina Ibarra Chávez de Chassale*	Inadmissible
	No. 468/82	*Raúl Cariboni da Silva*	Inadmissible
	No. 517/83	*Raúl Cariboni da Silva*	Inadmissible
	No. 627/84	*Mario Alberto Teti Izquierdo*	Settled
	No. 647/84	*"Cinco Días"*	Settled
	No. 648/84	*"Tribune Amplia"*	Settled
	No. 649/84	*"Somos Idea"*	Settled
	No. 650/84	*"Convicción"*	Settled

Viet Nam, Socialist Republic of	No. 434/82	*Duyen Ahn*	Inadmissible
	No. 544/83	*Bui Hoang Câm*	Settled
	No. 626/84	*Nguyên Hai Chi*	Settled
	No. 763/87	*Nguyên Dan Que*	Settled
	No. 764/87	*Truong Van Quynh*	Settled
	No. 765/87	*Doan Quôc Sy*	Settled
	No. 766/87	*Nguyên Chi Thien*	Settled
Yugoslavia	No. 478/82	*Franjo Tudjman*	
		Milovan Djilas et al.	Inadmissible
	No. 511/82	*Marko Veselica*	
		Milovan Djilas et al.	Inadmissible
	No. 655/84	*Jozo Gospodin Zovko* et al.	Inadmissible
	No. 676/85	*Jovan R. Gucič*	Settled
	No. 684/85	*Radomir Veljković*	Settled
	No. 685/85	*Vladimir Marković*	Inadmissible
	No. 686/85	*Božidar Todorović*	
		Božidar Todorović and Milica Todorović	Inadmissible/ Settled
	No. 687/85	*Slobodan Živković* et al.	Inadmissible
	No. 751/87	*Ismet Kasumagic*	Settled
	No. 772/87	*Uros Bukumira*	Inadmissible
	No. 779/88	*Bogdan Antić*	Inadmissible
Zaire	No. 472/82	*Ernest Wamba-dia-Wamba*	Settled
Zambia	No. 489/82	*Students expelled or suspended from the University of Zambia*	Inadmissible

Annex

(*b*) Communications examined under the 104 EX/Decision 3.3 Procedure of the Executive Board filed 1982-1988 (Cases)

ABC Color	*Paraguay*	No. 674/85
Abdi Ismail Younis	*Somalia*	No. 745/87
Abdulle Rage Taraweh	*Somalia*	No. 736/86
Abolfazl Ghassemi	*Iran*	No. 525/83
Achmad Zaini	*Indonesia*	No. 750/87
Adriana Susana Rondón González	*Chile*	No. 706/86
Al-Amin Muhamed Kassim Mazrui	*Kenya*	No. 546/83
Alberto Tessore	*Italy*	No. 677/85
Aldo Zuccolillo	*Paraguay*	No. 674/85
Alejandro Cedeño Leante	*Cuba*	No. 788/88
Aleksander Nicolaevich Bogoslovsky	*Union of Soviet Socialist Republics*	No. 694/85
Alexander Temkin	*Union of Soviet Socialist Republics*	No. 481/82
Alexandre Broussilovski	*Union of Soviet Socialist Republics*	No. 628/84
Alexandr Paritsky	*Union of Soviet Socialist Republics*	No. 442/82
Alexis Magarik	*Union of Soviet Socialist Republics*	No. 729/86
Alleged arrests of eminent personalities in the world of Iranian culture	*Islamic Republic of Iran*	No. 581/83
Alleged arrests of personalities in the world of Iranian culture	*Islamic Republuc of Iran*	No. 581/83
Alleged discrimination in education against the black American minority	*United States of America*	No. 613/84
Alleged discrimination in respect of admission to higher education courses in Moscow at the Faculty of Mechanics and Mathematics of the State University, the Institute of Physical Engineering, and the Physical-Technical Institute	*Union of Soviet Socialist Republics*	No. 483/82
Alleged discriminations against access to Jewish history, culture and art	*Union of Soviet Socialist Republics*	No. 754/87
Alleged discrimination with respect to education	*Union of Soviet Socialist Republics*	No. 651/84
Alleged discriminatory measures concerning university admissions	*Malta*	No. 623/84
Alleged discriminatory tuition fees imposed on foreign students under the New Zealand Education Amendment Act 1979	*New Zraland*	No. 602/84
Alleged medical tyranny as practised in the United States of America	*United States of America*	No. 656/84
Alleged medical tyranny in the United States of America	*United States of America*	No. 656/84

Annex

Alleged violations of human rights committed by Israel against the Lebanese and Palestinian peoples	*Israel*	No. 491/82
Alleged violations of human rights in El Salvador	*El Salvador*	No. 477/82
Anatoli Khazanov	*Union of Soviet Socialist Republics*	No. 561/83
Anatoli Raben	*Union of Soviet Socialist Republics*	No. 560/83
Anca Dragomir	*Romania*	No. 494/82
Andrei Sakharov	*Union of Soviet Socialist Republics*	No. 482/82
Andrei Sakharov	*Union of Soviet Socialist Republics*	No. 603/84
Arrest of leading figures in Iranian cultural life	*Islamic Republic of Iran*	No. 581/83
Arseny Borisovich Roginsky	*Union of Soviet Socialist Republics*	No. 470/82
Bärbel Bohley	*German Democratic Republic*	No. 640/84
Baro Orou Mora	*People's Republic of Benin*	No. 761/87
Basheva Hait Yelistratov	*Union of Soviet Socialist Republics*	No. 462/82
Bektaş Erdoğan	*Turkey*	No. 791/88
Bogdan Antić	*Yugoslavia*	No. 779/88
Božidarka Živković	*Yugoslavia*	No. 687/85
Božidar Todorović	*Yugoslavia*	No. 686/85
Bui Hoang Câm	*Socialist Republic of Viet Nam*	No. 544/83
Burhan Nedzhibov Hayrulov	*Bulgaria*	No. 748/87
Burhan Nedzhibov Hayrulov	*Bulgaria*	No. 776/88
Carlos Alfredo Andrade Vera	*Chile*	No. 559/83
Carlos Lira Moscoso	*Chile*	No. 590/83
Carlos Mario Lira Moscoso	*Chile*	No. 653/84
Carlos Ramirez	*Honduras*	No. 446/82
César Eugenio Leante González,	*Cuba*	No. 788/88
César Eugenio Leante Magaloni	*Cuba*	No. 788/88
Christian Schmidt	*Federal Republic of Germany*	No. 639/84
"Cinco Días"	*Uruguay*	No. 647/84
"Convicción"	*Uruguay*	No. 650/84
Delfin Guillermo Quiñones	*Chile*	No. 559/83
Discrimination in respect of admission to higher education courses in Moscow at the Faculty of Mechanics and Mathematics of the State University, the Institute of Physical Engineering, and the Physical-Technical Institute	*Union of Soviet Socialist Republics*	No. 483/82
Dismissal of teachers and withdrawal of the Shilchun Literary Company's publishing licence	*Republic of Korea*	No. 730/86
Doan Quôc Sy	*Socialist Republic of Viet Nam*	No. 765/87
Duyen Ahn	*Socialist Republic of Viet Nam*	No. 434/82
Edward Hertel	*Federal Republic of Germany*	No. 529/83
Eleven employees of the Banco Paraguayo de Datos and Estudio Gráfica	*Paraguay*	No. 582/83

Enrique Goossen Martens	*Paraguay*	No. 582/83
Enrique Ropert Gallet	*Chile*	No. 433/82
Erdal Atabek	*Turkey*	No. 606/84
Ernest Wamba-dia-Wamba	*Zaire*	No. 472/82
Evžen Freimann	*Czechoslovakia*	No. 787/88
Fernando Ramón Azula Ponce	*Chile*	No. 739/86
Filip Moyseyevich Gershkovich	*Union of Soviet Socialist Republics*	No. 449/82
Filomena Claros de Majano	*El Salvador*	No. 690/85
Francisco Javier Andrés Peña Torres	*Chile*	No. 731/86
Francisco Javier Lira Bianchi	*Chile*	No. 743/87
Franjo Tudjman	*Yugoslavia*	No. 478/82
František Lízna	*Czechoslovakia*	No. 451/82
Gennady Krochik	*Union of Soviet Socialist Republics*	No. 643/84
Germán Molina Valdivieso	*Chile*	No. 447/82
Gintautas Iesmantas	*Union of Soviet Socialist Republics*	No. 790/88
Grigory Rozenshtein	*Union of Soviet Socialist Republics*	No. 441/82
Gudrun Melchior-Dollinger	*Federal Republic of Germany*	No. 529/83
Giulia Arena	*Italy*	No. 719/86
Guillermo Vera Paulo	*Chile*	No. 559/83
Günay Avcı	*Turkey*	No. 784/88
Gyursel Hasanov Saadettinov	*Bulgaria*	No. 748/87
Halim Pasadzhov	*Bulgaria*	No. 752/87
Hanna Vasylivna Mykhaylenko	*Union of Soviet Socialist Republics*	No. 691/85
Hassan Kakar	*Afghanistan*	No. 630/84
Héctor Hernán Bravo Zamora	*Chile*	No. 543/83
Heinrich Häberlein	*Federal Republic of Germany*	No. 529/83
Helios Gürkov	*Federal Republic of Germany*	No. 540/83
History books and textbooks for pupils in the Soviet Union	*Union of Soviet Socialist Republics*	No. 758/87
Hüseyin Kolkesen	*Turkey*	No. 784/88
Hüseyin Sönmez	*Turkey*	No. 784/88
Hüseyin Sungur	*Turkey*	No. 784/88
Hüsrev Erginöz	*Turkey*	No. 784/88
Ignace Philippoussis	*Greece*	No. 744/87
Igor Guberman	*Union of Soviet Socialist Republics*	No. 564/83
Ikkevold Magazine	*Norway*	No. 642/84
Ion Caraion	*Romania*	No. 479/82
Ismet Abdulov	*Bulgaria*	No. 753/87
Ismet Kasumagic	*Yugoslavia*	No. 751/87
Ivan Dragićević	*Yugoslavia*	No. 655/84
Ivanka Ivanoković	*Yugoslavia*	No. 655/84
Jack Mapanje	*Malawi*	No. 781/88
Jakov Colo	*Yugoslavia*	No. 655/84
Jamil Omar	*Pakistan*	No. 535/83
Jan Hájek	*Czechoslovakia*	No. 671/85
Jaromir Šavrda	*Czechoslovakia*	No. 616/84
Jiří Wolf	*Czechoslovakia*	No. 638/84

Annex

Jorge Montes	*Chile*	No. 518/83
Jorge Segundo Insunza Becker	*Chile*	No. 543/83
José Hugo Pueller Bravo	*Chile*	No. 475/82
José Luis Rojas Valencia	*Chile*	No. 722/86
José Miguel Varas Morel	*Chile*	No. 608/84
Jovan R. Gucič	*Yugoslavia*	No. 676/85
Jozef Jablonicky	*Czechoslovakia*	No. 450/82
Jozo Gospodin Zovko	*Yugoslavia*	No. 655/84
Jozo Krizich	*Yugoslavia*	No. 655/84
Juan Guillermo López Carmona	*Chile*	No. 543/83
Julio Juan Piumato	*Argentina*	No. 465/82
Kai Mogens H. Lång	*Denmark*	No. 614/84
Karel Kyncl	*Czechoslovakia*	No. 443/82
Khamkhing Souvanlasy	*Lao People's Democratic Republic*	No. 480/82
Kim Jin Kyung	*Republic of Korea*	No. 730/86
Kishore Dehadrai	*Union of Soviet Socialist Republics*	No. 444/82
Krzysztof Śliwiński	*Poland*	No. 431/82
Lacrima Cofaru	*Romania*	No. 712/86
Ladislav Hejdánek	*Czechoslovakia*	No. 443/82
Ladislav Lis	*Czechoslovakia*	No. 595/83
Laura Leante González	*Cuba*	No. 788/88
Leaders of the Colombian Federation of Teachers	*Colombia*	No. 437/82
Ledy del Carmen Castro Urra	*Chile*	No. 773/88
Lee Tae-Bok	*Republic of Korea*	No. 780/88
Leonardo Cáceres Castro	*Chile*	No. 695/85
Léone Guyot	*France*	No. 637/84
Leonid Volvovski	*Union of Soviet Socialist Republics*	No. 725/86
Lev Blitshtein	*Union of Soviet Socialist Republics*	No. 461/82
Lev Dudkin	*Union of Soviet Socialist Republics*	No. 643/84
Liu De	*People's Republic of China*	No. 760/87
Liu Liping	*People's Republic of China*	No. 693/85
Luis Eduardo Labarca Goddard	*Chile*	No. 605/84
Luis Guillermo Deisler González	*Chile*	No. 530/83
Luis Ibacache Silva	*Chile*	No. 749/87
Luis José Godoy González	*Chile*	No. 618/84
Luis Ramón Contreras Parada	*Chile*	No. 559/83
Luis Ricardo Cedeño Felipe	*Cuba*	No. 788/88
Lyudmila Pavlovna Varigin	*France*	No. 755/87
Mahmut Dikerdem	*Turkey*	No. 606/84
Manfred Lehner-Wendt	*Federal Republic of Germany*	No. 529/83
Marek Benda	*Czechoslovakia*	No. 624/84
Marek Nowakowski	*Poland*	No. 631/84
Margarita Fréri	*Greece*	No. 746/87
Margono Bin Syafei	*Indonesia*	No. 750/87
María Marta Rivas de Gumucio	*Chile*	No. 543/83
María Ximena Mora Pozo	*Chile*	No. 705/86

Marija Pavlović	*Yugoslavia*	No. 655/83
Mario Alberto Teti Izquierdo	*Uruguay*	No. 627/84
Marko Veselica	*Yugoslavia*	No. 511/82
Mart Niklus	*Union of Soviet Socialist Republics*	No. 737/86
Milica Todorović	*Yugoslavia*	No. 686/85
Mirjana Dragićević	*Yugoslavia*	No. 655/84
Mirna Donoso Garcia	*Chile*	No. 583/83
Mithat Ünüvar	*Turkey*	No. 784/88
Mohamed Benrahhlate	*France*	No. 622/84
Mohamed Elyazghi	*Morocco*	No. 495/82
Mohamed Jaaidi	*Morocco*	No. 789/88
Natividad González Freire	*Cuba*	No. 788/88
Nguyên Chi Thien	*Socialist Republic of Viet Nam*	No. 766/87
Nguyên Dan Que	*Socialist Republic of Viet Nam*	No. 763/87
Nguyên Hai Chi	*Socialist Republic of Viet Nam*	No. 626/84
Novosibirsk Association for the Promotion of Friendship between the Peoples of the USSR and Israel	*Union of Soviet Socialist Republics*	No. 565/83
Oesmany al Hamidy	*Indonesia*	No. 734/86
Oleg Radzinsky	*Union of Soviet Socialist Republics*	No. 643/84
Olga Lusnikova	*Union of Soviet Socialist Republics*	No. 643/84
Olga Medvedkova	*Union of Soviet Socialist Republics*	No. 643/84
Omer Mustafov Kochandzhiev	*Bulgaria*	No. 748/87
Omer Mustafov Kochandzhiev	*Bulgaria*	No. 776/88
Orhan Apaydın	*Turkey*	No. 606/84
Osman Taraki Rustar	*Afghanistan*	No. 630/84
Osvaldo Hernán Rodrigues Musso	*Chile*	No. 543/83
"Radio Nanduti"	*Paraguay*	No. 669/85
Radomir Veljković	*Yugoslavia*	No. 684/85
Radu Dinculescu	*Romania*	No. 503/82
Rafael Gumucio	*Chile*	No. 543/83
Rasim Rezhebov	*Bulgaria*	No. 753/87
Raúl Cariboni da Silva	*Uruguay*	No. 468/82
Raúl Cariboni da Silva	*Uruguay*	No. 517/83
Raúl Manriquez	*Chile*	No. 632/84
Recep Marasli	*Turkey*	No. 762/87
Right of civil servants to lifelong education	*Morocco*	No. 528/83
Roald Zelichonok	*Union of Soviet Socialist Republics*	No. 721/86
Rosaura Mendoza Careaga	*Chile*	No. 559/83
Rose Fréri	*Greece*	No. 746/87
Sadun Aren	*Turkey*	No. 610/84
Salim Salimov	*Bulgaria*	No. 753/87
Sergio Spoerer	*Chile*	No. 484/82
Severo Augusto Samaniego Mesias	*Chile*	No. 543/83
Shukrullah Kohgadai	*Afghanistan*	No. 630/84
Slobodan Živković	*Yugoslavia*	No. 687/85

Annex

"Somos Idea"	*Uruguay*	No. 649/84
Song Ki Won	*Republic of Korea*	No. 730/86
Soviet scientists of Jewish origin who have filed applications to emigrate	*Union of Soviet Socialist Republics*	No. 645/84
Students expelled or suspended from the University of Zambia	*Zambia*	No. 489/82
Sushil Chandra Amatya	*Nepal*	No. 778/88
Syndicat national de la recherche et de l'enseignement supérieur	*Ivory Coast*	No. 473/82
Tai Solarin	*Nigeria*	No. 652/84
Tariq Ahsan	*Pakistan*	No. 539/83
Teachers belonging to the National Union of Secondary School Teachers of Côte d'Ivoire	*Côte d'Ivoire*	No. 768/87
Tengku Muhammad Usman Lampoh Awé	*Indonesia*	No. 487/82
Tomislav Ferdo Vlasich	*Yugoslavia*	No. 655/84
"Tribune Amplia"	*Uruguay*	No. 648/84
Truong Van Quynh	*Socialist Republic of Viet Nam*	No. 764/87
Twenty-eight personalities in the world of culture	*Islamic Republic of Iran*	No. 581/83
Twenty female activists for peace	*Hungary*	No. 641/84
Ulises Gómez	*Chile*	No. 601/84
Ulrike Poppe	*German Democratic Republic*	No. 640/84
Uros Bukumira	*Yugoslavia*	No. 772/87
Václav Benda	*Czechoslovakia*	No. 443/82
Valery Godyak	*Union of Soviet Socialist Republics*	No. 643/84
Various works by contemporary Soviet authors	*Union of Soviet Socialist Republics*	No. 759/87
Vicka Ivanoković	*Yugoslavia*	No. 655/84
Victor Blik	*Union of Soviet Socialist Republics*	No. 643/84
Victor Hugo de la Fuente	*Chile*	No. 577/83
Victoria Dragomir	*Romania*	No. 494/82
Victor Rapray Robles	*Peru*	No. 440/82
Victor Ulices Sandoval Alvarez	*Chile*	No. 439/82
Victor Yelistratov	*Union of Soviet Socialist Republics*	No. 462/82
Violation of human rights in El Salvador	*El Salvador*	No. 477/82
Violations of human rights committed by Israel against the Lebanese and Palestinian peoples	*Israel*	No. 491/82
Violations of human rights in El Salvador	*El Salvador*	No. 477/82
Vladimir Brodsky	*Union of Soviet Socialist Republics*	No. 643/84
Vladimir Lenin Chávez Rodriguez	*Chile*	No. 516/83
Vladimir Lifshits	*Union of Soviet Socialist Republics*	No. 726/86
Vladimir Marković	*Yugoslavia*	No. 685/85
Vladimir Raiz	*Union of Soviet Socialist Republics*	No. 441/82
Vladimir Raiz	*Union of Soviet Socialist Republics*	No. 500/82
Vladimir Yurevich Poresh	*Union of Soviet Socialist Republics*	No. 692/85

Annex

Withdrawal of academic diplomas	*Union of Soviet Socialist Republics*	No. 519/83
Withdrawal of academic diplomas and degrees	*Union of Soviet Socialist Republics*	No. 519/83
Živojin Živković	*Yugoslavia*	No. 687/85
Životа Živković	*Yugoslavia*	No. 687/85
Yolanda Catalina Ibarra Chávez de Chassale	*Uruguay*	No. 460/82
Yoon Jae Chul	*Republic of Korea*	No. 730/86
Yosif Z. Begun	*Union of Soviet Socialist Republics*	No. 536/83
Yosif Z. Begun	*Union of Soviet Socialist Republics*	No. 720/86
Yuli Edelshtein	*Union of Soviet Socialist Republics*	No. 728/86
Yuri Fedorovich Orlov	*Union of Soviet Socialist Republics*	No. 527/83
Yuri Hronopulo	*Union of Soviet Socialist Republics*	No. 643/84
Yuri Medvedkov	*Union of Soviet Socialist Republics*	No. 643/84

Executive Board
Two hundred and fourth session

United Nations
Educational, Scientific and
Cultural Organization

204 EX/CR/2
PARIS, 6 March 2018
Original: French

Distribution limited

COMMITTEE ON CONVENTIONS AND RECOMMENDATIONS

Item 17 of the provisional agenda

INFORMATION DOCUMENT

SUMMARY

This information document* comprises two parts:

I. Procedures for the examination of reports from Member States on the implementation of UNESCO's standard-setting instruments

II. Procedures for the examination of communications concerning the exercise of human rights in UNESCO's fields of competence

* At its 149th session (22 April-3 May 1996), the Executive Board decided that the Committee's procedural practice and the statistical information on its activities would be updated every two years, for the first session following the renewal of the membership of the Executive Board and of the Committee, in other words at the beginning of each biennium. At its 182nd session (7-23 September 2009), the Board requested the Secretariat to continue to update, every two years, the document that collates all texts relating to the two aspects of the Committee's terms of reference. This document updates and supplements document 199 EX/CR/2 Rev.

INTRODUCTION

Nature and membership of the CR

1. After the election of new Members of the Executive Board by the General Conference, the Board establishes from among its Members the permanent commissions and committees necessary to assist it in the execution of its tasks (Rule 16.1 of the Rules of Procedure of the Executive Board). The Committee on Conventions and Recommendations (CR) is one of the permanent subsidiary bodies of the Executive Board.[1] For 2017-2019, it is composed of 30 members from all the electoral groups: Finland, France, Greece, Italy and Spain (Group I); Albania, Bulgaria, Lithuania, Russian Federation and Slovenia (Group II); Cuba, Jamaica, Nicaragua, Paraguay and Venezuela (Bolivarian Republic of) (Group III); Bangladesh, China, Malaysia, Pakistan and Philippines (Group IV); Burundi, Ethiopia, Madagascar, Senegal and Zambia (Group V(a)); Egypt, Jordan, Morocco, Qatar and Sudan (Group V(b)).

2. The CR meets, in principle twice a year on the occasion of the sessions of the Executive Board. Extraordinary sessions may also be convened when the Executive Board considers it necessary.

Mandate of the CR

3. The mandate entrusted to the CR has two complementary components:

(a) on the one hand, the Committee considers all questions entrusted to the Executive Board concerning the implementation of UNESCO's standard-setting instruments, in accordance with Article 18.1 of the Rules of Procedure concerning recommendations to Member States and international conventions; accordingly, the CR examines reports received from Member States (Part I);

(b) on the other hand, the Committee examines communications relating to cases and questions concerning the exercise of human rights in UNESCO's fields of competence (Part II).

---

1 For more details on the background and development of this Committee, see the booklet "The Executive Board of UNESCO", 2018 edition.

I. PROCEDURES FOR THE EXAMINATION OF REPORTS FROM MEMBER STATES ON THE IMPLEMENTATION OF UNESCO's STANDARD-SETTING INSTRUMENTS

4. In accordance with Article VIII of the Constitution, each Member State submits to the Organization, at such times and in such manner as may be determined by the General Conference, reports on the action taken on recommendations and conventions.

5. At its 15th session, the General Conference invited the Executive Board "to make appropriate arrangements for reports by Member States on the implementation of conventions or recommendations to be examined by a subsidiary organ of the Board ..." (15 C/Resolution 12.2). The subsidiary organ in question is the CR.

6. At its 23rd session, the General Conference recommended to the Director-General that the draft questionnaires or forms sent to Member States with a view to the preparation of their reports should be submitted to the CR (23 C/Resolution 29.1).

7. At its 32nd session (2003), the General Conference in 32 C/Resolution 77 decided to amend Part VI of the Rules of Procedure concerning recommendations to Member States and international conventions, which now provides that the Executive Board, and in particular the Committee on Conventions and Recommendations, shall examine the reports on conventions and recommendations that it requests from Member States, with the exception of standard-setting instruments that provide for a specific monitoring mechanism. The CR reports on its work in this respect to the General Conference, ultimate addressee of reports from Member States.

8. At the request of the members of the Committee, a list of the conventions and recommendations that then fell within the competence of the Committee was drawn up by the Secretariat. The list comprises eight conventions (instead of the two in the previous system) and no less than 31 recommendations (instead of five formerly).[2]

9. At its 171st session (April 2005), the Board decided to strengthen and give fresh impetus to the first feature of the Committee's

2 See document 171 EX/21, Annex I, and 164 EX/23, Annex B.

mandate concerning the implementation of the standard-setting instruments.

10. For the monitoring of the implementation of UNESCO conventions and recommendations for which no specific institutional mechanism is provided, the Executive Board adopted at its 177th session (177 EX/Decision 35.I) the specific multi-stage procedure reproduced below, as subsequently amended at its 196th session (196 EX/Decision 20):

Specific multi-stage procedure for the monitoring of the implementation of UNESCO conventions and recommendations for which no specific institutional mechanism is provided (adopted by the Executive Board at its 177th session and amended at its 196th session)

Stage 1: ***Frequency of submission of reports on the monitoring of the implementation of UNESCO conventions and recommendations for which no specific institutional mechanism is provided***

In accordance with the provisions of Article IV, paragraph 4, and Article VIII of the Constitution, reports shall be submitted every four years unless the General Conference, in the case of specific conventions or recommendations, decides otherwise.

In this respect, the Secretariat shall prepare, at the start of each biennium, a timetable for submission of Member States' reports on measures taken to implement the conventions and recommendations for the period under consideration, while drawing attention to the frequency and dates of submission to the UNESCO General Conference of monitoring reports on the implementation of these instruments.

Stage 2: ***Transmission of conventions and recommendations to Member States***

Pursuant to the provisions of the Rules of Procedure concerning recommendations to Member States and international conventions covered by the terms of Article IV, paragraph 4, of the Constitution, while transmitting a certified copy of any convention or recommendation to Member States, the Director-General will formally remind them of their obligation to submit the convention or recommendation in question to their competent national authorities in accordance with Article IV, paragraph 4, of the Constitution, and will also draw their attention to the difference in the legal nature of conventions and recommendations.

The Secretariat will ensure that the standard-setting texts adopted by the General Conference are widely disseminated to Member States and the public.

Stage 3: ***Establishment of reports for monitoring the effective implementation of conventions and recommendations***

(a) Consultations concerning conventions

The Secretariat shall submit to the Executive Board its proposals concerning the modalities of consultation of Member States on any measures they have respectively adopted pursuant to Article IV, paragraphs 4 and 6, and Article VIII of the Constitution. To this effect, it shall prepare draft guidelines for the preparation of reports based on the framework guidelines adopted by the Executive Board, to which the Secretariat will add, in view of the wide variety of UNESCO's standard-setting instruments, specific questions on which additional information is sought in the light either of the conclusions of the previous consultation or of the information available.

The Executive Board shall entrust the examination of these proposals to its Committee on Conventions and Recommendations (CR).

After the guidelines have been approved by the Executive Board, the Director-General will invite the Member States to submit their report on the action taken on the convention, within a period of six months. Each Member State must submit such a report pursuant to Article 17, paragraph 1, of the Rules of Procedure concerning recommendations to Member States and international conventions covered by the terms of Article IV, paragraph 4, of the Constitution.

(b) Collection of information concerning recommendations

The Secretariat will collect from Member States and National Commissions and from the various partners of the Organization such as non-governmental organizations (NGOs), information on the implementation of the recommendation in question.

This collection of information may be conducted on the basis of the model guidelines and after consultation with the Committee on Conventions and Recommendations of the Executive Board.

(c) Preparation of reports

With regard to the conventions, the Member States shall prepare reports, with the cooperation and support of the National Commissions, in accordance with the model guidelines approved by the Board. Within the limit of available resources, the guidelines may be made accessible on the Internet to Member States to enable them to draw up and submit their report to the Secretariat by electronic means.

With regard to the recommendations, the Secretariat will prepare a report on their implementation by the Member States, on the basis of the information collected, in particular with regard to national legislation.

(d) Technical assistance provided by the Secretariat to Member States

In order to reduce their workload, the Secretariat, with the support of the field offices, will provide Member States, at their request or at the request of the General Conference, with technical assistance, which will focus both on a better understanding of the objectives of the convention or recommendation in question and on practical procedures for the preparation of their reports, in particular, the collection of information and the drafting of the reports.

Stage 4: Consideration by the Executive Board of the reports for monitoring the effective implementation of conventions and recommendations

The Secretariat will submit to the Executive Board a summary of the reports received from Member States on the measures taken for the implementation of the conventions. The Executive Board may, if it so desires, ask the Secretariat to submit to it for consideration all the reports for each country.

With regard to recommendations, the Secretariat will submit its consolidated report on the implementation of these instruments, prepared on the basis of the information collected.

The documents prepared by the Secretariat will be examined by the Executive Board, which will entrust the task to the Committee on Conventions and Recommendations. The debates and work of the Executive Board and the CR Committee arising from their consideration of the reports will take place in public meetings.

The Executive Board will transmit these documents to the General Conference, together with its observations or comments and any that the Director-General may make, following their consideration by the Executive Board.

Stage 5: ***Decision of the General Conference concerning the reports for monitoring the effective implementation of conventions and recommendations***

The General Conference may take, as necessary, a decision with regard to the implementation of the conventions and recommendations.

The Director-General shall regularly inform the General Conference and the Executive Board with respect to the implementation of the decisions taken by the General Conference.

11. At that very same session, the Board also adopted (177 EX/Decision 35.II) framework guidelines for the preparation of reports on the implementation of conventions for whose monitoring the CR Committee is responsible, which is reproduced below as subsequently amended at its 196th session (196 EX/Decision 20):

Framework Guidelines (adopted by the Executive Board at its 177th session and amended at its 196th session)

I. Information on the legislative, judicial, administrative and other measures taken by the State at the national level

(a) Pursuant to Article IV, paragraphs 4 and 6, and Article VIII of the Constitution, each State may provide information on its status in respect of UNESCO's conventions by indicating whether it plans to accede to the instruments to which it is not yet Party or which it has signed but not yet ratified.[1]

(b) States should describe the specific legal framework governing the protection on their territory of the rights guaranteed by the UNESCO convention to which they are Parties. They should indicate, inter alia, whether the rights set forth in the convention are protected by their constitution, by a basic legislative text or by any other national provision, and whether the UNESCO convention has been incorporated into national legislation, and should make reference to the legal, administrative or other authorities competent in relation to the rights guaranteed by the convention and the scope of such competence.

II. Information on the implementation of the convention (with reference to its provisions)

This part of the report provides States with an opportunity to concentrate on more specific questions pertaining to the implementation of the instrument concerned. It should contain the information requested by the Committee on Conventions and Recommendations in its most recent guidelines for the preparation of reports, and should set out the specific measures taken to respond to any concerns expressed by the Committee in its observations made at the conclusion of the examination of the State Party's previous report.

(a) Convention against Discrimination in Education

States should provide detailed information on:

(i) the means employed to proscribe discrimination in education based notably on grounds specified in the Convention, and to ensure equality of treatment in education;

1 In the case of the conventions on education, States Parties may wish to include information transmitted to the United Nations treaty bodies on their endorsement of other international human rights standards, in particular when such information is directly related to States' implementation of the provisions of UNESCO's conventions. States could indicate if they are Parties to regional human rights instruments.

(ii) the measures taken to ensure equal opportunities in education (in terms of access, participation and completion) including gender parity in education, and to implement strategies and programmes in order to achieve in the country the full exercise by all of the right to education without discrimination or exclusion;

(iii) progress made with respect to ensuring universal access to primary and secondary education and access to higher education based upon individual capacity, including technical and vocational education and training, the measures taken to enhance the quality of education and the status of teaching personnel, and the means employed to protect the right of national minorities to carry out their own educational activities.

(b) Convention on Technical and Vocational Education

States should provide detailed information on:

(i) the measures taken to develop evidence-based policies, strategies and frameworks for technical and vocational education and training (TVET) to foster equitable and inclusive lifelong learning opportunities for all young people and adults, designed for young people and adults, in relation to changing contexts and development strategies, and respective education, labour and other systems, specifying how these measures ensure the involvement of all relevant stakeholders;

(ii) the measures taken to develop effective mechanisms for assessing current and future skills needs at the various territorial levels and/or by sectors, and the main approaches used on a systematic and regular basis, specifying the extent of participation of employers' and employees' organizations;

(iii) the measures taken for the governance, regulation, management and financing of TVET, specifying how far governing structures at various levels are intersectoral, and how these measures ensure the involvement of all relevant stakeholders, including through social dialogue, partnerships and networks;

(iv) the measures taken to transform and expand TVET in all its forms to address the great diversity of learning and training needs, and the measures taken to periodically review and improve the quality and relevance of TVET staff, programmes, qualifications and curricula, information, guidance and counselling;(v) the measures taken to facilitate international cooperation in the area of TVET, through knowledge sharing and making full use of international and national networks, and to support the mutual recognition of outcomes of learning experiences and qualifications;

(vi) the measures taken, in the context of changing demands, to improve the knowledge and research base for TVET, including through monitoring and evaluation tools and mechanisms, to monitor the impact of TVET on expected outcomes including employability, lifelong learning, and social equity, including gender equality, and sustainable development.

III. Methods introduced to draw the attention of the various authorities in the country to the instrument and to remove obstacles encountered

(a) The report should contain an assessment of the effectiveness of the methods introduced to draw the attention of the various authorities of the country to the instrument and to remove obstacles encountered. It should highlight the difficulties encountered in implementing the key provisions of the convention, and the legal and practical obstacles encountered by States in implementing the convention.

(b) States should describe briefly the main issues that need to be resolved in order to promote the implementation of the key provisions of the convention in the country, or what measures have been taken to launch an awareness-raising campaign and to promote ratification.

(c) States should describe the measures taken to raise awareness of the basic principles of the convention, including their translation into national and, where necessary, local languages, and their national or local dissemination, in particular to non-governmental organizations. States should specify the activities undertaken or supported by the National Commission with a view to promoting the convention and fostering debate on critical issues, in relation to the rights enshrined in the convention.

12. Since five of the eight conventions had been superseded by the advent of new technologies, the Board also decided at its 177th session that the framework would apply to the three remaining conventions that were still being monitored regularly, namely the 1960 Convention against Discrimination in Education, the 1970 Convention on the Means of Prohibiting and Preventing the Illicit Import, Export and Transfer of Ownership of Cultural Property, and the 1989 Convention on Technical and Vocational Education.

13. In addition, at its 34th session (2007), the General Conference, in 34 C/Resolution 87, decided that of UNESCO's 31 recommendations, the Executive Board would primarily monitor the following 11 recommendations (requiring monitoring as a matter of priority): the 1960 Recommendation against Discrimination in Education, the 1996 Recommendation concerning the Status of Teachers, the 1974 Recommendation concerning Education for International Understanding, Cooperation and Peace and Education relating to Human Rights and Fundamental Freedoms, the 1974 Recommendation on the Status of Scientific Researchers, the 1976 Recommendation on the Development of Adult Education, the 1978 Revised Recommendation concerning the International Standardization of Educational Statistics, the 1980 Recommendation concerning the Status of the Artist, the 1993 Recommendation on the Recognition of Studies and Qualifications in Higher Education, the 1997 Recommendation concerning the Status of Higher-Education Teaching Personnel, the 2001 Revised Recommendation concerning Technical and Vocational, and the 2003 Recommendation concerning the Promotion and Use of Multilingualism and Universal Access to Cyberspace.

14. It is to be noted that since the adoption of 177 EX/Decision 35 and 34 C/Resolution 87, a specific institutional monitoring mechanism has been provided for the 1970 Convention on the Means of Prohibiting and Preventing the Illicit Import, Export and Transfer of Ownership of Cultural Property, as an outcome of the second Meeting of States Parties to the 1970 Convention. Furthermore, the

General Conference adopted in 2011 the Recommendation on the Historic Urban Landscape, including a glossary of definitions, and in 2015 the Recommendation concerning Technical and Vocational Education and Training (TVET) (superseding the above-mentioned Revised Recommendation of 2001), the Recommendation on Adult Learning and Education (superseding the above-mentioned Recommendation of 1976), the Recommendation concerning the Protection and Promotion of Museums and Collections, their Diversity and their Role in Society, and the Recommendation concerning the Preservation of, and Access to, Documentary Heritage, including in Digital Form. Lastly, in 2017, the General Conference adopted the Recommendation on Science and Scientific Researchers (replacing the abovementioned 1974 Recommendation on the Status of Scientific Researchers). The CR Committee is thus responsible for monitoring the implementation of the following two conventions and 14 recommendations:

- Convention against Discrimination in Education (Paris, 14 December 1960),
- Convention on Technical and Vocational Education (Paris, 10 November 1989),
- Recommendation against Discrimination in Education (14 December 1960),
- Recommendation concerning the Status of Teachers (5 October 1966),
- Recommendation concerning Education for International Understanding, Cooperation and Peace and Education relating to Human Rights and Fundamental Freedoms (19 November 1974),
- Revised Recommendation concerning the International Standardization of Educational Statistics (27 November 1978),
- Recommendation concerning the Status of the Artist (27 October 1980),
- Recommendation on the Recognition of Studies and Qualifications in Higher Education (13 November 1993),
- Recommendation concerning the Status of Higher-Education Teaching Personnel (11 November 1997),
- Recommendation concerning the Promotion and Use of Multilingualism and Universal Access to Cyberspace (15 October 2003),

- Recommendation on the Historic Urban Landscape, including a glossary of definitions (10 November 2011),
- Recommendation on Adult Learning and Education (13 November 2015),
- Recommendation concerning Technical and Vocational Education and Training (TVET) (13 November 2015),
- Recommendation concerning the Preservation of, and Access to Documentary Heritage, including in Digital Form (17 November 2015),
- Recommendation on the Protection and Promotion of Museums and Collections, their Diversity and their Role in Society (17 November 2015),
- Recommendation on Science and Scientific Researchers (13 November 2017).

II. PROCEDURES FOR THE EXAMINATION OF COMMUNICATIONS CONCERNING THE EXERCISE OF HUMAN RIGHTS IN UNESCO'S FIELDS OF COMPTENCE

15. At the request of the General Conference, the Executive Board adopted in 1978 the procedure laid down in 104 EX/Decision 3.3, and assigned the implementation therefore to the CR (see the text of the decision annexed to this document). That procedure was supplemented by a set of principles, rules and lines of conduct known as "the procedural practice" adopted by the Committee over the years (see para. 46 and Annex II to this document).

16. It has often been pointed out in the course of debates within the CR that, in accordance with paragraph 7 of the decision, "the aim of the Committee was not to condemn the governments concerned, nor a fortiori to sanction them, but to improve the situation of the alleged victims".[3] Bearing in mind paragraph 14(k) of the decision, its members emphasized at the 155th session that "in exercising its mandate, the Committee endeavoured, for humanitarian reasons, to establish a dialogue with the governments concerned in order to

3 Report of the working group on the methods of work of the Committee on Conventions and Recommendations, document 156 EX/CR/2, paragraph 7.

consider with them what might be done to promote human rights falling within the competence of UNESCO by seeking an amicable solution to cases brought to its attention".[4] At the 185th session, after emphasizing that Procedure 104 had "succeeded in contributing to alleviating the suffering of several victims of human rights violations and that it constitutes a useful tool in this regard", the Executive Board stressed that the CR was "working towards dialogue and good offices as a way to resolve matters that negatively affect the practices of human rights within the fields of competence of UNESCO and that the Committee is not of a judicial nature" (185 EX/Decision 22).

17. It follows that a proper understanding of the CR's mandate, methods of work and specific characteristics, both by the representatives serving on the CR and by their respective governments, guarantees that its tasks will be discharged in accordance with its responsibilities. Further background information on the development of the procedure is provided in a document published by UNESCO in 2008 on the occasion of the 30th anniversary of 104 EX/Decision 3.3: "UNESCO's procedure for the protection of human rights: the legislative history of the 104 EX/3.3 Procedure".

Treatment of communications

(i) Preliminary measures

18. Any communication that appears at first sight to be covered by the provisions of 104 EX/Decision 3.3 is dealt with in the following way:

(a) the Secretariat sends a letter to the author of the communication describing the procedure laid down in 104 EX/Decision 3.3. The letter draws the author's attention to the conditions governing the admissibility of communications and asks him or her to fill in a form and sign a declaration agreeing to the examination of the communication in

4 See Report of the Committee on Conventions and Recommendations, document 155 EX/3 PRIV., paragraph 198.

accordance with the procedure (see Annexes III and IV to this document);

(b) the communication is then sent to the government concerned informing it that any reply it may wish to make will be brought to the notice of the Committee and that it may attend meetings of the Committee in order to provide additional information or answer questions;

(c) the communications are transmitted to the members of the Committee, accompanied, where appropriate, by the reply from the government concerned and additional information provided by the author.

(ii) Time limits

19. It is to be noted that 104 EX/Decision 3.3 does not provide for any time limit in respect of the aforementioned measures.

20. The Secretariat deals with the communications as and when they arrive. The principal working document for the CR is normally ready one month before the opening of the session. Subsequent communications and additional information are reproduced in an addendum to the main document.

21. In order to allow the government concerned to assess fully the communication concerning it, the Committee has decided that the government should have at least one month to consider it before the opening of the session and that communications and any correspondence relating thereto should in general be addressed preferably to the permanent delegates to UNESCO of the States concerned, under cover of a letter from the Secretariat.

22. This time limit, although observed in practice, is not a hard-and-fast one, since the representatives of the governments concerned sometimes agree to leave it to the Committee to produce a detailed decision, while declaring their readiness to consider a communication in accordance with an emergency procedure. Where such is not the case, the representative of the government concerned can always request that consideration of a communication should be postponed until the following session, even if the one-month time

limit has been observed, when the appropriate authorities in his or her country have not been able to decide on their position.

23. For the authors of communications, the cases they submit to UNESCO are always important and urgent or indeed tragic. They submit them to UNESCO with confidence, in the hope that they will find a solution. For this reason, care had been taken not to set too strict a time limit for the transmission to the members of the CR of communications or additional information. Accordingly, it had been considered preferable, if need be, to postpone consideration of a late communication to a future session rather than not submit it to the Committee.

24. At the 156th session, the members of the Committee, looking into possible ways of speeding up the decision on admissibility of a communication, decided that any government concerned would in future be required to make its position known within a time limit of three months after the Secretariat had transmitted a new communication to it, failing which the Committee would proceed without further delay to examine the admissibility of the communication (see paragraph 31 of this document).

(iii) Examination of communications by the CR

25. The Committee examines at every session, in a private meeting, the communications transmitted to it by the Director-General, and also examines at every session the cases already before the Committee, unless it decides otherwise. The Committee has before it a confidential document setting out all the communications by country and clearly showing the stage reached in the consideration of each communication. The Director-General, represented by the Office of International Standards and Legal Affairs, submits at the beginning of each session of the Committee an oral report summarizing the communications which have not been considered transmittable to the Committee under the terms of the conditions outlined in paragraph 14 (a) of 104 EX/Decision 3.3 and which have been removed according to paragraph 6 of the procedural practice contained in Annex II to this document. The Secretariat makes the necessary arrangements to ensure that the communications relating to member(s) of the Committee would be examined at the end of each daily meeting. At the start of the consideration of each

communication, the Office of International Standards and Legal Affairs submits a summary of each of the cases, providing the most recent information received and particularly any information not included in the documents. The representative of the government concerned is then invited to give the members of the CR his or her views on the communication or communications in question. The members of the Committee have the opportunity to ask questions or seek further information. Deliberation on the content of the decision to be taken for each communication takes place without the presence of the representative of the State concerned. At the 140th session, "The Committee decided that members of the Committee representing countries about which a communication has been raised should not be present for the private discussions leading to a decision and recommendations when communications concerning their own country are considered. This would ensure:

- equal treatment of all States;
- recognizing the principle that States cannot be both judges and judged at the same time;
- assisting decision-making by consensus;
- maintaining confidentiality."[5]

At the 196th session, on the occasion of examination of the Committee's methods of work, the members of the Committee emphasized the importance that the Committee attached to the transmission of additional written information by the author of the communication and the government concerned prior to the Committee's session, and were also in favour of limiting the speaking time for the various speakers during examination of each communication, as follows: (i) at the start of the consideration of each communication, the representative of the Director-General must endeavour to limit the summary of each case to a reasonable duration; (ii) subsequently, the representative of the government concerned would also be invited to limit the presentation of each case to a reasonable duration, with the exception of new communications; (iii) lastly, at the end of each presentation, any questions from members of the Committee should be limited to 3 minutes for each case if a reply was to be given.

5 Report of the Committee on Conventions and Recommendations: document 140 EX/3 PRIV., paragraphs 151-154.

The members of the Committee also considered that the Committee should, to the extent possible, combine examination of similar communications for the same country, subject to the agreement of the representative of the government concerned. In this case, the Committee could ask the representative of the Director-General to submit an overall summary for these similar communications.[6]

26. The Committee's first task is indeed to determine whether the conditions of admissibility listed in paragraph 14(a) of 104 EX/Decision 3.3 have been met. At the 185th session, the members of the Committee emphasized that the CR Committee applies the criteria for the admissibility to each case, within the framework of 104 Procedure.

27. Communications must in particular relate to violations of human rights lying within UNESCO's competence. Those rights, as expressed in the Universal Declaration of Human Rights, are the following:

- the right to education (Article 26);
- the right to benefit from scientific progress (Article 27);
- the right to participate freely in cultural life (Article 27);
- the right to information, including freedom of opinion and expression (Article 19).

To those rights are added others which constitute their indispensable complement, namely the right to freedom of thought and conscience (Article 18), the right to seek, receive and impart, regardless of frontiers, information and ideas by any means whatsoever (Article 19), the right to protection of the moral and material interests deriving from any scientific, literary or artistic production (Article 27), and the right to freedom of assembly and association (Article 20) for activities connected with education, science, culture or information.

28. Such communications must be submitted either by individuals or by groups of individuals and non-governmental organizations possessing reliable knowledge of such violations, or by a person or persons presumed to have suffered an alleged violation of human

6 Report of the Committee on Conventions and Recommendations: document 196 EX/36, paragraph 12.

rights as specified in the preceding paragraph. Such persons may include teachers, students, researchers, artists, writers and journalists; in short, intellectuals who on account of their activity come within UNESCO's fields of competence.

29. If the information supplied by the author of the communication is not such that the Committee can reach a decision on its admissibility, it can keep it on its agenda and seek additional information, in particular from the government of the State concerned, which is always invited to send a representative to the Committee.

30. It is not uncommon, during consideration of a communication's admissibility, for the Committee to examine its substance. There are several reasons for this. The conditions governing the admissibility of a communication are not all conditions of form. Certain conditions require at least a preliminary substantive examination. The same therefore applies, for example, to the question of UNESCO's competence, which, to be determined, often requires thorough examination. Secondly, in practice, ruling that a communication is admissible simply because the conditions governing admissibility are met does not necessarily make it easy to settle the case, and it may sometimes seem advisable not to do so while already actually considering, at least to some extent, the substance of the communication. Lastly, deferring in this way the ruling on the admissibility of a communication may make it possible for the dialogue with the States concerned to continue, and a fresh opportunity may thus be afforded to those States to find a satisfactory solution tending to favour the promotion of human rights within UNESCO's fields of competence.

31. At the 156th session, on the occasion of examination of the Committee's methods of work, some members maintained that a purely procedural admissibility decision merely meant that the communication could be examined by the Committee on the grounds that it met the criteria set out in 104 EX/Decision 3.3. It was after that procedural decision had been taken that the discussion as to substance was held with the government concerned. They therefore considered it necessary to speed up that decision-making process, which in some cases had been drawn out over several years. The Committee decided to give the government concerned three months in which to respond to the allegations contained in a communication. If the government concerned did not contest the admissibility

of a communication, the CR would decide on such admissibility at the first meeting devoted to the examination of the communication in question. If on the other hand the government concerned did contest admissibility, the Committee would obviously examine the arguments put forward by the government concerned and would endeavour to take a decision at the first meeting. The CR stressed, however, that in declaring a communication admissible it was in no way implying any condemnation of the government concerned.[7]

32. At the 171st session of the Executive Board, the Committee, examining its methods of work, decided that more attention should be paid to the application of the criteria of admissibility of communications so as to ensure greater clarity and improve the work of the Committee in that field. To that end, when a communication is declared admissible, the Committee should specify, in the light of 104 EX/Decision 3.3, the criteria and conditions underlying the decision of admissibility.[8] At the 196th session of the Board, the Committee recalled the above and also considered it necessary that the Secretariat specify the criteria that it used for screening of communications according to procedural practice in this field.[9]

33. Having declared a communication to be admissible, the CR continues to examine it as to its substance while endeavouring to find a solution in accordance with 104 EX/Decision 3.3, paragraph 7, which provides that, in matters concerning human rights within its fields of competence, UNESCO, basing its efforts on moral considerations and its specific competence, should act in a spirit of international cooperation, conciliation and mutual understanding, and should not play the role of an international judicial body.

(iv) The terminology and the wording used

34. The Secretariat makes every effort to reflect faithfully the position of the author and the position of the government concerned.

---

7 Report of the Committee on Conventions and Recommendations: document 156 EX/52, paragraphs 9 and 10.

8 Report of the Committee on Conventions and Recommendations: document 171 EX/61, paragraphs 16 to 18.

9 Report of the Committee on Conventions and Recommendations: document 196 EX/36, paragraph 12.

35. The wording used to express the CR's position, in particular the wording of its decisions, takes account of the essential fact that the CR is not a court and cannot become one. The wording is therefore deliberately not very juridical in character. Paragraph 14(k) of 104 EX/Decision 3.3 is significant in this regard. At the 144th session, it was pointed out that the "appeal for clemency" was motivated by humanitarian considerations in keeping with the spirit and letter of 104 EX/Decision 3.3. For this reason, while being aware of the need to conform to human rights usage, the CR has always been careful not to confine itself to an over-rigid terminology. Pursuant to the Committee's wishes expressed at the 147th session,[10] a list of wording used by the Committee in each particular situation has been compiled by the Secretariat (see Annex V to this document: thematic list of wording used in the decisions of the Committee on Conventions and Recommendations). At the 185th session, it was decided that the Committee shall endeavour to avoid standard formulae when drafting its decisions (185 EX/Decision 22).

(v) The special character of the CR's meetings[11]

36. The concern for effectiveness in the search for an amicable solution means that communications are examined in the strictest confidence, in the Committee and also in the Board when it examines the report of the Committee. Nothing has ever been done to make public cases that have been considered and/or settled. Nevertheless, the Board has examined a communication in public meeting at the Committee's request.

37. Members of the Board who are not members of the CR shall refrain from attending the Committee's meetings when it is considering communications, in accordance with paragraph 14(c) of 104 EX/Decision 3.3. This custom, based on a well-established practice of the Board, shall be drawn to the attention of all the Members of the Board at the first session following the renewal of the membership of the Executive Board and of the Committee.

10 Report of the Committee on Conventions and Recommendations: document 147 EX/53, paragraph 8.

11 Report of the Committee on Conventions and Recommendations: document 180 EX/63, paragraphs 2 to 11.

38. Members of the Board not members of the CR who, exceptionally, wish to have observer status shall submit their request in writing to the Chairperson of the Committee, who will transmit it to the Committee for examination. In the exceptional case when an observer is thus admitted to one of its meetings, such observer shall not be present for the private discussions leading to a decision on a communication nor for the adoption of the decisions (180 EX/Decision 29, Annex).

(vi) Cases and questions

39. Certain communications sent to UNESCO do not allege individual cases of violations of human rights but a series of violations of human rights, so that there is some doubt as to whether they constitute a "question" within the meaning of 104 EX/Decision 3.3, that is to say, "massive, systematic or flagrant violations of human rights and fundamental freedoms which result either from a policy contrary to human rights applied de jure or de facto by a State or from an accumulation of individual cases forming a consistent pattern". "Questions" should be considered, in accordance with 104 EX/Decision 3.3, "by the Executive Board and the General Conference in public meetings". At the 116th session, after a long debate on the various aspects of the procedure for the examination of questions, the Committee decided to apply the rules contained in paragraph 34 of the procedural practice (Annex II to this document). It will be noted that, to date, use has never been made of this procedure whose effect would be to remove the communication from the jurisdiction of the Committee.

(vii) Adoption of draft decisions and of the report

40. The CR adopts the recommendations that it wishes to make regarding the action to be taken on the communications submitted to it for examination. The formal adoption of draft decisions takes place 48 hours after examination of the communications. On that occasion, members of the Committee check whether the wording of the decisions corresponds to the deliberations.

41. In keeping with a well-established practice, at this stage all Committee members may attend the meeting, including the member(s)

concerned by a communication, without reopening the debate. CR members have considered that this practice should continue on the ground that the Committee is not a judicial body but a good offices body based on good faith.

42. At the end of its proceedings, the CR also adopts a confidential report containing the decisions that it has adopted and all relevant information arising from its examination of the communications which it considers desirable to bring to the notice of the Executive Board.

43. It is customary for the Board to take note of the narrative part of the report and to endorse the wishes expressed by the CR in its decisions.

(viii) Implementation of the CR's decisions

44. After the session, the author of the communication and the government concerned are informed of the Committee's decisions. The author of the communication receives a letter containing a summary of the position taken by the government concerned and the Committee's decision. A copy of the relevant part of the report is sent to the government concerned.

45. The Committee's decisions are final. The Committee does not, however, decline to give fresh consideration to a communication on the basis of additional information or new material.

(ix) The procedural practice of the CR

46. In considering communications, the CR has formulated certain principles, rules or lines of conduct for the implementation of 104 EX/Decision 3.3. These principles, rules or lines of conduct together constitute what is referred to as "the procedural practice" of the CR. Although neither systematic nor all-embracing, the rules thus laid down provide useful guidelines for dealing with cases where circumstances are similar. Annex II to this document, updated every two years, illustrates the content and scope of these guidelines.

(x) Cooperation and coordination with other organizations set up to protect human rights

47. The fact that a case is being examined within another organization in the United Nations system or by another international organization does not prevent the CR from examining it as well. At the Committee's request, the Secretariat has, in addition, often had occasion to contact other international organizations, particularly when dealing with the same cases, in order to obtain information or to agree on the distribution of tasks.

48. On the occasion of the examination of the CR's methods of work at the 156th session of the Executive Board, stressing the special character of UNESCO's procedure as compared with similar United Nations procedures, most members observed that those procedures were not incompatible but, rather, complementary. They did not wish to change the Committee's practice. The CR decided that when a communication submitted to it for examination was being or had already been examined by another body in the United Nations system, the Secretariat would check with that other body that there was no unnecessary duplication or incompatibility, having due regard, in particular, for the Committee's humanitarian aims. Should there be any doubt, the Secretariat would submit the question to the Committee.

49. On examination of its methods of work at the 171st session, the Committee decided that contact would be made with other international organizations, in particular when they were dealing with the same cases, so as to obtain additional information. At the 185th session, the Committee decided that the Secretariat shall strive to obtain from the international organizations that have competence for the protection of human rights complementary information on the cases that are the subject of communications and transmit it to the members of the Committee.

The specific characteristics of UNESCO's procedure

50. The procedure laid down in 104 EX/Decision 3.3 of the Executive Board of UNESCO has specific characteristics in comparison with similar procedures in other organizations of the United Nations system. At the 185th session of the Executive Board, the members of the Committee stressed that Procedure 104 was unique and at

the same time complementary to other mechanisms of the United Nations system responsible for protecting human rights.

51. In accordance with 104 EX/Decision 3.3, a complaint may be directed at any Member State, for the very reason that it is a member of UNESCO;[12] and the complaint will be examined under a procedure that will preserve its individual character from beginning to end.

52. It will also be noted that the various aspects of UNESCO's procedure are not, taken separately, either very original or very new. It is the combination of these aspects and the spirit in which they are applied that give the procedure its originality. While the other procedures seem most often to take a conflictual and accusatory form, the UNESCO procedure – although it is largely similar – has from the very beginning been deliberately applied exclusively with a view to seeking a solution with the State concerned. For this reason, everything has always been done to avoid reaching the conclusion that a State has violated human rights. Such a conclusion would in fact mean a deadlock, preventing the continued search for a solution. This is the background against which the many and varied stages of the procedure before the CR must be understood, since each stage represents a further level of dialogue with the State concerned and, consequently, another opportunity to find a satisfactory solution. The desire shown by the Committee to take its decisions solely by consensus is no doubt a reflection of the same concern.

53. However, what is perhaps the overriding characteristic of the UNESCO procedure is the emphasis, or indeed the insistence, on its strictly confidential nature, even after cases have been settled. No publicity has ever been given to the successes achieved through the UNESCO procedure, in order to sustain the confidence of the State concerned and secure its cooperation. The desire for confidentiality has even been taken to the point of declaring inadmissible those communications whose confidentiality had clearly been breached by their authors.

54. However, confidentiality does not mean that any interested party cannot be fully informed about the procedure. Indeed the UNESCO monthly publication Sources has devoted a special issue to human

12 In practice, even non-Member States of UNESCO have of their own accord agreed to a communication concerning them being considered by the Committee.

rights and the CR's procedure (No. 16, June 1990). UNESCO's Internet site (http://www.unesco.org/en/la/cr) provides an outline of the procedure. At the 185th session, the Committee decided to invite the Director-General to enhance the visibility of 104 Procedure by making this procedure more easily accessible on the official website of UNESCO and by ensuring the promotion of the procedure by other appropriate means. At the 196th session, the members of the Committee also requested the Secretariat to send a circular every two years to the National Commissions encouraging them to bring the 104 procedure to the attention of bodies likely to be interested in it, such as non-governmental organizations.

55. At the 171st session of the Executive Board, the Committee examined its methods of work and decided that the documents of the Committee would be published or made accessible to the public after a period of 20 years, as provided for by Rule 29, paragraph 4, of the Rules of Procedure of the Executive Board, so as to ensure that the Committee's achievements were more widely known.

56. Among legal writings, the articles published by five members of the Committee, namely Mr Francesco Margiotta Broglio (Italy), member of the CR until 2014, Mr Georges-Henri Dumont (Belgium), Chairman of the CR from 1987 to 1989, Mr Karl Joseph Partsch (Germany), member of the CR until 1993, Mr Klaus Hüfner (Germany), member of the Committee until 2011, and Mr Pierre Michel Eisemann (France), are particularly interesting.[13]

---

13 F. MARGIOTTA BROGLIO, *"Protezione internazzionale dei diritti dell' uomo nei settori di competenza dell' UNESCO"* [International protection of human rights in UNESCO's fields of competence]. *Rassegna Quadrimestrale della Commissione Nazionale Italiana per l'UNESCO*, 1985, No. 3, p. 8-17.
G.H. DUMONT, "UNESCO's practical action on human rights". *International Social Sciences Journal*, vol. 122 (1989), p. 651-660.
K.J. PARTSCH, *La mise en œuvre des droits de l'homme par l'UNESCO*. Annuaire français de droit international, XXXVI, 1990, p. 482-506.
K.J. PARTSCH and K. HÜFNER, *UNESCO Procedures for the Protection of Humans Rights*. Human Rights: International Protection, Monitoring, edited by J. Symonides, Ashgate & UNESCO, 2003, p. 111-132.
K. HÜFNER, "How to File Complaints on Human Rights Violations", edited by the German Commission for UNESCO, 2000, p. 70-80, new edition: 2002, p. 79-88 as well as a CD-ROM, 2005.
K. HÜFNER, "UNESCO und Menschenrechte" [UNESCO and human rights]. Politikwissenschaft, Band 3, 2008, p. 21-78.
The German and the French Commissions for UNESCO. Claiming Human Rights: Guide to International Procedures Available in Cases of Human

57. The CR's competence to examine individual communications alleging violations of human rights in UNESCO's fields of competence has been gradually recognized by practically all UNESCO's Member States, and an increasing number of the governments concerned by the communications send representatives to the Committee and cooperate with it although they are under no legal obligation to do so. This is a tribute to the procedure established by the Executive Board in 104 EX/Decision 3.3 and to the way in which it has been applied for 40 years.

58. In establishing the terms of reference of the CR, the Executive Board recalled and confirmed the role that the Director-General has always played with regard to the promotion of human rights. In accordance with well-established practice, the Director-General has had occasion through the right of intercession vested in him by the General Conference, in particular in 19 C/Resolution 12.1, personally to make various humanitarian representations on behalf of persons who have allegedly been victims of human rights violations in UNESCO's fields of competence and whose cases have called for urgent consideration. Paragraphs 8 and 9 of 104 EX/Decision 3.3 recognize the important role of the Director-General in this regard:

"*8. Recognizing the important role of the Director-General, in:*

(a) seeking, continually to strengthen the action of UNESCO in the promotion of human rights, both through the settlement of cases and the elimination of massive, systematic or flagrant violations of human rights and fundamental freedoms; and,

(b) initiating consultations, in conditions of mutual respect, confidence and confidentiality, to help reach solutions to particular problems concerning human rights.

Rights Violations in Africa. Co-published by the national French and German Commissions for UNESCO with the support of the Foreign Offices of France and Germany on the occasion of the 60th anniversary of the Universal Declaration of Human Rights, July 2009. This publication is available at the following address: http://www.claiminghumanrights.org.

P. M. EISEMANN, "Quelques observations sur une procédure discrète de promotion des droits de l'homme : la « procédure 104 » de l'UNESCO" in "*L'homme dans la société internationale, Mélanges en hommage au professeur Paul Tavernier*", ed. Jean-François Akandji-Kombé, Bruylant, 2013, p. 707-732.

9. Invites the Director-General to pursue this role."

At the 185th session, the Committee decided to invite the Director-General to use her/his good offices in order to facilitate the emergence of solutions concerning the cases under examination by the Committee.

Summary of the results of the application of the procedure laid down by 104 EX/Decision 3.3

59. From 1978 to September 2017, 602 communications were considered by the Committee on Conventions and Recommendations. The results concerning alleged victims (or groups of alleged victims) for this period may be broken down as follows:

released before completion of sentence	231
released after completion of sentence	27
authorized to leave their country to go to study or teach	21
authorized to return to their country	35
able to resume their employment or activity falling within UNESCO's fields of competence	30
able to resume a banned publication or broadcast programme	14
able to resume normal life following a cessation of threats	5
able to benefit from changes in certain education laws which were discriminatory towards ethnic or religious minorities	16
able to obtain passports and/or grants, or to receive diplomas	12
able to resume studies	9
Total	**400**

(The remaining 202 cases concern communications that are inadmissible or whose examination has been suspended or is under way.)

ANNEX I

104 EX/DECISION 3.3

3.3 STUDY OF THE PROCEDURES WHICH SHOULD BE FOLLOWED IN THE EXAMINATION OF CASES AND QUESTIONS WHICH MIGHT BE SUBMITTED TO UNESCO CONCERNING THE EXERCISE OF HUMAN RIGHTS IN THE SPHERES OF ITS COMPETENCE, IN ORDER TO MAKE ITS ACTION MORE EFFECTIVE: REPORT OF THE WORKING PARTY OF THE EXECUTIVE BOARD (104 EX/3)

The Executive Board,

1. Mindful that the competence and role of UNESCO in the field of human rights derive primarily from Article I.1 of the Constitution of UNESCO, which states: "The purpose of the Organization is to contribute to peace and security by promoting collaboration among the nations through education, science and culture in order to further universal respect for justice, for the rule of law and for the human rights and fundamental freedoms which are affirmed for the peoples of the world, without distinction of race, sex, language or religion, by the Charter of the United Nations", and from the Charter of the United Nations,

2. Recalling the Universal Declaration of Human Rights, the international covenants on human rights and the various conventions and recommendations adopted by UNESCO,

3. Recalling 19 C/Resolution 6.113 concerning UNESCO's responsibilities in the field of human rights,

4. Recalling also 19 C/Resolution 12.1: "UNESCO's contribution to peace and its tasks with respect to the promotion of human rights and the elimination of colonialism and racialism – long-term programme of measures whereby UNESCO can contribute to the strengthening of peace"; and in particular paragraph 10 of the resolution, which invites the Executive Board and the Director-General:

   (a) "to examine with particular attention the general situation with regard to respect for human rights throughout the world in UNESCO's fields of competence;

(b) to study the procedures which should be followed in the examination of cases and questions which might be submitted to UNESCO concerning the exercise of human rights in the spheres to which its competence extends, in order to make its action more effective;

(c) to continue to establish, with a view to the implementation of subparagraphs (a) and (b), close cooperation and coordination with the relevant United Nations organs so as to take advantage of their work and the lessons that can be learned from them in this field";

5. Having considered the report of a working group of the Board set up by virtue of 102 EX/Decision 5.6.2 to carry out an in-depth study of document 102 EX/19, the analytical summary of discussions that took place at the 102nd session of the Board, and additional written comments provided by members of the Board,

6. Mindful of Article I.3 of the Constitution of UNESCO, which states: "With a view to preserving the independence, integrity and fruitful diversity of the cultures and educational systems of the States members of the Organization, the Organization is prohibited from intervening in matters which are essentially within their domestic jurisdiction".

7. Considering that, in matters concerning human rights within its fields of competence, UNESCO, basing its efforts on moral considerations and its specific competence, should act in a spirit of international cooperation, conciliation and mutual understanding; and recalling that UNESCO should not play the role of an international judicial body,

8. Recognizing the important role of the Director-General, in:

(a) seeking, continually to strengthen the action of UNESCO in the promotion of human rights, both through the settlement of cases and the elimination of massive, systematic or flagrant violations of human rights and fundamental freedoms, and,

(b) initiating consultations, in conditions of mutual respect, confidence and confidentiality, to help reach solutions to particular problems concerning human rights,

9. Invites the Director-General to pursue this role;

10. Considering that, in the exercise of its competence in the field of human rights, UNESCO is called upon to examine:

   (a) cases concerning violations of human rights which are individual and specific,

   (b) questions of massive, systematic or flagrant violations of human rights which result either from a policy contrary to human rights applied de jure or de facto by a State or from an accumulation of individual cases forming a consistent pattern,

11. Considering the terms of reference of the Committee on Conventions and Recommendations in Education,

12. Taking into account the tasks already entrusted to the Committee concerning human rights matters within the Organization's fields of competence,

13. Decides that the Committee will henceforth be designated "the Committee on Conventions and Recommendations";

14. Decides that the Committee will continue to carry out its functions with respect to conventions and recommendations and will consider communications received by the Organization concerning cases and questions of violations of human rights within UNESCO's fields of competence in accordance with the following conditions and procedures:

Conditions

(a) Communications shall be deemed admissible if they meet the following conditions:

   (i) the communication must not be anonymous;

   (ii) the communication must originate from a person or a group of persons who, it can be reasonably presumed, are victims of an alleged violation of any of the human rights referred to in paragraph (iii) below. It may also originate from any person, group of persons or non-governmental organization having reliable knowledge of those violations;

   (iii) the communication must concern violations of human rights falling within UNESCO's competence in the fields of education, science, culture and information and must not be motivated exclusively by other considerations;

(iv) the communication must be compatible with the principles of the Organization, the Charter of the United Nations, the Universal Declaration of Human Rights, the international covenants on human rights and other international instruments in the field of human rights;

(v) the communication must not be manifestly ill-founded and must appear to contain relevant evidence;

(vi) the communication must be neither offensive nor an abuse of the right to submit communications. However, such a communication may be considered if it meets all other criteria or admissibility, after the exclusion of the offensive or abusive parts;

(vii) the communication must not be based exclusively on information disseminated through the mass media;

(viii) the communication must be submitted within a reasonable time limit following the facts which constitute its subject matter or within a reasonable time limit after the facts have become known;

(ix) the communication must indicate whether an attempt has been made to exhaust available domestic remedies with regard to the facts which constitute the subject matter of the communication and the result of such an attempt, if any;

(x) communications relating to matters already settled by the States concerned in accordance with the human rights principles set forth in the Universal Declaration of Human Rights and the international covenants on human rights shall not be considered.

Procedures

(b) The Director-General shall:

(i) acknowledge receipt of communications and inform the authors thereof of the above-mentioned conditions governing admissibility;

(ii) ascertain that the author of the communication has no objection to his communication, after having been communicated to the government concerned, being brought to the notice of the Committee, and to his name being divulged;

(iii) upon receipt of an affirmative answer from the author of the communication, transmit the communication to the government concerned, informing it that the communication will be brought to the notice of the Committee, together with any reply the government may wish to make;

(iv) transmit the communication to the Committee, together with the reply, if any, of the government concerned and additional relevant information from the author, taking into account the need to proceed without undue delay;

(c) the Committee shall examine in private session the communications transmitted to it by the Director-General;

(d) the Committee shall decide on the admissibility of communications in accordance with the above-mentioned conditions;

(e) representatives of the governments concerned may attend meetings of the Committee in order to provide additional information or to answer questions from members of the Committee on either admissibility or the merits of the communication;

(f) the Committee may avail itself of the relevant information at the disposal of the Director-General;

(g) in consideration of a communication, the Committee may, in exceptional circumstances, request the Executive Board to authorize it under Rule 29[1] of the Rules of Procedure to take appropriate action;

(h) the Committee may keep a communication submitted to it on its agenda while seeking additional information it may consider necessary for the disposition of the matter;

1 Currently Article 30.

(i) the Director-General shall notify the author of the communication and the government concerned of the Committee's decision on the admissibility of the communication;

(j) the Committee shall dismiss any communication which, having been found admissible, does not, upon examination of the merits, appear to warrant further action. The author of the communication and the government concerned shall be notified accordingly;

(k) communications which warrant further consideration shall be acted upon by the Committee with a view to helping to bring about a friendly solution designed to advance the promotion of the human rights falling within UNESCO's fields of competence;

15. Decides further that the Committee shall submit confidential reports to the Executive Board at each session on the carrying out of its mandate under the present decision. These reports shall contain appropriate information arising from its examination of the communications which the Committee considers it useful to bring to the notice of the Executive Board. The reports shall also contain recommendations which the Committee may wish to make either generally or regarding the disposition of a communication under consideration;

16. Decides to consider confidential reports of the Committee in private session and to take further action as necessary in accordance with Rule 28[2] of the Rules of Procedure;

17. Decides also that communications transmitted to it by the Committee which testify to the existence of a question shall be dealt with in accordance with paragraph 18 below;

18. Considers that questions of massive, systematic or flagrant violations of human rights and fundamental freedoms – including, for example, those perpetrated as a result of policies of aggression, interference in the internal affairs of States, occupation of foreign territory and implementation of a policy of colonialism, genocide, apartheid, racialism, or national and social oppression – falling within UNESCO's fields of competence should be

2 Currently Article 29.

considered by the Executive Board and the General Conference in public meetings;

19. Decides to consider at its 105th session the report to be made by the Executive Board and the Director-General to the General Conference, at its twentieth session, on the implementation of Part II of 19 C/Resolution 12.1.

(104 EX/SR.6, 7)

Annex II

PROCEDURAL PRACTICE OF THE COMMITTEE ON CONVENTIONS AND RECOMMENDATIONS

[References between square brackets are to the relevant provisions of 104 EX/Decision 3.3]

1. The Committee is not a judicial or quasi-judicial body

[para. 7] This principle is constantly recalled by the Committee when a government asserts that the Committee cannot set itself up as a supreme international court with the power to review the final judgments passed by the competent courts of Member States. The Committee has stated that its sole object is, for purely humanitarian reasons, to establish dialogue with the governments concerned in order to consider with them what might be done on behalf of alleged victims in the event of their having suffered from violations of human rights in UNESCO's fields of competence. The Committee's aim is to promote those rights by seeking a friendly solution to human problems. Its work consists in seeking information and facilitating conciliation.

At the 185th session of the Executive Board, the members of the Committee stressed that the Committee was working towards dialogue and good offices as a way to resolve matters that negatively affected the practices of human rights within the field of competence of UNESCO and that the Committee is not of a judicial nature.

I. CONDITIONS OF ADMISSIBILITY OF COMMUNICATIONS

2. The concept of "reliable knowledge"

[para. 14(a)(ii)] A communication may originate from the presumed victims of an alleged violation of human rights and from any person or group of persons or non-governmental organizations having reliable knowledge of those violations. On the matter of "reliable knowledge", it has been noted that in all legal systems good faith is presumed. It has been considered that this rule should also apply in respect of the condition of admissibility provided for in paragraph 14(a)(ii).

3. When the profession of the alleged victim comes within UNESCO's fields of competence, there is a presumption at the stage of examination as to admissibility that there exists a link between the alleged violation and UNESCO's fields of competence

[para. 14 (a) (iii)] Such is the practice of the Committee, which has made it clear that this presumption cannot be considered to be a decisive factor justifying UNESCO's intervention. It counts only for the admissibility of the communication. UNESCO's competence is then determined *rationae personae*, according to the status of the alleged victim. Whenever there has been uncertainty as to that status, the alleged victim has always been given the benefit of the doubt.

4. The activity of which the alleged victim is accused, and not necessarily his or her profession, is decisive in determining whether or not a communication is admissible

[para. 14 (a) (iii)] The Committee laid down this principle when considering a communication concerning an alleged victim whose profession did not, on the face of it, have any link with of a manual worker who had published articles). It is by virtue of this principle that the Committee asks the government concerned for further information about the grounds on which the alleged victim has been convicted or in order to establish whether the activities of which he or she was accused included incitement to violence.

5. Rights that do not per se come within UNESCO's fields of competence

[para. 14 (a) (iii)] (a) Right of movement: Though this right, which is a fundamental human right, does not per se come within UNESCO's fields of competence, it might nevertheless do so when its exercise is linked to activities that do come within those fields, as for example going abroad in order to study, teach or engage in research. With regard to problems affecting the movement of scientists and other categories of persons within its fields of competence, the Committee considered at the 155th session that, while it could not remain indifferent to such problems, UNESCO was not the appropriate forum for examining communications concerning the granting of visas by a government to citizens of a foreign country which was a matter pertaining to national sovereignty.

(b) Right to emigrate: The Committee has decided that this right does not per se come within UNESCO's fields of competence. The admissibility of a communication concerning this right should be determined on the basis of other criteria, i.e. the profession of the alleged victim, and in the light of additional information provided by the government concerned and by the author of the communication.

(c) Right to freedom of association: On one occasion, the Committee decided that a communication that had been submitted to it did not come within its competence because it hinged on the exercise of the right to freedom of association per se and should consequently be declared inadmissible. It nevertheless requested the representative of the government concerned to inform the relevant authorities in his country of the humanitarian concerns voiced by some of its members.

(d) The problem of compensation for an alleged victim does not fall within UNESCO's competence.

6. Prior selection of communications by the Secretariat

[para. 14 (a) (iii)] In principle, the Secretariat is not authorized to weed out communications except in cases specified by the Committee, namely:

(a) Allegations manifestly not within UNESCO's competence. At the 105th session, the Committee decided to allow the Director-General to "proceed with a preliminary analysis of communications in order to exclude those which manifestly do not relate to the competence of UNESCO".

[para. 14 (a) (v)] (b) Allegations manifestly ill-founded or whose authors are mentally unbalanced. The Committee decided to authorize the Secretariat "not to deal with communications whose authors are mentally unbalanced or which are manifestly ill-founded". However, in 1996 the Committee reasserted the principle that, when in doubt, the Secretariat must inform the Chairperson of the Committee, who decides whether the communication should be transmitted to the Committee.

In addition, some communications submitted to the Committee for consideration contain, in part, material not concerning UNESCO's fields of competence. Since it is "free to judge certain parts of a communication inadmissible while accepting other parts", the Committee has had occasion to ask the Secretariat to review such communications in order to eliminate from them allegations not concerning human rights within the Organization's competence.

At the 182nd session of the Executive Board, the Committee requested the Secretariat to give the members of the CR Committee, in addition to the list of communications on its roll, a reasoned summary of the communications excluded by the Secretariat on the basis of present paragraph 6 of the procedural practice.

At the 185th session of the Board, the members of the Committee decided that the representative of the Director-General shall present, at the beginning of each session of the Committee, an oral report which summarized the communications which had not been considered transmissible to the Committee under the terms of the conditions outlined in paragraph 14 (a) of 104 EX/Decision 3.3 and which had been removed according to the present paragraph 6 of the procedural practice.

At the 196th session of the Board, the Committee considered that the Secretariat should specify the criteria that it used for screening of communications according to procedural practice in this field.

7. Emergency: derogation from certain human rights in accordance with Article 4 of the International Covenant on Civil and Political Rights

[para. 14 (a) (iv)] The Committee has recognized that, in accordance with Article 4 of the International Covenant on Civil and Political Rights, a State may, in time of public emergency, derogate from certain human rights to the extent strictly required by the exigencies of the situation. Consequently, it is not required to consider communications relating to such situations.

8. When there is doubt within the Committee regarding the condition laid down in paragraph 14(a)(v) of 104 EX/Decision 3.3 (a communication must not be manifestly ill-founded and must contain relevant evidence), the Committee asks the Secretariat to transmit the information provided by the government concerned to the author

[para. 14 (a) (v)] It should be made clear in this connection that the information supplied by the government concerned is transmitted to the author in summary form only after the Committee has taken cognizance of it. The Secretariat is thus not empowered to transmit that information upon receiving it. The Committee has also had occasion to ask the Secretariat to transmit to the author a record of its discussions concerning the communication *in extenso*, as contained in its report.

9. When a communication contains material calling into question the foundations of a Member State it is declared inadmissible

[para. 14 (a) (vi)] This concerns cases where, for example, the communication contains slanderous and offensive attacks against the social structure, constitution and legislation of a state.

As submitted, the communication cannot be considered, it being understood that the author of the communication might subsequently submit an amended communication not calling into question the foundations of a Member State.

10. The Committee concerns itself only with actual and not potential violations of human rights

[para. 14 (a) (vi)] A communication that concerns only a potential violation of human rights and not an actual violation is declared inadmissible. The Committee cannot presume in advance that a human rights violation might occur (e.g. case of a person living abroad who wanted to go back to his country but feared that criminal proceedings would be instituted against him on his return, when it could not be known whether the authorities concerned would indeed prosecute him if he returned).

11. It is the allegations contained in the communication form that must not be based exclusively on media reports

[para. 14 (a) (viii)]

12. A communication must be submitted within a reasonable time limit following the facts which constitute its subject matter or within a reasonable time limit after the facts have become known

[para. 14 (a) (viii)] A communication that has not been submitted within a reasonable time limit following the facts which constitute its subject-matter or after the facts have become known is declared inadmissible.

13. The author of a communication must indicate whether steps have been taken to exhaust all possible domestic remedies and what their outcome has been

[para. 14 (a) (ix)] Since the Committee is not a court of law, the author of a communication is not obliged to have exhausted domestic remedies, but to indicate whether steps have been taken to obtain them. The Committee has agreed that it should be flexible in this regard. Consequently, and contrary to the procedure applied by other authorities, a communication could therefore be admissible under the procedure established in 104 EX/Decision 3.3, even if domestic remedies have not been exhausted.

14. Submission of a communication to the CR or to another body in the United Nations system

[para. 14 (a) (ix)] At the 156th session of the Executive Board, most members of the Committee stressed the special character of UNESCO's procedure as compared with similar United Nations procedures, observing that those procedures were not incompatible but, rather, complementary. They did not wish to change the Committee's practice. The Committee specified that when a communication submitted to it for examination was being or had already been examined by another body in the United Nations system, the Secretariat would check with that other body that there was no unnecessary duplication or incompatibility, having due regard, in particular, for the Committee's humanitarian aims. Should there be any doubt, the Secretariat would submit the question to the Committee.

At the 171st session of the Executive Board, the Committee decided that contact would be made with other international organizations, in particular when they were dealing with the same cases, so as to obtain additional information.

At the 185th session of the Board, after stressing that 104 Procedure is unique and at the same time complementary to other mechanisms of the United Nations system responsible for protecting human rights, the members of the Committee decided that the Secretariat shall strive to obtain from the international organizations whose field of competence was the protection of human rights complementary information on the cases that are the subject of communications, and transmit it to the members of the Committee.

15. A communication considered to be settled may be struck by the Committee from its list, subject to the Secretariat receiving confirmation of the reason why the communication had been considered to be settled (e.g. confirmation that the alleged victim has indeed been authorized to return to his or her country)

[para. 14 (a) (x)] The Committee stated when adopting this decision that if such confirmation did not reach the Secretariat by the next session, the communication would then be placed on the agenda of the next session of the Committee.

16. Communication struck from the list ipso facto in the event of there being no reply from its author

[para. 14 (a) (x)] In cases where the author of the communication does not reply to requests for further information made by the Committee, the practice of the Committee is to grant a period of grace and to strike the communication from its list only if the author still fails to reply. This rule is valid even in cases where the government concerned has never produced any comments. The Committee has also had occasion to request the Secretariat to notify the author of a communication that, should he fail to seek administrative or judicial redress in the country concerned, notwithstanding having been informed of this by the Committee, it would strike the communication from its list ipso facto at its next session. At the 185th session of the Executive Board, the members of the Committee decided that the Committee might suspend the examination of a communication whose author has not transmitted new information during four successive sessions, but may resume its examination at any time.

II. PROCEDURES

17. Time limits for the transmission of an additional communication or additional information to the governments concerned

[para. 14 (b) (iii)] The Committee has taken the view that any further communication or additional information transmitted by the author of a communication to the Secretariat should reach the government concerned at least one month before the Committee's session. Otherwise, the representative of the government concerned should be able to ask for the communication not to be considered until the following session, to enable the relevant authorities in his or her country to determine their position in the light of this new or additional information. At the 156th session of the Executive Board, the Committee having decided that any government concerned would in future be required to make its position known within a time limit of three months after the Secretariat had transmitted a new communication to it, the time limit for transmission of the communication is modified.

18. Agreement of the Committee to a request to consider a communication submitted urgently on account of the seriousness of the matter

[para. 14 (b) (iv)] The Committee has made it clear in this connection that prior submission of the form is by no means a condition of admissibility. The sole purpose of the form is to make it easier for the author of the communication to set out his or her complaints and for the Committee to examine the communication.

19. Need to preserve the confidential character of communications

[para. 14 (c)] Confidentiality is considered to be essential for the success of the Committee's action. In cases where this principle is not observed by the author of the communication, it is up to the Committee to decide whether such indiscretion constitutes an abuse of the right to submit communications under the terms of paragraph 14(a) (vi) of 104 EX/Decision 3.3 and then to strike the communication from its list, as a kind of penalty. In practice, communications whose authors had clearly breached the confidential character of the procedure have been declared inadmissible (the Committee has sometimes instructed the Secretariat to remind the author of the need to preserve the confidential character of the Committee'swork).

At the 176th session of the Executive Board, the Committee encouraged the Director-General to take all necessary steps, based on the recommendations submitted to the Committee (confidential document 176 EX/CR/HR Add.2), to improve the security of procedures concerning the composition and distribution of the confidential documents, with a view to addressing the various concerns expressed by Committee members following the unauthorized disclosure of confidential information contained in CR documents.

20. A communication can only be declared admissible by express decision of the Committee

[para. 14 (d)] It is important to distinguish decisions on the "admissibility" of a communication, which are entirely the responsibility of the Committee, from those on the "transmissibility" of a complaint which, at the request of the Committee, are left to the discretion of the Secretariat. (See No. 6 above.)

21. Decision on the admissibility of a communication

At the 156th session of the Executive Board, the Committee stressed that in declaring a communication admissible it was in no way implying any condemnation of the government concerned. It was simply recognizing that the communication met the admissibility criteria set out in 104 EX/Decision 3.3 and that it might be examined as to its substance.

The Committee also agreed that, in order to speed up its decision-making on the admissibility of communications:

- any government concerned by a communication was required to make its position known within a time limit of three months after the Secretariat had transmitted a new communication to it, failing which the Committee would proceed without further delay to examine the admissibility of the communication;

- If the government concerned did not contest the admissibility of a communication, the CR would decide on such admissibility at the first meeting devoted to the examination of the communication in question. If on the other hand the government concerned did contest admissibility, the Committee would obviously examine the arguments put forward by the government concerned and would endeavour to take a decision at the first meeting.

At the 171st session of the Executive Board, the Committee decided that more attention should be paid to the application of the criteria of admissibility of communications so as to ensure greater clarity and improve the work of the Committee in that field. To that end, when a communication is declared admissible, the Committee should specify, in the light of 104 EX/Decision 3.3, the criteria and conditions underlying the decision of admissibility.

At the 185th session of the Executive Board, the members of the Committee emphasized that the CR Committee applies the criteria for the admissibility of communications to each case, within the framework of 104 Procedure.

At the 196th session of the Executive Board, on the basis of the outcomes of the examination of the working methods of the Committee at the 171st session, the Committee recalled that more attention should be paid to applying the admissibility criteria for communications to ensure greater clarity and improve the Committee's work in this field. In this regard, the Committee reaffirmed that when a communication was declared admissible the Committee should specify, in the light of 104 EX/Decision 3.3, the criteria and conditions underlying the admissibility decision.

22. The Committee may express its concern regarding a particularly serious case and still declare the communication inadmissible

[par 14 (d)] A communication may be struck from the Committee's list on the grounds that it does not satisfy the conditions for admissibility provided for in paragraph 14(a) of the decision (for instance, it does not come within one of UNESCO's fields of competence). However, the Committee can declare a communication inadmissible and at the same time express its strong concern about the seriousness of the human rights violation it refers to.

23. Cooperation of the government concerned

[para. 14 (e)] It is a constant rule of the Committee to invite the governments concerned to send representatives to the Committee, and they are always allowed to speak so that they can provide all the clarifications they consider appropriate. Even though the presence of a representative is not obligatory, the Committee has always considered it desirable that "solutions to human rights problems be sought through dialogue with the governments concerned". The Committee has therefore constantly drawn the attention of the governments concerned to the importance it attached to the presence of a representative.

Lack of cooperation from the government concerned has often prompted the Committee to request the Chairperson of the Committee or the Director-General to take steps to obtain the attendance of a government representative or at least a letter.

On one occasion, having noted for the third time that the government concerned by a communication had not replied or sent a representative, the Committee declared the communication to be admissible, after stressing that the procedure did not expressly require that government's attendance. It stated, however, that it should not be inferred from this that, in future, other communications would be automatically admitted when the government concerned did not send a representative. There has also been a case of the Committee considering submitting an individual report to the Executive Board so as to obtain the cooperation of the government concerned. At the 157th session, given the silence of the authorities, which on two occasions had not seen fit to reply to the letters which, at the Committee's request, the Director-General had addressed to the President of the Republic and to the Ambassador, Permanent Delegate of a country concerned, and failing any additional information supplied at the session by the representatives of the government concerned, the Executive Board, on the Committee's proposal, examined the communication in question at a private meeting, inviting the representative of the government concerned, in accordance with Rule 30, paragraph 3, of its Rules of Procedure.

24. Members of the Committee who represent the states concerned by a communication should not be present during the private discussions leading to a decision or to recommendations concerning that communication

[para. 14 (e)] This principle was clearly established at the 140th session of the Executive Board. The concern is to "ensure equal treatment of all states, recognizing the principle that states cannot be both judges and judged at the same time, assisting decision-making by consensus and maintaining confidentiality".

25. The Committee may defer consideration of a communication until it receives additional information regarding it

[para. 14 (h)] A communication may be kept on the Committee's agenda and consideration of it suspended until such time as a national court reaches a decision.

The Committee may request information on a communication from other United Nations bodies, and from bodies such as the International Committee of the Red Cross or the Inter-American Commission on Human Rights.

On various occasions the Committee has found itself unable to continue consideration of a communication because it has not obtained sufficient information. In such cases, the Committee has decided to put the communication "on hold", that is, to suspend consideration of it while maintaining it on its list, it being understood that it would be put before the Committee again if new information were provided.

26. Efforts to find a friendly solution

[para. 14 (k)] With the aim of seeking a humanitarian solution, on a friendly basis, to a case brought to its attention, the Committee has decided on several occasions to invite the Director-General, the Chairperson of the Committee or the Chairperson of the Executive Board to use their good offices, to consult or approach the governments concerned with appeals for clemency or to make contact with them with a view to achieving the desired result. The Committee has on four occasions decided to send a mission of good offices, with the agreement of the governments concerned.

At the 185th session of the Executive Board, the members of the Committee invited the Director-General to use her/his good offices in order to facilitate the emergence of solutions concerning the cases under examination by the Committee.

27. The Committee is vested with discretionary powers for the examination of a communication

[para. 14 (k)] The Committee has had occasion to recall this basic principle. Accordingly, when acceding to the request of one government to postpone examination of a communication until its next session, the Committee specified that that decision did not constitute a precedent, reserving the right to examine communications whether or not the governments concerned were represented.

28. Agreement of the Committee to the request to withdraw a communication made by its author

[para. 14 (k)] The Committee has had occasion to agree to withdraw a communication at the request of its author. It stressed, however, that this could not serve as a precedent for automatically granting such requests. The Committee reserves the right to check that the author has not come under any pressure. In such cases, the withdrawal must be regarded as a friendly solution within the meaning of paragraph 14(k) of 104 EX/Decision 3.3.

29. Fresh allegations justify the re-examination of a communication declared inadmissible

The Committee's decisions, in particular those declaring a communication inadmissible, are final. Nevertheless, the Committee does not refuse to re-examine a communication previously declared inadmissible if new facts relating to it are brought to its notice. In that event, the Secretariat must ask the author to fill out a new form.

30. Changes in the circumstances under which a communication had been submitted

If a number of circumstances that were relevant when the communication was submitted have changed in the meantime, the Committee has decided to suspend consideration of the communication in its present formulation.

31. The Committee strikes from its list cases of alleged violations of human rights concerning persons whose death has been proved, in view of the fact that its intervention could have no result

32. A government is normally responsible for the safety of its citizens and of all those under its jurisdiction

During the examination of communications relating to a period of disturbance in which the government concerned was not able to control a situation, the question has arisen of whether the alleged violations could be imputed to the government concerned. The

Committee has not been unconcerned by such situations and has considered that, "without taking any decision having the force of a rule ..., a government is normally responsible for the safety of its citizens and of all those under its jurisdiction".

33. The Committee is the only subsidiary body of the Executive Board empowered to take its own decisions (the others restricting themselves to making recommendations to the Board)

[para. 16]

Although the Executive Board can modify neither the decisions nor the narrative part of the Committee's report, Members of the Board can nevertheless comment on the Committee's report and ensure that the position of the representatives of the governments concerned is reflected accurately in the minutes of the Board session. The Executive Board takes note and may or may not endorse the decisions contained in the Committee's report, regardless of whether or not they are intended to have effect. If it disagrees with a decision by the Committee it can request it to reconsider the case.

34. Questions

[para. 10 (b), 17 and 18]

At the 116th session of the Executive Board, the Committee decided that:

(a) the sources of information for the purpose of deciding whether to describe a communication as a "question" would be the individual communications received by the Organization and such relevant information as the Director-General might provide, either at the request of the Committee or on her own initiative;

(b) the decision as to the designation of a communication as a "question" would be taken by the Committee only after a full examination of the substance of the communication, and then only if it was not possible to reach the friendly solution contemplated in paragraph 14(k) of 104 EX/Decision 3.3;

(c) it was for the Executive Board to decide whether or not to examine in public meetings any "question" forwarded to it by the Committee, but that in any event the Committee should be extremely cautious before deciding to forward a matter as a "question" to the Board and should do so only as a last resort.

Consequently, the Committee has always stressed the need to submit communications referring by name to individual cases.

35. Statistics on the procedure

At the 171st session of the Executive Board, the Committee decided, while recalling the principle of confidentiality which dominated the entire 104 EX/Decision 3.3 procedure, that the private documents of the Committee should be published or made accessible to the public after a period of 20 years, as provided for by Rule 29, paragraph 4, of the Rules of Procedure of the Executive Board, in order to give a higher profile to the Committee's achievements.

ANNEX III

STANDARD LETTER SENT BY THE OFFICE OF INTERNATIONAL STANDARDS AND LEGAL AFFAIRS TO THE AUTHORS OF COMMUNICATIONS EXAMINED UNDER 104 EX/DECISION 3.3

CONFIDENTIAL

...

On behalf of the Director-General, I acknowledge receipt of your letter of ... alleging violations of human rights. In so far as your communication concerns human rights falling within UNESCO's competence in the fields of education, science, culture or communication, it can be examined under the procedure approved by the Executive Board of UNESCO on 26 April 1978 in 104 EX/Decision 3.3, a copy of which is attached for your information.[1]

It must be stressed that in no case is UNESCO an international court nor can it become one. The rights falling within UNESCO's spheres of competence are essentially the following:

- the right to education (Article 26 of the Universal Declaration of Human Rights);
- the right to share in scientific advancement (Article 27);
- the right to participate freely in cultural life (Article 27);
- the right to information, including freedom of opinion and expression (Article 19).

These rights may imply the exercise of others, the most noteworthy of which are set out below:

- the right to freedom of thought, conscience and religion (Article 18);
- the right to seek, receive and impart information and ideas through any media and regardless of frontiers (Article 19);

1 This decision is reproduced in Annex I hereto.

– the right to the protection of the moral and material interests resulting from any scientific, literary or artistic production (Article 27);

– the right to freedom of assembly and association (Article 20) for the purposes of activities connected with education, science, culture and information.

In accordance with 104 EX/Decision 3.3, I wish to draw your attention to the conditions governing admissibility, which must be met before UNESCO can take action on your communication. They are listed in paragraph 14(a) of 104 EX/Decision 3.3. In order to enable the Director-General to complete the file on your communication, you are invited to fill in the enclosed form[2] and to return it to UNESCO, duly signed by yourself, as soon as possible.

The allegations should be set out in a concise statement, specifying which of the human rights is/are considered to have been violated and which of UNESCO's fields of competence is/are concerned. The date of the decisions complained of and the authority which took them should be clearly indicated, including, in particular, whatever legal remedies have been used (for instance, recourse to the courts in the country concerned) and the results of such action. There should also be an indication as to whether another international procedure has been used and, if so, before what body, the date on which the matter was referred to it and any results of this procedure.

You will notice that you are asked whether you have any objection to your name being divulged and to your communication being brought to the notice of the UNESCO Executive Board Committee on Conventions and Recommendations, after it has been transmitted to the government concerned. Failing an affirmative answer from you on this point, no action on your communication can be taken by UNESCO under the aforementioned decision.

Accept ... the assurances of my highest consideration.

Office of International Standards
and Legal Affairs

2 The form is reproduced in Annex IV hereto.

ANNEX IV

UNESCO

CONFIDENTIAL

UNESCO

FORM FOR COMMUNICATIONS CONCERNING HUMAN RIGHTS TO BE SUBMITTED TO UNESCO

For UNESCO use only:

Number of communication: ☐

Date of communication:
Date of dispatch of this form:

To be filled in by the author of the communication:

I. INFORMATION CONCERNING THE AUTHOR

Name: First name(s):

Nationality: Profession:

Date and place of birth:

Present address:

Address to be used for correspondence (if other than the present address)

Indicate, by ticking the appropriate box, in what capacity you are acting:

☐ victim of the violation or violations described below

☐ representative of the victim or victims of the violations described below

☐ person, group of persons or non-governmental organization with reliable knowledge of the violations described below

☐ In another capacity. Specify

II. INFORMATION CONCERNING THE VICTIM OR VICTIMS OF THE ALLEGED VIOLATIONS*

☐ If the author is the victim, tick here and pass directly to Part III.

Give the following particulars for each victim, adding as many pages as necessary.

Name: First name(s):
Nationality: Profession:
Date and place of birth:
Present address or whereabouts:

III. INFORMATION CONCERNING THE ALLEGED FACTS

Name of the country considered by the author to be responsible for the alleged violation.

Human rights allegedly violated (refer, if possible, to the Universal Declaration of Human Rights, the International Covenant on Economic, Social and Cultural Rights and the International Covenant on Civil and Political Rights).

Connection between the alleged violation and education, science, culture or information.

Facts of the claim.

IV. INFORMATION CONCERNING MEANS OF REDRESS USED

What steps have been taken to exhaust domestic remedies (recourse to the courts or other public authorities), by whom, when and with what results?

.

Has the matter been submitted to another international authority concerned with protection of human rights? If so, when and with what results?

V. PURPOSE AND AIM OF THIS COMMUNICATION

* N.B. This information is essential in cases where the communication concerns one or more individuals and specific cases of violation of human rights.

VI. DECLARATION BY THE AUTHOR

Does the author agree to his communication being examined in accordance with the procedure approved by the Executive Board of UNESCO in 104 EX/ Decision 3.3 and, in particular, is he willing for his name to be divulged and for the communication to be transmitted to the government concerned and brought to the notice of the UNESCO Executive Board Committee on Conventions and Recommendations?

☐ Yes ☐ No

Date:
Name, first name
Signature of author:

ANNEX V

THEMATIC LIST OF WORDING USED IN THE DECISIONS OF THE COMMITTEE ON CONVENTIONS AND RECOMMENDATIONS

INTRODUCTION

To facilitate decision-making by the Committee during the examination of communications, a list of wording used by the Committee is given below at the request of the Committee (147th session). For each situation, significant examples are given of the wording used in the past by the Committee in its decisions. Slight variations introduced by the Committee according to circumstances are also indicated.

I. COOPERATION OF THE GOVERNMENT CONCERNED WITH THE COMMITTEE

A. Examples of wording used by the Committee in situations in which the government concerned is cooperating with the Committee. The government has replied to the allegations of the author and has accepted the Committee's invitation to send a representative to attend the Committee's meetings

1. The Committee decided to thank the representative of the government concerned for his attendance and cooperation (147 EX/3 PRIV., para. 16).

2. The Committee decided to thank the representative of the government concerned for his attendance and his exemplary cooperation (131 EX/3 PRIV., para. 129).

3. The Committee decided to thank the representative of the government concerned for his attendance, cooperation and the information provided (146 EX/3 PRIV., para. 40).

4. The Committee decided to thank the government concerned for its spirit of cooperation in sending a representative to the Committee to enter into a dialogue (125 EX/3 PRIV., para. 15; 152 EX/3 PRIV., para. 75).

5. The Committee decided to express its appreciation for the attendance at the Committee of the Ambassador, Permanent Delegate of ... to UNESCO, the representative of the government concerned (154 EX/3 PRIV., para. 114).

6. The Committee decided to take note of the information which the government concerned had kindly supplied by letter and to thank its representative for his further clarifications (130 EX/3 PRIV., para. 70).

7. The Committee decided to note with interest the very detailed information provided by the representative of the government concerned, and the very full replies he gave to the many questions raised by members of the Committee (119 EX/35 PRIV., para. 185).

8. The Committee decided to take note of the statements by the representative of the government (137 EX/3 PRIV., para. 60).

9. The Committee decided to take note of the statements of the government concerned (117 EX/18 PRIV., para. 159).

10. The Committee decided to thank the representative of the government concerned for his attendance and cooperation, which reflected a significant change in the government's assessment of the Committee's competence in respect of human rights, and to express the wish that the dialogue thus initiated might continue (139 EX/3 PRIV., para. 180).

11. The Committee decided to thank the representative of the government concerned for his attendance and cooperation, which continued to reflect a growing recognition by the government of the Committee's competence in respect of human rights, and to express the wish that the dialogue might continue (140 EX/3 PRIV., para. 128).

B. Examples of wording used by the Committee in situations in which the government concerned has transmitted information in writing, but has not replied to the Committee's invitation to send a representative to attend its meetings

12. The Committee decided to thank the government concerned for the information it had provided by letter, while regretting that it had not sent a representative (130 EX/3 PRIV., para. 120).

13. The Committee decided to thank the government concerned for its letter, while again expressing its regret that it had once again been denied the benefit of the attendance of a representative of the government concerned, despite the wishes repeatedly expressed by the Committee (154 EX/3 PRIV., para. 138).

14. The Committee decided to express regret that the government concerned did not send a representative, and to take note of its letter of ... (147 EX/3 PRIV., para. 170).

15. The Committee decided to thank the representative of the government concerned for the very full information it had provided (142 EX/3 PRIV., para. 101).

16. The Committee decided to express its satisfaction at the information received (131 EX/3 PRIV., para. 144).

17. The Committee decided to thank the government concerned for its letter of ... (146 EX/3 PRIV., para. 222).

18. The Committee decided to thank the government concerned for its letters of ..., and to urge it to send a representative to attend the next session in order to hear the position of the government concerned and enable dialogue with the Committee (187 EX/3 PRIV., para. 167).

II. FAILURE OF THE GOVERNMENT CONCERNED TO COOPERATE WITH THE COMMITTEE

A. Examples of wording used by the Committee in situations in which the government concerned has not transmitted any information in writing and has not replied to the Committee's invitation

19. The Committee decided to express regret that it continued to be denied the presence and cooperation of a representative of the government concerned (144 EX/3 PRIV., para. 165).

20. The Committee decided to express its deep regret that it had once again been denied the benefit of the attendance of a representative of the government concerned, despite the wishes repeatedly

expressed by the Committee, a subsidiary organ of the Executive Board (152 EX/3 PRIV., para. 128).

21. The Committee decided to express its regret that no representative of that government had been able to attend its meeting, for that would have helped to initiate a fruitful dialogue (120 EX/15 PRIV., para. 109).

22. The Committee decided to express regret that the representative of the government concerned had not sent a representative (146 EX/3 PRIV., para. 144).

23. The Committee decided to express regret that the government concerned had not sent a representative (147 EX/3 PRIV., para. 97).

B. Examples of wording used by the Committee in situations in which the government concerned has not sent any information by letter and has repeatedly failed to reply to the Committee's invitation

(i) The Committee expresses its regret

24. The Committee decided to express its deep regret concerning this refusal to cooperate on the part of the government concerned (120 EX/15 PRIV., para. 208).

25. The Committee decided to express regret that the government concerned had again not seen fit to send a representative to the session (136 EX/3 PRIV., para. 15).

26. The Committee decided to express deep regret that it continued to be denied the presence and cooperation of a representative of the government concerned (146 EX/3 PRIV., para. 187).

27. The Committee decided deeply to deplore the persistent failure of the government concerned to be represented or to communicate any information (132 EX/3 PRIV., para. 177).

28. The Committee decided to deplore the persistent lack of interest shown by the government concerned in this communication (135 EX/3 PRIV., para. 41).

29. The Committee decided to deplore deeply the persistent failure of the government concerned to be represented or to communicate any information (147 EX/3 PRIV., para. 135).

(ii) The Committee urges the government concerned to cooperate

30. The Committee decided to urge the government concerned to cooperate with the Committee (135 EX/3 PRIV., para. 65).

31. The Committee decided once again to express regret that no representative of the government concerned had been present and again to urge the government to cooperate with the Committee, in particular by responding to the requests for information that the Committee had made to it at the previous sessions (136 EX/3 PRIV., para. 208).

(iii) The Committee stresses the importance of the participation of the government concerned

32. The Committee decided to reiterate to the government concerned that its failure to participate in the work of the Committee continued to cause the Committee great concern, for it considered that it was of the first importance to secure the active cooperation of the government in question in regard to its examination and analysis of this case (116 EX/48 PRIV., para. 285).

33. The Committee decided to request the Secretariat to call the attention of the authorities of the government concerned to the importance attached by the Committee to the presence of a representative of the government concerned by a communication at the meeting at which that communication would be examined so that, in accordance with 104 EX/Decision 3.3, paragraph 14(e), an open dialogue might be established with a view to achieving a friendly solution designed to advance the promotion of human rights (117 EX/18 PRIV., para. 92).

34. The Committee decided to draw the attention of the government concerned to the importance attached by the Committee to the attendance of a government representative (146 EX/3 PRIV., para. 137).

35. The Committee decided to reiterate the importance attached by the Committee to the attendance of a government representative (147 EX/3 PRIV., para. 97).

(iv) The Committee reminds the government concerned that the Committee is not a court of law

36. The Committee decided to point out to the government concerned that the Committee was not in any way trying to set itself up as an international supreme court, but was merely attempting, for purely humanitarian reasons, to establish a dialogue with the governments concerned in order to consider with them what might be done on behalf of alleged victims in the event of their having suffered violations of human rights in UNESCO's fields of competence (135 EX/3 PRIV., para. 156).

37. The Committee decided to remind the government concerned that the Committee had no ambition whatsoever to assume the authority of an international supreme court, but was simply endeavouring, for purely humanitarian reasons, to initiate a dialogue with the governments concerned in order to discuss what might be done on behalf of alleged victims in cases in which their human rights might have been violated in UNESCO's fields of competence (136 EX/3 PRIV., para. 208; 152 EX/3 PRIV., para. 139).

38. The Committee decided to recall that the Committee in no way set itself up as an international court of law, but that its aim was to promote human rights relating to UNESCO's fields of competence by seeking a friendly solution to specific human cases (134 EX/3 PRIV., para. 207).

(v) The Committee requests the Chairperson of the Committee or the Director-General to use their good offices

39. The Committee decided to ask its Chairperson to attempt to establish dialogue with the authorities of the country concerned (124 EX/3 PRIV., para. 168).

40. The Committee decided to express its regret that it had been unable to benefit from the presence of a representative of the

government concerned, and to request the Chairperson to send a letter in those terms to the permanent delegation of the government concerned (126 EX/3 PRIV., para. 203).

41. The Committee decided to express its regret at the continued failure of any representative of the government concerned to attend its meetings, despite the representations made to that end by its Chairperson at its request, to which there had been no response from the government (130 EX/3 PRIV., para. 53).

42. The Committee decided to request its Chairperson to pursue his efforts with the delegation of the government concerned in order to convey to the authorities of that country the importance attached by the Committee to the attendance of a representative of the government concerned by a communication (134 EX/3 PRIV., para. 75).

43. The Committee decided to ask its Chairperson to use his good offices with the ambassador of the country concerned (141 EX/3 PRIV., para. 181).

44. The Committee decided to request its Chairperson, given the urgency of the situation, to make representations to the Permanent Delegation of ... to UNESCO with a view to securing the cooperation of the government concerned, having regard to international human rights instruments (150 EX/3 PRIV., para. 88).

45. The Committee decided to request the Chairperson to make contact with the government concerned with a view to obtaining additional information on the alleged victim (144 EX/3 PRIV., para. 165).

46. The Committee decided to request the Director-General, in pursuance of paragraph 14(k) of 104 EX/Decision 3.3, to use his good offices to obtain greater collaboration in this matter from the government concerned (136 EX/3 PRIV., para. 161).

47. The Committee decided to request the Executive Board to ask the Director-General to use his good offices with the government concerned in order to secure new information ... on the alleged victim (121 EX/46 PRIV., para. 224).

48. The Committee decided to request the Director-General to continue his efforts to ensure that the government concerned cooperated in the case (149 EX/3 PRIV., para. 158).

49. The Committee decided to request the Director-General to write to the Head of Government concerned in order to draw his attention to the importance the Committee attaches to the attendance of a representative of the government concerned (152 EX/3 PRIV., para. 128).

(vi) The Committee may declare a communication admissible

50. The Committee decided to inform the government concerned that owing to the lack of adequate information, the Committee would be obliged at the next session to declare the communication admissible (131 EX/3 PRIV., para. 167).

51. The Committee decided that, failing receipt of the relevant information requested, it would be compelled at its next session to declare the communication admissible (127 EX/3 PRIV., para. 83).

52. The Committee decided to express its regret at having been denied the benefit of the attendance of a representative of the government concerned and at having received no information from it on this case and to declare the communication admissible (154 EX/3 PRIV., para. 192).

53. The Committee decided to express once again its regret that a representative of the government concerned had not been present and that it had received no information whatsoever, and to declare the communication admissible (131 EX/3 PRIV., para. 74).

54. The Committee decided to express regret that it continued to be denied the presence of a representative of the government concerned, and to declare this communication admissible (142 EX/3 PRIV., para. 139).

55. The Committee decided to declare the communication admissible, as the letter from the permanent delegation of the government concerned did not provide the information requested (131 EX/3 PRIV., para. 174).

(vii) The Committee decides to dispatch a mission of good offices

56. The Committee decided to request the Executive Board, after consultation with the government concerned and in agreement with it, to commission one of its members to visit ... and, with the assistance of the Director-General or his representative, to initiate discussions with the government concerned about the allegations made in the communications (120 EX/15 PRIV., para. 69).

(viii) On occasion, the Committee may consider submitting the communication to the Executive Board for public examination, in view of the persistent silence of the government concerned

57. The Committee decided to request the Secretariat to prepare a specific interim draft report for the Executive Board on this case (117 EX/18 PRIV., para. 207).

58. The Committee decided to ask the Secretariat to draw up a draft specific report for submission to the Executive Board in pursuance of paragraph 15 of 104 EX/Decision 3.3. This draft, together with an appropriate recommendation, will be examined and adopted by the Committee at the next session after being transmitted in advance to the government concerned for its comments and observations (115 EX/28 PRIV., para. 419).

59. The Committee decided that, in the absence of effective participation by the representative of the government concerned at the next session, it would be bound to consider as established the facts alleged in the communication and consequently to submit to the Executive Board a specific report on the case in question (119 EX/35 PRIV., para. 134).

60. The Committee informed the government concerned that, without its active cooperation and representation before the Committee, the Committee will decide at the next session to refer this communication to the Executive Board for public examination in accordance with the procedural practice of the Committee and for such further action as it deemed necessary (179 EX/3 PRIV., para. 226).

61. The Committee decided to recommend that the Executive Board, in accordance with 104 EX/Decision 3.3, paragraph 15, examine this communication in private meeting at the 157th session and to recommend also that the Board invite the representative of the government concerned in accordance with Rule 30, paragraph 3, of its Rules of Procedure (157 EX/3 PRIV., para. 115).

62. The Committee decided to request the Executive Board to examine this communication in the light of paragraph 16 of 104 EX/Decision 3.3 and to take further action as necessary (167 EX/PRIV., para. 274).

III. PRINCIPLE OF NON-INTERVENTION IN THE INTERNAL AFFAIRS OF STATES INVOKED BY THE GOVERNMENT CONCERNED

Examples of wording used by the Committee in situations in which the government concerned refers the Committee to the principle of non-intervention in a state's internal affairs:

63. The Committee decided to point out that the principle of non-interference in the internal affairs of states did not absolve those states of the duties incumbent on them as a result of their accession to the international instruments relating to human rights (136 EX/3 PRIV., para. 208).

64. The Committee decided to recall the procedure laid down in 104 EX/Decision 3.3, which defines the framework within which communications alleging violations of human rights in the fields of competence of UNESCO shall be dealt with by the Committee (134 EX/3 PRIV., para. 47).

65. The Committee decided to draw the attention of the government concerned to the international instruments relating to human rights to which that country is a party, in particular the International Covenant on Economic, Social and Cultural Rights and the International Covenant on Civil and Political Rights ... (135 EX/3 PRIV., para. 164).

66. The Committee decided to point out that respect for universally recognized fundamental human rights was a duty incumbent on the entire international community (139 EX/3 PRIV., para. 81).

67. The Committee decided to point out that the whole of the international community is duty-bound to respect fundamental universally recognized human rights; that those fundamental rights, enshrined in particular in the Universal Declaration of Human Rights, include the right to "freedom of opinion and expression; that this right includes freedom to hold opinions without interference and to seek, receive and impart information and ideas through any media"; and that the Universal Declaration of Human Rights admits only such limitations to the exercise of those rights as are determined by law, and then solely "for the purpose of securing due recognition and respect for the rights and freedoms of others and of meeting the just requirements of morality, public order and the general welfare" (140 EX/3 PRIV., para. 133).

IV. REQUESTS FOR FURTHER INFORMATION

A. Examples of wording used by the Committee in situations in which the Committee requires further information in order to continue its examination of a communication

68. The Committee decided to suspend the examination of this communication until further information was received (116 EX/48 PRIV., para. 129).

69. The Committee decided to defer consideration of the admissibility of this communication until the next session, in anticipation of the additional information which the representative of the government concerned proposed to provide (116 EX/48 PRIV., para. 34).

B. Examples of wording used by the Committee in situations in which the Committee is requesting the author of the communication to provide further information

70. The Committee decided to ask the author of the communication if he had further information to transmit to the Committee (130 EX/3 PRIV., para. 166).

71. The Committee decided to invite the author of the communication to bring up to date the information contained in it, to the extent that the situation of certain alleged victims seems to have changed (130 EX/3 PRIV., para. 172).

72. The Committee decided that it was necessary ... to ask the author of the communication to provide additional information, bearing in mind all the points raised in the Committee's discussion (119 EX/35 PRIV., para. 185).

73. The Committee decided to ask the author of the communication whether the alleged victim had engaged in scientific activities and could therefore be considered to be a scientist (137 EX/3 PRIV., para. 95).

74. The Committee decided to invite its Secretariat to ask the author of the communication about the grounds for its allegations (136 EX/3 PRIV., para. 104).

75. The Committee decided to request the author of the communication to supply more detailed information concerning the allegations (149 EX/3 PRIV., para. 99).

C. Examples of wording used by the Committee in situations in which the Committee is requesting further information from the government concerned

(i) Requests for general information

76. The Committee decided to request the government concerned to communicate to the Committee its observations concerning the allegations contained in Communication No. ... (135 EX/3 PRIV., para. 72).

77. The Committee decided to urge the government concerned to provide additional information concerning the alleged victim (144 EX/3 PRIV., para. 165).

78. The Committee decided to repeat the request for information it had addressed to the government concerned and to which the government had not yet replied (137 EX/3 PRIV., para. 163).

(ii) Requests for more specific information

79. The Committee decided to request the government concerned to provide it with additional information on the allegations (130 EX/3 PRIV., para. 13).

80. The Committee decided to request the government concerned to provide it with more detailed information on the factual and legal bases for the alleged victim's conviction (131 EX/3 PRIV., para. 85).

81. The Committee decided to make an immediate appeal to the government concerned to provide detailed information, particularly concerning the state of health of the alleged victim (144 EX/3 PRIV., para. 89).

82. The Committee decided once again to urge strongly the government concerned to provide more specific information on the factual and legal grounds for the convictions of the alleged victims, the conditions of their detention and their state of health (135 EX/3 PRIV., para. 13).

83. The Committee decided to request the government concerned to provide it with further information: about the conditions of the alleged victim's detention and the place where he was being held; about his state of health; about the offence he was said to have committed, particularly whether in expressing his opinions he had advocated violence; about the nature of his detention (whether administrative or penal) (135 EX/3 PRIV., para. 80).

84. The Committee decided to ask the government concerned also to let it know if the alleged victim had acted violently or preached violence while expressing his political opinions (135 EX/3 PRIV., para. 19).

85. The Committee decided to repeat its request to the government for information regarding the precise reasons for the alleged victim's being convicted, in particular whether he had been found guilty of violence or incitement to violence (130 EX/3 PRIV., para. 120).

86. The Committee decided to ask the government concerned to be good enough to provide details regarding the reasons for the alleged victim's sentence, and, more especially, whether the "counter-revolutionary" activities imputed to him included incitement to

violence, since it was the activity, which the alleged victim was accused of and not necessarily his profession, which was essential in determining the admissibility of the communication (130 EX/3 PRIV., para. 35).

87. The Committee decided to request the government concerned, in view of the extreme inadequacy of the information available on this case, to provide further particulars, firstly, regarding the precise grounds for the severe sentence passed on the alleged victim, and in particular as to whether he had simply made peaceful use of his right to freedom of expression or whether he had advocated violence, and, secondly, regarding the opportunities open to him to lodge an appeal (130 EX/3 PRIV., para. 135).

88. The Committee decided to request the government concerned to provide more precise information about the offence committed by the alleged victim and about the grounds of his sentence (145 EX/3 PRIV., para. 134).

89. The Committee decided to repeat its request for information particularly regarding the offence committed by the alleged victim and the grounds of his sentence (147 EX/3 PRIV., para. 105).

90. The Committee decided to request the government concerned to provide more detailed information on the alleged offence of the alleged victim, the sentence normally meted out for this offence and the domestic remedies available (130 EX/3 PRIV., para. 81).

91. The Committee decided to request the government concerned to provide it, before the next session, with additional and updated written information on the situation of the alleged victim, in particular on the precise facts for which he had been convicted, and written replies to the questions raised by the members of the Committee during the session and listed in the report (191 EX/3 PRIV., para. 238).

92. The Committee requested the government concerned to provide it, before the next session, with further written information on the situation of the alleged victim, in particular on his state of health as well as the cause and nature of the disciplinary measures taken against the alleged victim (200 EX/3 PRIV., para. 169).

93. The Committee decided to request the government concerned to provide the verdicts relating to this case in order to enable it to gain a better understanding of the situation (136 EX/3 PRIV., para. 77).

94. The Committee decided to request the government concerned to tell the Committee what steps had been taken to trace the alleged victim (135 EX/3 PRIV., para. 87).

95. The Committee decided also to request information from the government regarding the stage reached in the lawsuit still in progress (130 EX/3 PRIV., para. 120).

96. The Committee decided to request the government concerned to keep it informed of the final decisions taken by the military and civilian authorities with regard to the alleged victim (131 EX/3 PRIV., para. 21).

97. The Committee decided to request the government concerned to inform the Committee of the results of the recourse procedure concerning the alleged victim (145 EX/3 PRIV., para. 68).

D. Examples of wording used by the Committee in situations in which the Committee is requesting further information from other international or regional human rights bodies (United Nations bodies, the International Committee of the Red Cross, the Inter-American Commission on Human Rights)

98. The Committee decided to ask the Secretariat to seek more concrete information from other organs of the United Nations regarding this case (144 EX/3 PRIV., para. 165).

99. The Committee decided to request the Secretariat to make contact again with the United Nations Working Group on Enforced or Involuntary Disappearances in order to obtain any information it might have received (136 EX/3 PRIV., para. 104).

100. The Committee decided to request the Secretariat to ask the United Nations Working Group on Enforced or Involuntary

Disappearances to inform it of the reasons for its decision to close the file on this case (135 EX/3 PRIV., para. 87).

101. The Committee decided to request its Secretariat to approach the United Nations Commission on Human Rights[1] in order to obtain information on the current situation in the country concerned (136 EX/3 PRIV., para. 87).

102. The Committee decided to request the Secretariat to obtain from the United Nations Commission on Human Rights[2] any available information concerning these allegedly missing persons (130 EX/3 PRIV., para. 166).

103. The Committee decided to instruct the Secretariat to contact the International Committee of the Red Cross to ask it whether, at the Committee's request, it could investigate through its regional delegate the disappearance of the alleged victim (116 EX/48 PRIV., para. 81).

104. The Committee decided to invite the Secretariat once more to ask the International Committee of the Red Cross to make representations through its delegations in the countries concerned in an attempt to retrace the alleged victim's itinerary in those countries prior to his disappearance (130 EX/3 PRIV., para. 53).

105. The Committee decided to request the Secretariat to contact the International Committee of the Red Cross in order to obtain any available information on the case (192 EX/3 PRIV., para. 272).

106. The Committee decided to request the Secretariat to collect all possible information from the Inter-American Commission on Human Rights, to which the case had also been submitted (124 EX/3 PRIV., para. 84).

1 Pursuant to resolution A/RES/60/251 adopted on 3 April 2006 by the United Nations General Assembly, the Commission on Human Rights has been replaced by the Human Rights Council.

2 Idem.

V. PERSISTENT FAILURE TO REPLY TO REQUESTS FOR INFORMATION

A. Examples of wording used by the Committee in situations in which the Committee has not received from the author of the communication information for which it has made repeated requests

107. The Committee decided to give the author one last opportunity to reply, if he so wished, and to re-examine the case at the next session only in the event of the author providing this reply (116 EX/48 PRIV., para. 306).

108. The Committee decided to invite its Secretariat to make one last attempt to contact the author of the communication, who had remained silent since ... despite various promptings by the Committee, and to inform her that, failing some response on her part, the Committee would be compelled to strike the communication from its list (135 EX/3 PRIV., para. 41).

109. The Committee requested again the author of the communication to provide it with information on the case, in the absence of such information the Committee may decide to suspend further consideration of the communication at the next session (181 EX/3 PRIV., para. 25).

110. The Committee decided that, although the authors of the communication had been invited by registered letter to enter into contact with the Committee at four of the sessions, but had never done so, under those circumstances, it was not possible for it to continue to consider the communication, which should consequently be struck off its list (120 EX/15 PRIV., para. 215).

111. The Committee decided to strike the communication from its list, on the grounds of the continued silence of the author ... (141 EX/3 PRIV., para. 126).

112. The Committee decided to note that the author of the communication had not replied to the requests of the Committee and to strike this communication from its list (154 EX/3 PRIV., para. 22).

113. The Committee decided to delete the case of the alleged victim from its list since no new information concerning him had been received by the Committee for a long time (122 EX/21 PRIV., para. 111).

114. The Committee decided to strike these communications from its list in view of the fact that their authors had provided no further information for several years, it being understood that new communications may be submitted to the Committee if the authors consider that it is necessary to do so (157 EX/3 PRIV., para. 133).

115. The Committee decided to suspend consideration of this communication on its list because the author has not provided any new information on this case for several sessions (182 EX/3 PRIV., para. 27).

B. Examples of wording used by the Committee in situations in which, following repeated requests for further information made over very many sessions, the Committee finds itself unable to continue consideration of the communication (the case is put "on hold" pending the receipt of new information)

116. The Committee decided to suspend consideration of the communication and to resume it only when it had received new information (134 EX/3 PRIV., para. 172).

117. The Committee decided to resume consideration of this communication as soon as new information was made available to it (142 EX/3 PRIV., para. 15).

118. The Committee decided to resume consideration of the admissibility of these communications at one of the forthcoming sessions, once new facts had been communicated to the Director-General (115 EX/28 PRIV., para. 262).

119. The Committee decided to note with satisfaction the information provided by the representative of the government concerned, and to keep the communication on its list, it being understood that it would be put before the Committee again only if new information

were provided either by the author of the communication or by the government concerned (117 EX/18 PRIV., para. 148).

120. The Committee decided to keep this communication on its list, but to resume consideration of it only at such time as new information came into its possession which would enable it to continue with its work (139 EX/3 PRIV., para. 123).

121. The Committee decided to keep the communication on its list, but to resume consideration of it only at such time as new information on the status of the independent investigation on the case by the Secretary-General of the United Nations was provided either from the author of the communication, from the government concerned, or from the United Nations (192 EX/3 PRIV., para. 171).

122. The Committee decided to resume consideration of this communication at such time as any information is provided by the International Committee of the Red Cross or the United Nations Working Group on Enforced or Involuntary Disappearances or new information is provided by the government concerned or the author of the communication regarding the alleged victim (192 EX/3 PRIV., para. 261).

123. The Committee decided to resume consideration of this communication at the next session, with a view possibly to examining it subsequently at every other session in the light of the content of the further written information requested from the government concerned (190 EX/3 PRIV., para. 25)

VI. ASSERTION BY THE COMMITTEE OF ITS COMPETENCE WITH REGARD TO A COMMUNICATION

Examples of wording used by the Committee in situations in which, before ruling on the admissibility of a communication, the Committee asserts its competence with regard to that communication

124. The Committee decided to assert its competence in principle with regard to this communication (144 EX/3 PRIV., para. 89).

125. The Committee decided on the basis of the facts at its disposal, to assert its competence to examine this communication (132 EX/3 PRIV., para. 80).

126. The Committee decided to reaffirm its competence regarding this communication, given the information currently at its disposal (146 EX/3 PRIV., para. 100).

VII. DECLARATION BY THE COMMITTEE OF THE INADMISSIBILITY OF A COMMUNICATION

Examples of wording used by the Committee in situations in which it declares a communication inadmissible

(i) The Committee decides to strike the communication from its list

127. The Committee decided to strike this communication from its list as not falling within the field of competence of UNESCO, in accordance with paragraph 14(a)(iii) of 104 EX/Decision 3.3 (135 EX/3 PRIV., para. 126).

128. The Committee decided to declare the communication inadmissible since it did not fall within UNESCO's fields of competence as required under paragraph 14(a)(vi) of 104 EX/Decision 3.3 (161 EX/3 PRIV., para. 107).

129. The Committee decided to strike this communication from its list as manifestly ill-founded in the meaning of paragraph 14(a)(v) of 104 EX/Decision 3.3 (135 EX/3 PRIV., para. 31; 137 EX/3 PRIV., para. 125).

130. The Committee decided to strike the communication from its list, on the grounds that it was ill-founded (137 EX/3 PRIV., para. 125).

131. The Committee decided to declare the communication inadmissible in accordance with 104 EX/Decision 3.3, paragraph 14(a)(vii), on the grounds that it was based exclusively on information published in the press (130 EX/3 PRIV., para. 27).

132. The Committee decided to declare the communication inadmissible as being incompatible with the Organization's principles, ill-founded and offensive, by virtue of paragraph 14(a)(iv), (v) and (vi) of 104 EX/Decision 3.3 (127 EX/3 PRIV., para. 124).

133. The Committee decided to declare the communication inadmissible, a communication dealing with these two cases having been previously declared inadmissible by the Committee at the previous session and there being no new elements to justify its re-examination (129 EX/3 PRIV., para. 18).

(ii) The Committee decides to strike the communication from its list, but, in view of the particular gravity of the case, wishes to express its concern

134. The Committee decided to declare the communication inadmissible but, notwithstanding, to request the government concerned to keep the Committee informed of any further developments which might occur in this case (116 EX/48 PRIV., para. 154).

135. The Committee decided to express its grave preoccupation given the serious violation of human rights to which the communication attests, but nevertheless to strike it from its list, as not falling within UNESCO's fields of competence as required by 104 EX/Decision 3.3 (137 EX/3 PRIV., para. 90).

136. The Committee decided to declare the communication inadmissible in application of paragraph 14(a)(iii) of 104 EX/Decision 3.3 on the grounds that, given the information currently available, it did not fall within UNESCO's areas of competence, and to appeal to the authorities to show clemency by commuting the death penalty (141 EX/3 PRIV., para. 193).

VIII. FAILURE TO RESPECT THE PRINCIPLE OF CONFIDENTIALITY

Examples of wording used by the Committee in situations in which, in its consideration of a communication, the Committee finds that the author of the communication has failed to observe the principle of confidentiality of procedure

137. The Committee decided to express its regrets and its deep concern that the principle of confidentiality had not been respected,

and to strike this communication from its list (146 EX/3 PRIV., para. 112).

138. The Committee decided to ask the Secretariat to ensure that the letter sent to the authors of communications clearly explained the need for confidentiality and the consequences of breaches thereof (114 EX/38 PRIV., para. 650).

139. The Committee decided to request the Secretariat to draw the attention of the author to the need to preserve the confidentiality of any communication submitted to UNESCO under the procedure laid down in 104 EX/Decision 3.3 (159 EX/3 PRIV., para. 16).

140. The Committee decided to request the Secretariat to draw the author's attention to the need to preserve the confidentiality of a communication submitted to UNESCO under the procedure set out in 104 EX/Decision 3.3 and decided to strike this communication from the Committee's list, as the principle of confidentiality had been violated (179 EX/3 PRIV., para. 179).

IX. LEGAL PROCEEDINGS IN PROCESS

Examples of wording used by the Committee in situations in which legal proceedings against the alleged victim are still under way

141. The Committee decided to note the fact that legal proceedings involving the alleged victim were in progress, and accordingly, to defer examination of this communication to the next session of the Executive Board (141 EX/3 PRIV., para. 110).

142. The Committee decided to take note of the fact that the alleged victim's case was still before the Supreme Court, and to resume consideration of this communication at the next session (144 EX/3 PRIV., para. 124).

143. The Committee decided to suspend its consideration of this communication, awaiting the pronouncement of the Supreme Court (129 EX/3 PRIV., para. 108).

144. The Committee decided to keep the communication on its list pending the result of the current judicial investigation (132 EX/3 PRIV., para. 43).

145. The Committee decided to keep this communication on its list pending the result of the current judicial proceedings (160 EX/3 PRIV., para. 120).

146. The Committee decided to keep the communication on its list while awaiting the results of the current court proceedings (149 EX/3 PRIV., para. 18).

147. The Committee decided to keep the communication on its list until additional information had been received from the government concerned about the current proceedings against the alleged victim (156 EX/3 PRIV., para. 107).

148. The Committee decided in view of the judicial proceedings still under way, to comply with the request made by the government concerned and to postpone consideration of the communication until the next session (127 EX/3 PRIV., para. 50).

149. The Committee decided to note that the trial of the alleged victim was in progress and to express the wish that it would be held in a climate of understanding (154 EX/3 PRIV., para. 114).

X. PARTICULARLY ALARMING STATE OF HEALTH OF THE ALLEGED VICTIM

Examples of wording used by the Committee in situations in which the state of health of the alleged victim is a matter for concern

(i) The Committee expresses its concern

150. The Committee decided to express to the government in question its deep concern at the contradictory and disquieting, not to say tragic, information regarding the health of the alleged victim (132 EX/3 PRIV., para. 35).

151. The Committee decided to express to the government in question its deep concern about this case (145 EX/3 PRIV., para. 77).

152. The Committee decided to express to the government concerned its deep concern at the alarming state of health of the alleged victim (161 EX/3 PRIV., para. 293).

153. The Committee decided to express to the government concerned its deep concern regarding the state of health of the alleged victim and to request it to allow him to receive appropriate medical treatment (155 EX/3 PRIV., para. 47).

154. The Committee decided to voice its concern at the state of health of the alleged victim and consequently to request the government concerned to allow an independent medical team to examine them (154 EX/3 PRIV., para. 138).

155. The Committee decided to express to the government concerned its concern at the state of health of the alleged victim and to request it to allow him to receive additional specialized and urgent medical treatment (169 EX/3 PRIV., para. 92).

(ii) The Committee appeals for clemency[3] for the alleged victim

156. The Committee decided to appeal for clemency on behalf of the alleged victim, particularly on account of his state of health (129 EX/3 PRIV., para. 102).

3 At the 144th session, it was recalled that an "appeal for clemency" was a humanitarian step in keeping with the spirit and the letter of 104 EX/Decision 3.3. Some members of the Committee pointed out that an appeal for clemency, which was not the same thing as seeking a pardon, was much more than a purely legal matter, and reflected everyone's concern for respect for the individual, for the human being (144 EX/3 PRIV., para. 88). Other members felt that an appeal for clemency constituted recognition of the alleged victim's guilt. (The Committee began to make appeals for clemency at the 124th session of the Executive Board, in May 1986.)

157. The Committee decided to make a fresh appeal for clemency on behalf of the alleged victim, particularly in view of his poor state of health (130 EX/3 PRIV., para. 81).

158. The Committee decided to launch to the government concerned a new appeal for clemency for the alleged victim on humanitarian grounds (187 EX/3 PRIV., para. 112).

159. The Committee decided to reiterate its appeal for clemency with a view to the release of the alleged victim on humanitarian grounds, particularly in view of his poor health (145 EX/3 PRIV., para. 163).

160. The Committee decided to appeal for clemency with a view to obtaining the release of the alleged victim on humanitarian grounds, particularly in view of his poor state of health (154 EX/3 PRIV., para. 146).

161. The Committee decided to appeal to the government concerned on behalf of the alleged victim with a view to his release on humanitarian grounds in view of his age and state of health (157 EX/3 PRIV., para. 66).

162. The Committee decided to renew its appeal for clemency with a view to securing the immediate early release of the alleged victim, having regard to the gravity of her state of health (150 EX/3 PRIV., para. 81).

163. The Committee decided to appeal on humanitarian grounds to the government concerned to ensure that everything be done to safeguard the alleged victim's health (117 EX/18 PRIV., para. 155).

164. The Committee decided to appeal to the government concerned to treat the alleged victim humanely having regard to his state of health (147 EX/3 PRIV., para. 97).

165. The Committee decided to request the government concerned to continue treating the alleged victim humanely and provide him with the medical treatment necessitated by his state of health (160 EX/3 PRIV., para. 140).

166. The Committee decided to urge the government concerned to kindly treat the alleged victim humanely, having regard to his state of health, and to allow his own doctor to visit him (150 EX/3 PRIV., para. 88).

167. The Committee decided to appeal to the authorities concerned for the alleged victim to be transferred to a medical centre in keeping with the serious state of his health and for him to be granted an early release (154 EX/3 PRIV., para. 157).

(iii) The Committee requests the Chairperson of the Committee or the Director-General to use his or her good offices

168. The Committee decided to issue an urgent appeal to the government concerned to ensure that the alleged victim was treated with the clemency warranted by his critical state of health, and to request its Chairperson to make personal representations to the highest authorities and to the representative of the country concerned on the Executive Board (130 EX/3 PRIV., para. 108).

169. The Committee decided to ask the Executive Board to request the Director-General to make such representations as he might deem appropriate, having regard to the concern expressed by the members of the Committee as regards the health and conditions of detention of the alleged victim (117 EX/18 PRIV., para. 99).

XI. CONDITIONS OF CONFINEMENT AND VISITING RIGHTS

Examples of wording used by the Committee in situations in which the conditions under which the alleged victim is being detained are difficult

170. The Committee decided to request the government concerned to improve the conditions of confinement of the alleged victims, in particular by granting more frequent and extended visiting rights (151 EX/3 PRIV., para. 99).

171. The Committee decided to request the government concerned to improve the conditions under which the alleged victim

was being detained and to authorize his family to visit him more frequently (154 EX/3 PRIV., para. 157).

172. The Committee decided to request the government concerned to grant extended visiting rights to the alleged victims (152 EX/3 PRIV., para. 128).

173. The Committee decided to request the government concerned to transfer the alleged victim to a penal institution closer to his family (176 EX/3 PRIV., para. 144).

174. The Committee decided to request the government concerned to improve the conditions of detention of the alleged victim until his release (177 EX/3 PRIV., para. 75).

175. This Committee decided to request the government concerned to ensure that the alleged victim is treated during his detention according to international standards and that his physical safety is being ensured (179 EX/3 PRIV., para. 285).

176. The Committee decided to request the government concerned to allow the alleged victims to be granted family visits in prison under better conditions (192 EX/3 PRIV., para. 239).

177. The Committee decided to request the government concerned to continue to authorize the alleged victim to be granted family visits and to receive the literature necessary to continue his scientific studies (199 EX/3 PRIV., para. 208).

XII. CHANGES IN THE POLITICAL SITUATION OF THE COUNTRY

Examples of wording used by the Committee in situations in which the political situation of the country concerned has changed since action was first taken against the alleged victim

(i) The Committee requests the government concerned to review the case

178. The Committee decided once again to request the government concerned to review the case in the light of the changes that

had occurred in the country and not in the light of the exceptional circumstances obtained at the time of the events in question (136 EX/3 PRIV., para. 87).

(ii) The Committee makes a fresh appeal for clemency for the alleged victim

179. The Committee decided to renew its appeal for clemency in the light of the changes that have taken place in the country's political situation (137 EX/3 PRIV., para. 84).

180. The Committee decided to appeal again for clemency to the authorities, asking for a remission of sentence and the release of the alleged victim, in view of developments in the political situation of the country (139 EX/3 PRIV., para. 133).

181. The Committee decided to express the hope that the efforts currently being undertaken by the government concerned with regard to human rights might help to improve the situation of the alleged victim (157 EX/3 PRIV., para. 66).

(iii) The Committee decides to strike the communication from its list

182. The Committee decided to cease examination of this communication and to strike it from its list, in view of the return of democracy and the rule of law to the country concerned, the efforts of the government concerned to elucidate the case of the alleged victim and the fact that the Working Group of the Commission on Human Rights was continuing its examination of the case (129 EX/3 PRIV., para. 165).

183. The Committee decided in view of the favourable development of the human rights situation in the country, especially as regards human rights within UNESCO's fields of competence, to cease examination of the communication (116 EX/48 PRIV., para. 277).

XIII. PARTICULARLY DIFFICULT CASES: NO TRIAL, HARSHNESS OF THE SENTENCE PASSED ON THE ALLEGED VICTIM

Examples of wording used by the Committee in situations in which the alleged victim has received a particularly harsh sentence or has been detained without trial

(i) The Committee expresses its concern with regard to the communication

184. The Committee decided to express to the government its grave concern about the extreme length of the alleged victim's detention, apparently without trial, and at the particularly disquieting information regarding his state of health (135 EX/3 PRIV., para. 172).

185. The Committee decided to express to the government concerned its concern about the length of the alleged victim's detention without trial (155 EX/3 PRIV., para. 47).

186. The Committee decided to reiterate its humanitarian concern for the alleged victim (120 EX/15 PRIV., para. 112).

(ii) The Committee appeals for clemency

187. The Committee decided to appeal for clemency[4] to be shown to the alleged victim on account of the harshness of his sentence (131 EX/3 PRIV., para. 104).

XIV. REQUEST BY THE COMMITTEE FOR THE RELEASE OF THE ALLEGED VICTIM

Examples of wording used by the Committee in situations in which the Committee is attempting to obtain the release of the alleged victim

(i) The Committee requests a release

4 On several occasions, in view of the fact that the sentence being served by the alleged victim had nearly expired, members of the Committee have been of the view that only an appeal for clemency involving an amnesty or a reduction of the sentence would still serve a useful purpose.

188. The Committee decided to request the release of the alleged victim for humanitarian reasons, which are the major concern of the Committee (131 EX/3 PRIV., para. 74).

189. The Committee decided to request the immediate release of the alleged victim (145 EX/3 PRIV., para. 122).

(ii) The Committee <u>appeals for clemency</u>

190. The Committee decided to appeal for clemency with a view to the immediate release of the alleged victim (141 EX/3 PRIV., para. 181).

191. The Committee decided to renew its appeal for clemency with a view to the release of the alleged victims (147 EX/3 PRIV., para. 70).

192. The Committee decided to launch a pressing appeal for clemency with a view to the release of the alleged victim (150 EX/3 PRIV., para. 88).

193. The Committee decided to appeal to the government concerned for clemency for the alleged victim with a view to her release on humanitarian grounds, especially as she has already served more than half of her sentence (160 EX/3 PRIV., para. 130).

194. The Committee decided to renew its appeal for clemency in order that the alleged victim might be granted an early release in view of his advanced age, his exemplary conduct in detention and the fact that he had already served the greater part of his long sentence (135 EX/3 PRIV., para. 50).

195. The Committee decided to make to the government concerned another urgent appeal for clemency for the alleged victim with a view to his immediate release on humanitarian grounds and in view of the fact that he has served half of his sentence (157 EX/3 PRIV., para. 115).

196. The Committee decided to make a further appeal for clemency for the alleged victim with a view to having her sentence reduced (154 EX/3 PRIV., para. 94).

197. The Committee decided to appeal again for clemency to the authorities, asking for a remission of sentence for the person concerned, and for his release (135 EX/3 PRIV., para. 96).

198. The Committee decided to launch a fresh appeal for clemency in favour of the alleged victim, already held in administrative detention for over a year (130 EX/3 PRIV., para. 76).

199. The Committee decided to appeal again for clemency to be shown to the alleged victim, who had already been detained for almost 12 years (130 EX/3 PRIV., para. 142).

200. The Committee decided to make a humanitarian appeal on behalf of the alleged victim (131 EX/3 PRIV., para. 85).

201. The Committee decided to reiterate its appeal, on humanitarian grounds, to the government concerned for a solution to the case in question (122 EX/21 PRIV., para. 102).

(iii) The Committee <u>requests the Chairperson of the Committee and/or the Director-General and/or the Chairperson of the Executive Board to use their good offices</u>

202. The Committee decided to request the Chairperson of the Executive Board and the Director-General to intercede with the authorities for the release of the alleged victim (144 EX/3 PRIV., para. 139).

203. The Committee decided to request its Chairperson and the Director-General to attempt again ... to make representations to the President of the country concerned with a view to securing the lifting of the measures of restraint on the freedom of the alleged victim (141 EX/3 PRIV., para. 145).

204. The Committee decided to request the Executive Board, in view of the seriousness of the alleged violations, to ask the Director-General to continue his humanitarian action with a view to seeking a satisfactory solution to the serious problems raised by the communication, in accordance with 104 EX/Decision 3.3, paragraph 14(k) (122 EX/21 PRIV., para. 163).

205. The Committee decided to request the Director-General to continue to use his good offices on behalf of the persons who were the subject of the communication (130 EX/3 PRIV., para. 172).

206. The Committee decided to request the Director-General to use his good offices to appeal for clemency to the Head of State on behalf of the alleged victims and to keep the Committee informed of the outcome at the 161st session of the Executive Board (160 EX/3 PRIV., para. 180).

207. The Committee decided to request the Director-General to use his good offices to appeal to the Head of State for the immediate release of the alleged victim (146 EX/3 PRIV., para. 100).

208. The Committee decided to request the Director-General to use his good offices with the government concerned with a view to the release of the alleged victim, on humanitarian grounds (146 EX/3 PRIV., para. 187).

209. The Committee decided to request the Director-General to use his good offices to obtain greater cooperation in this matter from the government concerned (179 EX/3 PRIV., para. 303).

210. The Committee decided to request the Director-General to make a humanitarian appeal to the appropriate authorities, asking them to alleviate the lot of the alleged victim (119 EX/35 PRIV., para. 196).

211. The Committee decided to ask the Director-General to reissue his urgent appeal for clemency on behalf of the alleged victim to the Head of State concerned, asking for a pardon or at the very least a substantial reduction in his sentence (152 EX/3 PRIV., para. 102).

212. The Committee decided to request the Director-General to write without delay to the Head of State concerned to request him to pardon the alleged victim on humanitarian grounds (151 EX/3 PRIV., para. 76).

213. The Committee decided to request its Chairperson to use his good offices on behalf of the alleged victim at the forthcoming session of the General Conference (137 EX/3 PRIV., para. 19).

214. The Committee decided to request its Chairperson to make appropriate representations in favour of the alleged victim to the delegation in question at the forthcoming session of the General Conference (147 EX/3 PRIV., para. 97; 152 EX/3 PRIV., para. 139).

215. The Committee decided to request its Chairperson to send a personal letter to the Head of State concerned, pleading for clemency for the alleged victim with a view to his immediate release (142 EX/3 PRIV., para. 95).

216. The Committee decided to request the Director-General, in consultation with the Chairperson of the Committee, to take forthwith all necessary steps in favour of the alleged victim, including a visit to him by a UNESCO representative (156 EX/3 PRIV., para. 167).

217. The Committee decided to request the Director-General to examine the possibility of dispatching a UNESCO mission to monitor the progress of the Organization's projects and programmes, and to discuss other matters of mutual interest (154 EX/3 PRIV., para. 94).

218. The Committee decided to urge the Director-General to make representations to the United Nations and the International Committee of the Red Cross in order to examine the possibility of sending a mission to ... to visit the alleged victim (175 EX/3 PRIV., para. 235).

219. The Committee decided to request the Director-General to send, with the agreement of the government concerned, a special representative to visit the alleged victim (176 EX/3 PRIV., para. 133).

220. The Committee decided to request the government concerned to consider the possibility of allowing and organizing a visit by the International Committee of the Red Cross to the alleged victims in order to independently assess their conditions of detention and state of health (190 EX/3 PRIV., para. 232).

XV. DEATH OF THE ALLEGED VICTIM WHILE IN DETENTION

Examples of wording used by the Committee in situations in which the alleged victim has died while in detention

221. The Committee decided to express its sorrow at the death of the alleged victim (140 EX/3 PRIV., para. 143).

222. The Committee decided to express its profound sadness at the announcement of the recent death of the alleged victim (156 EX/3 PRIV., para. 100).

223. The Committee decided to express its profound dismay at learning that 10 of the alleged victims had been executed (134 EX/3 PRIV., para. 190).

224. The Committee decided to express its consternation at the death of the alleged victim (154 EX/3 PRIV., para. 157).

XVI. RELEASE OF THE ALLEGED VICTIM

A. Examples of wording used by the Committee in situations in which the alleged victim has been released before serving the full term (reduction of sentence, royal pardon, amnesty)

225. The Committee decided to take note, with satisfaction, of the release of the alleged victim, to consider the case of the alleged victim as settled, and accordingly to strike this communication from its list (147 EX/3 PRIV., para. 89).

226. The Committee decided to take note of the letter from the permanent delegation, to thank the government concerned for the information contained therein regarding the release of the alleged victim as a result of the reduction of his sentence, and to strike it from its list (131 EX/3 PRIV., para. 63).

227. The Committee decided after having determined that the objective of the communication had been effectively achieved by the release of the alleged victim, to consider the matter settled and to

strike the case from its list, in compliance with paragraph 14(a)(x) of 104 EX/Decision 3.3 (117 EX/18 PRIV., para. 130).

228. The Committee decided to take note with satisfaction of the amnesty from which, along with others, the alleged victim had benefited, and to strike this communication from its list, considering it to have been settled in accordance with paragraph 14(a)(x) of 104 EX/Decision 3.3 (132 EX/3 PRIV., para. 11).

229. The Committee decided to take note, with satisfaction, of the release of the alleged victim, to thank the government concerned for its humanitarian gesture and to strike this communication from its list (156 EX/3 PRIV., para. 126).

230. The Committee decided to warmly acknowledge the clemency shown by the ... authorities which had enabled the early release of the alleged victim (185 EX/3 PRIV., para 149).

231. The Committee decided to express its deep appreciation to His Excellency the President ... for his pardon which had enabled the early release of the alleged victims (191 EX/3 PRIV., para. 161).

B. Examples of wording used by the Committee in situations in which the alleged victim has been released after having served his sentence

232. The Committee decided to take note of the letter from the permanent delegation and to thank the government concerned for the information contained therein regarding the release of the alleged victim, who had served his sentence, and to declare that this communication had thus ceased to be relevant and to strike it from its list (131 EX/3 PRIV., para. 63).

233. The Committee decided to take note of the release of the alleged victim after having completed serving his sentence, and to strike the communication from its list (147 EX/3 PRIV., para. 70).

234. The Committee decided to take note of the release of the alleged victim after having served the full term of his sentence, and to strike the communication from its list (180 EX/3 PRIV., para. 27).

C. Examples of wording used by the Committee in situations in which the alleged victim has been granted a conditional release

235. The Committee decided to take note of his release (144 EX/3 PRIV., para. 170).

XVII. COMMUNICATIONS SETTLED

Examples of wording used by the Committee in situations in which the Committee considers a communication as settled (satisfactory outcome of a case)

(i) The Committee decides to strike the communication from its list

236. The Committee decided to note with satisfaction the happy outcome of this case, and to strike the communication from its list as being settled in accordance with paragraph 14(a)(x) of 104 EX/Decision 3.3 (130 EX/3 PRIV., para. 42).

237. The Committee decided to express its satisfaction at the outcome of this case, and to strike the communication from its list (130 EX/3 PRIV., para. 129).

238. The Committee decided to strike this communication from its list, and to consider it settled in accordance with paragraph 14(a)(x) of 104 EX/Decision 3.3 (135 EX/3 PRIV., para. 25).

239. The Committee decided in view of all the relevant information received, to strike this communication from its list (146 EX/3 PRIV., para. 40).

240. The Committee decided to express its satisfaction at the outcome of these cases and to strike these communications from its list (170 EX/3 PRIV., para. 270).

(ii) The Committee decides not to continue its examination of the communication

241. The Committee decided in view of all the relevant information received, not to continue the examination of this communication (144 EX/3 PRIV., para. 81).

242. The Committee decided in view of all the relevant information received, not to continue the examination of this communication (146 EX/3 PRIV., para. 164).

243. The Committee decided not to continue at this stage consideration of the communication (152 EX/3 PRIV., para. 63).

244. The Committee decided to keep these communications on its list, but to resume consideration of them only at such time as new information on the identity of the alleged victims is provided and their whereabouts is established, both of which would enable the Committee to continue its work (161 EX/3 PRIV., para. 100).

XVIII. COMMUNICATION SETTLED SUBJECT TO CONFIRMATION

Examples of wording used by the Committee in situations in which a communication is considered settled, but for which the Committee wishes to receive confirmation

245. The Committee decided to strike the communication from its list subject to confirmation that the travel permit had been available or was no longer needed (140 EX/3 PRIV., para. 53).

246. The Committee decided to strike the communication from its list in the event of the alleged victim being released, and, should she not be released, to resume consideration of this communication at the forthcoming session (132 EX/3 PRIV., para. 18).

247. The Committee decided to strike the communication from its list subject to receiving not later than the 164th session of the Executive Board confirmation by the authorities of the government concerned of the definitive release of the alleged victim, failing which it would renew consideration of the communication at its next meeting (162 EX/3 PRIV., para. 168).

XIX. RE-EXAMINATION OF A COMMUNICATION DECLARED TO BE INADMISSIBLE

Examples of wording used by the Committee in situations in which the re-examination of a communication declared to be inadmissible is justified by further allegations

248. The Committee decided:

- to point out that, at the session during the ... session of the Executive Board, the Committee had declared Communication No. ... submitted by the same authors and concerning the same alleged victim to be inadmissible;

- to note that Communication No. 989/99 contained no new information and consequently was not admissible either (159 EX/3 PRIV., para. 202).

249. The Committee decided to declare this communication inadmissible as it currently stands (185 EX/3 PRIV, para. 235).

Printed on recycled paper